Operations Research

OPERATIONS RESEARCH

Second Edition

Frederick S. Hillier
Stanford University

Gerald J. Lieberman
Stanford University

CBS PUBLISHERS & DISTRIBUTORS PVT. LTD.
New Delhi • Bengaluru • Chennai • Kochi • Mumbai • Pune

ISBN : 81-239-0939-X

First Indian Edition : 1994
Reprint : 2000

This edition has been reprinted in India by arrangement with Holden-Day Inc., USA

Published by Satish Kumar Jain and produced by V.K. Jain for
CBS Publishers & Distributors Pvt. Ltd.,
CBS Plaza, 4819/XI Prahlad Street, 24 Ansari Road, Daryaganj,
New Delhi - 110002, India. • Website: www.cbspd.com
e-mail: delhi@cbspd.com, cbspubs@airtelmail.in
Ph.: 23289259, 23266861, 23266867 • Fax: 011-23243014

Branches:

- ***Bengaluru:*** Seema House, 2975, 17th Cross, K.R. Road, Bansankari 2nd Stage, Bengaluru - 560070
  • Ph.: +91-80-26771678/79 • Fax: +91-80-26771680
  • E-mail: cbsbng@gmail.com, bangalore@cbspd.com
- ***Pune:*** Bhuruk Prestige, Sr. No. 52/12/2+1+3/2, Narhe, Haveli (Near Katraj-Dehu Road By-pass), Pune - 411041
  • Ph.: +91-20-64704058/59, 020-32392277 • E-mail: pune@cbspd.com
- ***Kochi:*** 36/14, Kalluvilakam, Lissie Hospital Road, Kochi - 682018, Kerala • Ph.: +91-484-4059061-65
  • Fax: +91-484-4059065 • E-mail: cochin@cbspd.com
- ***Chennai:*** 20, West Park Road, Shenoy Nagar, Chennai - 600030
  Ph.: +91-44-26260666, 26208620 • Fax: +91-44-42032115
  • E-mail: chennai@cbspd.com
- ***Mumbai:*** 83-C, Ist Floor, Dr. E. Moses Road, Worli, Mumbai-400 018, Maharashtra Ph.: +91-9833017933, 022-24902340/24902341
  • E-mail: mumbai@cbspd.com

Printed at :
J.S. Offset Printers, Delhi

Contents

PART 2 PROBABILISTIC MODELS

Preface

We continue to be deeply gratified by the widespread response to the first edition. However, the realization that many thousands of students are being introduced to operations research through our book each year also has given us a great sense of responsibility. Therefore, after receiving feedback from numerous instructors and students, we have expended as much time and energy in revising and refining this material for the second edition as we did in writing the entire first edition. However, when we are asked to describe the "big changes" in this revision, we have a difficult time doing so! The topics are largely unchanged. The orientation is still roughly the same. Many of the sections are not substantially changed. The only big change really is that there are innumerable small improvements. In the belief that the principle of additivity applies in this case, we hope and trust that these small changes add up to a markedly superior book that will both inspire and elucidate.

One of the most visible changes is that a new chapter on the application of linear programming has been added to emphasize the practical importance of this technique. Many chapters also have been completely rewritten to increase the simplicity and clarity of the material, and sections have been added or updated to reflect new trends and developments. The number of problems has been approximately doubled, with selected answers given in the back of the book. The interrelationship between the various techniques of operations research is stressed, with different ones applied to obtain solutions to the same problem. Finally, the only chapter containing completely new subject material is the short one on reliability. The authors feel that this topic is growing in importance and hence should be included.

Great care also has gone into developing many interesting and relatively realistic examples. Some of these involve contemporary social problems that have attracted the interest of today's generation of college students, and others concern more traditional kinds of large-scale business problems, and so on. However, they all are designed to appeal to a broad spectrum of students.

These examples should considerably improve the appeal and readability of the book for the more practically inclined student without much mathematical maturity. Somewhat more emphasis also has been placed on problem formulation and other practical considerations. However, we still feel that the essential theory of operations research can best be understood and appreciated by being presented from a mathematical viewpoint. Therefore the second edition still is aimed at the same audience as the first edition, namely, the broad spectrum of students in a variety of fields (engineering, business, mathematical sciences, and social sciences), who sometimes prefer a modest use of mathematics to an immoderate amount of verbosity.

However, the mathematics used has been kept at a relatively elementary level. Chapters 2 to 7 on mathematical programming (Part 1) require no mathematics beyond high school algebra. Somewhat more mathematical training is desirable in Part 2 (Chapters 8 to 15), which presents probabilistic models. Although portions of Part 2 can be covered without further prerequisites, a basic knowledge of elementary calculus is assumed in a few places, and the mathematical maturity that a student achieves through taking an elementary calculus course also is useful. Chapter 8 presents a primer or review of the probability theory needed, but a previous introduction to probability would be helpful. Part 3 (Chapters 16 to 18) on advanced topics in mathematical programming is meant for students who wish to go beyond elementary material in mathematical programming; it also requires the mathematical maturity achieved through knowledge of the calculus. In addition, some basic matrix manipulations (reviewed in an appendix) are used in portions of Part 3.

There are many ways to package the material in this text into a course. The book is divided into parts, with a gradation of levels of difficulty. Therefore it is well suited for a relatively wide range of student capabilities. It is aimed largely at the junior or senior undergraduate level and for first year (Master's level) graduate students. The book has great flexibility. Part 1 or Parts 1 and 3 (on mathematical programming) may be covered essentially independently of Part 2 (on probabilistic models) and vice versa. Furthermore, the chapters within Parts 1 and 3 are essentially independent, with the one exception that they all use basic material presented in Chapter 2. Within Part 2 there is considerable flexibility of coverage, although some integration of the material is available.

An elementary survey course covering mathematical programming and some probabilistic models can easily be presented in a quarter (40 hours) or semester by using some of the material in Chapters 1 to 15, for example, most of Chapters 1 to 7, 9 to 11, and 15. (This assumes a prerequisite of elementary probability theory for Chapters 9 to 15; otherwise, additional time will be required to cover the material in Chapter 8.) Most of the material in Chapters 1 to 15 (excluding Chapter 8) can be covered in a two-quarter survey sequence (60 hours). Chapters 1 to 4 and 16 form an excellent basis for a (one-quarter) course in linear programming. The material in Chapters 5 to 7 and 17 to 18 covers topics for another (one-quarter) course in other deterministic models. Finally, the material in Chapters 9 to 15 covers the subjects of probabilistic models suitable for presentation in a (one-quarter) course. In fact, these latter three courses (the material in the entire text) can be viewed as a basic 1-year sequence in the techniques of operations research, forming the core of a Master's program. Each course outlined is currently being presented at Stanford University, and this text has been used in the manner suggested. In the discussion of the chapters covered, Chapter 19, planning an operations research study, has not been specifically mentioned. Chapter 19 is similar to Chapter 2 in the first edition, but it is now presented at the end of the text rather than at the beginning. It is our feeling that a student is best prepared to understand how an operations research study is planned *after* he understands the techniques that can be brought to bear on a problem, rather than discuss such a study before the student knows what operations research is. Therefore we suggest that this chapter be covered at the end of each course outlined above to place the material previously presented into its proper perspective, but it can still be presented at the beginning if the instructor prefers.

We are deeply indebted to many people for their part in making this revision possible. Those making helpful comments on the first edition are literally too numerous to mention, but reviews by Colin Bell and Andrew Stedry were especially enlightening. We also particularly acknowledge the help of a number of people who read a portion of the manuscript for the second edition and made many valuable suggestions. These especially include David Butler, Richard Cottle, Cyrus Derman, Bruce Faaland, J. Michael Harrison, Donald Rosenfield, Sheldon Ross, and Andrew Shogan. They also include many of the students who used preliminary chapters of the revision and suggested clarifications. In addition, we express our appreciation to Gail Lemmond, Paula Matthews, and Chris Verhoeven for their typing of the final manuscript. We are also indebted to the Office of Naval Research and the National Science Foundation for supporting some of the research that led to results included in the chapters on queueing theory and reliability.

Finally, as in the first edition, we again thank our wives Ann and Helen for their editorial and typing assistance, and we thank both them and our children David, John, and Mark Hillier and Janet, Joanne, Michael, and Diana Lieberman for their encouragement and understanding in allowing us to devote so much of our time that really belonged to them on this revision.

FREDERICK S. HILLIER
GERALD J. LIEBERMAN

Stanford University
November 1973

1 Introduction

1 Introduction

1.1 THE ORIGINS OF OPERATIONS RESEARCH

Since the advent of the industrial revolution the world has seen a remarkable growth in the size and complexity of organizations. The artisans' small shops of an earlier era have evolved into the billion dollar corporations of today. An integral part of this revolutionary change has been a tremendous increase in the division of labor and segmentation of management responsibilities in these organizations. The results have been spectacular. However, along with its blessings, this increasing specialization has created new problems, problems that are still occurring in many organizations. One problem is a tendency for the many components of an organization to grow into relatively autonomous empires with their own goals and value systems, thereby losing sight of how their activities and objectives mesh with those of the overall organization. What is best for one component frequently is detrimental to another, so they may end up working at cross purposes. A related problem is that as the complexity and specialization in an organization increases it becomes more and more difficult to allocate its available resources to its various activities in a way which is most effective for the organization as a whole. These kinds of problems and the need to find a better way to resolve them provided the environment for the emergence of operations research.

The roots of operations research can be traced back many decades, when early attempts were made to use a scientific approach in the management of organizations. However, the beginning of the activity called operations research has generally been attributed to the military services early in World War II. Because of the war effort, there was an urgent need to allocate scarce resources to the various military operations and to the activities within each operation in an effective manner. Therefore the British and then the American military management called upon a large number of scientists to apply a scientific approach to dealing with this and other strategic and tactical problems. In effect they were asked to do research on (military) operations. These teams of scientists were the first operations research teams. Their efforts allegedly were instrumental in winning the Air Battle of Britain, the Island Campaign in the Pacific, the Battle of the North Atlantic, and so on.

Spurred on by the apparent success of operations research in the military, industry gradually became interested in this new field. As the industrial boom following the war was running its course, the problems caused by the increasing complexity and specialization in organizations were again coming to the forefront. It was becoming apparent to a growing number of people, including business consultants who had served on or with the operations research teams during the war, that these were basically the same problems but in a different context that had been faced by the military. In this way operations research began to creep into industry, business, and civil government. By 1951, it had already taken hold in Great Britain and was in the process of doing so in the United States. Since then the field has developed very rapidly, as will be described further in Sec. 1.3.

At least two other factors that played a key role in the rapid growth of operations research during this period can be identified. One was the substantial progress that was made early in improving the techniques available to operations research. After the war, many of the scientists who had participated on operations research teams or who had heard about this work were motivated to pursue research relevant to the field; important advancements in the state of the art resulted. A prime example is the simplex method for solving linear programming problems, developed by George Dantzig in 1947. Many of the standard tools of operations research, e.g., linear programming, dynamic programming, queueing theory, and inventory theory, were relatively well developed before the end of the 1950s. In addition to this rapid advancement in the theory of operations research, a second factor that gave great impetus to the growth of the field was the onslaught of the computer revolution. A large amount of computation usually is required to deal most effectively with the complex problems typically considered by operations research. Doing this by hand would often be out of the question. Therefore the development of the electronic digital computers, with their ability to perform arithmetic calculations thousands or even millions of times faster than a human being can, was a tremendous boon to operations research.

1.2 THE NATURE OF OPERATIONS RESEARCH

What is operations research? One way of trying to answer this question is to give a definition. For example, operations research may be described as a scientific approach to decision making that involves the operations of organizational systems. However, this description, like earlier attempts at a definition, is so general that it is equally applicable to many other fields as well. Therefore, perhaps the best way of grasping the unique nature of operations research is to examine its outstanding characteristics.

As its name implies, operations research involves "research on operations." This says something about both the approach and the area of application of the field. Thus operations research is applied to problems that concern how to conduct and coordinate the operations or activities within an organization. The nature of the organization is essentially immaterial, and, in fact, operations research has been applied extensively in business, industry, the military, civil government and agencies, hospitals, and so forth. Therefore the breadth of application is unusually wide. The approach of operations research is that of the scientific method. In particular, the process begins by carefully observing and formulating the problem and then constructing a scientific (typically mathematical) model that attempts to abstract the essence of the real problem. It is then hypothesized that this model is a sufficiently precise representation of the essential features of the situation, so that the conclusions (solutions) obtained from the model are also valid for the real problem. This hypothesis is then modified and verified by suitable experimentation. Thus, in a certain sense operations research involves creative scientific research into the fundamental properties of operations. However, there is more to it than this. Specifically, operations research also is concerned with the practical management of the organization. Therefore, to be successful it must also provide positive, understandable conclusions to the decision maker(s) when they are needed. In short, operations research involves research on operations but without the benefit of an ivory tower.

Still another characteristic of operations research is its broad viewpoint. As implied in the preceding section, operations research adopts an organizational point of view. Thus it attempts to resolve the conflicts of interest among the components of the organization in a way that is best for the organization as a whole. This does not imply that the study of each problem must give explicit consideration to all aspects of the organization; rather, the objectives being sought must be consistent with those of the overall organization. An additional characteristic that was mentioned in passing is that operations research attempts to find the best or optimal solution to the problem under consideration. Rather than being content with merely improving the status quo, the goal is to identify the best possible course of action. Although it must be interpreted carefully this "search for optimality" is a very important theme in operations research.

All these characteristics lead quite naturally to still another one. It is evident that no single individual should be expected to be an expert on all the many aspects of operations research work or the problems typically considered; this would require a group of individuals having diverse backgrounds and skills. Therefore, when undertaking a full-fledged operations research study of a new problem it is usually necessary to use a team approach. Such an operations research team typically needs to include individuals who collectively are highly trained in mathematics, statistics and probability theory, economics, business administration, electronic computing, engineering and the physical sciences, the behavioral sciences, and the special techniques of operations research. The team also needs to have the necessary experience and variety of skills to give appropriate consideration to the many ramifications of the problem throughout the organization and to execute effectively all the diverse phases of the operations research study.

In summary, operations research is concerned with optimal decision making in, and modeling of, deterministic and probabilistic systems that originate from real life. These applications, which occur in government, business, engineering, economics, and the natural and social sciences, are largely characterized by the need to allocate limited resources. In these situations, considerable insight can be obtained from scientific analysis such as that provided by operations research. The contribution from the operations research approach stems primarily from

1. The structuring of the real life situation into a mathematical model, abstracting the essential elements so that a solution relevant to the decision maker's objectives can be sought. This involves looking at the problem in the context of the entire system.

2. Exploring the structure of such solutions and developing systematic procedures for obtaining them.

3. Developing a solution, including the mathematical theory, if necessary, that yields an optimal value of the system measure of desirability (or possibly comparing alternative courses of action by evaluating their measure of desirability).

1.3 THE IMPACT OF OPERATIONS RESEARCH

Operations research has had an increasingly great impact on the management of organizations in recent years. Both the number and the variety of its applications continue to grow rapidly, and no slowdown is in sight. In fact, with the exception of the advent of the electronic computer, the extent of this impact seems to be unrivaled by that of any other recent development.

After their success with operations research during World War II, the British and American military services continued to have active operations research groups, often at different levels of command. As a result, there now exists a large number of people called "military operations researchers" who are applying an operations research approach to problems of national defense. For example, they engage in tactical planning for requirements and use of weapon systems as well as consider the larger problems of the allocation and integration of effort. Some of their techniques involve quite sophisticated ideas in political science, mathematics, economics, probability theory, and statistics.

Operations research is also being used widely in other types of organizations, including business and industry. Almost all the dozen or so largest corporations in the world, and a sizable proportion of the small industrial organizations, have well-established operations research groups. Many industries, including aircraft and missile, automobile, communication, computer, electric power, electronics, food, metallurgy, mining, paper, petroleum, and transportation, have made widespread use of operations research. Also financial institutions, governmental agencies, and hospitals are rapdily increasing their use of operations research.

To be more specific, consider some of the problems that have been solved by particular techniques of operations research. Linear programming has been used successfully in the solution of problems concerned with assignment of personnel, blending of materials, distribution and transportation, and investment portfolios. Dynamic programming has been successfully applied to such areas as planning advertising expenditures, distributing sales effort, and production scheduling. Queueing theory has had application in solving problems concerned with traffic congestion, servicing machines subject to breakdown, determining the level of a service force, air traffic scheduling, design of dams, production scheduling, and hospital operation. Other techniques of operation research, such as inventory theory, game theory, and simulation, also have been successfully applied to a variety of contexts.

In 1972, Turban[1] reported on a survey of operations research activities that provided a snapshot of activities in 1969. Mail questionnaires were sent to the Directors of Operations Research/Management Science of 475 companies. These companies were selected from *Fortune*'s list of the top 500, using the 300 largest industrial corporations, 50 industrial corporations drawn from the companies ranking between 300 and 500, and the 25 largest companies in each of the service categories, banks, utilities, merchandising, life insurance, and transportation. There were 107 questionnaires returned; of these, 47 (or nearly one-half) reported having a special department at their headquarters that is mainly engaged in O.R. activities. In addition, 13 companies indicated that they intended to establish such a department in the near future. Furthermore, the growth rates are impressive in that approximately 4 percent of these companies had departments established prior to 1950, 15 percent between 1951 and 1959, 50 percent between 1960 and 1965, and 30 percent after 1966. Another rather interesting finding is that almost all the departments reported to the company president, vice-president, or controller. The survey also indicated how widely the techniques of operations research had been applied to current projects; the results are shown in Table 1.1.

It is evident that statistical analysis, simulation, and linear programming were currently the most widely used techniques. Furthermore, the survey revealed that the computer was used in the majority of the projects reported.

Because of the great impact of operations research, professional societies devoted to this field and related activities have been founded in a number of countries throughout the world. In the United States, the Operations Research

[1] E. Turban, "A Sample Survey of Operations Research Activities at the Corporate Level," *Operations Research*, **20**:708–721, 1972.

Table 1.1 Use of Operations Research in Current Activities (Turban Survey)

Techniques	*No. of projects*	*Frequency of use (%)*
Statistical analysis†	63	29
Simulation	54	25
Linear programming	41	19
Inventory theory	13	6
PERT/CPM	13	6
Dynamic programming	9	4
Nonlinear programming	7	3
Queueing	2	1
Heuristic programming	2	1
Miscellaneous	13	6

† Includes probability theory, regression analysis, exponential smoothing, statistical sampling, and tests of hypotheses.

Society of America (ORSA), established in 1952, has approximately 8,000 members; The Institute of Management Sciences (TIMS), founded in 1953, has approximately 6,500 members. Each of these societies publishes a journal (*Operations Research* and *Management Science*, respectively) that now contains more than 1,000 pages per year reporting new research and applications in the field. In addition, there are many other similar journals published in such countries as the United States, England, France, India, Japan, Canada, and West Germany.

Operations research also has had considerable impact in the colleges and universities. Today most of the major American universities offer courses in this field, and many offer advanced degrees that are either in or with specialization in operations research. As a result, there are now thousands of students taking at least one course in operations research each year. Much of the basic research in the field is also being done in the universities.

1.4 TRAINING FOR A CAREER IN OPERATIONS RESEARCH

Because of the great growth of operations research, career opportunities in this field appear to be outstanding. The demand for trained people continues to far exceed the supply, and both attractive starting positions and rapid advancement are readily available. Because of the nature of their work, operations research groups tend to have a prominent staff position, with access to higher level management in the organization. The problems they work on tend to be important, challenging, and interesting. Therefore, any individual with a mathematics and science orientation who is also interested in the practical management of organizations is likely to find a career in operations research very rewarding.

Three complementary types of academic training are particularly relevant for a career in operations research. The first is a basic training in the fundamentals upon which operations research is based. This includes the basic methodology of mathematics and science as well as such topics as linear algebra and matrix theory, probability theory, statistical inference, stochastic processes, computer science, microeconomics, accounting and business administration, organization theory, and the behavioral sciences.

A second important type of training is in operations research per se, including special techniques of the field such as linear and nonlinear programming, dynamic programming, inventory theory, network flow theory, queueing models, reliability, game theory, and simulation. It should also include an introduction to the methodology of operations research, where the various techniques and their role in an operations research study involving specific problem areas would be placed in perspective. Often courses covering certain of these topics are offered in more than one department within a university, including Departments of Business, Industrial Engineering, Mathematics, Statistics, Computer Science, Economics, and Electrical Engineering. This is a natural reflection of the broad scope of application of the field. Since it does tread across traditional disciplinary lines, separate programs or departments in operations research also are being established in some universities.

Finally, it is also well to have specialized training in some field other than operation research, for example, mathematics, statistics, industrial engineering, business, or economics. This additional training provides one with an area of special competence for applying operations research, and it should make that person a more valuable member of an operations research team.

The early operations researchers were people whose primary training and work had been in some traditional field, such as physics, chemistry, mathematics, engineering, or economics. They tended to have little or no formal education in operations research per se. However, as the body of special knowledge has expanded, it has become increasingly more difficult to enter the field without

Table 1.2 Educational Background of Operations Research Personnel (Turban Survey)

Major field of study	Percentage of total at degree level: Bachelors	Masters	Doctorate	All degree levels
Operations research & management science	3	24	32	12
Mathematics & statistics	26	16	21	22
Business administration	20	27	2	22
Engineering	34	17	29	28
Other	17	16	16	16
Percentage of total	27	53	20	

considerable prior education in this area. As a result, although it is still common for new operations researchers to have their college degree(s) in a traditional field, they generally have specialized too in operations research as part of their academic program. The traditional fields that have most commonly served as a vehicle into operations research are indicated in Table 1.2, which is based on the 1972 survey by Turban described in the preceding section. However, present trends indicate that many operations researchers in the future will have both an undergraduate degree in a traditional field and a graduate degree in operations research itself.

1.5 THE ROAD AHEAD

As an introduction to operations research, this book is designed to acquaint students with the formulation, solution, and implementation of operations research models for analyzing complex systems problems in industry or government. Part 1 presents an introduction to mathematical programming, which is a very prominent area of operations research concerned largely with how to allocate limited resources among the various activities of an organization. Part 2 considers a number of probabilistic models that take into account the uncertainty associated with future events in order to analyze certain important types of problems. Part 3 then discusses some relatively advanced topics in mathematical programming that are important for anyone specializing in operations research.

Much of the material presented in Parts 1 and 2 can be described in terms of typical examples of situations that are encountered in practice. Synopses of several such examples are presented below, with detailed solutions given in successive chapters.

The technique of *linear programming* is illustrated by a company that operates a *reclamation center* which collects several types of solid waste materials and then treats them so they can be amalgamated into a saleable product. Different grades of this product can be made, depending upon the mix of the materials used. Although there is some flexibility in the mix for each grade, quality standards do specify a minimum or maximum percentage (by weight) of certain materials allowed in that product grade. Data are available on the cost of amalgamation and the selling price for each grade. The reclamation center collects its solid waste materials from some regular sources and so is normally able to maintain a steady production rate for treating these materials. Furthermore, the quantities available for collection and treatment each week, as well as the cost of treatment, for each type of material are known. Using the given information, the company is to determine just how much of each product grade to produce *and* the exact mix of materials to be used for each grade so as to maximize their total weekly profit (total sales income minus the total costs of *both* amalgamation and treatment).

Another example of linear programming concerns a steel producer who is facing an *air pollution problem* caused by pollutants emanating from the manufacturing plant. The three main types of pollutants in the airshed are particulate matter, sulfur oxides, and hydrocarbons. New standards require that the company reduce its annual emmission of these pollutants. The steel works has two primary sources of pollution, namely, the blast furnaces for making pig iron and the open-hearth furnaces for changing iron into steel. In both cases the engineers have decided that the most effective types of abatement methods are (1) increasing the height of the smoke stacks, (2) using filter devices (including gas traps) in the smoke stacks, and (3) including cleaner high-grade materials among the fuels for the furnaces. All these methods have known technological limits on how much emission they can eliminate. Fortunately the methods can be used at any fraction of their abatement capacities. A cost analysis results in estimates of the total annual cost that is incurred by each abatement method when used by blast and open-hearth furnaces (cost of less-than-full capacity use of a method is essentially proportional to its fractional capacity). Using the aforementioned data, the optimal plan (minimum cost) for pollution abatement is to be determined. This would consist of specifying which types of abatement methods would be used and at what fractions of their abatement capacities for the (1) blast furnaces and (2) open-hearth furnaces.

One of the important special types of linear programming problems is called the *transportation problem*; a typical example deals with a company producing canned peas. The peas are prepared at several distantly located canneries and then shipped by truck to distributing warehouses throughout the Western United States. Because the shipping costs are a major expense, management is initiating a study to reduce them as much as possible. For the upcoming season, an estimate has been made of what the output will be from each cannery, and each warehouse has been allocated a certain amount from the total supply of peas. This information (in units of truckloads), along with the shipping cost per truckload for each cannery-warehouse combination, is given. Using the data, the (optimal) plan for assigning these shipments to the various cannery-warehouse combinations that minimize total shipping costs is to be determined.

In addition to linear programming, there are a number of related mathematical programming techniques for dealing with similar kinds of problems. One of these is *dynamic programming*, which is concerned with making a sequence of interrelated decisions. It is illustrated by a job shop whose work load is subject to considerable seasonal fluctuation. However, machine operators are difficult to hire and costly to train, so the manager is reluctant to lay off workers during the slack seasons. He is likewise reluctant to maintain his peak payroll when it is not required. Furthermore, he is definitely opposed to overtime work on a regular basis. Because all work is done to custom orders, it is not possible to build up inventories during slack seasons. Therefore the manager is in a dilemma as to what his policy should be regarding employment levels. Estimates are available for the manpower requirements during the four seasons of the year for the forseeable future. Employment is not permitted to fall below these levels. Any employment above these levels is wasted. The salaries, hiring costs, and firing costs are known. Assuming that fractional levels of employment are possible because of a few part-time employees, the employment in each season that minimizes the total cost is to be determined.

Among the probabilistic models considered in Part 2 are some falling into the area of queueing (waiting line) theory. A *queueing theory* model is illustrated by a *hospital emergency room.* The emergency room provides quick medical care for emergency cases that are brought to the hospital by ambulance or private automobile. At any hour there is always one doctor on duty in the emergency room. However, because of a growing tendency for emergency cases to use these facilities rather than go to a private physician, the hospital has been experiencing a continuing increase in the number of emergency room visits each year. As a result, when patients arrive during peak usage hours (the early evening) they have to wait until it is their turn to be treated by the doctor. Therefore a proposal has been made that a second doctor should be assigned to the emergency room during these hours so that two emergency cases can be treated simultaneously. By recognizing that the emergency room is a queueing system, several alternative queueing theory models can be applied to predict the waiting characteristics of the system with one doctor and with two doctors that will aid the hospital in its evaluation of the proposal to add a second physician.

A similar queueing example in a very different context concerns determining the *optimal number of repairmen* for a group of machines. A company uses 10 identical machines in its production facility. However, because these machines break down and require repair frequently, the company only has enough operators to operate *eight* machines at a time, so two machines are available on a standby basis for use while other machines are down. Thus eight machines are always operating whenever no more than two machines are waiting to be repaired, but the number of operating machines is reduced by one for each additional machine waiting to be repaired. The probability distribution of the time until any given operating machine breaks down and the probability distribution of the time required to repair a machine are known from past history. Up until now the company has had just *one* repairman to repair these machines. However, this has frequently resulted in reduced productivity by having *less than eight* operating machines. Therefore consideration is being given to hiring a *second* repairman so that *two* machines can be repaired simultaneously. Thus the queueing system to be studied has the repairmen as its servers and the machines requiring repair as its customers, where the problem is to choose between having *one* or *two* servers (or possibly more). Given the cost of each repairman and the cost of inoperable machines, the optimal number of repairmen is to be determined.

Inventory theory is illustrated by a television manufacturing company that produces its own speakers which are used in the production of its television sets. The television sets are assembled on a continuous production line at a known monthly rate. The speakers are produced in batches because they do not warrant setting up a continuous production line, and relatively large quantities can be produced in a short time. The company is interested in determining when and how much to produce. Several costs must be considered: (1) Each time a batch is produced, a setup cost is incurred. This cost includes the cost of "tooling up", administrative costs, record keeping, and so on. (2) The production of speakers in large batch sizes leads to a large inventory, resulting in a monthly cost for keeping a speaker in stock. This cost includes the cost of capital tied up, storage space, insurance, taxes, protection, and so forth. (3) A cost of producing a single speaker (excluding the setup cost) is incurred. (4) Company policy prohibits deliberately planning for shortages of any of its components. However, a shortage of speakers occasionally occurs, resulting in a monthly cost for each speaker unavailable when required. This cost includes the cost of installing speakers after the television set is fully assembled, storage space, delayed revenue, record keeping, and so on. Given data on these costs, the optimal batch size (and period between production) is to be determined.

The use of *Markovian decision processes* can be described in terms of a production process that contains a machine which deteriorates rapidly in both quality and output under heavy usage so that it is inspected at the end of each day. Immediately after inspection the condition of the machine is noted and classified into one of four possible states: 0 (as good as new), 1 (operable—minor deterioration), 2 (operable—major deterioration), and 3 (inoperable—output of unacceptable quality). The state of the system is assumed to evolve according to some known probabilistic "laws of motion." At the end of each day, one of three decisions can be made: (1) leave the machine alone, (2) overhaul the machine, which results in leaving it operable with minor deterioration, and (3) replacing it, which results in a new machine. As a result of the state of the system found at the end of the day and the decision taken, a cost is incurred. Given these costs and a description of the probabilistic "laws of motion," an optimal maintenance policy is to be found.

Part 1
Mathematical Programming

2 Linear Programming

Many people rank the development of linear programming among the most important scientific advances of the mid-twentieth century, and we must agree with this assessment. Its impact since just 1950 has been extraordinary. Today it is a standard tool that has saved many thousands or millions of dollars for companies or businesses of even moderate size in the industrialized countries of the world, and its use in other sectors of society is rapidly spreading. Dozens of textbooks have been written about the subject, and *published* articles describing important applications now number well over 100. In fact, it has been estimated that 25 percent of all scientific computation on computers is devoted to the use of linear programming and closely related techniques.[1]

What is the nature of this remarkable tool, and what kinds of problems does it address? You will gain insight on this as you work through subsequent examples. However, a verbal summary may help provide perspective. Briefly, linear programming typically deals with the problem of allocating *limited resources* among *competing activities* in the best possible (i.e., *optimal*) way. This problem of allocation can arise whenever one must select the level of certain activities that must compete for certain scarce resources necessary to perform those activities. The variety of situations to which this description applies is diverse indeed, ranging from the allocation of production facilities to products to the allocation of national resources to domestic needs, from portfolio selection to the selection of shipping patterns, from production scheduling to the solution of parlor games, and so on, almost ad infinitum. However, the one common ingredient in each of these situations is the necessity for allocating resources to activities.

[1] Reported by a 1970 IBM study of computer usage.

Linear programming uses a mathematical model to describe the problem of concern. The adjective "linear" means that all the mathematical functions in this model are required to be linear functions. The word "programming" does not refer here to computer programming; rather, it is essentially a synonym for planning. Thus, linear programming involves the planning of activities to obtain an "optimal" result, i.e., a result that reaches the specified goal best (according to the mathematical model) among all feasible alternatives.

Because of its importance, we devote the next three chapters to linear programming. In this first chapter we provide a basic introduction to the general features of linear programming, including the form of the model and the solution procedure. The next chapter considers several special types of linear programming problems whose importance warrants individual study. Chapter 4 then concentrates on the application of linear programming, including more difficult formulation problems and sensitivity analysis. Relatively technical topics are reserved for Chap. 16. You can also look forward to seeing applications of linear programming to other areas of operations research in several other chapters.

We begin this chapter by developing a miniature prototype example of a linear programming problem. This example is small enough so that it can be solved graphically in a straightforward way. After presenting the general linear programming model and some additional examples, we shall then use this same prototype example to illustrate the principles and mechanics of the general solution procedure for linear programming (called the *simplex method*).

2.1 PROTOTYPE EXAMPLE

The *Wyndor Glass Co.* is a producer of high-quality glass products, including windows and glass doors. It has three plants. Aluminum frames and hardware are made in Plant 1, wood frames are made in Plant 2 and Plant 3 is used to produce the glass and assemble the products.

Because of declining earnings, top management has decided to revamp the product line. Several unprofitable products are being discontinued, and this will release production capacity to undertake one or both of two potential new products that have been in demand. One of these proposed products (product 1) is an 8-foot glass door with aluminum framing. The other product (product 2) is a large (4 × 6 foot) double-hung wood-framed window. The Marketing Department has concluded that the company could sell as much of either product as could be produced with the available capacity. However, because both products would be competing for the same production capacity in Plant 3, it is not clear which mix between the two products would be most profitable. Therefore management has asked the Operations Research Department to study this question.

After some investigation the O.R. Department determined (1) the percentage of each plant's production capacity that would be available for these products, (2) the percentages required by each product for each unit produced per minute, and (3) the unit profit for each product. This information is summarized in Table 2.1. Because whatever capacity is used by one product in Plant 3 becomes

Table 2.1 Data for Wyndor Glass Co.

Plant \ Product	Capacity used per unit production rate 1	2	Capacity Available
1	1	0	4
2	0	2	12
3	3	2	18
Unit profit	\$3	\$5	

unavailable for the other, the O.R. Department immediately recognized that this was a linear programming problem of the classic "product mix" type, and they next undertook its formulation and solution.

Formulation as a Linear Programming Problem To formulate the mathematical (linear programming) model for this problem, let x_1 and x_2 represent the number of units of product 1 and 2 produced per minute, and let Z be the resulting contribution to profit per minute. Thus, x_1 and x_2 are the ***decision variables*** for the model, and the objective is to choose their values so as to maximize

$$Z = 3x_1 + 5x_2,$$

subject to the restrictions imposed on their values by the limited plant capacities available. Table 2.1 implies that each unit of product 1 produced per minute would use 1 percent of Plant 1 capacity, whereas only 4 percent is available. This restriction is expressed mathematically by the inequality $x_1 \leq 4$. Similarly, Plant 2 imposes the restriction that $2x_2 \leq 12$. The percentage of Plant 3 capacity consumed by choosing x_1 and x_2 as the new products' production rates would be $3x_1 + 2x_2$. Therefore the mathematical statement of the Plant 3 restriction is $3x_1 + 2x_2 \leq 18$. And because production rates can not be negative, it is necessary to restrict the decision variables to be nonnegative: $x_1 \geq 0$ and $x_2 \geq 0$.

To summarize, in the mathematical language of linear programming the problem is to choose the values of x_1 and x_2 so as to

$$\text{Maximize} \quad Z = 3x_1 + 5x_2,$$

subject to the restrictions

$$\begin{aligned} x_1 \qquad\quad &\leq 4 \\ 2x_2 &\leq 12 \\ 3x_1 + 2x_2 &\leq 18 \end{aligned}$$

and

$$x_1 \geq, \; x_2 \geq 0.$$

(Notice how the layout of the coefficients of x_1 and x_2 in this linear programming model essentially duplicates the information that was summarized in Table 2.1.)

Graphical Solution This very small problem has only two decision variables, and therefore only two "dimensions," so a graphical procedure can be used to solve it. This procedure involves constructing a two-dimensional graph, with x_1 and x_2 as the axes. The first step is to identify the values of (x_1,x_2) that are permitted by the restrictions. This is done by drawing the lines that must border the range of permissible values. To begin, note that the nonnegativity restrictions $x_1 \geq 0$ and $x_2 \geq 0$ require (x_1,x_2) to lie on the positive side of the axes. Next, observe that the restriction $x_1 \leq 4$ means that (x_1,x_2) can not lie to the right of the line $x_1 = 4$. These results are shown in Fig. 2.1, where the shaded area contains the only values of (x_1,x_2) that are still allowed. In a similar fashion, the line $2x_2 = 12$ would be added to the boundary of the permissible region. The final restriction $3x_1 + 2x_2 \leq 18$ requires plotting the points (x_1, x_2) such that $3x_1 + 2x_2 = 18$ (another line) to complete the boundary. (Note that the points such that $3x_1 + 2x_2 \leq 18$ are those which lie underneath the line $3x_1 + 2x_2 = 18$, so this is the limiting line beyond which the inequality ceases to hold.) The resulting region of permissible values of (x_1,x_2) is shown in Fig. 2.2.

The final step is to pick out the point in this region that maximizes the value of $Z = 3x_1 + 5x_2$. This step becomes automatic after a little practice, but to discover the basis for it, it is instructive to proceed by trial and error. Try, for example, $Z = 10 = 3x_1 + 5x_2$ to see if there are any values of (x_1,x_2) in the permissible region that yield a value of Z as large as 10. By drawing the line $3x_1 + 5x_2 = 10$ it is seen that there are many points on this line which lie within the region. Therefore, try a larger value of Z, say, for example, $Z = 20 = 3x_1 + 5x_2$.

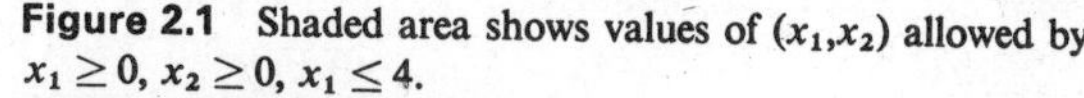

Figure 2.1 Shaded area shows values of (x_1,x_2) allowed by $x_1 \geq 0$, $x_2 \geq 0$, $x_1 \leq 4$.

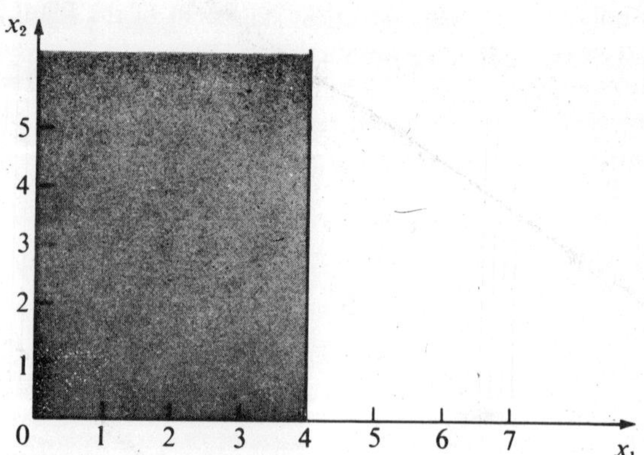

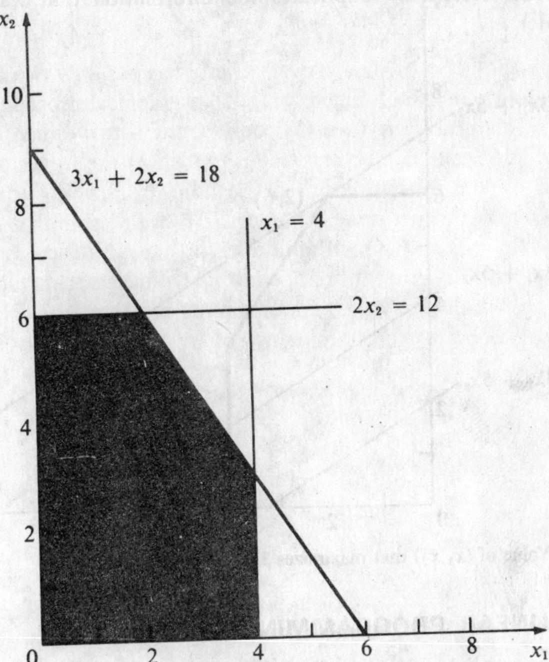

Figure 2.2 Shaded area shows permissible values of (x_1,x_2).

Again a segment of the line $3x_1 + 5x_2 = 20$ lies within the region, so that the maximum permissible value of Z must be at least 20. Notice that this line giving a larger value of Z is farther up and away from the origin than the first line and that the two lines are parallel. Thus this trial-and-error procedure involves nothing more than drawing a family of parallel lines[1] containing at least one point in the permissible region and selecting the line that is the greatest distance from the origin (in the direction of increasing values of Z). This line passes through the point (2,6), as indicated in Fig. 2.3, so that the equation is $3x_1 + 5x_2 = 3(2) + 5(6) = 36 = Z$. Hence the desired solution is $x_1 = 2$, $x_2 = 6$, which indicates that the Wyndor Glass Co. should produce products 1 and 2 at the rate of two per minute and six per minute, respectively, with a resulting profitability of \$36/minute. Furthermore, no other mix of the two products would be so profitable—*according to the model.*

At this point the O.R. Department now was ready to evaluate the validity of the model more critically (to be continued in Sec. 2.3) and to perform a sensitivity analysis on the effect of uncertain input data (such as the estimated unit profits) taking on other possible values (to be continued in Sec. 4.3).

[1] After a little practice, a simpler method is to actually draw just *one* of these lines to establish the slope and then to *visually* move this line parallel to itself.

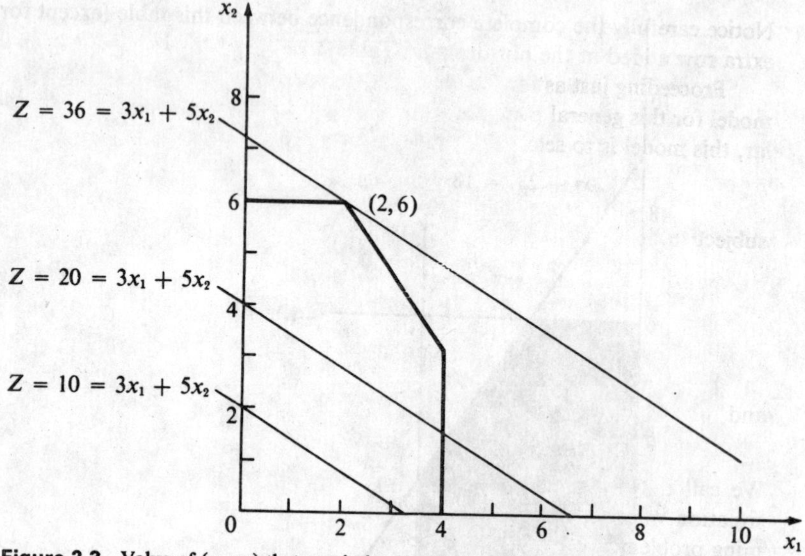

Figure 2.3 Value of (x_1,x_2) that maximizes $3x_1 + 5x_2$.

2.2 THE LINEAR PROGRAMMING MODEL

Let us begin generalizing from the Wyndor Glass Co. problem. In that example there were three limited resources (production capacities at the three plants) to be allocated among two competing activities (the two proposed products). Now suppose that there are any number (call it m) of limited resources of any kind to be allocated among any number (call it n) of competing activities of any kind. Assign number labels to the resources $(1,2, \ldots, m)$ and activities $(1,2, \ldots, n)$. Let x_j be the level of activity j (a decision variable) for $j = 1, 2, \ldots, n$, and let Z be the chosen overall measure of effectiveness. Then let c_j be the increase in Z that would result from each unit increase in x_j (for $j = 1,2, \ldots, n$). Next, let b_i denote the amount of resource i available for allocation (for $i = 1,2, \ldots, m$). Finally, define a_{ij} as the amount of resource i consumed by each unit of activity j (for $i = 1,2, \ldots, m$ and $j = 1,2, \ldots, n$). This set of data is summarized in Table 2.2.

Table 2.2 Data for Linear Programming Model

Activity / *Resource*	*Resource usage/unit* 1	2	$\cdots$	n	*Amount of resource available*
1	a_{11}	a_{12}	$\cdots$	a_{1n}	b_1
2	a_{21}	a_{22}	$\cdots$	a_{2n}	b_2
$\vdots$			$\vdots$		$\vdots$
m	a_{m1}	a_{m2}	$\cdots$	a_{mn}	b_m
ΔZ/*unit*	c_1	c_2	$\cdots$	c_n	
Level	x_1	x_2	$\cdots$	x_n	

Notice carefully the complete correspondence between this table (except for the extra row added at the bottom) and Table 2.1.

Proceeding just as for the example, we can now formulate the mathematical model for this general problem of allocating resources to activities. In particular, this model is to select the values for $x_1, x_2, \ldots, x_n$ so as to

$$\text{Maximize} \quad Z = c_1x_1 + c_2x_2 + \cdots + c_nx_n,$$

subject to the restrictions

$$\begin{aligned} a_{11}x_1 + a_{12}x_2 + \cdots + a_{1n}x_n &\leq b_1 \\ a_{21}x_1 + a_{22}x_2 + \cdots + a_{2n}x_n &\leq b_2 \\ &\vdots \\ a_{m1}x_1 + a_{m2}x_2 + \cdots + a_{mn}x_n &\leq b_m, \end{aligned}$$

and

$$x_1 \geq 0, x_2 \geq 0, \ldots, x_n \geq 0.$$

We call this *our standard form*[1] for the linear programming problem. Any situation whose mathematical formulation fits this model is a linear programming problem.

Common terminology for the linear programming model can now be summarized. The function being maximized, $c_1x_1 + c_2x_2 + \cdots + c_nx_n$, is called the *objective function*. The restrictions also are referred to as *constraints*. The first m constraints (those with a function $a_{i1}x_1 + a_{i2}x_2 + \cdots + a_{in}x_n$, representing the total usage of resource i, on the left) are sometimes called *functional constraints*. Similarly, the $x_j \geq 0$ restrictions are called *nonnegativity constraints*. As mentioned, the x_j variables are decision variables. The input constants—the a_{ij}, b_i, and c_j—may be referred to as *parameters* of the model.

We now hasten to add that the above model does not actually (immediately) fit all linear programming problems. The other *legitimate forms* are the following:

1. Minimizing rather than maximizing the objective function:

$$\text{Minimize} \quad Z = c_1x_1 + c_2x_2 + \cdots + c_nx_n,$$

2. Some functional constraints with a greater-than-or-equal-to inequality:

$$a_{i1}x_1 + a_{i2}x_2 + \cdots + a_{in}x_n \geq b_i, \text{ for some values of } i,$$

3. Some functional constraints in equation form:

$$a_{i1}x_1 + a_{i2}x_2 + \cdots + a_{in}x_n = b_i, \text{ for some values of } i,$$

4. Deleting the nonnegativity constraints for some decision variables:

$$x_j \text{ unrestricted in sign, for some values of } j.$$

Any problem that mixes some or all of these forms with the remaining parts of the above model is still a linear programming problem as long as they are the *only* new forms introduced. Our interpretation of allocating *limited resources* among competing activities may no longer apply very well, but regardless of the

[1] This is called *our* standard form rather than *the* standard form because some textbooks adopt other forms.

interpretation or context, all that is required is that the mathematical statement of the problem fit the allowable forms.

Later in the chapter (Sec. 2.10) we shall see that all these other four legitimate forms can be rewritten in an equivalent way to fit the above model. Thus every linear programming problem can be put into our standard form if so desired. We shall take advantage of this fact everywhere that procedures for solving linear programming problems are discussed (except Sec. 2.10) by assuming the problems are in our standard form.

(We recommend that you reread this section to review the symbols and terminology because they will be used frequently hereafter without redefinition.)

2.3 ASSUMPTIONS OF LINEAR PROGRAMMING

All the assumptions of linear programming actually are implicit in the model formulation given above. However, it is well to highlight these assumptions so you can more easily evaluate how well linear programming applies to any given problem. Furthermore, we still need to see why the O.R. Department of the Wyndor Glass Co. concluded that a linear programming formulation provided a satisfactory representation of their problem.

Proportionality

To explain the assumption of proportionality, consider the case where only one of the n activities is undertaken. Call it activity k, so that $x_j = 0$ for all $j = 1, 2, \ldots, n$ except $j = k$.

The assumption is that in this case (1) the measure of effectiveness Z equals $c_k x_k$, and (2) the usage of each resource i equals $a_{ik} x_k$; that is, both quantities are directly *proportional* to the level of each activity k conducted by itself ($k = 1,2, \ldots, n$). This implies that there is no extra start-up charge with beginning the activity and that the proportionality holds over the entire range of levels of the activity.

We shall see in Sec. 4.1 that a certain important kind of nonproportionality actually can still be handled by linear programming by reformulating the problem appropriately. Another approach to the case where there are start-up charges is given in Sec. 17.5 (the fixed-charge problem).

In the Wyndor Glass Co. problem there is actually an extra cost associated with arranging the distribution of each new product introduced. Thus the objective function $Z = 3x_1 + 5x_2$ should have this cost (amortized on a per minute basis) subtracted for each product j such that $x_j > 0$ (but not when $x_j = 0$). However, this cost spread over the life of the product was too negligible to warrant inclusion in the model. It was noted also that for each product production efficiency would increase slightly at higher production rates, thereby increasing the marginal unit profit and decreasing the usage of production capacity per unit increase in production rate. Nevertheless, it was concluded that, for practical purposes, proportionality could be assumed without serious distortion.

Additivity

The proportionality assumption is not enough to guarantee that the objective function and constraint functions are linear. "Cross-product terms" will arise if there are interactions between some of the activities that would change the total measure of effectiveness or the total usage of some resource. Therefore the additivity assumption requires that, given any activity levels $(x_1, x_2, \ldots, x_n)$, the total usage of each resource and the resulting total measure of effectiveness equal the *sum* of the corresponding quantities generated by each activity conducted by itself. (Models involving nonlinear functions are in the realm of *nonlinear programming*, which is discussed in Chap. 18.)

In the Wyndor Glass Co. problem, the two proposed new products would not be competitive, so profits would not be reduced by marketing both of them. They sometimes could be shipped together from Plant 3 to the same distributor, but this would be a very minor cost savings. On the production side, facilities reserved for one product might occasionally be used for the other product during otherwise idle periods, but this again was too negligible a factor to include in the model.

Divisibility

Sometimes the decision variables would have physical significance only if they have integer values. However, the solution obtained by linear programming often is not integer. Therefore, the divisibility assumption is that activity units can be *divided* into any fractional levels, so that noninteger values for the decision variables are permissible.

Frequently linear programming is still applied even when an integer solution is required. If the solution obtained is not integer, then the noninteger variables are merely rounded to integer values. This may be satisfactory, particularly if the decision variables are large, but it does have certain pitfalls, which we discuss at the beginning of Chap. 17. If this approach can not be used, then we are in the realm of *integer linear programming*, which is the topic of Chap. 17. However, it should be noted that linear programming *automatically* will obtain integer solutions to certain special types of problems, including some of those discussed in Chap. 3.

For the Wyndor Glass Co. problem, the decision variables represent production rates, which can have fractional values. Certain fractional values correspond to integer numbers of men and machines working fulltime on the product and so are more convenient than other values. However, the O.R. Dept. concluded that these minor adjustments could be made easily after using the model to analyze the big picture and identify approximately what the combination of production rates should be.

Deterministic

The deterministic assumption is that all the parameters of the model (the a_{ij}, q_i, and c_j values) are known constants. In real problems this assumption is seldom satisfied precisely. Linear programming models usually are formulated in order to select some future course of action. Therefore the parameters used would be based on a prediction of future conditions, which inevitably introduces some degree of uncertainty.

For this reason it usually is important to conduct a thorough sensitivity analysis after finding the linear programming solution with the assumed parameter values. The general purpose is to identify the relatively sensitive parameters (i.e., those that can not be changed much without changing the solution), to try to estimate these more closely, and then to select a solution which remains a good one over the ranges of likely values of the sensitive parameters. This is what the O.R. Department did for the Wyndor Glass Co. problem, as you will see in Sec. 4.3. However, it is necessary to acquire some more background before finishing that story. (Occasionally the degree of uncertainty in some parameters is so great that it is necessary to treat them as random variables. Formulations of this kind have been developed but are beyond the scope of this book.)

As you work through the examples in the next section, you will find it good practice to analyze how well each of the above assumptions applies to these problems.

2.4 ADDITIONAL EXAMPLES

The Wyndor Glass Co. problem is a prototype example of linear programming in several respects: It involves allocating limited resources among competing activities, its model fits our standard form, and its context is the traditional one of improved business planning. However, the applicability of linear programming is much wider. In this section we begin broadening our horizons. As you study the following examples, note that it is their underlying mathematical model rather than their context which characterize them as linear programming problems. Then give some thought as to how the same mathematical model could arise in many other contexts by merely changing the names of the activities, and so forth.

These examples have been kept very small (by linear programming standards) for ease of reading. However, much larger versions of the problems, involving hundreds of constraints and variables, are readily solvable by linear programming.

Regional Planning

One of the interesting social experiments in the Mediterranean region is the system of kibbutzim, or communal farming communities, in Israel. It is common for groups of kibbutzim to join together to share common technical services and to coordinate their production. Our first example concerns one such group of three kibbutzim, which we call the *Southern Confederation of Kibbutzim*.

Overall planning for the Southern Confederation of Kibbutzim is done in its Coordinating Technical Office. This office currently is planning agricultural production for the coming year.

The agricultural output of each kibbutz is limited by both the amount of available irrigable land and by the quantity of water allocated for irrigation by the Water Commissioner (a national government official). These data are given in Table 2.3.

Table 2.3 Resources Data for Southern Confederation of Kibbutzim

Kibbutz	*Usable land (acres)*	*Water allocation (acre feet)*
1	400	600
2	600	800
3	300	375

The crops suited for this region include sugar beets, cotton, and sorghum and are the only ones being considered for the upcoming season. These crops differ primarily in their expected net return per acre and their consumption of water. In addition, the Ministry of Agriculture has set a maximum quota for the total acreage than can be devoted to each of these crops by the Southern Confederation of Kibbutzim, as shown in Table 2.4.

Table 2.4 Crop Data for Southern Confederation of Kibbutzim

Crop	*Maximum quota (acres)*	*Water consumption (acre feet/acre)*	*Net return (dollars/acre)*
Sugar beets	600	3	400
Cotton	500	2	300
Sorghum	325	1	100

The three kibbutzim belonging to the Southern Confederation have agreed that every kibbutz will plant the same proportion of its available irrigable land. However, any combination of the crops may be grown at any of the kibbutzim. The job facing the Coordinating Technical Office is to plan how many acres to devote to each crop at the respective kibbutzim while satisfying the above restrictions. The objective is to maximize the total net return to the Southern Confederation as a whole.

Formulation as a Linear Programming Problem The quantities to be decided upon are the number of acres to devote to each of the three crops at each of the three kibbutzim. The decision variables x_j ($j = 1,2, \ldots, 9$) represent these nine quantities, as shown in Table 2.5.

Table 2.5 Decision Variables for Southern Confederation of Kibbutzim Problem

Crop \ Kibbutz	Allocation (acres) 1	2	3
Sugar beets	x_1	x_2	x_3
Cotton	x_4	x_5	x_6
Sorghum	x_7	x_8	x_9

Since the measure of effectiveness Z is total net return, the resulting linear programming model for this problem is

Maximize $Z = 400(x_1 + x_2 + x_3) + 300(x_4 + x_5 + x_6) + 100(x_7 + x_8 + x_9)$,

subject to the following constraints:

1. *Land:*

$$x_1 + x_4 + x_7 \leq 400$$
$$x_2 + x_5 + x_8 \leq 600$$
$$x_3 + x_6 + x_9 \leq 300$$

2. *Water:*

$$3x_1 + 2x_4 + x_7 \leq 600$$
$$3x_2 + 2x_5 + x_8 \leq 800$$
$$3x_3 + 2x_6 + x_9 \leq 375$$

3. *Crop:*

$$x_1 + x_2 + x_3 \leq 600$$
$$x_4 + x_5 + x_6 \leq 500$$
$$x_7 + x_8 + x_9 \leq 325$$

4. *Social:*

$$\frac{x_1 + x_4 + x_7}{400} = \frac{x_2 + x_5 + x_8}{600}$$
$$\frac{x_2 + x_5 + x_8}{600} = \frac{x_3 + x_6 + x_9}{300}$$
$$\frac{x_3 + x_6 + x_9}{300} = \frac{x_1 + x_4 + x_7}{400}$$

and

5. *Nonnegativity:*

$$x_j \geq 0, \text{ for } j = 1, 2, \ldots, 9.$$

This completes the model, except that the social constraints are not yet in an appropriate form for a linear programming model because some of the variables are on the right-hand side. Hence their final form[1] is

4. *Social:*

$$3(x_1 + x_4 + x_7) - 2(x_2 + x_5 + x_8) = 0$$

$$x_2 + x_5 + x_8 - 2(x_3 + x_6 + x_9) = 0$$

$$4(x_3 + x_6 + x_9) - 3(x_1 + x_4 + x_7) = 0.$$

The Coordinating Technical Office formulated this model and then applied the simplex method (developed in the following sections) to find the best solution. The solution they obtained is

$$(x_1, x_2, x_3, x_4, x_5, x_6, x_7, x_8, x_9) = (133\tfrac{1}{3}, 100, 25, 100, 250, 150, 0, 0, 0),$$

as shown in Table 2.6.

Table 2.6 Optimal Solution for Southern Confederation of Kibbutzim Problem

Crop \ Kibbutz	Best allocation (acres) 1	2	3
Sugar beets	133⅓	100	25
Cotton	100	250	150
Sorghum	0	0	0

The above example illustrates, among other things, how equality constraints can arise naturally in linear programming problems. One feature of the next example is the inclusion of two other nonstandard forms in the model, namely (1) minimizing the objective function and (2) functional constraints with $\geq$ inequalities.

Controlling Air Pollution

The Nori & Leets Co., one of the major producers of steel in its part of the world, is located in the city of Steeltown and is the only large employer there. Steeltown has grown and prospered along with the company, which now employs nearly 50,000 residents. Therefore the attitude of the townspeople always has been "What's good for Nori & Leets is good for the town." However, this is now changing; uncontrolled air pollution from the company's furnaces is ruining the appearance of the city and endangering the health of its residents.

[1] Actually, any one of these equations is redundant and can be deleted if desired. Because of these equations, any two of the land constraints also could be deleted.

A recent stockholders' revolt resulted in the election of a new enlightened Board of Directors for the company. These directors are determined to follow socially responsible policies, and they have been discussing with Steeltown city officials and citizens' groups what to do about the air pollution problem. Together they have worked out stringent air quality standards for the Steeltown airshed.

The three main types of pollutants in this airshed are particulate matter, sulfur oxides, and hydrocarbons. The new standards require that the company reduce its annual emission of these pollutants by the amounts shown in Table 2.7.

Table 2.7 Clean Air Standards for Nori & Leets Co.

Pollutant	*Required reduction in annual emission rate (million pounds)*
Particulates	60
Sulfur oxides	150
Hydrocarbons	125

The Board of Directors has instructed management to have the engineering staff determine how to achieve these reductions in the most economical way.

The steel works has two primary sources of pollution, namely, the blast furnaces for making pig iron and the open-hearth furnaces for changing iron into steel. In both cases the engineers have decided that the most effective types of abatement methods are (1) increasing the height of the smoke stacks, (2) using filter devices (including gas traps) in the smoke stacks, and (3) including cleaner high-grade materials among the fuels for the furnaces. All these methods have technological limits on how much emission they can eliminate, as shown (in millions of pounds per year) in Table 2.8.

Table 2.8 Reduction in Emission Rate from Maximum Feasible Use of Abatement Method for Nori & Leets Co.

	Taller smoke stacks		*Filters*		*Better fuels*	
Pollutant	*Blast furnaces*	*Open-hearth furnaces*	*Blast furnaces*	*Open-hearth furnaces*	*Blast furnaces*	*Open-hearth furnaces*
Particulates	12	9	25	20	17	13
Sulfur oxides	35	42	18	31	56	49
Hydrocarbons	37	53	28	24	29	20

However, the methods can be used at any fraction of their abatement capacities shown in this table. Because they operate independently, the emission reduction achieved by each method are not substantially affected by whether or not the other methods also are used.

After these data were developed, it became clear that no single method by itself can achieve all the required reductions. On the other hand, combining all three methods at full capacity (which would be prohibitively expensive if the company's products are to remain competitively priced) is much more than adequate. Therefore the engineers concluded that they would have to use some combination of the methods, perhaps with fractional capacities, based upon their relative costs. Furthermore, because of the differences between the blast and the open-hearth furnaces the two types probably should not use the same combination.

An analysis was conducted to estimate the total annual cost that would be incurred by each abatement method. In addition to increased operating and maintenance expenses, consideration was given also to the initial costs (converted to an equivalent annual basis) of the method as well as any resulting loss in efficiency of the production process. This analysis led to the total cost estimates (in millions of dollars) given in Table 2.9 for using the methods at their full abatement capacities.

Table 2.9 Total Annual Cost from Maximum Feasible Use of Abatement Method for Nori & Leets Co.

Abatement method	*Blast furnaces*	*Open-hearth furnaces*
Taller smoke stacks	8	10
Filters	7	6
Better fuels	11	9

It also was determined that the cost of lesser uses of a method is essentially proportional to its fractional capacity. Thus, for any given fraction used the total annual cost would be that fraction of the corresponding quantity in Table 2.9.

The stage now was set to develop the general framework of the company's plan for pollution abatement. This would consist of specifying which types of abatement methods would be used and at what fractions of their abatement capacities for (1) the blast furnaces and (2) the open-hearth furnaces. (Details on the individual methods can be worked out later.) Because of the combinatorial nature of the problem of finding which plan satisfies the requirements with the smallest possible cost, an operations research team was formed to solve it. The team adopted a linear programming approach, formulating the model summarized below.

FORMULATION AS A LINEAR PROGRAMMING PROBLEM This problem has six decision variables x_j ($j = 1,2, \ldots, 6$), each representing the usage of one of the three abatement methods for one of the two types of furnaces, expressed as a fraction of the abatement capacity. The ordering of these variables is shown in Table 2.10.

Table 2.10 Decision Variables (Fraction of Maximum Feasible Use of Abatement Method) for Nori & Leets Co.

Abatement method	*Blast furnaces*	*Open-hearth furnaces*
Taller smoke stacks	x_1	x_2
Filters	x_3	x_4
Better fuels	x_5	x_6

Because the objective is to minimize total cost while satisfying the emission reduction requirements, the model is

$$\text{Minimize} \quad Z = 8x_1 + 10x_2 + 7x_3 + 6x_4 + 11x_5 + 9x_6,$$

subject to the following constraints:

1. *Emission reduction:*

$$12x_1 + 9x_2 + 25x_3 + 20x_4 + 17x_5 + 13x_6 \geq 60$$
$$35x_1 + 42x_2 + 18x_3 + 31x_4 + 56x_5 + 49x_6 \geq 150$$
$$37x_1 + 53x_2 + 28x_3 + 24x_4 + 29x_5 + 20x_6 \geq 125$$

2. *Technological:*

$$x_j \leq 1, \text{ for } j = 1, 2, \ldots, 6$$

and

3. *Nonnegativity:*

$$x_j \geq 0, \text{ for } j = 1, 2, \ldots, 6.$$

The operations research team used this model[1] to find the minimum cost plan $(x_1, x_2, x_3, x_4, x_5, x_6) = (1, 0.623, 0.343, 1, 0.048, 1)$. Sensitivity analysis then was conducted, followed by detailed planning and managerial review. Soon after, this program for controlling air pollution was fully implemented by the company, and the citizens of Steeltown breathed deep sighs of relief.

Other Examples

The three linear programming examples you have seen so far are but a small sampling of the uses of this technique. Many more illustrations are given in the following two chapters; most involve business and industrial applications, but several others arise in different contexts. Chapter 3 focuses on special classes of linear programming problems that provide many important applications. Chapter 4 considers some examples that are more difficult to formulate, and it

[1] Another equivalent formulation is to express each decision variable in natural units for its abatement method; for example, x_1 and x_2 could represent the number of *feet* that the heights of the smoke stacks are increased.

also includes a case study involving the design of school attendance zones to achieve better racial balance. But before considering these topics, we next discuss how to solve linear programming problems.

2.5 PRINCIPLES OF THE SIMPLEX METHOD

We now are ready to begin studying the *simplex method*, the general procedure for solving linear programming problems. This is a remarkably efficient method that is routinely used to solve huge problems on today's computers. (Details on its computational capabilities are presented in Sec. 4.2) A computer always is used, except for very small problems, and codes are widely available. Nevertheless, it is important to learn something about how the method works in order to properly interpret the form of the final solution and, even more importantly, to understand how to perform sensitivity analysis on the model. Furthermore, the simplex method provides an excellent illustration of the *algorithms* (iterative solution procedures) that are so prevalent in operations research work.

In this section we concentrate on the principles underlying the simplex method, deferring details to later in the chapter. Because geometrical interpretation is emphasized, the graphical solution to the Wyndor Glass Co. example (Sec. 2.1) is used to illustrate general concepts. Thus we discuss the decision variables $(x_1, x_2, \ldots, x_n)$ for any linear programming problem while illustrating in two dimensions with the decision variables (x_1, x_2) for the Wyndor Glass Co. problem. To refresh your memory, the graph for this example is repeated in Fig. 2.4. The five constraint lines and their points of intersection are highlighted in this figure because they are the keys to the analysis. We begin by introducing some basic terminology for linear programming.

Figure 2.4 **Constraint lines for the Wyndor Glass Co. problem.**

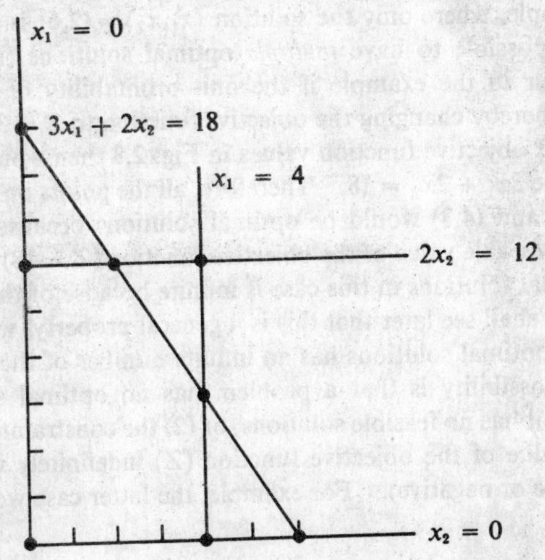

Terminology

You may be used to having the term **solution** mean the final answer to a problem, but the convention in linear programming (and its extensions) is quite different. Here, *any* specification of values for the decision variables ($x_1, x_2, \ldots, x_n$) is called a solution, regardless of whether it is a desirable or even an allowable choice. Different types of solutions are then identified by using an appropriate adjective, as you will see below.

A **feasible solution** is a solution for which *all* the constraints are satisfied.

In the example, the feasible solutions are the points within or on the boundary of the shaded area (sometimes called *feasible region*) in Fig. 2.4. Thus (2,3) and (4,1) are feasible solutions, but (−1,3) and (4,4) are *infeasible* solutions.

It is possible for a problem to have no feasible solutions. This would have happened in the example if the new products had been required to return a net profit of at least $50/minute to justify discontinuing part of the current product line. The corresponding constraint $3x_1 + 5x_2 \geq 50$ would eliminate the entire feasible region, so no mix of new products would be superior to the status quo.

Given that there are feasible solutions, the goal of linear programming is to find which one is "best," as measured by the value of the objective function in the model.

An **optimal solution** is a feasible solution that has the most favorable value of the objective function.

By most favorable value is meant the largest or smallest value, depending upon whether the objective is maximization or minimization. Thus an optimal solution maximizes/minimizes the objective function over the entire feasible region.

Frequently a problem will have just one optimal solution. This was the case in the example, where only the solution $(x_1,x_2) = (2,6)$ is optimal. However, it is also possible to have *multiple* optimal solutions (more than one). This would occur in the example if the unit profitability of product 2 were changed to $2, thereby changing the objective function to $Z = 3x_1 + 2x_2$. The lines for constant objective function values in Fig. 2.3 then would be parallel to the constraint line $3x_1 + 2x_2 = 18$. Therefore, all the points on the line segment connecting (2,6) and (4,3) would be optimal solutions because they all would have the most favorable value of the objective function ($Z = 18$). Note that the number of optimal solutions in this case is infinite because of the assumption of divisibility. We shall see later that this is a general property, viz., any problem having multiple optimal solutions has an infinite number of them.

The third possibility is that a problem has no optimal solutions. This occurs only if (1) it has no feasible solutions, or (2) the constraints do not prevent increasing the value of the objective function (Z) indefinitely in the favorable direction (positive or negative). For example, the latter case would result if the last two functional constraints were mistakenly deleted in the example. A discussion of how the simplex method identifies these unusual cases is included in Secs. 2.9 (for case 2) and 2.10 (for case 1); we assume until then that they do not arise.

It is very useful to identify the general characteristics of optimal solutions to narrow down the search for them. First, it may be quite intuitive to you from Fig. 2.3 that optimal solutions must lie on the boundary of the feasible region, and this is in fact a general property. We shall be able to say much more than this later, but let us begin here.

> The **boundary equation** for any constraint is obtained by replacing its $\leq$, $=$, or $\geq$ sign by an $=$ sign.

Thus the boundary equations for the five constraints of the example are the equations given for the five lines in Fig. 2.4. In general, the form of a constraint boundary equation is $a_{i1}x_1 + a_{i2}x_2 + \cdots + a_{in}x_n = b_i$ for functional constraints and $x_j = 0$ for nonnegativity constraints. These equations define a "flat" geometrical shape (called a *hyperplane*) in n-dimensional space analogous to the line in two-dimensional space and the plane in three-dimensional space. Thus our first conclusion is that the *boundary* of the feasible region consists of those feasible solutions which satisfy one or more of the constraint boundary equations (i.e., which lie on one or more of the bounding hyperplanes) and that the optimal solution(s) must be among them.

You may have noticed in the example that the optimal solution was not only on the boundary of the feasible region but that it also was at a corner of this region. This is no coincidence, as you will soon see, but first we must define what these corners are in n-dimensional space.

> A **corner-point feasible solution** is a feasible solution that does not lie on *any* line segment[1] connecting two *other* feasible solutions.

Thus (0,0), (0,6), (2,6), (4,3), and (4,0) are corner-point feasible solutions in the example. (Convince yourself of this by trying to draw line segments that work.) However, these are the only corner-point feasible solutions. For example, the solution (2,3) lies on the line segment between many pairs of feasible solutions, such as (1,4) and (3,2), and the solution (0,5) lies on the line segment between such pairs as (0,3) and (0,6).

With n decision variables ($n > 3$), this definition is not very convenient for identifying corner-point feasible solutions. Therefore it will prove most helpful to interpret them algebraically. In the example, each corner-point feasible solution lies at the intersection of two ($n = 2$) constraint lines; i.e., it is the *simultaneous solution* of a system of two constraint boundary equations. This is summarized in Table 2.11, where *defining equations* refer to the constraint boundary equations that yield (define) the indicated corner-point feasible solution.

[1] A formal definition of line segment is given in Appendix 1.

Table 2.11 Corner-point Feasible Solutions for Wyndor Glass Co. Problem

Corner-point feasible solution	*Defining equations*
(0,0)	$x_1 = 0$ $x_2 = 0$
(0,6)	$x_1 = 0$ $2x_2 = 12$
(2,6)	$2x_2 = 12$ $3x_1 + 2x_2 = 18$
(4,3)	$3x_1 + 2x_2 = 18$ $x_1 = 4$
(4,0)	$x_1 = 4$ $x_2 = 0$

Similarly, for any linear programming problem each corner-point feasible solution lies at the intersection of n constraint boundaries; i.e., it is the *simultaneous solution* of a system of n constraint boundary equations. However, this is not to say that *every* set of n boundary equations chosen from among the $(n + m)$ constraints yields a corner-point feasible solution. In particular, the simultaneous solution to such a system of equations might violate one or more of the other m constraints, in which case it is a corner-point *infeasible* solution. The example has three such solutions, as summarized in Table 2.12. (Check to see why they are infeasible.)

Table 2.12 Corner-point Infeasible Solutions for Wyndor Glass Co. Problem

Corner-point infeasible solution	*Defining equations*
(0,9)	$x_1 = 0$ $3x_1 + 2x_2 = 18$
(4,6)	$2x_2 = 12$ $x_1 = 4$
(6,0)	$3x_1 + 2x_2 = 18$ $x_2 = 0$

Furthermore, a system of n constraint boundary equations might have no solution at all. This occurs twice in the example with the pairs of equations (1) $x_1 = 0$ and $x_1 = 4$; (2) $x_2 = 0$ and $2x_2 = 12$. Such systems are of no interest to us. The final possibility (which never occurs in the example) is that a system has multiple solutions because of redundant equations. You need not be concerned with this case either because the simplex method circumvents its difficulties.

We need just one more definition to identify convenient groupings of corner-point feasible solutions for the simplex method:

Two corner-point feasible solutions are said to be **adjacent** if the line segment connecting them lies on (an edge of)[1] the boundary of the feasible region.

Thus, in the example the pairs of adjacent corner-point feasible solutions are (0,0) and (0,6); (0,6) and (2,6); (2,6) and (4,3); (4,3) and (4,0); and lastly, (4,0) and (0,0). The algebraic interpretation of these pairs is suggested by Table 2.11. Notice that in each case just *one* defining equation is different for adjacent corner-point solutions. For example, (0,6) is reached from (0,0) by deleting an intersecting line (defining equation) $x_2 = 0$ and moving away from it in the feasible direction ($x_2 \geq 0$) along the other line $x_1 = 0$ until the *first* new constraint boundary (defining equation) $2x_2 = 12$ is reached. It is important to stop at the first new constraint boundary because continuing on to the next one ($3x_1 + 2x_2 = 18$) yields a corner-point *infeasible* solution (0,9). Similarly, consider the other corner-point feasible solution that is adjacent to (0,0), namely, (4,0). It is reached from (0,0) by deleting the *other* intersecting line (defining equation) $x_1 = 0$ and moving away from it in the feasible direction ($x_1 \geq 0$) along the line $x_2 = 0$ until the *first* new constraint boundary (defining equation) $x_1 = 4$ is reached. Now convince yourself that each of the other corner-point feasible solutions also has two ($n = 2$) adjacent corner-point feasible solutions that are reached by moving away from one of the two constraint boundaries to the first new one.

These same conclusions also apply when $n > 2$. Recall that a corner-point feasible solution lies at the intersection of n constraint boundaries. Suppose that one of these constraint boundaries (defining equations) is deleted. The intersection of the remaining $(n - 1)$ constraint boundaries is a line. One segment of this line lies on the boundary of the feasible region, and the rest of it is not allowed by the other constraints. (The technical term used in the above definition for such a line segment is *edge*.) Now suppose that you move away from the corner-point feasible solution in the feasible direction along this line until the *first* new constraint boundary (defining equation) is reached. This new point is an *adjacent* corner-point feasible solution. Moving beyond it along the line to other new constraint boundaries only would lead to corner-point *infeasible* solutions. Thus a corner-point feasible solution has just n adjacent corner-point feasible solutions, each of which is reached in the fashion just described by deleting one of the n defining equations for this solution and replacing it by the appropriate new defining equation.

Analysis

We shall present now three key properties of corner-point feasible solutions that constitute the underlying principles of the simplex method. The first property relates these solutions to optimal solutions.

[1] This parenthetical phrase can be deleted until the next paragraph, where it is explained when it first becomes relevant.

Property 1 (*a*) If there is exactly one optimal solution, then it *must* be a corner-point feasible solution. (*b*) If there are multiple optimal solutions, then at least two *must* be adjacent corner-point feasible solutions.

The explanation for property 1 is a rather intuitive one. We present it first for case (*a*), which is illustrated by the example, where the one optimal solution (2,6) is indeed a corner-point feasible solution. However, note that there is nothing special about the example that led to this result. For *any* problem having just one optimal solution it always is possible to keep raising the objective function line (hyperplane) until it just touches one point (the optimal solution) at a corner of the feasible region.

The following algebraic viewpoint also clarifies why the property must hold in case (*a*). Let Z^* denote the value of the objective function for the one optimal solution. Now consider the implications if this solution is not a corner-point feasible solution. By definition it must lie on a line segment connecting two other feasible solutions; i.e., it is a weighted average of these other two feasible solutions. Let α $(0 < \alpha < 1)$ and $(1 - \alpha)$ denote the weights on these solutions, and let Z_1 and Z_2 be their values of the objective function. Thus, $Z^* = \alpha Z_1 + (1 - \alpha)Z_2$. Since these weights add up to 1, the only possibilities for how Z^*, Z_1, and Z_2 compare are (1) $Z^* = Z_1 = Z_2$, (2) $Z_1 < Z^* < Z_2$, and (3) $Z_1 > Z^* > Z_2$. The first possibility implies that the other two feasible solutions also are optimal, so there are multiple optimal solutions. Both the latter possibilities imply that the original solution actually is not optimal. The resulting conclusion is that it is impossible to have a single optimal solution which is not a corner-point feasible solution.

Now consider case (*b*), which was demonstrated earlier under the definition of *optimal solution* by changing the objective function in the example to $Z = 3x_1 + 2x_2$. What then happens in the graphical solution procedure is that the objective function line keeps getting raised until it contains the line segment connecting the two corner-point feasible solutions (2,6) and (4,3). The same thing would happen in higher dimensions except that now it would be an objective function *hyperplane* that keeps getting raised until it contains the line segment(s) connecting two (or more) adjacent corner-point feasible solutions. As a consequence, *all* optimal solutions can be obtained as weighted averages of optimal corner-point feasible solutions. (This is described further in Prob. 11 at the end of the chapter.)

The real significance of property 1 is that it greatly simplifies the search for an optimal solution because now only corner-point feasible solutions need be considered. The magnitude of this simplification is emphasized in property 2:

Property 2 There are only a *finite* number of corner-point feasible solutions.

This property certainly holds in the example, where there are just *five* corner-point feasible solutions. To see why the number is finite in general, recall that each corner-point feasible solution is the simultaneous solution of a system of n out of the $(m + n)$ constraint boundary equations. The number of different combinations of $(m + n)$ equations taken n at a time is

$$\frac{(m+n)!}{m!n!},$$

which is a finite number. This number, in turn, is an *upper bound* on the number of corner-point feasible solutions. In the example, $m = 3$ and $n = 2$, so there are 10 different systems of two equations, but only half of them yield corner-point feasible solutions.

Property 2 suggests that an optimal solution can be obtained just by exhaustive enumeration, i.e., find and compare all the finite number of corner-point feasible solutions. Unfortunately, there are finite numbers, and then there are finite numbers that (for all practical purposes) might as well be infinite. For example, a rather small linear programming problem with only $m = 50$ and $n = 50$ would have $(100!)/(50!)^2 \approx 10^{29}$ systems of equations to be solved! By contrast, the simplex method would need only to examine approximately 100 corner-point feasible solutions for a problem of this size. This tremendous saving can be obtained because of property 3:

PROPERTY 3 If a corner-point feasible solution is better[1] (as measured by Z) than all its *adjacent* corner-point feasible solutions, then it is better than all other corner-point feasible solutions (i.e., it is *optimal*).

Each corner-point feasible solution in the example has two adjacent corner-point feasible solutions. In the case of (0,0), where $Z = 0$, both its adjacent corner-point feasible solutions are better—(0,6) with $Z = 30$ and (4,0) with $Z = 12$. Three of the corner-point feasible solutions—(0,6), (4,0) and (4,3)—have one adjacent corner-point feasible solution that is better and one that is worse (check this). But only (2,6), with $Z = 36$, is better than both its adjacent corner-point feasible solutions—(0,6) with $Z = 30$ and (4,3) with $Z = 27$. By properties 3 and 1, this information alone is enough to guarantee that (2,6) is an optimal solution. (The basic reason that property 3 also holds for larger problems is that the feasible region always has the property of being *convex*, as defined in Appendix 1.)

The significance of property 3 is that it provides a convenient test of whether a corner-point feasible solution is optimal without having to enumerate all possible solutions. The simplex method exploits this fact by examining only a relatively few of the promising corner-point feasible solutions and stopping as soon as one passes this test for optimality. In particular, it repeatedly (iteratively) moves from the current corner-point feasible solution to a better adjacent corner-point feasible solution (which can be done very efficiently) until the current solution does not have any better[2] adjacent corner-point feasible solutions. This procedure is now summarized.

Outline of The Simplex Method

Initialization step Start at a corner-point feasible solution.

[1] "Better" can be interpreted either as "strictly better" or "at least as good as."

[2] The term "better" in the following description means "at least as good as."

Iterative step Move to a better adjacent corner-point feasible solution. (Repeat this step as often as needed.)

Stopping rule Stop when the current corner-point feasible solution is better than all its adjacent corner-point feasible solutions. It is an optimal solution.

This is the essence of the simplex method. However, it is helpful to specify a convenient way of choosing the new solution in both the initialization and iterative steps, and you will see in Secs. 2.7 and 2.8 that the complete statement of the simplex method does this. Using these choice rules, the simplex method proceeds as follows in the example:

Initialization step Start at (0,0).

Iteration 1 Move from (0,0) to (0,6).

Iteration 2 Move from (0,6) to (2,6).

Stopping rule (2,6) is better than both (0,6) and (4,3), so stop. (2,6) is optimal.

Even though the simplex method succeeds in this example, it may not yet be clear to you that it must eventually find an optimal solution for every linear programming problem that has one (or more). (Think about this before reading on.) The reasons this can be guaranteed are the following. First, because of properties 1 and 3, there is an optimal solution that is a corner-point feasible solution, but the stopping rule never stops the algorithm until such a solution is reached, and then it always stops it. Second, since the iterative step always moves to a better corner-point feasible solution, so the value of the objective function is continually improving, the algorithm can never repeat a corner-point feasible solution that has already been examined at a previous iteration.[1] Thus it keeps looking at *new* corner-point feasible solutions until an optimal one is found, so the number of iterations must be smaller than the number of corner-point feasible solutions. Third, because of property 2, the number of corner-point feasible solutions is finite. Therefore the simplex method must find an optimal solution in a *finite* number of iterations.

We commented earlier that just being finite is not very reassuring. The real key to the success of the simplex method is that it requires only a relatively small finite number of iterations. No mathematical proof can be offered for this—just the consistent results of more than two decades of solving real problems.

2.6 SETTING UP THE SIMPLEX METHOD

The preceding section stressed the geometrical concepts underlying the simplex method. However, this algorithm normally is run on a computer, which can follow only algebraic instructions. Therefore it is necessary to translate the

[1] The one possible exception is if the iterative step moves to an adjacent corner-point feasible solution that is equally as good as, but not strictly better than, the current corner-point feasible solution, so the value of the objective function stays the same. The fact that this technical point does not invalidate our conclusions here is discussed in Sec. 2.9.

conceptually geometrical procedure described above into a usable algebraic procedure. In this section we introduce the algebraic language of the simplex method and relate it to the concepts of the preceding section.

In an algebraic procedure it is much more convenient to deal with equations than inequality relationships. Therefore the first step in setting up the simplex method is to convert the functional inequality constraints into equivalent equality constraints. (The nonnegativity constraints can be left as inequalities because they are only used indirectly by the algorithm.) This is done by introducing **slack variables**. To illustrate, consider the first functional constraint in the example

$$x_1 \le 4.$$

The slack variable for this constraint is

$$x_3 = 4 - x_1,$$

which is just the slack between the two sides of the inequality. Thus

$$x_1 + x_3 = 4.$$

The original constraint $x_1 \le 4$ holds whenever $x_3 \ge 0$. Hence $x_1 \le 4$ is entirely *equivalent* to the set of constraints

$$x_1 + x_3 = 4$$

and

$$x_3 \ge 0,$$

so these more convenient constraints are used instead.

By introducing slack variables in an identical fashion for the other functional constraints, the original linear programming model for the example can now be replaced by the *equivalent* model

$$\text{Maximize} \quad Z = 3x_1 + 5x_2,$$

subject to

$$\begin{aligned}
&(1) \quad x_1 \quad\quad + x_3 \quad\quad\quad = 4\\
&(2) \quad\quad 2x_2 \quad + x_4 \quad = 12\\
&(3) \quad 3x_1 + 2x_2 \quad\quad + x_5 = 18
\end{aligned}$$

and

$$x_j \ge 0, \text{ for } j = 1, 2, \ldots, 5.$$

Although this problem is identical to the original, this form is much more convenient for algebraic manipulation and for identification of corner-point feasible solutions.

For any linear programming problem in our standard form,[1] the appearance

[1] The following discussion and definitions assume that nonstandard forms have been converted into our standard form, except that equality constraints may be retained as is without slack variables. In this case, what will be called defining variables are deleted for these equality constraints.

of the functional constraints after converting them into equality form is as follows:

$$
\begin{array}{lll}
(1) & a_{11}x_1 + a_{12}x_2 + \cdots + a_{1n}x_n + x_{n+1} & = b_1 \\
(2) & a_{21}x_1 + a_{22}x_2 + \cdots + a_{2n}x_n \qquad + x_{n+2} & = b_2 \\
 & \vdots & \\
(m) & a_{m1}x_1 + a_{m2}x_2 + \cdots + a_{mn}x_n \qquad\qquad + x_{n+m} & = b_m,
\end{array}
$$

where $x_{n+1}, x_{n+2}, \ldots, x_{n+m}$ are the slack variables. We call this the "equality form" of the problem, as opposed to the original "inequality form," in order to introduce the following definition:

> An **augmented solution** is a solution for the problem in inequality form $(x_1, x_2, \ldots, x_n)$ that has been augmented by the corresponding values of the slack variables $(x_{n+1}, x_{n+2}, \ldots, x_{n+m})$ for the problem in equality form, yielding $(x_1, x_2, \ldots, x_{n+m})$.

For example, augmenting the solution (3,2) in the example yields the augmented solution (3,2,1,8,5) because the corresponding values of the slack variables are $x_3 = 1$, $x_4 = 8$, $x_5 = 5$.

> **A basic solution** is an *augmented* corner-point solution.[1]

To illustrate, consider the corner-point (infeasible) solution (4,6) in the example. Augmenting it with the resulting values of the slack variables $x_3 = 0$, $x_4 = 0$, $x_5 = -6$ yields the corresponding basic solution $(4,6,0,0,-6)$. Basic solutions are allowed to be either feasible or infeasible, which implies the following definition:

> **A basic feasible solution** is an *augmented* corner-point feasible solution.

Thus the corner-point feasible solution (0,6) in the example is equivalent to the basic feasible solution (0,6,4,0,6) for the problem in equality form.

Since the terms *basic solution* and *basic feasible solution* are very important parts of the standard vocabulary of linear programming, we now need to clarify their algebraic properties. Recall that each corner-point solution is the simultaneous solution of a system of n constraint boundary equations, which we called its *defining equations*. The key question is "How do we tell whether a particular constraint boundary equation is one of the defining equations when the problem is in equality form?" The answer, fortunately, is a simple one. Since there now are $(n + m)$ variables, one for each of the $(n + m)$ constraints,[2] each constraint has exactly one variable which completely indicates (by whether its value is zero) whether or not that constraint's boundary equation is satisfied by the current solution. This is summarized in Table 2.13.

[1] When the problem includes equality constraints, the basic solutions are just the augmented corner-point solutions that satisfy all these constraints.

[2] These constraints consist of the m *functional* constraints and the n *nonnegativity* constraints on the original n variables.

Table 2.13 Indicating Variables for Constraint Boundary Equations

Constraint boundary equation	*Indicating variable*
$x_j = 0$	x_j
$a_{i1}x_1 + a_{i2}x_2 + \cdots + a_{in}x_n = b_i$	x_{n+i}

Variable $= 0 \Rightarrow$ equation satisfied
Variable $\neq 0 \Rightarrow$ equation violated

Thus, whenever a constraint boundary equation is one of the defining equations for a corner-point solution, its indicating variable has a value of zero in the equality form of the problem. For each defining equation for a corner-point solution, we thereby call its indicating variable a **defining variable** for the corresponding basic solution. The resulting conclusions and terminology are summarized below.

> Each **basic solution** has *n defining variables* (conventionally called **nonbasic variables**) set equal to zero. The values of the remaining *m* variables (called **basic variables**) are the simultaneous solution of the system of *m* equations for the problem in equality form (after setting the nonbasic variables to zero). This basic solution is the augmented corner-point solution whose *n defining equations* are those indicated by the defining variables.

Now consider the basic *feasible* solutions. Note that the only requirements for a solution to be feasible in the equality form of the problem are that it satisfy the system of equations and that *all* the variables be *nonnegative.*

> A **basic feasible solution** is a basic solution where all *m* basic variables are nonnegative (≥ 0). A basic feasible solution is said to be **degenerate** if any of these *m* variables equals zero.

Thus it is possible for a variable to be zero and still not be a defining variable (nonbasic variable) for the current basic feasible solution. (This corresponds to a corner-point feasible solution that satisfies another constraint boundary equation in addition to its *n* defining equations.) Therefore it is necessary to keep track of which is the current set of defining variables (or the current set of basic variables) rather than relying upon their zero values.

Note again that just as for the corner-point feasible solutions, not every set of *n* defining variables (nonbasic variables) yields a basic solution. The equations may not have a solution, or they may have multiple solutions. However, these cases are avoided by the simplex method.

To illustrate these definitions, consider the example once more. Its constraint boundary equations and *indicating variables* are shown in Table 2.14.

Table 2.14 Indicating Variables for Constraint Boundary Equations of Wyndor Glass Co. Problem

Constraint boundary equation	*Indicating variable*
$x_1 = 0$	x_1
$x_2 = 0$	x_2
$x_1 = 4$	x_3
$2x_2 = 12$	x_4
$3x_1 + 2x_2 = 18$	x_5

Variable $= 0 \Rightarrow$ equation satisfied
Variable $\neq 0 \Rightarrow$ equation violated

Augmenting each of the corner-point feasible solutions (see Table 2.11) yields the *basic feasible solutions* listed in Table 2.15.

Table 2.15 Basic Feasible Solutions for Wyndor Glass Co. Problem

Corner-point feasible solution	*Defining equations*	*Basic feasible solution*	*Defining variables*
(0,0)	$x_1 = 0$ $x_2 = 0$	(0,0,4,12,18)	x_1 x_2
(0,6)	$x_1 = 0$ $2x_2 = 12$	(0,6,4,0,6)	x_1 x_4
(2,6)	$2x_2 = 12$ $3x_1 + 2x_2 = 18$	(2,6,2,0,0)	x_4 x_5
(4,3)	$3x_1 + 2x_2 = 18$ $x_1 = 4$	(4,3,0,6,0)	x_5 x_3
(4,0)	$x_1 = 4$ $x_2 = 0$	(4,0,0,12,6)	x_3 x_2

Notice that in each case the defining variables (nonbasic variables) necessarily are the indicating variables for the defining equations. Thus *adjacent* basic feasible solutions differ by having just one different defining variable. Also notice that each basic feasible solution necessarily is the resulting simultaneous solution of the system of equations (1,2,3) for the problem in equality form when the defining variables are set equal to zero.

Similarly, the other three corner-point solutions (see Table 2.12) yield the remaining basic solutions shown in Table 2.16.

The other two sets of defining variables, (1) x_1 and x_3, (2) x_2 and x_4, do not yield a solution for the system of equations (1,2,3), as we pointed out in Sec. 2.5 for the corresponding sets of defining equations.

Table 2.16 Basic Infeasible Solutions for Wyndor Glass Co. Problem

Corner-point infeasible solution	*Defining equations*	*Basic infeasible solution*	*Defining variables*
(0,9)	$x_1 = 0$	(0,9,4,−6,0)	x_1
	$3x_1 + 2x_2 = 18$		x_5
(4,6)	$2x_2 = 12$	(4,6,0,0,−6)	x_4
	$x_1 = 4$		x_3
(6,0)	$3x_1 + 2x_2 = 18$	(6,0,−2,12,0)	x_5
	$x_2 = 0$		x_2

This completes the mechanics and terminology needed to set up and interpret the algebra of the simplex method—with two exceptions. First, if the linear programming problem is not in our standard form, then some additional adjustments are needed to set up and apply the simplex method. This subject is postponed to Sec. 2.10. The second exception is the following bookkeeping detail. It is convenient to consider and manipulate the objective function equation at the same time as the new constraint equations $(1, 2, \ldots, m)$. Therefore the equality form of the problem is rewritten in an equivalent way as

$$\text{Maximize} \quad Z,$$

subject to the system of equations

$$\begin{aligned}
&(0) \quad Z - c_1x_1 - c_2x_2 - \cdots - c_nx_n &&= 0\\
&(1) \quad a_{11}x_1 + a_{12}x_2 + \cdots + a_{1n}x_n + x_{n+1} &&= b_1\\
&(2) \quad a_{21}x_1 + a_{22}x_2 + \cdots + a_{2n}x_n \qquad + x_{n+2} &&= b_2\\
&\qquad \vdots\\
&(m) \quad a_{m1}x_1 + a_{m2}x_2 + \cdots + a_{mn}x_n \qquad\qquad + x_{n+m} &&= b_m,
\end{aligned}$$

and

$$x_j \geq 0, \text{ for } j = 1, 2, \ldots, n + m.$$

We call this the **equality representation** for any linear programming problem in our standard form. Thus the equality representation for the example is

$$\text{Maximize} \quad Z,$$

subject to

$$\begin{aligned}
&(0) \quad Z - 3x_1 - 5x_2 &&= 0\\
&(1) \quad x_1 + x_3 &&= 4\\
&(2) \quad 2x_2 + x_4 &&= 12\\
&(3) \quad 3x_1 + 2x_2 + x_5 &&= 18,
\end{aligned}$$

and

$$x_j \geq 0, \text{ for } j = 1, 2, \ldots, 5.$$

It is just as if Eq. (0) actually were one of the original constraints, but because it already is in equality form, no slack variable or indicating variable is needed. With this interpretation, the basic solutions would be unchanged except that Z would be viewed as a (permanent) additional basic variable.

2.7 THE ALGEBRA OF THE SIMPLEX METHOD[1]

The discussion in Sec. 2.5 of the principles of the simplex method did not get into the details of how the steps are performed. In particular, the following questions have not yet been answered completely (the parenthetical phrases restate the questions in the algebraic terminology of Sec. 2.6).

Initialization step How is the initial corner-point feasible solution (basic feasible solution) selected?

Iterative step (1) What is the criterion for selecting the defining equation (nonbasic variable) to be replaced?

(2) How is the replacement identified?

(3) How can the new solution be identified without completely resolving the new system of defining equations (the system of equations with the new set of nonbasic variables)?

Stopping rule How is the test for optimality performed?

In this section we answer these questions for any linear programming problem in our standard form such that $b_i > 0$ for all $i = 1, 2, \ldots, m$. (Other forms are treated in Sec. 2.10.) We continue to use the prototype example of Sec. 2.1, as rewritten at the end of the last section, for illustrative purposes.

Initialization Step

As indicated in Sec. 2.5, the simplex method can start at any corner-point feasible solution, so it chooses a convenient one. When the problem is in the form assumed above, this choice is the origin $(x_1, x_2, \ldots, x_n) = (0,0, \ldots, 0)$, or $(x_1, x_2) = (0,0)$ in the example. After introducing slack variables, this corresponds to choosing the original variables $(x_1, x_2, \ldots, x_n)$ as the *nonbasic* (defining) variables, and so the slack variables $(x_{n+1}, x_{n+2}, \ldots, x_{n+m})$ as the *basic* variables, for the initial basic feasible solution. This is illustrated below, where the basic variables are shown in darker type.

[1] The reader or instructor has several options at this point. If you do not have time to cover all the material in Chaps. 2 to 4, you could skip the details of the simplex method (Secs. 2.7 to 2.11) altogether, but then you must bypass the derivation of the dual problem (beginning of Sec. 2.12) and how to do sensitivity analysis (Sec. 4.3). Otherwise, you have the choice of studying the simplex method (1) in algebraic form (Sec. 2.7), which is more enlightening, or (2) in tabular form (Sec. 2.8), which is more straightforward, or (3) doing both because the tabular form follows directly from the algebraic form. (The tabular form is used primarily after Sec. 2.8.) Finally, if you are comfortable with linear and matrix algebra (briefly reviewed in Appendix 3), you also have the choice of studying the simplex method in matrix form (Sec. 16.4), which has the advantages of compactness and conforming to most computer codes.

$$\begin{array}{llr}
(1) & x_1 \qquad\qquad + x_3 & = 4 \\
(2) & \qquad 2x_2 \qquad + x_4 & = 12 \\
(3) & 3x_1 + 2x_2 \qquad\quad + x_5 & = 18
\end{array}$$

Since the nonbasic variables are set equal to zero, the remaining solution is read off as if they were not there, so $x_3 = 4$, $x_4 = 12$, $x_5 = 18$, giving the **initial basic feasible solution** (0,0,4,12,18).

Notice that the reason this solution could be read off immediately is that each equation has just one basic variable, which has a coefficient of +1, and this basic variable does not appear in any other equation. You will see soon that the simplex method algebraically manipulates the equations in such a way that they continue to have this convenient form for reading off every subsequent basic feasible solution as well.

Iterative Step

At each iteration, the simplex method moves from the current basic feasible solution (corner-point feasible solution) to a better *adjacent* basic feasible solution. This involves replacing one nonbasic variable (called the **entering basic variable**) by a new one (called the **leaving basic variable**) and identifying the new basic feasible solution.

QUESTION 1 What is the criterion for selecting the entering basic variable?

The candidates for entering basic variables are the n current nonbasic variables. The one chosen would be changed from a nonbasic to a basic variable, so its value would be increased from zero to some positive number (except in degenerate cases), and the others would be kept at zero. Since the new basic feasible solution is required to be an improvement (larger Z) over the current one, it is thus necessary that the net change in Z from increasing the entering basic variable be a positive one. This is determined by rewriting the objective function just in terms of the nonbasic variables [using the current Eq. (0) in the system of equations], so that the coefficient of each one is the rate at which Z would change as that variable is increased. The one that has the largest coefficient, and so would *increase* Z at the *fastest rate*, is chosen to be the entering basic variable.[1]

To illustrate, the two candidates for entering basic variable in the example are the current nonbasic variables x_1 and x_2. Since the objective function already is written only in terms of these nonbasic variables, it can be considered just as is:

$$Z = 3x_1 + 5x_2.$$

Both variables have positive coefficients, so increasing either one would increase

[1] Note that this criterion does not guarantee selecting the variable that would increase Z the most because the constraints may not allow increasing this variable as much as some of the others. However, the extra computations required to check this are not considered worthwhile.

Z, but at the different rates of 3 and 5 per unit increase in the variable. Since $3 < 5$, the choice for **entering basic variable** is x_2.

QUESTION 2 How is the leaving basic variable identified?

Recall from Sec. 2.5 that an adjacent corner-point feasible solution is reached from the current one by (1) deleting one constraint boundary (defining equation) from the set of n constraint boundaries defining the current solution, (2) moving away from the current solution in the *feasible* direction along the intersection of the remaining $(n - 1)$ constraint boundaries, and (3) stopping when the *first* new constraint boundary (defining equation) is reached. Moving beyond this first new constraint boundary only would lead to corner-point *infeasible* solutions.

Equivalently, in our new terminology, the simplex method reaches an adjacent basic feasible solution from the current one by (1) deleting one variable (the *entering basic variable*) from the set of n nonbasic variables defining the current solution, (2) moving away from the current solution by *increasing* this one variable from zero while keeping the remaining $(n - 1)$ nonbasic variables at zero, and (3) stopping when the *first* of the basic variables (the *leaving basic variable*) reaches a value of zero (its constraint boundary). Thus, having chosen the entering basic variable, the leaving basic variable is not a matter of choice because trying to use any other as the new nonbasic variable only would yield a basic *infeasible* solution. The variable that must be the leaving basic variable is the one whose nonnegativity constraint imposes the smallest upper bound on how much the entering basic variable can be increased, as illustrated below.

The possibilities for leaving basic variable in the example are the current basic variables x_3, x_4, and x_5. The most that the entering basic variable x_2 can be increased before each of these variables would become negative is summarized in Table 2.17. Since x_4 imposes the smallest upper bound on x_2, the

Table 2.17 Calculations for Determining First Leaving Basic Variable for Wyndor Glass Co. Problem

Basic variable	*Equation*	*Upper bound for x_2*
x_3	$x_3 = 4 - x_1$	No limit
x_4	$x_4 = 12 - 2x_2$	$x_2 \leq \frac{12}{2} = 6 \leftarrow$ minimum
x_5	$x_5 = 18 - 3x_1 - 2x_2$	$x_2 \leq \frac{18}{2} = 9$

leaving basic variable is x_4, so $x_4 = 0$ and $x_2 = 6$ in the new basic feasible solution.

QUESTION 3 How can the new basic feasible solution be identified most conveniently?

After identifying the entering and leaving basic variables (including the new value of the former variable), all that remains is to solve for the new values of the remaining basic variables. This requires converting the system of equations into the same convenient form we had in the initialization step (namely, each equation has just one basic variable, which has a coefficient of +1, and this basic variable does not appear in any other equation). This can be done by performing the following two kinds of algebraic operations:

(*a*) Multiplying an equation by a nonzero constant.
(*b*) Adding a multiple of one equation to another equation.

These operations are legitimate because they involve only (*a*) multiplying equals (both sides of an equation) by the same constant and (*b*) adding equals to equals. Therefore a solution will satisfy the system of equations after such operations if and only if it did so before.

To illustrate, consider the original set of equations, where the *new* basic variables are shown in darker type (with Z playing the role of the basic variable in the objective function equation):

$$
\begin{array}{ll}
(0) & \mathbf{Z} - 3x_1 - 5\mathbf{x_2} = 0 \\
(1) & x_1 + \mathbf{x_3} = 4 \\
(2) & 2\mathbf{x_2} + x_4 = 12 \\
(3) & 3x_1 + 2\mathbf{x_2} + \mathbf{x_5} = 18.
\end{array}
$$

Thus x_2 has replaced x_4 as the basic variable in Eq. (2). Since x_2 has a coefficient of +2 there, this equation would be multiplied by ½ to give its new basic variable a coefficient of +1. The resulting new Eq. (2) is

$$(2) \qquad \mathbf{x_2} + \frac{1}{2}x_4 = 6.$$

Next, x_2 must be eliminated from the other equations in which it appears [including Eq. (0), to set it up for the stopping rule]. Using the second kind of algebraic operation listed above, this is done as follows:

New Eq. (3) = old Eq. (3) + (−2) × new Eq. (2)
New Eq. (0) = old Eq. (0) + 5 × new Eq. (2).

This yields the second set of equations (which is completely equivalent algebraically to the first set), as given below.

$$
\begin{array}{ll}
(0) & \mathbf{Z} - 3x_1 + \frac{5}{2}x_4 = 30 \\
(1) & x_1 + \mathbf{x_3} = 4 \\
(2) & \mathbf{x_2} + \frac{1}{2}x_4 = 6 \\
(3) & 3x_1 - x_4 + \mathbf{x_5} = 6.
\end{array}
$$

For purposes of illustration, exchange the location of x_2 and x_4.

$$\begin{aligned}
&(0) \quad & Z - 3x_1 + \frac{5}{2}x_4 & & &= 30\\
&(1) \quad & x_1 & + x_3 & &= 4\\
&(2) \quad & \frac{1}{2}x_4 & + x_2 & &= 6\\
&(3) \quad & 3x_1 - x_4 & & + x_5 &= 6.
\end{aligned}$$

Now compare this set of equations with the initial set obtained under the initialization step, and notice that it is indeed in the same convenient form for immediately reading off the current basic feasible solution. Thus we now have our new basic feasible solution, $(x_1, x_2, x_3, x_4, x_5) = (0,6,4,0,6)$, which yields $Z = 30$.†

Stopping Rule

To determine whether the current basic feasible solution is optimal, the current Eq. (0) is used to rewrite the objective function just in terms of the current nonbasic variables. If all these variables have negative coefficients, so that increasing any of them would decrease Z, the current solution must be optimal (by property 3 of Sec. 2.5) and the algorithm stops. Otherwise the algorithm returns to the iterative step to find a better adjacent basic feasible solution.

To clarify the reasoning behind this stopping rule, consider the second basic feasible solution in the example (0,6,4,0,6). Is this solution optimal? As before, the answer is obtained by checking whether the objective function can be increased by increasing the value of one *nonbasic variable* (x_1 or x_4) while keeping the others at zero (but adjusting the values of the basic variables as needed to continue satisfying the constraints). However, this can no longer be determined simply by examining the objective function in its original form $Z = 3x_1 + 5x_2$. One reason is that increasing x_1 might affect the value of x_2 because x_2 is now a basic rather than a nonbasic variable fixed at zero. (Note, for example, that the values of two of the original basic variables, x_4 and x_5, were affected by increasing x_2 in the first iteration above.) Second, without x_4 in the objective function, no judgment can be made regarding its effect on Z resulting from the interactions of the constraints. Therefore the objective function must be rewritten in terms of all the nonbasic variables, but none of the basic variables, before one can test for optimality and (if necessary) select an entering variable. This is exactly what was accomplished by the above manipulations of Eq. (0), which yielded $Z = 30 + 3x_1 - 5x_4$ as the objective function. This objective function is completely equivalent to the original one, in view of the constraints, but is in a form convenient for the present analysis. It can now be concluded

† The algebraic method illustrated above for obtaining the simultaneous solution of a system of linear equations is called the *Gauss-Jordan method of elimination*. If it is not yet clear, we suggest you study the method further in Appendix 4.

that increasing the value of x_1 (with x_4 remaining nonbasic and therefore equal to zero) does indeed increase the value of Z, so that the current basic feasible solution is not optimal. Therefore, at least one more iteration is required.

Before proceeding with the next iteration, it is now possible to give a meaningful summary of the simplex method.

Summary of Simplex Method

Initialization step Introduce slack variables. If the model is not in the form being assumed in this section, see Sec. 2.11 for the necessary adjustments. Otherwise, select the original variables to be the nonbasic variables (so equal to zero) and the slack variables to be the basic variables (so equal to the right-hand side) in the initial basic feasible solution. Go to the stopping rule.

Iterative step

Part 1 Determine the entering basic variable: Select the nonbasic variable that, when increased, would increase Z at the fastest rate. This is done by checking the magnitude of the coefficients in the objective function rewritten just in terms of the nonbasic variables [obtained from the current Eq. (0)] and selecting the nonbasic variable whose coefficient is *largest*.[1] (See Sec. 2.9 regarding ties.)

Part 2 Determine the leaving basic variable: Select the basic variable that reaches zero first as the entering basic variable is increased. This is done by checking each equation to see how much the entering basic variable can be increased before the current basic variable in that equation reaches zero. A formal algebraic procedure for doing this is to let e denote the subscript of the entering basic variable, let a'_{ie} denote its current coefficient in Eq. (i), and let b'_i denote the current right-hand side for this equation ($i = 1,2, \ldots, m$). Then the upper bound for x_e in Eq. (i) is

$$x_e \leq \begin{cases} +\infty, & \text{if } a'_{ie} \leq 0 \\ \dfrac{b'_i}{a'_{ie}}, & \text{if } a'_{ie} > 0. \end{cases}$$

Therefore, determine the equation with the *smallest* such upper bound, and select the current basic variable in that equation as the leaving basic variable. (See Sec. 2.9 regarding ties, including the case where *all* upper bounds are $+\infty$.)

Part 3 Determine the new basic feasible solution: Starting from the current set of equations, solve for the basic variables and Z in terms of the nonbasic variables by the Gauss-Jordan method of elimination (see Appendix 4). Set the nonbasic variables equal to zero; each basic variable (and Z) equals the new right-hand side of the one equation in which it appears (with a coefficient of $+1$).

[1] Equivalently, the current Eq. (0) can be used directly, in which case the nonbasic variable with the largest *negative* coefficient would be selected. This is what is done in the tabular form of the simplex method presented in Sec. 2.8.

Stopping rule Determine whether this solution is optimal: Check if Z can be increased by increasing any nonbasic variable. This is done by rewriting the objective function just in terms of the nonbasic variables by bringing these variables to the right-hand side in the current Eq. (0) and then checking the sign of the coefficient of each nonbasic variable. If all these coefficients are nonpositive, then this solution is optimal, so stop.[1] (See Sec. 2.9 to interpret zero coefficients.) Otherwise, go to the iteration step.

To illustrate, apply this summary to the next iteration for the example.

Iteration 2 for Example

Part 1 Since the current Eq. (0) yields $Z = 30 + 3x_1 - 5/2 x_4$, increasing only x_1 would increase Z; that is, x_1 has the largest (and only) positive coefficient. Therefore x_1 is chosen as the new entering basic variable.

Part 2 The upper limits on x_1 before the basic variable in the respective equations reaches zero are shown in Table 2.18. Therefore x_5 must be chosen as the leaving basic variable.

Table 2.18 Calculations for Determining Second Leaving Basic Variable for Wyndor Glass Co. Problem

Basic variable	*Equation number*	*Upper bound for* x_1
x_3	1	$x_1 \leq \frac{4}{1} = 4$
x_2	2	No limit
x_5	3	$x_1 \leq \frac{6}{3} = 2 \leftarrow$ minimum

Part 3 After eliminating x_1 from all equations in the current set except Eq. (3), where x_1 replaces x_5 as the basic variable, the new set of equations is

$$(0) \quad Z \qquad + \frac{3}{2}x_4 + x_5 = 36$$

$$(1) \quad x_3 + \frac{1}{3}x_4 - \frac{1}{3}x_5 = 2$$

$$(2) \quad x_2 \quad + \frac{1}{2}x_4 \qquad = 6$$

$$(3) \quad x_1 \quad - \frac{1}{3}x_4 + \frac{1}{3}x_5 = 2.$$

Therefore the next basic feasible solution is (2,6,2,0,0), yielding $Z = 36$.

[1] Equivalently, the current Eq. (0) can be used directly, in which case all these coefficients have to be nonnegative (≥ 0) for the solution to be optimal. This is what is done in the tabular form of the simplex method presented in Sec. 2.8.

Stopping rule Since the new form of the objective function is $Z = 36 - \frac{3}{2}x_4 - x_5$, so that the coefficient of neither nonbasic variable is positive, the current basic feasible solution obtained above must be optimal. Therefore the desired solution to the original (inequality) form of the problem is $x_1 = 2$, $x_2 = 6$, which yields $Z = 36$.

2.8 THE SIMPLEX METHOD IN TABULAR FORM

The algebraic form of the simplex method presented in Sec. 2.7 may be the best one for learning the underlying logic of the algorithm. However, it is not the most convenient form for performing the required calculations. When you need to solve a problem by hand, we recommend the *tabular form* described in this section.[1]

The tabular form of the simplex method is *mathematically equivalent* to the algebraic form. However, instead of writing down each set of equations in full detail, we instead use a **simplex tableau** to record only the essential information, namely, (1) the coefficients of the variables, (2) the constants on the right-hand side of the equations, and (3) the basic variable appearing in each equation. This saves writing the symbols for the variables in each of the equations, but more importantly, it permits highlighting the numbers involved in arithmetic calculations and compactly recording the computations.

To introduce the tabular form, consider the *equality representation* for any linear programming problem in our standard form, as presented at the end of Sec. 2.6. This system of Eqs. (0 to m) can be expressed as shown in Table 2.19.

Table 2.19 Initial Simplex Tableau for Linear Programming

Equation number	Coefficient of: Z	x_1	x_2	$\cdots$	x_n	x_{n+1}	x_{n+2}	$\cdots$	x_{n+m}	*Right side of equation*
0	1	$-c_1$	$-c_2$	$\cdots$	$-c_n$	0	0	$\cdots$	0	0
1	0	a_{11}	a_{12}	$\cdots$	a_{1n}	1	0	$\cdots$	0	b_1
2	0	a_{21}	a_{22}	$\cdots$	a_{2n}	0	1	$\cdots$	0	b_2
$\vdots$	$\vdots$				$\vdots$				$\vdots$	$\vdots$
m	0	a_{m1}	a_{m2}	$\cdots$	a_{mn}	0	0	$\cdots$	1	b_m

This is the layout for our *simplex tableau*, except that the tableau has one more column (on the left) to indicate which basic variable appears in each equation for the current basic feasible solution. (We shall abbreviate also the headings for the first and last columns shown above.) The simplex method develops one such tableau for each new basic feasible solution obtained, until the optimal solution is reached. The procedure is outlined below for problems in our standard form, with $b_i > 0$ for all $i = 1, 2, \ldots, m$.† (Other forms are discussed

[1] A form more convenient for a *computer* is presented in Sec. 16.4.

† If you already understand the algebraic form of the simplex method, then you will not need to carefully study the following procedure, which is just a tabular representation of the algebraic procedure presented in Sec. 2.7.

in Sec. 2.10, and tie-breaking considerations are deferred to Sec. 2.9.) The Wyndor Glass Co. example (see the end of Sec. 2.6 for its equality representation) again is used for illustrative purposes.

Initialization step Introduce slack variables, obtaining the part of the simplex tableau shown above. Then select the original variables ($x_1, x_2, \ldots, x_n$) to be the initial nonbasic variables, set equal to zero, and the slack variables

$$(x_{n+1}, x_{n+2}, \ldots, x_{n+m})$$

to be the initial basic variables. This yields the initial simplex tableau for the example shown in Table 2.20. Since each equation contains just one basic

Table 2.20 Initial Simplex Tableau for Wyndor Glass Co. Problem

Basic variable	*Eq. no.*	*Coefficient of* Z	x_1	x_2	x_3	x_4	x_5	*Right side*
Z	0	1	−3	−5	0	0	0	0
x_3	1	0	1	0	1	0	0	4
x_4	2	0	0	2	0	1	0	12
x_5	3	0	3	2	0	0	1	18

variable, which has a coefficient of +1, each basic variable *equals* the constant on the right-hand side of its equation. (Part 3 of the iterative step develops this same property for each new basic feasible solution as well.) Thus the initial basic feasible solution for the example is (0,0,4,12,18). Go next to the stopping rule to determine if this solution is optimal.

Stopping rule The current basic feasible solution is optimal if and only if *every* coefficient in Eq. (0) is nonnegative (≥ 0). If it is, stop; otherwise go to the iterative step to obtain the next basic feasible solution—which involves changing one nonbasic variable to a basic variable (part 1) and vice versa (part 2) and then solving for the new solution (part 3).

The example has two negative coefficients in Eq. 0, -3 for x_1 and -5 for x_2, so go to the iterative step.

Iterative step

Part 1. Determine the *entering basic variable* by selecting the variable (automatically a nonbasic variable) with the *largest negative* coefficient in Eq. (0). Put a box around the column below this coefficient, and call this the **pivot column**.

In the example, the largest negative coefficient is -5 for x_2 ($5 > 3$), so x_2 is to be changed to a basic variable.

Part 2. Determine the *leaving basic variable* by (*a*) picking out each coefficient in the boxed column that is strictly positive (>0), (*b*) dividing each of these coefficients into "right side" for the same row, (*c*) identifying the equation that has the *smallest* of these ratios, and (*d*) selecting the basic variable for this equation. Put a box around this equation's row in the tableau to the right of the Z column, and call the boxed row the **pivot row.** (Hereafter we continue to use the term *row* to refer just to a row of numbers to the right of the Z column.) Also call the one number that is in *both* boxes the **pivot number.**

The result of parts 1 and 2 for the example (before boxing the row) is shown in Table 2.21.

Table 2.21 Calculations to Determine First Leaving Basic Variable for Wyndor Glass Co. Problem

Basic variable	Eq. no.	Coefficient of: Z	x_1	x_2	x_3	x_4	x_5	Right side	Ratio
Z	0	1	−3	−5	0	0	0	0	
x_3	1	0	1	[0]	1	0	0	4	
x_4	2	0	0	[2]	0	1	0	12	$\frac{12}{2} = 6 \leftarrow$ minimum
x_5	3	0	3	[2]	0	0	1	18	$\frac{18}{2} = 9$

Thus the leaving basic variable is x_4.

Part 3 Determine the new basic feasible solution by constructing a new simplex tableau below the current one. The first three columns are unchanged *except* that the leaving basic variable in the first column is replaced by the entering basic variable. To change the coefficient of the new basic variable to +1, the pivot row is changed by ***dividing*** the entire row (i.e., every number in that row including the right side) by the pivot number, so

$$\text{New pivot row} = \frac{\text{old pivot row}}{\text{pivot number}}.$$

The tableaux for the example at this point have the appearance shown in Table 2.22. To eliminate the new basic variable from the other equations, every

Table 2.22 Simplex Tableaux for Wyndor Glass Co. Problem after Revising First Pivot Row

Iteration	Basic variable	Eq. no.	Coefficient of: Z	x_1	x_2	x_3	x_4	x_5	Right side
0	Z	0	1	−3	−5	0	0	0	0
	x_3	1	0	1	[0]	1	0	0	4
	x_4	2	0	[0	2	0	1	0	12]
	x_5	3	0	3	[2]	0	0	1	18
1	Z	0	1						
	x_3	1	0						
	x_2	2	0	0	1	0	$\frac{1}{2}$	0	6
	x_5	3	0						

row[1] [including the one for Eq. (0)] *except* the pivot row is changed for the new tableau by using the following formula:

New row = old row − (pivot column coefficient) × new pivot row,

where "pivot column coefficient" is the number in this row that is in the pivot column. To illustrate, the new rows for the example are obtained below.

Row 0

$$\begin{array}{rl} & [-3 \quad -5 \quad 0 \quad 0 \quad 0, \quad 0] \\ -(-5) & \left[0 \quad 1 \quad 0 \quad \frac{1}{2} \quad 0, \quad 6\right] \\ \hline \text{new row} = & \left[-3 \quad 0 \quad 0 \quad \frac{5}{2} \quad 0, \quad 30\right]. \end{array}$$

Row 1 Unchanged because its pivot column coefficient is zero.

Row 3

$$\begin{array}{rl} & [3 \quad 2 \quad 0 \quad 0 \quad 1, \quad 18] \\ -(2) & \left[0 \quad 1 \quad 0 \quad \frac{1}{2} \quad 0, \quad 6\right] \\ \hline \text{new row} = & [3 \quad 0 \quad 0 \quad -1 \quad 1, \quad 6]. \end{array}$$

This yields the new tableau shown in Table 2.23 for iteration 1.

Table 2.23 First Two Simplex Tableaux for Wyndor Glass Co. Problem

Iteration	Basic variable	Eq. no.	Z	x_1	x_2	x_3	x_4	x_5	Right side
				Coefficient of					
0	Z	0	1	−3	−5	0	0	0	0
	x_3	1	0	1	0	1	0	0	4
	x_4	2	0	0	2	0	1	0	12
	x_5	3	0	3	2	0	0	1	18
1	Z	0	1	−3	0	0	$\frac{5}{2}$	0	30
	x_3	1	0	1	0	1	0	0	4
	x_2	2	0	0	1	0	$\frac{1}{2}$	0	6
	x_5	3	0	3	0	0	−1	1	6

Since each basic variable always equals the right side of its equation, the new basic feasible solution is (0,6,4,0,6), with $Z = 30$.

This completes the iterative step, so next return to the stopping rule to check whether the new solution is optimal. Since the new Eq. (0) still has a

[1] "Row" refers just to the part of a tableau row to the right of the Z column (this column never changes), including the right side number.

negative coefficient (-3 for x_1), the stopping rule indicates that the solution is not optimal, and so it directs the algorithm to return to the iterative step to obtain the next basic feasible solution. The iterative step then starts anew from the current tableau to find this new solution. Following the instructions for parts 1 and 2, we find x_1 as the entering basic variable and x_5 as the leaving basic variable, as shown below in the tableau for iteration 1 given in Table 2.24.

Table 2.24 Calculations to Determine Second Leaving Basic Variable for Wyndor Glass Co. Problem

											Ratio
	Z	0	1	-3	0	0	$\frac{5}{2}$	0	30		
1	x_3	1	0	1	0	1	0	0	4		$\frac{4}{1}=4$
	x_2	2	0	0	1	0	$\frac{1}{2}$	0	6		
	x_5	3	0	3	0	0	-1	1	6		$\frac{6}{3}=2\leftarrow$ minimum

Using the pivot number 3, the calculations to obtain the rows for the new tableau are

Row 3 Since this is the pivot row,

$$\text{new row} = \frac{1}{3}[3 \quad 0 \quad 0 \quad -1 \quad 1, \quad 6]$$

$$= \left[1 \quad 0 \quad 0 \quad -\frac{1}{3} \quad \frac{1}{3}, \quad 2\right]$$

Row 0

$$\left[-3 \quad 0 \quad 0 \quad \frac{5}{2} \quad 0, \quad 30\right]$$

$$-(-3)\left[1 \quad 0 \quad 0 \quad -\frac{1}{3} \quad \frac{1}{3}, \quad 2\right]$$

$$\text{new row} = \left[0 \quad 0 \quad 0 \quad \frac{3}{2} \quad 1, \quad 36\right]$$

Row 1

$$[1 \quad 0 \quad 1 \quad 0 \quad 0, \quad 4]$$

$$-(1)\left[1 \quad 0 \quad 0 \quad -\frac{1}{3} \quad \frac{1}{3}, \quad 2\right]$$

$$\text{new row} = \left[0 \quad 0 \quad 1 \quad \frac{1}{3} \quad -\frac{1}{3}, \quad 2\right]$$

Row 2 Unchanged because its pivot column coefficient is zero.

We now have the set of tableaux shown in Table 2.25.

Table 2.25 Complete Set of Simplex Tableaux for Wyndor Glass Co. Problem

Iteration	Basic variable	Eq. no.	Coefficient of: Z	x_1	x_2	x_3	x_4	x_5	Right side
0	Z	0	1	-3	-5	0	0	0	0
	x_3	1	0	1	0	1	0	0	4
	x_4	2	0	0	2	0	1	0	12
	x_5	3	0	3	2	0	0	1	18
1	Z	0	1	-3	0	0	$\frac{5}{2}$	0	30
	x_3	1	0	1	0	1	0	0	4
	x_2	2	0	0	1	0	$\frac{1}{2}$	0	6
	x_5	3	0	3	0	0	-1	1	6
2	Z	0	1	0	0	0	$\frac{3}{2}$	1	36
	x_3	1	0	0	0	1	$\frac{1}{3}$	$-\frac{1}{3}$	2
	x_2	2	0	0	1	0	$\frac{1}{2}$	0	6
	x_1	3	0	1	0	0	$-\frac{1}{3}$	$\frac{1}{3}$	2

Therefore the new basic feasible solution is (2,6,2,0,0), with $Z = 36$. Going to the stopping rule, we find that this solution is *optimal* because none of the coefficients in Eq. (0) are negative, so the algorithm is finished. Consequently, the optimal solution to the Wyndor Glass Co. problem (before introducing slack variables) is $x_1 = 2$, $x_2 = 6$.

2.9 TIE BREAKING IN THE SIMPLEX METHOD

You may have noticed in the preceding two sections that we did not say what to do if the various choice rules of the simplex method do not lead to a clear-cut decision, either because of ties or other similar ambiguities. These details are filled in below.

Tie for the Entering Basic Variable

Part 1 of the iterative step chooses the nonbasic variable having the *largest negative* coefficient in the current Eq. (0) as the entering basic variable. Now suppose that two or more nonbasic variables are tied for having the largest negative coefficient. For example, this would occur in the first iteration for the Wyndor Glass Co. problem if its objective function were changed to $Z = 3x_1 + 3x_2$, so that the initial Eq. (0) becomes $Z - 3x_1 - 3x_2 = 0$. How should this tie be broken?

The answer is that the selection between these contenders may be made arbitrarily. The optimal solution will be reached eventually, regardless of the tied variable chosen, and there is no convenient method for predicting in advance which choice will lead there sooner. Notice in Fig. 2.2 that the simplex method happens to reach the optimal solution (2,6) in three iterations with x_1 as the initial entering basic variable, versus two iterations if x_2 is chosen.

Tie for the Leaving Basic Variable—Degeneracy

Now suppose that two or more basic variables tie for being the leaving basic variable in part 2 of the iterative step. Does it matter which one is chosen? Theoretically it does, and in a very critical way. To illustrate the cause for concern, we modify the prototype example of Sec. 2.1 by replacing the third constraint $3x_1 + 2x_2 \leq 18$ by $3x_1 + 2x_2 \leq 12$. The resulting feasible region is shown in Fig. 2.5, where the changed constraint boundary $3x_1 + 2x_2 = 12$ now passes through two corner-point feasible solutions (0,6) and (4,0), which were each already defined by a pair of constraint boundaries.

Applying the simplex method (in tabular form) to this modified example yields the tableaux shown in Table 2.26, where the tie between x_4 and x_5 for being

Figure 2.5 Shaded area shows feasible region for the Wyndor Glass Co. problem, with $b_3 = 12$.

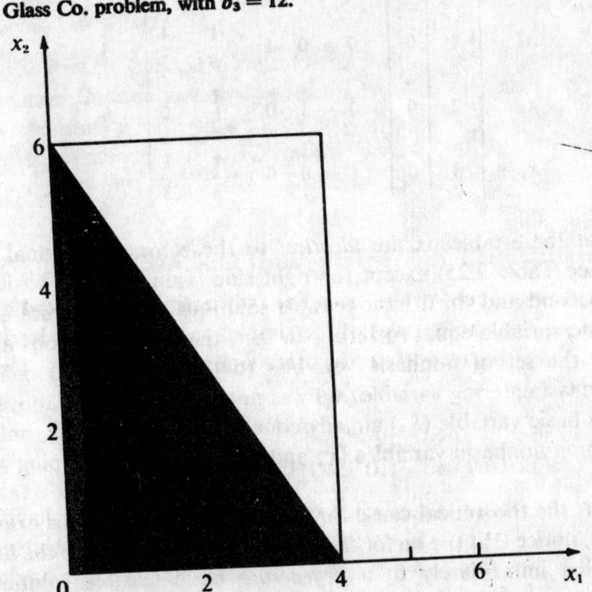

the initial leaving basic variable is broken arbitrarily by choosing the first of the tied variables (x_4).

Table 2.26 Complete Set of Simplex Tableaux for Wyndor Glass Co. Problem with $b_3 = 12$

Iteration	Basic variable	Eq. no.	Z	x_1	x_2	x_3	x_4	x_5	Right Side	Ratio
0	Z	0	1	-3	-5	0	0	0	0	
	x_3	1	0	0	0	1	0	0	4	
	x_4	2	0	0	2	0	1	0	12	$\frac{12}{2} = 6 \leftarrow$ minimum
	x_5	3	0	3	2	0	0	1	12	$\frac{12}{2} = 6 \leftarrow$ minimum
1	Z	0	1	-3	0	0	$\frac{5}{2}$	0	30	
	x_3	1	0	1	0	1	0	0	4	$\frac{4}{1} = 4$
	x_2	2	0	0	1	0	$\frac{1}{2}$	0	6	
	x_5	3	0	3	0	0	-1	1	0	$\frac{0}{3} = 0 \leftarrow$ minimum
2	Z	0	1	0	0	0	$\frac{3}{2}$	1	30	
	x_3	1	0	0	0	1	$\frac{1}{3}$	$-\frac{1}{3}$	4	
	x_2	2	0	0	1	0	$\frac{1}{2}$	0	6	
	x_1	3	0	1	0	0	$-\frac{1}{3}$	$\frac{1}{3}$	0	

Notice that these tableaux are *identical* to those for the original example in Sec. 2.8 (see Table 2.25) except for right side (values of the basic variables). Both the second and third basic feasible solutions are *degenerate* because they have a basic variable equal to zero. In fact, these two solutions are *identical*, except for the set of nonbasic variables (or basic variables) defining them, because the last entering variable (x_1) was not able to increase above zero when the leaving basic variable (x_5) already equaled zero. However, only the latter set of defining nonbasic variables (x_4 and x_5) passed the stopping rule test for optimality.

What is the theoretical cause for concern suggested by this example? To answer this, notice that the tie for the leaving basic variable (see the first tableau) inevitably led immediately to a *degenerate* basic feasible solution (see the second tableau) because the tied variable(s) not chosen must nevertheless take on a value of zero. If such a variable is subsequently chosen to be a leaving basic variable before its value is changed from zero, the corresponding entering basic variable must also remain zero, and the value of Z must remain unchanged (see the second and third tableaux). But if Z may remain the same rather than increase at each iteration, what is to prevent the simplex method from going round in a loop, repeating the same sequence of solutions periodically rather than eventually increasing Z toward the optimal solution? This did not happen in the example where the optimal solution had already been reached, but other examples have been artificially constructed so that they do become entrapped in just such a perpetual loop.

Fortunately, although it has been shown that such a perpetual loop is theoretically possible, it has rarely been known to occur in practical problems. If a loop were to occur, one could always get out of it by changing the choice of the leaving basic variable. Furthermore, special rules[1] have been constructed for breaking ties so that such loops are always avoided. However, such rules have been virtually ignored in actual application, and they will not be repeated here.

No Leaving Basic Variable—Unbounded Z

There is one other possible outcome in part 2 of the iterative step that we have not yet discussed, namely, that *no* variable qualifies to be the leaving basic variable.[2] This would occur if the entering basic variable can be increased *indefinitely* without giving negative values to *any* of the current basic variables. In the tabular form, this means that *every* coefficient in the pivot column [excluding Eq. (0)] is either negative or zero. This is illustrated in Table 2.27 by deleting the last two functional constraints of the prototype example.

Table 2.27 Initial Simplex Tableau for Wyndor Glass Co. Problem without Last Two Functional Constraints

Basic variable	*Eq. no.*	Z	x_1	x_2	x_3	*Right side*	Ratio
Z	0	1	−3	−5	0	0	
x_3	1	0	1	$\boxed{0}$	1	4	No minimum

The interpretation of such an occurrence is that the constraints do not prevent increasing the value of the objective function (Z) indefinitely in the favorable direction (positive or negative), so the simplex method would stop with the message that Z is unbounded. Since even linear programming has not discovered a way of making infinite profits, the real message for practical

[1] See, for example, A. Charnes, Optimality and Degeneracy in Linear Programming, *Econometrica*, **20**: 160–170, 1952.

[2] Note that the analogous case (no *entering* basic variable) can not occur in part 1 of the iterative step because of the stopping rule.

problems is that a mistake has been made! The model probably has been misformulated, either by omitting relevant constraints or by stating them incorrectly. Alternatively, a computational mistake may have occurred.

Multiple Optimal Solutions

We mentioned in Sec. 2.5 (under the definition of "optimal solution") that a problem can have more than one optimal solution. This was illustrated by changing the objective function in the prototype example to $Z = 3x_1 + 2x_1$, so that *every* point on the line segment between (2,6) and (4,3) is optimal. Based on property 1 in Sec. 2.5, we also know that every such problem has at least two optimal basic feasible solutions and that these solutions can be used to identify every other optimal solution (as described in Prob. 12).

In most applications it is important to know that the model being used has multiple optimal solutions. A mathematical model can not incorporate all the factors that are relevant in managerial decision making; all it can do is incorporate the basic economic and technological considerations. Therefore, after identifying the most attractive alternatives (some of the optimal solutions and perhaps some near-optimal solutions suggested by sensitivity analysis) on these grounds, the final choice among them should be left to management's judgment.

On the other hand, the stopping rule for the simplex method breaks the tie among optimal solutions by stopping with the first optimal (basic feasible) solution it finds. This raises two key questions. How can we then tell whether there exist other optimal basic feasible solutions (the only way there can be multiple optimal solutions) as well? How can these solutions be identified? Fortunately, they have the following rather simple answer:

> Whenever a problem has more than one optimal basic feasible solution, at least one of the nonbasic variables has a coefficient of *zero* in the final Eq. (0), so increasing any such variable would not change the value of Z. Therefore, these other optimal solutions usually can be identified by performing additional iterations of the simplex method, each time choosing a nonbasic variable with a zero coefficient as the entering basic variable.

To illustrate, consider the example where the objective function is $Z = 3x_1 + 2x_2$. The simplex method obtains the first three tableaux shown in Table 2.28 and stops with an optimal basic feasible solution. However, because a nonbasic variable (x_3) then has a zero coefficient in Eq. (0), we perform one more iteration in Table 2.28 to identify the other optimal basic feasible solution. Thus the two optimal basic feasible solutions are (4,3,0,6,0) and (2,6,2,0,0), each yielding $Z = 18$. Notice that the last tableau also has a *nonbasic* variable (x_4) with a zero coefficient in Eq. (0). This is inevitable because the extra iteration(s) does not change row 0, so each leaving basic variable necessarily retains its zero coefficient. Making x_4 an entering basic variable now would only lead back to the third tableau. (Check this.) Therefore these are the only two basic

Table 2.28 Complete Set of Simplex Tableaux to Obtain All Optimal Basic Feasible Solutions for Wyndor Glass Co. Problem with $c_2 = 2$

Iteration	Basic variable	Eq. no.	Coefficient of: Z	x_1	x_2	x_3	x_4	x_5	Right side	Solution Optimal?
0	Z	0	1	−3	−2	0	0	0	0	No
	x_3	1	0	1	0	1	0	0	4	
	x_4	2	0	0	2	0	1	0	12	
	x_5	3	0	3	2	0	0	1	18	
1	Z	0	1	0	−2	3	0	0	12	No
	x_1	1	0	1	0	1	0	0	4	
	x_4	2	0	0	2	0	1	0	12	
	x_5	3	0	0	2	−3	0	1	6	
2	Z	0	1	0	0	0	0	1	18	Yes
	x_1	1	0	1	0	1	0	0	4	
	x_4	2	0	0	0	3	1	−1	6	
	x_2	3	0	0	1	$-\frac{3}{2}$	0	$\frac{1}{2}$	3	
Extra	Z	0	1	0	0	0	0	1	18	Yes
	x_1	1	0	1	0	0	$-\frac{1}{3}$	$\frac{1}{3}$	2	
	x_3	2	0	0	0	1	$\frac{1}{3}$	$-\frac{1}{3}$	2	
	x_2	3	0	0	1	0	$\frac{1}{2}$	0	6	

feasible solutions that are optimal, and all *other* optimal solutions are a weighted average of these two.

2.10 ADAPTING TO OTHER MODEL FORMS

Thus far we have presented the details of the simplex method under the assumption that the problem is in our standard form (see Sec. 2.2), with $b_i > 0$ for all $i = 1, 2, \ldots, m$. In this section we point out how to make the adjustments required for other legitimate forms of the linear programming model. You will see that all these adjustments can be made in the initialization step, so that the rest of the simplex method can then be applied just as you have already learned it.

The only real problem that the other forms for functional constraints ($=$, $\geq$, or $b_i \leq 0$) introduce is in identifying an initial basic feasible solution. Before, this initial solution was found very conveniently by letting the slack variables be the initial basic variables, so that each one just equals the *positive* right-hand side of its equation. Now, something else must be done. The standard approach that is used for all these cases is the **artificial variable technique.** This technique constructs a more convenient *revised problem* by introducing into each constraint that needs one a dummy variable (called an *artificial variable*) just for the purpose of being the initial basic variable for that equation. The usual nonnegativity constraints are placed on these variables, and the objective function also is modified to impose an exorbitant penalty on their having values larger than zero. The iterations of the simplex method then automatically force the artificial variables to disappear (become zero) one at a time until they are all gone, after which the *real* problem is solved.

To illustrate the artificial variable technique, we first consider the case where the only nonstandard form in the problem is the presence of one or more equality constraints.

Equality Constraints

Any equality constraint

$$a_{i1}x_1 + a_{i2}x_2 + \cdots + a_{in}x_n = b_i$$

actually is equivalent to a pair of inequality constraints:

$$a_{i1}x_1 + a_{i2}x_2 + \cdots + a_{in}x_n \le b_i$$
$$a_{i1}x_1 + a_{i2}x_2 + \cdots + a_{in}x_n \ge b_i.$$

However, rather than making this substitution, and thereby increasing the number of constraints, it is more convenient to use the artificial variable technique instead, as described below.

Suppose that the Wyndor Glass Co. problem in Sec. 2.1 is modified to *require* that Plant 3 be used at full capacity. The only resulting change in the linear programming model is that the third constraint, $3x_1 + 2x_2 \le 18$, becomes an *equality* constraint, $3x_1 + 2x_2 = 18$, instead. Therefore the feasible region for this problem (see Fig. 2.2) now consists of *just* the line segment connecting (2,6) and (4,3).

After introducing the slack variables still needed for the *inequality* constraints, the original set of equations (see the end of Sec. 2.6) becomes

$$\begin{array}{llll}
(0) & Z - 3x_1 - 5x_2 & & = 0 \\
(1) & x_1 & + x_3 & = 4 \\
(2) & 2x_2 & + x_4 & = 12 \\
(3) & 3x_1 + 2x_2 & & = 18.
\end{array}$$

Unfortunately, these equations do not have an obvious initial basic feasible solution because there is no longer a slack variable to use as the initial basic variable for Eq. (3). The artificial variable technique circumvents this difficulty by introducing a nonnegative *artificial variable* (call it $\bar{x}_5$)† into this equation,

† We shall always label artificial variables by putting a bar over them.

just as if it were a slack variable! Thus this technique *revises* the problem by changing Eq. (3) to

$$(3) \qquad 3x_1 + 2x_2 + \bar{x}_5 = 18,$$

just as we had in the original Wyndor Glass Co. problem. Proceeding as before, we now have an initial basic feasible solution (for the *revised problem*) $(x_1, x_2, x_3, x_4, \bar{x}_5) = (0,0,4,12,18)$.

The effect of introducing an artificial variable is to *enlarge* the feasible region. In this case the feasible region expands from just the line segment connecting (2,6) and (4,3) to the entire shaded area shown in Fig. 2.2. A feasible solution for the *revised* problem is also feasible for the *original* problem if the artificial variable equals zero ($\bar{x}_5 = 0$).

Now suppose that the simplex method is permitted to proceed and obtain an *optimal* solution for the *revised* problem and that this solution happens to be *feasible* for the *original* problem. It can then be concluded that this solution must also be *optimal* for the *original* problem, so we are finished. (The reason is that this solution is the best one in the *entire* feasible region for the revised problem, which includes the feasible region for the original problem.)

Unfortunately, there is no guarantee that the optimal solution to the revised problem will also be feasible for the original problem. That is, there is no guarantee until *another* revision is made. Using the **Big *M* method**, this new revision amounts to assigning such an overwhelming penalty to being outside the feasible region for the original problem that the optimal solution to the revised problem must lie within this region. Recall that the revised problem coincides with the original problem when $\bar{x}_5 = 0$. Therefore, if the original objective function $Z = 3x_1 + 5x_2$ is changed to

$$Z = 3x_1 + 5x_2 - M\bar{x}_5,$$

where M denotes some *very* large number, then the maximum value of Z must occur when $\bar{x}_5 = 0$ ($\bar{x}_5$ can not be negative). After a little more setting up (discussed below), applying the simplex method to *this* revised problem automatically leads to the desired solution.

Using this revised objective function, Eq. (0) becomes

$$(0) \qquad Z - 3x_1 - 5x_2 + M\bar{x}_5 = 0,$$

or in tabular form,

$$R_0 = [-3 \quad -5 \quad 0 \quad 0 \quad M, \quad 0].$$

However, this R_0 can *not* be used for the initial tableau for applying the simplex method because both the stopping rule and part 1 of the iterative step require that *every* basic variable must have a coefficient of zero, and $\bar{x}_5$ is an initial basic variable. This requirement is normally fulfilled by part 3 of the iteration step, and the same method must be used here, proceeding as if the column for the artificial variable ($\bar{x}_5$) were the pivot column and its equality constraint were the pivot row. This is demonstrated below.

$$
\begin{array}{lrrrrrr}
\textit{Row 0} & [\;\; -3 & -5 & 0 & 0 & M, & 0\;\;] \\
-M & [\;\; 3 & 2 & 0 & 0 & 1, & 18\;\;] \\
\hline
\text{new row} = & [(-3M-3), & (-2M-5), & 0 & 0 & 0, & -18M].
\end{array}
$$

This completes the additional work required in the initialization step for problems of this type, and the rest of the simplex method proceeds just as before. The quantities involving M never appear anywhere except in row 0, so they need to be taken into account only in the stopping rule and part 1 of the iterative step. This could be done by assigning some particular (huge) numerical value to M and just working with the resulting numbers in row 0 in the usual way. However, this may result in significant round-off errors that invalidate the stopping rule. Therefore it is better to do what is shown above, namely, express each coefficient in row 0 as a linear function $aM + b$ of the *symbolic* quantity M by separately recording and updating the current numerical value of (1) the *multiplicative* factor a and (2) the *additive* factor b. Since M is assumed to be so large that b always is negligible compared to aM when $a \neq 0$, the decisions in the stopping rule and part 1 of the iterative step are made by using just the *multiplicative* factors in the usual way. The one exception is when this leads to a tie [for the stopping rule this means that the smallest multiplicative factor(s) equals zero], in which case the tie would be broken by using the corresponding *additive* factors.

Using this approach on the example yields the simplex tableaux shown in Table 2.29.

Thus the optimal solution is (2,6,2,0,0) or $x_1 = 2$, $x_2 = 6$, just as for the original Wyndor Glass Co. problem, so the Big M method was not even needed in this case. However, a different sequence of basic feasible solutions was obtained because a comparison of the initial multiplicative factors ($3 > 2$) led to choosing x_1 rather than x_2 as the initial entering basic variable. If the equality constraint had been $3x_1 + 3x_2 = 18$ instead, both multiplicative factors would have been -3, so then a comparison of the *additive* factors ($5 > 3$) would have led to choosing x_2 as before.

This example involved only *one* equality constraint. If a linear programming model has more than one, each would be handled in just this same way.[1] Thus each such constraint would be given an artificial variable to serve as its initial basic variable, each of these variables would be assigned a coefficient of $-M$ in the objective function, and the resulting row 0 would have subtracted from it M times each equality constraint row.

The approach to other kinds of constraints requiring artificial variables is

[1] This assumes that the equality constraint has a nonnegative right-hand side. Otherwise, multiply it through by (-1) first to satisfy this condition before introducing the artificial variable.

Table 2.29 Complete Set of Simplex Tableaux for Wyndor Glass Co. Problem with an Equality Constraint

Iteration	Basic variable	Eq. no.	Coefficient of: Z	x_1	x_2	x_3	x_4	$\bar{x}_5$	Right side
0	Z	0	1	$(-3M-3)$	$(-2M-5)$	0	0	0	$-18M$
	x_3	1	0	1	0	1	0	0	4
	x_4	2	0	0	2	0	1	0	12
	$\bar{x}_5$	3	0	3	2	0	0	1	18
1	Z	0	1	0	$(-2M-5)$	$(3M+3)$	0	0	$-6M+12$
	x_1	1	0	1	0	1	0	0	4
	x_4	2	0	0	2	0	1	0	12
	$\bar{x}_5$	3	0	0	2	-3	0	1	6
2	Z	0	1	0	0	$-\frac{9}{2}$	0	$\left(M+\frac{5}{2}\right)$	27
	x_1	1	0	1	0	1	0	0	4
	x_4	2	0	0	0	3	1	-1	6
	x_2	3	0	0	1	$-\frac{3}{2}$	0	$\frac{1}{2}$	3
3	Z	0	1	0	0	0	$\frac{3}{2}$	$(M+1)$	36
	x_1	1	0	1	0	0	$-\frac{1}{3}$	$\frac{1}{3}$	2
	x_3	2	0	0	0	1	$\frac{1}{3}$	$-\frac{1}{3}$	2
	x_2	3	0	0	1	0	$\frac{1}{2}$	0	6

completely analogous. To illustrate the adjustments for a variety of different forms, we modify the Wyndor Glass Co. model as follows.

MODIFIED EXAMPLE

$$\text{Minimize} \quad Z = 3x_1 + 5x_2,$$

subject to

$$\begin{aligned} x_1 \quad\quad &\leq 4 \\ 2x_2 &= 12 \\ 3x_1 + 2x_2 &\geq 18 \end{aligned}$$

and

$$x_1 \geq 0,\ x_2 \geq 0.$$

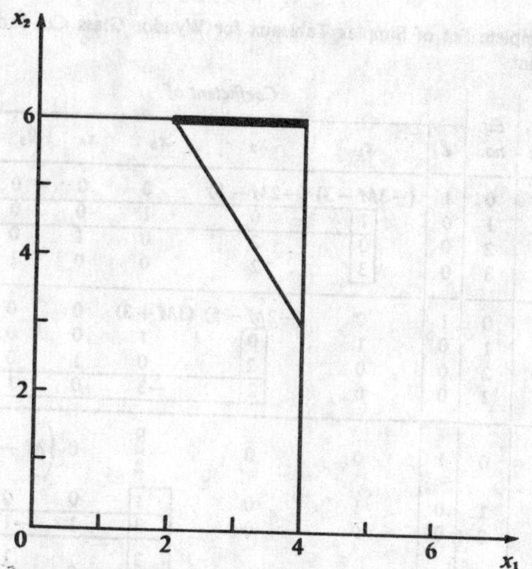

Figure 2.6 Constraint boundaries for modified example. Darker line segment is feasible region.

Figure 2.6 shows the constraint boundaries for this example. The feasible region consists of just the line segment connecting (2,6) and (4,6). Since we are now *minimizing* Z, the optimal solution again lies at (2,6).

Before solving the example in its entirety, the different kinds of adjustments required are discussed individually.

Minimization

One straightforward way of minimizing Z with the simplex method is to exchange the roles of the positive and negative coefficients in row 0 for both the stopping rule and part 1 of the iterative step. However, rather than changing our instructions for the simplex method, we instead present the following simple way of converting any minimization problem into an equivalent maximization problem:

Minimizing $\quad Z = \sum_{j=1}^{n} c_j x_j$ is equivalent to

maximizing $\quad (-Z) = \sum_{j=1}^{n} (-c_j) x_j$, that is, the two formulations yield the same optimal solution(s).

The reason the two formulations are equivalent is that the smaller Z is, the larger $(-Z)$ is, so the solution which gives the *smallest* value of Z in the entire feasible region must also give the *largest* value of $(-Z)$ in this region.

In the modified example, this means making the following change in the formulation:

$$\begin{aligned} &\text{Minimize} \quad Z = 3x_1 + 5x_2 \\ \rightarrow &\text{Maximize} \quad (-Z) = -3x_1 - 5x_2. \end{aligned}$$

≥ Inequality Constraints

The direction of an inequality always is reversed when both sides are multiplied by (−1). As a result, any functional constraint of the ≥ form can be converted into an *equivalent* constraint of our standard ≤ form by changing the signs of all the numbers on both sides.

Using this approach for the third constraint of the example,

$$\begin{aligned} &3x_1 + 2x_2 \geq 18 \\ \rightarrow &-3x_1 - 2x_2 \leq -18 \\ \rightarrow &-3x_1 - 2x_2 + x_5 = -18, \end{aligned}$$

where x_5 is the slack variable for this constant. However, one more change is still needed, as you will see next.

Negative Right-hand Sides

You may recall that the simplex method was presented in Secs. 2.7 and 2.8 under the assumption that $b_i > 0$ for all $i = 1, 2, \ldots, m$ so the slack variables could be selected for the initial basic variables (equal to the right-hand sides) and still yield a *nondegenerate* basic *feasible* solution. We have since pointed out in Sec. 2.9 that degeneracy (basic variables equal to zero) does not need to be avoided. However, a negative right-hand side, such as in the third constraint

$$-3x_1 - 2x_2 + x_5 = -18,$$

would give a negative value for the slack variable ($x_5 = -18$) in the initial solution, which is not allowed. Multiplying through the equation by (−1) makes the right-hand side positive:

$$3x_1 + 2x_2 - x_5 = 18,$$

but it also changes the coefficient of the slack variable to −1, so the variable still would be negative. However, in this form the constraint can be viewed as an *equality constraint* with a nonnegative right-hand side, so the *artificial variable technique* can be applied just as discussed earlier in this section. (In fact, this constraint is identical to our example of an equality constraint except that it includes one more term on the left-hand side.) Letting $\bar{x}_6$ be the nonnegative artificial variable for this constraint, its final form becomes

$$3x_1 + 2x_2 - x_5 + \bar{x}_6 = 18,$$

where $\bar{x}_6$ is used as the initial basic variable ($\bar{x}_6 = 18$) for this equation. The Big M method also would be applied just as before, as we shall demonstrate shortly.

As usual, introducing this artificial variable enlarges the feasible region. The original constraint allowed only solutions lying above or on the constraint boundary $3x_1 + 2x_2 = 18$. Now, it allows any solution lying below this constraint boundary as well because both x_5 and $\bar{x}_6$ are constrained only to be nonnegative, so their difference $(\bar{x}_6 - x_5)$ can be *any* positive or negative number. Therefore, the effect of including $\bar{x}_6$ is to *eliminate* this constraint at the outset (before the Big M method forces $\bar{x}_6$ to be zero). Considering the other constraints as well (see Fig. 2.6), this expands the feasible region for the *revised* problem to include the entire line segment connecting (0,6) and (4,6).

You may have noticed that we took a somewhat circuitous route in converting the third constraint from its original form $3x_1 + 2x_2 \geq 18$ to its final version $3x_1 + 2x_2 - x_5 + \bar{x}_6 = 18$. In fact, we multiplied through the constraint by (-1) twice along the way! Now that you have seen the motivation leading to the final form, we should point out the following shortcut:

$$\begin{aligned} &3x_1 + 2x_2 \geq 18 \\ &\rightarrow 3x_1 + 2x_2 - x_5 = 18 \qquad (x_5 \geq 0) \\ &\rightarrow 3x_1 + 2x_2 - x_5 + \bar{x}_6 = 18 \qquad (x_5 \geq 0, \bar{x}_6 \geq 0). \end{aligned}$$

In this form, x_5 is called a **surplus variable** because it subtracts the surplus of the left-hand side over the right-side to convert the constraint into an equivalent equation.

Solving the Modified Example

With the above adjustments in the model for the modified example, we now are almost ready to apply the iterative part of the simplex method. All that remains is to make the usual adjustment in the equality constraint $2x_2 = 12$ and to apply the Big M method. Letting $\bar{x}_4$ be the artificial variable for this constraint, it becomes

$$2x_2 + \bar{x}_4 = 12.$$

Since the entire set of equations now contains two artificial variables $\bar{x}_4$ and $\bar{x}_6$, the objective function becomes

$$\text{Minimize} \quad Z = 3x_1 + 2x_2 + M\bar{x}_4 + M\bar{x}_6,$$

or in maximization form,

$$\text{Maximize} \quad (-Z) = -3x_1 - 2x_2 - M\bar{x}_4 - M\bar{x}_6.$$

This latter form yields our preliminary Eq. (0):

$$(0) \qquad -Z + 3x_1 + 2x_2 + M\bar{x}_4 + M\bar{x}_6 = 0,$$

or in tabular form,

$$R_0 = [3 \;\; 2 \;\; 0 \;\; M \;\; 0 \;\; M, \;\; 0].$$

Table 2.30 Complete Set of Simplex Tableaux for Modified Example

Iteration	Basic variable	Eq. no.	Z	x_1	x_2	x_3	$\bar{x}_4$	x_5	$\bar{x}_6$	Right side
				Coefficient of						
0	Z	0	−1	$(-3M+3)$	$(-4M+5)$	0	0	M	0	$-30M$
	x_3	1	0	1	0	1	0	0	0	4
	$\bar{x}_4$	2	0	0	2	0	1	0	0	12
	$\bar{x}_6$	3	0	3	2	0	0	−1	1	18
1	Z	0	−1	$(-3M+3)$	0	0	$\left(2M-\frac{5}{2}\right)$	M	0	$-6M-30$
	x_3	1	0	1	0	1	0	0	0	4
	x_2	2	0	0	1	0	$\frac{1}{2}$	0	0	6
	$\bar{x}_6$	3	0	3	0	0	−1	−1	1	6
2	Z	0	−1	0	0	0	$\left(M-\frac{3}{2}\right)$	1	$(M-1)$	−36
	x_3	1	0	0	0	1	$\frac{1}{3}$	$\frac{1}{3}$	$-\frac{1}{3}$	2
	x_2	2	0	0	1	0	$\frac{1}{2}$	0	0	6
	x_1	3	0	1	0	0	$-\frac{1}{3}$	$-\frac{1}{3}$	$\frac{1}{3}$	2

Since $\bar{x}_4$ and $\bar{x}_6$ are to be initial basic variables, row 0 needs to be updated to reflect this.

$$
\begin{array}{lrcccccccc}
\textit{Row 0} & [& 3 & 5 & 0 & M & 0 & M, & 0\,] \\
 & -M[& 0 & 2 & 0 & 1 & 0 & 0, & 12\,] \\
 & -M[& 3 & 2 & 0 & 0 & -1 & 1, & 18\,] \\
\hline
\text{new row} = & [(-3M+3), & & (-4M+5), & 0 & 0 & M & 0, & -30M].
\end{array}
$$

The resulting initial simplex tableau and the subsequent iterations are shown in Table 2.30.

It is interesting to reflect on what the Big M method actually does, as illustrated by this example. It *essentially* can be interpreted as using the following two-phase approach.[1] In phase 1 the simplex method is used to *minimize* the *sum* (i.e., maximize the negative of the sum) of the artificial variables over the feasible region for the *revised* problem. For the example, this consists of minimizing $\bar{x}_4 + \bar{x}_6$ (this is essentially obtained by dividing $Z = 3x_1 + 5x_2 + M\bar{x}_4 + M\bar{x}_6$ by the huge quantity M). The "optimal" solution for phase 1 necessarily has all the artificial variables equal to zero (with the one exception discussed below), so this solution is *feasible* for the *original* problem. Phase 2 then solves the original problem by the simplex method, starting with this solution as the initial basic feasible solution. For the example, this initial solution (see the last tableau of Table 2.30) also happens to be optimal for the original problem, so no more iterations are needed. In our earlier example just for equality constraints (see Table 2.29), one iteration was required in phase 2.

No Feasible Solutions

So far in this section we have been concerned primarily with the basic problem of identifying an initial basic feasible solution when an obvious one is not available. You have seen how the artificial variable technique constructs an artificial problem and obtains an initial basic feasible solution for this revised problem instead. The Big M method then enables the simplex method to begin its pilgrimage toward the basic feasible solutions, and ultimately the optimal solution, for the *original* problem.

However, you should be wary of a certain pitfall with this approach. If there is no obvious choice for the initial basic feasible solution, this may be for the very good reason that there are no feasible solutions at all! Nevertheless, by constructing an artificial "feasible" solution there is nothing to prevent the simplex method from proceeding as usual and ultimately reporting a supposedly optimal solution.

[1] This approach is called the *two-phase method.* It is commonly used directly in computer codes rather than the Big M method. The two methods are essentially equivalent from a computational viewpoint.

Table 2.31 Complete Set of Simplex Tableaux for Example with No Feasible Solutions

Iteration	Basic variable	Eq. no.	Coefficient of Z	x_1	x_2	x_3	$\bar{x}_4$	x_5	$\bar{x}_6$	Right side
0	Z	0	-1	$(-3M+3)$	$(-4M+5)$	0	0	M	0	$-30M$
	x_3	1	0	1	0	1	0	0	0	1
	$\bar{x}_4$	2	0	0	2	0	1	0	0	12
	$\bar{x}_6$	3	0	3	2	0	0	-1	1	18
1	Z	0	-1	$(-3M+3)$	0	0	$\left(2M-\frac{5}{2}\right)$	M	0	$-6M-30$
	x_3	1	0	1	0	1	0	0	0	1
	x_2	2	0	0	1	0	$\frac{1}{2}$	0	0	6
	$\bar{x}_6$	3	0	3	0	0	-1	-1	1	6
2	Z	0	-1	0	0	$(3M-3)$	$\left(2M-\frac{5}{2}\right)$	M	0	$-3M-33$
	x_1	1	0	1	0	1	0	0	0	1
	x_2	2	0	0	1	0	$\frac{1}{2}$	0	0	6
	$\bar{x}_6$	3	0	0	0	-3	-1	-1	1	3

Fortunately the artificial variable technique provides the following signpost to indicate when this has happened:

If the original problem has *no feasible solutions*, then any optimal solution for the *revised* problem with the Big M method has at least one artificial variable *not* equal to zero. Otherwise, they *all* equal zero.

To illustrate, let us change the first constraint in the modified example (see Fig. 2.6) as follows:

$$x_1 \leq 4 \rightarrow x_1 \leq 1,$$

so that the problem no longer has any feasible solutions. Applying the simplex method just as before yields the tableaux shown in Table 2.31. Hence the indicated optimal solution is (1,6,0,0,0,3). However, since an artificial variable $\bar{x}_6 = 3 > 0$, the real message is that the problem has no feasible solutions.

Variables Allowed to be Negative

In most practical problems, negative values for the decision variables would have no physical meaning, so it is necessary to include nonnegativity constraints in the formulations of their linear programming models. However, this is not always the case. To illustrate, suppose that the Wyndor Glass Co. problem is changed so that product 1 already is in production, and the first decision variable x_1 represents the *increase* in its production rate. Therefore a negative value of x_1 would indicate that product 1 is to be cut back by that amount. Such reductions might be desirable to allow a larger production rate for the new more profitable product 2, so negative values should be allowed for x_1 in the model.

Since the iterative step (part 2) of the simplex method requires that all the variables have nonnegativity constraints, any problem containing variables allowed to be negative must be converted into an *equivalent* problem involving only nonnegative variables. Fortunately this can be done. The modification required for each variable depends upon whether it has a (negative) lower bound on the values allowed or not. Each of these two cases is now discussed.

VARIABLES WITH A BOUND ON THE NEGATIVE VALUES ALLOWED Consider any decision variable x_j that is allowed to have negative values, but only those that satisfy a constraint of the form

$$x_j \geq L_j,$$

where L_j is some negative constant. This constraint can be converted into a nonnegativity constraint by making the change of variables

$$x'_j = x_j - L_j, \text{ so } x'_j \geq 0.$$

Thus $(x'_j + L_j)$ would be substituted for x_j throughout the model, so that the redefined decison variable x'_j can not be negative.

To illustrate, suppose that the current production rate for product 1 in the Wyndor Glass Co. problem is 10. With the definition of x_1 given above, the complete model at this point is the same as given in Sec. 2.1 except that the nonnegativity constraint $x_1 \geq 0$ is replaced by

$$x_1 \geq -10.$$

To obtain the equivalent model needed for the simplex method, this decision variable would be redefined as the *total* production rate of product 1,

$$x_1' = x_1 + 10,$$

which yields the changes in the objective function and constraints as shown:

$$\boxed{\begin{array}{l} Z = 3x_1 + 5x_2 \\ x_1 \qquad\quad \leq 4 \\ \qquad 2x_2 \leq 12 \\ 3x_1 + 2x_2 \leq 18 \\ x_1 \geq -10,\ x_2 \geq 0 \end{array}} \rightarrow \boxed{\begin{array}{l} Z = 3(x_1' - 10) + 5x_2 \\ (x_1' - 10) \qquad \leq 4 \\ \qquad\qquad 2x_2 \leq 12 \\ 3(x_1' - 10) + 2x_2 \leq 18 \\ (x_1' - 10) \geq -10,\ x_2 \geq 0 \end{array}} \rightarrow \boxed{\begin{array}{l} Z = -30 + 3x_1' + 5x_2 \\ x_1' \qquad\quad \leq 14 \\ \qquad 2x_2 \leq 12 \\ 3x_1' + 2x_2 \leq 48 \\ x_1' \geq 0,\ x_2 \geq 0 \end{array}}$$

Variables with No Bound on the Negative Values Allowed In the case where x_j does *not* have a lower bound constraint in the model formulated, another approach is required: x_j is replaced throughout the model by the *difference* of two new *nonnegative* variables

$$x_j = x_j' - x_j'', \text{ where } x_j' \geq 0,\ x_j'' \geq 0.$$

Since x_j' and x_j'' can have any nonnegative values, this difference $(x_j' - x_j'')$ can have *any* value (positive or negative), so it is a legitimate substitute for x_j in the model. But after such substitutions, the simplex method can proceed with just nonnegative variables.

The new variables x_j' and x_j'' have a simple interpretation. Each basic feasible solution for the new form of the model necessarily has the property that *either* $x_j' = 0$ or $x_j'' = 0$ (or both). (You can see the reason why a positive constant can not be added to both variables, and still be a basic feasible solution, by referring to the geometrical definition of *corner-point feasible solution* in Sec. 2.5.) Therefore, at the optimal solution obtained by the simplex method,

$$x_j' = \begin{cases} x_j, & \text{if } x_j \geq 0 \\ 0, & \text{otherwise;} \end{cases}$$

$$x_j'' = \begin{cases} |x_j|, & \text{if } x_j \leq 0 \\ 0, & \text{otherwise;} \end{cases}$$

so that x_j' represents the *positive* part of the decision variable x_j and x_j'' its *negative* part.

To illustrate this approach, let us use the same example as for the bounded variable case above. However, now suppose that the $x_1 \geq -10$ constraint was not included in the original model because it clearly would not change the optimal solution. (In some problems, certain variables do not need explicit lower bound constraints because the functional constraints already prevent lower values.) Therefore, before applying the simplex method, x_1 would be replaced by the difference

$$x_1 = x_1' - x_1'', \text{ where } x_1' \geq 0, x_1'' \geq 0,$$

as shown:

Original model		Transformed model
Maximize $Z = 3x_1 + 5x_2$ $x_1 \leq 4$ $2x_2 \leq 12$ $3x_1 + 2x_2 \leq 18$ $x_2 \geq 0$ (only)	→	Maximize $Z = 3x_1' - 3x_1'' + 5x_2$ $x_1' - x_1'' \leq 4$ $2x_2 \leq 12$ $3x_1' - 3x_1'' + 2x_2 \leq 18$ $x_1' \geq 0, x_1'' \geq 0, x_2 \geq 0$

From a computational viewpoint, this approach has the disadvantage that the new equivalent model to be used has more variables than the original model. In fact, if *all* the original variables lack lower bound constraints, the new model will have *twice* as many variables. Fortunately the approach can be modified slightly so that the number of variables is increased by only *one*, regardless of how many original variables need to be replaced. This is done by replacing each such variable x_j by

$$x_j = x_j' - x'', \text{ where } x_j' \geq 0, x'' \geq 0,$$

instead, where x'' is the *same* variable for all relevant j. The interpretation of x'' in this case is that $-x''$ is the current value of the largest negative original variable, so that x_j' is the amount by which x_j exceeds this value. Thus the simplex method now can make some of the x_j' variables larger than zero even when $x'' > 0$.

2.11 A FUNDAMENTAL INSIGHT

We shall now focus on a property of the simplex method that provides the key to both duality theory (Sec. 2.12) and sensitivity analysis (Sec. 4.3), two very important parts of linear programming. This property involves the coefficients of the slack variables and the information they give. It is a direct result of the initialization step, where the *i*th slack variable (x_{n+i}) is given a coefficient of $+1$ in Eq. (i) and a coefficient of *zero* in *every other* equation [including Eq. (0)] for $i = 1, 2, \ldots, m$.†

PROPERTY For any row k in the *current* tableau[1] ($k = 0, 1, \ldots, m$), the coefficient of x_{n+i} ($i \neq k$) is the multiple of the *original* row i that has been added (directly or indirectly) to the *original* row k by the simplex method. (If $i = k$,

† If artificial variables are needed (as discussed in Sec. 2.10), then let x_{n+i} be the slack *or* artificial variable that is given a coefficient of $+1$ in Eq. (i) and a coefficient of zero in every other equation.

[1] If you studied the algebraic form of the simplex method but not the tabular form, then substitute the term "equation" for "row" and "set of equations" for "tableau" both here and in the following discussion.

then the coefficient of x_{n+k} is the constant by which the *original* row k has since been multiplied by the simplex method.)

To clarify the meaning of this property, let us first concentrate on the case $k = 0$ for the original Wyndor Glass Co. example as solved in Sec. 2.8. In the second tableau (the result of iteration 1) of Table 2.25, the coefficients of the slack variables—x_3, x_4, and x_5—are 0, 5/2, and 0, respectively. This indicates the fact that no multiple of either row 1 or row 3 has yet been added to row 0, but that 5/2 of the original row 2 has been added. This is correct because the current row 2 is 1/2 of the original row 2 (the coefficient of x_4 is 1/2) and 5 times the current row 2 was added to the original row 0.

In the third tableau of Table 2.25 the coefficients of the slack variables in row 0 are 0, 3/2, and 1. Thus the original row 1 still has not influenced row 0 (since it never has been a pivot row), but 1/3(3) = 1 times the original row 3 now has been added to row 0. The multiple for row 2 has changed from 5/2 to 3/2 because the original row 2 was subtracted from the original row 3, and this entire quantity (3 times the *current* row 3) has now been added to row 0. Thus 5/2 times the original row 2 has been added *directly* to row 0, but (−1) times the original row 2 has been added *indirectly* via row 3, so 5/2 − 1 = 3/2.

To express our conclusions *symbolically* (which will be very useful in Secs. 2.12 and 4.3), let

$\bar{R}_k$ = row k in *original* tableau,

R_k = row k in *current* tableau after any given iteration,

R_k^* = row k in *final* tableau (the one yielding an optimal solution),

for $k = 0, 1, \ldots, m$. Thus, in the example,

$$\begin{aligned}\bar{R}_0 &= [-3 \quad -5 \quad 0 \quad 0 \quad 0, \quad 0],\\ \bar{R}_1 &= [\ \ 1 \quad\ \ 0 \quad 1 \quad 0 \quad 0, \quad 4],\\ \bar{R}_2 &= [\ \ 0 \quad\ \ 2 \quad 0 \quad 1 \quad 0, \quad 12],\\ \bar{R}_3 &= [\ \ 3 \quad\ \ 2 \quad 0 \quad 0 \quad 1, \quad 18],\end{aligned}$$

while the R_k (for iteration 1) and R_k^* are the corresponding rows in the second and third tableaux. Also define the numbers in row 0 symbolically by

$$R_0 = [z_1 - c_1, z_2 - c_2, \ldots, z_n - c_n, y_1, y_2, \ldots, y_m, y_0].$$

Since the *original* row 0 is

$$\bar{R}_0 = [-c_1, -c_2, \ldots, -c_n, 0, 0, \ldots, 0, 0],$$

the interpretations of these new symbols are

z_j = net amount by which *original* coefficient of x_j in Eq. (0) has been *increased* by simplex method, for $j = 1, 2, \ldots, n$,

y_0 = current value of Z,

and by the property stated above,

y_i = multiple of *original* row i that has been added to row 0 by simplex method, for $i = 1, 2, \ldots, m$.

(When we are speaking specifically about the *final* row 0, R_0^*, we shall put an asterisk on each of these new symbols). Therefore our property and its direct implications can now be stated as follows for the case $k = 0$.

PROPERTY FOR ROW 0 $\quad R_0 = \bar{R}_0 + \sum_{i=1}^{m} \bar{R}_i y_i.$

Immediate consequences $\quad z_j - c_j = -c_j + \sum_{i=1}^{m} a_{ij} y_i$, for $j = 1, 2, \ldots, n$;

$$y_0 = \sum_{i=1}^{m} b_i y_i.$$

These consequences merely restate the property for just *one* number in R_0.

Now let us directly apply this property to the example (see Table 2.25), using only information about the $\bar{R}_i$ (given above) and the current values of the y_i.

Iteration 1 Since $y_1 = 0,\ y_2 = \frac{5}{2},\ y_3 = 0,$

$$\begin{aligned} R_0 &= [-3 \quad -5 \quad 0 \quad 0 \quad 0, \quad 0] \\ &\quad + \tfrac{5}{2}[\ 0 \quad 2 \quad 0 \quad 1 \quad 0, \quad 12] \\ &= \left[-3 \quad 0 \quad 0 \quad \tfrac{5}{2} \quad 0, \quad 30\right] \\ &\equiv [z_1 - c_1, z_2 - c_2, y_1, y_2, y_3, y_0]. \end{aligned}$$

Iteration 2 Since $y_1^* = 0,\ y_2^* = \frac{3}{2},\ y_3^* = 1,$

$$\begin{aligned} R_0^* &= [-3 \quad -5 \quad 0 \quad 0 \quad 0, \quad 0] \\ &\quad + \tfrac{3}{2}[\ 0 \quad 2 \quad 0 \quad 1 \quad 0, \quad 12] \\ &\quad + 1[\ 3 \quad 2 \quad 0 \quad 0 \quad 1, \quad 18] \\ &= \left[\ 0 \quad 0 \quad 0 \quad \tfrac{3}{2} \quad 1, \quad 36\right] \\ &\equiv [z_1^* - c_1, z_2^* - c_2, y_1^*, y_2^*, y_3^*, y_0^*]. \end{aligned}$$

Notice for both iterations how the $(z_j - c_j)$ and y_0 automatically satisfy the expressions given for them.

You will see in Sec. 2.12 that this property for row 0 provides the basis for the very useful duality theory of linear programming. Sensitivity analysis is based both on this property and the corresponding property for the other rows. Therefore, we now briefly turn our attention to the other rows to parallel the above development. The required notation is introduced only for the *final* tableau because this is all that is relevant for sensitivity analysis.

For each *final* row $k(R_k^*)$ except row 0, denote its numbers by

$$R_k^* = [a_{k1}^*, a_{k2}^*, \ldots, a_{kn}^*, s_{k1}^*, s_{k2}^*, \ldots, s_{km}^*, b_k^*], \text{ for } k = 1, 2, \ldots, m.$$

Thus, each a_{kj}^* or b_k^* represents the *same* entry in row k of the *final* tableau that a_{kj} or b_k represents in the *original* tableau (as shown at the beginning of Sec. 2.7). Similarly,

$$s_{ki}^* = \text{coefficient of } i\text{th slack variable } x_{n+i} \text{ in } \textit{final} \text{ Eq. } (k).$$

With this notation, we can now state mathematically the remainder of our property of the simplex method.

PROPERTY FOR R_k^* $\quad R_k^* = \sum_{i=1}^{m} \bar{R}_i s_{ki}^*$, for $k = 1, 2, \ldots, m$

Immediate consequences $\quad a_{kj}^* = \sum_{i=1}^{m} a_{ij} s_{ki}^*$, for $j = 1, 2, \ldots, n$;

$$b_k^* = \sum_{i=1}^{m} b_i s_{ki}^*.$$

Notice that this property for R_k^* is almost the same as the one above for R_0 because both s_{ki}^* and y_i are the coefficient of the ith slack variable (x_{n+i}) for the row under consideration. The only difference is that R_0 includes the extra $\bar{R}_0$ term on the right, but this difference is more form than substance because R_k^* can be rewritten as

$$R_k^* = \bar{R}_k + \sum_{i=1}^{m} \bar{R}_i (s_{ki}^* - s_{ki}),$$

where s_{ki} denotes the coefficient of x_{n+i} in the *original* Eq. (i) (so $s_{ki} = 0$ for all $i \neq k$ and $s_{kk} = 1$). Since the *original* row 0 has zero terms for *all* the slack variables, the difference $(s_{ki}^* - s_{ki})$ and y_i both give the *increase* (either positive or negative) in the coefficient of x_{n+i} for the row under consideration. These increases actually are the relevant quantities for our general property.

To illustrate the property for R_k^*, it is used below to derive the remaining rows of the final tableau for the example.

Row 1 Since $s_{11}^* = 1, s_{12}^* = \frac{1}{3}, s_{13}^* = -\frac{1}{3}$,

$$\begin{aligned} R_1^* = & \quad [1 \;\; 0 \;\; 1 \;\; 0 \quad 0, \quad 4] \\ & + \frac{1}{3}[0 \;\; 2 \;\; 0 \;\; 1 \quad 0, \quad 12] \\ & - \frac{1}{3}[3 \;\; 2 \;\; 0 \;\; 0 \quad 1, \quad 18] \\ = & \left[0 \;\; 0 \;\; 1 \;\; \frac{1}{3} \;\; -\frac{1}{3}, \;\; 2\right] \\ \equiv & \; [a_{11}^*, a_{12}^*, s_{11}^*, s_{12}^*, s_{13}^*, b_1^*]. \end{aligned}$$

Row 2 Since $s_{21}^* = 0, s_{22}^* = \frac{1}{2}, s_{23}^* = 0,$

$$\begin{aligned} R_2^* &= \frac{1}{2}[0 \;\; 2 \;\; 0 \;\; 1 \;\; 0, \;\; 12] \\ &= \left[0 \;\; 1 \;\; 0 \;\; \frac{1}{2} \;\; 0, \;\; 6\right] \\ &\equiv [a_{21}^*, a_{22}^*, s_{21}^*, s_{22}^*, s_{23}^*, b_3^*]. \end{aligned}$$

Row 3 Since $s_{31}^* = 0, s_{32}^* = -\frac{1}{3}, s_{33}^* = \frac{1}{3},$

$$\begin{aligned} R_3^* &= -\frac{1}{3}[0 \;\; 2 \;\; 0 \;\; 1 \;\; 0, \;\; 12] \\ &\quad + \frac{1}{3}[3 \;\; 2 \;\; 0 \;\; 0 \;\; 1, \;\; 18] \\ &= \left[1 \;\; 0 \;\; 0 \;\; -\frac{1}{3} \;\; \frac{1}{3}, \;\; 2\right] \\ &\equiv [a_{31}^*, a_{32}^*, s_{31}^*, s_{32}^*, s_{33}^*, b_3^*]. \end{aligned}$$

2.12 DUALITY THEORY

One of the most important discoveries in the early development of linear programming was the concept of duality and its many important ramifications. This discovery revealed that every linear programming problem has associated with it another linear programming problem called the *dual.* The relationships between the dual problem and the original problem (called the *primal*) prove to be extremely useful in a variety of ways.

We begin this section by showing how the dual problem arises and what its resulting form is. We then describe an economic interpretation for this problem, which is very useful for analyzing the primal problem. Following this, we discuss the relationships of the two problems and how they can be exploited. For greater clarity, all this is done under the assumption that the *primal* linear programming problem is in *our standard form,*[1] as shown below.

PRIMAL PROBLEM Find $x_1, x_2, \ldots, x_n$ so as to

$$\text{Maximize} \quad Z = \sum_{j=1}^{n} c_j x_j,$$

subject to

$$\sum_{j=1}^{n} a_{ij} x_j \le b_i, \text{ for } i = 1, 2, \ldots, m$$

[1] However, the model parameters, including the b_i, are allowed to have any positive *or* negative values.

and

$$x_j \geq 0, \text{ for } j = 1, 2, \ldots, n.$$

The changes for other forms are then mentioned at the end of the section.

Origin of the Dual Problem

Duality theory is based directly on the fundamental insight (particularly with regard to row 0) presented in Sec. 2.11. (If that material is not fresh in your mind, we recommend that you review it at this point.) To see why, we continue to use the notation introduced there. Thus, at any given iteration of the simplex method for the above primal problem, the current numbers in row 0 are denoted as shown in the (partial) tableau given in Table 2.32.

Table 2.32 Notation for Entries in Row 0 of Simplex Tableau

			Coefficient of									Right side
Iteration	*Basic variable*	*Eq. no.*	Z	x_1	x_2	$\cdots$	x_n	x_{n+1}	x_{n+2}	$\cdots$	x_{n+m}	
Any	Z	0	1	$(z_1 - c_1)$	$(z_2 - c_2)$	$\cdots$	$(z_n - c_n)$	y_1	y_2	$\cdots$	y_m	y_0

Also recall that the fundamental insight led to the following relationships between these quantities and the parameters of the original model:

$$y_0 = \sum_{i=1}^{m} b_i y_i$$

$$z_j = \sum_{i=1}^{m} a_{ij} y_i, \text{ for } j = 1, 2, \ldots, n.$$

The remaining key now is to express what the simplex method tries to accomplish (according to the stopping rule) in terms of these symbols. Specifically, it seeks a set of basic variables, and the corresponding basic feasible solution, such that *all* the coefficients in row 0 are *nonnegative*. It then stops with this optimal solution. This goal is expressed symbolically as follows:

CONDITION FOR OPTIMALITY $\quad z_j - c_j \geq 0, \text{ for } j = 1, 2, \ldots, n$

$$y_i \geq 0, \text{ for } i = 1, 2, \ldots, m.$$

After substituting the above expression for z_j, this says that the simplex method can be interpreted as seeking values for $y_1, y_2, \ldots, y_m$ such that

$$y_0 = \sum_{i=1}^{m} b_i y_i,$$

subject to

$$\sum_{i=1}^{m} a_{ij} y_i \geq c_j, \text{ for } j = 1, 2, \ldots, n$$

and

$$y_i \geq 0, \text{ for } i = 1, 2, \ldots, m.$$

But except for lacking an objective for y_0, this also is a linear programming problem! To complete the formulation, let us now explore what this objective should be.

Since y_0 is just the current value of Z, and the objective for the primal problem is to maximize Z, a natural first reaction is that y_0 should be maximized also. However, this is not correct for the following rather subtle reason: The only *feasible* solutions for this new problem are those that satisfy the condition for *optimality* for the primal problem. Therefore it is *only* the optimal solution for the primal problem that corresponds to a feasible solution for this new problem. As a consequence, the optimal value of Z in the primal problem is the *minimum* feasible value of y_0 in the new problem. (The complete justification for this conclusion is provided by the relationships we develop later in the section.) This gives the **dual problem** stated below.

DUAL PROBLEM Find $y_1, y_2, \ldots, y_m$ so as to

$$\text{Minimize} \quad y_0 = \sum_{i=1}^{m} b_i y_i,$$

subject to

$$\sum_{i=1}^{m} a_{ij} y_i \geq c_j, \text{ for } j = 1, 2, \ldots, n$$

and

$$y_i \geq 0, \text{ for } i = 1, 2, \ldots, m.$$

At this point you should carefully compare the *form* of the primal and dual problems. The **primal-dual table** for linear programming (Table 2.33) might

Table 2.33 Primal-dual Table for Linear Programming

			Primal problem					
			Coefficient of				*Right side*	
			x_1	x_2	$\cdots$	x_n		
Dual Problem	*Coefficient of*	y_1	a_{11}	a_{12}	$\cdots$	a_{1n}	$\leq b_1$	*Coefficients for objective function (minimize)*
		y_2	a_{21}	a_{22}	$\cdots$	a_{2n}	$\leq b_2$	
		$\vdots$	$\vdots$				$\vdots$	
		y_m	a_{m1}	a_{m2}	$\cdots$	a_{mn}	$\leq b_m$	
	Right side		$\geq c_1$	$\geq c_2$	$\cdots$	$\geq c_n$		
			Coefficients for objective function (maximize)					

be helpful in this regard. It shows all the linear programming parameters (the a_{ij}, b_i, and c_j) and how they are used to construct the two problems. All the horizontal headings are for the primal problem, whereas the headings for the dual problem are read by turning the book sideways. We suggest that you begin by looking at each problem *individually* by covering up the headings for the other problem with your hands. Then, after you see what the table is saying for the individual problems, compare them. Particularly notice how (1) the parameters for a *constraint* in either problem are the coefficients of a *variable* in the other problem, and (2) the coefficients for the *objective function* of either problem are the *right sides* for the other problem. Thus there is a direct correspondence between these entities in the two problems, as summarized in Table 2.34. These correspondences are a key to some of the applications of duality theory, including sensitivity analysis.

Table 2.34 Correspondence between Entities in Primal and Dual Problems

One problem		*Other problem*
Constraint i	⟷	variable i
Objective function	⟷	right sides

To be more concrete, let us now consider the Wyndor Glass Co. problem of Sec. 2.1. Substituting the parameters for this example into Table 2.33 yields Table 2.35 (after deleting the headings). The resulting primal and dual

Table 2.35 Primal-dual Table for Wyndor Glass Co. Problem

	x_1	x_2	
y_1	1	0	≤ 4
y_2	0	2	≤ 12
y_3	3	2	≤ 18
	≥ 3	≥ 5	

problems are shown side by side in Table 2.36. A close inspection of this dual linear programming problem reveals its optimal solution. (Try it, but be careful; it is not $y_1 = 3$, $y_2 = 5/2$, $y_3 = 0$.) Actually, we have already solved this problem! Go back to the *final* tableau for the primal problem (see Table 2.25), and check the values of y_1^*, y_2^*, y_3^* given there (the coefficients of the slack variables in row 0), $y_1^* = 0$, $y_2^* = 3/2$, $y_3^* = 1$. It is no coincidence that this is the answer. Rather, it is just one consequence of the relationships between the primal and dual problems developed later in this section.

Table 2.36 Primal and Dual Problems for Wyndor Glass Co.

Primal problem	*Dual problem*
Maximize $Z = 3x_1 + 5x_2$, subject to $x_1 \le 4$ $2x_2 \le 12$ $3x_1 + 2x_2 \le 18$ and $x_1 \ge 0,\ x_2 \ge 0$	Minimize $y_0 = 4y_1 + 12y_2 + 18y_3$, subject to $y_1 + 3y_3 \ge 3$ $2y_2 + 2y_3 \ge 5$ and $y_1 \ge 0,\ y_2 \ge 0,\ y_3 \ge 0$

You will see next that our derivation of the general dual problem has a natural economic interpretation that proves to be valuable for analyzing *primal* linear programming problems.

Economic Interpretation of the Dual Problem

The economic interpretation of the dual problem is based directly upon the interpretation for the primal problem (linear programming problem in our standard form) presented in Sec. 2.2. To refresh your memory, we have summarized this primal interpretation in Table 2.37.

Table 2.37 Economic Interpretation of Primal Problem

Quantity	*Interpretation*
x_j	Level of activity j ($j = 1,2, \ldots, n$)
c_j	Unit profit from activity j
Z	Total profit from all activities
b_i	Amount of resource i available ($i = 1,2, \ldots, m$)
a_{ij}	Amount of resource i consumed by each unit of activity j

To see the resulting interpretation for the dual problem, let us begin with the dual variables $y_1, y_2, \ldots, y_m$. Recall that

$$y_0 = b_1 y_1 + b_2 y_2 + \cdots + b_m y_m$$

and that y_0 is the current value of Z at any iteration of the simplex method. Therefore, given the values of $y_1, y_2, \ldots, y_m$ shown in row 0 at the current iteration (see Table 2.32),

y_i is current unit contribution to profit of resource i ($i = 1,2, \ldots, m$).

Thus, in the *final* tableau for the example (see Table 2.25), where $y_1^* = 0$, $y_2^* = 3/2$, $y_3^* = 1$, this says that each unit of the three resources (available production capacities in the three plants) contributes 0, \$1.50, and \$1.00, respectively, to the total profit of \$36/minute with the optimal solution for the Wyndor Glass Co.; that is,

$$36 = 4(0) + 12\left(\frac{3}{2}\right) + 18(1).$$

This allocation of the credit for the profit obtained may seem quite arbitrary, particularly in the example where Plant 1 receives no credit despite the fact that it must be used to implement the optimal solution. However, there actually is a precise rationalization for this allocation, as summarized below.

> More precisely, y_i is the *marginal value* of resource i, that is, the rate at which Z could be increased by increasing b_i, when using the current set of basic variables to obtain the primal solution.

To see how this interpretation applies to the example, we ask you to refer to Fig. 2.2 and check what happens when each b_i *individually* is increased by 1. Note how the optimal corner-point solution, $x_1 = 2$, $x_2 = 6$ with $Z = 36$, changes in the three respective cases ($i = 1,2,3$) to (1) $x_1 = 2$, $x_2 = 6$ with $Z = 36$ ($\Delta Z = 0 = y_1^*$); (2) $x_1 = 5/3$, $x_2 = 13/2$ with $Z = 37\frac{1}{2}$ ($\Delta Z = 3/2 = y_2^*$); and (3) $x_1 = 7/3$, $x_2 = 6$ with $Z = 37$ ($\Delta Z = 1 = y_3^*$). Also note that the interpretation may be relevant only for a relatively small increase in b_i because the current basic solution (corner-point solution) may become infeasible with a larger increase. In particular, since our current corner-point solution under consideration in the example (the optimal one) lies at the intersection of the constraint boundaries $2x_2 = 12$ and $3x_1 + 2x_2 = 18$, it becomes infeasible if either $b_2 = 12$ or $b_3 = 18$ is increased by more than 6.

This interpretation of the dual variables is extremely useful in many practical applications of linear programming. The reason is that even though the formulation of the general linear programming model assumes that the b_i are fixed constants, there frequently is some flexibility in the resource allocations in practice. In such cases the values of b_i used in the model represent the *anticipated* allocation of the resources to the set of activities under consideration. After obtaining an optimal solution for this model, the corresponding values (see Table 2.34) of the dual variables (often called **shadow prices** in this context) are then used to evaluate whether the resource allocations should be changed. The shadow price y_i^* for resource i represents the (maximum) unit price you should be willing to pay to increase the allocation of that resource. If the shadow price is greater than the actual unit cost, then the allocation should be increased until this relationship no longer holds.

In the Wyndor Glass Co. problem, management has ruled out any expansion of the production capacity in the three plants at this time. Nevertheless, the available capacities allocated to the two new products ($b_1 = 4$, $b_2 = 12$, $b_3 = 18$) can be increased by cutting back further on the current product line. The O.R. Dept. actually investigates this possibility as part of the sensitivity analysis study presented in Sec. 4.3.

Now let us turn our attention to the interpretation of the overall dual problem.[1] By directly applying the initial interpretation of the dual variables,

> $z_j = \sum_{i=1}^{m} a_{ij} y_i$ is current contribution to profit of resources that would be consumed by one unit of activity j ($j = 1,2, \ldots, n$).

[1] Actually, several slightly different interpretations have been proposed. The one presented here seems to us to be the most useful because it also directly interprets what the simplex method does in the primal problem.

Therefore, since c_j is interpreted as the unit profit from activity j, the functional constraints

$$\sum_{i=1}^{m} a_{ij} y_i \geq c_j$$

say that the contribution to profit of these resources must be at least as much as if they were used by this activity. Otherwise, we would not be making the best possible use of these resources. Similarly, the nonnegativity constraints

$$y_i \geq 0$$

say that the contribution to profit of resource i ($i = 1, 2, \ldots, m$) must be nonnegative. Otherwise, we would be better off not using this resource at all. The objective,

$$\text{Minimize} \quad y_0 = \sum_{i=1}^{m} b_i y_i,$$

can be viewed as minimizing the total implicit value of the resources consumed by the activities.

This interpretation can be sharpened somewhat by differentiating between *basic* and *nonbasic* variables in the primal problem. Recall that the *basic* variables (the only nonzero variables) *always* have a coefficient of *zero* in row 0. Therefore, for any basic feasible solution ($x_1, x_2, \ldots, x_{n+m}$),

$$\sum_{i=1}^{m} a_{ij} y_i = c_j, \text{ if } x_j > 0 \qquad (j = 1, 2, \ldots, n),$$

$$y_i = 0, \text{ if } x_{n+i} > 0 \qquad (i = 1, 2, \ldots, m).$$

(You will see later in the section that this *complementary slackness property* is one part of some fundamental relationships between the primal and dual problems.) The economic interpretation of the first statement is that whenever an activity j operates at a strictly positive level ($x_j > 0$), the marginal value of the resources it consumes *must* equal the profit from this activity. The second statement implies that the marginal value of resource i is *zero* ($y_i = 0$) whenever the supply of this resource is not exhausted by the activities ($x_{n+i} > 0$). In economic terminology, such a resource is a "free good"; the price of goods that are oversupplied must drop to zero by the law of supply and demand. This is what justifies interpreting the objective for the dual problem as minimizing the total implicit value of the resources *consumed*, rather than the resources *allocated*.

The interpretation of the dual problem also provides an economic interpretation of what the simplex method does in the primal problem. The goal of the simplex method is to find how to use the available resources in the most profitable feasible way. This requires reaching a basic feasible solution that satisfies all the requirements on profitable use of the resources (the constraints of the dual problem) which comprise the condition for optimality for the algorithm. For any given basic feasible solution, the requirements (dual constraints) associated with the *basic* variables are automatically satisfied (with equality). However, those associated with *nonbasic* variables may or may not be satisfied. In particular, if an *original* variable x_j is nonbasic, so that activity j is not used, then the current contribution to profits of the resources that would be required to undertake each unit of this activity

$$\sum_{i=1}^{m} a_{ij}y_i$$

may be either smaller ($<$) or larger ($\geq$) than the unit profit c_j obtainable from the activity. If it is smaller, so $(z_j - c_j) < 0$ in row 0 of the simplex tableau, then these resources can be used more profitably by initiating this activity. If it is larger, then these resources already are being assigned elsewhere in a more profitable way, so they should not be diverted to activity j. Similarly, if a *slack* variable x_{n+i} is nonbasic, so that the total allocation b_i of resource i is being used, then y_i is the current contribution to profit of this resource on a marginal basis. Hence, if $y_i < 0$, profit can be increased by cutting back on the use of this resource (i.e., increasing x_{n+i}). If $y_i \geq 0$, it is worthwhile to continue fully using this resource.

Therefore, what the simplex method does is to examine all the nonbasic variables in the current basic feasible solution to see which ones can provide a more profitable use of the resources by being increased. If *none* can, so that no feasible shifts or reductions in the current proposed use of the resources can increase profit, the current solution must be optimal. If one or more can, it selects the variable that, if increased by *1*, would improve the profitability of the use of the resources the most. It then actually increases this variable (the *entering basic variable*) as much as it can until the marginal values of the resources change. This results in a new basic feasible solution with a new row 0 (dual solution), and the whole process is repeated.

To solidify your understanding of this interpretation of the simplex method, we suggest that you apply it to the Wyndor Glass Co. problem, using both Fig. 2.2 and Table 2.25. (See Prob. 24.)

Although the economic interpretation of the dual problem considerably expands our ability to analyze the primal problem, you will see next that this is just a portion of the story about the useful relationships between the two problems.

Relationships between the Primal and Dual Problems

Since the dual problem is a linear programming problem, it also has corner-point solutions. Furthermore, by using the equality representation of the problem, these corner-point solutions can be expressed as basic solutions. Because the functional constraints have the $\geq$ form, this equality representation is obtained by *subtracting* the surplus

$$z_j - c_j = \sum_{i=1}^{m} a_{ij}y_i - c_j$$

from the left-hand side of each constraint j ($j = 1,2, \ldots, n$).† Thus $(z_j - c_j)$ plays the role of the *surplus variable* for constraint j (or its slack variable if the constraint is multiplied through by -1). Therefore each corner-point solution $(y_1, y_2, \ldots, y_m)$ yields a basic solution $(y_1, y_2, \ldots, y_m, z_1 - c_1, z_2 - c_2, \ldots, z_n - c_n)$ by using this expression for $(z_j - c_j)$. Since the equality representation has n functional constraints and $(n + m)$ variables, each basic solution has n basic variables and m nonbasic variables. (Note how m and n reverse their previous roles here because, as Table 2.34 indicates, dual constraints correspond to primal variables and dual variables correspond to primal constraints.)

One of the important relationships between the primal and dual problems is a direct correspondence between their basic solutions. To see this, look again at the partial tableau shown in Table 2.32. Such a row 0 can be constructed for *any* primal basic solution, feasible or not, by algebraically reducing the coefficients of all basic variables to zero (using the method employed by part 3 of the iterative step). Now note how a solution for the dual problem can be read directly from row 0. Thus, because of its coefficient in row 0, each variable in the primal problem has an associated variable in the dual problem, as summarized in Table 2.38. The remaining key insight is that the dual solution read from

Table 2.38 Association between Variables in Primal and Dual Problems

Primal variable		*Associated dual variable*	
(Original variable)	x_j	$(z_j - c_j)$	(surplus variable), $j = 1, 2, \ldots, n$
(Slack variable)	x_{n+i}	y_i	(original variable), $i = 1, 2, \ldots, m$

row 0 must also be a basic solution! The reason is that the m basic variables for the primal problem are required to have a coefficient of *zero* in row 0, which thereby requires the m associated dual variables to be zero, i.e., *nonbasic* variables for the dual problem. Selecting *any* set of the required number of variables to be nonbasic automatically yields a basic solution, provided the remaining variables possess a (unique) simultaneous solution to the system of equations. Since the system of equations in this case is just the above expression for $(z_j - c_j)$ for $j = 1, 2, \ldots, n$, such a solution is guaranteed by the fundamental insight presented in Sec. 2.9 (see the property for row 0 and its consequences).[1] Therefore the dual solution is indeed a basic solution.

Table 2.32 also reveals one more important fact about corresponding basic solutions in the two problems. Note that the first and last columns

† You might wonder why we do not also introduce *artificial variables* into these constraints as discussed in the preceding section. The reason is that these variables have no purpose other than to change the feasible region temporarily as a convenience in starting the simplex method. We are not interested now in applying the simplex method to the dual problem, and we do not want to change its feasible region.

[1] The uniqueness of this solution also relies on the fact that the selection of basic variables for the primal problem yields a unique solution; i.e., the columns in the initial tableau for these m variables are *linearly independent* (as defined in Appendix 3).

(basic variables and right side) indicate that y_0 is the value of the objective function Z for the current basic solution in the primal problem. Since the fundamental insight given in Sec. 2.11 has told us that y_0 also is the objective function value for the dual problem, including the basic solution read from row 0, we now can conclude that the corresponding basic solutions yield the *same* value for their respective objective functions.

Let us now summarize our conclusions about the correspondence between primal and dual basic solutions.

RELATIONSHIP 1 Each basic solution in the primal problem has a **complementary basic solution** in the dual problem, with the **complementary slackness** relationship between their associated variables shown in Table 2.39.

Table 2.39 Complementary Slackness Relationship for Complementary Basic Solutions

Primal variable	*Associated dual variable*	
Basic	Nonbasic	(m variables)
Nonbasic	Basic	(n variables)

Given row 0 of the simplex tableau for the primal basic solution, the coefficient of each variable equals the value of the associated dual variable in the complementary basic solution. Furthermore,

$$(Z =)\sum_{j=1}^{n} c_j x_j = \sum_{i=1}^{m} b_i y_i (= y_0).$$

We should mention here that this relationship between the two problems actually is a symmetrical one. At the end of this section we shall be in a position to conclude that, for any given primal problem and its dual problem, the dual problem for this dual problem is this primal problem. (Remember that *any* linear programming problem, even a dual problem, has its own dual problem.) Because of this, all our statements about the relationship of the dual problem to the primal problem also hold for the primal problem (put into minimization form) relative to the dual problem (put into maximization form). For relationship 1 this implies that there is a one-to-one correspondence between the basic solutions in the two problems. Therefore each pair may be referred to as *complementary basic solutions* because each solution is complementary to the other one.

The complementary slackness property in relationship 1 is an important one. It says (in part) that for each pair of associated variables, if one of them has *slack* in its nonnegativity constraint (a basic variable > 0), then the other one must have *no slack* (a nonbasic variable = 0). We mentioned earlier that this has a useful economic interpretation for linear programming problems.

To illustrate relationship 1, again consider the Wyndor Glass Co. problem.

All eight of its basic solutions (five feasible and three infeasible) are shown in Tables 2.15 and 2.16, along with the corresponding corner-point solutions. Thus its dual problem also must have eight basic solutions, each complementary to one of these primal solutions. This is indeed true, as summarized in Table 2.40. (You can verify this by finding the eight corner-point solutions for the dual problem; see Probs. 7 and 26.) At this point we ask you to refer back to the complete set of tableaux shown in Table 2.25 for the primal problem. The three basic solutions obtained there are the first, fifth, and sixth primal solutions shown in the above table. Now note how the three complementary basic solutions for the dual problem can be read directly from row 0 in these three tableaux, starting with the coefficients of the slack variables (x_3, x_4, x_5) and then the original variables (x_1, x_2). The other dual basic solutions also could be identified in this way by using part 3 of the iterative step (ignoring the rules in parts 1 and 2 for choosing the entering and leaving basic variables) to iterate to the tableau for the complementary basic solution in the primal problem. (For example, try starting from the final tableau, using x_5 as the entering basic variable and x_3 as the leaving basic variable, and you will obtain the next-to-last pair of complementary basic solutions in the table.) Alternatively, the *complementary slackness* property can be used to identify the defining (nonbasic) variables for the complementary dual basic solution, so that the equations can be solved directly. [For example, on the next-to-last primal basic solution, x_1, x_2, and x_5 being basic imply that $(z_1 - c_1)$, $(z_2 - c_2)$, and y_3 are nonbasic, so that the equations for the dual problem immediately yield $y_1 = 3$, $y_2 = 5/2$.] Finally, note how the complementary slackness property is satisfied for each of these pairs of complementary basic solutions.

Table 2.40 Complementary Basic Solutions for Wyndor Glass Co. Problem

	Primal problem			*Dual problem*	
No.	*Basic solution*	*Feasible?*	$Z = y_0$	*Feasible?*	*Basic solution*
1	(0,0,4,12,18)	Yes	0	No	$(0,0,0,-3,-5)$
2	(4,0,0,12,6)	Yes	12	No	$(3,0,0,0,-5)$
3	(6,0,−2,12,0)	No	18	No	$(0,0,1,0,-3)$
4	(4,3,0,6,0)	Yes	27	No	$\left(-\frac{9}{2},0,\frac{5}{2},0,0\right)$
5	(0,6,4,0,6)	Yes	30	No	$\left(0,\frac{5}{2},0,-3,0\right)$
6	(2,6,2,0,0)	Yes	36	Yes	$\left(0,\frac{3}{2},1,0,0\right)$
7	(4,6,0,0,−6)	No	42	Yes	$\left(3,\frac{5}{2},0,0,0\right)$
8	(0,9,4,−6,0)	No	45	Yes	$\left(0,0,\frac{5}{2},\frac{9}{2},0\right)$

We now turn our attention to the feasibility relationships between complementary basic solutions. The middle columns in Table 2.40 provide some valuable clues. For the pairs of complementary solutions, notice how the yes or no answers on feasibility also satisfy a complementary relationship in most cases. In particular, whenever one solution is feasible, the other is not. (It also is possible for *neither* solution to be feasible, as happened with the third pair.) The only exception is the sixth pair, where the primal solution is known to be optimal. The explanation is suggested by the $Z = y_0$ column. If the sixth dual solution also is optimal (as we hinted earlier), with $y_0 = 36$, then the first five dual solutions can not be feasible because $y_0 < 36$ (remember that the dual problem objective is to *minimize* y_0). By the same token, the last two primal solutions can not be feasible because $Z > 36$.

This explanation is verified by the general relationships given below. The first concerns *any* pair of solutions for the two problems, not just complementary basic solutions. It is stated for the original (inequality) representation of the two problems, but augmenting the solutions with the resulting values of the slack or surplus variables would not change anything.

RELATIONSHIP 2 If $(x_1, x_2, \ldots, x_n)$ is a feasible solution for the primal problem and $(y_1, y_2, \ldots, y_m)$ is a feasible solution for the dual problem, then

$$\sum_{j=1}^{n} c_j x_j \leq \sum_{i=1}^{m} b_i y_i.$$

This relationship actually is a direct consequence of the inequalities in the functional constraints of the two problems, as outlined below.

$$\begin{aligned}\sum_{j=1}^{n} x_j(c_j) &\leq \sum_{j=1}^{n} x_j\left(\sum_{i=1}^{m} a_{ij} y_i\right)\\ &= \sum_{i=1}^{m} y_i\left[\sum_{j=1}^{n} a_{ij} x_j\right]\\ &\leq \sum_{i=1}^{m} y_i[b_i].\end{aligned}$$

Since relationship 2 holds for *any* feasible solutions for the two problems, it also must hold for their *optimal* solutions. The important implication is that, given an optimal basic solution for the primal problem, if its complementary basic solution is feasible for the dual problem, then this must be an optimal dual solution. However, it does not guarantee that this complementary basic solution actually is feasible. (After all, the $\leq$ in relationship 2 only says *either* $<$ or $=$, even for optimal solutions.) This guarantee is instead provided by the *stopping rule* for the simplex method, as expressed earlier in this section in the *condition for optimality*.

RELATIONSHIP 3 If $(x_1^*, x_2^*, \ldots, x_{n+m}^*)$ is the optimal (basic) solution obtained by the simplex method for the primal problem, then its complementary basic solution $(y_1^*, y_2^*, \ldots, y_m^*, z_1^* - c_1, z_2^* - c_2, \ldots, z_n^* - c_n)$ must be feasible for the dual problem.

The condition for optimality requires that *all* these dual variables be *nonnegative*, which implies that this solution is feasible.

Thus, relationship 3 tells us that the objective function values in relationship 2 must be *equal* when the feasible solutions involved are the optimal solutions for the two problems. (This is true even when the problems have multiple optimal solutions because all of them must have the same objective function value.) This key conclusion is summarized in the following relationships.

RELATIONSHIP 4 If $(x_1^*, x_2^*, \ldots, x_n)$ and $(y_1^*, y_2^*, \ldots, y_m)$ are optimal solutions[1] for the primal and dual problems, respectively, then

$$\sum_{j=1}^{n} c_j x_j^* = \sum_{i=1}^{m} b_i y_i^*.$$

Relationship 4 usually is called the **dual theorem** because it is the fundamental theorem of duality theory. Note that it verifies our explanation for the very important feasibility relationships shown in the table of complementary basic solutions for the example. We shall summarize those relationships for any linear programming problem after a couple more definitions.

Basic solutions can be classified according to whether or not they satisfy each of two conditions. One is the condition for feasibility, namely, whether *all* the variables in the augmented solution are *nonnegative.* The other is the condition for optimality, namely, whether *all* the coefficients in row 0 (i.e., all the variables in the complementary basic solution) are nonnegative. Our names for the different types of basic solutions are summarized in Table 2.41.

Table 2.41 Classification of Basic Solutions

		Satisfies condition for optimality?	
		Yes	*No*
Feasible?	*Yes*	Optimal	Suboptimal
	No	Superoptimal	Neither feasible nor superoptimal

For example, in the table of complementary basic solutions, primal basic solutions 1, 2, 4, and 5 are suboptimal, 6 is optimal, 7 and 8 are superoptimal, and 3 is neither feasible nor superoptimal.

Using these definitions, the general relationships between complementary basic solutions are summarized in Table 2.42. The resulting range of possible (common) values for the objective functions ($Z = y_0$) for the first three pairs

[1] If either problem possesses at least one optimal solution, the other must also. The only ways in which both problems can have no optimal solutions are (1) both problems have no feasible solutions, or (2) one problem has no feasible solutions and the other problem has an unbounded feasible region that permits increasing the objective function value indefinitely in the favorable direction.

Table 2.42 Relationships between Complementary Basic Solutions

Primal basic solution	*Complementary dual basic solution*
Suboptimal	Superoptimal
Optimal	Optimal
Superoptimal	Suboptimal
Neither feasible nor superoptimal	Neither feasible nor superoptimal

given in Table 2.42 (the last pair can have any value) are shown in Fig. 2.7. Thus, while the simplex method is dealing directly with suboptimal basic solutions and working toward optimality in the primal problem, it is simultaneously dealing indirectly with complementary superoptimal solutions and working toward feasibility in the dual problem. Conversely, it sometimes is more convenient (or necessary) to work with superoptimal basic solutions and move toward feasibility in the primal problem, which is equivalent to using the simplex method to deal with suboptimal solutions and work toward optimality in the dual problem. These relationships prove very useful, particularly in sensitivity analysis, as you will see next.

Figure 2.7 Range of possible values of $Z = y_0$ for certain types of complementary basic solutions.

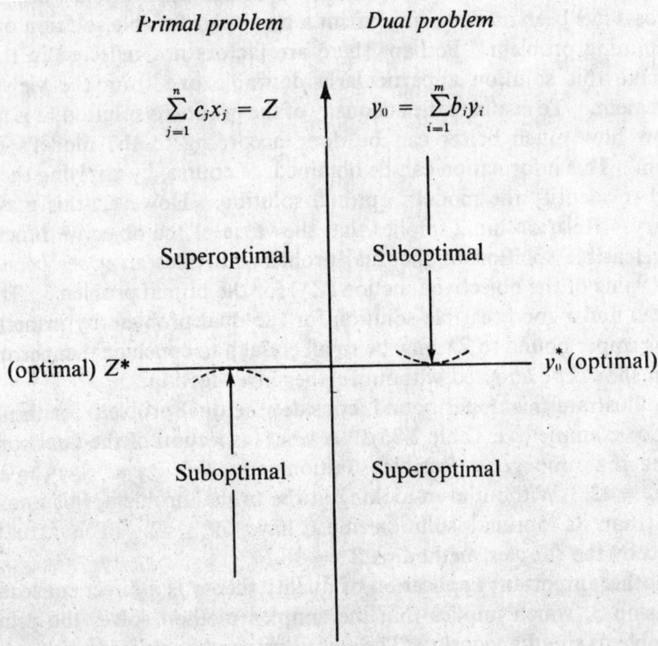

Applications

One important application of duality theory is the economic interpretation of the dual problem and the resulting insights for analyzing the primal problem that we presented earlier. The application to sensitivity analysis is quite similar. This analysis basically involves investigating the effect on the optimal solution of making changes in the values of the model parameters (the a_{ij}, b_i, and c_j). However, changing parameters in the *primal* problem also changes the corresponding parameters in the *dual* problem. Therefore you have your choice of which problem to use to investigate each change; the dual problem frequently is more convenient. Because of the above relationships, it is easy to move back and forth between the two problems as desired. We elaborate further in Sec. 4.3.

A related application is the *dual simplex method* presented in Sec. 16.2 for dealing with superoptimal basic solutions and working toward feasibility. This algorithm operates on the primal problem exactly as if the simplex method were being applied simultaneously to the dual problem. The dual simplex method sometimes is used instead of the simplex method when it is easier to find an initial superoptimal basic solution than an initial suboptimal one, particularly if it appears that fewer iterations will be required to reach an optimal solution. It also is valuable in sensitivity analysis when changes are made in the right-hand sides in such a way that the previously optimal basic solution becomes superoptimal. Starting the algorithm with this superoptimal solution usually leads quickly to a new optimal solution.

Relationship 2 above also provides a useful application. Suppose that a proposal has been made to implement a particular feasible solution of a linear programming problem. Perhaps there are factors not reflected in the model that make this solution a particularly desirable one from the viewpoint of management. To evaluate the adequacy of the proposed solution, it is necessary to know how much better can be done according to the model's objective function. This information can be obtained, of course, by applying the simplex method to identify the model's optimal solution. However, this may not be necessary. Relationship 2 implies that the value of the objective function (y_0) for *any* feasible solution of the dual problem provides an *upper bound* to the *optimal* value of the objective function (Z^*) for the primal problem. Therefore, if you can find a good feasible solution for the dual problem by inspection, the resulting upper bound to Z^* may be small enough to conclude that the proposed solution should be adopted without further investigation.

To illustrate this upper bound, consider the dual problem for the Wyndor Glass Co. example (see Table 2.36). A brief inspection of the dual constraints indicates that one good feasible solution is $y_1 = 3$, $y_2 = 5/2$, $y_3 = 0$, which yields $y_0 = 42$. Without even looking at the primal problem, this immediately implies that its optimal solution must have $Z^* \leq 42$. (The actual value, obtained by the simplex method, is $Z^* = 36$.)

Another important application of duality theory is a direct consequence of relationship 3, which implies that the simplex method solves the primal and dual problems simultaneously. The algorithm can be applied to either problem, and the final row 0 will yield an optimal solution to the other one. Therefore, if it appears that the *dual* problem would require less computational effort, then it should be solved directly instead.[1] Frequently a substantial reduction in computation time can be achieved in this way. We shall be discussing computational considerations in Sec. 4.2 and shall indicate then how to predict which problem should be easier.

Adapting to Other Forms

Thus far it has been assumed that the model for the primal problem is in *our standard form.* However, we indicated at the beginning of the section that *any* linear programming problem, whether in standard form or not, possesses a dual problem. Therefore let us now briefly consider how the dual problem changes for other forms.

Each *nonstandard* form was discussed in Sec. 2.10, and we pointed out how it is possible to convert each one into an *equivalent* standard form if so desired. To review, these conversions are summarized in Table 2.43. Hence you always

Table 2.43 Conversions to Standard Form for Linear Programming Models

Nonstandard form	*Equivalent standard form*
Minimize Z	Maximize $(-Z)$
$\sum_{j=1}^{n} a_{ij}x_j \geq b_i$	$-\sum_{j=1}^{n} a_{ij}x_j \leq -b_i$
$\sum_{j=1}^{n} a_{ij}x_j = b_i$	$\sum_{j=1}^{n} a_{ij}x_j \leq b_i$ *and* $-\sum_{j=1}^{n} a_{ij}x_j \leq -b_i$
x_j unconstrained in sign	$(x'_j - x''_j)$, $x'_j \geq 0$, $x''_j \geq 0$

have the option of converting any model into our standard form and *then* constructing its dual problem in the usual way. To illustrate, we do this for our standard *dual problem* (it must have a dual also) in Table 2.44. (If you prefer working with numbers, then do the same thing for the Wyndor Glass Co. dual problem, perhaps replacing y_0 by Z and y_1, y_2, y_3 by x_1, x_2, x_3 if you want; see Prob. 32.) Note that what we end up with is just our standard *primal problem*! Since *any* pair of primal and dual problems can be converted into these forms, this demonstrates the following key property of primal-dual relationships:

Symmetry Property For any primal problem and its dual problem, all relationships between them must be *symmetrical* because the dual of this dual problem is this primal problem.

[1] This is essentially equivalent to applying the *dual simplex method* to the primal problem except for the number of equations involved.

Table 2.44 Constructing The Dual of The Dual Problem

Dual problem

Minimize $y_0 = b_1y_1 + b_2y_2 + \cdots + b_my_m$,
subject to

$$\begin{aligned} a_{11}y_1 + a_{21}y_2 + \cdots + a_{m1}y_m &\geq c_1 \\ a_{12}y_1 + a_{22}y_2 + \cdots + a_{m2}y_m &\geq c_2 \\ &\vdots \\ a_{1n}y_1 + a_{2n}y_n + \cdots + a_{mn}y_m &\geq c_m \end{aligned}$$

and

$$y_1 \geq 0, y_2 \geq 0, \ldots, y_m \geq 0$$

→

Converted to standard form

Maximize $(-y_0) = -b_1y_1 - b_2y_2 - \cdots - b_my_m$,
subject to

$$\begin{aligned} -a_{11}y_1 - a_{21}y_2 - \cdots - a_{m1}y_m &\leq -c_1 \\ -a_{12}y_1 - a_{22}y_2 - \cdots - a_{m2}y_m &\leq -c_2 \\ &\vdots \\ -a_{1n}y_1 - a_{2n}y_2 - \cdots - a_{mn}y_m &\leq -c_m \end{aligned}$$

and

$$y_1 \geq 0, y_2 \geq 0, \ldots, y_m \geq 0$$

↓

Its dual problem

Minimize $(-Z) = -c_1x_1 - c_2x_2 - \cdots - c_nx_n$,
subject to

$$\begin{aligned} -a_{11}x_1 - a_{12}x_2 - \cdots - a_{1n}x_n &\geq -b_1 \\ -a_{21}x_1 - a_{22}x_2 - \cdots - a_{2n}x_n &\geq -b_2 \\ &\vdots \\ -a_{m1}x_1 - a_{m2}x_2 - \cdots - a_{mn}x_n &\geq -b_m \end{aligned}$$

and

$$x_1 \geq 0, x_2 \geq 0, \ldots, x_n \geq 0$$

←

Converted to standard form

Maximize $Z = c_1x_1 + c_2x_2 + \cdots + c_nx_n$,
subject to

$$\begin{aligned} a_{11}x_1 + a_{12}x_2 + \cdots + a_{1n}x_n &\leq b_1 \\ a_{21}x_1 + a_{22}x_2 + \cdots + a_{2n}x_n &\leq b_2 \\ &\vdots \\ a_{m1}x_1 + a_{m2}x_2 + \cdots + a_{mn}x_n &\leq b_m \end{aligned}$$

and

$$x_1 \geq 0, x_2 \geq 0, \ldots, x_n \geq 0$$

As a result, all the statements made earlier in this section about the relationships of the dual problem to the primal problem also hold in reverse.

Another consequence of the symmetry property is that it is immaterial which problem is called the primal and which is called the dual. In practice, you might see a linear programming problem fitting our standard form being referred to as the *dual* problem. The convention is that the model formulated to fit the actual problem is called the *primal problem*, regardless of its form.

Our illustration of how to construct the dual problem for a nonstandard primal problem did not involve either equality constraints or variables unconstrained in sign. Actually, for these two forms a shortcut is available. It is possible to show [see Probs. 30 and 34(b)] that an equality constraint in the primal problem should be treated just like an $\leq$ constraint in constructing the dual problem *except* that the nonnegativity constraint for the corresponding dual variable should be *deleted* (i.e., this variable is unconstrained in sign). By the symmetry property, this also says that deleting a nonnegativity constraint in the primal problem affects the dual problem only by changing the corresponding constraint into an equality constraint.

Because of these shortcuts, it is only necessary to convert the *primal problem* into the form shown in *either* column of Table 2.45. You then construct its *dual problem* in the usual way, using the form shown in the *other* column. However, beware of mixing the forms in the two columns (e.g., maximize Z with $\geq$ constraints) for defining the primal problem. It is not allowed for this purpose of constructing the dual problem.

Table 2.45 Corresponding Primal-dual Forms

Primal problem (or dual problem)	Dual problem (or primal problem)
Maximize Z (or y_0)	Minimize y_0 (or Z)
Constraint i	Variable y_i (or x_i)
$\leq$ form	$y_i \geq 0$
$=$ form	$y_i \geq 0$ deleted
Variable x_j (or y_j)	Constraint j
$x_j \geq 0$	$\geq$ form
$x_j \geq 0$ deleted	$=$ form

To illustrate this procedure, consider the *modified example* presented in Sec 2.10: Let it be our primal problem. To find its dual problem, we need to convert the model into one of the two allowable forms. The form in the second column of the table is obtained simply by multiplying through the first constraint $x_1 \leq 4$ by (-1). This is shown in Table 2.46, along with the resulting dual

Table 2.46 One Primal-dual Form for Modified Example of Sec. 2.10

Primal problem	Dual problem
Minimize $Z = 3x_1 + 5x_2$, subject to	Maximize $y_0 = -4y_1 + 12y_2 + 18y_3$, subject to
$-x_1 \geq -4$	$-y_1 + 3y_3 \leq 3$
$2x_2 = 12$	$2y_2 + 2y_3 \leq 5$
$3x_1 + 2x_2 \geq 18$	
and	and
$x_1 \geq 0, x_2 \geq 0$	$y_1 \geq 0, y_3 \geq 0$
	(y_2 unconstrained in sign)

problem. Equivalently, the form in the first column of the table can be used instead to set up the primal problem. (This is needed anyway to apply the simplex method as we have presented it.) This approach leads to the formulation of the two problems shown in Table 2.47. Note that the two versions of

Table 2.47 The Other Primal-dual Form for Modified Example of Sec. 2.10

Primal problem	Dual Problem
Maximize $(-Z) = -3x_1 - 5x_2$, subject to	Minimize $(-y_0) = 4y_1 + 12y_2' - 18y_3$, subject to
$x_1 \leq 4$	$y_1 - 3y_3 \geq -3$
$2x_2 = 12$	$2y_2' - 2y_3 \geq -5$
$-3x_1 - 2x_2 \leq -18$	
and	and
$x_1 \geq 0, x_2 \geq 0$	$y_1 \geq 0, y_3 \geq 0$
	(y_2' unconstrained in sign)

the primal and dual problems are *completely equivalent*, where $y_2' = -y_2$. This is inevitable because the differences only involve substituting equivalent forms.

When the simplex method is applied to the nonstandard primal forms, and the artificial technique is used to adapt to them, the duality interpretation of row 0 of the simplex tableau must be adjusted somewhat. The reason is that the artificial variables and M's *revise* the primal problem, which thereby changes its dual problem, so the complementary basic solutions shown in row 0 are for this *revised dual problem*. However, *after* the artificial variables have been eliminated (made nonbasic), so that the current solution is a legitimate basic feasible solution for the *original* primal problem, row 0 can still be used to identify the complementary basic solution for the original dual problem. We describe how to do this below.

Suppose that the form in the first column of Table 2.45 is being used. For each *equality* constraint i, its artificial variable plays the role of a slack variable, *except* that M has been added initially to the coefficient of this variable in row 0. Therefore the current value of the corresponding dual variable y_i is the current coefficient of this artificial variable *minus M*. If a $\leq$ constraint has a negative right-hand side initially (perhaps because it was converted from a $\geq$ constraint), so that it has been given an artificial variable, the dual variable corresponding to this constraint still equals the coefficient of its *slack* variable. The coefficient of the artificial variable would be ignored in this case. Finally, if a variable x_j is unconstrained in sign, so that it has been replaced by the difference of two nonnegative variables $(x_j' - x_j'')$, then the coefficient of x_j' $(z_j' - c_j)$ would be used just as for x_j. In other words,

$$z_j' = \sum_{i=1}^{m} a_{ij} y_i.$$

The coefficients of x_j'', $(z_j'' + c_j) = -(z_j' - c_j)$, would be ignored. Except for these cases, the coefficients in row 0 would be used just as before (see relationship 1) to give the values of the corresponding dual variables.

To illustrate this procedure, we ask you to refer to the set of simplex tableaux given in Table 2.30 for the modified example. The first two tableaux still have artificial variables as basic variables. However, this is not the case for the *final* tableau, so we can use its row 0 to identify the *optimal* solution for the dual problem shown in Table 2.47. The first primal constraint is a standard one, so y_1 is just the coefficient of the first slack variable (x_3), $y_1 = 0$. The second constraint is an equality constraint, so we refer to the coefficient of its artificial variable $(\bar{x}_4)$ to obtain

$$y_2' = \left(M - \frac{3}{2}\right) - M = -\frac{3}{2}.$$

The third constraint has a negative right-hand side, so we use the coefficient of its slack variable (x_5) to yield $y_3 = 1$. Similarly, the surplus variables are the coefficients of x_1 and x_2, so $(z_1 - c_1) = 0$, $(z_2 - c_2) = 0$. This completes the optimal dual solution (for the equality representation of the problem)

$$(y_1, y_2', y_3, z_1 - c_1, z_2 - c_2) = \left(0, -\frac{3}{2}, 1, 0, 0\right).$$

2.13 CONCLUSIONS

Linear programming is a powerful technique for dealing with the problem of allocating limited resources among competing activities as well as other problems having a similar mathematical formulation. It has become a standard tool of great importance for numerous business and industrial organizations. Furthermore, almost any social organization is concerned with allocating resources in some context, and there is a growing recognition of the extremely wide applicability of this technique. The simplex method provides an efficient and reliable algorithm for solving linear programming problems having many hundreds or even thousands of constraints and variables on a computer. The resulting solution can then be analyzed further by applying duality theory.

However, not all problems of allocating limited resources can be formulated to fit a linear programming model, even as a reasonable approximation. When one or more of the assumptions of linear programming are violated seriously, it may then be possible to apply another mathematical programming model instead, e.g., the models of integer programming (Chap. 17) or nonlinear programming (Chap. 18).

Selected References

1 Dantzig, George B.: *Linear Programming and Extensions*, Princeton University Press, Princeton, N.J., 1963.

2 Simmons, Donald M.: *Linear Programming for Operations Research*, Holden-Day, San Francisco, 1972.

3 Spivey, W. Allen and Robert M. Thrall: *Linear Optimization*, Holt, Rinehart & Winston, New York, 1970.

4 Strum, Jay E.: *Introduction to Linear Programming*, Holden-Day, San Francisco, 1972.

Problems[1]

1 A manufacturing firm has discontinued production of a certain unprofitable product line. This created considerable excess production capacity. Management is considering devoting this excess capacity to one or more of three products; call them products 1, 2, and 3. The available capacity on the machines that might limit output is summarized in the following table:

Machine type	*Available time (in machine hours per week)*
Milling machine	500
Lathe	350
Grinder	150

[1] Some additional *formulation* problems also are given at the end of Chap. 4.

The number of machine hours required for each unit of the respective products is

Productivity coefficient (in machine hours per unit)

Machine type	*Product 1*	*Product 2*	*Product 3*
Milling machine	9	3	5
Lathe	5	4	0
Grinder	3	0	2

The sales department indicates that the sales potential for products 1 and 2 exceeds the maximum production rate and that the sales potential for product 3 is 20 units per week.

The unit profit would be \$30, \$12, and \$15, respectively, on products 1, 2, and 3.

(*a*) Formulate the linear programming model for determining how much of each product the firm should produce to maximize profit.
(*b*) Solve this problem by the simplex method.
(*c*) Use a computer code of the simplex method to solve this problem.

2 A farmer is raising pigs for market, and he wishes to determine the quantities of the available types of feed that should be given to each pig to meet certain nutritional requirements at a *minimum cost*. The numbers of each type of basic nutritional ingredient contained within a pound of each feed type is given in the following table, along with the daily nutritional requirements and feed costs:

Nutritional ingredient	*Pound of corn*	*Pound of tankage*	*Pound of alfalfa*	*Minimum daily requirement*
Carbohydrates	9	2	4	20
Protein	3	8	6	18
Vitamins	1	2	6	15
Cost (¢)	7	6	5	

(*a*) Formulate the linear programming model for this problem.
(*b*) Rewrite this model in an equivalent way to fit our standard form given in Sec. 2.2.
(*c*) Construct the initial simplex tableau, introducing artificial variables and so forth as needed for applying the simplex method.
(*d*) Solve this problem by the simplex method.
(*e*) Use a computer code of the simplex method to solve this problem.

3 A certain corporation has three branch plants with excess production capacity. All three plants have the capability for producing a certain product, and management has decided to use some of the excess production capacity in this way. This product can be made in three sizes—large, medium, and small—that yield a net unit profit of \$35, \$30, and \$25, respectively. Plants 1, 2, and 3 have the excess manpower and equipment capacity to produce 750, 900, and 450 units per day of this product, respectively, regardless of the size or combination of sizes involved. However, the amount of available in-process storage space also imposes a limitation on the production rates. Plants 1, 2, and 3 have 13,000, 12,000, and 5,000 square feet of in-process storage space available for a day's production of this product. Each unit of the large, medium, and small sizes produced per day requires 20, 15, and 12 square feet, respectively.

Sales forecasts indicate that 900, 1200, and 750 units of the large, medium, and small sizes, respectively, can be sold per day.

To maintain a uniform work load among the plants and to retain some flexibility, management has decided that the additional production assigned to each plant must use the same percentage of the excess manpower and equipment capacity.

Management wishes to know how much of each of the sizes should be produced by each of the plants to maximize profit.

(*a*) Formulate the linear programming model for this problem.
(*b*) Use a computer code of the simplex method to solve this problem.

4 For each of the four assumptions of linear programming discussed in Sec. 2.3, write a one-paragraph analysis of how well you feel it applies to each of the following examples given in Sec. 2.4:

(*a*) Regional planning (Southern Confederation of Kibbutzim).
(*b*) Controlling air pollution (Nori & Leets Co.).

5 Use the graphical procedure illustrated in Sec. 2.1 to solve the problem

$$\text{Maximize } Z = 2x_1 + x_2,$$

subject to

$$x_2 \leq 10$$
$$2x_1 + 5x_2 \leq 60$$
$$x_1 + x_2 \leq 18$$
$$3x_1 + x_2 \leq 44$$

and

$$x_1 \geq 0, x_2 \geq 0.$$

6 Consider the problem

$$\text{Maximize } Z = 3x_1 + 2x_2,$$

subject to

$$2x_1 + 4x_2 \leq 22$$
$$-x_1 + 4x_2 \leq 10$$
$$2x_1 - x_2 \leq 7$$
$$x_1 - 3x_2 \leq 1$$

and

$$x_1 \geq 0, x_2 \geq 0.$$

(*a*) Solve this problem graphically. Identify the corner-point feasible solutions.
(*b*) Develop a table giving each of the corner-point feasible solutions and the corresponding defining equations, basic feasible solution, and defining (nonbasic) variables. Use just this information to identify the optimal solution.
(*c*) Develop the corresponding table for the corner-point infeasible solutions and so on. Also identify the sets of defining equations and defining (nonbasic) variables that do not yield a solution.

(*d*) Solve this problem by the simplex method.

7 Consider the linear programming problem given in Table 2.36 as the *dual problem* for the Wyndor Glass Co. example.

(*a*) Identify the 10 sets of defining equations for this problem. For each one, solve (if a solution exists) for the corresponding corner-point solution, and classify it as a corner-point feasible solution or corner-point infeasible solution.

(*b*) For each corner-point solution, give the corresponding basic solution and its set of defining (nonbasic) variables. (Compare with Table 2.40.)

8 Consider the problem

$$\text{Maximize} \quad Z = 4x_1 + 3x_2 + 6x_3,$$

subject to

$$3x_1 + x_2 + 3x_3 \leq 30$$
$$2x_1 + 2x_2 + 3x_3 \leq 40$$

and

$$x_1 \geq 0,\ x_2 \geq 0,\ x_3 \geq 0.$$

(*a*) Solve by the simplex method in algebraic form.
(*b*) Solve by the simplex method in tabular form.

9 Consider the problem

$$\text{Maximize} \quad Z = 2x_1 - x_2 + x_3,$$

subject to

$$3x_1 + x_2 + x_3 \leq 60$$
$$x_1 - x_2 + 2x_3 \leq 10$$
$$x_1 + x_2 - x_3 \leq 20$$

and

$$x_1 \geq 0,\ x_2 \geq 0,\ x_3 \geq 0.$$

(*a*) Solve by the simplex method in algebraic form.
(*b*) Solve by the simplex method in tabular form.

10 Consider the problem

$$\text{Maximize} \quad Z = 6x_1 + 2x_2 + 10x_3 + 8x_4,$$

subject to

$$3x_1 - 3x_2 + 2x_3 + 8x_4 \leq 25$$
$$5x_1 + 6x_2 - 4x_3 - 4x_4 \leq 20$$
$$4x_1 - 2x_2 + x_3 + 3x_4 \leq 10$$

and

$$x_1 \geq 0,\ x_2 \geq 0,\ x_3 \geq 0,\ x_4 \geq 0.$$

Use the simplex method to demonstrate that Z is unbounded.

11 A weighted average of N solutions, $(x_1^{(1)}, x_2^{(1)}, \ldots, x_n^{(1)}), \ldots, (x_1^{(N)}, x_2^{(N)}, \ldots, x_n^{(N)})$, is a solution $(x_1, x_2, \ldots, x_n)$ such that

$$x_j = \sum_{k=1}^{N} \alpha_k x_j^{(k)}, \text{ for } j = 1, 2, \ldots, n,$$

where the weights $\alpha_1, \alpha_2, \ldots, \alpha_N$ are nonnegative and sum to 1. If the feasible region is bounded, then every feasible solution can be expressed as a weighted average of some of the corner-point feasible solutions (perhaps in more than one way). Similarly, after augmenting solutions with slack variables, every feasible solution can be expressed as a weighted average of some of the basic feasible solutions.

(*a*) Show that *any* weighted average of corner-point feasible solutions must be a feasible solution.
(*b*) Use the result quoted in part (*a*) to show that *any* weighted average of basic feasible solutions must be a feasible solution.

12 Using the facts given in Prob. 11, show that the following statements must be true for any linear programming problem which has a bounded feasible region and multiple optimal solutions:

(*a*) Every weighted average of the optimal basic feasible solutions must be optimal.
(*b*) No *other* feasible solution can be optimal.

13 Consider the problem

$$\text{Maximize} \quad Z = x_1 + x_2 + x_3 + x_4,$$

subject to

$$x_1 + x_2 \leq 2$$
$$x_3 + x_4 \leq 5$$

and

$$x_j \geq 0, \text{ for } j = 1, 2, 3, 4.$$

(*a*) Use the simplex method to find *all* the optimal basic feasible solutions.
(*b*) Apply the information given in Probs. 11 and 12 to give an expression identifying all other optimal solutions.

14 Consider the problem

$$\text{Maximize} \quad Z = 2x_1 + 3x_2,$$

subject to

$$x_1 + 2x_2 \leq 4$$
$$x_1 + x_2 = 3$$

and

$$x_1 \geq 0, x_2 \geq 0.$$

(*a*) Solve this problem graphically.
(*b*) Construct the complete first simplex tableau for the simplex method and identify the corresponding initial (artificial) basic feasible solution. Also identify the initial entering basic variable and leaving basic variable.
(*c*) Solve by the simplex method.

15 Consider the problem

$$\text{Minimize} \quad Z = 4x_1 + 3x_2,$$

subject to

$$2x_1 + x_2 \geq 10$$
$$-3x_1 + 2x_2 \leq 6$$
$$x_1 + x_2 \geq 6$$

and

$$x_1 \geq 0, x_2 \geq 0.$$

(*a*) Solve this problem graphically.
(*b*) Construct the complete first simplex tableau for the simplex method and identify the corresponding initial (artificial) basic feasible solution. Also identify the initial entering basic variable and leaving basic variable.
(c) Solve by the simplex method.

16 Consider the problem

$$\text{Maximize} \quad Z = 3x_1 + 5x_2 + 2x_3,$$

subject to

$$-2x_2 + x_3 \geq 2$$
$$x_1 + 4x_2 + 2x_3 = 5$$

and

$$x_1 \geq 0, x_2 \geq 0, x_3 \geq 0.$$

(*a*) Construct the complete first simplex tableau for the simplex method and identify the corresponding initial (artificial) basic feasible solution. Also identify the initial entering basic variable and leaving basic variable.
(*b*) Solve by the simplex method.

17 Consider the problem

$$\text{Maximize} \quad Z = -x_1 + 4x_2,$$

subject to

$$-3x_1 + x_2 \leq 6$$
$$x_1 + 2x_2 \leq 4$$
$$x_2 \geq -3$$

(no lower bound constraint for x_1).

(*a*) Solve this problem graphically.
(*b*) Reformulate this problem so that it has only two functional constraints and all variables have nonnegativity constraints.
(*c*) Solve by the simplex method.

18 Consider the problem

$$\text{Maximize} \quad Z = x_1 + 2x_2 - x_3,$$

subject to

$$2x_1 + x_2 - 3x_3 \leq 5$$
$$-4x_1 - x_2 + x_3 \leq 4$$
$$x_1 + 3x_2 \leq 6$$

(no nonnegativity constraints).

(*a*) Reformulate this problem so all variables have nonnegativity constraints.
(*b*) Solve by the simplex method.

19 Consider the problem

$$\text{Maximize} \quad Z = 5x_1 + 3x_2 + 2x_3 + 4x_4,$$

subject to

$$5x_1 + x_2 + x_3 + 8x_4 = 10$$
$$2x_1 + 4x_2 + 3x_3 + 2x_4 = 10$$

and

$$x_j \geq 0, \text{ for } j = 1, 2, 3, 4.$$

(*a*) Construct the complete first simplex tableau for the simplex method and identify the corresponding initial (artificial) basic feasible solution. Also identify the initial entering and leaving basic variable.
(*b*) Solve by the simplex method.
(*c*) Find a basic feasible solution for the *real* problem by directly using the simplex method to minimize the sum of the artificial variables subject to the constraints as expressed in the simplex tableau obtained in part (*a*). (This is phase 1 of the *two-phase method* described on p. 70.)
(*d*) Obtain an optimal solution by using the solution obtained in part (*c*) as the initial basic feasible solution (deleting all artificial variables) for the simplex method. (This is phase 2 of the two-phase method.)

20 Consider the problem

$$\text{Minimize} \quad Z = 2x_1 + 3x_2 + x_3,$$

subject to

$$x_1 + 4x_2 + 2x_3 \geq 8$$
$$3x_1 + 2x_2 \geq 6$$

and

$$x_1 \geq 0, x_2 \geq 0, x_3 \geq 0.$$

(*a*) Reformulate this problem to fit our standard form for a linear programming model presented in Sec. 2.2.
(*b*) Construct the complete first simplex tableau for the simplex method and identify the corresponding initial (artificial) basic feasible solution. Also identify the initial entering basic variable and leaving basic variable.
(*c*) Solve by the simplex method.
(*d*) Find a basic feasible solution for the *real* problem by directly using the simplex method to minimize the sum of the artificial variables subject to the constraints as expressed in the simplex tableau obtained in part (*b*). (This is phase 1 of the *two-phase method*.)

(*e*) Obtain an optimal solution by using the solution obtained in part (*d*) as the initial basic feasible solution (deleting all artfiicial variables) for the simplex method. (This is phase 2 of the two-phase method.)

21 Consider the problem

$$\text{Minimize} \quad Z = 3x_1 - 4x_2 + x_3 - 2x_4,$$

subject to

$$\begin{aligned} 2x_1 + x_2 + 2x_3 + x_4 &= 10 \\ x_3 + 2x_4 &\leq 10 \\ x_1 - x_2 + x_4 &\geq -5 \\ 5 \leq 2x_1 + 3x_2 + x_3 + x_4 &\leq 20 \end{aligned}$$

and

$$x_1 \geq 0, \; x_2 \geq 0, \; x_3 \geq 0$$

(no nonnegativity constraint for x_4).

(*a*) Reformulate this problem (except for the equality constraint) to fit our standard form for a linear programming model presented in Sec. 2.2.
(*b*) Construct the complete first simplex tableau for the simplex method and identify the corresponding initial (artificial) basic feasible solution. Also identify the initial entering basic variable and leaving basic variable.
(*c*) Find a basic feasible solution for the *real* problem by applying the simplex method until all the artificial variables are zero.
(*d*) Find a basic feasible solution for the *real* problem by directly using the simplex method to minimize the sum of the artificial variables subject to the constraints as expressed in the simplex tableau obtained in part (*b*). (This is phase 1 of the *two-phase method.*)

22 Consider the problem

$$\text{Maximize} \quad Z = 10x_1 + 15x_2 + 12x_3,$$

subject to

$$\begin{aligned} 5x_1 + 3x_2 + x_3 &\leq 9 \\ -5x_1 + 6x_2 + 15x_3 &\leq 15 \\ 2x_1 + x_2 + x_3 &\geq 5 \end{aligned}$$

and

$$x_1 \geq 0, \; x_2 \geq 0, \; x_3 \geq 0.$$

Use the simplex method to demonstrate that this problem does not possess any feasible solutions.

23 Construct the primal-dual table and the dual problem for each of the following linear programming models fitting our standard form:

(*a*) Model given in Prob. 8.
(*b*) Model given in Prob. 9.

24 Consider the simplex tableaux for the Wyndor Glass Co. problem given in Table 2.25. For each tableau, give the economic interpretation of the following items:

(*a*) Each of the coefficients of the slack variables (x_3, x_4, x_5) in row 0.
(*b*) Each of the coefficients of the original variables (x_1, x_2) in row 0.
(*c*) The resulting choice for the entering basic variable (or the decision to stop after the final tableau).

25 Consider the problem

$$\text{Maximize} \quad Z = 6x_1 + 8x_2,$$

subject to

$$5x_1 + 2x_2 \leq 20$$
$$x_1 + 2x_2 \leq 10$$

and

$$x_1 \geq 0, \; x_2 \geq 0.$$

(*a*) Construct the dual problem for this primal problem.
(*b*) Solve both the primal problem and dual problem graphically. Identify the corner-point feasible solutions and corner-point infeasible solutions for both problems.
(*c*) Use the information obtained in part (*b*) to construct a table listing the complementary basic solutions and so forth for these problems. (Use the same column headings as for Table 2.40.)
(*d*) Solve the primal problem by the simplex method. After each iteration (including iteration 0), identify the basic feasible solution for this problem and the complementary basic solution for the dual problem. Also identify the corresponding corner-point solutions.

26 Consider the primal and dual problems for the Wyndor Glass Co. example given in Table 2.36. Using Tables 2.15, 2.16, 2.39, and 2.40, construct a new table giving the eight sets of defining (nonbasic) variables for the primal problem in column 1. the corresponding sets of associated variables for the dual problem in column 2, and the set of defining (nonbasic) variables for each complementary basic solution of the dual problem in column 3. Explain why this table demonstrates the complementary slackness property for this example.

27 Consider the problem

$$\text{Maximize} \quad Z = 4x_1 + 7x_2 + 2x_3,$$

subject to

$$x_1 + 2x_2 + x_3 \leq 10$$
$$2x_1 + 3x_2 + 3x_3 \leq 10$$

and

$$x_1 \geq 0, \; x_2 \geq 0, \; x_3 \geq 0.$$

(*a*) Construct the dual problem for this primal problem.
(*b*) Use the dual problem to demonstrate that the optimal value of Z for the primal problem can not exceed 25.
(*c*) It has been conjectured that x_1 and x_2 should be the basic variables for the optimal solution of the primal problem. Show that this is not true by directly

deriving this basic solution (applying only part 3 of the iterative step of the simplex method). Simultaneously derive and identify the complementary basic solution for the dual problem.

(*d*) Solve the dual problem graphically. Use this to identify the basic variables and the defining (nonbasic) variables for the optimal solution of the primal problem. Directly derive this solution (applying only part 3 of the iterative step of the simplex method).

28 Construct the dual problem for the linear programming problem given in Prob. 20.

29 For each of the following linear programming models, convert this primal problem into one of the two forms given in Table 2.45 and then construct its dual problem:

(*a*) Model given in Prob. 15.
(*b*) Model given in Prob. 16.
(*c*) Model given in Prob. 21.

30 Consider the model with equality constraints given in Prob. 19.

(*a*) Construct its dual problem by using the corresponding primal-dual form given in Table 2.45.

(*b*) Demonstrate that the answer in part (*a*) is correct (i.e., equality constraints yield dual variables without nonnegativity constraints) by first converting the primal problem to our standard form (see Table 2.43), then constructing its dual problem, and then converting this dual problem to the form obtained in part (*a*).

31 Consider the model without nonnegativity constraints given in Prob. 18.

(*a*) Construct its dual problem by using the corresponding primal-dual form given in Table 2.45.

(*b*) Demonstrate that the answer in part (*a*) is correct (i.e., variables without nonnegativity constraints yield equality constraints in the dual problem) by first converting the primal problem to our standard form (see Table 2.43), then constructing its dual problem, and then converting this dual problem to the form obtained in part (*a*).

32 Consider the dual problem for the Wyndor Glass Co. example given in Table 2.36. Demonstrate that *its* dual problem is the primal problem given in Table 2.36 by going through the conversion steps given in Table 2.44.

33 Consider the primal and dual problems in our standard form presented at the beginning of Sec. 2.12. Let $y_1^*, y_2^*, \ldots, y_m^*$ denote the optimal solution for this dual problem. Suppose that $b_1, b_2, \ldots, b_m$ are then replaced by $b_1', b_2', \ldots, b_m'$. Let $x_1', x_2', \ldots, x_n'$ denote the optimal solution for the new primal problem.

Prove that

$$\sum_{j=1}^{n} c_j x_j' \le \sum_{i=1}^{m} b_i' y_i^*.$$

34 Using matrix notation (see Appendix 3), if the primal problem is maximize cx subject to $Ax \le b$ and $x \ge 0$, then the dual problem is minimize $b^T y$ subject to $A^T y \ge c^T$ and $y \ge 0$. Use only this information from duality theory to prove each of the following independent statements:

(*a*) The dual of this dual problem is this primal problem.

(*b*) If the primal problem is maximize cx subject to $Ax = b$ and $x \geq 0$, then the dual problem is minimize $b^T y$ subject to $A^T y \geq c^T$ (with no sign restriction on y).

(*c*) If the primal problem (as given in the first sentence of the problem statement) has unbounded optimal solutions, then the dual problem has no feasible solutions.

3 Special Types of Linear Programming Problems

The early part of Chap. 2 emphasized the wide applicability of linear programming. We continue broadening our horizons in this chapter by discussing some particularly important types of linear programming problems. These special types share several key characteristics. The first is that they all arise frequently in practice in a variety of contexts. They also tend to require a very large number of constraints and variables, so a straightforward computer application of the simplex method may be very expensive or even computationally prohibitive. Fortunately, another characteristic is that most of the a_{ij} coefficients in the constraints are zeros, and the relatively few nonzero coefficients appear in a distinctive pattern. As a result, it has been possible to develop special streamlined versions of the simplex method that achieve dramatic computational savings by exploiting this *special structure* of the problem. Therefore it is important to become sufficiently familiar with these special types of problems so that you can recognize them when they arise and apply the proper computational procedure.

To describe special structures, we shall introduce the table (or matrix) of constraint coefficients shown in Fig. 3.1,

Figure 3.1 Table of constraint coefficients for linear programming.

$$A = \begin{bmatrix} a_{11} & a_{12} & \cdots & a_{1n} \\ a_{21} & a_{22} & \cdots & a_{2n} \\ \vdots & \vdots & & \vdots \\ a_{m1} & a_{m2} & \cdots & a_{mn} \end{bmatrix}$$

where a_{ij} is the coefficient of the jth variable in the ith functional constraint. Portions of the table containing only coefficients equal to zero will be indicated by leaving them blank, whereas blocks containing nonzero coefficients will be shaded darker.

Probably the most important special type of linear programming problem is the so-called *transportation problem*, and we shall describe it first. Its special solution procedure also will be presented, partially to illustrate the kind of streamlining of the simplex method that can be obtained by exploiting special structure in the problem. We next shall present two special types (the *transshipment problem* and the *assignment problem*) that are closely related to the transportation problem. Then comes a special type that frequently arises in multidivisional organizations, another that sometimes occurs in long-range planning, and a combination of the two.

3.1 THE TRANSPORTATION PROBLEM

Prototype Example

One of the main products of the *P & T Company* is canned peas. The peas are prepared at three canneries (near Bellingham, Washington, Eugene, Oregon, and Albert Lea, Minnesota) and then shipped by truck to four distributing warehouses (in Sacramento, California, Salt Lake City, Utah, Rapid City, South Dakota, and Albuquerque, New Mexico) in the Western United States, as shown in Fig. 3.2. Since the shipping costs are a major expense, management is initiating a study to reduce them as much as possible. For the upcoming season, an estimate has been made of what the output will be from each cannery, and each warehouse has been allocated a certain amount from the total supply of peas. This information (in units of truck loads), along with the shipping cost per truckload for each cannery-warehouse combination, is given in Table 3.1. Thus there are a total of 300 truckloads to be shipped. The problem

Table 3.1 Shipping Data for P&T Company

Shipping cost (\$) *per truckload*

	Warehouse 1	2	3	4	*Output*
Cannery 1	464	513	654	867	75
Cannery 2	352	416	690	791	125
Cannery 3	995	682	388	685	100
Allocation	80	65	70	85	

now is to determine which plan for assigning these shipments to the variables cannery-warehouse combinations would minimize total shipping costs.

This actually is a linear programming problem of the *transportation problem* type. To formulate it, let Z denote total shipping cost, and let x_{ij} ($i = 1,2,3;$

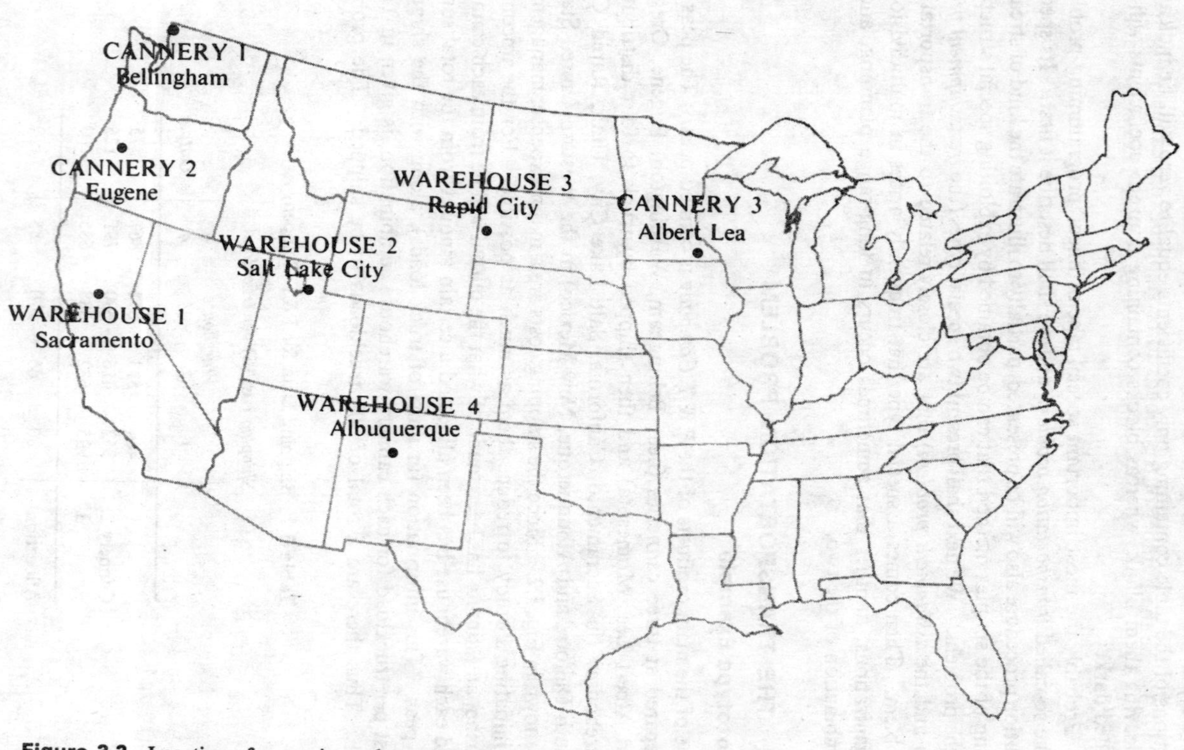

Figure 3.2 Location of canneries and warehouses for the P&T Company.

$j = 1,2,3,4$) be the number of truckloads to be shipped from cannery i to warehouse j. Thus the objective is to choose the values of these 12 decision variables (the x_{ij}) so as to

$$\text{Minimize} \quad Z = 464x_{11} + 513x_{12} + 654x_{13} + 867x_{14} + 352x_{21} + 416x_{22} + 690x_{23} + 791x_{24} + 995x_{31} + 682x_{32} + 388x_{33} + 685x_{34},$$

subject to the constraints

$$\begin{aligned}
x_{11} + x_{12} + x_{13} + x_{14} \qquad\qquad\qquad\qquad\qquad\qquad\qquad\qquad &= 75 \\
x_{21} + x_{22} + x_{23} + x_{24} \qquad\qquad\qquad\qquad &= 125 \\
x_{31} + x_{32} + x_{33} + x_{34} &= 100 \\
x_{11} \qquad\qquad + x_{21} \qquad\qquad + x_{31} \qquad\qquad &= 80 \\
x_{12} \qquad\qquad + x_{22} \qquad\qquad + x_{32} \qquad &= 65 \\
x_{13} \qquad\qquad + x_{23} \qquad\qquad + x_{33} \qquad &= 70 \\
x_{14} \qquad\qquad + x_{24} \qquad\qquad + x_{34} &= 85
\end{aligned}$$

and

$$x_{ij} \geq 0 \quad (i = 1,2,3; j = 1,2,3,4).$$

Note that the table of constraint coefficients is that shown in Fig. 3.3. As you will see next, it is this special structure that distinguishes this problem as a transportation problem, not its context.

By the way, the optimal solution for this problem is $x_{11} = 0$, $x_{12} = 20$, $x_{13} = 0$, $x_{14} = 55$, $x_{21} = 80$, $x_{22} = 45$, $x_{23} = 0$, $x_{24} = 0$, $x_{31} = 0$, $x_{32} = 0$, $x_{33} = 70$, $x_{34} = 30$. If you study the stopping rule in Sec. 3.2, you will be able to verify this yourself (see Prob. 6).

The Transportation Problem Model

To describe the general model for the transportation problem, we need to use terms that are considerably less specific than for the components of the prototype example. In particular, the general transportation problem is concerned

Figure 3.3 Table of constraint coefficients for the P&T Company.

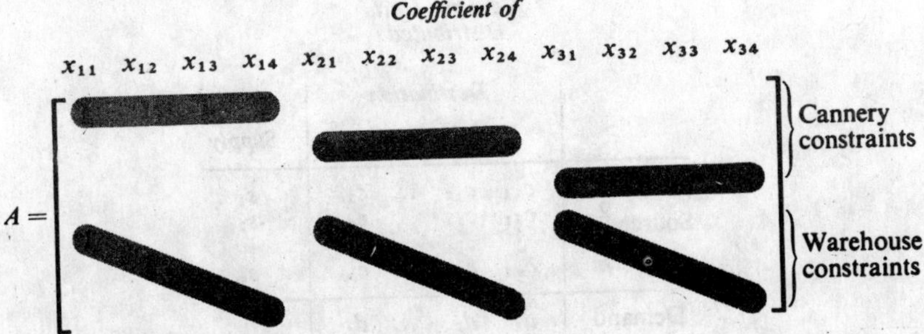

(literally or figuratively) with distributing *any* commodity from *any* group of supply centers, called **sources**, to *any* group of receiving centers, called **destinations**, in such a way as to minimize total distribution costs. The correspondence in terminology between the prototype example and general problem is summarized in Table 3.2. Thus, in general source i ($i = 1,2, \ldots, m$) has a supply

Table 3.2 Terminology for Transportation Problem

Prototype example	*General problem*
Truckloads of canned peas	Units of a commodity
Three canneries	m sources
Four warehouses	n destinations
Output from cannery i	s_i supply from source i
Allocation to warehouse j	d_j demand at destination j
Shipping cost per truckload from cannery i to warehouse j	c_{ij} cost per unit distributed from source i to destination j

of s_i units to distribute to the destinations, and destination j ($j = 1,2, \ldots, n$) has a demand for d_j units to be received from the sources. A basic assumption is that the cost of distributing units from source i to destination j is directly proportional to the number distributed, where c_{ij} denotes the cost per unit distributed. As for the prototype example, these input data can be summarized conveniently in the *cost and requirements table* shown in Fig. 3.4.

Letting Z be total distribution cost and x_{ij} ($i = 1, 2, \ldots, m$; $j = 1, 2, \ldots, n$) be the number of units to be distributed from source i to destination j, the linear programming formulation of this problem becomes

$$\text{Minimize} \quad Z = \sum_{i=1}^{m} \sum_{j=1}^{n} c_{ij} x_{ij},$$

Figure 3.4 Cost and requirements table for the transportation problem.

Cost per Unit Distributed

		Destination				
		1	*2*	...	*n*	*Supply*
Source	1	c_{11}	c_{12}	...	c_{1n}	s_1
	2	c_{21}	c_{22}	...	c_{2n}	s_2
	⋮	⋮	⋮	...	⋮	⋮
	m	c_{m1}	c_{m2}	...	c_{mn}	s_m
Demand		d_1	d_2	...	d_n	

subject to

$$\sum_{j=1}^{n} x_{ij} = s_i, \text{ for } i = 1, 2, \ldots, m$$

$$\sum_{i=1}^{m} x_{ij} = d_j, \text{ for } j = 1, 2, \ldots, n$$

and

$$x_{ij} \geq 0, \text{ for all } i \text{ and } j.$$

Note that the resulting table of constraint coefficients has the special structure shown in Fig. 3.5. *Any* linear programming problem that fits this special formulation is of the transportation problem type, regardless of its physical context. In fact, there have been numerous applications having nothing to do with transportation that have been fitted to this special structure, as we shall illustrate in the next example. (The *assignment problem* to be described in Sec. 3.4 is an additional example.) This is one of the reasons why the transportation problem is generally considered the most important special type of linear programming problem.

For many applications, the supply and demand quantities in the model (the s_i and d_j) will have integer values, and implementation will require that the distribution quantities (the x_{ij}) also be integer. Fortunately, because of the special structure shown in Fig. 3.5, if such a model has any feasible solution, it *always* will have an optimal solution with just integer values, and this solution will be found by the solution procedure described in Sec. 3.2. Therefore it is unnecessary to add a constraint to the model that the x_{ij} must be integer.

It should be carefully noted that the model has feasible solutions only if

$$\sum_{i=1}^{m} s_i = \sum_{j=1}^{n} d_j.$$

This may be verified by observing that the restrictions require that both

$$\sum_{i=1}^{m} s_i \quad \text{and} \quad \sum_{j=1}^{n} d_j \quad \text{equal} \quad \sum_{i=1}^{m} \sum_{j=1}^{n} x_{ij}.$$

Figure 3.5 Table of constraint coefficients for the transportation problem.

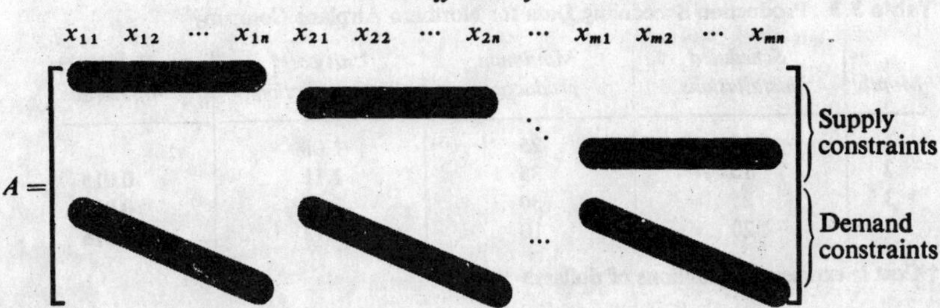

This condition that the total supply must equal the total demand merely requires that the system be in balance. If the problem has physical significance and this condition is not met, it usually means that either s_i or d_j actually represents a bound rather than an exact requirement. If this is the case, a fictitious "source" or "destination" can be introduced to take up the slack in order to convert the inequalities into equalities and satisfy the feasibility condition. The next two examples illustrate how to fit some other common variations into the transportation problem formulation.

Example—Production Scheduling

The *Northern Airplane Company* builds commercial airplanes for various airline companies around the world. The last stage in their production process is to produce the jet engines and then to install them (a very fast operation) in the completed airplane frame. The company has been working under some contracts to deliver a considerable number of airplanes in the near future, and the production of the jet engines for these planes must now be scheduled for the next 4 months.

To meet the contracted dates for delivery, it is necessary to supply engines for installation in the quantities indicated in the second column of Table 3.3. Thus the cumulative number produced by the end of month 1, 2, 3, and 4 must be at least 10, 25, 50, and 70, respectively. The facilities that will be available for producing the engines vary according to other production, maintenance, and renovation work scheduled during this period. The resulting monthly differences in the maximum number that can be produced and the cost (in millions of dollars) of producing each one are given in the third and fourth columns of Table 3.3. Because of the variations in production costs, it may well be worthwhile to produce some of the engines a month or more before they are scheduled for installation, and this possibility is being considered. The drawback is that such engines must be stored until the scheduled installation (the airplane frame will not be ready previously) at a storage cost of $15,000/month (including interest on expended capital), as shown in the last column of Table 3.3. Therefore the production manager wants a schedule developed for how many engines to produce in each of the 4 months so that the total of the production and storage costs will be minimized.

Table 3.3 Production Scheduling Data for Northern Airplane Company

Month	*Scheduled installations*	*Maximum production*	*Unit cost† of production*	*Unit cost† of storage*
1	10	25	1.08	
2	15	35	1.11	0.015
3	25	30	1.10	0.015
4	20	10	1.13	0.015

† Cost is expressed in millions of dollars.

By letting $x_j (j = 1,2,3,4)$ be the number of jet engines to be produced in month j, it is straightforward to formulate the problem in terms of only these decision variables as a linear programming problem that bears no apparent resemblance to the transportation problem type. (See Prob. 11 and its solution.) Nevertheless, by adopting a different viewpoint, the problem can indeed be formulated as a transportation problem that requires *much* less effort to solve. This viewpoint is to describe the problem in terms of sources and destinations and then to identify the corresponding x_{ij}, c_{ij}, s_i, and d_i. (See if you can do this before reading further.) Specifically, since the units being distributed are jet engines, each of which is to be scheduled for production in a particular month and then installed in a particular (perhaps different) month,

Source i = production of jet engines in month i ($i = 1,2,3,4$)

Destination j = installation of jet engines in month j ($j = 1,2,3,4$)

x_{ij} = number of engines produced in month i for installation in month j

c_{ij} = cost associated with each unit of x_{ij}

$$= \begin{cases} \text{cost per unit for production and any storage, if } i \leq j \\ ?, \text{ if } i > j \end{cases}$$

s_i = ?

d_j = number of scheduled installations in month j.

The corresponding (incomplete) cost and requirements table is given in Fig. 3.6. Thus it remains to identify the missing costs and the supplies.

Since it is impossible to produce engines in 1 month for installation in an earlier month, x_{ij} must be zero if $i > j$. Therefore there is no real cost that can be associated with such x_{ij}. Nevertheless, unless the solution procedure is to be executed manually with the prohibited allocations excluded from consideration, it is necessary to assign some value for the unidentified costs. Fortunately, the *Big M method* introduced in Sec. 2.10 may be used to do this.

Figure 3.6 Partial cost and requirements table for the Northern Airplane Company.

		Cost per Unit Distributed				
		Destination				
		1	*2*	*3*	*4*	*Supply*
Source	1	1.080	1.095	1.110	1.125	?
	2	?	1.110	1.125	1.140	?
	3	?	?	1.100	1.115	?
	4	?	?	?	1.130	?
Demand		10	15	25	20	

Thus a *very* large number (denoted by M for convenience) is assigned to the unidentified entries in the cost table to force the corresponding values of x_{ij} to be zero in the final solution.

The numbers to insert into the supply column are not obvious because the "supplies," the amount produced in the respective months, are not fixed quantities. In fact, the objective is to solve for the most desirable values of these production quantities. Nevertheless, it is necessary to assign some definite number to every entry in the table, including those in the supply column. A clue is provided by the fact that although the supply constraints are not present in the usual form, these constraints do exist in the form of upper bounds on the amount that can be supplied, namely,

$$x_{11} + x_{12} + x_{13} + x_{14} \leq 25,$$
$$x_{21} + x_{22} + x_{23} + x_{24} \leq 35,$$
$$x_{31} + x_{32} + x_{33} + x_{34} \leq 30,$$
$$x_{41} + x_{42} + x_{43} + x_{44} \leq 10.$$

The only change from the standard model for the transportation problem is that these constraints are in the form of inequalities instead of equations. To convert them to equations, the device employed in Sec. 2.6 of introducing *slack variables* should be used. In this context, the slack variables are allocations to a fictitional or *dummy destination* representing the unused production capacity in the respective months. This permits the supply to be the total production capacity in the given month. Furthermore, since the demand for the dummy destination is the total unused capacity, the sum of the supplies equals the sum of the demands, so that a feasible solution is obtainable. The cost entries associated with the dummy destination should be zero because there is no cost incurred by a fictional allocation.

The resulting final cost and requirements table is given in Fig. 3.7, with the dummy destination labeled as destination 5(*D*). Using this formulation, it is quite easy to find the optimal production schedule by the solution procedure described in Sec. 3.2. (See Prob. 10 and its answer.)

Figure 3.7 Complete cost and requirements table for the Northern Airplane Company.

Cost per Unit Distributed

		Destination					
		1	*2*	*3*	*4*	*5(D)*	*Supply*
Source	1	1.080	1.095	1.110	1.125	0	25
	2	M	1.110	1.125	1.140	0	35
	3	M	M	1.100	1.115	0	30
	4	M	M	M	1.130	0	10
Demand		10	15	25	20	30	

Example—Distribution of Water Resources

The *Metro Water District* is an agency that administers the distribution of water in a certain large geographical region. The region is fairly arid, so the District must purchase and bring in water from outside the region. The sources of this imported water are the Colombo, Sacron and Calorie Rivers. The District then resells the water to users in the region. Its main customers are the water departments of the cities of Berdoo, Los Devils, San Go, and Hollyglass. It is possible to supply any of these cities with water brought in from any of the three rivers, with the one exception that no provision has been made to supply Hollyglass with Calorie River water. However, because of the geographical layout of the viaducts and the cities in the region, the cost to the District of supplying water depends upon both the source of the water and the city being supplied. The variable cost per acre foot of water (in dollars) for each combination of river and city is given in Table 3.4. Despite these variations, the price per acre foot charged by the District is independent of the source of the water and is the same for all cities.

Table 3.4 Water Resources Data for Metro Water District

	Cost ($) per acre foot				
	Berdoo	*Los Devils*	*San Go*	*Hollyglass*	*Supply*
Colombo River	16	13	22	17	50
Sacron River	14	13	19	15	60
Calorie River	19	20	23	—	50
Min. needed:	30	70	0	10	(in units of
Requested:	50	70	30	∞	million acre feet)

The management of the District is now faced with the problem of how to allocate the available water during the upcoming summer season. Using units of 1 million acre feet, the amounts available from the three rivers are given in the right-hand column of Table 3.4. The District is committed to provide a certain minimum amount to meet the essential needs of each city (with the exception of San Go, which has an independent source of water), as shown in the min. needed row of the table. The requested row indicates that Los Devils desires no more, but that Berdoo would like to buy as much as 20 more, San Go would buy up to 30, and Hollyglass will take as much as it can get.

Management wishes to allocate *all* the available water from the three rivers to the four cities in such a way as to at least meet the essential needs of each city while minimizing the total cost to the District.

FORMULATION Table 3.4 already is close to the proper form for a cost and requirements table, with the rivers being the sources and the cities being the destinations. However, the one basic difficulty is that it is not clear what the demands at the destinations should be. The amount to be received at each destination (except Los Devils) actually is a decision variable, with both a lower and upper bound. (Although Hollyglass's insatiable thirst imposes no upper bound on its allocation, the supply quantities and the minimum needs at the other cities imply that a maximum of 60 million acre feet can be sent there.) Unfortunately, the demand quantities in the cost and requirements table of a transportation problem *must* be constants.

To begin resolving this difficulty, suppose temporarily that it is not necessary to satisfy the minimum needs from these rivers, so that the upper bounds represented by the amounts requested (including 60 for Hollyglass) are the only constraints on amounts to be allocated to the cities. In this circumstance, can the requested allocations be viewed as the demand quantities for a transportation problem formulation? After one adjustment, yes! (Do you see already what the needed adjustment is?) The situation is exactly analogous to the production scheduling problem of the P & T Company, where there was *excess supply capacity*. Now there is *excess demand capacity*. Consequently, rather than introducing a *dummy destination* to "receive" the unused supply capacity, the adjustment needed here is to introduce a **dummy source** to "send" the unused demand capacity. The imaginary supply quantity for this dummy source would be the amount by which the sum of the demands (requested) exceeds the sum of the real supplies: $(50 + 70 + 30 + 60) - (50 + 60 + 50) = 50$. This yields the cost and requirements table shown in Fig. 3.8, which uses units of million acre feet and million dollars. (Since Calorie River water can not be used to supply Hollyglass, the Big M method is used to prevent any such allocation.)

Now let us see how we can take each of the city's minimum needs into account in this kind of formulation. Since San Go has no minimum need, it is all set already. Similarly, the formulation for Hollyglass does not require any adjustments because its demand exceeds the dummy source's supply by 10, so

Figure 3.8 Cost and requirements table without minimum needs for Metro Water District.

		Cost per Unit Distributed				
		Destination				
		Berdoo	*Los Devils*	*San Go*	*Hollyglass*	*Supply*
Source	Colombo R.	16	13	22	17	50
	Sacron R.	14	13	19	15	60
	Calorie R.	19	20	23	M	50
	Dummy	0	0	0	0	50
	Demand	50	70	30	60	

		Cost per Unit Distribution					
		Destination					
		B.(min.) 1	*B.(extra)* 2	*L.D.* 3	*S.G.* 4	*H.* 5	*Supply*
Source	Col. R. 1	16	16	13	22	17	50
	Sac. R. 1	14	14	13	19	15	60
	Cal. R. 3	19	19	20	23	M	50
	Dummy 4(*D*)	M	0	M	0	0	50
	Demand	30	20	70	30	60	

Figure 3.9 Cost and requirements table for Metro Water District.

its minimum need for 10 from the rivers is guaranteed. (If this coincidence had not occurred, Hollyglass would need the same adjustments that we shall make for Berdoo.) Los Devil's minimum need equals its requested allocation, so its *entire* demand of 70 must be filled from the real sources rather than the dummy source. This calls for the Big M method! Assigning a hugh unit cost of M to the allocation from the dummy source to Los Devils ensures that this allocation will be zero in an optimal solution. Finally, consider Berdoo. Since the minimum need is 30, the dummy source must not contribute more than 20 to its demand of 50. This is accomplished by splitting Berdoo into two destinations, one having a demand of 30 with a unit cost of M for any allocation from the dummy source and the other having a demand of 20 with a unit cost of zero for the dummy source allocation. This gives the final cost and requirements table shown in Fig. 3.9.

This problem will be solved in the next section to illustrate the solution procedure presented there.

3.2 A STREAMLINED SIMPLEX METHOD FOR THE TRANSPORTATION PROBLEM

Since the transporation problem is just a special type of linear programming problem, it can be solved by applying the simplex method just as it was described in Chap. 2. However, you will see in this section that some tremendous computational shortcuts can be obtained in this method by exploiting the special structure shown in Fig. 3.5. We shall refer to this streamlined procedure as the *transportation simplex method.*

As you read on, particularly note how the special structure is exploited to achieve great computational savings. Then bear in mind that comparable savings sometimes can be achieved by exploiting other types of special structure as well, including those described later in the chapter.

Setting up the Transportation Simplex Method

To highlight the streamlining achieved by the transportation simplex method, let us first review how the general (unstreamlined) simplex method would set up the transportation problem in tabular form. After constructing the table of constraints (see Fig. 3.5), converting the objective function to maximization form, and using the Big M method to introduce artificial variables $z_1, z_2, \ldots, z_{m+n}$ into the $(m+n)$ respective equality constraints (see Sec. 2.10), typical columns of the simplex tableau would have the form shown in Table 3.5, where

Table 3.5 Original Simplex Tableau Before Applying Simplex Method to Transportation Problem

Basic variable	*Eq. no.*	*Coefficient of* Z	$\ldots x_{ij} \ldots$	$z_i \ldots$	$z_{m+j} \ldots$	*Right side*
Z	0	-1	c_{ij}	M	M	0
	1					
	⋮					
z_i	i	0	1	1		s_i
	⋮					
z_{m+j}	$m+j$	0	1		1	d_j
	⋮					
	$m+n$					

all entries *not* shown in *these* columns are zeros. [The one remaining adjustment before the first iteration of the simplex method would be to algebracially eliminate the nonzero coefficients of the initial (artificial) basic variables in row 0.] After any subsequent iteration, row 0 then would have the form shown in Table 3.6. Because of the pattern of zeros and 1s for the coefficients in

Table 3.6 Row 0 of Simplex Tableau When Applying Simplex Method to Transportation Problem

Basic variable	*Eq. no.*	*Coefficient of* Z	$\cdots$ x_{ij} $\cdots$	z_i $\cdots$	$z_{m+j} \cdots$	*Right side*
Z	0	-1	$c_{ij}-u_i-v_j$	$M-u_i$	$M-v_j$	$-\sum_{i=1}^{m} s_i u_i - \sum_{j=1}^{n} d_j v_j$

Table 3.6, the u_i and v_j would have the interpretation

u_i = multiple of *original* row i that has been subtracted (directly or indirectly) from *original* row 0 by simplex method,

v_j = multiple of *original* row $(m+j)$ that has been subtracted (directly or indirectly) from *original* row 0 by simplex method.

(This is one application of our fundamental insight in Sec. 2.11.) You might also recognize the u_i and v_j from Sec. 2.12 as being the dual variables.[1] If x_{ij} is a nonbasic variable, $(c_{ij} - u_i - v_j)$ is interpreted as the rate at which Z would change as x_{ij} is increased.

To lay the groundwork for simplifying this setup, recall what information is needed by the simplex method. In the initialization step, an initial basic feasible solution must be obtained, which is done artificially by introducing artificial variables as the initial basic variables and setting them equal to the s_i and d_j. The stopping rule and part 1 of the iterative step (selecting an entering basic variable) requires knowing the current row 0, which is obtained by subtracting a certain multiple of another row from the preceding row 0. Part 2 (determining the leaving basic variable) must identify the basic variable that reaches zero first as the entering basic variable is increased, which is done by comparing the current coefficients of the entering basic variable and the corresponding right side. Part 3 must determine the new basic feasible solution, which is found by subtracting certain multiples of one row from the other rows in the current simplex tableau.

Now, how does the *transportation simplex method* obtain the same information in much simpler ways? We shall describe and illustrate this in some detail soon, but a few comments now will help clarify how to set up the method. First, no artificial variables are needed because a simple and convenient procedure (with several variations) is available for constructing an initial basic feasible solution. Second, the current row 0 can be obtained without using any other row simply by calculating the current values of the u_i and v_j directly. Since each basic variable must have a coefficient of zero in row 0, the current u_i and v_j are obtained by solving the set of equations

$$c_{ij} - u_i - v_j = 0 \text{ for each } i \text{ and } j \text{ such that } x_{ij} \text{ is a basic variable,}$$

which can be done in a very straightforward way. (Note how the special structure in Table 3.5 makes possible this convenient way of obtaining row 0 by yielding $c_{ij} - u_i - v_j$ as the coefficient of x_{ij} in Table 3.6.) Third, the leaving basic variable can be identified in a simple way without (explicitly) using the coefficients of the entering basic variable. Again, this is because of the special structure of the problem, which makes it very easy to see how the solution must change as the entering basic variable is increased. As a result, the new basic feasible solution also can be identified immediately without any algebraic manipulations on the rows of the simplex tableau.

The grand conclusion from all this is that almost the entire simplex tableau (and the work of maintaining it) can be eliminated! Besides the input data (the c_{ij}, s_i, and d_j values), the only information needed by the transportation simplex method is the current basic feasible solution,[2] the current values of the

[1] This is easier to see by relabeling all these variables as y_i and then changing all the signs in row 0 of Table 3.6 by converting the objective function back to its original minimization form.

[2] Since nonbasic variables are automatically zero, the current basic feasible solution is fully identified by recording just the values of the basic variables. We shall be using this convention hereafter.

u_i and v_j, and the resulting values of $(c_{ij} - u_i - v_j)$ for nonbasic variables x_{ij}. When you solve a problem by hand, it is convenient to record this information for each iteration in a **transportation simplex tableau** such as shown in Table 3.7.

Table 3.7 Format of Transportation Simplex Tableau

		Destination					
		1	2	...	n	Supply	u_i
Source	1	c_{11}	c_{12}	...	c_{1n}	s_1	
	2	c_{21}	c_{22}	...	c_{2n}	s_2	
	⋮	⋮	⋮	⋮	⋮	⋮	
	m	c_{m1}	c_{m2}	...	c_{mn}	s_m	
Demand		d_1	d_2	...	d_m		
	v_j						

Additional information to be added in each cell:

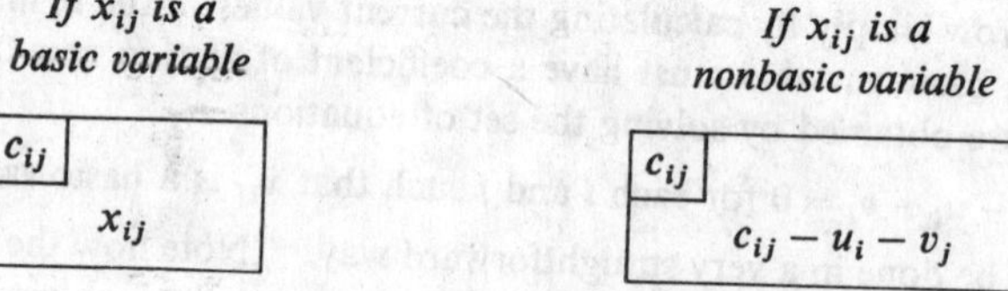

You can gain a fuller appreciation for the great difference in efficiency and convenience between the simplex and the transportation simplex methods by applying them both to the same small problem (see Prob. 12). However, the difference becomes even more pronounced for large problems that must be solved on a computer. This is suggested somewhat by comparing the sizes of the simplex and the transportation simplex tableaux. Thus, for a transportation problem having m sources and n destinations, the simplex tableau would have $(m + n + 1)$ rows and $(m + 1)(n + 1)$ columns (excluding those to the left of the x_{ij} columns), and the transportation simplex tableau would have m rows and n columns (excluding the two extra informational rows and columns). Now try plugging in various values for m and n (for example, $m = 10$ and $n = 100$ would be a rather typical middle-sized transportation problem), and note how the ratio of the number of cells in the simplex tableau to the number in the transportation simplex tableau increases as m and n increase.

Initialization Step

Recall that the objective of the initialization step is to obtain an initial basic feasible solution. Since all the functional constraints in the transportation problem are *equality* constraints, this could be done by introducing artificial variables and using them as the initial basic variables, as described in Sec. 2.10. This would give a basic solution that actually is feasible only for a revised version of the problem, and a number of iterations then would be needed to drive these variables to zero in order to reach the real basic feasible solutions. The transportation simplex method bypasses all this by instead using a simpler procedure to directly construct a real basic feasible solution on a transportation simplex tableau.

Before outlining this procedure we need to point out that the number of basic variables in any basic solution of a transportation problem is one less than you might have expected. Although there are $(m + n)$ functional constraints, the number of basic variables is just $m + n - 1$. The reason is that these are equality constraints, and this set of $(m + n)$ equations has one *extra* (or *redundant*) equation that can be deleted without changing the feasible region, i.e., any one of the constraints is automatically satisfied whenever the other $m + n - 1$ constraints are satisfied. (This can be verified by showing that any supply constraint exactly equals the sum of the demand constraints minus the sum of the *other* supply constraints, and correspondingly, any demand equation also can be reproduced by summing the supply equations and subtracting the other demand equations. See Prob. 13.) Therefore, any basic *feasible* solution would appear on a transportation simplex tableau with exactly $(m + n - 1)$ circled *nonnegative* allocations, where the sum of the allocations for each row or column equals its supply or demand.[1]

The procedure for constructing an initial basic feasible solution selects the $(m + n - 1)$ basic variables one at a time. After each selection, a value is assigned to that variable which will satisfy one additional constraint. Thus, after $(m + n - 1)$ selections an entire basic solution has been constructed in such a way as to satisfy all the constraints. A number of different criteria have been proposed for how to select the basic variables. We present and illustrate three of these criteria below after outlining the overall procedure.

Procedure[2] for Constructing An Initial Basic Feasible Solution

To begin All source rows and destination columns of the transportation simplex tableau are initially under consideration for providing a basic variable (allocation).

[1] This is not to say that any feasible solution with $(m + n - 1)$ nonzero variables necessarily is a basic solution because it might be the weighted average of two or more degenerate basic feasible solutions (i.e., basic feasible solutions having some basic variables equal to zero.) We need not be concerned about mislabeling such solutions as being basic, however, because the transportation simplex method constructs only legitimate basic feasible solutions.

[2] In Sec. 2.5 we pointed out that the simplex method is an example of the algorithms (iterative solution procedures) so prevalent in operations research work. Note that this procedure also is an algorithm, where each successive execution of the (three) steps constitutes an iteration.

Step 1 From among the rows and columns still under consideration, select the next basic variable (allocation) according to some criterion (see below).

Step 2 Make that allocation large enough to exactly use up the remaining supply in its row or the remaining demand in its column (whichever is smaller).

Step 3 Eliminate that row or column (whichever had the smaller remaining supply or demand)[1] from further consideration. If only one row or only one column remains under consideration, then the procedure is completed by selecting every *remaining* variable[2] associated with that row or column to be basic with the only feasible allocation. Otherwise, return to step 1.

Alternative Criteria for Step 1

1. *Northwest corner rule* Begin by selecting x_{11}. Thereafter, if x_{ij} was the last basic variable selected, then next select $x_{i,j+1}$ if source i has any supply remaining. Otherwise, select $x_{i+1,j}$ next.

2. *Vogel's approximation method* For each row and column remaining under consideration, calculate its *difference*, which is the arithmetic difference between the smallest and next-to-the-smallest unit cost (c_{ij}) still remaining in that row or column. Select the variable having the *smallest* remaining unit cost in that row or column having the *largest* difference.[3]

3. *Russell's approximation method* For each source row i remaining under consideration, determine its $\bar{u}_i$, which is the *largest* unit cost (c_{ij}) still remaining in that row. For each destination column j remaining under consideration, determine its $\bar{v}_j$, which is the *largest* unit cost (c_{ij}) still remaining in that column. For each variable x_{ij} not previously selected in these rows and columns, calculate $(c_{ij} - \bar{u}_i - \bar{v}_j)$. Select the variable having the *largest negative* value of $(c_{ij} - \bar{u}_i - \bar{v}_j)$.[†]

To make this description more concrete, let us now illustrate the procedure on the Metro Water District problem (see Fig. 3.9) with each of the three criteria. Since $m = 4$ and $n = 5$ in this case, the procedure should find an initial basic feasible solution having $m + n - 1 = 8$ basic variables.

With the northwest corner rule, the first allocation is $x_{11} = 30$, which exactly uses up the demand in column 1 (and eliminates this column from further consideration). This leaves a supply of 20 remaining in row 1, so next select $x_{1,1+1} = x_{12}$ to be a basic variable. Since this supply is no larger than the

[1] If the row and column have the *same* remaining supply and demand, then (arbitrarily) select the row as the one to be eliminated. (The column will be used later to provide a *degenerate* basic variable, i.e., a circled allocation of zero.)

[2] The remaining variables are those not previously selected to be basic or eliminated from consideration by eliminating its row or column.

[3] Ties for the largest difference may be broken arbitrarily.

† Ties may be broken arbitrarily.

Table 3.8 Initial Basic Feasible Solution from Northwest Corner Rule

		Destination					
	1	*2*	*3*	*4*	*5*	*Supply*	u_i
Source 1	16 (30) →	16 (20) ↓	13	22	17	50	
Source 2	14	14 (0) →	13 (60) ↓	19	15	60	
Source 3	19	19	20 (10) →	23 (30) →	M (10) ↓	50	
Source 4(D)	M	O	M	O	O (50)	50	
Demand	30	20	70	30	60		
v_j							

demand of 20 in column 2, all of it would be allocated, $x_{12} = 20$, and this row eliminated from further consideration (see footnote 1 on page 124). Therefore select $x_{1+1,2} = x_{22}$ next. Since the remaining supply of 0 in column 2 is less than the supply of 60 in row 2, allocate $x_{22} = 0$ and eliminate column 2. Continuing in this manner, we eventually obtain the initial basic feasible solution shown in Table 3.8, where arrows have been added to show the order in which the basic variables (allocations) have been selected.

With the criterion for Vogel's approximation method, we would use Fig. 3.9 (crossing out rows and columns and adjusting supplies and demands as we go along) to calculate the succession of information shown in Table 3.9, where the

Table 3.9 Initial Basic Feasible Solution from Vogel's Approximation Method

	Difference									
	Row				Column					
Iteration	*1*	*2*	*3*	*4(D)*	*1*	*2*	*3*	*4*	*5*	*Allocation*
1	3	1	0	0	2	14	0	(19)	15	$x_{44} = 30$
2	3	1	0	0	2	14	0		15	$x_{45} = 20$
3	(3)	1	0		2	2	0		2	$x_{13} = 50$
4		1	0		5	5	7		(M − 15)	$x_{25} = 40$
5		1	0		5	5	(7)			$x_{23} = 20$
		X								$x_{31} = 30$
										$x_{32} = 20$
										$x_{33} = 0$

largest difference for each iteration has been circled. Thus, at the first iteration, row 1 has a difference = 16 – 13 = 3, column 1 has a difference = 16 – 14 = 2, and so on. Since column 4 has the largest difference of 19, the variable having the smallest unit cost in the column ($c_{44} = 0$) is selected for the first allocation, $x_{44} = 30$. This exactly uses up the demand for column 4, so it is eliminated from further consideration. For the second iteration, the other differences happen to remain the same, so the column 5 difference of 15 leads to $x_{45} = 20$ being selected in a similar way. This exhausts the remaining supply for row 4, so it is now eliminated, which changes the difference for column 2 from 14 – 0 = 14 to 16 – 14 = 2. This leaves row 1 having the largest difference, so $x_{13} = 50$ is selected next. Since this exactly uses up the supply in row 1, it is eliminated from further consideration. This yields a difference of $M - 15$ for column 5 (where M represents a hugh positive number), so this difference automatically becomes the largest one for iteration 4, leading to $x_{25} = 40$. At iteration 5, the selection of $x_{23} = 20$ eliminates row 2 (see footnote 1 on page 124), so then the only row remaining under consideration is row 3. Therefore the procedure is completed by selecting x_{31}, x_{32}, and x_{33}, the only *remaining*

Table 3.10 Initial Basic Feasible Solution from Russell's Approximation Method

Iteration	$\bar{u}_1$	$\bar{u}_2$	$\bar{u}_3$	$\bar{u}_4$	$\bar{v}_1$	$\bar{v}_2$	$\bar{v}_3$	$\bar{v}_4$	$\bar{v}_5$	*Allocation*
1	22	19	M	M	M	19	M	23	M	$x_{45} = 50$
2	22	19	M		19	19	20	23	M	$x_{15} = 10$
3	22	19	23		19	19	20	23		$x_{13} = 40$
4		19	23		19	19	20	23		$x_{23} = 30$
5		19	23		19	19		23		$x_{21} = 30$
		X								(or $x_{22} = 30$)
										$x_{31} = 0$
										$x_{32} = 20$
										$x_{34} = 30$

variables associated with row 3 (x_{34} and x_{35} were eliminated previously by eliminating columns 4 and 5 from further consideration), to be basic. Even though the remaining demand in column 3 for x_{33} is zero, so x_{33} is just a *degenerate* basic variable, it is important to record this zero allocation. (You will see soon that the transportation simplex method must know *all* $m + n - 1$ basic variables in the current basic feasible solution.)

With the criterion for Russell's approximation method, we again would use and update Fig. 3.9 to obtain the information and sequence of basic variables (allocations) shown in Table 3.10. At iteration 1, the largest unit cost in row 1 is $\bar{u}_1 = 22$, the largest in column 1 is $\bar{v}_1 = M$, and so forth. Thus $(c_{11} - \bar{u}_1 - \bar{v}_1) = 16 - 22 - M = -6 - M$. Calculating all the $(c_{ij} - \bar{u}_i - \bar{v}_j)$ for $i = 1, 2, 3, 4$ and $j = 1, 2, 3, 4, 5$ shows that $(c_{45} - \bar{u}_4 - \bar{v}_5) = 0 - 2M$ has the *largest negative* value, so $x_{45} = 50$ is selected as the first basic variable (allocation). This exactly uses up the supply in row 4, so this row is eliminated from further consideration. (Note that this changes $\bar{v}_1$ and $\bar{v}_3$.) Therefore the second iteration requires recalculating all the $(c_{ij} - \bar{u}_i - \bar{v}_j)$ *except* for those where $i = 4$. The largest negative value now is $(c_{15} - \bar{u}_1 - \bar{v}_5) = 17 - 22 - M = -5 - M$, so $x_{15} = 10$ becomes the second basic variable (allocation), eliminating column 5 from further consideration. (The subsequent iterations proceed similarly, but you may want to test your understanding by verifying the remaining allocations given in Table 3.10.)

Now let us compare these three criteria. The main virtue of the Northwest corner rule is that it is quick and easy. However, because it pays no attention to unit costs (c_{ij}), usually the solution obtained will be far from optimal. (Note in Table 3.8 that $x_{35} = 10$ even though $c_{35} = M$.) Expending a little more effort to find a good initial basic feasible solution might greatly reduce the number of iterations then required by the transportation simplex method to reach an optimal solution (see Prob. 7). This is the objective of the other two criteria. Vogel's approximation method has been a popular criterion for many years.[1] Since *difference* represents the minimum extra unit cost incurred by failing to make an allocation to the cell having the smallest unit cost in that row or column, this criterion does take costs into account in an effective way. Russell's approximation method is a much more recently proposed criterion[2] that seems very promising. Although more experimentation is required to determine which is more effective *on the average*, this criterion *frequently* does obtain a better solution. (For a large problem, it may be worthwhile applying *both* criteria and then using the better solution obtained to start the iterations of the transportation simplex method.) One distinct advantage of Russell's approximation method is that it is patterned directly after part 1 of the iterative step for the transportation simplex method, which somewhat simplifies the overall computer code. In particular, the $\bar{u}_i$ and $\bar{v}_i$ have been defined in such a way that the relative values of the $(c_{ij} - \bar{u}_i - \bar{v}_j)$ *estimate* the relative values of the $c_{ij} - u_i - v_j$ that will be obtained when the transportation simplex method reaches the optimal solution.

We now shall use the initial basic feasible solution obtained in Table 3.10 by Russell's approximation method to illustrate the remainder of the transportation simplex method. Thus our *initial transportation simplex tableau* (before solving for the u_i and v_j) is the one shown in Table 3.11.

The next step is to check whether this initial solution is optimal by applying the *stopping rule*.

[1] N. V. Reinfeld and W. R. Vogel, *Mathematical Programming*. Prentice-Hall, Englewood Cliffs, N.J., 1958.

[2] Edward J. Russell, "Extension of Dantzig's Algorithm to Finding an Initial Near-Optimal Basis for the Transportation Problem," *Operations Research*, 17: 187–191, 1969. Subsequently, promising modifications of Russell's criterion also are being developed and tested. For example, see Benjamin L. Schwartz, "Initializing the Transportation Problem," tentatively scheduled for publication in *Operations Research* during 1974.

Table 3.11 Initial Transportation Simplex Tableau (Before Obtaining The $c_{ij} - u_i - v_j$) from Russell's Approximation Method

Iteration 0		*Destination* 1	2	3	4	5	*Supply*	u_i
	1	16	16	13 (40)	22	17 (10)	50	
	2	14 (30)	14	13 (30)	19	15	60	
Source	3	19 (0)	19 (20)	20	23 (30)	M	50	
	4(D)	M	0	M	0	0 (50)	50	
Demand		30	20	70	30	60		
v_j								

Stopping Rule

Recall that the purpose of the stopping rule is to determine whether the current basic feasible solution is optimal, so that the simplex method (or transportation simplex method now) can be stopped. Using the notation of Table 3.6, the standard test for optimality (see the stopping rule in Sec. 2.8) reduces to the following:

> CRITERION FOR OPTIMALITY A basic feasible solution is optimal if and only if $(c_{ij} - u_i - v_j) \geq 0$ for every (i, j) such that x_{ij} is nonbasic.[1]

Thus, the only work required by the stopping rule is to derive the value of the u_i and v_j for the current basic feasible solution and then to calculate these $(c_{ij} - u_i - v_j)$.

Since $(c_{ij} - u_i - v_j)$ is required to be zero if x_{ij} is a basic variable, the u_i and v_j satisfy the set of equations

$$c_{ij} = u_i + v_j \text{ for each } (i, j) \text{ such that } x_{ij} \text{ is basic.}$$

There are $(m + n - 1)$ basic variables, and so $(m + n - 1)$ of these equations. Since the number of unknowns (the u_i and v_j) is $(m + n)$, one of these variables can be assigned a value arbitrarily without violating the equations. (The rule we shall adopt is to select the u_i that has the largest number of allocations

[1] The one exception is that two or more equivalent degenerate basic feasible solutions (i.e., identical solutions having different degenerate basic variables equal to zero) can be optimal with only some of these basic solutions satisfying the criterion for optimality. This is illustrated later in the example.

in its row and assign it the value of zero.) Because of the simple structure of these equations, it is then very simple to solve for the remaining variables algebraically.

To demonstrate, each equation corresponding to a basic variable in our initial basic feasible solution is given:

$$\begin{array}{ll} x_{31}\colon 19 = u_3 + v_1 & x_{23}\colon 13 = u_2 + v_3 \\ x_{32}\colon 19 = u_3 + v_2 & x_{13}\colon 13 = u_1 + v_3 \\ x_{34}\colon 23 = u_3 + v_4 & x_{15}\colon 17 = u_1 + v_5 \\ x_{21}\colon 14 = u_2 + v_1 & x_{45}\colon\ 0 = u_4 + v_5 \end{array}$$

Setting $u_3 = 0$ and moving down the equations one at a time immediately gives $v_1 = 19$, $v_2 = 19$, $v_4 = 23$, $u_2 = 14 - 19 = -5$, $v_3 = 13 - (-5) = 18$, $u_1 = 13 - 18 = -5$, $v_5 = 17 - (-5) = 22$, and $u_4 = -22$.

Once you get the hang of it, you probably will find it even more convenient to solve these equations without even writing them down by working directly on the transportation simplex tableau. Thus in Table 3.11 you would begin by writing in the value $u_3 = 0$ and then picking out the circled allocations (x_{31}, x_{32}, x_{34}) in that row. For each one you would set $v_j = c_{3j}$ and then look for circled allocations in these columns (x_{21}). Mentally calculate $u_2 = c_{21} - v_1$, pick out x_{23}, set $v_3 = c_{23} - u_2$, and so on until you have filled in all the values for the u_i and v_j. (Try it.) Then calculate and fill in the value of $(c_{ij} - u_i - v_j)$ for each nonbasic variable x_{ij} (cell without a circled allocation), and you will have the completed initial transportation simplex tableau shown in Table 3.12.

Table 3.12 Completed Initial Transportation Simplex Tableau

Iteration 0	Destination 1	2	3	4	5	Supply	u_i
Source 1	16; +2	16; +2	13; (40)	22; +4	17; (10)	50	−5
2	14; (30)	14; 0	13; (30)	19; +1	15; −2	60	−5
3	19; (0)	19; (20)	20; +2	23; (30)	M; M − 22	50	0
4(D)	M; M + 3	0; +3	M; M + 4	0; −1	0; (50)	50	−22
Demand	30	20	70	30	60		
v_j	19	19	18	23	22		

We are now in a position to apply the criterion for optimality by checking the value of the $(c_{ij} - u_i - v_j)$ given in Table 3.12. Since two of these values, $(c_{25} - u_2 - v_5) = -2$ and $(c_{44} - u_4 - v_4) = -1$, are negative, we conclude that the current basic feasible solution is not optimal. Therefore the transportation simplex method must next go to the iterative step to find a better basic feasible solution.

Iterative step

As with the simplex method, the iterative step must determine an *entering basic variable* (part 1), a *leaving basic variable* (part 2), and then identify the resulting *new basic feasible solution* (part 3).

Part 1 Since $(c_{ij} - u_i - v_j)$ represents the rate at which the objective function would change as the nonbasic variable x_{ij} is increased, the entering basic variable must have a *negative* $(c_{ij} - u_i - v_j)$ to decrease the total cost Z. Thus the candidates in Tables 3.12 are x_{25} and x_{44}. To choose between the candidates, the rule used is to select the one having the *largest negative* value of $(c_{ij} - u_i - v_j)$ to be the *entering basic variable*, which is x_{25} in this case.

Part 2 Increasing the entering basic variable from zero sets off a chain reaction of compensating changes in other basic variables (allocations) in order to continue satisfying the supply and demand constraints. The first basic variable to be decreased to zero then becomes the *leaving basic variable.*

With x_{25} as the entering basic variable, the chain reaction in Table 3.12 is the relatively simple one summarized in Fig. 3.10. (We shall always indicate the entering basic variable by placing a boxed + sign in its cell.) Thus, increasing x_{25} requires decreasing x_{15} by the same amount to restore the demand of 60 in column 5, which in turn requires increasing x_{13} by this amount to restore the supply of 50 in row 1, which in turn requires decreasing x_{23} by this amount

Figure 3.10 Part of initial transportation simplex tableau showing the chain reaction caused by increasing the entering basic variable x_{25}.

			Destination		
		3	4	5	Supply
Source 1	...	13; (40) +	22; +4	17; (10) −	50
Source 2	...	13; (30) −	19; +1	15; [+] −2	60
	...	⋮	⋮	⋮	
Demand		70	30	60	

to restore the demand of 70 in column 3. This successfully completes the chain reaction because the decrease in x_{23} also restores the supply of 60 in row 2. (Equivalently, we could have started the chain reaction by restoring this supply in row 2 with the decrease in x_{23}, and then increase x_{13} and decrease x_{15}.) The net result is that cells (2,5) and (1,3) become **recipient cells**, each receiving its additional allocation from one of the **donor cells**, (1,5) and (2,3). (These are indicated in Fig. 3.10 by the + and − signs.) Note that cell (1,5) had to be the donor cell for column 5 rather than cell (4,5) because cell (4,5) would have no recipient cell in row 4 to continue the chain reaction. [Similarly, if the chain reaction had been started in row 2 instead, cell (2,1) could not be the donor cell for this row because the chain reaction could not then be completed successfully after necessarily choosing cell (3,1) as the next recipient cell and either cell (3,2) or (3,4) as its donor cell.]

Since each donor cell decreases its allocation by exactly the same amount the entering basic variable (and other recipient cells) is increased, cell (1,5) must reach a zero allocation first as x_{25} is increased. Therefore x_{15} becomes the leaving basic variable.

In general, there always is just one chain reaction (in either direction) that can be completed successfully to maintain feasibility when the entering basic variable is increased from zero. This chain reaction can be identified by selecting among the cells having a basic variable, first, the donor cell in the *column* having the entering basic variable, then the recipient cell in the row having this donor cell, then the donor cell in the column having this recipient cell, and so on until the chain reaction yields a donor cell in the *row* having the entering basic variable. When a column or row has more than one additional basic variable cell, it may be necessary to trace them all further to see which one must be selected to be the donor or recipient cell. After identifying the chain reaction, the donor cell having the *smallest* allocation automatically provides the leaving basic variable.[1]

Part 3 The *new basic feasible solution* is identified simply by adding the value of the leaving basic variable (before any change) to the allocation for each recipient cell and subtracting *this same amount* from the allocation for each donor cell. Since this amount is 10 in Fig. 3.10, this portion of the transportation simplex tableau changes as shown in Fig. 3.11 for the new solution. The leaving basic variable x_{15} now is nonbasic, so its allocation of zero no longer is given in the new tableau.

We now are in a position to point out a useful interpretation of the $(c_{ij} - u_i - v_j)$ quantities derived during the stopping rule. Because of the shift of 10 allocation units from the donor cells to the recipient cells, shown in Figs. 3.10 and 3.11, the total cost changes by $10(15 - 17 + 13 - 13) = 10(-2)$. Thus the effect of increasing the entering basic variable x_{25} from zero has been a cost change at the rate of -2 per unit increase in x_{25}. Now note that $(c_{25} - u_2$

[1] In the case of a tie for the donor cell having the smallest allocation, any one can be chosen arbitrarily to provide the leaving basic variable.

			Destination 3	4	5	Supply
Source	1	...	13 (50)	22	17	50
	2	...	13 (20)	19	15 (10)	60
		...	⋮	⋮	⋮	
Demand			70	30	60	

Figure 3.11 Part of second transportation simplex tableau showing the changes in the basic feasible solution.

$- v_5) = -2$ in Table 3.12; this is no coincidence. In fact, another (but less efficient) way of deriving $(c_{ij} - u_i - v_j)$ for each nonbasic variable x_{ij} is to identify the chain reaction caused by increasing this variable from zero to 1 and then calculate the resulting cost change. This intuitive interpretation sometimes is useful for checking calculations during the stopping rule.

Before completing the solution of the Metro Water District problem, let us now summarize the rules for the transportation simplex method.

Summary of Transportation Simplex Method

Initialization step Construct an initial basic feasible solution by the procedure outlined earlier in this section. Go to the stopping rule.

Iterative step

Part 1 Determine the entering basic variable: Select the nonbasic variable x_{ij} having the *largest negative* value of $(c_{ij} - u_i - v_j)$.

Part 2 Determine the leaving basic variable: Identify the chain reaction required to retain feasibility when the entering basic variable is increased. From among the donor cells, select the basic variable having the *smallest* value.

Part 3 Determine the new basic feasible solution: Add the value of the leaving basic variable to the allocation for each recipient cell. Subtract this value from the allocation for each donor cell.

Stopping rule Determine whether this solution is optimal. Derive the u_i and v_j by selecting the row having the largest number of allocations and setting its $u_i = 0$ and then solving the set of equations $c_{ij} = u_i + v_j$ for each (i, j) such that x_{ij} is basic. If $(c_{ij} - u_i - v_j) \geq 0$ for every (i, j) such that x_{ij} is *nonbasic*, then the current solution is optimal, so stop. Otherwise, go to the iterative step.

Continuing to apply this procedure to the Metro Water District problem yields the complete set of transportation simplex tableaux shown in Table 3.13. Since all the $(c_{ij} - u_i - v_j)$ are nonnegative in the fourth tableau, the stopping rule identifies the set of allocations ir this tableau as being optimal, which concludes the algorithm.

Table 3.13 Complete Set of Transportation Simplex Tableaux for The Metro Water District Problem

Iteration 0		Destination 1	2	3	4	5	Supply	u_i
Source	1	16 +2	16 +2	13 (40) +	22 +4	17 (10) −	50	−5
	2	14 (30)	14 0	13 (30) −	19 +1	15 [+] −2	60	−5
	3	19 (0)	19 (20)	20 +2	23 (30)	M $M-22$	50	0
	4(*D*)	M $M+3$	0 +3	M $M+4$	0 −1	0 (50)	50	−22
Demand		30	20	70	30	60		
v_j		19	19	18	23	22		

Iteration 1		Destination 1	2	3	4	5	Supply	u_i
Source	1	16 +2	16 +2	13 (50)	22 +4	17 +2	50	−5
	2	14 (30) −	14 0	13 (20)	19 +1	15 (10) +	60	−5
	3	19 (0) +	19 (20)	20 +2	23 (30) −	M $M-20$	50	0
	4(*D*)	M $M+1$	0 +1	M $M+2$	0 [+] −3	0 (50) −	50	−20
Demand		30	20	70	30	60		
v_j		19	19	18	23	20		

Table 3.13 Complete Set of Transportation Simplex Tableaux for The Metro Water District Problem (*Continued*)

Iteration 2	Source	Destination 1	2	3	4	5	Supply	u_i
Source	1	16; +5	16; +5	13; (50)	22; +7	17; +2	50	−8
	2	14; +3	14; +3	13; (20) −	19; +4	15; (40) +	60	−8
	3	19; (30)	19; (20)	20; [+] −1	23; (0) −	M; M − 23	50	0
	4(D)	M; M + 4	0; +4	M; M + 2	0; (30) +	0; (20) −	50	−23
Demand		30	20	70	30	60		
v_j		19	19	21	23	23		

Iteration 3	Source	Destination 1	2	3	4	5	Supply	u_i
Source	1	16; +4	16; +4	13; (50)	22; +7	17; +2	50	−7
	2	14; +2	14; +2	13; (20)	19; +4	15; (40)	60	−7
	3	19; (30)	19; (20)	20; (0)	23; +1	M; M − 22	50	0
	4(D)	M; M + 3	0; +3	M; M + 2	0; (30)	0; (20)	50	−22
Demand		30	20	70	30	60		
v_j		19	19	20	22	22		

It would be good practice for you to derive the values of the u_i and v_j given in the second, third, and fourth tableaux. Try doing this by working directly on the tableau. Also check out the chain reactions in the second and third tableaux, which are somewhat more complicated than the one you already have seen in Fig. 3.10. In addition, you should note the following special points that are illustrated by this example. First, the initial basic feasible solution is *degenerate* because the basic variable $x_{31} = 0$, but this causes no complication because cell (3,1) becomes a *recipient cell* in the second tableau, which increases x_{31} above zero. Second, another degenerate basic variable (x_{34}) arises in the third tableau because the basic variable for *two* donor cells in the second tableau, cells (2,1) and (3,4), *tie* for having the smallest value (30). (This tie is broken arbitrarily by selecting x_{21} as the leaving basic variable; if x_{34} had been selected instead, then x_{21} would have become the degenerate basic variable.) This does appear to create a complication subsequently because cell (3,4) becomes a *donor cell* in the third tableau but has nothing to donate! Fortunately, this actually is nothing to worry about. Since zero is the amount to be added or subtracted to the allocations for the recipient and donor cells, these allocations do not change. However, the degenerate basic variable does become the leaving basic variable, so it is replaced by the entering basic variable as the circled allocation of zero in the fourth tableau. This changes the values of the u_i and v_j. Therefore, if any of the $(c_{ij} - u_i - v_j)$ had been negative in the fourth tableau, the algorithm would have gone on to make *real* changes in the allocations whenever all donor cells have nondegenerate basic variables. Third, because none of the $(c_{ij} - u_i - v_j)$ turned out to be negative in the fourth tableau, the *equivalent* set of allocations in the third tableau is optimal also. Thus the algorithm executed one more iteration than necessary. This is a flaw that occasionally arises in both the transportation simplex method and simplex method because of degeneracy, but it is not sufficiently serious to warrant any adjustments in these algorithms.

3.3 THE TRANSSHIPMENT PROBLEM

One requirement of the transportation problem is that the way in which units would be distributed from each source i to each destination j be known in advance, so that the corresponding cost per unit (c_{ij}) can be determined. Sometimes, however, the best way is not clear because of the possibility of *transshipments*, whereby shipments would go through intermediate transfer points (which might be other sources or destinations). For example, rather than shipping a special cargo directly from port 1 to port 3, it may be cheaper to include it with regular cargoes from port 1 to port 2 and then from port 2 to port 3. Such possibilities could, of course, be investigated in advance to determine the cheapest route from each source to each destination. However, if there are many possible intermediate transfer points, this might be an extremely complicated and time-consuming task. Therefore it may be much more convenient to let a computer algorithm solve *simultaneously* for the amount to ship from each source to each destination *and* the route to follow for each shipment so as to minimize total shipping costs. This extension of the transportation problem to include the routing decisions is referred to as the *transshipment problem.*

Fortunately, there is a simple way of reformulating the transshipment problem to fit it back into the format of the transportation problem. Thus the transportation simplex method also can be used to solve the transshipment problem.

To clarify the structure of the transshipment problem, and the nature of this reformulation, we shall now extend the prototype example for the transportation problem to include transshipments.

Prototype Example

After further investigation, the *P&T Company* (see Sec. 3.1) has found that it can cut costs by discontinuing its own trucking operation and using common carriers instead to truck its canned peas. Since no single trucking company serves the entire area containing all the canneries and warehouses, many of the shipments will need to be transferred to another truck at least once along the way. These transfers can be made at intermediate canneries or warehouses, or at five other locations (Butte, Montana, Boise, Idaho, Cheyenne, Wyoming, Denver, Colorado, and Omaha, Nebraska) referred to as *junctions*, as shown in Fig. 3.12. The shipping cost per truckload between each of these points is given in Table 3.14, where a dash indicates that a direct shipment is not possible.

For example, a truckload of peas can still be sent from cannery 1 to warehouse 4 by direct shipment at a cost of $871. However, another possibility is to ship the truckload from cannery 1 to junction 2, transfer it to a truck going to warehouse 2, and then transfer it again to go to warehouse 4, at a cost of only ($286 + $207 + $341) = $834. This is only one of many possible indirect ways of shipping a truckload from cannery 1 to warehouse 4 that needs to be considered, if indeed this cannery should send anything to this warehouse. The overall problem is to determine how the output from all the canneries should be shipped to meet the warehouse allocations and minimize total shipping costs.

Now let us see how this *transshipment problem* can be reformulated as a transportation problem. The basic idea is to interpret the individual truck trips (as opposed to complete journeys for truckloads) as being the shipment from a source to a destination, and so label *all* the locations (canneries, junctions, and warehouses) as being *both* potential *destinations* and potential *sources* for these shipments. Thus we have 12 sources and 12 destinations, with the c_{ij} unit costs being given in Table 3.14 (use a huge cost M for the impossible shipments indicated by dashes). The number of truckloads transshipped through a location should be included in both the demand for that location as a destination and the supply for that location as a source. Since we do not know this number

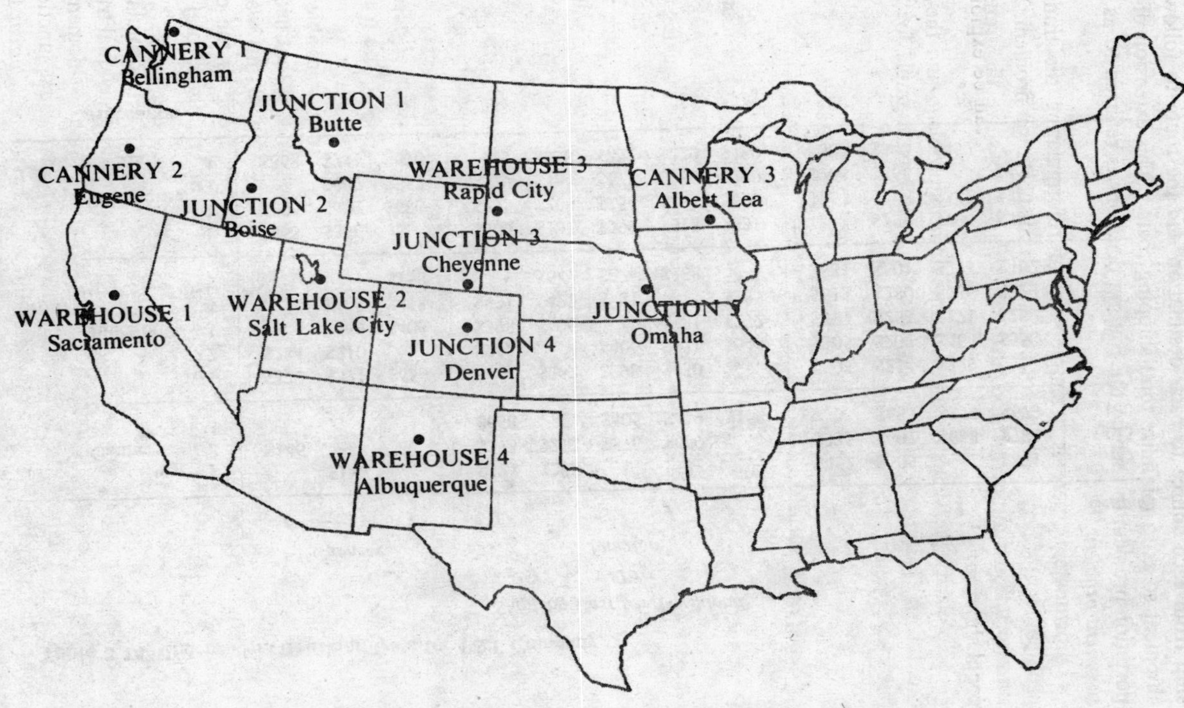

Figure 3.12 Location of canneries, warehouses, and junctions for the P&T Company.

Table 3.14 Independent Trucking Data for P&T Company

		Shipping Cost per Truckload												
		To												
		Cannery			*Junction*					*Warehouse*				
		1	*2*	*3*	*1*	*2*	*3*	*4*	*5*	*1*	*2*	*3*	*4*	*Output*
From Cannery	1		$146	....	$324	$286	....	....	....	$452	$505	....	$871	75
	2	$146		....	$373	$212	$570	$609	....	$335	$407	$688	$784	125
	3	....	....		$658	....	$405	$419	$158	....	$685	$359	$673	100
From Junction	1	$322	$371	$656		$262	$398	$430	....	$503	$234	$329	....	
	2	$284	$210	....	$262		$406	$421	$644	$305	$207	$464	$558	
	3	....	$569	$403	$398	$406		$ 81	$272	$597	$253	$171	$282	
	4	....	$608	$418	$431	$422	$ 81		$287	$613	$280	$236	$229	
	5	....	....	$158	....	$647	$274	$288		$831	$501	$293	$482	
From Warehouse	1	$453	$336	....	$505	$307	$599	$615	$831		$359	$706	$587	
	2	$505	$407	$683	$235	$208	$254	$281	$500	$357		$362	$341	
	3	....	$687	$357	$329	$464	$171	$236	$290	$705	$362		$457	
	4	$868	$781	$670	....	$558	$282	$229	$480	$587	$340	$457		
Allocation										80	65	70	85	

in advance, merely add a safe upper bound on this number to the demand and supply for that location and then introduce a slack variable into its demand and supply constraints to be allocated the excess. Since it never would pay to return a truckload to be transshipped through the same location more than once, a safe upper bound on this number for *any* location is the *total number of truckloads* (300), so we shall use this bound. The slack variable for both constraints for location i would be x_{ii}, the (fictional) number of truckloads shipped from this location to itself. Thus, $(300 - x_{ii})$ is the real number of truckloads transshipped through Location i. Since x_{ii} represents fictional shipments, let $c_{ii} = 0$ be the corresponding unit cost. This now gives us the complete cost and requirements table shown in Fig. 3.13 for the transportation problem formulation of our transshipment problem. Therefore, using the transportation simplex method to obtain an optimal solution for this transportation problem provides an optimal shipping plan (ignoring the x_{ii}) for the P&T Company (see Prob. 16).

GENERAL COMMENTS This prototype example illustrates all the general features of the transshipment problem and its relationship to the transportation problem. Thus the transshipment problem can be described in general terms as being concerned with how to allocate and route units (truckloads of canned peas in the example) from *supply centers* (canneries) to *receiving centers* (warehouses) via intermediate *transshipment points* (junctions, other supply centers, and other receiving centers). In addition to transshipping units, each supply center generates a given net surplus of units to be distributed, and each receiving center absorbs a given net deficit, whereas the junctions neither generate nor absorb any

igure 3.13 Cost and requirements table for the P&T Company transshipment problem formulated a transportation problem.

		Destination (Canneries)			(Junctions)					(Warehouses)				
		1	*2*	*3*	*4*	*5*	*6*	*7*	*8*	*9*	*10*	*11*	*13*	*Supply*
(Canneries)	1	0	146	*M*	324	286	*M*	*M*	*M*	452	505	*M*	871	375
	2	146	0	*M*	373	212	570	609	*M*	335	407	688	784	425
	3	*M*	*M*	0	658	*M*	405	419	158	*M*	685	359	673	400
ource (Junctions)	4	322	371	656	0	262	398	430	*M*	503	234	329	*M*	300
	5	284	210	*M*	262	0	406	421	644	305	207	464	558	300
	6	*M*	569	403	398	406	0	81	272	597	253	171	282	300
	7	*M*	608	418	431	422	81	0	287	613	280	236	229	300
	8	*M*	*M*	158	*M*	647	274	288	0	831	501	293	482	300
(Warehouses)	9	453	336	*M*	505	307	599	615	831	0	359	706	587	300
	10	505	407	683	235	208	254	281	500	357	0	362	341	300
	11	*M*	687	357	329	464	171	236	290	705	362	0	457	300
	12	868	781	670	*M*	558	282	229	480	587	340	457	0	300
Demand		300	300	300	300	300	300	300	300	380	365	370	385	

units. (The problem has feasible solutions only if the total net surplus generated at the supply centers *equals* the total net deficit to be absorbed at the receiving centers.) A positive cost c_{ij} is incurred for each unit sent *directly* from location i (a supply center, junction, or receiving center) to another location j. This direct shipment may be impossible ($c_{ij} = M$) for certain pairs of locations, and, in fact, certain supply centers and receiving centers may not be able to serve as transshipment points at all. The objective is to determine the plan for allocating and routing the units that minimizes total costs.

The resulting mathematical model for the transshipment problem (see Prob. 17) has a special structure slightly different from that for the transportation problem. As in the latter case, it has been found that some applications having nothing to do with transportation can be fitted to this special structure. However, regardless of the physical context of the application, this model always can be reformulated as an equivalent transportation problem in the manner illustrated by the prototype example.

3.4 THE ASSIGNMENT PROBLEM

The *assignment problem* is the special type of linear programming problem where the resources are being allocated to the activities on a *one-to-one basis*. Thus, each resource or *assignee* (e.g., an employee, machine, or time slot) is to be assigned uniquely to a particular activity or *assignment* (e.g., a task, site, or event). There is a cost c_{ij} associated with assignee i ($i = 1,2, \ldots, n$) performing assignment j ($j = 1,2, \ldots, n$), so that the objective is to determine how all the assignments should be made in order to minimize total costs.

Prototype Example

The *Job Shop Company* has purchased three new machines of different types. There are four available locations in the shop where a machine could be installed. Some of these locations are more desirable than others for particular machines because of their proximity to work centers that would have a heavy work flow to and from these machines. Therefore the objective is to assign the new machines to the available locations to minimize the total cost of materials handling. The estimated cost per unit time of materials handling involving each of the machines is given in Fig. 3.14 for the respective locations. Location 2

Figure 3.14 Materials-handling cost data for the Job Shop Company.

		Location			
		1	2	3	4
Machine	1	13	10	12	11
	2	15	×	13	20
	3	5	7	10	6

		Assignment			
		1	2	3	4
Assignee	1	13	10	12	11
	2	15	M	13	20
	3	5	7	10	6
	4(*D*)	0	0	0	0

Figure 3.15 Cost table for the Job Shop Company assignment problem.

is not considered suitable for machine 2. There would be no work flow between the new machines.

To formulate this problem as an assignment problem, a dummy machine must be introduced for the extra location. Also, an extremely large cost M should be attached to the assignment of machine 2 to location 2 to prevent this assignment in the optimal solution. The resulting assignment problem *cost table* is shown in Fig. 3.15.

The Job Shop Company can very easily obtain an optimal solution to this problem (or much larger versions of it) by using the *transportation simplex method*! (See Prob. 20.) In fact, this method can be used to solve any assignment problem, as will now be explained.

GENERAL COMMENTS The assignment problem is not only a special type of linear programming problem; it also turns out to be a special type of transportation problem. In particular, the assignees can be interpreted as transportation problem *sources*, each having a supply of 1. The assignments similarly are interpreted as *destinations* with a demand of 1. Therefore, after introducing any dummy assignees or assignments required to make the number of sources equal to the number of destinations ($m = n$), we would have the cost and requirements table shown in Fig. 3.16. Every basic feasible solution for this transportation problem would have $(n - 1)$ *degenerate* basic variables, but they also would have exactly one nondegenerate basic variable (allocation) $x_{ij} = 1$ for each destination column (as well as for each source row), which identifies the one source (assignee) being "assigned" to that destination (assignment).

Figure 3.16 Cost and requirements table for the assignment problem formulated as a transportation problem.

		Cost per Unit Distributed				
		Destination				
		1	*2*	⋯	*n*	*Supply*
Source	1	c_{11}	c_{12}	⋯	c_{1n}	1
	2	c_{21}	c_{22}	⋯	c_{2n}	1
	⋮	⋮	⋮		⋮	⋮
	m	c_{m1}	c_{m2}	⋯	c_{mn}	1
Demand		1	1	⋯	1	

Therefore, using the transportation simplex method to solve this transportation problem provides an optimal solution for the corresponding assignment problem.

Since computer codes for the transportation simplex method are widely available, this provides a very convenient way of solving any assignment problem. However, we also should point out that this formulation has *special* structure for a transportation problem (supplies and demands equal to 1) that can be exploited to streamline the solution procedure much further.[1] Therefore, if you need to solve many large assignment problems, it may be worthwhile to obtain or develop a computer code for one of these streamlined procedures.

3.5 MULTIDIVISIONAL PROBLEMS

Another important class of linear programming problems having exploitable special structure are the *multidivisional problems.* Their special feature is that they encompass several divisions of a *decentralized* organization, so that the divisions operate with considerable autonomy. Therefore the problem is *almost* decomposable into separate problems, where each division is concerned only with optimizing its own operation. However, some overall coordination is required in order to best divide certain organizational resources among the divisions.

As a result of this special feature, the *table of constraint coefficients* for multidivisional problems has the *angular structure* shown in Fig. 3.17. (Recall

Figure 3.17 Table of constraint coefficients for multidivisional problems.

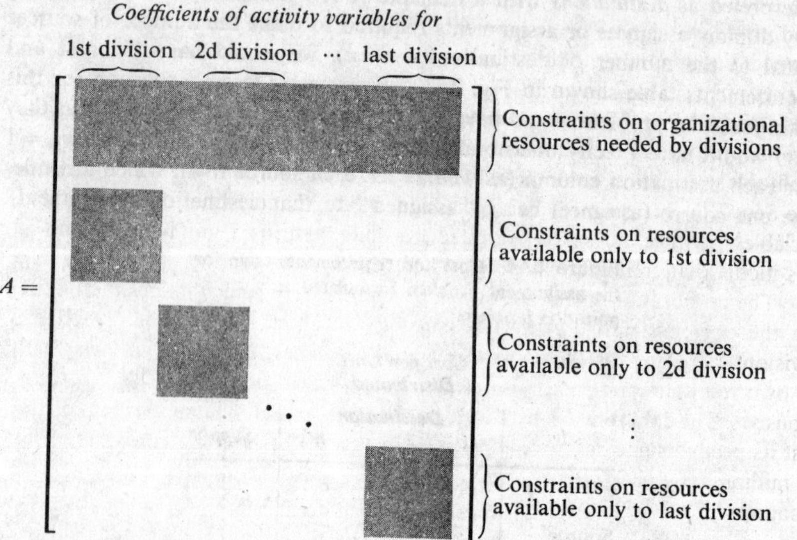

[1] See chap. 6 of Selected Reference 6 at the end of this chapter for a description of two special solution procedures for the assignment problem.

that shaded blocks represent the only portions of the table that have *any* nonzero a_{ij} coefficients.) Thus each smaller block contains the coefficients of the constraints for one *subproblem*, the problem of optimizing the operation of a division considered by itself. The long block at the top gives the coefficients of the *linking constraints* for the *master problem*, the problem of coordinating the activities of the divisions so as to obtain an overall optimal solution for the entire organization.

Because of their nature, multidivisional problems frequently are very large, containing many hundreds or even thousands of constraints and variables. Therefore it may be necessary to exploit the special structure in order to be able to solve such a problem with a reasonable expenditure of computer time, or even to solve it at all! The *decomposition principle* (described in Sec. 16.5) provides an effective way of doing this. Conceptually, this streamlined version of the simplex method can be thought of as having each division solve its subproblem and sending its proposal to "headquarters" (the master problem), where negotiations then coordinate the proposals from all the divisions to find the optimal solution for the overall organization. If the subproblems are of manageable size and the master problem is not too large (not more than 50 to 100 constraints), this approach has been successful in solving some *extremely* large multidivisional problems. It is particularly worthwhile when the total number of constraints is quite large (at least several hundred) and there are more than a few subproblems.

Prototype Example

The *Good Foods Corp.*, International is a very large producer and distributor of food products. It has three main divisions: the Processed Foods Division, the Canned Foods Division, and the Frozen Foods Division. Because costs and market prices change frequently in the food industry, Good Foods periodically uses a corporate linear programming model to revise the production rates for its various products in order to use its available production capacities in the most profitable way. This model is similar to that for the Wyndor Glass Co. problem (see Sec. 2.1), but on a much larger scale, having hundreds of constraints and variables. (Since our space is limited, we shall describe a simplified version of this model that combines the products or resources by types.)

The corporation grows its own high-quality corn and potatoes, and these are the only basic food materials currently in short supply used by all the divisions. Except for these organizational resources, each division only uses its own resources and so could determine its optimal production rates autonomously. The data for each division and the corresponding *subproblem* involving just its products and resources are given in Fig. 3.18 (where Z represents profit in millions of dollars per month), along with the data for the organizational resources.

Divisional Data

Processed foods division

Resource \ Product	1	2	3	Amount available
1	2	4	3	10
2	7	3	6	15
3	5	0	3	12
ΔZ/unit	8	5	6	
Level	x_1	x_2	x_3	

(Resource usage/unit)

Subproblem

Maximize $Z_1 = 8x_1 + 5x_2 + 6x_3$,
subject to

$$2x_1 + 4x_2 + 3x_3 \leq 10$$
$$7x_1 + 3x_2 + 6x_3 \leq 15$$
$$5x_1 \qquad + 3x_3 \leq 12$$

and

$$x_1 \geq 0, x_2 \geq 0, x_3 \geq 0.$$

Canned foods division

Resource \ Product	4	5	6	Amount available
4	3	1	2	7
5	2	4	3	9
ΔZ/unit	9	7	9	
Level	x_4	x_5	x_6	

(Resource usage/unit)

Maximize $Z_2 = 9x_4 + 7x_5 + 9x_6$,
subject to

$$3x_4 + x_5 + 2x_6 \leq 7$$
$$2x_4 + 4x_5 + 3x_6 \leq 9$$

and

$$x_4 \geq 0, x_5 \geq 0, x_6 \geq 0.$$

Frozen foods division

Resource \ Product	7	8	Amount available
6	8	5	25
7	7	9	30
8	6	4	20
ΔZ/unit	6	5	
Level	x_7	x_8	

(Resource usage/unit)

Maximize $Z_3 = 6x_7 + 5x_8$,
subject to

$$8x_7 + 5x_8 \leq 25$$
$$7x_7 + 9x_8 \leq 30$$
$$6x_7 + 4x_8 \leq 20$$

and

$$x_7 \geq 0, x_8 \geq 0.$$

Data for Organizational Resources

Resource \ Product	1	2	3	4	5	6	7	8	Available
Corn	5	3	0	2	0	3	4	6	30
Potatoes	2	0	4	3	7	0	1	0	20

Figure 3.18 Data for the Good Foods Corp. multidivisional problem.

The resulting linear programming problem for the corporation is

$$\text{Maximize } Z = 8x_1 + 5x_2 + 6x_3 + 9x_4 + 7x_5 + 9x_6 + 6x_7 + 5x_8,$$

subject to

$$\begin{array}{llllllllll}
5x_1 & + 3x_2 & & + 2x_4 & & + 3x_6 & + 4x_7 & + 6x_8 & \leq 30 \\
2x_1 & & + 4x_3 & + 3x_4 & + 7x_5 & & + x_7 & & \leq 20 \\
2x_1 & + 4x_2 & + 3x_3 & & & & & & \leq 10 \\
7x_1 & + 3x_2 & + 6x_3 & & & & & & \leq 15 \\
5x_1 & & + 3x_3 & & & & & & \leq 12 \\
 & & & 3x_4 & + x_5 & + 2x_6 & & & \leq 7 \\
 & & & 2x_4 & + 4x_5 & + 3x_6 & & & \leq 9 \\
 & & & & & & 8x_7 & + 5x_8 & \leq 25 \\
 & & & & & & 7x_7 & + 9x_8 & \leq 30 \\
 & & & & & & 6x_7 & + 4x_8 & \leq 20
\end{array}$$

and

$$x_j \geq 0, \text{ for } j = 1, 2, \ldots, 8.$$

Note how the corresponding table of constraint coefficients shown in Fig. 3.19 fits the special structure for multidivisional problems given in Fig. 3.17. Therefore the Good Foods Corp. can indeed solve this problem (or a more detailed version of it) by the streamlined version of the simplex method provided by the decomposition principle.

Important Special Cases

Some even simpler forms of the special structure exhibited in Fig. 3.17 arise quite frequently. Two particularly common forms are shown in Fig. 3.20. The first occurs when some or all of the variables can be divided into groups

Figure 3.19 Table of constraint coefficients for the Good Foods Corp. multidivisional problem.

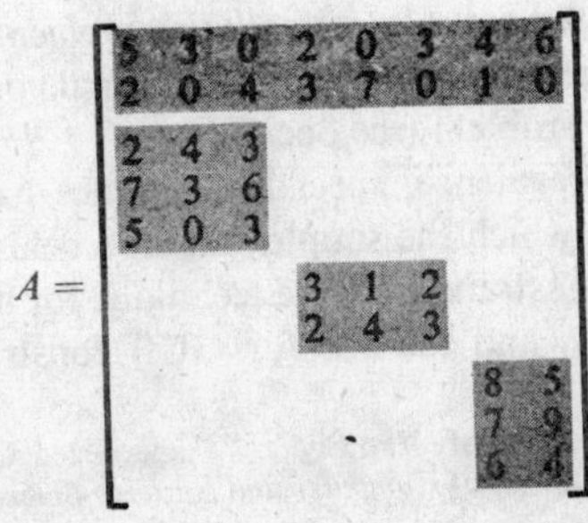

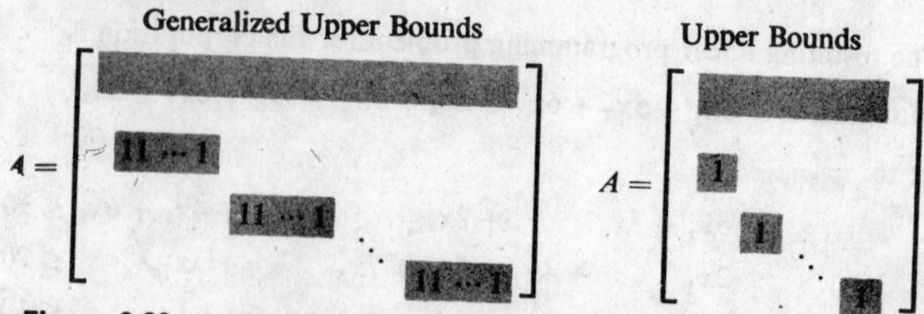

Figure 3.20 Table of constraint coefficients for important special cases of the structure for multidivisional problems given in Fig. 3.17.

such that the *sum* of the variables in *each* group must not exceed a specified upper bound for that group (or perhaps must equal a specified constant). Constraints of this form,

$$x_{j_1} + x_{j_2} + \cdots + x_{j_k} \le b_i$$
$$(\text{or} \quad x_{j_1} + x_{j_2} + \cdots + x_{j_k} = b_i),$$

usually are called either *generalized upper bound constraints* (*GUB constraints* for short) or *group constraints*. The second form shown in Fig. 3.20 occurs when some or all of the *individual* variables must not exceed a specified upper bound for that variable. These constraints,

$$x_j \le b_i,$$

normally are referred to as *upper bound constraints*.

Either GUB or upper bound constraints may occur because of the multidivisional nature of the problem. However, we should emphasize that they often arise in many other contexts as well. In fact, you already have seen several examples containing such constraints. Note in Fig. 3.5 that all the supply constraints in the *transportation problem* actually are GUB (group) constraints. (This fits the form in Fig. 3.20 by placing the supply constraints below the demand constraints.) Alternatively, the demand constraints can be taken to be the GUB constraints by reordering the variables. (Therefore a linear programming problem containing transportation problem constraints within it also fits the special structure in Fig. 3.20.) Either the land constraints or the crop constraints in the Southern Confederation of Kibbutzim *regional planning problem* (see Sec. 2.4) also are GUB constraints. The technological constraints in the Nori & Leets Co. *air pollution problem* (see Sec. 2.4) are upper bound constraints, as are two of the three functional constraints in the Wyndor Glass Co. product mix problem (see Sec. 2.1).

Because of their prevalence, special techniques have been developed for streamlining the way in which the simplex method deals with GUB constraints and with upper bound constraints. (The technique for upper bound constraints is described in Sec. 16.1, and the one for GUB constraints[1] is quite similar.)

[1] George B. Dantzig and Richard M. Van Slyke, "Generalized Upper Bounded Techniques for Linear Programming," *Journal of Computer and Systems Sciences*, **1**. 213–226, 1967.

If there are many such constraints, these techniques can drastically reduce the computation time for a problem.

3.6 MULTITIME PERIOD PROBLEMS

Any successful organization must plan ahead and take into account probable changes in its operating environment. For example, predicted future changes in sales because of *seasonal* variations or long run trends in demand might affect how the firm should operate currently. Such situations frequently lead to the formulation of *multitime period* linear programming problems for planning several time periods (e.g., days, months, or years) into the future. Just as for multidivisional problems, multitime period problems are *almost* decomposable into separate *subproblems*, where each subproblem in this case is concerned with optimizing the operation of the organization during one of the time periods. However, some overall planning is required to coordinate the activities in the different time periods.

The resulting special structure for multitime period problems is shown in Fig. 3.21. Each approximately square block gives the coefficients of the constraints for one *subproblem* concerned with optimizing the operation of the organization during a particular time period considered by itself. Each oblong block then contains the coefficients of the *linking variables* for those activities that affect two or more time periods. For example, the linking variables may describe inventories that are retained at the end of one time period for use in some later time period, as we shall illustrate in the prototype example.

As with multidivisional problems, the multiplicity of subproblems often causes multitime period problems to have a very large number of constraints

Figure 3.21 Table of constraint coefficients for multitime period problems.

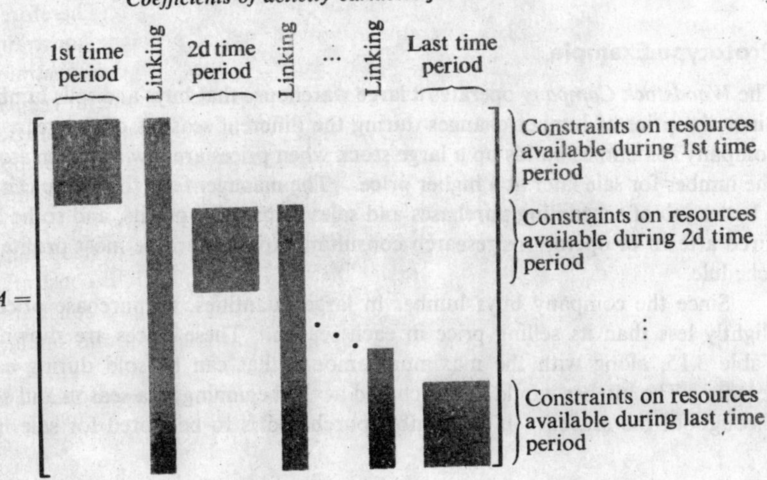

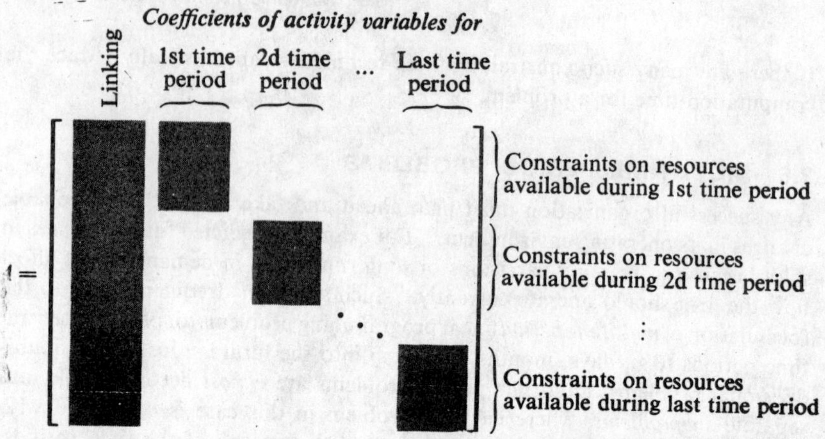

Figure 3.22 Table of constraint coefficients for multitime period problems after reordering the variables.

and variables, so again a method for exploiting the *almost decomposable* special structure of these problems is needed. Fortunately, the *same* method can be used for both types of problems! The idea is to reorder the variables in the multitime period problem to first list all the *linking variables*, as shown in Fig. 3.22, and then to construct its dual problem. This dual problem exactly fits the special *angular structure* shown in Fig. 3.17. (For this reason the special structure in Fig. 3.22 is referred to as the *dual angular structure*.) Therefore the *decomposition principle* for multidivisional problems can be used to solve this dual problem. Since directly applying even this streamlined version of the simplex method to the dual problem automatically identifies an optimal solution for the primal problem as a by-product, this provides an efficient way of solving any large multitime period problems.

Prototype Example

The *Woodstock Company* operates a large warehouse that buys and sells lumber. Since the price of lumber changes during the different seasons of the year, the company sometimes builds up a large stock when prices are low and then stores the lumber for sale later at a higher price. The manager feels that there can be a better job of scheduling purchases and sales to increase profits, and so he has hired a team of operations research consultants to develop the most profitable schedule.

Since the company buys lumber in large quantities, its purchase price is slightly less than its selling price in each season. These prices are shown in Table 3.15, along with the maximum amount that can be sold during each season. The lumber would be purchased at the beginning of a season and sold throughout the season. If the lumber purchased is to be stored for sale in a

Table 3.15 Price Data for the Woodstock Company

Season	*Purchase price†*	*Selling price†*	*Maximum sales‡*
Winter	410	425	1,000
Spring	430	440	1,400
Summer	460	465	2,000
Autumn	450	455	1,600

† Prices are in dollars per thousand board feet.
‡ Sales are in thousand board feet.

later season, a handling cost of \$7/1,000 board feet is incurred, as well as a storage cost (including interest on capital tied up) of \$10/1,000 board feet for each season stored. A maximum of 2 million board feet can be stored in the warehouse at any one time. (This includes lumber purchased for sale in the same period.) Since lumber should not age too long before sale, the manager wants it all sold by the end of the autumn (before the low winter prices go into effect).

The team of operations research consultants concluded that this problem should be formulated as a linear programming problem of the multitime period type. Numbering the seasons (1 = winter, 2 = spring, 3 = summer, 4 = autumn) and letting x_i be the number of 1,000 board feet purchased in season i, y_i be the number sold in season i, and z_{ij} be the number stored in season i for sale in season j, this formulation is

$$\begin{aligned}\text{Maximize}\quad Z = {} & -410x_1 + 425y_1 - 17z_{12} - 27z_{13} - 37z_{14} - 430x_2 + 440y_2 \\ & - 17z_{23} - 27z_{24} - 460x_3 + 465y_3 - 17z_{34} - 450x_4 + 455y_4,\end{aligned}$$

subject to

$$\begin{aligned}
x_1 - y_1 - z_{12} - z_{13} - z_{14} &= 0\\
x_1 &\le 2000\\
y_1 &\le 1000\\
z_{12} + x_2 - y_2 - z_{23} - z_{24} &= 0\\
z_{12} - y_2 &\le 0\\
z_{12} + z_{13} + z_{14} + x_2 &\le 2000\\
y_2 &\le 1400\\
z_{13} + z_{23} + x_3 - y_3 - z_{34} &= 0\\
z_{13} + z_{23} - y_3 &\le 0\\
z_{13} + z_{14} + z_{23} + z_{24} + x_3 &\le 2000\\
y_3 &\le 2000\\
z_{14} + z_{24} + z_{34} + x_4 - y_4 &= 0\\
y_4 &\le 1600
\end{aligned}$$

and

$$x_i \ge 0,\ y_i \ge 0,\ z_{ij} \ge 0, \text{ for } i = 1, 2, 3, 4, \text{ and } j = 2, 3, 4.$$

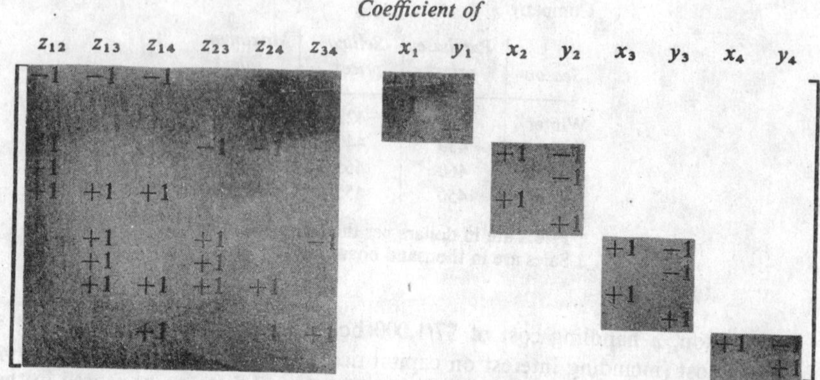

Figure 3.23 Table of constraint coefficients for the Woodstock Company multitime period problem after reordering the variables.

Thus this formulation contains four *subproblems*, where the subproblem for season i is obtained by deleting all variables except x_i and y_i from the overall problem. The storage variables (the z_{ij}) then provide the *linking variables* that interrelate these four time periods. Therefore, after reordering the variables to first list these linking variables, the corresponding table of constraint coefficients has the form shown in Fig. 3.23. Since this form fits the *dual angular structure* given in Fig. 3.22, the streamlined solution procedure for this kind of special structure can be used to solve the problem (or much larger versions of it).

3.7 MULTIDIVISIONAL MULTITIME PERIOD PROBLEMS

You saw in the preceding two sections how decentralized decision making can lead to *multidivisional problems* and how a changing operating environment can lead to *multitime period problems*. We discussed these two situations separately to focus on their individual special structures. However, we should now emphasize that it is fairly common for problems to possess *both* characteristics simultaneously. For example, because costs and market prices change frequently in the food industry, the Good Foods Corp. might want to expand their multidivisional problem to consider the effect of such predicted changes several time periods into the future. This would allow the model to indicate how to most profitably stock up on materials when costs are low and store portions of the food products until prices are more favorable. Similarly, if the Woodstock Company also owns several other warehouses, it might be advisable to expand their model to include and coordinate the activities of these divisions of their organization. (Also see Prob. 29 for another way in which the Woodstock Company problem might expand to include the multidivisional structure.)

The combined special structure for such *multidivisional multitime period problems* is shown in Fig. 3.24. It contains many subproblems (the approximately square blocks), each of which is concerned with optimizing the operation

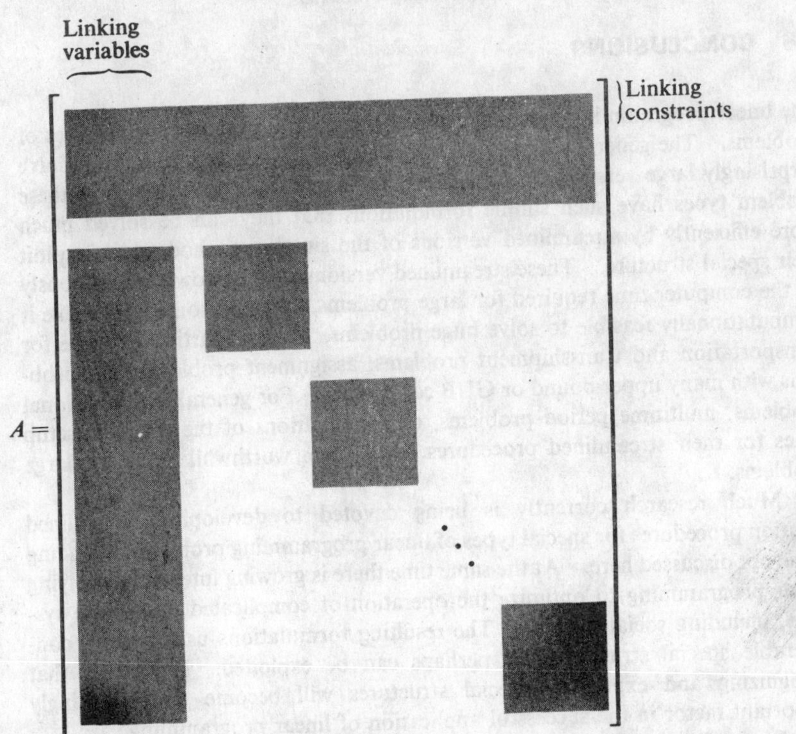

Figure 3.24 Table of constraint coefficients for multidivisional multitime period problems.

of one division during one of the time periods considered in isolation. However, it also includes *both* linking constraints and linking variables (the oblong blocks). The linking constraints coordinate the divisions by making them share the organizational resources available during one or more time periods. The linking variables coordinate the time periods by representing activities that affect the operation of a particular division (or possibly different divisions) during two or more time periods.

One way of exploiting the combined special structure of these problems is to apply an extended version of the decomposition principle for multidivisional problems. This involves treating everything but the linking constraints as one large subproblem and then using this decomposition principle to coordinate the solution for this subproblem with the *master problem* defined by the linking constraints. Since this large subproblem has the *dual angular structure* shown in Fig. 3.22, it would be solved by the special solution procedure for multitime period problems, which again involves using this decomposition principle.

Other procedures for exploiting this combined special structure also have been developed.[1] More experimentation is still needed to test the relative efficiency of the available procedures.

[1] For further information, see chap. 5 of Selected Reference 5 at the end of this chapter.

3.8 CONCLUSIONS

The linear programming model encompasses a wide variety of specific types of problems. The general simplex method is a powerful algorithm that can solve surprisingly large versions of any of these problems. However, some of these problem types have such simple formulations that they can be solved much more efficiently by streamlined versions of the simplex method which exploit their special structure. These streamlined versions can cut down tremendously on the computer time required for large problems, and they sometimes make it computationally feasible to solve huge problems. This is particularly true for transportation and transshipment problems, assignment problems, and problems with many upper bound or GUB constraints. For general multidivisional problems, multitime period problems, or combinations of the two, the setup times for their streamlined procedures make them worthwhile only for large problems.

Much research currently is being devoted to developing streamlined solution procedures for special types of linear programming problems, including some not discussed here. At the same time there is growing interest in applying linear programming to optimize the operation of complicated large-scale systems, including social systems. The resulting formulations usually have considerable special structure that perhaps can be exploited. It appears that recognizing and exploiting special structures will become an increasingly important factor in the successful application of linear programming.

We shall turn our attention in the next chapter to some other important considerations in applying linear programming.

Selected References

1 Cottle, Richard W. and Jakob Krarup (eds.): *Optimization Methods for Resource Allocation*, Proceedings of the NATO Conference on Applications of Optimization Methods for Large-Scale Resource-Allocation Problems (Elsinore, Denmark, July 5 to 9, 1971), English Universities Press, London, 1974.

2 Dantzig, George B.: *Linear Programming and Extensions*, chaps. 14–23, Princeton University Press, Princeton, N.J., 1963.

3 Driebeek, Norman J.: *Applied Linear Programming*, Addison-Wesley, Reading, Mass., 1969.

4 Geoffrion, Arthur M.: Elements of Large-Scale Mathematical Programming," *Management Science*, **16**:652–691, 1970.

5 Lasdon, Leon S.: *Optimization Theory for Large Systems*, Macmillan, New York, 1970.

6 Spivey, W. Allen and Robert M. Thrall: *Linear Optimization*, chaps. 6, 7, 10, Holt, Rinehart & Winston, New York, 1970.

7 Wismer, David A. (ed.): *Optimization Methods for Large-scale Systems with Applications*, McGraw-Hill, New York, 1971.

Problems

1 A company has three plants producing a certain product that is to be shipped to four distribution centers. Plants 1, 2, and 3 produce 12, 17, and 11 shipments per month, respectively. Each distribution center needs to receive 10 shipments per month. The distance from each plant to the respective distributing centers is given below in miles:

		Distribution Center			
		1	2	3	4
Plant	1	800	1,300	400	700
	2	1,100	1,400	600	1,000
	3	600	1,200	800	900

The freight cost for each shipment is $100 plus 50 cents/mile.

How much should be shipped from each plant to each of the distribution centers to minimize the total shipping costs?

(*a*) Formulate this problem as a *transportation problem* by constructing the appropriate cost and requirements table.
(*b*) Use the northwest corner rule to obtain an initial basic feasible solution.
(*c*) Use the transportation simplex method to obtain the optimal solution.

2 Tom would like exactly 3 pints of home brew today and at least an additional 4 pints of home brew tomorrow. Dick is willing to sell a maximum of 5 pints total at a price of 80 cents/pint today and 72 cents/pint tomorrow. Harry is willing to sell a maximum of 4 pints total at a price of 77 cents/pint today and 75 cents/pint tomorrow.

Tom wishes to know what his purchases should be to minimize his cost while satisfying his minimum thirst requirements.

(*a*) Formulate the *linear programming* model for this problem, and construct the initial simplex tableau (see Chap. 2).
(*b*) Formulate this problem as a *transportation problem* by constructing the appropriate cost and requirements table.
(*c*) Use the transportation simplex method to solve the problem as formulated in (*b*).

3 A corporation has decided to produce three new products. Five branch plants now have excess production capacity. The unit manufacturing cost of the first product would be $31, $29, $32, $28, and $29 in plants 1, 2, 3, 4, and 5, respectively. The unit manufacturing cost of the second product would be $45, $41, $46, $42, and $43 in plants 1, 2, 3, 4, and 5, respectively. The unit manufacturing cost of the third product would be $38, $35, and $40 in plants 1, 2, and 3, respectively, whereas plants 4 and 5 do not have the capability for producing this product. Sales forecasts indicate that 1,500, 2,500, and 2,000 units of products 1, 2, and 3, respectively, should be produced per day. Plants 1, 2, 3, 4, and 5 have the capacity to produce 2,000, 1,000, 2,000, 1,500, and 2,500 units daily, respectively, regardless of the product or combination of products involved. Assume that any plant having the capability and capacity can produce any combination of the products in any quantity.

Management wishes to know how to allocate the new products to the plants to minimize total manufacturing cost.

(*a*) Formulate this problem as a *transportation problem* by constructing the appropriate cost and requirements table.

(*b*) Use the transportation simplex method to solve the problem as formulated in (*a*).

4 Suppose that England, France, and Spain produce all the wheat, barley, and oats in the world. The world demand for wheat requires 125 million acres of land devoted to wheat production. Similarly, 60 million acres of land are required for barley and 75 million acres of land for oats. The total amount of land available for these purposes in England, France, and Spain is 70 million acres, 110 million acres, and 80 million acres, respectively. The number of hours of labor needed in England, France, and Spain to produce an acre of wheat is 18 hours, 13 hours, and 16 hours, respectively. The number of hours of labor needed in England, France, and Spain to produce an acre of barley is 15 hours, 12 hours, and 12 hours, respectively. The number of hours of labor needed in England, France, and Spain to produce an acre of oats is 12 hours, 10 hours, and 16 hours, respectively. The labor cost per hour in producing wheat is \$3.00, \$2.40, and \$3.30 in England, France, and Spain, respectively. The labor cost per hour in producing barley is \$2.70, \$3.00, \$2.80 in England, France, and Spain, respectively. The labor cost per hour in producing oats is \$2.30, \$2.50, and \$2.10 in England, France, and Spain, respectively. The problem is to allocate land use in each country so as to meet the world food requirement and minimize the total labor cost.

(*a*) Formulate this problem as a *transportation problem* by constructing the appropriate cost and requirements table.

(*b*) Use the transportation simplex method to solve this problem.

5 A firm producing a single product has three plants and four customers. The three plants will produce 3,000, 5,000, and 4,000 units, respectively, during the next time period. The firm has made a commitment to sell 4,000 units to customer 1, 3,000 units to customer 2, and at least 1,000 units to customer 3. Both customers 3 and 4 also want to buy as many of the remaining units as possible. The net profit associated with shipping a unit from plant i for sale to customer j is given by the following table:

	Customer			
	1	*2*	*3*	*4*
Plant 1	65	63	62	64
Plant 2	68	67	65	62
Plant 3	63	60	59	60

Management wishes to know how many units to sell to customers 3 and 4 and how many units to ship from each of the plants to each of the customers to maximize profit.

(*a*) Formulate this problem as a *transportation problem* by constructing the appropriate cost and requirements table.

(*b*) Use the transportation simplex method to solve the problem as formulated in (*a*).

6 Consider the prototype example for the transportation problem (the *P&T Company* problem) presented at the beginning of Sec. 3.1. Verify that the claimed optimal solution given there actually is optimal by applying just the *stopping rule* portion of the transportation simplex method (see Sec. 3.2) to this solution.

7 Consider the transportation problem having the following cost and requirements table:

		Destination				
		1	*2*	*3*	*4*	*Supply*
Source	1	3	7	6	4	5
	2	2	4	3	2	2
	3	4	3	8	5	3
Demand		3	3	2	2	

Use each of the criteria listed below to obtain an initial basic feasible solution. In each case apply the transportation simplex method, starting with this initial solution, to obtain an optimal solution. Compare the resulting number of iterations for the transportation simplex method.

(*a*) Northwest corner rule.
(*b*) Vogel's approximation method.
(*c*) Russell's approximation method.

8 Consider the transportation problem having the following cost and requirements table:

		Destination					
		1	*2*	*3*	*4*	*5*	*Supply*
Source	1	8	6	3	7	5	20
	2	5	*M*	8	4	7	30
	3	6	3	9	6	8	30
	4	0	0	0	0	0	20
Demand		25	25	20	10	20	

Use each of the following criteria to obtain an initial basic feasible solution. Compare the value of the objective function for these solutions.

(*a*) Northwest corner rule.
(*b*) Vogel's approximation method.
(*c*) Russell's approximation method.
(*d*) Use the best of these solutions to initialize the transportation simplex method to obtain an optimal solution.

9 Consider the transportation problem having the following cost and requirements table:

		Destination						
		1	*2*	*3*	*4*	*5*	*6*	*Supply*
Source	1	10	18	29	13	22	0	100
	2	13	M	21	14	16	0	120
	3	0	6	11	3	M	0	140
	4	9	11	23	18	19	0	80
	5	24	28	36	30	34	0	60
Demand		100	120	100	60	80	40	

Use each of the following criteria to obtain an initial basic feasible solution. Compare the value of the objective function for these solutions.

(*a*) Northwest corner rule.
(*b*) Vogel's approximation method.
(*c*) Russell's approximation method.
(*d*) Use the best of these solutions to initialize the transportation simplex method and then obtain the optimal solution.

10 Use the transportation simplex method to solve the *Northern Airplane Company* production scheduling problem as it is formulated in Fig. 3.7.

11 Consider the Northern Airplane Company production scheduling problem presented in Sec. 3.1 (see Table 3.3). Formulate this problem as a general linear programming problem by letting the decision variables be x_j = number of jet engines to be produced in month $j (j = 1,2,3,4)$. Construct the initial simplex tableau for this formulation, and then contrast the size of this tableau and the *transportation simplex tableaux* for the transportation problem formulation of the problem (see Fig. 3.7).

12 Consider the transportation problem having the following cost and requirements table:

		Destination		
		1	*2*	*Supply*
Source	1	6	4	2
	2	8	5	4
Demand		3	3	

(*a*) Solve this problem by the transportation simplex method.
(*b*) Reformulate this problem as a general *linear programming* problem, and then solve it by the simplex method. [Keep track of how long this takes you, and contrast it with the computation time for part (*a*).]

13 Consider the general linear programming formulation of the transportation problem (see Fig. 3.5). Verify the claim in Sec. 3.2 that the set of $(m + n)$ functional constraint equations (m supply constraints and n demand constraints) has one *redundant* equation, i.e., any one equation can be reproduced from a linear combination of the other $(m+n-1)$ equations.

14 Suppose that the air freight charge per ton between seven particular locations is given by the following table (except where no direct air freight service is available):

Location	*1*	*2*	*3*	*4*	*5*	*6*	*7*
1	...	21	50	62	93	77	...
2	21	...	17	54	67	...	48
3	50	17	...	60	98	67	25
4	62	54	60	...	27	...	38
5	93	67	98	27	...	47	42
6	77	...	67	...	47	...	35
7	...	48	25	38	42	35	...

A certain corporation must ship a certain perishable commodity from locations 1 to 3 to locations 4 to 7. A total of 70, 80, and 50 tons of this commodity are to be sent from locations 1, 2, and 3, respectively. A total of 30, 60, 50, and 60 tons are to be sent to locations 4, 5, 6, and 7, respectively. Shipments can be sent through intermediate locations at a cost equal to the sum of the costs for each of the legs of the journey. The problem is to determine the shipping plan that minimizes the total freight cost.

(*a*) Describe how this problem fits into the format of the general *transshipment problem.*

(*b*) Reformulate this problem as an equivalent *transportation problem* by constructing the appropriate cost and requirements table.

(*c*) Use *Vogel's approximation method* to obtain an initial basic feasible solution for the problem formulated in (*b*). Describe the corresponding shipping pattern.

(*d*) Use the transportation simplex method to obtain an optimal solution for the problem formulated in (*b*). Describe the corresponding optimal shipping pattern.

15 A student about to enter college away from home has decided that she will need an automobile during the next 4 years. But since funds are going to be very limited, she wants to do this in the cheapest possible way. However, considering both the initial purchase price and the operating and maintenance costs, it is not clear whether a very old car or just a moderately old car should be purchased. Furthermore, it is not clear whether she should plan to trade in her car at least once during the 4 years before the costs become too high.

The relevant data are

	Purchase price	*Operating and maintenance costs for year*				*Trade-in value at end of year*			
		1	*2*	*3*	*4*	*1*	*2*	*3*	*4*
Very old car	$250	$475	$550	$625	$700	$150	$100	$ 50	0
Moderately old car	$950	$250	$325	$425	$575	$550	$400	$300	$250

If the student trades in a car during the next 4 years, she would do it at the end of a year (during the summer) on another car of one of these two kinds. She definitely plans to trade in her car at the end of the 4 years on a much newer model. However, she needs to determine which plan for purchasing and (perhaps) trading in cars before then would minimize the *total* net cost for the 4 years.

(*a*) Describe how this problem can be fitted into the format of the *transshipment problem.*

(*b*) Reformulate this problem as an equivalent *transportation problem* by constructing the appropriate cost and requirements table.

(*c*) Use Russell's approximation method to obtain an initial basic feasible solution for the problem formulated in (*b*).

(*d*) Use the transportation simplex method to obtain an optimal solution for the problem formulated in (*b*).

16 Consider the *transshipment* problem for the *P&T Company* described in Sec. 3.3 (see Table 3.14). Use a computer code of the *transportation simplex method* to solve this problem as formulated in Fig. 3.13.

17 Without using x_{ii} variables to introduce fictional shipments from a location to itself, formulate the *linear programming* model for the general *transshipment problem* described at the end of Sec. 3.3. Identify the special structure of this model by constructing its *table of constraint coefficients* (similar to Fig. 3.5) showing the location and values of the nonzero coefficients.

18 Reconsider Prob. 3. Suppose that the sales forecasts have been revised downward to 600, 1,000, and 800 units per day of products 1, 2, and 3, respectively. Thus, each plant now has the capacity to produce all that is required of any one product. Therefore management has decided that each new product should be assigned to only one plant and that no plant should be assigned more than one product (so that three plants are each to be assigned one product, and two plants are to be assigned none). The objective is to make these assignments so as to minimize the *total* cost of producing these amounts of the three products.

(*a*) Formulate this problem as an *assignment problem* by constructing the appropriate cost matrix.

(*b*) Use the transportation simplex method to solve the problem as formulated in (*a*).

19 The coach of a certain swim team needs to assign swimmers to a 200-yard medley relay team to send to the Junior Olympics. Since most of his best swimmers are very fast in more than one stroke, it is not clear which swimmer should be assigned to each of the four strokes. The five fastest swimmers and the "best times" (in seconds) they have achieved in each of the strokes (for 50 yards) are:

Stroke	*Carl*	*Chris*	*David*	*Tony*	*Ken*
Backstroke	37.7	32.9	33.8	37.0	35.4
Breaststroke	43.4	33.1	42.2	34.7	41.8
Butterfly	33.3	28.5	38.9	30.4	33.6
Freestyle	29.2	26.4	29.6	28.5	31.1

The coach wishes to determine how to assign four swimmers to the four different strokes to minimize the sum of the corresponding "best times."

(*a*) Formulate this problem as an *assignment problem.*
(*b*) Use the transportation simplex method to solve this problem.

20 Use the transportation simplex method to solve the *Job Shop Company* assignment problem as formulated in Fig. 3.15.

21 Formulate the *linear programming* model for the general *assignment problem* described at the end of Sec. 3.4. How does its *table of constraint coefficients* differ from the one for the general *transportation problem* (Fig. 3.5)? In what other ways does it have more *special structure* than the general transportation problem?

22 Describe how the *Wyndor Glass Co.* problem formulated in Sec. 2.1 can be interpreted as a *multidivisional* linear programming problem. Identify the variables and constraints for the *master problem* and each *subproblem.*

23 Consider the linear programming problem

$$\text{Maximize} \quad Z = 4x_1 + x_2 + 2x_3 + 3x_4 - x_5 + 6x_6,$$

subject to

$$\begin{aligned} x_1 + 3x_2 + 2x_3 &\le 20 \\ 2x_5 - x_6 &\le 10 \\ 2x_1 - x_2 + 5x_3 + x_4 + 2x_5 + x_6 &\le 10 \\ 3 \le x_4 &\le 10 \\ x_5 + 3x_6 &\le 25 \\ 5x_1 - x_3 &\le 20 \\ 3x_1 + x_2 + 2x_4 + 3x_6 &\le 50 \\ -x_1 + 2x_2 + x_3 &\ge 10 \end{aligned}$$

and

$$x_j \ge 0, \text{ for } j = 1, 2, \ldots, 6.$$

(*a*) Rewrite this problem in a form that demonstrates that it possesses the special structure for *multidivisional problems.* Identify the variables and constraints for the *master problem* and each *subproblem.*
(*b*) Construct the corresponding *table of constraint coefficients* having the *angular structure* shown in Fig. 3.17. (Include only nonzero coefficients, and draw a box around each block of these coefficients to emphasize this structure.)

24 Consider the following table of *constraint coefficients* for a linear programming problem:

	Coefficient of						
Constraint	x_1	x_2	x_3	x_4	x_5	x_6	x_7
1		1			1		1
2				1			
3	2	1	−1	2	3		1
4			2			5	
5	1			1			
6		2	4		1	−2	3
7						1	
8		3			1		2
9	4			3			

(*a*) Show how this table can be converted into the *angular structure* for *multidivisional* linear programming shown in Fig. 3.17 (with three subproblems in this case) by reordering the variables and constraints appropriately.

(*b*) Identify the *upper bound constraints* and *generalized upper bound constraints* for this problem.

25 A corporation has two divisions (the *Eastern Division* and the *Western Division*) that operate semiautonomously, with each developing and marketing its own products. However, to coordinate their product lines and to promote efficiency, the divisions compete at the corporate level for investment funds for new *product development projects.* In particular, each division submits its proposals to corporate headquarters in September for new major projects to be undertaken the following year, and available funds are then allocated in such a way as to maximize the estimated total net discounted profits that will eventually result from the project.

For the upcoming year, each division is proposing three new major projects. Each project can be undertaken at any level, where the estimated net discounted profit would be *proportional* to the level. The relevant data on the projects are summarized below:

	Eastern division project			*Western division project*		
	1	*2*	*3*	*1*	*2*	*3*
Level	x_1	x_2	x_3	x_4	x_5	x_6
Required investment (in millions of dollars)	$16x_1$	$7x_2$	$13x_3$	$8x_4$	$20x_5$	$10x_6$
Net profitability	$5x_1$	$2x_2$	$4x_3$	$3x_4$	$6x_5$	$3x_6$
Facility restriction	$10x_1 + 3x_2 + 7x_3 \leq 50$			$6x_4 + 13x_5 + 9x_6 \leq 45$		
Manpower restriction	$4x_1 + 2x_2 + 5x_3 \leq 30$			$3x_4 + 8x_5 + 2x_6 \leq 25$		

A total of $40,000,000 is budgeted for investment in these projects.

(*a*) Formulate this problem as a *multidivisional* linear programming problem.

(*b*) Construct the corresponding *table of constraint coefficients* having the *angular structure* shown in Fig. 3.17.

26 Consider the following *table of constraint coefficients* for a linear programming problem:

Constraint	x_1	x_2	x_3	x_4	x_5	x_6	x_7	x_8	x_9	x_{10}
1	3	1								
2	1	2	−1							
3				1	5					
4			1	2	−1	−1	−1			
5					1					
6			1			1	1	1	3	2
7								2	−1	1

Show how this table can be converted into the *dual angular* structure for *multitime period* linear programming shown in Fig. 3.22 (with three time periods in this case) by reordering the variables and constraints appropriately.

27 Consider the *Wyndor Glass Co.* problem described in Sec. 2.1 (see Table 2.1). Suppose that decisions have been made to discontinue additional products in the future and to initiate other new products. Therefore the capacity available in each of the three plants will be different than shown in Table 2.1 after the first year. Furthermore, the unit profit (exclusive of storage costs) that can be realized from the sale of the two products being analyzed will vary from year to year as market conditions change. Therefore it may be worthwhile to *store* some of the units produced in 1 year for sale in a later year. The storage costs involved would be approximately $2 per unit per year for either product.

The relevant data for the next 3 years are summarized below.

		Capacity available in year		
		1	*2*	*3*
	1	4	6	3
Plant	2	12	12	10
	3	18	24	15
Unit profit, product 1		$3	$4	$5
Unit profit, product 2		$5	$4	$8

The capacities used by each product remains the same for each year as shown in Table 2.1. The objective is to determine how much of each product to produce in each year and what portion to store for sale in each subsequent year to maximize the total profit over the 3 years.

(*a*) Formulate this problem as a *multitime period* linear programming problem.

(*b*) Construct the corresponding *table of constraint coefficients* having the dual angular structure shown in Fig. 3.22.

28 Consider the following *table of constraint coefficients* for a linear programming problem:

Constraint	x_1	x_2	x_3	x_4	x_5	x_6	x_7	x_8	x_9	x_{10}
1	2			3				1		
2		1	1				2	2		
3	5	−1	2	−1	−1		−3			4
4						1		−1		
5		−1			2			−2	5	3
6	1			1						
7	2	1		3		2		1	−1	
8		−1	2				1	−1		
9					1				2	1
10		−1			4				1	5

Show how this table can be converted into the form for *multidivisional multitime period* problems shown in Fig. 3.24 (with two linking constraints, two linking variables, and four subproblems in this case) by reordering the variables and constraints appropriately.

29 Consider the *Woodstock Company* multitime period problem described in Sec. 3.6 (see Table 3.15). Suppose that the company has decided to expand its operations to also buy, store, and sell *plywood* in this warehouse. For the upcoming year, the relevant data for *raw lumber* are still as given in Sec. 3.6. The corresponding price data for plywood are

Season	*Purchase price*†	*Selling price*†	*Maximum sales*‡
Winter	680	705	800
Spring	715	730	1,200
Summer	760	770	1,500
Autumn	740	750	100

† Prices are in dollars per 1,000 board feet.
‡ Sales are in 1,000 board feet.

For plywood stored for sale in a later season, the handling cost is $6/1,000 board feet, and the storage cost is $18/1,000 board feet. The storage capacity of 2 million board feet now applies to the *total* for raw lumber and plywood. Everything should still be sold by the end of the autumn.

The objective now is to determine the most profitable schedule for buying and selling raw lumber *and* plywood.

(*a*) Formulate this problem as a *multidivisional multitime period* linear programming problem.

(*b*) Construct the corresponding *table of constraint coefficients* having the form shown in Fig. 3.24.

4 The Application of Linear Programming

Chapter 2 introduced the general nature of linear programming problems, the simplex method for solving them, and duality theory for analyzing them. We then discussed some particularly important special types of linear programming problems in Chap. 3. However, this is only a portion of the story. The most successful users of linear programming report that the key considerations on which they spend most of their time are problem formulation, computational considerations (including preparing input and output routines), and sensitivity analysis. So to provide you with a more complete perspective about the application of linear programming, we shall further introduce you to these topics in the next sections and then conclude with a case study.

4.1 PROBLEM FORMULATION

The formulation of linear programming problems is basically an art that is best learned by experience. You already have gained a little of this experience by studying the examples in the preceding two chapters and perhaps by working some of the formulation problems at the end of those chapters. In this section we shall expose you to somewhat more difficult formulation problems through three additional examples. These examples illustrate a number of formulation ideas, including some ways of reformulating nonlinearities to fit the linear programming format. (Such reformulations are very important in practical applications because the simplex method for linear programming is *much* more efficient and convenient than available algorithms for *nonlinear* programming.) The most important way of doing this is the *separable convex programming* technique, which is based on a rather subtle idea illustrated by the third example. The general features of this technique are discussed at the end of the section.

Example—Reclaiming Solid Wastes

The *Save-It Company* operates a reclamation center that collects four types of solid waste materials and then treats them so they can be amalgamated into a saleable product. Three different grades of this product can be made, depending upon the mix of the materials used. Although there is some flexibility in the mix for each grade, quality standards do specify a minimum or maximum percentage (by weight) of certain materials allowed in that product grade. These specifications are given in Table 4.1, along with the cost of amalgamation and the selling price for each grade.

Table 4.1 Product Data for The Save-It Company

Grade	*Specification*	*Amalgamation cost ($) per pound*	*Selling price ($) per pound*
A	Not more than 30% of material 1 Not less than 40% of material 2 Not more than 50% of material 3	3.00	8.50
B	Not more than 50% of material 1 Not less than 10% of material 2	2.50	7.00
C	Not more than 70% of material 1	2.00	5.50

The reclamation center collects its solid waste materials from some regular sources and so is normally able to maintain a steady production rate for treating these materials. Table 4.2 gives the quantities available for collection and treatment each week, as well as the cost of treatment, for each type of material.

Table 4.2 Solid Waste Materials Data for The Save-It Company

Material	*Pounds/week available*	*Treatment cost ($) per pound*
1	3,000	3
2	2,000	6
3	4,000	4
4	1,000	5

The problem facing the company is to determine just how much of each product grade to produce *and* the exact mix of materials to be used for each grade so as to maximize their total weekly profit (total sales income minus the total costs of *both* amalgamation and treatment).

FORMULATION Before attempting to construct a linear programming model, careful consideration should always be given to the proper definition of the decision variables. Although this is often obvious, it sometimes becomes the crux of the entire formulation. After clearly identifying what information is really desired and the most convenient form for conveying this information by means of decision variables, the objective function and the constraints on the values of these decision variables can then be developed.

In this particular problem, the decisions to be made are well defined, but the appropriate means of conveying this information may require some thought. (Try it and see if you first obtain the following *inappropriate* choice of decision variables.) Since one set of decisions is the *amount* of each product grade to produce, it would seem natural to define one set of decision variables accordingly. Proceeding tentatively along this line, define y_i ($i = A, B, C$) as the number of pounds of product grade i produced per week. The mixture of each grade is identified by the proportion of each material in the product. This would suggest defining the other set of decision variables, z_{ij} ($i = A, B, C$; $j = 1,2,3,4$), as the proportion of material j in product grade i. However, recall that both the treatment cost and the availability of the materials are by quantity, and that this information must be recorded in the objective function and the constraints, respectively. The total quantity of material 1 used, for example, is $z_{A1}y_A + z_{B1}y_B + z_{C1}y_C$. But this is *not* a linear function because it involves products of variables. Therefore a linear programming model can not be constructed with these decision variables.

Fortunately, there is another way of defining the decision variables that will fit the linear programming format. (Do you see how?) This is done by merely replacing each product of the old decision variables by a single variable! In other words, define $x_{ij} = z_{ij}y_i$ (for $i = A,B,C$; $j = 1,2,3,4$), and then let the x_{ij} be the decision variables. Thus x_{ij} is the total number of pounds of material j allocated to product grade i per week. The total amount of product grade i produced per week is then $x_{i1} + x_{i2} + x_{i3} + x_{i4}$. The proportion of material j in product grade i is $x_{ij}/(x_{i1} + x_{i2} + x_{i3} + x_{i4})$. Therefore this choice of decision variables conveys all the necessary information and proves to be well suited to the construction of the linear programming model given below. (Note particularly how the mixture constraints on the *nonlinear* proportion function are written in a linear form.)

The total profit Z is given by

$$\begin{aligned} Z = {} & 5.5(x_{A1} + x_{A2} + x_{A3} + x_{A4}) + 4.5(x_{B1} + x_{B2} + x_{B3} + x_{B4}) \\ & + 3.5(x_{C1} + x_{C2} + x_{C3} + x_{C4}) - 3(x_{A1} + x_{B1} + x_{C1}) \\ & - 6(x_{A2} + x_{B2} + x_{C2}) - 4(x_{A3} + x_{B3} + x_{C3}) - 5(x_{A4} + x_{B4} + x_{C4}). \end{aligned}$$

Thus, after combining common terms,

$$\begin{aligned} Z = {} & 2.5x_{A1} - 0.5x_{A2} + 1.5x_{A3} + 0.5x_{A4} + 1.5x_{B1} - 1.5x_{B2} + 0.5x_{B3} \\ & - 0.5x_{B4} + 0.5x_{C1} - 2.5x_{C2} - 0.5x_{C3} - 1.5x_{C4}. \end{aligned}$$

Hence the model is to maximize Z, subject to the constraints imposed by the availability of materials and the mixture specifications and by the restrictions that $x_{ij} \geq 0$ for $i = A, B, C$ and $j = 1, 2, 3, 4$. The availability constraints (see Table 4.2) are

$$x_{A1} + x_{B1} + x_{C1} \leq 3{,}000$$
$$x_{A2} + x_{B2} + x_{C2} \leq 2{,}000$$
$$x_{A3} + x_{B3} + x_{C3} \leq 4{,}000$$
$$x_{A4} + x_{B4} + x_{C4} \leq 1{,}000.$$

The mixture constraints for product grade A (see Table 4.1) can be written in a linear form as

$$x_{A1} \leq 0.3(x_{A1} + x_{A2} + x_{A3} + x_{A4})$$
$$x_{A2} \geq 0.4(x_{A1} + x_{A2} + x_{A3} + x_{A4})$$
$$x_{A3} \leq 0.5(x_{A1} + x_{A2} + x_{A3} + x_{A4}).$$

Since variables should be just on the left-hand side of constraints in a linear programming model, these constraints should be rewritten as

$$0.7x_{A1} - 0.3x_{A2} - 0.3x_{A3} - 0.3x_{A4} \leq 0$$
$$-0.4x_{A1} + 0.6x_{A2} - 0.4x_{A3} - 0.4x_{A4} \geq 0$$
$$-0.5x_{A1} - 0.5x_{A2} + 0.5x_{A3} - 0.5x_{A4} \leq 0.$$

Similarly, the final forms of the mixture constraints for product grades B and C are

$$0.5x_{B1} - 0.5x_{B2} - 0.5x_{B3} - 0.5x_{B4} \leq 0$$
$$-0.1x_{B1} + 0.9x_{B2} - 0.1x_{B3} - 0.1x_{B4} \geq 0$$
$$0.3x_{C1} - 0.7x_{C2} - 0.7x_{C3} - 0.7x_{C4} \leq 0.$$

A Model for Production and Employment Scheduling[1]

Many industrial firms face an unstable sales market and so must frequently make adjustments of some kind to compensate for predicted changes in the level of sales. When sales are increasing, these adjustments may take the form of increasing the employment level (hiring), using overtime, or using up existing (or future) inventories. Similarly, when sales are dropping, the firm might decrease its employment level (lay off), underutilize its current work force, or build up inventories. All these alternatives are costly in some way, especially when they are used to extremes. Often a firm will use some combination of these possible adjustments. However, it is very difficult to determine just which combination is least expensive, particularly when a series of adjustments are being planned to meet a series of predicted changes in sales. A considerable number of operations research models have been formulated for various versions of this problem, and several of these have been used successfully to achieve large cost savings. The one developed below is a rather convenient and useful linear programming model that illustrates a number of formulation ideas.

[1] This model was first developed by Fred Hanssmann and Sidney W. Hess in "A Linear Programming Approach to Production and Employment Scheduling," *Management Technology*, 1:46–52, 1960.

The model assumes that forecasts are available on the total volume of sales for the firm in each of the next T time periods (typically months). The decisions to be made are the total *work-force level* (number of employees), *production rate*, and net *inventory level* (amount stored minus back orders) to be scheduled for each of these time periods. These quantities shall be denoted as follows for time period t ($t = 1,2, \ldots, T$):

S_t = sales forecast.
W_t = work-force level.
P_t = production rate.
I_t = inventory level at the end of the time period.

If the firm produces more than one product, then S_t, P_t, and I_t each represent the *total* quantity aggregated over all the products, expressed in some common unit such as dollar value. To relate W_t and P_t, let k be the number of employees required to produce each unit of production per time period without using overtime, so that kP_t is the total work-force level that will achieve a production rate P_t when they are fully utilized on just regular time.[1] However, W_t does not necessarily equal kP_t because $W_t < kP_t$ if overtime is used, whereas $W_t > kP_t$ if the work force is not utilized to its full capacity on regular time.

Various kinds of costs need to be taken into account in the model. If the work-force level is increased ($W_t - W_{t-1} > 0$), then hiring costs are incurred due to training and reorganization. If it is decreased instead ($W_t - W_{t-1} < 0$), layoff costs result from terminal pay, reorganization, and undermining worker morale. There also are regular payroll costs for the continuing workers (even when they are not utilized to full capacity) as well as any overtime costs. If the net inventory level is positive ($I_t > 0$), inventory costs will be incurred because of various storage expenses and tieing up capital. If it is negative ($I_t < 0$), so that back orders have accumulated, shortage costs result from customer dissatisfaction and lost future sales.

The model assumes that each of these costs is *proportional* to the quantity involved *except* that it is zero if the quantity is negative. To express this mathematically, we shall let a superscript of + or − on any quantity q mean the following:

$$q^+ = \begin{cases} q, & \text{if } q \geq 0 \\ 0, & \text{if } q \leq 0, \end{cases}$$

$$q^- = \begin{cases} 0, & \text{if } q \geq 0 \\ |q|, & \text{if } q \leq 0. \end{cases}$$

Thus

$$q = q^+ - q^-,$$

[1] Note the implicit assumption here of proportionality (constant returns to scale), which does not always hold.

where either q^+ or q^- is zero, depending upon whether q is negative or positive. Using this notation, the costs for each time period t ($t = 1,2, \ldots, T$) are written as

$$\begin{aligned} \text{Hiring cost} &= c_h(W_t - W_{t-1})^+, \\ \text{Layoff cost} &= c_l(W_t - W_{t-1})^-, \\ \text{Regular payroll} &= c_r W_t, \\ \text{Overtime cost} &= c_o(kP_t - W_t)^+, \\ \text{Inventory cost} &= c_i I^+, \\ \text{Shortage cost} &= c_s I^-, \end{aligned}$$

where c_h, c_l, c_r, c_o, c_i, and c_s are the appropriate proportionality constants. Note that each of these costs except for regular payroll is a *nonlinear* function of the quantity involved because the function has a nonzero slope indicated by the proportionality constant when the quantity has one sign (positive or negative) but has a *zero* slope when the quantity has the other sign. Therefore, letting Z be the total cost over all T time periods, the "natural" formulation of the model is the *nonlinear* programming problem

$$\text{Minimize} \quad Z = \sum_{t=1}^{T} \{c_h(W_t - W_{t-1})^+ + c_l(W_t - W_{t-1})^- + c_r W_t + c_o(kP_t - W_t)^+ + c_i I^+ + c_s I^-\},$$

subject to

$$\left.\begin{aligned} &W_t \geq 0 \\ &P_t \geq 0 \\ &I_t = I_{t-1} + P_t - S_t \end{aligned}\right\} \text{ for } t = 1, 2, \ldots, T,$$

where the initial inventory level I_o and work-force level W_o are given.

Now let us see how this problem can be reformulated to fit the linear programming format.

Formulation As in the preceding example, the key to achieving a linear programming formulation of the problem is to define the decision variables appropriately. In this case, recall that each cost in the model is assumed to be *proportional* to the nonnegative value of the quantity involved. Therefore, by representing each quantity by a single nonnegative variable, the objective function can be made a *linear* function of these new decision variables! In particular, define

$$\begin{aligned} x_t &= (W_t - W_{t-1})^+, \\ y_t &= (W_t - W_{t-1})^-, \\ z_t &= (kP_t - W_t)^+, \\ w_t &= (kP_t - W_t)^-, \\ u_t &= I_t^+, \\ v_t &= I_t^-, \end{aligned}$$

for $t = 1, 2, \ldots, T$. The objective function then becomes

$$Z = \sum_{t=1}^{T} \{c_h x_t + c_l y_t + c_r W_t + c_o z_t + c_i u_t + c_s v_t\}.$$

You will see below that W_t also can be expressed as a linear function of the new variables to obtain the final form of the objective function.

For this new set of decision variables to work, we must be able to write the relevant constraints in terms of these new variables in a linear form. This can be done if the W_t, P_t, and $I_t (t = 1,2, \ldots, T)$ can be expressed as linear functions of these variables. This is easy to do for the I_t because they are simply

$$I_t = u_t - v_t.$$

Consequently, because

$$I_t = I_{t-1} + P_t - S_t,$$

or equivalently,

$$P_t = I_t - I_{t-1} + S_t,$$

we obtain

$$P_t = (u_t - v_t) - (u_{t-1} - v_{t-1}) + S_t.$$

(When $t = 1$, the known value of I_o should be substituted for $u_o - v_o$ in this expression.) Finally, since

$$z_t - w_t = kP_t - W_t,$$

this yields

$$\begin{aligned} W_t &= kP_t - (z_t - w_t) \\ &= k[(u_t - v_t) - (u_{t-1} - v_{t-1}) + S_t] - (z_t - w_t). \end{aligned}$$

It is this last expression that will enable rewriting the objective function just in terms of the new variables.

Now let us construct the constraints for the linear programming formulation. Since the equality constraints in the original formulation are being used to substitute $(I_t - I_{t-1} + S_t) = [(u_t - v_t) - (u_{t-1} - v_{t-1}) + S_t]$ for P_t in the model, these constraints need not be considered further. However, the $W_t \geq 0$ and $P_t \geq 0$ constraints need to be included in terms of the new variables

$$k[(u_t - v_t) - (u_{t-1} - v_{t-1}) + S_t] - (z_t - w_t) \geq 0$$
$$(u_t - v_t) - (u_{t-1} - v_{t-1}) + S_t \geq 0$$

for $t = 1, 2, \ldots, T$, where $u_o - v_o = I_o$. (For the final version of the model, we shall convert these constraints to $\leq$ form by multiplying through by -1 and then move the constant term involving S_t to the right-hand side.) Nonnegativity constraints on the new variables

$$x_t \geq 0, y_t \geq 0, z_t \geq 0, w_t \geq 0, u_t \geq 0, v_t \geq 0, \text{ for } t = 1, 2, \ldots, T,$$

also need to be included.

In addition, there is another less apparent set of constraints that must be added to the new formulation. These constraints arise because

$$x_t - y_t = W_t - W_{t-1},$$
$$z_t - w_t = k(I_t - I_{t-1} + S_t) - W_t,$$
$$u_t - v_t = I_t,$$

so that *both* the $(x_t - y_t)$ and $(z_t - w_t)$ are functions of W_t, and *both* the $(z_t - w_t)$ and $(u_t - v_t)$ are functions of the I_t. Therefore, $(x_t - y_t)$, $(z_t - w_t)$, $(u_t - v_t)$ for $t = 1, 2, \ldots, T$ can be allowed to take on *only* those combinations of values that could result by using the *same* W_t, I_t $(t = 1, 2, \ldots, T)$ values to determine all of them. To identify these feasible combinations we need to specify just how the individual quantities are related in terms of the original decision variables. This is done by the following *identity relationship* for each $t = 1, 2, \ldots, T$:

$$W_t - W_{t-1} = -(kP_t - W_t) + (kP_{t-1} - W_{t-1}) + k(P_t - P_{t-1}),$$

where

$$P_i = I_i - I_{i-1} + S_i, \text{ for } i = t-1, t,$$

which *must* hold for all possible values of the W_t and $I_t (t = 1, 2, \ldots, T)$. Therefore this relationship *must* still hold when the new variables are substituted in

$$x_t - y_t = -(z_t - w_t) + (z_{t-1} - w_{t-1}) + k[(u_t - v_t) - (u_{t-1} - v_{t-1}) + S_t]$$
$$-k[(u_{t-1} - v_{t-1}) - (u_{t-2} - v_{t-2}) + S_{t-1}], \text{ for } t = 1, 2, \ldots, T,$$

where

$$I_o \equiv u_o - v_o,$$
$$W_o \equiv -(z_o - w_o) + k[(u_o - v_o) - (u_{-1} - v_{-1}) + S_o].$$

After rearranging to bring the variables to the left-hand side and the constants to the right-hand side, these T equations provide the additional constraints needed for the new formulation.

To summarize, the complete linear programming formulation of this model for production and employment scheduling is

$$\text{Minimize } Z = \sum_{t=1}^{T} \{c_h x_t + c_l y_t + (c_o - c_r) z_t + c_r w_t + c_i u_t + c_s v_t\}$$
$$+ c_r k[(u_t - v_t) - I_o + \sum_{t=1}^{T} S_t],$$

subject to

$$\left.\begin{aligned}
&k[-(u_t - v_t) + (u_{t-1} - v_{t-1})] + (z_t - w_t) \le kS_t \\
&\quad -(u_t - v_t) + (u_{t-1} - v_{t-1}) \le S_t \\
&(x_t - y_t) + (z_t - w_t) - (z_{t-1} - w_{t-1}) \\
&\quad -k(u_t - v_t) + 2k(u_{t-1} - v_{t-1}) \\
&\quad -(u_{t-2} - v_{t-2}) = k(S_t - S_{t-1}) \\
&\text{and} \\
&x_t \ge 0, y_t \ge 0, z_t \ge 0, w_t \ge 0, u_t \ge 0, v_t \ge 0
\end{aligned}\right\} \text{for } t = 1, 2, \ldots, T,$$

where the given values of I_o and W_o are substituted for variables with subscripts of 0 and -1 as specified above. Thus this formulation has $6T$ variables and $3T$ functional constraints, which can be solved easily by the simplex method on a computer unless T is huge.

It might appear that there is still a flaw in this formulation. In particular, recall that q^+ and q^- were defined in such a way that at least one of these two variables must always be zero. Therefore this must also be true for each pair of variables (x_t, y_t), (z_t, w_t), and (u_t, v_t). However, none of the constraints in the linear programming formulation force this to be true, so there are many "feasible" solutions in this formulation that actually violate the definitions of q^+ and q^- for $q = (W_t - W_{t-1})$, $(kP_t - W_t)$, or I_t. This would seem to cause serious complications. But it does not at all! The reason is that the simplex method considers only *basic* feasible solutions, and all such solutions are legitimate feasible solutions satisfying these definitions. (You may recall this same property for basic feasible solutions occurring in Sec. 2.10, when variables with no bound on the negative values allowed each were replaced by the difference of two nonnegative variables.) Therefore, because of Property 1, Sec. 2.5, the optimal solution obtained by the simplex method will be a legitimate optimal solution for this production and employment scheduling model.

A Separable Convex Programming Example

The *Wyndor Glass Co.* (see Sec. 2.1) has received a special order for hand-crafted goods to be made in Plants 1 and 2 throughout the next 4 months. This will require borrowing certain employees from the work crews for the regular products, so the remaining workers would need to work overtime to utilize the full production capacity of the plant's machinery and equipment for these products. In particular, for the two new regular products discussed in Sec. 2.1, overtime would be required to utilize the last 25 percent of the production capacity available in Plant 1 for product 1, and for the last 50 percent of the capacity available in Plant 2 for product 2. The additional cost of using overtime work would reduce the profit for each unit involved from \$3 to \$2 for product 1, and from \$5 to \$1 for product 2, as shown in Fig. 4.1.

Management has decided to go ahead and use overtime work rather than hire additional workers during this temporary situation. However, it does insist that the work crew for each product be fully utilized on regular time before any overtime is used. Furthermore, it feels that the current production rates ($x_1 = 2$ for product 1 and $x_2 = 6$ for product 2) should be changed temporarily if this would improve overall profitability. Therefore it has instructed the O.R. Department to review products 1 and 2 again to determine the most profitable product mix during the next 4 months.

FORMULATION At first glance it may appear straightforward to modify the Wyndor Glass Co. linear programming model in Sec. 2.1 to fit this new situation. In particular, let the production rate for product 1 be $x_1 = x_{1R} + x_{1O}$, where

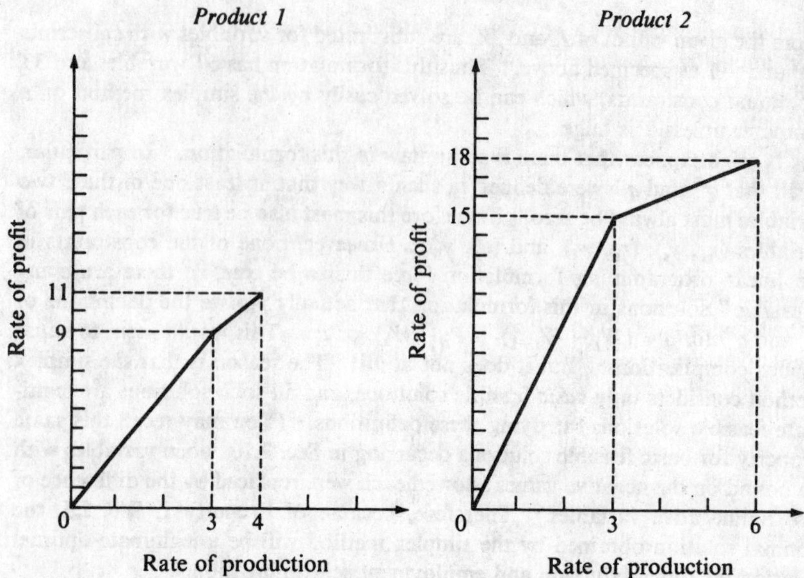

Figure 4.1 Profit data during the next 4 months for the Wyndor Glass Co.

x_{1R} is the production rate achieved on regular time and x_{1O} is the incremental production rate from using overtime. Define $x_2 = x_{2R} + x_{2O}$ in the same way for product 2. The new linear programming problem then is to determine the values of $x_{1R}, x_{1O}, x_{2R}, x_{2O}$ so as to

$$\text{Maximize} \quad Z = 3x_{1R} + 2x_{1O} + 5x_{2R} + x_{2O},$$

subject to

$$\begin{aligned} x_{1R} \qquad\qquad\qquad\qquad &\leq 3 \\ x_{1O} \qquad\qquad\qquad &\leq 1 \\ 2x_{2R} \qquad\quad &\leq 6 \\ 2x_{2O} &\leq 6 \\ 3(x_{1R} + x_{1O}) + 2(x_{2R} + x_{2O}) &\leq 18 \end{aligned}$$

and

$$x_{1R} \geq 0, x_{1O} \geq 0, x_{2R} \geq 0, x_{2O} \geq 0.$$

However, there is one important factor that is not taken into account in this formulation. Specifically, there is nothing in the model that requires all available regular time for a product to be fully utilized before any overtime is used for that product. In other words, it may be feasible to have $x_{1O} > 0$ even when $x_{1R} < 3$ and to have $x_{2O} > 0$ even when $x_{2R} < 3$. Such a solution would not, however, be acceptable to management.

Now we come to the real key of *separable convex programming*. Even though the model does not take this factor into account explicitly, it *is* taken into account implicitly! Despite the model having excess "feasible" solutions that actually are unacceptable, any *optimal* solution for the model is *guaranteed* to be a legitimate one that does not replace any available regular time work with overtime work. (The reasoning here is analogous to that for the *Big M method* discussed in Sec. 2.10, where excess feasible but *nonoptimal* solutions also were allowed in the model as a matter of convenience.) Therefore the simplex method can be safely applied to this model to find the most profitable acceptable product mix. The reason is twofold. First, the two decision variables for each product *always* appear together as a *sum*, $(x_{1R} + x_{1O})$ or $(x_{2R} + x_{2O})$, in *each* functional constraint (one in this case) other than the upper bound constraints on individual variables. Therefore it *always* is possible to convert an unacceptable feasible solution to an acceptable one having the same total production rates, $x_1 = x_{1R} + x_{1O}$ and $x_2 = x_{2R} + x_{2O}$, merely by replacing overtime production by regular time production as much as possible. Secondly, overtime production is less profitable than regular time production (i.e., the *slope* of each profit curve in Fig. 4.1 is a monotonically *decreasing* function of the rate of production), so converting an unacceptable feasible solution to an acceptable one in this way *must* increase the total rate of profit Z. Consequently, any feasible solution that uses overtime production for a product when regular time production is still available can *not* be optimal with respect to the model.

For example, consider the unacceptable feasible solution $x_{1R} = 1$, $x_{1O} = 1$, $x_{2R} = 1$, $x_{2O} = 3$, which yields a total rate of profit $Z = 13$. The acceptable way of achieving the same total production rates $x_1 = 2$ and $x_2 = 4$ would be $x_{1R} = 2$, $x_{1O} = 0$, $x_{2R} = 3$, $x_{2O} = 1$. This latter solution is still feasible, but it also increases Z by $(3 - 2)(1) + (5 - 1)(2) = 9$.

Similarly, the optimal solution for this model turns out to be $x_{1R} = 3$, $x_{1O} = 1$, $x_{2R} = 3$, $x_{2O} = 0$, which is an acceptable feasible solution.

ALTERNATIVE FORMULATION Notice that most of the functional constraints in the above model are *upper bound constraints*, i.e., constraints which simply specify the maximum value allowed for an individual variable. We mentioned at the end of Sec. 3.5 that there is a special streamlined version of the simplex method (presented in Sec. 16.1) for dealing with such constraints. When a computer code is available for this streamlined version it provides a very efficient way of solving even extremely large problems of this type. If the general simplex method must be used instead, however, the upper bound constraints would add essentially as much computation time as other constraints. In this situation it should be much more efficient (particularly for larger versions of this problem) to use an alternative formulation that has considerably fewer functional constraints.

The alternative formulation represents the total production rate for each product (x_1 and x_2) as

$$x_1 = 3w_{11} + 4w_{12},$$

$$x_2 = 3w_{21} + 6w_{22},$$

where the new decision variables w_{ij} may be interpreted as *interpolation weights* on the values of the abscissa specified in Fig. 4.1. For example, $w_{11} = \frac{1}{2}$, $w_{12} = 0$, $w_{21} = \frac{1}{2}$, $w_{22} = \frac{1}{2}$ would mean that x_1 is halfway between zero and the maximum regular time production rate (3) for product 1, whereas x_2 is halfway between the maximum regular time production rate (3) and the maximum total production rate (6) for product 2. To ensure that x_1 and x_2 remain within their bounds, the interpolation weights must satisfy the constraints

$$w_{11} + w_{12} \leq 1,$$

$$w_{21} + w_{22} \leq 1,$$

and

$$w_{11} \geq 0,\ w_{12} \geq 0,\ w_{21} \geq 0,\ w_{22} \geq 0.$$

Using these same interpolation weights on the values of the *ordinate* specified in Fig. 4.1, the total rate of profit Z can then be expressed as

$$Z = 9w_{11} + 11w_{12} + 15w_{21} + 18w_{22}.$$

The resulting overall model is to determine the values of $w_{11}, w_{12}, w_{21}, w_{22}$ so as to

$$\text{Maximize} \quad Z = 9w_{11} + 11w_{12} + 15w_{21} + 18w_{22},$$

subject to

$$\begin{aligned} w_{11} + w_{12} \qquad\qquad\qquad &\leq 1 \\ w_{21} + w_{22} &\leq 1 \\ 3(3w_{11} + 4w_{12}) + 2(3w_{21} + 6w_{22}) &\leq 18 \end{aligned}$$

and

$$w_{11} \geq 0,\ w_{12} \geq 0,\ w_{21} \geq 0,\ w_{22} \geq 0.$$

Once again, there appears to be an important factor that is not taken into account in this formulation. (Do you see what it is?) The difficulty is that the objective function assumes that the rate of profit for each product is obtained *just* by interpolating between the two ends of a *single* line segment in Fig. 4.1, whereas the constraints actually allow many other feasible solutions giving the same total production rates. For example, the objective function assumes that a total production rate of 4 for product 2 would be represented by $w_{21} = \frac{2}{3}$, $w_{22} = \frac{1}{3}$, so that

$$x_2 = \frac{2}{3}(3) + \frac{1}{3}(6) = 4,$$

$$\text{rate of profit for product } 2 = \frac{2}{3}(15) + \frac{1}{3}(18) = 16,$$

which is a point on the line segment between (3,15) and (6,18). However, the constraints also allow $w_{21} = 0$, $w_{22} = 2/3$, which involves interpolating between (0,0) and (6,18) to obtain

$$x_2 = \frac{1}{3}(0) + \frac{2}{3}(6) = 4,$$

$$\text{rate of profit for product 2} = \frac{1}{3}(0) + \frac{2}{3}(18) = 12.$$

They also allow $w_{21} = 1/3$, $w_{22} = 1/2$, which yields

$$x_2 = \frac{1}{6}(0) + \frac{1}{3}(3) + \frac{1}{2}(6) = 4,$$

$$\text{rate of profit for product 2} = \frac{1}{6}(0) + \frac{1}{3}(15) + \frac{1}{2}(18) = 14.$$

Thus the model has many excess feasible solutions that actually underestimate the profits obtainable from their total production rates. In fact, *every* such solution can be converted to a legitimate feasible solution having the *same* total production rates and a larger value of Z. (Again, this is due to the slope of each profit curve in Fig. 4.1 being a monotonically *decreasing* function of the rate of production.) Therefore, by the same reasoning as in the first formulation, any *optimal* solution for this model is *guaranteed* to be a legitimate one.

Incidentally, the first two constraints in this alternative formulation are *generalized upper bound constraints*. We pointed out at the end of Sec. 3.5 that there also is a streamlined version of the simplex method available for dealing with constraints of this kind.

Separable Convex Programming

Profit curves similar to those in Fig. 4.1 actually occur quite frequently. For example, it may be possible to sell just a limited amount of some product at a certain price, and then a further amount at a lower price, and perhaps finally a further amount at a still lower price. Similarly, it may be necessary to purchase raw materials from increasingly expensive sources. Another common situation is where a more expensive production process must be used (e.g., overtime rather than regular time work) to increase the production rate beyond a certain point.

These kinds of situations can lead to either type of profit curve shown in Fig. 4.2, where $f_j(x_j)$ represents the profit (or some other measure of performance) from activity j at the level x_j. In both cases the slope of the profit curve either stays the same or decreases (*never* increases) as x_j is increased. (Thus both curves represent *concave functions* as defined in Appendix 1.) However, in case 1 the slope decreases only at certain *break points*, so that $f_j(x_j)$ is a *piecewise linear function* (a sequence of connected line segments). For case 2, the slope may decrease continuously as x_j increases, so that $f_j(x_j)$ is a general *concave function*. Any such function can be approximated as closely as desired by a

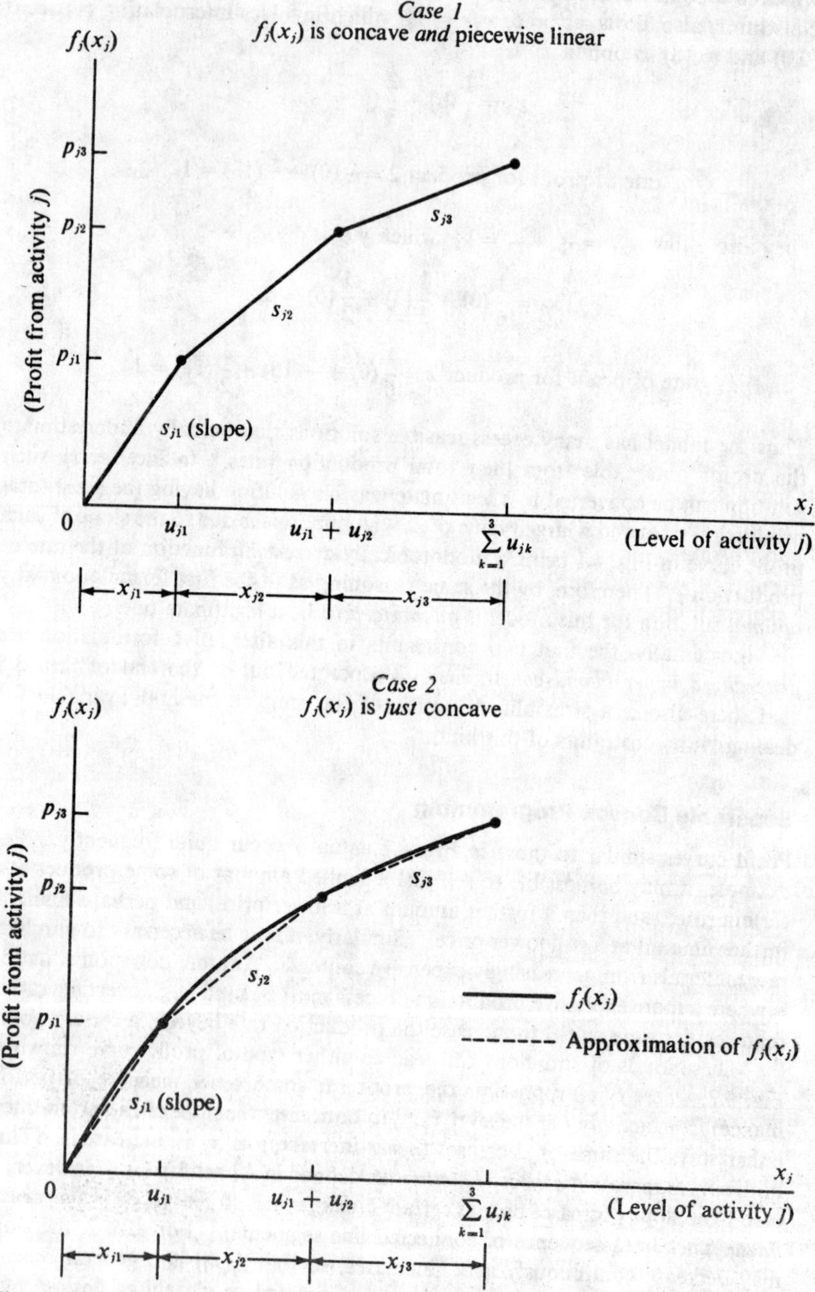

Figure 4.2 Shape of profit curves for separable convex programming.

piecewise linear function, and this is what would be done in the formulation. (Figure 4.2*b* shows an approximating function consisting of just three line segments, but the approximation can be made even better by just introducing additional break points.) This is a very convenient approximation because it simplifies the task of constructing the objective function, and it also permits the use of linear programming through the *separable convex programming technique*!

The separable convex programming technique is applicable to any problem of the form

$$\text{Maximize} \quad Z = \sum_{j=1}^{n} f_j(x_j),$$

subject to

$$\sum_{j=1}^{n} a_{ij} x_j \le b_i, \text{ for } i = 1, 2, \ldots, m$$

and

$$x_j \ge 0, \text{ for } j = 1, 2, \ldots, n,$$

where each $f_j(x_j)$ fits one of the two cases illustrated in Fig. 4.2. Thus the problem already is in the linear programming format, except for the objective function. However, each term in the objective function is, or can at least be closely approximated by, a piecewise linear function whose slope *decreases* at its break points.[1] Alternatively, the objective function for the problem can also be expressed in *minimization* form,

$$\text{Minimize} \quad -Z = \sum_{j=1}^{n} [-f_j(x_j)],$$

where each $f_j(x_j)$ still fits one of the two cases illustrated in Fig. 4.2. (Recall the relationship between minimization and maximization forms discussed in Sec. 2.10). Thus each objective function term $-f_j(x_j)$ now would be at least closely approximated by a piecewise linear function whose slope *increases* at its break points. (Consequently, $-f_j(x_j)$ would be *convex* as defined in Appendix 1.)

Incidentally, this technique was given its name because it is applicable when the objective function in minimization form is *separable* into a sum of *convex* functions of individual variables and the problem otherwise fits the linear *programming* format. By contrast, it is not applicable when a *nonlinear* objective function contains terms involving more than one variable (e.g., cross-product terms $x_j x_k$), or when the slope of the $f_j(x_j)$ functions *increases* at some points.

FORMULATION As in the preceding example, the first step in the formulation is to express x_j, the level of activity *j*, as a sum of variables

$$x_j = \sum_{k=1}^{n_j} x_{jk},$$

[1] Since $f_j(x_j) = c_j x_j$ can be viewed as a piecewise linear function having *no* break points, this statement does not rule out having some objective function terms that already fit the linear programming format.

where x_{jk} represents the level used of the kth most profitable segment of activity j, and n_j is the number of segments. (In Fig. 4.2, $n_j = 3$, so $x_j = x_{j1} + x_{j2} + x_{j3}$.) Thus, $f_j(x_j)$ (or the piecewise linear function approximating it) becomes

$$f_j(x_j) = \sum_{k=1}^{n_j} s_{jk} x_{jk},$$

where s_{jk} is the slope of the kth line segment. Each x_{jk} has an upper bound u_{jk}† and a lower bound zero, so these constraints must be included:

$$x_{jk} \le u_{jk} \text{ and } x_{jk} \ge 0, \text{ for } k = 1, 2, \ldots, n_j \text{ and } j = 1, 2, \ldots, n.$$

Since these constraints and functions fit the linear programming format, direct substitution into the original formulation yields the linear programming formulation

$$\text{Maximize} \quad Z = \sum_{j=1}^{n} \left(\sum_{k=1}^{n_j} s_{jk} x_{jk} \right),$$

subject to

$$\sum_{j=1}^{n} a_{ij} \left(\sum_{k=1}^{n_j} x_{jk} \right) \le b_i, \quad \text{for } i = 1, 2, \ldots, m,$$

$$x_{jk} \le u_{jk}, \text{ for } k = 1, 2, \ldots, n_j \text{ and } j = 1, 2, \ldots, n,$$

and

$$x_{jk} \ge 0, \quad \text{for } k = 1, 2, \ldots, n_j \text{ and } j = 1, 2, \ldots, n.$$

(The $\sum_{k=1}^{n_j} x_{jk} \ge 0$ constraints are deleted because they are ensured by the $x_{jk} \ge 0$ constraints.)

Now note that this formulation does not *explicitly* take into account the implied restriction on each $x_{jk} (k > 1)$ that

$$x_{jk} = 0 \text{ whenever } x_{j(k-1)} < u_{j(k-1)}.$$

(In some cases, the level of activity j can be increased in only one way, so this restriction must be satisfied for the x_{jk} to have physical meaning. Even in other cases, violating the restriction would only decrease profit.) Fortunately, this restriction is considered *implicitly* because it is *automatically* satisfied by any optimal solution to the above linear programming model. This is the key property of separable convex programming that makes it a particularly valuable technique. (This property holds by the same reasoning given in the last example, as we ask you to show in Prob. 7.)

The most efficient way of solving this formulation would be to use the streamlined version of the simplex method for dealing with *upper bound constraints* mentioned at the end of Sec. 3.5 (and described in Sec. 16.1). If only a

† The one exception is when x_j has no upper bound, so x_{jn_j} has no upper bound.

computer code for the general simplex method is available, it should be applied instead to the following equivalent formulation, which has fewer functional constraints.

Alternative Formulation The above formulation gives the profit for each activity j as the sum of the profit contributions from the respective line segments of the profit curve $(\sum_{k=1}^{n_j} s_j x_j)$. Because of the implied restriction on the x_{jk} discussed above, this can be viewed as moving up the profit curve from one break point to the next, and then just a proportion x_{jk}/u_{jk} up the last line segment that has $x_{jk} > 0$. Therefore an equivalent formulation would be to linearly *interpolate* along that line segment a proportion $w_{jk} = x_{jk}/u_{jk}$ of the way from its left-hand to its right-hand breakpoint. Thus, the profit $f_j(x_j)$ would be expressed as

$$f_j(x_j) = \sum_{k=1}^{n_j} p_{jk} w_{jk},$$

subject to the *explicit* constraints

$$\sum_{k=1}^{n_j} w_{jk} \leq 1$$

and

$$w_{jk} \geq 0, \text{ for } k = 1, 2, \ldots, n_j.$$

There also would be an *implied* restriction that if the interpolation is along the kth line segment $(k > 1)$, then

$$w_{j(k-1)} + w_{jk} = 1,$$

so the other variables would be zero. If the interpolation is along the *first* line segment, the implied restriction is that

$$w_{j1} \leq 1, \text{ with } w_{jk} = 0 \text{ for } k = 2, 3, \ldots, n_j.$$

These w_{jk} variables would be interpreted as *interpolation weights*, where the implicit restriction is that the interpolation must be between the two end points of a *single* line segment on the profit curve. Consequently, the value of x_j would be identified by using these same interpolation weights to interpolate between the *abscissa* values of the end points of this line segment,

$$x_j = \sum_{k=1}^{n_j} \sum_{l=1}^{k} u_{jl} w_{jk}.$$

The resulting linear programming formulation of the overall problem is

$$\text{Maximize} \quad Z = \sum_{j=1}^{n} \sum_{k=1}^{n_j} p_{jk} w_{jk},$$

subject to

$$\sum_{j=1}^{n} a_{ij}\left[\sum_{k=1}^{n_j}\left(\sum_{l=1}^{k} u_{jl}\right) w_{jk}\right] \le b_i, \text{ for } i = 1, 2, \ldots, m$$

$$\sum_{k=1}^{n_j} w_{jk} \le 1, \quad \text{for } j = 1, 2, \ldots, n$$

and

$$w_{jk} \ge 0, \quad \text{for } k = 1, 2, \ldots, n_j$$
$$\text{and } j = 1, 2, \ldots, n.$$

Notice that this model has just $(m + n)$ functional constraints (with n of these being the generalized upper bound constraints discussed at the end of Sec.3.5), as opposed to $[m + \sum_{j=1}^{n} n_j]$ functional constraints for the first formulation. You will see in the next section that such a reduction in the number of functional constraints is particularly helpful in substantially reducing computation time for the general simplex method.

Once again, because of the characteristics of separable convex programming, any *optimal* solution for this model is *guaranteed* to be a legitimate one that satisfies the implicit restriction on the w_{jk} variables. (As you saw in the last example, the reasoning behind this key property is completely analogous to that for the first formulation. See Prob. 8.)

4.2 COMPUTATIONAL CONSIDERATIONS

Computer codes for the simplex method now are widely available for essentially all modern computer systems. In fact, major computer manufacturers usually supply their customers with a rather sophisticated linear programming software package (Mathematical Programming System) that also includes many of the special procedures discussed in this book (e.g., the dual simplex method, transportation simplex method, upper bound or generalized upper bound technique, separable convex programming technique, systematic sensitivity analysis, and so on). Some very good linear programming software packages also have been developed by independent software development companies and service bureaus, and further progress is continuing to be made.[1]

These computer codes are being used routinely to solve surprisingly large linear programming problems. For example, a problem with 1,000 functional constraints and 10,000 variables usually can be solved in a few hours or less on a computer of recent vintage.[2] Problems with several times this number of

[1] For example, the Systems Optimization Laboratory of Stanford University is developing a particularly advanced mathematical programming system based on the latest research and computational techniques.

[2] On problems of this size, the computation time depends greatly upon the linear programming experience of the user and his familiarity with the problem because large savings can be achieved by using special techniques (e.g., "crashing techniques" for quickly finding an advanced initial basic feasible solution).

constraints and variables also have been successfully solved by the general simplex method. If the problem has some kind of special structure (as described in Chap. 3) that can be solved by a streamlined version of the simplex method, then even *much* larger sizes can sometimes be handled. For example, a problem with 50,000 functional constraints and 250,000 variables has been solved when all but 600 of these constraints were of a special kind (*generalized upper bound constraints* discussed at the end of Sec. 3.5).

There are several factors affecting how long the general simplex method will require to solve a linear programming problem. The most important one is the *number of ordinary functional constraints*. In fact, computation time tends to be roughly proportional to the *cube* of this number, so that doubling this number may multiply the computation time by a factor of approximately 8. By contrast, the number of variables is a relatively minor factor.[1] Thus, doubling the number of variables probably will not even double the computation time. A third factor of some importance is the *density* of the table of constraint coefficients (i.e., the *proportion* of the coefficients that are *not* zero) because this affects the computation time *per iteration*. One common rule of thumb for the *number of iterations* is that it tends to be roughly twice the number of functional constraints.

This brings us to one important application of the duality theory discussed in Sec. 2.12. Recall that the simplex method can be applied to either the original problem (the *primal problem*) or to its dual problem and will still identify an optimal solution for the other problem as well. Also recall that if the primal problem has m functional constraints and n variables, then the dual problem has n functional constraints and m variables. Therefore, if $m > n$, it usually will be more efficient to solve the problem of interest by applying the simplex method to its dual problem instead. If m is considerably larger than n, this can greatly reduce the computation time.

One difficulty in dealing with large linear programming problems is the tremendous amount of data involved. For example, a problem with just 1,000 functional constraints and variables would have 1 million constraint coefficients to be specified! Therefore most experienced practitioners make extensive use of the computer for data-processing purposes both before and after applying the simplex method. Frequently a *matrix generator* program will be written to convert the basic raw data into constraint coefficients in an appropriate format for the simplex method. The matrix generator will do the arithmetic required in this conversion, repeat recurring constraints (e.g., as in the multitime period problems discussed in Sec. 3.6), and fill in the zero coefficients (most of the coefficients usually are zeroes in large problems). It also should print out the key input data in an easily readable form so they can be shown to various people for checking and correcting. Another useful function of a matrix

[1] This assumes that the *matrix* form of the simplex method (called the *revised* simplex method) described in Sec. 16.4 is being used rather than the tabular form presented in Sec. 2.8. All production computer codes now use this matrix form.

generator is to scale the coefficients (by changing the units for the activities or resources) to approximately the same order of magnitude to avoid significant round-off error and so forth.

For many of the same reasons, it often is helpful to write an *output analyzer* program to convert the output of the simplex method into a useful form. An output analyzer (or *report writer*) has three major functions. One function is to compile and summarize relevant information for debugging the model. (Large linear programming problems seldom are correctly specified the first time they are formulated, and they may need to be partially or completely run at least once before the debugging of the data and formulation can be completed.) Another function is to provide useful data for analyzing the sensitivity of the optimal solution to the various estimated parameters of the model. (We shall discuss this further in the next section.) The third major purpose of an output analyzer is to develop a well-organized report presenting the relevant information about the proposed solution in the vernacular of management.

4.3 SENSITIVITY ANALYSIS

The work of the operations research team usually is not even nearly done when the simplex method has been successfully applied to identify an optimal solution for the model. As we pointed out at the end of Sec. 2.3, one assumption of linear programming is that all the parameters of the model (the a_{ij}, b_i, and c_j) are known constants. Actually, the parameter values used in the model normally are just estimates based on a prediction of future conditions. The data obtained to develop these estimates often are rather crude or nonexistent, so that the parameters in the original formulation may represent little more than quick rules of thumb provided by harassed line personnel. They may even represent deliberate overestimates or underestimates to protect the interests of the estimators.

Thus the successful manager and operations research staff will maintain a healthy skepticism about the original numbers coming out of the computer and in many cases will view them as only a starting point for further analysis of the problem. An "optimal" solution is optimal only with respect to the specific model being used to represent the real problem, and such a solution becomes a reliable guide for action only after it has been verified as performing well for other reasonable representations of the problem as well. Furthermore, the model parameters (particularly the b_i) sometimes are set as a result of policy decisions (e.g., the amount of certain resources to be made available to these activities), and these decisions should be reviewed after seeing their consequences on what can be achieved.

For these reasons it is important to perform a *sensitivity analysis* to investigate the effect on the optimal solution provided by the simplex method if the parameters take on other possible values. Usually there will be some parameters that can be assigned any reasonable value without affecting the optimality of this solution. However, there may also be parameters with likely values that would yield a new optimal solution. This is particularly serious if the original solution would then have a substantially inferior value of the objective function, or perhaps even be infeasible! Therefore the basic objective of sensitivity analysis is to identify these particularly sensitive parameters, so that special care can then be taken in estimating them more closely and in selecting a solution which performs well for most of their likely values.

Sensitivity analysis would be extremely expensive computationally if it were necessary to reapply the simplex method from the beginning to investigate each new change in a parameter value. Fortunately, the fundamental insight discussed in Sec. 2.11 provides an enormous shortcut here. The basic idea is that the fundamental insight reveals just how any changes in the original model would change the numbers in the final simplex tableau. Therefore, after making a few simple calculations to revise this tableau, it is then easy to check whether the original optimal basic feasible solution is now nonoptimal (or infeasible). If so, this solution would be used as the initial basic feasible solution to restart the simplex method (or dual simplex method). If the changes in the model were not too major, only a very few iterations should then be required to reach the new optimal solution from this "advanced" initial solution.

To describe this procedure more specifically, we need to ask you to review the notation and results for the fundamental insight. In particular, first see Table 2.19 in Sec. 2.8 to refresh your memory on how the parameters of the model appear in the *initial* simplex tableau. Then see in Sec. 2.11 how $z_j^* - c_j$, y_i^*, y_0^*, a_{kj}^*, s_{kj}^*, and b_i^* $(i, k = 1,2, \ldots, m; j = 1,2, \ldots, n)$ are used to denote the entries in the *final* simplex tableau (the one yielding an optimal solution), as summarized in Table 4.3. Finally, note in Sec. 2.11 how the fundamental

Table 4.3 Notation for Entries in The Final Simplex Tableau

Basic variable	*Eq. no.*	*Coefficient of* Z	x_1	x_2	$\cdots$	x_n	x_{n+1}	x_{n+2}	$\cdots$	x_{n+m}	*Right side*
Z	0	1	$z_1^* - c_1$	$z_2^* - c_2$	$\cdots$	$z_n^* - c_n$	y_1^*	y_2^*	$\cdots$	y_m^*	y_0^*
x_{B1}	1	0	a_{11}^*	a_{12}^*	$\cdots$	a_{1n}^*	s_{11}^*	s_{12}^*	$\cdots$	s_{1m}^*	b_1^*
x_{B2}	2	0	a_{21}^*	a_{22}^*	$\cdots$	a_{2n}^*	s_{21}^*	s_{22}^*	$\cdots$	s_{2m}^*	b_2^*
$\vdots$	$\vdots$	$\vdots$			$\vdots$				$\vdots$		$\vdots$
x_{Bm}	m	0	a_{m1}^*	a_{m2}^*	$\cdots$	a_{mn}^*	s_{m1}^*	s_{m2}^*	$\cdots$	s_{mn}^*	b_m^*

insight properties for rows 0 and i yield the following equations for most of these entries in terms of just the slack variable coefficients (the y_i^* and s_{ki}^*) and the parameters of the model:

$$y_0^* = \sum_{i=1}^{m} b_i y_i^*$$

$$b_k^* = \sum_{i=1}^{m} b_i s_{ki}^*, \qquad \text{for } k = 1, 2, \ldots, m$$

$$z_j^* - c_j = -c_j + \sum_{i=1}^{m} a_{ij} y_i^*, \text{ for } j = 1, 2, \ldots, n$$

$$a_{kj}^* = \sum_{i=1}^{m} a_{ij} s_{ki}^*$$

Therefore it is necessary to know only the y_i^* and s_{ki}^* (along with the a_{ij}, b_i, and c_j) to be able to construct the entire final simplex tableau. Because of the property of these coefficients given at the beginning of Sec. 2.11, this will provide the key to sensitivity analysis.

To illustrate this notation, consider again the Wyndor Glass Co. problem introduced in Sec. 2.1 and solved in tabular form in Sec. 2.8. For your convenience, the parameters of the model and the final simplex tableau are repeated in Table 4.4. Thus, for example, $z_2^* - c_2 = 0$, $y_2^* = 3/2$, $y_0^* = 36$, $a_{22}^* = 1$,

Table 4.4 Data for Performing Sensitivity Analysis for The Wyndor Glass Co. Problem

Model parameters
$c_1 = 3,\ c_2 = 5\ (n = 2)$
$a_{11} = 1, a_{12} = 0, b_1 = 4$
$a_{21} = 0, a_{22} = 2, b_2 = 12$
$a_{31} = 3, a_{32} = 2, b_3 = 18$

Final simplex tableau

Basic variable	Eq. no.	Z	x_1	x_2	x_3	x_4	x_5	Right side
		Coefficient of						
Z	0	1	0	0	0	$\frac{3}{2}$	1	36
x_3	1	0	0	0	1	$\frac{1}{3}$	$-\frac{1}{3}$	2
x_2	2	0	0	1	0	$\frac{1}{2}$	0	6
x_1	3	0	1	0	0	$-\frac{1}{3}$	$\frac{1}{3}$	2

$s_{22}^* = 1/2$, $b_2^* = 6$, and so on, as given in Sec. 2.11. We shall use this example to illustrate sensitivity analysis. First, however, we describe the overall procedure symbolically.

Consider the following situation. The simplex method has already been used to obtain an optimal solution to a linear programming model with specified values for the b_i, c_j, and a_{ij} parameters. To initiate sensitivity analysis, one or more of the parameters now are to be changed by a certain amount, namely,

$$b_i \to b_i + \Delta b_i, \text{ for } i = 1, 2, \ldots, m$$

$$c_j \to c_j + \Delta c_j, \text{ for } j = 1, 2, \ldots, n$$

$$a_{ij} \to a_{ij} + \Delta a_{ij},$$

where Δb_i, Δc_j, and Δa_{ij} denote the *change* in that parameter (zero in most cases). The first step is to simply revise the *final* simplex tableau to reflect these changes, assuming no changes in the y_i^* and s_{ki}^* entries. In other words, you can directly calculate the changes in the other entries that would result from applying the *same* sequence of arithmetic operations on the revised parameters that the simplex method already has applied to the original parameters. This is easy to do from the above equations. Specifically, the changes are

$$\Delta y_0^* = \sum_{i=1}^{m} \Delta b_i y_i^*$$

$$\Delta b_k^* = \sum_{i=1}^{m} \Delta b_i s_{ki}^*, \qquad \text{for } k = 1, 2, \ldots, m$$

$$\Delta(z_j^* - c_j) = -\Delta c_j + \sum_{i=1}^{m} \Delta a_{ij} y_i^*, \text{ for } j = 1, 2, \ldots, n$$

$$\Delta a_{kj}^* = \sum_{i=1}^{m} \Delta a_{ij} s_{ki}^*.$$

One possible consequence of these changes is that the current basic solution (originally the optimal solution) for the final simplex tableau may have changed its value. This occurs if any $\Delta b_i^* \neq 0$ because $b_i^* + \Delta b_i^*$ is the new value of the basic variable for row i. It may also occur if any $\Delta a_{kj}^* \neq 0$ for any basic variable x_j. The reason is that the basic variable for row i must have a coefficient of 1 in that row and a coefficient of *zero* in *every* other row (including row 0) for the tableau to be in the proper form for identifying and evaluating the current basic solution. Therefore, if the changes have violated this requirement, further changes must be made to restore this form. This is done by successively applying part 3 of the iterative step for the simplex method as if each violating basic variable were an entering basic variable. Note that this may also cause further changes in the right-side column, which gives the value of the current basic solution.

After converting the revised final simplex tableau to the proper form, the next step is to determine the status of the corresponding basic solution. The basic question is whether the revisions have caused any change in its previous status of being both *feasible* and *optimal.* Since this current solution still satisfies the functional constraints, the only way in which it may no longer be feasible is if some basic variables now violate their nonnegativity constraints. Therefore, if the right-side column (the values of the basic variables) has been revised in the final simplex tableau, it is necessary to check whether all these values are still nonnegative. If so, then the optimality status of this basic feasible solution would be checked in the usual way by examining the changed coefficients of the nonbasic variables in row 0. If all these coefficients are still nonnegative, then the solution is still optimal.

If the current basic solution fails either the test for feasibility or optimality, it may then be desirable to identify the new optimal solution. (It is often useful in sensitivity analysis to identify the solutions that are optimal for some set of likely values of the model parameters and then to determine which of these solutions most *consistently* performs well for the various likely parameter values.) The most efficient way of doing this usually is to use the current basic solution as the *initial* basic solution for restarting the simplex method (or dual simplex method), so that the revised *final* simplex tableau now becomes the initial simplex tableau. If this current basic solution is *not* feasible (but satisfies the condition for optimality), the *dual* simplex method described in Sec. 16.2 should be used rather than the simplex method (this is equivalent to applying the simplex method to the *dual* problem). If the solution fails *both* tests, so that the tableau has negative entries in both the right-side column and row 0, artificial variables can be introduced to convert the tableau to the proper form for an *initial* simplex tableau.[1]

This procedure simplifies somewhat when only certain kinds of model parameters are being changed at one time. Therefore, after summarizing the overall procedure, we shall describe and illustrate its application to each of the four basic types of parameter changes.

Summary of Procedure for Investigating The Effect on The Optimal Solution of Specific Changes in The Parameters of The Model

Step 1 Calculate the Δy_0^*, Δb_k^*, $\Delta(z_j^* - c_j)$, and Δa_{kj}^* using the above equations, and add them (when not zero) to the corresponding entries in the final simplex tableau.

Step 2 Convert this tableau to the proper form for identifying and evaluating the current basic solution by applying (as necessary) part 3 of the iterative step for the simplex method.

Step 3 Test this solution for feasibility by checking whether all its basic variable values in the right-side column of the tableau still are nonnegative.

Step 4 Test this solution for optimality (if feasible) by checking whether all its nonbasic variable coefficients in row 0 of the tableau still are nonnegative.

Step 5 If this solution fails either test, the new optimal solution can be obtained (if desired) by using the current tableau as the initial simplex tableau (making any necessary conversions) for the simplex method (or dual simplex method).

Sensitivity analysis often begins by investigating the effect of changes in the b_i, the amount of resource i ($i = 1,2, \ldots, m$) being made available for the activities under consideration. The reason is that there generally is more flexibility in setting and adjusting these values than for the other parameters of the model. The economic interpretation of the dual variables (the y_i) given in Sec. 2.12 is extremely useful for deciding which changes should be considered, and we suggest that you review this interpretation in conjunction with studying the first case below.

Case 1—Changes in The b_i

Suppose that the only changes in the current model are that one or more of the b_i parameters ($i = 1,2, \ldots, m$) have been changed by an amount Δb_i.

[1] There also exists a *primal-dual* algorithm that can be directly applied to such a simplex tableau without any conversion.

Summary of Procedure

Step 1 Calculate

$$\Delta y_0^* = \sum_{i=1}^{m} \Delta b_i y_i^*$$

$$\Delta b_k^* = \sum_{i=1}^{m} \Delta b_i s_{ki}^*, \text{ for } k = 1, 2, \ldots, m,$$

and add them to the respective entries in the right-side column of the final simplex tableau.

Step 2 Not applicable (the form of the tableau has not been changed).

Step 3 Test the current basic solution for feasibility by checking whether all its basic variable values in the right-side column of the tableau still are non-negative.

Step 4 If this solution is feasible, it must still be optimal (the nonbasic variable coefficients in row 0 of the tableau have not been changed).

Step 5 If this solution is not feasible (and so no longer optimal), the new optimal solution can be obtained (if desired) by using the current tableau as the initial simplex tableau for the dual simplex method.

EXAMPLE Sensitivity analysis has begun for the Wyndor Glass Co. problem by examining the optimal values of the y_i dual variables ($y_1^* = 0$, $y_2^* = 3/2$, $y_3^* = 1$), which give the marginal value of each resource i for the activities (two new products) under consideration. The equation for Δy_0^* suggests that the total profit from these activities ($Z = y_0^* + \Delta y_0^*$) can be increased by \$1.50/minute for each additional unit ($\Delta b_2 = 1$) of resource 2 (allocated production capacity in Plant 2) that is made available. This is indeed true for relatively small changes that do not affect the feasibility of the current basic solution (and so do not affect the values of the y_i^*). Consequently, the O.R. Department has investigated the marginal profitability from the other current uses of this resource to determine if any are less than \$1.50/minute. This reveals that one old product is far less profitable. The production rate for this product already has been reduced to the minimum amount that would justify its marketing expenses. However, it can be discontinued altogether, which would provide an additional 12 units of resource 2 for the new products. Thus the next step is to determine what profit could be obtained from the new products if this shift were to be made. This changes b_2 from 12 to 24 in the linear programming model, that is, $\Delta b_2 = 12$.

Applying the above procedure, the effect of $\Delta b_2 = 12$ on the final simplex tableau given in Table 4.4 is that the entries in the right-side column change by

$$\begin{aligned}
\Delta y_0^* &= 12 y_2^* = 18 \\
\Delta b_1^* &= 12 s_{12}^* = 4 \\
\Delta b_2^* &= 12 s_{22}^* = 6 \\
\Delta b_3^* &= 12 s_{32}^* = -4.
\end{aligned}$$

Thus the corresponding basic solution changes to

$$\begin{aligned} Z &= 36 + 18 = 54 \\ x_3 &= 2 + 4 = 6 \\ x_2 &= 6 + 6 = 12 \qquad (x_4 = 0, x_5 = 0) \\ x_1 &= 2 - 4 = -2, \end{aligned}$$

which is no longer feasible because x_2 is negative. (Note in Fig. 2.4 that this basic solution corresponds to a corner-point solution with defining equations $2x_2 = 24$ and $3x_1 + 2x_2 = 18$.) After making these changes in the right-side column in Table 4.4, the dual simplex method could be applied, starting with this simplex tableau to find the new optimal solution. This would lead in just one iteration to the new final simplex tableau shown in Table 4.5. (Alternatively, the simplex method could be applied from the beginning, which also would lead to this final tableau in just one iteration in this case.)

Based on these results, the relatively unprofitable old product will be discontinued. Since y_3^* still is positive, a similar study is made of the possibility of changing the allocation of resource 3, but the resulting decision is to retain the current allocation. Therefore the current linear programming model at this point has the parameter values shown in Table 4.5.

Table 4.5 Revised Data for The Wyndor Glass Co. Problem

Model parameters	*Final simplex tableau*: Basic variable	Eq. no.	Z	*Coefficient of*: x_1	x_2	x_3	x_4	x_5	Right side
$c_1 = 3,\ c_2 = 5\ (n = 2)$	Z	0	1	$\frac{9}{2}$	0	0	0	$\frac{5}{2}$	45
$a_{11} = 1, a_{12} = 0, b_1 = 4$	x_3	1	0	1	0	1	0	0	4
$a_{21} = 0, a_{22} = 2, b_2 = 24$	x_2	2	0	$\frac{3}{2}$	1	0	0	$\frac{1}{2}$	9
$a_{31} = 3, a_{32} = 2, b_3 = 18$	x_4	3	0	-3	0	0	1	-1	6

Case 2a—Changes in the Coefficients of a Nonbasic Variable

Consider a particular variable x_j that is a *nonbasic* variable in the optimal solution shown by the final simplex tableau. Case 2 is where the only changes in the current model are that one or more of the coefficients of this variable—c_j, a_{1j}, a_{2j}, ..., a_{mj}—have been changed by an amount Δc_j, Δa_{1j}, Δa_{2j}, ..., Δa_{mj}, respectively.

Summary of Procedure

Step 1 Calculate

$$\Delta(z_j^* - c_j) = -\Delta c_j + \sum_{i=1}^{m} \Delta a_{ij} y_i^*$$

$$\Delta a_{kj}^* = \sum_{i=1}^{m} \Delta a_{ij} s_{ki}^*, \text{ for } k = 1, 2, \ldots, m,$$

and add them to the respective entries in the x_j column of the final simplex tableau.

Step 2 Not applicable (the form of the tableau has not been changed).

Step 3 The current basic solution is unchanged and so (since $x_j = 0$) must still be feasible.

Step 4 Test this solution for optimality by checking whether the new coefficient of x_j in row 0 of the tableau still is nonnegative.

Step 5 If this solution is no longer optimal, the new optimal solution can be obtained (if desired) by using the current tableau as the initial simplex tableau for the simplex method (so that x_j will be the initial entering basic variable).

Note that the Δa_{kj}^* actually are needed only in step 5, so they need not be calculated to merely test for optimality.

EXAMPLE Since $x_1 = 0$ in the current optimal solution (see Table 4.5) for the Wyndor Glass Co. problem, the next step in its sensitivity analysis was to check whether any reasonable changes in the estimates of the coefficients of x_1 could still make it advisable to introduce product 1. One such set of changes would be to reset $c_1 = 4$ and $a_{31} = 2$, so that $\Delta c_1 = +1$ and $\Delta a_{31} = -1$. The resulting changes in the final simplex tableau of Table 4.5 would be

$$\Delta(z_j^* - c_j) = -(+1) + (-1)\frac{5}{2} = -\frac{7}{2}$$

$$\Delta a_{11}^* = (-1)0 = 0$$

$$\Delta a_{21}^* = (-1)\frac{1}{2} = -\frac{1}{2}$$

$$\Delta a_{31}^* = (-1)(-1) = +1.$$

Since the corresponding new coefficient of x_1 in row 0, $(z_1^* - c_1) = 9/2 + (-7/2) = +1$, still is nonnegative, the current solution with $x_1 = 0$ still would be optimal. In fact, the expression for $\Delta(z_j^* - c_j)$ indicates that the unit profit c_1 would need to exceed 5 ($\Delta c_1 > 2$), with $a_{31} = 2$ ($\Delta a_{31} = -1$), or to have a significantly larger reduction in a_{31} before x_1 should be positive.

Since a brief review of the data for product 1 indicates that such large changes in the estimates would be unrealistic, the O.R. Department concludes that the coefficients of x_1 are not particularly sensitive parameters in the current model.

Case 2b—Introduction of a New Variable

After solving for the optimal solution, it may be discovered that the linear programming formulation had not considered all the attractive alternative activities. Considering a new activity requires introducing a new variable with the appropriate coefficients into the objective function and constraints of the current model —which is Case 2*b*.

The convenient way to deal with this case is to treat it just as if it were Case 2*a*! This is done by pretending that the new variable x_j actually was in the original model with *all* its coefficients equal to *zero* and that x_j is a *nonbasic* variable in the current basic feasible solution. Therefore, by setting Δc_j and the Δa_{ij} equal to the corresponding new coefficients for this variable, the procedure does indeed become identical to that for Case 2*a*.

Case 3—Changes in the Coefficients of a Basic Variable

Now suppose that the variable x_j under consideration is a *basic* variable in the optimal solution shown by the final simplex tableau. Again let Δc_j and the Δa_{kj} $(k = 1,2, \ldots, m)$ denote the changes in the respective coefficients of this variable. Case 3 assumes that these are the only changes in the current model.

Case 3 differs from case 2*a* because of the requirement that a basic variable must have a coefficient of 1 in its row of the simplex tableau and a coefficient of *zero* in *every* other row (including row 0). Therefore, after calculating the changes—Δc_j^* and the Δa_{kj}^*—in these coefficients,[1] it probably will be necessary to apply part 3 of the iterative step to restore this form. This in turn probably will change the value of the current basic solution and may make it either infeasible or nonoptimal. Consequently, all five steps of the overall procedure are required for case 3.

EXAMPLE Since x_2 is a basic variable in Table 4.5 for the Wyndor Glass Co. problem, sensitivity analysis of its coefficients fits Case 3. One change considered was to reset $c_2 = 3$, $a_{22} = 3$, and $a_{32} = 4$, so that $\Delta c_2 = -2$, $\Delta a_{22} = +1$ and $\Delta a_{32} = +2$. The corresponding changes in the final simplex tableau are

$$\Delta(z_2^* - c_2) = -\Delta c_2 + \sum_{i=1}^{3} \Delta a_{i2}\, y_i^* = -(-2) + \left[0 + 0 + (2)\frac{5}{2}\right] = +7$$

$$\Delta a_{12}^* = \sum_{i=1}^{3} \Delta a_{i2}\, s_{1i}^* = 0$$

$$\Delta a_{22}^* = \sum_{i=1}^{3} \Delta a_{i2}\, s_{2i}^* = 0 + (2)\frac{1}{2} = +1$$

$$\Delta a_{32}^* = \sum_{i=1}^{3} \Delta a_{i2}\, s_{3i}^* = 0 + (1)1 + 2(-1) = -1.$$

[1] For the relatively sophisticated reader, we should point out a possible pitfall for case 3 that would be discovered at this point. Specifically, the Δa_{kj} changes *can* destroy the linear independence of the columns of coefficients of basic variables. This has occurred only if the unit coefficient of the basic variable x_j has been changed to *zero* at this point, in which case more extensive simplex method calculations must be used for case 3.

Adding these quantities to the respective coefficients of x_2 in Table 4.5 yields the first tableau shown in Table 4.6. Note that the new coefficients of this basic variable do not have the required values, so part 3 of the iterative step must next be applied. This involves dividing row 2 by 2, subtracting 7 times the new row 2 from row 0, and adding the new row 2 to row 3. The resulting second tableau in Table 4.6 gives the new value of the current basic solution, namely, $x_3 = 4$, $x_2 = 9/2$, $x_4 = 21/2$ ($x_1 = 0$, $x_5 = 0$). Since all these variables are nonnegative, the solution still is feasible. However, because of the negative coefficient of x_1 in row 0, we know it is no longer optimal. Therefore the simplex method would be applied to this tableau, with this solution as the initial basic feasible solution, to find the new optimal solution. The initial entering basic variable is x_1, with x_3 as the leaving basic variable. Just one iteration is needed in this case to reach the new optimal solution—$x_1 = 4$, $x_2 = 3/2$, $x_4 = 27/2$ ($x_3 = 0$, $x_5 = 0$)—as shown in the last tableau of Table 4.6.

Table 4.6 Sensitivity Analysis Procedure Applied to Case 3 Example

	Basic variable	Eq. no.	Coefficient of: Z	x_1	x_2	x_3	x_4	x_5	Right side
Revised final tableau after applying step 1 to tableau in Table 4.5	Z	0	1	$\frac{9}{2}$	7	0	0	$\frac{5}{2}$	45
	x_3	1	0	1	0	1	0	0	4
	x_2	2	0	$\frac{3}{2}$	2	0	0	$\frac{1}{2}$	9
	x_4	3	0	-3	-1	0	1	-1	6
Revised final tableau after applying step 2 (*Step 3* still feasible) (*Step 4* no longer optimal)	Z	0		$-\frac{3}{4}$	0	0	0	$\frac{3}{4}$	$\frac{27}{2}$
	x_3	1		1	0	1	0	0	4
	x_2	2		$\frac{3}{4}$	1	0	0	$\frac{1}{4}$	$\frac{9}{2}$
	x_4	3		$-\frac{9}{4}$	0	0	1	$-\frac{3}{4}$	$\frac{21}{2}$
New final tableau after applying step 5 (only one iteration of the simplex method needed in this case)	Z	0	1	0	0	$\frac{3}{4}$	0	$\frac{3}{4}$	$\frac{33}{2}$
	x_1	1	0	1	0	1	0	0	4
	x_2	2	0	0	1	$-\frac{3}{4}$	0	$\frac{1}{4}$	$\frac{3}{2}$
	x_4	3	0	0	0	$\frac{9}{4}$	1	$-\frac{3}{4}$	$\frac{39}{2}$

This analysis suggests that c_2, a_{22}, and a_{32} are relatively sensitive parameters. However, additional data for estimating them more closely can be obtained only by conducting a pilot run. Therefore the O.R. Department recommends that production of product 2 be initiated immediately on a small scale ($x_2 = 3/2$) and that this experience be used to guide the decision on whether the remaining production capacity should be allocated to product 2 or product 1.

Case 4—Introduction of a New Constraint

The last case is where a new constraint must be introduced into the model after it has already been solved. This may occur because the constraint was overlooked initially or because new considerations have arisen since the model was formulated originally. Another possibility is that the constraint was deleted purposely to decrease computational effort because it appeared to be less restrictive than other constraints already in the model, but now this impression needs to be checked with the optimal solution actually obtained.

Suppose for now that the new constraint is an *inequality* constraint. The overall procedure for this case begins by introducing a slack variable to convert the constraint to equality form and then introducing the constraint in this form as a *new row* in the *final* simplex tableau. (Just as for case 2*b*, you can think of this as having changed the new parameters from *zero* in the original model to their current values.) The slack variable is designated to be the basic variable for this new row. Because this new variable begins with zero coefficients in the other rows, no changes are needed in these other rows in either steps 1 or 2.

Summary of Procedure

Step 1 After introducing a slack variable for the new constraint, merely expand the final simplex tableau to include the new parameter values (including zero coefficients for this slack variable in the other rows), with the slack variable as the basic variable for the new row.

Step 2 For every *other* basic variable, convert its coefficient in the new row to zero by applying part 3 of the iterative step for the simplex method. The resulting basic variable value in the right-side column for the new row completes the otherwise unchanged current basic solution.

Step 3 Test this solution for feasibility by checking whether this additional basic variable is nonnegative.

Step 4 If this solution is feasible, it must still be optimal (the nonbasic variable coefficients in row 0 of the tableau have not been changed.)

Step 5 If this solution is not feasible (and so no longer optimal), the new optimal solution can be obtained (if desired) by using the current tableau as the initial simplex tableau for the dual simplex method.

If you want to see only if the current optimal solution would be affected by a potential new constraint, without introducing the constraint into the current tableau permanently, then a major shortcut is available. All you have to do is directly check whether the optimal solution satisfies the constraint. If it does, then it would still be the best feasible solution (i.e., the optimal solution), even if the constraint were added to the model. The reason is that a new constraint can only eliminate some previously feasible solutions without adding any new ones.

If the new constraint is an *equality* constraint, then there are two changes in the procedure summarized above. First, an artificial rather than a slack variable would be introduced into the constraint, with the artificial variable designated to be the basic variable for the new row. Second, using the Big M method, a coefficient of $+M$ would be introduced into row 0 for this variable. In step 2 this would additionally require subtracting M times the new row from row 0 to restore this coefficient to zero. Consequently it becomes necessary to test for optimality in step 4.

EXAMPLE To illustrate this case, suppose that the new constraint

$$2x_1 + 3x_2 \leq 24$$

is introduced into the model given in Table 4.5. Letting x_6 be the slack variable for this constraint, step 1 yields the first tableau shown in Table 4.7. Step 2 requires subtracting three times row 2 from the new row, which identifies the current basic solution—$x_3 = 4$, $x_2 = 9$, $x_4 = 6$, $x_6 = -3$ ($x_1 = 0$, $x_5 = 0$)—as shown in the second tableau. Since the additional basic variable x_6 is negative, step 3 concludes that this solution is *not* feasible. Step 5 then leads in just one iteration (more are sometimes needed) to the new optimal solution in the final tableau of Table 4.7.

Systematic Sensitivity Analysis—Parametric Programming

So far we have described how to test specific changes in the model parameters. Another common approach to sensitivity analysis is to vary one or more parameters continuously over some interval(s) to see when the optimal solution changes. For example, with the Wyndor Glass Co. problem, rather than beginning by testing the specific change from $b_2 = 12$ to $b_2 = 24$, we might instead set

$$b_2 = 12 + \theta,$$

and then vary θ continuously from 0 to 12 (the maximum value of interest). By using the expressions for y_0^* and b_i^*, it can be seen that the corresponding optimal solution is

$$Z = 36 + \frac{3}{2}\theta$$

$$x_3 = 2 + \frac{1}{3}\theta \qquad (x_4 = 0, x_5 = 0)$$

$$x_2 = 6 + \frac{1}{2}\theta$$

$$x_1 = 2 - \frac{1}{3}\theta$$

Table 4.7 Sensitivity Analysis Procedure Applied to Case 4 Example

	Basic variable	Eq. no.	Coefficient of: Z	x_1	x_2	x_3	x_4	x_5	x_6	Right side
Revised final tableau after applying step 1 to tableau in Table 4.5	Z	0	1	$\frac{9}{2}$	0	0	0	$\frac{5}{2}$	0	45
	x_3	1	0	1	0	1	0	0	0	4
	x_2	2	0	$\frac{3}{2}$	1	0	0	$\frac{1}{2}$	0	9
	x_4	3	0	-3	0	0	1	-1	0	6
	(x_6)	New	0	2	3	0	0	0	1	(24)
Revised final tableau after applying step 2 (*Step 3* not feasible)	Z	0	1	$\frac{9}{2}$	0	0	0	$\frac{5}{2}$	0	45
	x_3	1	0	1	0	1	0	0	0	4
	x_2	2	0	$\frac{3}{2}$	1	0	0	$\frac{1}{2}$	0	9
	x_4	3	0	-3	0	0	1	-1	0	6
	x_6	New	0	$-\frac{5}{2}$	0	0	0	$-\frac{3}{2}$	1	-3
New final tableau after applying step 5 (only one iteration of dual simplex method needed in this case)	Z	0	1	$\frac{1}{3}$	0	0	0	0	$\frac{5}{3}$	40
	x_3	1	0	1	0	1	0	0	0	4
	x_2	2	0	$\frac{2}{3}$	1	0	0	0	$\frac{1}{3}$	8
	x_4	3	0	$-\frac{4}{3}$	0	0	1	0	$-\frac{2}{3}$	8
	x_5	New	0	$\frac{5}{3}$	0	0	0	1	$-\frac{2}{3}$	2

for θ small enough that this solution still is feasible, i.e., for $\theta \leq 6$. For $\theta \geq 6$, the dual simplex method yields the tableau shown in Table 4.5, with $Z = 45$, $x_3 = 4$, $x_2 = 9$, and $x_4 = -6 + \theta$ ($x_1 = 0$, $x_5 = 0$). This information can then be used (along with other data not incorporated into the model on the effect of increasing b_2) to decide whether to retain the original optimal solution and, if not, how much to increase b_2.

In a similar way, the effect on the optimal solution of varying several parameters simultaneously can be investigated. When varying just b_i parameters, this would involve replacing each original right-hand side b_i (original) by $b_i = b_i$ (original) $+ \alpha_i \theta$ for $i = 1, 2, \ldots, m$, where the α_i are input constants specifying the desired rate of increase of the corresponding right-hand side as θ is increased. For example, it might be possible to shift some of the production of a current Wyndor Glass Co. product from Plant 2 to Plant 3, thereby increasing b_2 by decreasing b_3. If b_3 decreases twice as fast as b_2 increases, then

$$b_2 = 12 + \theta$$
$$b_3 = 18 - 2\theta,$$

where θ measures the amount of production shifted. (Thus, $\alpha_1 = 0$, $\alpha_2 = 1$, and $\alpha_3 = -2$ in this case.)

This way of continuously varying several parameters simultaneously is referred to as *parametric linear programming*. Section 16.3 presents the parametric linear programming procedure when just b_i parameters are being varied as well as the procedure for the analogous case where c_j parameters are being varied. Some mathematical programming computer codes also include routines for varying just the coefficients of a single variable or varying just the parameters of a single constraint. These procedures provide a convenient way of conducting sensitivity analysis systematically.

The Role of Duality Theory in Sensitivity Analysis

Recall from Sec. 2.12 that every linear programming problem has an associated *dual problem* which contains exactly the same parameter values (for different components of the model). Furthermore, these two problems possess certain close relationships, so that the properties of a basic solution for one problem provide considerable information about the complementary basic solution for the other problem. Therefore the effect of changing parameters for sensitivity analysis in one problem has a complementary effect in the other problem. Thus, you always have the choice of which problem to analyze *directly*, and it sometimes is more convenient to choose the dual problem. Furthermore, the dual problem provides useful economic interpretations for sensitivity analysis.

To illustrate, consider the example presented above for case 2*a*, where the changes in the parameters of Table 4.5 are $\Delta c_1 = 1$ and $\Delta a_{31} = -1$. The basic question is whether the current basic feasible solution for this problem (the *primal* problem) still is *optimal* after making these changes. As Tables 2.41 and 2.42 indicate, an *equivalent* question is whether the complementary basic solution for the *dual* problem ($y_1^* = 0$, $y_2^* = 0$, $y_3^* = 5/2$) still is *feasible* after making these changes. This solution was feasible previously, and the changes affect only the first constraint for the dual problem, which now is

$$y_1 + 2y_3 \geq 4.$$

Therefore we need only observe that this constraint still is satisfied,

$$0 + 2\left(\frac{5}{2}\right) \geq 4,$$

to answer *both* questions affirmatively!

4.4 A CASE STUDY—SCHOOL REZONING TO ACHIEVE RACIAL BALANCE[1]

The city of *Middletown* has three high schools, two of them attended primarily by white students and the other primarily by black students. Therefore the Middletown school board has decided to redesign the school attendance zones to reduce the racial isolation in these schools. The new zones will apply only to students entering high school in the future, so the goal is to achieve reasonable racial balance in 3 years without substantially increasing the distances that the students must travel to school.

The school district superintendent has read some articles about how operations research has been used to greatly aid the comprehensive planning of efficient zoning designs. On her recommendation, the school board has hired a team of operations research consultants to conduct the study and make their recommendations.

The consultants begin by defining and gathering the relevant data. For this purpose they divide the city geographically into 10 tracts. Since the current junior high population represents the anticipated high school population in 3 years, they then determine the number of white students and black students now in junior high from each tract. The distance the students must travel to school is a fundamental consideration, so they also determine the distance (in miles) from the center of each tract to each school. All this information is given in Table 4.8, along with the maximum number of students that can be assigned to each school.

The consultants next begin formulating a mathematical model for the problem. In this case (as for many practical problems) the objective is not too well defined. Instead, only two basic considerations have been articulated (racial balance and distance traveled to school), and the goal is to achieve a

Table 4.8 Data for Middletown Study

Tract	No. of whites	No. of blacks	Distance		
			School 1	*School 2*	*School 3*
1	300	150	1.2	1.5	3.3
2	400	0	2.6	4.0	5.5
3	200	300	0.7	1.1	2.8
4	0	500	1.8	1.3	2.0
5	200	200	1.5	0.4	2.3
6	100	350	2.0	0.6	1.7
7	250	200	1.2	1.4	3.1
8	300	200	3.5	2.3	1.2
9	150	250	3.2	1.2	0.7
10	350	100	3.8	1.8	1.0
		School capacity:	1,500	2,000	1,300

[1] Although this case study is a hypothetical one, it is similar to several actual studies that have been conducted recently.

"reasonable" tradeoff between them. A common approach in this kind of situation is to express one consideration in the objective function and the other in the constraints. Thus there is a choice between optimizing the racial balance subject to constraints on distance traveled or optimizing the distance traveled subject to constraints on racial balance. Since it is easier to express distance traveled in the objective function, and it seems more reasonable to (eventually) set minimal standards on racial balance for the constraints, the consultants choose the latter alternative. However, the objective of "optimizing the distance traveled" still needs to be stated more precisely. One possibility is to minimize the maximum distance that any student must travel. But this objective does not fit well into a mathematical programming format, and it also might lead to many students having to travel the maximum distance. Another more convenient objective that may yield a better overall result is to minimize the sum of the distances traveled by all students. If this should lead to a few unacceptable inequities, they can be eliminated during the sensitivity analysis phase by introducing constraints on distance traveled by groups of students having excessive distances in the original optimal solution. Therefore the structure chosen for the model is to minimize total distance traveled subject to constraints on racial balance and any other required constraints.

Ultimately decisions must be made about which individual students to assign to the respective schools. However, these detailed decisions on how to draw the boundaries of the school attendance zones can be worked out after making the broader decisions on how many students from each tract to assign to each school. Therefore the decision variables chosen for the model are

$$x_{ij} = \text{number of students in tract } i \text{ assigned to school } j \ (i = 1,2,\ldots,10; j = 1,2,3).$$

Rather than breaking down further these variables into the number of white students and the number of black students assigned, the simplifying assumption is made that the racial mixture in each tract will be maintained in the assignments to the respective schools. Using Table 4.8, the resulting formulation of the model is

$$\text{Minimize} \quad Z = 1.2x_{11} + 1.5x_{12} + \cdots + 1.0x_{10,3},$$

subject to the following constraints:

1. *Tract assignment*:

$$x_{11} + x_{12} + x_{13} = 450$$
$$x_{21} + x_{22} + x_{23} = 400$$
$$\vdots$$
$$x_{10,1} + x_{10,2} + x_{10,3} = 450$$

2. *School capacity*:

$$x_{11} + x_{21} + \cdots + x_{10,1} \leq 1{,}500$$
$$x_{12} + x_{22} + \cdots + x_{10,2} \leq 2{,}000$$
$$x_{13} + x_{23} + \cdots + x_{10,3} \leq 1{,}300$$

3. *Nonnegativity*:

$$x_{ij} \geq 0, \text{ for } i = 1, 2, \ldots, 10 \text{ and } j = 1, 2, 3$$

and

4. *Racial balance*:

Still to be developed.

The racial balance constraints need to specify that the fraction of students of a given race in a given school must fall within certain limits. After discussing the issue with the school board, it is decided that the same limits should apply to all the schools and that these limits should be symmetrical with respect to the races. Thus, for each school and either race, the fraction of students should fall within the limits

$$\frac{1}{2} - \theta \leq \text{fraction} \leq \frac{1}{2} + \theta,$$

so that θ represents the maximum allowable deviation from an equal distribution of races in a school. However, the school board does not wish to specify a value for θ at this point until they can see the consequences of their decision in terms of the distances that the students must travel. (Remember that they want to achieve a reasonable tradeoff between these two considerations.) Therefore the consultants conclude that they should use *parametric programming* (see Sec. 4.3) to determine how the optimal solution changes over the entire range of possible values of θ ($0 \leq \theta \leq \frac{1}{2}$).

To express the racial balance constraints mathematically, it is necessary to first express the fraction of students of each race in each school in terms of the decision variables. For example,

Fraction of white students in school 1

$$= \frac{(300/450)x_{11} + (400/400)x_{21} + \cdots + (350/450)x_{10,1}}{x_{11} + x_{21} + \cdots + x_{10,1}}$$

where each coefficient in the numerator is simply the number of white students in that tract (see Table 4.8) divided by the total number of students in that tract. Thus the lower limit constraint on this fraction is

$$L \leq \frac{(2/3)x_{11} + x_{21} + \cdots + (7/9)x_{10,1}}{x_{11} + x_{21} + \cdots + x_{10,1}},$$

where

$$L \equiv \frac{1}{2} - \theta.$$

Since constraints in this form would require the use of less efficient *nonlinear* programming algorithms, the consultants next convert these constraints into an equivalent form that fits the *linear* programming format. This is done by multiplying both sides by the denominator of the right-hand side to obtain

$$L(x_{11} + x_{21} + \cdots + x_{10,1}) \leq \frac{2}{3}x_{11} + x_{21} + \cdots + \frac{7}{9}x_{10,1},$$

and then subtracting this right-hand side from both sides to obtain

$$\left(L - \frac{2}{3}\right)x_{11} + (L-1)x_{21} + \cdots + \left(L - \frac{7}{9}\right)x_{10,1} \leq 0.$$

This same approach is used to develop the lower limit constraints for all six fractions, as summarized below:

4. *Racial balance*:

$$\left(L - \frac{2}{3}\right)x_{11} + (L-1)x_{21} + \cdots + \left(L - \frac{7}{9}\right)x_{10,1} \leq 0$$

$$\left(L - \frac{1}{3}\right)x_{11} + (L-0)x_{21} + \cdots + \left(L - \frac{2}{9}\right)x_{10,1} \leq 0$$

$$\left(L - \frac{2}{3}\right)x_{12} + (L-1)x_{22} + \cdots + \left(L - \frac{7}{9}\right)x_{10,2} \leq 0$$

$$\left(L - \frac{1}{3}\right)x_{12} + (L-0)x_{22} + \cdots + \left(L - \frac{2}{9}\right)x_{10,2} \leq 0$$

$$\left(L - \frac{2}{3}\right)x_{13} + (L-1)x_{23} + \cdots + \left(L - \frac{7}{9}\right)x_{10,3} \leq 0$$

$$\left(L - \frac{1}{3}\right)x_{13} + (L-0)x_{23} + \cdots + \left(L - \frac{2}{9}\right)x_{10,3} \leq 0.$$

This approach also could be used to develop the corresponding upper limit constraints representing the requirement that each fraction $\leq \frac{1}{2} + \theta$. However, since

Fraction of white students = 1 − fraction of black students,

the above lower limit constraints on both types of fractions *guarantee* that the upper limit requirements are satisfied also. Therefore no additional constraints are needed for the model.

One flaw in this formulation is that the x_{ij} (as well as the corresponding numbers of white students and black students from tract i assigned to school j) are allowed to take on *noninteger* values (the *divisibility* assumption of linear programming). However, considering the large numbers of students involved, the consultants feel that there will be no difficulty in adjusting a noninteger optimal solution to integer values during the subsequent analysis. They know from experience that a linear programming formulation has major computational advantages over an *integer* linear programming formulation, so this approximation seems well worthwhile.

The stage now is set to begin the computational phase of the study. When L is sufficiently small (that is, θ sufficiently close to ½), the racial balance constraints have no effect and can be deleted. The consultants also note that the problem without these constraints can be formulated as a *transportation problem* (a special class of linear programming problems described in Sec. 3.1), as shown in Fig. 4.3. Therefore, rather than using the simplex method, they begin by applying the much more efficient *transportation simplex method* (see Sec. 3.2) to this formulation. The resulting optimal solution has basic variables $x_{11} = 450$, $x_{21} = 400$, $x_{31} = 500$, $x_{42} = 500$, $x_{52} = 400$, $x_{62} = 450$, $x_{71} = 150$, $x_{72} = 300$, $x_{83} = 500$, $x_{92} = 50$, $x_{93} = 350$, $x_{10,3} = 450$, $x_{11,2} = 300$, with $Z = 4{,}965$. (Notice that this solution already is integer, which always occurs with transportation problems having integer supplies and demands.)

The next step is to determine when this solution also is optimal for the original model with the racial balance constraints included. This is done by checking how large L can be made before the solution violates any of the racial balance constraints, which turns out to be $L \leq 0.285$. Since the solution is feasible for this range of values of L, it must also be optimal for these values.

Given this information, the consultants next use parametric programming to determine how the optimal solution changes as L is increased continuously to ½, beginning with the above solution at $L = 0.285$. (This can be thought of as applying the sensitivity analysis procedure described in Sec. 4.3 on a continuing basis to determine the effect of introducing the racial balance constraints as needed and of changing the coefficients of the variables in these constraints.) However, they feel that the results in this form would be too complex to be considered effectively by the school board. Therefore, after a careful examination of the results, the consultants select a relatively small number of interesting

Figure 4.3 Cost and requirements table for transportation problem formulation of Middletown problem without racial balance constraints.

		Distance per Student			
		Destination			
		School 1	*School 2*	*School 3*	*Supply*
Source	Tract 1	1.2	1.5	3.3	450
	2	2.6	4.0	5.5	400
	3	0.7	1.1	2.8	500
	4	1.8	1.3	2.0	500
	5	1.5	0.4	2.3	400
	6	2.0	0.6	1.7	450
	7	1.2	1.4	3.1	450
	8	3.5	2.3	1.2	500
	9	3.2	1.2	0.7	400
	10	3.8	1.8	1.0	450
	Dummy 11(*D*)	0	0	0	300
Demand		1,500	2,000	1,300	

alternatives—$L = 0.285, 0.30, 0.35, 0.40$—that represent a cross section of trade-offs between racial balance and distance traveled (as summarized in Table 4.9).

Table 4.9 Summary of Results for Middletown Problem

θ	*Optimal Z*	*Average distance traveled (miles)*	*Percentage* < 1 mile	1.0–1.4 miles	1.5–1.9 miles	≥ 2 miles
0.215	4965	1.103	37.8	53.3	0	8.9
0.20	4983	1.107	38.9	51.1	1.1	8.9
0.15	5063	1.125	38.9	41.1	11.1	8.9
0.10	5182	1.152	38.9	36.1	16.1	8.9

These alternatives are analyzed in detail and appropriate refinements made in the "optimal solutions" obtained from the model. The consultants then present their basic data and conclusions for the four alternatives to the school board.

After considerable deliberation, the school board chooses the $\theta = 0.15$ alternative. However, they modify this alternative slightly to avoid reassigning a very small proportion of one tract to a new school. The resulting master plan allocates tracts 2, 3, and 7 to school 1, tracts 1, 4, 5, and 6 to school 2, and tracts 8 and 9 to school 3, with tract 10 split as follows: $x_{10,2} = 50$, $x_{10,3} = 400$. Since this yields $\theta = 0.155$, the school board officially announces the new policy as being that either race should form at least one-third the student body of any high school. They then instruct the superintendent to have her staff implement this policy, using the master plan as a basis for detailed planning.

4.5 CONCLUSIONS

This chapter has discussed some particularly relevant topics for the practical application of linear programming. This is good background, but the best teacher in this area is experience! Our goal has been to provide you with a solid foundation for dealing with real problems and for *continuing* to learn the art of linear programming.

Linear programming often is used as a supplementary tool in other areas of operations research. You will see examples of this in Chaps. 5, 7, 12, 17, and 18. Chapter 16 presents some more advanced topics in linear programming, with particular emphasis on algorithms.

Selected References

1 Beale, E. M. L. (ed.): *Applications of Mathematical Programming Techniques*, American Elsevier, New York, 1970.

2 ———: *Mathematical Programming in Practice*, Wiley, New York, 1968.

3 Daellenbach, Hans G. and Earl G. Bell: *User's Guide to Linear Programming*, Prentice-Hall, Englewood Cliffs, N.J., 1970.

4 Driebeek, Norman J.: *Applied Linear Programming*, Addison-Wesley, Reading, Mass., 1969.

5 House, William C. (ed.): *Operations Research—An Introduction to Modern Applications*, Auerbach, Princeton, N.J., 1972.
6 Orchard-Hays, William: *Advanced Linear-Programming Computing Techniques*, McGraw-Hill, New York, 1968.

Problems

1 A company desires to blend a new alloy of 30 percent lead, 20 percent zinc, and 50 percent tin from several available alloys having the following properties:

Property \ Alloy	1	2	3	4	5
Percentage lead	30	10	50	10	50
Percentage zinc	60	20	20	10	10
Percentage tin	10	70	30	80	40
Cost ($/lb)	8.5	6.0	8.9	5.7	8.8

The objective is to determine the proportions of these alloys that should be blended to produce the new alloy at a minimum cost.

Formulate the linear programming model for this problem.

2 A farm family owns 100 acres of land and has $15,000 in funds available for investment. Its members can produce a total of 3,500 man-hours worth of labor during the winter months (mid-September to mid-May) and 4,000 man-hours during the summer. If any of these man-hours are not needed, younger members of the family will use them to work on a neighboring farm for $1.80/hour during the winter months and $2.10/hour during the summer.

Cash income may be obtained from three crops and two types of livestock: dairy cows and laying hens. No investment funds are needed for the crops. However, each cow will require an investment outlay of $400, and each hen will require $3.

Each cow will require 1.5 acres of land, 100 man-hours of work during the winter months, and another 50 man-hours during the summer. Each cow will produce a net annual cash income of $400 for the family. The corresponding figures for each hen are: no acreage, 0.6 man-hours during the winter, 0.3 more man-hours during the summer, and an annual net cash income of $2. The chicken house can accommodate a maximum of 3,000 hens, and the size of the barn limits the herd to a maximum of 32 cows.

Estimated man-hours and income per acre planted in each of the three crops are

	Soybeans	*Corn*	*Oats*
Winter man-hours	20	35	10
Summer man-hours	50	75	40
Net annual cash income ($)	175	300	120

The family wishes to determine how much acreage should be planted in each of the crops and how many cows and hens should be kept to maximize its net cash income. Formulate the linear programming model for this problem.

3 A cargo plane has three compartments for storing cargo: front, center, and back. These compartments have capacity limits on both *weight* and *space*, as summarized below:

Compartment	*Weight capacity (tons)*	*Space capacity (cu ft)*
Front	8	5,000
Center	12	7,000
Back	7	3,000

Furthermore, the weight of the cargo in the respective compartments must be the same proportion of that compartment's weight capacity to maintain the balance of the airplane.

The following four cargoes have been offered for shipment on an upcoming flight as space is available:

Cargo	*Weight (tons)*	*Volume (cu ft/ton)*	*Profit ($/ton)*
1	14	500	100
2	11	700	130
3	18	600	115
4	9	400	90

Any portion of each of these cargoes can be accepted. The objective is to determine how much (if any) of each cargo should be accepted and how to distribute each among the compartments to maximize the total profit for the flight.

Formulate the linear programming model for this problem.

4 A lumber company has three sources of wood and five markets to be supplied. The annual availability of wood at sources 1, 2, and 3 are 10, 20, and 15 million board feet, respectively. The amount that can be sold annually at markets 1, 2, 3, 4, and 5 are 7, 12, 9, 10, and 8 million board feet, respectively.

In the past the company has shipped the wood by train. However, because shipping costs have been increasing, the alternative of using ships to make some of the shipments is being investigated. This alternative would require the company to invest in some ships. Except for these investment costs, the shipping costs in thousands of dollars per million board feet by rail and by water (when feasible) would be the following for each route:

Source \ Market	*Unit cost by rail*					*Unit cost by ship*				
	1	2	3	4	5	1	2	3	4	5
1	24.1	28.5	17.7	22.0	26.3	12.2	14.8	9.5	···	14.0
2	27.4	30.8	23.6	19.5	22.4	14.4	17.2	10.9	9.3	12.2
3	23.5	26.4	25.0	24.2	18.5	···	13.2	14.3	12.5	10.4

The capital investment (in thousands of dollars) in ships required for each million board feet to be transported annually by ship along each route is given below.

Source \ Market	Investment for ships 1	2	3	4	5
1	110	121	95	...	114
2	117	127	108	100	106
3	...	113	110	107	96

Considering the expected useful life of the ships and the time value of money, the equivalent uniform annual cost of these investments is one-tenth the amount given in the table. The company is only able to raise $2,500,000 to invest in ships. The objective is to determine the overall shipping plan that minimizes the total equivalent uniform annual cost while meeting this investment budget and the sales demand at the markets.

Formulate the linear programming model for this problem.

5 An investor has money-making activities *A* and *B* available at the beginning of each of the next 5 years (call them years 1 to 5). Each dollar invested in *A* at the beginning of 1 year returns $1.30 (a profit of $0.30) 2 years later (in time for immediate reinvestment). Each dollar invested in *B* at the beginning of 1 year returns $1.50 3 years later.

In addition, money-making activities *C* and *D* will each be available at one time in the future. Each dollar invested in *C* at the beginning of year 2 returns $1.70 at the end of year 5. Each dollar invested in *D* at the beginning of year 5 returns $1.20 at the end of year 5.

The investor begins with $10,000. He wishes to know which investment plan maximizes the amount of money he can accumulate by the beginning of year 6. Formulate the linear programming model for this problem.

6 A company needs to lease warehouse storage space over the next 5 months. It is known just how much space will be required in each of these months. However, since these space requirements are quite different, it may be most economical to lease only the amount needed each month on a month-by-month basis. On the other hand, the additional cost for leasing space for additional months is much less than for the first month, so it may be less expensive to lease the maximum amount needed for the entire 5 months. Another option is the intermediate approach of changing the total amount of space leased (by adding a new lease and/or having an old lease expire) at least once but not every month.

The space requirement (in thousands of square feet) and the leasing costs (in hundreds of dollars) for the various leasing periods are

Month	Required space	Leasing period (months)	Cost ($) per 1,000 sq ft leased
1	15	1	280
2	10	2	450
3	20	3	600
4	5	4	730
5	25	5	840

Two or more leases for different periods can begin at the same time. The objective is to determine the leasing schedule that provides the required amounts of space at a minimum cost.

Formulate the linear programming model for this problem.

7 For the first formulation of the separable convex programming technique presented in Sec. 4.1, there is an *implied* restriction on each x_{jk} $(k > 1)$ that $x_{jk} = 0$ whenever $x_{j(k-1)} < u_{j(k-1)}$. Even though this restriction is not explicitly included in the model, show that it is automatically satisfied by any optimal solution for the model. (*Hint*: Assume that there exists an optimal solution that violates this restriction, and then contradict this assumption by showing that there exists a better feasible solution.)

8 For the *alternative* formulation of the separable convex programming technique, Sec. 4.1 describes an *implied* restriction on the w_{jk} variables. Show that this restriction is automatically satisfied by any optimal solution for the model. (See the hint for Prob. 7.)

9 A spaceship is being designed to take astronauts to Mars and back. This ship will have three compartments, each with its own independent life support system. The key element in each of these life support systems is a small *oxidizer* unit that triggers a chemical process for producing oxygen. However, these units can not be tested in advance, and only some succeed in triggering this chemical process. Therefore it is important to have several backup units for each system. Because of differing requirements for the three compartments, the units needed for each have somewhat different characteristics. A decision must now be made on just *how many* units to provide for each compartment, taking into account design limitations on the *total* amount of *space*, *weight*, and *cost* that can be allocated to these units for the entire ship. The following table summarizes these limitations as well as the characteristics of the individual units for each compartment:

Compartment	*Space (cu in.)*	*Weight (lb)*	*Cost ($)*	*Probability of failure*
1	30	10	15,000	0.30
2	40	15	17,000	0.40
3	20	8	13,000	0.20
Limitation	400	150	200,000	

If all the units fail in just one or two of the compartments, the astronauts can occupy the remaining compartment(s) and continue their space voyage but with some loss in the amount of scientific information that can be obtained. However, if all units fail in all three compartments, then the astronauts can still return the ship safely, but the whole voyage must be completely aborted at great expense. Therefore the objective is to *minimize the probability* of this occurring, subject to the above limitations and the further restriction that each compartment have a probability of no more than 0.05 that all its units fail.

Formulate the linear programming model for this problem. (*Hint*: Use logarithms.)

10 One measure of the "quality" of water in a river is its dissolved oxygen (D.O) concentration. This is partly because certain minimum concentration levels of D.O. are necessary to permit fish and other aquatic animals to survive. A large portion of the waste released into streams is organic material. This material is a source of nutrients for many organisms found in streams. In the process of utilizing the organic material, the organisms withdraw D.O. contained in the stream. Thus, the larger the amount of these wastes, the larger the biochemical oxygen demand (B.O.D.).

Consider the river system depicted below consisting of two tributaries leading into the main stream. The daily flow rate of water at cities 1 to 4 are respectively

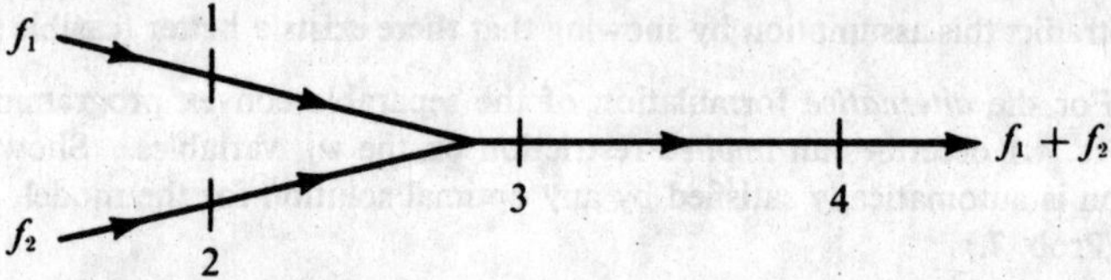

known to be $f_1, f_2, f_1+f_2, f_1+f_2$. Water at 1 or 2 requires 1 day to reach 3 and water at 3 requires 1 day to reach 4. Let D_i be the known D.O. concentration of the water just above city i ($i = 1,2$). Similarly, let B_i be the known waste concentration of the water, measured by its B.O.D. concentration, just above city i ($i = 1,2$). Wastes are discharged from cities 1 to 3 into the stream in known amounts w_1, w_2, w_3 per day. (These are negligible in comparison with f_1, f_2.)

If the waste discharged from city i ($i = 1,2,3$) is untreated, its B.O.D. concentration would be U_i. However, by using appropriate treatment processes, the B.O.D. concentration can be lowered to any level between L_i and U_i. The cost of reducing the B.O.D. concentration from U_i is c_i per unit reduction. However, some treatment is necessary at some or all of these cities to at least achieve a minimum standard S for the D.O. concentration at cities 3 and 4. The problem is to choose the B.O.D. concentration of wastes discharged from cities 1 to 3 that minimizes the cost of meeting this standard.

The following biochemical model has been developed to help solve problems of this type. Suppose that river water has a daily flow rate of f and a B.O.D. concentration of b and then has waste discharged at a rate of w per day with a B.O.D. concentration of x. The effect immediately down stream is to raise the B.O.D. concentration of the water to

$$v_0 = \frac{bf + xw}{f + w} \approx b + \left(\frac{w}{f}\right)x.$$

There is no immediate effect on the D.O. concentration. However, both the D.O. concentration and the B.O.D. concentration would change gradually down stream. In particular, if u_0 and v_0 are, respectively, the current D.O. and B.O.D. concentrations of the water at a particular location on a river, and no waste is added to this water, then the respective concentrations u_1, v_1 of D.O. and B.O.D. in this same water 1 day down stream becomes

$$u_1 = \alpha + \beta u_0 - \gamma v_0$$
$$v_1 = \delta + \varepsilon v_0,$$

where $\alpha, \beta, \gamma, \delta, \varepsilon$ are positive constants reflecting the various underlying physical and biochemical processes.

Formulate the linear programming model for this problem.

11 One of the most important problems in the field of *statistics* is the *linear regression problem.* Roughly speaking, this problem involves fitting a straight line to statistical data represented by points—(x_1, y_1), (x_2, y_2), ..., (x_n, y_n)—on a graph. Denoting the line by $y = a + bx$, the objective is to choose the constants a and b to provide the "best" fit according to some criterion. The criterion usually used is the *method of least squares*, but there are other interesting criteria where linear programming can be used to solve for the optimal values of a and b.

For each of the following criteria, formulate the linear programming model for this problem:

(*a*) Minimize the sum of the absolute deviations of the data from the line; that is,

$$\text{Minimize} \sum_{i=1}^{n} |y_i - (a + bx_i)|.$$

(*Hint*: Set $z_i = y_i - (a + bx_i)$, write a model with the z_i, a, and b as decision variables that are allowed to be negative, and then replace each of these variables by the difference of a pair of new nonnegative variables as described in Sec. 2.10.)

(*b*) Minimize the maximum absolute deviation of the data from the line; that is,

$$\text{Minimize} \quad \max_{i=1,2,\ldots,n} \quad |y_i - (a + bx_i)|.$$

12 A large paper manufacturing company has 10 paper mills and a large number (say, 1,000) customers to be supplied. It uses three alternative types of machines and four types of raw materials to make five different types of paper. Therefore the company needs to develop a detailed production-distribution plan on a monthly basis, with an objective of minimizing the total cost of producing and distributing the paper during the month. Specifically, it is necessary to jointly determine the amount of each type of paper to be made at each paper mill on each type of machine *and* the amount of each type of paper to be shipped from each paper mill to each customer.

The relevant data can be expressed symbolically as

D_{jk} = numbers of units of paper type k demanded by customer j,

r_{klm} = number of units of raw material m needed to produce one unit of paper type k on machine type l,

R_{im} = number of units of raw material m available at paper mill i,

c_{kl} = number of capacity units of machine type l that will produce one unit of paper type k,

C_{il} = number of capacity units of machine type l available at paper mill i,

P_{ikl} = production cost for each unit of paper type k produced on machine type l at paper mill i,

T_{ijk} = transportation cost for each unit of paper type k shipped from paper mill i to customer j.

(*a*) Using these symbols, formulate the linear programming model for this problem.

(*b*) Considering the special structure of this model, give your recommendation on how it should be solved.

(*c*) Since the model has over 5,000 functional constraints and over 150,000 variables, there are more than 750,000,000 coefficients for these constraints, which creates a storage problem for a computer solution of the model. Considering that over 99 percent of these coefficients are zeroes, give your recommendation on how to alleviate this problem.

(*d*) Since the number of *nonzero* coefficients is well over 100,000, even keypunching just this much input data for the model would be excessively time-consuming. Considering that the number of items of basic raw data is much smaller, give your recommendations on how to alleviate this problem.

13 A certain corporation is planning to produce and market three different products. Let x_1, x_2, and x_3 denote the number of units of the three respective products to be produced. The preliminary estimates of their potential profitability are as follows.

For the first 15 units produced of product 1, the unit profit would be approximately \$12. The unit profit would only be \$1 for any additional units of product 1. For the first 20 units produced of product 2, the unit profit is estimated at \$8. The unit profit would be \$4 for each of the next 20 units and \$3 for any additional units. For the first 10 units of product 3, the unit profit would be \$15. The unit profit would be \$10 for each of the next 5 units and \$6 for any additional units.

Certain limitations on the use of needed resources impose the following constraints on the production of the three products:

$$\begin{aligned} x_1 + x_2 + x_3 &\leq 60 \\ 3x_1 + 2x_2 &\leq 200 \\ x_1 + 2x_3 &\leq 70. \end{aligned}$$

Management wants to know what values of x_1, x_2, and x_3 should be chosen to maximize total profit.

(*a*) Use the first kind of separable convex programming formulation presented in Sec. 4.1 to formulate a linear programming model for this problem.

(*b*) Use the alternative formulation for the separable convex programming technique to formulate a linear programming model for this problem.

(*c*) Use a computer code of the simplex method to solve each of these models. In both cases, verify that the optimal solution satisfies the *implied* restriction for the model. Also verify that both optimal solutions correspond to the *same* solution for the original variables (x_1, x_2, x_3).

14 A certain company has received a contract from the government to supply three units of a product at the end of each of the next three time periods. Production data are

Period	*Maximum production, regular time*	*Maximum production, overtime*	*Production cost (\$) per unit, regular time*
1	2	3	50,000
2	4	2	60,000
3	1	3	55,000

The production cost per unit on overtime for each period is $7,000 more than on regular time. The cost of storage is $4,000 per unit for each extra period it is stored. There is already an inventory of two units on hand currently, and it is desired to retain one unit in inventory after the three time periods.

Management wishes to know how many units should be produced in each period to maximize profit. However, they also have imposed the restriction that overtime can not be used in any particular period unless regular time in that period is completely used up.

Without explicitly including management's restriction on the use of overtime, formulate this problem as a *transportation problem* by constructing the appropriate cost and requirements table. Explain why the logic of separable convex programming implies that this restriction will be satisfied automatically by any optimal solution for this transportation problem.

15 Consider the problem

$$\text{Maximize} \quad \{4x_1 + 6x_2 - x_1^3 - 2x_2^2\},$$

subject to

$$x_1 + 3x_2 \leq 8$$

$$5x_1 + 2x_2 \leq 14$$

and

$$x_1 \geq 0, x_2 \geq 0.$$

Treat this problem as a separable convex programming problem by formulating an *approximate* mathematical model that could be solved by the simplex method. Use the integers as the breakpoints of the piecewise linear functions.

(*a*) Use the first kind of separable convex programming formulation presented in Sec. 4.1.

(*b*) Use the alternative formulation for the separable convex programming technique.

(*c*) Use a computer code of the simplex method to solve each of these approximate models. In both cases verify that the optimal solution satisfies the *implied* restriction for the model. Also verify that both optimal solutions correspond to the *same* solution for the original variables (x_1, x_2). Compare this solution with the exact optimal solution for the original problem

$$(x_1, x_2) = \left(\frac{2}{\sqrt{3}}, \frac{3}{2}\right).$$

16 For each of the following linear programming models, give your recommendation on the most efficient way (probably) for obtaining an optimal solution (assuming the appropriate computer code is available). Explain.

(*a*) Maximize $Z = 10x_1 - 4x_2 + 7x_3$, subject to

$$3x_1 - x_2 + 2x_3 \leq 25$$

$$x_1 - 2x_2 + 3x_3 \leq 25$$

$$5x_1 + x_2 + 2x_3 \leq 40$$

$$x_1 + x_2 + x_3 \leq 90$$

$$2x_1 - x_2 + x_3 \leq 20$$

and

$$x_1 \geq 0, x_2 \geq 0, x_3 \geq 0.$$

(*b*) Maximize $Z = 2x_1 + 5x_2 + 3x_3 + 4x_4 + x_5$, subject to

$$x_1 + 3x_2 + 2x_3 + 3x_4 + x_5 \leq 6$$
$$4x_1 + 6x_2 + 5x_3 + 7x_4 + x_5 \leq 15$$

and

$$0 \leq x_j \leq 1, \text{ for } j = 1, 2, 3, 4, 5.$$

17 In the progressive country of Futureland, the government is taking firm action to control air pollution. Since this is a capitalistic country, it is using the tax structure rather than edict to induce industry to do what is best for society as a whole by doing what is economically best for them. Thus the government is imposing a progressive tax on the emission of pollutants of various types, where the rates are based on the cost of the damage caused to society by the pollution.

One of the cities in Futureland is *Steeltown*, which is the home of the *Nori & Leets Co.* discussed in Sec. 2.4. This company has already implemented the program of pollution abatement described in Sec. 2.4. However, they now are considering reducing their pollution emission further (by *increasing* some of the x_j in their linear programming model that are not yet at the upper bound of 1) to save taxes. The incremental rate of tax savings (in dollars per pound reduction in emission) when the additional reduction in the emission rate (in million pounds per year) is in various intervals is

Pollutant	*0–25*	*25–50*	*≥50*
Particulates	0.12	0.10	0.08
Sulfur oxides	0.17	0.13	0.09
Hydrocarbons	0.09	0.05	0.01

All the other data given in Sec. 2.4 still apply. The company's objective at this point would be to determine just how much to increase each of their abatement methods (decreases are not allowed) to maximize their *net* savings (i.e., their tax savings minus the additional abatement cost).

(*a*) Use separable convex programming (with the first type of formulation discussed) to formulate a linear programming model for this problem.
(*b*) Use a computer code of the simplex method (preferably with the upper bound technique) to solve this problem.
(*c*) Conduct sensitivity analysis from the viewpoint of the government to determine the effect on emission reductions from this company if each tax rate given in the table was individually increased by 0.01.
(*d*) Continue this sensitivity analysis to investigate the effect if government-sponsored research could provide this company with the technology to extend the maximum feasible use of each abatement method individually by 10 percent (so that the only change in the model of Sec. 2.4 is that two x_j variables have their upper bounds increased from 1 to 1.1).

18 Consider the problem

$$\text{Maximize} \quad Z = -5x_1 + 5x_2 + 13x_3,$$

subject to

$$-x_1 + x_2 + 3x_3 \le 20$$
$$12x_1 + 4x_2 + 10x_3 \le 90$$

and

$$x_j \ge 0 \ (j = 1,2,3).$$

Letting x_4 and x_5 be the slack variables for the respective constraints, the simplex method yields the following *final* set of equations:

$$
\begin{array}{llr}
(0) & Z \quad\quad + 2x_3 + 5x_4 & = 100. \\
(1) & -x_1 + x_2 + 3x_3 + x_4 & = 20. \\
(2) & 16x_1 \quad - 2x_3 - 4x_4 + x_5 & = 10.
\end{array}
$$

You are now to conduct sensitivity analysis by *independently* investigating each of the nine changes in the original model indicated below. For each change, use the sensitivity analysis procedure to convert this set of equations (in tableau form) to the proper form for identifying and evaluating the current basic solution, and then test this solution for feasibility and for optimality.

(*a*) Change the right-hand side of constraint 1 to $b_1 = 30$.

(*b*) Change the right-hand side of constraint 2 to $b_2 = 70$.

(*c*) Change the right-hand sides to $\begin{bmatrix} b_1 \\ b_2 \end{bmatrix} = \begin{bmatrix} 10 \\ 100 \end{bmatrix}$.

(*d*) Change the coefficient of x_3 in the objective function to $c_3 = 8$.

(*e*) Change the coefficients of x_1 to $\begin{bmatrix} c_1 \\ a_{11} \\ a_{21} \end{bmatrix} = \begin{bmatrix} -2 \\ 0 \\ 5 \end{bmatrix}$.

(*f*) Change the coefficients of x_2 to $\begin{bmatrix} c_2 \\ a_{12} \\ a_{22} \end{bmatrix} = \begin{bmatrix} 6 \\ 2 \\ 5 \end{bmatrix}$.

(*g*) Introduce a new variable x_6 with coefficients $\begin{bmatrix} c_6 \\ a_{16} \\ a_{26} \end{bmatrix} = \begin{bmatrix} 10 \\ 3 \\ 5 \end{bmatrix}$

(*h*) Introduce a new constraint $2x_1 + 3x_2 + 5x_3 \le 50$. (Denote its slack variable by x_6.)

(*i*) Change constraint 2 to $10x_1 + 5x_2 + 10x_3 \le 100$.

19 Consider the problem

$$\text{Maximize} \quad Z = 2x_1 + 7x_2 - 3x_3,$$

subject to

$$x_1 + 3x_2 + 4x_3 \le 30$$
$$x_1 + 4x_2 - x_3 \le 10$$

and

$$x_1 \ge 0, x_2 \ge 0, x_3 \ge 0.$$

Letting x_4 and x_5 be the slack variables for the respective constraints, the simplex method yields the following *final* set of equations:

$$
\begin{array}{llr}
(0) & Z \quad + x_2 + x_3 \qquad + 2x_5 = 20. \\
(1) & \quad - x_2 + 5x_3 + x_4 - x_5 = 20. \\
(2) & x_1 + 4x_2 - x_3 \qquad + x_5 = 10.
\end{array}
$$

You are now to conduct sensitivity analysis by *independently* investigating each of the seven changes in the original model indicated below. For each change, use the sensitivity analysis procedure to convert this set of equations (in tableau form) to the proper form for identifying and evaluating the current basic solution, and then test this solution for feasibility and for optimality.

(*a*) Change the right-hand sides to $\begin{bmatrix} b_1 \\ b_2 \end{bmatrix} = \begin{bmatrix} 10 \\ 20 \end{bmatrix}$.

(*b*) Change the coefficients of x_3 to $\begin{bmatrix} c_3 \\ a_{13} \\ a_{23} \end{bmatrix} = \begin{bmatrix} -2 \\ 3 \\ -2 \end{bmatrix}$.

(*c*) Change the coefficients of x_1 to $\begin{bmatrix} c_1 \\ a_{11} \\ a_{21} \end{bmatrix} = \begin{bmatrix} 4 \\ 3 \\ 2 \end{bmatrix}$.

(*d*) Introduce a new variable x_6 with coefficients $\begin{bmatrix} c_6 \\ a_{16} \\ a_{26} \end{bmatrix} = \begin{bmatrix} 3 \\ 1 \\ 2 \end{bmatrix}$.

(*e*) Change the objective function to $Z = x_1 + 5x_2 - 2x_3$.

(*f*) Introduce a new constraint $3x_1 + 2x_2 + 3x_3 \leq 25$. (Denote its slack variable by x_6.)

(*g*) Change constraint 2 to $x_1 + 2x_2 + 2x_3 \leq 40$.

20 Consider the problem

$$\text{Maximize} \quad Z = 2x_1 - x_2 + x_3,$$

subject to

$$
\begin{aligned}
3x_1 - 2x_2 + 2x_3 &\leq 15 \\
-x_1 + x_2 + x_3 &\leq 3 \\
x_1 - x_2 + x_3 &\leq 4
\end{aligned}
$$

and

$$x_1 \geq 0, x_2 \geq 0, x_3 \geq 0.$$

Letting x_4, x_5, and x_6 be the slack variables for the respective constraints, the simplex method yields the following *final* set of equations:

$$
\begin{array}{ll}
(0) & Z \qquad 2x_3 + x_4 + x_5 \qquad = 18. \\
(1) & \quad x_2 + 5x_3 + x_4 + 3x_5 \qquad = 24. \\
(2) & \qquad 2x_3 \qquad + x_5 + x_6 = 7. \\
(3) & x_1 \qquad + 4x_3 + x_4 + 2x_5 \qquad = 21.
\end{array}
$$

You are now to conduct sensitivity analysis by *independently* investigating each of the eight changes in the original model indicated below. For each change, use the sensitivity analysis procedure to convert this set of equations (in tableau form) to the proper form for identifying and evaluating the current basic solution, and then test this solution for feasibility and for optimality.

(*a*) Change the right-hand sides to $\begin{bmatrix} b_1 \\ b_2 \\ b_3 \end{bmatrix} = \begin{bmatrix} 20 \\ 4 \\ 2 \end{bmatrix}$.

(*b*) Change the coefficient of x_3 in the objective function to $c_3 = 2$.

(*c*) Change the coefficient of x_1 in the objective function to $c_1 = 3$.

(*d*) Change coefficients of x_3 to $\begin{bmatrix} c_3 \\ a_{13} \\ a_{23} \\ a_{33} \end{bmatrix} = \begin{bmatrix} 4 \\ 3 \\ 2 \\ 1 \end{bmatrix}$.

(*e*) Change coefficients of x_1 *and* x_2 to

$$\begin{bmatrix} c_1 \\ a_{11} \\ a_{21} \\ a_{31} \end{bmatrix} = \begin{bmatrix} 1 \\ 1 \\ -2 \\ 3 \end{bmatrix} \text{ and } \begin{bmatrix} c_2 \\ a_{12} \\ a_{22} \\ a_{23} \end{bmatrix} = \begin{bmatrix} -2 \\ -1 \\ 3 \\ 2 \end{bmatrix}, \text{ respectively.}$$

(*f*) Change the objective function to $Z = 5x_1 + x_2 + 3x_3$.

(*g*) Change constraint 1 to $2x_1 - x_2 + 4x_3 \leq 12$.

(*h*) Introduce a new constraint $2x_1 + x_2 + 2x_3 \leq 60$. (Denote its slack variable by x_7.)

21 Reconsider part (*d*) of Prob. 20. Use duality theory directly to determine if the original optimal solution is still optimal.

22 Consider the transportation problem formulation and solution of the Metro Water District problem presented in Secs. 3.1 and 3.2 (see Fig. 3.9 and Table 3.13). Adapt the sensitivity analysis procedure presented in Sec. 4.3 to conduct sensitivity analysis on this problem by *independently* investigating each of the four changes in the original model indicated below. For each change, convert (if necessary) the final transportation simplex tableau to the proper form for identifying and evaluating the current basic solution, and then test this solution for feasibility and for optimality.

(*a*) Change c_{34} from 23 to $c_{34} = 21$.

(*b*) Change c_{23} from 13 to $c_{23} = 15$.

(*c*) Decrease the supply from source 2 to 40 and decrease the demand at destination 5 to 40.

(*d*) Increase the supply at source 2 to 70 and increase the demand at destination 2 to 30.

5 Network Analysis, Including PERT-CPM

Network analysis has long played an important role in electrical engineering. However, there has been a growing awareness that certain concepts and tools of network theory are also very useful in many other contexts as well. For example, important applications of network analysis have been made in *information theory*, *cybernetics*, the study of *transportation systems*, and the planning and control of *research and development projects*. Other application areas include social-group structures, communication systems, production schedules, chemical-bond structures, and language structures. As a result, certain aspects of network analysis (commonly called *network flow theory*) are becoming an increasingly useful tool of operations research.

One basic problem of network theory that commonly arises in the study of transportation systems is finding the *shortest route* through a network. A similar problem is to choose a set of connections that provide a route between any two points of a network in such a way as to *minimize the total length of these connections*. Another fundamental problem involves allocating flows to *maximize the flow* through a network connecting a source and a destination. *Project planning and control* is a fourth problem area that has been attacked by network techniques, especially PERT (Program Evaluation and Review Technique) and CPM (Critical Path Method).

The first section introduces a prototype example that will be used subsequently to illustrate the approach to the first three of these problems. Section 5.2 presents some basic terminology for networks. The remainder of the chapter is then devoted to the four problems.

5.1 PROTOTYPE EXAMPLE

Seervada Park is a wilderness area that has recently been set aside for a limited amount of backpack hiking. Cars are not allowed into the park, but there is a narrow road system for trams and jeeps driven by the park rangers. This road system is shown (without the curves) in Fig. 5.1, where location O is the entrance into the park; other letters designate the location of ranger stations (and other limited facilities). The numbers give the distances of these winding roads in miles.

The long cross-country hike to another area begins at station T. A small number of trams are used to transport cross-country hikers from the park entrance to station T.

The park management currently is facing three problems. One is to determine which route from the park entrance to station T has the *smallest total distance* for the operation of the trams. (This is an example of the *shortest route problem* discussed in Sec. 5.3.)

A second problem is that telephone lines must be installed under the roads to establish telephone communication between all the stations (including the park entrance). Since the installation is both expensive and disturbing to the natural environment, lines will be installed under just enough roads to provide some connection between every pair of stations. The question is where the lines should be laid to accomplish this with a *minimum* total number of miles of line installed. (This is an example of the *minimal spanning tree problem* discussed in Sec. 5.4.)

The third problem is that more people desire the tram ride from the park entrance to station T than can be accommodated during the peak season. To avoid unduly disturbing the ecology and wildlife of the region, a strict ration has been placed on the number of loaded tram trips that can be made on each of the roads per day. (These limits differ for the different roads, as we shall describe in detail in Sec. 5.5.) Therefore, during the peak season, various

Figure 5.1 The road system for Seervada Park.

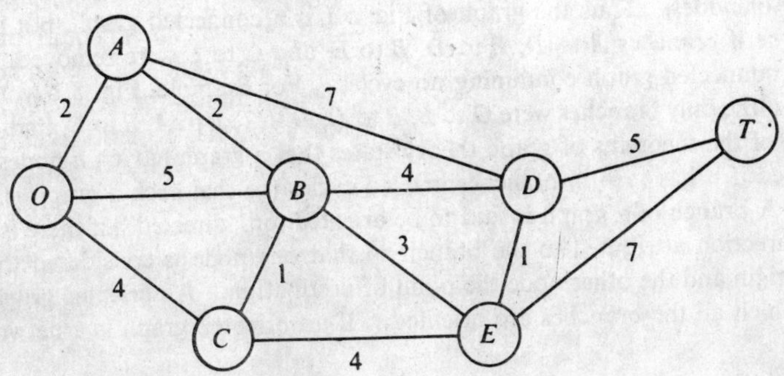

routes might be followed regardless of distance to increase the number of tram trips that can be made each day. The question is how to route the various trips to *maximize* the number of trips that can be made per day without violating the limits on any individual road. (This is an example of the *maximal flow problem* discussed in Sec. 5.5.)

You will see later in the chapter how each of these problems is solved.

5.2 THE TERMINOLOGY OF NETWORKS

According to the terminology of the *theory of graphs*, a **graph** consists of a set of junction points called **nodes**, with certain pairs of the nodes being joined by lines called **branches** (or "arcs," "links," or "edges"). Thus, Fig. 5.1 is an example of a graph, where the circles designating stations are the nodes and the roads connecting them are the branches. A **network** is considered to be a graph with a flow of some type in its branches. There are numerous examples of systems satisfying this definition of network, as suggested by Table 5.1.

Table 5.1 Components of Typical Networks

Nodes	*Branches*	*Flow*
Intersections	Roads	Vehicles
Airports	Air lanes	Aircraft
Switching points	Wires, channels	Messages
Pumping stations	Pipes	Fluid
Work centers	Materials-handling routes	Jobs

Additional terminology has been developed to describe graphs. A **chain** between nodes i and j is a sequence of branches connecting these two nodes. For example, one of the chains connecting nodes O and T in Fig. 5.1 is the sequence of branches O to B, B to D, D to T, or vice versa. When the direction of travel along the chain is also specified, it will be called a **path**. A **cycle** is a chain connecting a node to itself. Thus, A to D, D to B, and B to A form a cycle in Fig. 5.1.

A graph is said to be a **connected graph** if there is a chain connecting every pair of nodes. Thus the graph of Fig. 5.1 is a connected graph, but it would not be if branches A to D, B to D, B to E, and C to E were removed. A **tree** is a connected graph containing no cycles. For example, Fig. 5.1 would be a tree if the only branches were O to B, B to D, D to T, B to A, B to C, and D to E. One of the theorems of graph theory states that a graph having n nodes is connected if it has $(n - 1)$ branches and no cycles (so that such a graph is a tree).

A branch of a graph is said to be **oriented** (or "directed") if there is a sense of direction attributed to the branch so that one node is considered the point of origin and the other node the point of destination. An **oriented graph** is one in which all the branches are oriented. If an oriented graph is a network, the orientation of a branch is assumed to be the feasible direction of flow along the branch. However, a network need not be oriented because it may be feasible to have flow in either direction along a branch. The **flow capacity** of a branch in a specified direction is the upper limit to the feasible magnitude of the rate of flow (or total quantity of flow) in the branch in that direction. The flow capacity may be any nonnegative quantity, including infinity. A branch is oriented if the flow capacity is zero in one direction. A node may also have a limited flow capacity—although that possibility will be ignored here.

A node in a network is sometimes referred to as a **source** if every one of its branches has an orientation such that the flow moves away from that node. Similarly, it is sometimes called a **sink** if each of its branches is oriented toward that node. Thus sources may be thought of as the generators of the flow and sinks as the absorbers of that flow.

5.3 THE SHORTEST-ROUTE PROBLEM

The shortest-route problem is concerned with finding the *shortest route from an origin to a destination through a connecting network*, given the nonnegative distance associated with the respective branches of the network. Although various similar solution procedures have been proposed, the version to be described here is perhaps the shortest and simplest. The essence of this procedure is that it fans out from the origin, successively identifying the shortest route to each of the nodes of the network in the ascending order of their (shortest) distances from the origin, thereby solving the problem when the destination node is reached. We shall first develop the method and then illustrate it by solving the shortest route problem encountered by the *Seervada Park* management in Sec. 5.1.

Suppose that for a certain value of $n (n = 1, 2, \ldots)$ it is known which $(n - 1)$ nodes (excluding the origin) are nearest the origin along the shortest connecting chain, as well as the corresponding (shortest) routes and distances. [These $(n - 1)$ nodes plus the origin node will be referred to as the *original* nodes. All other nodes will be referred to as *new* nodes.] Given this information, how does one identify the node that has the nth smallest distance to the origin along its shortest route, i.e., *which of the new nodes is closest to the origin*? To qualify as a candidate, a new node must be connected by a branch to one of the original nodes. (Otherwise, the intervening new node would be closer to the origin.) Furthermore, it must be the *closest new node to one of the original nodes* to which it is connected by a single branch. (Otherwise, whichever route were taken to the origin, there would always be another new node that would have a head start.) Thus, since there are n original nodes, there are, at most, *n candidates* for the new node that is closest to the origin. To select the winning candidate, proceed as follows. *For each of the original nodes* connected by a branch to a new node, *compute the sum* of (1) the known (shortest) distance from the origin to that node and (2) the distance from that node to the nearest new node along a single branch. Each sum must be the distance along the corresponding route from the origin to this new node. Therefore the new node corresponding to the *smallest sum* must be the new node that is closest to the origin. Furthermore, its shortest route must be the route whose distance yielded this smallest sum.

Therefore, to find the shortest route from origin to destination, just repeat the above process of finding the *n*th nearest node to the origin successively for $n = 1, 2, 3$, and so on until the destination node is reached. This procedure is illustrated below.

Example

The *Seervada Park* management needs to find the shortest route from the park entrance (node *O*) to the embarkation point for cross-country hikes (node *T*) through their road system shown in Fig. 5.1. To begin, construct a list for each node of the branches leading out of that node in the order of the ascending branch distances. (It is not necessary to include branches *into* the origin node *O* or *out* of the destination node *T*.) Also record the branch distances.

(O)	(A)	(B)	(C)	(D)	(E)	(T)
OA-2	*AB*-2	*BC*-1	*CB*-1	*DE*-1	*ED*-1	
OC-4	*AD*-7	*BA*-2	*CE*-4	*DB*-4	*EB*-3	
OB-5		*BE*-3		*DT*-5	*EC*-4	
		BD-4		*DA*-7	*ET*-7	

$n = 1$ Since the origin is the only "original" node initially, only the *O* column needs to be considered at this point. Hence node *A* is immediately identified as the nearest node to the origin. To indicate this, circle the *OA*-2 entry. To prepare for the next iteration, write the distance to node *A* above the *A* column, and cross out branches leading into *A* in all columns in which they appear. The lists should now look like

	2					
(O)	(A)	(B)	(C)	(D)	(E)	(T)
(*OA*-2)	*AB*-2	*BC*-1	*CB*-1	*DE*-1	*ED*-1	
OC-4	*AD*-7	~~*BA*-2~~	*CE*-4	*DB*-4	*EB*-3	
OB-5		*BE*-3		*DT*-5	*EC*-4	
		BD-4		~~*DA*-7~~	*ET*-7	

$n = 2$ The candidates for the second nearest node to the origin are those *new* nodes nearest nodes *O* and *A*, namely, nodes *C* and *B*, respectively. Comparing their distances yields $(0 + 4) = 4$ for node *C* and $(2 + 2) = 4$ for node *B*. Since these distances are equal, nodes *C* and *B* are *tied* for being the *second closest* node to the origin. Therefore, circle both *OC*-4 and *AB*-2, write 4 above the *C* and *B* columns, and cross out all branches leading into either *C* or *B*. Since this exhausts the *O* column of new nodes, place an *X* above the branches to indicate that this column can be ignored henceforth. The resulting lists are

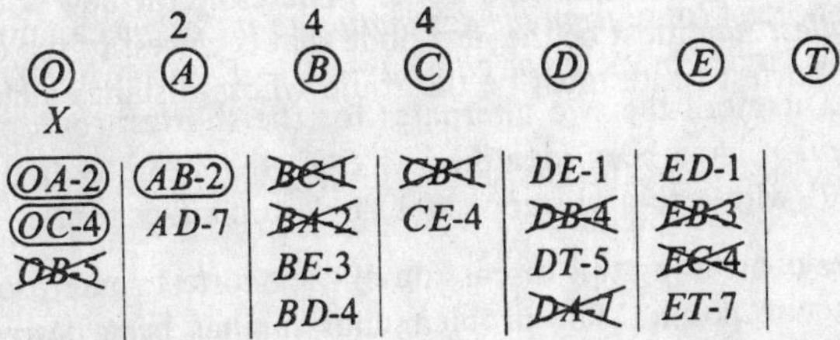

O	A	B	C	D	E	T
	2	4	4			
X						
(OA-2)	(AB-2)	~~BC-1~~	~~CB-1~~	DE-1	ED-1	
(OC-4)	AD-7	~~BA-2~~	CE-4	~~DB-4~~	~~EB-3~~	
~~OB-5~~		BE-3		DT-5	~~EC-4~~	
		BD-4		~~DA-7~~	ET-7	

$n = 4$ Since the *original* nodes at this point are O, A, B, and C (with O eliminated from further consideration), the candidates for the *fourth* nearest node to the origin are D (the *new* node nearest A) and E (nearest both B and C). The distances are $(2 + 7) = 9$ for node D via node A, $(4 + 3) = 7$ for node E via node B, and $(4 + 4) = 8$ for node E via node C. Therefore, node E (via node B) is the *fourth* nearest node, so circle BE-3, write 7 above the E column, and cross out all branches leading into E (which eliminates the C column from further consideration). This results in the following lists:

O	A	B	C	D	E	T
	2	4	4		7	
X			X			
(OA-2)	(AB-2)	~~BC-1~~	~~CB-1~~	~~DE-1~~	ED-1	
(OC-4)	AD-7	~~BA-2~~	~~CE-4~~	~~DB-4~~	~~EB-3~~	
~~OB-5~~		(BE-3)		DT-5	~~EC-4~~	
		BD-4		~~DA-7~~	ET-7	

$n = 5$ Compare $AD(2 + 7)$, $BD(4 + 4)$, and $ED(7 + 1)$, which identifies node D (via *either* B or E) as the *fifth* nearest node to the origin. Updating the lists accordingly yields

O	A	B	C	D	E	T
	2	4	4	8	7	
X	X	X	X			
(OA-2)	(AB-2)	~~BC-1~~	~~CB-1~~	~~DE-1~~	(ED-1)	
(OC-4)	~~AD-7~~	~~BA-2~~	~~CE-4~~	~~DB-4~~	~~EB-3~~	
~~OB-5~~		(BE-3)		DT-5	~~EC-4~~	
		(BD-4)		~~DA-7~~	ET-7	

$n = 6$ Compare $DT(8 + 5)$ and $ET(7 + 7)$, which indicates that the shortest route to the destination (node T) is via node D. The resulting ***final version*** of the lists is

O	A	B	C	D	E	T
	2	4	4	8	7	13
X	X	X	X	X	X	
(OA-2)	(AB-2)	~~BC-1~~	~~CB-1~~	~~DE-1~~	(ED-1)	
(OC-4)	~~AD-7~~	~~BA-2~~	~~CE-4~~	~~DB-4~~	~~EB-3~~	
~~OB-5~~		(BE-3)		(DT-5)	~~EC-4~~	
		(BD-4)		~~DA-7~~	~~ET-7~~	

The shortest route *from the destination to the origin* can now be traced back through the circled branches as *either* $T \to D \to E \to B \to A \to O$ or $T \to D \to B \to A \to O$. Therefore the two alternates for the shortest route *from the origin to the destination* have been identified as $O \to A \to B \to E \to D \to T$ and $O \to A \to B \to D \to T$, with a total distance of 13 miles on either route.

Before concluding this discussion of the shortest route problem we need to emphasize one point. The problem thus far has been described in terms of minimizing the *distance* from an origin to a destination. However, in actuality the network problem being solved is finding which path connecting two specified nodes minimizes the sum of the *branch values* on the path. There is no reason that these branch values need to represent *distances*, even indirectly. For example, the branches might correspond to *activities* of some kind, where the value associated with each branch is the *cost* of that activity. The problem then would be to find which sequence of activities accomplishing a specified objective minimizes the total *cost* involved. (See Prob. 2.) Another alternative is that the value associated with each branch is the *time* required for that activity. The problem then would be to find which sequence of activities accomplishing a specified objective minimizes the total *time* involved. (See Prob. 3.) Thus some of the most important applications of the shortest route problem have nothing to do with *routes* in the usual sense of the word.

5.4 THE MINIMAL SPANNING TREE PROBLEM

Now consider a variation of the shortest route problem known as the minimal spanning tree problem. As before, a set of nodes and the distances[1] between pairs of these nodes are given. However, the branches between the nodes are no longer specified. Thus, rather than finding a shortest route through a fully defined network, the problem involves *choosing the branches* for the network that have the *shortest total length* while providing a route between each pair of nodes. To achieve this, the branches would be chosen in such a way that the resulting network forms a *tree* (as defined in Sec. 5.2) that "spans" (i.e., connects to) all the given nodes. In short, the problem is to find the *spanning tree* with a minimum total branch length.

This problem has a number of important practical applications. For example, it can sometimes be helpful in the planning of *transportation networks*. The nodes would be terminals and the branches would be transportation lanes (highways, railroad tracks, air lanes, and so forth). In this context, the minimal spanning tree problem is to determine which transportation lanes would service all the terminals in a minimum total distance. Other examples where a comparable decision arises include the planning of large-scale *communication networks* and *distribution networks*.

[1] Once again, "distance" instead can be cost, time, or some other quantity.

The minimal spanning tree problem can be solved in a very straightforward way because it happens to be one of the few operations research problems where being *greedy* at each stage of the solution procedure will still lead to an overall optimal solution at the end! Thus, beginning with any node, the first stage involves choosing the shortest possible branch to another node, without worrying about the effect this would have on subsequent decisions. At the second stage, identify the unconnected node that is closest to either of these connected nodes, and then add the corresponding branch to the network. This process would be repeated, as summarized below, until all the nodes have been connected. The resulting network is guaranteed to be a "minimal spanning tree."

Summary of Solution Procedure

1. Select any node arbitrarily, and then connect it to the nearest distinct node.

2. Identify the unconnected node that is closest to a connected node, and then connect these two nodes. Repeat this until all nodes have been connected.

This procedure can be executed in a way very much like that for the shortest route problem. However, a graphical approach is even faster, as we shall now illustrate.

Example

The *Seervada Park* management (see Sec. 5.1) needs to determine under which roads telephone lines should be installed to connect all stations with a minimum total length of line. Using the data given in Fig. 5.1, the step-by-step solution of this problem is outlined below.

Nodes and distances for the problem are

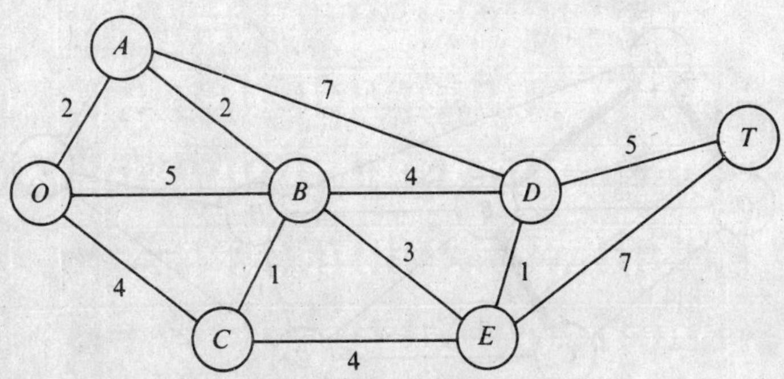

Arbitrarily select node O to start. The unconnected node closest to node O is node A. Connect node A to node O.

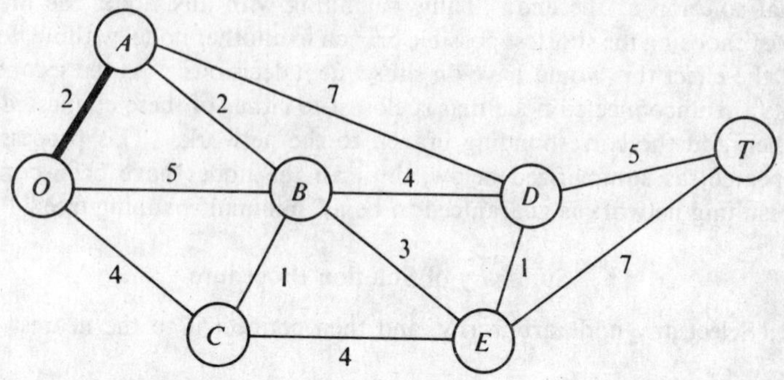

The unconnected node closest to node O or A is node B (closest to A). Connect node B to node A.

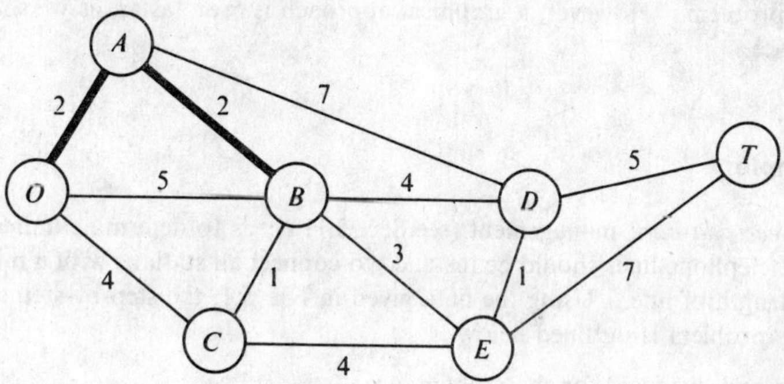

The unconnected node closest to node O, A, or B is node C (closest to B) Connect node C to node B.

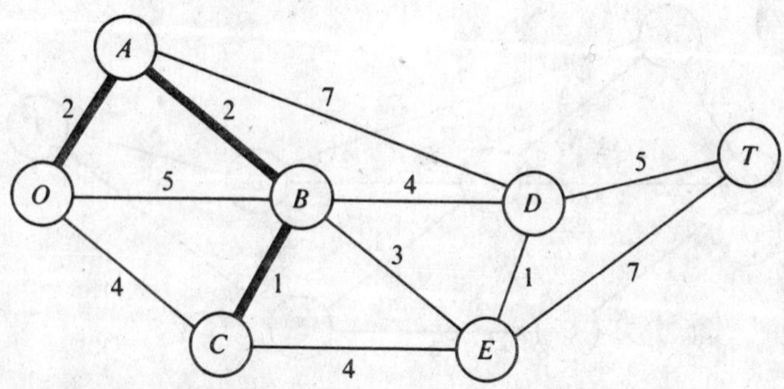

The unconnected node closest to node *O*, *A*, *B*, or *C* is node *E* (closest to *B*). Connect node *E* to node *B*.

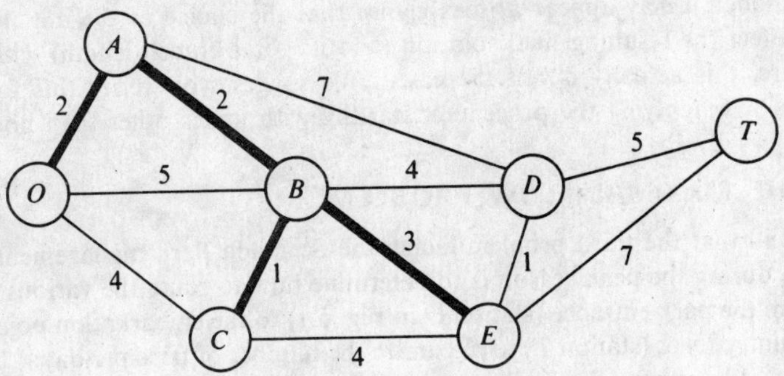

The unconnected node closest to node *O*, *A*, *B*, *C*, or *E* is node *D* (closest to *E*). Connect node *D* to node *E*.

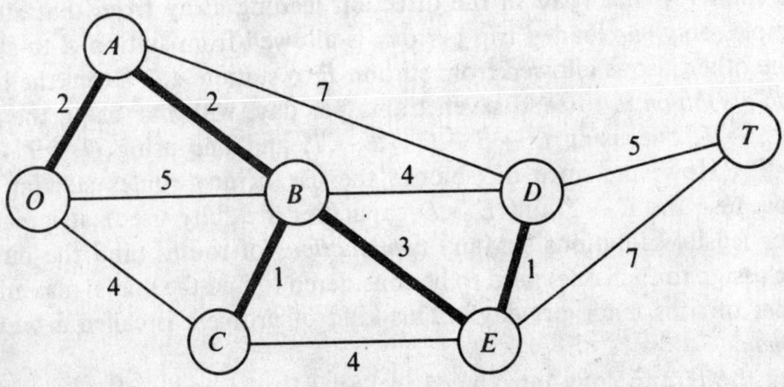

The only remaining unconnected node is node *T*. It is closest to node *D*. Connect node *T* to node *D*.

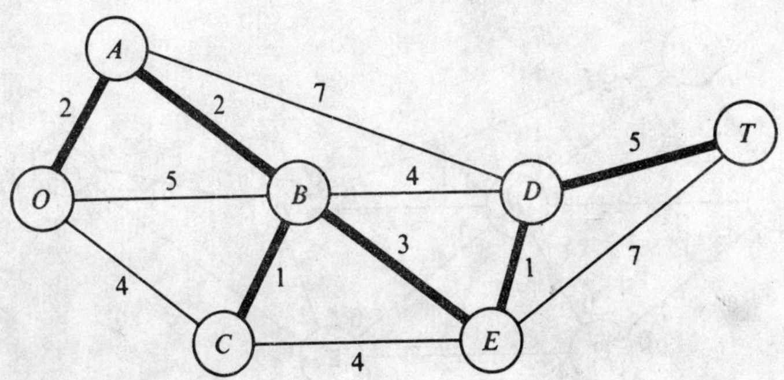

All nodes are now connected, so this is the desired solution to the problem. The total length of the branches is 14 miles.

Although it may appear at first glance that the choice of the initial node would affect the resulting final solution (and its total branch length) with this procedure, this actually is not the case. We suggest you verify this for the example by reapplying the procedure, starting with nodes other than node O.

5.5 THE MAXIMAL FLOW PROBLEM

Now recall that the third problem facing the Seervada Park management (see Sec. 5.1) during the peak season is to determine how to route the various tram trips from the park entrance (station O in Fig. 5.1) to the embarkation point for cross-country hikes (station T) to maximize the number of trips per day. Strict upper limits have been imposed on the number of loaded trips allowed in each direction on each individual road. (The limits are not applied to the unloaded return trips because of the greatly reduced weight and noise level.) These limits are shown in Fig. 5.2, where the number next to each station and road gives the limit for that road in the direction leading away from that station. For example, only *one* loaded trip per day is allowed from station A to station B, but one other also is allowed from station B to station A. Given the limits, one *feasible solution* is to send seven trams per day, with five using the route $O \to B \to E \to T$, one using $O \to B \to C \to E \to T$, and one using $O \to B \to C \to E \to D \to T$. However, since this blocks the use of any routes starting with $O \to C$ (because the $E \to T$ and $E \to D$ capacities are fully used), it is easy to find better feasible solutions. Many *combinations* of routes (and the number of trips to assign to each one) need to be considered to find the one(s) maximizing the number of trips made per day. This kind of problem is called a *maximal flow problem.*

Using the terminology introduced in Sec. 5.2, the maximal flow problem

Figure 5.2 Limits on the number of trips per day for the Seervada Park problem.

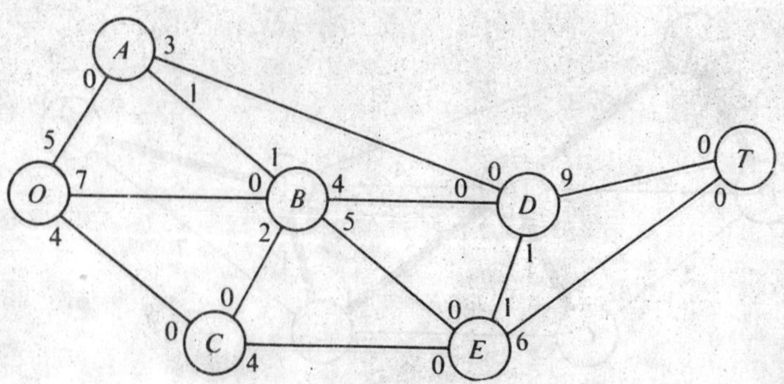

can be described formally as follows. Consider a connected network having a single *source* and a single *sink*. Assume *conservation of flow* (i.e., flow into the node equals flow out of the node) at each node other than the source and the sink. Suppose that the rate of flow along branch (i, j) from node i to node j can be any nonnegative quantity not exceeding the specified *flow capacity* c_{ij}. The objective is to determine the feasible steady-state pattern of flows through the network that *maximizes the total flow* from the source to the sink.

The maximal flow problem actually can be formulated as a *linear programming problem* (see Prob. 7), so it can be solved by the simplex method. However, an even more efficient solution procedure for this problem is available. Except for one refinement, this procedure says simply to repeatedly select *any* path from the source to the sink and assign the maximum feasible flow to that path, continuing this process until no more paths still have *strictly positive flow capacity*. (The flow capacity of a path equals the *smallest remaining flow capacity* for any branch on that path, which is just the maximum feasible flow that can be assigned to the path.) Since this indiscriminate selection of paths for assigning flows may prevent the use of a better combination of flow assignments, the purpose of the refinement is to *undo* a previous assignment to make room for a better one. It accomplishes this by merely modifying the process described above to *also* permit assigning fictional flows in the "wrong" direction along a branch (i.e., in a direction having zero flow capacity) when the real effect of this assignment is only to cancel out part or all of the previously assigned flow in the "right" direction. To permit this, whenever some amount of flow is assigned to a branch in one direction (thereby decreasing the remaining flow capacity by that amount), the remaining flow capacity in the *opposite* direction for that branch should be *increased* by the same amount. Therefore, each *iteration* of the solution procedure consists of the three steps summarized below.

Summary of Solution Procedure[1]

1. Find a path from source to sink with *strictly positive flow capacity*. (If none exists, the net flows already assigned constitute an optimal flow pattern.)

2. Search this path for the branch with the *smallest remaining flow capacity* (denote this capacity as c^*), and *increase* the flow in this path by c^*.

3. *Decrease* by c^* the *remaining flow capacity* of each branch in the path. *Increase* by c^* the *remaining flow capacity* in the opposite direction for each branch in the path. Return to step 1.

Applying this procedure to the *Seervada Park* problem (with an arbitrary selection of the path at each iteration) yields the results summarized below, where the numbers on the branches represent *remaining flow capacities*. (For the original network, see Fig. 5.2.)

[1] It is assumed that the flow capacities are either integers or rational numbers.

Iteration 1 Assign flow of 5 to $O \rightarrow B \rightarrow E \rightarrow T$. The resulting network is

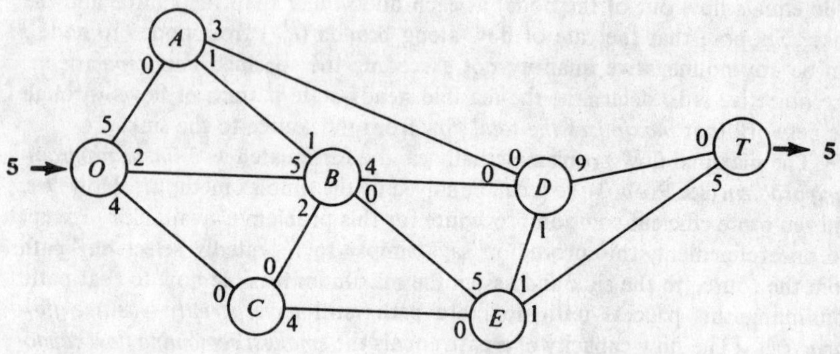

Iteration 2 Assign flow of 3 to $O \rightarrow A \rightarrow D \rightarrow T$. The resulting network is

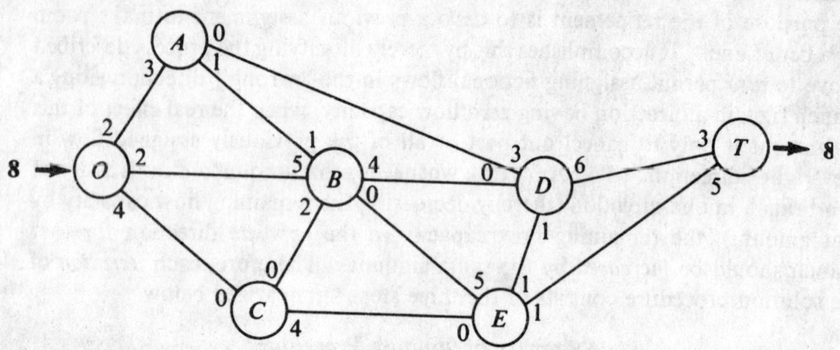

Iteration 3 Assign flow of 1 to $O \rightarrow A \rightarrow B \rightarrow D \rightarrow T$.

Iteration 4 Assign flow of 2 to $O \rightarrow B \rightarrow D \rightarrow T$. The resulting network is

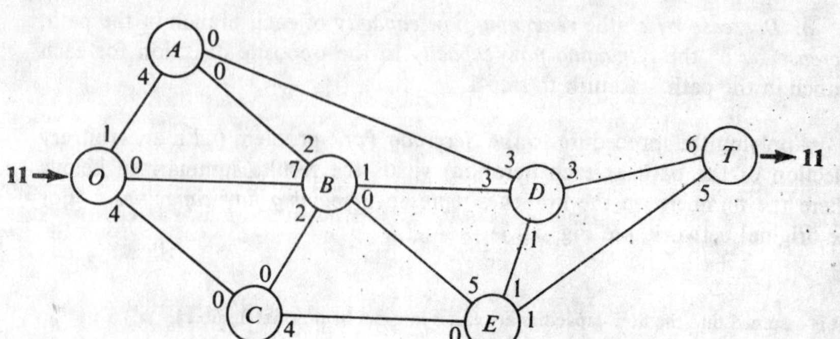

Iteration 5 Assign flow of 1 to $O \to C \to E \to D \to T$.

Iteration 6 Assign flow of 1 to $O \to C \to E \to T$. The resulting network is

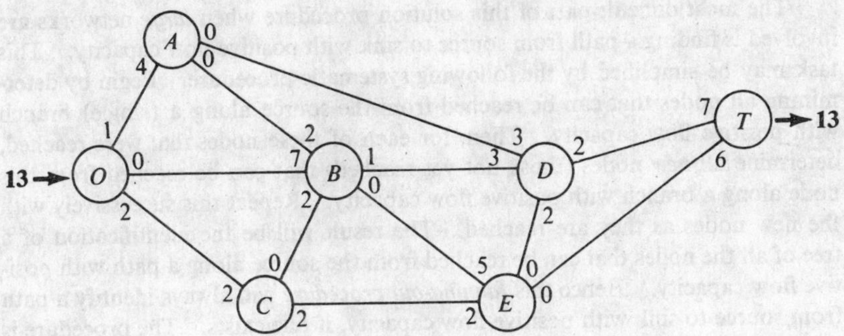

Iteration 7 Assign flow of 1 to $O \to C \to E \to B \to D \to T$. The resulting network is

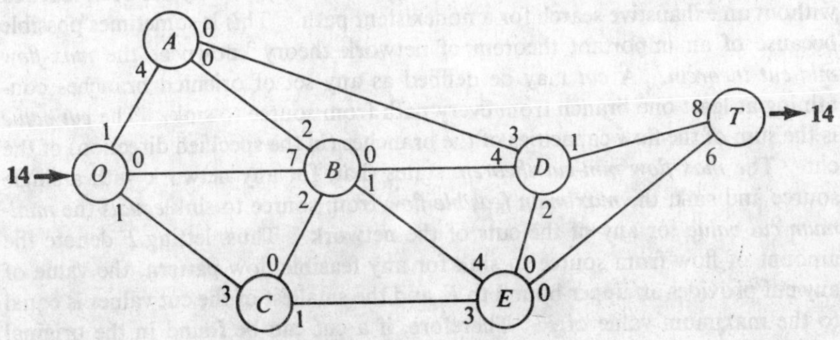

No paths with strictly positive flow capacity remain.
The current flow pattern is optimal.

The current flow pattern may be identified by either cumulating the flow assignments or by comparing the remaining flow capacities with the original flow capacities. Using the latter method, the direction of net flow in a branch would be in the direction of a branch whose remaining flow capacity is less than the original capacity. The magnitude of this flow would equal the amount by which this original flow capacity has been decreased.

This example nicely illustrates the role of the *refinement* in the solution procedure discussed above. Without the refinement, the first six iterations would be unchanged. However, at that point it would appear that no paths with strictly positive flow capacity remain (since the real flow capacity for $E \to B$ is *zero*). Therefore the refinement permits adding the flow assignment of 1 for $O \to C \to E \to B \to D \to T$ in *iteration 7*. In effect, this additional flow assignment cancels out one unit of flow assigned at *iteration 1* ($O \to B \to E \to T$) and replaces it by assignments of one unit of flow to *both* $O \to B \to D \to T$ and $O \to C \to E \to T$.

The most difficult part of this solution procedure when *large* networks are involved is finding a path from source to sink with positive flow capacity. This task may be simplified by the following systematic procedure. Begin by determining all nodes that can be reached from the source along a (single) branch with positive flow capacity. Then, for each of these nodes that were reached, determine all *new* nodes (those not yet reached) that can be reached from this node along a branch with positive flow capacity. Repeat this successively with the new nodes as they are reached. The result will be the identification of a tree of all the nodes that can be reached from the source along a path with positive flow capacity. Hence this *fanning-out procedure* will always identify a path from source to sink with positive flow capacity, if one exists. The procedure is illustrated in Fig. 5.3 for the network resulting from *iteration 6* for the above example.

Although the procedure illustrated in Fig. 5.3 is a relatively straightforward one, it would be helpful to be able to recognize when optimality has been reached without an exhaustive search for a nonexistent path. This is sometimes possible because of an important theorem of network theory known as the *max-flow min-cut theorem.* A *cut* may be defined as any set of oriented branches containing at least one branch from every path from source to sink. The *cut value* is the sum of the flow capacities of the branches (in the specified direction) of the cut. The *max-flow min-cut theorem* states that, for any network with a single source and sink, the *maximum feasible flow* from source to sink *equals* the *minimum cut value* for any of the cuts of the network. Thus, letting F denote the amount of flow from source to sink for any feasible flow pattern, the value of any cut provides an upper bound to F, and the smallest of the cut values is equal to the maximum value of F. Therefore, if a cut can be found in the original

Figure 5.3 Procedure for finding a path from source to sink with positive flow capacity for iteration 7 of the Seervada Park example.

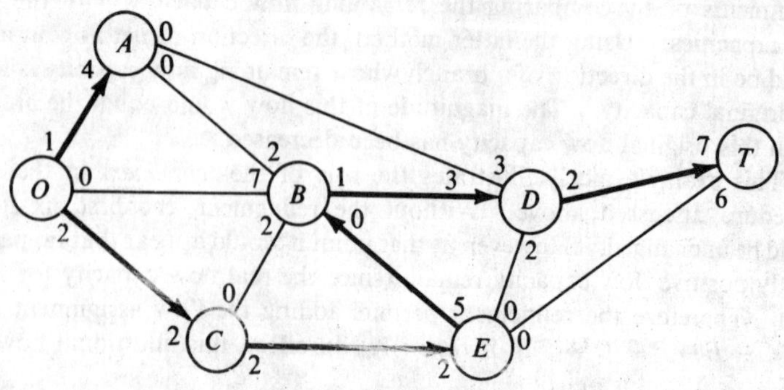

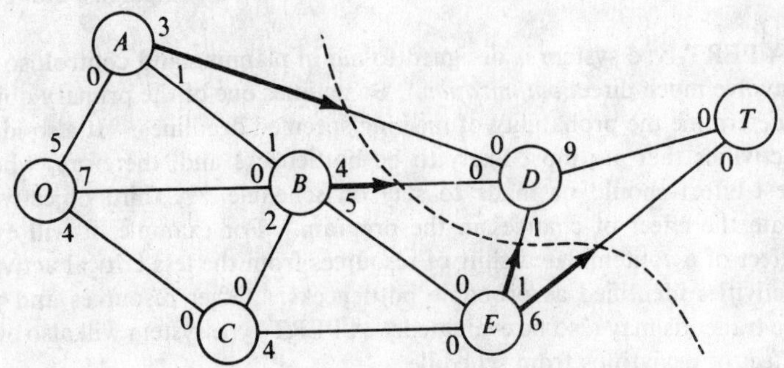

Figure 5.4 A minimal cut for the Seervada Park problem.

network whose value equals the value of F currently attained by the solution procedure, the current flow pattern must be *optimal*. Equivalently, optimality has been attained whenever there exists a cut in the *current* network whose value is zero with respect to the *remaining* flow capacities. To illustrate, consider the cut in the network of Fig. 5.2 indicated in Fig. 5.4.

Notice that the value of the cut in Fig. 5.4 is $(3 + 4 + 1 + 6) = 14$, which was found to be the maximum value of F, so this cut is a minimal cut. Notice also that, in the network resulting from iteration 7, where $F = 14$, the corresponding cut has a value of *zero* with respect to the *remaining* flow capacities. If this had been noticed, it would not have been necessary to search for additional paths for source to sink with positive flow capacity.

5.6 PROJECT PLANNING AND CONTROL WITH PERT-CPM

The successful management of large-scale projects requires careful *planning*, *scheduling*, and *coordinating* of numerous interrelated activities. To aid in these tasks, formal procedures based on the use of *networks* and *network techniques* were developed beginning in the late 1950s. The most prominent of these procedures have been PERT (Program Evaluation and Review Technique) and CPM (Critical Path Method), although there have been many variants under different names. As you will see later, there are a few important differences in these two procedures. However, the trend in recent years has been to merge the two approaches into what is usually referred to as a *PERT-type system*.

Although the original application of PERT-type systems was for evaluating the schedule for a research and development program, it is also being used to measure and control progress on numerous other types of special projects. Examples of these project types include construction programs, programming of computers, preparation of bids and proposals, maintenance planning, and the installation of computer systems. This kind of approach has even been applied to the production of motion pictures, political campaigns, and complex surgery.

A PERT-type system is designed to *aid* in planning and control, so it may not involve much direct *optimization*. Sometimes one of the primary objectives is to determine the probability of meeting specified deadlines. It also identifies the activities that are most likely to be bottlenecks and, therefore, where the greatest effort should be made to stay on schedule. A third objective is to evaluate the effect of changes in the program. For example, it will evaluate the effect of a contemplated shift of resources from the less critical activities to the activities identified as probable bottlenecks. Other resources and performance tradeoffs may also be evaluated. A PERT-type system will also evaluate the effect of deviations from schedule.

All PERT-type systems use a network to graphically portray the interrelationships among the elements of a project. This network representation of the project plan shows all the *precedence relationships* regarding the order in which tasks must be performed. This is illustrated by Fig. 5.5, which shows the initial project network for building a house.

In the terminology of PERT, each *branch* of the network represents an **activity**, which is one of the tasks required by the project. Each *node* represents an **event**, which usually is defined as the point when all activities leading into that node are completed. The *arrowheads* indicate the sequences in which the events must be achieved. Furthermore, an event must precede the initiation of the activities leading out of that node. (In reality, it is often possible to overlap successive phases of a project, so the network may represent an approximate idealization of the project plan.) The node toward which all activities lead (the sink of the network) is the event corresponding to the completion of the currently planned project. The network may represent either the plan for the project from its inception or, if the project has already begun, the plan for the completion of the project. In the latter case, each source of the network represents either the event of continuing a current activity or the event of initiating a new activity that may begin at any time.

Dashed-line arrows, called **dummies**, show precedence relationships only; they do not represent real activities. For example, there is a dummy branch from note 5 to node 8 in Fig. 5.5 because the rough exterior plumbing must be completed before the exterior painting can begin. A common rule for constructing these project networks is that two nodes can be directly connected by *no more than one* branch. Dummy activities can also be used to avoid violating this rule when there are two or more concurrent activities, as illustrated by the dummy branch from node 11 to node 12 in Fig. 5.5.

After developing the network for a project, the next step is to estimate the *time* required for each of the activities. These estimates for the house-construction example of Fig. 5.5 are shown by the darker numbers (in units of *work days*) next to the branches in Fig. 5.6. These times are used to calculate two basic quantities for *each event*, namely, its *earliest time* and its *latest time*.

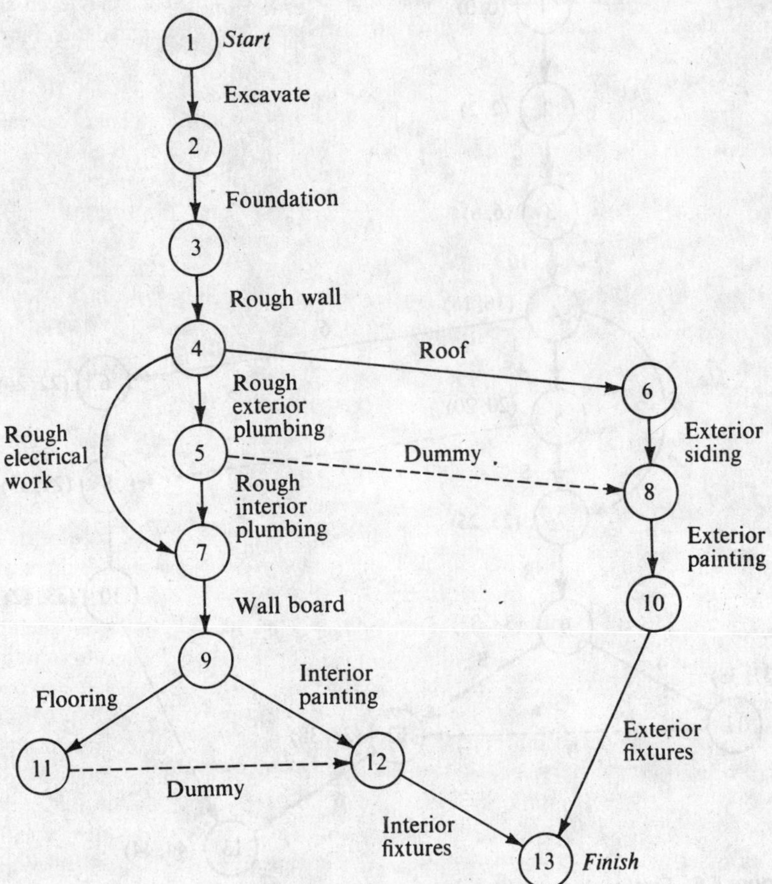

Figure 5.5 Initial *project network* for constructing a house.

DEFINITION The **earliest time** for an event is the (estimated) time at which the event will occur if the *preceding* activities are started *as early as possible.*

Using this definition, the earliest times are obtained successively for the events by making a *forward pass* through the network, starting with the initial events and working forward in time toward the final events. Labeling the initiation of the project as time 0, this process is shown in Table 5.2 for the example considered in Figs. 5.5 and 5.6. The resulting earliest times are recorded in Fig. 5.6 as the *first* of the two numbers given by each node.

DEFINITION The **latest time** for an event is the (estimated) last time at which the event can occur *without delaying the completion of the project* beyond its earliest time.

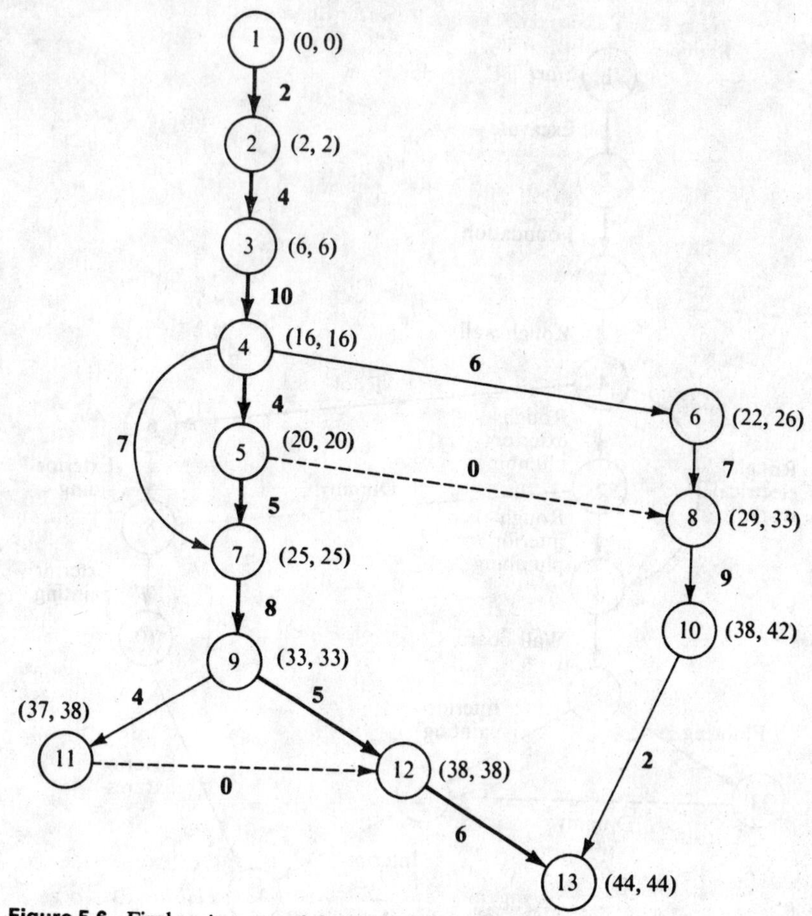

Figure 5.6 Final *project network* for constructing a house.

In this case the latest times are obtained successively for the events by making a *backward pass* through the network, starting with the final events and working backward in time toward the initial events. With 44 as the earliest time *and* latest time for the completion of the house-construction project, this process is illustrated in Table 5.3. The resulting latest times are recorded in Fig. 5.6 as the *second* of the two numbers given by each node.

DEFINITION The **slack** for an event is the *difference* between its latest and its earliest time.

Thus the slack indicates how much delay in reaching the event can be tolerated without delaying the project completion.

Table 5.2 Calculation of Earliest Times for House-construction Example

Event	*Immediately preceding event*	*Earliest time* + *Activity time*	*Maximum = Earliest time*
1	—	—	0
2	1	0 + 2	2
3	2	2 + 4	6
4	3	6 + 10	16
5	4	16 + 4	20
6	4	16 + 6	22
7	4	16 + 7	25
	5	20 + 5	
8	5	20 + 0	29
	6	22 + 7	
9	7	25 + 8	33
10	8	29 + 9	38
11	9	33 + 4	37
12	9	33 + 5	38
	11	37 + 0	
13	10	38 + 2	44
	12	38 + 6	

Table 5.3 Calculation of Latest Times for House-construction Example

Event	*Immediately following event*	*Latest time* − *Activity time*	*Minimum = Latest time*
13	—	—	44
12	13	44 − 6	38
11	12	38 − 0	38
10	13	44 − 2	42
9	12	38 − 5	33
	11	38 − 4	
8	10	42 − 9	33
7	9	33 − 8	25
6	8	33 − 7	26
5	8	33 − 0	20
	7	25 − 5	
4	7	25 − 7	16
	6	26 − 6	
	5	20 − 4	
3	4	16 − 10	6
2	3	6 − 4	2
1	2	2 − 2	0

DEFINITION A **critical path** for a project is a path through the network such that the events on this path have *zero slack*.

The critical path for the house-construction example is shown in Fig. 5.6 by the dark arrows.

This information on earliest and latest times, slack, and the critical path is invaluable for the project manager. Among other things, it enables him to investigate the effect of possible improvements in the project plan, to determine where special effort should be expended to stay on schedule, and to assess the impact of schedule slippages.

The PERT Three-estimate Approach

Thus far we have assumed that use is made of just one estimate of the time required for each *activity* of the project. However, there usually is considerable uncertainty about what the time will be; in actuality it is a *random variable* having some probability distribution. In recognition of this, the original version of PERT prescribed using *three* different types of estimates of the activity time to obtain basic information about its probability distribution. This information for all the activity times is then used to estimate the *probability* of completing the project by the scheduled date.

The three time estimates used by PERT for each activity are a *most likely* estimate, an *optimistic* estimate, and a *pessimistic* estimate. The **most likely estimate** (denoted by m) is intended to be the *most realistic* estimate of the time the activity might consume. Statistically speaking, it is an estimate of the *mode* (the highest point) of the probability distribution for the activity time. The **optimistic estimate** (denoted by a) is intended to be the *unlikely but possible time if everything goes well.* Statistically speaking, it is an estimate of essentially the *lower bound* of the probability distribution. The **pessimistic estimate** (denoted by b) is intended to be the *unlikely but possible time if everything goes badly.* Statistically speaking, it is an estimate of essentially the *upper bound* of the probability distribution. The intended location of these three estimates with respect to the probability distribution is shown in Fig. 5.7.

Two assumptions are made to convert m, a, and b into estimates of the *expected value* and *variance* of the elapsed time required by the activity. One is

Figure 5.7 Model of probability distribution for the PERT three-estimate approach. m = most likely estimate, a = optimistic estimate, and b = pessimistic estimate.

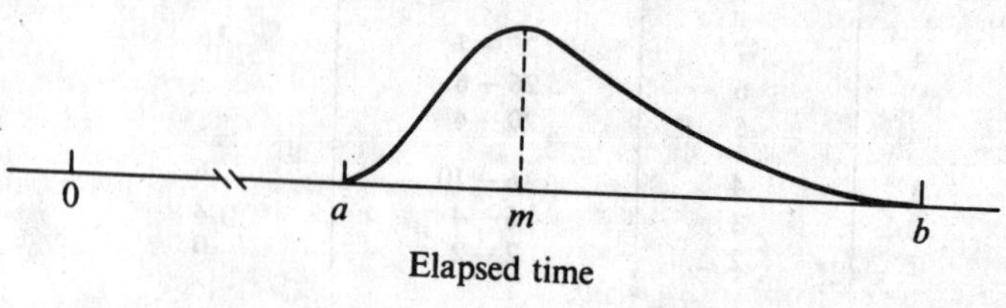

that σ, the standard deviation (square root of the variance), equals one-sixth the range of reasonably possible time requirements; that is,

$$\sigma^2 = \left[\frac{1}{6}(b-a)\right]^2$$

is the desired estimate of the variance. The rationale for this assumption is that the tails of many probability distributions (such as the normal distribution) are considered to lie at about 3 standard deviations from the mean, so that there would be a spread of about 6 standard deviations between the tails. For example the control charts commonly used for statistical quality control are constructed so that the spread between the control limits is estimated to be 6 standard deviations.

To obtain the estimated expected value, an assumption about the probability distribution of the time required for the activity is also required. This assumption is that the distribution is approximately *beta* (see the beta distribution in Sec. 8.7), where the mode is m, the lower bound is a, the upper bound is b, and $\sigma = (b-a)/6$. Such a distribution is shown in Fig. 5.7.

Using the model illustrated in Fig. 5.7, it can be derived that the expected value of the distribution (denoted by t_e in the PERT literature) is approximately

$$t_e = \frac{1}{3}\left[2m + \frac{1}{2}(a+b)\right].$$

This equation is therefore used to compute the *estimated expected value* of elapsed time required for an activity. Notice that the "midrange" $(a+b)/2$ lies midway between a and b, so that t_e is the weighted arithmetic mean of the mode and the midrange, the mode carrying two-thirds of the entire weight. Although the assumption of a beta distribution is an arbitrary one, it has served its purpose of locating the expected value with respect to m, a, and b in what seems to be a reasonable way.

After calculating the estimated *expected value* and *variance* for each of the activity times, three additional assumptions (or approximations) are needed to enable calculation of the probability of completing the project on schedule. One is that the activity times are *statistically independent*. A second is that the *critical path* (in terms of expected times) *always* requires a longer total elapsed time than any other path. The resulting implication is that the expected value and variance of *project time* are just the *sum* of the expected values and variances (respectively) of the times for the activities on the critical path.

The third assumption is that project time has a *normal distribution*. The rationale for this assumption is that this time is the sum of many independent random variables, and the general version of the central limit theorem (see Sec. 8.15) implies that such a sum is approximately normal under a wide range of conditions. Given the mean and variance, it is then straightforward (see the normal distribution in Sec. 8.7) to find the probability that this normal random variable (project time) will be less than the scheduled completion time.[1]

[1] The same procedure can also be used to find the probability that an *intermediate* event will be accomplished before a scheduled time.

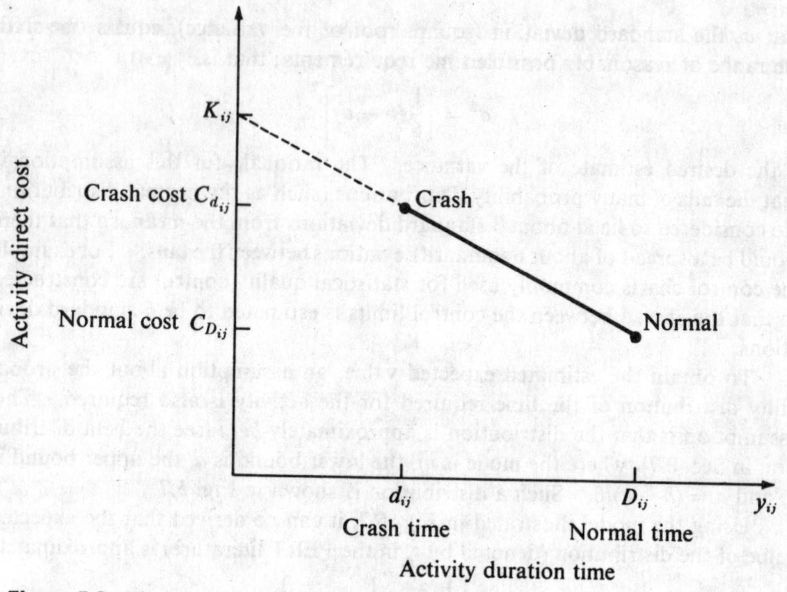

Figure 5.8 Time-cost curve for activity (i, j).

To illustrate, suppose that the house-construction project of Fig. 5.5 is scheduled to be completed after 50 working days and that *both* the expected value and variance of each activity time happens to equal the quantity given in Fig. 5.6. Therefore both the expected value and variance of *project time* are 44, so its standard deviation is $\sqrt{44} \approx 6.63$. Thus the scheduled completion time is approximately 0.9 standard deviations above the *expected* project time. Table A.5.1 then gives an approximate probability of $1 - 0.1841 \approx 0.82$ that this schedule will be met.

The CPM Method of Time-cost Tradeoffs

The original versions of CPM and PERT differ in two important ways. First, CPM assumes that activity times are *deterministic* (i.e., they can be reliably predicted without significant uncertainty), so that the three-estimate approach described above is not needed. Second, rather than primarily emphasizing time (explicitly), CPM places equal emphasis on *time and cost*. This is done by constructing a *time-cost curve* for each activity, such as shown in Fig. 5.8. This curve plots the relationship between the budgeted *direct cost*[1] for the activity and its resulting *duration time*. The plot normally is based on two points[2]:

[1] *Direct* cost includes the cost of the material, equipment, and direct labor required to perform the activity but *excludes* indirect project costs such as supervision and other customary overhead costs, interest charges, and so forth.

[2] More than two points also can be used under certain circumstances.

the *normal* and the *crash*. The normal point gives the cost and time involved when the activity is performed in the *normal* way *without* any extra costs (overtime labor, special time saving materials or equipment, and so on) being expended to speed up the activity. By contrast, the crash point gives the time and cost involved when the activity is performed on a *crash basis*, i.e., it is *fully expedited* with no cost spared to reduce the duration time as much as possible. As an approximation, it is then assumed that *all* intermediate *time-cost tradeoffs* also are possible and that they lie on the *line segment* between these two points (see the solid-line segment shown in Fig. 5.8). Thus the only estimates that need to be obtained from the project personnel are the cost and time for the two points.

The basic objective of CPM is to determine just *which* time-cost tradeoff should be used for each activity to *meet the scheduled project completion time at a minimum cost.* One way of doing this is by *linear programming.* To describe this approach we shall need to introduce considerable notation, some of which is summarized in Fig. 5.8. Thus, let activity (i, j) denote the activity going from event i to event j in the project network. Then let

$$D_{ij} = \textit{normal time} \text{ for activity } (i, j),$$

$$C_{D_{ij}} = \textit{normal (direct) cost} \text{ for activity } (i, j),$$

$$d_{ij} = \textit{crash time} \text{ for activity } (i, j),$$

$$C_{d_{ij}} = \textit{crash (direct) cost} \text{ for activity } (i, j).$$

The *decision variables* for the problem are the y_{ij}, where

$$y_{ij} = \textit{duration time} \text{ for activity } (i, j).$$

To express the direct cost for activity (i, j) as a (linear) function of y_{ij}, let

$$C_{ij} = \frac{C_{d_{ij}} - C_{D_{ij}}}{D_{ij} - d_{ij}},$$

which is the *incremental direct cost* for activity (i, j) *per unit decrease* in y_{ij}. Also define K_{ij} as the *intercept* with the *direct cost axis* of the line through the normal and crash points for activity (i, j), as shown in Fig. 5.8. Therefore,

$$\textit{Direct cost} \text{ for activity } (i, j) = K_{ij} - C_{ij} y_{ij}.$$

Consequently,

$$\text{Total direct cost for the project} = \sum_{(i, j)} (K_{ij} - C_{ij} y_{ij}),$$

where the summation is over *all* activities (i, j). We are now ready to state and formulate the problem mathematically.

THE PROBLEM For a given (maximum) project completion time λ, choose the y_{ij} so as to *minimize total direct cost* for the project.

Linear programming formulation To take the project completion time into account, the linear programming formulation of the problem requires one more variable for each event, namely,

T_k = (unknown) *earliest time* for event k, which is a deterministic function of the y_{ij}.

Label

$$\text{Event } 1 = \text{project start,}$$
$$\text{event } n = \text{project completion,}$$

so

$$T_1 = 0$$
$$T_n = \text{project completion time.}$$

Also note that $\sum K_{ij}$ is just a fixed constant that can be dropped from the objective function, so that minimizing total direct cost for the project is *equivalent* (see Sec. 2.10) to *maximizing* $\sum C_{ij} y_{ij}$. Therefore the linear programming problem is to find the y_{ij} (and the corresponding T_k) that

$$\text{Maximize} \quad Z = \sum_{(i,\, j)} C_{ij} y_{ij},$$

subject to

$$\left.\begin{aligned} y_{ij} &\geq d_{ij} \\ y_{ij} &\leq D_{ij} \\ T_i + y_{ij} - T_j &\leq 0 \end{aligned}\right\} \text{for all activities } (i, j)$$
$$T_n \leq \lambda.$$

From a computational viewpoint, this formulation can be improved somewhat by replacing each y_{ij} by

$$y_{ij} = d_{ij} + y'_{ij}$$

throughout the model, so that the first set of functional constraints ($y_{ij} \geq d_{ij}$) would be replaced by simple *nonnegativity constraints*

$$y'_{ij} \geq 0.$$

Nonnegativity constraints also can be introduced for the other variables as a convenience,

$$T_k \geq 0,$$

although these variables already are forced to be nonnegative by setting $T_1 = 0$ because of the $y'_{ij} \geq 0$ and $T_j \geq T_i + d_{ij} + y'_{ij}$ constraints.

The key to this formulation is the way that the T_k are introduced into the model to assign the value of T_n that it should have for any given values of the y_{ij}. To see why it works, consider any *particular* feasible values for the y_{ij}

and the corresponding *earliest times* for the events calculated by making a *forward pass* through the project network (as described earlier in the section). By setting $T_1 = 0$, the third group of constraints ($T_i + y_{ij} - T_j \leq 0$) *forces* the value of each T_j in the model to be *at least as large* as the true earliest time for event j. However, the linear programming formulation gives *no possible benefit* to making T_j any larger than it is forced to be. (In fact, having T_j larger can only be a *disadvantage* because this might ultimately force T_n to be larger than it needed to be.) Therefore the optimal solutions to the model will include a basic feasible solution with *all* T_j no larger than they are forced to be by the optimal y_{ij}, that is, these T_j will be true *earliest times* for the events.

The problem as stated above assumes that a specified deadline has been fixed (perhaps by contract) for the completion of the project. This frequently is not the case, so that it is not clear what value should be assigned to λ in the linear programming formulation. In such situations the decision on λ actually is a question of what is the *best tradeoff* between the *total cost* and the *total time* for the project. The basic information needed to address this question is how the *minimum total direct cost* changes as λ is changed in the above formulation, as illustrated in Fig. 5.9. This information can be obtained by using *parametric linear programming* (see Secs. 4.3 and 16.3) to solve for the optimal solution *as a function of* λ over its entire range.[1] However, for doing this there is available an even more efficient procedure that is commonly used instead. This procedure exploits the *special structure* of the problem by reducing the *dual problem* to a variation of the *maximal flow problem* described in the preceding section.[2] Computer codes for this procedure are quite widely available.

Figure 5.9 provides a useful basis for a managerial decision on λ (and the corresponding optimal solution for the y_{ij}) when some of the important effects of the project duration are largely intangible. However, when financial considerations are paramount, it would be appropriate to combine the minimum total direct cost curve of Fig. 5.9 with a curve of *minimum total indirect cost* (supervision, facilities, clerical, interest, contractual penalties) versus λ, as shown in Fig. 5.10. The *sum* of these curves thereby gives the *minimum total project cost* curve for the various values of λ. The *optimal* value of λ then is the one minimizing this total cost curve.

Choosing between PERT and CPM

The choice between the PERT *three-estimate approach* and the CPM *method of time-cost tradeoffs* depends primarily upon the *type of project* and *managerial objectives*. PERT is particularly appropriate when there is considerable uncertainty in predicting activity times, and it is important to effectively *control* the project schedule; for example, most *research and development* projects fall

[1] The *slope* of the time-cost curve changes at the points shown in Fig. 5.9 because the set of basic variables giving the optimal solution changes at these values of λ. This is discussed further in a more general context in Sec. 16.3.

[2] See Selected Reference 6, pages 218 to 235 for details on this procedure.

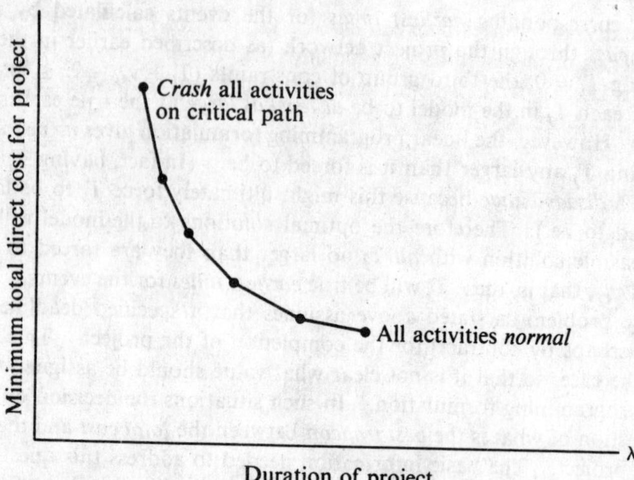

Figure 5.9 Time-cost curve for the overall project.

into this category. On the other hand, CPM is particularly appropriate when activity times can be predicted well (perhaps based on previous experience), but these times can be adjusted readily (e.g., by changing crew sizes), and it is important to plan an appropriate tradeoff between project *time* and *cost*. This is typified by most *construction* or *maintenance* projects.

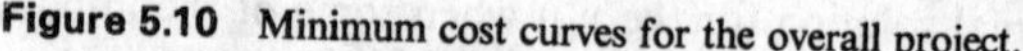

Figure 5.10 Minimum cost curves for the overall project.

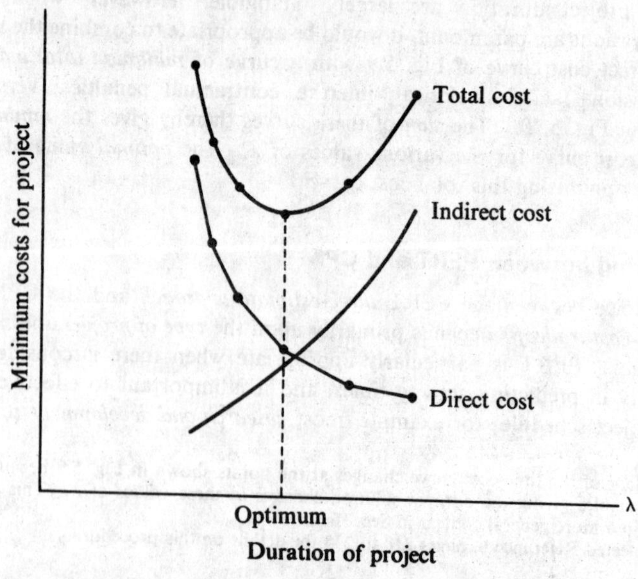

Actually, differences between *current* versions of PERT and CPM are not necessarily as pronounced as we have described them. Most versions of PERT now allow using only a *single* estimate (the most likely estimate) of each activity time and so omit the probabilistic investigation. A version called *PERT/Cost* also considers *time-cost tradeoffs* in a manner similar to CPM.

5.7 CONCLUSIONS

Networks of some type arise in a wide variety of contexts. *Network analysis* provides several useful techniques (especially optimization techniques) for the design and operation of network systems. However, because of the combinatorial nature of most network problems, efficient procedures are not available for solving many of these problems. Nevertheless, this is an active area of research, and progress is continuing to be made.

The most widely used network technique has been the *PERT-type system* for project planning and control. It has been very valuable for organizing the planning effort, testing alternative plans, revealing the overall dimensions and details of the project plan, establishing well-understood management responsibilities, and identifying realistic expectations for the project. It also lays the basis for *anticipatory* management action against potential trouble spots during the course of the project. Although it is not a panacea, and its serious pitfalls have not always been avoided,[1] it has greatly aided project management on numerous occasions.

Selected References

1 Berge, Claude and A. Ghouila-Houri: *Programming, Games and Transportation Networks*, (transl. from French by Maxine Merrington and C. Ramanujacharyulu), Methuen, London, and Wiley, New York, 1965.

2 Busacker, Robert G. and Thomas L. Saaty: *Finite Graphs and Networks: An Introduction with Applications*, McGraw-Hill, New York, 1965.

3 Ford, L. R., Jr., and D. R. Fulkerson: *Flows in Networks*, Princeton University Press, Princeton, N.J., 1962.

4 Frank, Howard and Ivan T. Frisch: *Communication, Transmission and Transportation Networks*, Addison-Wesley, Reading, Mass., 1971.

5 Fulkerson, D. R.: "Flow Networks and Combinatorial Operations Research" and Dreyfus, S. E.: "An Appraisal of Some Shortest-Path Algorithms," reprinted in Arthur M. Geoffrion (ed.), *Perspectives on Optimization: A Collection of Expository Articles*, pp. 197–238, Addison-Wesley, Reading, Mass., 1972.

6 Moder, Joseph J. and Cecil R. Phillips: *Project Management with CPM and PERT*, 2d ed., Van Nostrand, New York, 1970.

[1] For example, see J. W. Pocock, "PERT as an Analytical Aid for Program Planning—Its Payoff and Problems," *Operations Research*, **10**: 893–903, 1962.

Problems

1 Find the *shortest route* through networks (*a*) and (*b*), where the numbers represent actual distances between the corresponding nodes.

(*a*)

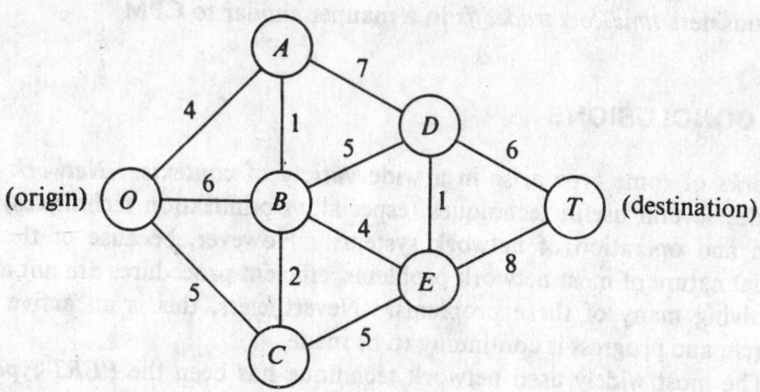

(*b*)

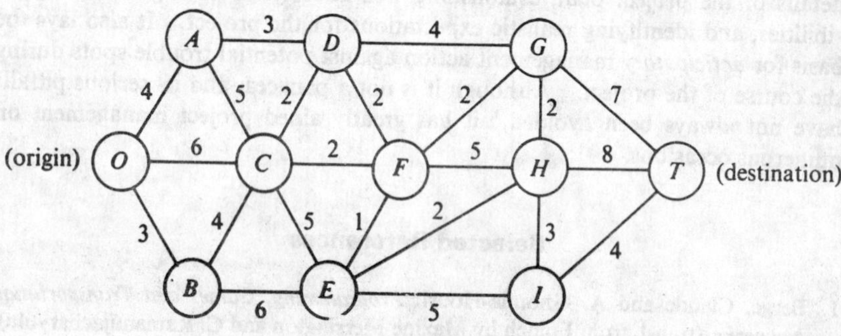

2 At a small but growing airport, the local airline company is purchasing a new tractor for a tractor-trailer train to bring luggage to and from the airplanes. A new mechanized luggage system will be installed in 3 years, so the tractor will not be needed after that. However, because it will receive heavy use, so that the running and maintenance costs will increase rapidly as it ages, it may still be more economical to replace the tractor after 1 or 2 years. The following table gives the total net discounted cost associated with purchasing a tractor (purchase price minus trade-in allowance, plus running and maintenance costs) at the end of year i and trading it in at the end of year j (where year 0 is now).

		j		
		1	2	3
	0	4	8	15
i	1		5	11
	2			6

The problem is to determine at what times (if any) the tractor should be replaced to minimize the total cost for the tractors over the 3 years.

(*a*) Formulate this problem as a shortest route problem.

(*b*) Use the procedure described in Sec. 5.3 to solve this shortest route problem.

3 A company has learned that a competitor is planning to come out with a new kind of product with great sales potential. This company has been working on a similar product, and research is nearly completed. It now wishes to rush the product out to meet the competition. There are four nonoverlapping phases left to accomplish this, including the remaining research that currently is being conducted at a normal pace. However, each phase can instead be conducted at a "priority" or "crash" level to expedite completion. The times required (in months) at these levels are

	Time			
Level	*Remaining research*	*Development*	*Design of manufacturing system*	*Initiate production and distribution*
Normal	5			
Priority	4	3	5	2
Crash	2	2	3	1

$10,000,000 is available for these phases. The cost (in millions of dollars) at the different levels is

	Cost			
Level	*Remaining research*	*Development*	*Design of manufacturing system*	*Initiate production and distribution*
Normal	1			
Priority	2	2	3	1
Crash	3	3	4	2

The problem is to determine at which level to conduct each of the four phases to minimize the total time until the product is marketed subject to the budget restriction.

(*a*) Formulate this problem as a shortest-route problem.

(*b*) Use the procedure described in Sec. 5.3 to solve this shortest route problem.

4 Reconsider the networks shown in Prob. 1. Assume that the nodes and actual distances between nodes are as shown there (where unspecified distances between nodes are greater than any of the given distances), but assume that the branches have not yet been specified. Find the minimal spanning tree for each of these networks.

5 A logging company will soon begin logging eight groves of trees in the same general area. Therefore it must develop a system of dirt roads that makes each grove accessible from every other grove. The distance (in miles) between every pair of groves is

Distance between Pairs of Groves

Grove	1	2	3	4	5	6	7	8
1	···	1.3	2.1	0.9	0.7	1.8	2.0	1.5
2	1.3	···	0.9	1.8	1.2	2.6	2.3	1.1
3	2.1	0.9	···	2.6	1.7	2.5	1.9	1.0
4	0.9	1.8	2.6	···	0.7	1.6	1.5	0.9
5	0.7	1.2	1.7	0.7	···	0.9	1.1	0.8
6	1.8	2.6	2.5	1.6	0.9	···	0.6	1.0
7	2.0	2.3	1.9	1.5	1.1	0.6	···	0.5
8	1.5	1.1	1.0	0.9	0.8	1.0	0.5	···

The problem is to determine between which pairs of groves to construct roads to connect all groves with a minimum total length of road.

(*a*) Describe how this problem fits the network description of the minimal spanning tree problem.

(*b*) Solve the problem.

6 For networks (*a*) and (*b*), find the maximal flow from the source to the sink, given that the flow capacity from node *i* to node *j* is the number along branch (*i*,*j*) nearest node *i*.

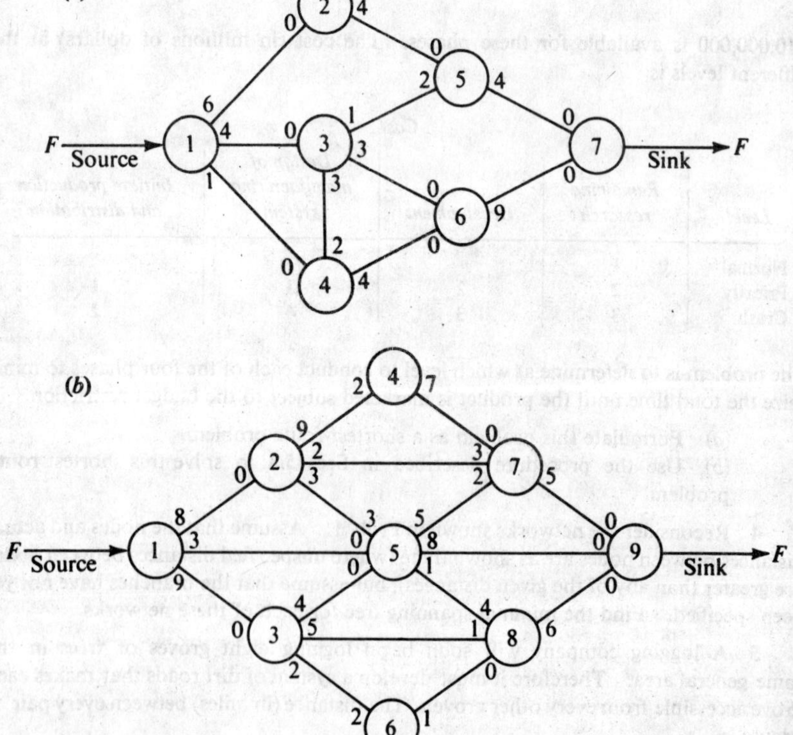

7 Formulate the maximal flow problem as a linear programming problem.

8 One track of the Eura Railroad system runs from the major industrial city of Faireparc to the major port city of Portstown. This track is heavily used by both express passenger and freight trains. The passenger trains are carefully scheduled and have priority over the slower freight trains (this is a European railroad), so that the freight trains must pull over onto a siding whenever a passenger train is scheduled to pass them soon. It is now necessary to increase the freight service even further, so the problem is to schedule the freight trains so as to maximize the number that can be sent each day without interfering with the fixed schedule for passenger trains.

Consecutive freight trains must maintain a schedule differential of at least 0.1 hours, and this is the time unit used for scheduling them (so that the daily schedule indicates the status of each freight train at times 0.0, 0.1, 0.2, ..., 23.9). There are S sidings between Faireparc and Portstown, where siding i is long enough to hold n_i freight trains ($i = 1, \ldots, S$). It requires t_i time units (rounded up to an integer) for a freight train to travel from siding i to siding $i+1$ (where t_0 is the time from the Faireparc station to siding 1 and t_S is the time from siding S to the Portstown station). A freight train is allowed to pass or leave siding i ($i = 0, 1, \ldots, S$) at time j ($j = 0.0, 0.1, \ldots, 23.9$) only if it would not be overtaken by a scheduled passenger train before reaching siding $i+1$ (let $\delta_{ij} = 1$ if it would not be overtaken, and let $\delta_{ij} = 0$ if it would be). A freight train also is required to stop at a siding if there will not be room for it at all subsequent sidings that would be reached before being overtaken by a passenger train.

Formulate this problem as a maximal flow problem by identifying every node (including the source and sink) as well as every branch and its flow capacity for the network representation of the problem. (*Hint:* Use a different set of nodes for each of the 240 times.)

9 Consider the following project network. Assume that the time required (in weeks) for each activity is a predictable constant and that it is given by the number along the corresponding branch. Find the earliest time, latest time, and slack for each event. Also identify the critical path.

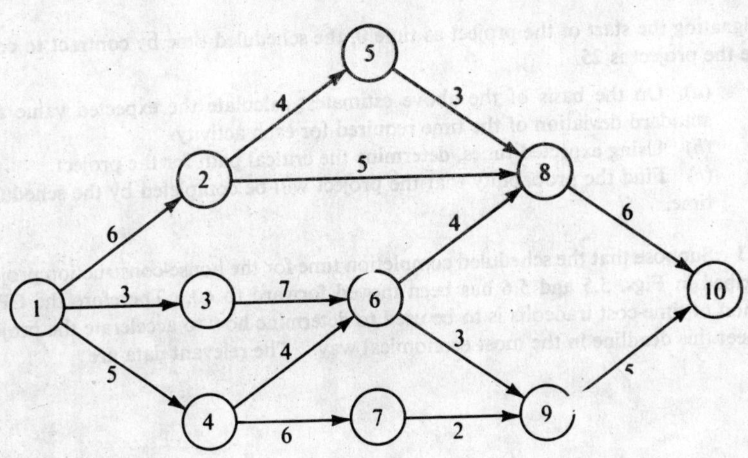

10 Consider the following project network:

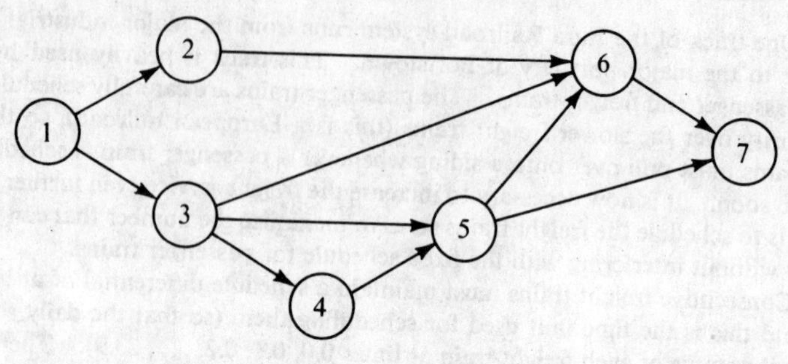

Using the PERT three-estimate approach, suppose that the usual three estimates fo the time required (in months) for each of these activities are

Activity	*Optimistic estimate*	*Most likely estimate*	*Pessimistic estimate*
1→2	7	8	9
1→3	5	7	8
2→6	6	9	12
3→4	4	4	4
3→5	7	8	10
3→6	10	13	19
4→5	3	4	6
5→6	4	5	7
5→7	7	9	11
6→7	3	4	8

Designating the start of the project as time 0, the scheduled time by contract to complete the project is 25.

(*a*) On the basis of the above estimates, calculate the expected value and standard deviation of the time required for each activity.

(*b*) Using expected times, determine the critical path for the project.

(*c*) Find the probability that the project will be completed by the scheduled time.

11 Suppose that the scheduled completion time for the house-construction project described in Figs. 5.5 and 5.6 has been moved forward to 40. Therefore the CPM method of time-cost tradeoffs is to be used to determine how to accelerate the project to meet this deadline in the most economical way. The relevant data are

Activity	*Normal time*	*Crash time*	*Normal cost, $*	*Crash cost, $*
1→2	2	1	1,200	1,500
2→3	4	3	2,500	2,700
3→4	10	7	5,500	6,400
4→5	4	2	3,400	4,100
4→6	6	4	1,900	2,200
4→7	7	5	1,400	1,600
5→7	5	3	1,100	1,400
6→8	7	4	9,300	9,900
7→9	8	6	4,600	4,800
8→10	9	5	1,300	1,700
9→11	4	3	900	1,000
9→12	5	3	1,800	2,100
10→13	2	1	300	400
12→13	6	3	2,600	3,000

Develop the linear programming model for this problem.

Dynamic Programming

Dynamic programming is a mathematical technique often useful for making a sequence of interrelated decisions. It provides a systematic procedure for determining the combination of decisions that maximizes overall effectiveness.

In contrast to linear programming, there does not exist a standard mathematical formulation of "the" dynamic programming problem. Rather, dynamic programming is a general type of approach to problem solving, and the particular equations used must be developed to fit each individual situation. Therefore a certain degree of ingenuity and insight into the general structure of dynamic programming problems is required to recognize when a problem can be solved by dynamic programming procedures and how it would be done. These abilities can probably best be developed by an exposure to a wide variety of dynamic programming applications and a study of the characteristics that are common to all these situations. A large number of illustrative examples are presented for this purpose.

6.1 PROTOTYPE EXAMPLE

A problem specially constructed[1] to illustrate the features and introduce the terminology of dynamic programming is the *stagecoach* problem; it concerns a mythical salesman who had to travel west by stagecoach through unfriendly Indian country about 100 years ago. Although his starting point and destination were fixed, he had considerable choice as to which *states* (or territories that subsequently became states) to travel through en route. The possible routes are shown in Fig. 6.1, where

[1] This problem was developed by Professor Harvey M. Wagner while he was at Stanford University.

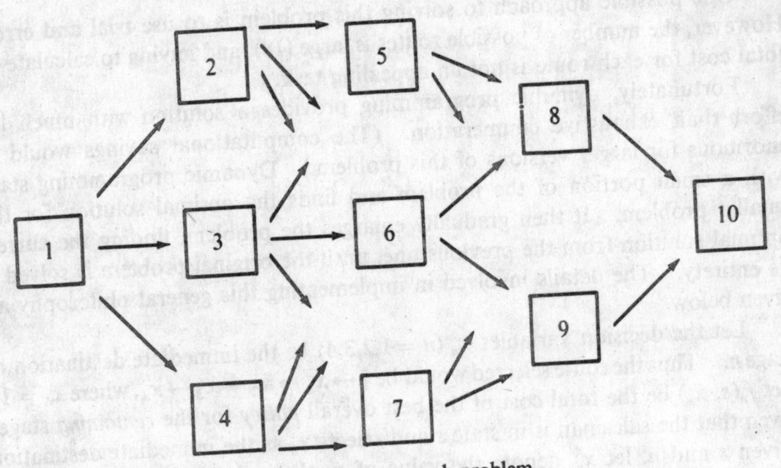

Figure 6.1 The road system for the stagecoach problem.

each state is represented by a numbered block. Thus four *stages* were required to travel from his point of embarkation in state 1 to his destination in state 10.

This salesman was a prudent man who was quite concerned about his safety on this trip. After some thought, a rather clever way of determining his safest route occurred to him. Life insurance policies were offered to stagecoach passengers. Since the cost of each *policy* was based on a careful evaluation of the safety of that run, the safest route should be the one with the cheapest life insurance policy.

The cost for the standard policy on the stagecoach run from state i to state j, which will be denoted by c_{ij}, is

	2	3	4
1	2	4	3

	5	6	7
2	7	4	6
3	3	2	4
4	4	1	5

	8	9
5	1	4
6	6	3
7	3	3

	10
8	3
9	4

Which route minimizes the total cost of the policy?

SOLUTION It should first be noted that making the decision which is best for each successive stage need not yield the overall optimal decision. Following this strategy of selecting the cheapest run offered by each successive stage would give the route $1 \rightarrow 2 \rightarrow 6 \rightarrow 9 \rightarrow 10$ at a total cost of 13. However, sacrificing a little on one stage may permit greater savings thereafter. For example, $1 \rightarrow 4 \rightarrow 6$ is cheaper overall than $1 \rightarrow 2 \rightarrow 6$.

One possible approach to solving this problem is to use trial and error.[1] However, the number of possible routes is large (18), and having to calculate the total cost for each route is not an appealing task.

Fortunately, dynamic programming provides a solution with much less effort than exhaustive enumeration. (The computational savings would be enormous for larger versions of this problem.) Dynamic programming starts with a small portion of the problem and finds the optimal solution for this smaller problem. It then gradually enlarges the problem, finding the current optimal solution from the previous one, until the original problem is solved in its entirety. The details involved in implementing this general philosophy are given below.

Let the decision variables x_n $(n = 1,2,3,4)$ be the immediate destination on stage n. Thus the route selected would be $1 \to x_1 \to x_2 \to x_3 \to x_4$, where $x_4 = 10$. Let $f_n(s, x_n)$ be the total cost of the best overall *policy* for the *remaining* stages, given that the salesman is in state s and selects x_n as the immediate destination. Given s and n, let x_n^* denote the value of x_n that minimizes $f_n(s, x_n)$, and let $f_n^*(s)$ be the corresponding minimum value of $f_n(s, x_n)$. Thus, $f_n^*(s) = f_n(s, x_n^*)$. The objective is to find $f_1^*(1)$ and the corresponding policy. Dynamic programming does this by successively finding $f_4^*(s)$, $f_3^*(s)$, $f_2^*(s)$ and then $f_1^*(1)$.†

When the salesman has only one more stage to go, his route is entirely determined by his final destination. Therefore the immediate solution to the one-stage problem is

s	$f_4^*(s)$	x_4^*
8	3	10
9	4	10

When the salesman has two more stages to go, the solution requires a few calculations. For example, assume that the salesman is in state 5. He must next go to either state 8 or 9 at a cost of 1 or 4, respectively. If he chooses state 8, the minimum additional cost after reaching there is given in the above table as 3, so that the total cost for this decision would be $1 + 3 = 4$. Similarly, the total cost if he chooses state 9 is $4 + 4 = 8$. Therefore he would choose state 8, $x_3^* = 8$, because it gives the minimum total cost, $f_3^*(5) = 4$. Proceeding similarly for $s = 6$ and $s = 7$ yields the following results for the two-stage problem:

[1] This problem also can be formulated as a *shortest route problem* (see Sec. 5.3), where the branch values represent *costs* rather than *distances*. The solution procedure presented in Sec. 5.3 actually uses the philosophy of dynamic programming. However, because the present problem has a fixed number of stages, the dynamic programming approach presented here is even better.

† Since this involves moving *backward* stage by stage, some writers also count n backward to denote the number of *remaining stages* to the destination. We are using the more natural *forward counting* for greater simplicity.

s \ x_3	$f_3(s, x_3) = c_{sx_3} + f_4^*(x_3)$: 8	9	$f_3^*(s)$	x_3^*
5	4	8	4	8
6	9	7	7	9
7	6	7	6	8

The solution for the three-stage problem is obtained in a similar fashion. In this case, $f_2(s, x_2) = c_{sx_2} + f_3^*(x_2)$. For example, if the salesman is in state 2 and chooses to go to state 5 next, the minimum total cost $f_2(2,5)$ would be the cost of the first stage $c_{25} = 7$ plus the minimum cost from state 5 onward, $f_3^*(5) = 4$, so that $f_2(2,5) = 7 + 4 = 11$. Similarly, $f_2(2,6) = 4 + 7 = 11$ and $f_2(2,7) = 6 + 6 = 12$, so that the minimum total cost from state 2 onward is $f_2^*(2) = 11$, and the immediate destination should be $x_2^* = 5$ or 6. The complete results for the three-stage problem are

s \ x_2	$f_2(s, x_2) = c_{sx_2} + f_3^*(x_2)$: 5	6	7	$f_2^*(s)$	x_2^*
2	11	11	12	11	5 or 6
3	7	9	10	7	5
4	8	8	11	8	5 or 6

Moving to the four-stage problem, the cost of the optimal policy given the immediate destination is again the sum of the cost of the first stage plus the minimum cost thereafter. The consequent results are

s \ x_1	$f_1(s, x_1) = c_{sx_1} + f_2^*(x_1)$: 2	3	4	$f_1^*(s)$	x_1^*
1	13	11	11	11	3 or 4

The optimal solution can now be written. The results for the four-stage problem indicate that the salesman should go initially to either state 3 or state 4. Suppose that he chooses $x_1^* = 3$. The three-stage problem result for $s = 3$ is $x_2^* = 5$. This leads to the two-stage problem, which gives $x_3^* = 8$ for $s = 5$, and the one stage problem yields $x_4^* = 10$ for $s = 8$. Hence one optimal route is $1 \to 3 \to 5 \to 8 \to 10$. Choosing $x_1^* = 4$ leads to the other two optimal routes, $1 \to 4 \to 5 \to 8 \to 10$ and $1 \to 4 \to 6 \to 9 \to 10$. They all yield a total cost of $f_1^*(1) = 11$.

You will see in the next section that the *special terms* describing the particular context of this problem—*stage, state, policy*—actually are part of the *general terminology* of dynamic programming with an analogous interpretation in other contexts.

6.2 CHARACTERISTICS OF DYNAMIC PROGRAMMING PROBLEMS

The stagecoach problem is a literal prototype of dynamic programming problems. In fact, this problem was purposely designed to provide a literal physical interpretation of the rather abstract structure of dynamic programming problems. Therefore, one way to recognize a situation which can be formulated as a dynamic programming problem is to notice that its basic structure is analogous to that of the stagecoach problem.

These basic features which characterize dynamic programming problems are presented and discussed below.

1. The problem can be divided into **stages**, with a **policy decision** required at each stage.

The stagecoach problem was literally divided into its four "stages" (stagecoaches) on the four legs of the journey. The policy decision at each stage was the destination for that particular stagecoach (i.e., which life insurance policy to choose). Other dynamic programming problems similarly require making a *sequence of interrelated decisions.*

2. Each stage has a number of **states** associated with it.

The states associated with each stage in the stagecoach problem were the states (or territories) in which the salesman could be located when embarking on that particular leg of the journey. In general, the states are the various *possible conditions* in which the system might be at that stage of the problem. The number of states may be either *finite* (as in the stagecoach problem) or *infinite* (as in some subsequent examples).

3. The effect of the policy decision at each stage is to *transform the current state into a state associated with the next stage* (possibly according to a probability distribution).

The salesman's decision as to his next destination led him from his current state to the next state on his journey. This suggests that dynamic programming problems can be interpreted in terms of the *networks* described in Chap. 5. Each *node* would correspond to a *state*. The network would consist of columns of nodes, with each *column* corresponding to a *stage*, so that flow from a node can go only to a node in the next column to the right. The value assigned to each branch connecting two nodes can sometimes be interpreted as the contribution to the objective function made by going from one state to the other corresponding to these nodes. If this is the case, the objective would be to find either the *shortest* or the *longest route* through the network.

4. Given the current state, an *optimal policy for the remaining stages* is *independent* of the policy adopted in *previous stages*.

Given the state in which the salesman is currently located, the optimal life insurance policy (and its associated route) from this point onward is independent of how he got there. For dynamic programming problems in general, knowledge of the current state of the system conveys all the information about its previous behavior necessary for determining the optimal policy henceforth. (This is the *Markovian property* discussed in Sec. 8.18.) This property is sometimes referred to as the *principle of optimality*.

5. The solution procedure begins by finding the optimal policy for each state of the *last* stage.

The solution of this one-stage problem is usually trivial, as it was for the stagecoach problem.

6. **A recursive relationship** that identifies the optimal policy for each state at stage n, given the optimal policy for each state at stage $(n+1)$, is available.

For the stagecoach problem, this recursive relationship was

$$f_n^*(s) = \min_{x_n}\{c_{sx_n} + f_{n+1}^*(x_n)\}.$$

Therefore, finding the *optimal policy* when starting in state s at stage n requires finding the minimizing value of x_n. This policy would consist of using this value of x_n and then following the optimal policy when starting in state x_n at stage $(n+1)$.

The precise form of the recursive relationship differs somewhat among dynamic programming problems. However, notation analogous to that introduced in the preceding section will continue to be used here. Thus, let the variable (or vector) x_n be the decision variable at stage n ($n = 1,2, \ldots, N$). Let $f_n(s,x_n)$ be the maximizing/minimizing value of the objective function, given that the system starts in state s at stage n and x_n is selected. [Thus $f_n(s,x_n) = c_{sx_n} + f_{n+1}^*(x_n)$ for the stagecoach problem.] Let $f_n^*(s)$ be the maximum/minimum value of $f_n(s,x_n)$ over all possible values of x_n. The recursive relationship will always be of the form

$$f_n^*(s) = \max_{x_n}/\min_{x_n}\{f_n(s,x_n)\},$$

where $f_n(s,x_n)$ would be written in terms of s, x_n, $f_{n+1}^*(\cdot)$ and probably some measure of the first-stage effectiveness/ineffectiveness of x_n.

7. Using this recursive relationship, the solution procedure moves ***backward*** stage by stage—each time finding the optimal policy for each state of that stage—until it finds the optimal policy when starting at the *initial* stage.

This was demonstrated by the stagecoach problem, where the optimal policy was successively found when beginning in each state at stage 4, 3, 2, and 1, respectively.[1] For all dynamic programming problems, a table such as the following would be obtained for each stage ($n = N, N-1, \ldots, 1$):

s	$f_n^*(s)$	x_n^*

[1] Actually, for this problem the solution procedure can move ***either*** backward or forward. However, for many problems (especially when the stages correspond to ***time periods***), the solution procedure ***must*** move backward.

When this table is finally obtained for the initial stage ($n = 1$), the problem of interest is solved. Since the initial state would be known, the initial decision is specified by x_1^* in this table. The optimal value of the other decision variables would then be specified by the other tables according to the state of the system at those stages.

6.3 DETERMINISTIC DYNAMIC PROGRAMMING

This section further elaborates upon the dynamic programming approach to *deterministic* problems, where the *state* at the *next stage* is *completely determined* by the *state* and *policy decision* at the *current stage*. The *probabilistic* case, where there is a probability distribution for what the next state will be, is discussed in the next section.

Deterministic dynamic programming can be described diagramatically, as shown in Fig. 6.2. Thus at stage n the process will be in some state s_n. Making policy decision x_n then moves the process to some state s_{n+1} at stage $(n + 1)$. From that point onward the objective function value for the optimal policy has been previously calculated to be $f_{n+1}^*(s_{n+1})$. The policy decision x_n also makes some contribution to the objective function. Combining these two quantities in an appropriate way provides the objective function value $f_n(s_n, x_n)$ beginning at stage n. Minimizing with respect to x_n then gives $f_n^*(s_n) = f_n(s_n, x_n^*)$. After doing this for each possible value of s_n, the solution procedure is ready to move back one stage.

One way of categorizing deterministic dynamic programming problems is by the *form of the objective function*. For example, the objective might be to *minimize* the *sum* of the contributions from the individual stages (as for the stagecoach problem), or to *maximize* such a sum, or to minimize a *product* of such terms, and so on. Another categorization is in terms of the nature of the *set of states* for the respective stages. In particular, the states s_n might be representable by a *discrete* state variable (as for the stagecoach problem), or by a *continuous* state variable, or perhaps a state *vector* (more than one variable) is required.

Several examples will be presented to illustrate these various possibilities. However, more importantly, they illustrate that these apparently major differences are actually quite inconsequential (except in terms of computational difficulty) because the underlying basic structure shown in Fig. 6.2 always remains the same.

Figure 6.2 The basic structure for deterministic dynamic programming.

Stage n — Stage $n+1$

State: s_n → s_{n+1}

$f_n(s_n, x_n)$ — Contribution of x_n — $f_{n+1}^*(s_{n+1})$

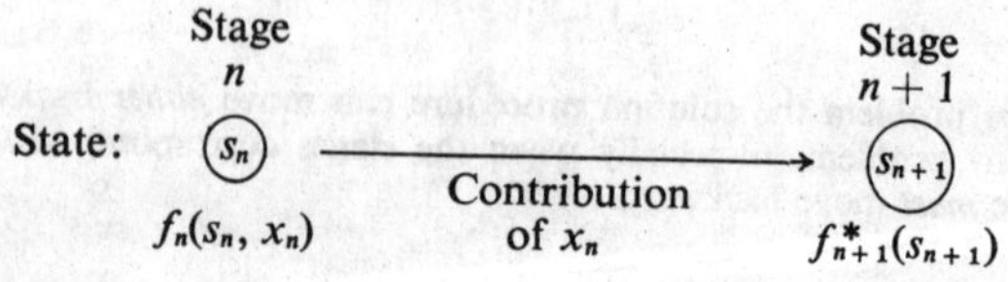

The first example arises in a much different context than the stagecoach problem, but it has the same *mathematical formulation* except that the objective is to *maximize* rather than minimize a sum.

Example 2

The *World Health Council* is devoted to improving health care in the underdeveloped countries of the world. It now has five *medical teams* available to allocate among three such countries to improve their medical care, health education, and training programs. Therefore the Council needs to determine how many teams (if any) to allocate to each of these countries to maximize the total effectiveness of the five teams. The measure of effectiveness being used is *additional man-years of life.* (For a particular country, this measure equals the country's *increased life expectancy* in years times its population.) Table 6.1 gives the estimated additional man-years of life (in multiples of 1,000) for each country for each possible allocation of medical teams.

Table 6.1 Data for World Health Council

	Thousands of additional man-years of life		
	Country		
No. of medical teams	*1*	*2*	*3*
0	0	0	0
1	45	20	50
2	70	45	70
3	90	75	80
4	105	110	100
5	120	150	130

SOLUTION This problem requires making three *interrelated decisions*, namely, how many medical teams to allocate to each of the three countries. Therefore, even though there is no fixed sequence, these three countries can be considered as the three *stages* in a dynamic programming formulation. The decision variables x_n $(n = 1,2,3)$ would be the number of teams to allocate to stage (country) n.

The identification of the *states* may not be readily apparent. To determine this, questions such as the following should be asked. What is it that changes from one stage to the next? Given that the decisions have been made at the previous stages, how can the status of the situation at the current stage be described? What information about the current state of affairs is necessary to determine the optimal policy hereafter? On these bases, an appropriate choice for the "state of the system" is the *number of medical teams still available for allocation* (i.e., the number not already allocated at previous stages).

Let $p_i(x_i)$ be the measure of effectiveness from allocating x_i medical teams to country i, as given in Table 6.1. Thus the objective is to choose x_1, x_2, x_3 so as to

$$\text{Maximize} \quad \sum_{i=1}^{3} p_i(x_i),$$

subject to

$$\sum_{i=1}^{3} x_i = 5$$

and

$$\text{the } x_i \text{ are nonnegative integers.}$$

Using the notation presented in Sec. 6.2, $f_n(s,x_n)$ then is

$$f_n(s,x_n) = p_n(x_n) + \text{maximum} \sum_{i=n+1}^{3} p_i(x_i)$$

$$\text{such that} \sum_{i=n}^{3} x_i = s,$$

$$\text{the } x_i \text{ are nonnegative integers,}$$

for $n = 1, 2, 3$. In addition,

$$f_n^*(s) = \max_{x_n=0,1,\ldots,s} f_n(s,x_n).$$

Therefore

$$f_n(s,x_n) = p_n(x_n) + f_{n+1}^*(s - x_n)$$

(with f_4^* defined to be *zero*). These basic relationships are summarized in Fig. 6.3.

Consequently, the ***recursive relationship*** relating the f_1^*, f_2^*, and f_3^* functions for this problem is

$$f_n^*(s) = \max_{x_n=0,1,\ldots,s} \{p_n(x_n) + f_{n+1}^*(s - x_n)\}, \text{ for } n = 1, 2.$$

For the last stage ($n = 3$),

$$f_3^*(s) = \max_{x_3=0,1,\ldots,s} p_3(x_3).$$

Figure 6.3 The basic structure for the World Health Council problem.

The resulting dynamic programming calculations are given below, beginning with the last stage ($n = 3$) and proceeding backward to the first stage ($n = 1$).

$n = 3$

s	$f_3^*(s)$	x_3^*
0	0	0
1	50	1
2	70	2
3	80	3
4	100	4
5	130	5

$n = 2$

s \ x_2	$f_2(s, x_2) = p_2(x_2) + f_3^*(s - x_2)$: 0	1	2	3	4	5	$f_2^*(s)$	x_2^*
0	0						0	0
1	50	20					50	0
2	70	70	45				70	0, 1
3	80	90	95	75			95	2
4	100	100	115	125	110		125	3
5	130	120	125	145	160	150	160	4

$n = 1$

s \ x_1	$f_1(s, x_1) = p_1(x_1) + f_2^*(s - x_1)$: 0	1	2	3	4	5	$f_1^*(s)$	x_1^*
5	160	170	165	160	155	120	170	1

Thus the optimal solution has $x_1^* = 1$, which makes $s = 5 - 1 = 4$ for $n = 2$, so $x_2^* = 3$, which makes $s = 4 - 3 = 1$ for $n = 3$, so $x_3^* = 1$. Since $f_1^*(5) = 170$, this (1,3,1) allocation of medical teams to the three countries will yield an estimated total of 170,000 *additional man-years of life*, which is at least 5,000 more than for any other allocation.

The *context* of the next example is somewhat similar to that for the World Health Council problem. However, its *mathematical formulation* differs in that its objective is to minimize a *product* of terms for the respective stages. At first glance this example may appear *not* to be a *deterministic* dynamic programming problem because probabilities are involved. However, it does indeed fit our definition because the state at the next stage is completely determined by the state and policy decision at the current stage.

Example 3

A government space project is conducting research on a certain engineering problem that must be solved before man can fly safely to Mars. Three research teams are currently trying three different approaches for solving this problem. The estimate has been made that, under present circumstances, the probability that the respective teams—call them 1, 2, and 3—will not succeed is 0.40, 0.60, and 0.80, respectively. Thus, the current probability that all three teams will fail is (0.40)(0.60)(0.80) = 0.192. Since the objective is to minimize this probability, the decision has been made to assign two more top scientists among the three teams to lower it as much as possible.

Table 6.2 gives the estimated probability that the respective teams will fail when 0, 1, or 2 additional scientists are added to that team. The problem is to determine how to allocate the two additional scientists to minimize the probability that all three teams will fail.

Table 6.2 Data on the Government Space Project Problem

	Probability of failure		
		Team	
No. of new scientists	*1*	*2*	*3*
0	0.40	0.60	0.80
1	0.20	0.40	0.50
2	0.15	0.20	0.30

SOLUTION The underlying structure of this problem is actually very similar to that of Example 2. In this case scientists replace medical teams and research teams replace countries. Therefore, instead of allocating medical teams to countries, scientists are to be allocated to research teams. The only basic difference between the two problems is in their objective functions.

With so few scientists and teams involved, this problem could be solved very easily by a process of exhaustive enumeration. However, the dynamic programming solution is presented for illustrative purposes. In this case the *stages* correspond to the research teams, and the *state* s is the number of new scientists still available for assignation at that stage. The decision variables x_n ($n = 1,2,3$) are the number of additional scientists allocated to stage (team) n. Let $p_i(x_i)$ denote the probability of failure for team i if it is assigned x_i additional scientists, as given by Table 6.2. Letting Π denote multiplication, the government's objective is to choose x_1, x_2, x_3 so as to

$$\text{Minimize} \quad \prod_{i=1}^{3} p_i(x_i) = p_1(x_1)p_2(x_2)p_3(x_3),$$

subject to

$$\sum_{i=1}^{3} x_i = 2$$

and

$$\text{the } x_i \text{ are nonnegative integers.}$$

Consequently,

$$f_n(s, x_n) = p_n(x_n) \cdot \text{minimum} \prod_{i=n+1}^{3} p_i(x_i)$$

$$\text{such that } \sum_{i=n}^{3} x_i = s,$$

$$\text{the } x_i \text{ are nonnegative integers,}$$

for $n = 1, 2, 3$. Thus

$$f_n^*(s) = \min_{x_n \leq s} f_n(s, x_n).$$

Hence

$$f_n(s, x_n) = p_n(x_n) \cdot f_{n+1}^*(s - x_n)$$

(with f_4^* defined to be *one*). Fig. 6.4 summarizes these basic relationships.

Thus the *recursive relationship* relating the f_1^*, f_2^*, and f_3^* functions in this case is

$$f_n^*(s) = \min_{x_n \leq s} \{p_n(x_n) \cdot f_{n+1}^*(s - x_n)\}, \text{ for } n = 1, 2,$$

and, when $n = 3$,

$$f_3^*(s) = \min_{x_3 \leq s} p_3(x_3).$$

The resulting dynamic programming calculations are

$n = 3$

s	$f_3^*(s)$	x_3^*
0	0.80	0
1	0.50	1
2	0.30	2

$n = 2$

s \ x_2	$f_2(s, x_2) = p_2(x_2) \cdot f_3^*(s - x_2)$: 0	1	2	$f_2^*(s)$	x_2^*
0	0.48			0.48	0
1	0.30	0.32		0.30	0
2	0.18	0.20	0.16	0.16	2

Figure 6.4 The basic structure for the government space project problem.

Stage n — Stage $n+1$

State: s → $s - x_n$ (transition $p_n(x_n)$)

$f_n(s, x_n) = p_n(x_n) \cdot f_{n+1}^*(s - x_n)$ — $f_{n+1}^*(s - x_n)$

$n = 1$ s \ x_1	$f_1(s, x_1) = p_1(x_1) \cdot f_2^*(s - x_1)$ 0	1	2	$f_1^*(s)$	x_1^*
2	0.064	0.060	0.072	0.060	1

Therefore the optimal solution must have $x_1^* = 1$, which makes $s = 1$ at stage 2, so that $x_2^* = 0$, which makes $s = 1$ at stage 3, so that $x_3^* = 1$. Thus, teams 1 and 3 should each receive one additional scientist. The new probability that all three teams will fail would then be 0.060.

All the examples thus far have had a *discrete* state variable s. Furthermore, they all have been *reversible* in the sense that the solution procedure actually could have moved *either* backward or forward stage by stage. The next example is different in both respects; rather than being restricted to *integer* values, its state variable s is a *continuous* variable that can take on *any* value over certain intervals. Since s now has an infinite number of values, it is no longer possible to consider each of its feasible values individually. Rather, the solution for $f_n^*(x)$ and x_n^* must be expressed as *functions* of s. Furthermore, this example is *not* reversible because its stages correspond to *time periods*, so the solution procedure *must* proceed backward.

Example 4

The work load for the *Local Job Shop* is subject to considerable seasonal fluctuation. However, machine operators are difficult to hire and costly to train, so the manager is reluctant to lay off workers during the slack seasons. He is likewise reluctant to maintain his peak season payroll when it is not required. Furthermore, he is definitely opposed to overtime work on a regular basis. Since all work is done to custom orders, it is not possible to build up inventories during slack seasons. Therefore the manager is in a dilemma as to what his policy should be regarding employment levels.

The following estimates are given for the manpower requirements during the four seasons of the year for the forseeable future:

Season	*Spring*	*Summer*	*Autumn*	*Winter*	*Spring*	...
Requirements	255	220	240	200	255	...

Employment will not be permitted to fall below these levels. Any employment above these levels is wasted at an approximate cost of $2,000 per man per season. It is also estimated that the hiring and firing costs are such that the total cost of changing the level of employment from one season to the next is $200 times the square of the difference in employment levels. Fractional levels of employment are possible because of a few part-time employees, and the above cost data also apply on a fractional basis.

The manager needs to determine what the employment level should be in each season to minimize total cost.

SOLUTION On the basis of the data available, it would not be worthwhile for the employment level to go above the peak season requirements of 255. Therefore spring employment should be at 255, and the problem reduces to finding the employment level for the other three seasons.

For a dynamic programming formulation, the seasons should be the *stages*. There is actually an indefinite number of stages because the problem extends into the indefinite future. However, each year begins an identical cycle, and because spring employment is known, it is possible to consider only one cycle of four seasons ending with the spring season.

The decision variables x_n ($n = 1,2,3,4$) are the employment levels at stage n. It is necessary that the spring season be the last stage because the optimal value of the decision variable for each state at the last stage must be either known or obtainable without considering other stages. For every other season, the solution for the optimal employment level must consider the effect on costs in the following season. Therefore x_1, x_2, x_3, and x_4 are the employment levels for summer, autumn, winter and spring, repectively, where $x_4 = 255$.

The cost at the current stage depends only upon the current decision x_n and the employment in the previous season. The preceding employment level is all the information about the current state of affairs that is required to determine the optimal policy henceforth. Therefore the *state s* is described by the employment level at the previous stage. Thus at stage n the state $s = x_{n-1}$ (where $x_0 = x_4 = 255$).

Let r_n denote the minimum manpower requirement at stage n, so that $r_1 = 220$, $r_2 = 240$, $r_3 = 200$, and $r_4 = 255$. The objective for the problem is to choose x_1, x_2, x_3, x_4 so as to

$$\text{Minimize} \quad \sum_{i=1}^{4} [200(x_i - x_{i-1})^2 + 2{,}000(x_i - r_i)],$$

subject to

$$r_i \le x_i \le 255, \text{ for } i = 1, 2, 3, 4.$$

Thus for stage n onward ($n = 1,2,3,4$),

$$\begin{aligned} f_n(s, x_n) = {} & 200(x_n - s)^2 + 2{,}000(x_n - r_n) \\ & + \text{minimum} \sum_{i=n+1}^{4} [200(x_i - x_{i-1})^2 + 2{,}000(x_i - r_i)] \\ & \text{such that } r_i \le x_i \le 255, \end{aligned}$$

since $s = x_{n-1}$. Also,

$$f_n^*(s) = \min_{r_n \le x_n \le 255} f_n(s, x_n).$$

Hence

$$f_n(s, x_n) = 200(x_n - s)^2 + 2{,}000(x_n - r_n) + f_{n+1}^*(x_n)$$

Stage n — State: s — $f_n(s, x_n)$ = sum — $200(x_n - s)^2 + 2{,}000(x_n - r_n)$ → Stage $n+1$ — x_n — $f^*_{n+1}(x_n)$

Figure 6.5 The basic structure for the Local Job Shop problem.

(with f_5^* defined to be *zero* because costs after stage 4 are irrelevant to the analysis). A summary of these basic relationships is given in Fig. 6.5.

Consequently, the *recursive relationship* relating the f_n^* functions is

$$f_n^*(s) = \min_{r_n \leq x_n \leq 255} \{200(x_n - s)^2 + 2{,}000(x_n - r_n) + f^*_{n+1}(x_n)\}.$$

The dynamic programming approach is to use this relationship to successively identify these functions—$f_4^*(s)$, $f_3^*(s)$, $f_2^*(s)$, $f_1^*(255)$—and the corresponding minimizing x_n.

Beginning at the *last* stage ($n = 4$), it has already been concluded that $x_4^* = 255$, so the necessary results are

$n=4$ s	$f_4^*(s)$	x_4^*
$200 \leq s \leq 255$	$200(255 - s)^2$	255

For the problem consisting of just the last *two* stages ($n = 3$), this recursive relationship reduces to

$$\begin{aligned} f_3^*(s) &= \min_{200 \leq x_3 \leq 255} f_3(s, x_3) \\ &= \min_{200 \leq x_3 \leq 255} \{200(x_3 - s)^2 + 2{,}000(x_3 - 200) + 200(255 - x_3)^2\}. \end{aligned}$$

One way to solve for the minimum of $f_3(s, x_3)$ for any particular value of s is the graphical approach illustrated in Fig. 6.6. However, a faster way is to use *calculus*. In particular, equate to zero the first (partial) derivative of $f_3(s, x_3)$ with respect to x_3,

$$\begin{aligned} \frac{\partial}{\partial x_3} f_3(s, x_3) &= 400(x_3 - s) + 2{,}000 - 400(255 - x_3) \\ &= 400(2x_3 - s - 250) \\ &= 0, \end{aligned}$$

which yields

$$x_3^* = \frac{s + 250}{2}.$$

Since the second derivative is positive, and this solution lies in the feasible interval for x_3, it is indeed the desired minimum. Using

$$f_3^*(s) = f_3(s, x_3^*) = 200\left(\frac{s+250}{2} - s\right)^2 + 200\left(255 - \frac{s+250}{2}\right)^2 + 2{,}000\left(\frac{s+250}{2} - 200\right)$$

and reducing this expression algebraically then completes the required results for the two-stage problem summarized below.

$n = 3$ s	$f_3^*(s)$	x_3^*
$240 \le s \le 255$	$50(250-s)^2 + 50(260-s)^2 + 1{,}000(s-150)$	$\frac{s+250}{2}$

The three-stage ($n = 2$) and four-stage problems ($n = 1$) are solved in a similar fashion. Thus for $n = 2$,

$$\begin{aligned} f_2(s, x_2) &= 200(x_2 - s)^2 + 2{,}000(x_2 - r_2) + f_3^*(x_2) \\ &= 200(x_2 - s)^2 + 2{,}000(x_2 - 240) \\ &\quad + 50(250 - x_2)^2 + 50(260 - x_2)^2 + 1{,}000(x_2 - 150) \end{aligned}$$

Figure 6.6 Graphical solution for $f_3^*(s)$ for the Local Job Shop problem.

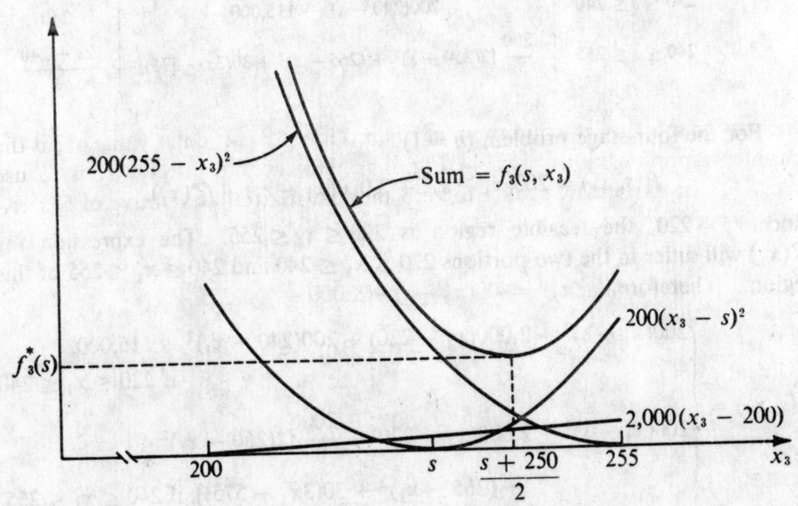

in the feasible region $240 \leq x_2 \leq 255$. The problem is to find the minimizing value of x_2 in this region, so that

$$f_2^*(s) = \min_{240 \leq x_2 \leq 255} f_2(s, x_2).$$

Setting

$$\frac{\partial}{\partial x_2} f_2(s, x_2) = 0$$

$$= 400(x_2 - s) + 2{,}000 - 100(250 - x_2) - 100(260 - x_2) + 1{,}000$$
$$= 200(3x_2 - 2s - 240)$$

yields

$$x_2 = \frac{2s + 240}{3}.$$

Since

$$\frac{\partial^2}{\partial x_2^2} f_2(s, x_2) = 600 > 0,$$

this is the desired minimizing value if $s \geq 240$. If $s < 240$ (so that the above x_2 is infeasible), then

$$\frac{\partial}{\partial x_2} f_2(s, x_2) > 0, \text{ for } 240 \leq x_2 \leq 255,$$

so that $x_2 = 240$ would be the minimizing value. The next step is to plug these values of x_2 into $f_2(s, x_2)$ to obtain $f_2^*(s)$ for $s \geq 240$ and $s < 240$. After some algebraic manipulation, the following results are obtained:

$n = 2$ s	$f_2^*(s)$	x_2^*
$220 \leq s \leq 240$	$200(240 - s)^2 + 115{,}000$	240
$240 \leq s \leq 255$	$\frac{200}{9}[2(250 - s)^2 + (265 - s)^2 + 30(3s - 575)]$	$\frac{2s + 240}{3}$

For the four-stage problem ($n = 1$),

$$f_1(s, x_1) = 200(x_1 - s)^2 + 2{,}000(x_1 - r_1) + f_2^*(x_1).$$

Since $r_1 = 220$, the feasible region is $220 \leq x_1 \leq 255$. The expression for $f_2^*(x_1)$ will differ in the two portions $220 \leq x_1 \leq 240$ and $240 \leq x_1 \leq 255$ of this region. Therefore,

$$f_1(s, x_1) = \begin{cases} 200(x_1 - s)^2 + 2{,}000(x_1 - 220) + 200(240 - x_1)^2 + 115{,}000, & \text{if } 220 \leq x_1 \leq 240 \\ 200(x_1 - s)^2 + 2{,}000(x_1 - 220) + \frac{200}{9}[2(250 - x_1)^2 + (265 - x_1)^2 + 30(3x_1 - 575)], & \text{if } 240 \leq x_1 \leq 255. \end{cases}$$

Considering first the case where $x_1 \le 240$,

$$\frac{\partial}{\partial x_1} f_1(s, x_1) = 400(x_1 - s) + 2{,}000 - 400(240 - x_1)$$
$$= 400(2x_1 - s - 235).$$

It is known that $s = 255$ (spring employment), so that

$$\frac{\partial}{\partial x_1} f_1(s, x_1) = 800(x_1 - 245)$$
$$< 0$$

for all $x_1 \le 240$. Therefore, $x_1 = 240$ is the minimizing value of $f_1(s,x_1)$ over the region $x_1 \le 240$.

When $240 \le x_1 \le 255$,

$$\frac{\partial}{\partial x_1} f_1(s, x_1) = 400(x_1 - s) + 2{,}000 - \frac{200}{9}[4(250 - x_1) + 2(265 - x_1) - 90]$$
$$= \frac{400}{3}(4x_1 - 3s - 225).$$

Since

$$\frac{\partial^2}{\partial x_1^2} f_1(s, x_1) > 0, \text{ for all } x_1,$$

set

$$\frac{\partial}{\partial x_1} f_1(s, x_1) = 0,$$

which yields

$$x_1 = \frac{3s + 225}{4}.$$

Since $s = 255$, $x_1 = 247.5$ therefore minimizes $f_1(s,x_1)$ over the region $240 \le x_1 \le 255$. Since this region includes $x_1 = 240$, which minimizes $f_1(s,x_1)$ over the region where $x_1 \le 240$, it follows that $x_1 = 247.5$ also minimizes $f_1(s,x_1)$ over the entire feasible region $220 \le x_1 \le 255$. Hence

$$f_1^*(255) = 200(247.5 - 255)^2 + 2{,}000(247.5 - 220)$$
$$+ \frac{200}{9}[s(250 - 247.5)^2 + (265 - 247.5)^2 + 30(742.5 - 575)]$$
$$= 185{,}000.$$

These results are summarized below.

$n = 1$ s	$f_1^*(s)$	x_1^*
255	185,000	247.5

Therefore the optimal policy is $x_1 = 247.5$, $x_2 = 245$, $x_3 = 247.5$, $x_4 = 255$, with a total estimated cost per cycle of \$185,000.

To conclude our illustrations of deterministic dynamic programming, we give one example that requires *more than one* variable to describe the state at each stage.

Example 5

Consider the linear programming problem

$$\text{Maximize} \quad Z = 3x_1 + 5x_2,$$

subject to

$$\begin{aligned} x_1 \qquad &\le 4 \\ 2x_2 &\le 12 \\ 3x_1 + 2x_2 &\le 18 \end{aligned}$$

and

$$x_1 \ge 0, x_2 \ge 0.$$

(You might recognize this as being the model for the *Wyndor Glass Co.* problem, which was the prototype example for linear programming in Chap. 2.) One way of solving small linear (or nonlinear) programming problems like this one is by dynamic programming, which is illustrated below.

SOLUTION This problem requires making two interrelated decisions, namely, the level of activity 1, x_1, and the level of activity 2, x_2. Therefore, these two activities can be interpreted as the two *stages* in a dynamic programming formulation. Although they can be taken in either order, let stage n = activity n ($n = 1,2$). Thus, x_n is the decision variable at stage n.

What are the states? In other words, given that the decision had been made at stage 1, what information is needed about the current state of affairs before making the decision at stage 2? Reflection might suggest that the required information is the *amount of slack* left in the constraints (other than the nonnegativity restrictions). To amplify, interpret the right-hand side of these constraints 4, 6, and 18 as the total available amount of resources 1, 2, and 3, respectively (as described in Sec. 2.1). Then the state s is the amount of the respective resources remaining to be allocated. Thus,

$$s = (R_1, R_2, R_3),$$

where R_i is the amount of resource i remaining to be allocated ($i = 1,2,3$).

Therefore, in contrast to the preceding examples, this problem has *three* state variables (i.e., a state vector with three components) rather than one. From a theoretical standpoint, this is not particularly serious. It only means that, instead of considering all possible values of the one state variable, it is necessary to consider all possible *combinations* of values of the several state variables. However, from the standpoint of computational efficiency, this tends to be a very serious complication. Since the number of combinations, in general, can be as large as the *product* of the number of possible values of the respective variables, the number of required calculations tend to "blow up" rapidly when additional decision variables are introduced. (This phenomenon has been given the apt name of *the curse of dimensionality*.)

Each of the three state variables is *continuous*. Therefore, rather than consider each possible combination of values separately, it is necessary to use the approach introduced in Example 4 of solving for the required information as a *function* of the state of the system.

Despite these complications, this problem is small enough so that it can still be solved without great difficulty. To do this, the usual dynamic programming notation needs to be introduced. Thus, interpreting Z as profit, $f_n(R_1,R_2,R_3,x_n)$ is the maximum total profit from stage n onward, *given* that the state and policy decision at stage n are (R_1,R_2,R_3) and x_n, respectively. Using the *general notation* of linear programming (see Sec. 2.2),

$$f_n(R_1,R_2,R_3,x_n) = c_n x_n + \text{maximum} \sum_{j=n+1}^{2} c_j x_j$$

$$\text{such that} \quad \sum_{j=n}^{2} a_{ij} x_j \leq R_i \ (i = 1,2,3),$$

$$\text{the } x_j \geq 0,$$

for $n = 1, 2$. In addition,

$$f_n^*(R_1,R_2,R_3) = \max_{x_n} f_n(R_1,R_2,R_3,x_n),$$

where this maximum is taken over the *feasible* values of x_n. Therefore

$$f_n(R_1,R_2,R_3, x_n) = c_n x_n + f_{n+1}^*(R_1 - a_{1n}x_n, R_2 - a_{2n}x_n, R_3 - a_{3n}x_n)$$

(with f_3^* defined to be *zero*). These basic relationships are summarized in Fig. 6.7.

Since the last two equations together define the *recursive relationship* relating f_1^* and f_2^*, the preparations for performing the dynamic programming calculations are completed. To solve at the last stage ($n = 2$), note that

$$f_2(R_1,R_2,R_3,x_2) = 5x_2,$$

Figure 6.7 The basic structure for the Wyndor Glass Co. linear programming problem.

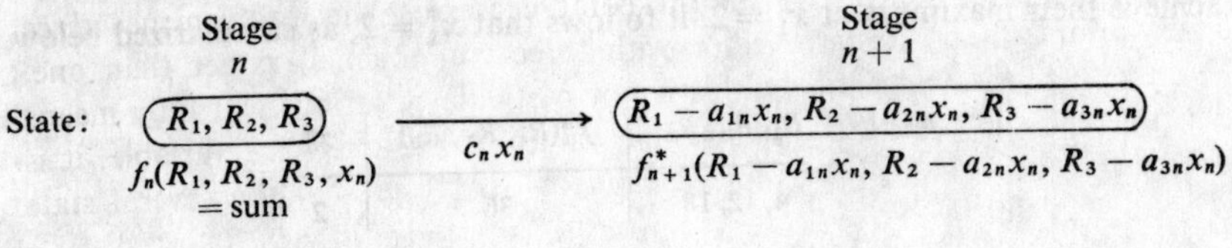

	Stage n		Stage $n+1$
State:	(R_1, R_2, R_3)	$\xrightarrow{c_n x_n}$	$(R_1 - a_{1n}x_n, R_2 - a_{2n}x_n, R_3 - a_{3n}x_n)$
	$f_n(R_1, R_2, R_3, x_n) = \text{sum}$		$f_{n+1}^*(R_1 - a_{1n}x_n, R_2 - a_{2n}x_n, R_3 - a_{3n}x_n)$

where the feasible values of x_2 are those satisfying the set of restrictions $2x_2 \leq R_2$, $2x_2 \leq R_3$, $x_2 \geq 0$. Therefore

$$f_2^*(R_1,R_2,R_3) = \max_{\substack{2x_2 \leq R_2 \\ 2x_2 \leq R_3 \\ x_2 \geq 0}} \{5x_2\}.$$

Thus, the resulting solution is

$n = 2$ R_1, R_2, R_3	$f_2^*(R_1, R_2, R_3)$	x_2^*
$R_i \geq 0$	$5 \min\left\{\frac{R_2}{2}, \frac{R_3}{2}\right\}$	$\min\left\{\frac{R_2}{2}, \frac{R_3}{2}\right\}$

For the two-stage problem ($n = 1$),

$$f_1(R_1,R_2,R_3,x_1) = 3x_1 + f_2^*(R_1 - x_1, R_2, R_3 - 3x_1),$$

where the feasible values of x_1 are those satisfying the set of restrictions $x_1 \leq R_1$, $3x_1 \leq R_3$, $x_1 \geq 0$. Therefore, because it is known that $R_1 = 4$, $R_2 = 12$, $R_3 = 18$ at the first stage, the desired recursive relationship is

$$f_1^*(4,12,18) = \max_{\substack{x_1 \leq 4 \\ 3x_1 \leq 18 \\ x_1 \geq 0}} \{3x_1 + f_2^*(4 - x_1, 12, 18 - 3x_1)\}$$

$$= \max_{0 \leq x_1 \leq 4} \left\{3x_1 + 5 \min\left\{\frac{12}{2}, \frac{18 - 3x_1}{2}\right\}\right\}.$$

Notice that

$$\min\left\{\frac{12}{2}, \frac{18 - 3x_1}{2}\right\} = \begin{cases} 6, & \text{if } 0 \leq x_1 \leq 2 \\ 9 - \frac{3}{2}x_1, & \text{if } 2 \leq x_1 \leq 4, \end{cases}$$

so that

$$3x_1 + 5 \min\left\{\frac{12}{2}, \frac{18 - 3x_1}{2}\right\} = \begin{cases} 3x_1 + 30, & \text{if } 0 \leq x_1 \leq 2 \\ 45 - \frac{9}{2}x_1, & \text{if } 2 \leq x_1 \leq 4. \end{cases}$$

Since both

$$\max_{0 \leq x_1 \leq 2} \{3x_1 + 30\} \text{ and } \max_{2 \leq x_1 \leq 4} \left\{45 - \frac{9}{2}x_1\right\}$$

achieve their maximum at $x_1 = 2$, it follows that $x_1^* = 2$, as summarized below.

$n = 1$ R_1, R_2, R_3	$f_1^*(R_1, R_2, R_3)$	x_1^*
4, 12, 18	36	2

Therefore the optimal solution for this problem is

$$x_1 = 2 \text{ and } x_2 = \min\left\{6, \frac{18 - 3(2)}{2}\right\} = 6,$$

with a total profit of 36.

6.4 PROBABILISTIC DYNAMIC PROGRAMMING

Probabilistic dynamic programming differs from deterministic dynamic programming in that the state at the next stage is *not* completely determined by the state and policy decision at the current stage. Rather, there is a *probability distribution* for what the next state will be. However, this probability distribution still is completely determined by the state and policy decision at the current stage. The resulting basic structure for probabilistic dynamic programming is described diagramatically in Fig. 6.8, where N denotes the number of possible states at stage $n + 1$; $(p_1, p_2, \ldots, p_N)$ is the probability distribution of what the state will be, given the state s_n and decision x_n at stage n; and C_i is the resulting contribution to the objective function from stage n if the state turns out to be state i.

When Fig. 6.8 is expanded to include all the possible states and decisions at all the stages, it is sometimes referred to as a **decision tree.** If the decision tree is not too large, it provides a useful way of summarizing the various possibilities that may occur.

Because of the probabilistic structure, the relationship between $f_n(s_n, x_n)$ and the $f^*_{n+1}(s_{n+1})$ necessarily is somewhat more complicated than for deterministic dynamic programming. The precise form of this relationship will

Figure 6.8 The basic structure for probabilistic dynamic programming.

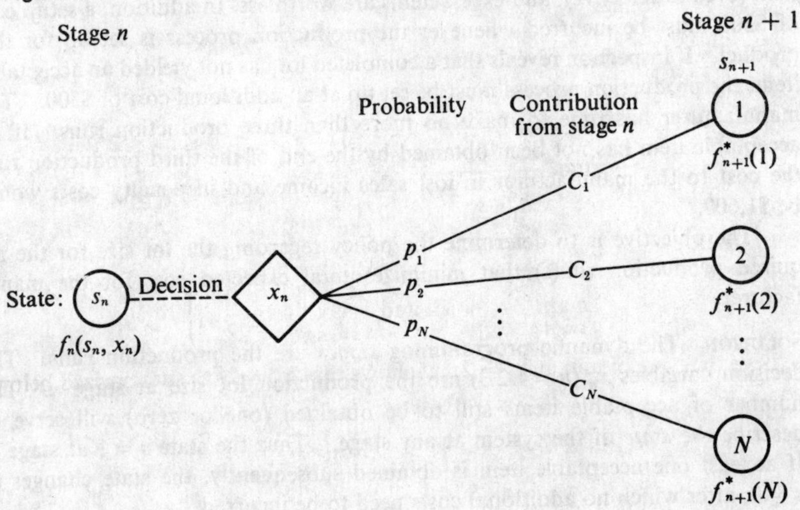

depend upon the form of the overall objective function. To illustrate, suppose that the objective is to *minimize* the *expected sum* of the contributions from the individual stages. In this case $f_n(s_n, x_n)$ would represent the minimum expected sum from stage n onward, *given* that the state and policy decision at stage n are s_n and x_n, respectively. Consequently,

$$f_n(s_n, x_n) = \sum_{i=1}^{N} p_i[C_i + f_{n+1}^*(i)],$$

with

$$f_{n+1}^*(s_{n+1}) = \min_{x_{n+1}} f_{n+1}(s_{n+1}, x_{n+1}),$$

where this minimization is taken over the *feasible* values of x_{n+1}.

Example 6 has this same form; Example 7 will illustrate another form.

Example 6

The *Hit-and-Miss Manufacturing Company* has received an order to supply one item of a particular type. However, the customer has specified such stringent quality requirements that the manufacturer may have to produce more than one item to obtain an acceptable one. The manufacturer estimates that each item of this type that he produces will be *acceptable* with probability ½ and *defective* (without possibility for rework) with probability ½. Thus the number of acceptable items produced in a lot of size L will have a binomial distribution (see binomial distribution in Sec. 8.6); that is, the probability of producing *zero* acceptable items in such a lot is $(\frac{1}{2})^L$.

Marginal production costs for this product are estimated to be \$100 per item (even if defective), and excess items are worthless. In addition, a setup cost of \$300 must be incurred whenever the production process is set up for this product. If inspection reveals that a completed lot has not yielded an acceptable item, the production process must be set up at an additional cost of \$300. The manufacturer has time to make no more than three production runs. If an acceptable item has not been obtained by the end of the third production run, the cost to the manufacturer in lost sales income and in penalty costs would be \$1,600.

The objective is to determine the policy regarding the lot size for the required production run(s) that minimizes total expected cost for the manufacturer.

SOLUTION The dynamic programming *stages* are the production runs. The decision variables x_n ($n = 1,2,3$) are the production lot size at stage n. The number of acceptable items still to be obtained (one or zero) will serve to describe the *state* of the system at any stage. Thus the state $s = 1$ at stage 1. If at least one acceptable item is obtained subsequently, the state changes to $s = 0$, after which no additional costs need to be incurred.

Although a complicated expression can be given for the overall objective function, it is more straightforward to define $f_n(s, x_n)$ directly. In this case $f_n(s, x_n)$ is the *minimum total expected cost* for stage n onward, *given* that the state and policy decision at stage n are s and x_n, respectively. Furthermore,

$$f_n^*(s) = \min_{x_n=0,1,\ldots} f_n(s, x_n),$$

where $f_n^*(0) = 0$. Using \$100 as the unit of money, the contribution to cost from stage n is $(K + x_n)$ regardless of the next state, where

$$K = \begin{cases} 0, & \text{if } x_n = 0 \\ 3, & \text{if } x_n > 0. \end{cases}$$

Therefore, for $s = 1$,

$$\begin{aligned} f_n(1, x_n) &= K + x_n + \left(\frac{1}{2}\right)^{x_n} f_{n+1}^*(1) + \left[1 - \left(\frac{1}{2}\right)^{x_n}\right] f_{n+1}^*(0) \\ &= K + x_n + \left(\frac{1}{2}\right)^{x_n} f_{n+1}^*(1) \end{aligned}$$

[where $f_4^*(1)$ is defined to be 16, the terminal cost if no acceptable items have been obtained]. A summary of these basic relationships is given in Fig. 6.9.

Consequently, the *recursive relationship* for the dynamic programming calculations is

$$f_n^*(1) = \min_{x_n=0,\,1,\,\ldots} \left\{K + x_n + \left(\frac{1}{2}\right)^{x_n} f_{n+1}^*(1)\right\}$$

for $n = 1, 2, 3$. These calculations are summarized below.

$n=3$	$s \backslash x_3$	$f_3(1, x_3) = K + x_3 + 16\left(\frac{1}{2}\right)^{x_3}$: 0	1	2	3	4	$f_3^*(s)$	x_3^*
	0	0					0	0
	1	16	12	9	8	8	8	3 or 4

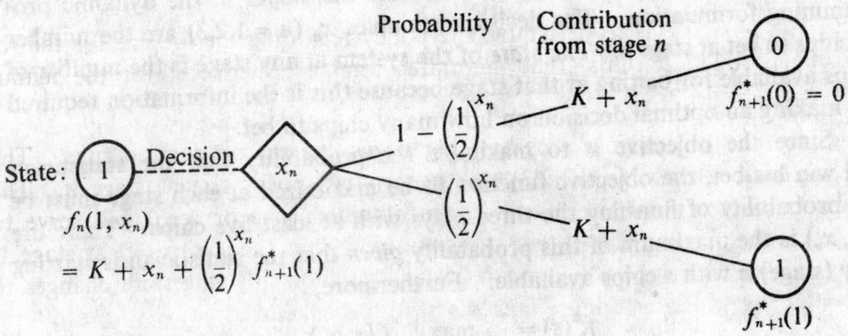

Figure 6.9 The basic structure for the Hit-and-Miss Manufacturing Company problem.

$n = 2$

s \ x_2	$f_2(1, x_2) = K + x_2 + \left(\frac{1}{2}\right)^{x_2} f_3^*(1)$					$f_2^*(s)$	x_2^*
	0	1	2	3	4		
0	0					0	0
1	8	8	7	7	$7\frac{1}{2}$	7	2 or 3

$n = 1$

s \ x_1	$f_1(1, x_1) = K + x_1 + \left(\frac{1}{2}\right)^{x_2} f_2^*(1)$					$f_1^*(s)$	x_1^*
	0	1	2	3	4		
1	7	$7\frac{1}{2}$	$6\frac{3}{4}$	$6\frac{7}{8}$	$7\frac{1}{16}$	$6\frac{3}{4}$	2

Thus the optimal policy is to produce *two* items on the first production run; if none are acceptable, then produce either *two* or *three* items on the second production run; if none are acceptable, then produce either *three* or *four* items on the third production run. The *total expected cost* for this policy is \$675.

Example 7

An enterprising young statistician believes that he has developed a system for winning a popular Las Vegas game. His colleagues do not believe that this is possible, so they make a large bet with him that, starting with three chips, he will not have five chips after three plays of the game. Each play of the game involves betting any desired number of available chips and then either winning or losing this number of chips. The statistician believes that his system will give him a probability of $\frac{2}{3}$ of winning a given play of the game.

Assuming the statistician is correct, determine his optimal policy regarding how many chips to bet (if any) at each of the three plays of the game. The decision at each play should take into account the results of earlier plays. The objective is to maximize the probability of winning his bet with his colleagues.

SOLUTION The plays of the game constitute the *stages* in the dynamic programming formulation. The decision variables x_n $(n = 1,2,3)$ are the number of chips to bet at stage n. The *state* of the system at any stage is the number of chips available for betting at that stage because this is the information required for making an optimal decision on how many chips to bet.

Since the objective is to maximize the probability that the statistician will win his bet, the objective function to be maximized at each stage must be the probability of finishing the three plays with at least five chips. Therefore $f_n(s, x_n)$ is the maximum of this probability *given* that the statistician is starting play (stage) n with s chips available. Furthermore,

$$f_n^*(s) = \max_{x_n = 0, 1, \ldots, s} f_n(s, x_n).$$

The expression for $f_n(s, x_n)$ must reflect the fact that it may still be possible to eventually accumulate five chips even if the statistician should lose the next play. If he should lose, the state at the next stage would be $(s - x_n)$, and the probability of finishing with at least five chips would then be $f^*_{n+1}(s - x_n)$. If he should win the next play instead, the state would become $(s + x_n)$, and the corresponding probability would be $f^*_{n+1}(s + x_n)$. Since the alleged probability of winning a given play is ⅔, it now follows that

$$f_n(s, x_n) = \frac{1}{3} f^*_{n+1}(s - x_n) + \frac{2}{3} f^*_{n+1}(s + x_n)$$

[where $f^*_4(s)$ is defined to be *zero* for $s < 5$ and 1 for $s \geq 5$]. Thus there is no direct contribution to the objective function from stage n in addition to the effect of being in the next state. These basic relationships are summarized in Fig. 6.10.

Therefore the ***recursive relationship*** for this problem is

$$f^*_n(s) = \max_{x_n = 0, 1, \ldots, s} \left\{ \frac{1}{3} f^*_{n+1}(s - x_n) + \frac{2}{3} f^*_{n+1}(s + x_n) \right\}$$

for $n = 1, 2, 3$. This leads to the computational results given below.

$n = 3$ s	$f^*_3(s)$	x^*_3
0	0	....
1	0	....
2	0	....
3	$\frac{2}{3}$	2 (or more)
4	$\frac{2}{3}$	1 (or more)
≥ 5	1	0 (or $\leq s - 5$)

Figure 6.10 The basic structure for the Las Vegas problem.

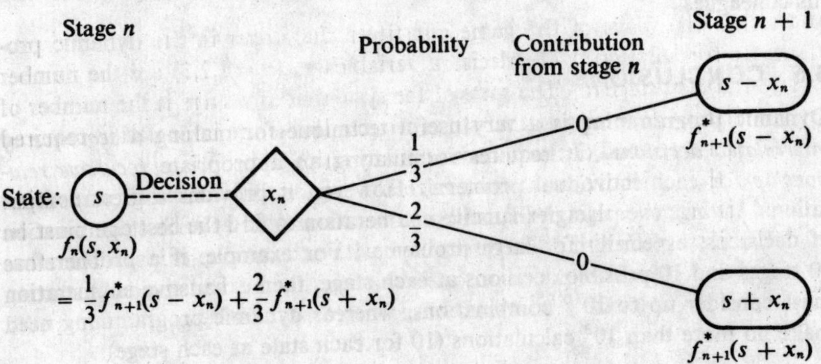

$n = 2$

$$f_2(s, x_2) = \frac{1}{3} f_3^*(s - x_2) + \frac{2}{3} f_3^*(s + x_2)$$

s \ x_2	0	1	2	3	4	$f_2^*(s)$	x_2^*
0	0					0	....
1	0	0				0	....
2	0	$\frac{4}{9}$	$\frac{4}{9}$			$\frac{4}{9}$	1, 2
3	$\frac{2}{3}$	$\frac{4}{9}$	$\frac{2}{3}$	$\frac{2}{3}$		$\frac{2}{3}$	0, 2, 3
4	$\frac{2}{3}$	$\frac{8}{9}$	$\frac{2}{3}$	$\frac{2}{3}$	$\frac{2}{3}$	$\frac{8}{9}$	1
≥ 5	1					1	0 (or $\leq s - 5$)

$n = 1$

$$f_1(s, x_1) = \frac{1}{3} f_2^*(s - x_1) + \frac{2}{3} f_2^*(s + x_1)$$

s \ x_1	0	1	2	3	$f_1^*(s)$	x_1^*
3	$\frac{2}{3}$	$\frac{20}{27}$	$\frac{2}{3}$	$\frac{2}{3}$	$\frac{20}{27}$	1

Therefore the optimal policy is

$$x_1^* = 1 \begin{cases} \text{if win, } x_2^* = 1 \begin{cases} \text{if win, } x_3^* = 0 \\ \text{if lose, } x_3^* = 2, 3 \end{cases} \\ \text{if lose, } x_2^* = 1 \text{ or } 2 \begin{cases} \text{if win, } x_3^* = 2, 3, \text{ or } 1, 2, 3, 4 \\ \text{if lose, bet is lost.} \end{cases} \end{cases}$$

This policy gives the statistician a probability of 20/27 of winning his bet with his colleagues.

6.5 CONCLUSIONS

Dynamic programming is a very useful technique for making a *sequence of interrelated decisions.* It requires formulating an appropriate *recursive relationship* for each individual problem. However, it provides a great computational savings over using exhaustive enumeration to find the best combination of decisions, especially for large problems. For example, if a problem has 10 stages and 10 possible decisions at each stage, then exhaustive enumeration must consider up to 10^{10} combinations, whereas dynamic programming need make no more than 10^3 calculations (10 for each state at each stage).

This chapter has considered only dynamic programming with a *finite* number of stages. Chapter 12 is devoted to a general kind of model for probabilistic dynamic programming where the stages continue recurring indefinitely, namely, *Markovian decision processes.*

Selected References

1 Bellman, Richard and Stuart Dreyfus: *Applied Dynamic Programming*, Princeton University Press, Princeton, N.J., 1962.
2 Howard, Ronald A.: "Dynamic Programming," *Management Science*, **12**: 317–345, 1966.
3 Kaufmann, A. and R. Cruon: *Dynamic Programming: Sequential Scientific Management*, (trans. from French by Henry C. Sneyd), Academic Press, New York, 1967.
4 Nemhauser, George L.: *Introduction to Dynamic Programming*, Wiley, New York, 1966.
5 White, D. J.: *Dynamic Programming*, Oliver & Boyd, Edinburgh, and Holden-Day, San Francisco, 1969.

Problems

1 The owner of a chain of three grocery stores has purchased five crates of fresh strawberries. The estimated probability distribution of potential sales of the strawberries before spoilage differs among the three stores. Therefore the owner wishes to know how he should allocate the five crates to the three stores to maximize expected profit.

For administrative reasons, the owner does not wish to split crates between stores. However, he is willing to distribute zero crates to any of his stores.

The following table gives the estimated expected profit at each store when it is allocated various numbers of crates:

Number of crates	*Stores* 1	2	3
0	0	0	0
1	3	5	4
2	7	10	6
3	9	11	11
4	12	11	12
5	13	11	12

Use dynamic programming to determine how many of the five crates should be assigned to each of the three stores to maximize the total expected profit.

2 A county chairwoman of a certain political party is making plans for an upcoming presidential election. She has received the services of six volunteer workers for precinct work, and she wishes to assign them to four precincts in such a way as to maximize their effectiveness. She feels that it would be inefficient to assign a worker to more than one precinct, but she is willing to assign no workers to any one of the precincts if they can accomplish more in other precincts.

The following table gives the estimated increase in the plurality (positive or negative) of the party's candidate in each precinct if it were allocated various numbers of workers:

Number of workers	Precinct 1	2	3	4
0	0	0	0	0
1	20	25	18	28
2	42	45	39	47
3	60	57	61	65
4	75	65	78	74
5	85	70	90	80
6	90	73	95	85

Use dynamic programming to determine how many of the six workers should be assigned to each of the four precincts to maximize the total estimated increase in the plurality of the party's candidate.

3 Use dynamic programming to solve the Northern Airplane Company production scheduling problem presented in Sec. 3.1 (see Table 3.3). Assume that production quantities must be integer multiples of 5.

4 A company will soon be introducing a new product into a very competitive market and so is currently planning its marketing strategy. The decision has been made to introduce the product in three phases. Phase 1 will feature making a special introductory offer of the product to the public at a greatly reduced price to attract first-time buyers. Phase 2 will involve an intensive advertising campaign to persuade these first-time buyers to continue purchasing the product at a regular price. It is known that another company will be introducing a new competitive product at about the time phase 2 will end. Therefore phase 3 will involve a follow-up advertising and promotion campaign to try to keep the regular purchasers from switching to the competitive product.

A total of $5 million has been budgeted for this marketing campaign. The problem now is to determine how to most effectively allocate this money to the three phases. Let m denote the initial share of the market (expressed as a percentage) attained in phase 1, f_2 the fraction of this market share that is retained in phase 2, and f_3 the fraction of the remaining market share that is retained in phase 3. Given the data outlined below, use dynamic programming to determine how to allocate the $5 million to maximize the *final share* of the market for the new product, i.e., to maximize mf_2f_3.

(*a*) Assume that the money must be spent in integer multiples of $1 million in each phase where the following table gives the estimated effect of expenditures in each phase:

Millions of dollars expended	Effect on market share m	f_2	f_3
0	..	0.30	0.50
1	10	0.50	0.70
2	15	0.70	0.85
3	22	0.80	0.90
4	27	0.85	0.93
5	30	0.90	0.95

(*b*) Now assume that *any* amount within the total budget can be spent in each phase, where the estimated effect of spending an amount x_i (in units of *millions* of dollars) in phase i $(i=1,2,3)$ is

$$m = 10x_1 - x_1^2$$

$$f_2 = 0.40 + 0.10x_2$$

$$f_3 = 0.60 + 0.70x_3\,.$$

[*Hint:* After solving for the $f_3^*(s)$ and $f_2^*(s)$ functions analytically, solve for x_1^* graphically.]

5 Consider an electronic system consisting of four components, each of which must function for the system to function. The reliability of the system can be improved by installing several parallel units in one or more of the components. The following table gives the probability that the respective components will function if they consist of one, two, or three parallel units:

Number of parallel units	Probability of functioning			
	Component 1	*Component 2*	*Component 3*	*Component 4*
1	0.70	0.50	0.70	0.60
2	0.80	0.70	0.90	0.70
3	0.90	0.80	0.95	0.90

The probability that the system will function is the product of the probabilities that the respective components will function.

The cost of installing one, two, or three parallel units in the respective components is given by the following table:

Number of parallel units	Cost, $			
	Component 1	*Component 2*	*Component 3*	*Component 4*
1	10	20	10	20
2	20	40	30	30
3	30	50	40	40

Because of budget limitations, a maximum of $100 can be expended.

Use dynamic programming to determine how many parallel units should be installed in each of the four components to maximize the probability that the system will function.

6 Resolve the *Local Job Shop* employment scheduling problem (Example 4) when the total cost of changing the level of employment from one season to the next is changed to $100 times the square of the difference in employment levels.

7 Consider the following nonlinear programming problem:

$$\text{Maximize} \quad Z = 12x_1 + 3x_1^2 - 2x_1^3 + 12x_2 - x_2^3,$$

subject to

$$x_1 + x_2 \leq 3$$

and

$$x_1 \geq 0, x_2 \geq 0.$$

Use dynamic programming to solve this problem.

8 Consider the following "fixed-charge" problem:

$$\text{Maximize} \quad Z = x_1 + 2x_2 + f(x_3),$$

subject to

$$x_1 + 3x_2 + 2x_3 \leq 6$$
$$x_1 + x_2 \leq 5$$

and

$$x_1 \geq 0, x_2 \geq 0, x_3 \geq 0,$$

where

$$f(x_3) = \begin{cases} 0, & \text{if } x_3 = 0 \\ -3 + 3x_3, & \text{if } x_3 > 0. \end{cases}$$

Use dynamic programming to solve this problem.

9 Imagine that you have $1,000 to invest and that you will have the opportunity to invest that amount in either of two investments (*A* or *B*) at the beginning of each of the next 3 years. Both investments have uncertain returns. For investment *A* you will either lose your money entirely or (with higher probability) get $2,000 back (a profit of $1,000) at the end of the year. For investment *B* you will either get just your $1,000 back or (with low probability) $2,000 back at the end of the year. The probabilities for these events are

Investment	*Amount returned* ($)	*Probability*
A	0	0.4
	2,000	0.6
B	1,000	0.9
	2,000	0.1

You are only allowed to make (at most) *one* investment each year and can only invest $1,000 each time. (Any additional money accumulated is left idle.)

(*a*) Use dynamic programming to find the investment policy that maximizes the *expected amount of money* you will have after the 3 years.

(*b*) Use dynamic programming to find the investment policy that maximizes the *probability* that you will have at least $2,000 after the 3 years.

10 Suppose that the situation for the Hit-and-Miss Manufacturing Co. problem (Example 6) has changed somewhat. After a more careful analysis, it is now estimated that each item produced will be *acceptable* with probability $\frac{2}{3}$, rather than $\frac{1}{2}$, so that the probability of producing *zero* acceptable items in a lot of size L is $(\frac{1}{3})^L$. Furthermore, there now is only enough time available to make *two* production runs. Use dynamic programming to determine the new optimal policy for this problem.

11 Reconsider Example 7. Suppose that the bet is changed to "Starting with two chips, he will not have five chips after *five* plays of the game." By referring to the previous computational results, make additional calculations to determine what the new optimal policy is for the enterprising young statistician.

12 The Profit & Gambit Company has a major product that has been losing money recently because of declining sales. In fact, during the current quarter of the year sales will be 4 million units below the *break-even point*. Since the *marginal* revenue for each unit sold exceeds the *marginal* cost by \$1, this amounts to a loss of \$4 million for the quarter. Therefore management must take action quickly to rectify this situation. Two alternative courses of action are being considered. One is to abandon the product immediately, incurring a cost of \$4 million for shutting down. The other alternative is to undertake an intensive advertising campaign to increase sales and then abandon the product (at the cost of \$4 million) only if the campaign is not sufficiently successful. Tentative plans for this advertising campaign have been developed and analyzed. It would extend over the next three quarters (subject to early cancellation), and the cost would be \$6 million in each of the three quarters. It is estimated that the increase in sales would be approximately 3 million units in the first quarter, another 2 million units in the second quarter, and another 1 million units in the third quarter. However, because of a number of unpredictable market variables, there is considerable uncertainty as to what impact the advertising actually would have, and careful analysis indicates that the estimate for each quarter could turn out to be off by as much as 2 million units in either direction. (To quantify this uncertainty, assume that the additional increase in sales in the three quarters are independent random variables having a uniform distribution with a range from 1 to 5 million, from 0 to 4 million, and from -1 to 3 million, respectively.) If the actual increases are too small, the advertising campaign can be discontinued and the product abandoned at the end of either of the next two quarters.

If the intensive advertising campaign were to be initiated and continued to its completion, it is estimated that the sales for some time thereafter would continue to be at about the same level as in the third (last) quarter of the campaign. Therefore, if the sales in that quarter still are below the break-even point, the product would be abandoned. Otherwise, it is estimated that the expected discounted profit thereafter would be \$8 for each unit sold over the break-even point in the third quarter.

Use dynamic programming to determine the optimal policy maximizing expected profit.

7 Game Theory

7.1 INTRODUCTION

Life is full of conflict and competition. Numerous examples involving adversaries in conflict include parlor games, military battles, political campaigns, advertising and marketing campaigns by competing business firms, and so forth. A basic feature in many of these situations is that the final outcome depends primarily upon the combination of strategies selected by the adversaries. *Game theory* is a mathematical theory that deals with the general features of competitive situations like these in a formal, abstract way. It places particular emphasis on the decision-making process of the adversaries.

Much of the research on game theory has been on *two-person zero-sum games*. As the name implies, these games involve only two adversaries or *players* (who may be armies, teams, firms, and so on). They are called *zero-sum* because one player wins whatever the other one loses, so that the sum of their net winnings is zero. The discussion hereafter concentrates on this kind of game, although other types are also mentioned at the end of the chapter.

To illustrate the basic characteristics of a game theory model, consider a simplified version of the game called "two-finger morra." In this version, each player simultaneously shows either one or two fingers. If the number of fingers match, then player I wins, say, $1 from player II. If they do not match, player I would pay $1 to player II. Thus each player has two *strategies*: to show either one or two fingers. The resulting payoff to player I in dollars is shown in the *payoff table* given in Table 7.1.

In general, a game is characterized by

1. The strategies of player I,
2. The strategies of player II,
3. The payoff table.

Table 7.1 Payoff Table for Simplified Version of Two-finger Morra

		II: 1	II: 2
I	1	1	−1
	2	−1	1

A *strategy* may involve only a simple action, as in this example. On the other hand, in more complicated games involving a series of moves, a strategy is a *predetermined rule that specifies completely how one intends to respond to each possible circumstance at each stage of the game.* Before the game begins, each player knows the strategies available to himself, the ones available to his opponent, and the payoff table. The actual play of the game consists of the players simultaneously choosing a strategy without knowing their opponent's choice.

The *payoff table* usually is given only for player I because the table for player II is just the negative of this one, due to the zero-sum nature of the game. The entries in the payoff may be in any units desired, such as dollars, provided that they accurately represent the "utility" to player I of the corresponding outcome. It should be noted that utility is not necessarily proportional to the amount of money (or of many other commodities) when large quantities are involved. For example, \$2 million (after taxes) is probably worth much less than twice as much as \$1 million to a poor man. In other words, given the choice between (1) a 50 percent chance of receiving \$2 million rather than nothing, and (2) being sure of getting \$1 million, he probably would much prefer the latter. On the other hand, the outcome corresponding to an entry of 2 in a payoff table should be "worth twice as much" to player I as the outcome corresponding to an entry of 1. Thus, given the choice, he should be indifferent between a 50 percent chance of receiving the former outcome (rather than nothing) and definitely receiving the latter outcome instead.

A primary objective of game theory is to develop *rational criteria* for selecting a strategy. This is done under the assumption that both players are rational, and that each will uncompromisingly attempt to do as well as possible, relative to his opponent. This is in contrast to decision theory (see Chap. 14), which essentially assumes that the decision maker is playing a game with a passive opponent, nature, which chooses its "strategies" in some random fashion. Instead, game theory assumes that both players are actively trying to promote their own welfare in opposition to that of the opponent.

We shall develop the standard game theory criteria for choosing strategies by means of illustrative examples. In particular, the next section presents a prototype example that illustrates the formulation of a game and its solution in some simple situations. A more complicated variation of this game is then carried into Sec. 7.3 to develop a more general criterion. Sections 7.4 and 7.5

describe a *graphical procedure* and a *linear programming formulation* for solving such games; extensions of game theory to cover situations other than two-person zero-sum games are then discussed briefly in Sec. 7.6.

7.2 SOLVING SIMPLE GAMES—A PROTOTYPE EXAMPLE

Two politicians are running against each other for the United States Senate. Campaign plans must now be made for the final 2 days before the election, which are expected to be crucial because of the closeness of the race. Therefore both politicians want to spend these days campaigning in two key cities: *Bigtown* and *Megalopolis.* To avoid wasting campaigning time they plan to travel at night and either spend one full day in each city or two full days in just one of the cities. However, since the necessary arrangements must be made in advance, neither politician will learn his opponent's campaign schedule until after he has finalized his own. Therefore each politician has asked his campaign manager in each of these cities to assess what the impact would be (in terms of votes won or lost) from the various possible combinations of days spent there by himself and by his opponent. He then wishes to use this information to choose his best strategy on how to use these 2 days.

FORMULATION To formulate this problem as a two-person zero-sum game it is necessary to identify the two *players* (obviously the two politicians), the *strategies* for each player, and the *payoff table.*

As the problem has been stated, each player has the following three strategies:

Strategy 1 = spend 1 day in each city.
Strategy 2 = spend both days in Bigtown.
Strategy 3 = spend both days in Megalopolis.

However, by contrast, these would *not* be the strategies if each politician could learn where his opponent will spend his first day before he finalizes his own plans for his second day. In that case, each politician would have *eight* strategies (since two choices of city for his first day *and* two choices for his second day given *each* of the two possible first-day choices by his opponent provides $2 \times 2 \times 2 = 8$ combinations).

Each entry in the payoff table for player I represents the *utility* to player I (or the negative utility to player II) of the outcome resulting from the corresponding strategies used by the two players. From the politician's viewpoint, the objective is to *win votes*, and each additional vote (before learning the outcome of the election) is of equal value to him. Therefore the appropriate entries for their payoff table are the *total net votes won* from the opponent (i.e., the sum of the net vote changes in the two cities) resulting from these 2 days of campaigning. This formulation is summarized in Table 7.2.

Table 7.2 Formulation of Payoff Table for The Political Campaign Problem

Strategy \ Strategy		Total net votes won by politician I (in units of 1,000 votes)		
		Politician II		
		1	*2*	*3*
Politician I	1			
	2			
	3			

However, we should also point out that this would *not* be the appropriate payoff table if additional information were available to the politicians. In particular, if they knew exactly how the populace was planning to vote 2 days before the election, the only significance of the data prescribed by Table 7.2 would be to indicate which politician would win the election with each combination of strategies. Since the ultimate goal is to win the election, and the siz of the plurality is relatively inconsequential, the utility entries in the table then should be some positive constant (say, $+\frac{1}{2}$) when politician I would win and $-\frac{1}{2}$ when he would lose. Even if only a *probability* of winning can be determined for each combination of strategies, the appropriate entries would be these probabilities minus $\frac{1}{2}$ because they then would represent *expected* utilities. However, sufficiently accurate data to do this usually are not available. Using the form given in Table 7.2, three alternative sets of data for the payoff table are given below to illustrate how to solve three different kinds of games.

Variation 1

Given that Table 7.3 is the payoff table for the two politicians (players), which strategy should *player I* play? A brief inspection indicates that the answer ***must*** be strategy 1 because it *dominates* strategies 2 and 3, that is, it is at least as good

Table 7.3 Payoff Table for Variation 1 of The Political Campaign Problem

		II		
		1	*2*	*3*
	1	2	1	4
I	2	2	0	1
	3	−1	−2	0

as either of these other strategies regardless of what the opponent does. Similarly, *player II* would automatically discard his strategy 3 from consideration because it is dominated by another strategy (strategy 2), which has *uniformly lower payoffs to player I.* Since both players are assumed to be rational, player II would further deduce that player I will play strategy 1 and that he should therefore play strategy 2 to minimize his losses. As a result, player I will always receive a payoff of 1 from player II (i.e., politician I will gain 1,000 votes from politician II), so that the *value* of this game is said to be 1. It is only when a game has a value of zero that it is said to be a *fair game*.

Thus the concept of a *dominated strategy* is a very useful one for reducing the size of the payoff table that needs to be considered and, in cases like this one, actually identifying the optimal solution to the game.

Variation 2

Now suppose that the current data give Table 7.4 as the payoff table for the politicians (players). This game does not have dominated strategies, so it is not obvious what the players should do. What line of reasoning does game

Table 7.4 Payoff Table for Variation 2 of The Political Campaign Problem

		II			
		1	*2*	*3*	Minimum
I	1	−3	−2	6	−3
	2	2	0	2	0 ← Maximin strategy for I
	3	5	−2	−4	−4
	Maximum:	5	0	6	
			↑ Minimax strategy for II		

theory say they should use? Consider player I: By selecting strategy 1, he could win 6 or he could lose as much as 3. However, since player II is rational, and so will protect himself from large payoffs to I, it seems probable that playing strategy 1 would result in a loss to I. Similarly, by selecting strategy 3, player I could win 5, but more probably his intelligent opponent would avoid this and administer him a loss, which could be as large as 4. On the other hand, if player I selects strategy 2, he is guaranteed not to lose anything, and he could even win something. Therefore, since it provides a *better guarantee* than the others, strategy 2 seems to be a "rational" choice for player I against his rational opponent. By arguing in a similar manner, player II would see that he could lose as much as 5, 0, and 6 by using strategies 1, 2, and 3, respectively, so the apparent "rational" choice is strategy 2. Furthermore, even when either player learns the other's strategy he can not improve by changing his own, so this strategy can be used safely and (given the opportunity) repeatedly.

The end product of the line of reasoning described above is that each player should play in such a way as to *minimize his maximum losses* whenever this would not give an advantage to the opponent. This so-called *minimax criterion* is a standard criterion proposed by game theory for selecting a strategy. In terms of the payoff table it implies that *player I* should select the strategy whose *minimum payoff* is *largest*, whereas *player II* should choose the one whose *maximum payoff to I* is the *smallest*. This is illustrated in payoff table 7.4, where strategy 2 is identified as the "maximin" strategy for player I, and strategy 2 is the minimax strategy for player II. The maximin and minimax values, which are both zero here, are referred to as the *lower value* and the *upper value* of the game, respectively. When they are equal, the common quantity is called the *value* of the game. It is zero here, so the game is *fair*.

Notice the interesting fact that the same entry in this payoff table yields both the lower and the upper values. The reason is that this entry is both the minimum in its row and the maximum in its column. The position of any such entry is called a *saddle point*.

The fact that this game possesses a saddle point was actually crucial in determining how it should be played. Because of the saddle point, neither player can take advantage of the opponent's strategy to improve his own position. In particular, when player II predicts or learns that player I is using strategy 2, player II would only increase his losses if he were to change from his original plan of using his strategy 2. Similarly, player I would only worsen his position if he were to change his plan. Thus neither player has any motive to consider changing strategies, either to take advantage of his opponent or to prevent the opponent from taking advantage of him. Therefore, since this solution is a *stable* one, players I and II should exclusively use their maximin and minimax strategies, respectively.

As the next variation illustrates, some games do not possess a saddle point, in which case a more complicated analysis is required.

Variation 3

Late developments in the campaign result in the *final* payoff table for the two politicians (players) given by Table 7.5. How should this game be played? Suppose that both players attempt to apply the *minimax criterion* in the same way as was done in variation 2.

Table 7.5 Payoff Table for Variation 3 of The Political Campaign Problem

		II *1*	*2*	*3*	Minimum
	1	0	−2	2	−2 ← Lower value of the game
I	2	5	4	−3	−3
	3	2	3	−4	−4
	Maximum:	5	4	2 ↑ Upper value of the game	

Player I would notice that the lower value of the game is -2, so he can guarantee that he will lose no more than 2 by playing strategy 1. Similarly, since the upper value of the game is 2, player II can guarantee that he will not lose more than 2 by playing strategy 3.

However, notice that there is no value of the game and therefore no saddle point. What are the resulting consequences if both players should plan to use the strategies derived above? It can be seen that player I would win 2 from player II, which would make player II unhappy. Since he is rational and can therefore foresee this outcome, player II would then conclude that he can do much better, actually winning 2 rather than losing 2, by playing strategy 2 instead. Since player I is also rational, he would anticipate this switch and conclude that he can improve considerably, from -2 to 4, by changing to strategy 2. Realizing this, player II would then consider switching back to strategy 3 to convert a loss of 4 to a gain of 3. This would cause player I to again consider using strategy 1, and then the whole cycle would start over again. In short, the originally suggested solution (player I to play strategy 1 and player II to play strategy 3) is *unstable*, so it is necessary to develop a more satisfactory solution. But what kind of solution should it be?

The key fact seems to be that whenever one player's strategy is predictable, the opponent here can take great advantage of this information to improve his position. Therefore, an essential feature of a "rational" plan for playing a game such as this one is that neither player should be able to deduce which strategy the other will use. Hence, rather than applying some known criterion for determining a single strategy that will definitely be used, it is necessary to choose among alternative acceptable strategies on some kind of random basis. By doing this, neither player knows in advance which of his own strategies will be used, let alone what his opponent will do.

This suggests, in very general terms, the kind of approach that is required for games lacking a saddle point. The next section discusses this approach more fully. Given this foundation, attention is then turned to procedures for finding an optimal way of playing such games. This particular variation of the political campaign problem will continue to be used to illustrate these ideas as they are developed.

7.3 GAMES WITH MIXED STRATEGIES

Whenever a game does not possess a saddle point, game theory advises each player to assign a probability distribution over his set of strategies. To express this mathematically, let

$$x_i = \text{probability that player I will use strategy } i \ (i = 1,2, \ldots, m),$$

$$y_j = \text{probability that player II will use strategy } j \ (j = 1,2, \ldots, n),$$

where m and n are the respective numbers of available strategies. Thus player I would specify his plan for playing the game by assigning values to $x_1, x_2, \ldots, x_m$. Since these values are probabilities, they would need to be nonnegative and add up to 1. Similarly, the plan for player II would be described by the values he assigned to his decision variables $y_1, y_2, \ldots, y_n$. These plans $(x_1, x_2, \ldots, x_m)$ and $(y_1, y_2, \ldots, y_n)$ are usually referred to as **mixed strategies**, and the original strategies would then be called *pure strategies*. When actually playing the game it is necessary for each player to use one of his pure strategies. However, this one would be chosen by using some random device to obtain a random observation from the probability distribution specified by the mixed strategy, where this observation would indicate which particular pure strategy to use.

To illustrate, suppose that players I and II in *variation* 3 of the political campaign problem (see Table 7.5) select the mixed strategies $(x_1, x_2, x_3) = (\frac{1}{2}, \frac{1}{2}, 0)$ and $(y_1, y_2, y_3) = (0, \frac{1}{2}, \frac{1}{2})$, respectively. This would say that player I is giving an equal chance (probability of $\frac{1}{2}$) to choosing either (pure) strategy 1 or 2, but he is discarding strategy 3 entirely. Similarly, player II is randomly choosing between his last two pure strategies. To play the game, each player could then flip a coin to determine which of his two acceptable pure strategies he will actually use.

Although no completely satisfactory quantity is available for evaluating mixed strategies, a very useful one is the *expected payoff* (in the statistical sense described in Sec. 8.8). Applying the definition of expected value, this quantity would be

$$\text{Expected payoff} = \sum_{i=1}^{m} \sum_{j=1}^{n} p_{ij} x_i y_j,$$

where p_{ij} is the payoff if player I uses pure strategy i and player II uses pure strategy j. It does not disclose anything about the "risks" involved in playing the game, but it does indicate what the average payoff will tend to be if the game were to be played many times. Thus in the above example there are four possible payoffs ($-2, 2, 4$, and -3), each occurring with a probability of $\frac{1}{4}$, so the expected payoff is $\frac{1}{4}(-2 + 2 + 4 - 3) = \frac{1}{4}$.

The time has now come to extend the concept of the minimax criterion to games having mixed strategies. In this context, the *minimax criterion* says that a given player should select the strategy that maximizes the minimum *expected* payoff (i.e., that minimizes the maximum expected loss) to himself. By minimum expected payoff is meant the smallest possible expected payoff that can result from any mixed strategy with which the opponent can counter. Thus the mixed strategy for player I that is *optimal* according to this criterion is the one that guarantees him the largest possible expected payoff, regardless of which mixed strategy player II might use. The value of this "maximin" *expected* payoff is called the *lower value* of the game and is denoted by $\underline{v}$. Similarly, the *optimal* strategy for player II is the one that guarantees him the smallest possible expected loss, regardless of what player I does. The corresponding value of the *expected* payoff to player I is the *upper value* of the game, $\bar{v}$.

Recall that when only pure strategies were being used, games not having a saddle point turned out to be unstable. The reason essentially was that

$\underline{v} < \bar{v}$, so that the players would want to change their strategy to improve their position. Similarly, for games with mixed strategies it is necessary that $\underline{v} = \bar{v}$ for the optimal solution to be stable. Fortunately, according to the *minimax theorem* of game theory this condition always holds for such games, as indicated below.

MINIMAX THEOREM: If mixed strategies are allowed, there always exists a value of the game, that is, $\underline{v} = \bar{v} = v$.

Thus if both players use their mixed strategy that is optimal according to the minimax criterion, the expected payoff would be v, and neither player can do better by unilaterally changing his strategy. One proof of this theorem is included in Sec. 7.5.

Although the concept of mixed strategies is quite intuitive if the game is to be played *repeatedly*, it requires some interpretation when the game is to be played just *once*. In this case, using a mixed strategy still involves selecting and using *one* pure strategy (randomly selected from the specified probability distribution), so it might seem more sensible to ignore this randomization process and just choose the one "best" pure strategy to be definitely used. However, we have already illustrated for variation 3 in the preceding section that a player must *not* allow his opponent to deduce what his strategy will be (i.e., the solution procedure under the rules of game theory must not *definitely* identify which pure strategy will be used when the game is unstable).

Furthermore, even if the opponent is able to use his knowledge of the tendencies of the first player to deduce *probabilities* for the pure strategy chosen that are different from those for the *optimal* mixed strategy, then he can take advantage of this to reduce the expected payoff to the first player. Therefore, the only way to *guarantee* attaining the optimal *expected* payoff v is to *randomly* select the pure strategy to be used from the probability distribution for the optimal mixed strategy. (Valid statistical procedures for making such a random selection are discussed in Chap. 15.) It now remains to show how to find the optimal mixed strategy for each player. There are several methods of doing this. One is a graphical procedure that may be used whenever one of the players has only two (undominated) pure strategies; this approach is described in the next section. When larger games are involved, the usual method is to transform the problem into a linear programming problem, which would then be solved by the simplex method on a computer; Sec. 7.5 discusses this approach.

7.4 GRAPHICAL SOLUTION PROCEDURE

Consider any game with mixed strategies such that, after eliminating dominated strategies, one of the players has only two pure strategies. To be specific, let this player be player I. Since his mixed strategies are (x_1, x_2) and $x_2 = 1 - x_1$, it is only necessary for him to solve for the optimal value of x_1. However, it is straightforward to plot the expected payoff as a function of x_1 for each of his opponent's pure strategies. This graph can then be used to identify the point that maximizes the minimum expected payoff. The opponent's minimax mixed strategy can also be identified from the graph.

To illustrate this procedure, consider *variation 3* of the political campaign problem (see Table 7.5). Notice that the third pure strategy for player I is dominated by his second, so the payoff table can be reduced to the form given in Table 7.6. Therefore, for each of the pure strategies available to player II the

Table 7.6 Reduced Payoff Table for Variation 3 of The Political Campaign Problem

			II		
		Probability	y_1	y_2	y_3
	Probability	*Pure strategy*	*1*	*2*	*3*
I	x_1	1	0	−2	2
	$1-x_1$	2	5	4	−3

expected payoff for player I would be

(y_1, y_2, y_3)	*Expected payoff*
(1,0,0)	$0x + 5(1-x_1) = 5 - 5x_1$
(0,1,0)	$-2x_1 + 4(1-x_1) = 4 - 6x_1$
(0,0,1)	$2x_1 - 3(1-x_1) = -3 + 5x_1$

Now plot these expected payoff lines on a graph, as shown in Fig. 7.1.(p. 290). For any given value of x_1 and of (y_1, y_2, y_3), the expected payoff will be the appropriate weighted average of the corresponding points on these three lines. In particular,

$$\text{Expected payoff} = y_1(5 - 5x_1) + y_2(4 - 6x_1) + y_3(-3 + 5x_1).$$

Thus, given x_1, the minimum expected payoff is given by the corresponding point on the "bottom" line. According to the minimax (or maximin) criterion, player I should select the value of x_1 giving the *largest* minimum expected payoff, so that

$$\underline{v} = v = \max_{0 \le x_1 \le 1} \{\min(-3 + 5x_1, 4 - 6x_1)\}.$$

Therefore the optimal value of x_1 is the one at the intersection of the two lines $(-3 + 5x_1)$ and $(4 - 6x_1)$. Solving algebraically,

$$-3 + 5x_1 = 4 - 6x_1,$$

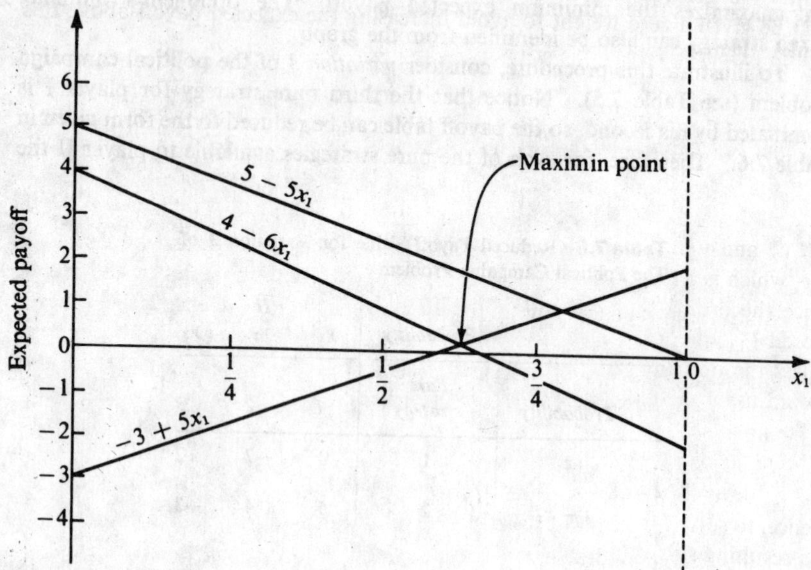

Figure 7.1 Graphical procedure for solving games.

so that $x_1 = 7/11$; thus $(x_1, x_2) = (7/11, 4/11)$ is the optimal mixed strategy for player I, and

$$\underline{v} = v = -3 + 5\left(\frac{7}{11}\right) = \frac{2}{11}$$

is the value of the game.

To find the corresponding optimal mixed strategy for player II, one would now reason as follows. According to the definition of upper value and the minimax theorem, the expected payoff resulting from this strategy $(y_1, y_2, y_3) = (y_1^*, y_2^*, y_3^*)$ will satisfy the condition,

$$y_1^*(5 - 5x_1) + y_2^*(4 - 6x_1) + y_3^*(-3 + 5x_1) \leq \bar{v} = v = \frac{2}{11}$$

for all values of $x_1 (0 \leq x_1 \leq 1)$; furthermore, when player I is playing optimally (that is, $x_1 = 7/11$), this inequality will be an equality, so that

$$\frac{20}{11} y_1^* + \frac{2}{11} y_2^* + \frac{2}{11} y_3^* = v = \frac{2}{11}.$$

Since (y_1, y_2, y_3) is a probability distribution, it is also known that

$$y_1^* + y_2^* + y_3^* = 1.$$

Therefore $y_1^* = 0$ because $y_1^* > 0$ would violate the next-to-last equation, i.e., the expected payoff on the graph at $x_1 = 7/11$ would be above the maximin point. (In general, any line that does not pass through the maximin point must be given a zero weight to avoid increasing the expected payoff above this point.) Hence,

$$y_2^*(4-6x_1)+y_3^*(-3+5x_1)\begin{cases}\leq \dfrac{2}{11}, \text{ for } 0 \leq x_1 \leq 1\\[2ex] = \dfrac{2}{11}, \text{ for } x_1 = \dfrac{7}{11}.\end{cases}$$

But y_2^* and y_3^* are numbers, so the left-hand side is the equation of a straight line, which is a fixed weighted average of the two "bottom" lines on the graph. Since the ordinate of this line must equal $2/11$ at $x_1 = 7/11$, and it must never exceed $2/11$, the line necessarily is horizontal. (This conclusion is always true, unless the optimal value of x_1 is either zero or 1, in which case player II also should use a single pure strategy.) Therefore

$$y_2^*(4-6x_1)+y_3^*(-3+5x_1)=\frac{2}{11}, \text{ for } 0 \leq x_1 \leq 1.$$

Hence, to solve for y_2^* and y_3^*, select two values of x_1 (say, zero and 1), and solve the resulting two simultaneous equations. Thus

$$4y_2^* - 3y_3^* = \frac{2}{11},$$

$$-2y_2^* + 2y_3^* = \frac{2}{11},$$

so that $y_3^* = 6/11$ and $y_2^* = 5/11$. Therefore the optimal mixed strategy for player II is $(y_1, y_2, y_3) = (0, 5/11, 6/11)$.

If, in another problem, there should happen to be more than two lines passing through the maximin point, so that more than two of the y_j^* can be greater than zero, this would imply that there are many ties for the optimal mixed strategy for player II. One such strategy can then be identified by arbitrarily setting all but two of these y_j^* equal to zero and solving for the remaining two in the manner described above.

Although this graphical procedure has been illustrated for only one particular problem, essentially the same reasoning can be used to solve any game with mixed strategies that has only two undominated pure strategies for one of the players.

7.5 SOLVING BY LINEAR PROGRAMMING

Any game with mixed strategies can be solved rather easily by transforming the problem into a linear programming problem. As you will see, this requires little more than applying the definitions of lower value and upper value and the minimax theorem.

First consider how to find the optimal mixed strategy for player I. As indicated in Sec. 7.3,

$$\text{Expected payoff} = \sum_{i=1}^{m} \sum_{j=1}^{n} p_{ij} x_i y_j$$

and the strategy $(x_1, x_2, \ldots, x_m)$ is optimal if

$$\sum_{i=1}^{m} \sum_{j=1}^{n} p_{ij} x_i y_j \geq \underline{v} = v$$

for all opposing strategies $(y_1, y_2, \ldots, y_n)$. Thus this inequality will need to hold, for example, for each of the pure strategies of player II, so that

$$\begin{aligned} p_{11} x_1 + p_{21} x_2 + \cdots + p_{m1} x_m &\geq v \\ p_{12} x_1 + p_{22} x_2 + \cdots + p_{m2} x_m &\geq v \\ &\vdots \\ p_{1n} x_1 + p_{2n} x_2 + \cdots + p_{mn} x_m &\geq v. \end{aligned}$$

However, notice that these inequalities imply that

$$\sum_{j=1}^{n} y_j \left(\sum_{i=1}^{m} p_{ij} x_i \right) \geq \sum_{j=1}^{n} y_j v = v$$

since

$$\sum_{j=1}^{n} y_j = 1,$$

so that imposing this set of m linear inequalities is equivalent to requiring the original inequality to hold for all strategies $(y_1, y_2, \ldots, y_n)$. But these are legitimate linear programming constraints, as are the additional constraints

$$x_1 + x_2 + \cdots + x_m = 1$$
$$x_i \geq 0, \text{ for } i = 1, 2, \ldots, m$$

that are required to ensure that the x_i are probabilities. Therefore, any solution $(x_1, x_2, \ldots, x_m)$ that satisfies this entire set of linear programming constraints is the desired optimal mixed strategy. The two remaining problems are (1) v is unknown and (2) the linear programming problem has no objective function. Fortunately, both these problems can be solved at one stroke by replacing the unknown constant v by the variable x_{m+1}, and then *maximizing* x_{m+1}, so that x_{m+1} automatically will *equal* v (by definition) at the *optimal* solution to the linear programming problem!

To summarize, player I would find his optimal mixed strategy by solving the *linear programming* problem

subject to

$$p_{11}x_1 + p_{21}x_2 + \cdots + p_{m1}x_m - x_{m+1} \geq 0$$
$$p_{12}x_1 + p_{22}x_2 + \cdots + p_{m2}x_m - x_{m+1} \geq 0$$
$$\vdots$$
$$p_{1n}x_1 + p_{2n}x_2 + \cdots + p_{mn}x_m - x_{m+1} \geq 0$$
$$-(x_1 + x_2 + \cdots + x_m) = -1$$

and

$$x_i \geq 0, \text{ for } i = 1, 2, \ldots, m.$$

(The objective function and equality constraint have been rewritten here in an equivalent way for later convenience.) A close examination of this formulation reveals one flaw, namely, that x_{m+1} is not restricted to be nonnegative, but this is easily rectified, as will be discussed shortly.

Now consider player II. He obviously could find his optimal mixed strategy by rewriting the payoff table as the payoff to himself rather than player I and then proceeding exactly as described above. However, it is enlightening to summarize his formulation in terms of the original payoff table. By proceeding in a way that is completely analogous to that described above, player II would conclude that his optimal mixed strategy is given by the optimal solution to the *linear programming* problem

$$\text{Maximize } (-y_{n+1}),$$

subject to

$$p_{11}y_1 + p_{12}y_2 + \cdots + p_{1n}y_n - y_{n+1} \leq 0$$
$$p_{21}y_1 + p_{22}y_2 + \cdots + p_{2n}y_n - y_{n+1} \leq 0$$
$$\vdots$$
$$p_{m1}y_1 + p_{m2}y_2 + \cdots + p_{mn}y_n - y_{n+1} \leq 0$$
$$-(y_1 + y_2 + \cdots + y_n) = -1$$

and

$$y_j \geq 0, \text{ for } j = 1, 2, \ldots, n.$$

Now notice the key fact that this linear programming problem and the one given for player I are *dual* to each other in the sense described in Sec. 2.12. (In particular, this problem is in the form given for the "primal" problem, and the one for player I is the corresponding dual problem.) This has several important implications. One is that the optimal mixed strategies for both players can be found by solving only one of the linear programming problems because the optimal dual solution is an automatic by-product of the simplex method calculations to find the optimal primal solution. A second is that this brings all duality theory (described in Sec. 2.12) to bear upon the interpretation and analysis of games. A related implication is that this provides a very simple proof of the minimax theorem. Let x^*_{m+1} and y^*_{n+1} denote the value of x_{m+1} and y_{n+1} in the optimal solution of the respective linear programming problems. It is known from the dual theorem given in Sec. 2.12 (see relationship 4) that

$-x_{m+1}^* = -y_{n+1}^*$, so that $x_{m+1}^* = y_{n+1}^*$. However, it is evident from the definition of lower value and upper value that $\underline{v} = x_{m+1}^*$ and $\bar{v} = y_{n+1}^*$, so it follows that $\underline{v} = \bar{v}$ as claimed by the minimax theorem.

One remaining loose end needs to be tied up, namely, what to do about x_{m+1} and y_{n+1} being unrestricted in sign in the linear programming formulations. To apply the simplex method to solve such a problem, all the variables involved need to be *nonnegative*. If it is clear that $v \geq 0$, so that the optimal value of x_{m+1} and y_{n+1} is nonnegative, then it is safe to restrict these variables to nonnegative values for purposes of solving the problem. However, if $v < 0$, then an adjustment needs to be made. One possibility is to use the approach described in Sec. 2.10 for applying the simplex method when a variable is allowed to be negative. Another is to reverse players I and II so that the payoff table would be rewritten as the payoff to the original player II, which would make the corresponding value of v positive. A third, and the most commonly used, procedure is to add a sufficiently large fixed constant to all the entries in the payoff table so that the new value of the game will be positive. (For example, setting this constant equal to minus the largest negative entry will suffice.) Since this same constant is added to every entry, this adjustment can not alter the optimal mixed strategies in any way, so they would now be obtained in the usual manner. The indicated value of the game would be increased by the amount of the constant, but this can be readjusted after the solution has been obtained.

7.6 EXTENSIONS

Although this chapter has considered only *two-person zero-sum games* with a *finite* number of pure strategies, it would be incorrect to conclude that game theory is limited solely to this kind of game. In fact, some research has been done on several more complicated types of games, which are summarized below.

One such type is the *n-person game*, where more than two players may participate in the game. This is a particularly important generalization because, in many kinds of competitive situations, there frequently are more than two competitors involved. This is often the case, for example, in competition among business firms, in international diplomacy, and so forth. Unfortunately, the existing theory for such games is less satisfactory than for two-person games.

Another generalization is the *nonzero-sum game*, where the sum of the payoffs to the players need not be zero (or any other fixed constant). This reflects the fact that many competitive situations include noncompetitive aspects that contribute to the mutual advantage or mutual disadvantage of the players. For example, the advertising strategies of competing companies can affect not only how they will split the market but also the total size of the market for their competing products. Since mutual gain is possible, nonzero-sum games are further classified in terms of the degree to which the players are permitted to cooperate. At one extreme is the *noncooperative game*, where there is no preplay communication between the players. At the other extreme is the *cooperative game*, where preplay discussions and binding agreements are permitted. For example, competitive situations involving trade regulations between countries, or collective bargaining between labor and management, might be formulated as cooperative games. When there are more than two players, cooperative games also allow some or all of the players to form coalitions.

Still another extension is to the class of *infinite games*, where the players have an infinite number of pure strategies available to them. These games are designed for the kind of situation where the strategy to be selected can be represented by a *continuous* decision variable. For example, this decision variable might be the time at which to take a certain action, or the proportion of one's resources to allocate to a certain activity, in a competitive situation. Much research has been concentrated on such games in recent years.

However, the analysis required in these extensions beyond the two-person zero-sum finite game is relatively complex and will not be pursued further here.

7.7 CONCLUSIONS

The general problem of how to make decisions in a competitive environment is a very common and important one. The fundamental contribution of game theory is that it provides a basic conceptual framework for formulating and analyzing such problems in simple situations. However, there is a considerable gap between what the theory can handle and the complexity of most competitive situations arising in practice. Therefore the conceptual tools of game theory usually play just a supplementary role in dealing with these situations.

Because of the importance of the general problem, research is continuing with some success to extend the theory to more complex situations

Selected References

1 Glicksman, Abraham M.: *An Introduction to Linear Programming and the Theory of Games*, Wiley, New York, 1963.
2 Luce, R. Duncan and Howard Raiffa: *Games and Decisions*, Wiley, New York, 1957.
3 May, Francis B.: *Introduction to Games of Strategy*, Allyn and Bacon, Boston, 1970.
4 McKinsey, J. C. C.: *Introduction to the Theory of Games*, McGraw-Hill, New York, 1952.
5 Owen, Guillermo: *Game Theory*, W. B. Saunders, Philadelphia, 1968.
6 Williams, J. D.: *The Compleat Strategyst*, rev. ed., McGraw-Hill, New York, 1966.

Problems

1 Consider the game having the following payoff table. Determine the optimal strategy for each player by successively eliminating dominated strategies.

		II		
		1	*2*	*3*
	1	−3	1	2
I	*2*	1	2	1
	3	1	0	−2

2 Find the saddle point for the game having the following payoff table:

		II			
		1	*2*	*3*	*4*
	1	2	−1	0	−3
I	*2*	1	0	3	2
	3	−3	−2	−1	4

3 The labor union and management of a particular company have been negotiating a new labor contract. However, negotiations have now come to an impasse, with management making a "final" offer of a wage increase of 20 cents/hour and the union making a "final" demand of a 25 cents/hour increase. Therefore both sides have agreed to have an impartial arbitrator set the wage increase somewhere between 20 and 25 cents/hour (inclusively).

The arbitrator has asked each side to submit to him a confidential proposal for a fair and economically reasonable wage increase (rounded to the nearest integer). From past experience both sides know that this arbitrator normally accepts the proposal of the side that gives in the most from its "final" figure. If neither side changes its final figure, or if they both give in the same amount, then the arbitrator normally compromises halfway between (22½ cents in this case). Each side now needs to determine what wage increase to propose for its own maximum advantage.

(*a*) Formulate this problem as a *two-person zero-sum game.*

(*b*) Use the concept of dominated strategies to determine the best strategy for each side.

(*c*) Without eliminating dominated strategies, use the minimax criterion to determine the best strategy for each side.

4 Two politicians soon will be starting their campaigns against each other for a certain political office. Each must now select the main issue he will emphasize as the theme of his campaign. Each has three advantageous issues from which to choose, but the relative effectiveness of each one would depend upon the issue chosen by his opponent. In particular, the estimated increase in the vote for politician I (expressed as a percentage of the total vote) resulting from each combination of issues is

		Issue for politician II		
		1	*2*	*3*
Issue for politician I	*1*	7	−1	3
	2	1	0	2
	3	−5	−3	1

However, since considerable staff work is required to research and formulate the issue chosen, each politician must make his own choice before learning his opponent's choice. Which issue should he choose?

For each of the situations described below, formulate this problem as a *two-person zero-sum game*, and then determine which issue should be chosen by each politician according to the specified criterion.

(*a*) The current preferences of the voters are very uncertain, so each additional percent of votes won by one of the politicians has the same value to him. Use the *minimax* criterion.

(*b*) Based on a reliable poll, it has been found that the percentage of the voters currently preferring politician I (before the issues have been raised) lies between 45 and 50 percent. (Assume a uniform distribution over this range.) Use the concept of *dominated strategies*, beginning with the strategies for politician I.

(*c*) Suppose that the percentage described in part (*b*) actually were 45 percent. Should politician I use the minimax criterion? Explain. Which issue would you recommend? Why?

5 Two manufacturers currently are competing for sales in two different but equally profitable product lines. In both cases the sales volume for manufacturer II is three times as large as that for manufacturer I. Because of a recent technological breakthrough, both manufacturers will be making a major improvement in both products. However, they are uncertain as to what development and marketing strategy they should follow.

If both product improvements are developed simultaneously, either manufacturer can have them ready for sale in 12 months. Another alternative is to have a "crash program" to develop only one product first to try to get it marketed ahead of the competition. By doing this, manufacturer II could have one product ready for sale in 9 months, whereas manufacturer I would require 10 months (because of previous commitments for its production facilities). For either manufacturer, the second product could then be ready for sale in an additional 9 months.

For either product line, if both manufacturers market their improved models simultaneously, it is estimated that manufacturer I would increase its share of the total future sales of this product by 8 percent of the total (from 25 to 33 percent). Similarly, manufacturer I would increase its share by 20, 30, and 40 percent of the total if it markets the product sooner than manufacturer II by 2, 6, and 8 months, respectively. On the other hand, manufacturer I would lose 4, 10, 12, and 14 percent of the total if manufacturer II markets it sooner by 1, 3, 7, and 10 months, respectively.

Formulate this problem as a two-person zero-sum game, and then determine which strategy the respective manufacturers should use according to the minimax criterion.

6 Consider the game having the following payoff table:

		II	
		1	*2*
I	*1*	−1	1
	2	2	−1

Use the graphical procedure described in Sec. 7.4 to determine the value of the game and the optimal *mixed* strategy for each player according to the minimax criterion. Check your answer for player II by constructing *his* payoff table and applying the graphical procedure directly to this table.

7 For each of the following payoff tables, use the graphical procedure described in Sec. 7.4 to determine the value of the game and the optimal *mixed* strategy for each player according to the minimax criterion:

(*a*)

		II		
		1	*2*	*3*
I	*1*	4	3	1
	2	0	1	2

(*b*)

		II		
		1	*2*	*3*
I	*1*	3	−2	5
	2	−3	6	−1
	3	1	−1	4
	4	0	4	2

8 Consider the following parlor game between two players. It begins when a referee flips a coin, notes whether it comes up heads or tails, and then shows this result to only player I. Player I may then either (1) pass and thereby pay \$1 to player II, or (2) he may bet. If player I passes, the game is terminated. However, if he bets, the game continues, in which case player II may then either (1) pass and thereby pay \$1 to player I, or (2) he may call. If player II calls, the referee then shows him the coin; if it came up heads, player II pays \$2 to player I; if it came up tails, player II receives \$2 from player I.

(*a*) Give the pure strategies for each player. (*Hint*: Player I will have four pure strategies, each one specifying how he would respond to each of the two results the referee can show him; player II will have two pure strategies, each one specifying how he will respond if player I bets.)
(*b*) Develop the payoff table for this game, using expected values for the entries when necessary. Determine whether it has a saddle point or not.
(*c*) Use the graphical procedure described in Sec. 7.4 to determine the optimal *mixed* strategy for each player according to the minimax criterion. Also give the corresponding value of the game.

9 Two companies share the bulk of the market for a particular kind of product. They each are now planning their new marketing plans for the next year in an attempt to wrest some sales away from the other company. (The total sales for the product are relatively fixed, so that one company can only increase its sales by winning them away from the other.) Each company is considering three possibilities: (1) better packaging of the product, (2) increased advertising, and (3) a slight reduction in price. The cost for the three alternatives are quite comparable and sufficiently large enough so that each company will select just one. The estimated effect of each combination of alternatives on the *increased percentage of the sales* for company I is

		II		
		1	*2*	*3*
I	*1*	1	−1	−2
	2	3	0	−1
	3	2	−1	2

Each company must make its selection before learning the decision of the other company.

(*a*) Eliminate dominated strategies, and then use the graphical procedure described in Sec. 7.4 to solve for the optimal *mixed* strategy for each company.
(*b*) Discuss the practical relevance of the concept of *mixed* strategies for these companies.

10 Consider the game having the following payoff table:

		II			
		1	*2*	*3*	*4*
I	*1*	5	0	3	1
	2	2	4	3	2
	3	3	2	0	4

Use the approach described in Sec. 7.5 to formulate the problem of finding the optimal *mixed* strategies according to the minimax criterion as a *linear programming* problem.

11 For each of the following payoff tables, transform the problem of finding the minimax *mixed* strategies into an equivalent *linear programming problem.*

(*a*)

		II		
		1	*2*	*3*
I	*1*	7	4	1
	2	2	−1	5
	3	3	8	0

(*b*)

		II				
		1	*2*	*3*	*4*	*5*
I	*1*	−5	−9	4	−4	1
	2	−2	3	−8	−1	−5
	3	−2	−4	−9	−6	0
	4	4	−5	−2	3	−7

12 Consider variation 3 of the political campaign problem (see Table 7.6), which was solved by the graphical procedure in Sec. 7.4. Now formulate this problem as a *linear programming* problem. Ignoring the objective function variable, plot the *feasible region* for the *other* variables graphically (as described in Sec. 2.1). Given the optimal solution identified in Sec. 7.4, mark the location of this solution in the feasible region. Now use the objective function variable to explain why the optimal solution for the other variables has this location in the feasible region.

13 The A. J. Swim Team soon will have an important swim meet with the G. N. Swim Team. Each team has a star swimmer (John and David, respectively) who can swim very well in the 100-yard butterfly, backstroke, and breaststroke events. However, the rules prevent them from being used in more than *two* nonrelay events. Therefore their coaches now need to decide how to use them to maximum advantage.

The following table gives the "best time" previously achieved by John and David in each of these events as well as the best times for the other swimmers who will definitely enter each event.

	A. J. Swim Team			*G. N. Swim Team*		
	Entry				*Entry*	
Event	*1*	*2*	*John*	*David*	*1*	*2*
Fly	59.7	1 : 03.2	57.1	58.6	1 : 01.4	1 : 04.8
Back	1 : 07.2	1 : 08.4	1 : 03.2	1 : 01.5	1 : 04.7	1 : 06.5
Breast	1 : 14.1	1 : 15.5	1 : 10.3	1 : 12.6	1 : 13.4	1 : 16.9

The points awarded are 5 points for 1st place, 3 for 2nd place, 1 for 3rd place, and none for lower places. Both coaches believe that all swimmers will essentially equal their best times in this meet.

(*a*) The coaches must submit all their entries before the meet without knowing the entries for the other team, and no changes are permitted later. The outcome of the meet is very uncertain, so each additional point has equal value for the coaches. Formulate this problem as a *two-person zero-sum* game. Eliminate dominated strategies, and then use the graphical procedure described in Sec. 7.4 to find the optimal *mixed* strategy for each team according to the minimax criterion.

(*b*) The situation and assignment is the same as in part (*a*), except that both coaches now believe that the A. J. Swim Team would win the swim meet if they can win 13 or more points in these three events, but would lose with less than 13 points. [Compare the resulting optimal mixed strategies with those obtained in part (*a*).]

(*c*) Now suppose that the coaches submit their entries during the meet one event at a time. When submitting his entries for an event, the coach does not know who will be swimming that event for the other team, but he does know who has swum *preceding* events. The three key events discussed above are swum in the order listed in the table. Once again, the A. J. Swim Team needs 13 points in these events to win the swim meet. Formulate this problem as a *two-person zero-sum* game. Then use the concept of dominated strategies to determine the best strategy for each team according to the minimax criterion.

14 Consider the general $m \times n$ two-person zero-sum game. Let P_{ij} denote the payoff to player I if he plays his strategy i $(i = 1, \ldots, m)$ and player II plays his strategy j $(j = 1, \ldots, n)$. Strategy 1 (say) for player I is said to be *weakly dominated* by strategy 2 (say) if $P_{1j} \leq P_{2j}$ for $j = 1, \ldots, n$ and $P_{1j} = P_{2j}$ for one or more values of j.

(*a*) Assume that the payoff table possesses one or more *saddle points*, so that the players have corresponding optimal pure strategies under the minimax criterion. Prove that eliminating *weakly dominated* strategies from the payoff table can not eliminate all these saddle points and can not produce any new ones.

(*b*) Assume that the payoff table does not possess any saddle points, so that the optimal strategies under the minimax criterion are *mixed* strategies. Prove that eliminating weakly dominated pure strategies from the payoff table can not eliminate all optimal mixed strategies and can not produce any new ones.

15 Briefly describe what you feel are the advantages and disadvantages of the minimax criterion.

Part 2

Probabilistic Models

8 Probability Theory

8.1 INTRODUCTION

In decision-making problems, one is often faced with making decisions based upon phenomena that have uncertainty associated with them. This uncertainty is caused by inherent variation due to sources of variation that elude control or the inconsistency of natural phenomena. Rather than treat this variability qualitatively, one can incorporate it into the mathematical model and thus handle it quantitatively. This generally can be accomplished if the natural phenomena exhibit some degree of regularity, so that their variation can be described by a probability model. The ensuing sections are concerned with methods for characterizing these probability models.

8.2 SAMPLE SPACE

Suppose the demand for a product over a period of time, say a month, is of interest. From a realistic point of view, demand is not generally constant but exhibits the type of variation alluded to in the previous section. Suppose an experiment that will result in observing the demand for the product during the month is run. Whereas the outcome of the experiment can not be predicted exactly, each *possible* outcome can be described. The demand during the period can be any one of the values 0, 1, 2, ..., that is, the entire set of nonnegative integers. The set of all possible outcomes of the experiment is called the sample space and will be denoted by Ω. Each outcome in the sample space is called a point and will be denoted by ω. Actually, in the experiment just described, the possible demands may be bounded from above by N, where N would represent the size of the population that has any use for the product. Hence the sample space would then consist of the set of the integers 0, 1, 2, ..., N. Strictly speaking, the sample space is much more complex than just described. In fact, it may be extremely difficult to characterize precisely. Associated with this experiment are such factors as the dates and times that the demands occur, the prevailing weather, the disposition of the personnel meeting the demand, and so on. Many more factors could be listed, most of which are irrelevant. Fortunately, as noted in the next section, it is not necessary to describe completely the sample space, but only to record those factors that appear to be necessary for the purposes of the experiment.

Another experiment may be concerned with the time until the first customer arrives at a store. Since the first customer may arrive at any time until the store closes (assuming an 8-hour day), for the purpose of this experiment the sample space can be considered to be all points on the real line between zero and 8 hours. Thus Ω consists of all points ω such that

$$0 \le \omega \le 8.\dagger$$

Now consider a third example. Suppose that a modification of the first experiment is made by observing the demands during the first 2 months. The sample space Ω consists of all points (x_1,x_2), where x_1 represents the demand during the first month, $x_1 = 0, 1, 2, \ldots$, and x_2 represents the demand during the second month, $x_2 = 0, 1, 2, \ldots$. Thus Ω consists of the set of all possible points ω, where ω represents a pair of nonnegative integer values (x_1,x_2). The point $\omega = (3,6)$ represents a possible outcome of the experiment where the demand in the first month is 3 units and the demand in the second month is 6 units. In a similar manner, the experiment can be extended to observing the demands during the first n months. In this situation Ω consists of all possible points $\omega = (x_1, x_2, \ldots, x_n)$, where x_i represents the demand during the ith month.

The experiment that is concerned with the time until the first arrival appears can also be modified. Suppose an experiment that measures the times of the arrival of the first customer on each of 2 days is performed. The set of all possible outcomes of the experiment Ω consists of all points (x_1,x_2), $0 \le x_1, x_2 \le 8$, where x_1 represents the time the first customer arrives on the first day, and x_2 represents the time the first customer arrives on the second day. Thus Ω consists of the set of all possible points ω, where ω represents a point in two space lying in the square shown in Fig. 8.1.

This experiment can also be extended to observing the times of the arrival of the first customer on each of n days. The sample space Ω consists of all points $\omega = (x_1, x_2, \ldots, x_n)$, such that $0 \le x_i \le 8$ $(i = 1, 2, \ldots, n)$, where x_i represents the time the first customer arrives on the ith day.

An event is defined as a set of outcomes of the experiment. Thus there are many events that can be of interest. For example, in the experiment concerned with observing the demand for a product in a given month, the set $\{\omega = 0, \omega = 1, \omega = 2, \ldots, \omega = 10\}$ is the event that the demand for the product does not

† It will be assumed that at least one customer arrives each day.

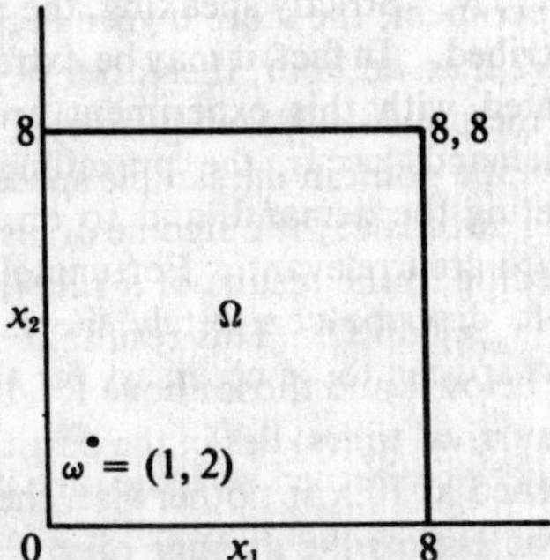

Figure 8.1 Sample space of the arrival time experiment.

exceed 10 units. Similarly, the set $\{\omega = 0\}$ denotes the event of no demand for the product during the month. In the experiment which measures the times of the arrival of the first customer on each of 2 days, the set $\{\omega = (x_1, x_2);\ x_1 < 1, x_2 < 1\}$, is the event that the first arrival on each day occurs before the first hour. It is evident that any subset of the sample space, e.g., any point, collection of points, or the entire sample space, is an event.

Events may be combined, thereby resulting in the formation of new events. For any two events E_1 and E_2, the new event $E_1 \cup E_2$, referred to as the union of E_1 and E_2, is defined to contain all points in the sample space that are in either E_1 or E_2, or in both E_1 and E_2. Thus the event $E_1 \cup E_2$ will occur if either E_1 or E_2 occurs. For example, in the demand experiment, let E_1 be the event of a demand in a single month of zero or 1 unit, and let E_2 be the event of a demand in a single month of 1 or 2 units. The event $E_1 \cup E_2$ is just $\{\omega = 0, \omega = 1, \omega = 2\}$, which is just the event of a demand of 0, 1, or 2 units.

The intersection of two events E_1 and E_2 is denoted by $E_1 \cap E_2$ (or equivalently by E_1E_2). This new event $E_1 \cap E_2$ is defined to contain all points in the sample space that are in both E_1 and E_2. Thus the event $E_1 \cap E_2$ will occur only if both E_1 and E_2 occur. In the aforementioned example, the event $E_1 \cap E_2$ is $\{\omega = 1\}$, which is just the event of a demand of 1 unit.

Finally, the events E_1 and E_2 are said to be mutually exclusive (or disjoint) if their intersection does not contain any points. In the example, E_1 and E_2 are not disjoint. However, if the event E_3 is defined to be the event of a demand of 2 or 3 units, then $E_1 \cap E_3$ is disjoint. Events that do not contain any points, and therefore can not occur, are called null events. (Of course, all these definitions can be extended to any finite number of events.)

8.3 RANDOM VARIABLES

It may occur frequently that in performing an experiment one is not interested directly in the entire sample space or in events defined over the sample space. For example, suppose that the experiment which measures the times of the first arrival on 2 days was performed to determine at what time to open the store.

Prior to performing the experiment, the store owner decides that if the average of the arrival times is greater than an hour, thereafter he will not open his store until 10 A.M. (9 A.M. being the previous opening time). The average of x_1 and x_2 (the two arrival times) is not a point in the sample space, and hence he can not make his decision by looking directly at the outcome of his experiment. Instead, he makes his decision according to the results of a rule that assigns the average of x_1 and x_2 to *each point* (x_1,x_2) in Ω. This resultant set is then partitioned into two parts: those points below 1 and those above 1. If the observed result of this rule (average of the two arrival times) lies in the partition with points greater than 1, the store will be opened at 10 A.M.; otherwise, the store will continue to open at 9 A.M. The rule that assigns the average of x_1 and x_2 to each point in the sample space is called a random variable. Thus, a *random variable is a numerically valued function defined over the sample space.* Note that a function is, in a mathematical sense, just a rule that assigns a number to each value in the domain of definition, in this context the sample space.

Random variables play an extremely important role in probability theory. Experiments are usually very complex and contain information that may or may not be superfluous. For example, in measuring the arrival time of the first customer, the color of his shoes may be pertinent. Although this is unlikely, the prevailing weather may certainly be relevant. Hence the choice of the random variable enables the experimenter to describe the factors of importance to him and permits him to discard the superfluous characteristics that may be extremely difficult to characterize.

There is a multitude of random variables associated with each experiment. In the experiment concerning the arrival of the first customer on each of 2 days, it has been pointed out already that the average of the arrival times $\overline{X}$ is a random variable. Notationally, random variables will be characterized by capital letters, and the values the random variable takes on will be denoted by lowercase letters. Actually, to be precise, $\overline{X}$ should be written as $\overline{X}(\omega)$, where ω is any point shown in the square in Fig. 8.1 because $\overline{X}$ is a function. Thus $\overline{X}(1,2) = (1 + 2)/2 = 1.5$, $\overline{X}(1.6,1.8) = (1.6 + 1.8)/2 = 1.7$, $\overline{X}(1.5,1.5) = (1.5 + 1.5)/2 = 1.5$, $\overline{X}(8,8) = (8 + 8)/2 = 8$. The values that the random variable $\overline{X}$ takes on are the set of values $\bar{x}$ such that $0 \le \bar{x} \le 8$. Another random variable, X_1, can be described as follows: For each ω in Ω, the random variable (numerically valued function) disregards the x_2 coordinate and transforms the x_1 coordinate into itself. This random variable, then, represents the arrival time of the first customer on the first day. Hence $X_1(1,2) = 1$, $X_1(1.6,1.8) = 1.6$, $X_1(1.5,1.5) = 1.5$, $X_1(8,8) = 8$. The values the random variable X_1 takes on are the set of values x_1 such that $0 \le x_1 \le 8$. In a similar manner, the random variable X_2 can be described as representing the arrival time of the first customer on the second day. A third random variable, S^2, can be described as follows: For each ω in Ω, the random variable computes the sum of squares of the deviations of the coordinates about their average; that is, $S^2(\omega) = S^2(x_1, x_2) = (x_1 - \bar{x})^2 + (x_2 - \bar{x})^2$. Hence $S^2(1,2) = (1 - 1.5)^2 + (2 - 1.5)^2 = 0.5$, $S^2(1.6,1.8) = (1.6 - 1.7)^2 + (1.8 - 1.7)^2 = 0.02$, $S^2(1.5,1.5) = (1.5 - 1.5)^2 +$

$(1.5 - 1.5)^2 = 0$, $S^2(8,8) = (8 - 8)^2 + (8 - 8)^2 = 0$. It is evident that the values the random variable S^2 takes on are the set of values s^2 such that $0 \leq s^2 \leq 32$.

All the random variables just described are called continuous random variables because they take on a continuum of values. Discrete random variables are those that take on a finite or countably infinite set of values.[1] An example of a discrete random variable can be obtained by referring to the experiment dealing with the measurement of demand. Let the discrete random variable X be defined as the demand during the month. (The experiment consists of measuring the demand for 1 month.) Thus $X(0) = 0$, $X(1) = 1$, $X(2) = 2, \ldots,$ so that the random variable takes on the set of values consisting of the integers. Note that Ω and the set of values the random variable takes on are identical, so that this random variable is just the identity function.

From the above paragraphs it is evident that any function of a random variable is itself a random variable because a function of a function is also a function. Thus, in the previous examples $\bar{X} = (X_1 + X_2)/2$ and $S^2 = (X_1 - \bar{X})^2 + (X_2 - \bar{X})^2$ can also be recognized as random variables by noting that they are functions of the random variables X_1 and X_2.

This text is concerned with random variables that are real-valued functions defined over the real line or a subset of the real line.

8.4 PROBABILITY AND PROBABILITY DISTRIBUTIONS

Returning to the example of the demand for a product during a month, note that the actual demand is not a constant; instead, it can be expected to exhibit some "variation." In particular, this variation can be described by introducing the concept of probability defined over events in the sample space. For example, let E be the event $\{\omega = 0, \omega = 1, \omega = 2, \ldots, \omega = 10\}$. Then intuitively one can speak of $P\{E\}$, where $P\{E\}$ is referred to as the probability of having a demand of 10 or less units. Note that $P\{E\}$ can be thought of as a numerical value associated with the event E. If $P\{E\}$ is known for all events E in the sample space, then some "information" is available about the demand that can be expected to occur. Usually these numerical values are difficult to obtain, but nevertheless their existence can be postulated. To define the concept of probability rigorously is beyond the scope of this text. However, for most purposes it is sufficient to postulate the existence of numerical values $P\{E\}$ associated with events E in the sample space. The value $P\{E\}$ is called the probability of the occurrence of the event E. Furthermore, it will be assumed that $P\{E\}$ satisfies the following reasonable properties:

[1] A countably infinite set of values is a set whose elements can be put into one-to-one correspondence with the set of positive integers. The set of odd integers is countably infinite. The 1 can be paired with 1, 3 with 2, 5 with 3, ..., $2n - 1$ with n. The set of all real numbers between 0 and ½ is not countably infinite because there are too many numbers in the interval to pair with the integers.

1. $0 \leq P\{E\} \leq 1$. This implies that the probability of an event is always nonnegative and can never exceed 1.

2. If E_0 is an event that can not occur (a null event) in the sample space, then $P\{E_0\} = 0$. Let E_0 denote the event of obtaining a demand of -7 units. Then $P\{E_0\} = 0$.

3. $P\{\Omega\} = 1$. If the event consists of obtaining a demand between 0 and N, that is, the entire sample space, the probability of having some demand between 0 and N is certain.

4. If E_1 and E_2 are disjoint (mutually exclusive) events in Ω, then $P\{E_1 \cup E_2\} = P\{E_1\} + P\{E_2\}$. Thus, if E_1 is the event of 0 or 1, and E_2 is the event of a demand of 4 or 5, then the probability of having a demand of 0, 1, 4, or 5, that is, $\{E_1 \cup E_2\}$, is given by $P\{E_1\} + P\{E_2\}$.

Although these properties are rather formal, they do conform to one's intuitive notion about probability. Nevertheless, these properties can not be used to obtain values for $P\{E\}$. Occasionally the determination of exact values, or at least approximate values, is desirable. Approximate values, together with an interpretation of probability, can be obtained through a frequency interpretation of probability. This may be stated precisely as follows. Denote by n the number of times an experiment is performed and by m the number of successful occurrences of the event E in the n trials. Then $P\{E\}$ can be interpreted as

$$P\{E\} = \lim_{n\to\infty} \frac{m}{n},$$

assuming the limit exists for such a phenomena. The ratio m/n can be used to approximate $P\{E\}$. Futhermore, m/n satisfies the properties required of probabilities; that is,

1. $0 \leq m/n \leq 1$.

2. $0/n = 0$. (If the event E can not occur, then $m = 0$.)

3. $n/n = 1$. (If the event E must occur every time the experiment is performed, then $m = n$.)

4. $(m_1 + m_2)/n = m_1/n + m_2/n$ if E_1 and E_2 are disjoint events. (If the event E_1 occurs m_1 times in the n trials and the event E_2 occurs m_2 times in the n trials, and E_1 and E_2 are disjoint, then the total number of successful occurrences of the event E_1 *or* E_2 is just $m_1 + m_2$.)

Since these properties are true for a finite n, it is reasonable to expect them to be true for

$$P\{E\} = \lim_{n\to\infty} \frac{m}{n}.$$

The trouble with the frequency interpretation as a definition of probability is that it is not possible to actually determine the probability of an event E because the question "How large must n be?" can not be answered. Furthermore, such a definition does not permit a logical development of the theory of probability. However, a rigorous definition of probability, or finding methods for determining exact probabilities of events, is not of prime importance here.

The existence of probabilities, defined over events E in the sample space, has been described, and the concept of a random variable has been introduced. Finding the relation between probabilities associated with events in the sample space and "probabilities" associated with random variables is a topic of considerable interest.

Associated with every random variable is a cumulative distribution function (CDF). To define a CDF it is necessary to introduce some additional notation. Define the symbol $E_b^X = \{\omega \mid X(\omega) \le b\}$ (or equivalently, $\{X \le b\}$) as the set of outcomes ω in the sample space forming the event E_b^X such that the random variable X takes on values less than or equal to b.† Then $P\{E_b^X\}$ is just the probability of this event. Note that this probability is well defined because E_b^X is an event in the sample space, and this event depends upon both the random variable that is of interest and the value of b chosen. For example, suppose the experiment that measures the demand for a product during a month is performed. Let $N = 99$, and assume that the events $\{0\}, \{1\}, \{2\}, \ldots, \{99\}$ each has probability equal to $1/100$; that is, $P\{0\} = P\{1\} = P\{2\} = \cdots = P\{99\} = 1/100$. Let the random variable X be the square of the demand, and choose b equal to 150. Then

$$E_{150}^X = \{\omega \mid X(\omega) \le 150\} = \{X \le 150\}$$

is the set $E_{150}^X = \{0,1,2,3,4,5,6,7,8,9,10,11,12\}$ (since the square of these numbers is less than 150). Furthermore,

$$P\{E_b^X\} = \frac{1}{100} + \frac{1}{100} + \frac{1}{100} + \frac{1}{100} + \frac{1}{100} + \frac{1}{100} + \frac{1}{100} + \frac{1}{100} + \frac{1}{100} + \frac{1}{100} + \frac{1}{100} + \frac{1}{100} + \frac{1}{100} = \frac{13}{100}.$$

Thus $P\{E_b^X\} = P\{X \le b\} = 13/100$.

For a given random variable X, $P\{X \le b\}$, denoted by $F_X(b)$, is called the CDF of the random variable X and is defined for all real values of b. Where there is no ambiguity, the CDF will be denoted by $F(b)$; that is,

$$F(b) = F_X(b) = P\{E_b^X\} = P\{\omega \mid X(\omega) \le b\} = P\{X \le b\}.$$

Although $P\{X \le b\}$ is defined through the event E_b^X in the sample space, it will often be read as the "probability" that the random variable X takes on a value less than or equal to b. The reader should interpret this statement properly, i.e., in terms of the event E_b^X.

† The notation $\{X \le b\}$ suppresses the fact that this is really an event in the sample space. However, it is simpler to write, and the reader is cautioned to interpret it properly, i.e., as the set of outcomes ω in the sample space, $\{\omega \mid X(\omega) \le b\}$.

As mentioned, each random variable has a cumulative distribution function associated with it. This is not an arbitrary function but is induced by the probabilities associated with events of the form E_b^X defined over the sample space Ω. Furthermore, the CDF of a random variable is a numerically valued function defined for all b, $-\infty \leq b \leq \infty$, having the following properties:

1. $F_X(b)$ is a nondecreasing function of b,
2. $\lim_{b \to -\infty} F_X(b) = F_X(-\infty) = 0$,
3. $\lim_{b \to +\infty} F_X(b) = F_X(+\infty) = 1$.

The CDF is a versatile function. Events of the form

$$\{\omega \mid a < X(\omega) \leq b\},$$

that is, the set of outcomes ω in the sample space such that the random variable X takes on values greater than a but not exceeding b, can be expressed in terms of events of the form E_b^X. In particular, E_b^X can be expressed as the union of two disjoint sets; that is,

$$E_b^X = E_a^X \cup \{\omega \mid a < X(\omega) \leq b\}.$$

Thus $P\{\omega \mid a < X(\omega) \leq b\} = P\{a < X \leq b\}$ can easily be seen to be

$$F_X(b) - F_X(a).$$

As another example, consider the experiment that measures the times of the arrival of the first customer on each of 2 days. Ω consists of all points (x_1, x_2) such that $0 \leq x_1, x_2 \leq 8$, where x_1 represents the time the first customer arrives on the first day, and x_2 represents the time the first customer arrives on the second day. Consider all events associated with this experiment, and assume that the probabilities of such events can be obtained. Suppose $\bar{X}$, the average of the two arrival times, is chosen as the random variable of interest and that $E_b^{\bar{X}}$ is the set of outcomes ω in the sample space forming the event $E_b^{\bar{X}}$ such that $\bar{X} \leq b$. Hence $F_{\bar{X}}(b) = P\{E_b^{\bar{X}}\} = P\{\bar{X} \leq b\}$. To illustrate how this can be evaluated, suppose that $b = 4$ hours. All the values of x_1, x_2 are sought such that $(x_1 + x_2)/2 \leq 4$ or $x_1 + x_2 \leq 8$. This is shown by the shaded area in Fig. 8.2. Hence $F_{\bar{X}}(b)$ is just the probability of a successful occurrence of the event given by the shaded area in Fig. 8.2. Presumably $F_{\bar{X}}(b)$ can be evaluated if probabilities of such events in the sample space are known.

Another random variable associated with this experiment is X_1, the time of the arrival of the first customer on the first day. Thus, $F_{X_1}(b) = P\{X_1 \leq b\}$, which can be obtained simply if probabilities of events over the sample space are given.

There is a simple frequency interpretation for the cumulative distribution function of a random variable. Suppose an experiment is repeated n times, and the random variable X is observed each time. Denote by $x_1, x_2, \ldots, x_n$ the

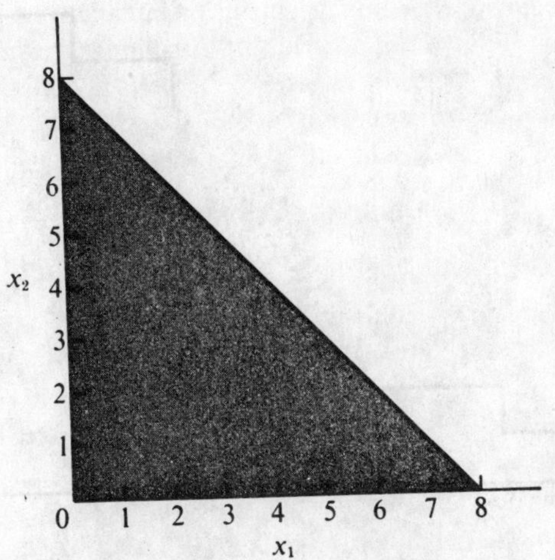

Figure 8.2 Shaded area represents the event $E_6^{\bar{X}} = \{\bar{X} \leq 4\}$.

outcomes of these n trials. Order these outcomes, letting $x_{(1)}$ be the smallest observation, $x_{(2)}$ the second smallest, . . . , $x_{(n)}$ the largest. Plot the following step function $F_n(x)$:

For $x < x_{(1)}$, let $F_n(x) = 0$.

For $x_{(1)} \leq x < x_{(2)}$, let $F_n(x) = \dfrac{1}{n}$.

For $x_{(2)} \leq x < x_{(3)}$, let $F_n(x) = \dfrac{2}{n}$.

⋮

For $x_{(n-1)} \leq x < x_{(n)}$, let $F_n(x) = \dfrac{n-1}{n}$.

For $x \geq x_n$, let $F_n(x) = \dfrac{n}{n} = 1$.

Such a plot is given in Fig. 8.3 and is seen to "jump" at the values that the random variable takes on.

$F_n(x)$ can be interpreted as the fraction of outcomes of the experiment less than or equal to x and is called the sample CDF. It can be shown that as the number of repetitions n of the experiment gets large, the sample CDF approaches the CDF of the random variable X.

In most problems encountered in practice, one is not concerned with events in the sample space and their associated probabilities. Instead, interest is

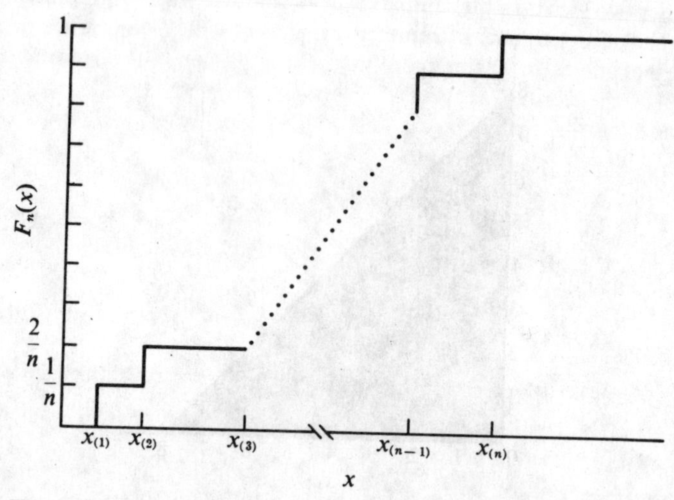

Figure 8.3 Sample cumulative distribution function.

focused on random variables and their associated cumulative distribution functions. Generally, a random variable (or random variables) is chosen, and some assumption is made about the form of the CDF or about the random variable. For example, the random variable X_1, the time of the first arrival on the first day, may be of interest, and an assumption may be made that the form of its CDF is exponential. Similarly, the same assumption about X_2, the time of the first arrival on the second day, may also be made. If these assumptions are valid, then the CDF of the random variable $\overline{X} = (X_1 + X_2)/2$ can be derived. Of course, these assumptions about the form of the CDF are not arbitrary and really imply assumptions about probabilities associated with events in the sample space. Hopefully, they can be substantiated by either empirical evidence or theoretical considerations.

8.5 CONDITIONAL PROBABILITY AND INDEPENDENT EVENTS

Often experiments are performed so that some results are obtained early in time and some later in time. This is the case, for example, when the experiment consists of measuring the demand for a product during each of 2 months; the demand during the first month is observed at the end of the first month. Similarly, the arrival times of the first two customers on each of 2 days are observed sequentially in time. This early information can be useful in making predictions about the subsequent results of the experiment. Such information need not necessarily be associated with time. If the demand for two products during a month is investigated, knowing the demand of one may be useful in assessing the demand for the other. To utilize this information the concept of "conditional probability," defined over events occurring in the sample space, is introduced.

Consider two events in the sample space E_1 and E_2, where E_1 represents the event that has occurred, and E_2 represents the event whose occurrence or nonoccurrence is of interest. Furthermore, assume that $P\{E_1\} > 0$. The conditional probability of the occurrence of the events E_2, given that the event E_1 has occurred, $P\{E_2|E_1\}$, is defined to be

$$P\{E_2|E_1\} = \frac{P\{E_1 \cap E_2\}}{P\{E_1\}},$$

where $\{E_1 \cap E_2\}$ represents the event consisting of all points ω in the sample space common to *both* E_1 and E_2. For example, consider the experiment that consists of observing the demand for a product over each of 2 months. Suppose the sample space Ω consists of all points $\omega = (x_1, x_2)$, where x_1 represents the demand during the first month, and x_2 represents the demand during the second month, $x_1, x_2 = 0, 1, 2, \ldots, 99$. Furthermore, it is known that the demand during the first month has been 10. Hence the event E_1, which consists of the points (10,0), (10,1), (10,2), . . . , (10,99), has occurred. Consider the event E_2, which represents a demand for the product in the second month that does not exceed 1 unit. This event consists of the points (0,0), (1,0), (2,0), . . . , (10,0), . . . , (99,0), (0,1), (1,1), (2,1), . . . , (10,1), . . . , (99,1). The event $\{E_1 \cap E_2\}$ consists of the points (10,0) and (10,1). Hence the probability of a demand which does not exceed 1 unit in the second month, given that a demand of 10 units occurred during the first month, that is, $P\{E_2|E_1\}$, is given by

$$\begin{aligned} P\{E_2|E_1\} &= \frac{P\{E_1 \cap E_2\}}{P\{E_1\}} \\ &= \frac{P\{\omega = (10,0), \omega = (10,1)\}}{P\{\omega = (10,0), \omega = (10,1), \ldots, \omega = (10,99)\}}. \end{aligned}$$

The definition of conditional probability can be given a frequency interpretation. Denote by n the number of times an experiment is performed, and let n_1 be the number of times the event E_1 has occurred. Let n_{12} be the number of times that the event $E_1 \cap E_2$ has occurred in the n trials. The ratio n_{12}/n_1 is the proportion of times that the event E_2 occurs when E_1 has also occurred; that is, n_{12}/n_1 is the conditional relative frequency of E_2, given that E_1 has occurred. This relative frequency n_{12}/n_1 is then equivalent to $(n_{12}/n)/(n_1/n)$. Using the frequency interpretation of probability for large n, n_{12}/n is approximately $P\{E_1 \cap E_2\}$, and n_1/n is approximately $P\{E_1\}$, so that the conditional relative frequency of E_2, given E_1, is approximately $P\{E_1 \cap E_2\}/P\{E_1\}$.

In essence, if one is interested in conditional probability, he is working with a reduced sample space, i.e., from Ω to E_1, modifying other events accordingly. Also note that conditional probability has the four properties described in Sec. 8.4; that is,

1. $0 \leq P\{E_2|E_1\} \leq 1$.
2. If E_2 is an event that can not occur, then $P\{E_2|E_1\} = 0$.

3. If the event E_2 is the entire sample space Ω, then $P\{\Omega | E_1\} = 1$.
4. If E_2 and E_3 are disjoint events in Ω, then

$$P\{(E_2 \cup E_3) | E_1\} = P\{E_2 | E_1\} + P\{E_3 | E_1\}.$$

In a similar manner, the conditional probability of the occurrence of the event E_1, given that the event E_2 has occurred, can be defined. If $P\{E_2\} > 0$, then

$$P\{E_1 | E_2\} = P\{E_1 \cap E_2\}/P\{E_2\}.$$

The concept of conditional probability was introduced so that advantage could be taken of information about the occurrence or nonoccurrence of events. It is conceivable that information about the occurrence of the event E_1 yields no information about the occurrence or nonoccurrence of the event E_2. If $P\{E_2 | E_1\} = P\{E_2\}$, or $P\{E_1 | E_2\} = P\{E_1\}$, then E_1 and E_2 are said to be independent events. It then follows that if E_1 and E_2 are independent and $P\{E_1\} > 0$, then $P\{E_2 | E_1\} = P\{E_1 \cap E_2\}/P\{E_1\} = P\{E_2\}$, so that $P\{E_1 \cap E_2\} = P\{E_1\}\, P\{E_2\}$. This can be taken as an alternative definition of independence of the events E_1 and E_2. It is usually difficult to show that events are independent by using the definitions of independence. Instead, it is generally simpler to use the information available about the experiment to postulate whether events are independent. This is usually based upon physical considerations. For example, if the demand for a product during a month is "known" *not* to affect the demand in subsequent months, then the events E_1 and E_2 defined previously can be said to be independent, in which case

$$\begin{aligned}
P\{E_2 | E_1\} &= \frac{P\{E_1 \cap E_2\}}{P\{E_1\}} \\
&= \frac{P\{\omega = (10,0), \omega = (10,1)\}}{P\{\omega = (10,0), \omega = (10,1), \ldots, \omega = (10,99)\}}, \\
&= \frac{P\{E_1\}P\{E_2\}}{P\{E_1\}} = P\{E_2\}, \\
&= P\{\omega = (0,0), \omega = (1,0), \ldots, \omega = (99,0), \omega = (0,1), \\
&\qquad \omega = (1,1), \ldots, \omega = (99,1)\}.
\end{aligned}$$

The definition of independence can be extended to any number of events. $E_1, E_2, \ldots, E_n$ are said to be independent events if for *every* subset of these events $E_1^*, E_2^*, \ldots, E_k^*$,

$$P\{E_1^* \cap E_2^* \cap \cdots \cap E_k^*\} = P\{E_1^*\}P\{E_2^*\} \cdots P\{E_k^*\}.$$

Intuitively, this implies that knowledge of the occurrence of any of these events has no effect on the probability of occurrence of any other event.

8.6 DISCRETE PROBABILITY DISTRIBUTIONS

It was pointed out that one is usually concerned with random variables and their associated probability distributions, and discrete random variables are those which take on a finite or countably infinite set of values. Furthermore, the CDF for a random variable is given by

$$F_X(b) = P\{\omega \mid X(\omega) \leq b\}.$$

For a discrete random variable X, the event $\{\omega \mid X(\omega) \leq b\}$ can be expressed as the union of disjoint sets; that is,

$$\{\omega \mid X(\omega) \leq b\} = \{\omega \mid X(\omega) = x_1\} \cup \{\omega \mid X(\omega) = x_2\} \cup \cdots \cup \{\omega \mid X(\omega) = x_{[b]}\},$$

where $x_{[b]}$ denotes the largest integer value of the x's less than or equal to b. It then follows that for the discrete random variable X, the CDF can be expressed as

$$\begin{aligned} F_X(b) &= P\{\omega \mid X(\omega) = x_1\} + P\{\omega \mid X(\omega) = x_2\} + \cdots + P\{\omega \mid X(\omega) = x_{[b]}\} \\ &= P\{X = x_1\} + P\{X = x_2\} + \cdots + P\{X = x_{[b]}\}. \end{aligned}$$

This last expression can also be expressed as

$$F_X(b) = \sum_{\text{all } k \leq b} P\{X = k\},$$

where k is an index that ranges over all the possible x values which the random variable X can take on.

Let $P_X(k)$ denote the probabilities $P\{X = k\}$, so that

$$F_X(b) = \sum_{\text{all } k \leq b} P_X(k).$$

The $P_X(k)$ are called the probability distribution of the discrete random variable X. When no ambiguity exists, $P_X(k)$ may be denoted by $P(k)$.

As an example, consider the discrete random variable that represents the demand for a product in a given month. Let $N = 99$. If it is assumed that $P_X(k) = P\{X = k\} = 1/100$ for all $k = 0, 1, \ldots, 99$, then the CDF for this discrete random variable is given in Fig. 8.4. The probability distribution of this discrete random variable is shown in Fig. 8.5. Of course, the heights of the vertical lines in Fig. 8.5 are all equal because $P_X(0) = P_X(1) = P_X(2) = \cdots = P_X(99)$ in this case. For other random variables X, the $P_X(k)$ need not be equal, and hence the vertical lines will not be constant. In fact, all that is required for the $P_X(k)$ to form a probability distribution is that $P_X(k)$ be nonnegative and

$$\sum_{\text{all } k} P_X(k) = 1.$$

There are several important discrete probability distributions used in operations research work. The remainder of this section is devoted to a study of these distributions.

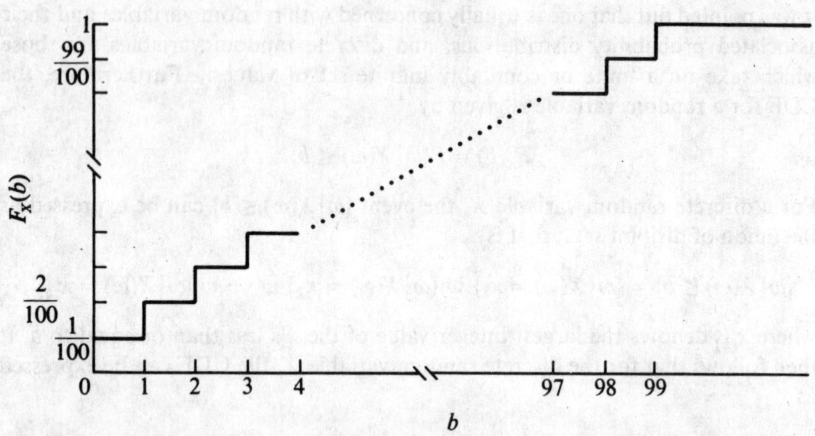

Figure 8.4 CDF of a discrete random variable.

Binomial Distribution

A random variable X is said to have a binomial distribution if its probability distribution can be written as

$$P\{X = k\} = P_X(k) = \frac{n!}{k!(n-k)!} p^k(1-p)^{n-k},$$

where p is a constant lying between zero and 1, n is any positive integer, and k is also an integer such that $0 \leq k \leq n$. It is evident that $P_X(k)$ is always nonnegative, and it is easily proven that

$$\sum_{k=0}^{n} P_X(k) = 1.$$

Figure 8.5 Probability distribution of a discrete random variable.

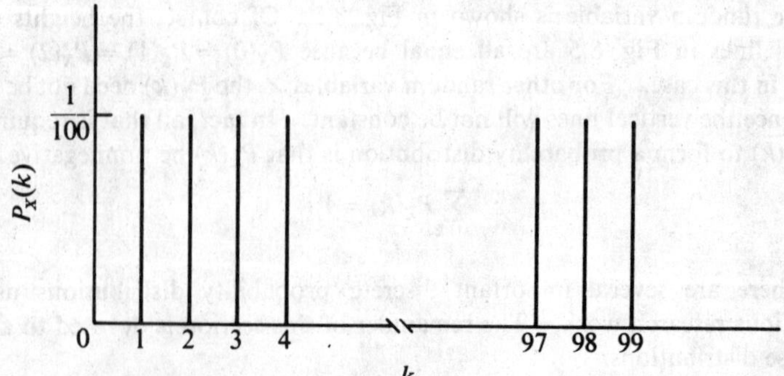

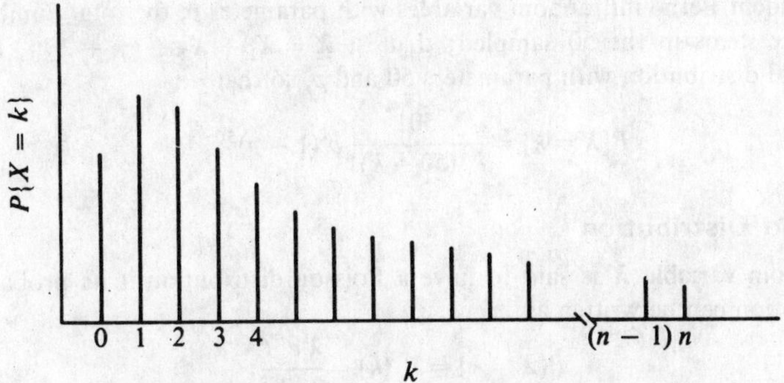

Figure 8.6 Binomial distribution with parameters n and p.

Note that this distribution is a function of the two parameters n and p. The probability distribution of this random variable is shown in Fig. 8.6. An interesting interpretation of the binomial distribution is obtained when $n = 1$:

$$P\{X = 0\} = P_X(0) = 1 - p,$$

and

$$P\{X = 1\} = P_X(1) = p.$$

Such a random variable is said to have a Bernoulli distribution. Thus, if a random variable takes on two values, say, 0 or 1, with probability $1 - p$ or p, respectively, a Bernoulli random variable is obtained. The upturned face of a flipped coin is such an example: If a head is denoted by assigning it the number 0 and a tail by assigning it a 1, and if the coin is "fair" (the probability that a head will appear is ½), the upturned face is a Bernoulli random variable with parameter $p = ½$. Another example of a Bernoulli random variable is the quality of an item. If a defective item is denoted by 1 and a nondefective item by 0, and if p represents the probability of an item being defective, and $1 - p$ represents the probability of an item being nondefective, then the "quality" of an item (defective or nondefective) is a Bernoulli random variable.

If $X_1, X_2, \ldots, X_n$ are independent[1] Bernoulli random variables, each with parameter p, then it can be shown that the random variable

$$X = X_1 + X_2 + \cdots + X_n$$

is a binomial random variable with parameters n and p. Thus, if a fair coin is flipped 10 times, with the random variable X denoting the total number of tails (which is equivalent to $X_1 + X_2 + \cdots + X_{10}$), then X has a binomial distribution with parameters 10 and ½; that is,

$$P\{X = k\} = \frac{10!}{k!(10-k)!}\left(\frac{1}{2}\right)^k\left(\frac{1}{2}\right)^{10-k}$$

[1] The concept of independent random variables is introduced in Sec. 8.13. For the present purpose, random variables can be considered independent if their outcomes do not affect the outcomes of the other random variables.

Similarly, if the quality characteristics (defective or nondefective) of 50 items are independent Bernoulli random variables with parameter p, the total number of defective items in the 50 sampled; that is, $X = X_1 + X_2 + \cdots + X_{50}$, has a binomial distribution with parameters 50 and p, so that

$$P\{X = k\} = \frac{50!}{k!(50-k)!} p^k (1-p)^{50-k}.$$

Poisson Distribution

A random variable X is said to have a Poisson distribution if its probability distribution can be written as

$$P\{X = k\} = P_X(k) = \frac{\lambda^k e^{-\lambda}}{k!},$$

where λ is a positive constant (the parameter of this distribution), and k is any nonnegative integer. It is evident that $P_X(k)$ is nonnegative, and it is easily shown that

$$\sum_{k=0}^{\infty} \frac{\lambda^k e^{-\lambda}}{k!} = 1.$$

An example of a probability distribution of a Poisson random variable is shown in Fig. 8.7. (The CDF of the Poisson random variable is tabulated in Table A5.4 of Appendix 5.)

The Poisson distribution is often used in operations research. Heuristically speaking, this distribution is appropriate in many situations where an "event" occurs over a period of time, like the arrival of a customer; when it is as likely that this "event" will occur in one interval as in any other; also the occurrence of an event has no effect on whether or not another occurs. Then the number of customer arrivals in a fixed time is often assumed to have a Poisson distribution. Similarly, the demand for a given product is also often assumed to have this distribution.

Figure 8.7 Poisson distribution.

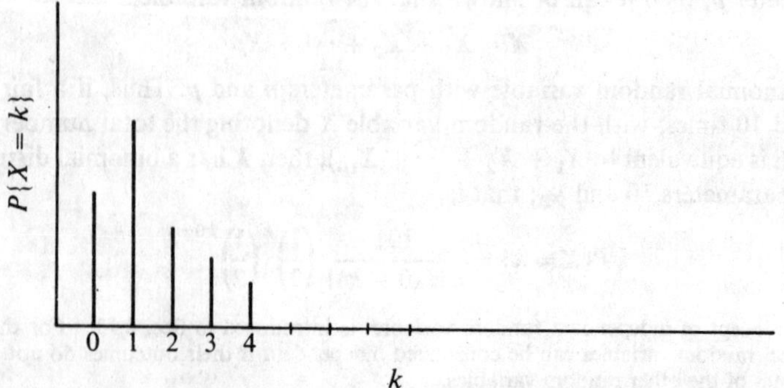

Geometric Distribution

A random variable X is said to have a geometric distribution if its probability distribution can be written as

$$P\{X = k\} = P_X(k) = p(1 - p)^{k-1},$$

where the parameter p is a constant lying between 0 and 1, and k takes on the values 1, 2, 3, ... It is clear that $P_X(k)$ is nonnegative, and it is easy to show that

$$\sum_{k=1}^{\infty} p(1 - p)^{k-1} = 1.$$

The geometric distribution is useful in the following situation. Suppose an experiment is performed that leads to a sequence of independent[1] Bernoulli random variables, each with parameter p; that is, $P\{X_i = 1\} = p$ and $P\{X_i = 0\} = 1 - p$, for all i. The random variable X, which is the number of trials occurring until the first Bernoulli random variable takes on the value 1, has a geometric distribution with parameter p.

8.7 CONTINUOUS PROBABILITY DISTRIBUTIONS

Section 8.3 defined continuous random variables as those random variables that take on a continuum of values. The CDF for a continuous random variable $F_X(b)$ can usually be written as

$$F_X(b) = P\{X(\omega) \le b\} = \int_{-\infty}^{b} f_X(y)\, dy,$$

where $f_X(y)$ is known as the density function of the random variable X. From a notational standpoint, the subscript X is used to indicate the random variable that is under consideration. When there is no ambiguity, this subscript may be deleted, and $f_X(y)$ will be denoted by $f(y)$. It is evident that the CDF can be obtained if the density function is known. Furthermore, a knowledge of the density function enables one to calculate all sorts of probabilities, for example

$$P\{a < X \le b\} = F(b) - F(a) = \int_{a}^{b} f_X(y)\, dy.$$

Note that strictly speaking the symbol $P\{a < X \le b\}$ relates to the probability that the outcome ω of the experiment belongs to a particular event in the sample space, namely, that event such that $X(\omega)$ is between a and b whenever ω belongs to the event. However, the reference to the event will be suppressed, and the symbol P will be used to refer to the probability that X falls between a and b. It becomes evident from the previous expression for $P\{a < X \le b\}$ that this

[1] The concept of independent random variables is introduced in Sec. 8.13. For now, random variables can be considered independent if their outcomes do not affect the outcomes of the other random variables.

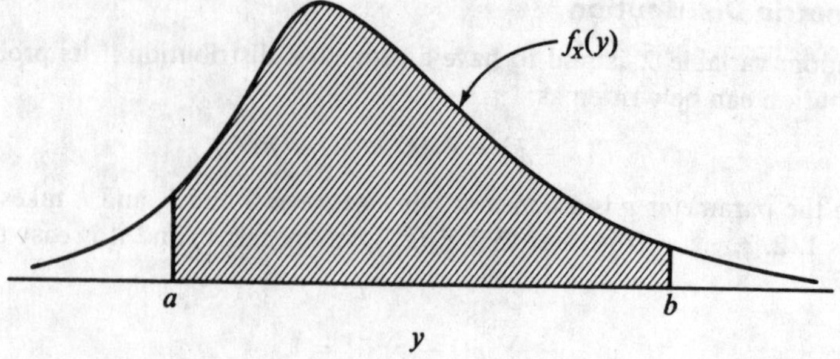

Figure 8.8 Density function of a random variable.

probability can be evaluated by obtaining the area under the density function between a and b, as illustrated by the shaded area under the density function shown in Fig. 8.8. Finally, if the density function is known, it will be said that the probability distribution of the random variable is determined.

Naturally, the density function can be obtained from the CDF by using the relation

$$\frac{dF_X(y)}{dy} = \frac{d}{dy}\int_{-\infty}^{y} f_X(t)\,dt = f_X(y).$$

For a given value c, $P\{X = c\}$ has not been defined in terms of the density function. However, because probability has been interpreted as an area under the density function, $P\{X = c\}$ will be taken to be zero for all values of c. Having $P\{X = c\} = 0$ does not mean that the appropriate event E in the sample space (E contains those ω such that $X(\omega) = c$) is an impossible event. Rather, the event E can occur, but it occurs with probability zero. Since X is a continuous random variable, it takes on a continuum of possible values, so that selecting correctly the actual outcome before experimentation would be rather startling. Nevertheless, some outcome is obtained, so that it is not unreasonable to assume that the preselected outcome has probability zero of occurring. It then follows from $P\{X = c\}$ being equal to zero for all values c that for continuous random variables, and any a and b,

$$P\{a \leq X \leq b\} = P\{a < X \leq b\} = P\{a \leq X < b\} = P\{a < X < b\}.$$

Of course, this is not true for discrete random variables.

In defining the CDF for continuous random variables, it was implied that $f_X(y)$ was defined for values of y from minus to plus infinity because

$$F_X(b) = \int_{-\infty}^{b} f_X(y)\,dy.$$

This causes no difficulty, even for random variables that can not take on negative values (e.g., the arrival time of the first customer) or are restricted to other regions, because $f_X(y)$ can be defined to be zero over the inadmissible segment of the real line. In fact, the only requirements of a density function are that

1. $f_X(y)$ be nonnegative.
2. $\int_{-\infty}^{\infty} f_X(y)\,dy = 1$.

It has already been pointed out that $f_X(y)$ can not be interpreted as $P\{X = y\}$ because this probability is always zero. However, $f_X(y)\,dy$ can be interpreted as the probability that the random variable X lies in the infinitesimal interval $(y, y + dy)$, so that, loosely speaking, $f_X(y)$ is a measure of the frequency with which the random variable will fall into a "small" interval near y.

There are several important continuous probability distributions that are used in operations research work. The remainder of this section is devoted to a study of these distributions.

The Exponential Distribution

A continuous random variable whose density is given by

$$f_X(y) = \begin{cases} \dfrac{1}{\theta} e^{-y/\theta}, & \text{for } y \geq 0 \\ 0, & \text{for } y < 0 \end{cases}$$

is known as an exponentially distributed random variable. The exponential distribution is a function of the single parameter θ, where θ is any positive constant. $f_X(y)$ is a density function because it is nonnegative and integrates to 1; that is,

$$\int_{-\infty}^{\infty} f_X(y)\,dy = \int_0^{\infty} \frac{1}{\theta} e^{-y/\theta}\,dy = -e^{-y/\theta}\Big|_0^{\infty} = 1.$$

The exponential density function is shown in Fig. 8.9.

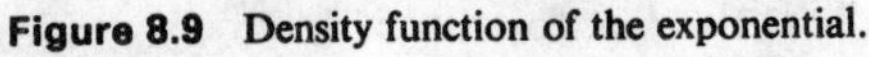
Figure 8.9 Density function of the exponential.

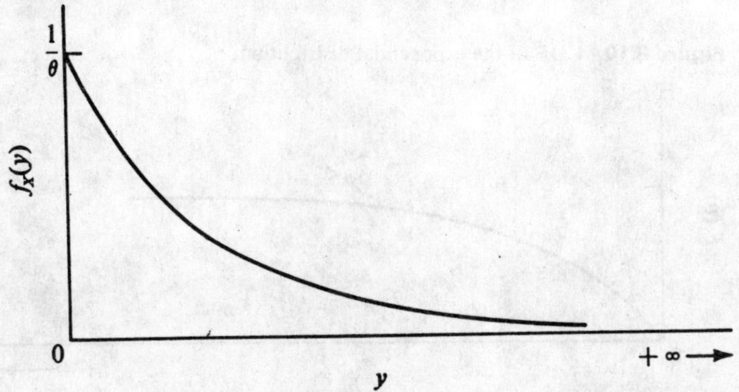

The CDF of an exponentially distributed random variable $F_X(b)$ is given by

$$F_X(b) = \int_{-\infty}^{b} f_X(y)\,dy$$

$$= \begin{cases} 0, & \text{for } b < 0 \\ \int_0^b \frac{1}{\theta} e^{-y/\theta}\,dy = 1 - e^{-b/\theta}, & \text{for } b \geq 0, \end{cases}$$

and is shown in Fig. 8.10.

The exponential distribution has had widespread use in operations research. The time between customer arrivals, the length of time of telephone conversations, and the life of electronic components are often assumed to have an exponential distribution. Such an assumption has the important implication that the random variable does not "age." For example, suppose that the life of a vacuum tube is assumed to have an exponential distribution. If the tube has lasted 1,000 hours, the probability of lasting an additional 50 hours is the same as the probability of lasting an additional 50 hours, given that the tube has lasted 2,000 hours. In other words, a brand new tube is no "better" than one that has lasted 1,000 hours. This implication of the exponential is quite important and is often overlooked in practice.

The Gamma Distribution

A continuous random variable whose density is given by

$$f_X(y) = \begin{cases} \frac{1}{\Gamma(\alpha)\beta^\alpha} y^{(\alpha-1)} e^{-y/\beta}, & \text{for } y \geq 0 \\ 0, & \text{for } y < 0 \end{cases}$$

is known as a gamma-distributed random variable. This density is a function of the two parameters α and β, both of which are positive constants. $\Gamma(\alpha)$ is defined as

$$\Gamma(\alpha) = \int_0^\infty t^{\alpha-1} e^{-t}\,dt, \text{ for all } \alpha > 0.$$

Figure 8.10 CDF of the exponential distribution.

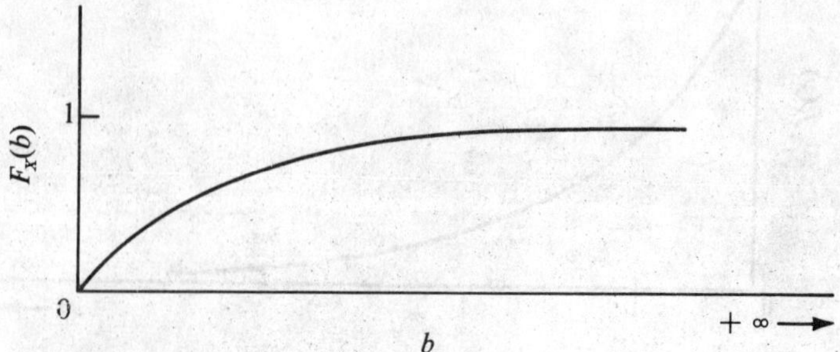

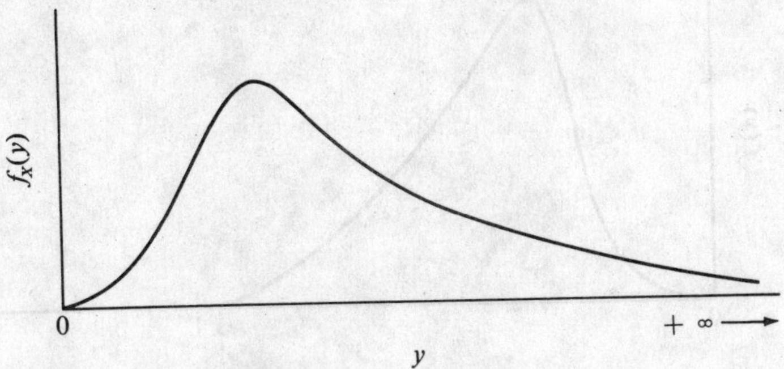

Figure 8.11 Gamma density function.

If α is an integer, then repeated integration by parts yields

$$\Gamma(\alpha) = (\alpha - 1)! = (\alpha - 1)(\alpha - 2)(\alpha - 3) \cdots 3 \cdot 2 \cdot 1.$$

A graph of a typical gamma density function is given in Fig. 8.11.

A random variable having a gamma density is useful in its own right as a mathematical representation of physical phenomena, or it may arise as follows: Suppose a customer's service time has an exponential distribution with parameter θ. The random variable T, the total time to service n (independent) customers, has a gamma distribution with parameters n and θ (replacing α and β, respectively); that is,

$$P\{T < t\} = \int_0^t \frac{1}{\Gamma(n)\theta^n} y^{(n-1)} e^{-y/\theta} \, dy.$$

Note that when $n = 1$ (or $\alpha = 1$) the gamma density becomes the density function of an exponential random variable. Thus sums of independent, exponentially distributed random variables have a gamma distribution.

Another important distribution, the chi square, is related to the gamma distribution. If X is a random variable having a gamma distribution with parameters $\beta = 1$ and $\alpha = v/2$ (v is a positive integer), then a new random variable $Z = 2X$ is said to have a chi-square distribution with v degrees of freedom. The density function is given in Table 8.1. The percentage points of the chi-square distribution are given in Table A5.3 of Appendix 5. Percentage points of the distribution of a random variable Z are the values z_α such that

$$P\{Z > z_\alpha\} = \alpha.$$

z_α is said to be the 100α percentage point of the distribution of the random variable Z.

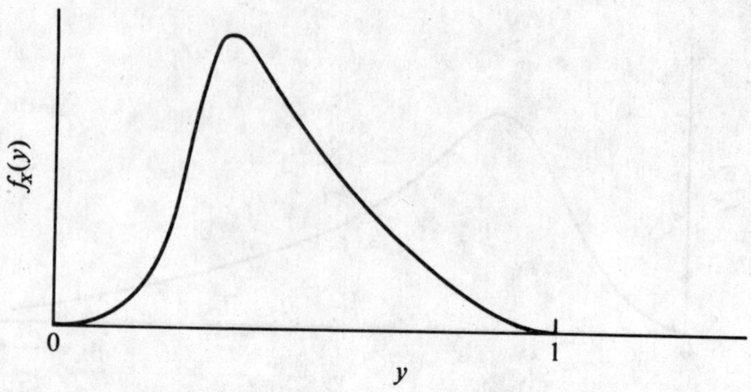

Figure 8.12 Beta density function.

The Beta Distribution

A continuous random variable whose density function is given by

$$f_X(y) = \begin{cases} \dfrac{\Gamma(\alpha+\beta)}{\Gamma(\alpha)\Gamma(\beta)} y^{(\alpha-1)}(1-y)^{(\beta-1)}, & \text{for } 0 \le y \le 1 \\ 0, & \text{elsewhere} \end{cases}$$

is known as a beta-distributed random variable. This density is a function of the two parameters α and β, both of which are positive constants. A graph of a typical beta density function is given in Fig. 8.12.

Beta distributions form a useful class of distributions when a random variable is restricted to the unit interval. In particular, when $\alpha = \beta = 1$, the beta distribution is called the *uniform distribution* over the unit interval. Its density function is shown in Fig. 8.13, and it can be interpreted as having all the values between zero and 1 equally likely to occur. The CDF for this random variable is given by

$$F_X(b) = \begin{cases} 0, \text{ for } b < 0 \\ b, \text{ for } 0 \le b \le 1 \\ 1, \text{ for } b > 1. \end{cases}$$

If the density function is to be constant over some other interval, such as the interval $[c, d]$, a uniform distribution over this interval can also be obtained.[1] The density function is given by

$$f_X(y) = \begin{cases} \dfrac{1}{d-c}, & \text{for } c \le y \le d \\ 0, & \text{otherwise.} \end{cases}$$

Although such a random variable is said to have a uniform distribution over the interval $[c, d]$, it is no longer a special case of the beta distribution.

[1] The beta distribution can also be generalized by defining the density function over some fixed interval, other than the unit interval.

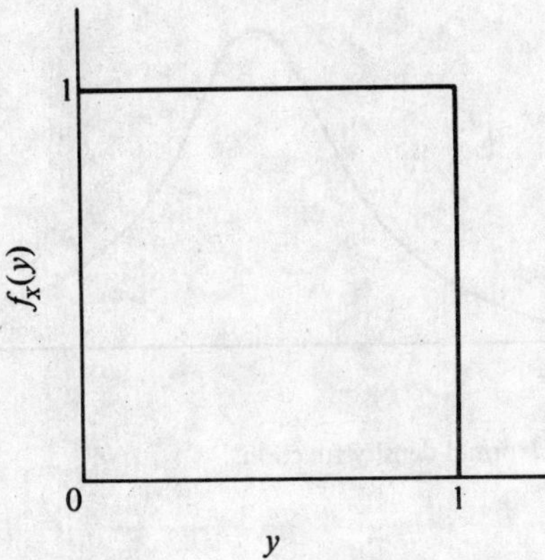

Figure 8.13 Uniform distribution over the unit interval.

Another important distribution, Students t, is related to the beta distribution. If X is a random variable having a beta distribution with parameters $\alpha = \frac{1}{2}$ and $\beta = v/2$ (v is a positive integer), then a new random variable $Z = \sqrt{vX/(1-X)}$ is said to have a Students t (or t) distribution with v degrees of freedom. The percentage points of the t distribution are given in Table A5.2 of Appendix 5.

A final distribution related to the beta distribution is the F distribution. If X is a random variable having a beta distribution with parameters $\alpha = v_1/2$ and $\beta = v_2/2$ (v_1 and v_2 are positive integers), then a new random variable $Z = v_2 X/v_1(1-X)$ is said to have an F distribution with v_1 and v_2 degrees of freedom. The percentage points of the F distribution are given in Table A5.5 of Appendix 5.

The Normal Distribution

One of the most important distributions in operations research is the normal distribution. A continuous random variable whose density function is given by

$$f_X(y) = \frac{1}{\sqrt{2\pi}\,\sigma} e^{-(y-\mu)^2/2\sigma^2}, \text{ for } -\infty < y < \infty$$

is known as a normally distributed random variable. The density is a function of the two parameters μ and σ, where μ is any constant, and σ is positive. A graph of a typical normal density function is given in Fig. 8.14. This density function is a bell-shaped curve that is symmetric around μ. The CDF for a normally distributed random variable is given by

$$F_X(b) = \int_{-\infty}^{b} \frac{1}{\sqrt{2\pi}\,\sigma} e^{-(y-\mu)^2/2\sigma^2}\, dy.$$

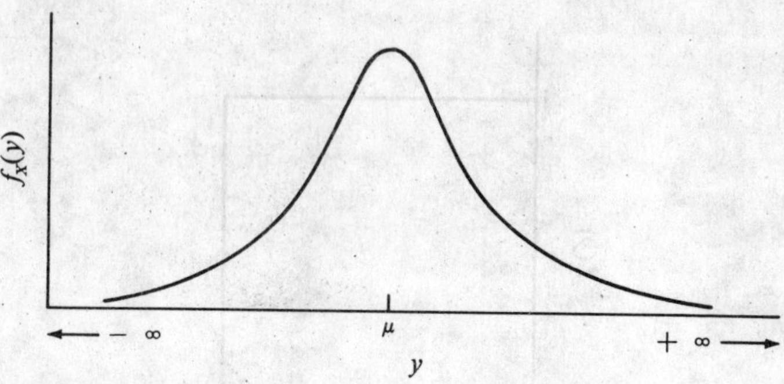

Figure 8.14 Normal density function.

By making the transformation $z = (y - \mu)/\sigma$, the CDF can be written as

$$F_X(b) = \int_{-\infty}^{(b-\mu)/\sigma} \frac{1}{\sqrt{2\pi}} e^{-z^2/2}\, dz.$$

Hence, although this function is not integrable, it is easily tabulated. Table A5.1 presented in Appendix 5 is a tabulation of

$$\alpha = \int_{K_\alpha}^{\infty} \frac{1}{\sqrt{2\pi}} e^{-z^2/2}\, dz$$

as a function of K_α. Hence, to find $F_X(b)$ (and any probability derived from it), Table A5.1 is entered with $K_\alpha = (b - \mu)/\sigma$, and

$$\alpha = \int_{K_\alpha}^{\infty} \frac{1}{\sqrt{2\pi}} e^{-z^2/2}\, dz$$

is read from it. $F_X(b)$ is then just $1 - \alpha$. Thus, if $P\{14 < X \leq 18\} = F_X(18) - F_X(14)$ is desired, where X has a normal distribution with $\mu = 10$ and $\sigma = 4$, Table A5.1 is entered with $(18 - 10)/4 = 2$, and $1 - F_X(18) = 0.0228$ is obtained. The table is then entered with $(14 - 10)/4 = 1$, and $1 - F_X(14) = 0.1587$ is read. From these figures, $F_X(18) - F_X(14) = 0.1359$ is found. If K_α is negative, use can be made of the symmetry of the normal distribution because

$$F_X(b) = \int_{-\infty}^{(b-\mu)/\sigma} \frac{1}{\sqrt{2\pi}} e^{-z^2/2}\, dz = \int_{-(b-\mu)/\sigma}^{\infty} \frac{1}{\sqrt{2\pi}} e^{-z^2/2}\, dz.$$

In this case $-(b - \mu)/\sigma$ is positive, and $F_X(b) = \alpha$ is thereby read from the table by entering it with $-(b - \mu)/\sigma$. Thus, suppose it is desired to evaluate the expression

$$P\{2 < X \leq 18\} = F_X(18) - F_X(2).$$

$F_X(18)$ has already been shown to be equal to $1 - 0.0228 = 0.9772$. To find

$F_X(2)$ it is first noted that $(2-10)/4=-2$ is negative. Hence Table A5.1 is entered with $K_\alpha=+2$, and $F_X(2)=0.0228$ is obtained. Thus

$$F_X(18)-F_X(2)=0.9772-0.0228=0.9544.$$

As indicated previously, the normal distribution is a very important one. In particular, it can be shown that if $X_1, X_2, \ldots, X_n$ are independent,[1] normally distributed random variables with parameters (μ_1, σ_1), (μ_2, σ_2), $\ldots$, (μ_n, σ_n), respectively, then $X=X_1+X_2+\cdots+X_n$ is also a normally distributed random variable with parameters

$$\sum_{i=1}^{n}\mu_i$$

and

$$\sqrt{\sum_{i=1}^{n}\sigma_i^2}.$$

In fact, even if $X_1, X_2, \ldots, X_n$ are not normal, then under very weak conditions

$$X=\sum_{i=1}^{n}X_i$$

tends to be normally distributed as n gets large. This is discussed further in Sec. 8.15.

Finally, if C is any constant and X is normal with parameters μ and σ, then the random variable CX is also normal with parameters $C\mu$ and $C\sigma$. Hence it follows that if $X_1, X_2, \ldots, X_n$ are independent, normally distributed random variables, each with parameters μ and σ, the random variable

$$\bar{X}=\sum_{i=1}^{n}\frac{X_i}{n}$$

is also normally distributed with parameters μ and $\sigma/\sqrt{n}$.

8.8 EXPECTATION

Although knowledge of the probability distribution of a random variable enables one to make all sorts of probability statements, a single value that may characterize the random variable and its probability distribution is often desirable. Such a quantity is the *expected value* of the random variable. One may speak of the expected value of the demand for a product or the expected value of the time of the first customer arrival. In the experiment where the arrival time of the first customer on two successive days was measured, the expected value of the average arrival time of the first customers on two successive days may be of interest.

[1] The concept of independent random variables is introduced in Sec. 8.13. For now, random variables can be considered independent if their outcomes do not affect the outcomes of the other random variables.

Formally, the expected value of a random variable X is denoted by $E(X)$ and is given by

$$E(X) = \begin{cases} \sum_{\text{all } k} kP\{X = k\} = \sum_{\text{all } k} kP_X(k), & \text{if } X \text{ is a discrete random variable} \\ \int_{-\infty}^{\infty} y f_X(y)\, dy, & \text{if } X \text{ is a continuous random variable.} \end{cases}$$

For a discrete random variable it is seen that $E(X)$ is just the sum of the products of the possible values the random variable X takes on and their respective associated probabilities. In the example of the demand for a product, where $k = 0, 1, 2, \ldots, 98, 99$ and $P_X(k) = 1/100$ for all i, the expected value of the demand is

$$E(X) = \sum_{k=0}^{99} kP_X(k) = \sum_{k=0}^{99} k \frac{1}{100} = 49.5.$$

Note that $E(X)$ need not be a value that the random variable can take on.

If X is a binomial random variable with parameters n and p, the expected value of X is given by

$$E(X) = \sum_{k=0}^{n} k \frac{n!}{k!\,(n-k)!} p^k(1-p)^{n-k}$$

and can be shown to equal np.

If the random variable X has a Poisson distribution with parameter λ,

$$E(X) = \sum_{k=0}^{\infty} k \frac{\lambda^k e^{-\lambda}}{k!}$$

and can be shown to equal λ.

Finally, if the random variable X has a geometric distribution with parameter p,

$$E(X) = \sum_{k=1}^{\infty} kp(1-p)^{k-1}$$

and can be shown to equal $1/p$.

For continuous random variables, the expected value can also be obtained easily. If X has an exponential distribution with parameter θ, the expected value is given by

$$E(X) = \int_{-\infty}^{\infty} y f_X(y)\, dy = \int_{0}^{\infty} y \frac{1}{\theta} e^{-y/\theta}\, dy.$$

This integral is easily evaluated to be

$$E(X) = \theta.$$

If the random variable X has a gamma distribution with parameter α and β the expected value of X is given by

$$\int_{-\infty}^{\infty} y f_X(y)\, dy = \int_0^{\infty} y \frac{1}{\Gamma(\alpha)\beta^\alpha} y^{(\alpha-1)} e^{-y/\beta}\, dy = \alpha\beta.$$

If the random variable X has a beta distribution with parameters α and β, the expected value of X is given by

$$\int_{-\infty}^{\infty} y f_X(y)\, dy = \int_0^1 y \frac{\Gamma(\alpha+\beta)}{\Gamma(\alpha)\Gamma(\beta)} y^{(\alpha-1)}(1-y)^{(\beta-1)}\, dy = \frac{\alpha}{\alpha+\beta}.$$

Finally, if the random variable X has a normal distribution with parameters μ and σ, the expected value of X is given by

$$\int_{-\infty}^{\infty} y f_X(y)\, dy = \int_{-\infty}^{\infty} y \frac{1}{\sqrt{2\pi}\,\sigma} e^{-(y-\mu)^2/2\sigma^2}\, dy = \mu.$$

The expectation of a random variable is quite useful in that it not only provides some characterization of the distribution, but it also has meaning in terms of the average of a sample. In particular, if a random variable is observed again and again and the arithmetic mean $\overline{X}$ is computed, then $\overline{X}$ tends to the expectation of the random variable X as the number of trials becomes large. A precise statement of this property is given in Sec. 8.14. Thus, if the demand for a product takes on the values $k = 0, 1, 2, \ldots, 98, 99$, each with $P_X(k) = 1/100$ for all k, and if demands of $x_1, x_2, \ldots, x_n$ are observed on successive days, then the average of these values, $(x_1 + x_2 + \cdots + x_n)/n$, should be close to $E(X) = 49.5$ if n is sufficiently large.

It is not necessary to confine the discussion of expectation to discussion of the expectation of a random variable X. If Z is some function of X, say, $Z = g(X)$, then $g(X)$ is also a random variable. The expectation of $g(X)$ can be defined as

$$E[g(X)] = \begin{cases} \sum_{\text{all } k} g(k)P\{X = k\} = \sum_{\text{all } k} g(k)P_X(k), & \text{if } X \text{ is a discrete random variable} \\ \int_{-\infty}^{\infty} g(y) f_X(y)\, dy, & \text{if } X \text{ is a continuous random variable.} \end{cases}$$

An interesting theorem, known as the "theorem of the unconscious statistician"[1] states that if X is a continuous random variable having density $f_X(y)$ and $Z = g(X)$ is a function of X having density $h_Z(y)$, then

$$E(Z) = \int_{-\infty}^{\infty} y h_Z(y)\, dy = \int_{-\infty}^{\infty} g(y) f_X(y)\, dy.$$

Thus the expectation of Z can be found by using its definition in terms of the density of Z or, alternatively, by using its definition as the expectation of a function of X with respect to the density function of X. The identical theorem is true for discrete random variables.

[1] The name for this theorem is motivated by the fact that a statistician often uses its conclusions without consciously worrying about whether the theorem is true.

8.9 MOMENTS

If the function g described in the previous section is given by

$$Z = g(X) = X^j,$$

where j is a positive integer, then the expectation of X^j is called the jth moment about the origin of the random variable X and is given by

$$E(X^j) = \begin{cases} \sum_{\text{all } k} k^j P_X(k), & \text{if } X \text{ is a discrete random variable} \\ \int_{-\infty}^{\infty} y^j f_X(y)\, dy, & \text{if } X \text{ is a continuous random variable.} \end{cases}$$

Note that when $j = 1$ the first moment coincides with the expectation of X. This is usually denoted by the symbol μ and is often called the mean or average of the distribution.

Using the theorem of the unconscious statistician, the expectation of $Z = g(X) = CX$ can easily be found, where C is a constant. If X is a continuous random variable, then

$$E(CX) = \int_{-\infty}^{\infty} Cyf_X(y)\, dy = C\int_{-\infty}^{\infty} yf_X(y)\, dy = CE(X).$$

Thus the expectation of a constant times a random variable is just the constant times the expectation of the random variable. This is also true for discrete random variables.

If the function g described in the previous section is given by $Z = g(X) = (X - E(X))^j = (X - \mu)^j$, where j is a positive integer, then the expectation of $(X - \mu)^j$ is called the jth moment about the mean of the random variable X and is given by

$$E(X - E(X))^j = E(X - \mu)^j = \begin{cases} \sum_{\text{all } k} (k - \mu)^j P_X(k), \\ \qquad \text{if } X \text{ is a discrete random variable} \\ \int_{-\infty}^{\infty} (y - \mu)^j f_X(y)\, dy, \\ \qquad \text{if } X \text{ is a continuous random variable.} \end{cases}$$

Note that if $j = 1$, then $E(X - \mu) = 0$. If $j = 2$, then $E(X - \mu)^2$ is called the variance of the random variable X and is often denoted by σ^2. The square root of the variance σ is called the standard deviation of the random variable X. It is easily shown, in terms of definitions, that $\sigma^2 = E(X - \mu)^2 = E(X^2) - \mu^2$; that is, the variance can be written as the second moment about the origin minus the square of the mean.

It has already been shown that if $Z = g(X) = CX$, then $E(CX) = CE(X) = C\mu$, where C is any constant and μ is $E(X)$. The variance of the random variable $Z = g(X) = CX$ is also easily obtained. By definition, if X is a continuous random variable, the variance of Z is given by

$$E(Z - E(Z))^2 = E(CX - CE(X))^2 = \int_{-\infty}^{\infty} (Cy - C\mu)^2 f_X(y)\, dy$$

$$= C^2 \int_{-\infty}^{\infty} (y - \mu)^2 f_X(y)\, dy = C^2\sigma^2.$$

Thus the variance of a constant times a random variable is just the square of the constant times the variance of the random variable. This is also true for discrete random variables. Finally, the variance of a constant is easily seen to be zero.

It has already been shown that if the demand for a product takes on the values 0, 1, 2, ..., 99, each with probability $1/100$, then $E(X) = \mu = 49.5$. Similarly,

$$\sigma^2 = \sum_{k=0}^{99} (k - \mu)^2 P_X(k) = \sum_{k=0}^{99} k^2 P_X(k) - \mu^2$$

$$= \sum_{k=0}^{99} \frac{k^2}{100} - (49.5)^2 = 833.25.$$

Table 8.1 gives the means and variances of the random variables that are often useful in operations research. Note that for some random variables a single moment, the mean, provides a complete characterization of the distribution, e.g., the Poisson random variable. For some random variables the mean and variance provide a complete characterization of the distribution, e.g., the normal. In fact, if all the moments of a probability distribution are known, this is usually equivalent to specifying the entire distribution.

It was seen that the mean and variance may be sufficient to completely characterize a distribution, e.g., the normal. However, what can be said, in general, about a random variable whose mean μ and variance σ^2 are known, but nothing else about the form of the distribution is specified? This can be expressed in terms of *Chebyshev's inequality*, which states that for any positive number c,

$$P\{\mu - C\sigma \leq X \leq \mu + C\sigma\} > 1 - \frac{1}{C^2},$$

where X is any random variable having mean μ and variance σ^2. For example, if $C = 3$, it follows that $P\{\mu - 3\sigma \leq X \leq \mu + 3\sigma\} > 1 - 1/9 = 0.8889$. However, if X is known to have a normal distribution, then $P\{\mu - 3\sigma \leq X \leq \mu + 3\sigma\} = 0.9973$. Note that the Chebyshev inequality only gives a lower bound on the probability (usually a very conservative one), so there is no contradiction here.

Table 8.1 Table of Common Distributions

Distribution of random variable X	*Form*	*Para-meters*	*Expected value*	*Variance*	*Range of random variable*
Binomial	$P_X(k) = \frac{n!}{k!(n-k)!} p^k(1-p)^{n-k}$	n, p	np	$np(1-p)$	$0, 1, 2 \ldots, n$
Poisson	$P_X(k) = \frac{\lambda^k e^{-\lambda}}{k!}$	λ	λ	λ	$0, 1, 2, \ldots.$
Geometric	$P_X(k) = p(1-p)^{k-1}$	p	$\frac{1}{p}$	$\frac{1-p}{p^2}$	$1, 2, \ldots.$
Exponential	$f_X(y) = \frac{1}{\theta} e^{-y/\theta}$	θ	θ	θ^2	$(0, \infty)$
Gamma	$f_X(y) = \frac{1}{\Gamma(\alpha)\beta^\alpha} y^{(\alpha-1)} e^{-y/\beta}$	α, β	$\alpha\beta$	$\alpha\beta^2$	$(0, \infty)$
Beta	$f_X(y) = \frac{\Gamma(\alpha+\beta)}{\Gamma(\alpha)\Gamma(\beta)} y^{(\alpha-1)}(1-y)^{(\beta-1)}$	α, β	$\frac{\alpha}{\alpha+\beta}$	$\frac{\alpha\beta}{(\alpha+\beta)^2(\alpha+\beta+1)}$	$(0,1)$
Normal	$f_X(y) = \frac{1}{\sqrt{2\pi}\,\sigma} e^{-(y-\mu)^2/2\sigma^2}$	μ, σ	μ	σ^2	$(-\infty, \infty)$
Students *t*	$f_X(y) = \frac{1}{\sqrt{\pi\nu}} \frac{\Gamma([\nu+1]/2)}{\Gamma(\nu/2)} (1 + y^2/\nu)^{-(\nu+1)/2}$	ν	$0 (\text{for } \nu > 1)$	$\nu/(\nu-2) (\text{for } \nu > 2)$	$(-\infty, \infty)$
Chi square	$f_X(y) = \frac{1}{2^{\nu/2}\Gamma(\nu/2)} y^{(\nu-2)/2} e^{-y/2}$	ν	ν	2ν	$(0, \infty)$
F	$f_X(y) = \frac{\Gamma\left(\frac{\nu_1+\nu_2}{2}\right)\nu_1^{\nu_1/2}\nu_2^{\nu_2/2}}{\Gamma\left(\frac{\nu_1}{2}\right)\Gamma\left(\frac{\nu_2}{2}\right)} \frac{(y)^{(\nu_1/2)-1}}{(\nu_2+\nu_1 y)^{(\nu_1+\nu_2)/2}}$	ν_1, ν_2	$\frac{\nu_2}{\nu_2-2}$ for $\nu_2 > 2$.	$\frac{\nu_2^2(2\nu_2+2\nu_1-4)}{\nu_1(\nu_2-2)^2(\nu_2-4)}$ for $\nu_2 > 4$.	$(0, \infty)$

8.10 BIVARIATE PROBABILITY DISTRIBUTION

Thus far the discussion has been concerned with the probability distribution of a single random variable, e.g., the demand for a product during the first month or the demand for a product during the second month. In an experiment that measures the demand during the first 2 months, it may well be important to look at the probability distribution of the vector random variable (X_1,X_2), the demand during the first month, and the demand during the second month, respectively.

Define the symbol

$$E_{b_1,b_2}^{X_1,X_2} = \{\omega \mid X_1(\omega) \le b_1, X_2(\omega) \le b_2\},$$

or equivalently,

$$E_{b_1,b_2}^{X_1,X_2} = \{X_1 \le b_1, X_2 \le b_2\},$$

as the set of outcomes ω in the sample space forming the event $E_{b_1,b_2}^{X_1,X_2}$, such that the random variable X_1 takes on values less than or equal to b_1 ,and X_2 takes on values less than or equal to b_2. Then $P\{E_{b_1,b_2}^{X_1,X_2}\}$ denotes the probability of this event. In the above example of the demand for a product during the first 2 months, suppose that the sample space Ω consists of the set of all possible points ω, where ω represents a pair of nonnegative integer values (x_1,x_2). Assume that x_1 and x_2 are bounded by 99. Thus there are $(100)^2\omega$ points in Ω. Suppose further that each point ω has associated with it a probability equal to $1/(100)^2$, except for the points $\omega=(0,0)$ and $\omega=(99,99)$. The probability associated with the event $\{0,0\}$ will be $1.5/(100)^2$, that is, $P\{0,0\}=1.5/(100)^2$, and the probability associated with the event $\{99,99\}$ will be $0.5/(100)^2$; that is, $P\{99,99\}=0.5/(100)^2$. Thus, if there is interest in the "bivariate" random variable (X_1, X_2), the demand during the first and second months, respectively, then the event

$$\{X_1 \le 1, X_2 \le 3\}$$

is the set

$$E_{1,3}^{X_1,X_2} = \{(0,0), (0,1), (0,2), (0,3), (1,0), (1,1), (1,2), (1,3)\}.$$

Furthermore,

$$P\{E_{1,3}^{X_1,X_2}\} = \frac{1.5}{(100)^2} + \frac{1}{(100)^2} + \frac{1}{(100)^2} + \frac{1}{(100)^2} + \frac{1}{(100)^2} + \frac{1}{(100)^2} + \frac{1}{(100)^2} + \frac{1}{(100)^2}$$

$$= \frac{8.5}{(100)^2},$$

so that

$$P\{X_1 \le 1, X_2 \le 3\} = P\{E_{1,3}^{X_1,X_2}\} = \frac{8.5}{(100)^2}.$$

A similar calculation can be made for any value of b_1 and b_2.

For any given bivariate random variable (X_1,X_2), $P\{X_1 \leq b_1,\ X_2 \leq b_2\}$ is denoted by $F_{X_1X_2}(b_1,b_2)$ and is called the joint cumulative distribution function (CDF) of the bivariate random variable (X_1,X_2) and is defined for all real values of b_1 and b_2. Where there is no ambiguity the joint CDF may be denoted by $F(b_1, b_2)$. Thus, attached to every bivariate random variable is a joint CDF. This is not an arbitrary function but is induced by the probabilities associated with events defined over the sample space Ω such that $\{\omega \mid X_1(\omega) \leq b_1, X_2(\omega) \leq b_2\}$.

The joint CDF of a random variable is a numerically valued function defined for all b_1, b_2, such that $-\infty \leq b_1, b_2 \leq \infty$, having the following properties:

1. $F_{X_1X_2}(b_1,\infty) = P\{X_1 \leq b_1,\ \ X_2 \leq \infty\} = P\{X_1 \leq b_1\} = F_{X_1}(b_1)$, where $F_{X_1}(b_1)$ is just the CDF of the univariate random variable X_1.
2. $F_{X_1X_2}(\infty,b_2) = P\{X_1 \leq \infty,\ \ X_2 \leq b_2\} = P\{X_2 \leq b_2\} = F_{X_2}(b_2)$, where $F_{X_2}(b_2)$ is just the CDF of the univariate random variable X_2.
3. $F_{X_1X_2}(b_1, -\infty) = P\{X_1 \leq b_1, X_2 \leq -\infty\} = 0$,
   $F_{X_1X_2}(-\infty, b_2) = P\{X_1 \leq -\infty, X_2 \leq b_2\} = 0$.
4. $F_{X_1X_2}(b_1+\Delta_1,\ b_2+\Delta_2) - F_{X_1X_2}(b_1+\Delta_1,\ b_2) - F_{X_1X_2}(b_1,\ b_2+\Delta_2) + F_{X_1X_2}(b_1, b_2) \geq 0$, for every $\Delta_1, \Delta_2 \geq 0$, and b_1, b_2.

Using the definition of the event $E_{b_1,\,b_2}^{X_1,\,X_2}$, events of the form

$$\{a_1 < X_1 \leq b_1, a_2 < X_2 \leq b_2\}$$

can be described as the set of outcomes ω in the sample space such that the bivariate random variable (X_1,X_2) takes on values such that X_1 is greater than a_1 but does not exceed b_1 *and* X_2 is greater than a_2 but does not exceed b_2. $P\{a_1 < X_1 \leq b_1, a_2 < X_2 \leq b_2\}$ can easily be seen to be

$$F_{X_1X_2}(b_1, b_2) - F_{X_1X_2}(b_1, a_2) - F_{X_1X_2}(a_1, b_2) + F_{X_1X_2}(a_1, a_2).$$

It was noted that single random variables are generally characterized as discrete or continuous random variables. A bivariate random variable can be characterized in a similar manner. A bivariate random variable (X_1, X_2) is called a discrete bivariate random variable if both X_1 and X_2 are discrete random variables. Similarly, a bivariate random variable (X_1, X_2) is called a continuous bivariate random variable if both X_1 and X_2 are continuous random variables. Of course, bivariate random variables that are neither discrete nor continuous can exist, but these will not be important in this book.

The joint CDF for a discrete random variable $F_{X_1X_2}(b_1, b_2)$ is given by

$$\begin{aligned} F_{X_1X_2}(b_1, b_2) &= P\{\omega \mid X_1(\omega) \leq b_1, X_2(\omega) \leq b_2\} \\ &= \sum_{\text{all } k \leq b_1} \sum_{\text{all } l \leq b_2} P\{\omega \mid X_1(\omega) = k, X_2(\omega) = l\} \\ &= \sum_{\text{all } k \leq b_1} \sum_{\text{all } l \leq b_2} P_{X_1X_2}(k, l), \end{aligned}$$

where $\{\omega | X_1(\omega) = k, X_2(\omega) = l\}$ is the set of outcomes ω in the sample space, such that the random variable X_1 takes on the value k, and the variable X_2 takes on the value l; and $P\{\omega | X_1(\omega) = k, X_2(\omega) = l\} = P_{X_1X_2}(k, l)$ denotes the probability of this event. The $P_{X_1X_2}(k, l)$ are called the joint probability distribution of the discrete bivariate random variable (X_1, X_2). Thus, in the previous example, $P_{X_1X_2}(k, l) = 1/(100)^2$ for all k, l that are integers between 0 and 99, except for $P_{X_1X_2}(0,0) = 1.5/(100)^2$ and $P_{X_1X_2}(99,99) = 0.5/(100)^2$.

For a continuous random variable, the joint CDF $F_{X_1X_2}(b_1, b_2)$ can usually be written as

$$F_{X_1X_2}(b_1,b_2) = P\{\omega | X_1(\omega) \le b_1, X_2(\omega) \le b_2\} = \int_{-\infty}^{b_1} \int_{-\infty}^{b_2} f_{X_1X_2}(s, t)\, ds\, dt,$$

where $f_{X_1X_2}(s,t)$ is known as the joint density function of the bivariate random variable (X_1,X_2). A knowledge of the joint density function enables one to calculate all sorts of probabilities, for example,

$$P\{a_1 < X_1 \le b_1, a_2 < X_2 \le b_2\} = \int_{a_1}^{b_1} \int_{a_2}^{b_2} f_{X_1X_2}(s, t)\, ds\, dt.$$

Finally, if the density function is known, it is said that the probability distribution of the random variable is determined.

The joint density function can be viewed as a surface in three dimensions, where the volume under this surface over regions in the s, t plane correspond to probabilities. Naturally, the density function can be obtained from the CDF by using the relation

$$\frac{\partial^2 F_{X_1X_2}(s, t)}{\partial s\, \partial t} = \frac{\partial^2}{\partial s\, \partial t} \int_{-\infty}^{s} \int_{-\infty}^{t} f_{X_1X_2}(u, v)\, du\, dv = f_{X_1X_2}(s, t).$$

In defining the joint CDF for a bivariate random variable, it was implied that $f_{X_1X_2}(s, t)$ was defined over the entire plane because

$$F_{X_1X_2}(b_1, b_2) = \int_{-\infty}^{b_1} \int_{-\infty}^{b_2} f_{X_1X_2}(s, t)\, ds\, dt$$

(which is analogous to what was done for a univariate random variable). This causes no difficulty, even for bivariate random variables having one or more components that can not take on negative values or are restricted to other regions. In this case, $f_{X_1X_2}(s, t)$ can be defined to be zero over the inadmissible part of the plane. In fact, the only requirements for a function to be a bivariate density function are that

1. $f_{X_1X_2}(s, t)$ be nonnegative, and
2. $\int_{-\infty}^{\infty} \int_{-\infty}^{\infty} f_{X_1X_2}(s, t)\, ds\, dt = 1.$

8.11 MARGINAL AND CONDITIONAL PROBABILITY DISTRIBUTIONS

In Sec. 8.11 the discussion was concerned with the joint probability distribution of a bivariate random variable (X_1,X_2). However, there may also be interest in the probability distribution of the random variables X_1 and X_2 considered separately. It was shown that if $F_{X_1X_2}(b_1, b_2)$ represents the joint CDF of (X_1,X_2), then $F_{X_1}(b_1) = F_{X_1X_2}(b_1, \infty) = P\{X_1 \leq b_1, \ X_2 \leq \infty\} = P\{x_1 \leq b_1\}$ is the CDF for the univariate random variable X_1, and $F_{X_2}(b_2) = F_{X_1X_2}(\infty, b_2) = P\{X_1 \leq \infty, \ X_2 \leq b_2\} = P\{X_2 \leq b_2\}$ is the CDF for the univariate random variable X_2.

If the bivariate random variable (X_1, X_2) is discrete, it was noted that the

$$P_{X_1X_2}(k, l) = P\{X_1 = k, X_2 = l\}$$

describe its joint probability distribution. The probability distribution of X_1 individually, $P_{X_1}(k)$, now called the marginal probability distribution of the discrete random variable X_1, can be obtained from the $P_{X_1X_2}(k, l)$. In particular,

$$F_{X_1}(b_1) = F_{X_1X_2}(b_1,\infty) = \sum_{\text{all } k \leq b_1} \sum_{\text{all } l} P_{X_1X_2}(k, l) = \sum_{\text{all } k \leq b_1} P_{X_1}(k),$$

so that

$$P_{X_1}(k) = P\{X_1 = k\} = \sum_{\text{all } l} P_{X_1X_2}(k, l).$$

Similarly, the marginal probability distribution of the discrete random variable X_2 is given by

$$P_{X_2}(l) = P\{X_2 = l\} = \sum_{\text{all } k} P_{X_1X_2}(k, l).$$

If the experiment (described previously) which measures the demand for a product during the first 2 months is considered, it is seen that the marginal distribution of X_1 is given by

$$\begin{aligned}
P_{X_1}(0) &= \sum_{\text{all } l} P_{X_1X_2}(0, l) \\
&= P_{X_1X_2}(0,0) + P_{X_1X_2}(0,1) + \cdots + P_{X_1X_2}(0,99) \\
&= \frac{1.5}{(100)^2} + \frac{1}{(100)^2} + \cdots + \frac{1}{(100)^2} = \frac{100.5}{(100)^2},
\end{aligned}$$

$$\begin{aligned}
P_{X_1}(1) = P_{X_1}(2) = \cdots = P_{X_1}(98) &= \sum_{\text{all } l} P_{X_1X_2}(k, l), \ k = 1, 2, \ldots, 98 \\
&= \frac{100}{(100)^2},
\end{aligned}$$

$$\begin{aligned}
P_{X_1}(99) &= \sum_{\text{all } l} P_{X_1X_2}(99, l) \\
&= P_{X_1X_2}(99,0) + P_{X_1X_2}(99,1) + \cdots + P_{X_1X_2}(99,99) \\
&= \frac{1}{(100)^2} + \frac{1}{(100)^2} + \cdots + \frac{0.5}{(100)^2} = \frac{99.5}{(100)^2}.
\end{aligned}$$

Note that this is indeed a probability distribution in that

$$P_{X_1}(0) + P_{X_1}(1) + \cdots + P_{X_1}(99) = \frac{100.5}{(100)^2} + \frac{100}{(100)^2} + \cdots + \frac{99.5}{(100)^2} = 1.$$

Similarly, the marginal distribution of X_2 is given by

$$\begin{aligned} P_{X_2}(0) &= \sum_{\text{all } k} P_{X_1X_2}(k, 0) \\ &= P_{X_1X_2}(0,0) + P_{X_1X_2}(1,0) + \cdots + P_{X_1X_2}(99,0) \\ &= \frac{1.5}{(100)^2} + \frac{1}{(100)^2} + \cdots + \frac{1}{(100)^2} = \frac{100.5}{(100)^2}, \end{aligned}$$

$$\begin{aligned} P_{X_2}(1) = P_{X_2}(2) = \cdots = P_{X_2}(98) &= \sum_{\text{all } k} P_{X_1X_2}(k, l),\ l = 1, 2, \ldots, 98 \\ &= \frac{100}{(100)^2}, \end{aligned}$$

$$\begin{aligned} P_{X_2}(99) &= \sum_{\text{all } k} P_{X_1X_2}(k, 99) \\ &= P_{X_1X_2}(0,99) + P_{X_1X_2}(1,99) + \cdots + P_{X_1X_2}(99,99) \\ &= \frac{1}{(100)^2} + \frac{1}{(100)^2} + \cdots + \frac{0.5}{(100)^2} = \frac{99.5}{(100)^2}. \end{aligned}$$

If the bivariate random variable (X_1, X_2) is continuous, then $f_{X_1X_2}(s, t)$ represents the joint density. The density function of X_1 individually, $f_{X_1}(s)$, now called the marginal density function of the continuous random variable X_1, can be obtained from the $f_{X_1X_2}(s, t)$. In particular,

$$F_{X_1}(b_1) = F_{X_1X_2}(b_1, \infty) = \int_{-\infty}^{b_1} \int_{-\infty}^{\infty} f_{X_1X_2}(s, t)\, dt\, ds = \int_{-\infty}^{b_1} f_{X_1}(s)\, ds,$$

so that

$$f_{X_1}(s) = \int_{-\infty}^{\infty} f_{X_1X_2}(s, t)\, dt.$$

Similarly, the marginal density function of the continuous random variable X_2 is given by

$$f_{X_2}(t) = \int_{-\infty}^{\infty} f_{X_1X_2}(s, t)\, ds.$$

As indicated in Section 8.5, experiments are often performed where some results are obtained early in time and further results later in time. For example, in the previously described experiment that measures the demand for a product during the first two months, the demand for the product during the first month is observed at the end of the first month. This information can be utilized in making probability statements about the demand during the second month.

In particular, if the bivariate random variable (X_1,X_2) is discrete, the conditional probability distribution of X_2, given X_1, can be defined as

$$P_{X_2|X_1=k}(l) = P\{X_2 = l \mid X_1 = k\} = \frac{P_{X_1X_2}(k, l)}{P_{X_1}(k)}, \text{ if } P_{X_1}(k) > 0,$$

and the conditional probability distribution of X_1, given X_2, as

$$P_{X_1|X_2=l}(k) = P\{X_1 = k \mid X_2 = l\} = \frac{P_{X_1X_2}(k, l)}{P_{X_2}(l)}, \text{ if } P_{X_2}(l) > 0.$$

Note that for a given $X_2 = l$, $P_{X_1|X_2=l}(k)$ satisfies all the conditions for a probability distribution for a discrete random variable. $P_{X_1|X_2=l}(k)$ is nonnegative, and furthermore,

$$\sum_{\text{all } k} P_{X_1|X_2=l}(k) = \sum_{\text{all } k} \frac{P_{X_1X_2}(k, l)}{P_{X_2}(l)} = \frac{P_{X_2}(l)}{P_{X_2}(l)} = 1.$$

Again, returning to the demand for a product during the first 2 months, if it were known that there was no demand during the first month, then

$$P_{X_2|X_1=0}(l) = P\{X_2 = l \mid X_1 = 0\} = \frac{P_{X_1X_2}(0, l)}{P_{X_1}(0)} = \frac{P_{X_1X_2}(0, l)}{100.5/(100)^2}.$$

Hence

$$P_{X_2|X_1=0}(0) = \frac{P_{X_1X_2}(0,0)}{(100.5)/(100)^2} = \frac{1.5}{100.5},$$

and

$$P_{X_2|X_1=0}(l) = \frac{1}{100.5} \qquad l = 1, 2, \ldots, 99.$$

If the bivariate random variable (X_1,X_2) is continuous with joint density function $f_{X_1X_2}(s, t)$, and the marginal density function of X_1 is given by $f_{X_1}(s)$, then the conditional density function of X_2, given $X_1 = s$, is defined as

$$f_{X_2|X_1=s}(t) = \frac{f_{X_1X_2}(s, t)}{f_{X_1}(s)}, \text{ if } f_{X_1}(s) > 0.$$

Similarly, if the marginal density function of X_2 is given by $f_{X_2}(t)$, then the conditional density function of X_1, given $X_2 = t$, is defined as

$$f_{X_1|X_2=t}(s) = \frac{f_{X_1X_2}(s, t)}{f_{X_2}(t)}, \text{ if } f_{X_2}(t) > 0.$$

Note that, given $X_1 = s$ and $X_2 = t$, the conditional density functions, $f_{X_2|X_1=s}(t)$ and $f_{X_1|X_2=t}(s)$, respectively, satisfy all the conditions for a density function. They are nonnegative, and furthermore,

$$\int_{-\infty}^{\infty} f_{X_2|X_1=s}(t)\,dt = \int_{-\infty}^{\infty} \frac{f_{X_1X_2}(s,t)\,dt}{f_{X_1}(s)}$$

$$= \frac{1}{f_{X_1}(s)} \int_{-\infty}^{\infty} f_{X_1X_2}(s,t)\,dt = \frac{f_{X_1}(s)}{f_{X_1}(s)} = 1,$$

and

$$\int_{-\infty}^{\infty} f_{X_1|X_2=t}(s)\,ds = \int_{-\infty}^{\infty} \frac{f_{X_1X_2}(s,t)\,ds}{f_{X_2}(t)}$$

$$= \frac{1}{f_{X_2}(t)} \int_{-\infty}^{\infty} f_{X_1X_2}(s,t)\,ds = \frac{f_{X_2}(t)}{f_{X_2}(t)} = 1.$$

As an example of the use of these concepts for a continuous bivariate random variable, consider an experiment that measures the time of the first arrivals at a store on each of two successive days. Suppose that the joint density function for the random variable (X_1, X_2), which represents the arrival time on the first and second days, respectively, is given by

$$f_{X_1X_2}(s,t) = \begin{cases} \dfrac{1}{\theta^2}\, e^{-(s+t)/\theta}, & \text{for } s, t \geq 0 \\ 0, & \text{otherwise.} \end{cases}$$

The marginal density function of X_1 is given by

$$f_{X_1}(s) = \begin{cases} \displaystyle\int_0^{\infty} \frac{1}{\theta^2}\, e^{-(s+t)/\theta}\,dt = \frac{1}{\theta}\, e^{-s/\theta}, & \text{for } s \geq 0 \\ 0, & \text{otherwise,} \end{cases}$$

and the marginal density function of X_2 is given by

$$f_{X_2}(t) = \begin{cases} \displaystyle\int_0^{\infty} \frac{1}{\theta^2}\, e^{-(s+t)/\theta}\,ds = \frac{1}{\theta}\, e^{-t/\theta}, & \text{for } t \geq 0 \\ 0, & \text{otherwise.} \end{cases}$$

If it is announced that the arrival time of the first customer on the first day occurred at time s, the conditional density of X_2, given $X_1 = s$, is given by

$$f_{X_2|X_1=s}(t) = \frac{f_{X_1X_2}(s,t)}{f_{X_1}(s)} = \frac{(1/\theta^2)e^{-(s+t)/\theta}}{(1/\theta)e^{-s/\theta}} = \frac{1}{\theta}\, e^{-t/\theta}.$$

It is interesting to note at this point that the conditional density of X_2, given $X_1 = s$, is independent of s and, furthermore, is the same as the marginal density of X_2.

8.12 EXPECTATIONS FOR BIVARIATE DISTRIBUTIONS

Section 8.8 defined the expectation of a function of a univariate random variable. The expectation of a function of a bivariate random variable (X_1,X_2) may be defined in a similar manner. Let $g(X_1,X_2)$ be a function of the bivariate random variable (X_1, X_2). Let

$$P_{X_1X_2}(k, l) = P\{X_1 = k, X_2 = l\}$$

denote the joint probability distribution if (X_1,X_2) is a discrete random variable, and let $f_{X_1X_2}(s, t)$ denote the joint density function if (X_1,X_2) is a continuous random variable. The expectation of $g(X_1,X_2)$ is now defined as

$$E[g(X_1,X_2)] = \begin{cases} \sum_{\text{all } k,\, l} g(k, l)P_{X_1X_2}(k, l), & \text{if } X_1, X_2 \text{ is a discrete random variable} \\ \int_{-\infty}^{\infty}\int_{-\infty}^{\infty} g(s, t)f_{X_1X_2}(s, t)\, ds\, dt, & \text{if } X_1, X_2 \text{ is a continuous random variable.} \end{cases}$$

An alternate definition can be obtained by recognizing that $Z = g(X_1, X_2)$ is itself a univariate random variable and hence has a density function if Z is continuous and a probability distribution if Z is discrete. The expectation of Z for these cases has already been defined in Sec. 8.8. Of particular interest here is the extension of the theorem of the unconscious statistician, which states that if (X_1, X_2) is a continuous random variable and if Z has a density function $h_Z(y)$, then

$$E(Z) = \int_{-\infty}^{\infty} yh_Z(y)\, dy = \int_{-\infty}^{\infty}\int_{-\infty}^{\infty} g(s, t)f_{X_1X_2}(s,t)\, ds\, dt.$$

Thus the expectation of Z can be found by using its definition in terms of the density of the univariate random variable Z or, alternatively, by use of its definition as the expectation of a function of the bivariate random variable (X_1,X_2) with respect to its joint density function. The identical theorem is true for a discrete bivariate random variable, and, of course, both results are easily extended to n variate random variables.

There are several important functions g that should be considered. All the results will be stated for continuous random variables, but equivalent results also hold for discrete random variables.

If $g(X_1,X_2) = X_1$, it is easily seen that

$$E(X_1) = \int_{-\infty}^{\infty}\int_{-\infty}^{\infty} sf_{X_1X_2}(s, t)\, ds\, dt = \int_{-\infty}^{\infty} sf_{X_1}(s)\, ds.$$

Note that this is just the expectation of the univariate random variable X_1 with respect to its marginal density.

In a similar manner, if $g(X_1,X_2) = [X_1 - E(X_1)]^2$, then

$$\begin{aligned} E[X_1 - E(X_1)]^2 &= \int_{-\infty}^{\infty}\int_{-\infty}^{\infty} [s - E(X_1)]^2 f_{X_1X_2}(s, t)\, ds\, dt \\ &= \int_{-\infty}^{\infty} [s - E(X_1)]^2 f_{X_1}(s)\, ds, \end{aligned}$$

which is just the variance of the univariate random variable X_1 with respect to its marginal density.

If $g(X_1,X_2) = [X_1 - E(X_1)][X_2 - E(X_2)]$, then $E[g(X_1,X_2)]$ is called the covariance of the random variable (X_1, X_2); that is,

$$E[X_1 - E(X_1)][X_2 - E(X_2)] = \int_{-\infty}^{\infty} \int_{-\infty}^{\infty} [s - E(X_1)][t - E(X_2)] f_{X_1X_2}(s, t)\, ds\, dt.$$

An easy computational formula is provided by the identity

$$E[X_1 - E(X_1)][X_2 - E(X_2)] = E(X_1X_2) - E(X_1)E(X_2).$$

The correlation coefficient between X_1 and X_2 is defined to be

$$\rho = \frac{E[X_1 - E(X_1)][X_2 - E(X_2)]}{\sqrt{E[X_1 - E(X_1)]^2 E[X_2 - E(X_2)]^2}}.$$

It is easily shown that $-1 \le \rho \le +1$.

The final results pertain to a linear combination of random variables. Let $g(X_1, X_2) = C_1X_1 + C_2X_2$, where C_1 and C_2 are constants. Then

$$\begin{aligned} E[g(X_1, X_2)] &= \int_{-\infty}^{\infty} \int_{-\infty}^{\infty} (C_1 s + C_2 t) f_{X_1X_2}(s, t)\, ds\, dt, \\ &= C_1 \int_{-\infty}^{\infty} s f_{X_1}(s)\, ds + C_2 \int_{-\infty}^{\infty} t f_{X_2}(t)\, dt, \\ &= C_1E(X_1) + C_2E(X_2). \end{aligned}$$

Thus, the expectation of a linear combination of univariate random variables is just the sum of the respective coefficient times the expectations of the random variables. It easily follows that

$$E[C_1X_1 + C_2X_2 + \cdots + C_nX_n] = C_1E(X_1) + C_2E(X_2) + \cdots + C_nE(X_n).$$

If

$$g(X_1, X_2) = [C_1X_1 + C_2X_2 - \{C_1E(X_1) + C_2E(X_2)\}]^2,$$

then

$$\begin{aligned} E[g(X_1, X_2)] &= \text{variance } (C_1X_1 + C_2X_2) \\ &= C_1^2E[X_1 - E(X_1)]^2 + C_2^2E[X_2 - E(X_2)]^2 \\ &\quad + 2C_1C_2E[X_1 - E(X_1)][X_2 - E(X_2)], \\ &= C_1^2 \text{ variance } (X_1) + C_2^2 \text{ variance } (X_2) \\ &\quad + 2C_1C_2 \text{ covariance } (X_1X_2). \end{aligned}$$

For n univariate random variables, the variance of a linear combination $C_1X_1 + C_2X_2 + \cdots + C_nX_n$ is given by

$$\sum_{i=1}^{n} C_i^2 \text{ variance } (X_i) + 2\sum_{j=2}^{n} \sum_{i=1}^{j-1} C_iC_j \text{ covariance } (X_iX_j).$$

8.13 INDEPENDENT RANDOM VARIABLES AND RANDOM SAMPLES

The concept of independent events has already been defined; that is, E_1 and E_2 are independent events if, and only if,

$$P\{E_1 \cap E_2\} = P\{E_1\}P\{E_2\}.$$

From this definition the very important concept of independent random variables can be introduced. For a bivariate random variable (X_1,X_2) and constants b_1 and b_2, denote by E_1 the event containing those ω such that $X_1(\omega) \leq b_1$, $X_2(\omega)$ is anything; that is,

$$E_1 = \{\omega \mid X_1(\omega) \leq b_1,\ X_2(\omega) \leq \infty\}.$$

Similarly, denote by E_2 the event containing those ω such that $X_1(\omega)$ is any thing and $X_2(\omega) \leq b_2$; that is,

$$E_2 = \{\omega \mid X_1(\omega) \leq \infty,\ X_2(\omega) \leq b_2\}.$$

Furthermore, the event $E_1 \cap E_2$ is given by

$$E_1 \cap E_2 = \{\omega \mid X_1(\omega) \leq b_1,\ X_2(\omega) \leq b_2\}.$$

The random variables X_1 and X_2 are said to be independent if events of the form given by E_1 and E_2 are independent events for all b_1 and b_2. Using the definition of independent events, then, the random variables X_1 and X_2 are called independent random variables if

$$P\{X_1 \leq b_1,\ X_2 \leq b_2\} = P\{X_1 \leq b_1\}P\{X_2 \leq b_2\}$$

for all b_1 and b_2. Therefore X_1 and X_2 are independent if

$$\begin{aligned} F_{X_1X_2}(b_1, b_2) &= P\{X_1 \leq b_1,\ X_2 \leq b_2\} = P\{X_1 \leq b_1\}P\{X_2 \leq b_2\} \\ &= F_{X_1}(b_1)F_{X_2}(b_2). \end{aligned}$$

Thus the independence of the random variables X_1 and X_2 implies that the joint CDF factors into the product of the CDF's of the individual random variables. Furthermore, it is easily shown that if (X_1,X_2) is a discrete bivariate random variable, then X_1 and X_2 are independent random variables if, and only if, $P_{X_1X_2}(k, l) = P_{X_1}(k)P_{X_2}(l)$; in other words, $P\{X_1 = k,\ X_2 = l\} = P\{X_1 = k\}P\{X_2 = l\}$, for all k and l. Similarly, if (X_1, X_2) is a continuous bivariate random variable, then X_1 and X_2 are independent random variables if, and only if,

$$f_{X_1X_2}(s, t) = f_{X_1}(s)f_{X_2}(t),$$

for all s and t. Thus, if X_1, X_2 are to be independent random variables, the joint density (or probability) function must factor into the product of the marginal density functions of the random variables. Using this result, it is easily seen that if X_1, X_2 are independent random variables, then the covariance of X_1, X_2 must be zero. Hence the results on the variance of linear combinations of random variables given in Sec. 8.12 can be simplified when the random variables are independent; that is,

$$\text{Variance}\left(\sum_{i=1}^{n} C_i X_i\right) = \sum_{i=1}^{n} C_i^2 \text{ variance } (X_i)$$

when the X_i are independent.

Another interesting property of independent random variables can be deduced from the factorization property. If (X_1, X_2) is a discrete bivariate random variable, then X_1 and X_2 are independent if, and only if,

$$P_{X_1|X_2=l}(k) = P_{X_1}(k), \text{ for all } k \text{ and } l.$$

Similarly, if (X_1, X_2) is a continuous bivariate random variable, then X_1 and X_2 are independent if, and only if,

$$f_{X_1|X_2=t}(s) = f_{X_1}(s), \text{ for all } s \text{ and } t.$$

In other words, if X_1 and X_2 are independent, a knowledge of the outcome of one, say, X_2, gives no information about the probability distribution of the other, say, X_1. It was noted in the example in Sec. 8.11 on the time of first arrivals that the conditional density of the arrival time of the first customer on the second day, given that the first customer on the first day arrived at time s, was equal to the marginal density of the arrival time of the first customer on the second day. Hence X_1 and X_2 were independent random variables. In the example of the demand for a product during two consecutive months it was seen that

$$P_{X_2|X_1=0}(0) = \frac{1.5}{100.5} \neq P_{X_2}(0) = \frac{100.5}{(100)^2}.$$

Hence the demands during each month were dependent (not independent) random variables.

The definition of independent random variables generally does not lend itself to determine whether or not random variables are independent in a probabilistic sense by looking at their outcomes. Instead, by analyzing the physical situation the experimenter usually is able to make a judgment about whether the random variables are independent by ascertaining if the outcome of one will affect the probability distribution of the other.

The definition of independent random variables is easily extended to three or more random variables. For example, if the joint CDF of the n-dimensional random variable $(X_1, X_2, \ldots, X_n)$ is given by $F_{X_1X_2\cdots X_n}(b_1, b_2, \ldots, b_n)$ and $F_{X_1}(b_1), F_{X_2}(b_2), \ldots, F_{X_n}(b_n)$ represents the CDF's of the univariate random variables $X_1, X_2, \ldots, X_n$, respectively, then $X_1, X_2, \ldots, X_n$ are independent random variables if, and only if,

$$F_{X_1X_2\cdots X_n}(b_1, b_2, \ldots, b_n) = F_{X_1}(b_1)F_{X_2}(b_2)\cdots F_{X_n}(b_n), \text{ for all } b_1, b_2, \ldots, b_n.$$

Having defined the concept of independent random variables, we can now introduce the term *random sample*. A random sample simply means a sequence of independent and identically distributed random variables. Thus $X_1, X_2, \ldots, X_n$ constitute a random sample of size n if the X_i are independent and identically distributed random variables. For example, in Sec. 8.6 it was pointed out that if $X_1, X_2, \ldots, X_n$ are independent Bernoulli random variables, each with parameter p (that is, if the X's are a random sample), then the random variable

$$X = \sum_{i=1}^{n} X_i$$

has a binomial distribution with parameters n and p.

8.14 LAW OF LARGE NUMBERS

Section 8.8 pointed out that the mean of a random sample tends to converge to the expectation of the random variables as the sample size increases. In particular, suppose the random variable X, the demand for a product, may take on one of the possible values $k = 0, 1, 2, \ldots, 98, 99$, each with $P_X(k) = 1/100$ for all k. Then $E(X)$ is easily seen to be 49.5. If a random sample of size n is taken, i.e., the demands are observed for n days, with each day's demand being independent and identically distributed random variables, it was noted that the random variable $\overline{X}$ should take on a value close to 49.5 if n is large. This result can be stated precisely as the *law of large numbers.*

Law of Large Numbers

Let the random variables $X_1, X_2, \ldots, X_n$ be independent, identically distributed random variables (a random sample of size n), each having mean μ. Consider the random variable that is the sample mean $\overline{X}$:

$$\overline{X} = \frac{X_1 + X_2 + \cdots + X_n}{n}.$$

Then for any constant $\varepsilon > 0$,

$$\lim_{n\to\infty} P\{|\overline{X} - \mu| > \varepsilon\} = 0.$$

The interpretation of the law of large numbers is that the sample size increases, the probability is "close" to 1 that $\overline{X}$ is "close" to μ. Assuming that the variance of each X_i is $\sigma^2 < \infty$, this result is easily proved by using Chebyshev's inequality (stated in Sec. 8.9). Since each X_i has mean μ and variance σ^2, $\overline{X}$ also has mean μ, but its variance is σ^2/n. Hence, applying Chebyshev's inequality to the random variable $\overline{X}$, it is evident that

$$P\left\{\mu - \frac{C\sigma}{\sqrt{n}} \le \overline{X} \le \mu + \frac{C\sigma}{\sqrt{n}}\right\} > 1 - \frac{1}{C^2}.$$

This is equivalent to

$$P\left\{|\bar{X} - \mu| > \frac{C\sigma}{\sqrt{n}}\right\} < \frac{1}{C^2}.$$

Let $C\sigma/\sqrt{n} = \varepsilon$, so that $C = \varepsilon\sqrt{n}/\sigma$. Thus

$$P\{|\bar{X} - \mu| > \varepsilon\} < \frac{\sigma^2}{\varepsilon^2 n},$$

so that

$$\lim_{n\to\infty} P\{|\bar{X} - \mu| > \varepsilon\} = 0,$$

as was to be proved.

8.15 CENTRAL LIMIT THEOREM

Section 8.7 pointed out that sums of independent normally distributed random variables are themselves normally distributed, and that even if the random variables are *not* normally distributed, the distribution of their sum still tends toward normality. This latter statement can be made precise by means of the *central limit theorem.*

Central Limit Theorem

Let the random variables $X_1, X_2, \ldots, X_n$ be independent with means $\mu_1, \mu_2, \ldots, \mu_n$, respectively, and variance $\sigma_1^2, \sigma_2^2, \ldots, \sigma_n^2$, respectively. Consider the random variable Z_n,

$$Z_n = \frac{\sum_{i=1}^n X_i - \sum_{i=1}^n \mu_i}{\sqrt{\sum_{i=1}^n \sigma_i^2}}.$$

Then, under certain regularity conditions, Z_n is approximately normally distributed with zero mean and unit variance in the sense that

$$\lim_{n\to\infty} P\{Z_n \le b\} = \int_b^\infty \frac{1}{\sqrt{2\pi}} e^{-y^2/2}\, dy.$$

Note that if the X_i form a random sample, with each X_i having mean μ and variance σ^2, then $Z_n = (\bar{X} - \mu)\sqrt{n}/\sigma$.† Hence sample means from random samples tend toward normality in the sense just described by the central limit theorem even if the X_i are not normally distributed.

It is difficult to give sample sizes beyond which the central limit theorem applies, and approximate normality can be assumed for sample means. This, of course, does depend upon the form of the underlying distribution. From a practical point of view, moderate sample sizes, like 10, are often sufficient.

† Under these conditions the central limit theorem actually holds without assuming any other regularity conditions.

8.16 FUNCTIONS OF RANDOM VARIABLES

Section 8.8 introduced the theorem of the unconscious statistician and pointed out that if a function $Z = g(X)$ of a continuous random variable is considered, its expectation can be taken with respect to the density function $f_X(y)$ of X or the density function $h_Z(y)$ of Z. In discussing this choice, it was implied that the density function of Z was known. In general, then, given the cumulative distribution function $F_X(b)$ of a random variable X, there may be interest in obtaining the cumulative distribution function $H_Z(b)$ of a random variable $Z = g(X)$. Of course, it is always possible to go back to the sample space and determine $H_Z(b)$ directly from probabilities associated with the sample space. However, alternate methods for doing this are desirable.

If X is a discrete random variable, the values k that the random variable X takes on and the associated $P_X(k)$ are known. If $Z = g(X)$ is also discrete, denote by m the values that Z takes on. The probabilities $Q_Z(m) = P\{Z = m\}$ for all m are required. The general procedure is to enumerate for each m all the values of k such that

$$g(k) = m.$$

$Q_Z(m)$ is then determined as

$$Q_Z(m) = \sum_{\substack{\text{all } k \\ \text{such that} \\ g(k)=m}} P_X(k).$$

To illustrate, consider again the example involving the demand for a product in a single month. Let this random variable be noted by X, and let $k = 0, 1, \ldots, 99$ with $P_X(k) = 1/100$, for all k. Consider a new random variable Z that takes on the value of 0 if there is no demand and 1 if there is *any* demand. This random variable may be useful for determining whether any is needed for shipping. The probabilities

$$Q_Z(0) \text{ and } Q_Z(1)$$

are required. If $m = 0$, the only value of k such that $g(k) = 0$ is $k = 0$. Hence

$$Q_Z(0) = \sum_{\substack{\text{all } k \\ \text{such that} \\ g(k)=0}} P_X(k) = P_X(0) = \frac{1}{100}.$$

If $m = 1$, the values of k such that $g(k) = 1$ are $k = 1, 2, 3, \ldots, 98, 99$. Hence

$$Q_Z(1) = \sum_{\substack{\text{all } k \\ \text{such that} \\ g(k)=1}} P_X(k)$$

$$= P_X(1) + P_X(2) + P_X(3) + \cdots + P_X(98) + P_X(99) = \frac{99}{100}.$$

If X is a continuous random variable, then both the CDF $F_X(b)$ and the density function $f_X(y)$ may be assumed to be known. If $Z = g(X)$ is also a continuous random variable, either the CDF $H_Z(b)$ or the density function $h_Z(y)$ is sought. To find $H_Z(b)$, note that

$$H_Z(b) = P\{Z \leq b\} = P\{g(X) \leq b\} = P\{A\},$$

where A consists of all points such that $g(X) \leq b$. Thus $P\{A\}$ can be determined from the density function or CDF of the random variable X. For example, suppose that the CDF for the time of the first arrival in a store is given by

$$F_X(b) = \begin{cases} 1 - e^{-b/\theta}, & \text{for } b \geq 0 \\ 0, & \text{for } b < 0, \end{cases}$$

where $\theta > 0$. Suppose further that the random variable $Z = g(X) = X + 1$, which represents an hour after the first customer arrives, is of interest, and the CDF of Z, $H_Z(b)$, is desired. To find this CDF note that

$$H_Z(b) = P\{Z \leq b\} = P\{X + 1 \leq b\} = P\{X \leq b - 1\}$$
$$= \begin{cases} 1 - e^{-(b-1)/\theta}, & \text{for } b \geq 1 \\ 0, & \text{for } b < 1. \end{cases}$$

Furthermore, the density can be obtained by differentiating the CDF; that is,

$$h_Z(y) = \begin{cases} \dfrac{1}{\theta} e^{-(y-1)/\theta}, & \text{for } y \geq 1 \\ 0, & \text{for } y < 1. \end{cases}$$

Another technique can be used to find the density function directly if $g(X)$ is monotone and differentiable; it can be shown that

$$h_Z(y) = f_X(s) \left| \frac{ds}{dy} \right|,$$

where s is expressed in terms of y. In the example, $Z = g(X) = X + 1$, so that y, the value the random variable Z takes on, can be expressed in terms of s, the value the random variable X takes on; that is, $y = g(s) = s + 1$. Thus

$$s = y - 1, f_X(s) = \frac{1}{\theta} e^{-s/\theta} = \frac{1}{\theta} e^{-(y-1)/\theta}, \text{ and } \frac{ds}{dy} = 1.$$

Hence

$$h_Z(y) = \frac{1}{\theta} e^{-(y-1)/\theta} |1| = \frac{1}{\theta} e^{-(y-1)/\theta},$$

which is the result previously obtained.

All the discussion in this section concerned functions of a single random variable. If (X_1, X_2) is a bivariate random variable, there may be interest in the probability distribution of such functions as $X_1 + X_2$, $X_1 X_2$, X_1/X_2, and so on. If (X_1, X_2) is discrete, the technique for single random variables is easily extended. A detailed discussion of the techniques available for continuous bivariate random variables is beyond the scope of this text; however, a few notions related to independent random variables will be discussed.

If (X_1, X_2) is a continuous bivariate random variable, and X_1 and X_2 are independent, then its joint density is given by

$$f_{X_1X_2}(s, t) = f_{X_1}(s)f_{X_2}(t).$$

Consider the function

$$Z = g(X_1, X_2) = X_1 + X_2.$$

The CDF for Z can be expressed as $H_Z(b) = P\{Z \leq b\} = P\{X_1 + X_2 \leq b\}$. This can be evaluated by integrating the bivariate density over the region such that $s + t \leq b$; that is

$$H_Z(b) = \iint_{s+t \leq b} f_{X_1}(s)f_{X_2}(t)\, ds\, dt$$

$$= \int_{-\infty}^{\infty} \int_{-\infty}^{b-t} f_{X_1}(s)f_{X_2}(t)\, ds\, dt.$$

Differentiating with respect to b yields the density function

$$h_Z(y) = \int_{-\infty}^{\infty} f_{X_2}(t)f_{X_1}(y - t)\, dt.$$

This can be written alternately as

$$h_Z(y) = \int_{-\infty}^{\infty} f_{X_1}(s)f_{X_2}(y - s)\, ds.$$

Note that the integrand may be zero over part of the range of the variable, as shown in the following example.

Suppose that the times of the first arrival on two successive days, X_1 and X_2, are independent, identically distributed random variables having density

$$f_{X_1}(s) = \begin{cases} \frac{1}{\theta} e^{-s/\theta}, & \text{for } s \geq 0 \\ 0, & \text{otherwise.} \end{cases}$$

$$f_{X_2}(t) = \begin{cases} \frac{1}{\theta} e^{-t/\theta}, & \text{for } t \geq 0 \\ 0, & \text{otherwise.} \end{cases}$$

To find the density of $Z = X_1 + X_2$, note that

$$f_{X_1}(s) = \begin{cases} \frac{1}{\theta} e^{-s/\theta}, & \text{for } s \geq 0 \\ 0, & \text{for } s < 0, \end{cases}$$

and

$$f_{X_2}(y-s) = \begin{cases} \dfrac{1}{\theta} e^{-(y-s)/\theta}, & \text{if } y - s \geq 0 \text{ so that } s \leq y \\ 0, & \text{if } y - s < 0 \text{ so that } s > y. \end{cases}$$

Hence

$$f_{X_1}(s) f_{X_2}(y-s) = \begin{cases} \dfrac{1}{\theta} e^{-s/\theta} \dfrac{1}{\theta} e^{-(y-s)/\theta} = \dfrac{1}{\theta^2} e^{-y/\theta}, & \text{if } 0 \leq s \leq y \\ 0, & \text{otherwise.} \end{cases}$$

Hence

$$h_Z(y) = \int_{-\infty}^{\infty} f_{X_1}(s) f_{X_2}(y-s)\, ds = \int_0^y \frac{1}{\theta^2} e^{-y/\theta}\, ds$$
$$= \frac{y}{\theta^2} e^{-y/\theta}.$$

Note that this is just a gamma distribution, with parameters $\alpha = 2$ and $\beta = \theta$. Hence, as indicated in Sec. 8.7, the sum of two independent, exponentially distributed random variables has a gamma distribution. This example illustrates how to find the density function for finite sums of independent random variables. Combining this result with those for univariate random variables leads to easily finding the density function of linear combinations of independent random variables.

A final result on the distribution of functions of random variables concerns functions of normally distributed random variables. The chi-square and the t and F distributions, introduced in Sec. 8.7, can be generated from functions of normally distributed random variables. These distributions are particularly useful in the study of statistics. In particular, let $X_1, X_2, \ldots, X_\nu$ be independent, normally distributed random variables having zero mean and unit variance. The random variable

$$\chi^2 = X_1^2 + X_2^2 + \cdots + X_\nu^2$$

can be shown to have a chi-square distribution with ν degrees of freedom. A random variable having a t distribution may be generated as follows. Let X be a normally distributed random variable having zero mean and unit variance and χ^2 be a chi-square random variable (independent of X) with ν degrees of freedom. The random variable

$$t = \frac{\sqrt{\nu} X}{\sqrt{\chi^2}}$$

can be shown to have a t distribution with ν degrees of freedom. Finally, a random variable having an F distribution can be generated from a function of two independent chi-square random variables. Let χ_1^2 and χ_2^2 be independent chi-square random variables, with ν_1 and ν_2 degrees of freedom, respectively. The random variable

$$F = \frac{\chi_1^2/\nu_1}{\chi_2^2/\nu_2}$$

can be shown to have an F distribution with ν_1 and ν_2 degrees of freedom.

8.17 STOCHASTIC PROCESS

A stochastic process is defined to be simply an indexed collection of random variables $\{X_t\}$, where the index t runs through a given set T. Often T is taken to be the set of nonnegative integers, and X_t represents a measurable characteristic of interest at time t. For example, the stochastic process, $X_1, X_2, X_3, \ldots$, can represent the collection of weekly (or monthly) inventory levels of a given product, or it can represent the collection of weekly (or monthly) demands for this product.

There are many stochastic processes that are of interest. A consideration of the behavior of a system operating for some period of time often leads to the analysis of a stochastic process with the following structure. At particular points of time t labeled $0, 1, \ldots$, the system is found in exactly one of a finite number of mutually exclusive and exhaustive categories or *states* labeled $0, 1, \ldots, M$. The points in time may be equally spaced, or their spacing may depend upon the overall behavior of the physical system in which the stochastic process is *imbedded*, e.g., the time between occurrences of some phenomenon of interest. Although the states may constitute a qualitative as well as quantitative characterization of the system, no loss of generality is entailed by the numerical labels $0, 1, \ldots, M$, which are used henceforth to denote the possible states of the system. Thus the mathematical representation of the physical system is that of a stochastic process $\{X_t\}$, where the random variables are observed at $t = 0, 1, 2, \ldots$, and where each random variable may take on any one of the $(M + 1)$ integers $0, 1, \ldots, M$. These integers are a characterization of the $(M + 1)$ states of the process.

As an example, consider the following inventory problem. A camera store stocks a particular model camera that can be ordered weekly. Let $D_1, D_2, \ldots$, represent the demand for this camera during the first week, second week, ..., respectively. It is assumed that the D_i are independent and identically distributed random variables having a known probability distribution. Let X_0 represent the number of cameras on hand at the outset, X_1 the number of cameras on hand at the end of week one, X_2 the number of cameras on hand at the end of week two, and so on. Assume that $X_0 = 3$. On Saturday night the store places an order that is delivered in time for the opening of the store on

Monday. The store uses the following (s, S) ordering policy:[1] If the number of cameras on hand at the end of the week is less than $s = 1$ (no cameras in stock), the store orders (up to) $S = 3$. Otherwise, the store does not order (if there are any cameras in stock, no order is placed). It is assumed that sales are lost when demand exceeds the inventory on hand. Thus $\{X_t\}$ for $t = 0, 1, \ldots$, is a stochastic process of the form described above. The possible states of the process are the integers 0, 1, 2, 3 representing the possible number of cameras on hand at the end of the week. In fact, the random variables X_t are clearly dependent and may be evaluated iteratively by the expression

$$X_{t+1} = \begin{cases} \max\{(3 - D_{t+1}), 0\}, & \text{if } X_t < 1 \\ \max\{(X_t - D_{t+1}), 0\}, & \text{if } X_t \geq 1, \end{cases}$$

for $t = 0, 1, 2, \ldots$. This example is used for illustrative purposes throughout many of the following sections. Section 8.18 further defines the type of stochastic process considered in this chapter.

8.18 MARKOV CHAINS

Assumptions regarding the joint distribution of $X_0, X_1, \ldots$, are necessary to obtain analytical results. One assumption which leads to analytical tractability is that the stochastic process is a Markov chain (defined below), which has the following key property: A stochastic process $\{X_t\}$ is said to have the *Markovian property* if $P\{X_{t+1} = j \mid X_0 = k_0, X_1 = k_1, \ldots, X_{t-1} = k_{t-1}, X_t = i\} = P\{X_{t+1} = j \mid X_t = i\}$, for $t = 0, 1, \ldots$ and every sequence $i, j, k_0, k_1, \ldots, k_{t-1}$.

This Markovian property can be shown to be equivalent to stating that the conditional probability of any future "event," given any past "event" and the present state $X_t = i$, is *independent* of the past event and depends upon only the present state of the process. The conditional probabilities $P\{X_{t+1} = j \mid X_t = i\}$ are called transition probabilities. If, for each i and j,

$$P\{X_{t+1} = j \mid X_t = i\} = P\{X_1 = j \mid X_0 = i\}, \text{ for all } t = 0, 1, \ldots,$$

then the (one step) transition probabilities are said to be *stationary* and are usually denoted by p_{ij}. Thus, having stationary transition probabilities implies that the transition probabilities do not change in time. The existence of stationary (one step) transition probabilities also implies that, for each i, j, and n $(n = 0, 1, 2, \ldots)$,

$$P\{X_{t+n} = j \mid X_t = i\} = P\{X_n = j \mid X_0 = i\},$$

for all $t = 0, 1, \ldots$. These conditional probabilities are usually denoted by $p_{ij}^{(n)}$† and are called n-step transition probabilities. Thus $p_{ij}^{(n)}$ is just the

[1] In general, an (s, S) policy is a periodic review policy that calls for ordering up to S units whenever the inventory level dips below s $(S \geq s)$. If the inventory level is s or greater then no order is placed. These policies are discussed in detail in Chap. 11.

† For $n = 0$, $p_{ij}^{(0)}$ is just $P\{X_0 = j \mid X_0 = i\}$ and hence is 1 when $i = j$ and 0 when $i \neq j$. For $n = 1$, $p_{ij}^{(1)}$ is just the (one step) transition probability and is denoted by p_{ij}.

conditional probability that the random variable X, starting in state i, will be in state j after exactly n steps (time units).

Since the $p_{ij}^{(n)}$ are conditional probabilities, they must satisfy the properties

$$p_{ij}^{(n)} \geq 0, \text{ for all } i \text{ and } j, \text{ and } n = 0, 1, 2, \ldots$$

$$\sum_{j=0}^{M} p_{ij}^{(n)} = 1, \text{ for all } i \text{ and } n = 0, 1, 2, \ldots.$$

A convenient notation for representing the transition probabilities is the matrix form

$$\mathbf{P}^{(n)} = \begin{array}{c|cccc} \text{State} & 0 & 1 & & M \\ \hline 0 & p_{00}^{(n)} & \cdots & & p_{0M}^{(n)} \\ 1 & \vdots & & & \vdots \\ \vdots & \vdots & & & \vdots \\ M & p_{M0}^{(n)} & \cdots & & p_{MM}^{(n)} \end{array}, \text{ for } n = 0, 1, 2, \ldots.$$

or equivalently

$$\mathbf{P}^{(n)} = \begin{bmatrix} p_{00}^{(n)} & \cdots & p_{0M}^{(n)} \\ \vdots & & \\ p_{M0}^{(n)} & & p_{MM}^{(n)} \end{bmatrix}.$$

It is now possible to define a Markov chain. A stochastic process $\{X_t\}$ $(t = 0, 1, \ldots)$ is said to be a *finite-state Markov chain*[1] if it has the following:

1. A finite number of states,
2. The Markovian property,
3. Stationary transition probabilities,
4. A set of initial probabilities $P\{X_0 = i\}$ for all i.

Returning to the inventory example developed in the preceding section, it is easily seen that $\{X_t\}$ where X_t is the number of cameras in stock at the end of the tth week (before an order is received), is a Markov chain. Now consider how to obtain the (one step) transition probabilities, i.e., the elements of the (one step) *transition matrix*

$$\mathbf{P} = \begin{bmatrix} p_{00} & p_{01} & p_{02} & p_{03} \\ p_{10} & p_{11} & p_{12} & p_{13} \\ p_{20} & p_{21} & p_{22} & p_{23} \\ p_{30} & p_{31} & p_{32} & p_{33} \end{bmatrix},$$

assuming that each D_t has a Poisson distribution with parameter $\lambda = 1$.

To obtain p_{00} it is necessary to evaluate $P\{X_t = 0 \mid X_{t-1} = 0\}$. If $X_{t-1} = 0$, then $X_t = \max\{(3 - D_t), 0\}$. Therefore, if $X_t = 0$, then the demand during the

[1] The definitions of Markovian property and Markov chain are more restrictive than the usages of these terms in the literature because the discussion is confined to a discrete time parameter and finite-state space.

week has to be 3 or more. Hence $p_{00} = P\{D_t \geq 3\}$. This is just the probability that a Poisson random variable with parameter $\lambda = 1$ takes on a value of 3 or more, which is obtained from Table A5.4 of Appendix 5, so that $p_{00} = 0.08$. $p_{10} = P\{X_t = 0 | X_{t-1} = 1\}$ can be obtained in a similar way. If $X_{t-1} = 1$, then $X_t = \max\{(1 - D_t), 0\}$. To have $X_t = 0$, the demand during the week has to be 1 or more. Hence $p_{10} = P\{D_t \geq 1\} = 0.632$ (from Table A5.4 of Appendix 5). To find $p_{21} = P\{X_t = 1 | X_{t-1} = 2\}$, note that $X_t = \max\{(2 - D_t), 0\}$ if $X_{t-1} = 2$. Therefore, if $X_t = 1$, then the demand during the week has to be exactly 1. Hence $p_{21} = P\{D_t = 1\} = 0.368$ (from Table A5.4 of Appendix 5). The remaining entries are obtained in a similar manner, which yield the following (one step) transition matrix:

$$\mathbf{P} = \begin{bmatrix} 0.080 & 0.184 & 0.368 & 0.368 \\ 0.632 & 0.368 & 0 & 0 \\ 0.264 & 0.368 & 0.368 & 0 \\ 0.080 & 0.184 & 0.368 & 0.368 \end{bmatrix}.$$

8.19 CHAPMAN-KOLMOGOROV EQUATIONS

Section 8.18 introduced the n-step transition probability $p_{ij}^{(n)}$. This transition probability can be useful when the process is in state i and the probability that the process will be in state j after n periods is desired. The *Chapman-Kolmogorov equations* provide a method for computing these n-step transition probabilities:

$$p_{ij}^{(n)} = \sum_{k=0}^{M} p_{ik}^{(v)} p_{kj}^{(n-v)}, \text{ for all } i, j, n, \text{ and } 0 \leq v \leq n.$$

These equations merely point out that in going from state i to state j in n steps the process will be in some state k after exactly v (less than n) steps. Thus $p_{ik}^{(v)}\, p_{kj}^{(n-v)}$ is just the conditional probability that, starting from state i, the process goes to state k after v steps and then to state j in $n - v$ steps. Therefore, summing these conditional probabilities over all possible k must yield $p_{ij}^{(n)}$. The special cases of $v = 1$ and $v = n - 1$ lead to the expressions

$$p_{ij}^{(n)} = \sum_{k=0}^{M} p_{ik}\, p_{kj}^{(n-1)}$$

and

$$p_{ij}^{(n)} = \sum_{k=0}^{M} p_{ik}^{(n-1)} p_{kj},$$

for all i, j, n. It then becomes evident that the n-step transition probabilities can be obtained from the one-step transition probabilities recursively. This recursive relationship is best explained in matrix notation (see Appendix 3). For $n = 2$, these expressions become

$$p_{ij}^{(2)} = \sum_{k=0}^{M} p_{ik}\, p_{kj}, \text{ for all } i, j.$$

Note that the $p_{ij}^{(2)}$ are the elements of the matrix $\mathbf{P}^{(2)}$. However, it must also be noted that these elements

$$\sum_{k=0}^{M} p_{ik} p_{kj}$$

are obtained by multiplying the matrix of one-step transition probabilities by itself; that is,

$$\mathbf{P}^{(2)} = \mathbf{P} \cdot \mathbf{P} = \mathbf{P}^2.$$

More generally, it follows that the matrix of n-step transition probabilities can be obtained from the expression

$$\mathbf{P}^{(n)} = \mathbf{P} \cdot \mathbf{P} \cdots \mathbf{P} = \mathbf{P}^n = \mathbf{P}\mathbf{P}^{n-1} = \mathbf{P}^{n-1}\mathbf{P}.$$

Thus the n-step transition probability matrix can be obtained by computing the nth power of the one-step transition matrix. For values of n that are not too large, the n-step transition matrix can be calculated in the manner described above. However, when n is large, such computations are often tedious, and furthermore, round-off errors may cause inaccuracies.

Returning to the inventory example, the two-step transition matrix is given by

$$\mathbf{P}^{(2)} = \mathbf{P}^2 = \begin{bmatrix} 0.080 & 0.184 & 0.368 & 0.368 \\ 0.632 & 0.368 & 0 & 0 \\ 0.264 & 0.368 & 0.368 & 0 \\ 0.080 & 0.184 & 0.368 & 0.368 \end{bmatrix} \begin{bmatrix} 0.080 & 0.184 & 0.368 & 0.368 \\ 0.632 & 0.368 & 0 & 0 \\ 0.264 & 0.368 & 0.368 & 0 \\ 0.080 & 0.184 & 0.368 & 0.368 \end{bmatrix}$$

$$= \begin{bmatrix} 0.249 & 0.286 & 0.300 & 0.165 \\ 0.283 & 0.252 & 0.233 & 0.233 \\ 0.351 & 0.319 & 0.233 & 0.097 \\ 0.249 & 0.286 & 0.300 & 0.165 \end{bmatrix}.^{\dagger}$$

Thus, given that there is one camera left in stock at the end of a week, the probability is 0.283 that there will be no cameras in stock 2 weeks later; that is, $p_{10}^{(2)} = 0.283$. Similarly, given that there are two cameras left in stock at the end of a week, the probability is 0.097 that there will be three cameras in stock 2 weeks later; that is, $p_{23}^{(2)} = 0.097$.

The four-step transition matrix can also be obtained as follows:

$$\mathbf{P}^{(4)} = \mathbf{P}^4 = \mathbf{P}^{(2)} \cdot \mathbf{P}^{(2)}$$

$$= \begin{bmatrix} 0.249 & 0.286 & 0.300 & 0.165 \\ 0.283 & 0.252 & 0.233 & 0.233 \\ 0.351 & 0.319 & 0.233 & 0.097 \\ 0.249 & 0.286 & 0.300 & 0.165 \end{bmatrix} \begin{bmatrix} 0.249 & 0.286 & 0.300 & 0.165 \\ 0.283 & 0.252 & 0.233 & 0.233 \\ 0.351 & 0.319 & 0.233 & 0.097 \\ 0.249 & 0.286 & 0.300 & 0.165 \end{bmatrix}$$

$$= \begin{bmatrix} 0.289 & 0.286 & 0.261 & 0.164 \\ 0.282 & 0.285 & 0.268 & 0.166 \\ 0.284 & 0.283 & 0.263 & 0.171 \\ 0.289 & 0.286 & 0.261 & 0.164 \end{bmatrix}$$

† Note that round-off errors already appear in the row corresponding to state 1.

Thus, given that there is one camera left in stock at the end of a week, the probability is 0.282 that there will be no cameras in stock 4 weeks later; that is, $p_{10}^{(4)} = 0.282$. Similarly, given that there are two cameras left in stock at the end of a week, the probability is 0.171 that there will be three cameras in stock 4 weeks later; that is, $p_{23}^{(4)} = 0.171$.

It was pointed out that the one- or n-step transition probabilities are conditional probabilities, for example, $P\{X_n = j \mid X_0 = i\} = p_{ij}^{(n)}$. If the unconditional probability $P\{X_n = j\}$ is desired, it is necessary to have specified the probability distribution of the initial state. Denote this probability distribution by $Q_{X_0}(i)$, where

$$Q_{X_0}(i) = P\{X_0 = i\}, \text{ for } i = 0, 1, \ldots, M.$$

It then follows that

$$P\{X_n = j\} = Q_{X_0}(0)p_{0j}^{(n)} + Q_{X_0}(1)p_{1j}^{(n)} + \cdots + Q_{X_0}(M)p_{Mj}^{(n)}.$$

In the inventory example it was assumed that initially there were 3 units in stock; that is, $X_0 = 3$. Thus

$$Q_{X_0}(0) = Q_{X_0}(1) = Q_{X_0}(2) = 0, \text{ and } Q_{X_0}(3) = 1.$$

Hence the (unconditional) probability that there will be three cameras in stock 2 weeks after the inventory system began is 0.165; that is, $P\{X_2 = 3\} = (1)p_{33}^{(2)}$. If, instead, it were given that $Q_{X_0}(i) = 1/4$, for $i = 0, 1, 2, 3$, then

$$P\{X_2 = 3\} = \left(\frac{1}{4}\right)0.165 + \left(\frac{1}{4}\right)0.233 + \frac{1}{4}(0.097) + \frac{1}{4}(0.165) = 0.165.$$

The fact that the same answer is obtained using these two initial probability distributions is purely coincidental.

8.20 FIRST PASSAGE TIMES

Section 8.19 dealt with finding n-step transition probabilities [i.e., given that the process is in state i, determining the (conditional) probability that the process will be in state j after n periods]. It is often desirable to make probability statements about the number of transitions made by the process in going from state i to state j *for the first time*. This length of time is called the *first passage time* in going from state i to state j. When $j = i$, this first passage time is just the number of transitions until the process returns to the initial state i. In this case, the first passage time is called the *recurrence time* for state i.

To illustrate these definitions, reconsider the inventory example developed in the preceding sections. Recall that the initial inventory (X_0) contains three cameras. Suppose that it turns out that there are two cameras at the end of the first week (X_1 takes on the value 2), one camera at the end of the second week (X_2 takes on the value 1), no cameras in stock at the end of the third week (X_3 takes on the value 0), three cameras at the end of the fourth week (X_4 takes on the value 3), and one camera at the end of the fifth week (X_5 takes on the value 1). In this case, the first passage time in going from state 3 to state 1 is 2 weeks, the first passage time in going from state 3 to state 0 is 3 weeks, and the recurrence time of state 3 is 4 weeks.

In general, the first passage times are random variables and hence have probability distributions associated with them. These probability distributions depend upon the transition probabilities of the process. In particular, let $f_{ij}^{(n)}$ denote the probability that the first passage time from state i to j is equal to n. It can be shown that these probabilities satisfy the following recursive relationships:

$$f_{ij}^{(1)} = p_{ij}^{(1)} = p_{ij},$$
$$f_{ij}^{(2)} = p_{ij}^{(2)} - f_{ij}^{(1)} p_{jj},$$
$$\vdots$$
$$f_{ij}^{(n)} = p_{ij}^{(n)} - f_{ij}^{(1)} p_{jj}^{(n-1)} - f_{ij}^{(2)} p_{jj}^{(n-2)} \cdots - f_{ij}^{(n-1)} p_{jj}.$$

Thus the probability of a first passage time from state i to state j in n steps can be computed recursively from the one-step transition probabilities. In the inventory example, the probability distribution of the first passage time in going from state 3 to state 0 is obtained as follows:

$$f_{30}^{(1)} = 0.080$$
$$f_{30}^{(2)} = (0.249) - (0.080)(0.080) = 0.243$$
$$\vdots$$

For fixed i and j, the $f_{ij}^{(n)}$ are nonnegative numbers such that

$$\sum_{n=1}^{\infty} f_{ij}^{(n)} \leq 1.$$

Unfortunately, this sum may be strictly less than 1, which implies that a process initially in state i may never reach state j. When the sum does equal 1, $f_{ij}^{(n)}$ (for $n = 1,2, \ldots$) can be considered as a probability distribution for the random variable, the first passage time.

If $i = j$ and

$$\sum_{n=1}^{\infty} f_{ii}^{(n)} = 1,$$

then state i is called a *recurrent state* because this implies that once the process is in state i, it will return to state i. A special case of a recurrent state is an *absorbing state*. A state i is said to be an *absorbing state* if the (one step) transition probability p_{ii} equals 1. Thus, if a state is an absorbing state, the process will never leave it once it enters.

If

$$\sum_{n=1}^{\infty} f_{ii}^{(n)} < 1,$$

then state i is called a *transient state* because this implies that once the process is in state i, there is a strictly positive probability that it will never return to state i.

It is not generally possible to calculate the probabilities of first passage time for all n so that it is not always evident whether a state should be classified as recurrent or transient. For example, although all states in the inventory example are recurrent (as shown in Sec. 8.21), it is not simple to prove that

$$\sum_{n=1}^{\infty} f_{ii}^{(n)} = 1.$$

As another example, suppose that a Markov process has the following transition matrix:

$$\mathbf{P} = \begin{array}{c} \\ \text{State} \end{array} \begin{array}{c} \\ 0 \\ 1 \\ 2 \\ 3 \\ 4 \end{array} \overset{\text{State}}{\begin{array}{c} \begin{array}{ccccc} 0 & 1 & 2 & 3 & 4 \end{array} \\ \begin{bmatrix} \frac{1}{4} & \frac{3}{4} & 0 & 0 & 0 \\ \frac{1}{2} & \frac{1}{2} & 0 & 0 & 0 \\ 0 & 0 & 1 & 0 & 0 \\ 0 & 0 & \frac{1}{3} & \frac{2}{3} & 0 \\ 1 & 0 & 0 & 0 & 0 \end{bmatrix} \end{array}}$$

It is evident that state 2 is an absorbing state (and hence a recurrent state) because once the process enters state 2 (third row of the matrix), it will never leave. States 3 and 4 are transient states because once the process is in state 3, there is a positive probability that it will never return. The probability is ⅓ that the process will go from state 3 to state 2 on the first step. Once the process is in state 2, it remains in state 2. Once a process leaves state 4, it can never return. States 0 and 1 are recurrent states. As indicated earlier, to show that states 0 and 1 are recurrent it is sufficient to show that

$$\sum_{n=1}^{\infty} f_{00}^{(n)} = 1 \text{ and } \sum_{n=1}^{\infty} f_{11}^{(n)} = 1.$$

This is generally difficult, and an alternative test is desired. A necessary and sufficient condition that state i be recurrent is that

$$\sum_{n=1}^{\infty} p_{ii}^{(n)}$$

should diverge. Unfortunately, this criterion is also difficult to apply, so that another criterion is given in Sec. 8.21. However, observe that the n-step transition matrix always has the appearance

$$\mathbf{P}^{(n)} = \begin{bmatrix} * & * & 0 & 0 & 0 \\ * & * & 0 & 0 & 0 \\ 0 & 0 & 1 & 0 & 0 \\ 0 & 0 & * & * & 0 \\ * & * & 0 & 0 & 0 \end{bmatrix},$$

where the symbol * represents positive numbers. Hence it is intuitively evident that once the process is in state 0 it will return to state 0 (possibly passing through state 1) after some number of steps. A similar argument holds for state 1.

Whereas calculating $f_{ij}^{(n)}$ for all n may be difficult, it is relatively simple to obtain the expected first passage time from state i to state j. Denote this expectation by μ_{ij}, which is defined by the expressions

$$\mu_{ij} = \begin{cases} \infty, & \text{if } \sum_{n=1}^{\infty} f_{ij}^{(n)} < 1 \\ \sum_{n=1}^{\infty} n f_{ij}^{(n)}, & \text{if } \sum_{n=1}^{\infty} f_{ij}^{(n)} = 1. \end{cases}$$

Whenever

$$\sum_{n=1}^{\infty} f_{ij}^{(n)} = 1,$$

then μ_{ij} satisfies uniquely the equation

$$\mu_{ij} = 1 + \sum_{k \neq j} p_{ik} \mu_{kj}.$$

For the inventory example, these equations can be used to compute the expected time until the cameras are out of stock, assuming the process is started when three cameras are available; i.e., the expected first passage time, μ_{30}, can be obtained. Assuming that all the states are recurrent (as is shown soon), the system of equations leads to the expressions

$$\begin{aligned} \mu_{30} &= 1 + p_{31}\mu_{10} + p_{32}\mu_{20} + p_{33}\mu_{30}, \\ \mu_{20} &= 1 + p_{21}\mu_{10} + p_{22}\mu_{20} + p_{23}\mu_{30}, \\ \mu_{10} &= 1 + p_{11}\mu_{10} + p_{12}\mu_{20} + p_{13}\mu_{30}, \end{aligned}$$

or

$$\begin{aligned} \mu_{30} &= 1 + 0.184\mu_{10} + 0.368\mu_{20} + 0.368\mu_{30}, \\ \mu_{20} &= 1 + 0.368\mu_{10} + 0.368\mu_{20}, \\ \mu_{10} &= 1 + 0.368\mu_{10}. \end{aligned}$$

The simultaneous solution to this system of equations is

$$\begin{aligned} \mu_{10} &= 1.58 \text{ weeks}, \\ \mu_{20} &= 2.51 \text{ weeks}, \\ \mu_{30} &= 3.50 \text{ weeks}, \end{aligned}$$

so that the expected time until the cameras are out of stock is 3.50 weeks. In making these calculations, μ_{20} and μ_{10} are also obtained.

When $j = i$, the expected first passage time is called the *expected recurrence time*. The recurrent state is called a *null recurrent* state if $\mu_{ii} = \infty$, and it is called a *positive recurrent* state if $\mu_{ii} < \infty$. In a finite-state Markov chain there are no null recurrent states (only positive recurrent states and transient states).

8.21 CLASSIFICATION OF STATES OF A MARKOV CHAIN

Section 8.20 classified states of a Markov chain as recurrent (positive or null) or transient. Some further concepts and definitions concerning these states are required.

State j is said to be *accessible* from state i if $p_{ij}^{(n)} > 0$ for some $n \geq 0$. Recall that $p_{ij}^{(n)}$ is just the conditional probability of being in state j after n steps, starting in state i. It is easily shown then that state j is accessible from state i if, and only if, it is possible for the system to enter state j starting from state i. In the inventory example, $p_{ij}^{(2)} > 0$ for all i, j, so that every state is accessible from every other state. Obviously a sufficient condition for *all* states to be accessible is that these exists a value of n, not dependent upon i and j, for which $p_{ij}^{(n)} > 0$ for all i and j.

If state j is accessible from state i, and, in addition, state i is accessible from state j, then states i and j are said to *communicate*. In the inventory example, all states communicate. In general, (1) any state communicates with itself [since $p_{ii}^{(0)} = P\{X_0 = i \mid X_0 = i\} = 1$]; (2) if state i communicates with state j, then state j communicates with state i; and furthermore, (3) if state i communicates with state j, and state j communicates with state k, then state i communicates with state k.

As a result of these three properties of communication the state space may be partitioned into disjoint classes, with two states communicating said to belong in the same class. Thus the states of a Markov chain may consist of one or more disjoint classes (a class may consist of a single state). If there is only one class, i.e., all the states communicate, the Markov chain is said to be *irreducible*. In the inventory example, the Markov chain is irreducible. The transition matrix presented in Sec. 8.20 contains four classes. States 0 and 1, recurrent states, form one class in that they communicate with one another. State 2 is an absorbing (and recurrent) state and hence forms a class because it communicates with itself. State 3, a transient state, communicates with itself and also forms a class. State 4, also a transient state, forms the final class.

In a finite-state Markov chain the members of a class are either all transient states or all positive recurrent states. Many Markov chains encountered in practice consist entirely of states that all communicate with each other; these irredicible Markov chains contain only positive recurrent states.[1] As indicated

[1] The only possible alternative for such a chain is that it contains all transient states, which is not possible for a finite-state Markov chain.

above, to determine if all states of a chain communicate with each other, it is sufficient to show that there exists a value of n not dependent upon i and j for which $p_{ij}^{(n)} > 0$ for all i and j. This is, then, the alternative criterion alluded to in Sec. 8.20 for determining if states are recurrent. In the inventory example, $p_{ij}^{(2)}$ is positive for all i and j, so that all states communicate and hence is an irreducible Markov chain. Therefore this chain must contain states that are all positive recurrent.

A final property of Markov chains that is to be considered is the property of *periodicities*. A state i is said to have period t $(t > 1)$ if $p_{ii}^{(n)} = 0$ whenever n is not divisible by t, and t is the smallest integer with this property. For example, it may be possible for the process to enter state i only at the time 0, 2, 4, ..., in which case this state has period 2. If there are two consecutive numbers, s and $(s+1)$, such that the process can be in state i at times s and $(s+1)$, the state is said to have period, 1 and is called an *aperiodic* state. If state i in a class is aperiodic, then all states in the class are aperiodic. Positive recurrent states that are aperiodic are called *ergodic* states.

8.22 LONG-RUN PROPERTIES OF MARKOV CHAINS

Steady-state Probabilities

In Sec. 8.19 the four-step transition matrix for the inventory example was obtained. It will now be instructive to examine the eight-step transition probabilities given by the matrix

$$\mathbf{P}^{(8)} = \mathbf{P}^8 = \mathbf{P}^4 \cdot \mathbf{P}^4 = \begin{bmatrix} 0.286 & 0.285 & 0.264 & 0.166 \\ 0.286 & 0.285 & 0.264 & 0.166 \\ 0.286 & 0.285 & 0.264 & 0.166 \\ 0.286 & 0.285 & 0.264 & 0.166 \end{bmatrix}$$

Notice the rather remarkable fact that each of the four rows has identical entries. This implies that the probability of being in state j after 8 weeks appears to be independent of the initial level of inventory. In other words, it appears that there is a limiting probability that the system will be in state j after a large number of transitions, and this probability is independent of the initial state. An important result related to the long-run behavior of finite state Markov processes follows.

For an irreducible ergodic Markov chain it can be shown that $\lim\limits_{n\to\infty} p_{ij}^{(n)}$ exists and is independent of i. Furthermore,

$$\lim_{n\to\infty} p_{ij}^{(n)} = \pi_j,$$

where the π_j's uniquely satisfy the following steady-state equations:

$$\pi_j > 0,$$

$$\pi_j = \sum_{i=0}^{M} \pi_i p_{ij}, \text{ for } j = 0, 1, \ldots, M,$$

$$\sum_{j=0}^{M} \pi_j = 1.$$

The π_j's are called the steady-state probabilities of the Markov chain and are equal to the reciprocal of the expected recurrence time; that is,

$$\pi_j = \frac{1}{\mu_{jj}}, \text{ for } j = 0, 1, \ldots, M.$$

The term *steady-state* probability means that the probability of finding the process in a certain state, say, j, after a large number of transitions tends to the value π_j, independent of the initial probability distribution defined over the states. It is important to note that steady-state probability does *not* imply that the process settles down into one state. On the contrary, the process continues to make transitions from state to state, and at any step n the transition probability from state i to state j is still p_{ij}.

The π_j's can also be interpreted as stationary probabilities (not to be confused with stationary transition probabilities). If the initial absolute probability of being in state j is given by π_j (that is, $P\{X_0 = j\} = \pi_j$) for all j, then the absolute probability of finding the process in state j at time $n = 1, 2, \ldots,$ is also given by π_j (that is, $P\{X_n = j\} = \pi_j$).

It should be noted that the steady-state equations consist of $(M+2)$ equations in $(M+1)$ unknowns. Since it has a unique solution, at least one equation must be redundant and can, therefore, be deleted, It can not be the equation

$$\sum_{j=0}^{M} \pi_j = 1$$

because $\pi_j = 0$ for all j will satisfy the other $(M+1)$ equations. Furthermore, the solutions to the other $(M+1)$ steady-state equations have a unique solution up to a multiplicative constant, and it is the final equation that forces the solution to be a probability distribution.

Returning to the inventory example, the steady-state equations can be expressed as

$$\begin{aligned}
\pi_0 &= \pi_0 p_{00} + \pi_1 p_{10} + \pi_2 p_{20} + \pi_3 p_{30}, \\
\pi_1 &= \pi_0 p_{01} + \pi_1 p_{11} + \pi_2 p_{21} + \pi_3 p_{31}, \\
\pi_2 &= \pi_0 p_{02} + \pi_1 p_{12} + \pi_2 p_{22} + \pi_3 p_{32}, \\
\pi_3 &= \pi_0 p_{03} + \pi_1 p_{13} + \pi_2 p_{23} + \pi_3 p_{33}, \\
1 &= \pi_0 \quad + \pi_1 \quad + \pi_2 \quad + \pi_3.
\end{aligned}$$

Substituting values for p_{ij} into these equations leads to the equations

$$\begin{aligned}
\pi_0 &= (0.080)\pi_0 + (0.632)\pi_1 + (0.264)\pi_2 + (0.080)\pi_3, \\
\pi_1 &= (0.184)\pi_0 + (0.368)\pi_1 + (0.368)\pi_2 + (0.184)\pi_3, \\
\pi_2 &= (0.368)\pi_0 \qquad\qquad\qquad + (0.368)\pi_2 + (0.368)\pi_3, \\
\pi_3 &= (0.368)\pi_0 \qquad\qquad\qquad\qquad\qquad\quad + (0.368)\pi_3, \\
1 &= \quad \pi_0 + \quad \pi_1 + \quad \pi_2 + \quad \pi_3.
\end{aligned}$$

Solving the last four equations provides the simultaneous solutions

$$\pi_0 = 0.285,$$
$$\pi_1 = 0.285,$$
$$\pi_2 = 0.264,$$
$$\pi_3 = 0.166,$$

which are essentially the results that appear in the matrix $\mathbf{P}^{(8)}$. Thus, after many weeks the probability of finding zero, one, two, and three cameras in stock tends to 0.285, 0.285, 0.264, and 0.166, respectively. The corresponding expected recurrence times are

$$\mu_{00} = \frac{1}{\pi_0} = 3.51 \text{ weeks},$$
$$\mu_{11} = \frac{1}{\pi_1} = 3.51 \text{ weeks},$$
$$\mu_{22} = \frac{1}{\pi_2} = 3.79 \text{ weeks},$$
$$\mu_{33} = \frac{1}{\pi_3} = 6.02 \text{ weeks}.$$

There are other important results concerning steady-state probabilities. In particular, if i and j are recurrent states belonging to different classes, then

$$p_{ij}^{(n)} = 0, \text{ for all } n.$$

This result follows from the definition of a class.

Similarly, if j is a transient state, then

$$\lim_{n\to\infty} p_{ij}^{(n)} = 0, \text{ for all } i.$$

This implies that the probability of finding the process in a transient state after a large number of transitions tends to zero.

Expected Average Cost per Unit Time

The previous section dealt with Markov chains whose states were ergodic (positive recurrent and aperiodic). If the requirement that the states be aperiodic is relaxed, then the limit

$$\lim_{n\to\infty} p_{ij}^{(n)}$$

may not exist. To illustrate this, consider the two-state transition matrix

$$\mathbf{P} = \begin{bmatrix} 0 & 1 \\ 1 & 0 \end{bmatrix}.$$

If the process starts in state 0 at time 0, it will be in state 0 at times 2, 4, 6, ..., and in state 1 at times 1, 3, 5, ... Thus $p_{00}^{(n)} = 1$ if n is even and $p_{00}^{(n)} = 0$ if n is odd, so that

$$\lim_{n \to \infty} p_{00}^{(n)}$$

does not exist. However, the following limit always exists: For an irreducible Markov chain with positive recurrent states, e.g., a finite-state chain, then

$$\lim_{n \to \infty} \left\{ \frac{1}{n} \sum_{k=1}^{n} p_{ij}^{(k)} \right\} = \pi_j,$$

where the π_j's satisfy the steady-state equations presented in Sec. 8.22.

This result is extremely important in computing the long-run average cost per unit time associated with a Markov chain. Suppose that a cost (or other penalty function) $C(X_t)$ is incurred when the process is in state X_t at time t, for $t = 0, 1, 2, \ldots$. Note that $C(X_t)$ is a random variable which takes on any one of the values $C(0), C(1), \ldots, C(M)$, and the function $C(\cdot)$ is independent of t. The expected average cost incurred over the first n periods is given by the expression

$$E\left[\frac{1}{n} \sum_{t=1}^{n} C(X_t)\right].$$

Using the result that

$$\lim_{n \to \infty} \left\{ \frac{1}{n} \sum_{k=1}^{n} p_{ij}^{(k)} \right\} = \pi_j,$$

it is simple to show that the (long run) *expected average cost per unit time* is given by

$$\lim_{n \to \infty} \left\{ E\left[\frac{1}{n} \sum_{t=1}^{n} C(X_t)\right] \right\} = \sum_{j=0}^{M} C(j)\pi_j.$$

As an example, suppose the camera store finds that a storage charge is being allocated for each camera remaining on the shelf at the end of the week. The cost is charged as follows: If $X_t = 0$, then $C(0) = 0$. If $X_t = 1$, then $C(1) = 2$. If $X_t = 2$, then $C(2) = 8$. Finally, if $X_t = 3$, then $C(3) = 18$. The long-run expected average holding cost per week can then be obtained from the preceding equation; that is,

$$\lim_{n \to \infty} \left\{ E\left[\frac{1}{n} \sum_{t=1}^{n} C(X_t)\right] \right\} = 0(0.285) + 2(0.285) + 8(0.264) + 18(0.166) = 5.67.$$

It should be noted that an alternative measure to the (long run) expected average cost per unit time is the (long run) *actual average cost per unit time*. It can be shown that this latter measure is given by

$$\lim_{n \to \infty} \left\{ \frac{1}{n} \sum_{t=1}^{n} C(X_t) \right\} = \sum_{j=0}^{M} \pi_j C(j)$$

for almost all paths of the process. Thus either measure leads to the same result. These results can also be used to interpret the meaning of the π_j's. To do this, let

$$C(X_k) = \begin{cases} 1, & \text{if } X_k = j \\ 0, & \text{if } X_k \neq j. \end{cases}$$

The (long run) expected fraction of times the system is in state j is then given by

$$\lim_{n\to\infty} \left\{ E\left[\frac{1}{n} \sum_{t=1}^{n} C(X_t) \right] \right\} = \lim_{n\to\infty} \{E[\text{fraction of times system is in state } j]\} = \pi_j.$$

Similarly, π_j can also be interpreted as the (long run) actual fraction of times that the system is in state j.

Expected Average Cost per Unit Time for Complex Cost Functions

In the preceding section the cost function was based solely on the state that the process is in at time t. In many important problems encountered in practice the cost may depend upon another random variable as well as upon the state that the process is in. For example, in the inventory example developed in this chapter, suppose that the costs to be considered are the ordering cost and the penalty cost for unsatisfied demand (storage costs will be ignored). It is reasonable to assume that the number of cameras ordered depends only upon the state of the process (the number of cameras in stock) when the order is placed. The cost for unsatisfied demand may be assumed to depend upon the demand during the week as well as upon the state of the process at the beginning of the week. The charges for period t will be made at the end of the week and will include the cost of the order delivered on the Monday of that week and the cost of unsatisfied demand during the week. Thus the cost incurred for period t can be described as a function of X_{t-1} and D_t, that is, $C(X_{t-1}, D_t)$. Note that the demands $D_t, D_{t+1}, \ldots$, during successive weeks are assumed to be independent and identically distributed random variables. Furthermore, recall that the (s, S) policy, (1,3), is being used. X_{t-1}, the stock level at the end of period $t-1$ (before ordering), is defined iteratively by the expression given in Sec. 8.17. Thus it follows that $(X_0, X_1, X_2, \ldots, X_{t-1})$ and D_t are independent random variables because $X_0, X_1, X_2, \ldots, X_{t-1}$ are functions only of $X_0, D_1, \ldots, D_{t-1}$, which are independent of D_t. Under these conditions, it can be shown that the (long run) *expected average cost per unit time* is given by

$$\lim_{n\to\infty} \left\{ E\left[\frac{1}{n} \sum_{t=1}^{n} C(X_{t-1}, D_t) \right] \right\} = \sum_{j=0}^{M} k(j)\pi_j,$$

where

$$k(j) = E[C(j, D_t)],$$

and this latter (conditional) expectation is taken with respect to the probability distribution of the random variable D_t (given the state). Similarly, the (long run) actual average cost per unit time is given by

$$\lim_{n\to\infty}\left\{\frac{1}{n}\sum_{t=1}^{n} C(X_{t-1}, D_t)\right\} = \sum_{j=0}^{M} k(j)\pi_j.$$

Suppose that the following costs are associated with the (s, S) inventory policy given earlier. If $z > 0$ cameras are ordered, the cost incurred is $10 + 25z$ dollars. If no cameras are ordered, no ordering cost is incurred. For each unit of unsatisfied demand (lost sales), there is a penalty of \$50 per unit. If the $(s = 1, S = 3)$ ordering policy is followed, then the cost in week t is given by $C(X_{t-1}, D_t)$, where

$$C(X_{t-1}, D_t) = \begin{cases} 10 + (25)(3) + 50\max\{(D_t - 3), 0\}, & \text{if } X_{t-1} < 1 \\ 50\max\{(D_t - X_{t-1}), 0\}, & \text{if } X_{t-1} \geq 1. \end{cases}$$

for $t = 1, 2, \ldots$.

Hence

$$C(0, D_t) = 85 + 50\max\{(D_t - 3), 0\},$$

so that

$$\begin{aligned} k(0) = E[C(0, D_t)] &= 85 + 50E[\max\{(D_t - 3), 0\}] \\ &= 85 + 50[1P_D(4) + 2P_D(5) + 3P_D(6) + \cdots], \end{aligned}$$

where $P_D(i)$ is the probability that the demand equals i and has been assumed to have a Poisson distribution with parameter $\lambda = 1$. Hence $k(0) = 86.2$. Similar calculations lead to the results

$$\begin{aligned} k(1) = E[C(1, D_t)] &= 50E[\max\{(D_t - 1), 0\}] \\ &= 50[1P_D(2) + 2P_D(3) + 3P_D(4) + \cdots] \\ &= 18.4, \\ k(2) = E[C(2, D_t)] &= 50E[\max\{(D_t - 2), 0\}] \\ &= 50[1P_D(3) + 2P_D(4) + 3P_D(5) + \cdots] \\ &= 5.2, \end{aligned}$$

and

$$\begin{aligned} k(3) = E[C(3, D_t)] &= 50E[\max\{(D_t - 3), 0\}] \\ &= 50[1P_D(4) + 2P_D(5) + \cdots] \\ &= 1.2. \end{aligned}$$

Thus the (long run) expected average inventory cost per week is given by

$$\sum_{j=0}^{3} k(j)\pi_j = (86.2)(0.285) + (18.4)(0.285) + (5.2)(0.264) + (1.2)(0.166) = 31.4.$$

This is the cost associated with the (s, S) policy, $(s, S) = (1,3)$. The cost of other (s, S) policies can be evaluated in a similar way to identify the policy that minimizes the expected average inventory cost per week.

The results of this section were presented only in terms of the inventory example. However, the (nonnumerical) results still hold for other problems as long as the following conditions are satisfied:

1. $\{X_t\}$ is an irreducible Markov chain whose states are positive recurrent.
2. Associated with this Markov chain is a sequence of random variables $\{D_t\}$, each of which is independent and identically distributed.
3. For a fixed $m = 0, \pm 1, \pm 2, \ldots$, a cost $C(X_t, D_{t+m})$, is incurred at time t, for $t = 0, 1, 2, \ldots$.
4. The sequence $(X_0, X_1, X_2, \ldots, X_t)$ must be independent of D_{t+m}.

In particular, it these conditions are satisfied then

$$\lim_{n\to\infty}\left\{E\left[\frac{1}{n}\sum_{t=1}^{n} C(X_t, D_{t+m})\right]\right\} = \sum_{j=0}^{M} k(j)\pi_j,$$

where

$$k(j) = E[C(j, D_{t+m})],$$

and this latter conditional expectation is taken with respect to the probability distribution of the random variable D_t (given the state). Furthermore,

$$\lim_{n\to\infty}\left\{\frac{1}{n}\sum_{t=1}^{n} C(X_t, D_{t+m})\right\} = \sum_{j=0}^{M} k(j)\pi_j,$$

for almost all paths of the process.

8.23 ABSORPTION STATES

It was pointed out that a state k is called an absorbing state if $p_{kk} = 1$, so tha once the chain visits k it remains there forever. If k is an absorbing state, the first passage probability from i to k is called the probability of absorption into k, having started at i. When there are two or more absorbing states in a chain, and it is evident that the process will be absorbed into one of these states, it is desirable to find these probabilities of absorption. These probabilities can be obtained by solving a system of linear equations. Suppose that the Markov chain is such that ultimately one of the absorbing states will be reached. If the state k is an absorbing state, then the set of absorption probabilities f_{ik} satisfies the system of equations

$$f_{ik} = \sum_{j=0}^{M} p_{ij} f_{jk}, \text{ for } i = 0, 1, \ldots, M,$$

subject to the conditions

$$f_{kk} = 1,$$
$$f_{ik} = 0, \text{ if state } i \text{ is recurrent and } i \neq k.$$

Absorption probabilities are important in "random walks." A *random walk* is a Markov chain with the property that if the system is in a state i, then in a single transition the system either remains at i or moves to one of the states immediately adjacent to i. For example, a random walk often is used as a model for situations involving gambling. To illustrate, suppose that two players, each having \$2, agree to keep playing a game betting \$1 at a time until one is broke. The amount of money that player A has after n plays of the game forms a Markov chain with transition matrix

$$\mathbf{P} = \begin{bmatrix} 1 & 0 & 0 & 0 & 0 \\ 1-p & 0 & p & 0 & 0 \\ 0 & 1-p & 0 & p & 0 \\ 0 & 0 & 1-p & 0 & p \\ 0 & 0 & 0 & 0 & 1 \end{bmatrix}$$

If p represents the probability of A winning a single encounter, then the probability of absorption into state 0 (A losing all his money) can be obtained from the above system of equations. It can be shown that this leads to the alternate expressions (for general M rather than $M = 4$ as in this example)

$$1 - f_{i0} = \frac{\sum_{m=0}^{i-1} \rho^m}{\sum_{m=0}^{M-1} \rho^m}, \text{ for } i = 1, 2, \ldots, M.$$

where $\rho = (1-p)/p$.
For $M = 4$ and $i = 2$, the probability of A going broke is given by

$$f_{20} = \frac{\rho^2 + \rho^3}{1 + \rho + \rho^2 + \rho^3}.$$

8.24 CONTINUOUS PARAMETER MARKOV CHAINS

All the previous sections assumed that the time parameter t was discrete (that is, $t = 0,1,2, \ldots$). Such an assumption is suitable for many problems, but there are certain cases (such as for some queueing models) where a continuous time parameter is required.

Let $\{X(t)\}$, where $t \geq 0$, be a Markov chain with $M + 1$ discrete states $0, 1, \ldots, M$ and stationary transition probability function

$$p_{ij}(t) = P\{X(t+s) = j \mid X(s) = i\}, \text{ for } i, j = 0, 1, \ldots, M.$$

This function is assumed to be continuous at $t = 0$ with

$$\lim_{t \to 0} p_{ij}(t) = \begin{cases} 1, & \text{if } i = j \\ 0, & \text{if } i \neq j. \end{cases}$$

Just as the discrete time parameter models satisfy the Chapman-Kolmogorov equations, the continuous time transition probability function also satisfies these equations; i.e., for any state i and j, and positive numbers t and v $(0 \leq v \leq t)$,

$$p_{ij}(t) = \sum_{k=0}^{M} p_{ik}(v) p_{kj}(t - v).$$

A pair of states i and j are said to communicate if there are times t_1 and t_2 such that $p_{ij}(t_1) > 0$ and $p_{ji}(t_2) > 0$. All states that communicate are said to form a class. If all states in a chain form a single class (irreducible chain), then

$$p_{ij}(t) > 0, \text{ for all } t > 0 \text{ and all states } i \text{ and } j.$$

Furthermore,

$$\lim_{t\to\infty} p_{ij}(t) = \pi_j$$

always exists and is independent of the initial state of the chain, for $i = 0, 1, \ldots, M$. The π_j satisfy the equations

$$\pi_j = \sum_{i=0}^{M} \pi_i p_{ij}(t), \text{ for } j = 0, 1, \ldots, M, \text{ and for every } t \geq 0.$$

Just as the one-step transition probabilities played a major role in describing the Markov process for a discrete time parameter chain, the analogous role for a continuous time parameter chain is played by the transition intensities. The *transition intensity* is defined by

$$u_j = -\frac{d}{dt} p_{jj}(0) = \lim_{t\to 0} \frac{1 - p_{jj}(t)}{t}, \text{ for } j = 0, 1, \ldots, M,$$

and

$$u_{ij} = \frac{d}{dt} p_{ij}(0) = \lim_{t\to 0} \frac{p_{ij}(t)}{t}, \qquad \text{for all } i \neq j,$$

provided that these limits exist and are finite. u_j is called the *intensity of passage*, given that the Markov chain is in state j, and u_{ij} is called the *intensity of transition* to state j from the state i.

These transition intensities also satisfy the equation

$$\pi_j u_j = \sum_{i \neq j} \pi_i u_{ij}, \text{ for } j = 0, 1, \ldots, M.$$

The transition intensities can be interpreted as follows. The probability of transition from state i to j during the interval of length Δt, $p_{ij}(\Delta t)$, is equal to $u_{ij}\,\Delta t$ plus a remainder that when divided by Δt tends to zero as $\Delta t \to 0$. Similarly, $1 - p_{jj}(\Delta t)$, the probability of a transition from a state j to some other state during the interval of length Δt, is equal to $u_j\,\Delta t$ plus a remainder that when divided by Δt tends to zero as $\Delta t \to 0$. Thus, for small Δt, the probabilities of transition within a time interval of length Δt are essentially proportional to Δt, the proportionality constants being the transition intensities.

As an example, consider the following repairman problem that is discussed in detail in Chap. 9 (queueing theory). There are M machines serviced by a single repairman. A machine that breaks down is serviced immediately unless the repairman is servicing another machine, in which case a waiting line is formed. A system is said to be in state n if n machines are not working. If the process is in state n, where $1 \le n \le M$, this means that one machine is being serviced and $(n-1)$ are in the waiting line waiting to be repaired. If the process is in state 0, then all machines are working, and the repairman is idle. Let $X(t)$ be the number of machines not working at time t. Suppose the transition intensities satisfy the condition that if i and j are states such that $|i-j| \ge 2$, then $u_{ij} = 0$. It can be shown that $\{X(t)\}$ is a continuous parameter Markov process which changes states only through transitions from a state to its immediate neighbors. The transition intensities can be written as

$$u_{j,j+1} = (M-j)\lambda, \qquad \text{if } j = 0, 1, 2, \ldots, M,$$

$$u_{j,j-1} = \begin{cases} \mu, & \text{if } j = 1, 2, \ldots, M \\ 0, & \text{if } j = 0, \end{cases}$$

$$u_j = \begin{cases} (M-j)\lambda + \mu, & \text{if } j = 1, \ldots, M \\ M\lambda, & \text{if } j = 0. \end{cases}$$

More explicitly,

$$\lim_{t\to 0} \left\{ \frac{p_{j,j+1}(t)}{t} = (M-j)\lambda, \qquad \text{for } j = 0, 1, 2, \ldots, M, \right.$$

$$\lim_{t\to 0} \left\{ \frac{p_{j,j-1}(t)}{t} = \begin{cases} \mu, & \text{for } j = 1, 2, \ldots, M \\ 0, & \text{for } j = 0, \end{cases} \right.$$

$$\lim_{t\to 0} \left\{ \frac{1 - p_{jj}(t)}{t} = \begin{cases} (M-j)\lambda + \mu, & \text{for } j = 1, 2, \ldots, M \\ M\lambda, & \text{for } j = 0. \end{cases} \right.$$

Thus, these equations indicate that in a small time interval the number of machines working either decreases by 1, increases by 1, or stays the same. The conditional probability of an increase of 1 is denoted by $(M-j)\lambda$; the conditional probability of a decrease by 1 is denoted by μ. Substituting these results into the system of equations that the π_j satisfy, that is,

$$\pi_j u_j = \sum_{i \ne j} \pi_i u_{ij},$$

the following system of equations is obtained:

$$\pi_0 M\lambda = \pi_1 \mu,$$

$$\pi_j[(M-j)\lambda + \mu] = \pi_{j-1}(M-j+1)\lambda + \pi_{j+1}\mu, \text{ for } j = 1, \ldots, M-1.$$

$$\pi_M \mu = \pi_{M-1}\lambda, \qquad \text{for } j = M.$$

Solving this system of equations leads to the steady-state probability distribution of $X(t)$ which is given in Sec. 9.6 (basic model with a limited source); that is,

$$P_0 = 1 \Big/ \sum_{j=0}^{M} \left[\frac{M!}{(M-j)!} \left(\frac{\lambda}{\mu}\right)^j \right]$$

$$P_j = \frac{M!}{(M-j)!} \left(\frac{\lambda}{\mu}\right)^j P_0, \text{ for } j = 1, 2, \ldots, M.$$

Selected References

1 Chung, K. L.: *Markov Chains with Stationary Transition Probabilities*, Springer-Verlag, Berlin, 1960.
2 Derman, C. and M. Klein: *Probability and Statistical Inference for Engineers*, Oxford University Press, New York, 1959.
3 Feller, W.: *An Introduction to Probability Theory and its Applications*, vol. 1, 2d ed., Wiley, New York, 1957.
4 Kemeny, J. G. and J. L. Snell: *Finite Markov Chains*, Van Nostrand, New York, 1959.
5 Meyer, P. L.: *Introductory Probability and Statistical Applications*, Addison-Wesley, Reading, Mass., 1965.
6 Parzen, E.: *Modern Probability Theory and its Applications*, Wiley, New York, 1960.
7 ———: *Stochastic Processes*, Holden-Day, San Francisco, 1962.
8 Ross, S.: *Introduction to Probability Models*, Academic Press, New York, 1972.

Problems

1 A cube has its six sides colored red, white, blue, green, yellow, and violet. It is assumed that these six sides are equally likely to show when the cube is tossed. The cube is tossed once.

(*a*) Describe the sample space.
(*b*) Consider the random variable that assigns the number 0 to red and white, the number 1 to green and blue, and the number 2 to yellow and violet. What is the distribution of this random variable?
(*c*) Let $Y=(X+1)^2$, where X is the random variable in part (*b*). Find $E(Y)$.

2 Suppose the sample space Ω consists of the four points

$$\omega_1, \omega_2, \omega_3, \omega_4,$$

and the associated probabilities over the events are given by

$$P\{\omega_1\}=\frac{1}{3}, P\{\omega_2\}=\frac{1}{4}, P\{\omega_3\}=\frac{1}{4}, P\{\omega_4\}=\frac{1}{6}.$$

Define the random variable X_1 by

$$X_1(\omega_1)=1,$$
$$X_1(\omega_2)=1,$$
$$X_1(\omega_3)=4,$$
$$X_1(\omega_4)=5,$$

and the random variable X_2 by

$$X_2(\omega_1)=1,$$
$$X_2(\omega_2)=1,$$
$$X_2(\omega_3)=1,$$
$$X_2(\omega_4)=5.$$

(*a*) Find the probability distribution of X_1, that is, $P_{X_1}(i)$.
(*b*) Find $E(X_1)$.
(*c*) Find the probability distribution of the random variable $X_1 + X_2$, that is, $P_{X_1+X_2}(i)$.
(*d*) Find $E(X_1 + X_2)$ and $E(X_2)$.
(*e*) Find $F_{X_1X_2}(b_1, b_2)$.
(*f*) Compute the correlation coefficient between X_1 and X_2.
(*g*) Compute $E[2X_1 - 3X_2]$.

3 During the course of a day a machine turns out two items, one in the morning and one in the afternoon. The quality of each item is measured as good (*G*), mediocre (*M*), or bad (*B*). The long-run fraction of good items the machine produces is ½, the fraction of mediocre items is ⅜, and the fraction of bad items is ⅛.

(*a*) In a column, write the sample space for the experiment that consists of observing the day's production.
(*b*) Assume a good item returns a profit of \$2, a mediocre item a profit of \$1, and a bad item yields nothing. Let *X* be the random variable describing the total profit for the day. In a column adjacent to the column in part (*a*), write the value of this random variable corresponding to each point in the sample space.
(*c*) Assuming that the qualities of the morning and afternoon items are independent, in a third column associate with every point in the sample space a probability for that point.

(*d*) Write the set of all possible outcomes for the random variable *X*. Give the probability distribution function for the random variable.
(*e*) What is the expected value of the day's profit?

4 The random variable *X* has density function *f* given by

$$f_X(y) = \begin{cases} \theta, & \text{for } 0 \le y \le \theta \\ K, & \text{for } \theta < y \le 1 \\ 0, & \text{elsewhere.} \end{cases}$$

(*a*) Determine *K* in terms of θ.
(*b*) Find $F_X(b)$, the CDF of *X*.
(*c*) Find $E(X)$.

(*d*) Suppose $\theta = \frac{1}{3}$. Is $P\left\{X - \frac{1}{3} < a\right\} = P\left\{-\left(X - \frac{1}{3}\right) < a\right\}$?

5 Let *X* be a discrete random variable, with probability distribution

$$P\{X = x_1\} = \frac{1}{3}$$

and

$$P\{X = x_2\} = \frac{2}{3}.$$

(*a*) Determine x_1 and x_2, so that

$$E(X) = 0 \text{ and variance } (X) = 10.$$

(*b*) Sketch the CDF of *X*.

6 The life X, in hours, of a certain kind of radio tube has a probability density function given by

$$f_X(y) = \begin{cases} \dfrac{100}{y^2}, & \text{for } y \geq 100 \\ 0, & \text{for } y < 100. \end{cases}$$

(*a*) What is the probability that a tube will survive 200 hours of operation?
(*b*) Find the expected value of the random variable.

7 The random variable X can take on only the values 0, ± 1, ± 2, and

$$P\{-1 < X < 2\} = 0.4, \qquad P\{X = 0\} = 0.3,$$
$$P\{|X| \leq 1\} = 0.6, \qquad P\{X \geq 2\} = P\{X = 1 \text{ or } -1\}.$$

(*a*) Find the probability distribution of X.
(*b*) Graph the CDF of X.
(*c*) Compute $E(X)$.

8 Let X be a random variable with density

$$f_X(y) = \begin{cases} K(1 - y^2), & \text{for } -1 < y < 1 \\ 0, & \text{otherwise.} \end{cases}$$

(*a*) What value of K will make $f_X(y)$ a true density?
(*b*) What is the CDF of X?
(*c*) Find $E(2X - 2)$.
(*d*) Find variance (X).
(*e*) Find the approximate value of $P\{\bar{X} > 0\}$, where $\bar{X}$ is the sample mean from a random sample of size $n = 100$ from the above distribution. (*Hint*: Note that n is "large.")

9 The distribution of X, the life of a transistor, in hours, is approximated by a triangular distribution as follows:

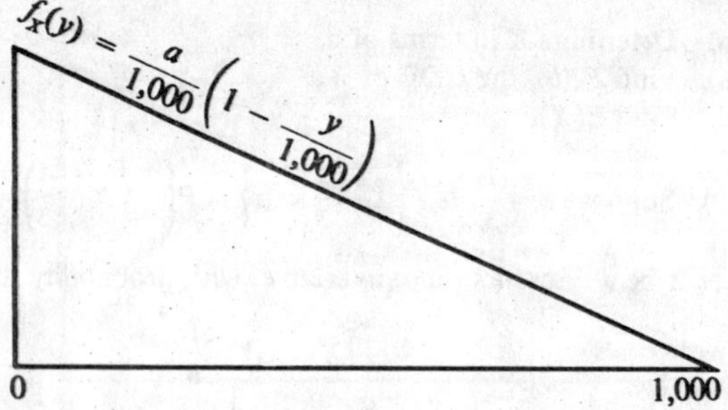

(*a*) What is the value of α?
(*b*) Find the expected value of the life of transistors.
(*c*) Find the CDF, $F_X(b)$, for this density. Note that this must be defined for all b between plus and minus infinity.
(*d*) If X represents the random variable the life of a transistor, let $Z = 2X$ be a new random variable. Using the results of (*c*), find the CDF of Z.

10 The number of orders per week, X, for radios can be assumed to have a Poisson distribution with parameter $\lambda = 25$.

(*a*) Find $P\{X \geq 25\}$ and $P\{X = 20\}$.
(*b*) If the number of radios in the inventory is 30, what is the probability of a shortage occurring in a week?

11 Consider the following game. Player A flips a fair coin until a head appears. She pays player B 2^n dollars, where n is the number of tosses required until a head appears. For example, if a head appears on the first trial, player A pays player B \$2. If the game results in 4 tails followed by a head, player A pays player B $2^5 = \$32$. Therefore the payoff to player B is a random variable that takes on the values 2^n for $n = 1, 2, \ldots$ and whose probability distribution is given by $(\frac{1}{2})^n$ for $n = 1, 2, \ldots$, that is, if X denotes the payoff to player B,

$$P(X = 2^n) = \left(\frac{1}{2}\right)^n \quad \text{for } n = 1, 2, \ldots.$$

The usual definition of a fair game between two players is for each player to have equal expectation for the amount to be won.

(*a*) How much should player B pay to player A so that this game will be fair?
(*b*) What is the variance of X?
(*c*) What is the probability of player B winning no more than \$8 in one play of the game?

12 The demand D for a product in a week is a random variable taking on the values of -1, 0, 1 with probabilities $\frac{1}{8}$, $\frac{4}{8}$, and $C/8$, respectively. A demand of -1 implies that an item is returned.

(*a*) Find C, $E(D)$, and variance D.
(*b*) Find $E(e^{D^2})$.
(*c*) Sketch the CDF of the random variable D, labeling all the necessary values.

13 In a certain chemical process three bottles of a standard fluid are emptied into a larger container. A study of the individual bottles shows that the mean value of the contents is 15 ounces and the standard deviation is 0.07 ounces. If three bottles form a random sample,

(*a*) Find the expected value and the standard deviation of the volume of liquid emptied into the larger container.
(*b*) If the content of the individual bottles is normally distributed, what is the probability that the volume of liquid emptied into the larger container will be in excess of 45.2 ounces?

14 Consider the density function of a random variable X defined by

$$f_X(y) = \begin{cases} 0, & \text{for } \quad y < 0 \\ 6y(1-y), & \text{for } 0 \leq y \leq 1 \\ 0, & \text{for } \quad 1 < y. \end{cases}$$

(*a*) Find the CDF corresponding to this density function. (Be sure you describe it completely.)
(*b*) Calculate the mean and variance.

(c) What is the probability that a random variable having this density will exceed 0.5?

(d) Consider the experiment where five independent random variables are observed, each random variable having the density function given above. What is the expected value of the sample mean of these observations?

(e) What is the variance of the sample mean described in part (d)?

15 A transistor radio operates on two $1\frac{1}{2}$ volt batteries, so that nominally it operates on 3 volts. Suppose the actual voltage of a single new battery is normally distributed with mean $1\frac{1}{2}$ volts and variance 0.04. The radio will not operate "properly" at the outset if the voltage falls outside the range $2\frac{3}{4}$ to $3\frac{1}{4}$ volts.

(a) What is the probability that the radio will not operate "properly?"

(b) Suppose that the assumption of normality is not valid. Give a bound on the probability that the radio will not operate "properly."

16 The life of electric light bulbs is known to be a normally distributed random variable with unknown mean μ and standard deviation 200 hours. The value of a lot of 1,000 bulbs is (1,000)(1/5,000) μ dollars. A random sample of n bulbs is to be drawn by a prospective buyer, and 1,000(1/5,000) $\bar{X}$ dollars paid to the manufacturer. How large should n be so that the probability is 0.95 that the buyer does not overpay or underpay the manufacturer by more than $15?

17 A joint random variable (X_1, X_2) is said to have a bivariate normal distribution if its joint density is given by

$$f_{X_1,X_2}(s,t) = \frac{1}{2\pi\sigma_{X_1}\sigma_{X_2}\sqrt{1-\rho^2}} \exp\left\{-\frac{1}{2(1-\rho^2)}\left[\left(\frac{s-\mu_{X_1}}{\sigma_{X_1}}\right)^2 - 2\rho\frac{(s-\mu_{X_1})(t-\mu_{X_2})}{\sigma_{X_1}\sigma_{X_2}} + \left(\frac{t-\mu_{X_2}}{\sigma_{X_2}}\right)^2\right]\right\}$$

for $-\infty < s < \infty$ and $-\infty < t < \infty$.

(a) Show that $E(X_1) = \mu_{X_1}$ and $E(X_2) = \mu_{X_2}$.

(b) Show that variance $(X_1) = \sigma_{X_1}^2$, variance $(X_2) = \sigma_{X_2}^2$, and the correlation coefficient is ρ.

(c) Show that marginal distributions of X_1 and X_2 are normal.

(d) Show that the conditional distribution of X_1, given $X_2 = x_2$, is normal with mean

$$\mu_{X_1} + \rho\frac{\sigma_{X_1}}{\sigma_{X_2}}(x_2 - \mu_{X_2})$$

and variance $\sigma_{X_1}^2(1-\rho^2)$.

18 The joint demand for a product over 2 months is a continuous random variable (X_1, X_2) having a joint density given by

$$f_{X_1,X_2}(s,t) = \begin{cases} c, & \text{if } 100 \le s \le 150, \text{ and } 50 \le t \le 100 \\ 0, & \text{otherwise.} \end{cases}$$

(a) Find c.

(b) Find $F_{X_1X_2}(b_1, b_2)$, $F_{X_1}(b_1)$, and $F_{X_2}(b_2)$.

(c) Find $f_{X_2|X_1=s}(t)$.

19 Two machines produce a certain item. The capacity per day of machine 1 is 1 unit and that of machine 2 is 2 units. Let (X_1, X_2) be the discrete random variable that measures the actual production on each machine per day. Each entry in the table below represents the joint probability, for example, $P_{X_1X_2}(0,0) = \frac{1}{8}$.

X_2 \ X_1	0	1
0	$\frac{1}{8}$	0
1	$\frac{1}{4}$	$\frac{1}{8}$
2	$\frac{1}{8}$	$\frac{3}{8}$

(*a*) Find the marginal distributions of X_1 and X_2.
(*b*) Find the conditional distribution of X_1, given $X_2 = 2$.
(*c*) Are X_1 and X_2 independent random variables?
(*d*) Find $E(X_1)$, $E(X_2)$, variance (X_1), and variance (X_2).
(*e*) Find the probability distribution of $(X_1 + X_2)$.

20 Suppose that $E_1, E_2, \ldots, E_m$ are mutually exclusive events such that $E_1 \cup E_2 \cup \cdots \cup E_m = \Omega$; that is, exactly one of the E events will occur. Denote by F any event in the sample space. Note that

$$F = FE_1 \cup FE_2 \cup \cdots \cup FE_m\dagger$$

and that FE_i, $i = 1, 2, \ldots, m$ are also mutually exclusive.

(*a*) Show that $P(E) = \sum_{i=1}^{m} P(FE_i) = \sum_{i=1}^{m} P(F|E_i)P(E_i)$.

(*b*) Show that $P\{E_i|F\} = P\{F|E_i\}P\{E_i\} \Big/ \sum_{i=1}^{m} P\{F|E_i\}P\{E_i\}$.

(This result is called Bayes' formula and is useful when it is known that the event F has occurred and there is interest in determining which one of the E_i also occurred.)

21 Assume that the probability of rain tommorrow is 0.8 if it is raining today, and assume that the probability of it being clear tomorrow is 0.9 if it is clear today.

(*a*) Determine the one-step transition matrix of the Markov chain.
(*b*) Find the steady-state probabilities.

† Recall that FE_1 is the same as $F \cap E_1$, that is, the intersection of the two events F and E_1.

22 Determine the classes of the Markov chains and whether or not they are recurrent.

$$\begin{bmatrix} 0 & 0 & \frac{1}{4} & \frac{3}{4} \\ 1 & 0 & 0 & 0 \\ 0 & 1 & 0 & 0 \\ 0 & 1 & 0 & 0 \end{bmatrix} \qquad \begin{bmatrix} 1 & 0 & 0 & 0 \\ 0 & \frac{1}{2} & \frac{1}{2} & 0 \\ 0 & \frac{1}{2} & \frac{1}{2} & 0 \\ \frac{1}{2} & 0 & 0 & \frac{1}{2} \end{bmatrix}$$

23 Consider the following gambler's ruin problem. A gambler bets one unit on each play of a game. She has a probability p of winning and $q=1-p$ of losing. She will continue to play until she goes broke or nets a fortune of T units. Let X_n denote the gambler's fortune on the nth play of the game. Then

$$X_{n+1} = \begin{cases} X_n + 1, \text{ with probability } p \\ X_n - 1, \text{ with probability } q = 1 - p \end{cases}, \quad \text{for } 0 < X_n < T.$$

$$X_{n+1} = X_n, \qquad \text{for } X_n = 0 \text{ or } T.$$

$\{X_n\}$ is a Markov chain. Assume that successive plays of the game are independent, and the gambler has an initial fortune of X_0.

(*a*) Determine the one-step transition matrix of the Markov chain.
(*b*) Find the classes of the Markov chain.
(*c*) Let $T=3$ and $p=0.4$. Find $f_{10}, f_{1T}, f_{20}, f_{2T}$.
(*d*) Let $T=3$ and $p=0.6$. Find $f_{10}, f_{1T}, f_{20}, f_{2T}$.
What can you conclude from (*c*) and (*d*)?

24 Suppose that a communications network transmits numbers in a binary system, that is, 0 or 1. In passing through the network, there is a probability q that the number will be received incorrectly at the next stage. If X_0 denotes the number entering the system, X_1 the number recorded after the first transmission, X_2 the number recorded after the second transmission, ..., then $\{X_n\}$ is a Markov chain. Find the one-step and steady-state transition matrix.

25 A transition matrix **P** is said to be doubly stochastic if the sum over each column equals 1; that is,

$$\sum_{i=0}^{M} p_{ij} = 1, \text{ for all } j.$$

If such a chain is irreducible, aperiodic, and consists of $M+1$ states, show that

$$\pi_j = \frac{1}{M+1}, \text{ for } j = 0, 1, \ldots, M.$$

26 A particle moves on a circle, through points that have been marked 0, 1, 2, 3, 4 (in a clockwise order). The particle starts at point 0. At each step it has probability q of moving to the right (clockwise) and $1-q$ to the left (counterclockwise). Let X_n ($n \geq 0$) denote its location on the circle. $\{X_n\}$ is a Markov chain.

(*a*) Find the transition probability matrix.
(*b*) Find the steady-state probabilities.

27 Using ordering costs and unsatisfied demand costs, evaluate the expected average inventory cost per week for the inventory example introduced in Sec. 8.22, using the (s, S) policy, $(s, S) = (2,3)$.

28 Consider the inventory example introduced in Sec. 8.17. Instead of following an (s, S) policy, a (q, Q) policy will be used. If the stock level at the end of each period is less than $q = 2$ units, $Q = 2$ additional units will be ordered. Otherwise, no ordering will take place. This is a (q, Q) policy with $q = 2$ and $Q = 2$. Let X_t denote the number of units on hand at the end of the tth period. Assume that demand which is not filled results in lost sales. $\{X_n\}$ is a Markov chain (assume $X_0 = 0$). Using the cost values and demand distribution given for the inventory example in the text,

(*a*) Find the steady-state probabilities.
(*b*) Find the long-run expected average cost per unit time.

29 Consider the following (k, Q) inventory policy. Let $D_1, D_2, \ldots$ be the demand for a product in periods 1, 2, ..., respectively. If the demand during a period exceeds the number of items available, this unsatisfied demand is backlogged; i.e., it is filled when the next order is received. Let Z_n $(n = 0,1, \ldots)$ denote the amount of inventory on hand minus the number of units backlogged before ordering at the end of period n $(Z_0 = 0)$. If Z_n is zero or positive, no orders are backlogged. If Z_n is negative, then $-Z_n$ represents the number of backlogged units and no inventory is on hand. If at the beginning of period n, $Z_n < k = 1$, an order is placed for $2m$ (Qm in general) units, where m is the smallest integer such that $Z_n + 2m \geq 1$. (The amount ordered is the smallest integral multiple of 2, which brings the level to at least 1 unit.) Let D_n be independent and identically distributed random variables taking on the values, 0, 1, 2, 3, 4, each with probability ⅕. Let X_n denote the amount of stock on hand *after* ordering at the end of period n $(X_0 = 2)$. It is evident that

$$X_n = \begin{cases} X_{n-1} - D_n + 2m, & \text{if } X_{n-1} - D_n < 1 \\ X_{n-1} - D_n, & \text{if } X_{n-1} - D_n \geq 1 \end{cases} \qquad (n = 1, 2, \ldots),$$

and $\{X_n\}$ $(n = 0,1, \ldots)$ is a Markov chain with only two states: 1 and 2. [The only time that ordering will take place is when $Z_n = 0, -1$, or -2, in which case 2, 2, and 4 units are ordered, respectively, leaving $X_n = 2, 1, 2$, respectively. In general, for any (k, Q) policy, the possible states are $k, k+1, k+2, \ldots, k+Q-1$.]

(*a*) Find the one-step transition matrix.
(*b*) Find the stationary probabilities (see Prob. 25).
(*c*) Suppose that the ordering cost is given by $(3 + 2m)$ if an order is placed and zero otherwise. The holding cost per period is Z_n if $Z_n \geq 0$ and zero otherwise. The shortage cost per period is $-4Z_n$ if $Z_n < 0$ and zero otherwise. Find the (long run) expected average cost per unit time.

30 An important unit consists of two components placed in parallel. The unit performs satisfactorily if one of the two components is operating. A component breaks down in a given period with probability q. Assume that the component breaks down only at the end of a period. When this occurs, the parallel component takes over, if available, beginning at the next period. Only one serviceman is assigned to service each component in need of repair, and it takes two periods to complete the servicing. Let X_t be a vector consisting of two elements U and V. U represents the number of components operating at the end of the tth period. V takes on the value 1 is the serviceman requires only one additional period to complete a repair, if he is so engaged, and zero otherwise. Thus, the state space consists of the four states (2,0), (1,0), (0,1), and (1,1). For example, the state (1,1) implies that one component is operative and the other component needs an additional period for repair before becoming operative. Denote these four states by 0, 1, 2, 3, respectively. $\{X_t\}$ $(t = 0, 1, \ldots)$ is a Markov chain. [Assume that X_0 is the vector (2,0); that is, $X_0 = 0$] with transition matrix,

$$\mathbf{P} = \begin{bmatrix} 1-q & q & 0 & 0 \\ 0 & 0 & q & 1-q \\ 0 & 1 & 0 & 0 \\ 1-q & q & 0 & 0 \end{bmatrix}.$$

(*a*) What is the probability that there is a waiting line of length 1 (a unit needing service but not being worked on) at the end of a current service period?
(*b*) What are the steady-state probabilities?
(*c*) If it costs \$10,000 per period when the unit is inoperable (both components down) and zero othrewise, what is the (long-run) expected average cost per period?

31 Consider a single-server queueing system, in which customers arrive according to a Poisson input process with parameter λ (see Sec. 9.6), and the service times for the respective calling units are independent and identically distributed random variables. For $n = 1, 2, \ldots$, let X_n denote the number of calling units in the system at the moment t_n when the nth calling unit to be served (over a certain time interval) has finished being served. The sequence of time $\{t_n\}$ corresponding to the moments when successive calling units depart service are called *regeneration points*. Furthermore, $\{X_n\}$, which represents the number of calling units in the system at the corresponding sequence of time $\{t_n\}$, is a Markov chain and is known as an *imbedded Markov chain*. Imbedded Markov chains are useful for studying the properties of continuous time parameter stochastic processes.

Now consider the particular special case where the service time of successive calling units is a fixed constant, say, 10 minutes, and the mean arrival rate is one every 50 minutes. To obtain a *finite* number of states, assume as an approximation that, if there are 4 calling units in the system, the system becomes saturated so that additional arrivals are turned away. Therefore, $\{X_n\}$ is an imbedded Markov chain with states 0, 1, 2, or 3. (Since there are never more than 4 calling units in the system, there can never be more than 3 in the system at a regeneration point.) Since the system is observed at successive departures, X_n can never decrease by more than 1. Furthermore, the probabilities of transitions that result in increases in X_n are obtained directly from the Poisson distribution.

(*a*) Find the one-step transition matrix. (In obtaining the transition probability from state 3 to state 3, use the probability of one or more arrivals rather than just one arrival, and similarly for other transitions to state 3.)
(*b*) Find the steady-state probabilities for the number of calling units in the system at regeneration points.
(*c*) Compute the expected number of calling units in the queueing system at regeneration points, and compare it to the value of L for the single-server model in Sec. 9.7.

9 Queueing Theory

Queueing theory involves the mathematical study of "queues," or waiting lines. The formation of waiting lines is, of course, a common phenomenon which occurs whenever the current demand for a service exceeds the current capacity to provide that service. Decisions regarding the amount of capacity to provide must be made frequently in industry and elsewhere. However, since it is often impossible to accurately predict when units will arrive to seek service and/or how much time will be required to provide that service, these decisions often are difficult ones. Providing too much service would involve excessive costs. On the other hand, not providing enough service capacity would cause the waiting line to become excessively long at times. Excessive waiting also is costly in some sense, whether it be a social cost, the cost of lost customers, the cost of idle employees, or so forth. Therefore the ultimate goal is to achieve an economic balance between the cost of service and the cost associated with waiting for that service. Queueing theory itself does not directly solve this problem; however, it does contribute vital information required for such a decision by predicting such various characteristics of the waiting line as the average waiting time.

Queueing theory provides a large number of alternative mathematical models for describing a waiting-line situation. Mathematical results predicting some of the characteristics of the waiting line often are available for these models. After some general discussion, this chapter presents most of the more elementary models and their basic results. Chapter 10 discusses how the information provided by queueing theory might be used for making decisions.

9.1 PROTOTYPE EXAMPLE

The emergency room of *County Hospital* provides quick medical care for emergency cases brought to the hospital by ambulance or private automobile. At any hour there is always one doctor on duty in the emergency room. However, because of a growing tendency for emergency cases to use these facilities rather than go to a private physician, the hospital has been experiencing a continuing increase in the number of emergency room visits each year. As a result, it has become quite common that patients arriving during peak usage hours (the early evening) have to wait until it is their turn to be treated by the doctor. Therefore a proposal has been made that a second doctor should be assigned to the emergency room during these hours, so that two emergency cases can be treated simultaneously. The hospital's Management Engineer has been assigned to study this question.[1]

The Management Engineer began by gathering the relevant historical data and then projecting these data into the next year. Recognizing that the emergency room is a queueing system, he then applied several alternative queueing theory models to predict the waiting characteristics of the system with one doctor and with two doctors—as you will see in the latter sections of this chapter.

9.2 BASIC STRUCTURE OF QUEUEING MODELS

The Basic Queueing Process

The basic process assumed by most queueing models is the following. "Customers" requiring service are generated over time by an "input source." These customers enter the *queueing system* and join a *queue*. At certain times a member of the queue is selected for service by some rule known as the *service discipline*. The required service is then performed for the customer by the *service mechanism*, after which the customer leaves the queueing system. This process is depicted in Fig. 9.1.

There are many alternative assumptions that can be made about the various elements of the queueing process; these are discussed below.

Input Source (Calling Population)

One characteristic of the input source or calling population is its "size." The size is the total number of customers that might require service from time to time, i.e., the total number of distinct potential customers. It may be assumed to be either *infinite* or *finite*. Since the calculations are far easier for the infinite case, this assumption often is made even when the actual size is some relatively large finite number. The finite case is more difficult analytically because the number of customers in the queueing system affects the number of potential

[1] For one actual case study of this kind, see W. Blaker Bolling, "Queueing Model of a Hospital Emergency Room," *Industrial Engineering*, pp. 26–31, September 1972.

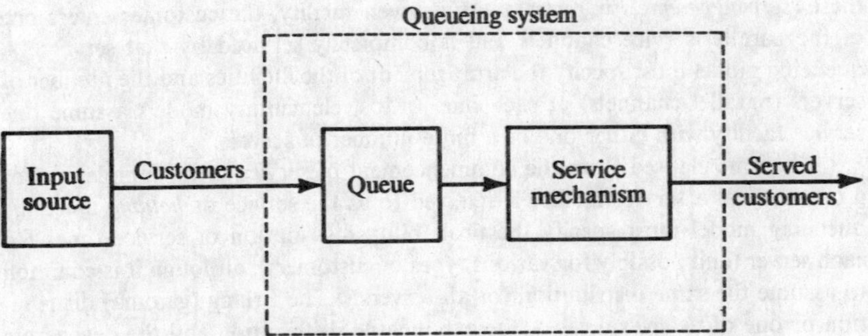

Figure 9.1 The basic queueing process.

customers outside the system at any time. However, the finite assumption must be made if the rate at which the input source generates new customers is significantly affected by the number of customers in the queueing system.

The statistical pattern by which customers are generated over time must also be specified. The common assumption is that they are generated according to a *Poisson process*, i.e., the number of customers generated until any specific time has a Poisson distribution (see Sec. 8.6). This is the case where arrivals to the queueing system occur "randomly" but at a certain average rate. An equivalent assumption is that the probability distribution of the time between consecutive arrivals is an *exponential* distribution (see Sec. 8.7). The time between consecutive arrivals is referred to as the **interarrival time**.

Any unusual assumptions about the behavior of the customers must also be specified. One example is *balking*, where the customer refuses to enter the system and is lost if the queue is too long.

Queue

A queue is characterized by the maximum permissible number of customers that it can contain. Queues are called *infinite* or *finite*, according to whether this number is infinite or finite.

Service Discipline

The service discipline refers to the order in which members of the queue are selected for service. For example, it may be first-come-first-served, random, according to some priority procedure, or so on. First-come-first-served usually is implicitly assumed by queueing models unless stated otherwise.

Service Mechanism

The service mechanism consists of one or more *service facilities*, each of which contains one or more *parallel service channels*, called **servers**. If there is more than one service facility, the customer may receive service from a sequence of these (*service channels in series*). At a given facility, the customer enters one of the parallel service channels and is completely serviced by that server. A queueing model must specify the arrangement of the facilities and the number of servers (parallel channels) at each one. Most elementary models assume one service facility with either one or a finite number of servers.

The time elapsed from the commencement of service to its completion for a customer at a service facility is referred to as the service or *holding time*. A queueing model must specify the probability distribution of service times for each server (and possibly for various types of customers), although it is common to assume the same distribution for all servers. The Erlang (gamma) distribution or one of its special cases, the exponential distribution and the degenerate distribution (constant service time), is frequently selected.

An Elementary Queueing Process

As suggested in the previous sections, queueing theory has studied many different types of waiting-line situations. However, it has concentrated primarily on the following situation: A single waiting line (which may be empty at times) forms in the front of a single service facility, within which are stationed one or more servers. Each customer generated by an input source is serviced by one of the servers, perhaps after some waiting in the queue (waiting line). The queueing system involved is depicted in Fig. 9.2.

Notice that the queueing process in the illustrative example of Sec. 9.1 is of this type. The input source generates customers in the form of emergency cases requiring medical care. The emergency room is the service facility, and the doctors are the servers.

Figure 9.2 An elementary queueing system (each customer is indicated by a *C* and each server by an *S*).

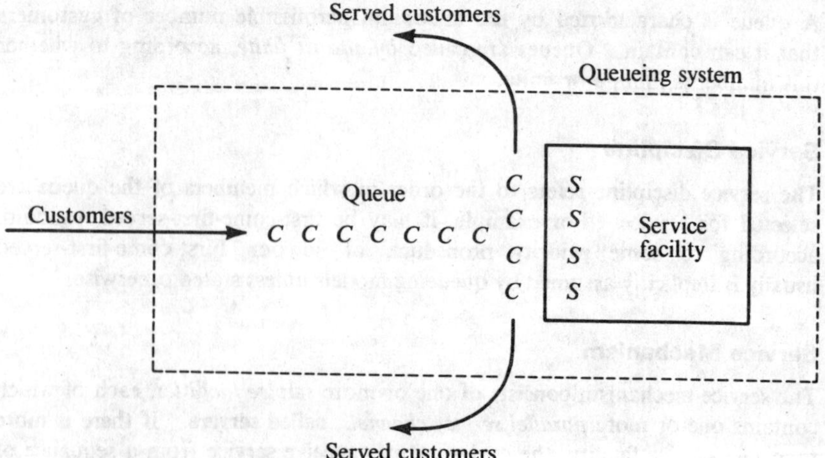

A server need not be a single individual; it may be a group of persons, e.g., a repair crew, who combine forces to perform simultaneously the required service for a customer. Furthermore, servers need not even be people. In many cases a server may be a machine or a piece of equipment, e.g., a forklift truck, which performs a given service on call (although probably with human guidance). By the same token, the customers in the waiting line need not be people. For example, they be items waiting for a certain operation by a given type of machine, or they may be cars waiting in front of a toll booth.

It is not necessary that there actually be a physical waiting line forming in front of a physical structure that constitutes the service facility. That is, the members of the queue may be scattered throughout an area waiting for a server to come to them, e.g., machines waiting to be repaired. The server or group of servers assigned to a given area would constitute the service facility for that area. Queueing theory would still give the average number waiting, the average waiting time, and so on because it is irrelevant whether or not the customers wait together in a group. The only essential requirement for queueing theory to be applicable is that changes in the number of customers waiting for a given service should occur just as though the physical situation described in Fig. 9.2 (or a legitimate counterpart) prevailed.

All the queueing models discussed in Secs. 9.6 to 9.8 are of the elementary type described in this section.

Terminology and Notation

Unless otherwise noted, the following standard terminology and notation will be used henceforth:

State of the system = number of customers in queueing system.

Queue length = number of customers waiting for service = state of system minus number of customers being served.

$N(t)$ = number of customers in queueing system at time $t (t \geq 0)$.

$P_n(t)$ = probability that exactly n customers are in queueing system at time t, given number at time 0.

s = number of servers (parallel service channels) in queueing system.

λ_n = mean arrival rate (expected number of arrivals per unit time) of new customers when n customers are in system.

μ_n = mean service rate for overall system (expected number of customers completing service per unit time) when n customers are in system. *Note*: μ_n represents *combined* rate at which all *busy* servers (those serving customers) achieve service completions.

When λ_n is a constant for all n, this constant is denoted by λ; when the mean service rate *per busy server* is a constant for all $n \geq 1$, this constant is denoted by μ (in this case $\mu_n = s\mu$ when $n \geq s$ so that all s servers are busy). Under these circumstances $1/\lambda$ and $1/\mu$ are the *expected interarrival time* and the *expected service time*, respectively. Also, $\rho = \lambda/s\mu$ is the *utilization factor* for the service facility, i.e., the expected fraction of time the servers are busy because $\lambda/s\mu$ represents the fraction of the system's service capacity ($s\mu$) that is being *utilized* on the average by arriving customers (λ).

Certain notation also is required to describe *steady-state* results. When a queueing system has recently begun operation, the state of the system (number of customers in the system) will be greatly affected by the initial state and the time that has since elapsed. The system is now said to be a *transient* condition. However, after sufficient time has elapsed, the state of the system becomes essentially independent of the initial state and the elapsed time (except under unusual circumstances[1]). The system has now essentially reached a steady-state condition. Queueing theory has tended to focus largely on the steady-state condition, partially because the transient case is more difficult analytically. (Some transient results exist, but they are generally beyond the technical scope of this book.) The following notation assumes that the system is in a *steady-state condition*:

P_n = probability that exactly n customers are in queueing system.

L = expected number of customers in queueing system.

L_q = expected queue length.

W = expected waiting time in system (includes service time).

W_q = expected waiting time in queue (excludes service time).

Relationship between L and W

Assume that λ_n is a constant λ for all n. It has been proven[2] that in a steady-state queueing process,

$$L = \lambda W.$$

Furthermore, the same proof also shows that

$$L_q = \lambda W_q.$$

If the λ_n are not equal, then λ can be replaced in these equations by $\bar{\lambda}$, the *average* arrival rate over the long run. (We shall show later how $\bar{\lambda}$ can be determined for some basic cases.)

[1] When λ and μ are defined, the usual requirement is that $\rho < 1$. Otherwise, the state of the system tends to grow continually larger as time goes on.

[2] John D. C. Little, "A Proof for the Queueing Formula: $L = \lambda W$," *Operations Research*, 9(3):383–387, 1961; Shaler Stidham, Jr., "A Last Word on $L = \lambda W$," *Operations Research*, 22(2):417–421, 1974.

Now assume that the mean service time is a constant, $1/\mu$, for all $n \geq 1$. It then follows that

$$W = W_q + \frac{1}{\mu}.$$

These relationships are extremely important because they enable all four of the fundamental quantities L, W, L_q, and W_q to be immediately determined as soon as one of them is found analytically. This is fortunate because some of these quantities often are much easier to find that others when solving a queueing model from basic principles.

9.3 EXAMPLES OF REAL QUEUEING SYSTEMS

It may appear that our description of queueing systems in the preceding section is relatively abstract and applicable to only rather special practical situations. To the contrary—queueing systems are surprisingly prevalent in a wide variety of contexts. To broaden your horizons on the applicability of queueing theory we shall briefly mention various examples of real queueing systems.

One important class of queueing systems that we all encounter in our daily lives is **commercial service systems**, where customers receive service from commercial organizations. Many of these involve person-to-person service at a fixed location, such as a *barber shop* (the barbers are the servers), *bank teller* service, *checkout stands* at a grocery store, and a *cafeteria line* (service channels in series). However, many others do not, such as *home appliance repairs* (the repairman server travels to the customers), a *vending machine* (so the server is a machine), and a *gas station* (the cars can be viewed as the customers).

Another important class is **transportation service systems**. For some of these systems the vehicles are the customers, such as *cars* waiting at a *toll booth* or *traffic light*, a *truck* or *ship* waiting to be loaded or unloaded by a crew (the server), and *airplanes* waiting to land or take off from a runway (the server). (A specific example of this kind is a *parking lot*, where the cars are the customers and the parking spaces are the servers, but there is no queue because arriving customers go elsewhere to park if the lot is full.) In other cases the vehicles are the servers, such as *taxicabs*, *fire trucks*, and *elevators*.

In recent years queueing theory probably has been applied most to **business-industrial service systems**. These include *materials-handling systems*, where materials-handling units (the servers) move loads (the customers); *maintenance systems*, where maintenance crews (the servers) repair machines (the customers); and *inspection stations*, where quality control inspectors (the servers) inspect items (the customers). *Employee facilities* and a *typing pool* also fit into this category. In addition, *machines* can be viewed as servers whose customers are the jobs being processed. A related example of great importance is a *computer facility*, where the computer is viewed as the server.

There is now growing recognition that queueing theory also is applicable to **social service systems**. For example, a *judicial system* is a queueing network, where the courts are service facilities, the judges (or panels of judges) are the servers, and the cases waiting to be tried are the customers. A *legislative system* is a similar queueing network, where the customers now are the congressional bills waiting to be processed. Various *health-care systems* also are queueing systems. You already have seen one example in Sec. 9.1 (a hospital emergency room), but you can also view *ambulances*, *x-ray machines*, and *hospital beds* as servers in their own queueing systems. Similarly, families waiting for low- and moderate-income housing, or other social services, can be viewed as customers in a queueing system.

Although these are four broad classes of queueing systems, they still do not exhaust the list. In fact, queueing theory first began early in this century with applications to *telephone engineering*, and this still remains an important area of application. Furthermore, we all have our own *personal queues*—homework assignments, books to be read, and so forth. However, these examples are sufficient to suggest that queueing systems do indeed pervade various areas of society.

9.4 THE ROLE OF THE EXPONENTIAL DISTRIBUTION

The operating characteristics of queueing systems are largely determined by two statistical properties, namely, the probability distribution of *interarrival times* (see input source in Sec. 9.2) and the probability distribution of *service times* (see service mechanism in Sec. 9.2). For real queueing systems, these distributions can take on almost any form. (The only restriction is that negative values can not occur.) However, to formulate a queueing-theory *model* as a representation of the real system it is necessary to specify the assumed form of each of these distributions. To be useful, the assumed form should be *sufficiently realistic*, so that the model provides *reasonable predictions* while, at the same time, being *sufficiently simple*, so that the model is *mathematically tractable*. On these bases, the most important probability distribution is queueing theory is the *exponential distribution*.

Suppose that a random variable T represents either *interarrival* or *service times*. (We shall refer to the occurrences marking the end of these times—arrivals or service completions—as *incidents*.) Recall (see the exponential distribution in Sec. 8.7) that T is said to have an *exponential distribution with parameter* α† if its probability density function is

$$f_T(t) = \begin{cases} \alpha e^{-\alpha t}, & \text{for } t \geq 0 \\ 0, & \text{for } t > 0, \end{cases}$$

as shown in Fig. 8.10. In this case, the cumulative probabilities are

$$\begin{aligned} P\{T \leq t\} &= 1 - e^{-\alpha t}, \\ P\{T > t\} &= e^{-\alpha t}, \end{aligned} \qquad (t \geq 0)$$

† The parameter α is the *reciprocal* of the parameter θ used in the exponential distribution in Sec. 8.7 to be consistent with conventional queueing-theory notation.

and the expected value and variance of T are

$$E(T) = \frac{1}{\alpha},$$

$$\text{var}(T) = \frac{1}{\alpha^2}.$$

What are the implications of assuming that T has an exponential distribution for a queueing model? To explore this, let us examine five key properties of the exponential distribution.

PROPERTY 1 $f_T(t)$ is a strictly *decreasing* function of t $(t \geq 0)$.

One consequence of property 1 is that

$$P\{0 \leq T \leq \Delta t\} > P\{t \leq T \leq t + \Delta t\}$$

for any strictly positive values of Δt and t. [This follows from the fact that these probabilities are the area under the $f_T(t)$ curve over the indicated interval of length Δt, and the average height of the curve is less for the second probability than for the first.] Therefore it is not only possible but relatively likely that T will take on a small value near zero. In fact,

$$P\left\{0 \leq T \leq \frac{1}{2}\frac{1}{\alpha}\right\} = 0.393,$$

whereas

$$P\left\{\frac{1}{2}\frac{1}{\alpha} \leq T \leq \frac{3}{2}\frac{1}{\alpha}\right\} = 0.383,$$

so that the value T takes on is more likely to be "small" [i.e., less than half of $E(T)$] than "near" its expected value [i.e., no further away than half of $E(T)$].

Is this really a reasonable propery for T in a queueing model? If T represents *service times*, the answer depends upon the general nature of the service involved, as discussed below.

If the service required is essentially identical for each customer, with the server always performing the same sequence of service operations, then the actual service times would tend to be near the expected service time. Small deviations from the mean may occur, but usually only because of minor variations in the efficiency of the server. A small service time far below the mean would be essentially impossible because a certain minimum amount of time is needed to perform the required service operations even when the server is working at top speed. The exponential distribution clearly would not provide a close approximation to the service-time distribution for this type of situation.

On the other hand, consider the type of situation where the specific tasks required of the server differ among the customers. The broad nature of the service may be the same, but the specific type and amount of service differ. For example, this would be the case in the *County Hospital* emergency room problem discussed in Sec. 9.1. The doctors encounter a wide variety of medical problems. In most cases they can provide the required treatment rather quickly, but an occasional patient requires extensive care. Similarly, bank tellers and grocery store checkout clerks are other servers of this general type, where the required service is often brief but must occasionally be extensive. An exponential service-time distribution would seem quite plausible for this type of service situation.

If T represents *interarrival times,* property 1 rules out situations where potential customers approaching the queueing system tend to postpone their entry if they see another customer entering ahead of them. On the other hand, it is entirely consistent with the common phenomenon of arrivals occurring "randomly," described by subsequent properties.

PROPERTY 2 Lack of memory.

This property can be stated mathematically as

$$P\{T > t + \Delta t \mid T > \Delta t\} = P\{T > t\}$$

for any positive quantities t and Δt. In other words, the probability distribution of the *remaining* time until the incident (arrival or service completion) occurs always is the same, regardless of how much time (Δt) already has passed. In effect, the process "forgets" its history. (This surprising phenomenon occurs with the exponential distribution because

$$\begin{aligned} P\{T > t + \Delta t \mid T > \Delta t\} &= \frac{P\{T > \Delta t, T > t + \Delta t\}}{P\{T > \Delta t\}} \\ &= \frac{P\{T > t + \Delta t\}}{P\{T > \Delta t\}} \\ &= \frac{e^{-\alpha(t+\Delta t)}}{e^{-\alpha \Delta t}} \\ &= e^{-\alpha t}.) \end{aligned}$$

For *interarrival times,* this property describes the common situation where the time until the next arrival is completely uninfluenced by when the last arrival occurred. For *service times,* the property is more difficult to interpret. We should not expect it to hold in a situation where the server must perform the same fixed sequence of operations for each customer because then a long elapsed service should imply that probably little remains to be done. On the other hand, in the type of situation where the required service operations differ among the customers, the mathematical statement of the property may be quite realistic. For this case, if considerable service has already elapsed for a customer, the only implication may be that this particular customer requires more extensive service than most.

PROPERTY 3 The *minimum* of several independent exponential random variables has an exponential distribution.

To state this property mathematically, let $T_1, T_2, \ldots, T_n$ be *independent* exponential random variables with parameters $\alpha_1, \alpha_2, \ldots, \alpha_n$, respectively. Also let U be the random variable that takes on the value equal to the *minimum* of the values actually taken on by $T_1, T_2, \ldots, T_n$; that is,

$$U = \min\{T_1, T_2, \ldots, T_n\}.$$

Thus, if T_i represents the time until a particular kind of incident will occur, then U represents the time until the *first* of the n different incidents will occur. Now note that for any $t \geq 0$,

$$\begin{aligned} P\{U > t\} &= P\{T_1 > t, T_2 > t, \ldots, T_n > t\} \\ &= P\{T_1 > t\}P\{T_2 > t\} \cdots P\{T_n > t\} \\ &= e^{-\alpha_1 t}e^{-\alpha_2 t} \cdots e^{-\alpha_n t} \\ &= \exp\left\{-\sum_{i=1}^{n} \alpha_i t\right\}, \end{aligned}$$

so that U indeed has an exponential distribution with parameter

$$\alpha = \sum_{i=1}^{n} \alpha_i .$$

This property has some implications for *interarrival times* in queueing models. In particular, suppose that there are several (n) *different* types of customers, but the interarrival times for *each* type (type i) have an exponential distribution with parameter $\alpha_i (i = 1,2, \ldots, n)$. By property 2, the *remaining* time from any specified instant until the next arrival of a customer of type i would have this same distribution. Therefore, let T_i be this remaining time measured from the instant a customer of *any* type arrives. Property 3 then tells us that U, the interarrival times for the queueing system as a whole, has an exponential distribution with parameter α defined by the above equation. As a result, you can choose to ignore the distinction between customers and still have exponential interarrival times for the queueing model.

However, the implications are even more important for *service times* in queueing models having more than one server. For example, consider the situation where all the servers have the same exponential service-time distribution with parameter μ. For this case let n be the number of servers *currently* providing service, and let T_i be the *remaining* service time for server i ($i = 1,2, \ldots, n$), which also has an exponential distribution with parameter $\alpha_i = \mu$. It then follows that U, the time until the *next* service completion from any of these servers, has an exponential distribution with parameter $\alpha = n\mu$. In effect, the queueing system *currently* would be performing just like a *single*-server system, where service times have an exponential distribution with parameter $n\mu$. We shall make frequent use of this implication for analyzing multiple-server models later in the chapter.

PROPERTY 4 Relationship to the Poisson distribution.

Suppose that the *time* between consecutive occurrences of some particular kind of incident (e.g., arrivals, or service completions by a continuously busy server) has an *exponential distribution* with parameter α. Property 4 then has to do with the resulting implication about the probability distribution of the *number* of times this kind of incident occurs over a specified length of time. In particular, let $X(t)$ be the number of occurrences by time t $(t > 0)$, where time 0 designates the instant at which the count begins. The implication is that

$$P\{X(t) = n\} = \frac{(\alpha t)^n e^{-\alpha t}}{n!}, \quad \text{for } n = 0, 1, 2, \ldots;$$

that is, $X(t)$ has a *Poisson distribution* (see Sec. 8.6) with parameter αt. For example, with $n = 0$,

$$P\{X(t) - 0\} = e^{-\alpha t},$$

which is just the probability from the exponential distribution that the *first* incident occurs after time t. The mean of this Poisson distribution is

$$E\{X(t)\} = \alpha t,$$

so that the expected number of incidents *per unit time* is α. Thus α is said to be the mean rate at which the incidents occur. When the incidents are counted on a continuing basis, the counting process $\{X(t); t > 0\}$ is said to be a *Poisson process* with parameter α (the mean rate).

This property provides useful information about *service completions* when service times have an exponential distribution with parameter μ. This is done by defining $X(t)$ as the number of service completions achieved by a *continuously busy* server in elapsed time t, where $\alpha = \mu$. For *multiple*-server queueing models, $X(t)$ can also be defined as the number of service completions achieved by n continuously busy servers in elapsed time t, where $\alpha = n\mu$.

The property is particularly useful for describing the probabilistic behavior of *arrivals* when interarrival times have an exponential distribution with parameter λ. In this case $X(t)$ would be the *number* of arrivals in elapsed time t, where $\alpha = \lambda$ is the *mean arrival rate*. Therefore, arrivals occur according to a *Poisson input process*. Such queueing models also are described as assuming a *Poisson input*.

Arrivals sometimes are said to occur *randomly*, meaning that they occur in accord with a Poisson input process. One intuitive interpretation of this phenomenon is that every time period of fixed length has the *same* chance of having an arrival regardless of when the preceding arrival occurred, as suggested by the following property.

PROPERTY 5 For all positive values of t, $P\{T \leq t + \Delta t \mid T > t\} \approx \alpha\, \Delta t$, for small Δt.

For a random variable T that has an exponential distribution with parameter α, property 2 implies that

$$
\begin{aligned}
P\{T \leq t + \Delta t \mid T > t\} &= P\{T \leq \Delta t\} \\
&= 1 - e^{-\alpha \Delta t}
\end{aligned}
$$

for any positive quantities t and Δt. Therefore, since the series expansion of e^x for any exponent x is

$$
e^x = 1 + x + \sum_{n=2}^{\infty} \frac{x^n}{n!},
$$

it follows that

$$
\begin{aligned}
P\{T \leq t + \Delta t \mid T > t\} &= 1 - 1 + \alpha \,\Delta t - \sum_{n=2}^{\infty} \frac{(-\alpha \,\Delta t)^n}{n!} \\
&\approx \alpha \,\Delta t, \text{ for small } \Delta t,\dagger
\end{aligned}
$$

because the summation terms become relatively negligible for sufficiently small values of $\alpha \,\Delta t$. Note that the value of t actually does not affect this probability at all.

As indicated previously, T might represent either *interarrival* or *service times* in queueing models. Therefore this property provides a convenient approximation of the probability that the incident of interest (arrival or service completion) occurs in the next small interval (Δt) of time. (Analysis based on this approximation also can be made exact by taking appropriate limits as $\Delta t \to 0$.) The property also shows that this probability is essentially proportional to Δt for small values of Δt.

9.5 THE BIRTH-AND-DEATH PROCESS

Most elementary queueing models assume that the inputs (arriving customers) and outputs (leaving customers) of the queueing system occur according to the *birth-and-death process.* This important process in probability theory has application in various areas. However, in the context of queueing theory, the term **birth** refers to the *arrival* of a new customer into the queueing system, and **death** refers to the *departure* of a served customer. The *state* of the system at time t ($t \geq 0$) is given by $N(t)$ (defined in terminology and notation in Sec. 9.2). Thus the birth-and-death process describes *probabilistically* how $N(t)$ changes as t increases. Broadly speaking, it says that *individual* births and deaths occur *randomly*, where their mean occurrence rates depend only upon the current

† More precisely,

$$
\lim_{\Delta t \to 0} \frac{P\{T \leq t + \Delta t \mid T > t\}}{\Delta t} = \alpha.
$$

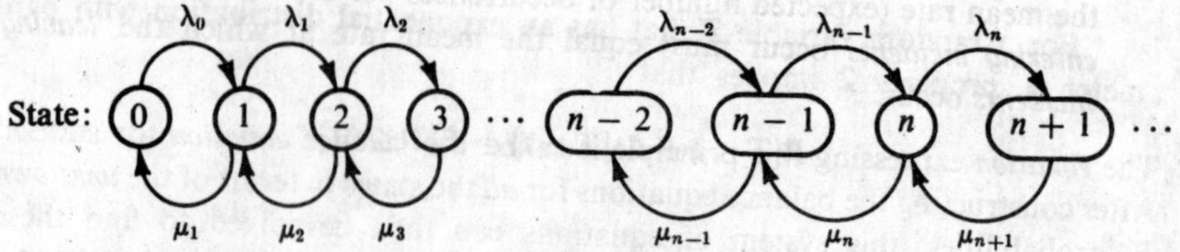

Figure 9.3 Rate diagram for the birth-and-death process.

state of the system. More precisely, the assumptions of the birth-and-death process are the following:

ASSUMPTION 1 Given $N(t) = n$, the current probability distribution of the *remaining* time until the next *birth* (arrival) is *exponential* with parameter λ_n $(n = 0,1,2,\ldots)$.

ASSUMPTION 2 Given $N(t) = n$, the current probability distribution of the *remaining* time until the next *death* (service completion) is *exponential* with parameter μ_n $(n = 1,2,\ldots)$.

ASSUMPTION 3 Only *one* birth or death can occur at a time.

Since property 4 for the exponential distribution (see Sec. 9.4) implies that the λ_n and μ_n are *mean rates*, we can summarize these assumptions by the *rate diagram* shown in Fig. 9.3. The arrows in this diagram show the only possible *transitions* in the state of the system (as specified by assumption 3), and the entry for each arrow gives the mean rate for that transition (as specified by assumptions 1 and 2) when the system is in the state at the base of the arrow.

Except for a few special cases, analysis of the birth-and-death process is very difficult when the system is in a *transient* condition. Some results about the probability distribution of $N(t)$† have been obtained, but they are too complicated to be of much practical use. On the other hand, it is relatively straightforward to derive this distribution *after* the system has reached a *steady-state* condition (assuming that this condition can be reached). This can be done directly from the rate diagram, as outlined below.

Consider any particular state of the system n $(n = 0,1,2,\ldots)$. Suppose that we were to start counting the number of times that the process *enters* this state and the number of times it *leaves* this state. Since the two types of incidents (entering and leaving) must alternate, these two numbers must always be either *equal* or differing by just 1. This possible difference of 1 would *eventually* cause only a *negligible* difference in the *average rates* (total number of occurrences per unit time) at which these two types of incidents have occurred (that is, $1/t \to 0$ as $t \to \infty$). Therefore these two rates *must* be *equal* in the long run. This yields the following key principle:

† S. Karlin and J. McGregor, "Many Server Queueing Processes with Poisson Input and Exponential Service Times," *Pacific Journal of Mathematics*, **8**: 87–118, 1958.

RATE IN = RATE OUT PRINCIPLE For any state of the system n ($n = 0,1,2,\ldots$), the mean rate (expected number of occurrences per unit time) at which the *entering incidents* occur must equal the mean rate at which the *leaving incidents* occur.

The *equation* expressing this principle is called the *balance equation* for state n. After constructing the balance equations for *all* the states in terms of the *unknown* P_n probabilities, this system of equations can then be solved to find these probabilities.

To illustrate a balance equation, consider state 0. The process enters this state *only* from state 1. Thus the steady-state probability of being in state 1 (P_1) represents the proportion of time that it would be *possible* for the process to enter state 0. *Given* that the process is in state 1, the mean rate of entering state 0 is μ_1. (In other words, for each cumulative unit of time that the process spends in state 1, the expected number of times that it would leave state 1 to enter state 0 is μ_1.) From any *other* state, this mean rate is 0. Therefore the overall mean rate at which the process leaves its current state to enter state 0 (the *mean occurrence rate* of the entering incidents) is

$$\mu_1 P_1 + 0(1 - P_1) = \mu_1 P_1.$$

By the same reasoning, the mean occurrence rate of the leaving incidents must be $\lambda_0 P_0$, so the balance equation for state 0 is

$$\mu_1 P_1 = \lambda_0 P_0.$$

For every other state there are *two* possible transitions both into and out of the state. Therefore each side of the balance equations for these states represents the *sum* of the mean rates for the two transitions involved. Otherwise, the reasoning is just the same as for state 0. These balance equations are summarized in Table 9.1.

Table 9.1 Balance Equations for Birth-and-Death Process

State	*Rate in = rate out*
0	$\mu_1 P_1 = \lambda_0 P_0$
1	$\lambda_0 P_0 + \mu_2 P_2 = (\lambda_1 + \mu_1) P_1$
2	$\lambda_1 P_1 + \mu_3 P_3 = (\lambda_2 + \mu_2) P_2$
$\vdots$	$\vdots$
$n-1$	$\lambda_{n-2} P_{n-2} + \mu_n P_n = (\lambda_{n-1} + \mu_{n-1}) P_{n-1}$
n	$\lambda_{n-1} P_{n-1} + \mu_{n+1} P_{n+1} = (\lambda_n + \mu_n) P_n$
$\vdots$	$\vdots$

Notice that the first balance equation contains two variables for which to solve (P_0 and P_1); the first two equations contain three variables (P_0, P_1, and P_2) and so on, so that there always is one "extra" variable. Therefore the procedure in solving these equations is to solve in terms of one of the variables, the most convenient one being P_0. Thus the first equation is used to solve for P_1 in terms of P_0, this result and the second equation is then used to solve for P_2 in terms of P_0, and so forth. At the end, the requirement that the sum of all the probabilities must equal 1 can be used to evaluate P_0.

Applying this procedure yields the following results:

State

$$
\begin{aligned}
0 &: P_1 = \frac{\lambda_0}{\mu_1} P_0 \\
1 &: P_2 = \frac{\lambda_1}{\mu_2} P_1 + \frac{1}{\mu_2}(\mu_1 P_1 - \lambda_0 P_0) = \frac{\lambda_1}{\mu_2} P_1 = \frac{\lambda_1 \lambda_0}{\mu_2 \mu_1} P_0 \\
2 &: P_3 = \frac{\lambda_2}{\mu_3} P_2 + \frac{1}{\mu_3}(\mu_2 P_2 - \lambda_1 P_1) = \frac{\lambda_2}{\mu_3} P_2 = \frac{\lambda_2 \lambda_1 \lambda_0}{\mu_3 \mu_2 \mu_1} P_0 \\
&\ \vdots \\
n-1 &: P_n = \frac{\lambda_{n-1}}{\mu_n} P_{n-1} + \frac{1}{\mu_n}(\mu_{n-1} P_{n-1} - \lambda_{n-2} P_{n-2}) = \frac{\lambda_{n-1}}{\mu_n} P_{n-1} = \frac{\lambda_{n-1}\lambda_{n-2} \cdots \lambda_0}{\mu_n \mu_{n-1} \cdots \mu_1} P_0 \\
n &: P_{n+1} = \frac{\lambda_n}{\mu_{n+1}} P_n + \frac{1}{\mu_{n+1}}(\mu_n P_n - \lambda_{n-1} P_{n-1}) = \frac{\lambda_n}{\mu_{n+1}} P_n = \frac{\lambda_n \lambda_{n-1} \cdots \lambda_0}{\mu_{n+1} \mu_n \cdots \mu_1} P_0 \\
&\ \vdots
\end{aligned}
$$

To simplify notation, let

$$C_n = \frac{\lambda_{n-1} \lambda_{n-2} \cdots \lambda_0}{\mu_n \mu_{n-1} \cdots \mu_1}, \text{ for } n = 1, 2, \ldots .$$

Thus the steady-state probabilities are

$$P_n = C_n P_0, \text{ for } n = 1, 2, \ldots .$$

The requirement that

$$\sum_{n=0}^{\infty} P_n = 1$$

implies that

$$\left[1 + \sum_{n=1}^{\infty} C_n\right] P_0 = 1,$$

so that

$$P_0 = \frac{1}{1 + \sum_{n=1}^{\infty} C_n}.$$

Given this information,

$$L = \sum_{n=0}^{\infty} n P_n .$$

Also, since the number of servers s represents the number of customers that can be served (and so removed from the queue) simultaneously,

$$L_q = \sum_{n=s}^{\infty} (n-s)P_n.$$

Furthermore, the relationships given in Sec. 9.2 yield

$$W = \frac{L}{\bar{\lambda}}, \; W_q = \frac{L_q}{\bar{\lambda}},$$

where $\bar{\lambda}$ is the *average* arrival rate over the long run. Since λ_n is the mean arrival rate while the system is in state n ($n = 0,1,2,\ldots$), and P_n is the proportion of time that the system is in this state,

$$\bar{\lambda} = \sum_{n=0}^{\infty} \lambda_n P_n.$$

Several of the expressions given above involve summations with an infinite number of terms. Fortunately, these summations have analytic solutions for a number of interesting special cases,[1] as seen in the next section. Otherwise, they can be approximated by summing a finite number of terms on an electronic computer.

These steady-state results have been derived under the assumption that the λ_n and μ_n parameters have values such that the process actually can *reach* a steady-state condition. This assumption *always* holds if $\lambda_n = 0$ for some value of n, so that only a finite number of states (those less than this n) are possible. It also *always* holds when λ and μ are defined (see terminology and notation in Sec. 9.2) and $\rho = \lambda/s\mu < 1$. It does *not* hold if $\sum_{n=1}^{\infty} C_n = \infty$.

9.6 QUEUEING MODELS BASED ON THE BIRTH-AND-DEATH PROCESS

Since each of the mean rates $\lambda_0, \lambda_1, \ldots$ and $\mu_1, \mu_2, \ldots$ for the birth-and-death process can be assigned any nonnegative value, this provides great flexibility in modeling a queueing system. Probably the most widely used models in queueing theory are based directly upon this process. Because of assumptions 1 and 2 (and property 4 for the exponential distribution), these models are said to have a **Poisson input** and **exponential service times**. The models differ only in their assumptions about how the λ_n and the μ_n change with n. We present four of these models in this section for four important types of queueing systems.

[1] These solutions are based on the following known results for the sum of any geometric series:

$$\sum_{n=0}^{N} x^n = \frac{1-x^{N+1}}{1-x}, \text{ for any } x,$$

$$\sum_{n=0}^{\infty} x^n = \frac{1}{1-x}, \text{ if } |x| < 1.$$

The Basic Model (Constant Arrival Rate and Service Rate)

It is quite common for a queueing system's *mean arrival rate* and *mean service rate per busy server* to be essentially constant (λ and μ, respectively) regardless of the state of the system. Therefore the basic model makes this assumption. When the system has just a *single server* ($s = 1$), this implies that the parameters for the birth-and-death process are $\lambda_n = \lambda\ (n = 0,1,2,\ldots)$ and $\mu_n = \mu\ (n = 1,2,\ldots)$. The resulting *rate diagram* is shown in Fig. 9.4*a*.

However, when the system has *multiple servers* ($s > 1$), the μ_n can not be expressed this simply. Keep in mind that μ_n represents the mean service rate for the *overall* queueing system (i.e., the mean rate at which service completions occur, so that customers leave the system) when there are n customers currently in the system. As mentioned for property 4 of the exponential distribution (see Sec. 9.4), when the mean service rate per busy server is μ, the overall mean service rate for n busy servers must be $n\mu$. Therefore $\mu_n = n\mu$ when $n \leq s$, whereas $\mu_n = s\mu$ when $n \geq s\mu$ so that all s servers are busy. The rate diagram for this case is shown in Fig. 9.4*b*.

When the maximum mean service rate ($s\mu$) exceeds the mean arrival rate (λ), that is, when

$$\rho = \frac{\lambda}{s\mu} < 1,$$

a queueing system fitting this model will eventually reach a steady-state condition. In this situation the steady-state results derived in Sec. 9.5 for the general birth-and-death process are directly applicable. However, these

Figure 9.4 Rate diagrams for the basic model.

(*a*) *Single-server case* ($s = 1$) $\lambda_n = \lambda$, for $n = 0, 1, 2, \ldots$
$\mu_n = \mu$, for $n = 1, 2, \ldots$

λ λ λ λ λ λ

State: 0 1 2 3 $\cdots$ $n-2$ $n-1$ n $n+1$ $\cdots$

μ μ μ μ μ μ

(*b*) *Multiple-server case* ($s > 1$) $\lambda_n = \lambda$, for $n = 0, 1, 2, \ldots$

$$\mu_n = \begin{cases} n\mu, & \text{for } n = 1, 2, \ldots, s \\ s\mu, & \text{for } n = s, s+1, \ldots \end{cases}$$

λ λ λ λ λ λ

State: 0 1 2 3 $\cdots$ $s-2$ $s-1$ s $s+1$ $\cdots$

μ 2μ 3μ $(s-1)\mu$ $s\mu$ $s\mu$

results simplify considerably for this model and yield closed form expressions for the P_n, L, L_q, and so forth, as shown below.

RESULTS FOR THE SINGLE-SERVER CASE ($s = 1$) For $s = 1$, the C_n factors for the birth-and-death process reduce to

$$C_n = \left(\frac{\lambda}{\mu}\right)^n = \rho^n, \text{ for } n = 1, 2, \ldots .$$

Therefore

$$P_n = \rho^n P_0, \qquad \text{for } n = 1, 2, \ldots,$$

where

$$\begin{aligned} P_0 &= \frac{1}{1 + \sum_{n=1}^{\infty} \rho^n} \\ &= \left(\sum_{n=0}^{\infty} \rho^n\right)^{-1} \\ &= \left(\frac{1}{1-\rho}\right)^{-1} \\ &= 1 - \rho. \end{aligned}$$

Thus

$$P_n = (1 - \rho)\rho^n, \text{ for } n = 0, 1, 2, \ldots .$$

Consequently,

$$\begin{aligned} L &= \sum_{n=0}^{\infty} n(1-\rho)\rho^n \\ &= (1-\rho)\rho \sum_{n=0}^{\infty} \frac{d}{d\rho}(\rho^n) \\ &= (1-\rho)\rho \frac{d}{d\rho}\left(\sum_{n=0}^{\infty} \rho^n\right) \\ &= (1-\rho)\rho \frac{d}{d\rho}\left(\frac{1}{1-\rho}\right) \\ &= \frac{\rho}{1-\rho} = \frac{\lambda}{\mu - \lambda}. \end{aligned}$$

Similarly,

$$\begin{aligned} L_q &= \sum_{n=1}^{\infty} (n-1)P_n \\ &= L - 1(1 - P_0) \\ &= \frac{\lambda^2}{\mu(\mu - \lambda)}. \end{aligned}$$

When $\lambda \geq \mu$, so that the mean arrival rate exceeds the mean service rate, the above solution "blows up" (since the summation for computing P_0 diverges). For this case the queue would "explode" and grow without bound.

Assuming again that $\lambda < \mu$, it is now possible to derive the probability distribution of waiting time. In particular, let the random variable $\mathscr{W}$ be the waiting time in the system (*including* service) for a random arrival when the service discipline is first-come-first-served. If this arrival finds n customers already in the system, he will have to wait through $(n + 1)$ exponential service times. (For the customer currently being served, recall the lack of memory property for the exponential distribution discussed in Sec. 9.4.) Therefore, let $T_1, T_2, \ldots$ be independent service time random variables having an exponential distribution with parameter μ, and let

$$S_{n+1} = T_1 + T_2 + \cdots + T_{n+1}, \text{ for } n = 0, 1, 2, \ldots,$$

so that S_{n+1} represents the *conditional* waiting time given n customers already in the system. As discussed in Sec. 8.7, S_{n+1} is known to have a *gamma distribution*[1] with the cumulative distribution function given there. Since the probability that the random arrival will find n customers in the system is P_n, it follows that

$$P\{\mathscr{W} > t\} = \sum_{n=0}^{\infty} P_n P\{S_{n+1} > t\},$$

which reduces after considerable algebraic manipulation to

$$P\{\mathscr{W} > t\} = e^{-\mu(1-\rho)t}, \text{ for } t \geq 0.$$

The surprising conclusion is that $\mathscr{W}$ has an *exponential* distribution with parameter $\mu(1 - \rho)$. Therefore

$$W = E(\mathscr{W}) = \frac{1}{\mu(1 - \rho)} = \frac{\mu}{\mu - \lambda}.$$

These results *include* service time in the waiting time. In some contexts (e.g., the County Hospital emergency room problem), the more relevant waiting time is just until service begins. Thus, let the random variable $\mathscr{W}_q$ be the waiting time in the queue (*excluding* service time) for a random arrival when the service discipline is first-come-first-served. If this arrival finds *no* customers already in the system, he begins being served immediately, so

$$P\{\mathscr{W}_q = 0\} = P_0 = 1 - \rho.$$

[1] When the distribution arises in this way, it also is commonly referred to in queueing theory as the *Erlang distribution*. The relevance of this distribution in queueing theory is discussed further in Sec. 9.7.

If he finds $n > 0$ customers already there instead, then he has to wait through n exponential service times until his own service begins, so

$$\begin{aligned} P\{\mathscr{W}_q > t\} &= \sum_{n=1}^{\infty} P_n P\{S_n > t\} \\ &= \sum_{n=1}^{\infty} (1-\rho)\rho^n P\{S_n > t\} \\ &= \rho \sum_{n=0}^{\infty} P_n P\{S_{n+1} > t\} \\ &= \rho P\{\mathscr{W} > t\} \\ &= \rho e^{-\mu(1-\rho)t}, \quad \text{for } t \geq 0. \end{aligned}$$

By deriving the mean of this distribution [or applying either $L_q = \lambda W_q$ or $W_q = W - (1/\mu)$],

$$W_q = E(\mathscr{W}_q) = \frac{\lambda}{\mu(\mu - \lambda)}.$$

Results for the Multiple-server case ($s > 1$) When $s > 1$. the C_n factors become

$$C_n = \frac{(\lambda/\mu)^n}{n!}, \qquad \text{for } n = 1, 2, \ldots, s,$$

and

$$C_n = \frac{(\lambda/\mu)^s}{s!}\left(\frac{\lambda}{s\mu}\right)^{n-s} = \frac{(\lambda/\mu)^n}{s!s^{n-s}}, \text{ for } n = s, s+1, \ldots.$$

Consequently, if $\lambda < s\mu$, then

$$\begin{aligned} P_0 &= 1\Bigg/\left[\sum_{n=0}^{s-1} \frac{(\lambda/\mu)^n}{n!} + \frac{(\lambda/\mu)^s}{s!} \sum_{n=s}^{\infty} \left(\frac{\lambda}{s\mu}\right)^{n-s}\right] \\ &= 1\Bigg/\left[\sum_{n=0}^{s-1} \frac{(\lambda/\mu)^n}{n!} + \frac{(\lambda/\mu)^s}{s!} \frac{1}{1-(\lambda/s\mu)}\right], \end{aligned}$$

and

$$P_n = \begin{cases} \dfrac{(\lambda/\mu)^n}{n!} P_0, & \text{if } 0 \leq n \leq s \\[2ex] \dfrac{(\lambda/\mu)^n}{s!s^{n-s}} P_0, & \text{if } n \geq s. \end{cases}$$

Using the notation $\rho = \lambda/\mu s$,

$$\begin{aligned}
L_q &= \sum_{n=s}^{\infty}(n-s)P_n \\
&= \sum_{j=0}^{\infty} jP_{s+j} \\
&= \sum_{j=0}^{\infty} j\frac{(\lambda/\mu)^s}{s!}\rho^j P_0 \\
&= P_0\frac{(\lambda/\mu)^s}{s!}\rho\sum_{j=0}^{\infty}\frac{d}{d\rho}(\rho^j) \\
&= P_0\frac{(\lambda/\mu)^s}{s!}\rho\frac{d}{d\rho}\left(\sum_{j=0}^{\infty}\rho^j\right) \\
&= P_0\frac{(\lambda/\mu)^s}{s!}\rho\frac{d}{d\rho}\left(\frac{1}{1-\rho}\right) \\
&= \frac{P_0(\lambda/\mu)^s\rho}{s!(1-\rho)^2}.
\end{aligned}$$

$$W_q = \frac{L_q}{\lambda};$$

$$W = W_q + \frac{1}{\mu};$$

$$L = \lambda\left(W_q + \frac{1}{\mu}\right) = L_q + \frac{\lambda}{\mu}.$$

Figures 9.5 and 9.6 show how P_0 and L change with ρ for various values of s.

The single-server method for finding the probability distribution of waiting times also can be extended to the multiple-server case. This yields[1] (for $t \geq 0$)

$$P\{\mathcal{W} > t\} = e^{-\mu t}\left[1 + \frac{P_0(\lambda/\mu)^s}{s!(1-\rho)}\left(\frac{1-e^{-\mu t(s-1-\lambda/\mu)}}{s-1-\lambda/\mu}\right)\right]$$

and

$$P\{\mathcal{W}_q > t\} = [1 - \text{[illegible]} {}^{-s\mu(1-\rho)t},$$

where

$$P\{\mathcal{W}_q = 0\} = \sum_{n=0}^{s-1} P_n.$$

[1] When $s - 1 - \lambda/\mu = 0$, $(1 - e^{-\mu t(s-1-\lambda/\mu)})/(s - 1 - \lambda/\mu)$ should be replaced by μt.

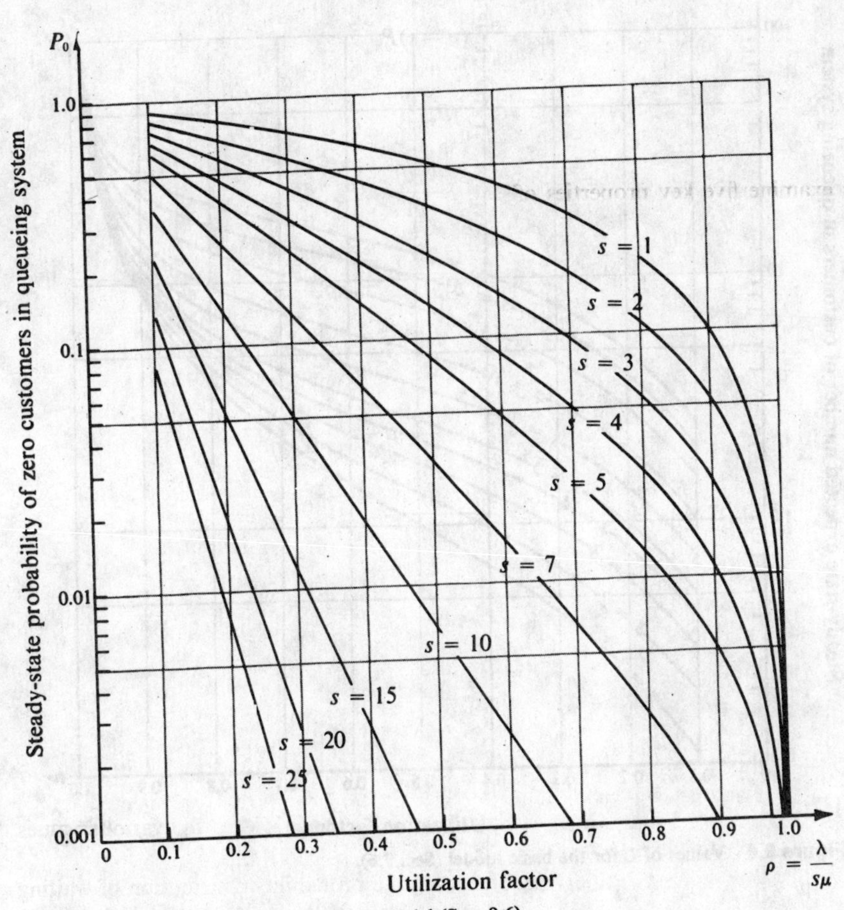

Figure 9.5 Values of P_0 for the basic model (Sec. 9.6).

If $\lambda \geq s\mu$, so that the mean arrival rate exceeds the maximum mean service rate, the queue grows without bound, so the above steady-state solutions are not applicable.

Example For the *County Hospital* emergency room problem (see Sec. 9.1), the Management Engineer has concluded that the emergency cases arrive pretty much at random (a *Poisson input process*) and that the time spent by a doctor treating the cases approximately follows an *exponential distribution*. Therefore he has chosen this basic model for a preliminary study of this queueing system.

By projecting the available data for the early evening shift into next year, it appears that patients will arrive at an *average* rate of one every half-hour.

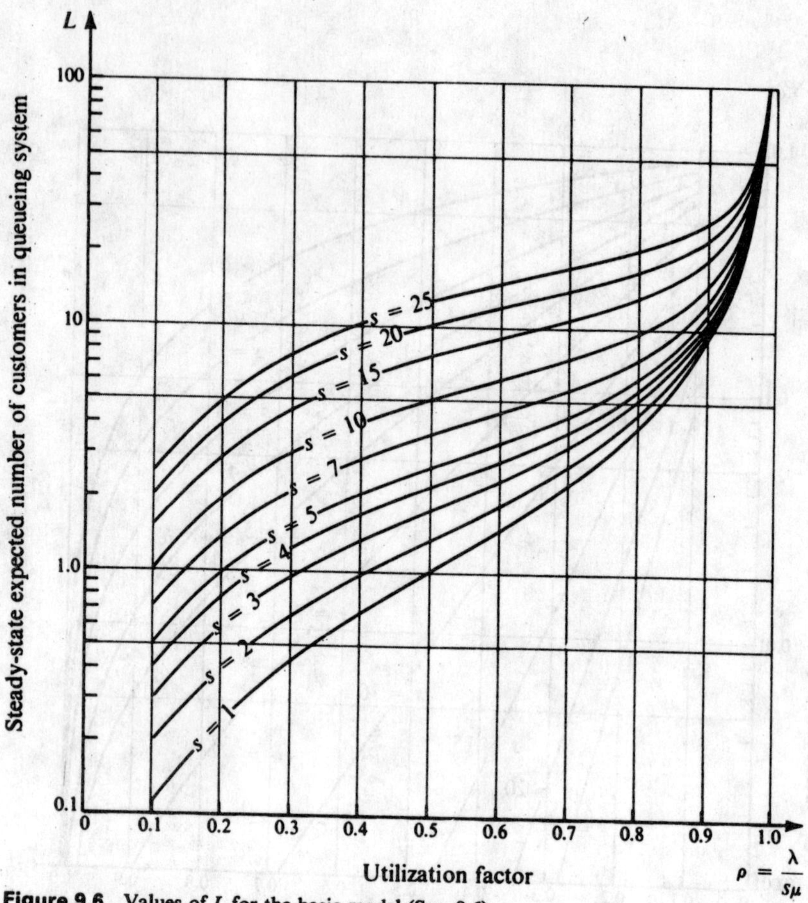

Figure 9.6 Values of L for the basic model (Sec. 9.6).

A doctor requires an average of 20 minutes to treat each patient. Thus, using an hour as the unit of time,

$$\frac{1}{\lambda} = \frac{1}{2} \text{ hours per customer}$$

$$\frac{1}{\mu} = \frac{1}{3} \text{ hours per customer,}$$

so

$$\lambda = 2 \text{ customers per hour}$$

$$\mu = 3 \text{ customers per hour.}$$

The two alternatives being considered are to continue having just one doctor during this shift ($s = 1$) or to add a second doctor ($s = 2$). In both cases

$$\rho = \frac{\lambda}{s\mu} < 1,$$

so that the system should approach a steady-state condition. (Actually, since λ is somewhat different during other shifts, the system will never truly reach a steady-steady condition, but the Management Engineer feels that steady-state results will provide a good approximation.) Therefore the above equations are used to obtain the results shown in Table 9.2.

On the basis of these results, it was tentatively concluded that a single doctor would be inadequate next year for providing the relatively prompt treat-

Table 9.2 Steady-state Results from Basic Model for County Hospital Problem

	$s = 1$	$s = 2$
ρ	$\frac{2}{3}$	$\frac{1}{3}$
P_0	$\frac{1}{3}$	$\frac{1}{2}$
P_1	$\frac{2}{9}$	$\frac{1}{3}$
$P_n(n \geq 2)$	$\frac{1}{3}\left(\frac{2}{3}\right)^n$	$\left(\frac{1}{3}\right)^n$
L_q	$\frac{4}{3}$	$\frac{1}{12}$
L	2	$\frac{3}{4}$
W_q	$\frac{2}{3}$	$\frac{1}{24}$ (in hours)
W	1	$\frac{3}{8}$ (in hours)
$P\{\mathscr{W}_q > 0\}$	0.667	0.167
$P\left\{\mathscr{W}_q > \frac{1}{2}\right\}$	0.404	0.022
$P\{\mathscr{W}_q > 1\}$	0.245	0.003
$P\{\mathscr{W}_q > t\}$	$\frac{2}{3}e^{-t}$	$\frac{1}{6}e^{-4t}$
$P\{\mathscr{W} > t\}$	e^{-t}	$\frac{1}{2}e^{-3t}(3 - e^{-t})$

ment needed in a hospital emergency room. You will see later how the Management Engineer checked this conclusion by applying two other queueing models that provide better representations of the real queueing system in some ways.

The Basic Model with a Finite Queue

We mentioned in the discussion of a queue in Sec. 9.2 that queueing systems sometimes have a *finite queue*, i.e., the number of customers in the system is not permitted to exceed some specified number (denoted by M). Any customer that arrives while the queue is "full" is refused entry into the system and so leaves forever. From the viewpoint of the birth-and-death process, the *mean input rate* into the system becomes zero at these times. Therefore the one modification needed in the basic model to introduce a finite queue is to change the λ_n parameters to

$$\lambda_n = \begin{cases} \lambda, & \text{for } n = 0, 1, 2, \ldots, M-1 \\ 0, & \text{for } n \geq M. \end{cases}$$

Since $\lambda_n = 0$ for some values of n, a queueing system fitting this model will eventually reach a steady-state condition.

The usual physical interpretation for this model is that there is only *limited waiting room* that will accommodate a maximum of M customers in the system. For example, with the *County Hospital* emergency room problem, this system actually would have a finite queue if there were only M cots for the patients and the policy were to send arriving patients to another hospital whenever there are no empty cots.

Another possible interpretation is that arriving customers will leave and "take their business elsewhere" whenever they find too many customers (M) ahead of them in the system because they are not willing to incur a long wait. This *balking* phenomenon is quite common in *commercial service systems*. However, there are other models available (e.g., see Prob. 5) that fit this interpretation even better.

The *rate diagram* for this model is identical to that shown in Fig. 9.4 for the basic model, *except* that it stops with state M.

RESULTS FOR THE SINGLE-SERVER CASE ($s = 1$) For this case

$$C_n = \begin{cases} \left(\dfrac{\lambda}{\mu}\right)^n = \rho^n, & \text{for } n = 1, 2, \ldots, M \\ 0, & \text{for } n > M. \end{cases}$$

Therefore

$$P_0 = \frac{1}{\sum_{n=0}^{M} (\lambda/\mu)^n}$$

$$= 1 \bigg/ \left[\frac{1-(\lambda/\mu)^{M+1}}{1-(\lambda/\mu)}\right]$$

$$= \frac{1-\rho}{1-\rho^{M+1}},$$

so that

$$P^n = \left(\frac{1-\rho}{1-\rho^{M+1}}\right)\rho^n, \text{ for } n = 0, 1, 2, \ldots M.$$

Hence

$$\begin{aligned} L &= \sum_{n=0}^{M} nP_n \\ &= \frac{1-\rho}{1-\rho^{M+1}}\rho\sum_{n=0}^{M}\frac{d}{d\rho}(\rho^n) \\ &= \frac{1-\rho}{1-\rho^{M+1}}\rho\frac{d}{d\rho}\left(\sum_{n=0}^{M}\rho^n\right) \\ &= \left(\frac{1-\rho}{1-\rho^{M+1}}\right)\rho\frac{d}{d\rho}\left(\frac{1-\rho^{M+1}}{1-\rho}\right) \\ &= \rho\frac{-(M+1)\rho^M + M\rho^{M+1} + 1}{(1-\rho^{M+1})(1-\rho)} \\ &= \frac{\rho}{1-\rho} - \frac{(M+1)\rho^{M+1}}{1-\rho^{M+1}}. \end{aligned}$$

As usual (when $s = 1$),

$$L_q = L - (1 - P_0).$$

Notice that the above results do not require that $\lambda < \mu$.

It can be verified that the second term in the final expression for L converges to zero as $M \to \infty$, so that the above results converge to the results of the first basic model of Sec. 9.6.

The waiting-time distributions can be derived by using the same reasoning as for the basic model (see Prob. 14). However, no simple expressions are obtained in this case, so computer calculations would be required Fortunately, the *expected* waiting times for customers entering the system can be obtained directly from the expressions given at the end of Sec. 9.5,

$$W = \frac{L}{\bar{\lambda}}, \quad W_q = \frac{L_q}{\bar{\lambda}},$$

where

$$\begin{aligned} \bar{\lambda} &= \sum_{n=0}^{\infty} \lambda_n P_n \\ &= \sum_{n=0}^{M-1} \lambda P_n \\ &= \lambda(1 - P_M). \end{aligned}$$

RESULTS FOR THE MULTIPLE-SERVER CASE ($s > 1$) Since this model does not allow more than M customers in the system, M is the maximum number of servers that could ever be used. Therefore, assume that $s \leq M$. In this case C_n becomes

$$C_n = \frac{(\lambda/\mu)^n}{n!}, \qquad \text{for } n = 1, 2, \ldots, s,$$

$$C_n = \frac{(\lambda/\mu)^s}{s!}\left(\frac{\lambda}{s\mu}\right)^{n-s} = \frac{(\lambda/\mu)^n}{s!s^{n-s}}, \text{ for } n = s, s+1, \ldots, M,$$

$$C_n = 0, \qquad \text{for } n > M.$$

Hence

$$P_n = \begin{cases} \dfrac{(\lambda/\mu)^n}{n!} P_0, \text{ for } n = 1, 2, \ldots, s \\ \dfrac{(\lambda/\mu)^n}{s!s^{n-s}} P_0, \text{ for } n = s, s+1, \ldots, M \\ 0, \qquad \text{for } n > M, \end{cases}$$

where

$$P_0 = 1 \Big/ \left[1 + \sum_{n=1}^{s} \frac{(\lambda/\mu)^n}{n!} + \frac{(\lambda/\mu)^s}{s!} \sum_{n=s+1}^{M} \left(\frac{\lambda}{s\mu}\right)^{n-s}\right].$$

Adapting the derivation of L_q in the first basic model of Sec. 9.6 to this case (see Prob. 17) yields

$$L_q = \frac{P_0(\lambda/\mu)^s \rho}{s!(1-\rho)^2}[1 - \rho^{M-s} - (M-s)\rho^{M-s}(1-\rho)],$$

and it can then be shown (see Prob. 26) that

$$L = \sum_{n=0}^{s-1} nP_n + L_q + s\left(1 - \sum_{n=0}^{s-1} P_n\right).$$

W and W_q are obtained from these quantities just as shown for the single-server case.

The Basic Model with a Limited Source

Now assume that the only deviation from the first basic model of Sec. 9.6 is that the *input source* is *limited*, i.e., the size of the *calling population* is *finite*. For this case let M denote the size of the calling population. Thus, when the number of customers in the queueing system is n ($n = 0,1,2, \ldots, M$), there are only ($M - n$) *potential* customers remaining in the input source.

The most important application of this model has been to *machine servicing*, where one or more repairmen (or operators) are assigned the responsibility of maintaining (or operating) a certain group of M machines. These machines constitute the calling population. Each one is considered to be a customer in the queueing system when it is down waiting for service (or being serviced), whereas it is outside the queueing system while it is running.

Note that each member of the calling population alternates between being *inside* and *outside* the queueing system. Therefore the analog of the basic model which fits this situation assumes that *each* member's *outside time* (i.e., the elapsed time from leaving the system until returning for the next time) has an *exponential distribution* with parameter λ. When n of the members are *inside*, and so $(M-n)$ members are *outside*, the current probability distribution of the *remaining* time until the next arrival to the queueing system is the distribution of the *minimum* of the *remaining outside times* for the latter $(M-n)$ members. Properties 2 and 3 for the exponential distribution imply that this distribution must be exponential with parameter $\lambda_n = (M-n)\lambda$. Hence this model is just the special case of the birth-and-death process with the rate diagram shown in Fig. 9.7.

Since $\lambda_n = 0$ for $n = M$, a queueing system fitting this model will eventually reach a steady-state condition. The available steady-state results are summarized below.

Results for the single-server case ($s = 1$) When $s = 1$, the C_n factors in Sec. 9.5 reduce to

$$C_n = M(M-1)\cdots(M-n+1)\left(\frac{\lambda}{\mu}\right)^n = \frac{M!}{(M-n)!}\left(\frac{\lambda}{\mu}\right)^n, \text{ for } n = 1, 2, \ldots, M$$

$$C_n = 0, \text{ for } n > M,$$

Figure 9.7 Rate diagrams for the basic model with a limited source.

(*a*) *Single-server case* ($s = 1$) $\lambda_n = \begin{cases}(M-n)\lambda, & \text{for } n = 0, 1, 2, \ldots, M \\ 0, & \text{for } n \geq M\end{cases}$

$\mu_n = \mu,$ for $n = 1, 2, \ldots, M$

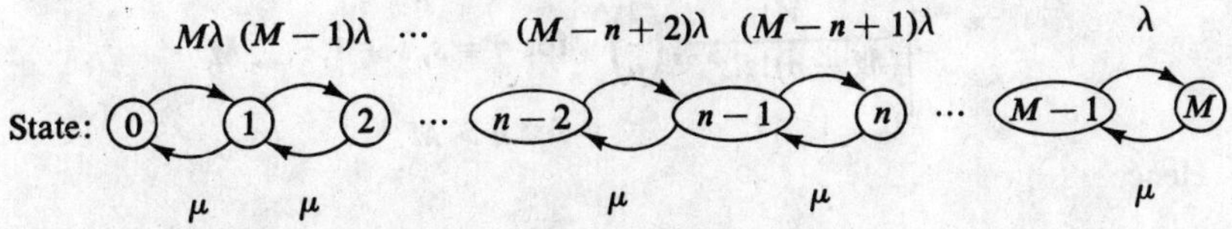

(*b*) *Multiple-server case* ($s > 1$) $\lambda_n = \begin{cases}(M-n)\lambda, & \text{for } n = 0, 1, 2, \ldots, M \\ 0, & \text{for } n \geq M \ (n \geq M)\end{cases}$

$\mu_n = \begin{cases} n\mu, & \text{for } n = 1, 2, \ldots, s \\ s\mu, & \text{for } n = s, s+1, \ldots\end{cases}$

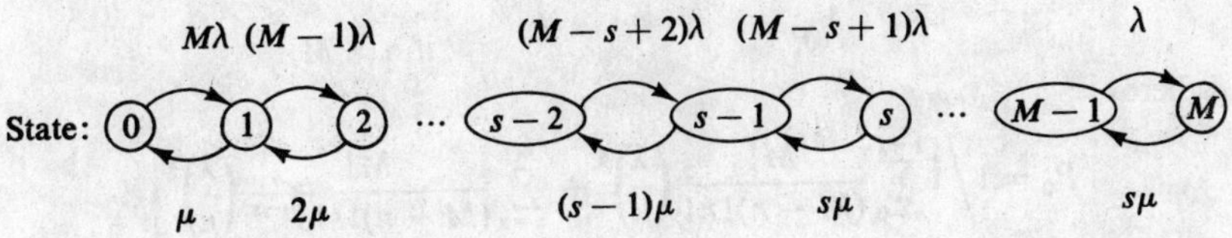

for this model. Therefore

$$P_0 = 1 \Bigg/ \sum_{n=0}^{M} \left[\frac{M!}{(M-n)!} \left(\frac{\lambda}{\mu}\right)^n \right];$$

$$P_n = \frac{M!}{(M-n)!} \left(\frac{\lambda}{\mu}\right)^n P_0, \text{ if } n = 1, 2, \ldots M;$$

$$L_q = \sum_{n=1}^{M} (n-1) P_n,$$

which can be made to reduce to

$$L_q = M - \frac{\lambda + \mu}{\lambda}(1 - P_0);$$

$$L = \sum_{n=0}^{M} n P_n = L_q + (1 - P_0)$$

$$= M - \frac{\mu}{\lambda}(1 - P_0).$$

Finally,

$$W = \frac{L}{\bar{\lambda}}, \qquad W_q = \frac{L_q}{\bar{\lambda}},$$

where

$$\bar{\lambda} = \sum_{n=0}^{\infty} \lambda_n P_n = \sum_{n=0}^{M} (M-n)\lambda P_n$$

$$= \lambda(M - L).$$

Results for the multiple-server case ($s > 1$) For $s > 1$,

$$C_n = \begin{cases} \dfrac{M!}{(M-n)!n!}\left(\dfrac{\lambda}{\mu}\right)^n, & \text{for } n = 1, 2, \ldots, s \\ \dfrac{M!}{(M-n)!s!s^{n-s}}\left(\dfrac{\lambda}{\mu}\right)^n, & \text{for } n = s, s+1, \ldots, M \\ 0, & \text{for } n > M. \end{cases}$$

Hence

$$P_n = \begin{cases} P_0 \dfrac{M!}{(M-n)!n!}\left(\dfrac{\lambda}{\mu}\right)^n, & \text{if } 0 \le n \le s \\ P_0 \dfrac{M!}{(M-n)!s!s^{n-s}}\left(\dfrac{\lambda}{\mu}\right)^n, & \text{if } s \le n \le M \\ 0, & \text{if } n > M, \end{cases}$$

where

$$P_0 = 1 \Bigg/ \left[\sum_{n=0}^{s-1} \frac{M!}{(M-n)!\,n!}\left(\frac{\lambda}{\mu}\right)^n + \sum_{n=s}^{M} \frac{M!}{(M-n)!\,s!\,s^{n-s}}\left(\frac{\lambda}{\mu}\right)^n \right].$$

Finally,

$$L_q = \sum_{n=s}^{M} (n-s)P_n,$$

$$L = \sum_{n=0}^{s-1} nP_n + L_q + s\left(1 - \sum_{n=0}^{s-1} P_n\right),$$

which then yield W and W_q by the same equations as in the single-server case.

Extensive tables of computational results are available[1] for this model for both the single-server and multiple-server cases.

A Model with State-dependent Service Rate and/or Arrival Rate

All the models thus far have assumed that the mean service rate is always a constant, regardless of how many customers are in the system. Unfortunately, this often is not the case in real queueing systems. When there is a large backlog of work (i.e., a long queue), it is quite likely that a server will tend to work faster than when the backlog is small or nonexistent. This increase in the service rate may result merely because the server increases his effort when he is under the pressure of a long queue. However, it may also result partly because the quality of the service is compromised or because assistance is obtained on certain service phases.

Given that the mean service rate does increase as the queue size is increased, it would be desirable to develop a theoretical model which seems to describe the pattern by which it increases. This model not only should be a reasonable approximation of the actual pattern, but it also should be simple enough to be practical for implementation. One such model is formulated below. We then show how the same results apply when the *arrival rate* is affected by the queue size in an analogous way.

FORMULATION FOR THE SINGLE-SERVER CASE ($s = 1$) Let

$$\mu_n = n^c \mu_1, \text{ for } n = 1, 2, \ldots,$$

where n = number of customers in system.
μ_n = mean service rate when there are n customers in system.
$1/\mu_1$ = expected "normal" service time—expected time to service customer when that customer is only one in system.
c = "pressure coefficient"—positive constant that indicates degree to which service rate of system is affected by system state.

Thus, selecting $c = 1$, for example, hypothesizes that the mean service rate is directly proportional to the line length n; $c = \frac{1}{2}$ implies that the mean service rate is proportional to the square root of n; and so on. The preceding queueing models in Sec. 9.6 have implicitly assumed that $c = 0$.

[1] L. G. Peck and R. N. Hazelwood, *Finite Queueing Tables*, Wiley, New York, 1958.

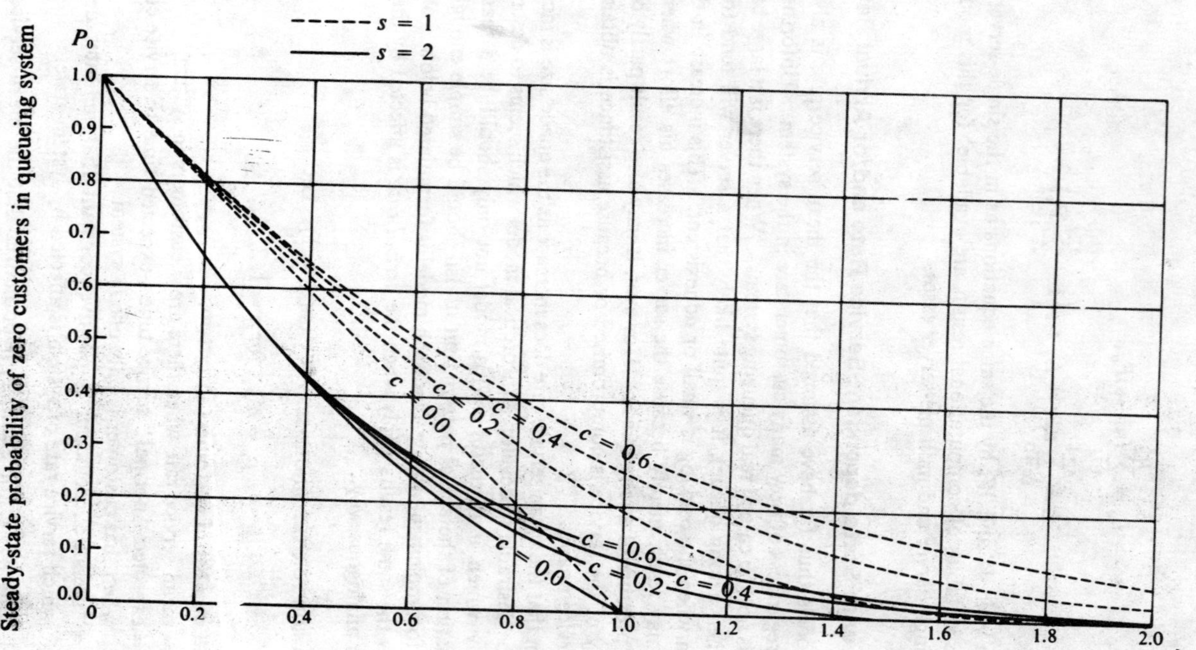

Figure 9.8 Values of P_0 for the state-dependent model (Sec. 9.6).

Now assume additionally that the queueing system has a Poisson input with $\lambda_n = \lambda$ (for $n = 0,1,2,\ldots$) and exponential service times with μ_n as given above. This is now a special case of the birth-and-death process, where

$$C_n = \frac{(\lambda/\mu_1)^n}{(n!)^c}, \text{ for } n = 1, 2, \ldots.$$

Thus, all the steady-state results given in Sec. 9.5 are applicable to this model. (A steady-state condition always can be reached when $c > 0$.) Unfortunately analytical expressions are not available for the summations involved. However, nearly exact values of P_0 and L have been tabulated[1] for various values of c and λ/μ_1 by summing a finite number of terms on an electronic computer. A small portion of these results also are shown in Figs. 9.8 and 9.9.

[1] Richard W. Conway and William L. Maxwell, "A Queueing Model with State Dependent Service Rate," *Journal of Industrial Engineering*, **12**: 132–136, 1961.

Figure 9.9 Values of L for the state-dependent model (Sec. 9.6).

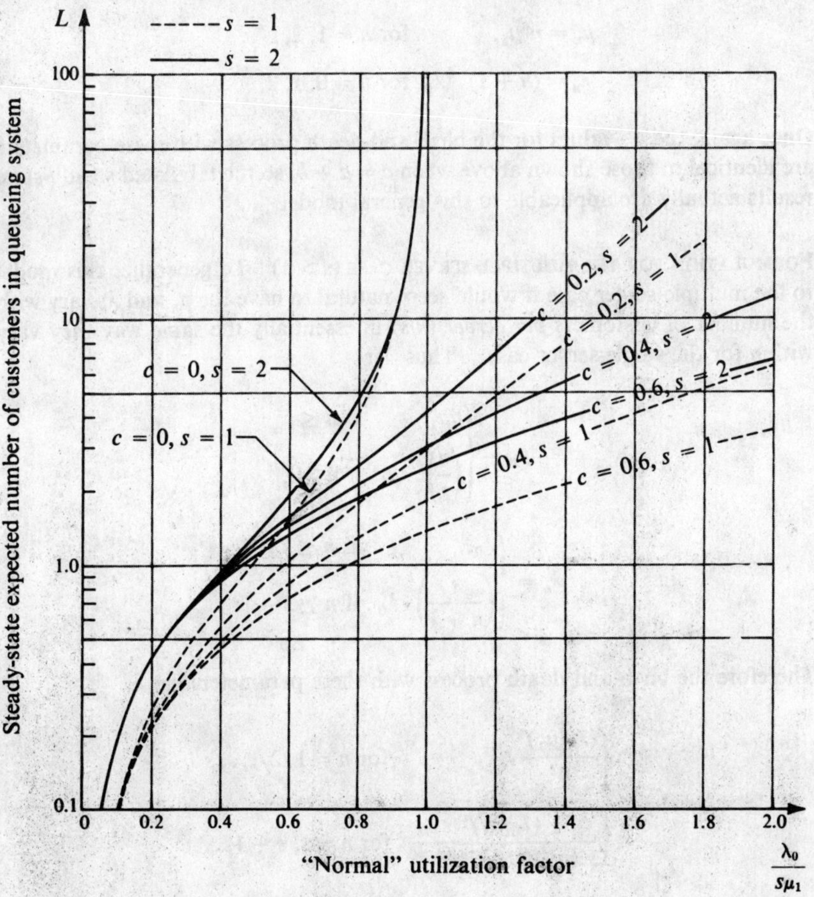

Rather than increasing the service rate, a queueing system may react to a long queue by decreasing the arrival rate instead. (This may be done, for example, by diverting some of the customers requiring service to another service facility.) The corresponding model for describing mean arrival rates for this case is to let

$$\lambda_n = (n+1)^{-b}\lambda_0, \text{ for } n = 0, 1, 2, \ldots,$$

where b is a constant whose interpretation is analogous to that for c. The C_n values for the birth-and-death process with these λ_n (and with $\mu_n = \mu$ for $n = 1, 2, \ldots$) are *identical* to those shown above (replacing λ by λ_0) for the state-dependent service rate model when $c = b$, so the steady-state results also are the same.

A more general model that combines these two patterns can also be used when both the mean arrival and the mean service rates are state-dependent. Thus, let

$$\mu_n = n^a \mu_1, \qquad \text{for } n = 1, 2, \ldots,$$
$$\lambda_n = (n+1)^{-b}\lambda_0, \text{ for } n = 0, 1, 2, \ldots.$$

Once again, the C_n values for the birth-and-death process with these parameters are identical to those shown above when $c = a + b$, so the tabulated steady-state results actually are applicable to this general model.

FORMULATION FOR THE MULTIPLE-SERVER CASE ($s > 1$) To generalize this model to the multiple-server case it would seem natural to have the μ_n and λ_n vary with the number of customers *per server* (n/s) in essentially the same way they vary with n for the single-server case. Thus let

$$\mu_n = \begin{cases} n\mu_1, & \text{if } n \le s \\ \left(\dfrac{n}{s}\right)^a s\mu_1, & \text{if } n \ge s, \end{cases}$$

$$\lambda_n = \begin{cases} \lambda_0, & \text{if } n \le s-1 \\ \left(\dfrac{s}{n+1}\right)^b \lambda_0, & \text{if } n \ge s-1. \end{cases}$$

Therefore the birth-and-death process with these parameters has

$$C_n = \begin{cases} \dfrac{(\lambda_0/\mu_1)^n}{n!}, & \text{for } n = 1, 2, \ldots, s \\ \dfrac{(\lambda_0/\mu_1)^n}{s!(n!/s!)^c s^{(1-c)(n-s)}}, & \text{for } n = s, s+1, \ldots. \end{cases}$$

Computational results for P_0, L_q, and L have been tabulated[1] for various values of c, (λ_0/μ_1), and s. Some of these results also are given in Figs. 9.8 and 9.9.

Example After gathering additional data for the *County Hospital* emergency room, the Management Engineer has found that the time a doctor spends with a patient tends to decrease as the number of patients waiting increases. This occurs partially because the doctor simply works faster, but the main reason is that he turns over more of the treatment to a nurse to complete. The pattern of the μ_n (the mean rate at which a doctor treats patients while there are a total of n patients to be treated in the emergency room) seems to reasonably fit the *state-dependent service rate model* presented here. Therefore the Management Engineer has decided to apply this model.

The new data indicate that the average time a doctor spends treating a patient is 24 minutes if no other patients are waiting, whereas this average becomes 12 minutes when he has six patients (so five are waiting their turn). Thus, with just a single doctor on duty,

$$\mu_1 = 2\tfrac{1}{2} \text{ customers per hour,}$$

$$\mu_6 = 5 \text{ customers per hour.}$$

Therefore the pressure coefficient c (or a in the general model) must satisfy the relationship

$$\mu_6 = 6^c \mu_1, \text{ so } 6^c = 2.$$

Using logarithms to solve for c yields $c = 0.4$. Since $\lambda = 2$ from before, this completes the specification of parameter values for this model.

To compare the two alternatives of having *one* doctor ($s = 1$) or *two* doctors ($s = 2$) on duty, the Management Engineer developed the various measures of performance shown in Table 9.3. The values of P_0, L, and (for $s = 2$) L_q were obtained directly from the tabulated results for this model. These values were then used to calculate

$$P_1 = C_1 P_0,$$

$$L_q = L - (1 - P_0), \text{ if } s = 1,$$

$$W_q = \frac{L_q}{\lambda}, \quad W = \frac{L}{\lambda},$$

$$P\{\mathscr{W}_q > 0\} = 1 - \sum_{n=0}^{s-1} P_n.$$

The fact that some of the results in Table 9.3 do not deviate substantially from those in Table 9.2 reinforced the tenative conclusion that a single doctor would be inadequate next year.

[1] F. S. Hillier, R. W. Conway, and W. L. Maxwell, "A Multiple Server Queueing Model with State Dependent Service Rate," *Journal of Industrial Engineering*, **15**: 153–157, 1964.

Table 9.3 Steady-state Results from State-dependent Service Rate Model for County Hospital Problem

	$s = 1$	$s = 2$
$\dfrac{\lambda}{s\mu_1}$	0.8	0.4
$\dfrac{\lambda}{s\mu_{6s}}$	0.4	0.2
P_0	0.367	0.440
P_1	0.294	0.352
L_q	0.618	0.095
L	1.251	0.864
W_q	0.309	0.048 (in hours)
W	0.626	0.432 (in hours)
$P\{\mathcal{W}_q > 0\}$	0.633	0.208

9.7 QUEUEING MODELS INVOLVING NONEXPONENTIAL DISTRIBUTIONS

Since all the queueing theory models in the preceding section are based on the birth-and-death process, both their interarrival and service times are required to have *exponential* distributions. As discussed in Sec. 9.4, this type of probability distribution has many convenient properties for queueing theory, but it provides a reasonable fit for only certain kinds of queueing systems. In particular, the assumption of exponential *interarrival times* implies that arrivals occur *randomly* (a Poisson input process), which is at least a reasonable approximation in many situations, but *not* when the arrivals are carefully scheduled or regulated. More significantly, the actual *service-time* distribution frequently deviates greatly from the exponential form, particularly when the service requirements of the customers are quite similar. Therefore it is important to have other queueing models available that use alternative distributions.

Unfortunately, the mathematical analysis of queueing models with nonexponential distributions is much more difficult. However, it has been possible to obtain some useful results for a few such models. The analysis is beyond the level of this book, but we shall summarize the models and describe the available results in this section.

Single-server Model with Poisson Input and Any Service-time Distribution

Suppose that a queueing system has a *single* server and a *Poisson* input process with a *fixed* mean arrival rate λ. As usual, it is assumed that the customers have *independent* service times with the *same* probability distribution. However, *no* restrictions are imposed on what this service-time distribution can be. In fact, it is only necessary to know (or estimate) the mean $1/\mu$ and variance σ^2 of this distribution.

Any such queueing system can eventually reach a *steady-state condition* if $\rho = \lambda/\mu < 1$. The readily available steady-state results[1] for this general model are the following:

$$P_0 = 1 - \rho,$$

$$L_q = \frac{\lambda^2\sigma^2 + \rho^2}{2(1-\rho)},$$

$$L = \rho + L_q,$$

$$W_q = \frac{L_q}{\lambda},$$

$$W = W_q + \frac{1}{\mu}.$$

For any fixed expected service time $1/\mu$, notice that L_q, L, W_q, and W all increase as σ^2 is increased. This is an important result because it indicates that, in addition to his average speed, the consistency of the server also has an important bearing on the performance of the service facility.

When the service-time distribution is exponential, $\sigma^2 = 1/\mu^2$, and the above results will reduce to the corresponding results in the first basic model of Sec. 9.6.

The complete flexibility in the service-time distribution provided by this model is extremely useful, so it is unfortunate that efforts to derive similar results for the *multiple-server* case have been unsuccessful. However, some multiple-server results have been obtained for the important special cases described by the following two models.

Poisson Input and Constant Service Times

When the service consists of essentially the same routine task to be performed for all customers, there tends to be little variation in the service time required. A queueing model that often provides a reasonable representation for this kind of situation assumes that all service times actually equal some fixed *constant* (the *degenerate* service-time distribution), along with a *Poisson* input process with a fixed mean arrival rate λ.

When there is just a *single* server, this model is just the special case of the preceding one where $\sigma^2 = 0$, so that

$$L_q = \frac{\rho^2}{2(1-\rho)}$$

[1] Equations also are available for calculating the probability distribution of the number of customers in the system or of the waiting time in the queue or system. However, these require the use of advanced techniques, including inverting the Laplace-Stieltjes transform of the service-time distribution.

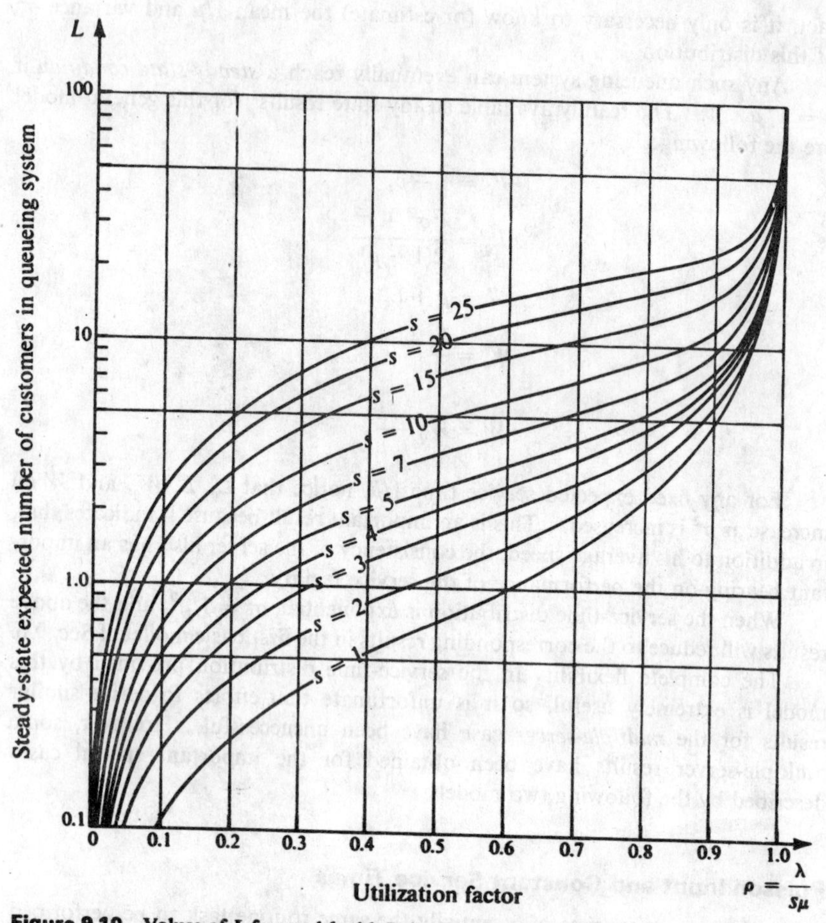

Figure 9.10 Values of L for model with Poisson input and constant service times (Sec.9.7).

and so forth for L, W_q, and W. (Notice that this L_q and W_q are exactly half as large as for the exponential service-time case of Sec. 9.6.)

For the multiple-server version of this model, there is a complicated method available[1] for deriving the steady-state probability distribution of the number of customers in the system and its mean (assuming $\rho = \lambda/s\mu < 1$). However, these results have been tabulated for numerous cases,[2] and the means (L) also are given graphically in Fig. 9.10.

[1] See N. U. Prabhu, *Queues and Inventories*, pp. 32–34, Wiley, New York, 1965.
[2] F. S. Hillier and O. S. Yu, *Tables for Multiple-Server Queueing Systems*, Technical Report, Department of Operations Research, Stanford University, late 1974.

Poisson Input and Erlang Service Times

The preceding model assumes *zero* variation in the service times ($\sigma = 0$), whereas the *exponential* service-time distribution assumes a very high degree of variability ($\sigma = 1/\mu$). Between these two rather extreme cases lies a long middle ground ($0 < \sigma < 1/\mu$), where most *actual* service-time distributions fall. Another kind of theoretical service-time distribution that fills in this middle ground is the *Erlang* distribution (named after an early pioneer in queueing theory).

The probability density function for the Erlang distribution is

$$f(t) = \frac{(\mu k)^k}{(k-1)!} t^{k-1} e^{-k\mu t}, \text{ for } t \geq 0,$$

where μ and k are strictly positive parameters of the distribution, and k is further restricted to be *integer*. (Except for this integer restriction, and the definition of the parameters, this distribution is *identical* to the *gamma* distribution discussed in Sec. 8.7.) Its mean and standard deviation are

$$\text{Mean} = \frac{1}{\mu},$$

$$\text{standard deviation} = \frac{1}{\sqrt{k}} \frac{1}{\mu}.$$

Thus, k is the parameter that specifies the degree of variability of the service times relative to the mean.

The Erlang distribution is a very important distribution in queueing theory for two reasons. To describe the first one, suppose that $T_1, T_2, \ldots, T_k$ are k independent random variables with an identical *exponential* distribution whose mean is $1/k\mu$. Then their sum,

$$T = T_1 + T_2 + \cdots + T_k,$$

has an *Erlang* distribution with parameters μ and k. The discussion of the exponential distribution in Sec. 9.4 suggested that the time required to perform certain kinds of tasks might well have an exponential distribution. However, the total service required by a customer may involve the server performing not just one specific task but a sequence of k tasks. If the respective tasks have an identical exponential distribution for their duration, the total service time would have an Erlang distribution. This would be the case, for example, if the server must perform the same exponential task k times for each customer.

The Erlang distribution is very useful also because it is a large (two-parameter) family of distributions permitting only nonnegative values. Hence empirical service-time distributions can usually be reasonably approximated by an Erlang distribution. In fact, both the *exponential* and the *degenerate* (constant) distributions are special cases of the Erlang distribution, with $k = 1$ and

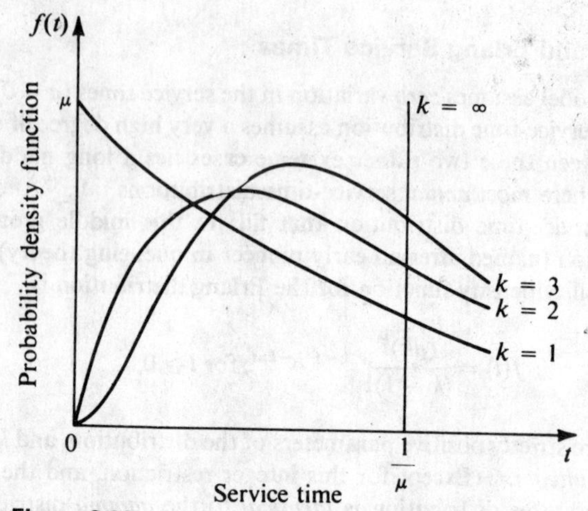

Figure 9.11 A family of Erlang distributions with constant mean $1/\mu$.

$k = \infty$, respectively. Intermediate values of k provide intermediate distributions with mean $= 1/\mu$, mode $= (k - 1)/\mu k$, and variance $= 1/k\mu^2$, as suggested by Fig. 9.11.

For the *single-server* version of the model, the results on page 415 with $\sigma^2 = 1/k\mu^2$ yield

$$L_q = \frac{\lambda^2/k\mu^2 + \rho^2}{2(1-\rho)} = \frac{1+k}{2k}\,\frac{\lambda^2}{\mu(\mu-\lambda)},$$

$$W_q = \frac{1+k}{2k}\,\frac{\lambda}{\mu(\mu-\lambda)},$$

$$W = W_q + \frac{1}{\mu},$$

$$L = \lambda W.$$

With *multiple* servers, the relationship of the Erlang distribution to the exponential distribution described above can be exploited to formulate a *modified* birth-and-death process in terms of individual exponential service phases (k per customer) rather than complete customers. However, it has not been possible to derive a general steady-state solution (when $\rho = \lambda/s\mu < 1$) for the probability distribution of the number of customers in the system as we did in Sec. 9.5. Instead, advanced theory is required to numerically solve individual cases. Once again, these results have been obtained and tabulated for numerous cases.[1] The means (L) also are given graphically in Fig. 9.12 for some cases where $s = 2$.

[1] F. S. Hillier and F. D. Lo, *Tables for Multiple-Server Queueing Systems Involving Erlang Distributions*, Technical Report No. 14, NSF GK-2925, Department of Operations Research, Stanford University, December 28, 1971.

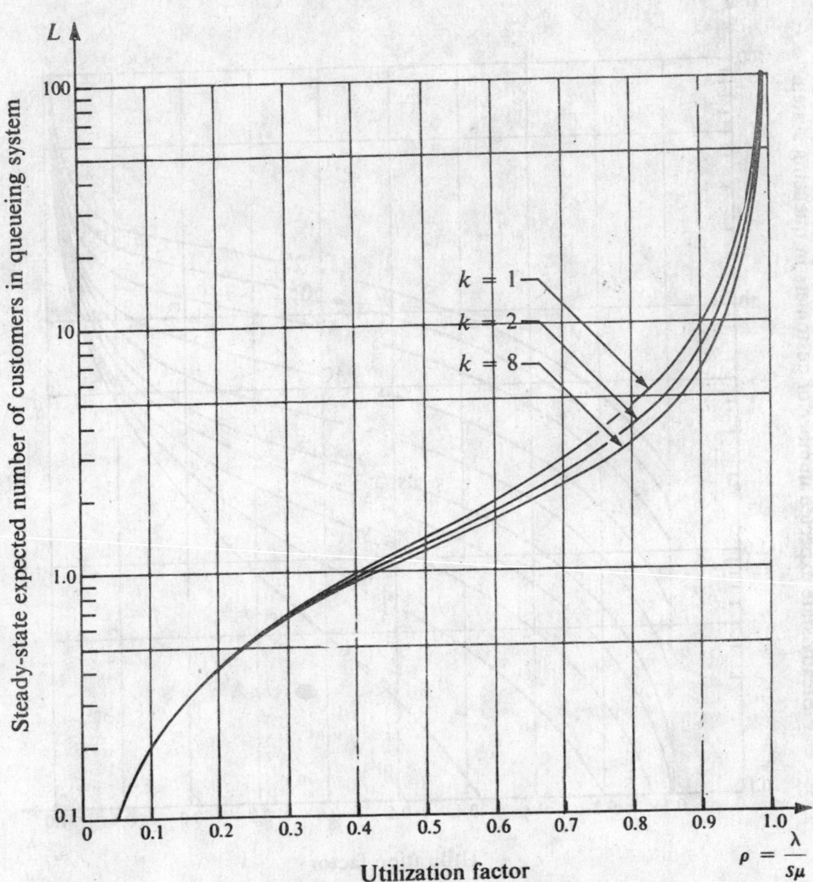

Figure 9.12 Values of L for model with Poisson input and Erlang service times (Sec. 9.7) with $s = 2$.

Models without a Poisson Input

All the queueing models presented thus far have assumed a Poisson input process. However, this assumption would be violated if the arrivals definitely are not occurring randomly for the queueing system under study, so another model would be needed.

As long as the service times have an *exponential* distribution with a fixed parameter, three such models are readily available. These models are obtained by merely *reversing* the assumed distributions of the *interarrival* and *service times* in the preceding three models. Thus the first new model imposes *no* restriction on what the *interarrival time* distribution can be. In this case there

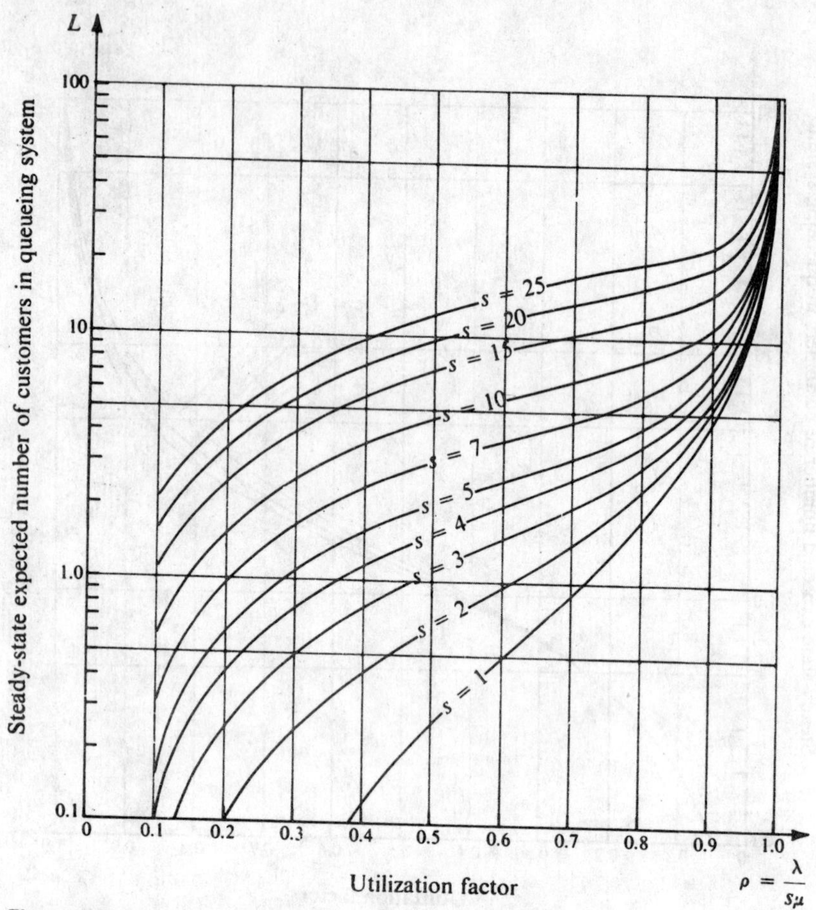

Figure 9.13 Values of L for model with constant interarrival and exponential service times (see Sec. 9.7).

are some steady-state results available[1] (particularly in regard to waiting-time distributions) for *both* the single-server and multiple-server versions of the model, but these results are not nearly as convenient as the simple expressions given for the single-server model on page 415. The second new model assumes that all interarrival times equal some fixed *constant*, which would represent a queueing system where arrivals are *scheduled* at regular intervals. The third new model assumes an *Erlang* interarrival time distribution, which provides a middle ground between *regularly scheduled* (constant) and *completely random*

[1] S. Karlin, *A First Course in Stochastic Processes*, pp. 445–448, 453–460, Academic Press, New York, 1966.

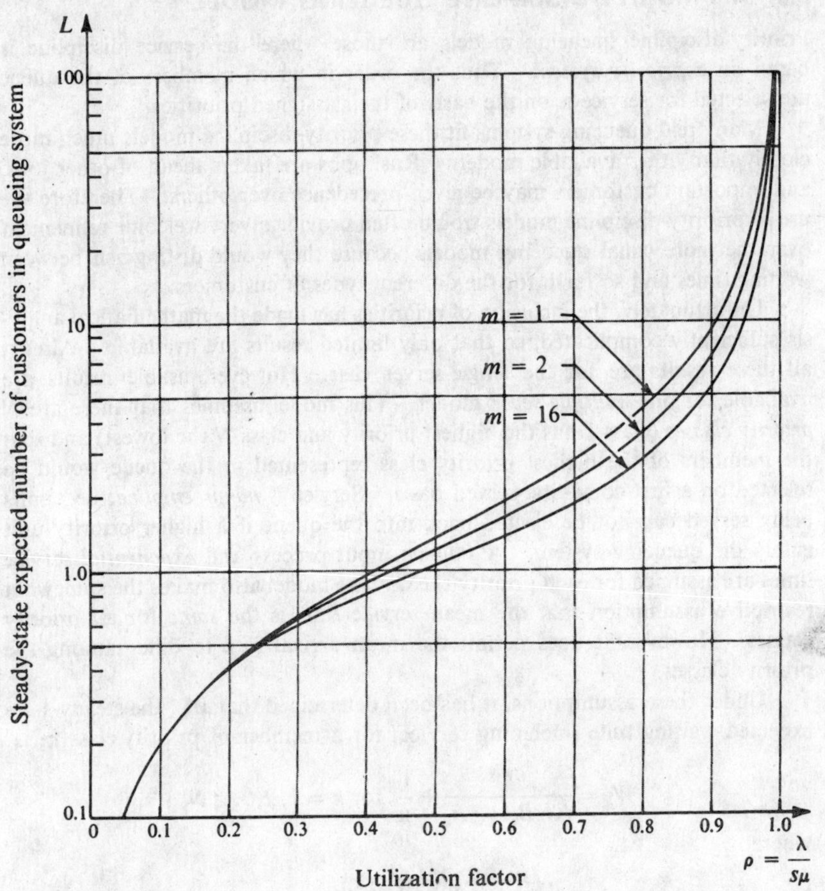

Figure 9.14 Values of L for model with Erlang interarrival and exponential service times (see Sec. 9.7) with $s = 2$.

(exponential) arrivals. Extensive computational results have been tabulated[1] for these latter two models, including the values of L given graphically in Figs. 9.13 and 9.14.

If *neither* the interarrival nor the service times for a queueing system have an *exponential* distribution, then there are three additional queueing models for which computational results also are available.[2] One of these models assumes an *Erlang* distribution for *both* these times. The other two models assume that *one* of these times has an *Erlang* distribution and the *other* time equals some fixed *constant*.

[1] F. S. Hillier and O. S. Yu, *op. cit.*; F. S. Hillier and F.-D. Lo, *op. cit.*

[2] *Ibid.*

9.8 A PRIORITY-DISCIPLINE QUEUEING MODEL

Priority-discipline queueing models are those where the service discipline is based on a *priority system.* Thus the order in which members of the queue are selected for service is on the basis of their assigned priorities.

Many real queueing systems fit these priority-discipline models much more closely than other available models. Rush jobs are taken ahead of other jobs, and important customers may be given precedence over others. Therefore the use of priority-discipline models would often provide a very welcome refinement over the more usual queueing models because they would distinguish between waiting times and so forth for the different types of customers.

Unfortunately, the inclusion of priorities has made the mathematical analysis sufficiently complicated, so that only limited results are available. Almost all these results are for the single-server case. However, usable results are available for one *multiple-sever* model. This model assumes that there are N *priority classes* (class 1 has the highest priority and class N the lowest) and that the members of the highest priority class represented in the queue would be selected on a first-come-first-served basis. Service is *nonpreemptive*; i.e., units being served can not be ejected back into the queue if a higher priority unit enters the queueing system. A *Poisson* input process and *exponential* service times are assumed for each priority class. The model also makes the somewhat restrictive assumption that the mean service time is the *same* for all priority classes. However, it does permit the mean arrival rate to differ among the priority classes.

Under these assumptions, it has been determined that W_k, the steady-state expected waiting time (including service) for a member of priority class k, is

$$W_k = \frac{1}{A \cdot B_{k-1} \cdot B_k} + \frac{1}{\mu}, \text{ for } k = 1, 2, \ldots, N,$$

where

$$A = s!\left(\frac{s\mu - \lambda}{\rho^s}\right)\sum_{j=0}^{s-1}\frac{\rho^j}{j!} + s\mu,$$

$$B_0 = 1,$$

$$B_k = 1 - \frac{\sum_{i=1}^{k}\lambda_i}{s\mu}, \qquad \text{for } k = 1, 2, \ldots, N$$

and

s = number of servers,

μ = mean service rate per busy server,

λ_i = mean arrival rate for priority class i, for $i = 1, 2, \ldots, N$,

$$\lambda = \sum_{i=1}^{N}\lambda_i,$$

$$\rho = \frac{\lambda}{\mu}.$$

(These results assume

$$\sum_{i=1}^{k} \lambda_i < \mu,$$

so that priority class k can reach a steady-state condition.)
It is also known that L_k, the steady-state expected number of members of priority class k in the queueing system (including those being served), is

$$L_k = \lambda_k W_k, \text{ for } k = 1, 2, \ldots, N.$$

To determine the expected waiting time excluding service for priority class k, merely subtract $1/\mu$ from W_k; the corresponding expected queue length would again be obtained by multiplying by λ_k. For the special case where $s = 1$, the expression for A reduces to $A = \mu^2/\lambda$.

Now consider the case where service is *preemptive*, so that the lowest priority customer being served is ejected back into the queue whenever a higher priority customer enters the queueing system. A server is thereby freed to begin servicing the new arrival immediately. If the other assumptions of the above model are retained, it has been found that when $s = 1$,

$$W_k = \frac{1/\mu}{B_{k-1} \cdot B_k}, \text{ for } k = 1, 2, \ldots, N$$

for this preemptive service case. Because of the lack of memory property of the exponential distribution, this result holds whether service for the preempted customer can resume at the point of interruption or must start at the beginning again. As usual,

$$L_k = \lambda_k W_k, \text{ for } k = 1, 2, \ldots, N,$$

The corresponding results excluding service time are obtained just as for the preceding model.

Some results are also available[1] for a few other single-server priority-discipline models involving other service-time distributions and/or unequal expected service times.

Example For the *County Hospital* emergency room problem, the Management Engineer has noticed that the patients are not treated on a first-come-first-served basis. Rather, the admitting nurse seems to roughly divide the patients into three categories: (1) *critical* cases, where prompt treatment is vital for survival; (2) *serious* cases, where early treatment is important to prevent further deterioration; and (3) *stable* cases, where treatment can be delayed without adverse medical consequences. Patients are then treated in this order of priority, where those in the same category would normally be taken on a first-come-first-served basis. A doctor normally will interrupt treatment of a patient if a new case in a higher priority category arrives. Approximately 10 percent of the patients fall into the first category, 30 percent into the second, and 60 percent into the

[1] N. K. Jaiswal, *Priority Queues*, Academic Press, New York, 1968.

third. Since the more serious cases will be sent into the hospital for further care after receiving emergency treatment, the average treatment time by a doctor in the emergency room actually does not differ greatly between these categories.

The Management Engineer has decided to use the priority-discipline queueing model described above as a reasonable representation of this queueing system, where the three categories of patients constitute the three priority classes in the model. Since treatment is interrupted by the arrival of a higher priority case, the *preemptive service* version of this model is the appropriate one. Given the available data (see the first basic model in Sec. 9.6), $\mu = 3$ and $\lambda = 2$, so $\lambda_1 = 0.2$, $\lambda_2 = 0.6$, $\lambda_3 = 1.2$. Table 9.6 gives the resulting expected waiting times *excluding* treatment time (in hours) for the respective priority classes[1] when there is one doctor ($s = 1$) or two doctors ($s = 2$) on duty. (The corresponding results for the *nonpreemptive service* version of the model also are given in Table 9.4 to show the effect of preempting.)

Table 9.4 Steady-state Results from Priority-discipline Model for County Hospital Problem

	Preemptive service		*Nonpreemptive service*	
	$s = 1$	$s = 2$	$s = 1$	$s = 2$
A	.....	....	4.5	36
B_1	0.933	....	0.933	0.967
B_2	0.733	....	0.733	0.867
B_3	0.333	....	0.333	0.667
$W_1 - \frac{1}{\mu}$	0.024	0.00037	0.238	0.029
$W_2 - \frac{1}{\mu}$	0.154	0.00793	0.325	0.033
$W_3 - \frac{1}{\mu}$	1.033	0.06542	0.889	0.048

These preemptive service results for $s = 2$ were obtained as follows. Since the waiting times for priority class 1 customers are completely unaffected by the presence of customers in lower priority classes, W_1 would be the same for any other values of λ_2 and λ_3, including $\lambda_2 = 0$, $\lambda_3 = 0$. Therefore W_1 must equal W for the corresponding *one-class* model in Sec. 9.6 with $s = 2$, $\mu = 3$ and $\lambda = \lambda_1 = 0.2$, which yields

$$\begin{aligned} W_1 &= W \text{ for } \lambda = 0.2 \\ &= 0.33370. \end{aligned}$$

[1] **Note** that these expected times can no longer be interpreted as the expected time until treatment begins when $k > 1$ because treatment may be interrupted at least once, causing additional waiting time, before being completed.

Now consider the first *two* priority classes. Again note that customers in these classes are completely unaffected by lower priority classes (just priority class 3 in this case), which can therefore be ignored in the analysis. Let $\overline{W}_{1-2}$ be the expected waiting time (including service time) of a *random arrival* in *either* of these two classes, so the probability is $\lambda_1/(\lambda_1+\lambda_2) = \frac{1}{4}$ that this arrival is in class 1 and $\lambda_2/(\lambda_1+\lambda_2) = \frac{3}{4}$ that it is in class 2. Therefore $\overline{W}_{1-2} = \frac{1}{4}W_1 + \frac{3}{4}W_2$. Furthermore, since *expected* waiting time is the same for *any* service discipline, $\overline{W}_{1-2}$ must also equal W for the first basic model in Sec. 9.6 with $s = 2$, $\mu = 3$ and $\lambda = \lambda_1 + \lambda_2 = 0.8$, which yields

$$\overline{W}_{1-2} = W \text{ for } \lambda = 0.8$$
$$= 0.33937.$$

Combining these facts gives

$$W_2 = \frac{4}{3}\left[0.33937 - \frac{1}{4}(0.33370)\right]$$
$$= 0.34126.$$

Finally let $\overline{W}_{1-3}$ be the expected waiting time (including treatment time) for a *random arrival* in *any* of the three priority classes, so the probabilities are 0.1, 0.3, and 0.6 that it is in class 1, 2, and 3, respectively.. Therefore

$$\overline{W}_{1-3} = 0.1W_1 + 0.3W_2 + 0.6W_3.$$

Furthermore, $\overline{W}_{1-3}$ must also equal W for the first basic model in Sec. 9.6 with $s = 2$, $\mu = 3$, and $\lambda = \lambda_1 + \lambda_2 + \lambda_3 = 2$, so that (from Table 9.2)

$$\overline{W}_{1-3} = W \text{ for } \lambda = 2$$
$$= 0.375.$$

Consequently,

$$W_3 = \frac{1}{0.6}[0.375 - 0.1(0.33370) - 0.3(0.34126)]$$
$$= 0.39875.$$

The corresponding W_q results for the first basic model in Sec. 9.6 also could have been used in exactly the same way to derive the $[W_k - (1/\mu)]$ quantities directly.

Since the $[W_k - (1/\mu)]$ values in Table 9.4 represent *statistical expectations*, and so some patients would have to wait considerably longer than this average (preemptive service case) for his priority class, the Management Engineer recommended that there be *two* doctors on duty in the emergency room during the early evening hours next year. The *Board of Directors* for County Hospital adopted this recommendation, and simultaneously raised the charge for using the emergency room!

9.9 QUEUEING NETWORKS

Thus far we have considered only queueing systems having just a *single* service facility with one or more servers. However, queueing systems encountered in operations research studies are sometimes actually *queueing networks*, i.e., networks of service facilities where customers must receive service at some or all of these facilities. For example, orders being processed through a job shop must be routed through a sequence of machine groups (service facilities). It is therefore necessary to study the entire network to obtain such information as expected total waiting time, expected number of customers in the entire system, and so forth.

Analytical results on queueing networks have been quite limited because of the difficulty of the problem. Essentially all the work has been confined to the case of a Poisson input process and exponential service times. Most of the results that have been obtained[1] have necessarily been quite involved and unsuitable for general routine use.

However, there is one simple result available which is of such fundamental importance for queueing networks that it warrants special attention here. This result is the following *equivalence property* for the *input process* of arriving customers and the *output process* of departing customers for certain queueing systems.

EQUIVALENCE PROPERTY Assume that a service facility with s servers has a Poisson input with parameter λ and the same exponential service-time distribution for each server, where $s\mu > \lambda$. Then the steady-state *output* of this service facility is also a Poisson process with parameter λ.†

Notice that this property makes no assumption about the type of service discipline used. Therefore, if the model for a service facility corresponds to either of the basic models discussed in Secs. 9.6 (the first model) and 9.8, the served customers will leave the service facility according to a Poisson distribution. The crucial implication of this for queueing networks is that if these units must then go to another service facility for further service, this second facility *also* will have a *Poisson* input. Thus suppose that customers must all receive service at a series of service facilities in a fixed sequence. Assume further that the customers arrive at the first facility according to a Poisson process with parameter λ and that each facility has the same exponential service-time distribution for its servers. It then follows from the equivalence property that (under steady-state conditions) each service facility has a Poisson input with parameter λ. Therefore the elementary models of Secs. 9.6 (the first model) or 9.8 can be used to analyze each service facility independently of the others! (The equivalence property can even be used to draw essentially the same conclusion when the customers pass through a network of service facilities in different sequences

[1] See Thomas L. Saaty, *Elements of Queueing Theory with Applications*, chap. 12, McGraw-Hill, New York, 1961, for a survey.

† For a proof see Saaty, *ibid*.

according to transition probabilities.[1]) The expected total waiting time and the expected number of customers in the entire system can then be obtained by merely summing the corresponding quantities obtained at the respective facilities.

Unfortunately, the equivalence property and its implications do not hold for the case of finite queues discussed in Sec. 9.6. This case is actually quite important in practice because there is often a definite limitation on the queue length in front of service facilities in networks. The facilities must be analyzed jointly in this case, and only limited results have been obtained.

9.10 CONCLUSIONS

Queueing systems are prevalent throughout society. The adequacy of these systems can have an important effect on the quality of life and productivity.

Queueing theory studies queueing systems by formulating mathematical models of their operation and then using these models to derive measures of performance. This provides vital information for effectively designing queueing systems that achieve an appropriate balance between the cost of providing a service and the cost associated with waiting for that service.

This chapter presented the most basic models of queueing theory for which particularly useful results are available. However, these models far from exhaust the list. In fact, over 2,000 research papers formulating and/or analyzing queueing models have already appeared in the technical literature, and many more are being published each year!

The exponential distribution plays a fundamental role in queueing theory for representing the distribution of interarrival and service times. Useful analytical results have been obtained for only a relatively few queueing models making other assumptions. Thus there actually remain many potentially useful queueing models that have so far been mathematically intractable. When no tractable model that provides a reasonable representation of the queueing system under study is available, a common approach is to obtain relevant performance data by developing a computer program for *simulating* the operation of the system. This technique will be discussed in Chap. 15.

Chapter 10 describes how queueing theory can be used to help design effective queueing systems.

Selected References

1 Beckmann, Petr: *Introduction to Elementary Queueing Theory and Telephone Traffic*, Golem Press, Boulder, Colo., 1968.

2 Cohen, J. W.: *The Single-Server Queue*, North-Holland, Amsterdam, 1969.

3 Cooper, Robert B.: *Introduction to Queueing Theory*, Macmillan, New York, 1972.

4 Jaiswal, N. K.: *Priority Queues*, Academic Press, New York, 1968.

5 Prabhu, N. U.: *Queues and Inventories: A Study of Their Basic Stochastic Processes*, Wiley, New York, 1965.

[1] See James R. Jackson, "Jobshop-Like Queueing Systems," *Management Science*, **10**(1): 131–142. 1963.

Problems[1]

1 Consider a typical barber shop. Demonstrate that it is a queueing system by describing its components.

2 Identify the customers and the servers in the queueing system representation of each of the following situations:

(*a*) The checkout stand in a grocery store.
(*b*) A fire station.
(*c*) The toll booth for a bridge.
(*d*) A bicycle repair shop.
(*e*) A shipping dock.
(*f*) A group of semiautomatic machines assigned to one operator.
(*g*) The materials-handling equipment in a factory area.
(*h*) A plumbing shop.
(*i*) A job shop producing to custom orders.
(*j*) A secretarial typing pool.

3 Suppose that a queueing system has *two* servers, an *exponential* interarrival time distribution with a mean of 1 hour, and an *exponential* service-time distribution with a mean of 1 hour. Furthermore, a customer has just arrived at 12:00 noon.

(*a*) What is the probability that the *next* arrival will come before 1:00 P.M.? Between 1:00 and 2:00 P.M.? After 2:00 P.M.?

(*b*) Suppose that *no* additional customers arrive before 1:00 P.M. Now what is the probability that the next arrival will come between 1:00 and 2:00 P.M.?

(*c*) What is the probability that the *number* of arrivals between 1:00 and 2:00 P.M. will be *zero*? *One*? *Two or more*?

(*d*) Suppose that both servers are serving customers at 1:00 P.M. What is the probability that *neither* customer will have its service completed before 2:00 P.M.? Before 1:10 P.M.? Before 1:01 P.M.?

4 The jobs to be performed on a particular machine arrive according to a Poisson input process with a mean rate of two per hour. Suppose that the machine breaks down and will require 1 hour to be repaired. What is the probability that the number of new jobs that will arrive during this time is (*a*) zero, (*b*) two, (*c*) five or more?

5 A service station has one gasoline pump. Cars wanting gasoline arrive according to a *Poisson* process at a mean rate of 20 per hour. However, if the pump already is being used, these potential customers may *balk* (drive on to another service station). In particular, if there are n cars already at the service station, the probability that an arriving potential customer will balk is $n/4$ for $n = 1, 2, 3, 4$. The time required to service a car has an *exponential* distribution with a mean of 3 minutes.

(*a*) Construct the rate diagram for this queueing system.
(*b*) Develop the balance equations.
(*c*) Solve these equations to find the steady-state probability distribution of the number of cars at the station. Verify that this solution is the same as given by the general solution for the *birth-and-death process*.
(*d*) Find the expected waiting time (including service) for those cars that stay.

[1] Also see the end of Chap. 10 for problems involving the application of queueing theory.

6 A certain small grocery store has a single checkout stand with a full-time cashier manning it. Customers arrive at the stand "randomly" (i.e., a Poisson input process) at a mean rate of 30 per hour. When there is only one customer at the stand, he is processed by the cashier alone, with an expected service time of 1.5 minutes. However, the stock boy has been given standard instructions that whenever there is more than one customer at the stand he is to help the cashier by boxing the groceries. This reduces the expected time required to process a customer to 1 minute. In both cases the service-time distribution is exponential.

(*a*) Construct the rate diagram for this queueing system.

(*b*) What is the steady-state probability distribution of the number of customers at the checkout stand?

(*c*) Derive L for this system. Use this information to determine L_q, W, and W_q.

7 For each of the following models, write the *balance equations* and show that they are satisfied by the solution given in the indicated section:

(*a*) The *basic model* (first model in Sec. 9.6), with $s = 2$.

(*b*) The *basic model with a finite queue* (Sec. 9.6), with $s = 2$ and $M = 4$.

(*c*) The *basic model with a limited source* (Sec. 9.6), with $s = 2$ and $M = 4$.

8 Consider a queueing system with a *Poisson* input and *exponential* service times.

(*a*) Suppose there is *one* server and the expected service time is exactly 6 seconds. Compare L for the cases where the mean arrival rate is 5.0, 9.0, and 9.9 customers per minute, respectively. Do the same for L_q, W, W_q, and $P\{\mathcal{W} > 5\}$.

(*b*) Now suppose there are *two* servers and the expected service time is exactly 12 seconds. Make the same comparisons as for part (*a*).

9 A bank employs three tellers to serve its customers. Customers arrive according to a *Poisson* process at a mean rate of four per minute. If a customer finds all tellers busy, he joins a queue that is serviced by all tellers; that is, there are no lines in front of each teller but rather one line waiting for the first available teller. The transaction time between the teller and customer has an exponential distribution with a mean of ½ minute.

(*a*) Construct the rate diagram for this queueing system.

(*b*) Find the steady-state probability distribution of the number of customers in the bank.

(*c*) Find L_q, W_q, W, and L.

10 Jobs arrive at a particular work center according to a Poisson input process at a mean rate of two per day, and the operation time has an exponential distribution with a mean of ¼ day. Enough in-process storage space is provided at the work center to accommodate three jobs in addition to the one being processed. Determine the proportion of time that this storage space will be adequate to accommodate all waiting jobs.

11 It is necessary to determine how much in-process storage space to allocate to a particular work center in a new factory. Jobs would arrive at this work center according to a *Poisson* process with a mean rate of three per hour, and the time required to perform the necessary work has an *exponential* distribution with a mean of 0.3 hours.

If each job would require 1 square foot of floor space while in in-process storage at the work center, how much space must be provided to accommodate all waiting jobs (*a*) 50 percent, (*b*) 90 percent, (*c*) 99 percent of the time? (*Hint:* The sum of a geometric series is

$$\sum_{n=0}^{N} x^n = \frac{1 - x^{N+1}}{1 - x}.)$$

12 Section 9.6 gives the following equations for the single-server version of the *basic model*:

$$P\{\mathscr{W} > t\} = \sum_{n=0}^{\infty} P_n P\{S_{n+1} > t\}. \tag{1}$$

$$P\{\mathscr{W} > t\} = e^{-\mu(1-\rho)t}. \tag{2}$$

Show that Eq. (1) reduces algebraically to Eq. (2).

13 Derive W_q directly for the following cases by developing and reducing an expression analogous to Eq. (1), Prob. 12.

(*a*) The single-server version of the *basic model* presented in Sec. 9.6.
(*b*) The multiple-server version of the *basic model* presented in Sec. 9.6.

14 For the single-server version of the *basic model with a finite queue* presented in Sec. 9.6, develop an expression analogous to Eq. (1), Prob. 12 for the following probabilities:

(*a*) $P\{\mathscr{W} > t\}$.
(*b*) $P\{\mathscr{W}_q > t\}$.

15 An airline ticket office has two ticket agents answering incoming phone calls for flight reservations. In addition, one caller can be put on "hold" until one of the agents is available to take the call. If all three phone lines (both agent lines and the hold line) are busy, a potential customer gets a busy signal, and it is assumed she calls another ticket office, so that her business is lost. The calls and attempted calls occur *randomly* (i.e., according to a *Poisson* process) at a mean rate of one per minute. The length of a telephone conversation has an *exponential* distribution with a mean of ½ minute.

(*a*) Construct the rate diagram for this queueing system.
(*b*) Find the steady-state probability that
  (*i*) A caller will get to talk to an agent immediately,
  (*ii*) The caller will be put on hold,
  (*iii*) The caller will get a busy signal.

16 Plans are being made for opening a small car-wash operation, and the decision must be made as to how much space to provide for waiting cars. It is estimated that customers would arrive randomly (i.e., a *Poisson* input process) with a mean rate of one every 4 minutes, unless the waiting area is full, in which case the customer would take his car elsewhere. The time that can be attributed to washing one car has an exponential distribution with a mean of 3 minutes. Compare the expected fraction of potential customers that would be *lost* because of inadequate waiting space if (*a*) zero, (*b*) two, or (*c*) four spaces (not including the car being washed) were to be provided.

17 Consider the multiple-server version of the *basic model with a finite queue* presented in Sec. 9.6. Derive the expression for L_q given there.

18 Suppose that one repairman has been assigned the responsibility of maintaining three machines. For each machine the probability distribution of the running time before a breakdown is *exponential*, with a mean of 9 hours. The repair time also has an *exponential* distribution with a mean of 2 hours.

(*a*) Calculate the steady-state probability distribution and the expected number of machines that are not running.

(*b*) As a crude approximation, it could be assumed that the calling population is infinite, so that the input process is *Poisson* with a mean arrival rate of *three* every 9 hours. Compare the result from part (*a*) with that obtained by making this approximation using (i) the corresponding infinite queue model, (ii) the corresponding finite queue model.

(*c*) Now suppose that a second repairman is made available whenever more than one of these three machines requires repair. Calculate the information specified in part (*a*).

19 Plans are currently being developed for a new factory. One department has been allocated a large number of automatic machines of a certain type, and it is now desired to determine how many machines should be assigned to each operator for servicing (loading, unloading, adjusting, setup and so on). For the purpose of this analysis, the following information has been provided.

The running time (time between completing service and requiring service again) of each machine has an *exponential* distribution, with a mean of 120 minutes. The service time has an *exponential* distribution, with a mean of 12 minutes. An operator must attend to his own machines; he can not give help to or receive help from other operators. For the department to achieve the required production rate, the machines must be running at least 87.5 percent of the time on the average.

What is the maximum number of machines that can be assigned to an operator while still achieving the required production rate?

20 Consider a single-server queueing system. It has been observed that this server seems to speed up as the number of customers in the system increases, and that the pattern of acceleration seems to fit the fourth model presented in Sec. 9.6. Furthermore, it is estimated that the expected service time is 4 minutes when there is only *one* customer in the system. Determine the pressure coefficient c for the fourth model of Sec. 9.6 for the following cases:

(*a*) The expected service time is estimated to be 2 minutes when there are *four* customers in the system.

(*b*) The expected service time is estimated to be 3 minutes when there are *four* customers in the system.

21 For the *state-dependent model* presented in Sec. 9.6, show the effect of the *pressure coefficient* c by using Fig. 9.9 to construct a table giving the *ratio* (expressed as a decimal number) of L for this model to L for the first *basic model* presented in Sec. 9.6 (that is, with $c = 0$). Tabulate these ratios for $\lambda_0/s\mu_1 = 0.5, 0.9, 0.99$ when $c = 0.2, 0.4, 0.6$ and $s = 1, 2$.

22 Consider a single-server queueing system with a *Poisson* input with known mean arrival rate λ. Suppose that the service-time distribution is unknown but that the expected service time $1/\mu$ is known.

(*a*) Compare the expected waiting time in the queue if the service-time distribution were (*i*) exponential, (*ii*) constant, (*iii*) Erlang with the amount of variation (i.e., the standard deviation) halfway between the constant and exponential cases.

(*b*) What is the effect on the expected waiting time in the queue, and expected queue length, if both λ and μ are doubled and the scale of the service-time distribution is changed accordingly?

23 Consider a queueing system with a *Poisson* input, where the server must perform two distinguishable tasks in sequence for each customer, so the total service time is the sum of the two task times (which are statistically independent).

(*a*) Suppose that the first task time has an *exponential* distribution with a mean of 1 minute, and the second task time has an *Erlang* distribution with a mean of 3 minutes and with the shape parameter $k = 3$. Which queueing theory model should be used to represent this system?

(*b*) Suppose that part (*a*) is modified so that the first task time also has an *Erlang* distribution with the shape parameter $k = 3$ (but with the mean still equal to 1 minute). Which queueing theory model should be used to represent this system?

24 An airline maintenance base only has facilities for overhauling one airplane engine at a time. Therefore to return the airplanes into use as soon as possible the policy has been to stagger the overhauling of the four engines of each airplane. In other words, only one engine is overhauled each time an airplane comes into the shop. Under this policy, airplanes have arrived according to a *Poisson* process at a mean rate of one per day. The time required for an engine overhaul (once work has begun) has an *exponential* distribution with a mean of ½ day.

A proposal has been made to change the policy so as to overhaul all four engines consecutively each time an airplane comes into the shop. It is pointed out that although this would quadruple the expected service time, each plane would need to come into the shop only one-fourth times as often.

Use queueing theory to compare the two alternatives on a meaningful basis.

25 Consider a single-server queueing system with *any* service-time distribution and distribution of interarrival times. Use only basic definitions and the relationships given in Sec. 9.2 to verify the following general relationships:

(*a*) $L = L_q + (1 - P_0)$.

(*b*) $L = L_q + \rho$.

(*c*) $P_0 = 1 - \rho$.

26 Show that

$$L = \sum_{n=0}^{s-1} nP_n + L_q + s\left(1 - \sum_{n=0}^{s-1} P_n\right)$$

by using the statistical definitions of L and L_q in terms of the P_n.

27 A company currently has *two* tool cribs, each with a *single* clerk, in its manufacturing area. One tool crib handles only the tools for the heavy machinery; the second one handles all other tools. However, for each crib the mechanics arrive to obtain tools at a mean rate of 24 per hour, and the expected service time is 2 minutes.

Because of complaints that the mechanics coming to the tool cribs have to wait too long, the proposal has been made to combine the two tool cribs so that either clerk can handle either kind of tool as the demand arises. It is believed that the mean arrival rate to the combined two-clerk tool crib would double to 48 per hour, and the expected service time would continue to be 2 minutes. However, information is not available on the *form* of the probability distributions for *interarrival* and *service times*, so it is not clear which queueing model would be most appropriate.

Compare the status quo and the proposal with respect to the total expected number of mechanics at the tool crib(s) and the expected waiting time (including service) for each mechanic. Do this by tabulating these data for the five queueing models considered in Figs. 9.6, 9.10, and 9.12 to 9.14 (use $k = 2$ when an Erlang distribution is appropriate).

28 A particular work center in a job shop can be represented as a single-server queueing system, where jobs arrive according to a *Poisson* process with a mean rate of eight per day. Although the arriving jobs are of three distinct types, the time required to perform any of these jobs has the same *exponential* distribution, with a mean of 0.1 working days. The practice has been to work on arriving jobs on a first-come-first-served basis. However. it is important that jobs of type 1 do not have to wait very long, whereas this is only moderately important for jobs of type 2 and relatively unimportant for jobs of type 3. These three types arrive with a mean rate of two, four, and two per day, respectively. Since all three types have been experiencing rather long delays on the average, it has been proposed that the jobs be selected according to an appropriate priority discipline instead.

Compare the expected waiting time (including service) for each of the three types of jobs if the service discipline were (*a*) first-come-first-served, (*b*) nonpreemptive priority, or (*c*) preemptive priority.

29 One inspector has been assigned the full-time task of inspecting the output from a group of 10 identical machines. Jobs to be done by any one of the machines arrive according to a *Poisson* process at a mean rate of 70 per hour. The time required by a machine to perform each job has an *exponential* distribution with a mean of 8 minutes. Thus when all 10 machines are being used, the jobs are completed ready for inspection at a mean rate of 75 per hour. Unfortunately, the inspector is able to inspect them at a mean rate of only 80 per hour. (In particular, his inspection time has an *Erlang* distribution with a mean of 0.75 minutes and a shape parameter $k = 25$.) This has resulted in a substantial amount of in-process inventory at the inspection station on the average (i.e., the expected number of jobs waiting to start inspection is fairly large), which is expensive for the company. Therefore the production manager has made two alternative proposals to reduce this average level of in-process inventory. Proposal 1 is to use slightly less power for the machines (which would increase their expected time to perform a job to 8.4 minutes), so that the inspector can keep up with their output better. Proposal 2 is to use a certain younger inspector for this task instead. He is somewhat faster (albeit more variable in his inspection times because of less experience), so should keep up better. (His inspection time would have an *Erlang* distribution with a mean of 0.72 minutes and a shape parameter $k = 2$.)

The production manager has asked you to "use the latest O.R. techniques to see how much each proposal would cut down in-process inventory."

(*a*) What would be the effect of proposal 1? Why? How would you explain this to the production manager?

(*b*) Determine the effect of proposal 2. How would you explain this outcome to the production manager?

(*c*) What suggestions would you make for reducing the average level of in-process inventory at the inspection station?

30 Consider the queueing-theory model with a *preemptive priority* service discipline presented in Sec. 9.8. Suppose that $s = 1$, $N = 2$, and $(\lambda_1 + \lambda_2) < \mu$, and let P_{ij} be the steady-state probability that there are i members of the higher priority class and j members of the lower priority class in the queueing system ($i = 0,1,2,\ldots; j = 0,1,2,\ldots$). Use a method analogous to that presented in Sec. 9.5 to derive a system of linear equations whose simultaneous solution is the P_{ij}. Do not actually obtain this solution.

31 Consider a single-server queueing system with a *Poisson* input, *Erlang* service times, and a *finite* queue. In particular, suppose that $k = 2$, the mean arrival rate is two customers per hour, the expected service time is 0.25 hours, and the maximum permissible number of customers in the system is two. Derive the steady-state probability distribution of the number of customers in the system, and then calculate the expected number. Compare this with the corresponding results when the service-time distribution is *exponential* instead.

10 The Application of Queueing Theory

Queueing theory has enjoyed a prominent place among the modern analytical techniques of operations research. However, the emphasis thus far has been on developing a mathematical *descriptive* theory. Thus queueing theory is not directly concerned with achieving the goal of operations research: *optimal decision making.* Rather, it develops *information* on the *behavior* of queueing systems. This provides *part* of the information needed to conduct an operations research study attempting to find the *best* design for a queueing system.

This chapter discusses the *application* of queueing theory in the broader context of an overall operations research study. It begins by introducing three examples that will be used for illustration throughout the chapter. Section 10.2 discusses the basic considerations for *decision making* in this context. The following two sections then develop *decision* models for the *optimal* design of queueing systems. The last model requires the incorporation of *travel-time models,* which are presented in Sec. 10.5. Section 10.6 then describes how to estimate the parameters of a queueing model that represents a real queueing system.

10.1 EXAMPLES

Example 1—How Many Repairmen?

Simulation, Inc., a small company that makes gidgets for analog computers, has 10 gidget-making machines. However, because these machines break down and require repair frequently, the company has only enough operators to operate *eight* machines at a time, so two machines are available on a standby basis for use while other machines are down. Thus eight machines are always operating whenever no more than two machines are waiting to be repaired, but the number of operating machines is reduced by 1 for each additional machine waiting to be repaired.

The time until any given operating machine breaks down has an exponential distribution, with a mean of 20 days. The time required to repair a machine also has an exponential distribution, with a mean of 2 days. Until now the company has had just *one* repairman to repair these machines. However, this has frequently resulted in reduced productivity by having *less than eight* operating machines. Therefore, consideration is being given to hiring a *second* repairman, so that *two* machines can be repaired simultaneously.

Thus the queueing system to be studied has the repairmen as its servers and the machines requiring repair as its customers, where the problem is to choose between having *one* or *two* servers. (Notice the analogy between this problem and the *County Hospital* emergency room problem described in Sec. 9.1.) This system fits a slight variation of the *basic model with a limited source* presented in Sec. 9.6, where $M = 10$ machines, $\lambda = \frac{1}{20}$ customers per day (for each operating machine), and $\mu = \frac{1}{2}$ customers per day. The variation is that the λ_0 and λ_1 parameters of the birth-and-death process are changed from $\lambda_0 = 10\lambda$ and $\lambda_1 = 9\lambda$ to $\lambda_0 = 8\lambda$ and $\lambda_1 = 8\lambda$. (All the other parameters are the same as given in Sec. 9.6.) Therefore the C_n factors for calculating the P_n probabilities change accordingly (see Sec. 9.5).

Each repairman costs the company approximately $70/day. However, the estimated *lost profit* from not having a machine operating to produce gidgets is $100/day. (The company could sell the full output from eight operating machines, but not much more).

The analysis of this problem will be pursued in Secs. 10.3 and 10.4.

Example 2—Which Computer?

Emerald University currently has one large computer that is shared by everyone on campus. Because students have been experiencing long turnaround times, the university now is planning to lease an additional small batch-processing computer for the exclusive use of its students, while reserving the large computer for the other users. Two models are being considered: one from the MBI Corporation and the other from the EG Company. The MBI computer costs more but is somewhat faster than the EG computer. In particular, if a sequence of typical student programs were run continuously for 1 hour, the number completed would have a Poisson distribution with a mean of 30 and 25 for the MBI and EG computer, respectively. A statistical study has shown that the student population actually submits programs to be run every 3 minutes on the average during all operating hours and that the time from one submission to the next has an exponential distribution with this mean. The leasing cost per operating hour would be $100 for the MBI computer and $75 for the EG computer.

Thus the queueing system of concern has the new small computer as its (single) server and the students' programs as its customers. Furthermore, this system fits the single-server version of the *basic model* (Poisson input and exponential service times) presented in Sec. 9.6. With 1 hour as the unit of time, $\lambda = (60 \text{ min/hr})/(3 \text{ min/customer}) = 20$ customers per hour, whereas $\mu = 30$ and 25 customers per hour with the MBI and EG computer, respectively. You will see in Secs. 10.3 and 10.4 how the decision between the two computers was made.

Example 3—How Many Tool Cribs?

The *Mechanical Company* is designing a new plant. This plant will need to include one or more tool cribs in the factory area to store tools required by the shop mechanics. The tools will be handed out by clerks as the mechanics arrive and request them and returned to the clerks when no longer needed. In existing plants there have been frequent complaints from foremen that their mechanics have had to waste too much time traveling to tool cribs and waiting to be served, so it appears that there should be *more* tool cribs and clerks in the new plant. On the other hand, management is exerting pressure to reduce overhead in the new plant, which would lead to *less* tool cribs and clerks. To resolve these conflicting pressures, an operations research study is to be conducted to determine just how many tool cribs and clerks should be provided in the new plant.

Each tool crib constitutes a queueing system, with the clerks as its servers and the mechanics as its customers. Based on previous experience, it is estimated that the time required by a tool-crib clerk to service a mechanic has an exponential distribution, with a mean of ½ minute. Judging from the anticipated number of mechanics in the entire factory area, it is also predicted that they would require this service *randomly* but at a mean rate of two mechanics per minute. Therefore it was decided to use the first *basic model* of Sec. 9.6 with Poisson input and exponential service times to represent each queueing system. With 1 hour as the unit of time, $\mu = 120$. If only one tool crib were to be provided, λ also would be 120. With more than one tool crib, this mean arrival rate would be divided among the different queueing systems.

The net cost to the company of each tool crib clerk is about \$5/hour. The capital recovery costs, upkeep costs, and so forth associated with each tool crib provided is estimated to be \$4 per working hour. While a mechanic is busy, the value to the company of his output averages about \$12/hour.

Sections 10.3 and 10.5 include discussions of how this (and additional) information were used to make the required decisions.

10.2 DECISION MAKING

Queueing-type situations requiring decision making arise in a wide variety of contexts. For this reason it is not possible to present a meaningful decision-making procedure applicable to all these situations. Instead, this section attempts to give a broad conceptual picture of the general approach to a predominant group of waiting-line problems.

A large proportion of waiting-line problems that arise in practice involve making one or a combination of the following decisions:

1. Number of servers at a service facility.
2. Efficiency of the servers.
3. Number of service facilities.

When such problems are formulated in terms of a queueing model, the corresponding decision variables usually would be s (number of servers at each facility), μ (mean service rate per busy server), and λ (mean arrival rate at each facility). The *number of service facilities* is directly related to λ because, assuming a uniform work load among the facilities, λ equals the total mean arrival rate to all facilities divided by the number of facilities.

The three examples of Sec. 10.1 respectively illustrate situations involving these three decisions. The first kind of decision is particularly common. However, the other two also arise frequently, particularly for *business-industrial* queueing systems. One example illustrating a decision on the *efficiency of the servers* is the selection of the type of materials-handling equipment (the servers) to purchase to transport certain kinds of loads (the customers). Still another such example arises when selecting the size of a maintenance crew (where the entire crew is one server). A decision as to the *number of service facilities* to distribute throughout an area may be required for such facilities as restrooms, first-aid centers, drinking fountains, storage areas, reproduction equipment, and so on.

All the specific decisions discussed above involve the general question of the *appropriate level of service* to provide in a queueing system. As mentioned at the beginning of Chap. 9, decisions regarding the amount of service capacity to provide usually are based primarily on two considerations: (1) the cost incurred by providing the service, as shown in Fig. 10.1, and (2) the amount of waiting for

Figure 10.1 Service cost as a function of service level.

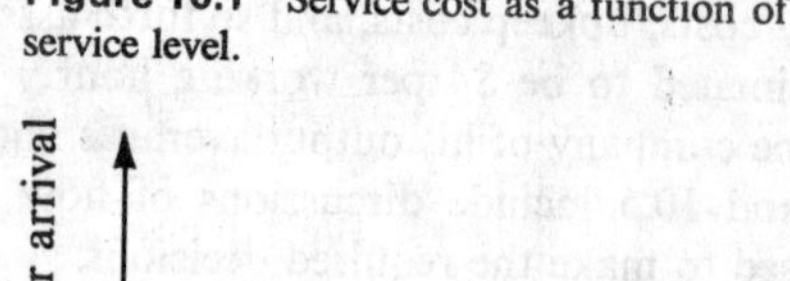

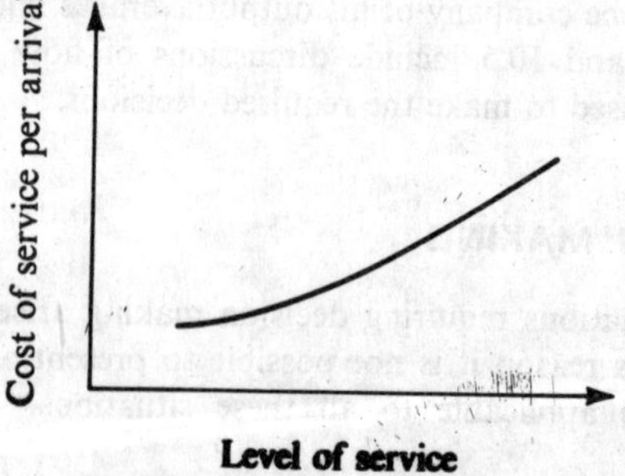

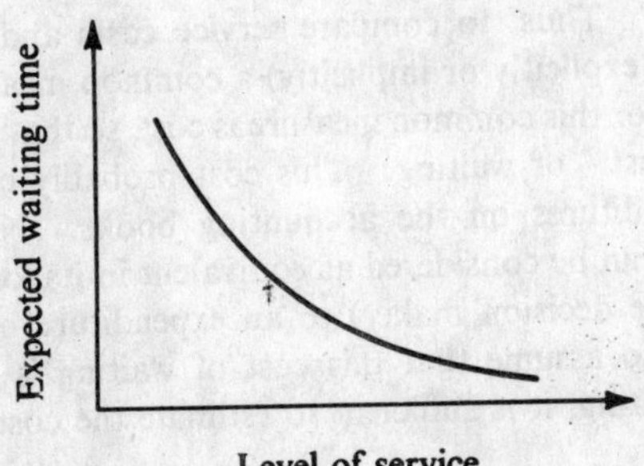

Figure 10.2 Expected waiting time as a function of service level.

that service, as suggested in Fig. 10.2. Figure 10.2 would be obtained by using the appropriate waiting-time equation from queueing theory.

It is readily apparent that these two considerations create conflicting pressures on the decision maker. The objective of reducing service costs recommends a minimal level of service. On the other hand, long waiting times are undesirable, which recommends a high level of service. Therefore it is necessary to strive for some type of compromise. To assist in this endeavor, Figs. 10.1 and 10.2 may be combined, as shown in Fig. 10.3. The problem is thereby reduced to selecting the point on the curve of Fig. 10.3 which gives the best balance between the average delay in being serviced and the cost of providing that service. Reference to Figs. 10.1 and 10.2 would indicate the corresponding level of service.

Unfortunately, it is all too easy to terminate further analysis and make a quick subjective judgment on the basis of Fig. 10.3 (or less). Actually, the most crucial portion of the analysis still lies ahead. An intelligent decision on the proper balance between delays and service costs can be made only after the relative seriousness of delays and service costs has been established. This requires obtaining answers to such questions as "How much expenditure on service is equivalent (in its detrimental impact) to a customer being delayed

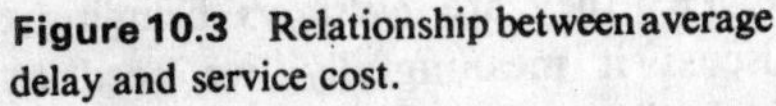

Figure 10.3 Relationship between average delay and service cost.

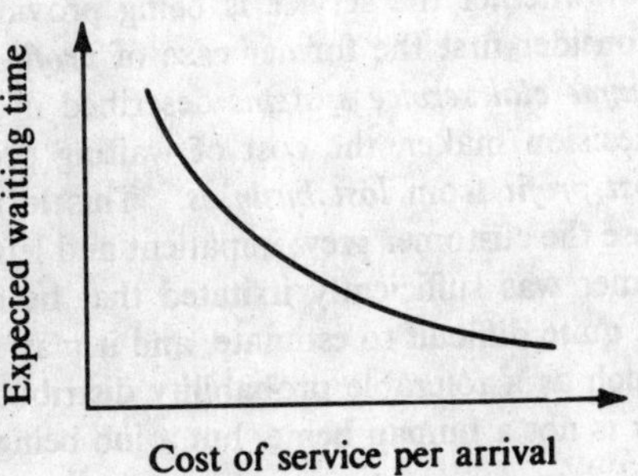

one unit of time?" Thus, to compare service costs and waiting times, it is necessary to adopt (explicitly or implicitly) a common measure of their impact. The natural choice for this common measure is cost, so that it becomes necessary to estimate the "cost" of waiting. This cost probably can not be identified entirely with expenditures on the accounting books. Nevertheless, a given amount of waiting can be considered as equivalent in its long-run impact (from the viewpoint of the decision maker) to an expenditure of a certain amount. If it is reasonable to assume that this cost of waiting is proportional to the total amount of waiting, it is sufficient to estimate the cost of waiting per unit time per arrival.

A common viewpoint in practice is that the cost of waiting is often too intangible to be amenable to estimation; hence the decision must instead be based on more tangible, even if less fundamental, criteria such as the desired expected waiting time in Fig. 10.3. The fallacy in this viewpoint is that it is impossible to avoid doing the equivalent of estimating waiting costs when analyzing the problem rationally. Whether it is done explicitly or implicitly, any comparison of waiting times and service costs must inevitably reduce to estimating the cost that is equivalent to the waiting. The only question is whether the estimation should be done explicitly or implicitly. This depends, in part, upon the time and cost required to develop a reasonable explicit estimate as opposed to the potential savings. However, it seems evident that performing the penetrating analysis required to obtain this explicit estimate should provide a sounder basis for the required decision than superficial criteria that are ultimately based on these same cost considerations in a very imprecise and intuitive way. In addition to using a better estimate, this explicit procedure permits using rigorous mathematical analysis to accurately identify the decision that minimizes total estimated expected cost.

Granted that an explicit estimate of the cost of waiting would be desirable, the next question is how to develop this estimate. Because of the diversity of waiting-line situations, no single estimating process is generally applicable. However, we shall discuss the basic considerations involved for several types of situations.

One broad category is where the customers are *external* to the organization providing the service, i.e., they are *outsiders* bringing their business to the organization. To discuss it meaningfully, we need to further divide this category in terms of whether the service is being provided *for profit* or on a *nonprofit basis*. Consider first the former case of *profit-making* organizations (typified by the *commercial service systems* described in Sec. 9.3). From the viewpoint of the decision maker, the cost of waiting probably would consist primarily of the *lost profit* from *lost business*. This lost business may occur immediately (because the customer grew impatient and left) and/or in the future (because the customer was sufficiently irritated that he did not come again). This kind of cost is quite difficult to estimate, and it may be necessary to revert to other criteria, such as a tolerable probability distribution of waiting times. When the customer is not a human being, but a job being performed on order, there may also be more readily identifiable costs incurred, such as those caused by idle in-process inventories or increased expediting and administrative effort.

Now consider the type of situation where service is provided on a *non-profit* to customers *external* to the organization (typical of *social service systems* and some *transportation service systems*). In this case the cost of waiting usually is a *social cost* of some kind. Thus it is necessary to evaluate the consequences of the waiting for the individuals involved and/or for society as a whole and to try to impute a monetary value to avoiding these consequences. (We shall illustrate this in the next section with Example 2—the Emerald University computer problem—which most closely fits this type of situation.) Once again, this kind of cost is quite difficult to estimate, and it may be necessary to revert to other criteria.

A situation that may be more amenable to estimating waiting costs is one in which the customers are *internal* to the organization providing the service (typical of *business-industrial service systems*). For example, the customers may be machines (as in Example 1) or employees (as in Example 3) of a firm. Therefore it may be possible to directly identify some or all of the costs associated with the idleness of these customers. A detailed discussion of the estimating process for this situation is available elsewhere.[1] However, to illustrate the underlying rationale (and to warn against a common pitfall), consider the case where the customers are machine operators. At first glance it is easy to jump to the conclusion that the relevant cost to the firm if such an employee waits in a queue is his wage during the waiting time. However, this would imply that the net reduction in the earnings of the firm because an operator has to wait is equal to his wage. There is no reason why this particular relationship should hold in general. Perhaps one reason this approach is sometimes used in practice is the misconception that what is being "wasted" by the waiting is the operator's wage. But he will receive the same wage regardless of the waiting, and what is instead being lost is the contribution to the firm's earnings that the operator would have made otherwise. Furthermore, the worker does not work in a vacuum; rather, he is the catalyst that causes the efforts of all the economic resources involved (machinery and equipment, materials, managerial skill, capital, and so on) to result in one of the changes in the product necessary to make it salable. Thus, although the output of the machine operator and his colleagues is essential if a salable product is to be produced, the sale of that product must not only pay their wages but must also pay for the other necessary economic resources. Therefore, when the operator is idle because he is waiting in a queue, what is being wasted is productive output that would have helped pay the fixed expenses of the firm in addition to the operator's wage. In short, rather than focusing solely on the value of the one economic resource that physically waits in the queue, the emphasis instead should be on finding the value of all the economic resources that would be idled as a consequence of this

[1] See chap. 12 of Selected Reference 1.

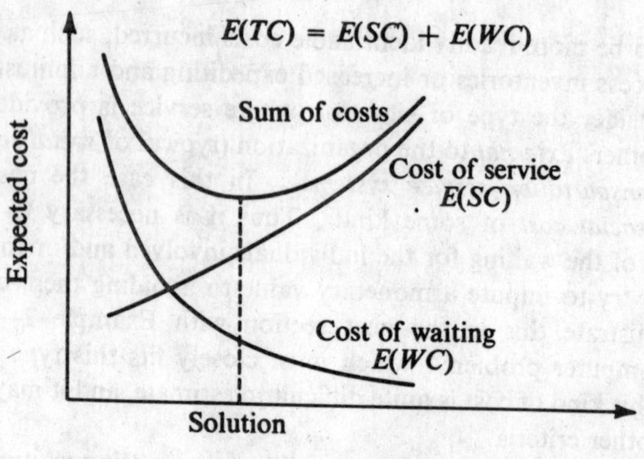

Figure 10.4 Conceptual solution procedure for many waiting-line problems.

waiting. This frequently boils down to evaluating the *lost profit* from *all lost productivity*.

Given that the cost of waiting has been evaluated explicitly, the remainder of the analysis is conceptually straightforward. The objective would be to determine the level of service which minimizes the total of the expected cost of service and the expected cost of waiting for that service. This concept is depicted in Fig. 10.4, where *WC* denotes *waiting cost*, *SC* denotes *service cost*, and *TC* denotes *total cost*. Thus the mathematical statement of the objective is to

$$\text{Minimize} \quad E(TC) = E(SC) + E(WC).$$

Sections 10.3 to 10.5 are concerned with the *application* of this concept to various types of problems. Thus Sec. 10.3 describes how $E(WC)$ can be expressed mathematically. Section 10.4 then focuses on $E(SC)$ to formulate the overall objective function $E(TC)$ for several basic design problems (including some with multiple decision variables, so that the level of service axis in Fig. 10.4 actually requires more than one dimension). This section also introduces the fact that when a decision on the number of service facilities is required, time spent in traveling to and from a facility should be included in the analysis (as part of the total time waiting for service)—Sec. 10.5 discusses how to do this.

10.3 FORMULATION OF WAITING-COST FUNCTIONS

To express $E(WC)$ mathematically, it is first necessary to formulate a *waiting-cost function* that describes how the actual waiting cost being incurred varies with the current behavior of the queueing system. The form of this function depends upon the context of the individual problem. However, most situations can be represented by one of the two basic forms described below.

The $g(N)$ Form

Consider first the situation discussed in the preceding section where the queueing system *customers* are *internal* to the organization providing the service, and so the primary cost of waiting may be the *lost profit from lost productivity*. The *rate* at which productive output is lost sometimes is essentially *proportional* to the number of customers in the queueing system. However, in many cases there is not enough productive work available to keep all the members of the calling population continuously busy. Therefore little productive output may be lost by having just a few members idle waiting for service in the queueing system, whereas the loss may increase greatly if a few more members are idled requiring service. Consequently, the primary property of the queueing system that determines the *current rate* at which waiting costs are being incurred is N, the *number of customers* in the system. Thus the form of the waiting-cost function for this kind of situation is that illustrated in Fig. 10.5, namely, a function of N. We shall denote this form by $g(N)$.

The $g(N)$ function would be constructed for a particular situation by estimating $g(n)$, the waiting cost rate incurred when $N = n$, for $n = 1, 2, \ldots,$ where $g(0) = 0$. After computing the P_n probabilities for a given design of the queueing system,

$$E(WC) = E\{g(N)\}$$

can then be calculated. Since N is a random variable, this is done by using the equation for the expected value of a *function* of a *discrete* random variable (see Sec. 8.8); that is,

$$E(WC) = \sum_{n=0}^{\infty} g(n)P_n.$$

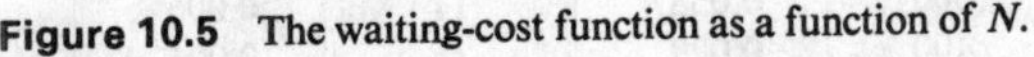

Figure 10.5 The waiting-cost function as a function of N.

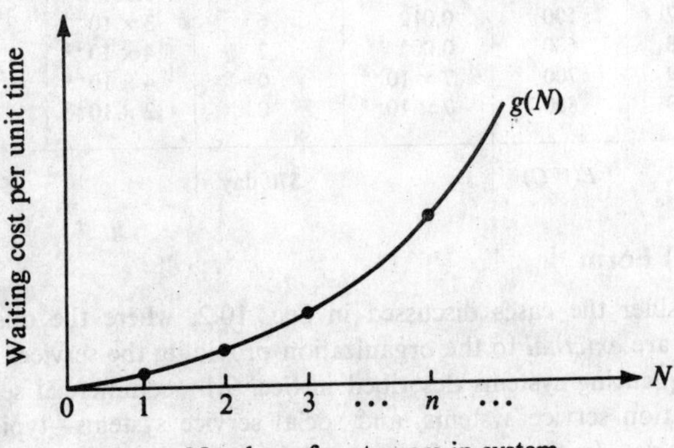

When $g(N)$ is a *linear* function (i.e., the waiting-cost rate is proportional to N), then

$$g(N) = C_w N,$$

where C_w is the cost of waiting per unit time for each customer. In this case $E(WC)$ reduces to

$$E(WC) = C_w \sum_{n=0}^{\infty} nP_n = C_w L.$$

EXAMPLE 1—HOW MANY REPAIRMEN? For Example 1, Sec. 10.1, *Simulation, Inc.*, has two *standby* gidget-making machines, so there is *no* lost productivity as long as the number of customers (machines requiring repair) in the system does not exceed *two*. However, for each *additional* customer (up to the maximum of 10 total), the estimated lost profit is \$100/day. Therefore

$$g(n) = \begin{cases} 0, & \text{for } n = 0, 1, 2 \\ 100(n-2), & \text{for } n = 3, 4, \ldots, 10, \end{cases}$$

as shown in Table 10.1. Consequently, $E(WC)$ is calculated by summing the last column of Table 10.1 for each of the two cases of interest, namely, having *one* repairman ($s = 1$) or *two* repairmen ($s = 2$).

Table 10.1 Calculation of $E(WC)$ for Example 1

		$s = 1$		$s = 2$	
$N = n$	$g(n)$	P_n	$g(n)P_n$	P_n	$g(n)P_n$
0	0	0.271	0	0.433	0
1	0	0.217	0	0.346	0
2	0	0.173	0	0.139	0
3	100	0.139	14	0.055	6
4	200	0.097	19	0.019	4
5	300	0.058	17	0.006	2
6	400	0.029	12	0.001	0
7	500	0.012	6	3×10^{-4}	0
8	600	0.003	2	4×10^{-5}	0
9	700	7×10^{-4}	0	4×10^{-6}	0
10	800	7×10^{-5}	0	2×10^{-7}	0
	$E(WC)$		\$70/day		\$12/day

The $h(\mathscr{W})$ Form

Now consider the cases discussed in Sec. 10.2, where the queueing system *customers* are *external* to the organization providing the service. Three major types of queueing systems described in Sec. 9.1—commercial service systems, transportation service systems, and social service systems—typically fall into this category. In the case of *commercial service systems*, the primary cost of waiting may be the *lost profit from lost future business.* For *transportation service systems* and *social systems*, the primary cost of waiting may be in the form of a *social cost.* However, for either type of cost, its magnitude tends to be affected greatly by the size of the waiting times experienced by the customers. Thus the primary property of the queueing system that determines the waiting costs currently being incurred is $\mathscr{W}$, the waiting time in the system for the *individual* customers. Consequently, the form of the waiting-cost function for this kind of situation is that illustrated in Fig. 10.6, namely, a function of $\mathscr{W}$. We shall denote this form by $h(\mathscr{W})$.

One way of constructing the $h(\mathscr{W})$ function is to estimate $h(w)$ (the waiting cost incurred when a customer's waiting time $\mathscr{W} = w$) for several different values of w and then to fit a polynomial to these points. The expectation of this *function* of a *continuous* random variable (see Sec. 8.7) is then defined as

$$E\{h(\mathscr{W})\} = \int_0^\infty h(w) f_{\mathscr{W}}(w)\, dw,$$

where $f_{\mathscr{W}}(w)$ is the probability density function of $\mathscr{W}$. However, since $E\{h(\mathscr{W})\}$ is the expected waiting cost *per customer* and $E(WC)$ is the expected waiting cost *per unit time*, these two quantities are not equal in this case. To relate them it is necessary to multiply $E\{h(\mathscr{W})\}$ by the expected *number of customers per unit time* entering the queueing system. In particular, if the mean arrival rate is a constant λ, then

$$E(WC) = \lambda E\{h(\mathscr{W})\} = \lambda \int_0^\infty h(w) f_{\mathscr{W}}(w)\, dw.$$

EXAMPLE 2—WHICH COMPUTER? Since the students of *Emerald University* would experience different turnaround times with the two computers under consideration (see Sec. 10.1), the choice between them required an evaluation of

Figure 10.6 The waiting-cost function as a function of $\mathscr{W}$.

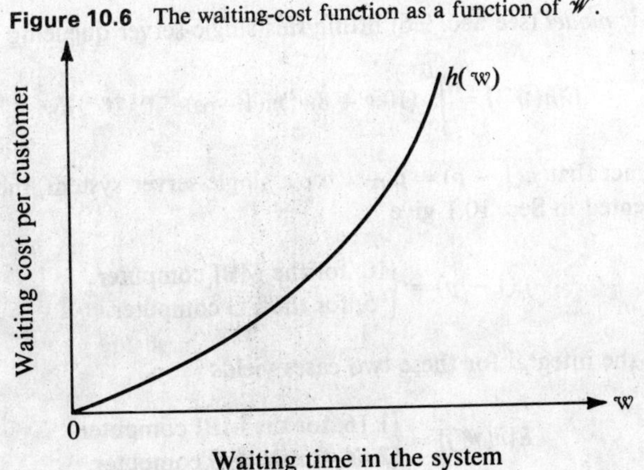

the *consequences* of making students wait for their programs to be run. This evaluation led to the following conclusions.

From the university's viewpoint there are two primary consequences of making students wait. First, it decreases the time available for the student to pursue other academic endeavors because little effective studying can be done during the wait. Second, it detracts from the efficiency and academic value of doing the computer assignment because it breaks the continuity in dealing with the problem and it may prevent the student from fully completing the assignment to his/her satisfaction.

To evaluate the first consequence, an estimate was made that an average student studies at only one-third of full efficiency during the wait. Furthermore, by calculating the total expenditures from all sources for a student's college education, a monetary figure of \$15/hour was placed on the value of being able to study at *full* efficiency. Therefore this component of waiting cost was estimated to be \$10/hour, that is, $10\mathscr{W}$, where $\mathscr{W}$ is expressed in units of *hours*.

To evaluate the second consequence, two groups of students were interviewed just after experiencing turnaround times of ½ hour and 1 hour, respectively. They were asked to estimate how much additional time working on the assignment had been caused by the break in the continuity and what the effect of the wait on their ability to complete the assignment satisfactorily was. On this basis, averages of \$2 and \$8 were imputed to the value of a student being able to avoid this consequence entirely rather than having a wait of ½ hour and 1 hour, respectively. Therefore this component of waiting cost was estimated to be $8\mathscr{W}^2$.

This analysis yields

$$h(\mathscr{W}) = 10\mathscr{W} + 8\mathscr{W}^2.$$

Since

$$f_{\mathscr{W}}(w) = \mu(1-\rho)e^{-\mu(1-\rho)w}$$

for the *basic model* (see Sec. 9.6) fitting this single-server queueing system,

$$E\{h(\mathscr{W})\} = \int_0^\infty (10w + 8w^2)\mu(1-\rho)e^{-\mu(1-\rho)w}\,dw.$$

Using the fact that $\mu(1-\rho) = \mu - \lambda$ for a single-server system, the values of μ and λ presented in Sec. 10.1 give

$$\mu(1-\rho) = \begin{cases} 10, & \text{for the MBI computer} \\ 5, & \text{for the EG computer.} \end{cases}$$

Evaluating the integral for these two cases yields

$$E\{h(\mathscr{W})\} = \begin{cases} 1.16, & \text{for the MBI computer} \\ 2.64, & \text{for the EG computer.} \end{cases}$$

This represents the expected waiting cost (in dollars) for each student arriving with a computer program to be run. Since $\lambda = 2$, the total expected waiting cost per hour becomes

$$E(WC) = \begin{cases} \$23.20/\text{hr, for the MBI computer} \\ \$52.80/\text{hr, for the EG computer.} \end{cases}$$

The Linear Case When $h(\mathcal{W})$ is a *linear* function

$$h(\mathcal{W}) = C_w \mathcal{W},$$

$E(WC)$ reduces to

$$E(WC) = \lambda E(C_w \mathcal{W}) = C_w(\lambda W) = C_w L.$$

Note that this is identical to the result when $g(N)$ is a linear function. Consequently, when the total waiting cost incurred by the queueing system is simply *proportional* to the total waiting time, it does not matter whether the $g(N)$ or the $h(\mathcal{W})$ form is used for the waiting-cost function.

EXAMPLE 3—HOW MANY TOOL CRIBS? As indicated in Sec. 10.1, the value to the *Mechanical Company* of a busy mechanic's output averages about \$12/hour. Thus $C_w = 12$. Consequently, *for each tool crib* the expected waiting cost per hour is

$$E(WC) = 12L,$$

where L represents the expected number of mechanics waiting (or being served) at the tool crib.

10.4 DECISION MODELS

We mentioned in Sec. 10.2 that three common decision variables in designing queueing systems are s (number of servers), μ (mean service rate for each server), and λ (mean arrival rate at each service facility). We shall now formulate models for making some of these decisions.

Model 1—Unknown s

Model 1 is designed for the case where both μ and λ are fixed at a particular service facility, but a decision must be made on the number of servers to have on duty at the facility.

FORMULATION OF MODEL 1

Definition: C_s = marginal cost of a server per unit time.

Given: μ, λ, C_s.

To Find: s.

Objective: Minimize $E(TC) = sC_s + E(WC)$.

Since only a few alternative values of s normally need to be considered, the usual way of solving this model is to calculate $E(TC)$ for these values of s and select the minimizing one.

EXAMPLE 1—HOW MANY REPAIRMEN? For Example 1 of Sec. 10.1, each repairman (server) costs *Simulation Inc.* approximately \$70/day. Thus, with a day as the unit of time, $C_s = 70$. Using the values of $E(WC)$ calculated in Table 10.1 then yields the results shown in Table 10.2, which indicate that the company should continue having just *one* repairman.

Table 10.2 Calculation of $E(TC)$ for Example 1

s	sC_s	$E(WC)$	$E(TC)$
1	70	70	\$140/day ← minimum
2	140	12	\$152/day
≥ 3	≥ 210	≥ 0	$\geq$ \$210/day

Model 2—Unknown μ and s

Model 2 is designed for the case where both the *efficiency* of service, measured by μ, and the *number* of servers s at a service facility need to be selected. Alternative values of μ may be available because there is a choice on the *quality* of the servers. (One example is where both the *type* and *quantity* of materials-handling equipment to transport certain kinds of loads must be selected for purchase.) Another possibility is that the *speed* of the servers can be adjusted mechanically. (For example, the speed of machines frequently can be adjusted by changing the amount of power consumed, which also changes the cost of operation.) Still another type of example is the selection of the number of crews (the servers) and the size of each crew (which determines μ) for jointly performing a certain task, e.g., maintenance work, loading and unloading operations, inspection work, setup of machines, and so forth. In many cases only a few alternative values of μ are available, e.g., the efficiency of the alternative types of materials-handling equipment or the efficiency of the alternative crew sizes.

FORMULATION OF MODEL 2

Definitions: $f(\mu)$ = marginal cost of server per unit time when mean service rate is μ.

A = set of feasible values of μ.

Given: $\lambda, f(\mu), A$.

To find: μ, s.

Objective: Minimize $E(TC) = sf(\mu) + E(WC)$, subject to $\mu \in A$.

EXAMPLE 2—WHICH COMPUTER? As indicated in Sec. 10.1, $\mu = 30$ for the *MBI computer* and $\mu = 25$ for the *EG computer*, where 1 hour is the unit of time.

These are the only two computers being considered by Emerald University, so

$$A = \{25, 30\}.$$

Since the leasing cost per operating hour would be \$75 for the *EG* computer ($\mu = 25$) and \$100 for the MBI computer ($\mu = 30$),

$$f(\mu) = \begin{cases} 75, & \text{for } \mu = 25 \\ 100, & \text{for } \mu = 30. \end{cases}$$

The computer chosen will be the only one available for student use, so the number of servers (computers) for this queueing system is restricted to be $s = 1$. Hence

$$E(TC) = f(\mu) + E(WC),$$

where $E(WC)$ is given in Sec. 10.3 for the two alternatives. Thus

$$\begin{aligned} E(TC) &= 75 + 52.80 \\ &= \$127.80/\text{hr}, \text{ for EG computer;} \\ E(TC) &= 100 + 23.20 \\ &= \$123.20/\text{hr}, \text{ for MBI computer.} \end{aligned}$$

Consequently, the decision was made to lease the MBI computer.

This example illustrates a case where the number of feasible values of μ is *finite* but the value of s is fixed. If s were not fixed, a two-stage approach can be used to solve such a problem. First, for each individual value of μ, set $C_s = f(\mu)$, and solve for the value of s that minimizes $E(TC)$ for model 1. Second, compare these minimum $E(TC)$ for the alternative values of μ, and select the one giving the overall minimum.

When the number of feasible values of μ is *infinite* (as when mechanically setting the speed of a machine or piece of equipment within some feasible interval), another two-stage approach sometimes can be used to solve the problem. First, for each individual value of s, *analytically* solve for the value of μ that minimizes $E(TC)$. [This requires setting to zero the derivative of $E(TC)$ with respect to μ and then solving this equation for μ, which can be done only when analytical expressions are available for both $f(\mu)$ and $E(WC)$.] Second, compare these minimum $E(TC)$ for the alternative values of s, and select the one giving the overall minimum.

This analytical approach frequently is relatively straightforward for the case of $s = 1$ (see Prob. 11). However, since far fewer and less convenient analytical results are available for *multiple-server* versions of queueing models, this approach is either difficult (requiring computer calculations with numerical methods to solve the equation for μ) or completely impossible when $s > 1$. Therefore a more practical approach is to consider only a relatively small number of representative values of μ and to use available tabulated results for the appropriate queueing model to obtain (or approximate) $E(TC)$ for these μ.

Fortunately, under certain fairly common circumstances described below, $s = 1$ (and its minimizing value of μ) *must* yield the overall minimum $E(TC)$ for model 2, so $s > 1$ cases need not be considered at all.

Optimality of a Single Server Under certain conditions, $s = 1$ *necessarily is optimal* for model 2.

The primary conditions[1] are

1. The value of μ minimizing $E(TC)$ for $s = 1$ is feasible;
2. $f(\mu)$ is either a *linear* function or a *concave* function (as defined in Appendix 1).

In effect, this optimality result indicates that it is better to concentrate service capacity into one *fast* server rather than dispersing it among several *slow* servers. Condition 2 says that this concentrating of a given amount of service capacity can be done without increasing the cost of service Condition 1 says that it must be possible to make μ sufficiently large so that a single server can be used to full advantage.

To motivate why this result holds, consider *any* other solution to model 2, $(s, \mu) = (s^*, \mu^*)$, where $s^* > 1$. The service capacity of this system would be $s^*\mu^*$. We shall now compare this solution with the corresponding *single-server* solution $(s, \mu) = (1, s^*\mu^*)$ having the *same* service capacity. In particular, Table 10.3 compares the *mean rate* at which service completions would occur for each given number of customers in the system $N = n$. Table 10.3 shows

Table 10.3 Comparison of Service Efficiency for Model 2 Solutions

$N = n$	*Mean rate of service completions* (s^*, μ^*) *vs.* ($1, s^*\mu^*$) *for* (s, μ), *where* $s^* > 1$		
$n = 0$	0	=	0
$n = 1, 2, \ldots, s^* - 1$	$n\mu^*$	<	$s^*\mu^*$
$n \geq s^*$	$s^*\mu^*$	=	$s^*\mu^*$

that the service efficiency of the (s^*, μ^*) solution sometimes is worse but is never better than for the $(1, s^*\mu)$ solution because it can use the full service capacity only when there are at least s^* customers in the system, whereas the single-server solution uses the full service capacity whenever there are *any* customers in the system. Since this lower service efficiency can only increase waiting in the system, $E(WC)$ must be *larger* for (s^*, μ^*) than $(1, s^*\mu^*)$. Furthermore, the expected service cost must be *at least as large* because condition 2 [and $f(0) = 0$] imply that

$$s^*f(\mu^*) \geq f(s^*\mu^*).$$

Therefore $E(TC)$ is *larger* for (s^*, μ^*) than $(1, s^*\mu^*)$. Finally, note that condition 1 implies that there is a *feasible* solution with $s = 1$ that is *at least as good*

[1] There also are minor restrictions on the queueing model and the waiting-cost function. However, any of the constant service-rate queueing models presented in Chap. 9 for $s \geq 1$ are allowed. If the $g(N)$ form is used for the waiting-cost function, it can be any *increasing* function. If the $h(\mathscr{W})$ form is used, it can be any *linear* function or any *convex* function (as defined in Appendix 1), which fits most cases of interest.

as $(1, s^*\mu^*)$. The conclusion is that *any* $s > 1$ solution can *not* be optimal for model 2, so $s = 1$ must be.[1]

This result is still of some use even when one or both conditions fail to hold. If μ can not be made sufficiently large to permit a single server, it still suggests that a *few* fast servers should be preferred to many slow ones. If condition 2 does not hold, we still know that $E(WC)$ is minimized by concentrating any given amount of service capacity into a single server, so the best $s = 1$ solution must be at least nearly optimal unless it causes a ***substantial*** increase in service cost.

Model 3—Unknown λ and s

Model 3 is designed especially for the case where it is necessary to select both the *number of service facilities* and the *number of servers* (s) at each one. The typical situation would be where a population (such as the employees in an industrial building) must be provided with a certain service, so a decision must be made on what proportion of the population (and therefore what value of λ) should be assigned to each service facility. Examples of such facilities include *employee facilities* (drinking fountains, vending machines, and restrooms), *storage facilities*, and *reproduction equipment*. It may sometimes be clear that only a single server should be provided at each facility (e.g., one drinking fountain or one Xerox machine), but s often is also a decision variable.

To simplify our presentation, we shall require in model 3 that λ and s must be the same for all service facilities. However, it should be recognized that a slight improvement in the indicated solution might be achieved by permitting minor deviations in these parameters at individual facilities. This should be investigated as part of the detailed analysis that generally follows the application of the mathematical model.

FORMULATION OF MODEL 3

Definitions: C_s = marginal cost of server per unit time.
C_f = fixed cost of service per service facility per unit time.
λ_p = mean arrival rate for entire population.
n = number of service facilities = λ_p/λ.

Given: μ, C_s, C_f, λ_p.

To find: λ, s.

Objective: Minimize $E(TC)$, subject to $\lambda = \lambda_p/n$, where $n = 1, 2, \ldots$.

It might appear at first glance that the appropriate expression for the expected total cost per unit time of all the facilities should be

$$E(TC) \stackrel{?}{=} n[(C_f + sC_s) + E(WC)],$$

[1] For a rigorous proof of this result, see Shaler Stidham, Jr., "On the Optimality of Single-Server Queueing Systems," *Operations Research*, **18**: 708–732, 1970.

where $E(WC)$ here represents the expected waiting cost per unit time for *each* facility. However, if this expression actually were valid, it would imply that $n = 1$ *necessarily* is optimal for model 3. [The reasoning is completely analogous to that for the optimality of a single server result for model 2, namely, any solution $(n, s) = (n^*, s^*)$ with $n^* > 1$ has higher service costs than the $(n, s) = (1, n^*s^*)$ solution, and it *also* has a higher expected waiting cost because it sometimes makes less effective use of the available service capacity. In particular, it sometimes has idle servers at one facility while customers are waiting at another facility, so the mean rate of service completions would be less than if the customers had access to *all* the servers at one common facility.] Since there are many situations where it obviously would *not* be optimal to have just *one* service facility (e.g., the number of restrooms in the Pentagon), something must be wrong with this expression. The deficiency is that it considers only the cost of service and the cost of waiting at the *service facilities* and totally ignores the cost of the time wasted in *traveling to and from* the facilities. Since travel time would be prohibitive with only one service facility for a large population, enough separate facilities must be distributed throughout the population to hold down travel time to a reasonable level.

Thus, letting the *random variable* T be the round trip *travel time* for a customer coming to one of the service facilities, the *total time lost* by the customer actually is $(\mathscr{W} + T)$. (Recall from Chap. 9 that $\mathscr{W}$ is the waiting time in the queueing system *after* the customer arrives.) Therefore a customer's *total* cost for time lost should be based on $(\mathscr{W} + T)$ rather than just $\mathscr{W}$. To simplify the analysis, we shall separate this total cost into the *sum* of the *waiting-time cost* based on $\mathscr{W}$ (or N) and the *travel-time cost* based on T. We shall also assume that the travel-time cost is *proportional* to T, where C_t is the cost of each unit of travel time for each customer. For ease of presentation, suppose that the probability distribution of T is the same for each service facility, so that $C_t E(T)$ is the *expected travel cost* for each arrival at any of the service facilities. The resulting expression for $E(TC)$ would be

$$E(TC) = n[(C_f + sC_s) + E(WC) + \lambda C_t E(T)]$$

because λ is the expected number of arrivals *per unit time* at each facility. Consequently, if $E(T)$ could be evaluated for each case of interest, model 3 can be solved by calculating $E(TC)$ for various values of s for each n and then selecting the solution giving the overall minimum. The next section discusses how to evaluate $E(T)$ and also solves an example (Example 3) fitting model 3.

10.5 THE EVALUATION OF TRAVEL TIME

$E(T)$ can be interpreted as the *average travel time* spent by customers in coming both to and from a given service facility. Therefore the value of $E(T)$ depends very much upon the characteristics of the individual situation. However, we shall illustrate a rather general approach to evaluating $E(T)$ by developing a basic travel-time model and then calculating $E(T)$ for a particular example involving a more complicated situation. In both cases it is assumed that the portion of the population assigned to the service facility under consideration is *distributed uniformly* throughout the assigned area, that each arrival returns to its *original location* after receiving service, and that the average speed of travel does *not* depend upon the distance traveled. Another basic assumption is that all travel is *rectilinear*, i.e., it progresses along a system of *orthogonal* paths (aisles, streets, highways, and so on) that are *parallel* to the main sides of the area under consideration.

A Basic Travel-time Model

Description: Rectangular area and rectilinear travel, as shown in Fig. 10.7.

Definitions: T = travel time (round trip) for an arrival.
v = average velocity (speed) of customers in traveling to and from facility.
a, b, c, d = respective distances from facility to boundary of area assigned to facility, as shown in Fig. 10.7.

Given: v, a, b, c, d.

To find: Expected value of T, $E(T)$.

Using an orthogonal (x, y) coordinate system, Fig. 10.7 shows the coordinates (x, y) of the location of a *particular* customer. The x and y coordinates of the location from which a *random* arrival comes actually are *random variables* X and Y, where X ranges from $-a$ to c and Y ranges from $-b$ to d. Since the total distance traveled (round trip) by the random arrival is

$$D = 2(|X| + |Y|)$$

and

$$T = \frac{D}{v},$$

Figure 10.7 Graphical representation of a basic travel-time model, where the service facility is at (0, 0) and a random arrival comes from (and returns to) some location (x, y).

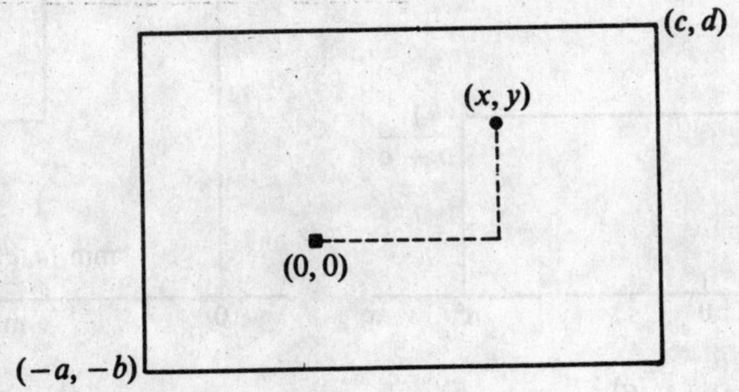

it follows that

$$E(T) = \frac{2}{v}(E\{|X|\} + E\{|Y|\}).$$

Thus the problem is reduced to identifying the probability distributions of $|X|$ and $|Y|$ and then calculating their means.

First consider $|X|$. Its probability distribution can be obtained directly from the probability of X. Since the customers are assumed to be distributed uniformly throughout the assigned area, and the *height* of the rectangular area is the *same* for all possible values of $X = x$, X must have a *uniform distribution* between $-a$ and c, as shown in Fig. 10.8*a*. Since $|x| = |-x|$, adding the probability density function values at x and $-x$ then yields the probability distribution of $|X|$ shown in Fig. 10.8*b*.

Therefore

$$\begin{aligned} E\{|X|\} &= \int_0^{\max\{a,c\}} x\, f_{|X|}(x)\, dx \\ &= \int_0^{\min\{a,c\}} \frac{2x}{a+c}\, dx + \int_{\min\{a,c\}}^{\max\{a,c\}} \frac{x}{a+c}\, dx \\ &= \frac{1}{2}\frac{1}{a+c}[(\min\{a,c\})^2 + (\max\{a,c\})^2] \\ &= \frac{a^2+c^2}{2(a+c)}. \end{aligned}$$

The analysis for $|Y|$ is completely analogous, where the *width* of the rectangular area for possible values of $Y = y$ now determines the probability distribution of Y. The result is that

$$E\{|Y|\} = \frac{b^2+d^2}{2(b+d)}.$$

Figure 10.8 Probability density functions of (*a*) X; (*b*) $|X|$.

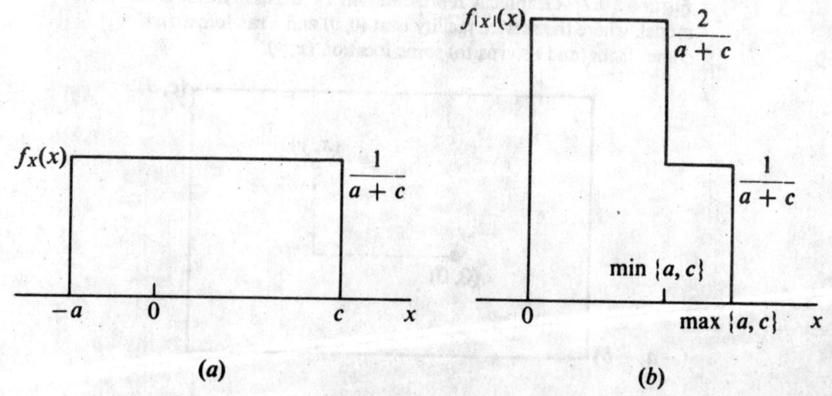

Consequently,

$$E(T) = \frac{1}{v}\left(\frac{a^2 + c^2}{a + c} + \frac{b^2 + d^2}{b + d}\right).$$

EXAMPLE 3—HOW MANY TOOL CRIBS? For the new plant being designed for the *Mechanical Company* (see Sec. 10.1), the layout of the portion of the factory area where the mechanics would work is shown in Fig. 10.9. The three *possible* locations for tool cribs are identified as Loc. 1, Loc. 2, and Loc. 3, where access to these locations would be provided by a system of orthogonal aisles parallel to the sides of the indicated area. The coordinates are given in units of *feet*. The mechanics will be distributed quite uniformly throughout the area shown, and each mechanic will be assigned to the *nearest* tool crib. It is estimated that the mechanics would walk to and from a tool crib at an average speed of slightly less than 3 miles/hour, so v is set at $v = 15{,}000$ feet/hour.

The three basic alternatives being considered are to have *three* tool cribs in the indicated locations, to have just *one* tool crib in Loc. 2, and to have ***two*** tool cribs in Locs. 1 and 3. The calculation of $E(T)$ for each alternative is given next, followed by the use of model 3 to make the choice between them.

$n = 3$ By using all three locations, ***each*** tool crib would be servicing a **300** × 300 foot *square* area. Therefore this is just a special case of the **basic** travel-time model presented above, where $a = c = 150$ and $b = d = 150$.

Figure 10.9 Layout for Example 3.

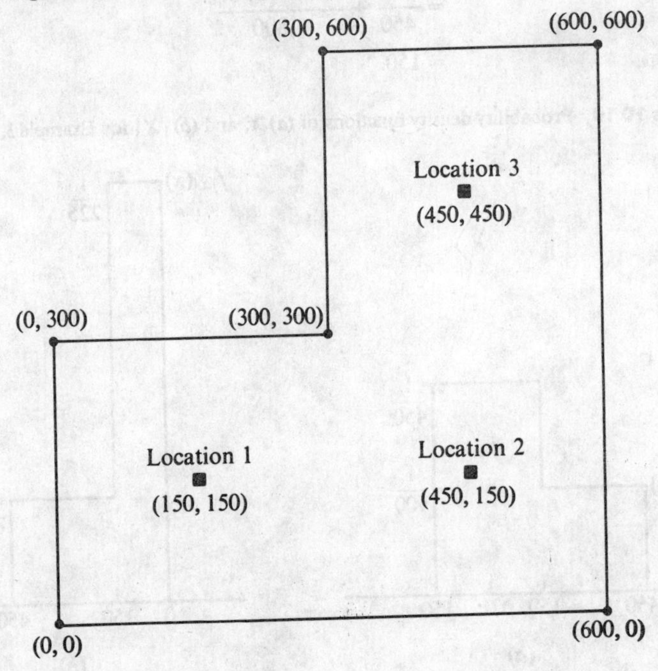

Consequently,

$$E(T) = \frac{1}{15{,}000 \text{ ft/hr}} \left(\frac{150^2 + 150^2}{150 + 150} + \frac{150^2 + 150^2}{150 + 150} \right) \text{ft}$$
$$= \frac{1}{15{,}000 \text{ ft/hr}} (300 \text{ ft})$$
$$= 0.02 \text{ hr.}$$

n = 1 With just *one* tool crib to service the entire area shown in Fig. 10.9, the derivation of $E(T)$ is a little more complicated than for the basic travel-time model. The first step is to relabel Loc. 2 as the origin (0,0) for an (x, y) coordinate system, so that 450 would be subtracted from the first coordinates shown and 150 would be subtracted from the second coordinates. The probability density function for X is then obtained by dividing the *height* for each possible value of $X = x$ by the total area (so that the area under the probability density function curve equals 1), as given in Fig. 10.10*a*. Combining the values for x and $-x$ then yields the probability distribution of $|X|$ shown in Fig. 10.10*b*.

Hence

$$E\{|X|\} = \int_0^{450} x \, f_{|X|}(x) \, dx$$
$$= \int_0^{150} x \left(\frac{1}{225} \right) dx + \int_{150}^{450} x \left(\frac{1}{900} \right) dx$$
$$= \frac{150^2}{450} + \frac{450^2 - 150^2}{1{,}800}$$
$$= 150.$$

Figure 10.10 Probability density functions of (*a*) X, and (*b*) $|X|$ for Example 3, with $n = 1$.

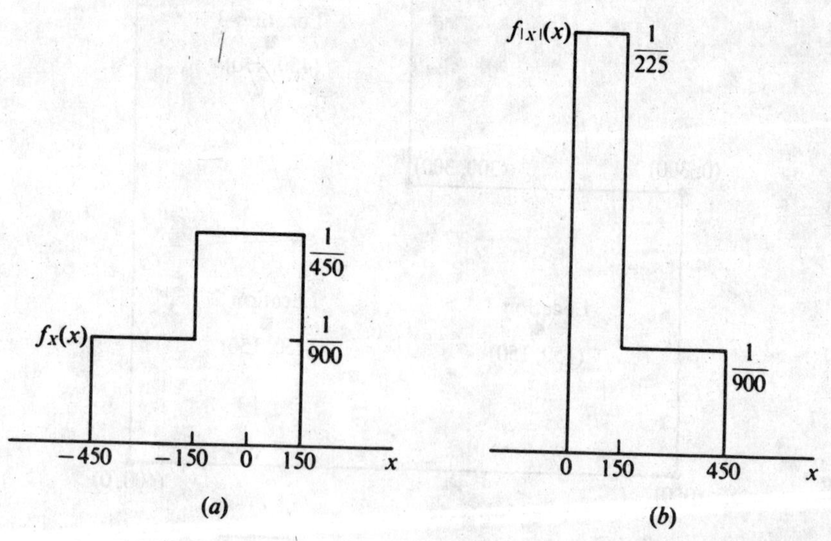

We suggest that you now try the same approach (but using the *width* of the area rather than height) to derive $E\{|Y|\}$. You will find that the probability distribution of $|Y|$ is *identical* to that for $|X|$, so $E\{|Y|\} = 150$. As a result,

$$E(T) = \frac{2}{15{,}000}(150 + 150)$$
$$= 0.04 \text{ hr.}$$

$n = 2$ With tool cribs just in Locs. 1 and 3, the areas assigned to them would be divided by a line segment between (300,300) and (600,0) in Fig. 10.9. Notice that the two areas and their tool cribs are located symmetrically with respect to this line segment. Therefore $E(T)$ is the same for both, so we shall derive it just for the tool crib in Loc. 1. (You might try it for the other tool crib for practice.)

Proceeding just as for the $n = 1$ case, relabel Loc. 1 as the origin (0,0) for an (x, y) coordinate system, so that 150 would be subtracted from all coordinates shown in Fig. 10.9. This leads directly to the probability density function of X, and then of $|X|$, shown in Fig. 10.11.

As a result,

$$E\{|X|\} = \frac{1}{225}\int_0^{150} x\,dx + \frac{1}{300}\int_{150}^{450}\left(1 - \frac{x}{450}\right)x\,dx$$
$$= \frac{1}{225}\left[\frac{x^2}{2}\right]_0^{150} + \frac{1}{300}\left[\frac{x^2}{2} - \frac{x^3}{1{,}350}\right]_{150}^{450}$$
$$= \frac{1}{225}\frac{150^2}{2} + \frac{1}{300}\left[\frac{450^2}{2} - \frac{450^3}{1{,}350}\right] - \frac{1}{300}\left[\frac{150^2}{2} - \frac{150^3}{1{,}350}\right]$$
$$= 133\tfrac{1}{3}.$$

Figure 10.11 Probability density functions of (*a*) X, and (*b*) $|X|$ for Example 3, with $n = 2$ (Loc. 1).

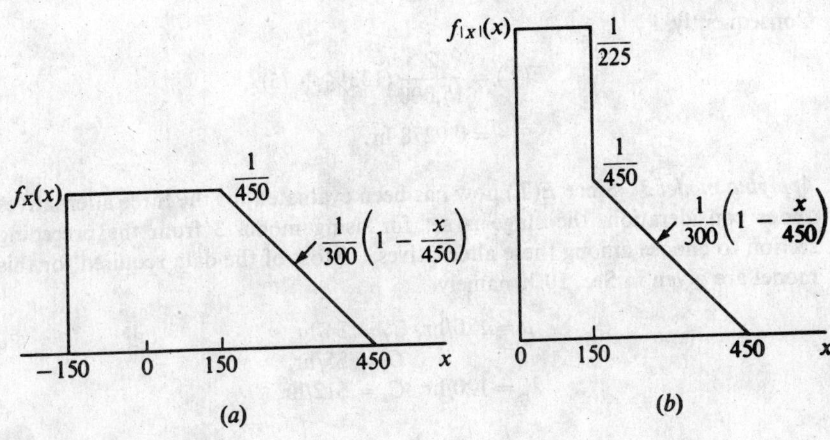

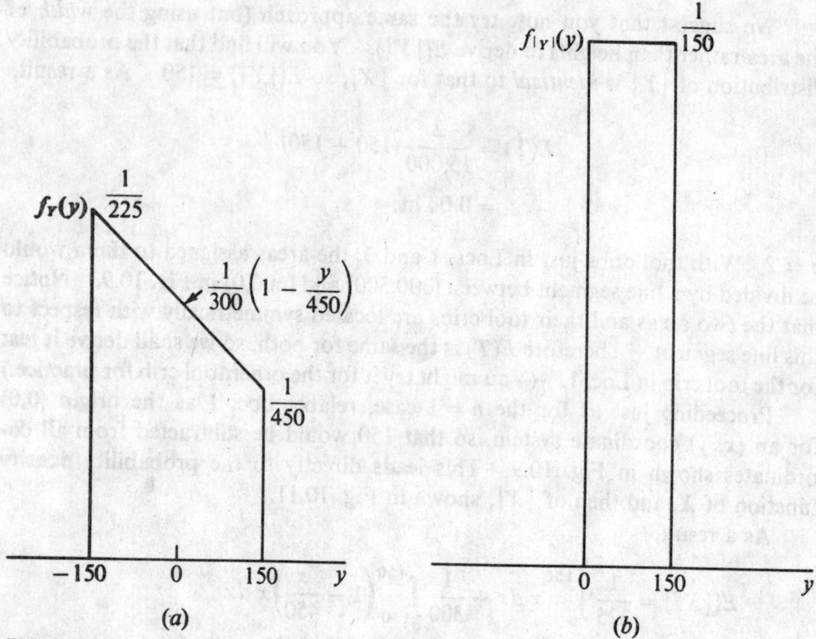

Figure 10.12 Probability density functions of (*a*) Y, and (*b*) $|Y|$ for Example 3, with $n = 2$ (Loc. 1).

Next, the probability density function of Y is obtained by using the *width* of the area assigned to the Loc. 1 tool crib for each possible value of $Y = y$ and then dividing by the size of the area, as given in Fig. 10.12*a*. This then yields the *uniform* distribution of $|Y|$ shown in Fig. 10.12*b*. Thus

$$E\{|Y|\} = \int_0^{150} y\,dy$$
$$= 75.$$

Consequently,

$$E(T) = \frac{2}{15{,}000}(133\tfrac{1}{3} + 75)$$
$$= 0.0278 \text{ hr.}$$

Applying model 3 Since $E(T)$ now has been evaluated for the three alternatives under consideration, the stage is set for using model 3 from the preceding section to choose among these alternatives. Most of the data required for this model are given in Sec. 10.1, namely,

$$\mu = 120/\text{hr}, \quad C_f = \$4/\text{hr},$$
$$C_s = \$5/\text{hr},$$
$$\lambda_p = 120/\text{hr}, \quad C_t = \$12/\text{hr},$$

where the first basic queueing model given in Sec. 9.6 would be used to calculate L and so on. In addition, the end of Sec. 10.3 gives $E(WC) = 12L$ in dollars per hour. Therefore

$$E(TC) = n\left[(4 + 5s) + 12L + \frac{120}{n}\,12E(T)\right].$$

The resulting calculation of $E(TC)$ for various s for each n is given in Table 10.4, which indicates that the *overall minimum* $E(TC)$ is obtained by having *three* tool cribs (so $\lambda = 40$ for each), with *one* clerk at *each* tool crib.

Table 10.4 Calculation of $E(TC)$ in \$/hr for Example 3

n	λ	s	L	$E(T)$	$C_f + sC_s$	$E(WC)$	$\lambda C_t E(T)$	$E(TC)$
1	120	1	∞	0.04	9.00	∞	57.60	∞
1	120	2	1.333	0.04	14.00	16.00	57.60	87.60
1	120	3	1.044	0.04	19.00	12.53	57.60	89.13
2	60	1	1.000	0.0278	9.00	12.00	20.00	82.00
2	60	2	0.534	0.0278	14.00	6.41	20.00	80.82
3	40	1	0.500	0.02	9.00	6.00	9.60	73.80
3	40	2	0.344	0.02	14.00	4.13	9.60	83.19

10.6 ESTIMATING MODEL PARAMETERS

All the results derived in Chap. 9 were expressed in terms of the parameters of the interarrival time and service-time distributions. In most practical situations these parameters are unknown, and hence estimates must be obtained. Little research has been done on deriving optimal statistical estimators of the parameters of various queueing models.[1] However, this section suggests a few convenient estimating procedures. The assumption is made throughout that statistical data regarding arrivals and service times can be obtained, so that estimates of the model parameters can be obtained.

Consider a queueing system where the mean arrival rate and the mean service rate per busy server are both fixed constants (λ and μ, respectively). To estimate λ, one approach is to count the number of customers N that enter the queueing system over a time interval of specified length t†; *an unbiased estimator* of λ would then be

$$\hat{\lambda} = \frac{N}{t}.$$

An alternative approach is to instead fix the number of customers observed rather than the length of the time interval. Thus let T be the total elapsed time

[1] One of the few research papers on this topic is H. W. Lilliefors, "Some Confidence Intervals for Queues," *Operations Research*, **14**: 723–727, 1966.

† Fixed constants are being denoted by a lowercase letter, whereas random variables are being denoted by uppercase letters.

that the system is observed until the last of the specified number of arrivals n has entered the system. T is then the sum of the n interarrival times. An estimator of $1/\lambda$ is given by T/n, so that

$$\hat{\hat{\lambda}} = \frac{n}{T}$$

is an estimator of λ. If the system has a Poisson input, then either $\hat{\lambda}$ or $\hat{\hat{\lambda}}$ is a *maximum likelihood estimator* of λ, depending upon how the data are recorded. To estimate μ it might seem reasonable to tabulate both the total number of units served, M, and the sum of the busy times (time spent servicing a customer of the servers, B, over a time interval of specified length; an estimator of μ would then be

$$\hat{\mu} = \frac{M}{B}.$$

However, it is unclear how to count units that are in the process of being served at the beginning or end of the time interval, and it would create a bias to consider only the number and service times of the units that are completely served during the time interval. Therefore it is usually preferable to use the alternative approach of fixing the number of customers observed rather than the length of the time interval. Thus let B be the sum of the service times of the first m customers that begin service after initiating the observation of the system, where m is a prespecified number. (In a multiple-server system it may be more convenient to record the sum of m service times for only *one* of the servers, which is also permissible.) An estimator of $1/\mu$ is then given by B/m, so that

$$\hat{\hat{\mu}} = \frac{m}{B}$$

is an estimator of μ. If the service-time distribution is exponential, then $\hat{\hat{\mu}}$ is a *maximum likelihood estimator* of μ.

The *utilization factor* $\rho = \lambda/s\mu$ plays a particularly important role in queueing theory. An estimator $\hat{\rho}$ of this parameter can be obtained from

$$\hat{\rho} = \frac{\hat{\hat{\lambda}}}{s\hat{\hat{\mu}}} = \frac{n/T}{sm/B} = \frac{B/m}{sT/n}.$$

For the *basic model* described in Sec. 9.6 (Poisson input and exponential service times), $\hat{\rho}$ is a *maximum likelihood estimator* of ρ.

For this basic model, utilization of distributional properties of the random variables B and T can lead to the calculation of a *confidence interval estimator* for ρ. Since T is the sum of n independent exponentially distributed (each with mean $1/\lambda$) interarrival times, $2\lambda T$ has a chi-square distribution with $2n$ degrees of freedom.[1] Similarly, since B is the sum of m independent exponentially distributed (each with mean $1/\mu$) service times, $2\mu B$ has a chi-square

[1] See Secs. 8.7 (the gamma distribution) and 8.16.

distribution with $2m$ degrees of freedom. Furthermore, B and T are assumed to be independent. Hence it follows that

$$\frac{\mu B/m}{\lambda T/n} = \hat{\rho}/\rho$$

has an F distribution with $2m$ and $2n$ degrees of freedom.[1]

A confidence interval estimator for ρ can now be obtained. Since $\hat{\rho}/\rho$ has an F distribution,

$$P\{F_{1-\alpha/2;\,2m,\,2n} \le \hat{\rho}/\rho \le F_{\alpha/2;\,2m,\,2n}\} = 1 - \alpha,$$

where $F_{\gamma;\,\nu_1,\,\nu_2}$ is the 100α percentage point of the F distribution, with ν_1 and ν_2 degrees of freedom, and is tabulated in Table A5.5 of Appendix 5. This probability statement is equivalent to

$$P\{F\frac{\hat{\rho}}{\alpha/2;\,2m,\,2n} \le \rho \le \hat{\rho} F_{\alpha/2;\,2n,\,2m}\},\dagger$$

so that

$$\underline{\rho} = \frac{\hat{\rho}}{F_{\alpha/2;\,2m,\,2n}}, \qquad \bar{\rho} = \hat{\rho} F_{\alpha/2;\,2n,\,2m}$$

is a 100 $(1 - \alpha)$ percent confidence interval for ρ.

These results are also useful for obtaining a confidence interval estimator for any *monotone increasing* function of ρ, say, $H(P)$.‡ The appropriate 100 $(1 - \alpha)$ percent confidence interval for $H(\rho)$ is given by

$$H(\underline{\rho}) \le H(\rho) \le H(\bar{\rho}).$$

Some important cases of monotone increasing functions that $H(\rho)$ can represent are L, L_q, and P_0.

For example, when $s = 1$, $L = \rho/(1 - \rho)$. Since $\rho/(1 - \rho)$ is monotone increasing, the 100 $(1 - \alpha)$ percent confidence interval is given by

$$\frac{\underline{\rho}}{1 - \underline{\rho}}, \qquad \frac{\bar{\rho}}{1 - \bar{\rho}}.$$

The corresponding confidence intervals for L_q and P_0 are shown in Table 9.1. The same approach also can be used for $s > 1$, as illustrated by the two-server results given in Table 10.5. A similar derivation yields the confidence intervals given in the last part of Table 10.5 for the model described in Sec. 9.7 (Poisson input, Erlang service times) when $s = 1$.

[1] See Secs. 8.7 (the beta distribution) and 8.16.

† It can be shown that

$$F_{1-\gamma;\,\nu_1,\,\nu_2} = \frac{1}{F_{\gamma;\,\nu_2,\,\nu_1}}$$

‡ The results are also applicable for monotone decreasing functions, in which case the limits are reversed.

Example

Assume that the queueing model calls for Poisson input, exponential service times, and a single server. Twenty observations on the interarrival times and service times are obtained, and a 95 percent confidence interval on L is desired. Assume the data indicate that

$$\hat{\rho} = \frac{\hat{\lambda}}{\hat{\mu}} = \frac{B/m}{T/n} = \frac{300/20}{600/20} = \frac{1}{2}.$$

Since $L = \rho/(1 - \rho)$, then the maximum likelihood estimate for L is 1. To find the 95 percent confidence interval for L, $F_{0.025;\,40,40}$ must be obtained from Table A5.5 of Appendix 5. Thus

$$F_{0.025,40,40} = 1.88,$$

so that

$$\underline{\rho} = \frac{1/2}{1.88} = 0.266$$

Table 10.5 Confidence Interval Estimators for Parameters of Queueing Systems[1]

	Parameter	*100 (1 − α) percent confidence interval*
Poisson input	$L = \dfrac{\rho}{1-\rho}$	$\dfrac{\underline{\rho}}{1-\underline{\rho}}, \dfrac{\bar{\rho}}{1-\bar{\rho}}$
Exponential service	$L_q = \dfrac{\rho^2}{1-\rho}$	$\dfrac{\underline{\rho}^2}{1-\underline{\rho}}, \dfrac{\bar{\rho}^2}{1-\bar{\rho}}$
Single server	$P_0 = 1-\rho$	$1-\bar{\rho}, 1-\underline{\rho}$
Poisson input	$L = \dfrac{2\rho}{1-\rho}$	$\dfrac{2\underline{\rho}}{1-\underline{\rho}}, \dfrac{2\bar{\rho}}{1-\bar{\rho}}$
Exponential service	$L_q = \dfrac{4\rho^3}{1-2\rho^2}$	$\dfrac{4\underline{\rho}^3}{1-2\underline{\rho}^2}, \dfrac{4\bar{\rho}^3}{1-2\bar{\rho}^2}$
Two servers	$P_0 = \dfrac{1-\rho}{1+\rho}$	$\dfrac{1-\bar{\rho}}{1+\bar{\rho}}, \dfrac{1-\underline{\rho}}{1+\underline{\rho}}$
Poisson input	$L = \dfrac{k+1}{2k}\,\dfrac{\rho^2}{1-\rho} + \rho$	$\dfrac{k+1}{2k}\,\dfrac{\underline{\rho}^2}{1-\underline{\rho}} + \underline{\rho}, \dfrac{k+1}{2k}\,\dfrac{\bar{\rho}^2}{1-\bar{\rho}} + \bar{\rho}$
Erlang service Single server	$L_q = \dfrac{k+1}{2k}\,\dfrac{\rho^2}{1-\rho}$	$\dfrac{k+1}{2k}\,\dfrac{\underline{\rho}^2}{1-\underline{\rho}}, \dfrac{k+1}{2k}\,\dfrac{\bar{\rho}^2}{1-\bar{\rho}}$

[1] For all models, $\rho = \lambda/s\mu$. For the cases of exponential service time, $\underline{\rho} = \hat{\rho}/F_{\alpha/2;2m,2n}$ and $\bar{\rho} = \hat{\rho}F_{\alpha/2;2n,2m}$. For Erlang service times with parameters μ and k, $\underline{\rho} = \hat{\rho}/F_{\alpha/2;2mk,2n}$ and $\bar{\rho} = \hat{\rho}\,F_{\alpha/2;2n,2mk}$. For either case

$$\hat{\rho} = \frac{\hat{\lambda}}{s\hat{\mu}} = \frac{B/m}{sT/n}.$$

and

$$\bar{\rho} = \frac{1}{2} 1.88 = 0.94.$$

Hence the 95 percent confidence interval for L is given by

$$\frac{0.266}{1-0.266} = 0.362, \qquad \frac{0.94}{1-0.94} = 16.$$

This interval is very wide, so little can be concluded yet about how well the queueing system would perform on the average with the current single server and input source. Much more data would be needed to obtain a relatively precise estimator for L.

Now suppose that the mean service rate per busy server varies with queue size, as described in Sec. 9.6, so that $\mu_n = (n/s)^c s\mu_1$ if $n \geq s$. Hence, $\log \mu_n = c \log(n/s) + \log(s\mu_1)$, if $n \geq s$. Assuming an exponential service-time distribution, a *maximum likelihood estimator* of μ_n is the observed number of units that completed service while n units were in the system divided by the total observed time n units were in the system. After obtaining these estimates, $\hat{\mu}_n$ $(n - s = 0,1,2, \ldots)$, plot $\log \hat{\mu}_n$ versus $\log(n/s)$. The slope c and the intercept $\log(s\mu_1)$ of the $\log \mu_n$ line can then be estimated by the *method of least squares*. Confidence intervals for $\log \mu_n$ can also be obtained from *linear regression theory*.

10.7 CONCLUSIONS

This chapter has discussed the application of queueing theory for *designing* queueing systems. Every individual problem has its own special characteristics, so no standard procedure can be prescribed to fit every situation. Therefore the emphasis has been on introducing fundamental considerations and approaches that can be adapted to most cases. We have focused on three particularly common decision variables (s, μ, and λ) as a vehicle for introducing and illustrating these concepts. However, there are many other possible decision variables (e.g., the size of a waiting room for a queueing system) and many more complicated situations (e.g., designing a *priority* queueing system) that can also be analyzed in a similar way.

The time required to *travel* to and from a service facility sometimes is an important consideration. A rather general approach to evaluating expected travel time has been introduced by applying it to some relatively simple cases. However, once again, many more complicated situations can also be analyzed quite similarly. We have discussed the incorporation of travel-time information into the overall analysis only in the context of determining the *number* of service facilities to provide when *customers* must travel to the nearest facility. But travel-time models also can be very useful when the *servers* must travel to the customer from the service facility (e.g., fire trucks and ambulances), as well as in other contexts.

Another potentially useful area for the application of queueing theory is the development of policies for *controlling* queueing systems, e.g., for *dynamically* adjusting the number of servers or the service rate to compensate for changes in the number of customers in the system. Considerable research is being conducted in this area, but the theory and computational results have not yet progressed far enough to permit widespread use.

Queueing theory has proven to be a very useful tool, and we anticipate that its use will continue to grow as recognition of the many guises of queueing systems grows.

Selected References

1 Buffa, Elwood S. (ed.): *Readings in Production and Operations Management*, chaps. 12–15, Wiley, New York, 1966.

2 Conway, Richard W., William L. Maxwell, and Louis W. Miller: *Theory of Scheduling*, Addison-Wesley, Reading, Mass., 1967.

3 Cruon, R. (ed.): *Queueing Theory (Recent Developments and Applications)*, American Elsevier, New York, 1967.

4 Lee, Alec M.: *Applied Queueing Theory*, St. Martin's Press, New York, 1966.

5 Newell, Gordon F.: *Applications of Queueing Theory*, Chapman and Hall, London, 1971.

6 Wolff, Ronald W.: "Problems of Statistical Inference for Birth-and-Death Queueing Models," *Operations Research*, **13**: 343–357, 1965.

Problems

1 For each kind of queueing system listed in Prob. 2, Chap. 9, briefly describe the nature of the *cost of service* and the cost *of waiting* that would need to be considered in designing the system.

2 Suppose that a queueing system fits the first *basic model* described in Sec. 9.6, with $s = 1$, $\lambda = 2$, $\mu = 4$. Evaluate the expected waiting cost per unit time $E(WC)$ for this system when its waiting cost function has the form

(*a*) $g(N) = 10N + 2N^2$.

(*b*) $g(N) = \begin{cases} 2N, & \text{for } N = 0, 1, 2 \\ N^2, & \text{for } N = 3, 4, 5 \\ \frac{1}{5}N^3, & \text{for } N > 5. \end{cases}$

(*c*) $h(\mathscr{W}) = 25\mathscr{W} + \mathscr{W}^3$.

(*d*) $h(\mathscr{W}) = \begin{cases} 4\mathscr{W}, & \text{for } 0 \le \mathscr{W} \le 2 \\ \mathscr{W}^2, & \text{for } \mathscr{W} \ge 2. \end{cases}$

3 A certain queueing system has a *Poisson* input, with a mean arrival rate of four customers per hour. The service-time distribution is *exponential*, with a mean of 0.2 hours. The marginal cost of providing each server is \$6/hour, where it is estimated that the cost which is incurred by having each customer *idle* (i.e., in the queueing system) is \$100/hour for the first customer and \$150 for each additional customer. Determine the ***number of servers*** **that should be assigned to the system to minimize the**

expected total cost per hour. [*Hint*: Express $E(WC)$ in terms of L, P_0, and ρ and then use Figs. 9.5 and 9.6.]

4 The problem is to choose between two types of materials-handling equipment, A and B, for transporting certain types of goods between certain producing centers in a job shop. Calls for the materials-handling unit to move a load would come essentially at random (i.e., according to a *Poisson* input process) at a mean rate of two per hour. The total time required to move a load has an *exponential* distribution, where the expected time is 24 minutes for A and 15 minutes for B. The total equivalent uniform hourly cost (capital recovery cost plus operating cost) would be \$10 for A and \$20 for B. The estimated cost of idle goods (waiting to be moved or in transit) because of increased in-process inventory is \$10 per load per hour. Furthermore, the scheduling of the work at the producing centers allows for just 1 hour from the completion of a load at one center to the arrival of that load at the next center. Therefore an additional \$20 per load per hour of delay (including transit time) *after the first hour* is to be charged for lost production because of idle personnel and equipment, extra costs of expediting and supervision, and so forth.

Assuming that only one materials-handling unit is to be purchased, which type of unit should be selected?

5 A railroad considers it necessary to paint its cars once a year. Alternative 1 is to provide two paint shops, where painting is done by hand (one car at a time), for a total annual cost of \$200,000. The painting time for a car is 6 hours. Alternative 2 is to provide one spray shop involving an annual cost of \$250,000. In this case the painting time for a car is 3 hours. For both alternatives, the cars arrive according to a *Poisson* input, with a mean arrival rate of one every 8 hours. The cost of idle time per car is \$60/hour. Which alternative should the railroad choose? Assume that the paint shops are always open; i.e., they work (24) (365) = 8,760 hours/year.

6 An airline maintenance base wishes to make a change in its overhaul operation. The present situation is that only one airplane can be repaired at a time, and the expected repair time is 30 hours, whereas the expected time between arrivals is 45 hours. This has led to frequent and prolonged delays in repairing incoming planes, even though the base operates continuously. The average cost of an idle plane to the airline is \$2,000/hour. It is estimated that each plane goes into the maintenance shop five times per year. It is believed that the input process for the base is essentially *Poisson* and that the probability distribution of repair times is *Erlang*, with shape parameter $k = 2$. Alternative A is to provide a duplicate maintenance shop, so that two planes can be repaired simultaneously. The cost, depreciated over a period of 5 years, is \$400,000 per airplane per year.

Alternative B is to replace the present maintenance equipment by the most efficient (and expensive) equipment available, thereby reducing the expected repair time to 18 hours. The cost, depreciated over a period of 5 years, is \$450,000 per airplane per year.

Which alternative should the airline choose?

7 A particular in-process inspection station is used to inspect subassemblies of a certain kind. At present there are two inspectors at the station, and they work together in inspecting each subassembly. The inspection time has an *exponential* distribution, with a mean of 15 minutes. The cost of providing this inspection system is \$20/hour.

A proposal has been made to streamline the inspection procedure so that it can be handled by only one inspector. This inspector would begin by visually inspecting the exterior of the subassembly, and he would then use new efficient equipment to complete the inspection. The times required for these two phases of the inspection have independent *Erlang* distributions, with shape parameter $k = 2$ and means of 6 and 12 minutes, respectively. The capitalized cost of providing this inspection system would be $15/hour.

The subassemblies arrive at the inspection station according to a Poisson process at a mean rate of three per hour. The cost of having the subassemblies wait at the inspection station (thereby increasing in-process inventory and disrupting subsequent production) is estimated to be $10/hour.

Determine whether to continue the status quo or adopt the proposal in order to minimize expected total cost per hour.

8 A certain small car-wash business is currently being analyzed to see if costs can be reduced. Customers arrive according to a *Poisson* process at a mean rate of 10 per hour, and only one car can be washed at a time. At present the time required to wash a car has an *exponential* distribution, with a mean of 6 minutes. It also has been noticed that if there are already four cars waiting (including the one being washed), then any additional arriving customers leave and take their business elsewhere instead. The lost incremental profit from each such lost customer is $1.

Two proposals have been made. Proposal 1 is to add certain equipment, at a capitalized cost of $1/hour, which would reduce the expected washing time to 5 minutes. In addition, each arriving customer would be given a guarantee that if he has to wait longer than ½ hour (according to a time slip he receives upon arrival) before his car is ready, then he receives rather than pays the price of his car wash (a net actual loss of $3 for the company). This would be well posted and advertised, so it is believed that no arriving customers would be lost.

Proposal 2 is to obtain the most advanced equipment available, at an increased cost of $2/hour, where each car would be sent through two cycles of the process in succession. The time required for a cycle has an *exponential* distribution, with a mean of 2 minutes, so total expected washing time would be 4 minutes. Because of the increased speed and effectiveness, it is believed that essentially no arriving customers would be lost.

The owner also feels that because of the loss of customer good will (and consequent lost future buisness) when customers have to wait, a cost of 5 cents for each minute that a customer has to wait before his car wash begins should be included in the analysis of all alternatives.

Evaluate the expected total cost per hour of the status quo proposal 1, and proposal 2 to determine which one should be chosen.

9 A single crew is provided for unloading and/or loading each truck that arrives at the loading dock of a warehouse. These trucks arrive according to a *Poisson* input process at a mean rate of one per hour. The time required by a crew to unload and/or load a truck has an *exponential* distribution (regardless of the crew size). The expected time required by a one-man crew would be 1 hour.

The cost of providing each additional member of the crew is $10/hour. The cost that is attributable to having a truck not in use (i.e., a truck standing at the loading dock) is estimated to be $15/hour.

(*a*) Assume that the mean service rate of the crew is proportional to its size. What should the size be to minimize the expected total cost per hour?

(*b*) Assume that the mean service rate of the crew is proportional to the square root of its size. What should the size be to minimize expected total cost per hour?

10 A machine shop contains a grinder for sharpening the machine cutting tools. A decision must now be made on the speed at which to set the grinder.

The grinding time required by a machine operator to sharpen his cutting tool has an *exponential* distribution, where the mean $1/\mu$ can be set at anything from ½ to 2 minutes, depending upon the speed of the grinder. The running and maintenance costs goes up rapidly with the speed of the grinder, so the estimated cost per minute for providing a mean of $1/\mu$ is $\$(0.10\mu^2)$.

The machine operators arrive to sharpen their tools according to a *Poisson* process at a mean rate of one every 2 minutes. The estimated cost of an operator being away from his machine to the grinder is \$0.20/minute.

Plot the expected total cost per minute $E(TC)$ vs. μ over the feasible range for μ to solve graphically for the minimizing value of μ.

11 Consider the special case of model 2, where any $\mu > \lambda/s$ is feasible, and both $f(\mu)$ and the waiting-cost function are *linear* functions, so that

$$E(TC) = s\,C_r\,\mu + C_w L,$$

where C_r is the marginal cost per unit time for each unit of a server's mean service rate and C_w is the cost of waiting per unit time for each customer. The optimal solution is $s = 1$ (by the optimality of a single server result), and

$$\mu = \lambda + \sqrt{\frac{\lambda C_w}{C_r}}$$

for any queueing system fitting the *basic model* presented in Sec. 9.6.1.

Show that this μ is indeed optimal.

12 Consider a factory whose floor area is a square 400 feet on each side. Suppose that one service facility of a certain kind is provided in the center of the factory. The employees are distributed uniformly throughout the factory, and they walk to and from the facility at an average speed of 3 miles/hour along a system of orthogonal aisles.

Compute the expected travel time $E(T)$ per arrival.

13 Suppose that the calling population for a particular service facility is uniformly distributed over each area shown below, where the service facility is located at (0,0). Making the same assumptions as in Sec. 10.5, derive the expected travel time (round trip) per arrival $E(T)$ in terms of the average velocity v and the distance r.

(*a*)

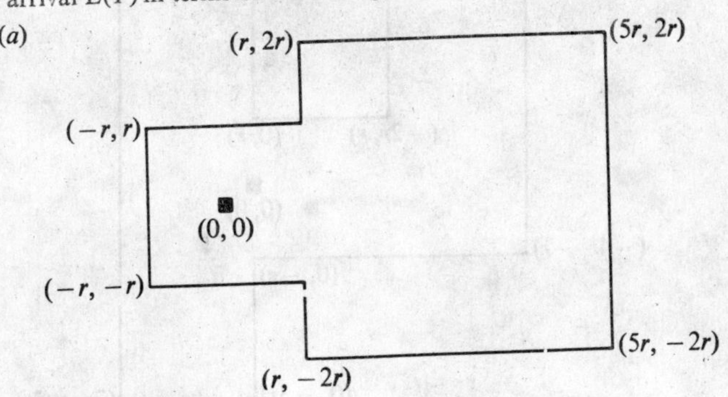

(*b*)

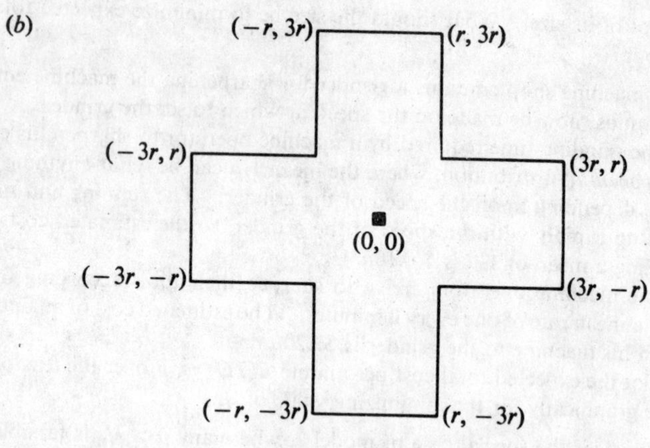
(−r, 3r)
(r, 3r)
(−3r, r)
(3r, r)
(0, 0)
(−3r, −r)
(3r, −r)
(−r, −3r)
(r, −3r)

(*c*)

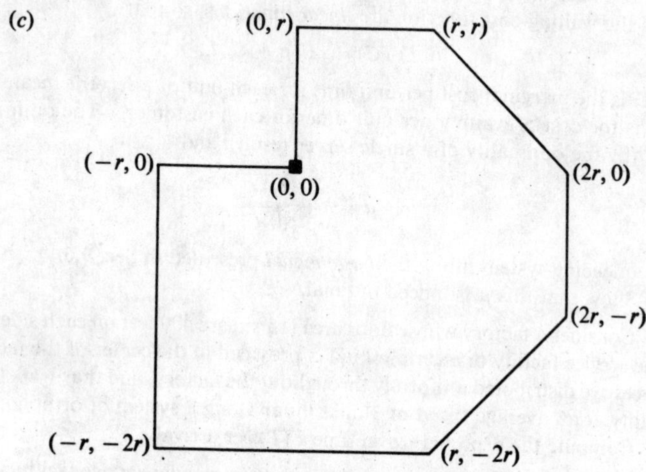
(0, r)
(r, r)
(−r, 0)
(0, 0)
(2r, 0)
(2r, −r)
(−r, −2r)
(r, −2r)

(*d*)

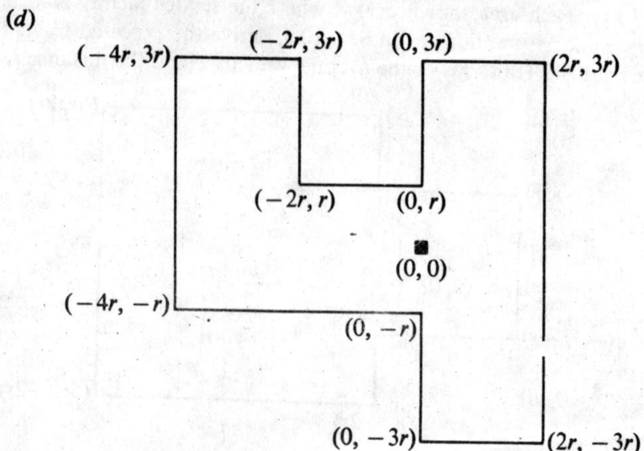
(−4r, 3r)
(−2r, 3r)
(0, 3r)
(2r, 3r)
(−2r, r)
(0, r)
(0, 0)
(−4r, −r)
(0, −r)
(0, −3r)
(2r, −3r)

14 A certain large shop doing light fabrication work uses a single central storage facility (dispatch station) for material in-process storage. The typical procedure is that each employee personally delivers his finished work (by hand, tote box, or hand cart) and receives new work and materials at the facility. Although this procedure had worked well in earlier years when the shop was smaller, it appears that it may now be advisable to divide the shop into two semi-independent parts, with a separate storage facility for each one. You have been assigned the job of comparing the use of two facilities and of one facility from a cost standpoint.

The factory has the shape of a rectangle 150 by 100 yards. Thus, letting 1 yard be the unit of distance, the (x, y) coordinates of the corners would be (0,0), (150,0), (150,100), and (0,100). Using this coordinate system, the existing facility is located at (50,50), and the location available for the second facility is (100,50).

Each facility would be operated by a single clerk. The time required by a clerk to service a caller has an *exponential* distribution, with a mean of 2 minutes. Employees arrive at the present facility according to a *Poisson* input process at a mean rate of 24 per hour. The employees are rather uniformly distributed throughout the shop, and if the second facility were installed, each employee would normally use the nearer of the two facilities. Employees walk at an average speed of about 5,000 yards/hour. All aisles are parallel to the outer walls of the shop. The net cost of providing each facility is estimated to be about $18/hour, plus $7/hour for the clerk. The estimated total cost of an employee being idled by traveling or waiting at the facility is $15/hour.

Given the preceding cost factors, which alternative minimizes expected total cost?

15 A job shop is being laid out in a square area 600 feet on a side, and one of the decisions to be made is the *number* of facilities for the storage and shipping of final inventory. The capitalized cost associated with providing each facility would be $10/hour. There are just four potential locations available for these facilities, one in the middle of each of the four sides of the square area (as shown in the following figure):

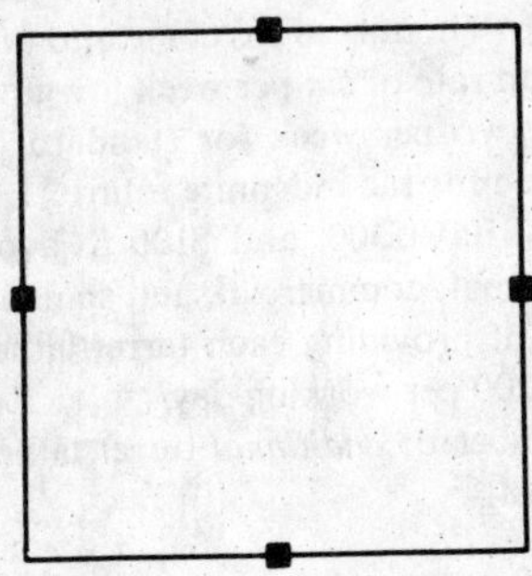

The loads to be moved to a storage and shipping facility would be distributed uniformly throughout the shop area, and they become available according to a *Poisson* process at a mean rate of 30 per hour. Each time a load becomes available, an appropriate materials-handling vehicle would be sent from the *nearest* facility to pick it up (with an expected loading time of 3 minutes) and bring it there, where the cost would be $10/hour for time spent in traveling, loading, and waiting to be unloaded. The vehicles would travel at a speed of 20,000 feet/hour along a system of orthogonal aisles parallel to the sides of the shop area.

Another decision to be made is the number of men (m) to provide at each storage and shipping facility for unloading an arriving vehicle. These m men would work together on each vehicle, and the time required to unload it would have an *exponential* distribution, with a mean of $6/m$ minutes. The cost of providing each man is $5/hour.

Determine the number of facilities, and the value of m at each, that will minimize expected total cost per hour.

16 Consider the formulation of the *County Hospital* emergency room problem as a preemptive priority queueing system, as presented in Sec. 9.8. Suppose that the following imputed costs were assigned to making patients wait (*excluding* treatment time): $10/hour for *stable* cases, $1,000/hour for *serious* cases, and $100,000/hour for *critical* cases. The cost associated with having an additional doctor on duty would be $40/hour. Determine on an expected total cost basis whether there should be *one* or *two* doctors on duty.

17 A certain job shop has been experiencing long delays in jobs going through the turret lathe department because of inadequate capacity. The foreman contends that five machines are required, as opposed to the three machines that he now has. However, because of pressure from management to hold down capital expenditures, only one additional machine will be authorized unless there is solid evidence that a second one is necessary.

This shop does three kinds of jobs, namely, government jobs, commercial jobs, and standard products. Whenever a turret lathe finishes a job, it starts a government job if one is waiting; if not, it starts a commercial job if any are waiting; if not, it starts on a standard product if any are waiting. Jobs of the same type are taken on a first-come-first-served basis.

Although much overtime work is required currently, management wants the turret lathe department to operate on an 8-hour, 5-day-a-week basis. The probability distribution of the time required by a turret lathe for a job appears to be approximately *exponential*, with a mean of 10 hours. Jobs come into the shop according to a *Poisson* input process, but at a mean rate of six per week for government jobs, four per week for commercial jobs, and two per week for standard products. (These figures are expected to remain the same for the indefinite future.)

It is worth about $500, $300, and $100 to avoid a delay of one additional (working) day in a government, commercial, and standard job, respectively. The incremental capitalized cost of providing each turret lathe (including the operator and so on) is estimated to be $200 per working day.

Determine the number of *additional* turret lathes that should be obtained to minimize expected total cost.

18 A certain single-server queueing system has been under observation to determine which theoretical model should be used to represent this system. The following service times (in minutes) have been recorded:

0.47, 0.22, 1.42, 0.72, 0.38, 2.85, 0.09, 0.85, 0.72,
0.27, 1.39, 0.32, 0.55, 0.13, 0.25, 2.20, 0.81, 1.03,
0.16, 0.61

Assuming that the service-time distribution is exponential, estimate the **mean** service rate μ.

19 A single-server queueing system has a Poisson input and an exponential service-time distribution. The system is under study. The total elapsed time that the system is observed until the last of 30 arrivals has entered the system is 535 minutes. Similarly, the sum of the service times of these first 30 customers that began service after initiating the observation of the system is 428 minutes.

(*a*) Find the maximum likelihood estimate of the utilization factor.
(*b*) Find a 95 percent confidence interval for the utilization factor.
(*c*) Find a 95 percent confidence interval for L, L_q and P_0.

20 Solve Prob. 19 by using the data given, except that the results are based upon observing 60 customers.

21 Solve Prob. 19 by assuming that there are two servers.

22 Solve Prob. 19 by assuming that the service-time distribution has an Erlang distribution with $k = 2$.

23 Solve Prob. 19 by assuming that there are two servers, and the results are based upon observing 60 customers.

Inventory Theory

11.1 INTRODUCTION

Keeping an inventory (stock of goods) for future sale or use is very common in business. Retail firms, wholesalers, manufacturing companies—and even blood banks—generally have a stock of goods on hand. How does such a facility decide upon its "inventory policy"; i.e., when and how much does it replenish? In a small firm the manager may keep track of his inventory and make these decisions. However, since this may not be feasible even in small firms, many companies have saved large sums of money by using "scientific inventory management." In particular, they

1. Formulate a mathematical model describing the behavior of the inventory system,

2. Derive an optimal inventory policy with respect to this model,

3. Frequently use a computer to maintain a record of the inventory levels and to signal when and how much to replenish.

There are several basic considerations involved in determining an inventory policy that must be reflected in the mathematical inventory model; these are illustrated in the following examples.

EXAMPLE 1 A television manufacturing company produces its own speakers, which are used in the production of its television sets. The television sets are assembled on a continuous production line at a rate of 8,000 per month. The speakers are produced in batches because they do not warrant setting up a continuous production line, and relatively large quantities can be produced in a short time. The company is interested in determining when and how much to produce. Several costs must be considered:

1. Each time a batch is produced, a setup cost of $12,000 is incurred. Thus cost includes the cost of "tooling up," administrative costs, record keeping, and so forth. Note that the existence of this cost argues for producing speakers in large batches.

2. The production of speakers in large batch sizes leads to a large inventory. It is estimated that the cost of keeping a speaker in stock is 30 cents/month. This cost includes the cost of capital tied up, storage space, insurance, taxes, protection, and so on. The existence of a storage or holding cost argues for producing in small batches.

3. The production cost of a single speaker (excluding the setup cost) is $10 and can be assumed to be a unit cost independent of the batch size produced. (In general, however, the unit production cost need not be constant and may decrease with batch size.)

4. Company policy prohibits deliberately planning for shortages of any of its components. However, a shortage of speakers occasionally crops up, and it has been estimated that each speaker unavailable when required cost $1.10/month. This cost includes the cost of installing speakers after the television set is fully assembled, storage space, delayed revenue, record keeping, and so forth.

EXAMPLE 2. A wholesale distributor of bicycles is having trouble with shortages of the most popular 10-speed model and is currently reviewing the inventory policy for this model. The distributor purchases this model bicycle from the manufacturer monthly and then supplies them to various bicycle shops in the Western United States. Upon request from shops, the distributor wholesales bicycles to the individual shops in its region. The distributor has analyzed his costs and has determined that the following are important:

1. The shortage cost, i.e., the cost of not having a bicycle on hand when needed. Most models are easily reordered from the manufacturer, and stores usually accept a delay in delivery. Still, although shortages are permissible, the distributor feels that he incurs a loss, which he estimates to be $15 per bicycle. This cost represents an evaluation of the cost of the loss of good will, additional clerical costs incurred, and the cost of the delay in revenue received. On a very few competitive (in price) models, stores do not accept a delay, resulting in lost sales. In this case the cost of lost revenue must be included in the shortage cost.

2. The holding cost, i.e., the cost of maintaining an inventory, is $1 per bicycle remaining at the end of the month. This cost represents the cost of capital tied up, warehouse space, insurance, taxes, and so on.

3. The ordering cost, i.e., the cost of placing an order plus the cost of the bicycle, consists of two components: The paper work involved in placing an order is estimated as $200, and the actual cost of a bicycle is $35.

These two examples indicate that there exists a tradeoff between the costs involved; the next section will discuss the basic cost components of inventory models.

11.2 COMPONENTS OF INVENTORY MODELS

Since inventory policies obviously affect "profitability," the choice among policies depends upon their relative profitability. Some of the costs that determine this profitability are (1) the costs of ordering or manufacturing, (2) holding or storage costs, (3) unsatisfied demand or shortage penalty costs, (4) revenues, (5) salvage costs, and (6) discount rate. [Costs (1)to (3) were encountered in Examples 1 and 2.]

The cost of ordering or manufacturing an amount z can be represented by a function $c(z)$. The simplest form of this function is one that is directly proportional to the amount ordered, that is, $c \cdot z$, where c represents the unit price paid. Another common assumption is that $c(z)$ is composed of two parts: a term that is directly proportional to the amount ordered and a term that is constant K for z positive and zero for $z = 0$. For this case, if z is positive, the ordering, or production cost, is given by $K + c \cdot z$. The constant K is often referred to as the setup cost and generally includes the administrative cost of ordering, the preliminary labor, and other expenses of starting a production run. There are other assumptions that can be made about this ordering function, but this chapter is restricted to the two cases described above. In Example 1, the speakers are manufactured, and the setup cost for the production run is $12,000. Furthermore, each speaker cost $10, so that the *production* cost is given by

$$c(z) = 12{,}000 + 10z, \text{ for } z > 0.$$

In Example 2, the distributor orders bicycles from the manufacturer, and the *ordering* cost is given by

$$c(z) = 200 + 35z, \text{ for } z > 0.$$

The holding or storage costs represent the costs associated with the storage of the inventory until it is sold or used. They may include the cost of capital tied up, space, insurance, protection, and taxes attributed to storage. This cost may be a function of the maximum quantity held during a period, the average amount held, or the cumulated excess of supply over the amount required (demand). The latter viewpoint is usually taken in this chapter. In the bicycle example, the holding cost was $1 per bicycle remaining at the end of the month. This can be interpreted as the interest lost in keeping capital tied up in an "unnecessary" bicycle for a month, cost of extra storage space, insurance, and so forth.

The unsatisfied demand or shortage penalty cost is incurred when the amount of the commodity required (demand) exceeds the available stock. This cost depends upon the structure of the model. One such case occurs when (1) the demand exceeds the available inventory, and it is met by a priority shipment, or (2) is not met at all. In (1) the penalty cost can be viewed as the difference between the cost of priority shipment and the cost of routine delivery. In (2), the situation where the unsatisfied demand is lost, the penalty cost can be viewed as the loss in revenue. Either situation is known as "no backlogging of unsatisfied demand." The scenario of the bicycle example implies that there exists a few competitive (in price) bicycle models where unsatisfied demand is lost, thereby resulting in lost revenue, and hence is an example where unsatisfied demand is not backlogged. The second case of demand not being fulfilled out of stock assumes that it is satisfied when the commodity next becomes available. The penalty cost can be interpreted as the loss of customer's good will, his subsequent reluctance to do business with the firm, the cost of delayed revenue, and extra record keeping. This case is known as "backlogging" of unsatisfied demand. The speaker example calls for backlogging of unsatisfied demand. If a shortage occurs, the final assembly of the television sets awaits the production of the next batch of speakers. Usually the unsatisfied demand cost is a function of the excess of demand over supply.

The revenue cost may or may not be included in the model If it is assumed that both the price and the demand for the product are not under the control of the company, the revenue from sales is independent of the firm's inventory policy and may be neglected. However, if revenue is neglected in the model, the *loss in revenue* must then be included in the unsatisfied demand penalty cost whenever the firm can not meet the demand and the sale is lost. This point is discussed at length in the 10-speed bicycles example presented on page 494. Furthermore, even in the case where demand is backlogged, the cost of the delay in revenue must also be included in the unsatisfied demand cost. With these interpretations, revenue will not be considered as a separate cost in the remainder of this chapter.

The salvage value of an item is the value of a leftover item at the termination of the inventory period. If the inventory policy is carried on for an indefinite number of periods, and there is no obsolescence, there are no leftover items. What is left over at the end of one period is the amount available at the beginning of the next period. On the other hand, if the policy is to be carried out for only one period, the salvage value represents the disposal value of the item to the firm, say, the selling price. The negative of the salvage value is called the salvage cost. If there is a cost associated with the disposal of an item, the salvage cost may be positive. Since the storage costs generally are assumed to be a function of excess of supply over demand, the salvage costs can be combined with this cost and hence are usually neglected in this chapter.

Finally, the discount rate takes into account the time value of money. When a firm ties up capital in inventory it is prevented from using this money for alternative purposes. For example, it could invest this money in secure investments, say, government bonds, and have a return on investment a year hence of, say, 7 percent. Thus a dollar invested today would be worth \$1.07 a year hence, or alternatively, a dollar profit a year hence is equivalent to $\alpha = 1/\$1.07$ today. The quantity α is known as the discount factor. Thus, in considering "profitability" of an inventory policy, the profit or costs a year hence should be multiplied by α; 2 years hence, by α^2; and so on.

Of course, the convention of choosing a discount factor α that is based upon the current value of a dollar delivered *1 year* hence is arbitrary, and any time period could have been used, for example, 1 month. It is also evident that in problems having "short-time horizons," α may be assumed to be 1 (and thereby neglected) because the current value of a dollar delivered during this short-time horizon does not change very much. However, in problems having long-time horizons the discount factor must be included.

In using quantitative techniques to seek optimal inventory policies, the criterion of minimizing the total (expected) discounted cost will be used. Under the assumption that the price and demand for the product are not under the control of the company, and including the lost or delayed revenue in the shortage penalty cost, minimizing cost is equivalent to maximizing net income. Another criterion to be considered, although nonquantitative but nevertheless important in practice, is that the resultant inventory policy be simple; i.e., the rule for indicating *when to order* and *how much to order* must be easily described. Most of the policies considered will possess this property.

Inventory models are usually classified according to whether the demand for a period is known (deterministic demand) or whether it is a random variable having a known probability distribution (nondeterministic or random demand). The production of batches of speakers is an example of deterministic demand because it is assumed that they are used in television assemblies at a rate of 8,000 per month. The bicycle shops' purchases of bicycles from the distributor is an example of random demand. This classification is frequently coupled with whether or not there exists time lags in the delivery of the items ordered or produced. In both the speaker and bicycle examples there was an implication that the items appeared "immediately" after an order was placed. In fact, the production of speakers may require some time, and similarly, the delivery of bicycles may not be instantaneous, so that time lags may have to be incorporated into the inventory model.

Another possible classification relates to how the inventory is reviewed, continuously or periodically. In continuous review an order is placed as soon as the stock level falls below the prescribed reorder point, whereas in the periodic review case the inventory level is checked at discrete intervals, e.g., at the end of each week, and ordering decisions are made only at these times even if the inventory level dips below the reorder point during the preceding period. The production of speakers is an example of a continuous review, whereas the bicycle problem is an example of periodic review. Incidently, in practice a periodic review policy can be used to approximate a continuous review policy by making the time interval sufficiently small.

In this chapter inventory policies will be classified according to whether the demand is deterministic or random, and models will be developed for instantaneous delivery and delivery-lag cases and for continuous and periodic review policies.

11.3 DETERMINISTIC MODELS

This section is concerned with inventory problems, where the actual demand is assumed to be known. Several models are considered, including the well-known economic lot-size formulation.

Continuous Review—Uniform Demand

The most common inventory problem faced by manufacturers, retailers, or wholesalers is concerned with the case where stock levels are depleted with time and then are replenished by the arrival of new items. A simple model representing this situation is given by the economic lot-size model. Items are assumed to be withdrawn continuously and at a known constant rate denoted by a; that is, a units are required per unit time, say, per month. It is further assumed that items are produced (or ordered) in equal numbers, Q at a time, and all Q items arrive simultaneously when desired (fixed delivery lags will be considered later). The only costs to be considered are the setup cost K, charged at the time of the production (or ordering), a production cost (or purchase cost) of c dollars per item, and an inventory holding cost of h dollars per item per unit of time. The inventory problem is to determine how often to make a production run and what size it should be so that the cost per unit of time is a minimum. This is a continuous review inventory policy. It will first be assumed that shortages are not allowed, and then this assumption will be relaxed. The example of production of speakers in television sets satisfies this model.

SHORTAGES NOT PERMITTED A cycle can be viewed as the time between production runs. Thus, if 24,000 speakers are produced at each production run and are used at the rate of 8,000 per month, then the cycle length is 24,000/8,000 = 3 months. In general, the cycle length is Q/a. Figure 11.1 illustrates how the inventory level varies over time.

The cost per unit time is obtained as follows: The production cost per cycle is given by

$$\begin{cases} 0, & \text{if } Q = 0 \\ K + cQ, & \text{if } Q > 0. \end{cases}$$

The holding cost per cycle is easily obtained. The average inventory level during a cycle is $(Q + 0)/2 = Q/2$ items per unit of time, and the corresponding

Figure 11.1 Diagram of inventory level as a function of time—no shortages permitted.

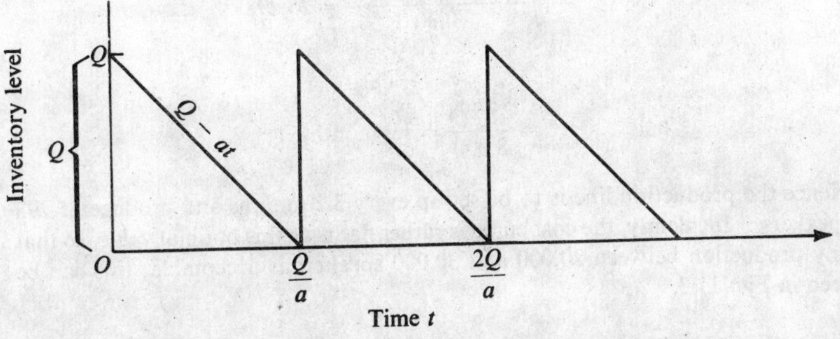

cost is $hQ/2$ per unit of time. Since the cycle length is Q/a, the holding cost per cycle is given by

$$\frac{hQ^2}{2a}.$$

Therefore the total cost per cycle is

$$K + cQ + \frac{hQ^2}{2a},$$

and the total cost per unit of time is

$$T = \frac{K + cQ + hQ^2/2a}{Q/a} = \frac{aK}{Q} + ac + \frac{hQ}{2}.$$

It is evident that the value of Q, say, Q^*, which minimizes T is found from $dT/dQ = 0$. $dT/dQ = -aK/Q^2 + h/2 = 0$, so that

$$Q^* = \sqrt{\frac{2aK}{h}},$$

(since $d^2T/dQ^2 > 0$) which is the well-known economic lot-size result. Similarly, the time it takes to withdraw this optimum value of Q^*, say, t^*, is given by

$$t^* = \frac{Q^*}{a} = \sqrt{\frac{2K}{ah}}.$$

These results will now be applied to the speaker example. The appropriate parameters are

$$K = 12{,}000$$
$$h = 0.30$$
$$a = 8{,}000,$$

so that

$$Q^* = \sqrt{\frac{(2)(8{,}000)(12{,}000)}{0.30}} = 25{,}298$$

and

$$t^* = \frac{25{,}298}{8{,}000} = 3.2 \text{ months}.$$

Hence the production line is to be set up every 3.2 months and produce 25,298 speakers. Incidently, the cost curve is rather flat near this optimal value, so that any production between 20,000 and 30,000 speakers is acceptable; this can be seen in Fig. 11.3.

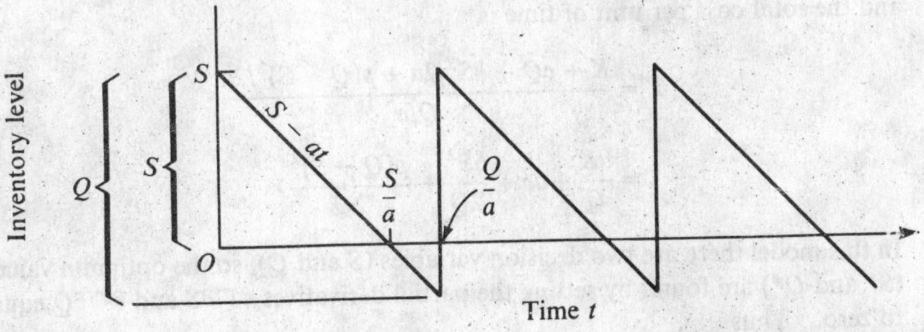

Figure 11.2 Diagram of inventory level as a function of time—shortages permitted.

SHORTAGES PERMITTED It may be "profitable" to permit shortages to occur because the cycle length can be increased with a resultant saving in setup costs. However, this benefit may be offset by the cost that is incurred when shortages occur, and hence a detailed analysis is required.

If shortages are allowed and are priced out at a cost of p dollars for each unit of demand unfilled for one unit of time, results similar to the no shortage case can be obtained. Denote by S the stock on hand at the beginning of a cycle. The problem is summarized in Fig. 11.2.

The cost per unit time is obtained as follows: The production cost per cycle is given by

$$\begin{cases} 0, & \text{if } Q = 0 \\ K + cQ, & \text{if } Q > 0. \end{cases}$$

The holding cost per cycle is easily obtained. Note that the inventory level is positive for a time of S/a. The average inventory level *during this time* is $(S + 0)/2 = S/2$ items per unit of time, and the corresponding cost is $hS/2$ per unit of time. Hence the total holding cost incurred over the time the inventory level is positive is the holding cost per cycle, which is given by

$$\frac{hS}{2}\frac{S}{a} = \frac{hS^2}{2a}.$$

Similarly, shortages occur for a time $(Q - S)/a$. The average amount of shortages *during this time* is $[0 + (Q - S)]/2 = (Q - S)/2$ items per unit of time, and the corresponding cost is $p(Q - S)/2$ per unit of time. Hence the total shortage cost incurred over the time shortages exist is the shortage cost per cycle, which is given by

$$\frac{p(Q - s)}{2}\frac{(Q - S)}{a} = \frac{p(Q - S)^2}{2a}.$$

Therefore the total cost per cycle is

$$K + cQ + \frac{hS^2}{2a} + \frac{p(Q - S)^2}{2a},$$

and the total cost per unit of time is

$$T = \frac{K + cQ + hS^2/2a + p(Q-S)^2/2a}{Q/a}$$

$$= \frac{aK}{Q} + ac + \frac{hS^2}{2Q} + \frac{p(Q-S)^2}{2Q}.$$

In this model there are two decision variables (S and Q), so the optimum values (S^* and Q^*) are found by setting the partial derivatives $\partial T/\partial S$ and $\partial T/\partial Q$ equal to zero. Thus

$$\frac{\partial T}{\partial S} = \frac{hS}{Q} - \frac{p(Q-S)}{Q} = 0.$$

$$\frac{\partial T}{\partial Q} = -\frac{aK}{Q^2} - \frac{hS^2}{2Q^2} + \frac{p(Q-S)}{Q} - \frac{p(Q-S)^2}{2Q^2} = 0.$$

Solving these equations simultaneously leads to

$$S^* = \sqrt{\frac{2aK}{h}}\sqrt{\frac{p}{p+h}},$$

$$Q^* = \sqrt{\frac{2aK}{h}}\sqrt{\frac{p+h}{p}}.$$

The optimal period length t^* is given by

$$t^* = \frac{Q^*}{a} = \sqrt{\frac{2K}{ah}}\sqrt{\frac{p+h}{p}}.$$

The maximum shortage is expressed as

$$Q^* - S^* = \sqrt{\frac{2aK}{p}}\sqrt{\frac{h}{p+h}}.$$

Further, from Fig. 11.2, the fraction of time that no shortage exists is given by

$$\frac{S^*/a}{Q^*/a} = \frac{p}{p+h},$$

which is independent of K.

If shortages are permitted in the speaker example, their cost was estimated as $p = \$1.10$ per speaker. Again

$$K = 12{,}000$$

$$h = 0.30$$

$$a = 8{,}000,$$

so that

$$S^* = \sqrt{\frac{(2)(8{,}000)(12{,}000)}{0.30}} \sqrt{\frac{1.1}{1.1 + 0.3}} = 22{,}424,$$

$$Q^* = \sqrt{\frac{(2)(8{,}000)(12{,}000)}{0.30}} \sqrt{\frac{1.1 + 0.3}{1.1}} = 28{,}540,$$

and

$$t^* = \frac{28{,}540}{8{,}000} = 3.6 \text{ months.}$$

Hence when shortages are permitted the production line is to be set up every 3.6 months and produce 28,540 speakers. A shortage of 6,116 speakers is permitted. Note that Q^* and t^* are not very different from the "no shortage" case.

QUANTITY DISCOUNTS, SHORTAGES NOT PERMITTED The models considered have assumed that the unit cost of an item was the same, independent of the quantity produced. In fact, this assumption resulted in the optimal solutions being independent of this unit cost. Suppose, however, that there exist cost breaks; i.e., the unit cost varies with the quantity ordered. For example, suppose the unit cost of producing a speaker is $c_1 = \$11$ if less than 10,000 speakers are produced, $c_2 = \$10$ if production falls between 10,000 and 80,000 speakers, and $c_3 = \$9.50$ if production exceeds 80,000 speakers. What is the optimal policy? The solution to this specific problem will reveal the general method.

From the results of the previously considered economic lot-size model (shortages not permitted), the total cost per unit time if the production cost is c_j is given by

$$T_j = \frac{aK}{Q} + ac_j + \frac{hQ}{2}, \text{ for } j = 1, 2, 3.$$

A plot of T_j versus Q is shown in Fig. 11.3

The feasible values of Q are shown by the solid lines, and it is only these regions that must be investigated. For each curve, the value of Q that minimizes T_j is easily found by the methods used in the previously considered economic lot-size model. For $K = 12{,}000$, $h = 0.30$, and $a = 8{,}000$, this value is

$$\sqrt{\frac{(2)(8{,}000)(12{,}000)}{0.30}} = 25{,}298.$$

This number is a feasible value for the cost function T_2. Since it is evident that for fixed Q, $T_j < T_{j-1}$ for all j, T_1 can be eliminated from further consideration. However, T_3 can not be immediately discarded. Its minimum feasible value (which occurs at $Q = 80{,}000$) must be compared to T_2 evaluated at 25,298 (which is \$87,389). Since T_3 evaluated at 80,000 equals \$89,200, it is better to produce in quantities of 25,298, and thus this is the optimal value for

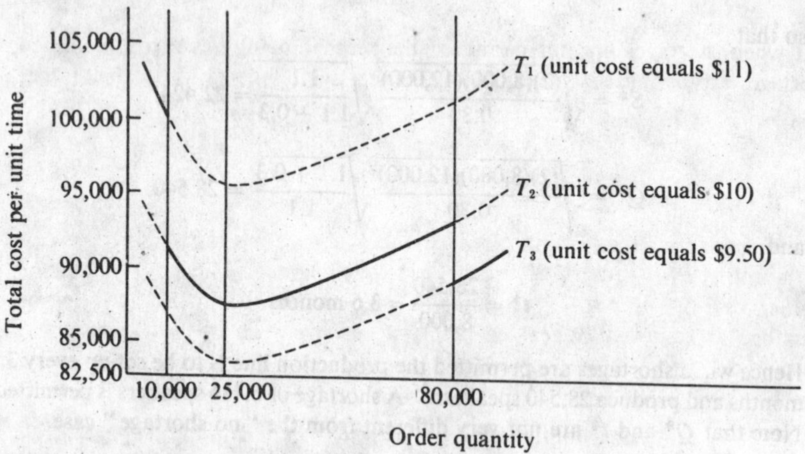

Figure 11.3 Total cost per unit time for speaker example with quantity discounts.

this set of quantity discounts. If the quantity discount led to a cost of $9 (instead of $9.50) when production exceeds 80,000, then T_3 evaluated at 80,000 would equal 85,200, and the optimal production quantity becomes 80,000.

Although this analysis concerned a very specific problem, its extension to a general problem is evident. Furthermore, a similar analysis can be made for other types of quantity discounts such as incremental quantity discounts, where a cost c_0 is incurred for the first q_0 items, c_1 for the next q_1 items, and so on.

Remarks There are several remarks that can be made about economic lot-size models:

1. If it is assumed that the production (or purchase) cost of an item is constant throughout time, it does not appear in the optimal solution. This is evident because no matter what policy is used, the same quantity is required, and hence this cost is fixed.

2. It was previously assumed that Q, the number of units produced, was constant from cycle to cycle. A little reflection will reveal that this is a result rather than an assumption.

3. These models can be viewed as a special case of an (s, S) policy. An (s, S) policy is usually used in the context of a periodic review policy, where at review time an order is placed to bring the inventory level up to S if the current inventory is less than or equal to s. Otherwise, no order is placed.[1] The symbol S then denotes the reorder level, and s denotes the reorder point. In the economic lot-size models, s denotes the inventory level when items are ordered, so

[1] Usually (s,S) policies are described as ordering when the inventory level is less than s rather than when the inventory level is less than or equal to s. However, the costs are often the same if an optimal policy is followed.

that when shortages are not permitted the reorder point s is zero, and when shortages are permitted, s is equal to the negative of the maximum shortage; that is,

$$s = -\sqrt{\frac{2aK}{p}}\sqrt{\frac{h}{p+h}}.$$

Furthermore, since the economic lot-size models are continuously reviewed, when the inventory level equals s an order is placed, bringing the inventory up to the reorder level S. Hence, for economic lot-size models the (s,S) policy can be described as follows: When the inventory level reaches the reorder point s, place an order to bring the inventory level up to reorder level S; that is, order $Q = S - s$.

4. It is evident from the analysis presented that the reorder point will never be positive. A policy that calls for $s > 0$ can not be optimal because it is dominated by a policy which calls for ordering the same Q, but only when the reorder point reaches zero. It is dominated in that the latter policy has the same setup and purchase costs but has a uniformly smaller holding cost.

5. A known fixed delivery lag is easily accommodated. Denote by λ the lead time between the placing and receiving of the order. It shall be assumed that λ is constant over time and independent of the size of the order. It is evident that if it is desired to have the order arrive the moment the inventory level reaches s, then the order must be placed λ periods earlier. Thus the reorder point is simply

$$s + \lambda a,$$

where s is determined for the no-lag situation.[1]

Periodic Review—A General Model for Production Planning

The last section explored the economic lot-size model. The results were dependent upon the assumption of a constant demand rate. When this is relaxed, i.e., when the amounts required from period to period are allowed to vary, the square root formula no longer ensures a minimum cost solution.

Consider the following model due to Wagner and Whitin.[2] As before, the only costs to be considered are the setup cost K, charged at the beginning of the period, a production cost (or purchase cost) of c dollars per item, and an inventory holding cost of h dollars per item, which is charged (arbitrarily) at the end of the time period. The choice of charging the inventory at the end of the period, and hence as a function of the excess of the supply over the requirement,

[1] This result holds only when $\lambda a < Q$.

[2] H. M. Wagner and T. M. Whitin, "Dynamic Version of the Economic Lot Size Model," *Management Science*, **5**(1): 89–96. 1958

is somewhat different from the holding charge incurred in the economic lot-size models. In the latter case the average cost per unit of time was charged. Clearly, different policies can result from alternative ways of dealing with holding costs. In addition, r_i, $i = 1, 2, \ldots, n$, represents the requirements at time i, and it is assumed that these requirements must be met. Initially there is no stock on hand. For a horizon of n periods, the inventory problem is to determine how much should be produced at the beginning of each time period (assumed to be instantaneous) so as to minimize the total cost incurred over the n periods.

The model can be illustrated by the following variation of the speaker example.

EXAMPLE A market survey conducted by the television manufacturer has indicated that the demand for television sets is seasonal rather than uniform. In particular, a sales of 30,000 sets is forecast for the Christmas season (October to December), 20,000 during the winter slack season (January to March), 30,000 during the "new model" season (April to June), and 20,000 during the summer season (July to September). Because of the necessity of meeting the increased demand during the peak seasons, the television set production line was revamped. This enabled the company to introduce new equipment as well as redesign some of its components, including the speakers. Hence the setup cost for speaker production is now \$20,000, but the unit cost is down to \$1. Furthermore, the holding cost of a speaker has also been reduced to 20 cents per (3 month) period. Finally, the labor and equipment costs are such that the speakers must be produced in increments of 10,000. It shall be assumed that production of the television sets is completed and ready for shipment in the 3-month period prior to the season in which it is required. Thus the 30,000 sets required for the Christmas season are to be assembled during the July to September period. The speaker is the last component added to the television set, and it is easily installed. Furthermore, large quantities of speakers can be produced in a very short time period so that their production and subsequent installation can be viewed as instantaneous. The problem is to determine how much to produce in each period satisfying the requirements and minimizing the total cost. A solution, though not optimal, is given in Fig. 11.4; this policy calls for producing 30,000 speakers at the beginning of the first period (Christmas season), 60,000 speakers at the beginning of the second period, and 10,000 speakers at the beginning of the fourth period.

One approach to the solution of this model is to enumerate, for each of the 2^{n-1} combinations of either producing or not producing in each period, the possible quantities that can be produced. This is rather cumbersome, even for moderate-sized n. Hence a more efficient method is desirable. In particular, the method of dynamic programming introduced in Chap. 6, will be applied, followed by the introduction of an algorithm (in the ensuing section) that exploits the structure. Finally, a mathematical programming solution will be presented.

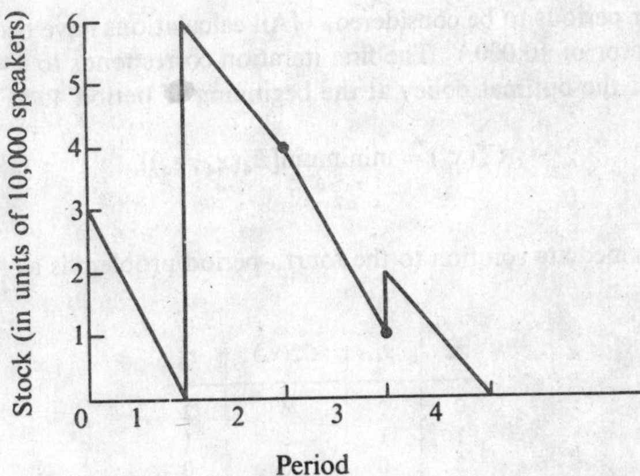

Figure 11.4 Production schedule that satisfies requirements.

THE DYNAMIC PROGRAMMING SOLUTION Following the notation introduced for dynamic programming (Chap. 6), and interpreting the variables in the inventory context, the ith stage corresponds to the ith period; the state corresponds to the inventory entering period i and will be denoted by x_i; and the decision variable corresponds to the quantity produced (or ordered) at the beginning of period i and will be denoted by z_i.†

Let $B_i(x_i, z_i)$ denote the costs incurred in period i, given the entering inventory and the quantity produced. Recall that the only costs considered are the setup cost K, charged at the beginning of the period, a production cost (or purchase cost) of c dollars per item, and an inventory holding cost of h dollars per item charged at the end of the time period. The requirements for period i is r_i. Then $B_i(x_i, z_i)$ is given by

$$B_i(x_i, z_i) = \begin{cases} K + cz_i + h(x_i + z_i - r_i), & \text{if } z_i > 0 \\ h(x_i - r_i), & \text{if } z_i = 0. \end{cases}$$

Denote by $C_i(x_i, z_i)$ the total cost of the best overall policy from the beginning of period i to the end of the planning horizon, given that the inventory level entering period i is x_i and z_i is chosen to be produced; and let $C_i^*(x_i)$ denote the corresponding minimum value of $C_i(x_i, z_i)$, subject to the constraints that $z_i \geq 0$ and that the requirements for the periods are met. Therefore

$$C_i^*(x_i) = \underset{\substack{z_i \geq 0 \\ z_i \geq r_i - x_i}}{\text{minimum}}[B_i(x_i, z_i) + C_{i+1}^*(x_i + z_i - r_i)],$$

for $i = 1, 2, \ldots, n$, and $C_{n+1}^*(\cdot)$ is defined to be zero. In the speaker example,

† For the notation in this chapter to be consistent with that used in inventory theory, in general it may differ somewhat from the notation introduced in Chap. 6.

there are four periods to be considered. (All calculations have been reduced in scale by a factor of 10,000.) The first iteration corresponds to $i = 4$, that is, a description of the optimal policy at the beginning of period 4. For this case

$$C_4^*(x_4) = \underset{\substack{z_4 \geq 0 \\ z_4 \geq 2 - x_4}}{\text{minimum}}[B_4(x_4, z_4)],$$

so that the immediate solution to the fourth-period problem is as follows:

x_4	z_4	$C_4^*(x_4)$	z_4^*
0	2	4	2
1	1	3	1
2	0	0	0

The second iteration requires finding the optimal policy from the beginning of period 3 to the end of period 4. For this case

$$C_3^*(x_3) = \underset{\substack{z_3 \geq 0 \\ z_3 \geq 3 - x_3}}{\text{minimum}}[B_3(x_3, z_3) + C_4^*(x_3 + z_3 - 3)],$$

so that the solution to the problem beginning at period 3 is as follows:

	$B_3(x_3, z_3) + C_4^*(x_3 + z_3 - 3)$							
x_3 \ z_3	0	1	2	3	4	5	$C_3^*(x_3)$	z_3^*
0	···	···	···	9.0	9.2	7.4	7.4	5
1	···	···	8	8.2	6.4	···	6.4	4
2	···	7	7.2	5.4	···	···	5.4	3
3	4.0	6.2	4.4	···	···	···	4.0	0
4	3.2	3.4	···	···	···	···	3.2	0
5	0.4	···	···	···	···	···	0.4	0

A typical entry can be verified. Let $x_3 = 2$ and $z_3 = 3$. Then 3 units are produced, given an initial inventory of 2. The cost of production is then $2 + 1(3) = 5$, and the inventory holding cost is $\frac{1}{5}(2 + 3 - 3) = 0.4$. The entering inventory in period 4 is then 2, so that $C_4^*(2) = 0$. Hence the total cost is given by $5 + 0.4 = 5.4$, which is the value given above.

The third iteration requires finding the optimal policy from the beginning of period 2 to the end of period 4. For this case

$$C_2^*(x_2) = \underset{\substack{z_2 \geq 0 \\ z_2 \geq 2 - x_2}}{\text{minimum}}[B_2(x_2, z_2) + C_3^*(x_2 + z_2 - 2)],$$

so that the solution to the problem beginning at period 2 is as follows:

x_2 \ z_2	$B_2(x_2, z_2) + C_3^*(x_2 + z_2 - 2)$ 0	1	2	3	4	5	6	7	$C_2^*(x_2)$	z_2^*
0	...	...	11.4	11.6	11.8	11.6	12.0	10.4	10.4	7
1	...	10.4	10.6	10.8	10.6	11.0	9.4	...	9.4	6
2	7.4	9.6	9.8	9.6	10.0	8.4	...	...	7.4	0
3	6.6	8.8	8.6	9.0	7.4	...	...	...	6.6	0
4	5.8	7.6	8.0	6.4	...	...	...	...	5.8	0
5	4.6	7.0	5.4	...	...	...	...	...	4.6	0
6	4.0	4.4	...	...	...	...	...	...	4.0	0
7	1.4	...	...	...	...	...	...	...	1.4	0

Finally, the last iteration requires finding the optimal policy from the beginning of period 1 to the end of period 4. For this case

$$C_1^*(0) = \underset{z_1 \geq 3}{\text{minimum}}[B_1(0, z_1) + C_2^*(z_1 - 3)],$$

so that the solution to the production planning problem is as follows:

x_1 \ z_1	$B_1(0,z_1) + C_2^*(z_1 - 3)$ 0	1	2	3	4	5	6	7	8	9	10	$C_1^*(x_1)$	z_1^*
0	...	...	...	15.4	15.6	14.8	15.2	15.6	15.6	16.2	14.8	14.8	5 or 10

Therefore the optimal production schedule is to produce all the speakers at the beginning of the first period, or produce 50,000 speakers (5 units) at the beginning of the first period and 50,000 speakers (5 units) at the beginning of the third period. The minimum cost is $148,000.

It should be noted that the unit cost c is irrelevant to the problem because over all the time periods, all policies use the same number of items at the same total cost. Hence this cost could have been neglected, and the same optimal policies would have been obtained. Different costs in different periods are easily handled by this method of solution. For example, during the peak production periods (when 30,000 speakers are produced), the workers are fully engaged in the assembly of television sets, so that the speakers must be produced during overtime hours. Hence the unit cost is increased. This would be reflected in the calculations of $C_3^*(x_3)$ and $C_1^*(x_1)$

Periodic Review—Production Planning—An Algorithm

In the previous section dynamic programming was applied to solve the production planning model. Alternatively, by streamlining the dynamic programming approach an algorithm will be developed that exploits the structure of the model. Initially the production planning model considered will be the same as that presented in the previous section, i.e., arbitrary demand requirement, a fixed setup cost, and linear production and holding costs.

The following result characterizes an optimal policy:

For an arbitrary demand requirement, a fixed setup cost, and linear production and holding costs, there is an optimum policy that produces only when the inventory level is zero.

To show why this result is true, choose any policy. Consider the time from the beginning of a period, when production from zero is made to the first time production is made, when the stock is not zero. For the policy given in Fig. 11.4 this interval starts at the beginning of period 2 and ends at the beginning of period 4, when one item is produced. This time period is also shown by the solid lines in Fig. 11.5.

Consider the alternate policy, which implies production of 50,000 speakers at the beginning of period 2 and production of 20,000 speakers at the beginning of period 4. This policy is shown by the dotted lines in Fig. 11.5. This policy, B, dominates policy A in that the total cost is smaller. The setup and the production costs for both policies are the same. It is evident that the holding cost for B is smaller than that for A because there is always less stock on hand at the end of a period. Therefore B is better than A, so that A can not be optimal.

This characterization of optimal policies can be used to determine which policies are not optimal. In addition, because it implies that the amount produced at the beginning of the ith period must be either 0, r_i, $r_i + r_{i+1}$, ..., $r_i + r_{i+1} \cdots + r_n$, it can be exploited to obtain an efficient algorithm.

Figure 11.5 Production schedules.

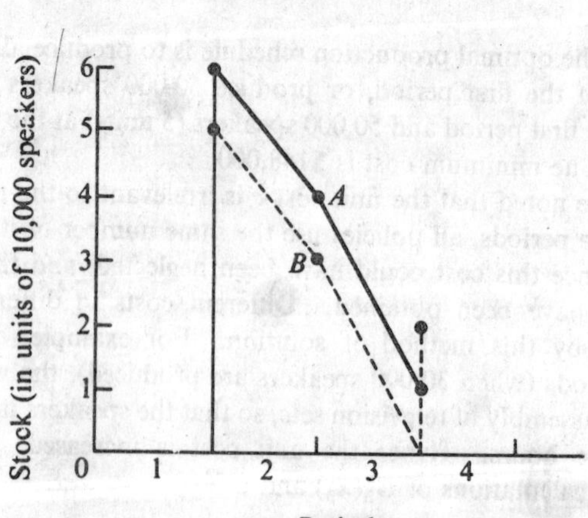

Suppose an optimal policy is presented. Consider the time from the initial production at the beginning of the first period to the first time the inventory level is again zero. The total cost of the subsequent periods must be a minimum for this reduced problem because the overall policy is optimal. Therefore, in the context of the speaker example, if the inventory level is zero for the first time (after the initial production) at the end of the second period, and an optimal policy is being followed, all that remains is to determine the optimal policy for the last two periods (periods 3 and 4) having a requirement of 30,000 speakers for period 3 and 20,000 speakers for period 4.

Let C_i denote the total cost of the best overall policy from the beginning of period i, when no stock is available, to the end of the planning horizon, $i = 1, 2, \ldots, n$. A recursive relationship for C_i is given by

$$C_i = \underset{j=i,\,i+1,\ldots,n}{\text{minimum}} \left[C_{j+1} + K + c(r_i + r_{i+1} + \cdots + r_j) + h(r_{i+1} + 2r_{i+2} + 3r_{i+3} + \cdots + (j-i)r_j)\right],$$

where j can be viewed as an index that denotes the (end of the) period that the inventory reaches a zero level for the first time after the production at the beginning of period i. The cost C_{n+1} is 0, $c(r_i + r_{i+1} + \cdots + r_j)$ is the cost of the production from period i until the inventory level next reaches zero, and the quantity $h(\ )$ is the total holding cost of the inventory resulting from the production from period i and remaining until the inventory level next reaches zero. This latter cost is charged at the end of every period as a function of the excess, if any, over the requirement.

The solution of this algorithm is much simplier than the dynamic programming approach. As in dynamic programming, C_n, C_{n-1}, $\ldots$, C_2 must be found before C_1 is obtained. However, the number of calculations is much smaller, and the number of possible production values is greatly reduced.

EXAMPLE Returning to the speaker example, first consider the case of finding C_4, the cost of the optimal policy from the beginning of period 4 to the end of the planning horizon:

$$C_4 = C_5 + 2 + 1(2) = 0 + 2 + 2 = 4.0.$$

In finding C_3 there are two cases to consider; i.e., the first time after period 3 the inventory reaches a zero level can occur at (1) the end of the third period or (2) the end of the fourth period. In the recurrence relationship j may range over 3 or 4, resulting in the costs $C_3^{(3)}$ or $C_3^{(4)}$, respectively. The cost C_3 is then the minimum of $C_3^{(3)}$ and $C_3^{(4)}$. These are reflected by the policies given in Fig. 11.6.

$$C_3^{(3)} = C_4 + 2 + 1(3) = 4 + 2 + 3 = 9,$$

and

$$C_3^{(4)} = C_5 + 2 + 1(3 + 2) + \frac{1}{5}(2) = 0 + 2 + 5 + 0.4 = 7.4.$$

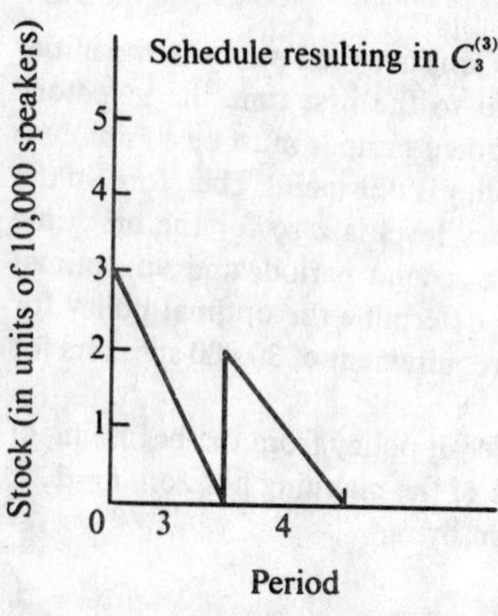

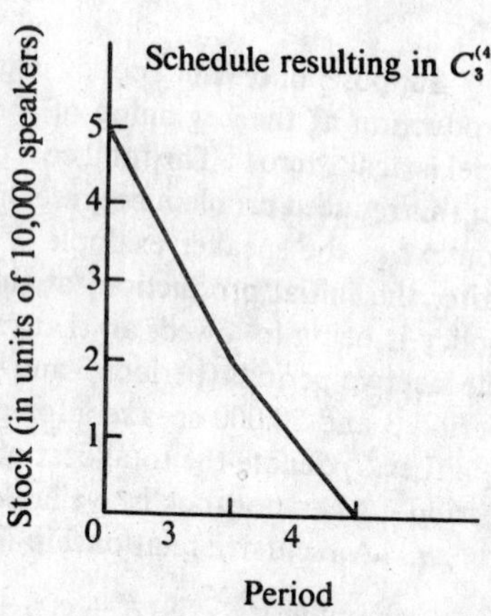

Figure 11.6 Alternate production schedules when production is required at the beginning of period 3.

Hence

$$C_3 = \min(7.4, 9.0) = 7.4.$$

In finding C_2 there are three cases to consider; i.e., the first time after period 2 the inventory reaches a zero level can occur at (1) the end of the second period, (2) the end of the third period, or (3) the end of the fourth period. In the recursive relationship j may range over 2, 3, or 4, resulting in costs $C_2^{(2)}$, $C_2^{(3)}$, or $C_2^{(4)}$, respectively. The cost C_2 is then the minimum of $C_2^{(2)}$, $C_2^{(3)}$, and $C_2^{(4)}$.

$$C_2^{(2)} = C_3 + 2 + 1(2) \qquad = 7.4 + 2 + 2 = 11.4,$$

$$C_2^{(3)} = C_4 + 2 + 1(2+3) + \frac{1}{5}(3) \qquad = 4 + 2 + 5 + 0.6 = 11.6,$$

and

$$C_2^{(4)} = C_5 + 2 + 1(2+3+2) + \frac{1}{5}[3 + 2(2)] = 0 + 2 + 7 + 1.4 = 10.4.$$

Hence

$$C_2 = \min(11.4, 11.6, 10.4) = 10.4.$$

Finally, in finding C_1 there are four cases to consider; i.e., the first time after period 1 the inventory reaches zero can occur at (1) the end of the first period, (2) the end of the second period, (3) the end of the third period, or (4) the end of the fourth period. In the recursive relationship j may range over 1, 2, 3, or 4, resulting in the costs $C_1^{(1)}$, $C_1^{(2)}$, $C_1^{(3)}$, $C_1^{(4)}$. The cost C_1 is then the minimum of $C_1^{(1)}$, $C_1^{(2)}$, $C_1^{(3)}$, and $C_1^{(4)}$.

$$C_1^{(1)} = C_2 + 2 + 1(3) \qquad = 10.4 + 2 + 3 = 15.4,$$

$$C_1^{(2)} = C_3 + 2 + 1(3 + 2) + \frac{1}{5}(2) \qquad = 7.4 + 2 + 4 + 0.4 = 14.8,$$

$$C_1^{(3)} = C_4 + 2 + 1(3 + 2 + 3) + \frac{1}{5}[2 + 2(3)] \qquad = 4 + 2 + 8 + 1.6 = 15.6,$$

and

$$C_1^{(4)} = C_5 + 2 + 1(3 + 2 + 3 + 2)$$
$$+ \frac{1}{5}[2 + 2(3) + 3(2)] = 0 + 2 + 10 + 2.8 = 14.8.$$

Hence

$$C_1 = \min(15.4, 14.8, 15.6, 14.8) = 14.8,$$

so that the optimal production schedule is to produce all the speakers at the beginning of the first period, or produce 50,000 speakers at the beginning of the first period and 50,000 speakers at the beginning of the third period (the same solution as obtained previously).

Again it should be noted that the unit cost c is irrelevant to the problem because over all the time periods, all policies use the same number of items at the same total cost. Hence this cost could have been neglected, and the same optimal policies would have been obtained.

The characterization of the optimal policy, and the subsequent algorithm for finding an optimal policy, depended upon the assumption that the holding and production costs were linear. This constraint can be relaxed to include *concave production and holding costs*. In fact, any increasing function of the holding cost will serve as an alternative condition if the production cost is linear. However, these alternate conditions require a modification in the algorithm for finding an optimal policy. If the production cost function is denoted by $c[\cdot]$ and holding cost function $h[\cdot]$, the recursive relationship for C_i becomes

$$C_i = \underset{j=i,\, i+1,\ldots,n}{\text{minimum}} \{C_{j+1} + K + c[r_i + r_{i+1} + \cdots + r_j]$$
$$+ h[r_{i+1} + r_{i+2} + r_{i+3} + \cdots + r_j]$$
$$+ h[r_{i+2} + r_{i+3} + \cdots + r_j] + \cdots + h[r_j]\},$$

where $C_{n+1} = 0$.†

A natural extension of the production planning model is to permit shortages to occur. This has been studied by Zangwill[1] and differs from the production planning model studied in that shortage costs are incurred for each unit of

† In the expression for C_i there is no holding cost when $j = i$.

[1] W. I. Zangwill, "A Deterministic Multi-Period Production Scheduling Model with Backlogging," *Management Science*, 13(1): 105–119, 1966.

demand unfilled for one unit of time. Zangwill characterizes the form of the optimal policy and gives an efficient recursive relationship for finding the optimal policy. These results apply when the production, holding, and shortage costs, per period, are concave functions (thereby including the case of linear costs).

Other results have been obtained for this production planning model under the assumption that the production, holding, and shortage costs are convex. Convex production costs arise, for example, where there are several sources of limited production at different unit costs in a period. If one uses these sources up to capacity in order of ascending unit cost (as is optimal), the resulting production cost is convex in the total amount produced. Such an assumption about the production cost precludes the use of the setup charge.

Periodic Review—Production Planning—Integer Programming Formulation

The final technique for solving the production planning model is to formulate it as an integer programming problem. Instead of presenting the general solution, the speaker production example will be solved.

Again, let z_i denote the quantity produced at the beginning of period i.† The costs to be considered are

$$\text{Production costs} = \text{setup costs} + c(z_1 + z_2 + z_3 + z_4)$$

and

$$\begin{aligned}\text{Holding costs} \\ &= h(z_1 - r_1) + h(z_1 + z_2 - r_1 - r_2) \\ &\quad + h(z_1 + z_2 + z_3 - r_1 - r_2 - r_3) \\ &= 3h(z_1 - r_1) + 2h(z_2 - r_2) + h(z_3 - r_3) \\ &= 0.20[3(z_1 - 3) + 2(z_2 - 2) + (z_3 - 3)].\end{aligned}$$

Hence the problem to be solved is to minimize the sum of the production and holding costs, that is,

$$\text{Minimize} \quad W = \text{setup cost} + 1(z_1 + z_2 + z_3 + z_4) + 0.20[3(z_1 - 3) + 2(z_2 - 2) + (z_3 - 3)],$$

subject to

$$\begin{aligned} z_1 &\le r_1 + r_2 + r_3 + r_4 = 10 \\ z_2 &\le r_2 + r_3 + r_4 = 7 \\ z_3 &\le r_3 + r_4 = 5 \\ z_4 &\le r_4 = 2 \end{aligned}$$

† Again, all values are expressed in units of 10,000 speakers.

$$z_1 \geq r_1 = 3$$
$$z_1 + z_2 \geq r_1 + r_2 = 5$$
$$z_1 + z_2 + z_3 \geq r_1 + r_2 + r_3 = 8$$
$$z_1 + z_2 + z_3 + z_4 = r_1 + r_2 + r_3 + r_4 = 10$$

and

$$z_1 \geq 0, z_2 \geq 0, z_3 \geq 0, z_4 \geq 0, \text{ and integer valued.}$$

Unfortunately, this is not an integer linear programming model because the objective function is not linear because of the "setup costs" term that appears in the objective function. However, this can be resolved as follows:

Define variables v_1, v_2, v_3, and v_4 such that

$$v_1 \leq 1, v_2 \leq 1, v_3 \leq 1, v_4 \leq 1,$$
$$v_1 \geq 0, v_2 \geq 0, v_3 \geq 0, v_4 \geq 0,$$

and

$$v_1, v_2, v_3, \text{ and } v_4 \text{ are integers } (v_i \text{ is then 0 or 1}).$$

Add the following constraints to the problem:

$$z_1 \leq \left(\sum_{i=1}^{4} r_i\right) v_1 = 10v_1$$
$$z_2 \leq \left(\sum_{i=2}^{4} r_i\right) v_2 = 7v_2$$
$$z_3 \leq \left(\sum_{i=3}^{4} r_i\right) v_3 = 5v_3$$
$$z_4 \leq r_4 v_4 = 2v_4 .$$

Thus, if $v_i = 0$, then $z_i = 0$, and if $v_i = 1$, then z_i is less than or equal to the maximum production in period i. The objective function can now be written as a linear function subject to linear constraints; that is,

$$\text{Minimize} \quad W = K(v_1 + v_2 + v_3 + v_4) + 1(z_1 + z_2 + z_3 + z_4) + 0.20[3(z_1 - 3) + 2(z_2 - 2) + (z_3 - 3)],$$

subject to

$$z_1 \leq 10v_1$$
$$z_2 \leq 7v_2$$
$$z_3 \leq 5v_3$$
$$z_4 \leq 2v_4$$
$$z_1 \geq 3$$
$$z_1 + z_2 \geq 5$$
$$z_1 + z_2 + z_3 \geq 8$$
$$z_1 + z_2 + z_3 + z_4 = 10$$

and

$$\begin{cases} z_1 \geq 0, z_2 \geq 0, z_3 \geq 0, z_4 \geq 0, \text{ and integer valued,} \\ v_1 \geq 0, v_2 \geq 0, v_3 \geq 0, v_4 \geq 0, \\ v_1 \leq 1, v_2 \leq 1, v_3 \leq 1, v_4 \leq 1, \text{ and integer valued.} \end{cases}$$

The solution to this problem may be obtained by using an integer programming algorithm; it yields the same solution as obtained previously, i.e., produce 100,000 speakers at the beginning of the first period ($z_1 = 10$, $v_1 = 1$, and all other z_i and v_i equal zero), or produce 50,000 speakers at the beginning of the first period and 50,000 speakers at the beginning of the third period ($z_1 = z_3 = 5$, $v_1 = v_3 = 1$, and all other z_i and v_i equal zero).

11.4 STOCHASTIC MODELS

This section is concerned with inventory problems, where the demand for a period is a random variable having a known probability distribution. Both single-period and multiperiod models are analyzed.

A Single-period Model with No Setup Cost

The second example discussed in Sec. 11.1 is concerned with a wholesale distributor of 10-speed bicycles. Suppose that this distributor is offered very favorable terms on the purchase of a model of a name-brand bicycle whose production is to be discontinued. This opportunity appears to be ideal for the forthcoming Christmas season, where, because production has been discontinued, the stores have been informed that no reorders are possible. The cost of each bicycle is \$20, and it will be assumed that there is no setup cost incurred. The cost of maintaining an inventory is $-\$9$ per bicycle. This cost includes \$1, which represents the cost of capital tied up, warehouse space, and so on, and $-\$10$, which is what the distributor can get for each bicycle remaining in the inventory after the Christmas season (the salvage value). Note that this cost of maintaining an inventory is obtained by combining the bicycle storage cost with the bicycle salvage value and results in a negative "holding" cost.

Each bicycle is sold for \$45, with a profit of \$25. If the demand exceeds the supply available, then the unit cost of unsatisfied demand must be interpreted as the lost revenue of \$45 per bicycle and not just the lost profit. A little reflection will indicate that this procedure is reasonable. Suppose one adopts the point of view that revenue should be added as a (negative) cost to the model being considered. Minimizing total cost is then equivalent to maximizing net income. Suppose further that there is no loss in good will, no cost of delayed revenue, and so on, in not meeting demand, so that this penalty cost can be neglected. Of course, the ordering and holding costs continue to be included. The revenue received is \$45 times the demand *less* \$45 times the unsatisfied demand whenever a shortage occurs. Note that the former is independent of the inventory policy and hence can be neglected, whereas the latter is just the lost revenue when a shortage occurs. Thus the lost revenue can be interpreted as the unsatisfied demand cost. Of course, if there are additional costs associated with unsatisfied demand (e.g., loss of good will), they can be added to lost revenue. Another explanation of interpreting the cost of unsatisfied demand as lost revenue is as follows. Suppose the West Coast distributor is forced to meet the unsatisfied demand by purchasing bicycles from the Midwest distributor at the same cost that bicycles are sold to the retail outlets ($45). The appropriate penalty cost is then at least $45 per bicycle.

The previous discussion was concerned with the costs involved in the model, and little attention was paid to the concept of the demand for the bicycles. Unfortunately, the distributor does not know what the demand for these bicycles will be from the stores in the Western United States, i.e., the demand is a random variable, and hence he does not know how many bicycles will be required. However, an optimal inventory policy can be obtained if information about the probability distribution of demand is available. Let D represent the random variable demand, and denote by $P_D(d)$ the probability that the demand equals d; that is,

$$P_D(d) = P\{D = d\}.$$

It will be assumed that $P_D(d)$ is known for all values of d; that is, the probability distribution is specified.

In general, the following inventory model is being considered. Items are purchased (or produced) for a *single period* at a cost of c dollars per item. The holding cost, the net unit cost of storing leftover items minus their salvage value, is given by h dollars per item and charged as a function of excess stock over the amount required. The cost of unsatisfied demand, e.g., lost revenue from sales or the cost of supplying a required unit, is given by p dollars per unit ($p > c$). It is assumed that there is no initial inventory on hand. Denote by y the quantity purchased (or produced) at the beginning of the period,[1] and let D be a random variable that denotes the demand during the period.

This single-period model may represent the inventory of an item that (1) becomes obsolete quickly such as the bicycle in the example, or a daily newspaper; (2) spoils quickly, such as vegetables; (3) is stocked only once, such as spare parts for a single production run of a new model airplane; or (4) has a future that is uncertain beyond a single period.

With the aforementioned structure, the question of how much inventory to have becomes relevant. More than the expected demand is probably desirable, but certainly less than the maximum demand is required. A tradeoff is needed between (1) the risk of being short and thereby incurring shortage costs and (2) the risk of having an excess and thereby incurring wasted costs of ordering and

[1] In the previous models the symbol z was used to denote the quantity produced, and x represented the inventory level at the beginning of the period. The symbol y is introduced here to denote the inventory level to be achieved after the ordering decision is made; that is, y is the amount ordered up to, so that $y = x + z$. Since the initial inventory level is assumed to be zero, that is, $x = 0$, y and z are the same.

holding of excess units. One reasonable criterion is to choose the inventory level that minimizes the expected value (in the statistical sense) of the sums of these costs.

The amount sold is given by

$$\begin{cases} D, \text{ if } D < y \\ y, \text{ if } D \geq y \end{cases} = \min(D, y).$$

Hence the cost incurred if the demand is D and y is stocked is given by

$$C(D, y) = cy + p \max(0, D - y) + h \max(0, y - D).$$

Since the demand is a random variable [with probability distribution $P_D(d)$], this cost is also a random variable. The expected cost is then given by $C(y)$, where

$$\begin{aligned} C(y) = E[C(D, y)] &= \sum_{d=0}^{\infty} [cy + p \max(0, d - y) + h \max(0, y - d)]P_D(d) \\ &= cy + \sum_{d=y}^{\infty} p(d - y)P_D(d) + \sum_{d=0}^{y-1} h(y - d)P_D(d). \end{aligned}$$

It is evident that $C(y)$ depends upon the probability distribution $P_D(d)$. Frequently a representation of this probability distribution is difficult to find, particularly when the demand ranges over a large number of possible values. Hence this discrete random variable is often approximated by a continuous random variable. Furthermore, when demand ranges over a large number of possible values, this approximation will generally yield small differences in numerical values in the optimal amounts of inventory to stock. In addition, when discrete demand is used the resulting expressions may become slightly more difficult to solve analytically. Hence, unless otherwise stated, continuous demand will be assumed throughout the remainder of this chapter. The probability *density* function of this *continuous* random variable will be denoted by $\varphi_D(\xi)$. The expected cost $C(y)$ is then expressed as

$$\begin{aligned} C(y) = E[C(D, y)] &= \int_0^{\infty} [cy + p \max(0, \xi - y) + h \max(0, y - \xi)]\varphi_D(\xi)\, d\xi \\ &= cy + \int_y^{\infty} p(\xi - y)\varphi_D(\xi)\, d\xi + \int_0^{y} h(y - \xi)\varphi_D(\xi)\, d\xi\dagger \\ &= cy + L(y), \end{aligned}$$

where $L(y)$ is often called the expected shortage plus holding cost. It then

† The notation introduced in Chap. 8 is being followed. If X is a random variable having density function $f_X(y)$, and $g(X)$ is a function of X, then

$$E[g(X)] = \int_{-\infty}^{\infty} g(y) f_X(y)\, dy.$$

Thus the expected cost is given by $C(y)$.

becomes necessary to find the value of y, say y°, which minimizes $C(y)$. *The optimal quantity to order, y°, is that value which satisfies*

$$\Phi(y^\circ) = \frac{p - c}{p + h},$$

where the function $\Phi(a)$ is the cumulative distribution function of the demand random variable; that is,

$$\Phi(a) = \int_0^a \varphi_D(\xi)\, d\xi.$$

The derivation of this solution is given on page 499.

If D is assumed to be a discrete random variable having cumulative distribution function

$$F_D(b) = \sum_{d=0}^{b} P_D(d),$$

a similar result for the optimal order quantity is obtained. In particular, *the optimal quantity to order, y°, is the smallest integer such that*

$$F_D(y^\circ) \geq \frac{p - c}{p + h}.$$

Example Returning to the bicycle example described in this section, assume that the demand has an exponential distribution given by

$$\varphi_D(\xi) = \begin{cases} \dfrac{1}{10{,}000} e^{-\xi/10{,}000}, & \xi \geq 0 \\ 0, & \text{otherwise.} \end{cases}$$

From the data given,

$$c = 20$$
$$p = 45$$
$$h = -9.$$

Since the demand density is exponential,

$$\Phi(a) = \int_0^a \frac{1}{10{,}000} e^{-\xi/10{,}000}\, d\xi = 1 - e^{-a/10{,}000}.$$

The optimum quantity to order, y°, is that value which satisfies

$$1 - e^{-y^0/10{,}000} = \frac{45 - 20}{45 - 9} = 0.6944,$$

or alternatively,

$$y^0 = 11{,}856.$$

Therefore the distributor should stock 11,856 bicycles in the Christmas season. Note that this is slightly more than the expected demand.

Whenever the demand is exponential with expectation λ, y^0 can easily be obtained from the relation

$$y^0 = -\lambda \ln \left(\frac{c+h}{p+h}\right).$$

MODEL WITH INITIAL STOCK LEVEL As a slight variation of the previous model, suppose that the distributor has 500 bicycles of the aforementioned type on hand. How does this influence the optimal inventory policy? In particular, suppose that the initial stock level is given by x, and the problem is to determine how much is to be made available, y, at the beginning of the period. Thus, $(y - x)$ is to be ordered so that

Amount available (y) = initial stock (x) + amount produced $(y - x)$.

The cost equation presented earlier remains identical except for the term that was previously cy. This term now becomes $c(y - x)$, so that minimizing the expected cost is given by

$$\underset{y \geq x}{\text{minimum}}\left[c(y-x) + \int_y^\infty p(\xi - y)\varphi_D(\xi)\,d\xi + \int_0^y h(y-\xi)\varphi_D(\xi)\,d\xi\right].$$

The constraint $y \geq x$ must be added because it is assumed that items on hand at the beginning of the period can not be depleted or returned. The optimum policy is described as follows.

The inventory policy which satisfies, for $p > c$,

$$\underset{y \geq x}{\text{minimum}}\left[-cx + \left\{\int_y^\infty p(\xi - y)\varphi_D(\xi)\,d\xi + \int_0^y h(y-\xi)\varphi_D(\xi)\,d\xi + cy\right\}\right]$$

is given by $y = \begin{cases} y^\circ \\ x \end{cases}$*, so that*

If $x < y^\circ$, *order up to* y° *(order* $y^\circ - x$*),*
If $x \geq y^\circ$, *do not order,*

where y° *satisfies*

$$\Phi(y^\circ) = \frac{p-c}{p+h}.$$

Thus, in the bicycle example, if there are 500 bicycles on hand, the optimal policy is to order up to 11,856 bicycles (which implies ordering 11,356 additional bicycles). On the other hand, if there are 12,000 bicycles already on hand, the optimal policy is not to order.

MODEL WITH NONLINEAR PENALTY COSTS Similar results for these models can be obtained for other than linear holding and shortage penalty costs. Denote the holding cost by

$$\begin{cases} h[y - D], & \text{if } y \geq D \\ 0, & \text{if } y < D, \end{cases}$$

where $h[\cdot]$ is a mathematical function, not necessarily linear.

Similarly, the shortage penalty cost can be denoted by

$$\begin{cases} p[D-y], & \text{if } D \geq y \\ 0, & \text{if } D < y, \end{cases}$$

where $p[\cdot]$ is also a function, not necessarily linear.

Thus the total expected cost is given by

$$c(y-x) + \int_y^\infty p[\xi - y]\varphi_D(\xi)\,d\xi + \int_0^y h[y-\xi]\varphi_D(\xi)\,d\xi,$$

where x is the amount on hand.

If $L(y)$ is defined as the expected shortage plus holding cost, that is,

$$L(y) = \int_y^\infty p[\xi - y]\varphi_D(\xi)\,d\xi + \int_0^y h[y-\xi]\varphi_D(\xi)\,d\xi,$$

then the total expected cost can be written as

$$c(y-x) + L(y).$$

The optimal policy is obtained by minimizing this expression, subject to the constraint that $y \geq x$, that is,

$$\underset{y \geq x}{\text{minimum}}\ [c(y-x) + L(y)].$$

If $L(y)$ is strictly convex[1] *[a sufficient condition being that the shortage and holding costs each are convex and $\varphi_D(\xi) > 0$], then the optimal policy is given by*

$$\begin{cases} \text{if } x < y^\circ, \text{ order up to } y^\circ, \\ \text{if } x \geq y^\circ, \text{ do not order,} \end{cases}$$

where y° is the value of y that satisfies the expression

$$\frac{dL(y)}{dy} + c = 0.$$

DERIVATION OF RESULTS FOR THE SINGLE-PERIOD MODEL WITH NO SETUP COST AND LINEAR SHORTAGE AND HOLDING COSTS[2] A useful result for finding policies that minimizes the expected cost is as follows:

Let D be a random variable having a density function

$$\begin{cases} \varphi_D(\xi), & \text{if } \xi \geq 0 \\ 0, & \text{otherwise.} \end{cases}$$

Denote by $\Phi(a)$ the cumulative distribution function; that is,

$$\Phi(a) = \int_0^a \varphi_D(\xi)\,d\xi.$$

[1] See Appendix 1 for the definition of a convex function.

[2] This section may be omitted by the less mathematically inclined reader.

Let $g(\xi, y)$ be defined as

$$g(\xi, y) = \begin{cases} c_1(y - \xi), \text{ if } y > \xi,\ c_1 > 0 \\ c_2(\xi - y), \text{ if } y \le \xi,\ c_2 > 0, \end{cases}$$

and

$$G(y) = \int_0^\infty g(\xi, y)\varphi_D(\xi)\, d\xi + cy,$$

where $c > 0$. Then $G(y)$ is minimized at $y = y^\circ$, where y° is the solution to

$$\Phi(y^\circ) = \frac{c_2 - c}{c_2 + c_1}.$$

To see why this value of y° minimizes $G(y)$, note that by definition

$$G(y) = c_1 \int_0^y (y - \xi)\varphi_D(\xi)\, d\xi + c_2 \int_y^\infty (\xi - y)\varphi_D(\xi)\, d\xi + cy.$$

Taking the derivative (see Appendix 2) and setting it equal to zero leads to

$$\frac{dG(y)}{dy} = c_1 \int_0^y \varphi_D(\xi)\, d\xi - c_2 \int_y^\infty \varphi_D(\xi)\, d\xi + c = 0.$$

This implies that

$$c_1\Phi(y^\circ) - c_2[1 - \Phi(y^\circ)] + c = 0$$

because

$$\int_0^\infty \varphi_D(\xi)\, d\xi = 1.$$

Solving this expression results in

$$\Phi(y^\circ) = \frac{c_2 - c}{c_2 + c_1}.$$

Checking the second derivative indicates that

$$\frac{d^2G(y)}{dy^2} = (c_1 + c_2)\varphi_D(y) \ge 0$$

for all y, so that the result is obtained.

To apply this result, it is sufficient to show that

$$C(y) = cy + \int_y^\infty p(\xi - y)\varphi_D(\xi)\, d\xi + \int_0^y h(y - \xi)\varphi_D(\xi)\, d\xi$$

has the form of $G(y)$.

Clearly $c_1 = h$, $c_2 = p$, and $c = c$, so that the optimal quantity to order, y°, is that value which satisfies

$$\Phi(y^\circ) = \frac{p - c}{p + h}.$$

In deriving the results for the case where the initial stock level is x, recall that it is necessary to solve the relationship

$$\min_{y \geq x}\left[-cx + \left\{\int_y^\infty p(\xi - y)\varphi_D(\xi)\,d\xi + \int_0^y h(y-\xi)\varphi_D(\xi)\,d\xi + cy\right\}\right].$$

Note that the expression in braces has the form of a $G(y)$, with $c_1 = h$, $c_2 = p$, and $c = c$. Hence the cost function to be minimized can be written as

$$\min_{y \geq x}\,[-cx + G(y)].$$

It is clear that $-cx$ is a constant, so that it is sufficient to find the y which minimizes the expression

$$\min_{y \geq x} G(y).$$

Hence the value of y° that minimizes $G(y)$ satisfies

$$\Phi(y^\circ) = \frac{p-c}{p+h}.$$

Furthermore, $G(y)$ must be a convex function because

$$\frac{d^2G(y)}{dy^2} \geq 0.$$

Also,

$$\lim_{y\to 0}\frac{dG(y)}{dy} = c - p,$$

which is negative,[1] and

$$\lim_{y\to\infty}\frac{dG(y)}{dy} = h + c,$$

which is positive. Hence $G(y)$ must be as shown in Fig. 11.7
Thus the optimal policy must be given by the following:

If $x < y^\circ$, order up to y° because y° can be achieved together with the minimum value $G(y^\circ)$,

If $x \geq y^\circ$, do not order because any $G(y)$, with $y > x$, must exceed $G(x)$.

A similar argument can be constructed for obtaining optimal policies with nonlinear penalty costs when $L(y)$ is strictly convex.

[1] If $c - p$ is nonnegative, $G(y)$ will be a monotone increasing function. This implies that the item should not be stocked; that is, $y^0 = 0$.

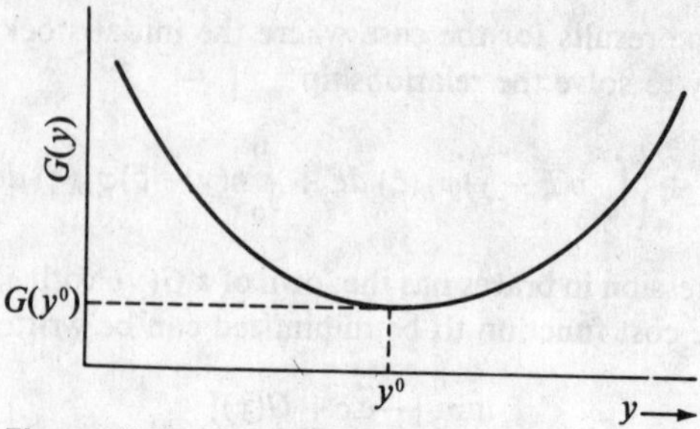

Figure 11.7 Graph of $G(y)$.

A Single-period Model with A Setup Cost

In discussing the bicycle example in this section, it was assumed that there was no fixed cost incurred in ordering the bicycles for the Christmas season. In actual fact, the cost of placing this special order is \$800, and this cost should be included in the analysis of the model. In fact, inclusion of the setup cost generally causes major changes in the results.

In general, the setup cost will be denoted by K. To begin with, the shortage and holding costs will each be assumed to be linear. Their resultant effect is then given by $L(y)$, where

$$L(y) = p \int_y^\infty (\xi - y)\varphi_D(\xi)\, d\xi + h \int_0^y (y - \xi)\varphi_D(\xi)\, d\xi.$$

Thus the total expected cost incurred if one orders up to y is given by

$$\begin{cases} K + c(y - x) + L(y), & \text{if } y > x \\ L(x), & \text{if } y = x. \end{cases}$$

Note that $cy + L(y)$ is the same expected cost considered in the previous section when the setup cost was omitted. If $cy + L(y)$ is drawn as a function of y, it will appear as shown in Fig. 11.8.† Define S as the value of y that minimizes $cy + L(y)$, and define s as the smallest value of y for which $cs + L(s) = K + cS + L(S)$. From Fig. 11.8 it is evident that if $x > S$, then $K + cy + L(y) > cx + L(x)$, for all $y > x$. Hence $K + c(y - x) + L(y) > L(x)$, where the left-hand side of the inequality represents the expected total cost if one orders up to y, and the right-hand side of the inequality represents the expected total cost if no ordering occurs. Hence the optimum policy indicates that if $x > S$, do not order. If $s \le x \le S$, it is again evident from Fig. 11.8 that

$$K + cy + L(y) \ge cx + L(x), \text{ for all } y > x,$$

so that

$$K + c(y - x) + L(y) \ge L(x).$$

† In the derivation of results for the single-period model with no setup cost and linear shortage and holding costs, $cy + L(y)$ was denoted by $G(y)$ and rigorously shown to be a convex function of the form plotted in Fig. 11.8.

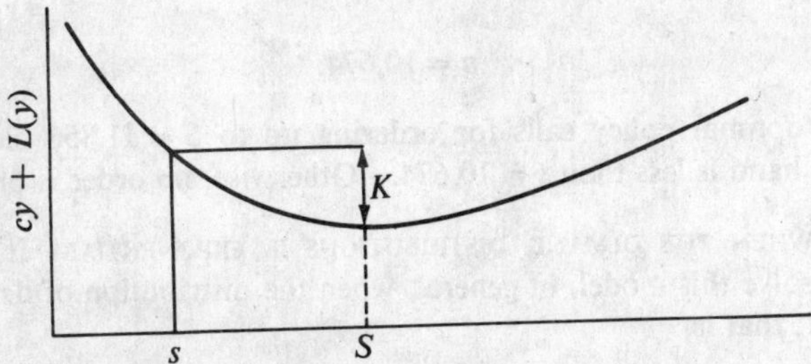

Figure 11.8 Graph of $cy + L(y)$.

Again, no ordering is less expensive than ordering. Finally, if $x < s$, it follows from Fig. 11.8 that

$$\min_{y \geq x} [K + cy + L(y)] = K + cS + L(S) < cx + L(x),$$

or

$$\min_{y \geq x} [K + c(y - x) + L(y)] = K + c(S - x) + L(S) < L(x),$$

so that it pays to order. The minimum cost is incurred if one orders up to S.

Thus the optimum ordering policy can be summarized as follows:

$$\begin{cases} \textit{if } x < s, \textit{ order up to } S \\ \textit{if } x \geq s, \textit{ do not order.} \end{cases}$$

The value of S is obtained from

$$\Phi(S) = \frac{p - c}{p + h},$$

and s is the smallest value that satisfies the expression

$$cs + L(s) = K + cS + L(S).$$

This is an (s, S) policy mentioned previously, and has had extensive use in industry.

EXAMPLE Referring to the bicycle example of the previous section,

$$y^\circ = S = 11{,}856.$$

If $K = 800$, $c = 20$, $p = 45$, and $h = -9$, s is obtained from

$$20s + 45 \int_s^\infty (\xi - s) \frac{1}{10{,}000} e^{-\xi/10{,}000} \, d\xi - 9 \int_0^s (s - \xi) \frac{1}{10{,}000} e^{-\xi/10{,}000} \, d\xi$$

$$= 800 + 45(11{,}856) + 45 \int_{11{,}856}^\infty (\xi - 11{,}856) \frac{1}{10{,}000} e^{-\xi/10{,}000} \, d\xi$$

$$-9 \int_0^{11{,}856} (11{,}856 - \xi) \frac{1}{10{,}000} e^{-\xi/10{,}000} \, d\xi,$$

so that

$$s = 10{,}674.$$

Hence the optimal policy calls for ordering up to $S = 11{,}856$ bicycles if the amount on hand is less than $s = 10{,}674$. Otherwise, no order is placed.

SOLUTION WHEN THE DEMAND DISTRIBUTIONS IS EXPONENTIAL It may be of interest to solve this model, in general, when the distribution of demand, D, is exponential; that is,

$$\varphi_D(\xi) = \frac{1}{\lambda} e^{-\xi/\lambda}.$$

If Δ is defined as $S - s$, then Δ is the solution to the equation

$$e^{\Delta/\lambda} = \frac{K}{\lambda(c+h)} + \frac{\Delta}{\lambda} + 1.$$

Furthermore, a good approximation for Δ is given by

$$\Delta \simeq \sqrt{\frac{2\lambda K}{c+h}}.$$

Note that

$$s = S - \Delta.$$

These results are easily obtained. From the no-setup cost results

$$1 - e^{-S/\lambda} = \frac{p-c}{p+h} \text{ or } S = \lambda \ln\left(\frac{h+p}{h+c}\right).$$

For any y,

$$\begin{aligned} cy + L(y) &= cy + h\int_0^y (y-\xi)\frac{1}{\lambda} e^{-\xi/\lambda}\, d\xi + p\int_y^\infty (\xi - y)\frac{1}{\lambda} e^{-\xi/\lambda}\, d\xi \\ &= (c+h)y + \lambda(h+p)e^{-y/\lambda} - \lambda h. \end{aligned}$$

Evaluating $cy + L(y)$ at the point $y = s$ and $y = S$ leads to

$$(c+h)s + \lambda(h+p)e^{-s/\lambda} - \lambda h = K + (c+h)S + \lambda(h+p)e^{-S/\lambda} - \lambda h,$$

or

$$(c+h)s + \lambda(h+p)e^{-s/\lambda} = K + (c+h)S + \lambda(c+h).$$

By letting $\Delta = S - s$, the last equation yields

$$e^{\Delta/\lambda} = \frac{K}{\lambda(c+h)} + \frac{\Delta}{\lambda} + 1.$$

If Δ/λ is close to zero, $e^{\Delta/\lambda}$ can be expanded into a Taylor series around zero. If the terms beyond the quadratic term are neglected, the result becomes

$$1 + \frac{\Delta}{\lambda} + \frac{\Delta^2}{2\lambda^2} \simeq \frac{K}{\lambda(c+h)} + \frac{\Delta}{\lambda} + 1,$$

so that

$$\Delta \simeq \sqrt{\frac{2\lambda K}{c+h}}.$$

Using the approximation in the bicycle example results in

$$\Delta = \sqrt{\frac{(2)(10{,}000)(800)}{20-9}} = 1{,}206,$$

which is quite close to the exact value of $\Delta = 1{,}182$.

MODEL WITH NONLINEAR PENALTY COSTS Again it is evident that these results can be extended easily to any strictly convex expected shortage plus holding cost, $L(y)$. This results in a strictly convex $cy + L(y)$, similar to Fig. 11.8. Hence the optimal ordering policy is of the form

$$\begin{cases} \textit{if } x < s, \textit{ order up to } S \\ \textit{if } x \geq s, \textit{ do not order,} \end{cases}$$

where S is the value of y that satisfies

$$c + \frac{dL(y)}{dy} = 0,$$

and s is the smallest value which satisfies the expression

$$cs + L(s) = K + cS + L(S).$$

Multiperiod Models—An Overview[1]

The single-period model was illustrated with a bicycle example, where the distributor had only one opportunity to place an order. In many situations an opportunity to place an order occurs periodically, e.g., monthly, and the inventory manager must make a decision about whether and how much to stock. He may be interested in these decisions for a horizon of the next 2 months, 12 months, 18 months, or even possibly forever. Even for a horizon of 2 months, the periodic review policy of using the optimal one-period solution twice is not generally the optimal policy for the two-period problem. Smaller costs can usually be achieved by viewing the problem from a two-period viewpoint and then using the methods of dynamic programming introduced in Chap. 6

[1] This section surveys many of the important multiperiod stochastic models, without deriving any of the results. Derivations appear in Sec. 11.5.

to obtain the best inventory policy. In fact, the only difference in concept in the dynamic programming approach for solving the inventory problem compared to the material in Chap. 6 is the probabilistic aspects introduced by the random demand.

TWO-PERIOD MODEL—NO SETUP COST Suppose that the bicycle distributor is permitted to make at most one reorder, to occur on November 15, after placing his initial order for the special type 10-speed bicycle on October 15. The assumptions about the costs are similar to those presented before. Assume that the purchase leads to immediate delivery; shortages at the end of the first period are to be made up, if they exist (backlogging of orders is possible at the end of the first period, but not at the end of the second period); no disposal of stock is permitted. Furthermore, the demands D_1, D_2 for the two periods are independent, identically distributed random variables having density $\varphi_D(\xi)$. The purchase cost is linear, that is, cz, where z is the amount ordered (no setup cost), and the expected (one period) shortage plus holding penalty cost $L(y)$ is strictly convex [which is the case if each cost is linear and $\varphi_D(\xi) > 0$].

As indicated earlier, the solution to this problem is not to use the optimal one-period solution twice. Smaller costs can be achieved by viewing the problem from a two-period dynamic programming viewpoint. Order the time periods so that the beginning of time period 1 implies that there are two periods left in the horizon. Similarly, the beginning of time period 2 implies that there is one period left in the horizon (the last period is beginning). The problem is to find critical numbers that describe the optimal ordering policy. It can be shown that these are single critical numbers denoted by y_1° and y_2°, respectively, for each period.[1] Although the numbers y_1° and y_2° are relatively difficult to obtain numerically (using the methods of dynamic programming), the optimal policy is easily characterized, i.e.,

At the beginning of period 1,

$$\begin{cases} \textit{order up to } y_1^\circ \textit{ (order } y_1^\circ - x_1\textit{)}, & \textit{if } x_1 < y_1^\circ \\ \textit{do not order}, & \textit{if } x_1 \geq y_1^\circ. \end{cases}$$

At the beginning of period 2,

$$\begin{cases} \textit{order up to } y_2^\circ \textit{ (order } y_2^\circ - x_2\textit{)}, & \textit{if } x_2 < y_2^\circ \\ \textit{do not order}, & \textit{if } x_2 \geq y_2^\circ. \end{cases}$$

MULTIPERIOD MODEL—NO SETUP COST This model is an extension of the two-period problem. Suppose there exists an horizon of n periods, for which it is required to determine the optimal inventory policy. As before, assume that the production leads to immediate delivery; shortages are to be backlogged except at the final period when they are lost; no disposal of stock is permitted. Furthermore, the demands for the n periods are independent, identically distributed

[1] The mathematical derivation for finding the optimal policy for this particular model is given in the discussion of a two-period inventory model with no setup cost in Sec. 11.5.

random variables having density $\varphi_D(\xi)$. The purchase cost is linear, that is, cz, where z is the amount ordered (no setup cost), and the expected (one period) shortage plus holding penalty cost $L(y)$ is strictly convex [which is the case if each cost is linear and $\varphi_D(\xi) > 0$]. A cost discounting factor will be included; it is denoted by α, $0 < \alpha < 1$.

Again the time periods are ordered so that the beginning of time period 1 implies that there are n periods left in the horizon. Similarly, the beginning of time period n implies there is one period left in the horizon (the last period is beginning). The problem is to find critical numbers that describe the optimal ordering policy.[1] As in the two-period model, the numbers $y_1^\circ, y_2^\circ, \ldots, y_n^\circ$ are difficult to obtain numerically, but it can be shown that the optimal policy has the form

At the beginning of period i, i = 1, 2, . . . , n

$$\begin{cases} \textit{order up to } y_i^\circ \ (\textit{order } y_i^\circ - x_i), & \textit{if } x_i < y_i^\circ \\ \textit{do not order}, & \textit{if } x_i \geq y_i^\circ. \end{cases}$$

Furthermore,

$$y_n^0 \leq y_{n-1}^0 \leq \cdots \leq y_2^0 \leq y_1^0.$$

For the infinite-period model (where the inventory decisions are made indefinitely), there exists a single critical period number y°, so that the optimal policy now has the form

At the beginning of period i, i = 1, 2, . . .

$$\begin{cases} \textit{order up to } y^\circ \ (\textit{order } y^\circ - x_i), & \textit{if } x_i < y^\circ \\ \textit{do not order}, & \textit{if } x_i \geq y^\circ. \end{cases}$$

Furthermore, y° is easily obtained because y° is the value of y that satisfies the expression

$$\frac{dL(y)}{dy} + c(1 - \alpha) = 0.$$

A VARIATION OF THE MULTIPERIOD INVENTORY MODEL—NO SETUP COST A slight modification of the aforementioned model leads to some simple, but interesting, results.[2] Consider the n-period model, but now assume that stock left over at the end of the final period can be salvaged with a return of the initial purchase cost c. Similarly, if there is a shortage at this time, the items are supplied also at the purchase price c. These two changes may lead to more realism in the

[1] Mathematical results for finding the optimal policy for this particular model (and the infinite-period model) are given in the discussion of a multiperiod inventory model with no setup cost in Sec. 11.5.

[2] This formulation is due to A. F. Veinott, Jr., "The Optimal Inventory Policy for Batch Orderings," *Operations Research*, **13**(3): 424–432, 1965.

model, but, as important, they lead to rather simple optimal policies. In particular, the same single critical number y^0 is used for *all* periods, and, furthermore, the optimal policy is the same as that just presented in the infinite-period model; i.e.,

At the beginning of period i, $i = 1, 2, \ldots, n$

$$\begin{cases} \textit{order up to } y^0 \ (\textit{order } y^0 - x_i), & \textit{if } x_i < y^0 \\ \textit{do not order,} & \textit{if } x_i \geq y^0, \end{cases}$$

where y^0 satisfies the expression

$$\frac{dL(y)}{dy} + c(1 - \alpha) = 0.$$

Of course, this same result also holds for the infinite-period model.

EXAMPLE OF A MULTIPERIOD MODEL Example 2, Sec. 11.1 concerned the Western distributor of bicycles who is having trouble with shortages of the most popular 10-speed model. The unit shortage cost p was estimated to be \$15. The holding cost h was determined to be \$1 per bicycle remaining at the end of the month. The actual cost of a bicycle is \$35. Orders may be placed on the first working day of each month. The distributor always places an order for some model bicycles each month, so that he is willing to assume that the marginal setup cost is zero for this most popular model. The discount factor may be assumed to be $\alpha = 0.995$. From past history the distribution of demand can be approximated by a uniform distribution given by

$$\varphi_D(\xi) = \begin{cases} \dfrac{1}{800}, & \text{if } 0 \leq \xi \leq 800 \\ 0, & \text{otherwise.} \end{cases}$$

The distributor expects to stock this model indefinitely, so that the infinite-period model is appropriate.

Recall that y^0 satisfies the equation

$$\frac{dL(y)}{dy} + c(1 - \alpha) = 0,$$

where

$$L(y) = p\int_y^\infty (\xi - y)\varphi_D(\xi)\,d\xi + h\int_0^y (y - \xi)\varphi_D(\xi)\,d\xi$$

$$= \frac{p(800 - y)^2}{2(800)} + \frac{hy^2}{2(800)} = 6{,}000 - 15y + \frac{y^2}{100}.$$

Now,

$$\frac{dL(y)}{dy} = -15 + \frac{y}{50},$$

so that y^0 satisfies

$$-15 + \frac{y}{50} + 35(0.005) = 0,$$

or

$$y^0 = 741.$$

Thus, if the number of bicycles on hand, x, at the first of each month is less than 741, the optimal policy calls for ordering up to 741 (ordering $741 - x$ bicycles). Otherwise, no order is placed. Note that if this policy is to be in effect for only a finite number of months, say 24, and if (1) bicycles remaining in stock after 24 months can be salvaged at \$35 per bicycle and (2) unsatisfied demand remaining at the end of 24 months can be supplied to the Western distributor from, say, the Eastern distributor, at \$35 per bicycle, then the policy of ordering up to 741 bicycles each month is still optimal.

MULTIPERIOD MODEL WITH SETUP COST The introduction of a fixed setup cost K which is incurred when ordering, often adds more realism to the model. Unfortunately, however, the mathematics becomes very cumbersome, and the results available are primarily those that characterize the form of the optimal policy. In particular, if the ordering cost is assumed to be $K + cz$ for $z > 0$ and zero for $z = 0$, and if $L(y)$ is strictly convex, then the optimal policy has the form

At the beginning of period i, $i = 1, 2, \ldots, n$

order up to S_i (order $S_i - x_i$), if $x_i < s_i$

do not order, if $x_i \geq s_i$.

This is the familiar (s, S) policy alluded to earlier in the discussion of one-period models. As previously mentioned, unfortunately exact computations of s_i and S_i for the finite- or infinite-horizon model are extremely difficult. However, the importance of this result can not be minimized. Even if the exact s_i and S_i are unknown, it is important to know that one should consider using policies of this form rather than a policy from another class.

(k,Q) POLICIES FOR A MULTIPERIOD MODEL WITHOUT SETUP COST In the discussion of the previous models, any quantity could be ordered at the time of inventory review. Suppose that an additional constraint is placed on the ordering policy; i.e., each order for stock must be some nonnegative integral multiple of Q, a fixed positive constant.

As before, the demands for the n periods are assumed to be independent, identically distributed random variables having density $\varphi_D(\xi)$. The purchase cost is linear, and the expected (one period) shortage plus holding penalty cost $L(y)$ is strictly convex. α is the cost discounting factor, $0 < \alpha < 1$. At the beginning of each period the system is reviewed. An order may be placed for any nonnegative integral multiple of Q, a fixed positive number. Thus orders must be placed in multiples of some standard batch size, e.g., a case or a truckload.

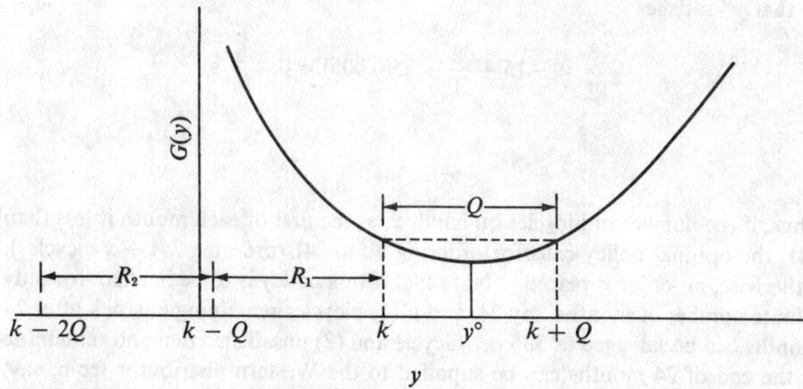

Figure 11.9 Plot of the $G(y)$ function.

When the demand exceeds the inventory on hand the excess demand is backlogged until it is subsequently filled by a delivery. In addition, it is assumed that stock left over at the end of the final period n can be salvaged with a return of the initial purchase cost c. Similarly, if there is a shortage at this time, the items are backlogged also at the purchase price c. This model was introduced by Veinott, Jr.[1] He shows that a (k,Q) policy is optimal. A (k,Q) policy is described as follows:

> *If at the beginning of a period the stock on hand is less than k, an order should be placed for the smallest multiple of Q that will bring the stock level to at least k (and probably higher); otherwise, an order should not be placed. The same parameter k is used in each period.*

The parameter k is chosen as follows: Let y^0 be the minimum of $G(y) = (1-\alpha)cy + L(y)$. $G(y)$ must be of the shape (convex) shown in Fig. 11.9. Then k is any number for which $k \le y^0 \le k + Q$ and $G(k) = G(k+Q)$. Referring to Fig. 11.9, if a "ruler" of length Q is placed horizontally into the "valley," k is found to be that value of the abscissa, to the left of y^0, where the ruler intersects the valley. Note that if the initial inventory on hand lies in R_1, then Q is ordered; if it lies in R_2, then $2Q$ is ordered; and so on.

It should be noted that the same value of the parameter k is used for each period of a finite-horizon model as well as for the infinite-horizon model. In the latter situation this is the same optimal policy that would have been obtained if salvage costs and backlogging *at the last period* were omitted.

MULTIPRODUCT INVENTORY MODELS The previous sections dealt with inventory systems for single-product models. But most real inventory systems involve many products with various types of interactions such as joint storage and

[1] *Ibid.*

budget limitations and product substitutability. However, an important motivation for the study of single-product models is that it provides insight into solving multiproduct problems, and, furthermore, it is often possible to "factor" an N-product problem into N one-product problems without loss of optimality. (This occurs if the demand and cost for each product can be treated independently of the other products.) There has been some work on multiproduct models in which such "factorization" is not possible. In these models stocks of a single product at different locations or echelons of a supply system can also be conveniently viewed as stocks of different products.[1] A multiproduct model was proposed by Veinott, Jr.,[2] which is a direct analog of the single-product multiperiod inventory model with no setup cost presented earlier. This multiproduct model considers N products and m different classes of demands for these products. The demand classes in a period may be classified by such caracteristics as time of occurrence, essentiality, products desired, and acceptable substitutes. Under the usual restrictions on the form of the costs, the optimal policy is a single critical number policy for each product; i.e., if x_{ik} is the amount on hand of product k at period i, order up to y_{ik} if $x_{ik} < y_{ik}$; otherwise, do not order (assuming initially that $x_{1k} \leq y_{1k}$ for all k).

This model has many useful applications. For example, suppose there are two products, with product 1 serving as a substitute for product 2, and all unsatisfied demands are lost. By appropriately choosing a stocking policy, which for this model supplies unsatisfied demand for product 2 with excess stock from product 1, if available, the optimal critical numbers can be obtained. This example can be interpreted as a two-echelon inventory model with demands for a single product that can not be satisfied at echelon 2 being transmitted up to echelon 1.

A second application concerns two products that serve as substitutes for each other. Again, all unsatisfied demands are assumed to be lost. The stocking policy supplies unsatisfied demand for one product, with excess stock from the other, if available. This example can be interpreted as a two-location inventory model with an end-of-period redistribution of excess stock (if any) at one location to satisfy a shortage (if one exists) at the other location.

A different variation of the two-product inventory models was presented by Iglehart.[3] Inventories of product 2 are maintained to provide capability for production of product 1. For example, if product 1 is a car, product 2 might be machinery or labor. An optimal policy describes the amount of product 1 and product 2 to produce in period i to minimize the total cost, subject to certain constraints.

[1] An excellent summary of the status of inventory theory is given in a paper by A. F. Veinott, Jr., "The Status of Mathematical Inventory Theory," *Management Science*, **12**(11): 745–777, 1966.

[2] A. F. Veinott, Jr., "Optimal Policy for a Multi-Product, Dynamic Non-Stationary Inventory Problem," *Management Science*, **12**(3): 206–222, 1965.

[3] D. Iglehart, "Capital Accumulation and Production for the Firm: Optimal Dynamic Policies," *Management Science*, **12**(3): 193–205, 1965.

11.5 ADVANCED MATHEMATICAL TOPICS IN MULTIPERIOD STOCHASTIC MODELS

This section will consider some of the models presented in the discussion of multiperiod stochastic models and derive the results presented. The reader who is not interested in mathematical derivations may skip this section.

A Two-period Inventory Model with No Setup Cost

Suppose a run of a particular part is to be made twice before the part becomes obsolete. Assume that the production (or purchase) leads to immediate delivery; shortages at the end of the first period must be made up, if they exist (backlogging of orders is possible at the end of the first period, but not at the end of the second period); no disposal of stock is permitted. Furthermore, the demands D_1, D_2 for the two periods are independent, identically distributed random variables having density $\varphi_D(\xi)$. The purchase cost is linear; that is, cz, where z is the amount ordered, and the expected (one period) shortage plus holding penalty cost $L(y)$ is strictly convex [which is the case if each is linear and $\varphi_D(\xi) > 0$].

The solution to this problem is not to use the optimal one-period solution twice. Smaller costs can be achieved by viewing the problem from a two-period dynamic programming viewpoint. Order the time periods so that the beginning of time period 1 implies that there are two periods left in the horizon. Similarly, the beginning of time period 2 implies that there is one period left in the horizon (the last period is beginning). The problem is to find critical numbers that describe the optimum ordering policy. It will be shown that these are single critical numbers for each period. These numbers will be denoted by y_1^0 and y_2^0. Furthermore, y_1 and y_2 (without the superscript) represent any amount of stock ordered up to at the beginning of the respective period.

Denote by $C_1(x_1)$ the expected cost of following an optimum policy (minimum cost) from the beginning of period 1 to the end of period 2, given that there are x_1 units on hand. Similarly, denote by $C_2(x_2)$ the expected cost of following an optimum policy (minimum cost) from the beginning of period 2, given that there are x_2 units on hand. $C_1(x_1)$ is the expression sought because this is obtained by following the optimum policy for the entire (two period) horizon. To obtain $C_1(x_1)$ it is necessary to first find $C_2(x_2)$. From the results for the single-period model, the optimal policy for a one-period problem is given by a single critical number found from

$$c + L'(y_2^0) = 0;$$

that is, if x_2 is the amount available at the beginning of the last period, then

$$\begin{cases} \text{order } (y_2^0 - x_2^0), & \text{if } x_2 < y_2^0 \\ \text{do not order,} & \text{if } x_2 \ge y_2^0. \end{cases}$$

The cost of this optimum policy can be expressed as

$$C_2(x_2) = \begin{cases} L(x_2), & \text{if } x_2 \geq y_2^0 \\ c(y_2^0 - x_2) + L(y_2^0), & \text{if } x_2 < y_2^0, \end{cases}$$

where y_2^0 is the single critical number determined above.

At the beginning of period 1 the costs incurred consist of the purchase cost $c(y_1 - x_1)$, the expected shortage plus holding cost $L(y_1)$, and the costs associated with following an optimal policy during the second period. Thus the expected cost of following the optimal policy for two periods is given by

$$C_1(x_1) = \underset{y_1 \geq x_1}{\text{minimum}} \{c(y_1 - x_1) + L(y_1) + E[C_2(x_2)]\},$$

where $E[C_2(x_2)]$ is obtained as follows: Note that x_2 is a random variable which depends upon the amount of stock on hand at the beginning of period two; that is, $x_2 = y_1 - D_1$. Thus

$$C_2(x_2) = C_2(y_1 - D_1) = \begin{cases} L(y_1 - D_1), & \text{if } y_1 - D_1 \geq y_2^0 \\ c(y_2^0 - y_1 + D_1) + L(y_2^0), & \text{if } y_1 - D_1 < y_2^0. \end{cases}$$

Hence $C_2(x_2)$ is a random variable, and its expected value is given by

$$E[C_2(x_2)] = \int_0^\infty C_2(y_1 - \xi)\varphi_D(\xi)\,d\xi = \int_0^{y_1 - y_2^0} L(y_1 - \xi)\varphi_D(\xi)\,d\xi$$
$$+ \int_{y_1 - y_2^0}^\infty [c(y_2^0 - y_1 + \xi) + L(y_2^0)]\varphi_D(\xi)\,d\xi.$$

Note that because shortages are permitted, $(y_1 - \xi)$ can be negative; further note that $E[C_2(x_2)]$ is just a function of y_1 and y_2^0, with y_2^0 obtained from the solution to the single-period problem. Thus $C_1(x_1)$ can now be expressed as

$$C_1(x_1) = \underset{y_1 \geq x_1}{\text{minimum}} \Big\{ c(y_1 - x_1) + L(y_1) + \int_0^{y_1 - y_2^0} L(y_1 - \xi)\varphi_D(\xi)\,d\xi$$
$$+ \int_{y_1 - y_2^0}^\infty [c(y_2^0 - y_1 + \xi) + L(y_2^0)]\varphi_D(\xi)\,d\xi \Big\}.$$

Again note that $C_1(x_1)$ is just a function of x_1, the amount of stock on hand. Furthermore, it is easily shown that the expression in the braces in the equation for $C_1(x_1)$ is strictly convex, so that there is a unique minimum, with this minimum occurring at y_1^0. Hence the optimal policy is as follows:

At the beginning of period 1,

$$\begin{cases} \text{order up to } y_1^0 (\text{order } y_1^0 - x_1), & \text{if } x_1 < y_1^0 \\ \text{do not order}, & \text{if } x_1 \geq y_1^0. \end{cases}$$

At the beginning of period 2,

$$\begin{cases} \text{order up to } y_2^0 \ (\text{order } y_2^0 - x_2), & \text{if } x_2 < y_2^0 \\ \text{do not order}, & \text{if } x_2 \geq y_2^0. \end{cases}$$

If a discount factor α is incurred at the beginning of period 2, $C_1(x_1)$ is given by

$$C_1(x_1) = \underset{y_1 \geq x_1}{\text{minimum}}\{c(y_1 - x_1) + L(y_1) + \alpha E[C_2(x_2)]\},$$

where $0 \leq \alpha \leq 1$.

Example Consider the following example: The cost of producing an item is \$10 per item ($c = 10$). If any excess inventory remains at the end of a period, it is charged at \$10 per item ($h = 10$); if no excess appears, there is no holding charge. If a shortage occurs within a period, there is a penalty cost of \$15 per item ($p = 15$). The density function of demand is given by

$$\varphi_D(\xi) = \begin{cases} \dfrac{1}{10}, & \text{if } 0 \leq \xi \leq 10 \\ 0, & \text{otherwise.} \end{cases}$$

It is necessary to find the optimum two-period policy. For linear costs, the equation for the optimal single-period model becomes

$$\Phi(y_2^0) = \frac{p - c}{p + h} = \frac{15 - 10}{15 + 10} = \frac{1}{5}.$$

Hence, since $\Phi(y_2^0) = y_2^0/10$,

$$y_2^0 = 2.$$

Furthermore,

$$L(z) = \int_z^{10} \frac{15(\xi - z)}{10}\, d\xi + \int_0^z \frac{10(z - \xi)}{10}\, d\xi$$

$$= 75 - 15z + \frac{5}{4} z^2.$$

Substituting into the equation for $E[C_2(x_2)]$ yields

$$E[C_2(x_2)] = \int_0^{y_1 - 2} \left[75 + 15(y_1 - \xi) + \frac{5}{4}(y_1 - \xi)^2\right] \frac{1}{10}\, d\xi$$

$$+ \int_{y_1 - 2}^{10} \left[10(2 - y_1 + \xi) + 75 - (15)(2) + \frac{5}{4}\, 2^2\right] \frac{1}{10}\, d\xi$$

$$= \int_0^{y_1 - 2} \left[75 - 15(y_1 - \xi) + \frac{5}{4}(y_1 - \xi)^2\right] \frac{1}{10}\, d\xi$$

$$+ \int_{y_1 - 2}^{10} [70 - 10(y_1 - \xi)] \frac{1}{10}\, d\xi$$

$$= \frac{y_1^3}{24} - \frac{y_1^2}{4} - \frac{19y_1}{2} + \frac{359}{3}.$$

Thus $C_1(x_1)$ becomes

$$C_1(x_1) = \underset{y_1 \geq x_1}{\text{minimum}} \left\{10(y_1 - x_1) + 75 - 15y_1 + \frac{5}{4}(y_1)^2 + \frac{y_1^3}{24} - \frac{y_1^2}{4} - \frac{19y_1}{2} + \frac{359}{3}\right\}$$

$$= \underset{y_1 \geq x_1}{\text{minimum}} \left\{-10x_1 + \frac{y_1^3}{24} + (y_1)^2 - \frac{29y_1}{2} + \frac{584}{3}\right\}.$$

Taking the derivative, with respect to y_1, of the expression in braces and setting it equal to zero lead to

$$\frac{d\{\ \}}{dy_1} = \left[-\frac{29}{2} + 2y_1^0 + \frac{1}{8}(y_1^0)^2\right] = 0,$$

so that

$$y_1^0 = 5.42 \text{ (discarding the negative root)}.$$

Substituting $y_1^0 = 5$ and $y_1^0 = 6$ into $C_1(x_1)$ leads to a smaller value, with $y_1^0 = 5$. Thus the optimal policy can be described as follows: If the initial amount of stock on hand does not exceed 5, order up to 5 units (order $5 - x_1$ units). Otherwise, do not order. After a period has elapsed, and at the beginning of the last period, if the amount on hand does not exceed 2 units, order up to 2 units (order $2 - x_2$ units, where x_2 may be negative).

This two-period model has been solved by using the same penalty shortage cost for each of the two periods, even though unsatisfied demand is backlogged at the end of the first period and lost at the end of the second period. This is a deficiency of the model as presented, but it can be remedied by using different penalty shortage costs in each period. The computational procedure of the modified model is similar, and no additional difficulties are added.

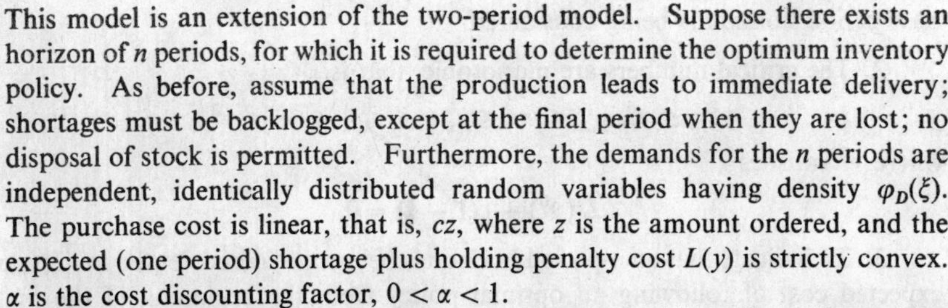

Multiperiod Inventory Model with No Setup Cost

This model is an extension of the two-period model. Suppose there exists an horizon of n periods, for which it is required to determine the optimum inventory policy. As before, assume that the production leads to immediate delivery; shortages must be backlogged, except at the final period when they are lost; no disposal of stock is permitted. Furthermore, the demands for the n periods are independent, identically distributed random variables having density $\varphi_D(\xi)$. The purchase cost is linear, that is, cz, where z is the amount ordered, and the expected (one period) shortage plus holding penalty cost $L(y)$ is strictly convex. α is the cost discounting factor, $0 < \alpha < 1$.

$C_1(x_1)$ is defined as the minimum expected cost of following an optimum policy from the beginning of the first period to the end of the horizon (period n), given that there are x_1 units on hand now. Similarly, define $C_2(x_2)$, $C_3(x_3)$, ..., $C_{n-1}(x_{n-1})$, $C_n(x_n)$.

At the beginning of period 1, a decision about the inventory is made; that is, $y_1 - x_1$ is ordered ($y_1 \geq x_1$), and a cost incurred. This is given by

$$c(y_1 - x_1) + L(y_1).$$

During this first period, a demand D_1 occurs, so that at the beginning of the second period, the amount on hand, x_2, is a random variable equal to $(y_1 - D_1)$. If an optimum policy is carried on from the beginning of the second period to the end of the horizon, the discounted (discounted to the beginning of period 1) expected minimum cost of the future $(n - 1)$ periods is given by

$$\alpha E[C_2(x_2)] = \alpha E[C_2(y_1 - D_1)] = \alpha \int_0^\infty C_2(y_1 - \xi)\varphi_D(\xi)\, d\xi.$$

Thus the expected cost of following the optimal policy for the n-period horizon is obtained and is given by

$$C_1(x_1) = \underset{y_1 \geq x_1}{\text{minimum}}\{c(y_1 - x_1) + L(y_1) + \alpha E[C_2(y_1 - D_1)]\}.$$

This dynamic programming approach can be used to obtain the expected cost of following an optimal policy from the beginning of any period i, $i = 1, 2, \ldots, n$, to the end of period n, given that there are x_i units on hand; that is,

$$C_i(x_i) = \underset{y_i \geq x_i}{\text{minimum}}\{c(y_i - x_i) + L(y_i) + \alpha E[C_{i+1}(y_i - D_i)]\},$$

where $C_{n+1}(x_{n+1}) = 0$. In principle then it is possible to reach a solution by first finding $C_n(x_n)$, given that $C_{n+1}(x_{n+1}) = 0$, then finding $C_{n-1}(x_{n-1})$ from a knowledge of $C_n(x_n)$, and so on until $C_1(x_1)$ is obtained. This is rather cumbersome, and some qualitative results would be useful.

This model has the following properties, which are stated without proof but can be found in the work of Arrow, Karlin, and Scarf (see Selected References at the end of the chapter):

1. The optimal ordering policy in each period is a single critical number $y_{1,n}^0, y_{2,n}^0, \ldots, y_{n-1,n}^0, y_{n,n}^0$, where the second subscript is used to indicate that an n-period horizon is being considered.

2. The critical numbers are monotonic, that is,

$$y_{n,n}^0 \leq y_{n-1,n}^0 \leq \cdots \leq y_{2,n}^0 \leq y_{1,n}^0 \leq \cdots \leq y^0,$$

where y^0 satisfies

$$L'(y^0) + c(1 - \alpha) = 0.$$

3. To indicate that an n-period horizon is being considered, let the minimum expected cost of following an optimal policy from the beginning of the first period to the end period n, given that there are x units on hand, now be denoted by $C_{1,n}(x)$. Then for every x the sequence $C_{1,n}(x)$ converges. Hence, one may define a function

$$C(x) = \lim_{n \to \infty} C_{1,n}(x).$$

The limit function satisfies the equation

$$C(x) = \min_{y \geq x}\{c(y - x) + L(y) + \alpha \int_0^\infty C(y - \xi)\varphi_D(\xi)\, d\xi\}.$$

5. The value of y that satisfies (4) is the maximum of y^0 and x, where y^0 is obtained from the equation in (2).

6. $\lim_{n\to\infty} y^0_{1,n} = y^0$.

7. $\lim_{n\to\infty} |(y^0 - y^0_{1,n})/\alpha^n| \leq 2c/L''(y^0)$. This indicates how fast the $y^0_{1,n}$ converge to y^0.

The solution referred to in (5) for the infinite-stage model, which is given in (2), is readily obtained if one is willing to assume that the form of the solution is a single critical number and $x \leq y$.† The total cost can be written as

$$c(y - x) + L(y) + \alpha[cD_1 + L(y)] + \alpha^2[cD_2 + L(y)] + \cdots + \alpha^i[cD_i + L(y)] + \cdots,$$

where D_i is the demand during the ith period. Since $D_i \geq 0$, one always orders up to y, and, hence the expected holding and shortage cost for each period is $L(y)$. The total expected cost is then obtained as

$$cy - cx + L(y)(1 + \alpha + \alpha^2 + \cdots) + cE(D)\alpha[1 + \alpha + \alpha^2 + \cdots]$$

or

$$cy - cx + \frac{L(y)}{1 - \alpha} + \frac{cE(D)\alpha}{1 - \alpha}.$$

Taking the derivative with respect to y and setting it equal to zero lead to

$$L'(y^0) + c(1 - \alpha) = 0.$$

For the example of the two-period model, it is of interest to find y^0 for the infinite-period model. α is now included and is chosen equal to 0.75:

$$L'(y^0) = h\Phi(y^0) - p[1 - \Phi(y^0)] = \frac{10}{10}y^0 - 15\left[1 - \frac{y^0}{10}\right] = \frac{5}{2}y^0 - 15.$$

Therefore y^0 satisfies

$$\frac{5}{2}y^0 - 15 = -10(0.25)$$

or

$$y^0 = 5.$$

Hence the infinite-period model says that if the amount on hand does not exceed 5, order up to 5 units. Furthermore, from property (2), for any finite-stage model the critical numbers are always less than or equal to 5.

† If $x > y$ and $E(D) > 0$, the law of large numbers ensures that eventually $x \leq y$.

Just as in the case of the two-period model, the multiperiod model has been solved by using the same penalty shortage cost for each period, even though unsatisfied demand is backlogged at the end of each period, except at the end of the nth period, where it is assumed to be lost. Again, this is a deficiency of the model as presented, but it can be remedied by either using a different penalty shortage cost in the last period or by letting $C_{n+1}(x_{n+1})$ denote the additional cost of the lost demand. In either case the dynamic programming model can be solved, at least in principle. Of course the qualitative result presented above about the form of the optimal policy may no longer be valid, but the optimal policy will still be represented by single critical numbers. Furthermore, if the original formulation of the multiperiod model is retained, and if the number of periods is large, then the effect of the handling of the shortage cost incurred in the last period may be negligible because of discounting.

A Variation of the Multiperiod Inventory Model with No Setup Cost

There is another interesting formulation due to Veinott, Jr.,[1] which avoids the aforementioned problem with the shortage cost and also leads to the same optimal policy as obtained before. Consider the n-period model presented earlier, but now assume that stock left over at the end of the final period can be salvaged with a return of the initial purchase cost c. Similarly, if there is a shortage at this time, the items are supplied also at the purchase price c. These two changes could lead to more realism in the model, but, as important, they lead to rather simple optimal policies. In particular, the optimal ordering policy for the n- and infinite-period models is a single critical number policy of the form

$$\begin{cases} \text{order up to } y^0, & \text{if } x_i < y^0 \\ \text{do not order,} & \text{if } x_i \geq y^0 \end{cases} \quad \text{for all } i,$$

where y^0 satisfies the equation

$$L'(y^0) + c(1 - \alpha) = 0.$$

These results are rather striking because a slight modification in the model leads to the same single critical number for *all* periods, both finite and infinite. It should also be noted that for the infinite-stage model the two models, with or without including salvage value, are equivalent because of the discount factor.

In deriving the results for this model, recall that stock left over at the end of period n can be salvaged with a return of the initial purchase cost c. Similarly, if there is a shortage at this time, the items are supplied also at the purchase price c. It will again be assumed that the expected shortage plus holding penalty cost $L(y)$ is strictly convex. If y_i and x_i are the amount of stock ordered up to and the amount of stock available, respectively, at the beginning of the ith

[1] A. F. Veinott, Jr., "The Optimal Inventory Policy for Batch Orderings," *loc. cit.*

period, the total cost of producing items (including salvage or backlogging at the end of the horizon but not shortage and holding costs) can be written as

$$c(y_1 - x_1) + \alpha c(y_2 - x_2) + \cdots + \alpha^{n-1}c(y_n - x_n) - \alpha^n c(y_n - D_n)$$
$$= \sum_{i=1}^{n} \alpha^{i-1}c(y_i - x_i) - \alpha^n c(y_n - D_n),$$

where D_n represents the demand during the last period. In general let D_i be the demand during the ith period, so that

$$x_i = y_{i-1} - D_{i-1}, \text{ for } i = 2, 3, \ldots, n.$$

The total cost of producing the items may be written as

$$c(y_1 - x_1) + \sum_{i=2}^{n} \alpha^{i-1}c(y_i - y_{i-1} + D_{i-1}) - \alpha^n \cdot c(y_n - D_n)$$
$$= cy_1 - cx_1 + \sum_{i=2}^{n} \alpha^{i-1}cy_i - \sum_{i=2}^{n} \alpha^{i-1}cy_{i-1} + \sum_{i=2}^{n} \alpha^{i-1}cD_{i-1} - \alpha^n cy_n + \alpha^n cD_n$$
$$= -cx_1 + \sum_{i=1}^{n} \alpha^{i-1}cy_i - \sum_{i=2}^{n+1} \alpha^{i-1}cy_{i-1} + \sum_{i=2}^{n+1} \alpha^{i-1}cD_{i-1}$$
$$= -cx_1 + (1 - \alpha)\sum_{i=1}^{n} \alpha^{i-1}cy_i + \sum_{i=1}^{n} \alpha^i cD_i.$$

The expected total cost of production is then given by

$$c\left\{-x_1 + (1 - \alpha)\sum_{i=1}^{n} \alpha^{i-1}y_i + E\left[\sum_{i=1}^{n} \alpha^i D_i\right]\right\}$$
$$= c(1 - \alpha)\sum_{i=1}^{n} \alpha^{i-1}y_i + \left\{-cx_1 + cE(D)\sum_{i=1}^{n} \alpha^i\right\}.$$

Notice that the bracketed quantity on the right, in the expression for the expected total cost of production, in no way depends upon the decision variables $y_1, \ldots, y_n$ and hence may be ignored in the minimization that follows.

Since the expected shortage plus holding cost in period i is given by $L(y_i)$, the total expected cost is given by

$$\sum_{i=1}^{n} \alpha^{i-1}G(y_i) + \left[-cx_1 + cE(D)\sum_{i=1}^{n} \alpha^i\right],$$

where

$$G(y_i) = (1 - \alpha)cy_i + L(y_i).$$

To minimize this total expected cost one need only minimize

$$\sum_{i=1}^{n} \alpha^{i-1}G(y_i).$$

If it can be shown that this sum is minimized term by term, that is,

$$\min_{y \geq x} G(y) = \begin{cases} G(y^0), \text{ if } y^0 > x \\ G(x), \text{ if } y^0 \leq x, \end{cases}$$

where y^0 is defined through

$$G'(y^0) = (1 - \alpha)c + L'(y^0) = 0,$$

the following result holds:

The optimal ordering policy for the n- and infinite-period models is a single critical number policy of the form

$$\begin{cases} \textit{order up to } y^0, \textit{ if } x_k < y^0 \\ \textit{do not order}, \quad \textit{if } x_k \geq y^0 \end{cases} \quad \textit{for all } k,$$

where y^0 satisfies the equation

$$L'(y^0) + c(1 - \alpha) = 0.$$

To show that y^0 does indeed have this property note that under the assumption that $L(y)$ is strictly convex, $G(y)$ must also be strictly convex and appear as shown in Fig. 11.10. Now, consider any policy other than the single critical number policy described above. Let $y_n, y_{n-1}, \ldots, y_1$ be the inventory levels associated with it and $y'_n, y'_{n-1}, \ldots, y'_1$ the inventory levels associated with the single critical number policy.

Case 1 Suppose $y'_i \leq y^0$.
The single critical number policy calls for ordering up to y^0, so that $G(y'_i) = G(y^0)$.
Hence

$$G(y'_i) \leq G(y_i).$$

Case 2 Suppose $y'_i > y^0$.
If $y'_i > y^0$, so is every other earlier y'_i. In fact,

$$y'_1 \geq y'_2 \geq \cdots \geq y'_i.$$

Figure 11.10 Plot of the $G(y)$ function.

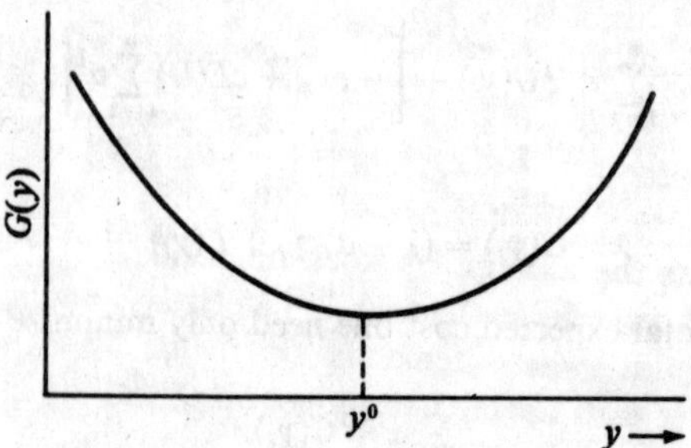

Hence no ordering ever took place under the single critical number policy, so that $x_i' = x_1 - D_1 - D_2 - \cdots - D_{i-1}$.

Furthermore,

$$x_i = x_1 - D_1 - D_2 - \cdots - D_{i-1} + \text{any amount ordered},$$

so that

$$y_i \geq x_i \geq x_i' = y_i'$$

or

$$y_i \geq y_i'.$$

Hence

$$G(y_i) \geq G(y_i').$$

In both cases the inventory levels associated with following the single critical number policy lead to total expected costs which are no greater (and possibly smaller) than that obtained by following a different policy. Hence the single critical number policy must be optimal.

The results easily extend to the infinite-case model.

Dynamic Inventory Models with Lead Times

Up to now it has been assumed that stock is obtained instantaneously after ordering. This assumption is now relaxed, and a lead time, λ, between the placing and receiving of an order is considered. λ is assumed constant over time and independent of the size of the order. Again, backlogging is permitted. One-period costs are a function of the stock on hand at the beginning of the period *after* delivery of old orders but before the placing of a new one. Under these assumptions, it can be shown that the optimal policy can be obtained from the dynamic programming expressions

$$C_i(u_i) = \underset{y_i \geq u_i}{\text{minimum}}\left\{K\delta(y_i - u_i) + c(y_i - u_i) + \alpha^\lambda \int_0^\infty L(y_i - \eta)\varphi_D^{(\lambda)}(\eta)\, d\eta \right.$$
$$\left. + \alpha \int_0^\infty C_{i+1}(y_i - \xi)\varphi_D(\xi)\, d\xi \right\},$$

where

$$K\delta(y_i - u_i) = \begin{cases} K, & \text{if } y_i > u_i \\ 0, & \text{if } y_i = u_i, \end{cases}$$

and u_i represents the amount of stock on hand at the beginning of period i, plus the amount on order in the next $\lambda - 1$ periods. $\varphi_D^{(\lambda)}(\eta)$ is the density of the sum of λ demands, where demands are independent, identically distributed random variables each having density $\varphi_D(\xi)$.

It is evident that $C_i(u_i)$ is the usual zero lead time equation with a modified expected shortage plus holding cost $\mathscr{L}(y)$, where

$$\alpha^\lambda \mathscr{L}(y) = \alpha^\lambda \int_0^\infty L(y-\eta)\varphi_D^{(\lambda)}(\eta)\, d\eta.$$

The optimal policies for this model are exactly the same as the zero lead time models given previously. For example, for the infinite-stage dynamic inventory model with no setup cost, the critical number is obtained from the solution of

$$L'(y^0) + c(1-\alpha) = 0.$$

The solution to this problem with a λ-period lead time is found from

$$\alpha^\lambda \mathscr{L}'(y^0) + c(1-\alpha) = 0,$$

where $\alpha^\lambda \mathscr{L}(y)$ is obtained as indicated above. If $\varphi_D(\xi)$ is exponential with parameter μ, then $\varphi_D^{(\lambda)}(\eta)$ has a gamma distribution with parameters μ and λ.

11.6 FORECASTING

The previous sections of this chapter were concerned with finding optimal inventory policies. These policies were derived from inventory models and are, in part, dependent upon some forecast of sales or use of the items of interest. Sales forecasts of many different products often play an even more important role in making key company decisions. Hence there is a need for forecasting procedures that can be routinely mechanized. There exist many approaches to forecasting, ranging from an educated guess from sales management or the sales force itself to consumer surveys. This section will concentrate on *statistical forecasts*; i.e., it will be assumed that there exists historical data on the item being forecast, that these are the only input available, and that past performance is relevant for predicting future sales.

For example, the West Coast distributor of 10-speed bicycles may make quarterly sales forecasts for planning purposes. He has data on sales during previous quarters; i.e., he has the values the random variable quarterly sales takes on, and he would like to forecast the sales that will occur during the forthcoming quarter or subsequent quarters. Recognizing the fact that the sales during subsequent quarters are themselves random variables, accompanied by their associated variability, the distributor is willing to "settle" for an *estimate* of the expected sales during the present quarter, which will be used as the forecast of sales for future periods. In the absence of trends, seasonal adjustments, and so on, this estimate (presumably based upon many previous observations and not only on sales during the current period) will provide a "good" forecast for sales during subsequent quarters.

In general, the forecasting problem can be stated as follows. There exists a sequence of random variables $X_1, X_2, \ldots$ (a stochastic process) having expected values given by $E(X_1), E(X_2), \ldots$. The distribution of each of these random variables may be the same, or they may be changing (e.g., shifting) according to some pattern. The random variables may be independent or dependent. Observations on these random variables $X_1, X_2, \ldots, X_t$ have been taken, and their values are denoted by $x_1, x_2, \ldots, x_t$. Based upon these previous outcomes, $E(X_t)$ is to be estimated; the estimate, which will be used as the forecast for subsequent periods, will be denoted by $\hat{E}(X_t)$.

There are several potential forecasting procedures. To begin with, suppose the underlying process is relatively stable; i.e., distributions are almost the same, and there exists little dependence.

1. *Last value.* The bicycle distributor may use the sales during last quarter to estimate $E(X_t)$ and serve as the forecast of the sales for future quarters. Hence $\hat{E}(X_t) = x_t$. This estimator has the disadvantage of being imprecise; i.e., its variance is large because it is based upon a sample of size 1. It is worth considering only if the conditional distribution has very small variance and/or the process is changing so rapidly that anything before time t is almost irrelevant or may even be misleading.

2. *Average.* The bicycle distributor may use *all* his past quarterly data to forecast the sales for future quarters; i.e., he may choose

$$\hat{E}(X_t) = \sum_{i=1}^{t} \frac{x_i}{t}.$$

This is an excellent estimate if the process is entirely stable. However, besides being cumbersome in using large masses of data, one does not want to use data that are too old because occasional shifts are to be expected.

3. *Moving average.* In using a moving-average estimate, the bicycle distributor uses only the last n periods; that is,

$$\hat{E}(X_t) = \sum_{i=t-n+1}^{t} \frac{x_i}{n}.$$

Not only does this estimator use all the "relevant" history in the last n periods, but it is easily updated from period to period; i.e., the first observation is lopped off and the last one added. The moving-average estimator combines the advantages of the previous estimators in that it uses only recent history and represents multiple observations. A disadvantage of this procedure is that it places as much weight on x_{t-n+1} as on x_t, and intuitively one would expect a good procedure to place more weight on the most recent observation.

4. *Exponential smoothing.* If the bicycle distributor uses exponential smoothing, then

$$\hat{E}(X_t) = \alpha x_t + (1-\alpha)\hat{E}(X_{t-1}),$$

where $0 < \alpha < 1$ is called the smoothing constant. Thus the forecast is just a weighted sum of the last observation and the previous forecast. The choice of α

will be discussed later. Note that the exponential smoothing technique represents a recursive relationship and can be expressed alternatively as

$$\hat{E}(X_t) = \alpha x_t + \alpha(1-\alpha)x_{t-1} + \alpha(1-\alpha)^2 x_{t-2} + \cdots.$$

In this form it becomes evident that exponential smoothing gives most weight to x_t and decreasing weights to earlier observations. Furthermore, the first form reveals that the forecast is simple to calculate because the data prior to x_{t-1} need not be retained; all that is required is x_t and the previous forecast $\hat{E}(X_{t-1})$. Another alternative form for the exponential smoothing technique is given by

$$\hat{E}(X_t) = \hat{E}(X_{t-1}) + \alpha[x_t - \hat{E}(X_{t-1})],$$

which gives a hueristic justification for this procedure. Finally, a measure of effectiveness of exponential smoothing can be obtained under the assumption that the process is completely stable; that is, X_1, X_2, ... are independent, identically distributed random variables with variance σ^2. It then follows that

$$\text{var}[\hat{E}(X_t)] \approx \frac{\alpha\sigma^2}{2-\alpha} = \frac{\sigma^2}{(2-\alpha)/\alpha},$$

so that the variance is statistically equivalent to a moving average with $(2-\alpha)/\alpha$ observations. If α is chosen equal to 0.1, then $(2-\alpha)/\alpha = 19$. Thus the exponential smoothing technique is "equivalent" to a moving-average procedure that uses 19 observations. However, it must be noted that when the aforementioned underlying assumptions are violated, exponential smoothing will "react" more quickly with superior "tracking."

An important drawback of exponential smoothing is that it lags behind a continuing trend; i.e., if the mean is increasing steadily, then the forecast will be several periods behind. However, the procedure can be easily adjusted for trend (and even seasonably adjusted). Another disadvantage of exponential smoothing is the problem of choosing an appropriate smoothing constant α. Exponential smoothing can be viewed as a statistical filter that inputs "raw" data from a stochastic process and outputs "smoothed" estimates of a mean varying with time. If α is chosen to be small, response to change is slow, with resultant smooth estimators. Similarly if α is chosen to be large, response to change is fast, with resultant large variability in the output. Hence there is a need to compromise, depending upon the stability of the process. Furthermore, a "good" value of the smoothing constant depends upon the underlying stochastic process and the choice of a criterion to use in comparing constants. It has been suggested that a reasonable choice for α is approximately 0.1. Of course, it can be increased, perhaps temporarily, if an unusual change is expected, or when starting. When starting, a reasonable approach is to choose $\hat{E}(X_1)$ according to

$$\hat{E}(X_1) = \alpha x_1 + (1-\alpha) \text{ (initial estimate)}.$$

In the presence of past history, another procedure for choosing α is to run a retrospective simulation of the process; i.e., for a fixed value of α and using the past history, compare the forecasted quantity with the actual outcome, and choose that value of α which is in some sense optimal. Hopefully, the future process will behave in the same manner as the past history.

5. *Exponential smoothing adjusted for trend.* As indicated earlier, the procedure outlined in (4) lags behind a continuing trend. Suppose that $E(X_t)$ is linear with *known* slope S. The slope is the trend factor, and it represents the units per period that the expected sales rate is increasing or decreasing. Then instead of using the previous expression for $\hat{E}(X_t)$, the new expression

$$\hat{E}(X_t) = \alpha x_t + (1 - \alpha)[\hat{E}(X_{t-1}) + S]$$

is substituted. However, S is usually not known, so that it must also be estimated, and exponential smoothing can again be used for this purpose; that is,

$$\hat{E}(S_t) = \beta[\hat{E}(X_t) - \hat{E}(X_{t-1})] + (1 - \beta)\hat{E}(S_{t-1}),$$

where $0 < \beta < 1$ is another (possibly different from α) smoothing constant.[1] Hence $\hat{E}(X_t)$ can now be expressed as

$$\hat{E}(X_t) = \alpha x_t + (1 - \alpha)[\hat{E}(X_{t-1}) + \hat{E}(S_{t-1})],$$

and this now becomes the estimate of $E(X_t)$. Unlike exponential smoothing without trend, $\hat{E}(X_t)$ is only a "good" estimate for $E(X_t)$ and is *not* a forecast for future periods. This is caused by the increasing or decreasing trend, and hence the forecast of sales for the $(t + T)$th period based upon past data through the tth period is given by $X_{t,T}$, where

$$X_{t,T} = \hat{E}(X_t) + T\hat{E}(S_t)$$

and

$$T = 0, 1, 2, \ldots .$$

The forecasting procedure (in the context of sales) can now be summarized as follows:

(*a*) Using the actual sales occuring during the tth period x_t, the estimate of the last period's expected sales $\hat{E}(X_{t-1})$, and trend rate $\hat{E}(S_{t-1})$, the estimate of the tth period's expected sales is given by

$$\hat{E}(X_t) = \alpha x_t + (1 - \alpha)[\hat{E}(X_{t-1}) + \hat{E}(S_{t-1})].$$

(*b*) From the estimate of this periods expected sales $\hat{E}(X_t)$ [calculated in (*a*)], last period's estimate of expected sales $\hat{E}(X_{t-1})$, and trend rate $\hat{E}(S_{t-1})$, the estimate of the tth period trend rate is given by

$$\hat{E}(S_t) = \beta[\hat{E}(X_t) - \hat{E}(X_{t-1})] + (1 - \beta)\hat{E}(S_{t-1}).$$

(*c*) Forecasts of sales for the $(t + T)$th period are given by

$$X_{t,T} = \hat{E}(X_t) + T\hat{E}(S_t).$$

[1] The previous discussion concerning the choice of α is relevant to the choice of β.

EXAMPLE Suppose quarterly sales for bicycles were 2,800, 2,925, and 3,040, respectively. The initial estimate of the expected sales is 2,750, and the initial estimate of the trend is 100. Use exponential smoothing based upon the first three observations to forecast sales for the fifth period, using $\alpha = \beta = 0.1$. From (*a*), and using the initial estimates of expected sales and trend,

$$\hat{E}(X_1) = 0.1(2{,}800) + 0.9(2{,}750 + 100) = 2{,}845.$$

The initial estimate of sales can also be used to update the trend in (*b*); that is,

$$\hat{E}(S_1) = 0.1(2{,}845 - 2{,}750) + 0.9(100) = 99.5.$$

Repeating this procedure for the second observation leads to

$$\hat{E}(X_2) = 0.1(2{,}925) + 0.9(2{,}845 + 99.5) = 2{,}943$$

and

$$\hat{E}(S_2) = 0.1(2{,}943 - 2{,}845) + 0.9(99.5) = 99.4.$$

Finally, the third observation results in

$$\hat{E}(X_3) = 0.1(3{,}040) + 0.9(2{,}943 + 99.4) = 3{,}041$$

and

$$\hat{E}(S_3) = 0.1(3{,}041 - 2{,}943) + 0.9(99.4) = 99.3.$$

Therefore, the forecast of sales for the fifth period is

$$X_{3,2} = 3{,}041 + 2(99.3) = 3{,}240.$$

11.7 CONCLUSIONS

The inventory models presented are rather simplified, but they serve the purpose of introducing the general nature of inventory models. Furthermore, they are sufficiently accurate enough representations of many actual inventory situations so that they frequently are useful in practice. For example, the economic lot-size formulas particularly have been widely used, although sometimes modified to include some type of stochastic demand. The multiperiod models with stochastic demand have been important in characterizing the type of policies to follow, for example, (s,S) policies, even though the optimal values of s and S are difficult to obtain. Nevertheless, there are many inventory situations that possess complications which must still be taken into account, e.g., interaction between products. Several complex models have been formulated in an attempt to fit such situations, but they still leave a wide gap between practice and theory. Continued growth is anticipated in computerization of inventory data processing, with accompanying growth in scientific inventory management.

Selected References

1 Arrow, K. J., S. Karlin, and H. Scarf: *Studies in the Mathematical Theory of Inventory and Production*, Stanford Univ. Press, Stanford, Calif., 1958.
2 Brown, R. G.: *Smoothing, Forecasting, and Prediction*, Prentice-Hall, Englewood Cliffs, N.J., 1963.
3 Buchan, J. and E. Koenigsberg: *Scientific Inventory Management*, Prentice-Hall, Englewood Cliffs, N.J., 1963.
4 Hadley, G. and T. Whitin: *Analysis of Inventory Systems*, Prentice-Hall, Englewood Cliffs, N.J., 1963.
5 Starr, M. and D. Miller: *Inventory Control: Theory and Practice*, Prentice-Hall, Englewood Cliffs, N.J., 1962.
6 Veinott, A. F., Jr.: "The Status of Mathematical Inventory Theory," *Management Science*, **12**(11): 745–777, 1966.

Problems

1 Suppose that the demand for a product is 20 units per month, and the items are withdrawn uniformly. The setup cost each time a production run is made is $15. The production cost is $1 per item, and the inventory holding cost is $0.30 per item per month.

(*a*) Assuming shortages are not allowed, determine how often to make a production run and what size it should be.
(*b*) If shortages cost $1.50 per item per month, determine how often to make a production run and what size it should be.

2 The demand for a product is 500 units per week, and the items are withdrawn uniformly. The items are ordered, and the setup cost is $25. The unit cost of each item is $3, and the inventory holding cost is $0.05 per item per week.

(*a*) Assuming shortages are not allowed, determine how often to order and what size should it be.
(*b*) If shortages cost $2 per item per week, determine how often to order and what size it should be.

3 Solve Prob. 2 with shortages permitted and assume a delivery lag of 1 week.

4 Solve the economic lot-size model problem presented in Sec. 11.3, when shortages are permitted but cost $1.25 per speaker.

5 A taxi company uses gasoline at the rate of 8,000 gallons/month. The gasoline costs 35 cents/gallon, with a setup cost of $1,000. The inventory holding cost is 1 cent/gallon/month.

(*a*) Assuming shortages are not allowed, determine how often and how much to order.
(*b*) If shortages cost 10 cents/gallon/month, determine how often and how much to order.

6 Solve Prob. 5*a* by assuming that the cost of gasoline drops to 30 cents/gallon if at least 50,000 gallons are purchased.

7 Solve Prob. 5*a* if the cost of gasoline is 40 cents/gallon for the first 20,000 gallons purchased, 35 cents for the next 20,000 gallons, and 30 cents/gallon thereafter.

8 Suppose the requirement for the next 5 months is given by $r_1 = 2$, $r_2 = 4$, $r_3 = 2$, $r_4 = 2$, and $r_5 = 3$. Items are ordered, and the setup cost is \$4, the purchase cost is \$1, and the holding cost is \$0.25. Determine the optimal production schedule satisfying the monthly requirements. Use dynamic programming.

9 Solve Prob. 8 by assuming that the production costs are given by $\$3(1 + \log_e X)$, where X is the amount produced in a month.

10 Solve Prob. 8 by using the algorithm presented in Sec. 11.3.

11 Solve Prob. 9 by using the algorithm presented in Sec. 11.3.

12 Formulate Prob. 8 as an integer programming problem.

13 Solve the production planning model for the production of speakers when the requirements are increased by 1 unit in each period.

14 Solve the production planning model for the production of speakers when the unit costs during the first and third periods are increased to \$1.30. Use dynamic programming.

15 Develop an algorithm to solve the production planning model that uses forward induction. (*Hint:* If an optimal policy is being followed and if the time of the *last* production is known for this optimal policy, the total cost of the previous periods must be a minimum for this reduced problem because the overall policy is optimal.)

16 Consider a situation where a particular product is produced and placed in in-process inventory until it is needed in a subsequent production process. The number of units required in each of the next 3 months, as well as the setup cost and regular time unit production cost that would be incurred in each month, are

Month	*Requirements*	*Setup cost (\$)*	*Regular time unit cost (\$)*
1	1	5	8
2	3	10	10
3	2	5	9

There currently is 1 unit in inventory, and it is desired to have 2 units in inventory at the end of the 3 months. A maximum of 3 units can be produced on regular-time production in each month, although one additional unit can be produced on overtime at a cost that is \$2 larger than the regular time unit production cost. The cost of storage is \$2 per unit for each extra month that it is stored.

Use dynamic programming to determine how many units should be produced in each month to minimize total cost.

17 A newspaper stand purchases newspapers for 7 cents and sells them for 10 cents. The shortage cost is 10 cents per newspaper (since the dealer buys papers at retail price to satisfy shortages). The holding cost is 0.1 cent. The demand distribution is a uniform distribution between 200 and 300. Find the optimal number of papers to buy.

18 Suppose the demand D for a spare airplane part has an exponential distribution with parameter $\frac{1}{50}$; that is,

$$\varphi_D(\xi) = \begin{cases} \frac{1}{50} e^{-\xi/50}, & \xi \geq 0 \\ 0, & \text{otherwise.} \end{cases}$$

This airplane will be obsolete in 1 year, and hence all production is to take place at the present time. The production costs now are \$1,000 per item, that is, $c = 1{,}000$, but they become \$10,000 per item if they must be supplied at later dates, that is, $p = 10{,}000$. The holding costs, charged on the excess after the end of the period, are \$100 per item. Determine the required number of spare parts.

19 A bread manufacturer distributes bread to grocery stores daily. The cost of the bread is 12 cents per loaf. The company sells the bread to the stores for 20 cents per loaf sold provided that it is disposed of as fresh bread (sold on the day it is baked). Bread not sold is returned to the company. The company has a store outlet that sells bread a day or more old for 10 cents per loaf. This salvage cost represents the holding cost. The unsatisfied demand cost is estimated to be 25 cents per loaf. If the demand has a uniform distribution between 1,000 and 2,000 loaves, find the optimal daily number of loaves that the manufacturer should produce.

20 A student majoring in operations research enjoys optimizing his personal decisions. He is analyzing one such decision currently, namely, how much money to take out of his savings account (if any) to buy travelers checks before leaving on a summer vacation trip to Europe.

He already has used the money he did have in his checking account to buy travelers checks worth \$1,200, but this may not be enough. In fact, he has estimated the probability distribution of what he will need as shown in the following table:

Amount needed (\$)	1,000	1,100	1,200	1,300	1,400	1,500	1,600	1,700
Probability	0.05	0.10	0.15	0.20	0.20	0.15	0.10	0.05

If he turns out to have less than he needs, then he would have to leave Europe 1 week early for every \$100 short. Since he places a value of \$150 on each week in Europe, each week lost would thereby represent a net inputed loss of \$50 to him. However, every \$100 travelers check costs an extra \$1. Furthermore, *each* such check left over at the end of the trip (which would be redeposited in the savings account) represents a loss of \$2 in interest that could have been earned in the savings account during the trip, so he does not want to purchase too many.

Using these data, determine the optimal decision on how many additional \$100 travelers checks (if any) the student should purchase from his savings account money.

21 Find the optimal ordering policy for a one-period model, where the demand has a probability density

$$\varphi_D(\xi) = \begin{cases} \frac{1}{20}, & \text{if } 0 \leq \xi \leq 20 \\ 0, & \text{otherwise,} \end{cases}$$

and the costs are

$$\text{Holding} = \$1 \text{ per item}$$
$$\text{Shortage} = \$3 \text{ per item,}$$
$$\text{Setup} = 90 \text{ cents}$$
$$\text{Production} = \$2 \text{ per item.}$$

22 Consider the following inventory model, which is a single-period model with known density of demand $\varphi_D(\xi) = e^{-\xi}$, for $\xi > 0$ and zero elsewhere. There are two costs connected with the model: The first is the purchase cost, given by $c \cdot (y - x)$; the second is the unsatisfied demand cost, which is just a constant, p (independent of the amount of unsatisfied demand).

(*a*) If x units are available and goods are ordered up to y, write the expression for the expected loss, and describe completely the optimal policy.

(*b*) If a fixed cost K is also incurred whenever an order is placed, describe the optimal policy.

23 Using the approximation for finding the optimal policy for a single-period model when the density of demand has an exponential distribution, find this policy when

$$\varphi_D(\xi) = \begin{cases} \dfrac{1}{25} e^{-\xi/25}, & \text{if } \xi \geq 0 \\ 0, & \text{otherwise,} \end{cases}$$

and the costs are

$$\text{Holding} = 30 \text{ cents per item,}$$
$$\text{Shortage} = \$1.50 \text{ per item,}$$
$$\text{Purchase price} = \$1 \text{ per item,}$$
$$\text{Setup} = \$10.$$

24 There are production processes for which the difference between the cost of producing the maximum number of units allowed by some capacity restriction an[d the] cost of producing any number of units less than this maximum is negligible; [and] ordering is by batches. Consider a one-stage model, where the only two costs a[re] holding costs given by

$$h(y - D) = \left(\frac{3}{10}\right)(y - D)$$

and the penalty cost of unsatisfied demand given by

$$p(D - y) = \left(\frac{3}{2}\right)(D - y).$$

The density function for demand is given by

$$\varphi_D(\xi) = \begin{cases} \dfrac{e^{-\xi/25}}{25}, & \text{for } \xi \geq 0 \\ 0, & \text{otherwise.} \end{cases}$$

If you order, you must order in batches of 100 units of product, and this quantity is delivered instantaneously. Thus, if x denotes the quantity on hand, and you do not order, then $y = x$. If you order one batch, then $y = x + 100$. Let $G(y)$ denote the total expected cost of this inventory problem when there are y units available for the period (after you have ordered).

(a) Write the expression for $G(y)$.
(b) What is the optimal ordering policy?

25 In a single-stage inventory situation ordering must be in batches of size b, that is, order b, $2b$, $3b$, ... Suppose that for a fixed amount x of material on hand the expected loss is given by $G(x)$. If b units are ordered, the expected loss is given by $G(x + b)$. For example, if $x = x_0$ and no ordering is done, the loss incurred is $G(x_0)$,

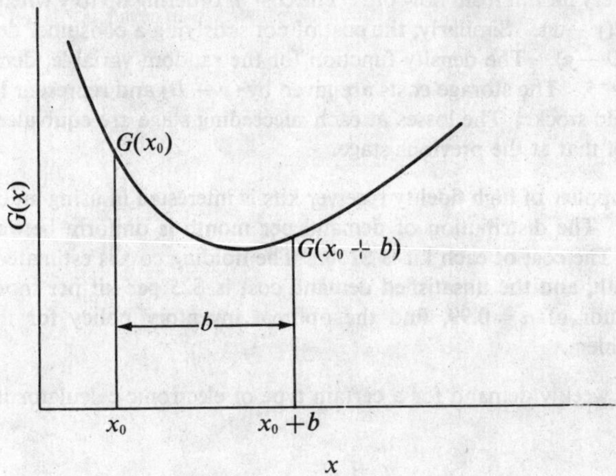

whereas if b units are ordered, the loss is $G(x_0 + b)$. In the above figure it is clearly better to order the b units. Describe the optimal ordering procedure.

26 Consider the following inventory situation. Demands are independent with common density $\varphi_D(\xi) = 1/10$, $0 < \xi < 10$. Orders may be placed at the start of each period without setup cost and at a price of $c = 10$. There is a holding cost of 10 per unit remaining in stock at the end of each period and a penalty cost of 15 per unit quantity backlogged.

(a) Find the optimal one-period policy.
(b) Find the optimal two-period policy. Use a discount factor $\alpha = 3/4$.

27 Find the optimal inventory policy for the following two-period model by using a discount factor of $\alpha = 0.9$. Let the density of the demand D be given by

$$\varphi_D(\xi) = \begin{cases} \dfrac{1}{25} e^{-\xi/25}, & \text{if } \xi \geq 0 \\ 0, & \text{otherwise,} \end{cases}$$

and the costs are

$$\text{Holding} = 30 \text{ cents per item},$$
$$\text{Shortage} = \$1.50 \text{ per item},$$
$$\text{Purchase price} = \$1 \text{ per item}.$$

Stock left over at the end of the final period is salvaged for $1 per item, and shortages remaining at this time are also available at $1 per item.

28 Solve Prob. 27 for a four-period model by using a discount factor of $\alpha = 0.90$.

29 Solve Prob. 27 for an infinite-period model by using a discount factor of $\alpha = 0.90$.

30 Determine the optimum inventory policy when the goods are to be ordered at the end of every month from now on. The cost of ordering up to y when x is available is given by $2(y - x)$. Similarly, the cost of not satisfying a consumer demand of D is given by $5(D - y)$. The density function for the random variable, demand, is given by $\varphi_D(\xi) = e^{-\xi}$. The storage costs are given by $(y - D)$ and represent the expense of storing unsold stock. The losses at each succeeding stage are equivalent to a loss of 95 percent of that at the previous stage.

31 A supplier of high fidelity receiver kits is interested in using an optimal inventory policy. The distribution of demand per month is uniform between 2,000 and 3,000 kits. The cost of each kit is $150. The holding cost is estimated to be $2 per kit per month, and the unsatisfied demand cost is $25 per kit per month. Using a discount factor of $\alpha = 0.99$, find the optimal inventory policy for this "infinite" horizon problem.

32 The weekly demand for a certain type of electronic calculator is estimated to be given by

$$\varphi_D(\xi) = \begin{cases} \dfrac{1}{1{,}000} e^{-\xi/1{,}000}, & \xi \geq 0 \\ 0, & \text{otherwise.} \end{cases}$$

The cost of these calculators is $75. The holding cost is 50 cents per calculator per week. The unsatisfied demand cost is $15 per calculator per week. Using a discount factor of $\alpha = 0.995$, find the optimal inventory policy for this infinite-horizon problem.

33 Consider an infinite-period inventory model in which the demands are independent, identically distributed random variables. Denote the expected demand in a period by μ. Assume the cost of ordering z units ($z \geq 0$) is $c \cdot z$ ($c > 0$). Let α ($0 < \alpha < 1$) be the discount factor. Assume that all unsatisfied demand is backlogged. Finally, suppose that when y is the inventory on hand after ordering but before the occurrence of a demand of size D in a period, a cost $(y - D)^2$ is incurred. When $y > D$, the cost is a charge for carrying the inventory; when $y < D$, the cost is a charge for backlogging demand. Describe the optimal ordering policy, and give simple formulas for its parameters in terms of c, α, and μ.

34 Find the optimal (k, Q) policy for Prob. 24 for an infinite-period model by using a discount factor of $\alpha = 0.95$.

35 In Sec. 11.4 the critical number y^0 for the optimal ordering policy for an infinite-period model was shown to satisfy the equation

$$\int_0^{y^0} \varphi_D(\xi)\, d\xi = \Phi(y^0) = \frac{p - c(1-\alpha)}{p+h}$$

when the ordering, shortage, and holding costs are linear, and the demand D is a continuous random variable with density function $\varphi_D(\xi)$. Show that these results are valid for demands which are discrete random variables, provided that the integral is replaced by a summation.

36 Solve the forecasting example presented in Sec. 11.6 by using $\alpha = 0.1$ and $\beta = 0.2$. Forecast sales for the fourth period.

37 Solve the forecasting example presented in Sec. 11.6 by using $\alpha = 0.2$ and $\beta = 0.1$. Forecast sales for the sixth period.

12 Markovian Decision Processes and Applications

12.1 INTRODUCTION

Section 8.17 introduced the concept of a dynamic system evolving over time. The behavior of such a system resulted in an analysis of a particular type of stochastic process. The ideas presented can be illustrated by considering the following maintenance-model example. A production process contains a machine that deteriorates rapidly in both quality and output, under heavy usage, so that it is inspected periodically, say, at the end of each day. Immediately after inspection, the condition of the machine is noted and classified into one of four possible states:

State	*Condition*
0	Good as new
1	Operable—minor deterioration
2	Operable—major deterioration
3	Inoperable—output of unacceptable quality

Let X_t denote the observed state of the machine after inspection at the end of the tth day. It is reasonable to assume that the state of the system evolves according to some probabilistic "laws of motion," so that the sequence of states $\{X_t\}$ can be viewed as a stochastic process. Furthermore, it will be assumed that the stochastic process is a finite-state Markov chain (see Sec. 8.18), with known transition matrix given by

State	0	1	2	3
0	0	$\frac{7}{8}$	$\frac{1}{16}$	$\frac{1}{16}$
1	0	$\frac{3}{4}$	$\frac{1}{8}$	$\frac{1}{8}$
2	0	0	$\frac{1}{2}$	$\frac{1}{2}$
3	0	0	0	1

From this transition matrix it becomes evident that once the machine becomes inoperable (enters state 3), it remains inoperable. Therefore the analysis of this stochastic process is probably uninteresting because state 3 is an absorbing state and eventually the machine will enter this state and just remain there; i.e., after some time period, X_t will always equal 3. Clearly, from a practical point of view this model is intolerable because a machine that is inoperable can not continue to remain in the production process and must be replaced (or repaired). This action of replacement alters the behavior of the system, so that the system now evolves over time according to the joint effect of the probabilistic laws of motion and the action of replacing an inoperable machine. Note that the action of replacing an inoperable machine can be thought of as defining a maintenance policy.

When a machine becomes inoperable and is replaced, the replacement machine is "as good as new"; i.e., the machine is found to be in state 0 at the time of the regular inspection at the end of the next day. As a practical matter, the replacement process can be thought of as taking 1 day to complete, so that production is lost for this period.

The costs incurred while this system evolves contains several components. When the system is in state 0, 1, or 2, defective items may be produced during the next day, and the expected costs are given by

State	*Expected cost due to producing defective items*
0	0
1	\$1,000
2	\$3,000

If the machine is replaced, a replacement cost of \$4,000 is incurred, together with a cost of lost production (lost profit) of \$2,000. Hence the total cost incurred whenever the system is in state 3 is \$6,000.

The stochastic process resulting from the system with the aforementioned maintenance policy, i.e., repairing an inoperable machine, is still a finite-state Markov chain but with transition matrix now given by

State	*0*	*1*	*2*	*3*
0	0	$\frac{7}{8}$	$\frac{1}{16}$	$\frac{1}{16}$
1	0	$\frac{3}{4}$	$\frac{1}{8}$	$\frac{1}{8}$
2	0	0	$\frac{1}{2}$	$\frac{1}{2}$
3	1	0	0	0

It may be of interest to evaluate the cost of this "maintenance policy." If the (long run) expected average cost per day or the (long run) actual average cost per day is an appropriate measure, the results appearing in Sec. 8.22 (under subsections expected average cost per unit time or expected average cost per unit time for complex cost functions) are appropriate.

By noting that $p_{ij}^{(4)} > 0$ for all i and j, it is evident that every state is positive recurrent and belongs to one class. The steady-state equations can be written as

$$\pi_0 = \pi_3,$$

$$\pi_1 = \frac{7}{8}\pi_0 + \frac{3}{4}\pi_1,$$

$$\pi_2 = \frac{1}{16}\pi_0 + \frac{1}{8}\pi_1 + \frac{1}{2}\pi_2,$$

$$\pi_3 = \frac{1}{16}\pi_0 + \frac{1}{8}\pi_1 + \frac{1}{2}\pi_2,$$

$$1 = \pi_0 + \pi_1 + \pi_2 + \pi_3.$$

The simultaneous solution is

$$\pi_0 = \frac{2}{13}$$

$$\pi_1 = \frac{7}{13}$$

$$\pi_2 = \frac{2}{13}$$

$$\pi_3 = \frac{2}{13}.$$

Hence the (long run) expected average cost per day is given by

$$0\,\pi_0 + 1{,}000\pi_1 + 3{,}000\pi_2 + 6{,}000\pi_3 = \frac{25{,}000}{13} = \$1{,}923.08,$$

and this represents the cost of this maintenance policy.

12.2 MARKOVIAN DECISION MODELS

The previous section introduced an example of a maintenance model for a machine and presented a maintenance policy; i.e., when a machine becomes inoperable it is replaced; otherwise, the machine is left alone. In other words, a decision is made to take the action replace the machine when it is found to be in state 3, whereas a decision is made to take the action leave the machine as is when it is found to be in states 0, 1, or 2. Even when these two actions are the only permissible ones, there are still other "policies" that can be generated; e.g., when the machine becomes inoperable or is found to be operable but with major deterioration (machine is in state 2 or 3), replace it; otherwise leave the machine as is. Note that this policy generates a different transition matrix, i.e.,

State	*0*	*1*	*2*	*3*
0	0	$\frac{7}{8}$	$\frac{1}{16}$	$\frac{1}{16}$
1	0	$\frac{3}{4}$	$\frac{1}{8}$	$\frac{1}{8}$
2	1	0	0	0
3	1	0	0	0

To make the machine-maintenance example more realistic, suppose that a third action is permitted: overhaul. When a machine is overhauled the machine is returned to state 1 (operable—minor deterioration) at the time of the regular inspection at the end of the next day. As a practical matter, like replacement, the overhaul process can be thought of as requiring a day to complete, so that production is lost for this period. Overhauling the machine will not be considered as a viable decision when the machine becomes inoperable.

In viewing this dynamic system it is evident that the system evolves over time according to the joint effect of the probabilitsic laws of motion and the sequence of decisions made (actions taken). In particular, the machine is inspected at the end of each day and its state recorded. A decision as to which action to take must be made, i.e.,

Decision	*Action*
1	Do nothing
2	Overhaul (return system to state 1)
3	Replace (return system to state 0)

For the general model it will be assumed that a system is observed at time $t = 0, 1, \ldots$ and classified into one of a finite number of states labeled $0, 1, \ldots, M$.

Let $\{X_t, t = 0,1, \ldots\}$ denote the sequence of observed states. After each observation, one of K (finite) possible decisions (actions), labeled 1, 2, ..., K, is taken.[1] Let $\{\Delta_t, t = 0,1 \ldots\}$ denote the sequence of actual decisions made.

A policy, denoted by R, is a rule for making decisions at each point in time. In principle a policy could use all the previously observed information up to time t, that is, the entire "history" of the system consisting of $X_0, X_1, \ldots, X_t$ and $\Delta_0, \Delta_1, \Delta_2, \ldots, \Delta_{t-1}$. However, for most problems encountered in practice it is sufficient to confine consideration to those policies that depend upon only the observed state of the system at time t, X_t, and the possible decisions available. Hence a policy R can be viewed as a rule that prescribes decision $d_i(R)$ when the system is in state i, $i = 0, 1, \ldots, M$. Thus R is completely characterized by the values

$$\{d_0(R), d_1(R), \ldots, d_M(R)\}.$$

Note that this description assumes that whenever the system is in state i, the decision to be made is the same for all values of t. Policies possessing this property are called stationary policies.

In the example, the interesting policies are

Policy	*Verbal description*	$d_0(R)$	$d_1(R)$	$d_2(R)$	$d_3(R)$
R_a	Replace in state 3	1	1	1	3
R_b	Replace in state 3 overhaul in state 2	1	1	2	3
R_c	Replace in states 2, 3	1	1	3	3
R_d	Replace in states 1, 2, 3	1	3	3	3

Note that policy R_a is the policy described in the previous section, and R_c is the policy alluded to earlier in this section. Furthermore, recall that each policy results in a different transition matrix.

It has been noted that a system evolves over time according to the joint effect of the probabilistic laws of motion and the sequence of decisions made; its path is dependent upon its initial state, X_0. It shall be assumed that whenever the system is in state i and decision $d_i(R) = k$ is made, the system moves to a new state j, with known transition probability $p_{ij}(k)$, for all $i, j = 0, 1, \ldots, M$ and $k = 1, 2, \ldots, K$. Thus, if a given policy R is followed, the resultant stochastic process is a Markov chain with a known transition matrix (dependent upon the policy chosen). Unless otherwise noted, thoughout this chapter it will be assumed for technical reasons that the Markov chain associated with every transition matrix is irreducible.

[1] In general, the number of possible decisions may depend upon the state of the system. Such a case is considered in Sec. 12.7.

In the example the following transition matrices are obtained:

	R_a			
State	*0*	*1*	*2*	*3*
0	0	$\frac{7}{8}$	$\frac{1}{16}$	$\frac{1}{16}$
1	0	$\frac{3}{4}$	$\frac{1}{8}$	$\frac{1}{8}$
2	0	0	$\frac{1}{2}$	$\frac{1}{2}$
3	1	0	0	0

	R_b			
State	*0*	*1*	*2*	*3*
0	0	$\frac{7}{8}$	$\frac{1}{16}$	$\frac{1}{16}$
1	0	$\frac{3}{4}$	$\frac{1}{8}$	$\frac{1}{8}$
2	0	1	0	0
3	1	0	0	0

	R_c			
State	*0*	*1*	*2*	*3*
0	0	$\frac{7}{8}$	$\frac{1}{16}$	$\frac{1}{16}$
1	0	$\frac{3}{4}$	$\frac{1}{8}$	$\frac{1}{8}$
2	1	0	0	0
3	1	0	0	0

	R_d			
State	*0*	*1*	*2*	*3*
0	0	$\frac{7}{8}$	$\frac{1}{16}$	$\frac{1}{16}$
1	1	0	0	0
2	1	0	0	0
3	1	0	0	0

To summarize then, given a distribution $P\{X_0 = i\}$ over the initial states of the system and a policy R, a system evolves over time according to the joint effect of the probabilistic laws of motion and the sequence of decisions made (actions taken). In particular, when the system is in state i and decision $d_i(R) = k$ is made, then the probability that the system is in state j at the next observed time period is given by $p_{ij}(k)$. This results in a sequence of observed states X_0, $X_1, \ldots$ and a sequence of decisions made, $\Delta_0, \Delta_1, \ldots$. This sequence of observed states and sequence of decisions made is called a *Markovian decision process.* The term Markovian is used because of the underlying assumptions made about the probabilistic laws of motion.

Four maintenance policies have been described, but their properties have not been evaluated. Questions like "Which one is 'best'?" remain to be answered. To pursue this avenue, it is necessary to introduce a cost structure. When the system is in state i and decision $d_i(R) = k$ is made following policy R, a known cost C_{ik} is incurred. This cost may represent an expected rather than an actual cost. For example, in the maintenance problem the cost of leaving a machine as is depends upon the random variable, the number of defectives produced during the next time period. The expected value of this cost function taken with respect to the distribution of the number of defectives will result in the desired cost C_{ik}.† It is important to reiterate that this cost depends upon only the state the system is found in and the decision made; that is,

$$C_{ik} = \text{known (expected) cost incurred during next transition if system is in state } i \text{ and decision } k \text{ is made.}$$

For the four maintenance policies the costs can be obtained from the following information:

Decision	State \ Cost	Expected cost due to producing defective items	Maintenance cost	Cost (lost profit) from lost production	Total cost per day
1. Leave machine as is	0	0	0	0	0
	1	\$1,000	0	0	\$1,000
	2	\$3,000	0	0	\$3,000
	3	∞†	0	0	∞
2. Overhaul	0, 1, 2	0	\$2,000	\$2,000	\$4,000
	3	0	∞†	\$2,000	∞
3. Replace	0, 1, 2, 3	0	\$4,000	\$2,000	\$6,000

† Since leaving the machine in an inoperable condition or overhauling it when it is inoperable is prohibited by assumption, a cost of infinity is being assigned. An alternate approach would be to omit these decisions from the set of possible decisions when the machine is found to be in state 3.

Note that the costs incurred when the decision is made to replace is independent of the state of the system. This is evident because no production takes place during the ensuing day when this action is taken. Finally, the total expected costs incurred per day is summarized as follows:

State \ Decision	C_{ik} (in thousands of dollars) 1	2	3
0	0	4	6
1	1	4	6
2	3	4	6
3	∞	∞	6

To compare policies it is necessary to settle on an appropriate cost measure. One such measure associated with a policy is the (long run) expected average

† See Sec. 8.22, under subsection expected average cost per unit time for complex cost functions, for an additional example.

cost per unit time; this will be the one used.[1] The results appearing in Sec. 8.22 are appropriate; i.e., for any policy the (long run) expected average cost per unit time, $E(C)$, can be calculated from the expression

$$E(C) = \sum_{i=0}^{M} C_{ik}\,\pi_i,$$

where $k = d_i(R)$ for each i, and $(\pi_0, \pi_1, \ldots, \pi_M)$ represents the steady-state distribution of the state of the system under the policy R being evaluated. Thus, the policy that minimizes $E(C)$ is sought. Using this criterion, it is evident that the distribution over the initial states of the system is not important because the long-run effect of the cost of the initial decision is negligible. In the maintenance example it is necessary to solve for $(\pi_0, \pi_1, \ldots, \pi_M)$ under each of the four "interesting" policies and then use these results to obtain $E(C)$. The necessary calculations for R_a are given in Sec. 12.1; all are now summarized:

Policy	$\pi_0, \pi_1, \pi_2, \pi_3$	$E(C)$
R_a	$\left(\frac{2}{13}, \frac{7}{13}, \frac{2}{13}, \frac{2}{13}\right)$	$\frac{1}{13}[2(0) + 7(1) + 2(3) + 2(6)] = \frac{25}{13} = 1.923$
R_b	$\left(\frac{2}{21}, \frac{5}{7}, \frac{2}{21}, \frac{2}{21}\right)$	$\frac{1}{21}[2(0) + 15(1) + 2(4) + 2(6)] = \frac{35}{21} = 1.667$ min.
R_c	$\left(\frac{2}{11}, \frac{7}{11}, \frac{1}{11}, \frac{1}{11}\right)$	$\frac{1}{11}[2(0) + 7(1) + 1(6) + 1(6)] = \frac{19}{11} = 1.727$
R_d	$\left(\frac{1}{2}, \frac{7}{16}, \frac{1}{32}, \frac{1}{32}\right)$	$\frac{1}{32}[16(0) + 14(6) + 1(6) + 1(6)] = \frac{96}{32} = 3$

It is evident that policy R_b is the best. Among the four policies considered, the policy that calls for replacing the machine when it is found to be in state 3 and overhauling it when it is found to be in state 2 is the best, and the (long run) expected average cost per day is $1,667.

The technique described above is just an exhaustive enumeration of a given set of possible policies. It is evident that direct enumeration becomes cumbersome when the number of policies is large and algorithms for finding optimal policies are desirable. The next three sections will each consider such algorithms.

12.3 LINEAR PROGRAMMING AND OPTIMAL POLICIES

Section 12.2 defined a policy. It was observed that a policy R can be viewed as a rule which prescribes decision $d_i(R)$ when the system is in state i. Thus R is characterized by the values

$$\{d_0(R), d_1(R), \ldots, d_M(R)\}.$$

[1] The ensuing results are also valid for the (long run) actual average cost per unit time measure as noted in Sec. 8.22.

Alternatively, R can be characterized by assigning values $D_{ik} = 0$ or 1 in the matrix

$$\text{State}\quad \begin{array}{c} \\ 0 \\ 1 \\ \vdots \\ M \end{array} \overset{\displaystyle \text{Decision, } k}{\overset{\begin{array}{cccc} 1 & 2 & \cdots & K \end{array}}{\begin{bmatrix} D_{01} & D_{02} & \cdots & D_{0K} \\ D_{11} & D_{12} & \cdots & D_{1K} \\ \vdots & \vdots & \vdots & \vdots \\ D_{M1} & D_{M2} & \cdots & D_{MK} \end{bmatrix}}},$$

where each row must contain a single 1 with the rest of the elements zero (i.e., each row sums to 1). When an element $D_{ik} = 1$, it can be interpreted as calling for decision k when the system is in state i. In the maintenance-model example the policy R_b can be characterized by the matrix

$$\text{State}\quad \begin{array}{c} 0 \\ 1 \\ 2 \\ 3 \end{array} \overset{\displaystyle \text{Decision, } k}{\overset{\begin{array}{ccc} 1 & 2 & 3 \end{array}}{\begin{bmatrix} 1 & 0 & 0 \\ 1 & 0 & 0 \\ 0 & 1 & 0 \\ 0 & 0 & 1 \end{bmatrix}}};$$

i.e., replace the machine when it is in state 3, overhaul the machine when it is in state 2, and leave the machine as is when it is in states 0 or 1. This interpretation of the D_{ik} provides motivation for a linear programming formulation. Hopefully, the expected cost of a policy can be expressed as a linear function of the D_{ik}, or a related variable, subject to linear constraints. Unfortunately, the D_{ik} are integers (zero or 1), and continuous variables are required for a linear programming formulation. This can be handled by expanding the interpretation of a policy. The previous definition calls for making the same decision every time the system is in state i. The new interpretation of a policy will call for determining a probability distribution for the decision to be made when the system is in state i. Thus D_{ik} can now be viewed as

$$D_{ik} = P\{\text{decision} = k \mid \text{state} = i\},\dagger \quad \begin{array}{l} k = 1, 2, \ldots, K, \\ i = 0, 1, \ldots, M. \end{array}$$

Such a policy is called a randomized policy, whereas the policy calling for $D_{ik} = 0$ or 1 can be called a deterministic policy. Randomized policies can again be characterized by the matrix

† The right-hand side of this equation is read as the conditional probability that the decision k is made, given the system is in state i.

$$
\begin{array}{cc}
 & \text{Decision, } k \\
 & \begin{array}{cccc} 1 & 2 & \cdots & K \end{array} \\
\text{State} \begin{array}{c} 0 \\ 1 \\ \vdots \\ M \end{array} &
\begin{bmatrix} D_{01} & D_{02} & \cdots & D_{0K} \\ D_{11} & D_{12} & \cdots & D_{1K} \\ & & \vdots & \\ D_{M1} & D_{M2} & \cdots & D_{MK} \end{bmatrix},
\end{array}
$$

where each row sums to 1, and now

$$0 \leq D_{ik} \leq 1.$$

Note that each row $(D_{i1}, D_{i2}, \ldots, D_{ik})$ is the probability distribution for the decision to be made when the system is in state i. As an example, suppose that a new policy, R_e, is to be used in the maintenance model. This is a randomized policy and is given by the matrix

$$
\begin{array}{cc}
 & \text{Decision, } k \\
 & \begin{array}{ccc} 1 & 2 & 3 \end{array} \\
\text{State} \begin{array}{c} 0 \\ 1 \\ 2 \\ 3 \end{array} &
\begin{bmatrix} 1 & 0 & 0 \\ 1 & 0 & 0 \\ \frac{1}{4} & \frac{1}{4} & \frac{1}{2} \\ 0 & \frac{1}{2} & \frac{1}{2} \end{bmatrix}.
\end{array}
$$

This policy calls for observing the state of the machine at the end of the day. If it is found to be in state 0 or 1, it is left as is. If it is found to be in state 2, it is left as is with probability ¼, overhauled with probability ¼, and replaced with probability ½. Presumably, a random device with these probabilities (possibly a table of random numbers) can be used to make the actual decision. Finally, if the machine is found to be in state 3, it is overhauled with probability ½ and replaced with probability ½.

The linear programming formulation is best expressed in terms of a variable y_{ik}, which is related to D_{ik} as follows. Let y_{ik} be the (steady state) unconditional probability that the system is in state i *and* decision k is made; that is,

$$y_{ik} = P\{\text{state} = i \text{ and decision} = k\}.$$

Note that y_{ik} can be interpreted as the steady-state probability of being in state i when operating under a given policy. From the rules of conditional probability,

$$y_{ik} = \pi_i D_{ik}.$$

Furthermore

$$\pi_i = \sum_{k=1}^{K} y_{ik},$$

so that

$$D_{ik} = \frac{y_{ik}}{\pi_i} = \frac{y_{ik}}{\sum_{k=1}^{K} y_{ik}}.$$

There exists several constraints on y_{ik}:

1. $\sum_{i=0}^{M} \pi_i = 1$, so that $\sum_{i=0}^{M} \sum_{k=1}^{K} y_{ik} = 1$.
2. From results on steady-state probabilities (see Sec. 8.22),
$$\pi_j = \sum_{i=0}^{M} \pi_i p_{ij}, \text{ so that } \sum_{k=1}^{K} y_{jk} = \sum_{i=0}^{M} \sum_{k=1}^{K} y_{ik} p_{ij}(k),\dagger \text{ for } j = 0, 1, \ldots, M.$$
3. $y_{ik} \geq 0$, $i = 0, 1, \ldots, M$ and $k = 1, 2, \ldots, K$.

The (long run) expected average cost per unit time is given by

$$E(C) = \sum_{i=0}^{M} \sum_{k=1}^{K} \pi_i C_{ik} D_{ik} = \sum_{i=0}^{M} \sum_{k=1}^{K} C_{ik} y_{ik}.$$

Hence the problem is to choose the y_{ik} that

$$\text{Minimizes } \sum_{i=0}^{M} \sum_{k=1}^{K} C_{ik} y_{ik},$$

subject to the constraints

(1) $$\sum_{i=0}^{M} \sum_{k=1}^{K} y_{ik} = 1$$

(2) $$\sum_{k=1}^{K} y_{jk} - \sum_{i=0}^{M} \sum_{k=1}^{K} y_{ik} p_{ij}(k) = 0, \text{ for } j = 0, 1, \ldots, M,$$

(3) $$y_{ik} \geq 0 \qquad i = 0, 1, \ldots, M;\ k = 1, 2, \ldots, K.$$

This is clearly a linear programming problem that can be solved by the simplex method. Once the y_{ik} are obtained, D_{ik} is easily found from

$$D_{ik} = \frac{y_{ik}}{\sum_{k=1}^{K} y_{ik}}.$$

The solution has some interesting properties. It will contain $(M+1)$ basic variables $y_{ik} \geq 0$ (there is one redundant constraint). It can be shown that $y_{ik} > 0$ for at least one $k = 1, \ldots, K$, for each $i = 0, 1, \ldots, M$. Therefore it follows that $y_{ik} > 0$ for only *one* k for each $i = 0, 1, \ldots, M$; that is, $D_{ik} = 0$ or 1. In other words, the optimal policy is deterministic rather than randomized. Finally, since there are $(M+2)$ functional constraints and $K(M+1)$ original variables, "practical" problems tend to be large under this formulation, so that solutions may not be obtainable even with the simplex method.

† The k is introduced in $p_{ij}(k)$ to indicate that the appropriate transition probability depends upon the decision k.

EXAMPLE As an example, the machine maintenance problem can be formulated as a linear program; i.e.,

$$\begin{aligned}\text{Minimize}\quad & 4{,}000y_{02} + 6{,}000y_{03} + 1{,}000y_{11} + 4{,}000y_{12} + 6{,}000y_{13} \\ & + 3{,}000y_{21} + 4{,}000y_{22} + 6{,}000y_{23} + M_1 y_{31} + M_2 y_{32} \\ & + 6{,}000y_{33},\end{aligned}$$

where M_1 and M_2 are taken to be large numbers,

subject to

$$\sum_{i=0}^{3}\sum_{k=1}^{3} y_{ik} = 1$$

$$\sum_{k=1}^{3} y_{0k} - (y_{03} + y_{13} + y_{23} + y_{33}) = 0$$

$$\sum_{k=1}^{3} y_{1k} - \left(\frac{7}{8}y_{01} + y_{02} + \frac{3}{4}y_{11} + y_{12} + y_{22} + y_{32}\right) = 0$$

$$\sum_{k=1}^{3} y_{2k} - \left(\frac{1}{16}y_{01} + \frac{1}{8}y_{11} + \frac{1}{2}y_{21}\right) = 0$$

$$\sum_{k=1}^{3} y_{3k} - \left(\frac{1}{16}y_{01} + \frac{1}{8}y_{11} + \frac{1}{2}y_{21} + y_{31}\right) = 0$$

and

$$y_{ik} \geq 0,\ i = 0, 1, 2, 3 \text{ and } k = 1, 2, 3.$$

This linear program can be solved by using the simplex method.

The results yield all y_{ik} equal to zero, except for $y_{01} = 2/21$, $y_{11} = 5/7$, $y_{22} = 2/21$, and $y_{33} = 2/21$. Note that these values are just the steady-state probabilities for policy R_b, which is now seen to be the optimal policy. The corresponding

$$D_{ik} = \frac{y_{ik}}{\sum_{k=1}^{3} y_{ik}}$$

are given by

$$D_{01} = D_{11} = D_{22} = D_{33} = 1,$$

and all the remaining $D_{ik} = 0$. This policy calls for leaving the machine as is when it is in state 0 or 1, overhauling it when in state 2, and replacing it when in state 3.

12.4 POLICY-IMPROVEMENT ALGORITHMS FOR FINDING OPTIMAL POLICIES

A second algorithm for finding optimal policies is given by a policy-improvement technique. The algorithm to be presented is useful in that it often leads to finding the optimal policy quickly and also is applicable under more general conditions than previously specified; e.g., under certain assumptions, the number of states may be countably infinite rather than finite.

Following the model of Sec. 12.2, and as a joint result of the current state i of the system, and the decision $d_i(R) = k$ when operating under policy R, two things occur. An (expected) cost C_{ik} is incurred, which depends upon only the observed state of the system and the decision made. The system moves to a new state j at the next observed time period, with transition probability given by $p_{ij}(k)$. If, in fact, a cost is incurred that depends upon both the initial and transited states, it is treated as follows. Denote by $q_{ij}(k)$ the (expected) cost incurred when the system is in state i and decision k is made, and then evolves to state j at the next observed time period. Then

$$C_{ik} = \sum_{j=0}^{M} q_{ij}(k)\, p_{ij}(k).$$

When a system operates as described above under policy R, it can be shown that there exist values $g(R)$, $v_0(R)$, $v_1(R)$, ..., $v_M(R)$ which satisfy

$$g(R) + v_i(R) = C_{ik} + \sum_{j=0}^{M} p_{ij}(k)\, v_j(R), \text{ for } i = 0, 1, 2, \ldots, M.$$

A heuristic justification for these relationships, and an interpretation for these values, are desirable. Denote by $v_i^n(R)$ the total expected cost of a system starting in state i (at the first observed time period) and evolving for n time periods. Then $v_i^n(R)$ consists of two components, namely, (1) C_{ik}, the cost incurred at the first observed time period as a result of the current state i and the decision $d_i(R) = k$ when operating under policy R and (2) $\sum_{j=0}^{M} p_{ij}(k) v_j^{n-1}(R)$, the total expected cost of the system evolving over the remaining $n - 1$ time periods. Thus the recursive equation

$$v_i^n(R) = C_{ik} + \sum_{j=0}^{M} P_{ij}(k) v_i^{n-1}(R),$$

for $i = 0, 1, 2, \ldots, M$ and $v_i^1(R) = C_{ik}$ for all i, is obtained. It is of interest to explore the behavior of the total expected cost $v_i^n(R)$ as n gets large. Now, it is known that the (long run) expected average cost *per unit time* following any policy R can be expressed as

$$g(R) = \sum_{i=0}^{M} \pi_i C_{ik},$$

which is independent of the starting state i. Hence $v_i^n(R)$ behaves approximately as $ng(R)$ for large n, and, in fact, can be expressed (neglecting certain fluctuations) as the sum of two components, one of which is independent of the initial state and one which depends upon it; that is,

$$v_i^n(R) \approx ng(R) + v_i(R),$$

where $v_i(R)$ can be interpreted as the effect on the total expected cost due to starting in state i. Thus

$$v_i^n(R) - v_j^n(R) \approx v_i(R) - v_j(R),$$

so that $v_i(R) - v_j(R)$ is a measure of the effect of starting in state i rather than state j.

Substituting this linear approximation for $v_i^n(R)$ (which is assumed to be valid for large n) into the recursive equation for $v_i^n(R)$ leads to

$$g(R) + v_i(R) = C_{ik} + \sum_{j=0}^{M} p_{ij}(k)v_j(R),$$

for $i = 0, 1, \ldots, R$, so that these values satisfy the expressed equations.

Note that there are $M + 1$ equations with $M + 2$ unknowns, so that one of these variables may be chosen arbitrarily. By convention, $v_M(R)$ will be chosen equal to zero. Therefore, by solving a system of linear equations, the (long run) expected average cost per unit time following policy R, $g(R)$, can be obtained. In principle, all policies can be enumerated, and that policy which minimizes $g(R)$ can be found. However, even for a moderate number of states and decisions this technique is cumbersome. Fortunately there exists an algorithm that can be used to evaluate policies and find the optimum one without complete enumeration. The algorithm begins by choosing an arbitrary policy R_1 and calculates the values of $g(R_1)$, $v_0(R_1)$, $v_1(R_1)$, $\ldots$, $v_{M-1}(R_1)$ [recall that $v_M(R_1)$ is chosen equal to zero]. This is called *value determination*. A "better" policy denoted by R_2, is then constructed. This is called *policy improvement*. Using the new policy R_2, the value-determination step is repeated. This continues until two successive iterations lead to identical policies, which signifies that the optimal policy has been obtained. In particular, the following steps are to be followed:

Step 1 Value determination For an arbitrarily chosen policy R_1, use $p_{ij}(k_1)$, C_{ik_1}, and $v_M(R_1) = 0$ to solve the set of $(M + 1)$ equations

$$g(R_1) = C_{ik_1} + \sum_{j=0}^{M} p_{ij}(k_1)v_j(R_1) - v_i(R_1),\ i = 0, 1, \ldots, M$$

for all $(M + 1)$ unknown values of $g(R_1)$, $v_0(R_1)$, $v_1(R_1)$, $\ldots$, $v_{M-1}(R_1)$.

Step 2 Policy improvement Using the current values of $v_i(R_1)$ computed for policy R_1, find the alternative policy R_2 such that, for each state i, $d_i(R_2) = k_2$ is the decision which makes

$$C_{ik_2} + \sum_{j=0}^{M} p_{ij}(k_2)v_j(R_1) - v_i(R_1)$$

a minimum. That is, for *each* state i, find the appropriate value of k_2 that

$$\underset{k_2 = 1, 2, \ldots, K}{\text{Minimizes}} \left\{C_{ik_2} + \sum_{j=0}^{M} p_{ij}(k_2)v_j(R_1) - v_i(R_1)\right\},$$

and then set $d_i(R_2)$ = minimizing value of k_2. This defines a new policy R_2.

If R_2 does not equal R_1, then return to step 1, using R_2 instead of R_1, and solve for $g(R_2)$, $v_0(R_2)$, $v_1(R_2), \ldots, v_{n-1}(R_2)$. Using these values, go to step 2 and find R_3. Continue in this fashion until two successive R's are found to be equal. When this occurs the optimal policy is achieved, and the algorithm terminates. In fact, it can be shown that

1. $$g(R_{j+1}) \leq g(R_j), \text{ for } j = 1, 2, \ldots,$$

and

2. The algorithm terminates with the optimal solution in a finite number of iterations.

EXAMPLE As an example of this algorithm, the maintenance model presented in Sec. 12.2 will be solved. Recall that the machine can be in one of four states: state 0, signifying the machine is as good as new; state 1, signifying the machine is operable—with minor deterioration; state 2, signifying the machine is operable—with major deterioration; and state 3, signifying the machine is inoperable. There exist three possible decisions: decision 1 implies leaving the machine as is; decision 2 implies overhaul, which returns it to state 1; and decision 3 implies replacement, which returns it to state 0. Each decision necessitates an action that affects the transition matrix, and there are costs C_{ik} associated with making decision k when the system is in state i. To find the optimal policy, step 1 of the algorithm calls for choosing a policy arbitrarily. Choose the policy that calls for replacement of the machine when it is found to be in state 3; otherwise, leave the machine as is. Denote this policy by R_1. The transition matrix for this policy is given by

State	*0*	*1*	*2*	*3*
0	0	$\frac{7}{8}$	$\frac{1}{16}$	$\frac{1}{16}$
1	0	$\frac{3}{4}$	$\frac{1}{8}$	$\frac{1}{8}$
2	0	0	$\frac{1}{2}$	$\frac{1}{2}$
3	1	0	0	0

The costs incurred following policy R_1 are given by

State	C_{ik_1}
0	0
1	1,000
2	3,000
3	6,000

With this policy, the value-determination step requires solving the following four equations simultaneously for $g(R_1)$, $v_0(R_1)$, $v_1(R_1)$, and $v_2(R_1)$ [recall that $v_3(R_1)$ is arbitrarily taken to be zero]:

$$g(R_1) = C_{0k_1} + \sum_{j=0}^{3} p_{0j}(k_1)v_j(R_1) - v_0(R_1)$$

$$g(R_1) = C_{1k_1} + \sum_{j=0}^{3} p_{1j}(k_1)v_j(R_1) - v_1(R_1)$$

$$g(R_1) = C_{2k_1} + \sum_{j=0}^{3} p_{2j}(k_1)v_j(R_1) - v_2(R_1)$$

$$g(R_1) = C_{3k_1} + \sum_{j=0}^{3} p_{3j}(k_1)v_j(R_1) - v_3(R_1),$$

or alternatively [with $v_3(R_1) = 0$],

$$g(R_1) = \qquad + \frac{7}{8}v_1(R_1) + \frac{1}{16}v_2(R_1) - v_0(R_1)$$

$$g(R_1) = 1{,}000 + \frac{3}{4}v_1(R_1) + \frac{1}{8}v_2(R_1) - v_1(R_1)$$

$$g(R_1) = 3{,}000 \qquad + \frac{1}{2}v_2(R_1) - v_2(R_1)$$

$$g(R_1) = 6{,}000 + v_0(R_1).$$

The simultaneous solution to this system of equations yields

$$g(R_1) = \frac{25{,}000}{13} = 1{,}923$$

$$v_0(R_1) = -\frac{53{,}000}{13} = -4{,}077$$

$$v_1(R_1) = -\frac{34{,}000}{13} = -2{,}615$$

$$v_2(R_1) = \frac{28{,}000}{13} = 2{,}154.$$

Step 2 can now be applied. It is necessary to find the "improved" policy R_2, which has the property that $d_0(R_2) = k_2^0$, $d_1(R_2) = k_2^1$, $d_2(R_2) = k_2^2$, and $d_3(R_2) = k_2^3$ minimize the following expressions:

(0) $C_{0k_2^0} - p_{00}(k_2^0)4{,}077 - p_{01}(k_2^0)2{,}615 + p_{02}(k_2^0)2{,}154 + 4{,}077$

(1) $C_{1k_2^1} - p_{10}(k_2^1)4{,}077 - p_{11}(k_2^1)2{,}615 + p_{12}(k_2^1)2{,}154 + 2{,}615$

(2) $C_{2k_2^2} - p_{20}(k_2^2)4{,}077 - p_{21}(k_2^2)2{,}615 + p_{22}(k_2^2)2{,}154 - 2{,}154$

(3) $C_{3k_2^3} - p_{30}(k_2^3)4{,}077 - p_{31}(k_2^3)2{,}615 + p_{32}(k_2^3)2{,}154.$

To find k_2^0, the "best" decision when the machine is in state 0, it is necessary to evaluate the first expression for all possible decisions. Note that the appropriate transition probabilities and the costs C_{0k} depend upon the decisions made. A summary of the necessary calculations follows:

Decision	$p_{00}(k_2)$	$p_{01}(k_2)$	$p_{02}(k_2)$	$p_{03}(k_2)$	C_{0k_2}	*Value of expression 0*
1	0	$\frac{7}{8}$	$\frac{1}{16}$	$\frac{1}{16}$	0	1,923
2	0	1	0	0	4,000	5,462
3	1	0	0	0	6,000	6,000

It is clear that $d_0(R_2) = k_2^0 = 1$ minimizes this first expression, so that under R_2 the appropriate decision when the system is in state 0 is to leave the machine as is.

Similar calculations are required to find $d_1(R_2) = k_2^1$, $d_2(R_2) = k_2^2$, and $d_3(R_2) = k_2^3$; these are summarized below.

State 1

Decision	$p_{10}(k_2)$	$p_{11}(k_2)$	$p_{12}(k_2)$	$p_{13}(k_2)$	C_{1k_2}	*Value of expression 1*
1	0	$\frac{3}{4}$	$\frac{1}{8}$	$\frac{1}{8}$	1,000	1,923
2	0	1	0	0	4,000	4,000
3	1	0	0	0	6,000	4,538

State 2

Decision	$p_{20}(k_2)$	$p_{21}(k_2)$	$p_{22}(k_2)$	$p_{23}(k_2)$	C_{2k_2}	*Value of expression 2*
1	0	0	$\frac{1}{2}$	$\frac{1}{2}$	3,000	1,923
2	0	1	0	0	4,000	−769
3	1	0	0	0	6,000	−231

State 3

Decision	$p_{30}(k_2)$	$p_{31}(k_2)$	$p_{32}(k_2)$	$p_{33}(k_2)$	C_{3k_2}	*Value of expression 3*
1	0	0	0	1	∞	∞
2	0	1	0	0	∞	∞
3	1	0	0	0	6,000	1,923

Thus $d_1(R_2) = k_2^1 = 1$, $d_2(R_2) = k_2^2 = 2$, and $d_3(R_2) = k_2^3 = 3$. Hence policy R_2 calls for leaving the machine alone when it is in state 0 or 1, overhauling it when it is in state 2, and replacing it when it is in state 3. Furthermore, since R_2 differs from R_1, at least one more iteration is required. The equations that must now be solved are given by [again setting $v_3(R_2) = 0$]

$$\begin{aligned}
g(R_2) &= \qquad\quad + \frac{7}{8}v_1(R_2) + \frac{1}{16}v_2(R_2) - v_0(R_2)\\
g(R_2) &= 1{,}000 \quad + \frac{3}{4}v_1(R_2) + \frac{1}{8}v_2(R_2) - v_1(R_2)\\
g(R_2) &= 4{,}000 \quad + v_1(R_2) \qquad\qquad - v_2(R_2)\\
g(R_2) &= 6{,}000 + v_0(R_1).
\end{aligned}$$

The simultaneous solution to these equations yields

$$\begin{aligned}
g(R_2) &= \frac{5{,}000}{3} = 1{,}667\\
v_0(R_2) &= -\frac{13{,}000}{3} = -4{,}333\\
v_1(R_2) &= \qquad -3{,}000\\
v_2(R_2) &= -\frac{2{,}000}{3} = -667
\end{aligned}$$

Step 2 can now be applied. An improved policy R_3 is sought which has the property that $d_0(R_3) = k_3^0$, $d_1(R_3) = k_3^1$, $d_2(R_3) = k_3^2$, and $d_3(R_3) = k_3^3$ minimizes the following expressions:

(0) $C_{0k_3{}^0} - p_{00}(k_3^0)4{,}333 - p_{01}(k_3^0)3{,}000 - p_{02}(k_3^0)667 + 4{,}333$

(1) $C_{1k_3{}^1} - p_{10}(k_3^1)4{,}333 - p_{11}(k_3^1)3{,}000 - p_{12}(k_3^1)667 + 3{,}000$

(2) $C_{2k_3{}^2} - p_{20}(k_3^2)4{,}333 - p_{21}(k_3^2)3{,}000 - p_{22}(k_3^2)667 + 667$

(3) $C_{3k_3{}^3} - p_{30}(k_3^3)4{,}333 - p_{31}(k_3^3)3{,}000 - p_{32}(k_3^3)667.$

The first iteration provides most of the necessary data (the transition probabilities and C_{ik}) required for determining the new policy, except for the values of each of the four expressions. These values are found to be

Decision	*Value of expression 0*	*Value of expression 1*	*Value of expression 2*	*Value of expression 3*
1	1,667	1,667	3,333	∞
2	5,333	4,000	1,667	∞
3	6,000	4,667	2,334	1,667

Thus $d_0(R_3) = k_3^0 = 1$, $d_1(R_3) = k_3^1 = 1$, $d_2(R_3) = k_3^2 = 2$, and $d_3(R_3) = k_3^3 = 3$, so that this policy is identical to R_2. Since the policies obtained on two successive iterations are the same, the optimal policy has been obtained. This optimal policy calls for leaving the machine as is when it is in state 0 or 1, overhauling it when it is in state 2, and replacing it when it is in state 3. Of course, this is the same result as found in Sec. 12.3.

12.5 CRITERION OF DISCOUNTED COSTS

Throughout this chapter policies were measured on the basis of (long run) expected average cost per unit time or (long run) actual average cost per unit time. An alternative measure is to find the expected long-run total discounted cost. A discount factor $\alpha < 1$ is specified, so that the present value of 1 unit of cost m periods in the future is α^m. α can be interpreted as equal to $1/(1 + i)$, where i is the current interest rate. This measure was used extensively in Chap. 11. A policy is sought that minimizes the expected long-run total discounted cost.

Policy-improvement Algorithm

The description of the Markovan decision process is as described previously. Given a distribution $P\{X_0 = i\}$ over the initial states of the system and a policy R, a system evolves over time according to the joint effect of the probabilistic laws of motion and the sequence of decisions made (actions taken). In particular, when the system is in state i and decision $d_i(R) = k$ is made, then the probability that the system is in state j at the next observed time period is given by $p_{ij}(k)$. Furthermore, a known (expected) cost C_{ik} is incurred. Denote by $V_i^n(R)$ the expected total discounted cost of a system starting in state i (at the first observed time period) and evolving for n time periods. Then $V_i^n(R)$ consists of two components, namely, (1) C_{ik}, the cost incurred at the first observed time period as a result of the current state i and the decision $d_i(R) = k$ when operating under policy R, and (2) $\alpha \sum_{j=0}^{M} p_{ij}(k)\, V_j^{n-1}(R)$, the expected total discounted cost of the system evolving over the remaining $n - 1$ time periods. Thus the recursive equation

$$V_i^n(R) = C_{ik} + \alpha \sum_{j=0}^{M} p_{ij}(k) V_j^{n-1}(R),$$

for $i = 0, 1, 2, \ldots, M$ and $V_i^1(R) = C_{ik}$ for all i, is obtained. This policy can be evaluated by using the techniques associated with dynamic programming. It can be shown that as n approaches infinity, this expression converges to

$$V_i(R) = C_{ik} + \alpha \sum_{j=0}^{M} p_{ij}(k) V_j(R), \text{ for } i = 0, 1, \ldots, M,$$

where $V_i(R)$ can now be interpreted as the expected long-run total discounted cost for a system starting in state i and continuing indefinitely. There are $M + 1$ equations and $M + 1$ unknowns, and hence $V_i(R)$ may be obtained by standard methods. For example, the machine-maintenance model will be solved by using the policy which calls for leaving the machine as is when in state 0 and 1, overhauling it when it is in state 2, and replacing it when it is in state 3, that is, policy R_b. The discount factor will be chosen to be $\alpha = 0.9$. The following set of equations is obtained:

$$V_0(R) = \qquad +0.9\left[\frac{7}{8}V_1(R) + \frac{1}{16}V_2(R) + \frac{1}{16}V_3(R)\right]$$

$$V_1(R) = 1{,}000 + 0.9\left[\frac{3}{4}V_1(R) + \frac{1}{8}V_2(R) + \frac{1}{8}V_3(R)\right]$$

$$V_2(R) = 4{,}000 + 0.9\,[\qquad V_1(R) \qquad]$$

$$V_3(R) = 6{,}000 + 0.9\,[V_0(R) \qquad].$$

The simultaneous solution to this system of equations yields

$$V_0(R) = 14{,}949$$
$$V_1(R) = 16{,}262$$
$$V_2(R) = 18{,}636$$
$$V_3(R) = 19{,}454.$$

Thus, assuming that the system started in state 0, the expected long-run total discounted cost is \$14,949.

The aforementioned procedure not only evaluates a given policy but is also suggestive of an algorithm to determine the optimal policy. The calculations are similar to those required in the value-determination step (step 1) of the policy-improvement technique presented in Sec. 12.4. Indeed, an algorithm very similar to that presented in Sec. 12.4 is available. In particular, the following steps are to be followed:

Step 1 Value determination For an arbitrarily chosen policy R_1, use $p_{ij}(k_1)$ and C_{ik_1} to solve the set of $(M+1)$ equations

$$V_i(R_1) = C_{ik_1} + \alpha \sum_{j=0}^{M} p_{ij}(k_1)V_j(R_1), \; i = 0, 1, \ldots, M$$

for all $(M+1)$ unknown values of $V_i(R_1)$.

Step 2 Policy improvement Using the current values of $V_i(R_1)$, find the alternative policy R_2 such that, for each state i, $d_i(R_2) = k_2$ is the decision that makes

$$C_{ik_2} + \alpha \sum_{j=0}^{M} p_{ij}(k_2)V_j(R_1)$$

a minimum. That is, for *each* state i, find the appropriate value of k_2 that

$$\underset{k_2=1,2,\ldots,K}{\text{Minimizes}} \left\{C_{ik_2} + \alpha \sum_{j=0}^{M} p_{ij}(k_2)V_j(R_1)\right\},$$

and then set $d_i(R_2)$ = minimizing value of k_2. This defines a new policy R_2.

If R_2 does not equal R_1, then return to step 1 by using R_2 instead of R_1, and solve for $V_i(R_2)$, $i = 0, 1, \ldots, M$. Using these values, go to step 2 and find R_3. Continue in this fashion until two successive R's are found to be equal. When this occurs, the optimal policy is achieved, and the algorithm terminates. In fact, it can be shown that

1. $V_i(R_{j+1}) \leq V_i(R_j)$, for $i = 0, 1, \ldots, M$ and $j = 1, 2, \ldots,$

2. The algorithm terminates with the optimal solution in a finite number of iterations,

and

3. The algorithm is valid without the assumptions that the Markov chain associated with every transition matrix is irreducible.

Example As an example, the optimal policy for the machine-maintenance problem will be obtained. The discount factor is chosen to be 0.9. The first step, the value-determination step, has already been carried out earlier in this section if the arbitrary policy chosen, R_1, calls for leaving the machine as is when it is in state 0 or 1, overhauling it when it is in state 2, and replacing it when it is in state 3. The appropriate V's are

$$V_0(R_1) = 14{,}949$$

$$V_1(R_1) = 16{,}262$$

$$V_2(R_1) = 18{,}636$$

$$V_3(R_1) = 19{,}454.$$

Step 2 can now be applied. An improved policy R_2 is sought which has the property that $d_0(R_2) = k_2^0$, $d_1(R_2) = k_2^1$, $d_2(R_2) = k_2^2$, and $d_3(R_2) = k_2^3$ minimizes the following expressions:

(0) $C_{0k_2^0} + 0.9[p_{00}(k_2^0)14{,}949 + p_{01}(k_2^0)16{,}262 + p_{02}(k_2^0)18{,}636 + p_{03}(k_2^0)19{,}454]$

(1) $C_{1k_2^1} + 0.9[p_{10}(k_2^1)14{,}949 + p_{11}(k_2^1)16{,}262 + p_{12}(k_2^1)18{,}636 + p_{13}(k_2^1)19{,}454]$

(2) $C_{2k_2^2} + 0.9[p_{20}(k_2^2)14{,}949 + p_{21}(k_2^2)16{,}262 + p_{22}(k_2^2)18{,}636 + p_{23}(k_2^2)19{,}454]$

(3) $C_{3k_2^3} + 0.9[p_{30}(k_2^3)14{,}949 + p_{31}(k_2^3)16{,}262 + p_{32}(k_2^3)18{,}636 + p_{33}(k_2^3)19{,}454]$.

Most of the necessary data can be taken from the first iteration of the example in Sec. 12.4 (the transition probabilities and C_{ik}). Using these data, the values of each of the four expressions are obtained below.

Decision	*Value of expression 0*	*Value of expression 1*	*Value of expression 2*	*Value of expression 3*
1	14,949	16,262	20,140	∞
2	18,636	18,636	18,636	∞
3	19,454	19,454	19,454	19,454

Thus $d_0(R_2) = k_2^0 = 1$, $d_1(R_2) = k_2^1 = 1$, $d_2(R_2) = k_2^2 = 2$, and $d_3(R_2) = k_2^3 = 3$, so that this policy is identical to R_1. Since the policies obtained on two successive iterations are the same, the optimal policy has been obtained. Again, the optimal policy calls for leaving the machine as is when it is in state 0 or 1, overhauling it when it is in state 2, and replacing it when it is in state 3—the same policy that was obtained by using the long-run expected average cost per day criterion.

Linear Programming Formulation

Just as there is a policy-improvement algorithm for the expected long-run total discounted cost criterion, there is also a linear programming formulation. The statement of the linear programming problem is to choose the y_{ik} that

$$\text{Minimizes} \quad \sum_{i=0}^{M} \sum_{k=1}^{K} C_{ik}\, y_{ik},$$

subject to the constraints

1. $$\sum_{k=1}^{K} y_{jk} - \alpha \sum_{i=0}^{M} \sum_{k=1}^{K} y_{ik}\, p_{ij}(k) = \beta_j, \text{ for } j = 0, 1, \ldots, M,$$

where β_j are given constants such that $\beta_j > 0$ and $\sum_{j=0}^{M} \beta_j = 1$,

2. $$y_{ik} \geq 0,\ i = 0, 1, \ldots, M;\ k = 1, 2, \ldots, K.$$

As in Sec. 12.4, the D_{ik} are related to the y_{ik} and, in fact, again

$$P\{\text{decision} = k \mid \text{state} = i\} = D_{ik} = \frac{y_{ik}}{\sum_{k=1}^{K} y_{ik}}.$$

The y_{ik} can be interpreted as a weighted (in a discounted sense) average of the probability of being in state i and making decision k, when $P\{X_0 = j\} = \beta_j$; that is, if

$$z_{ik} = P\{\text{state} = i \text{ and decision} = k\},$$

then

$$y_{ik} = z_{ik} + \alpha z_{ik} + \alpha^2 z_{ik} + \alpha^3 z_{ik} + \cdots = \frac{z_{ik}}{(1-\alpha)}.$$

Again, it can be shown that the optimal policy is deterministic, that is, $D_{ik} = 0$ or 1. Furthermore, the technique is valid without the assumption that the Markov chain associated with every transition matrix is irreducible.

EXAMPLE Returning to the machine-maintenance model (with $\alpha = 0.9$), the linear program can be formulated as

$$\begin{aligned} \text{Minimize} \quad & 4{,}000y_{02} + 6{,}000y_{03} + 1{,}000y_{11} + 4{,}000y_{12} + 6{,}000y_{13} \\ & + 3{,}000y_{21} + 4{,}000y_{22} + 6{,}000y_{23} + M_1 y_{31} + M_2 y_{32} + 6{,}000y_{33}, \end{aligned}$$

where M_1 and M_2 are taken to be large numbers,

subject to

$$\sum_{k=1}^{3} y_{0k} - 0.9(y_{03} + y_{13} + y_{23} + y_{33}) = \frac{1}{4}$$

$$\sum_{k=1}^{3} y_{1k} - 0.9\left(\frac{7}{8} y_{01} + y_{02} + \frac{3}{4} y_{11} + y_{12} + y_{22} + y_{32}\right) = \frac{1}{4}$$

$$\sum_{k=1}^{3} y_{2k} - 0.9\left(\frac{1}{16} y_{01} + \frac{1}{8} y_{11} + \frac{1}{2} y_{21}\right) = \frac{1}{4}$$

$$\sum_{k=1}^{3} y_{3k} - 0.9\left(\frac{1}{16} y_{01} + \frac{1}{8} y_{11} + \frac{1}{2} y_{21} + y_{31}\right) = \frac{1}{4}$$

and

$$y_{ik} \geq 0, i = 0, 1, 2, 3; k = 1, 2, 3,$$

where $\beta_0, \beta_1, \beta_2, \beta_3$ are arbitrarily chosen to be ¼.

The optimal solution yields all y_{ik} equal to zero, except for $y_{01} = 1.210$, $y_{11} = 6.656$, $y_{22} = 1.067$, and $y_{33} = 1.067$. The corresponding

$$D_{ik} = \frac{y_{ik}}{\sum_{k=1}^{3} y_{ik}}$$

are given by $D_{01} = D_{11} = D_{22} = D_{33} = 1$, and all the remaining $D_{ik} = 0$. This solution is the same as that obtained earlier in this section and calls for leaving the machine as is when it is in state 0 or 1, overhauling it when it is in state 2, and replacing it when it is in state 3. The minimizing value of the objective function is \$17,325 and is seen to be related to the V's of the optimal policy found in the discussion of the discounted cost policy-improvement algorithm. Because $P\{X_0 = j\}$ was chosen to equal ¼ for all j,

$$17{,}325 = \frac{1}{4}[V_0(R) + V_1(R) + V_2(R) + V_3(R)]$$

$$= \frac{1}{4}[14{,}949 + 16{,}262 + 18{,}636 + 19{,}454].$$

Finite-period Markovian Decision Processes and the Method of Successive Approximations

Chapter 6 introduced the concept of dynamic programming and characterized deterministic dynamic programming problems and their solution. Many of these concepts have analogous interpretations with Markovian decision processes. In particular, suppose one seeks the expected total discounted cost of a system starting in state i and evolving for n time periods when an optimal policy is followed. Note that a finite number of time periods is now being considered. This problem is analogous to deterministic dynamic programming, except that the Markov system evolves according to some probabilistic laws of motion rather than evolving in a deterministic fashion. The deterministic dynamic programming solution is suggestive of the solution to this "probabilistic" dynamic programming problem. Denote by V_i^n the expected total discounted cost of a system starting in state i and evolving for n time periods when an optimal policy is followed.[1] Using the "principle of optimization," it follows that this cost function satisfies the recursive relationship

$$V_i^{n+1} = \min_k \left\{ C_{ik} + \alpha \sum_{j=0}^{M} p_{ij}(k) V_j^n \right\}, \; i = 0, 1, \ldots, M.$$

Using this recursive relationship, the solution procedure moves backward period by period—each time finding the optimal policy for that period model—until it finds the optimal policy for the original problem. In particular, it is usually assumed that $V_0^0, V_1^0, \ldots, V_M^0$ is zero, so that V_i^1 can be obtained from

$$V_i^1 = \min_k \{C_{ik}\}, \; i = 0, 1, \ldots, M,$$

with the corresponding optimal decisions becoming known. If this optimal policy is followed, V_i^1 is the minimum expected total discounted cost of a system starting in state i and evolving for one time period.

The V_i^2 can now be obtained from

$$V_i^2 = \min_k \left\{ C_{ik} + \alpha \sum_{j=0}^{M} p_{ij}(k) V_j^1 \right\}, \; i = 0, 1, \ldots, M,$$

with the corresponding optimal decisions becoming known. If this optimal policy is followed, V_i^2 is the minimum expected total discounted cost of a system starting in state i and evolving for two time periods.

In a similar manner, the V_i^T can be obtained from

$$V_i^T = \min_k \left\{ C_{ik} + \alpha \sum_{j=0}^{M} p_{ij}(k) V_j^{T-1} \right\}, \; i = 0, 1, \ldots, M,$$

with the corresponding optimal decisions becoming known. If this optimal policy is followed, V_i^T is the minimum expected total discounted cost of a system starting in state i and evolving for T time periods. Thus, solving a five-period problem requires solving the four-, three-, two-, and one-period problems also. An example of a three-period version of the machine-maintenance model will be solved later in this section. It should be noted that α can be set equal to 1 (no discounting) for finite-period problems, in which case the cost criterion becomes the expected total cost.

[1] This notation V_i^n for cost is now being used instead of the notation introduced in Chap. 6 to be consistent with the material introduced in the current chapter. In accordance with the notation of Chap. 6, the subscript (i) is the state variable, and the superscript (n) is equivalent to the stage, except that the stage is now measured by the system having "n periods to go" rather than being in period n. This change is due to the need to also treat the infinite-period problem.

Until now this section has dealt with a finite-period version of a Markov decision process. When the criterion of discounted costs is utilized, it can be shown that the V_i^n converges to V_i as n approaches infinity, where V_i is the expected (long run) total discounted cost of a system starting in state i and continuing indefinitely when an *optimal* policy is followed and satisfies

$$V_i = \min_k \left\{ C_{ik} + \alpha \sum_{j=0}^{M} p_{ij}(k) V_j \right\}, \; i = 0, 1, \ldots, M.$$

Furthermore, the optimal policy is obtained by making the appropriate decisions so as to minimize the right-hand side of the above equation. This solution is, indeed, the solution to the Markov decision process considered throughout earlier sections of this chapter.

Finding V_i and the corresponding optimal decisions is generally difficult, but it is relatively simple to approximate V_i and obtain the corresponding policy. This is what the *method of successive approximations* does. It utilizes the recursive relationship of the finite-period problem presented earlier; that is,

$$V_i^{n+1} = \min_k \left\{ C_{ik} + \alpha \sum_{j=0}^{M} p_{ij}(k) V_j^n \right\}.$$

The first step is to arbitrarily choose a set of values, $V_0^0, V_1^0, V_2^0, \ldots, V_M^0$, usually taken to be zero, as will be assumed from here on in. Using the expression for V_i^{n+1}, V_i^1 can be obtained from

$$V_i^1 = \min_k \{C_{ik}\}, \; i = 0, 1, \ldots, M$$

with the corresponding decisions becoming known. This can be viewed as the first approximation to the optimal policy, and as noted earlier the V_i^1 can be interpreted as the expected total discounted cost of a system starting in state i and evolving for one period when an optimal policy is followed.

The next iteration uses the $V_0^1, V_1^1, V_2^1, \ldots, V_M^1$ found from the previous step. From the recurrence relationship presented, V_i^2 can be obtained from

$$V_i^2 = \min_k \left\{ C_{ik} + \alpha \sum_{j=0}^{M} p_{ij}(k) V_j^1 \right\},$$

with the corresponding decisions becoming known. This policy can be viewed as the second approximation to the optimal policy, and as noted earlier the V_i^2 can be interpreted as the expected total discounted cost of a system starting in state i and evolving for two periods when an optimal policy is followed.

Further iterations can be obtained by using the recursive relationship. For the Tth iteration, V_i^T can be interpreted as the expected total discounted cost of a system starting in state i and evolving for T periods when an optimal policy is followed. The number T can be made large, and V_i^T will become "close" to the optimal expected long-run total discounted cost, and for sufficiently large T the optimal policy will be obtained. However, there is no procedure for deciding when to terminate the method of successive approximations. A check can be made at any time to see if the current iteration satisfies the policy-improvement equations, which would signify that an optimal procedure has been obtained.

Although the method of successive approximations may not lead to an optimal policy (using a finite number of iterations), it has one distinct advantage over the policy-improvement and linear programming techniques, namely, it never requires the solution of a system of simultaneous equations, and hence each iteration can be performed simply and quickly.

EXAMPLE As an example of the method of successive approximations, the machine maintenance model will be solved ($\alpha = 0.9$). Let $V_0^0 = V_1^0 = V_2^0 = V_3^0 = 0$. Then

$$V_0^1 = \min_k \{C_{0k}\} = 0 \qquad (k = 1)$$

$$V_1^1 = \min_k \{C_{1k}\} = 1{,}000 \ (k = 1)$$

$$V_2^1 = \min_k \{C_{2k}\} = 3{,}000 \ (k = 1)$$

$$V_3^1 = \min_k \{C_{3k}\} = 6{,}000 \ (k = 3).$$

Thus the first approximation calls for making decision 1 (leave the machine alone) when the system is in state 0, 1, or 2. When the system is in state 3, decision 3 (replace) is made.

The second iteration leads to

$$V_0^2 = \min\left\{0 + 0.9\left[\frac{7}{8}(1{,}000) + \frac{1}{16}(3{,}000) + \frac{1}{16}(6{,}000)\right],\right.$$
$$\left. 4{,}000 + 0.9[1(1{,}000)],\ 6{,}000 + 0.9[1(0)]\right\} = 1{,}294 \ (k = 1)$$

$$V_1^2 = \min\left\{1{,}000 + 0.9\left[\frac{3}{4}(1{,}000) + \frac{1}{8}(3{,}000) + \frac{1}{8}(6{,}000)\right],\right.$$
$$\left. 4{,}000 + 0.9[1(1{,}000)],\ 6{,}000 + 0.9[1(0)]\right\} = 2{,}688 \ (k = 1)$$

$$V_2^2 = \min\left\{3{,}000 + 0.9\left[\frac{1}{2}(3{,}000) + \frac{1}{2}(6{,}000)\right],\right.$$
$$\left. 4{,}000 + 0.9[1(1{,}000)],\ 6{,}000 + 0.9[1(0)]\right\} = 4{,}900 \ (k = 2)$$

$$V_3^2 = 6{,}000 + 0.9[1(0)] = 6{,}000 \ (k = 3).$$

Thus the second approximation calls for leaving the machine as is when it is in state 0 or 1, overhauling it when it is in state 2, and replacing it when it is in state 3. Note that this is the optimal policy, even though the optimal cost has not been obtained.

The third iteration leads to

$$V_0^3 = \min\left\{0 + 0.9\left[\frac{7}{8}(2{,}688) + \frac{1}{16}(4{,}900) + \frac{1}{16}(6{,}000)\right],\right.$$

$$\left.4{,}000 + 0.9[1(2{,}688)],\ 6{,}000 + 0.9[1(1{,}294)]\right\} = 2{,}730\ (k = 1)$$

$$V_1^3 = \min\left\{1{,}000 + 0.9\left[\frac{3}{4}(2{,}688) + \frac{1}{8}(4{,}900) + \frac{1}{8}(6{,}000)\right],\right.$$

$$\left.4{,}000 + 0.9[1(2{,}688)],\ 6{,}000 + 0.9[1(1{,}294)]\right\} = 4{,}041\ (k = 1)$$

$$V_2^3 = \min\left\{3{,}000 + 0.9\left[\frac{1}{2}(4{,}900) + \frac{1}{2}(6{,}000)\right],\right.$$

$$\left.4{,}000 + 0.9[1(2{,}688)],\ 6{,}000 + 0.9[1(1{,}294)]\right\} = 6{,}419\ (k = 2)$$

$$V_3^3 = \qquad 6{,}000 + 0.9[1(1{,}294)] = 7{,}165\ (k = 3).$$

Again the optimal policy is achieved, and the costs are getting closer to those of the optimal policy. This procedure can be continued, and V_0^n, V_1^n, V_2^n, and V_3^n will converge to 14,949, 16,262, 18,636, and 19,454, respectively. It should be noted that termination of the method of successive approximations after the second iteration would have resulted in an optimal policy, although there is no way to know this without solving the problem by other methods.

As indicated earlier, the method of successive approximation solves a finite-period Markovian decision problem. In particular, the optimal solution to the one-period machine maintenance model calls for leaving the machine alone when it is in state 0, 1, or 2, and replacing it when it is in state 3. The minimum expected total discounted cost of the system starting in state i, $i = 0$, 1, 2, 3, and evolving for one period is given by 0, 1,000, 3,000, and 6,000, respectively. The optimal solution to the two-period machine maintenance model is

Period 1 Leave machine alone when in state 0 or 1.
Overhaul machine when in state 2.
Replace machine when in state 3.

Period 2 Leave machine alone when in state 0, 1, 2.
Replace machine when in state 3.

The minimum expected total discounted cost of the system starting in state i, $i = 0, 1, 2, 3$, and evolving for two periods is given by 1,294, 2,688, 4,900, 6,000, respectively. Finally, the optimal solution to the three period model is

Period 1 Leave machine alone when in state 0 or 1.
and Overhaul machine when in state 2.
Period 2 Replace when in state 3.

Period 3 Leave machine alone when in state 0, 1, or 2.
Replace when in state 3.

The minimum expected total discounted costs over three periods, if the system starts in state i, $i = 0, 1, 2, 3$, are given by 2,730, 4,041, 6,419, 7,165, respectively.

12.6 A WATER-RESOURCE MODEL

A multipurpose dam is used for generating electric power as well as for flood control. The capacity of the dam is 3 units. The probability distribution of the quantity of water, W_t, that flows into the dam during month t (for $t = 0, 1, \ldots$) is given by $P_W(m)$, where

$$P_W(0) = P\{W = 0\} = \frac{1}{6}$$

$$P_W(1) = P\{W = 1\} = \frac{1}{3}$$

$$P_W(2) = P\{W = 2\} = \frac{1}{3}$$

$$P_W(3) = P\{W = 3\} = \frac{1}{6}.$$

For the purpose of generating electric power, 1 unit of water is required. At the beginning of each month water is released from the dam. The first unit is used to generate the electric power and then used for irrigation purposes, the latter function being worth \$100,000. If additional units are released, they can also be used for irrigation purposes, and each unit is worth \$100,000. If the dam contains less than 1 unit at the beginning of a month, additional power must be purchased at a cost of \$300,000. If at any time the water in the dam exceeds the capacity of 3 units, the excess water is released through the spillways at no cost or gain.

A release policy is sought. Policies are to be compared on the basis of expected discounted cost, with discount factor $\alpha = 0.99$. The policy-improvement algorithm will be used.

Let X_t denote the amount of water in the dam at time t. Then $X_t = 0, 1, 2, 3$. The "natural laws of motion" for this system (no water released) is given by the transition matrix

State	0	1	2	3
0	$\frac{1}{6}$	$\frac{1}{3}$	$\frac{1}{3}$	$\frac{1}{6}$
1	0	$\frac{1}{6}$	$\frac{1}{3}$	$\frac{1}{2}$
2	0	0	$\frac{1}{6}$	$\frac{5}{6}$
3	0	0	0	1

For example, the element in the second row and fourth column, p_{13}, is obtained as follows: If the dam contains 1 unit of water now, then for it to contain 3 units of water a month later, 2 or 3 units of water must flow into the dam during the month (recall that dam capacity is 3 units, so that a flow of 3 units will result in 1 unit being released through the spillways). This occurs with probability $\frac{1}{3} + \frac{1}{6} = \frac{1}{2}$.

There are three possible decisions that can be made at the beginning of each month:

Decision	Action
1	Release 1 unit
2	Release 2 units
3	Release 3 units

It is clear that releasing no units is not a sensible action because 1 unit is needed for electric power generation anyway. Thus a policy calls for determining how many units to release as a function of the quantity of water found in the dam. A typical policy R_1 might call for releasing all the water in the dam if it contains 0, 1, or 2 units, and releasing 2 units if it contains 3 units. The resultant transition matrix is given by

State	0	1	2	3
0	$\frac{1}{6}$	$\frac{1}{3}$	$\frac{1}{3}$	$\frac{1}{6}$
1	$\frac{1}{6}$	$\frac{1}{3}$	$\frac{1}{3}$	$\frac{1}{6}$
2	$\frac{1}{6}$	$\frac{1}{3}$	$\frac{1}{3}$	$\frac{1}{6}$
3	0	$\frac{1}{6}$	$\frac{1}{3}$	$\frac{1}{2}$

Of course, a policy that calls for releasing 3 units when there is only 1 unit in the dam is to be interpreted as calling for releasing all the available water. Necessary cost information can be obtained from the following data:

State	*Decision*	*Cost (in hundred thousand)*
0	1	3
	2	3
	3	3
1	1	−1
	2	−1
	3	−1
2	1	−1
	2	−2
	3	−2
3	1	−1
	2	−2
	3	−3

The policy R_1 will be used in the value-determination step (step 1) of the policy-improvement algorithm. Using the cost information given earlier, the values of C_{ik_1} are

$$C_{0k_1} = 3$$
$$C_{1k_1} = -1$$
$$C_{2k_1} = -2$$
$$C_{3k_1} = -2.$$

The following four equations must be solved:

$$V_0(R_1) = 3 + 0.99\left[\frac{1}{6}V_0(R_1) + \frac{1}{3}V_1(R_1) + \frac{1}{3}V_2(R_1) + \frac{1}{6}V_3(R_1)\right]$$

$$V_1(R_1) = -1 + 0.99\left[\frac{1}{6}V_0(R_1) + \frac{1}{3}V_1(R_1) + \frac{1}{3}V_2(R_1) + \frac{1}{6}V_3(R_1)\right]$$

$$V_2(R_1) = -2 + 0.99\left[\frac{1}{6}V_0(R_1) + \frac{1}{3}V_1(R_1) + \frac{1}{3}V_2(R_1) + \frac{1}{6}V_3(R_1)\right]$$

$$V_3(R_1) = -2 + 0.99\left[\qquad \frac{1}{6}V_1(R_1) + \frac{1}{3}V_2(R_1) + \frac{1}{2}V_3(R_1)\right]$$

The simultaneous solution of these equations results in the values $V_0(R_1) = -103.881$, $V_1(R_1) = -107.881$, $V_2(R_1) = -108.881$, and $V_3(R_1) = -110.358$.

Step 2 can now be applied. An improved policy R_2 is sought which has the property that $d_0(R_2) = k_2^0$, $d_1(R_2) = k_2^1$, $d_2(R_2) = k_2^2$, and $d_3(R_2) = k_2^3$ minimizes the following expressions:

$$(0)\quad C_{0k_2{}^0} + 0.99[-103.881p_{00}(k_2^0) - 107.881p_{01}(k_2^0) - 108.881p_{02}(k_2^0) - 110.358p_{03}(k_2^0)]$$

(1) $C_{1k_2^1} + 0.99[-103.881p_{10}(k_2^1) - 107.881p_{11}(k_2^1) - 108.881p_{12}(k_2^1) - 110.358p_{13}(k_2^1)]$

(2) $C_{2k_2^2} + 0.99[-103.881p_{20}(k_2^2) - 107.881p_{21}(k_2^2) - 108.881p_{22}(k_2^2) - 110.358p_{23}(k_2^2)]$

(3) $C_{3k_2^3} + 0.99[-103.881p_{30}(k_2^3) - 107.881p_{31}(k_2^3) - 108.881p_{32}(k_2^3) - 110.358p_{33}(k_2^3)]$.

To find k_2^0, the best decision when the system is in state 0, it is necessary to evaluate the first expression for all possible decisions. It is clear that when the system is in state 0 (dam empty) there is no choice among the decisions because they all are equivalent. The data for the necessary calculations for evaluating expression (0) follow:

State 0

Decision	$p_{00}(k_2)$	$p_{01}(k_2)$	$p_{02}(k_2)$	$p_{03}(k_2)$	C_{0k_2}	*Total value of expression 0*
1, 2, 3	$\frac{1}{6}$	$\frac{1}{3}$	$\frac{1}{3}$	$\frac{1}{6}$	3	−103.881

Similarly, for state 1 there is no choice among the decisions because they are all equivalent. The data for the necessary calculations for evaluating follow:

State 1

Decision	$p_{10}(k_2)$	$p_{11}(k_2)$	$p_{12}(k_2)$	$p_{13}(k_2)$	C_{1k_2}	*Total value of expression 1*
1, 2, 3	$\frac{1}{6}$	$\frac{1}{3}$	$\frac{1}{3}$	$\frac{1}{6}$	−1	−107.881

For the remaining two states, the appropriate transition probabilities and costs generally depend upon the decisions made. The data for the necessary calculations for finding the best decisions, given the dam is in states 2 and 3, follow:

State 2

Decision	$p_{20}(k_2)$	$p_{21}(k_2)$	$p_{22}(k_2)$	$p_{23}(k_2)$	C_{2k_2}	*Total value of expression 2*
1	0	$\frac{1}{6}$	$\frac{1}{3}$	$\frac{1}{2}$	−1	−109.358
2, 3	$\frac{1}{6}$	$\frac{1}{3}$	$\frac{1}{3}$	$\frac{1}{6}$	−2	−108.881

State 3

Decision	$p_{30}(k_2)$	$p_{31}(k_2)$	$p_{32}(k_2)$	$p_{33}(k_2)$	C_{3k_2}	Total value of expression 3
1	0	0	$\frac{1}{6}$	$\frac{5}{6}$	−1	−110.011
2	0	$\frac{1}{6}$	$\frac{1}{3}$	$\frac{1}{2}$	−2	−110.358
3	$\frac{1}{6}$	$\frac{1}{3}$	$\frac{1}{3}$	$\frac{1}{6}$	−3	−109.881

Thus $d_0(R_2) = k_2^0 = d_1(R_2) = k_2^1 = 1$, 2, or 3; $d_2(R_2) = k_2^2 = 1$, and $d_3(R_2) = k_2^3 = 2$. Hence policy R_2 calls for releasing all the water when there is 1 unit in the dam, 1 unit of water when there are 2 units available in the dam, and 2 units when there are 3 units available in the dam. This policy differs from R_1, so that another iteration is required. For the value-determination step, the equations that must now be solved are

$$V_0(R_2) = 3 + 0.99\left[\frac{1}{6}V_0(R_2) + \frac{1}{3}V_1(R_2) + \frac{1}{3}V_2(R_2) + \frac{1}{6}V_3(R_2)\right]$$

$$V_1(R_2) = -1 + 0.99\left[\frac{1}{6}V_0(R_2) + \frac{1}{3}V_1(R_2) + \frac{1}{3}V_2(R_2) + \frac{1}{6}V_3(R_2)\right]$$

$$V_2(R_2) = -1 + 0.99\left[\frac{1}{6}V_1(R_2) + \frac{1}{3}V_2(R_2) + \frac{1}{2}V_3(R_2)\right]$$

$$V_3(R_2) = -2 + 0.99\left[\frac{1}{6}V_1(R_2) + \frac{1}{3}V_2(R_2) + \frac{1}{2}V_3(R_2)\right].$$

The simultaneous solution of these equations results in the values $V_0(R_2) = -119.642$, $V_1(R_2) = -123.642$, $V_2(R_2) = -125.119$, and $V_3(R_2) = -126.119$.

Step 2 can now be applied. An improved policy R_3 is sought which has the property that $d_0(R_3) = k_3^0$, $d_1(R_3) = k_3^1$, $a_2(R_3) = k_3^2$, and $d_3(R_3) = k_3^3$ minimizes the following expressions:

(0) $C_{0k_3^0} + 0.99[-119.642p_{00}(k_3^0) - 123.642p_{01}(k_3^0) - 125.119p_{02}(k_3^0) - 126.119p_{03}(k_3^0)]$

(1) $C_{1k_3^1} + 0.99[-119.642p_{10}(k_3^1) - 123.642p_{11}(k_3^1) - 125.119p_{12}(k_3^1) - 126.119p_{13}(k_3^1)]$

(2) $C_{2k_3^2} + 0.99[-119.642p_{20}(k_3^2) - 123.642p_{21}(k_3^2) - 125.119p_{22}(k_3^2) - 126.119p_{23}(k_3^2)]$

(3) $C_{3k_3^3} + 0.99[-119.642p_{30}(k_3^3) - 123.642p_{31}(k_3^3) - 125.119p_{32}(k_3^3) - 126.119p_{33}(k_3^3)]$.

The data on the transition matrices and the costs from the previous iteration can again be used; the resulting values of the expression are

Decision	Value of expression (0)	Value of expression (1)	Value of expression (2)	Value of expression (3)
1	−119.642	−123.642	−125.119	−125.693
2	−119.642	−123.642	−124.642	−126.119
3	−119.642	−123.642	−124.642	−125.642

Thus $d_0(R_3) = k_3^0 = d_1(R_3) = k_3^1 = 1$, 2, or 3; $d_2(R_3) = k_3^2 = 1$, and $d_3(R_3) = k_3^3 = 2$. Hence policy R_3 and policy R_2 are identical, and the optimal release policy calls for releasing all the water when there is 1 unit in the dam, 1 unit of water when there are 2 units available in the dam, and 2 units when there are 3 units available in the dam.

Of course, direct enumeration would have been just as simple a technique to use in this situation, but the policy-improvement algorithm was used for illustrative purposes.

12.7 INVENTORY MODEL

In Chap. 8 the following inventory problem was considered. A camera store stocks a particular model camera that can be ordered weekly. Let $D_1, D_2, \ldots,$ represent the demand for this camera during the first week, second week, ..., respectively. It is assumed that the D_i are independent, identically distributed random variables having a Poisson distribution with parameter λ equal to 1. Let X_0 represent the number of cameras on hand at the outset, X_1 the number of cameras on hand at the end of week one, X_2 the number of cameras on hand at the end of week two, and so forth. On Saturday night the store places an order that is delivered in time for the opening of the store on Monday. The store uses an (s, S) ordering policy. If the number of cameras on hand at the end of the week is less than $s = 1$ (no cameras in stock), the store orders (up to) $S = 3$. Otherwise, the store does not order (if there are any cameras in stock, no order is placed). It is assumed that sales are lost when demand exceeds the inventory on hand (no backlogging). The cost structure considered calls for incurring a penalty cost of \$50 per unit for each unit of unsatisfied demand (lost sales). If $z > 0$ cameras are ordered, the cost incurred is $10 + 25z$ dollars. If no cameras are ordered, no ordering cost is incurred. Holding costs are to be neglected.

In Sec. 8.22 this policy was evaluated by using the (long run) expected average cost per unit time as the criterion. It is not evident that this policy is optimal and the purpose of this section is to find the optimal policy. Even though it is known that the optimal policy must be of the (s, S) form, all possible policies will be considered, although it will be assumed that three cameras is the maximum number of cameras that the store will stock. The policy-improvement algorithm will be used first, followed by the linear programming formulation.

Since X_t represents the state of the system, i.e., the number of cameras on hand at the end of week t (before ordering), then $X_t = 0, 1, 2, 3$. Similarly, there are four possible decisions:

Decision	*Action*
0	Do not order
1	Order 1 camera
2	Order 2 cameras
3	Order 3 cameras

The possible transitions are given by[1]

Decision 0

State	*0*	*1*	*2*	*3*
0	1	0	0	0
1	$P\{D \geq 1\}$	$P\{D = 0\}$	0	0
2	$P\{D \geq 2\}$	$P\{D = 1\}$	$P\{D = 0\}$	0
3	$P\{D \geq 3\}$	$P\{D = 2\}$	$P\{D = 1\}$	$P\{D = 0\}$

Decision 1

State	*0*	*1*	*2*	*3*
0	$P\{D \geq 1\}$	$P\{D = 0\}$	0	0
1	$P\{D \geq 2\}$	$P\{D = 1\}$	$P\{D = 0\}$	0
2	$P\{D \geq 3\}$	$P\{D = 2\}$	$P\{D = 1\}$	$PD\{= 0\}$
3	Decision 1 not permitted			

Decision 2

State	*0*	*1*	*2*	*3*
0	$P\{D \geq 2\}$	$P\{D = 1\}$	$P\{D = 0\}$	0
1	$P\{D \geq 3\}$	$P\{D = 2\}$	$P\{D = 1\}$	$P\{D = 0\}$
2, 3	Decision 2 not permitted			

Decision 3

State	*0*	*1*	*2*	*3*
0	$P\{D \geq 3\}$	$P\{D = 2\}$	$P\{D = 1\}$	$P\{D = 0\}$
1, 2, 3	Decision 3 not permitted			

[1] Note that in this example the set of possible decisions varies with the states.

Recalling that the demand D is a Poisson random variable with parameter $\lambda = 1$, and using appendix Table A.5.4, these transitions can now be expressed as

Decision 0

State	0	1	2	3
0	1	0	0	0
1	0.632	0.368	0	0
2	0.264	0.368	0.368	0
3	0.080	0.184	0.368	0.368

Decision 1

State	0	1	2	3
0	0.632	0.368	0	0
1	0.264	0.368	0.368	0
2	0.080	0.184	0.368	0.368
3	Decision 1 not permitted			

Decision 2

State	0	1	2	3
0	0.264	0.368	0.368	0
1	0.080	0.184	0.368	0.368
2, 3	Decision 2 not permitted			

Decision 3

State	0	1	2	3
0	0.080	0.184	0.368	0.368
1, 2, 3	Decision 3 not permitted			

The cost information required is similar to that given in Sec. 8.22, and the reader is urged to review this material. A summary is given by

State	Decision	*Actual cost per week*	*Expected cost per week,* C_{ik}
0	0	$50D$	$50E(D) = 50$
	1	$35 + 50 \max\{(D-1),0\}$	$35 + 50[1P\{D=2\} + 2P\{D=3\} + \cdots] = 53.4$
	2	$60 + 50 \max\{(D-2),0\}$	$60 + 50[1P\{D=3\} + 2P\{D=4\} + \cdots] = 65.2$
	3	$85 + 50 \max\{(D-3),0\}$	$85 + 50[1P\{D=4\} + 2P\{D=5\} + \cdots] = 86.2$
1	0	$50 \max\{(D-1),0\}$	$50[1P\{D=2\} + 2P\{D=3\} + \cdots] = 18.4$
	1	$35 + 50 \max\{(D-2),0\}$	$35 + 50[1P\{D=3\} + 2P\{D=4\} + \cdots] = 40.2$
	2	$60 + 50 \max\{(D-3),0\}$	$60 + 50[1P\{D=4\} + 2P\{D=5\} + \cdots] = 61.2$
	3	Decision 3 not permitted	
2	0	$50 \max\{(D-2),0\}$	$50[1P\{D=3\} + 2P\{D=4\} + \cdots] = 5.2$
	1	$35 + 50 \max\{(D-3),0\}$	$35 + 50[1P\{D=4\} + 2P\{D=5\} + \cdots] = 36.2$
	2, 3	Decisions 2, 3 not permitted	
3	0	$50 \max\{(D-3),0\}$	$50[1P\{D=4\} + 2P\{D=5\} + \cdots] = 1.2$
	1, 2, 3	Decisions 1, 2, 3 not permitted	

Choose the (s, S) policy already introduced as the initial policy for carrying out the value determination step (step 1) of the policy-improvement algorithm. This policy, R_1, calls for ordering (up to) 3 units whenever the system is in state 0 (no other cameras on hand); otherwise, no order is placed. With this policy, the following four equations must be solved simultaneously for $g(R_1)$, $v_0(R_1)$, $v_1(R_1)$, and $v_2(R_1)$ [recall that $v_3(R_1)$ is arbitrarily taken to be zero]:

$$g(R_1) = C_{0k_1} + \sum_{j=0}^{3} p_{0j}(k_1)v_j(R_1) - v_0(R_1)$$

$$g(R_1) = C_{1k_1} + \sum_{j=0}^{3} p_{1j}(k_1)v_j(R_1) - v_1(R_1)$$

$$g(R_1) = C_{2k_1} + \sum_{j=0}^{3} p_{2j}(k_1)v_j(R_1) - v_2(R_1)$$

$$g(R_1) = C_{3k_1} + \sum_{j=0}^{3} p_{3j}(k_1)v_j(R_1) - v_3(R_1),$$

or alternatively,

$$\begin{aligned}
g(R_1) &= 86.2 + 0.080v_0(R_1) + 0.184v_1(R_1) + 0.368v_2(R_1) - v_0(R_1)\\
g(R_1) &= 18.4 + 0.632v_0(R_1) + 0.368v_1(R_1) \qquad\qquad\qquad - v_1(R_1)\\
g(R_1) &= 5.2 + 0.264v_0(R_1) + 0.368v_1(R_1) + 0.368v_2(R_1) - v_2(R_1)\\
g(R_1) &= 1.2 + 0.080v_0(R_1) + 0.184v_1(R_1) + 0.368v_2(R_1).
\end{aligned}$$

The simultaneous solution of this system of equations yields

$$\begin{aligned}
g_1(R_1) &= 31.43\\
v_0(R_1) &= 85.00\\
v_1(R_1) &= 64.38\\
v_2(R_1) &= 31.49.
\end{aligned}$$

Step 2 can now be applied. It is necessary to find the improved policy R_2, which has the property that $d_0(R_2) = k_2^0, d_1(R_2) = k_2^1, d_2(R_2) = k_2^2$, and $d_3(R_2) = k_2^3$ minimizes the following expressions:

$$\begin{aligned}
&(0) \qquad C_{0k_2^0} + p_{00}(k_2^0)85 + p_{01}(k_2^0)64.38 + p_{02}(k_2^0)31.49 - 85\\
&(1) \qquad C_{1k_2^1} + p_{10}(k_2^1)85 + p_{11}(k_2^1)64.38 + p_{12}(k_2^1)31.49 - 64.38\\
&(2) \qquad C_{2k_2^2} + p_{20}(k_2^2)85 + p_{21}(k_2^2)64.38 + p_{22}(k_2^2)31.49 - 31.49\\
&(3) \qquad C_{3k_2^3} + p_{30}(k_2^3)85 + p_{31}(k_2^3)64.38 + p_{32}(k_2^3)31.49.
\end{aligned}$$

To find the optimal decisions, the following data are required:

State 0

Decision	$p_{00}(k_2)$	$p_{01}(k_2)$	$p_{02}(k_2)$	C_{0k_2}	Total value of expression (0)
0	1	0	0	50	50
1	0.632	0.368	0	53.4	45.81
2	0.264	0.368	0.368	65.2	37.92
3	0.080	0.184	0.368	86.2	31.43

State 1

Decision	$p_{10}(k_2)$	$p_{11}(k_2)$	$p_{12}(k_2)$	C_{1k_2}	Total value of expression (1)
0	0.632	0.368	0	18.4	31.43
1	0.264	0.368	0.368	40.2	33.54
2	0.080	0.184	0.368	61.2	27.05

State 2

Decision	$p_{20}(k_2)$	$p_{21}(k_2)$	$p_{22}(k_2)$	C_{2k_2}	Total value of expression (2)
0	0.264	0.368	0.368	5.2	31.43
1	0.080	0.184	0.368	36.2	34.94

State 3

Decision	$p_{30}(k_2)$	$p_{31}(k_2)$	$p_{32}(k_2)$	C_{3k_2}	Total value of expression (3)
0	0.080	0.184	0.368	1.2	31.43

Thus $d_0(R_2) = k_2^0 = 3$, $d_1(R_2) = k_2^1 = 2$, $d_2(R_2) = k_2^2 = d_3(R_2) = k_2^3 = 0$. Hence policy R_2 calls for ordering up to three cameras whenever there are 0 or 1 cameras in stock; otherwise, no ordering is done; i.e., if the number of cameras on hand at the end of the week is less than $s = 2$ cameras, the store orders up to $S = 3$ cameras. Since policy R_2 differs from policy R_1, another iteration is required. The following four equations must be solved simultaneously for $g(R_2)$, $v_0(R_2)$, $v_1(R_2)$, and $v_2(R_2)$:

$$g(R_2) = 86.2 + 0.080v_0(R_2) + 0.184v_1(R_2) + 0.368v_2(R_2) - v_0(R_2)$$
$$g(R_2) = 61.2 + 0.080v_0(R_2) + 0.184v_1(R_2) + 0.368v_2(R_2) - v_1(R_2)$$
$$g(R_2) = 5.2 + 0.264v_0(R_2) + 0.368v_1(R_2) + 0.368v_2(R_2) - v_2(R_2)$$
$$g(R_2) = 1.2 + 0.080v_0(R_2) + 0.184v_1(R_2) + 0.368v_2(R_2).$$

The simultaneous solution of this system of equations yields

$$g_1(R_2) = 30.33$$
$$v_0(R_2) = 85.00$$
$$v_1(R_2) = 60.00$$
$$v_2(R_2) = 30.68.$$

Step 2 can now be applied. It is necessary to find the improved policy R_3, which has the property that $d_0(R_3) = k_3^0$, $d_1(R_3) = k_3^1$, $d_2(R_3) = k_3^2$, and $d_3(R_3) = k_3^3$ minimizes the following expressions:

(0) $$C_{0k_3^0} + p_{00}(k_3^0)85 + p_{01}(k_3^0)60 + p_{02}(k_3^0)30.68 - 85$$

(1) $C_{1k_3^1} + p_{10}(k_3^1)85 + p_{11}(k_3^1)60 + p_{12}(k_3^1)30.68 - 60$

(2) $C_{2k_3^2} + p_{20}(k_3^2)85 + p_{21}(k_3^2)60 + p_{22}(k_3^2)30.68 - 30.68$

(3) $C_{3k_3^3} + p_{30}(k_3^3)85 + p_{31}(k_3^3)60 + p_{32}(k_3^3)30.68.$

Using the data from the previous iteration, the relevant calculations are

Decision	*Total value of expression (0)*	*Total value of expression (1)*	*Total value of expression (2)*	*Total value of expression (3)*
0	50	34.20	30.33	30.33
1	44.20	36.01	34.65	.....
2	36.01	30.33	.....	.....
3	30.33	.....	.....	.....

Thus $d_0(R_3) = k_3^0 = 3$, $d_1(R_3) = k_3^1 = 2$, $d_2(R_3) = k_3^2 = d_3(R_3) = k_3^3 = 0$. Hence policy R_3 and policy R_2 are identical, so that the optimal policy calls for ordering up to three cameras when there are 0 or 1 cameras in stock; otherwise, no ordering is done.

The linear programming formulation calls for finding the y_{ik} that

$$\text{Minimize} \quad 50y_{00} + 53.4y_{01} + 65.2y_{02} + 86.2y_{03} + 18.4y_{10} + 40.2y_{11} + 61.2y_{12} + 5.2y_{20} + 36.2y_{21} + 1.2y_{30},$$

subject to

$$y_{00} + y_{01} + y_{02} + y_{03} + y_{10} + y_{11} + y_{12} + y_{20} + y_{21} + y_{30} = 1,$$

$$y_{00} + y_{01} + y_{02} + y_{03} - [y_{00} + y_{01}(0.632) + y_{02}(0.264) + y_{03}(0.080) + y_{10}(0.632) + y_{11}(0.264) + y_{12}(0.080) + y_{20}(0.264) + y_{21}(0.080) + y_{30}(0.080)] = 0,$$

$$y_{10} + y_{11} + y_{12} - [y_{01}(0.368) + y_{02}(0.368) + y_{03}(0.184) + y_{10}(0.368) + y_{11}(0.368) + y_{12}(0.184) + y_{20}(0.368) + y_{21}(0.184) + y_{30}(0.184)] = 0,$$

$$y_{20} + y_{21} - [y_{02}(0.368) + y_{03}(0.368) + y_{11}(0.368) + y_{12}(0.368) + y_{20}(0.368) + y_{21}(0.368) + y_{30}(0.368)] = 0,$$

$$y_{30} - [y_{30}(0.368) + y_{12}(0.368) + y_{21}(0.368) + y_{30}(0.368)] = 0,$$

and

$$y_{00}, y_{01}, y_{02}, y_{03}, y_{10}, y_{11}, y_{12}, y_{20}, y_{21}, y_{30} \geq 0.$$

This linear program can be solved by using the simplex method. The results yield all y_{ik} equal to zero, except for

$$y_{03} = 0.148, y_{12} = 0.252, y_{20} = 0.368, y_{30} = 0.233.$$

The corresponding D_{ik} are given by

$$D_{03} = D_{10} = D_{20} = D_{30} = 1,$$

and all the remaining $D_{ik} = 0$.

12.8 CONCLUSIONS

The material presented in this chapter represents a powerful tool for formulating models and finding the optimal policies for controlling a large class of systems—those that are Markovian decision processes. These techniques are applicable to the solution of problems in such areas as queueing theory, inventory, maintenance, and probabilistic dynamic programming, in general.

Two algorithms were presented, the policy improvement and linear programming, for finding optimal policies. It is evident from the examples that data-collection requirements are high. Even if the solution converges rapidly in the policy-improvement algorithm, for systems with a large number of states completing step 2 requires considerable calculation. Using the linear programming formulation with, say, 50 states and 25 decisions leads to 1,250 variables and 51 constraints (excluding the nonnegativity constraints), which represents a large linear program. Nevertheless, these two methods of solution are useful for solving real-world problems. When the cost criterion is the expected discounted cost, the method of successive approximations provides a valuable tool for approximating the optimal solution. Much simpler calculations are required for this algorithm than for the policy-improvement or linear programming methods.

Considerable research activities have been devoted to the field of Markovian decision processes in recent years. Derman[1] has shown that in the expected average cost per unit time case, the optimal policy is deterministic (calls for always taking a particular action when the system is in a given state). Similarly, he has shown[2] that in the expected discounted cost case, the optimal policy is also deterministic. The policy improvement algorithm is due to Howard.[3] For the expected average cost per unit time case, he presents not only the algorithm for the situation where all the states belong to one class but also an algorithm that is applicable when there is more than one (a finite number) class of states. He also considers the continuous-time case. The linear programming formulation using the expected average cost per unit time was first given by Manne,[4] who treated the case where all the states belong to one class. The linear programming formulation using the expected discounted cost was first given by d'Epenoux.[5] Finally, although the results presented in this chapter

[1] C. Derman, "On Sequential Decisions and Markov Chains," *Management Science*, **9**:16–24, 1962.

[2] C. Derman, "Markovian Sequential Control Processes—Denumberable State Space," *Journal Mathematical Analysis and Applications*, **10**:295–302, 1965.

[3] R. Howard, *Dynamic Programming and Markov Processes*, Technology Press, Cambridge, Mass., and Wiley, New York, 1960.

[4] A. S. Manne, "Linear Programming and Sequential Decisions," *Management Science*, **6**:259–267, 1960.

[5] F. d'Epenoux, "Sur un Probleme de Production et de Stockage dans l'a Léatoire," *Rev. Française Information Recherche Opérationnelle*, **14**:3–16, 1960. English translation: *Management Science*, **10**:98–108, 1963.

assumed the state space to be finite, most of the results are applicable to the case of a countable state space.

Selected References

1 Derman, C.: *Finite State Markovian Decision Processes*, Academic Press, New York, 1970.
2 Howard, R.: *Dynamic Programming and Markov Processes*, M.I.T. Press, Cambridge, Mass., 1960.
3 Ross, S. M.: *Applied Probability Models with Optimization Applications*, Holden-Day, San Francsico, 1970.
4 White, D. J.: *Dynamic Programming*, Holden-Day, San Francisco, 1969.

Problems

1 During any period, a potential customer arrives at a certain facility with probability $\frac{1}{2}$. If there are two people at the facility already (including the one being served), the potential customer leaves the facility immediately and never returns. However, if there is one or fewer people, he enters the facility and becomes an actual customer. The manager of the facility has two types of service rates available. If he uses his "slow" service rate at a cost of \$2.00 during a period, a customer will be served and leave the facility with probability $\frac{3}{5}$. If he uses his "fast" service rate at a cost of \$6.00 during a period, a customer will be served and leave the facility with probability $\frac{4}{5}$. Note that the probability of more than one customer arriving or more than one customer being served in a period is zero. A profit of \$40 is earned when a customer is served. Use policy improvement to determine the policy the manager should follow to minimize his expected long-run average cost per period. (*Hint:* In computing the costs for services when two customers are at a facility, do not forget the opportunity cost of losing a potential customer.)

2 Formulate Prob. 1 as a linear programming problem.

3 A person often finds that she is up to 1 hour late for work. If she is from 1 to 30 minutes late, \$4 is deducted from her paycheck; if she is from 31 to 60 minutes late for work, \$8 is deducted from her paycheck. If she drives to work at her normal speed (which is well under the speed limit), she can arrive in 20 minutes. However, if she exceeds the speed limit a little here and there on her way to work, she can get there in 10 minutes, but she runs the risk of getting a speeding ticket. With probability $\frac{1}{8}$ she will get caught speeding and not only get fined \$20 but also get delayed 10 minutes, so that it takes 20 minutes to reach work.

Let s be the time she finds she has to reach work before being late; that is, $s = 10$ means she has 10 minutes to get to work and $s = -10$ means she is already 10 minutes late for work. For simplicity, she considers s to be in one of four intervals: $(20,\infty)$, $(10,19)$, $(-10,9)$, and $(-20,-11)$.

The transition probabilities for s tomorrow if she does not speed today are given by

	$(20, \infty)$	$(10, 19)$	$(-10, 9)$	$(-20, -11)$
$(20, \infty)$	$\frac{3}{8}$	$\frac{1}{4}$	$\frac{1}{4}$	$\frac{1}{8}$
$(10, 19)$	$\frac{1}{2}$	$\frac{1}{4}$	$\frac{1}{8}$	$\frac{1}{8}$
$(-10, 9)$	$\frac{5}{8}$	$\frac{1}{4}$	$\frac{1}{8}$	0
$(-20, -11)$	$\frac{3}{4}$	$\frac{1}{4}$	0	0

The transition probabilities for s tomorrow if she speeds to work today are given by

	$(20, \infty)$	$(10, 19)$	$(-10, 9)$	$(-20, -11)$
$(20, \infty)$				
$(10, 19)$	$\frac{3}{8}$	$\frac{1}{4}$	$\frac{1}{4}$	$\frac{1}{8}$
$(-10, 9)$				
$(-20, -11)$	$\frac{5}{8}$	$\frac{1}{4}$	$\frac{1}{8}$	0

Note that there are no transition probabilities for $(20, \infty)$ and $(-10, 9)$ because she will get to work on time and from 1 to 30 minutes late, respectively, regardless of whether she speeds or not. Hence speeding when in these states would not be a logical choice.

Also note that the transition probabilities imply that the later she is for work and the more she has to rush to get there, the likelier she is to leave for work earlier the next day.

Use policy improvement to determine when she should speed and when she should take her time getting to work.

4 Formulate Prob. 3 as a linear programming problem.

5 Every Saturday night a man plays poker, much to the dismay of his wife. Regardless of the kind of mood his wife is in, if he takes her out to dinner (at an expected cost of \$14) before going to play poker, she will be in a good mood, with probability ⅞, and a bad mood, with probability ⅛ next Saturday night. However, if he goes to play poker without taking her out to dinner first, she will be in a good mood next Saturday, with probability ⅛, and a bad mood, with probability ⅞, regardless of her mood this week. Furthermore, if she happens to be in a bad mood and he does not take her to dinner, she will go to an exclusive store and buy a new clothes outfit (at an expected cost of $50). Use the policy-improvement method to find the policy that the man should follow to minimize his long-run expected average cost per week.

6 Formulate Prob. 5 as a linear programming problem.

7 When a tennis player serves, he gets two chances to serve in bounds. If he fails to do so twice, he loses the point (1 unit). If he attempts to serve an ace, he serves in bounds, with probability ⅜. If he serves a lob, he serves in bounds, with probability ⅞. If he serves an ace in bounds, he wins the point (1 unit), with probability ⅔. With an inbounds lob he wins the point (1 unit), with probability ⅓. Use the policy improvement method to determine the optimal strategy. (*Hint:* Let state 1 denote point over, two serves to go on next point; and let state 2 denote one serve left.)

8 Formulate Prob. 7 as a linear programming problem.

9 A student is concerned about her car and does not like to get it dented. When she drives to school she has a choice of parking in the street in a street space, taking up two spaces in the street, or parking in the lot. If she parks in the street, her car gets dented, with probability 1/10. If she takes two spaces, probability of a dent is 1/50 and probability of a $10 ticket is 3/10. Parking in a lot costs $5, but she will not get the car dented. If her car gets dented, she can have it repaired at the dealer, in which case it is out of commission for a day and costs her $50 in fees and cab fares. She can also drive her car dented, but she feels that the loss of pride and shame is worth about $9 a day. Using the policy-improvement method, determine the optimal policy.

10 Formulate Prob. 9 as a linear programming problem.

11 Each year Mr. Merrill has the chance of investing in two different no-load mutual funds: The Go-Go Fund or Go-Slow Mutual Fund. At the end of each year Mr. Merrill liquidates his holdings, takes his profits, and then reinvests. The yearly profits of the mutual funds are dependent upon how the market reacts each year. Recently the market has been oscillating around the 1,000 mark, according to the probabilities given in the following matrix:

$$\begin{array}{c} \\ 900 \\ 1{,}000 \\ 1{,}100 \end{array}\begin{array}{c} \begin{array}{ccc} 900 & 1{,}000 & 1{,}100 \end{array} \\ \begin{bmatrix} 0.3 & 0.5 & 0.2 \\ 0.1 & 0.5 & 0.4 \\ 0.1 & 0.4 & 0.5 \end{bmatrix} \end{array}$$

Each year the market moves up (or down) 100 points, the Go-Go fund has profits (or losses) of $20, while the Go-Slow Fund has profits (or losses) of $10. If the market moves up (or down) 200 points in a year, the Go-Go fund has profits (or losses) of $50, while the Go-Slow fund has profits (or losses) of only $20. If the market does not change, there is no profit or loss for either fund. Use the policy-improvement method to determine how Mr. Merrill should invest each year.

12 Formulate Prob. 11 as a linear programming problem.

13 Suppose a person wishes to dispose of a car. She receives an offer each month and must decide immediately whether or not to accept the offer. Once rejected, the offer is lost. The possible offers are \$600, \$800, and \$1,000 made with probabilities ⅝, ¼, and ⅛ respectively (it may be assumed that successive offers are independent of each other). Suppose that there is a maintenance cost of \$60 per month and a discount factor of $\alpha = 0.99$ is specified. Using the policy-improvement method, find a policy that minimizes the expected long run total discounted cost. (*Hint:* There are two actions; accept or reject the offer. Let the state space at time t denote the offer at time t, augmented by the state ∞. The process goes to state ∞ whenever an offer is accepted, and it remains there at a monthly cost of 0.) Find the optimal policy using the policy-improvement method.

14 Formulate Prob. 13 as a linear programming problem.

15 In Prob. 13, use three iterations of the method of successive approximations to approximate the optimal solution.

16 The price of a certain stock is fluctuating among the prices \$10, \$20, and \$30 from month to month. Market analysts have predicted that if the stock is at \$10 during any month, it will be at \$10 or \$20 next month, with probabilities ⁹⁄₁₀ and ⅒ respectively; if the stock is at \$20, it will be at \$10, \$20, or \$30, with probabilities ¼, ¼, and ½ respectively; and if the stock is at \$30, it will be at \$20 or \$30, with probabilities ⅞ and ⅛ respectively. Given a discount factor of 0.9, use policy improvement to determine when to sell and when to hold the stock to maximize the expected long-run total discounted profits. (*Hint:* Augment the state space with a state that is reached with probability 1 when the stock is sold and with probability 0 when the stock is held.)

17 Formulate Prob. 16 as a linear programming problem.

18 In Prob. 16, use three iterations of the method of successive approximations to approximate the optimal solution.

19 A person is in the market for a house. Until he finds one he lives in a hotel for \$40 a day. When he buys one, he pays immediately and moves in the next day. He can look at a house (if he chooses to) at most once a day, and when he does look at a house, he pays a broker's fee of \$25. The houses can cost \$35,000, \$40,000, and \$45,000, and these costs each occur with probability ⅓ on any given day when he looks at a house. There is a daily discount factor of 0.999. Use the policy-improvement method to find the optimal policy.

20 Formulate Prob. 19 as a linear programming problem.

21 In Prob. 19, use three iterations of the method of successive approximations to approximate the optimal solution.

22 A farmer raises corn. Each year that he has a sucessful crop he grosses \$17,000 on expenses for seed and labor of \$5,000. Sometimes his crop fails and he grosses only \$8,000. Each year the farmer has a chance of using two types of fertilizers: type *A* at a cost of \$2,000 guarantees that there is a 60 percent chance of having a successful crop the next year, and type *B* at a cost of \$3,000 guarantees that there is an 80 percent chance of a good crop next year. Using the policy-improvement algorithm with a discount factor of 0.5, determine when the farmer should use fertilizer *A* and *B*.

23 Formulate Prob. 22 as a linear programming problem.

24 In Prob. 22, use three iterations of the method of successive approximations to approximate the optimal solution.

25 A chemical company produces two chemicals, denoted by 0 and 1. Each month a decision is made as to which chemical will be produced that month. Since the demand for each chemical is predictable, it is known that if 1 is produced this month, there is a 60 percent chance that it will also be produced next month. Similarly, if 0 is produced this month, there is only a 20 percent chance that it will be produced again next month.

To combat the emissions of pollutants, the chemical company has two processes, process *A*, which is efficient in combating the pollution from the production of 1 but not from 0, and process *B*, which is efficient in combating the pollution from the production of 0 but not from 1. The amount of pollution from the production of each chemical under both processes is

	0	*1*
A	100	10
B	10	30

Unfortunately, there is a time delay in setting up the pollution-control processes, so that a decision as to which process to use must be made in the month prior to the production decision. Use the policy-improvement method to determine a pollution control policy that will minimize the present value of all future pollution at a discount factor of $\alpha = 0.5$.

26 Formulate Prob. 25 as a linear programming problem.

27 In Prob. 25, use two iterations of the method of successive approximations to approximate the optimal solution.

28 A man is playing a slot machine at $1 per play. Each time that he wins the jackpot of $10 he finds that if he pulls the lever hard, he has a 10 percent chance of winning on the next round. But if he pulls the lever gently, he has a 20 percent chance of hitting the jackpot on the next round. If he loses and then pulls the lever hard, he has an 80 percent chance of losing on the next round also. But if he pulls the lever softly, he has a 95 percent chance of losing again. Use the policy-improvement algorithm with a discount factor of 0.9 to determine how hard the player should pull the lever.

29 Formulate Prob. 28 as a linear programming problem.

30 In Prob. 28, use two iterations of the method of successive approximations to approximate the optimal solution.

31 Solve Prob. 19 as a four-period model.

32 Solve Prob. 22 as a four-period model.

33 Solve Prob. 25 as a three-period model.

34 Solve Prob. 28 as a three-period model.

35 Formulate the water-resource model presented in Sec. 12.6 as a linear programming problem.

36 Use three iterations of the method of successive approximations to approximate the optimal solution to the water-resource model presented in Sec. 12.6.

37 Solve the inventory model presented in Sec. 12.7 using expected discounted cost as the cost criterion, with a discount factor of $\alpha = 0.99$.

38 Use three iterations of the method of successive approximations to approximate the optimal solution to Prob. 37.

39 Find the optimal solution to a four-period machine maintenance model using the data from the example presented in the chapter. (Use a discount factor of $\alpha = 0.9$.)

40 Solve the inventory model presented in Sec. 12.7 as a four-period problem.

41 Solve the water-resource model presented in Sec. 12.6 as a three-period problem.

13 Reliability

13.1 INTRODUCTION

Many definitions of reliability exist, depending upon the viewpoint of the user. However, they all have a common core which contains the statement that reliability, $R(t)$, is the probability that a device performs adequately over the interval $[0,t]$. In general, it is assumed that unless repair or replacement occurs adequate performance at time t implies adequate performance during the interval $[0,t]$. The device under consideration may be an entire system, a subsystem, or a component.[1] Although this definition is simple, the systems to which it is applied are generally very complex. In principle, it is possible to break down the system into black boxes, with each black box being in one of two states: good or bad. Mathematical models of the system can then be abstracted from the physical processes and the theory of combinatorial probability utilized to predict the reliability of the system. The black boxes may be independent of, or be very dependent upon, each other. For any reasonable system such a probability analysis generally becomes so cumbersome that it must be considered impractical. Hence other methods that either simplify the calculations or provide bounds on the reliability of the entire complex system are sought.

As an example, consider an automobile. There are a large number of functional parts, wiring, and joints. These may be broken into subsystems, with each subsystem having a reliability associated with it. Possible subsystems are the engine, transmission, exhaust, body, carburator, and brakes. A mathematical model of the automobile system can be abstracted, and the theory of combinatorial probability utilized to predict the reliability of the automobile.

[1] A subsystem can be viewed as containing one or more components.

13.2 STRUCTURAL FUNCTION OF A SYSTEM

Suppose an automobile can be divided into n components (subsystems). The performance of each component can be denoted by a random variable X_i, which takes on the value $x_i = 1$ if the component performs satisfactorily for the desired time and $x_i = 0$ if the component fails during this time. In general then, X_i is a binary random variable defined by

$$X_i = \begin{cases} 1, & \text{if component } i \text{ performs satisfactorily during time } [0,t] \\ 0, & \text{if component } i \text{ fails during time } [0,t]. \end{cases}$$

The "performance" of the system is measured by the binary random variable $\phi(X_1, X_2, \ldots, X_n)$,† where

$$\phi(X_1, X_2, \ldots, X_n) = \begin{cases} 1, & \text{if system performs satisfactorily during time } [0,t] \\ 0, & \text{if system fails during time } [0,t]. \end{cases}$$

The function ϕ is called the structure function of the system and is just a function of the n-component random variables. Thus the performance of the automobile is a function of its n components and takes on the value 1 if the automobile functions properly for the desired time and 0 if it does not. Since the performance of each component in the automobile takes on the value 1 or 0, then the function ϕ is defined over 2^n points, with each point resulting in a 1 if the automobile performs satisfactorily and a 0 if the automobile fails.

There are several important structure functions to consider, depending upon how the components are assembled. Three will be discussed in detail.

Series System

The series system is the simplest and most common of all configurations. For a series system, the system fails if any component of the system fails; i.e., it performs satisfactorily if and only if all the components perform satisfactorily. The structure function for a series system is given by

$$\phi(X_1, X_2, \ldots, X_n) = X_1 X_2 \cdots X_n = \min\{X_1, X_2, \ldots, X_n\}.$$

This follows because each X_i is either 1 or 0. Hence the structure function takes on the value 1 if each X_i equals 1, or alternatively, if the minimum of the X_i equals 1. For example, suppose the automobile is divided into only two components: the engine (X_1) and the transmission (X_2). Then it is reasonable to assume that the automobile will perform satisfactorily for the desired time period if and only if the engine and transmission perform satisfactorily. Hence

$$\phi(X_1, X_2) = X_1 X_2,$$

and

$$\phi(1,1) = 1, \phi(1,0) = \phi(0,1) = \phi(0,0) = 0.$$

† Note that X_i and ϕ are functions of the time t, but t will be surpressed for ease of notation.

Parallel System

A parallel system of n components is defined to be a system that fails if all components fail, or alternatively, the system performs satisfactorily if at least one of the n components performs satisfactorily (with all n components operating simultaneously). This property of parallel systems is often called "redundancy" (i.e., there are alternative components, existing within the system, to help the system operate successfully in case of failure of one or more components). The structure function for a parallel system is given by

$$\phi(X_1, X_2, \ldots, X_n) = 1 - (1 - X_1)(1 - X_2) \cdots (1 - X_n) = \max\{X_1, X_2, \ldots, X_n\}.$$

This again follows because each X_i is either 1 or 0. The structure function takes on the value 1 if at least one of the X_i equals 1, or alternatively, if the largest X_i equals 1. In the automobile example, cars are equipped with front disk (X_1) and rear drum (X_2) brakes. The automobile will perform successfully if either the front or rear brakes operate properly.[1] If one is concerned with the structure function of the brake subsystem, then

$$\phi(X_1, X_2) = 1 - (1 - X_1)(1 - X_2) = X_1 + X_2 - X_1 X_2,$$

and

$$\phi(1,1) = \phi(1,0) = \phi(0,1) = 1, \phi(0,0) = 0.$$

k Out of n System

Some systems are assembled such that the system operates if k out of n components function properly. Note that the series system is a k out of n system, with $k = n$, and the parallel system is a k out of n system, with $k = 1$. The structure function for a k out of n system is given by

$$\phi(X_1, X_2, \ldots, X_n) = \begin{cases} 1, \text{ if } \sum_{i=1}^{n} X_i \geq k \\ 0, \text{ if } \sum_{i=1}^{n} X_i < k. \end{cases}$$

In the automobile example, consider a large truck equipped with eight tires. The structure function for the tire system is an example of a four out of eight system (although the system performance may be degraded if less than eight tires are operating, rearrangement of the tire configuration will result in adequate performance as long as at least four tires are useable).

It is reasonable to expect the performance of an automobile to improve if the performance of one or more components are improved. This can be reflected in the characterization of the structure function, where, for example,

[1] It is evident that the loss of the front or rear brakes will affect the braking capability of the automobile, but the definition of "perform successfully" may allow for either set working.

one would expect $\phi(1,0,0,1)$ to be no less than $\phi(1,0,0,0)$. Hence it will be assumed that if $x_i \le y_i$, for $i = 1, 2, \ldots, n$, then

$$\phi(y_1, y_2, \ldots, y_n) \ge \phi(x_1, x_2, \ldots, x_n).$$

A system possessing this property (ϕ is an increasing function of x) is called a *coherent* (*or monotone*) system.

13.3 SYSTEM RELIABILITY

The structure function of a system containing n components is a binary random variable that takes on the value 1 or 0. Furthermore, the reliability of this system can be expressed as

$$R = P\{\phi(X_1, X_2, \ldots, X_n) = 1\}.\dagger$$

Thus, for a series system, the reliability is given by

$$R = P\{X_1 X_2 \cdots X_n = 1\} = P\{X_1 = 1, X_2 = 1, \ldots, X_n = 1\}.$$

When the usual terms for conditional probability are employed,

$$R = P\{X_1 = 1\}P\{X_2 = 1 \mid X_1 = 1\}P\{X_3 = 1 \mid X_1 = 1, X_2 = 1\} \cdots P\{X_n = 1 \mid X_1 = 1, \ldots, X_{n-1} = 1\}.$$

In general, such conditional probabilities require careful analysis. For example, $P\{X_2 = 1 \mid X_1 = 1\}$ is the probability that component 2 will perform successfully, given that component 1 performs successfully. Consider a system where the heat from component 1 affects the temperature of component 2 and thereby its probability of success. The performance of these components are then dependent, and the evaluation of the conditional probability is extremely difficult. If, on the other hand, the performance characteristics of these components do not interact, e.g., temperature of the component does not affect the performance of the other component, then the components can be said to be independent. The expression for the reliability then simplifies and becomes

$$R = P\{X_1 = 1\}P\{X_2 = 1\} \cdots P\{X_n = 1\}.$$

When components of a series system are assumed to be independent, it should be noted that the reliability is a function of the probability distribution of the X_i. This phenomenon is true for any system structure.

Unless otherwise specified it will be assumed throughout the remainder of this chapter that the component performances are independent. Hence the probability distribution of the binary random variables X_i can be expressed as

$$P\{X_i = 1\} = p_i,$$

and

$$P\{X_i = 0\} = 1 - p_i.$$

† The time t is now suppressed in the notation. Recall that the time is implicitly included in determining whether or not the ith component performs satisfactorily.

Thus, for systems composed of independent components, the reliability becomes a function of the p_i; that is,

$$R = R(p_1, p_2, \ldots, p_n).$$

Reliability of Series Systems

As previously indicated, for a series structure

$$\begin{aligned} R(p_1, p_2, \ldots, p_n) &= P\{\phi(X_1, X_2, \ldots, X_n) = 1\} \\ &= P\{X_1 X_2 \cdots X_n = 1\} \\ &= P\{X_1 = 1, X_2 = 1, \ldots, X_n = 1\} \\ &= P\{X_1 = 1\}P\{X_2 = 1\} \cdots P\{X_n = 1\} \\ &= p_1 p_2 \cdots p_n. \end{aligned}$$

Thus, returning to the automobile example, if the probability that the engine performs satisfactorily is 0.95 and the probability that the transmission performs satisfactorily equals 0.99, then the reliability of this automobile series subsystem is given by $R = (0.95)(0.99) = 0.94$.

Reliability of Parallel Systems

The structure function for a parallel system is

$$\phi(X_1, X_2, \ldots, X_n) = \max(X_1, X_2, \ldots, X_n),$$

and the reliability is given by

$$\begin{aligned} R(p_1, p_2, \ldots, p_n) &= P\{\max(X_1, X_2, \ldots, X_n) = 1\} \\ &= 1 - P\{\text{all } X_i = 0\} \\ &= 1 - P\{X_1 = 0, X_2 = 0, \ldots, X_n = 0\} \\ &= 1 - (1 - p_1)(1 - p_2) \cdots (1 - p_n). \end{aligned}$$

Thus, if the probability that the front disk brakes and the rear drum brakes perform satisfactorily are each 0.99, the subsystem reliability is given by

$$R = 1 - (0.01)(0.01) = 0.9999.$$

Reliability of k Out of n Systems

The structure function for a k out of n system is

$$\phi(X_1, X_2, \ldots, X_n) = \begin{cases} 1, \text{ if } \sum_{i=1}^{n} X_i \geq k \\ 0, \text{ if } \sum_{i=1}^{n} X_i < k, \end{cases}$$

and the reliability is given by

$$R(p_1, p_2, \ldots, p_n) = P\left\{\sum_{i=1}^{n} X_i \geq k\right\}.$$

The evaluation of this expression is, in general, quite difficult except for the case of $p_1 = p_2 = \cdots = p_n = p$. Under this assumption $\sum_{i=1}^{n} X_i$ has a binomial distribution with parameters n and p, so that

$$R(p, p, \ldots, p) = \sum_{i=k}^{n} \binom{n}{i} p^i (1-p)^{n-i}.$$

For the truck tire example, if each tire has a probability of 0.95 of performing satisfactorily, then the reliability of a four out of eight system is given by

$$R = \sum_{i=4}^{8} \binom{8}{i} (0.95)^i (0.05)^{8-i} = 0.9999.$$

For general structures the system reliability calculations can become quite tedious. A technique for computing reliabilities for this general case will be presented in the next section. However, the final result of this section is to indicate that the reliability function of a system of independent components can be shown to be an increasing function of the p_i; that is, if $p_i \leq q_i$ for $i = 1, 2, \ldots, n$, then

$$R(q_1, q_2, \ldots, q_n) \geq R(p_1, p_2, \ldots, p_n).$$

This result is analogous to, and dependent upon, the assumption that the structure function of the system is coherent. The implication of this intuitive result is that the reliability of the automobile will improve if the reliability of one or more components is improved.

13.4 CALCULATION OF EXACT SYSTEM RELIABILITY

A representation of the structure of a system can be expressed in terms of a network, and some of the material presented in Chap. 5 is relevant. For example, consider the system that can be represented by the network in Fig. 13.1.

Figure 13.1 A five-component system.

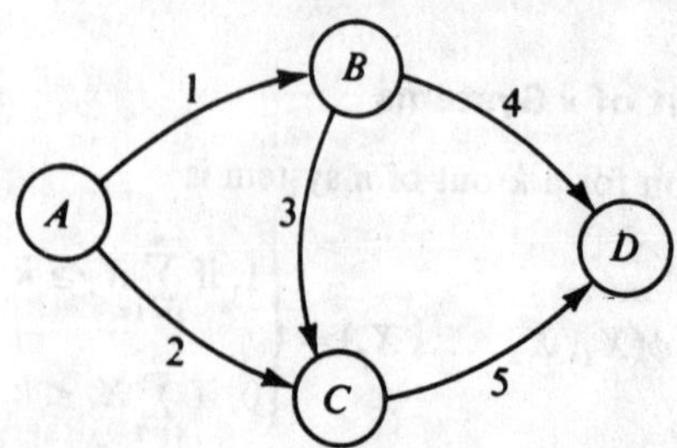

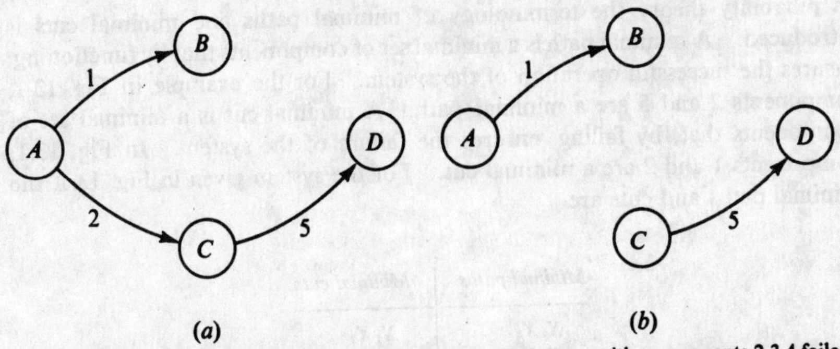

Figure 13.2 (*a*) System with components 3,4 failed; (*b*) system with components 2,3,4 failed.

This system consists of five components, connected in a somewhat complex manner. According to the network diagram, the system will operate successfully if there exists a "flow" from A (source) to D (sink) through the directed graph, i.e., if components 1 and 4 operate successfully, or components 2 and 5 operate successfully, or components 1, 3, and 5 operate successfully. In fact, each arc can be viewed as having capacity 1 or 0, depending upon whether or not the component is operating. If an arc has a 0 attached to it (the component fails), then the network would lose that arc, and the system would operate successfully if and only if there was a path from the source to sink in the resultant network. This is illustrated in Fig. 13.2, where the system still operates if components 3 and 4 fail but becomes inoperable if components 2, 3, and 4 fail. This suggests a possible method for computing the exact system reliability. Again, denote the performance of the ith component by the binary random variable X_i. Then X_i takes on the value 1 with probability p_i and 0 with probability $(1 - p_i)$. For each realization, $X_1 = x_1$, $X_2 = x_2$, $X_3 = x_3$, $X_4 = x_4$, $X_5 = x_5$, (there are 2^5 such realizations) it is determined whether or not the system will operate, i.e., whether or not the structure function equals 1. The network consisting of those arcs with X_i equal to 1 contains at least one path if and only if the corresponding structure function equals 1. If a path is formed, the probability of obtaining this configuration is obtained. For the realization in Fig. 13.2*a*, a path is formed, and

$$P\{X_1 = 1, X_2 = 1, X_3 = 0, X_4 = 0, X_5 = 1\} = p_1 p_2 (1 - p_3)(1 - p_4) p_5 .$$

Since each realization is disjoint, the system reliability is just the sum of the probabilities of those realizations that contain a path. Unfortunately, even for this simple system, 32 different realizations must be evaluated, and other techniques are desirable.

Another possible procedure for finding the exact reliability is to note that the reliability $R(p_1, p_2, \ldots, p_n)$ can be expressed as

$$R(p_1, p_2, \ldots, p_n) = P\,\{\text{maximum flow from source to sink} \geq 1\}.$$

This allows the concept of paths and cuts presented in Chap. 5 to be used.

In reliability theory the terminology of minimal paths and minimal cuts is introduced. A minimal path is a minimal set of components that by functioning, ensures the successful operation of the system. For the example in Fig. 13.1, components 2 and 5 are a minimal path. A minimal cut is a minimal set of components that, by failing, ensures the failure of the system. In Fig. 13.1, components 1 and 2 are a minimal cut. For the system given in Fig. 13.1, the minimal paths and cuts are

Minimal paths	*Minimal cuts*
$X_1 X_4$	$X_1 X_2$
$X_1 X_3 X_5$	$X_4 X_5$
$X_2 X_5$	$X_2 X_3 X_4$
	$X_1 X_5$

Utilizing all the minimal paths, there are two ways to obtain the exact system reliability. Since the system will operate if all the components in at least one of the minimal paths operate, the system reliability can be expressed as

$$\begin{aligned} R(p_1, p_2, p_3, p_4, p_5) &= P\{\phi(X_1, X_2, X_3, X_4, X_5) = 1\} \\ &= P\{(X_1 X_4 = 1) \cup (X_1 X_3 X_5 = 1) \cup (X_2 X_5 = 1)\}. \end{aligned}$$

Using the algebra of sets,

$$\begin{aligned} R(p_1, p_2, p_3, p_4, p_5) &= P\{X_1 X_4 = 1\} + P\{X_1 X_3 X_5 = 1\} \\ &\quad + P\{X_2 X_5 = 1\} - P\{X_1 X_3 X_4 X_5 = 1\} \\ &\quad - P\{X_1 X_2 X_4 X_5 = 1\} - P\{X_1 X_2 X_3 X_5 = 1\} \\ &\quad + P\{X_1 X_2 X_3 X_4 X_5 = 1\} \\ &= p_1 p_4 + p_1 p_3 p_5 + p_2 p_5 - p_1 p_3 p_4 p_5 \\ &\quad - p_1 p_2 p_4 p_5 - p_1 p_2 p_3 p_5 + p_1 p_2 p_3 p_4 p_5 \\ &= 2p^2 + p^3 - 3p^4 + p^5, \text{ when } p_i = p. \end{aligned}$$

Notice that there are $2^3 - 1 = 7$ terms in the expansion of the reliability function (in general, if there are r paths then there are $2^r - 1$ terms in the expansion), so that this calculation is not simple.

The second method of determining the system reliability from paths is as follows: For the minimal path containing components 1 and 4, $X_1 X_4 = 1$ if and only if both components function. This is similarly true for the other three minimal paths. However, the system will operate if all the components in at least one of the minimal paths operate. Hence paths operate as a parallel system, so that

$$\begin{aligned} \phi(X_1, X_2, X_3, X_4, X_5) &= \max[X_1 X_4, X_1 X_3 X_5, X_2 X_5] \\ &= 1 - (1 - X_1 X_4)(1 - X_1 X_3 X_5)(1 - X_2 X_5). \end{aligned}$$

Since $X_i^2 = X_i$, then

$$\phi(X_1, X_2, X_3, X_4, X_5) = X_1X_4 + X_1X_3X_5 + X_2X_5 - X_1X_3X_4X_5 - X_1X_2X_4X_5 - X_1X_2X_3X_5 + X_1X_2X_3X_4X_5.$$

Noting that ϕ is a binary random variable taking on the values 1 and 0,

$$E[\phi(X_1, X_2, X_3, X_4, X_5)] = P\{\phi(X_1, X_2, X_3, X_4, X_5) = 1\} = R(p_1, p_2, p_3, p_4, p_5).$$

Therefore

$$\begin{aligned} R(p_1, p_2, p_3, p_4, p_5) &= E[X_1X_4 + X_1X_3X_5 + X_2X_5 - X_1X_3X_4X_5 - X_1X_2X_4X_5 \\ &\qquad - X_1X_2X_3X_5 + X_1X_2X_3X_4X_5] \\ &= p_1p_4 + p_1p_3p_5 + p_2p_5 - p_1p_3p_4p_5 - p_1p_2p_4p_5 - p_1p_2p_3p_5 \\ &\qquad + p_1p_2p_3p_4p_5. \end{aligned}$$

This is the same result as obtained earlier and requires essentially the same amount of calculation.

Utilizing all the minimal cuts, there are also two ways to obtain the exact system reliability. Since the system will fail if and only if all the components in at least one of the minimal cuts fail, the system reliability can be expressed as

$$\begin{aligned} R(p_1, p_2, p_3, p_4, p_5) &= 1 - P\{\phi(X_1, X_2, X_3, X_4, X_5) = 0\} \\ &= 1 - P\{(X_1 = 0, X_2 = 0) \cup (X_4 = 0, X_5 = 0) \\ &\qquad \cup (X_2 = 0, X_3 = 0, X_4 = 0) \cup (X_1 = 0, X_5 = 0)\} \\ &= 1 - P\{X_1 = 0, X_2 = 0\} - P\{X_4 = 0, X_5 = 0\} \\ &\quad - P\{X_2 = 0, X_3 = 0, X_4 = 0\} - P\{X_1 = 0, X_5 = 0\} \\ &\quad + P\{X_1 = 0, X_2 = 0, X_4 = 0, X_5 = 0\} \\ &\quad + P\{X_1 = 0, X_2 = 0, X_3 = 0, X_4 = 0\} \\ &\quad + P\{X_1 = 0, X_2 = 0, X_5 = 0\} \\ &\quad + P\{X_2 = 0, X_3 = 0, X_4 = 0, X_5 = 0\} \\ &\quad + P\{X_1 = 0, X_4 = 0, X_5 = 0\} \\ &\quad + P\{X_1 = 0, X_2 = 0, X_3 = 0, X_4 = 0, X_5 = 0\} \\ &\quad - P\{X_1 = 0, X_2 = 0, X_3 = 0, X_4 = 0, X_5 = 0\} \\ &\quad - P\{X_1 = 0, X_2 = 0, X_4 = 0, X_5 = 0\} \\ &\quad - P\{X_1 = 0, X_2 = 0, X_3 = 0, X_4 = 0, X_5 = 0\} \\ &\quad - P\{X_1 = 0, X_2 = 0, X_3 = 0, X_4 = 0, X_5 = 0\} \\ &\quad + P\{X_1 = 0, X_2 = 0, X_3 = 0, X_4 = 0, X_5 = 0\} \\ &= 1 - q_1q_2 - q_4q_5 - q_2q_3q_4 - q_1q_5 + q_1q_2q_3q_4 \\ &\quad + q_1q_2q_5 + q_2q_3q_4q_5 + q_1q_4q_5 - q_1q_2q_3q_4q_5, \end{aligned}$$

where $\qquad q_i = 1 - p_i.$

This is, of course, algebraically equivalent to the same result as obtained previously and involves $2^4 - 1 = 15$ terms in the expansion of the reliability function. In general, if there are s cuts, there are $2^s - 1$ terms in the expansion.

The second method of determining the system reliability from cuts is: For the minimal cut containing components 1 and 2, $1 - (1 - X_1)(1 - X_2) = 0$ if and only if both components fail. This is similarly true for the other three cuts. However, the system will operate if at least one of the components in *each* cut operates. Hence cuts operate as a series system, so that

$$\begin{aligned}\phi(X_1, X_2, X_3, X_4, X_5) &= \min[1 - (1 - X_1)(1 - X_2), 1 - (1 - X_4)(1 - X_5),\\ &\quad 1 - (1 - X_2)(1 - X_3)(1 - X_4), 1 - (1 - X_1)(1 - X_5)]\\ &= ([1 - (1 - X_1)(1 - X_2)][1 - (1 - X_4)(1 - X_5)]\\ &\quad [1 - (1 - X_2)(1 - X_3)(1 - X_4)][1 - (1 - X_1)(1 - X_5)])\\ &= 1 - (1 - X_1)(1 - X_2) - (1 - X_4)(1 - X_5)\\ &\quad - (1 - X_2)(1 - X_3)(1 - X_4) - (1 - X_1)(1 - X_5)\\ &\quad + (1 - X_1)(1 - X_2)(1 - X_3)(1 - X_4)\\ &\quad + (1 - X_1)(1 - X_2)(1 - X_5)\\ &\quad + (1 - X_2)(1 - X_3)(1 - X_4)(1 - X_5)\\ &\quad + (1 - X_1)(1 - X_4)(1 - X_5)\\ &\quad - (1 - X_1)(1 - X_2)(1 - X_3)(1 - X_4)(1 - X_5).\end{aligned}$$

Taking expectations on both sides leads to the desired expression for the reliability. *Again*, this method requires essentially the same amount of calculation as required for the first procedure using cuts.

Although the results presented in this section were based upon the example, the extension to any system is easily obtained. All minimal paths and/or cuts must be found and one of the four methods presented chosen.

As previously mentioned, if there are r paths and s cuts in the network, then calculating the exact reliability using paths will involve summing $2^r - 1$ terms, and using cuts will involve $2^s - 1$ terms. Hence the method using paths should be used if and only if $r \leq s$. Generally, however, it is simpler to find minimal paths rather than minimal cuts, so that the method using paths may have to be used because finding all cuts is computationally infeasible. It is evident that finding the exact reliability of a system is quite difficult and bounds would be desirable, provided that the calculations are substantially reduced.

13.5 BOUNDS ON SYSTEM RELIABILITY

It is evident that the calculations required to compute exact system reliability are numerous, and that other methods, such as obtaining upper and lower bounds are desirable.

There exists a well-known result concerning binary random variables, i.e.,

If $X_1, X_2, \ldots, X_n$ are independent binary random variables that take on the values 1 *or* 0, *and $Y_i = \prod_{j \in J_i} X_j$, where the product ranges over all j which are elements in the set J_i, $i = 1, 2, \ldots, r$, then*

$$P\{Y_1 = 0, Y_2 = 0, \ldots, Y_r = 0\} \geq P\{Y_1 = 0\}P\{Y_2 = 0\} \cdots P\{Y_r = 0\}.$$

Returning to the example of Sec. 13.4, it was pointed out that the system will operate if all the components in at least one of the minimal paths operate, so that

$$\begin{aligned} R(p_1, p_2, p_3, p_4, p_5) &= P\{\phi(X_1, X_2, X_3, X_4, X_5) = 1\} \\ &= 1 - P\{\text{all paths fail}\} \\ &= 1 - P\{X_1X_4 = 0, X_1X_3X_5 = 0, X_2X_5 = 0\}. \end{aligned}$$

From the aforementioned result on binary random variables,

$$\begin{aligned} R(p_1, p_2, p_3, p_4, p_5) &\leq 1 - P\{X_1X_4 = 0\}P\{X_1X_3X_5 = 0\}P\{X_2X_5 = 0\} \\ &= 1 - (1 - p_1p_4)(1 - p_1p_3p_5)(1 - p_2p_5) \\ &= 1 - (1 - p^2)^2(1 - p^3), \text{ when } p_i = p, \end{aligned}$$

so that an upper bound is obtained. Similarly, in Sec. 13.4 it was pointed out that the system will operate if at least one of the components in *each* cut operates, so that

$$\begin{aligned} &R(p_1, p_2, p_3, p_4, p_5) \\ &\quad = P\{\phi(X_1, X_2, X_3, X_4, X_5) = 1\} = P\{\text{at least one of } X_1, X_2 \text{ operates; at least one of } X_4, X_5 \text{ operates; at least one of } X_2, X_3, X_4 \text{ operates; at least one of } X_1, X_5 \text{ operates}\} \\ &\quad = P\{[1 - (1 - X_1)(1 - X_2)] = 1, [1 - (1 - X_4)(1 - X_5)] = 1, \\ &\qquad [1 - (1 - X_2)(1 - X_3)(1 - X_4)] = 1, [1 - (1 - X_1)(1 - X_5)] = 1\} \\ &\quad = P\{(1 - X_1)(1 - X_2) = 0, (1 - X_4)(1 - X_5) = 0, \\ &\qquad (1 - X_2)(1 - X_3)(1 - X_4) = 0, (1 - X_1)(1 - X_5) = 0\}. \end{aligned}$$

Now $(1 - X_i)$ are independent binary random variables which take on the values 1 and 0, so that the result on binary random variables is again applicable; that is,

$$\begin{aligned} &R(p_1, p_2, p_3, p_4, p_5) \\ &\quad \geq (P\{(1 - X_1)(1 - X_2) = 0\}P\{(1 - X_4)(1 - X_5) = 0\} \\ &\qquad P\{(1 - X_2)(1 - X_3)(1 - X_4) = 0\}P\{(1 - X_1)(1 - X_5) = 0\}) \\ &\quad = ([1 - (1 - p_1)(1 - p_2)][1 - (1 - p_4)(1 - p_5)] \\ &\qquad [1 - (1 - p_2)(1 - p_3)(1 - p_4)][1 - (1 - p_1)(1 - p_5)]) \\ &\quad = [1 - (1 - p)^2]^3[1 - (1 - p)^3], \text{ when } p_i = p, \end{aligned}$$

so that a lower bound is obtained.

Thus an upper bound on the reliability based upon paths is obtained, and a lower bound based upon cuts is also found. For example, if $p_i = p = 0.9$, then

$$0.9693 = [1 - (0.1)^2]^3[1 - (0.1)^3] \leq R(0.9,0.9,0.9,0.9,0.9)$$
$$\leq 1 - [1 - (0.9)^2]^2[1 - (0.9)^3] = 0.9902.$$

Furthermore, the exact reliability obtained from the expressions in Sec. 13.4 is given by

$$R(0.9,0.9,0.9,0.9,0.9) = 2(0.9)^2 + (0.9)^3 - 3(0.9)^4 + (0.9)^5 = 0.9712.$$

In general, this technique provides useful results in that the bounds are frequently quite narrow.

13.6 BOUNDS ON RELIABILITY BASED UPON FAILURE TIMES

The previous sections considered systems that performed successfully for a designated period or failed during this period. An alternative way of viewing systems is to view their performance as a function of time.

Consider a component (or system) and its associated random variable, the time to failure, T. Denote the probability distribution of the time to failure of the component by F and its density function by f. In terms of the previous discussion, the random variables X and T are related in that X takes on the values

$$\begin{aligned} &1, \text{ if } T \geq t \\ &0, \text{ if } T < t. \end{aligned}$$

Then

$$R(t) = P\{X = 1\} = 1 - F(t) = \int_t^\infty f(y)\, dy.$$

An appealing intuitive property in reliability is the failure rate. The failure rate $r(t)$ is defined for those values of t for which $F(t) < 1$ by

$$r(t) = \frac{f(t)}{R(t)}.$$

This function has a useful probabilistic interpretation; namely, $r(t)\, dt$ represents the conditional probability that an object surviving to age t will fail in the interval $[t, t + dt]$. This function is sometimes called the hazard rate.

In many applications there is every reason to believe that the failure rate tends to increase because of the inevitable deterioration which occurs. Such a failure rate that remains constant or increases with age is said to have an increasing failure rate (IFR).

In some applications the failure rate tends to decrease. It would be expected to decrease initially, for instance, for materials that exhibit the phenomenon of "work hardening." Certain solid-state electronic devices are also believed to have a decreasing failure rate. Thus a failure rate that remains constant or decreases with age is said to have a decreasing failure rate (DFR).

The failure rate possesses some interesting properties. The time to failure distribution is completely determined by the failure rate. In particular, it is easily shown that

$$R(t) = 1 - F(t) = \exp\left[-\int_0^t r(\xi)\, d\xi\right].$$

Thus an assumption made about the failure rate has direct implications on the time to failure distribution. As an example, consider a component whose failure distribution is given by the exponential; that is,

$$F(t) = P\{T \le t\} = 1 - e^{-t/\theta}.$$

Thus $R(t)$ is given by $e^{-t/\theta}$, and the failure rate is given by

$$r(t) = \frac{\frac{1}{\theta} e^{-t/\theta}}{e^{-t/\theta}} = \frac{1}{\theta}$$

Note that the exponential has a constant failure rate and hence is both IFR and DFR. In fact, using the expression relating the time to failure distribution and the failure rate, it is evident that a component having a constant failure rate must have a time to failure distribution that is exponential.

Bounds for IFR Distributions

Under either IFR or DFR assumptions, it is possible to obtain sharp bounds on the reliability in terms of moments and percentiles: In particular, such bounds can be derived from statements based upon the mean time to failure. This is particularly important because many design engineers present specifications in terms of mean time to failure.

Because the exponential distribution with constant failure rate is the boundary distribution between IFR and DFR distributions, it provides natural bounds on the survival probability of IFR and DFR distributions. In particular, it can be shown that if all that is known about the failure distribution is that it is IFR and has mean μ, then the greatest lower bound on the reliability which can be given is

$$R(t) \ge \begin{cases} e^{-t/\mu}, & \text{for } t < \mu \\ 0, & \text{for } t \ge \mu \end{cases}$$

and the inequality is sharp, i.e., the exponential distribution with mean μ attains the lower bound for $t < \mu$, and the degenerate distribution concentrating at μ attains the lower bound for $t \ge \mu$. This can be represented graphically as shown in Fig. 13.3.

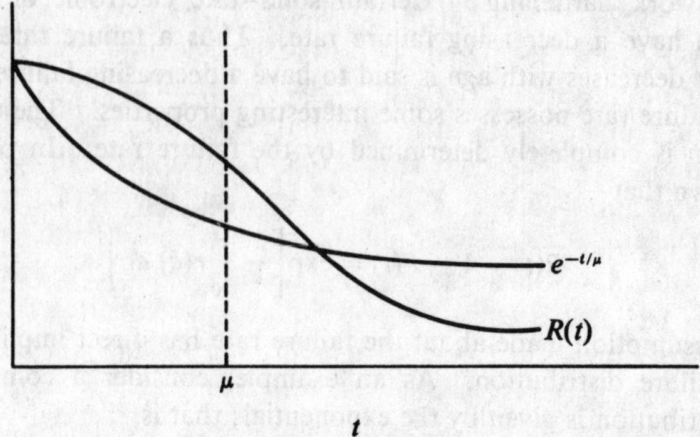

Figure 13.3 A lower bound on reliability for IFR distributions.

The least upper bound on $R(t)$ which can be obtained knowing only that F is IFR with mean μ is given by

$$R(t) \leq \begin{cases} 1, & \text{for } t \leq \mu \\ e^{-\omega t}, & \text{for } t > \mu, \end{cases}$$

where ω depends on t and satisfies $1 - \omega\mu = e^{-\omega t}$. It is important to note that the ω in the term $e^{-\omega t}$ is a function of t, so that a different ω must be found for each t. For fixed t and μ, this is obtained by finding the intersection of the linear function $(1 - \omega\mu)$ and the exponential function $e^{-\omega t}$. It can be shown that for $t > \mu$, such an intersection always exists.

Thus $R(t)$ for an IFR distribution with mean μ can be bounded above and below, as shown in Fig. 13.4. Note that the lower bound is the only one of consequence for $t < \mu$, and that the upper bound is the only one of consequence for $t > \mu$.

Figure 13.4 Upper and lower bounds on reliability for IFR distributions.

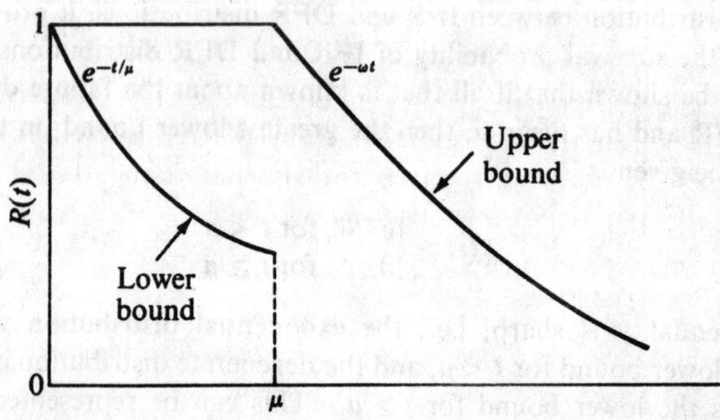

Increasing-failure-rate Average

Now that bounds on the reliability of a component have been obtained, what can be said about the preservation of monotone failure rate; i.e., what structures have the IFR property when their individual components have this property? Series structures of independent IFR (DFR) components are also IFR(DFR). k out of n structures consisting of n identical independent components, each having an IFR failure distribution, is also IFR; however, parallel structures of independent IFR components are not IFR unless they are composed of identical components. Thus it is evident that even for some simple systems there may not be a preservation of the monotone failure rate.

Instead of using the failure rate as a means for characterizing the reliability

$$R(t) = \exp\left[-\int_0^t r(\xi)\, d\xi\right],$$

a somewhat less appealing characterization can be obtained from the failure-rate average function

$$\int_0^t \frac{r(\xi)\, d\xi}{t} = -\frac{\log R(t)}{t}.$$

A distribution F such that $F(0) = 0$ is called IFRA (increasing failure rate average) is and only if

$$\int_0^t \frac{r(\xi)\, d\xi}{t}$$

is nondecreasing in $t \geq 0$. A similar definition is given for DFRA. It can be shown that a coherent system of independent components, each of which has an IFRA failure distribution, has a system failure distribution which is also IFRA.

As with IFR systems, there are bounds for systems that are IFRA. It is easily shown that IFR distributions are also IFRA (but not the reverse), and the same upper bound as given for IFR distributions is applicable here. A sharp lower bound for IFRA distributions with mean μ is given by

$$R(t) \geq \begin{cases} 0, & \text{for } t \geq \mu \\ e^{-bt}, & \text{for } t < \mu, \end{cases}$$

where b depends upon t and is defined by $e^{-bt} = b(\mu - t)$.

As an example, a monotone system containing only independent components, each of which are exponential (thereby IFRA), is itself IFRA, and the aforementioned bounds are applicable. Furthermore, these bounds are dependent only upon the system mean time to failure.

13.7 CONCLUSIONS

In recent years delivering systems that perform adequately for a specified period of time in a given environment has become an important goal for both industry and government. In the space program, higher system reliability meant the difference between life and death. In general, the cost of maintaining and/or repairing electronic equipment during the first year of operation often exceeds the purchase cost, giving impetus to the study and development of reliability techniques.

This chapter has been concerned with determining system reliability (or bounds) from a knowledge of component reliability or characteristics of components such as failure rate or mean time to failure. Even the desirable state of knowing these values may lead to cumbersome and sometimes crude results. However, it must be emphasized that these values, e.g., component reliabilities or mean time to failure, are *not* known and are often just the design engineers' educated guess. Furthermore, except in the case of the exponential distribution, knowledge of the mean time to failure leads to nothing but bounds. Also, it is evident that the reliability of components or systems depends heavily upon the failure rate, and the assumption of constant failure rate, which appears to be used frequently in practice, should not be made without careful analysis.

The contents of the chapter were not concerned with the statistical aspects of reliability, i.e., estimating reliability from test data. This was omitted because of the emphasis of this text on probability models rather than a reflection on its importance. The statistical aspects of reliability may very well be the important problem. Statistical estimation of component reliability is well in hand, but estimation of system reliability from component data is virtually an unsolved problem.

Selected References

1 Barlow, R. E. and F. Proschan: *Mathematical Theory of Reliability*, Wiley, New York, 1965.
2 ——— and ———: *Statistical Theory of Reliability and Life Testing*, Holt, Reinhart & Winston, New York, 1974.
3 Gnedenko, B. V., Yu. K. Belyayev, and A. D. Solovyev: *Mathematical Methods of Reliability Theory*, Academic Press, New York, 1969.
4 Lieberman, G. J.: "The Status and Impact of Reliability Methodology," *Naval Research Logistics Quarterly*, **16**(1): 17–35, 1969.
5 Ross, S.: *Introduction to Probability Models*, Academic Press, New York, 1972.
6 Shooman, M. L.: *Probabilistic Reliability—An Engineering Approach*, McGraw-Hill, New York, 1968.

Problems

1 Show that the structure function for a system, consisting of 3 components which functions if and only if component 1 functions and at least one of the components 2 or 3 function, is given by

$$\begin{aligned}\phi(X_1 X_2 X_3) &= X_1 \max(X_2, X_3)\\ &= X_1[1-(1-X_2)(1-X_3)].\end{aligned}$$

2 Show that the structure function for a system, consisting of 4 components which functions if and only if component 1 and 2 function and at least one of the components 3 or 4 function, is given by

$$\phi(X_1, X_2, X_3) = X_1 X_2 \max(X_3, X_4).$$

3 Find the reliability of the structure function given in Prob. 1 when each component has probability p_i of performing successfully.

4 Find the reliability of the structure function given in Prob. 2 when each component has probability p_i of performing successfully.

5 Suppose that there exists three different type components, with 2 units of each type. Each unit operates independently, and each type has probability p_i of performing successfully. Either one or two systems can be built. One system can be assembled as follows: The two units of each type component are put together in parallel, and the three types are then assembled to operate in series. Alternatively, two subsystems are assembled, each consisting of the three different type components assembled in series. The final system is obtained by putting the two subsystems together in parallel. Which system has higher reliability?

6 Consider the following network:

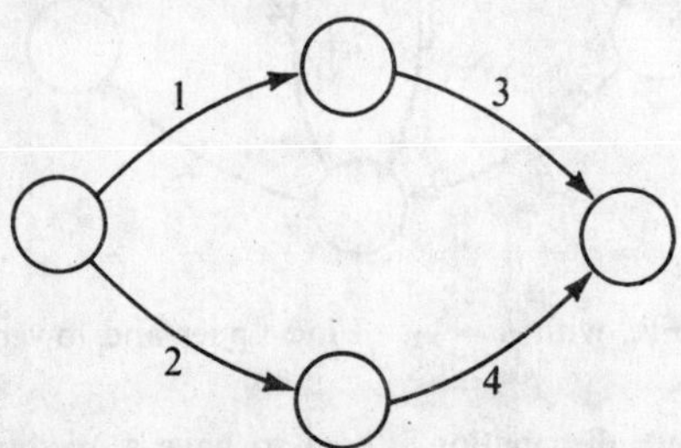

Assume that each component is independent with probability p_i of performing satisfactorily.

(*a*) Find all the minimal paths and cuts.
(*b*) Compute the exact system reliability, and evaluate it when $p_i = p = 0.9$.
(*c*) Find upper and lower bounds on the reliability, and evaluate them when $p_i = p = 0.9$.

7 Solve Prob. 6 by using the following network:

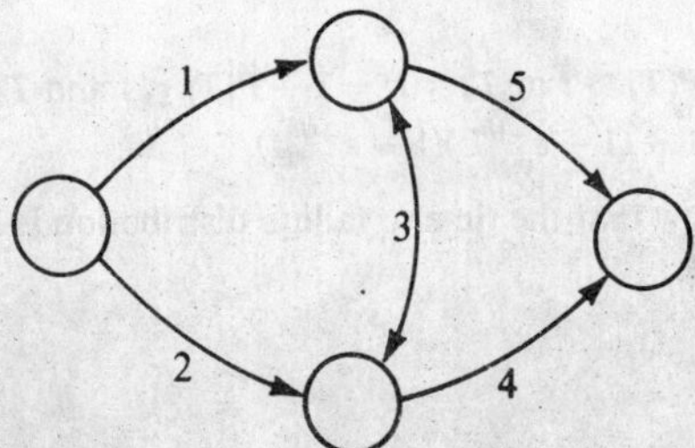

Note that component 3 flows in either direction.

8 Solve Prob. 6 by using the following network:

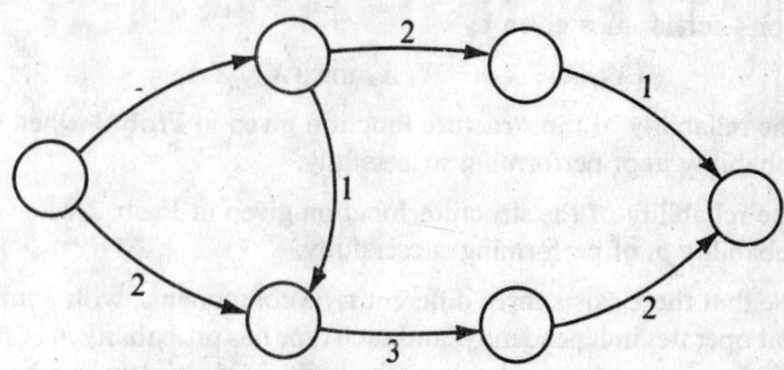

9 Solve Prob. 6 by using the following network containing three components:

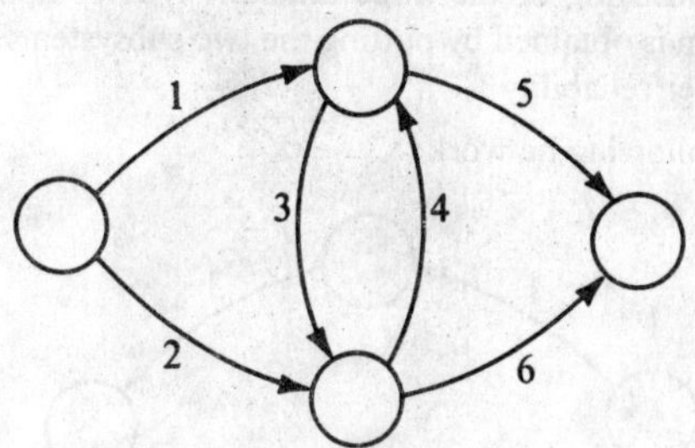

10 Suppose F is IFR, with $\mu = \frac{1}{2}$. Find upper and lower bounds on $R(t)$ for (*a*) $t = \frac{1}{4}$ and (*b*) $t = 1$.

11 A time to failure distribution is said to have a Weibull distribution if the cumulative distribution function is given by

$$F(t) = 1 - e^{-t^{\beta}/\eta,\ \eta,\ \beta > 0}.$$

Find the failure rate, and show that the Weibull is IFR when $\beta \geq 1$ and DFR when $0 < \beta \leq 1$.

12 Consider a parallel system consisting of two independent components whose time to failure distributions are exponential with parameters μ_1 and μ_2, respectively ($\mu_1 \neq \mu_2$). Show that the time to failure distribution is not IFR.
Hint:

$$\begin{aligned} R(t) &= P\{T_1 > t \text{ or } T_2 > t\} = 1 - P\{T_1 \leq t \text{ and } T_2 \leq t\} \\ &= 1 - (1 - e^{-t/\mu_1})(1 - e^{-t/\mu_2}). \end{aligned}$$

13 In Prob. 12, show that the time to failure distribution is IFRA

14 Decision Analysis

14.1 INTRODUCTION

Chapter 8 introduced the basic notions of probability theory. Little mention was made of decision making because the discussion was concerned with describing natural phenomena in terms of a probabilistic model. Random variables and their associated probability distributions were always assumed to be completely specified. Even in this situation, and in the absence of experimentation, decisions may be required.

A more common occurrence involves decision making when experimentation is possible; this is the concern of statistics. Statistics is a science that deals with making decisions from observed data in the face of uncertainty. This chapter presents a framework for making decisions when (1) experimentation is infeasible and (2) experimentation is possible, resulting in the availability of sample data.

EXAMPLE Consider the following situation. An oil company has some land that is purported to contain oil. The company classifies such land into four categories by the total number of barrels that are expected to be obtained from the well, i.e., a 500,000-barrel well, a 200,000-barrel well, a 50,000-barrel well, or a dry well. The company is faced with deciding whether to drill for oil, to unconditionally lease the land, or to conditionally lease the land at a rate depending upon the oil strike. The cost of drilling a producing well is \$100,000, and the cost of drilling a dry well is \$75,000. For producing wells the profit per barrel of oil is \$1.50 (after deducting all production costs). Under the unconditional lease agreement, the company receives \$45,000 for the land, whereas under the conditional lease arrangement the company receives 50 cents for each barrel of oil extracted, provided the land yields a 200,000- or 500,000-barrel strike; otherwise it receives nothing.

The possible profits for the oil company are shown in Table 14.1.

Table 14.1 Table of Profits for Oil Company

	500,000-barrel well	*200,000-barrel well*	*50,000-barrel well*	*Dry well*
Drill for oil	650,000	200,000	−25,000	−75,000
Unconditionally lease	45,000	45,000	45,000	45,000
Conditionally lease	250,000	100,000	0	0

14.2 DECISION MAKING WITHOUT EXPERIMENTATION

General Framework

Before seeking a solution to the aforementioned problem, it is worthwhile to formulate a general framework for decision making. The decision maker must choose an action a from a set A of possible actions. In the oil-drilling example, the set A consists of three points, a_1, a_2, a_3, corresponding to drilling for oil, unconditionally leasing the land, and conditionally leasing the land, respectively. In taking an action the decision maker must be aware of its consequences, which will usually also be a function of the "state of nature." A state of nature θ is a representation of the actual real-world situation to which the action will apply. Generally, the states of nature are an enumeration, within the model according to some set of indices, of possible alternative representations of the physical phenomenon being studied. The set of possible values that θ can assume will be denoted by Θ. In the oil-drilling example Θ consists of four points, θ_1, θ_2, θ_3, and θ_4, with θ_1 corresponding to the land yielding a 500,000-barrel well, θ_2 corresponding to a 200,000-barrel well, θ_3 corresponding to a 50,000-barrel well, and θ_4 corresponding to a dry well. Very often the states of nature are characterized by a parameter of a family of probability distributions. In the context of the oil-drilling example, the potential strikes might be viewed as the expected value of the random variable, oil yield, having an assumed form of probability distribution. Thus a representation of the model of this oil-drilling problem is that the oil yield in the site is a random variable with an unknown expected value. The company is willing to approximate this expected value by one of four values: 500,000 barrels, 200,000 barrels, 50,000 barrels and no barrels (dry). Thus the states of nature become these possible values of the expected value of the random variable, oil yield.

To measure the consequences of a decision maker's action, it will be assumed that there exists a *loss function* $l(a, \theta)$ which reflects the loss from taking action a when the state of nature is θ and which is defined for each combination of a and θ. If the problem is formulated in terms of gains, a gain can be termed as a negative loss. The loss function is generally measured in monetary terms, although other "utility" functions can be used. Note that $l(a, \theta)$ is assumed to be a function only of a and θ. The loss function for the oil-drilling example is

Table 14.2 Loss Function for Oil-drilling Example

Action \ State of nature	θ_1: *500,000-barrel well*	θ_2: *200,000-barrel well*	θ_3: *50,000-barrel well*	θ_4 *dry well*
a_1: drill for oil	−650,000	−200,000	25,000	75,000
a_2: unconditionally lease	−45,000	−45,000	−45,000	−45,000
a_3: conditionally lease	−250,000	−100,000	0	0

easily obtained from Table 14.1 and is given in Table 14.2.† Although the loss function is easily obtained directly from the action and state of nature in this example, occasionally the loss depends upon the outcome of a random variable whose probability distribution depends upon the true state of nature. For example, this would occur in the oil-drilling example if the "profit" was expressed directly in terms of the random variable, oil yield. The loss would then be a random variable, and $l(a, \theta)$ is then to be interpreted as the expected value of the loss incurred when action a is taken and the true state of nature is θ. Hence, even here the loss function depends upon only a and θ. In general, in formulating the problem, if the state of nature is defined so broadly that observing its value resolves all uncertainty relevant to the decision at hand, then the loss can always be expressed as a (deterministic) function of θ and the action a. If this is not the case, meaning that observation of θ would still leave some uncertainty as to the ultimate consequence of a given action a, the loss function $l(a, \theta)$ is computed as the expected loss, given state θ and action a.

Minimax Criterion

If the true state of nature were known, it would be simple to choose the correct action, i.e., that action which has minimum loss. Unfortunately, the true state of nature is not generally known, and choosing a "correct action" is not simple. In the oil-drilling example, if $\theta = \theta_1$, a 500,000-barrel well, the best action is to drill for oil, whereas if $\theta = \theta_4$, a dry well, the best action is to unconditionally lease. This decision-theory formulation has the appearance of game theory described in detail in Chap. 7, with the two players being the decision maker and nature. The "actions" correspond to the pure strategies of the decision maker, and the states of nature correspond to the pure strategies of nature. The payoff matrix in game theory is analogous to the loss table. An approach for obtaining solutions to game theory problems is through the minimax principle. This principle tells the decision maker to find the maximum loss for each of his actions and choose that action which has the smallest maximum loss. Similarly, the decision maker's opponent, nature in this case, should find the

† In discussing this example throughout the chapter many negative values will appear. These are to be interpreted as gains or profit and should not cause the reader any trouble.

minimum loss to the decision maker for each one of his possible states of nature and present to the decision maker that state of nature which maximizes this minimum loss. If these loss values are equal, the game is said to have a "value." If a game has a "value," and each player follows his optimal strategy, the decision maker can guarantee that his loss will never exceed the value. Furthermore, if the decision maker follows his optimal strategy and nature deviates from his, the loss to the decision maker can only be decreased. Unfortunately, in this context a value does not always exist. However, it does exist in the oil-drilling example. By using the minimax criterion the decision maker should choose action a_2 and guarantee that his loss will not exceed $-45{,}000$. Similarly, nature should choose state $\theta = \theta_3$ or $\theta = \theta_4$ and can guarantee that the decision maker's loss will be at least $-45{,}000$. Thus, this "game" does indeed have a value, and the minimax strategy for the decision maker is to unconditionally lease.

A fundamental theorem in the theory of games states that if mixed strategies are allowed, and the minimax principle followed, the game always has a value. A mixed strategy for the decision maker is a probability distribution defined over the action space. The actual choice of strategy is dependent upon the outcome of a random device having the probability distribution associated with the action space. Thus, choosing a mixed strategy is equivalent to choosing a probability distribution. Similarly, a mixed strategy for nature is a probability distribution defined over the possible states of nature. Pure strategies are just special cases of mixed strategies, where the probability assigned to the chosen action is 1 and 0 to the others. Since both the action and the state of nature are random variables, the loss incurred is also a random variable, and again "expected loss" is the criterion.

However, even though the minimax principle has some attractive properties, it is seldom used in games against nature because it is an extremely conservative criterion in this context. The actions taken by using this principle assume that nature is a conscious opponent who wishes to inflict on the decision maker as much "damage" as possible. Generally, nature is not a malevolent opponent, and it is unlikely that the decision maker has to guard against such an occurrence.

Bayes' Criterion

The previous section pointed out that the minimax principle says to proceed as if nature will select a probability distribution, defined over the possible states of nature, which is "least favorable" to the decision maker. It was also noted that this is a very conservative approach because there is no reason to expect nature to use this distribution. As a matter of fact, in some situations the decision maker will actually have some advance information about θ that contradicts this assumption about what nature will do. When this happens, the decision maker certainly should take this information into account. Such information can usually be translated into a probability distribution, acting as though the state of nature is a random variable, in which case this distribution is referred to as a *prior* distribution. Prior distributions are often subjective in that they may depend upon the experience or intuition of an individual.

For example, in the oil-drilling problem, the company has had some experience with wells in similar geographical areas and has concluded that about 10 percent of the strikes are 500,000-barrel wells, 15 percent are 200,000-barrel wells, 25 percent are 50,000-barrel wells, and 50 percent are dry wells. Hence these data can be translated into the prior distribution

$$P\{\theta = \theta_1\} = P_\theta(1) = 0.10$$
$$P\{\theta = \theta_2\} = P_\theta(2) = 0.15$$
$$P\{\theta = \theta_3\} = P_\theta(3) = 0.25$$
$$P\{\theta = \theta_4\} = P_\theta(4) = 0.50.$$

A procedure for utilizing the prior distribution to aid in the selection of an action is the Bayes' criterion. The *Bayes' principle* tells the decision maker to select that action (called the *Bayes' decision procedure*) which minimizes the expected loss. The expected loss $l(a)$ is evaluated with respect to the prior distribution which is defined over the possible states of nature; that is,

$$l(a) = E[l(a, \theta)] = \begin{cases} \sum_{\text{all } k} l(a, k)P_\theta(k), & \text{if } \theta \text{ is discrete} \\ \int_{-\infty}^{\infty} l(a, y)P_\theta(y)\, dy, & \text{if } \theta \text{ is continuous.} \end{cases}$$

Thus, for the oil-drilling example, the expected loss $l(a)$ for each action is given by

$$\begin{aligned} l(a_1) = E[l(a_1, \theta)] &= -650{,}000(0.10) - 200{,}000(0.15) + 25{,}000(0.25) \\ &\quad + 75{,}000(0.50) \\ &= -\$51{,}250, \\ l(a_2) = E[l(a_2, \theta)] &= -45{,}000(0.10) - 45{,}000(0.15) - 45{,}000(0.25) \\ &\quad - 45{,}000(0.50) \\ &= -\$45{,}000, \\ l(a_3) = E[l(a_3, \theta)] &= -250{,}000(0.10) - 100{,}000(0.15) \\ &= -\$40{,}000. \end{aligned}$$

Hence the Bayes' principle leads to selecting action a_1, that is, drill for oil, and the associated expected loss is $-\$51{,}250$ (profit). It is interesting to speculate on whether the decision maker could have improved upon this expected loss by making use of a mixed strategy rather than a pure strategy (since nature is using the mixed strategy specified by the prior distribution). It can be shown that the decision maker can not improve his position by using mixed strategies, so that it is sufficient for him to consider only pure strategies.

14.3 DECISION MAKING WITH EXPERIMENTATION

The previous sections assumed that the decision maker was to make his decision without experimentation. However, if some experimentation is possible (possibly at a cost), the data derived from this experimentation should be incorporated into the decision-making process. For example, returning to the oil-drilling example, suppose that it is possible to obtain seismic soundings at a cost of $12,000. This information leads to four possible seismic classifications, denoted by (1), (2), (3), and (4). The classification (1) denotes that there is definitely a closed geological structure to the site (a very favorable outcome if the presence of oil is desired); the classification (2) denotes that there is probably a closed structure to the site; the classification (3) denotes that there is a nonclosed structure (a relatively unfavorable report); the classification (4) denotes that there is no structure to the site (an unfavorable condition). Based upon past examination of similar geological areas (100 such examinations) the data presented in Table 14.3 are obtained.[1] The values in parenthesis in each cell

Table 14.3 Frequency of Seismic Classifications

Seismic classification	θ_1: *500,000-barrel well*	θ_2: *200,000-barrel well*	θ_3: *50,000-barrel well*	θ_4: *dry well*
1	$7\left(\frac{7}{12}\right)$	$9\left(\frac{9}{16}\right)$	$11\left(\frac{11}{24}\right)$	$9\left(\frac{9}{48}\right)$
2	$4\left(\frac{4}{12}\right)$	$3\left(\frac{3}{16}\right)$	$6\left(\frac{6}{24}\right)$	$13\left(\frac{13}{48}\right)$
3	$1\left(\frac{1}{12}\right)$	$2\left(\frac{2}{16}\right)$	$3\left(\frac{3}{24}\right)$	$15\left(\frac{15}{48}\right)$
4	$0\left(\frac{0}{12}\right)$	$2\left(\frac{2}{16}\right)$	$4\left(\frac{4}{24}\right)$	$11\left(\frac{11}{48}\right)$

can be interpreted as conditional probabilities, given the state of nature, e.g., if the well is a 200,000-barrel well, then $3/16$ can be interpreted as the conditional probability that the seismic reading is classified as (2) (probably a closed structure to the site); if the well is dry, then $15/48$ can be interpreted as the conditional probability that the seismic reading is classified as 3 (a nonclosed structure to the site); and so on. Before proceeding with the example, a general method for incorporating these data will be discussed.

[1] Although the actual fraction of wells historically falling into the four categories differs slightly from the prior distribution, the prior probabilities given under Bayes' criterion in Sec. 14.2 are thought to be more representative of what to expect in the future and will be used subsequently.

Let X denote the information made available by experimentation obtained from a random sample. X is then a random variable and may be viewed as a function of the sample data; for example, X may denote a sample mean, the maximum of the sample, a vector of the sample observations, the third observation in a sample, and so forth. The decision maker is to choose a decision procedure rule, or strategy, which tells him the form and amount of experimentation and what action to take for each possible value that X may take on. Denote this function to be chosen as $d[x]$, so that if the random variable X takes on the value x, then $a = d[x]$ would be the action to be taken. The decision maker, then, is interested in choosing a function d from among the many possible decision functions that are, in some sense, optimal. (Indeed, part of the problem here is to choose a good working definition for the term "optimal.") To evaluate a decision function, its consequences must be explored. Since the action taken, a, is a function of the outcome of the random variable X, then $d[X]$ is also a random variable, and the loss associated with that action also depends upon the outcome of this random variable. An appropriate measure of the consequences of taking action $a = d[X]$, when the true state of nature is θ, is then given by the expected value of the loss. This quantity will be known as the *risk function* $R(d, \theta)$; that is,

$$R(d, \theta) = E[l(d[X], \theta)],$$

where the expectation is taken with respect to the probability distribution of the random variable X, and the loss function includes the cost of experimentation.

Now consider how to apply this approach to the oil-drilling example. Suppose the following decision rule, d_1, is to be evaluated. If the seismic reading is classified as (1), take action a_1; if the seismic reading is classified as (2) or (3), take action a_3; and if the seismic reading is classified as (4), take action a_2; that is,

$$d_1[x] = a_1, \text{ for } x = 1$$
$$d_1[x] = a_2, \text{ for } x = 4$$
$$d_1[x] = a_3, \text{ for } x = 2 \text{ or } x = 3.$$

Therefore

$$R(d_1, \theta_1) = -650{,}000\left(\frac{7}{12}\right) - 45{,}000(0) - 250{,}000\left[\frac{4}{12} + \frac{1}{12}\right] + 12{,}000$$
$$= -\$471{,}333,$$

$$R(d_1, \theta_2) = -200{,}000\left(\frac{9}{16}\right) - 45{,}000\left(\frac{2}{16}\right) - 100{,}000\left(\frac{3}{16} + \frac{2}{16}\right) + 12{,}000$$
$$= -\$137{,}375,$$

$$R(d_1, \theta_3) = 25{,}000\left(\frac{11}{24}\right) - 45{,}000\left(\frac{4}{24}\right) + 0\left(\frac{6}{24} + \frac{3}{24}\right) + 12{,}000$$
$$= \$15{,}958,$$

$$R(d_1, \theta_4) = 75{,}000\left(\frac{9}{48}\right) - 45{,}000\left(\frac{11}{48}\right) + 0\left(\frac{13}{48} + \frac{15}{48}\right) + 12{,}000$$
$$= \$15{,}750.$$

Note that the 12,000 represents the cost of obtaining the seismic data.

Thus it is evident how the risk function for a given decision procedure is evaluated. The risk function provides a means for defining "optimality." An optimal decision function might be defined as one that will minimize the risk for every value of θ. However, it is evident that an optimal decision function (in this sense) may not always exist and, in fact, does not exist in most cases. Thus the above definition is inadequate. Hence another definition of optimality is considered in the next section.

Bayes' Procedures

Even when data are available, there is no best definition of "optimal procedures." With data, it is still possible to use a minimax criterion or a minimax decision function, but it too suffers from the same disadvantages as when no data are available; i.e., it assumes that nature will act as a conscious opponent and confront the decision maker with the least favorable distribution of θ.

If the decision maker has some advance information about the states of nature that can be described in terms of a prior distribution, then the Bayes' principle can be applied to the risk function. If the states of nature are discrete, the Bayes' risk corresponding to a decision function d and a prior probability distribution of θ, $P_\theta(k)$, is given by

$$B(d) = \sum_{\text{all } k} R(d, k)P_\theta(k).$$

If the states of nature are continuous, the Bayes' risk corresponding to a prior probability density function of θ, $P_\theta(y)$, is given by

$$B(d) = \int_{-\infty}^{\infty} R(d, y)P_\theta(y)\, dy.$$

The Bayes' risk provides another means for defining optimality for decision rules using the *Bayes' principle*. The *Bayes' principle* tells the decision maker to select that function d (called the *Bayes' decision procedure*) which minimizes $B(d)$. A method for finding Bayes' decision procedures is presented below.

When no data were available, the Bayes' procedure selected that action which minimized the expected loss; this expectation was evaluated with respect to the prior distribution of θ. Now that data are available, additional information is available about the state of nature. For example, if the seismic data is classified as (4), this is "evidence" that the strike will not be a 500,000-barrel well and probably not a 200,000-barrel well. Hence, after observing the experimental data, the prior distribution should be updated by using more timely information about the probability distribution of the state of nature. Such updated information is called the *posterior distribution* of θ, given the prior distribution and the data $X = x$. The posterior distribution of θ is just the conditional distribution of θ, given $X = x$. If θ is discrete the posterior distribution will be denoted by $h_{\theta|X=x}(k)$, and if θ is continuous, then the posterior distribution will be denoted by $h_{\theta|X=x}(y)$. The method for calculating the posterior distribution is given later. However, if the method used for calculating the Bayes' procedure when no data are available is followed (selecting that action which minimizes the *expected loss*), with this expectation now evaluated with respect to the *posterior distribution* of θ, given $X = x$, this decision procedure minimizes $B(d)$. Hence, it is the Bayes' procedure. This is not an obvious statement, but it can easily be proved. Thus, to find the Bayes' procedure, the decision maker computes the posterior distribution of θ, given $X = x$. He then chooses that action which minimizes the expected loss[1] $l_h(a)$ (including the cost of experimentation) with this expectation evaluated with respect to the ***posterior*** distribution of θ, given $X = x$, where

$$l_h(a) = E[l(a, \theta)] = \begin{cases} \sum_{\text{all } k} l(a, k) h_{\theta|X=x}(k), & \text{if } \theta \text{ is discrete} \\ \int_{-\infty}^{\infty} l(a, y) h_{\theta|X=x}(y)\, dy, & \text{if } \theta \text{ is continuous.} \end{cases}$$

In the oil-drilling example, the posterior distribution can be calculated by methods to be discussed later in this section and is given in Table 14.4.

Table 14.4 Values of $h_{\theta|X=x}(k)$, The Posterior Distribution of θ

x \ k	θ_1	θ_2	θ_3	θ_4
1	0.166	0.240	0.327	0.267
2	0.129	0.108	0.241	0.522
3	0.039	0.087	0.146	0.728
4	0	0.107	0.238	0.655

Suppose that the seismic reading is classified as (3) (the geographical site has a nonclosed structure). To obtain the Bayes' procedure, the expected loss is computed with respect to the posterior distribution of θ, given $X = 3$ for each of the actions as follows:

$$\begin{aligned} l_h(a_1) = E[l(a_1, \theta)] &= -650{,}000(0.039) - 200{,}000(0.087) + 25{,}000(0.146) \\ &\quad + 75{,}000(0.728) + 12{,}000 \\ &= \$27{,}500, \end{aligned}$$

$$l_h(a_2) = E[l(a_2, \theta)] = -45{,}000 + 12{,}000 = -\$33{,}000,$$

$$\begin{aligned} l_h(a_3) = E[l(a_3, \theta)] &= -250{,}000(0.039) - 100{,}000(0.087) + 12{,}000 \\ &= -\$6{,}450. \end{aligned}$$

[1] Note that loss is used rather than risk.

The Bayes' procedure selects action a_2 (since this minimizes the expected loss), which implies that the company should unconditionally lease the land. Thus it is seen that the experimental data change the action of the decision maker. Without experimentation, the Bayes' procedure was to drill for oil, whereas the information obtained from the seismic data leads the company to unconditionally lease the land. Incidentally, although Table 14.4 was obtained for all values of x, it was necessary to obtain the values only for $x = x_3$. In fact, this method of computing Bayes' procedures has the important advantage that it is only necessary to compute $d[x]$ for the single point corresponding to the outcome of the experiment. Using the basic formula for $B(d)$ to find the Bayes' procedure requires the determination of the entire function $d[x]$, which is generally more difficult.

Calculation of the Posterior Distribution

Sections 8.10 and 8.11 introduced bivariate probability distributions and marginal and conditional probability distributions. In the context of the present section, (θ, X) is a bivariate random variable having a joint probability distribution. Consider the case where (θ, X) is a discrete bivariate random variable, with joint probability distribution given by $P_{\theta X}(k, j)$. The random variables θ and X each have marginal distributions. In fact, $P_\theta(k)$, the prior distribution of θ, is the marginal distribution of θ. The usual expression given as the probability distribution of the random variable X actually corresponds to the conditional probability distribution of X, given θ. For example, if X has a Poisson distribution with parameter $\lambda = 24$, then $e^{-24}24^j/j!$ is just the conditional probability distribution function of X, given $\lambda = 24$. To indicate that this is a "conditional distribution," the notation

$$Q_{X|\theta=k}(j) = P\{X = j | \theta = k\}$$

is introduced. Thus

$$Q_{X|\theta=24}(j) = P\{X = j | \theta = 24\} = \frac{e^{-24}24^j}{j!}$$

represents the conditional probability distribution of X, given that $\theta = 24$, and has the form of a Poisson distribution with parameter $\lambda = 24$.

If the joint distribution of (θ, X) is of interest, the expression

$$P_{\theta X}(k, j) = Q_{X|\theta=k}(j)P_\theta(k)$$

can be used to evaluate it. $Q_X(j)$, the marginal distribution of X, can also be obtained; that is,

$$Q_X(j) = \sum_{\text{all } k} P_{\theta X}(k, j) = \sum_{\text{all } k} Q_{X|\theta=k}(j)P_\theta(k).$$

Finally, the only remaining probability distribution that has not been discussed is the conditional distribution of θ, given $X = j$, that is, the posterior distribution of θ, given $X = j$, $h_{\theta|X=j}(k)$. An alternative expression for the joint probability distribution of (θ, X) is given by

$$P_{\theta X}(k, j) = h_{\theta|X=j}(k) Q_X(j).$$

Equating the two expressions for $P_{\theta X}(k, j)$, and letting $j = x$ (the outcome of the experiment), leads to the important result from which the posterior distribution can be calculated; that is,

$$h_{\theta|X=x}(k) = \frac{Q_{X|\theta=k}(x) P_\theta(k)}{Q_X(x)}.$$

Thus, in summary, the posterior distribution can be calculated by using the above expression. $P_\theta(k)$ is the prior distribution. $Q_{X|\theta=k}(x)$ is the ordinary expression for the probability distribution of the random variable X evaluated at $X = x$, but it is written in this form to show the dependence upon the value of the parameter θ. The function $Q_X(x)$ is the marginal distribution of the random variable X evaluated at $X = x$ and is obtained from

$$Q_X(x) = \sum_{\text{all } k} Q_{X|\theta=k}(x) P_\theta(k).$$

Returning to the oil-drilling example, suppose that the seismic reading is classified as x_3 (the geographical site has a nonclosed structure). Recall that the prior distribution of the classification of the land is assumed to be

$$P\{\theta = \theta_1\} = P_\theta(1) = 0.10$$
$$P\{\theta = \theta_2\} = P_\theta(2) = 0.15$$
$$P\{\theta = \theta_3\} = P_\theta(3) = 0.25$$
$$P\{\theta = \theta_4\} = P_\theta(4) = 0.50.$$

It is necessary to evaluate the expressions $h_{\theta|X=3}(1)$, $h_{\theta|X=3}(2)$, $h_{\theta|X=3}(3)$, and $h_{\theta|X=3}(4)$, where

$$h_{\theta|X=3}(k) = \frac{Q_{X|\theta=k}(3) P_\theta(k)}{Q_X(3)}, \text{ for } k = 1, 2, 3, \text{ and } 4.$$

In this case $Q_{X|\theta=k}(3) = P\{X = 3 | \theta = k\}$ is just the probability that the seismic reading will be classified as (3), given that the well is a θ_k barrel well, and these values can be obtained directly from Table 14.3. Hence

$$Q_{X|\theta=1}(3) = \frac{1}{12},\ Q_{X|\theta=2}(3) = \frac{1}{8},\ Q_{X|\theta=3}(3) = \frac{1}{8},\ Q_{X|\theta=4}(3) = \frac{5}{16}.$$

The marginal distribution of the random variable X evaluated at $X = 3$ can now be obtained; that is,

$$Q_X(3) = Q_{X|\theta=1}(3) P_\theta(1) + Q_{X|\theta=2}(3) P_\theta(2) + Q_{X|\theta=3}(3) P_\theta(3) + Q_{X|\theta=4}(3) P_\theta(4)$$
$$= \left(\frac{1}{12}\right)(0.1) + \frac{1}{8}(0.15) + \frac{1}{8}(0.25) + \frac{5}{16}(0.50) = 0.215,$$

so that the posterior distribution can now be calculated; that is,

$$h_{\theta|X=3}(1) = \frac{(\frac{1}{12})(0.1)}{0.215} = 0.039$$

$$h_{\theta|X=3}(2) = \frac{(\frac{1}{8})(0.15)}{0.215} = 0.087$$

$$h_{\theta|X=3}(3) = \frac{(\frac{1}{8})(0.25)}{0.215} = 0.146$$

$$h_{\theta|X=3}(4) = \frac{(\frac{5}{16})(0.50)}{0.215} = 0.728.$$

The expression for the posterior distribution has been given, where θ and X are both discrete random variables. If θ is discrete and X is continuous, the posterior distribution $h_{\theta|X=x}(k)$ is given by

$$h_{\theta|X=x}(k) = \frac{f_{X|\theta=k}(x)P_\theta(k)}{f_X(x)}$$

where $P_\theta(k)$ is the prior distribution of θ, and $f_{X|\theta=k}(x)$ is the ordinary expression for the density function of the random variable X, but it is written in this form to show the dependence upon the value of the parameter θ. The function $f_X(x)$ is the marginal density of the random variable X and is obtained from

$$f_X(x) = \sum_{\text{all } k} f_{X|\theta=k}(x)P_\theta(k).$$

If both θ and X are continuous, the posterior distribution $h_{\theta|X=x}(y)$ is given by

$$h_{\theta|X=x}(y) = \frac{f_{X|\theta=y}(x)P_\theta(y)}{f_X(x)},$$

where $P_\theta(y)$ is the prior density function of θ. The function $f_{X|\theta=y}(x)$ has been defined previously. $f_X(x)$ is the marginal density of the random variable X and is obtained from

$$f_X(x) = \int_{-\infty}^{\infty} f_{X|\theta=y}(x)P_\theta(y)\,dy.$$

Finally, if θ is continuous and X is discrete the posterior distribution $h_{\theta|X=x}(y)$ is given by

$$h_{\theta|X=x}(y) = \frac{Q_{X|\theta=y}(x)P_\theta(y)}{Q_X(x)},$$

where $P_\theta(y)$ is the prior density function of θ. The function $Q_{X|\theta=y}(x)$ is the ordinary expression for the probability distribution of the random variable X, that is, $P\{X = x | \theta = y\}$, but it is written in this form to show the dependence upon the value of the parameter θ. $Q_X(x)$ is the marginal distribution of the random variable X and is obtained from

$$Q_X(x) = \int_{-\infty}^{\infty} Q_{X|\theta=y}(x)P_\theta(y)\,dy.$$

Value of Experimentation

Before performing any experiment it is desirable to determine its potential value. Suppose the experiment can lead to perfect information about the state of nature. What is it worth? In the oil-drilling example, seismic information, which is *imperfect*, costs \$12,000. If perfect information "saves" say only \$10,000, seismatic information should be foregone because it is too expensive. If one knew that the strike would be a 500,000-barrel well (state of nature is θ_1), then by examining Table 14.2 the best action to take is clearly a_1, drill for oil, leading to a loss of $-$\$650,000. Similarly, if one knew that the strike would be a 200,000-barrel well (state of nature is θ_2), the best action is again a_1, with a corresponding loss of $-$\$200,000. However, if one knew that the strike would be a 50,000-barrel well (state of nature is θ_3), the best action is a_2, unconditionally lease the land, and the corresponding loss is $-$\$45,000. Finally, if one knew that the well was dry (state of nature is θ_4), the best action is again a_2, and the loss is also $-$\$45,000. Since the (prior) probabilities of each of these states are known, the expected loss with perfect information available about the state of nature $E(PI)$ is given by

$$\begin{aligned} E(PI) &= -650{,}000(0.1) - 200{,}000(0.15) - 45{,}000(0.25) - 45{,}000(0.50) \\ &= -\$128{,}750. \end{aligned}$$

The Bayes' solution (without any data) provided for an expected loss of $-$\$51,250, which is substantially more than the expected loss with perfect information, so that experimentation can lead to potential savings. In fact, the experimenter should be willing to pay a cost for perfect information up to $-51{,}250 + 128{,}750 = \$77{,}500$.

Now that experimentation may be desirable, it is useful to determine the value of obtaining seismic data. It has been shown that if the seismic data is classified as (3), the optimal (Bayes) action is a_2, with a corresponding loss of $-$\$33,000. Using the same techniques, the optimal (Bayes) actions can be obtained if the seismic data is classified as (1), (2), or (4). These results are summarized in Table 14.5. Since the entries for the expected loss depend upon the outcome of the experiment x, the overall measure of the effectiveness of the experiment requires obtaining a weighted sum, weighted with respect to the marginal probability distribution of the random variable X of the Bayes' losses. The calculations required for obtaining this marginal distribution, $Q_X(x)$, are described earlier in the section dealing with the calculation of the posterior distribution, where $Q_X(3)$ was obtained. Other values are given in Table 14.5.

Table 14.5 Bayes' Actions, Expected Losses, and Marginal Distribution for Oil Example

x	*Bayes' action*	*Expected loss*	*Marginal distribution* $Q_X(x)$
1	a_1	−115,700	0.351
2	a_1	−48,275	0.259
3	a_2	−33,000	0.215
4	a_2	−33,000	0.175

Hence the weighted sum of the Bayes' losses, called the unconditional expected loss with experimentation, is given by

$$-115{,}700(0.351) - 48{,}275(0.259) - 33{,}000(0.215) - 33{,}000(0.175) = -\$65{,}984.$$

The "value" of the experiment (beyond its cost of $12,000) is then given by the difference between this weighted sum and the Bayes' loss without data, that is,

$$-65{,}984 + 51{,}250 = -\$14{,}734,$$

indicating an expected savings of $14,734 due to following an optimal decision procedure with experimentation. Hence, obtaining seismic soundings does reduce the total expected cost.

In fact, if the nonoptimal procedure, d_1, presented earlier in this section is followed, its weighted risk is given by

$$-471{,}333(0.1) - 137{,}375(0.15) + 15{,}958(0.25) + 15{,}750(0.50) = -\$55{,}875.$$

Thus an expected savings of $10,109 (−65,984 + 55,875) is obtained by using the (optimal) Bayes' procedure rather than the procedure d_1.

14.4 DECISION TREES

An alternative method to the analysis presented in this chapter is through the use of *decision trees.* A decision tree is a graphical method of expressing, in chronological order, the alternative actions that are available to the decision maker and the choices determined by chance. For example, the decision tree for the oil-drilling problem is given in Fig. 14.1, and the reader is urged to refer to this figure throughout the ensuing discussion. Initially the decision maker has a choice of not utilizing seismic soundings or utilizing seismic soundings. Either action triggers some consequences. If the decision not to take seismic soundings is made, he is led down the appropriate path, arriving at a fork (node) with branches marked: drill, unconditionally lease, and conditionally lease the site. He must choose one of these branches on which to continue. If he chooses to drill, he is led down the appropriate path, arriving at a fork with branches marked: 500,000-barrel well, 200,000-barrel well, 50,000 barrel-well, and dry well. The choice of the branch on which to continue is a chance event.

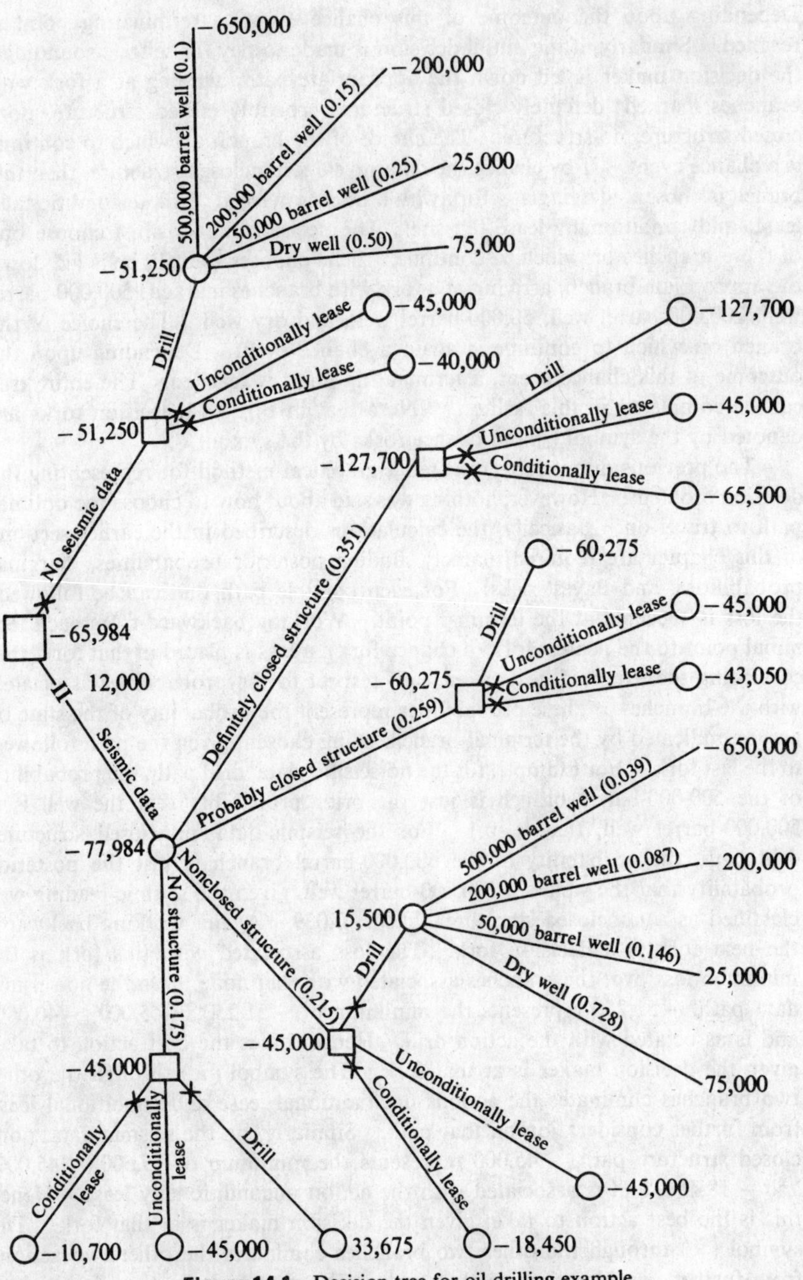

Figure 14.1 Decision tree for oil-drilling example.

Depending upon the outcome of this chance event, a terminating point is reached. Similarly, if the initial decision is made to pay for seismic soundings, the decision maker is led down the appropriate path, arriving at a fork with branches marked: definitely closed structure, probably closed structure, nonclosed structure, no structure. The choice of the branch on which to continue is a chance event. If by chance the data reveal a nonclosed structure, then this branch is chosen, arriving at a fork with branches marked: drill, unconditionally lease, and conditionally lease the site. The decision maker must choose one of these branches on which to continue. If he chooses to drill, he is led down the appropriate branch, arriving at a fork with branches marked: 500,000-barrel well, 200,000-barrel well, 50,000-barrel well, and dry well. The choice of the branch on which to continue is again a chance event. Depending upon the outcome of this chance event, a terminating point is reached. The entire tree can be completed in this fashion.[1] Note that in Fig. 14.1 decision forks are denoted by the symbol □ and chance forks by the symbol ○.

The previous discussion presented a graphical method for representing the decision problem. However, nothing was said about how to choose the optimal path to travel on. Basically, the calculations described in the earlier sections of this chapter are required, namely, finding posterior probabilities, marginal probabilities, and Bayes' risks. For each possible path that can be followed, the loss is specified at the terminal point. Working backward from each terminal point to the nearest fork (a chance fork), a loss is placed in that fork, this cost being the expected cost taken with respect to the probabilities associated with the branches. These probabilities represent the probability of the state of nature, indicated by the terminal branch, being chosen, given the path followed to the last fork. For example, for the no-seismic data, drill path, the probability of the 500,000-barrel branch is just the prior probability that the well is a 500,000-barrel well, that is, 0.1. For the seismic-data, nonclosed structure, drill path, the probability of the 500,000-barrel branch is just the posterior probability that the well is a 500,000-barrel well, given the seismic reading was classified as a nonclosed structure, that is, 0.039. Again, working backward, the next fork is a decision fork. The loss associated with this fork is the minimum loss over the branches associated with that node. On the no-seismic data path, $-51{,}250$ represents the minimum of $-51{,}250$, $-45{,}000$, $-40{,}000$, and is associated with the action drill. Hence this is the best action to take, given the decision maker is at that fork. The symbol ($\times$) through the other two branches eliminates the actions unconditional lease and conditional lease from further consideration on that path. Similarly, on the seismic data, nonclosed structure path, $-45{,}000$ represents the minimum of 15,500, $-45{,}000$, and $-18{,}450$, and is associated with the action unconditionally lease. Hence this is the best action to take, given the decision maker is at that fork. The symbol ($\times$) through the other two branches eliminates the other two actions from further consideration on that path. The next fork on the seismic data

[1] In Fig. 14.1 only part of the tree is presented, but all other branches are easily drawn.

path is a chance fork. The loss associated with this fork is the expected cost taken with respect to the probabilities associated with the branches. These probabilities represent the (unconditional) probability that the seismic reading, indicated by the branch, is obtained, given the path followed to this fork. For the seismic data path, the probability that the seismic reading will lead to the nonclosed structure branch is just the unconditional probability that it will be classified as a nonclosed structure, that is, 0.215. Finally, the beginning fork has a loss associated with it of −65,984. This is the minimum of −51,250 that is associated with the no-seismic data branch and −65,984, which is associated with the seismic data branch (and obtained by adding the cost of taking seismic soundings, 12,000, to the −77,984 attached to the branch). Note that the cost of taking seismic soundings is denoted by the symbol II on the branch. Hence the no-seismic data branch is eliminated, and the optimal procedure is to follow the seismic data path, and the expected loss is −65,984, which is, of course, the solution obtained earlier. Again, it is worthwhile noting that the calculations required by using the decision-tree analysis are identical to those required by using the previously described analytical methods.

14.5 UTILITY FUNCTION

The oil-drilling example assumed that expected loss (profit) in monetary terms was the appropriate measure of the consequences of taking an action, given a state of nature. However, there are many situations where this is inappropriate. For example, suppose that an individual was offered the choice of accepting (1) a 50–50 chance of winning $10,000 or nothing or (2) receiving $4,000 with certainty. Many people would prefer the $4,000 even though the expected payoff on the 50–50 chance of winning $10,000 is $5,000. A company may be unwilling to invest a large sum of money in a new product even if the expected profit is substantial if there is a risk of loosing their investment and thereby becoming bankrupt. People buy insurance even though it is a poor investment because the insurance company must pay expenses and make a profit. Do these examples invalidate the previous material? Fortunately, there is a way of transforming monetary values into an appropriate scale that reflects the decision makers' preferences. This scale is called the *utility scale*, and it becomes the appropriate measure of the consequences of taking an action, given a state of nature. A detailed discussion of utilities can be found in the references at the end of this chapter.

14.6 CARNIVAL EXAMPLE

A carnival is sheduled to appear in a city on a given date. The profits obtained are heavily dependent upon the weather. In particular, if the weather is rainy, the carnival looses $15,000; if cloudy, the carnival looses $5,000; and if sunny, the carnival makes a profit of $10,000. The carnival has to set up equipment for its show but can cancel the show prior to setting up its equipment. This action results in a loss of \$1,000. Furthermore, by incurring an additional cost of \$1,000 the carnival can postpone its setup decision until the day before the scheduled performance. At this time they can obtain the local weather report. The Weather Bureau has compiled data based upon its predictions; it is given in Table 14.6. Furthermore, the Weather Bureau has compiled a prior distribution of the weather. In particular, the probabilities of rain, clouds, and sun are 0.1, 0.3, and 0.6, respectively.

Table 14.6 Weather Bureau Data

Probability that forecast is	Actual Weather		
	Rain	*Clouds*	*Sun*
Rain (R)	0.7	0.2	0.1
Clouds (C)	0.2	0.6	0.2
Sun (S)	0.1	0.2	0.7

Note that there are two actions: set-up (a_1) and no set-up (a_2). There are three states of nature: Rain (R), Clouds (C), and Sun (S). The loss function is presented in Table 14.7. The problem will be solved by first assuming the local Weather Bureau report is unavailable (no data). The expected loss $l(a)$ for each action is given by

Table 14.7 Loss Function for Carnival Example

Actions	State of nature		
	Rain	*Clouds*	*Sun*
a_1: set-up	15,000	5,000	−10,000
a_2: no set-up	1,000	1,000	1,000

$$l(a_1) = 15{,}000(0.1) + 5{,}000(0.3) - 10{,}000(0.6) = -\$3{,}000,$$
$$l(a_2) = 1{,}000(0.1) + 1{,}000(0.3) + 1{,}000(0.6) = \$1{,}000.$$

Hence the Bayes' principle leads to selecting action a_1, that is, setting up, and the associated expected loss is $-\$3{,}000$ (profit).

Now, the Weather Bureau report will be assumed to be available but at a cost of \$1,000. The posterior distribution can be obtained and is given in Table 14.8. A typical entry will be obtained. The posterior distribution that the weather will be sunny, given that the forecast is for rain is given by

$$\frac{(0.1)(0.6)}{(0.7)(0.1) + (0.2)(0.3) + (0.1)(0.6)} = 0.316.$$

Table 14.8 The Posterior Distribution for the Carnival Example

Weather forecast	State of nature		
	Rain	*Clouds*	*Sun*
R	0.368	0.316	0.316
C	0.062	0.563	0.375
S	0.020	0.123	0.857

The optimal Bayes' actions, given the various forecasts, are presented in Table 14.9. A typical entry in Table 14.9 will be obtained. Given that the forecast is for rain,

$$l_h(a_1) = (0.368)(15{,}000) + (0.316)(5{,}000) - (0.316)(10{,}000) + 1{,}000$$
$$= \$4{,}940$$

$$l_h(a_2) = \$1{,}000 + 1{,}000 = \$2{,}000.$$

Hence the Bayes' action is a_2, and the corresponding expected loss is \$2,000. Similarly, the marginal probability that the forecast will be rain is given by

$$(0.7)(0.1) + (0.2)(0.3) + (0.1)(0.6) = 0.19.$$

Hence, if the Weather Bureau reports are to be used, the Bayes' actions call for setting up if the forecast is for clouds or sun but not setting up if the forecast is for rain.

Table 14.9 Table of Bayes' actions, Expected Losses, and Marginal Distribution for Carnival Example

Forecast	*Bayes' action*	*Expected loss*	*Marginal distribution*
R	a_2	2,000	0.19
C	a_1	995	0.32
S	a_1	−6,655	0.49

Is utilization of the Weather Bureau data desirable? This calls for computing the unconditional expected loss with experimentation (weighted sum of the Bayes' losses); that is,

$$2{,}000(0.19) + 995(0.32) - 6{,}655(0.49) = -2{,}563.$$

Thus the "value" of Weather Bureau data is given by

$$-2{,}563 + 3{,}000 = 437,$$

(which is an actual loss relative to the no-data case), so that the Weather Bureau data is not worth the \$1,000 cost.

Finally, what is the most that the carnival would be willing to pay for any type of information about the weather? The expected loss with perfect information is given by

$$1{,}000(0.1) + 1{,}000(0.3) - 10{,}000(0.6) = -\$5{,}600,$$

so that some type of experimentation may lead to a potential saving, with a decision maker being willing to pay a "cost" for perfect information up to

$$-3{,}000 + 5{,}600 = \$2{,}600.$$

14.7 CONCLUSIONS

Decision analysis has become an important technique in the solution of business problems. It can be applied to broad problems facing management, such as determining whether or not to enter a new product field, or it can be used to solve smaller problems, such as that illustrated by the oil-drilling example. It is characterized by the decision maker enumerating all the available courses of action, expressing his utilities, and quantifying his subjective probabilities. When these data are available, decision analysis becomes a powerful tool in determining an optimal course of action. Of course, this approach also has its limitations because the data required, e.g., subjective probabilities, utilities, and so on, may be either impossible to obtain or heavily dependent upon the judgment of a single individual.

Selected References

1 Chernoff, H. and L. E. Moses: *Elementary Decision Theory*, Wiley, New York, 1959.

2 Hadley, G.: *Introduction to Probability and Statistical Decision Theory*, Holden-Day, San Francisco, 1967.

3 Pratt, J. W., H. Raiffa, and R. O. Schlaifer: *Introduction to Statistical Decision Theory* (preliminary edition), McGraw-Hill, New York, 1965.

4 Raiffa, H.: *Decision Analysis*, Addison-Wesley, Reading, Mass., 1968.

5 Schlaifer, R. O.: *Introduction to Statistics for Business Decisions*, McGraw-Hill, New York, 1961.

Problems

1 A new type of airplane is to be purchased by the Air Force, and the number of spare engines accompanying the order must be determined. The Air Force must order these spare engines in batches of 5 and can only choose among 15, 20, or 25 spares. The supplier of these engines has two plants, and the Air Force must make its decision prior to knowing which plant will be used. From past experience it is known that the number of spare engines required when production takes place at plant A is approximated by a Poisson distribution with parameter $\lambda = 21$, whereas the number of spare engines required when production takes place at plant B is approximated by a

Poisson distribution with parameter $\lambda = 24$. The cost of a spare engine purchased now is \$250,000, whereas the cost of purchasing a spare engine at a later date will be \$500,000. Holding costs and interest are to be neglected. Spares must always be supplied if they are demanded, and unused engines will be scrapped when the airplanes become obsolete. The loss function is given as

Action \ State of nature	$\theta_1: \lambda = 21$	$\theta_2: \lambda = 24$
a_1: order 15	6.8265×10^6	8.265×10^6
a_2: order 20	6.178×10^6	7.270×10^6
a_3: order 25	6.514×10^6	7.002×10^6

The Air Force know from past experience that ⅔ of all types of airplane engines are produced in plant *A* and only ⅓ in plant *B*. Furthermore, it is known that a similar type of engine was produced for an earlier version of the current airplane under consideration. The order size for this earlier type was the same as for the current model. Furthermore, its nonobsolete life is identical with that planned for the present version. The engine for the current order will be produced in the same plant as the previous model, although the Air Force is not aware of which of the two plants this is. The reason for this lack of knowledge is due to the haste in which the spare engine decision must be made. The Air Force has access to the data on the number of spares actually required for the older version (which had a Poisson distribution), but it does not have time to determine the production location.

(*a*) What is the Bayes' action, assuming that the information on the old airplane model is unavailable?

(*b*) How much money can be paid for "perfect information?"

(*c*) Assuming that cost of data on the old airplane model is free and 30 spares were required, determine the Bayes' action.

2 A large mill is faced with the problem of extending \$100,000 credit to a new customer, a dress manufacturer. The mill classifies typical companies into the categories: poor risk, average risk, and good risk. Their experience indicates that 30 percent of similar companies are poor risks, 50 percent are average risks, and 20 percent are good risks. If credit is extended, the expected profit for poor risks is −\$15,000, for average risks \$10,000, and for good risks \$20,000. If credit is not extended, the dress manufacturers will turn to another mill. The mill is able to consult a credit-rating organization for a fee of \$2,000. Their experience with this credit-rating company is given by

Credit company evaluation	*Actual credit rating, %*		
	Poor	*Average*	*Good*
Poor	50	40	20
Average	40	50	40
Good	10	10	40

(*a*) What is the Bayes' action, assuming the credit rating company is not used?
(*b*) How much money can be paid for "perfect information?"
(*c*) What is the optimal expected loss if the credit rating company data is used? Does it pay to utilize these data?
(*d*) What is the Bayes' action if the credit-rating company determines the dress manufacturer to be a poor risk?

3 A manufacturer produces items having a probability p of being defective. These items are formed into lots of 150. Past experience indicates that p is either 0.05 or 0.25, and, furthermore, in 80 percent of the lots produced p equals 0.05 (and in 20 percent of the lots p equals 0.25). These items are then used in an assembly, and ultimately their quality is determined before the final assembly leaves the plant. The manufacturer can initially screen each item in a lot at a cost of $10 per item, replacing defective items found, or use the items directly without screening. If the latter action is chosen, the cost of rework is ultimately $100 per defective item. The costs per lot are given by

	$p = 0.05$	$p = 0.25$
Screen	1,500	1,500
Do not screen	750	3,750

Because screening requires scheduling of inspectors and equipment, the decision to screen or not screen must be made 2 days before the potential screening takes place. However, one item can be taken from the lot and sent to a laboratory, and its quality (defective or nondefective) can be reported before the screen, no-screen decision must be made. The cost of this initial inspection is $125.

(*a*) What is the Bayes' action without looking at the single item?
(*b*) How much money can be paid for "perfect information?"
(*c*) What is the optimal expected cost if the quality of an item is determined before the screen, no-screen decision is made?
(*d*) What is the Bayes' action if the quality of an item is determined and found to be defective?

4 Assume that there are two weighted coins. Coin 1 has a probability of 0.3 of turning up heads, and coin 2 has a probability of 0.6 of turning up heads. The decision maker must decide which coin was tossed. The probability that coin 1 was tossed is 0.6, and the probability that coin 2 was tossed is 0.4. The loss matrix is

	Coin 1 tossed	*Coin 2 tossed*
a_1: say coin 1 tossed	0	1
a_2: say coin 2 tossed	1	0

(*a*) What is the Bayes' procedure (action) before the coin is tossed?
(*b*) What is the Bayes' procedure if the coin is tossed once and the outcome is heads? What if it is tails?

5 A new type of film for ordinary 35-millimeter cameras has been developed. It is packaged in sets of 5 sheets, each sheet providing an instantaneous snapshot. Since this is a new process, the manufacturer has attached an additional sheet to the package, so that the store may test 1 before the package of 5 is sold. In promoting the film, an offer to refund the entire purchase price of the film if 1 of the 5 is defective has been made. This refund must be paid by the camera store, and the selling price has been fixed at $1 if this guarantee is to be valid. The camera store may sell the film for 50 cents if the above guarantee is replaced by one that pays 10 cents for each defective sheet. The cost of the film to the camera store is 25 cents and is not returnable. The store may take three actions:

a_1: scrap the film,

a_2: sell the film for $1,

a_3: sell the film for 50 cents.

(*a*) If the six states of nature correspond to 0, 1, 2, 3, 4, 5 defective sheets in the package, complete the following loss table:

a \ θ	*0*	*1*	*2*	*3*	*4*	*5*
a_1	0.25					
a_2	−0.75		0.25			
a_3	−0.25	−0.15		0.05		

(*b*) The store has accumulated the following information on sales of 60 such packages:

Quality of attached sheet	*Defectives in box* 0	1	2	3	4	5
Good	10	8	6	4	2	0
Bad	0	2	4	6	8	10
Total	10	10	10	10	10	10

These data indicated that each state of nature is equally likely, so that this prior can be assumed. What is the Bayes' procedure (before testing the attached sheet) for a package of film?

(*c*) What is the optimal expected loss for a package of film if the attached sheet is tested? What is the Bayes' action if the sheet is good? If it is bad?

6 Solve the oil-drilling example if the profit per barrel of oil is increased to $2.

7 Solve the oil-drilling example by using the prior distribution formed from the data in Table 14.3.

8 Solve the carnival example if the cost of utilizing the Weather Bureau data is reduced to $500.

Simulation

The technique of simulation has long been an important tool of the designer, whether he be simulating airplane flight in a wind tunnel, simulating plant layouts with scale models of machines, or simulating lines of communication with an organization chart. With the advent of the high-speed digital computer with which to conduct simulated experiments, this technique also has become increasingly important to the operations researcher. Thus simulation has become an *experimental arm of operations research.*

The emphasis in the preceding chapters was on formulating and solving mathematical models that represent real systems. One of the main strengths of this approach is that it abstracts the essence of the problem and reveals its underlying structure, thereby providing insight into the cause-and-effect relationships within the system. Therefore, if it is possible to construct a mathematical model that is both a reasonable idealization of the problem and amenable to solution, this analytical approach usually is superior to simulation. However, many problems are so complex that they can not be solved analytically. Thus, even though it tends to be a relatively expensive procedure, simulation often provides the only practical approach to a problem.

Within operations research simulation typically also involves the construction of a model that is largely mathematical in nature. Rather than directly describing the overall behavior of the system, the *simulation model* describes the operation of the system in terms of *individual events* of the individual components of the system. In particular, the system is divided into elements whose behavior can be predicted, at least in terms of probability distributions, for each of the various possible states of the system and its inputs. The interrelationships between the elements also are built into the model. Thus simulation provides a means of dividing the model-building job into smaller component parts (where it may be possible to formulate each of these parts by methods described in other chapters) and then combining these parts in their natural order and allowing the computer to present the effect of their interaction on each other. After constructing the model, it is then activated (by generating input data) to simulate the actual operation of the system over time and record its aggregate behavior. By repeating this for the various alternative design configurations and comparing their performances, the most promising configurations can be identified. Because of statistical error, it is impossible to guarantee that the configuration yielding the best simulated performance is indeed the optimal one, but it should be at least near optimal if the simulated experiment was designed properly.

Thus simulation typically is nothing more or less than the technique of performing *sampling experiments* on the model of the system. The experiments are done on the model rather than on the real system itself only because the latter would be too inconvenient, expensive, and time consuming. Otherwise, simulated experiments should be viewed as virtually indistinguishable from ordinary statistical experiments, so that they also should be based upon sound statistical theory. Even though simulated experiments usually are executed on a digital computer, this is only because of the vast amount of data being generated and processed, rather than any inherent relationship.

15.1 ILLUSTRATIVE EXAMPLES

Example 1

Suppose you were offered the chance to play a game whereby you would repeatedly flip an unbiased coin until the difference between the number of heads tossed and the number of tails tossed is three. You would be required to pay $1 for each flip of the coin, but you would receive $8 at the end of each play of the game. You are not allowed to quit during a play of a game. Thus you win money if the number of flips required is less than eight, but you lose money if more than eight flips are required. How would you decide whether or not to play this game?

Many people would base this decision on simulation, although they probably would not call it by that name. (There is also an analytical solution for this game, but it is not a particularly elementary one.) In this case simulation would amount to nothing more than playing the game alone many times until it becomes clear whether it is worthwhile playing for stakes. Half an hour spent in repeatedly flipping a coin and recording the earnings or losses that would have resulted might be sufficient.

How would this simulated experiment be executed on a digital computer? Although the computer can not flip coins, it can generate numbers. Therefore it would generate (or be given) a sequence of random digits, each of which would correspond to a flip of a coin. (The generation of random numbers is discussed in Sec. 15.2.) The probability distribution for the outcome of a flip is that the probability of a head is ½ and the probability of a tail is ½, whereas there are 10 possible values of a random digit, each having a probability of $\frac{1}{10}$. Therefore, five of these values (say, 0,1,2,3,4) would be assigned an association with a head and the other five (say, 5,6,7,8,9) with a tail. Thus the computer would simulate the playing of the game by examining each new random digit generated and labeling it a head or a tail, according to its value. It would continue doing this, recording the outcome of each simulated play of the game, as long as desired.

To illustrate the computer approach to this simulated experiment, suppose that the computer had generated the following sequence of random digits:

8, 1, 3, 7, 2, 7, 1, 6, 5, 5, 7, 9, 0, 0, 3, 4, 3, 5, 6, 8, 5,
8, 9, 4, 8, 0, 4, 8, 6, 5, 3, 5, 9, 2, 5, 7, 9, 7, 2, 9, 3, 9,
8, 5, 8, 9, 2, 5, 7, 6, 9, 7, 6, 0, 7, 3, 9, 8, 2, 7, 1, 0, 3,
2, 6, 2, 7, 1, 3, 7, 0, 4, 4, 1, 8, 3, 2, 1, 3, 9, 5, 9, 0, 5,
0, 3, 8, 7, 8, 9, 5, 4, 0, 8, 3, 8, 0, 1.

Thus, denoting a head by H and a tail by T, the first simulated play of the game is $THHTHTHTTTT$, requiring 11 simulated flips of a coin. The subsequent simulated plays of the game require 5, 5, 9, 7, 7, 5, 3, 17, 5, 5, 3, 9, and 7 simulated flips, respectively, for an overall average of 7. This sample average would seem to indicate that, on the average, you should win about $1 for each play of the game. Therefore, if you do not have a relatively high aversion to risk, it appears that you should choose to play this game, preferably a large number of times. However, beware! One of the common errors in the use of simulation is that conclusions are based on overly small samples because the statistical analysis was inadequate or totally lacking. In this case the sample standard deviation is 3.67, so that the estimated standard deviation of the sample average is $3.67/\sqrt{14} \approx 0.98$. Therefore, even if it is assumed that the probability distribution of the number of flips required for a play of the game is a normal distribution (which is a gross assumption because the true distribution is skewed), any reasonable confidence interval for the true mean of this distribution would extend far above 8. Hence a much larger sample is required to draw a valid conclusion at a reasonable level of statistical significance. Unfortunately, since the standard deviation of a sample average is inversely proportional to the *square root* of the sample size, a large increase in the sample size is required to yield a relatively small increase in the precision of the estimate of the true mean. In this case it appears that perhaps an additional 100 simulated plays of the game would be adequate.

It so happens that the true mean of the number of flips required for a play of this game is 9. Thus, in the long run, you actually would lose about $1 for each play of the game.

Example 2

Consider the first single-server queueing theory model with Poisson input and exponential service times that was discussed in Sec. 9.6. Although this model already has been solved analytically, it will be instructive to consider how to use simulation to study it.

To summarize the physical operation of the system, arriving customers enter the queue, eventually are serviced by the server, and then leave. Thus it is necessary for the simulation model to describe and synchronize the arrival of customers and the servicing of customers. The two methods for handling such synchronization in a digital computer are *fixed-time incrementing* and *next-event incrementing*. They will be described in turn.

With fixed-time incrementing the following two-step procedure is used, beginning with the system in its initial state at a given point in time. First, *advance time* by a small *fixed amount*; add 1 to a register that serves as the "master clock" for the system to record the passage of this time. Second, *update the system* by determining what events occurred during this elapsed time unit and what the resulting state of the system is. Repeat these two steps for as many time units as desired.

For the queueing-theory model under consideration, only two types of events can occur during each of these elapsed time units, namely, one or more customers can *arrive* and one or more customers can *complete being served*. Furthermore, the probability of two or more arrivals or of two or more service completions during a time unit is negligible for this model if the time unit is relatively short. Thus the only two possible events during a time unit that need to be investigated are the arrival of one customer and the completion of service for one customer. Each of these events has a known probability. Therefore, just as in Example 1, to simulate whether an event occurs or not the computer only needs to generate a random number. For example, suppose that the probability that a customer will arrive during an elapsed time unit is 0.007. The computer would need to generate 1 of the 1,000 possible three-digit numbers (000,001,...,999) at random. By associating seven of the possible numbers (say, 000,...,006) with the event occurring, and the remaining numbers with the event not occurring, the random number generated determines the actual simulated outcome for that time unit. If a customer were in the process of being served, the computer would be programmed to use this same method to determine if a simulated service completion occurs or not during the elapsed time unit, given the probability of such a completion. However, if no customer were being served, the computer would decide automatically that no service completion had occurred during the elapsed time unit. To implement this, the computer would use an indicator that would be given one of two numerical values, depending upon whether the server was busy servicing a customer or not. Similarly, a counter would be used to record the current number of customers in the queue waiting to be served.

Thus, updating the system after an elapsed time unit amounts to updating the numbers that should be inserted into the indicator and the counter. At the same time, the computer would record the desired information about the aggregate behavior of the system during this time unit. For example, it could record the number of customers in the queueing system and the waiting time of any customer who just completed his wait. If it is sufficient to estimate only the mean rather than the probability distribution of each of these random variables, the computer would merely add the value (if any) for the current time unit to a cumulative sum. The sample averages would be obtained after the simulation run is completed by dividing these sums by the total elapsed time and the total number of customers, respectively.

Next-event incrementing differs from fixed-time incrementing in that the master clock is incremented by a variable amount rather than by a fixed amount each time. Conceptually, the next-event incrementing procedure is to keep the simulated system running without interruption until an event occurs, at which point the computer pauses momentarily to record the change in the system. To implement this conceptual idea, the computer actually proceeds by keeping track of when the next few simulated events are scheduled to occur, jumping in simulated time to the first of these events, and updating the system. This cycle is repeated as many times as desired.

For this example the computer needs to keep track of two future events, namely, when the next customer will arrive and when the server will finish servicing his current customer (if any). These times are obtained by taking a random observation from the probability distribution of interarrival and service times, respectively. As before, the computer takes such a random observation by generating and using a random number. (The technique for doing this is discussed subsequently in Sec. 15.2.) Thus, each time an arrival or service completion occurs, the computer first determines how long it will be until the next time this event will occur and then adds this to the current clock time.[1] This sum is then stored in a computer file. To determine which event will occur next, the computer finds the minimum of the clock times stored in the file. This procedure will be illustrated in Sec. 15.4 (see Table 15.8) for a specific single-server queueing system.

Several pertinent questions about how to conduct a simulation study of this type still remain to be answered. These answers are presented in a broader context in subsequent sections.

15.2 FORMULATING AND IMPLEMENTING A SIMULATION MODEL

Constructing the Model

The first step in a simulation study is to develop a model representing the system to be investigated. It is apparent that this requires the analyst to become thoroughly familiar with the operating realities of the system and the objectives of the study. Given this, the analyst probably would attempt to reduce the real system to a logical flow diagram. The system is thereby broken

[1] If the service completion leaves no customers left in the system, then the generation of the time until the next service completion is postponed until the next arrival occurs.

down into a set of components linked together by a master flow diagram, where the components themselves may be broken down into subcomponents and so on. Ultimately the system is decomposed into a set of elements for which operating rules may be given. These operating rules predict the events that will be generated by the corresponding elements, perhaps in terms of probability distributions. After specifying these elements, rules, and logical linkages, the model should be thoroughly tested piece by piece. This can be done partially by performing a gross version of the simulation on a desk calculator and checking whether each input is received from the appropriate source and each output is acceptable to the next submodel. However, the individual components of the model also should be tested alone to verify that their internal performance is reasonably consistent with reality.

It should be emphasized that, like any operations research model, the simulation model need not be a completely realistic representation of the real system. In fact, it appears that most simulation models err on the side of being overly realistic rather than overly idealized. With the former approach, the model easily degenerates into a mass of trivia and meandering details, so that a great deal of programming and computer time is required to obtain a small amount of information. Furthermore, failing to strip away trivial factors to get down to the core of the system may obscure the significance of those results that are obtained.

If the behavior of an element can not be predicted exactly, given the state of the system, it is better to take random observations from the probability distributions involved than to use averages to simulate this performance. This is true even when one is only interested in the average aggregate performance of the system because combining average performances for the individual elements may result in something far from average for the overall system.

One question that may arise when choosing probability distributions for the model is whether to use frequency distributions of historical data or to seek the theoretical probability distribution which best fits these data. The latter alternative usually is preferable because it would seem to come closer to predicting expected future performance rather than reproducing the idiosyncrasies of a certain period of the past.

Generating Random Numbers

As the example in Sec. 15.1 demonstrated, implementing a simulation model requires random numbers to obtain random observations from probability distributions. One method for generating such random numbers is to use a physical device such as a spinning disk or an electronic randomizer. Several tables of random numbers have been generated in this way, including one containing 1 million random digits, published by the Rand Corporation. An excerpt from the Rand table is given in Table 15.1.

Various relatively sophisticated statistical procedures have been proposed for testing whether a sequence of numbers constitutes a sample of random num-

Table 15.1 Table of Random Digits†

09656	96657	64842	49222	49506	10145	48455	23505	90430	04180
24712	55799	60857	73479	33581	17360	30406	05842	72044	90764
07202	96341	23699	76171	79126	04512	15426	15980	88898	06358
84575	46820	54083	43918	46989	05379	70682	43081	66171	38942
38144	87037	46626	70529	27918	34191	98668	33482	43998	75733
48048	56349	01986	29814	69800	91609	65374	22928	09704	59343
41936	58566	31276	19952	01352	18834	99596	09302	20087	19063
73391	94006	03822	81845	76158	41352	40596	14325	27020	17546
57580	08954	73554	28698	29022	11568	35668	59906	39557	27217
92646	41113	91411	56215	69302	86419	61224	41936	56939	27816
07118	12707	35622	81485	73354	49800	60805	05648	28898	60933
57842	57831	24130	75408	83784	64307	91620	40810	06539	70387
65078	44981	81009	33697	98324	46928	34198	96032	98426	77488
04294	96120	67629	55265	26248	40602	25566	12520	89785	93932
48381	06807	43775	09708	73199	53406	02910	83292	59249	18597
00459	62045	19249	67095	22752	24636	16965	91836	00582	46721
38824	81681	33323	64086	55970	04849	24819	20749	51711	86173
91465	22232	02907	01050	07121	53536	71070	26916	47620	01619
50874	00807	77751	73952	03073	69063	16894	85570	81746	07568
26644	75871	15618	50310	72610	66205	82640	86205	73453	90232

† Reproduced with permission from The Rand Corporation, *A Million Random Digits with 100,000 Normal Deviates*. Copyright, The Free Press, Glencoe, Ill., 1955, top of p. 182.

bers or not.[1] Basically the requirements are that each successive number in the sequence must have an equal probability of taking on any one of the possible values, and it must be statistically independent of the other numbers in the sequence. In other words, the numbers need to be random observations from a (discretized) *uniform distribution*.

If a digital computer is to be used for executing the simulation, the random numbers it needs could be fed into the computer from one of the available tables. (In fact, the Rand table already is available on punched cards.) However, it is more common to have the computer itself generate the random numbers. There are a number of methods for doing this, of which the most popular are the *congruential methods* (additive, multiplicative, and mixed). The *mixed congruential method* has become probably the most widely used in recent years, so we shall focus on this approach.

The **mixed congruential method** generates a *sequence* of random numbers by always calculating the next random number from the last one obtained, given an initial random number x_0 (called the *seed*), which may be obtained from some published source such as the Rand table. In particular, it calculates the $(n + 1)$st random number x_{n+1} from the nth random number x_n by using the recurrence relation

$$x_{n+1} \equiv (ax_n + c)(\text{modulo } m),$$

[1] The interested reader is referred to Selected References 4 and 6 for a description of these tests and for more details about the generation of random numbers.

where a, c, and m are positive integers ($a < m$, $c < m$). This mathematical notation signifies that x_{n+1} is the *remainder* when $(ax_n + c)$ is divided by m. Thus, the *possible* values of x_{n+1} are 0, 1, ..., $m - 1$, so that m represents the desired number of *different* values that could be generated for the random numbers. To illustrate, suppose that $m = 8$ (so that eight different possible values are desired), $a = 5$, $c = 7$, and $x_0 = 4$. The resulting sequence of random numbers are calculated in Table 15.2. (The sequence can not be continued

Table 15.2 Illustration of Mixed Congruential Method

n	x_n	$5x_n + 7$	$\frac{5x_n + 7}{8}$	x_{n+1}
0	4	27	$3 + \frac{3}{8}$	3
1	3	22	$2 + \frac{6}{8}$	6
2	6	37	$4 + \frac{5}{8}$	5
3	5	32	$4 + \frac{0}{8}$	0
4	0	7	$0 + \frac{7}{8}$	7
5	7	42	$5 + \frac{2}{8}$	2
6	2	17	$2 + \frac{1}{8}$	1
7	1	12	$1 + \frac{4}{8}$	4

further because it would just begin repeating the numbers in the same order.) Note that this sequence includes each of the eight possible numbers exactly once. This is a desirable property, but it does not occur with some choices of a and c. (Try $a = 4$, $c = 7$, $x_0 = 3$.) Fortunately, there are rules available for choosing values of a and c that will guarantee this property. (There are no restrictions on the seed x_0 because it only affects where the sequence begins and not the progression of numbers.)

For a binary computer with a word size of b bits, the usual choice for m is $m = 2^b$ because this is the total number of nonnegative integers that can be expressed within the capacity of the word size. (Any undesired integers that arise in the sequence of random numbers would then just not be used.) With this choice of m, the above property can be ensured by selecting any of the values $a = 1, 5, 9, 13, \ldots$ and $c = 1, 3, 5, 7, \ldots$. For a decimal computer with a word size of d digits ,the usual choice for m is $m = 10^d$, and the same property is ensured by selecting any of the values $a = 1, 21, 41, 61, \ldots$ and $c = 1, 3, 7, 9, 11, 13, 17, 19, \ldots$ (that is, all positive *odd* integers *except* those ending with the digit 5). The specific selection can be made on the basis of the *serial correlation* between successively generated numbers, which differs considerably among these alternatives.[1]

Frequently random numbers with only a relatively small number of digits are desired. For example, suppose that only three digits are desired, so that the possible values can be expressed as 000, 001, ..., 999. In such a case the usual procedure still is to use $m = 2^b$ or $m = 10^d$, so that an extremely large number of random numbers can be generated before the sequence starts repeating itself. However, except for purposes of calculating the next random number, all but three digits of each random number would be discarded. One convention is to take the *last* three digits (i.e., the three trailing digits).

The *multiplicative congruential method* is just the special case of the mixed congruential method, where $c = 0$. The *additive congruential method* also is similar, but it sets $a = 1$ and replaces c by some random number preceding x_n in the sequence, for example, x_{n-1} (so that more than one seed is required to start calculating the sequence).

Strictly speaking, the numbers generated by the computer should not be called random numbers because they are predictable and reproducible (which sometimes is advantageous). Therefore, they are sometimes given the name *pseudorandom numbers.* However, the important point is that they satisfactorily play the role of random numbers in the simulation if the method used to generate them is valid.

Generating Random Observations from a Probability Distribution

Given a sequence of random numbers, how can one generate a sequence of random observations from a given probability distribution?

For simple discrete distributions one answer is quite evident, as demonstrated by the examples of Sec. 15.2. Merely allocate the possible values of a random number to the various numbers in the probability distribution in direct proportion to the respective probabilities of those numbers. For example, consider the probability distribution of the outcome of a throw of two dice. It is known that the probability of throwing a 2 is $1/36$ (as is the probability of a 12), the probability of a 3 is $2/36$, and so on. Therefore $1/36$ of the possible values of a random number should be associated with throwing a 2, $2/36$ of the values with throwing a 3, and so forth. Thus, if two digit random numbers are being used, 72 of the 100 values would be selected for consideration, so that a random number would be rejected if it took on any one of the other 28 values.

[1] See R. R. Coveyou, "Serial Correlation in the Generation of Pseudo-Random Numbers," *Journal of the Association of Computing Machinery*, 7:72–74, 1960.

Then, 2 of the 72 possible values (say, 00 and 01) would be assigned an association with throwing a 2, 4 of them (say, 02, 03, 04, and 05) would be assigned to throwing a 3, and so on.

For more complicated distributions, the answer still is essentially the same although the procedure is slightly more involved. The *first step* is to construct the cumulative distribution function $F(x) = P\{X \leq x\}$, where X is the random variable involved. This can be done by *writing the equation* for this function, *graphically plotting* the function, or by *developing a table* giving the value of x for uniformly spaced values of $F(x)$ from 0 to 1. The *second step* is to generate a random decimal number between 0 and 1. This is done by obtaining a random integer number having the desired number of digits (including any leading zeros) and then placing a decimal point in front of it. The *final step* is to set $P\{X \leq x\}$ equal to the random decimal number and solve for x. This value of x is the desired random observation from the probability distribution. This procedure is illustrated in Fig. 15.1 for the case where the cumulative distribution function is plotted graphically and the random decimal number happens to be 0.5269.

When the given probability distribution is continuous, the procedure outlined above actually approximates this continuous distribution by a discrete distribution whose irregularly spaced points have equal probabilities. However, this is not particularly serious because the approximation can be made as accurate as desired by using a sufficiently large number of digits for the random number. Perhaps the greatest danger is that the approximation will be adequate everywhere except in the extreme tails of the distribution. For example, suppose that three-digit random numbers are being used. Then the values of $P\{X \leq x\}$ that will be sampled range from 0.000 to 0.999. However, it may be that those rare occurrences when the actual value taken on by X falls outside the range permitted in the simulation would have a critical impact on the

Figure 15.1 Illustration of procedure for obtaining a random observation from a given probability distribution.

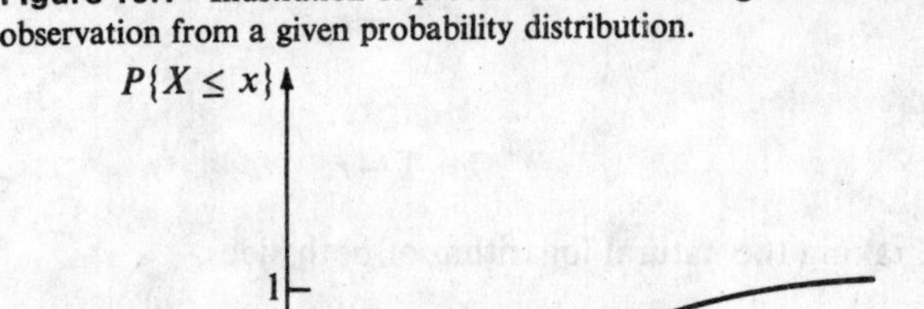

system. One refinement that would rectify this is to generate a second random number whenever the first one is (for the case of three-digit random numbers) 000 or 999 to select a value of $P\{X \leq x\}$ within the range from 0.000000 to 0.000999 or from 0.999000 to 0.999999.

Although the graphical procedure illustrated by Fig. 15.1 is convenient if the simulation is done manually, the digital computer must revert to some alternative approach such as the two mentioned earlier. One of these involved using a table of the cumulative distribution function. Having the computer do this is essentially equivalent to using the graphical procedure manually. The disadvantages of this *table look-up approach* are the great amount of work required to develop the required tables and the limitations on accuracy because of computer storage limitations. The other approach mentioned earlier requires *writing the equation* for the cumulative distribution function and then solving for the point where this function equals the random decimal number. This approach leads to a simple explicit solution for several important probability distributions, as illustrated below for the exponential and Erlang distributions. For other cases, time-consuming numerical methods would be required to obtain the solution. Fortunately, for each of several important probability distributions, special techniques have been developed for efficiently generating random observations from that particular distribution. Two of the simplest of these techniques that are applicable to the normal distribution and the chi-square distribution, repectively, are described at the end of this section.

Consider the *exponential distribution* (see Sec. 9.4) that has the cumulative distribution function

$$P\{X \leq x\} = 1 - e^{-\alpha x}, \text{for } x \geq 0,$$

where $1/\alpha$ is the mean of the distribution. Applying the procedure outlined above, set this function equal to a *random decimal number* between 0 and 1 denoted by r. Thus

$$1 - e^{-\alpha x} = r,$$

so

$$e^{-\alpha x} = 1 - r.$$

Therefore, taking the natural logarithm of both sides,

$$\ln(e^{-\alpha x}) = \ln(1 - r),$$

so that

$$-\alpha x = \ln(1 - r),$$

which yields

$$x = \frac{\ln(1 - r)}{-\alpha}$$

as the desired random observation from the exponential distribution. (It should be noted that other, more complicated techniques have also been developed for the exponential distribution, which may be faster for the computer to use than calculating a logarithm.)

A natural extension of the above procedure can also be used to generate a random observation from an *Erlang* (gamma) *distribution* (see Sec. 9.7). The sum of k independent exponential random variables, each with mean $1/k\alpha$, has the Erlang distribution with shape parameter k and mean $1/\alpha$. Therefore, given a sequence of k random decimal numbers between 0 and 1, say, $r_1, r_2, \ldots, r_k$, the desired random observation from the Erlang distribution is

$$x = \sum_{i=1}^{k} \frac{\ln(1 - r_i)}{-k\alpha},$$

which reduces to

$$x = -\frac{1}{k\alpha} \ln\left\{\prod_{i=1}^{k} (1 - r_i)\right\},$$

where $\prod$ denotes multiplication.

Since a random decimal number between 0 and 1 is just a random observation from a (discretized) *uniform distribution* between 0 and 1, $(1 - r)$ and the $(1 - r_i)$ in the above expressions are themselves random decimal numbers. Therefore, to save a subtraction it is common in practice to substitute r and r_i for these respective quantities.

A particularly simple technique for generating a random observation from a *normal distribution* (see Sec. 8.7) is obtained by applying the central limit theorem (presented in Sec. 8.15). Since a random decimal number has a *uniform distribution* from 0 to 1, it has mean ½ and standard deviation $1/\sqrt{12}$. Therefore this theorem implies that the sum of n random decimal numbers has approximately a normal distribution with mean $n/2$ and standard deviation $\sqrt{n/12}$. Thus, if $r_1, r_2, \ldots, r_n$ are a sample of random decimal numbers, then

$$x = \frac{\sigma}{2n/12} \sum_{i=1}^{n} r_i + \left(\mu - \frac{n}{2} \frac{\sigma}{2n/12}\right)$$

is a random observation from an approximately normal distribution with mean μ and standard deviation σ. This approximation is an excellent one (except in the tails of the distribution), even with small values of n. Thus values of n from 5 to 10 often are used; $n = 12$ also is a convenient value because it eliminates the square root terms from the above expression.

Various other approximate or exact techniques for generating random observations from a normal distribution have also been developed.

A simple method for handling the *chi-square distribution* (see Table 8.1) is to use the fact that it is obtained by summing squares of standardized normal random variables. Thus, if $y_1, y_2, \ldots, y_n$ are a sample of random observations from a normal distribution with mean 0 and standard deviation 1, such as could be obtained (approximately) by the technique described above, then

$$x = \sum_{i=1}^{n} y_i^2$$

is a random observation from a chi-square distribution with n degrees of freedom.

Preparing a Simulation Program

A number of detailed decisions confront the person who must write the computer program for executing a simulation. Although an extensive discussion of these issues is beyond the scope of this book, we shall mention several major considerations.

The basic purpose of most simulation studies is to compare alternatives. Therefore the simulation program must be flexible enough to readily accommodate the alternatives that will be considered. Since it often is impossible to predict exactly what interesting alternatives will be uncovered during the course of the study, it is essential that flexibility and provision for rapid, simple modifications be built into the program.

Most of the instructions in a simulation program are logical operations, whereas the relatively little actual arithmetic work required usually is of a very simple type. This should be reflected in the choice of computer equipment and programming language to be used.

The considerations mentioned above actually provided part of the motivation for an important breakthrough in the art of simulation that occurred during the early 1960s, namely, the development of general *simulation programming languages*. These languages are designed expecially to expedite the type of programming (and reprogramming) unique to simulation. Their specific purposes include the following. One objective is to provide a convenient means of describing the elements that commonly appear in simulation models. A second is to expedite changing the design configuration of the system being simulated, so that a large number of configurations (including some suggested during the course of the study) can be considered easily. Another service provided by the simulation languages is some type of internal timing and control mechanism, with related commands, to assist in the kind of bookkeeping that is required when executing a simulation run. They also are designed to conveniently obtain data and statistics on the aggregate behavior of the system being simulated. Finally, these languages provide simple operational procedures, such as introducing changes into the simulation model, initializing the state of the model, altering the kind of output data to be generated, and stacking a series of simulation runs.

For all these reasons a simulation program almost always should be written in one of these simulation languages rather than a general programming language. The tremendous savings in programming time ordinarily provided by the simulation languages usually compensates for any slight loss in computer running time. The two most widely used general simulation languages are GPSS and SIMSCRIPT, although several others also are available.[1]

Finally, it should be emphasized that the strategy of the simulation study should be planned carefully before finishing the simulation program. Merely letting the computer compile masses of data in a blind search for attractive alternatives is far from adequate. Simulation basically is a means for conducting an experimental investigation. Therefore, just as with a physical experiment, careful attention should be given to the construction of a theory of formal hypothesis to be tested and to the skillful design of a statistical experiment that will yield valid conclusions. This is the subject of discussion in Secs. 15.3 and 15.4.

Validating the Model

The typical simulation model consists of a high number of elements, rules, and logical linkages. Therefore, even when the individual components have been carefully tested, numerous small approximations can still cumulate into gross distortions in the output of the overall model. Consequently, after writing and debugging the computer program it is important to test the *validity* of the model for reasonably predicting the aggregate behavior of the system being simulated.

When some form of the real system has already been in operation, its performance data should be compared with the corresponding output data from the model. Standard statistical tests can sometimes be used to determine whether the differences in the means, variances, and probability distributions generating the two sets of data are statistically significant. The time-dependent behavior of the data might also be compared statistically. If the data are not amenable to statistical analysis, another approach is to ask personnel familiar with the behavior of the real system if they can discriminate between the two sets of data.

If the model is intended to simulate alternative design configurations or operating policies for a proposed system for which no actual data are available, it may be worthwhile to conduct a *field test* to collect some real data to compare with the output of the model. This might involve constructing a small prototype of some version of the proposed system and placing it into operation. Another possibility might be to temporarily alter an existing system to correspond to one of the proposals.

However, field tests frequently are too expensive and time consuming to be used. Without any real data as a standard of comparison, the only way to validate the overall model is to have knowledgeable people carefully check the credibility of output data for a variety of situations. Even when no basis exists

[1] A comparison of these languages is given by Howard S. Krasnow and Reino A. Merikallio, "The Past, Present, and Future of General Simulation Languages," *Management Science*, 11(2): 236–267, 1964. Also see Selected References 1, 3, 5, and 6.

for checking the reasonableness of the data for a *single* situation, some conclusions usually can be drawn about how the *relative* performance of the system should change as various parameters are changed. It is especially important to convince the *decision maker* of the credibility of the model, so he will be willing to use it to at least *aid* his decisions. If the model may be used again in the future, careful records should be kept of its predictions and of actual results to continue the validation process.

15.3 EXPERIMENTAL DESIGN FOR SIMULATION

Selecting a Statistical Procedure[1]

The underlying statistical theory applicable to *simulated* experimentation is essentially indistinguishable from that for *physical* experimentation. Thus the design of a simulated experiment should be based upon the large body of knowledge comprising the science of statistics.

There are, however, differences between physical and simulated experimentation regarding the emphasis placed on using the various types of statistical procedures. Physical experiments frequently involve testing hypotheses about the value of a population parameter or about whether several population means are equal. Simulated experiments typically place more emphasis on *optimization*. It probably is taken for granted that alternative design configurations have different population means for the index of performance of the system. Instead, the objective of the simulation study often is to find the alternative yielding the greatest mean index of performance[2]. Hence *multiple decision tests* and complete or partial *ordering procedures* frequently are appropriate for simulated experiments. Furthermore, *sequential procedures* tend to be useful, both because the evolution of the experiments may be difficult to predict and because a simulated experiment often can be resumed relatively easily.

Another difference between these two types of experiments is the degree to which conditions (under which alternatives are compared) can be made as identical as possible. Only simulated experiments can control the variability in the behavior of the elements of the system during the course of the experiment. By reproducing the same sequence of random numbers for each alternative simulated, it often is possible to reproduce an identical sequence of events. This sharpens the contrast between alternatives by reducing the residual variation in the differences in the aggregate performance of the system, so that much smaller sample sizes are required to detect statistically significant differences. Therefore this approach usually is far superior to generating new random

[1] This subsection assumes some knowledge of statistical procedures.

[2] In some cases, however, the objective is just to *describe* the performance of proposed systems or policies for management's evaluation and decision making, so *point estimates* and *confidence intervals* probably would be obtained. Simulated experiments also are occasionally conducted to determine which factors significantly influence the performance of the system (perhaps to guide subsequent experimentation), in which case *analysis of variance* probably would be used.

numbers for each alternative. The fact that reproducing the same random numbers does not yield statistically independent results should not be of great concern. The correct procedure for comparing only two alternatives is to pair the results regarding the aggregate performance of the system that were produced by the same events. Since these pairs of results are obtained under the same experimental conditions, the differences between them become the relevant sample observations. This sample would be used to test the hypothesis that the mean of these differences is zero and to obtain a confidence interval estimate of this mean. This would thereby indicate whether there is a statistically significant difference between the means of the performance index of the system for the two alternatives. If more than two alternatives need to be compared, the *Bonferroni inequality* can be used to construct *simultaneous confidence intervals* on the means of the differences for the various pairs of alternatives.[1]

Often it is possible to express the alternatives in terms of the values of one or more continuous design variables. In these cases there actually is an infinite number of alternatives (although the differences among some of them are minute). Since it would be impossible to simulate all of them, it is necessary to take a selective sample of these alternatives and then estimate the value of the design variables that will maximize some index of performance for the system. There now exists considerable literature giving efficient procedures for experimentally determining the maximum of a mathematical function to within a specified accuracy.[2]

Variance Reducing Techniques

Since considerable computer time usually is required for simulation runs, it is important to obtain as much and as precise information as possible from the amount of simulation that can be done. Unfortunately there has been a tendency in practice to apply simulation uncritically without giving adequate thought to the efficiency of the experimental design. This has been true despite the fact that considerable progress has been made in developing special techniques for increasing the precision (i.e., decreasing the variance) of sample estimators.

These variance reducing techniques often are called *Monte Carlo* techniques (a term sometimes applied to simulation in general). Since they tend to be rather sophisticated, it is not possible to explore them deeply here. However, we shall attempt to impart the flavor of these techniques and the great increase in precision they sometimes provide by presenting two of them in the following example.

Consider the *exponential distribution* whose parameter has a value of 1. Thus its probability density function is $f(x) = e^{-x}$, as shown in Fig. 15.2, and its

[1] See Albert H. Bowker and Gerald J. Lieberman, *Engineering Statistics*, 2d ed., pp. 304–308, Prentice-Hall, Englewood Cliffs, N.J., 1972.

[2] A survey of the procedures available for this problem is given by Douglass J. Wilde, *Optimum Seeking Methods*, Prentice-Hall, Englewood Cliffs, N.J., 1963.

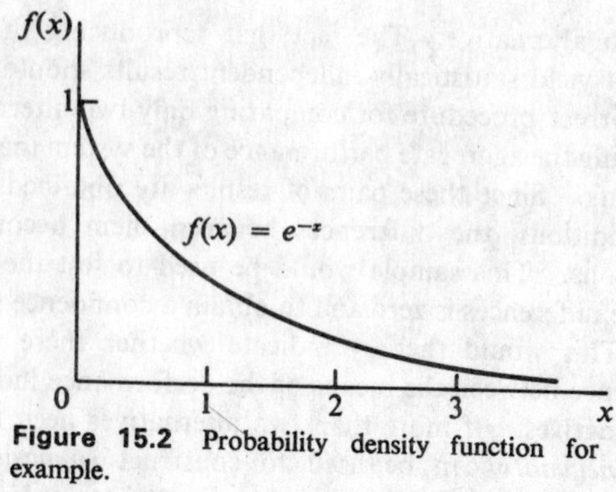

Figure 15.2 Probability density function for example.

cumulative distribution function is $F(x) = 1 - e^{-x}$. It is known that the mean of this distribution is 1. However, suppose this were not known and that it is desired to estimate this mean by using simulation.

To provide a standard of comparison for the two variance-reducing techniques, consider first the straightforward simulation approach, sometimes called the *crude Monte Carlo* technique. This approach involves generating some *random observations* from the exponential distribution under consideration and then using the *average* of these observations to estimate the mean. As described in Sec. 15.2, these random observations would be

$$x_i = -\ln(1 - r_i), \text{ for } i = 1, 2, \ldots, n,$$

where $r_1, r_2, \ldots, r_n$ are random decimal numbers between 0 and 1. Using a portion of Table 15.1 to obtain 10 such random decimal numbers, the resulting random observations are shown in Table 15.3. (These same random numbers also are used to illustrate the variance-reducing techniques to sharpen the comparison.) Notice that the sample average is 0.779, as opposed to the true mean of 1.000. However, because the standard deviation of the sample average happens to be $1/\sqrt{n}$, or $1/\sqrt{10}$ in this case (as could be estimated from the sample), an error of this amount or larger would occur approximately one-half of the time. Furthermore, since the standard deviation of a sample average always is inversely proportional to $\sqrt{n}$, this sample size would need to be quadrupled to reduce this standard deviation by one-half. These somewhat disheartening facts suggest the need for other techniques that would obtain such estimates more precisely and more efficiently.

A relatively simple Monte Carlo technique for obtaining better estimates is **stratified sampling.** There are two shortcomings of the crude Monte Carlo approach that are rectified by stratified sampling. First, by the very nature of randomness, a random sample may not provide a particularly uniform cross section of the distribution. For example, the random sample given in Table 15.3 has no observations between 0.014 and 0.328 even though the probability that a random observation will fall inside this interval is greater than ¼.

Table 15.3 Example for Crude Monte Carlo Technique

i	Random number r_i†	Random observation $x_i = -\ln(1 - r_i)$
1	0.495	0.684
2	0.335	0.408
3	0.791	1.568
4	0.469	0.633
5	0.279	0.328
6	0.698	1.199
7	0.013	0.014
8	0.761	1.433
9	0.290	0.343
10	0.693	1.183
		Total = 7.793
		Estimate of mean = 0.779

† Actually, 0.0005 was added to the indicated value for each of the r_i so that the range of their possible values would be from 0.0005 to 0.9995 rather than from 0.000 to 0.999.

Second, certain portions of a distribution may be more critical than others for obtaining a precise estimate, but random sampling gives no special priority to obtaining observations from these portions. For example, the tail of an exponential distribution is especially critical in determining its mean. However, the random sample in Table 15.3 includes no observations larger than 1.568, even though there is at least a small probability of *much* larger values. This is the basic explanation for this particular sample average being far below the true mean. Stratified sampling circumvents these difficulties by dividing the distribution into portions called *strata*, where each stratum would be sampled individually with disproportionately heavy sampling of the more critical strata.

To illustrate, suppose that the distribution is divided into *three* strata in the manner shown in Table 15.4. These strata were chosen to correspond to

Table 15.4 Formulation of Stratified Sampling example

Stratum	Portion of distribution	Stratum random no.	Sample size	Sampling weight
1	$0 \le F(x) \le 0.64$	$r_i' = 0 + 0.64r_i$	4	$w_i = \frac{4/10}{0.64} = \frac{5}{8}$
2	$0.64 \le F(x) \le 0.96$	$r_i' = 0.64 + 0.32r_i$	4	$w_i = \frac{4/10}{0.32} = \frac{5}{4}$
3	$0.96 \le F(x) \le 1$	$r_i' = 0.96 + 0.04r_i$	2	$w_i = \frac{2/10}{0.04} = 5$

observations approximately from 0 to 1, from 1 to 3, and from 3 to infinity, respectively. To ensure that the random observations generated for each stratum actually lie in that portion of the distribution, the random decimal numbers must be converted into the indicated range for $F(x)$, as shown in the third column of Table 15.4. The number of observations to be generated from each stratum is given in the fourth column.[1] The last column then shows the resulting *sampling weight* for each stratum, i.e., the *ratio* of the *sampling proportion* (the fraction of the total sample to be drawn from the stratum) to the *distribution proportion* (the probability of a random observation falling inside the stratum). These sampling weights roughly reflect the relative importance of the respective strata in determining the mean.

Given the formulation of the stratified sampling approach shown in Table 15.4, the same random numbers used in Table 15.3 yield the observations given in the fifth column in Table 15.5. However, it would not be correct to use the unweighted average of these observations to estimate the mean because certain portions of the distributions have been sampled more than others. Therefore, before taking the average, the observations from each stratum should be divided by the sampling weight for that stratum to give porportionate weightings to the different portions of the distribution, as shown in the last column of Table 15.5. The resulting *weighted* average of 0.948 provides the desired estimate of the mean.

The second variance-reducing technique we shall mention is the method of **complementary random numbers.**[2] The motivation for this method is that the "luck of the draw" on the random decimal numbers generated may cause the average of the resulting random observations to be substantially on one side of the true mean, whereas the *complements* of those random decimal numbers (which are themselves random decimal numbers) would have tended to yield a nearly opposite result. (For example, the random decimal numbers in Table 15.3 average less than 0.5, and none are as large as 0.8, which led to an estimate substantially below the true mean.) Therefore, using *both* the original random decimal numbers *and* their complements to generate random observations and then calculating the *combined* sample average should provide a more precise estimator of the mean. This is illustrated in Table 15.6,† where the first three columns come from Table 15.3 and the last two columns use the complementary random decimal numbers, which results in a combined sample average of 0.920.

This example has suggested that the variance-reducing techniques provide

[1] These sample sizes are roughly based on a recommended guideline that they be proportional to the *product* of the *probability* of a random observation falling inside the corresponding stratum *times* the *standard deviation* within this stratum.

[2] This method is a special case of the method of *antithetic variates*, which attempts to generate *pairs* of random observations having a high *negative* correlation, so that the combined average will tend to be closer to the mean.

† It should be noted that 20 calculations of a logarithm were required in this case, in contrast to the 10 that were required by each of the preceding techniques.

Table 15.5 Example for Stratified Sampling

Stratum	i	Random number r_i	Stratum random no. r_i'	Stratum random observation $x_i' = -\ln(1 - r_i')$	Sampling weight w_i	$\frac{x_i'}{w_i}$
1	1	0.495	0.317	0.381	$\frac{5}{8}$	0.610
	2	0.335	0.215	0.242	$\frac{5}{8}$	0.387
	3	0.791	0.507	0.707	$\frac{5}{8}$	1.131
	4	0.469	0.300	0.357	$\frac{5}{8}$	0.571
2	5	0.279	0.729	1.306	$\frac{5}{4}$	1.045
	6	0.698	0.864	1.995	$\frac{5}{4}$	1.596
	7	0.013	0.644	1.033	$\frac{5}{4}$	0.826
	8	0.761	0.884	2.154	$\frac{5}{4}$	1.723
3	9	0.290	0.9716	3.561	5	0.712
	10	0.693	0.9877	4.398	5	0.880

Total = 9.481
Estimate of mean = 0.948

Table 15.6 Example for Method of Complementary Random Numbers

i	Random number r_i	Random observation $x_i = -\ln(1 - r_i)$	Complementary random number $r_i' = 1 - r_i$	Random observation $x_i' = -\ln(1 - r_i')$
1	0.495	0.684	0.505	0.702
2	0.335	0.408	0.665	1.092
3	0.791	1.568	0.209	0.234
4	0.469	0.633	0.531	0.756
5	0.279	0.328	0.721	1.275
6	0.698	1.199	0.302	0.359
7	0.013	0.014	0.987	4.305
8	0.761	1.433	0.239	0.272
9	0.290	0.343	0.710	1.236
10	0.693	1.183	0.307	0.366
		Total: 7.793		10.597

Estimate of mean = $\frac{1}{2}(0.799 + 1.060) = 0.920$

a much more precise estimator of the mean than does straightforward simulation. These results definitely were not a coincidence, as a derivation of the variance of the estimators would show. In comparison with straightforward simulation, these techniques (including several more complicated ones not presented here) do indeed provide a much more precise estimator with the same amount of computer time, or as precise an estimator with much less computer time. Despite the fact that additional analysis may be required to incorporate one or more of these techniques into the simulation study, the rewards should not be foregone readily.

Although this example was a particularly simple one, it is often possible, though more difficult, to apply these techniques to much more complex problems. For example, suppose that the objective of the simulation study is to estimate the mean waiting time of customers in a queueing system (such as those described in Chap. 10). Since both the probability distribution of time between arrivals and the probability distribution of service times are involved, and since consecutive waiting times are not statistically independent, this problem may appear to be beyond the capabilities of the variance-reducing techniques. However, as has been described in detail elsewhere,[1] these techniques and others can indeed be applied to this type of problem very advantageously. For example, the method of *complementary random numbers* can be applied simply by repeating the original simulation run, substituting the complements of the original random decimal numbers to generate the corresponding random observations.

Tactical Problems

There are several special *tactical* issues that arise in connection with gathering the data from simulated experiments. We shall briefly describe these here and then subsequently elaborate on certain ways of dealing with them.

Many simulation studies are concerned with investigating systems that operate continually in a steady-state condition. Unfortunately, a simulation model can not be operated this way; it must be started and stopped. Because of the artificiality introduced by the abrupt beginning of operation, the performance of the simulated system does not become representative of the corresponding real-world system until it too has essentially reached a steady-state condition (i.e., until the probability distribution of the state of the simulated system has essentially reached a limiting *equilibrium* distribution). Thus one tactical problem is how to obtain data that are relevant for predicting the *steady-state* behavior of the real system.

The traditional way of dealing with this problem is to run the simulation model for some time without collecting data until it is believed that the simulated

[1] S. Ehrenfeld and S. Ben-Tuvia, "The Efficiency of Statistical Simulation Procedures," *Technometrics*, 4(2): 257–275, 1962. Also see chap. 10 of Selected Reference 5. Selected Reference 2 includes a general introduction to the theory and application of various variance-reducing techniques.

system has essentially reached a steady-state condition. Unfortunately, it is difficult to estimate just how long this *stabilization period* needs to be. Furthermore, available analytical results suggest that a surprisingly long period is required, so that a great deal of unproductive computer time must be expended. Section 15.4 presents a new statistical approach that eliminates these difficulties.

A related tactical issue is the selection of the *starting conditions* for the simulated system. The traditional recommendation is that the simulated system should be started in a state as representative of steady-state conditions as possible to minimize the required length of the stabilization period. However, the underlying objective of the simulated experiment is to *estimate* these conditions, so little advance information may be available to guide the selection in this way. The procedure is Sec. 15.4 also eliminates this difficulty.

Most statistical sampling procedures assume that the experimental output data are in the form of a collection of distinct and statistically independent random observations from some underlying probability distribution. By contrast, because of the nature of the problems for which simulation is used, the observations from a simulated experiment are likely to be highly correlated. For example, there is a high correlation between the waiting times of consecutive customers in a queueing system. Furthermore, many measures of performance are such that the simulated experiment yields this measure continuously as a function of time rather than as a sequence of separate observations. Thus another tactical problem is how to collect the data so as to circumvent these difficulties.

One traditional method is to execute a series of completely separate and independent simulation runs of equal length and use the average measure of performance for each run (excluding the initial stabilization period) as an individual observation. The main disadvantage is that each run requires an initial stabilization period for approaching a steady-state condition, so that much of the simulation time is unproductive. The second traditional method eliminates this disadvantage by making the runs consecutively, using the ending condition of one run as the steady-state starting condition for the next run. In other words, there is only one continuous overall simulation run that (except for the one initial stabilization period) is divided for bookkeeping purposes into a series of equal portions (runs). The average measure of performance for each portion is then treated as an individual observation. The disadvantage of this method is that it does not eliminate the correlation between observations entirely, even though it may reduce it considerably by making the portions sufficiently long.

Once again, these difficulties are eliminated by the new statistical approach in Sec. 15.4.

15.4 THE CYCLE METHOD OF STATISTICAL ANALYSIS

The subsection on tactical problems in Sec. 15.3 described several difficult tactical problems in gathering data from simulated experiments and the shortcomings of traditional statistical procedures in dealing with these problems.

We shall now present a recently developed statistical approach[1] that is especially designed to eliminate these problems.

The basic concept underlying this approach is that a simulation run for many systems can be divided into a series of **cycles** such that the behavior of the system during different cycles are both *statistically independent* and *identically distributed.* Thus, by calculating some *statistic* to summarize the behavior of interest within each cycle, these statistics for the respective cycles constitute a series of independent and identically distributed observations that can be analyzed by standard statistical procedures. Since the system keeps going through these independent and identically distributed cycles whether or not it is yet in a steady-state condition, these observations are directly applicable from the outset for estimating the steady-state behavior of the system.

For cycles to possess these properties they must each begin at the same *regeneration point*, i.e., at the point where the system again enters a certain special state from which the simulation can proceed without any knowledge of its past history. The system can be viewed as *regenerating* itself at this point in the sense that the probabilistic structure of the future behavior of the system depends upon only being at this point and not on anything that happened previously. (This is the *Markovian property* described in Sec. 8.18 for Markov chains.) A cycle *ends* when the system again reaches the regeneration point (when the next cycle begins). Thus the length of a cycle is just the elapsed time between consecutive occurrences of the regeneration point, which is a random variable depending upon the evolution of the system.

When *next-event incrementing* is being used, a typical regeneration point is a point at which an event has just occurred but no future events have yet been scheduled. Thus nothing needs to be known about the history of previous schedulings, and the simulation can start from scratch in scheduling future events. When fixed-time incrementing is being used, a regeneration point is a point at which the probabilities of possible events occurring during the next unit of time do not depend upon when any past events occurred but only on the current state of the system.

Not every system possesses regeneration points, so this *cycle method* of collecting data can not always be used. Furthermore, even when there are regeneration points, the one chosen to define the beginning and ending points of the cycles must recur frequently enough so that at least several cycles will be obtained with a reasonable amount of computer time.[2] Thus some care must be taken in choosing a suitable regeneration point.

EXAMPLE Suppose that information needs to be obtained about the steady-state behavior of a system that can be formulated as a *single-server queueing*

[1] Michael A. Crane and Donald L. Iglehart, "Statistical Analysis of Discrete-Event Simulations," *Proceedings of the 1974 Winter Simulation Conference*, Washington, D.C., January 1974. Also see articles by these authors appearing in the *Journal of the Association of Computing Machinery*, in approximately 1974.

[2] The theoretical requirements for the method are that the expected cycle length be *finite* and that the number of cycles would go to infinity if the system continued operating indefinitely.

system (see Sec. 9.2). However, both the interarrival and service times have a *uniform distribution* with a range from 5 to 25 and from 0 to 20, respectively, so that analytical results are not available. Therefore simulation with *next-event incrementing* is to be used to obtain the desired results.

Except for the distributions involved, the general approach is the same as described in Sec. 15.1 for Example 2. Suppose that *one-digit* random numbers are used to generate the random observations from the distributions, as shown in Table 15.7. Beginning the simulation run with *zero* customers in the system

Table 15.7 Correspondence between Random Numbers and Random Observations for Queueing System Example

Random number	*Interarrival time*	*Service time*
0	6	1
1	8	3
⋮	⋮	⋮
9	24	19

then yields the results summarized in Table 15.8 and Fig. 15.3, where the random numbers are obtained sequentially as needed from the tenth row of Table 15.1.†

For this system, one *regeneration point* is where an *arrival* occurs with *no* previous customers left. At this point the probabilistic structure of when future arrivals and service completions will occur is completely independent of any previous history. The only relevant information is that the system has just entered the special state of having had *zero* customers and the time until the next arrival reach *zero*. The simulation run would not previously have scheduled any future events but would now generate *both* the next interarrival time and service times.

The only other regeneration points for this system are where an arrival and service completion occur simultaneously with a prespecified number of customers in the system. These points would occur only rarely[1] for the real system because its distributions for interarrival and service times are *continuous*. However, they would occur with some frequency in the simulation run because Table 15.7 *discretizes* the distributions actually used to generate the random observations. Therefore, one of these points actually could be chosen to define a *cycle*. However, the regeneration point described in the preceding paragraph occurs much more frequently and so is a better choice. With this selection, the five complete cycles of the simulation run are those shown in Fig. 15.3.

† When both an interarrival and a service time need to be generated at the same time, the interarrival time has been obtained first.

[1] More precisely, the probability is *zero* than an arrival and service completion will occur at *exactly* the same time.

Table 15.8 Simulation Run for Queueing System Example

Time	Number of customers	Random number	Next arrival	Next service completion
0	0	9	24	...
24	1	2,6	34	37
34	2	4	48	37
37	1	6	48	50
48	2	4	62	50
50	1	1	62	53
53	0	...	62	...
62	1	1,1	70	65
65	0	..	70	...
70	1	3,9	82	89
82	2	1	90	89
89	1	4	90	98
90	2	1	98	98
98	2	1,5	106	109
106	3	6	124	109
109	2	2	124	114
114	1	1	124	117
117	0	...	124	...
124	1	5,6	140	137
137	0	..	140	...
140	1	9,3	164	147
147	0	...	164	...
164	1			

Figure 15.3 Outcome of the simulation run for the queueing system example.

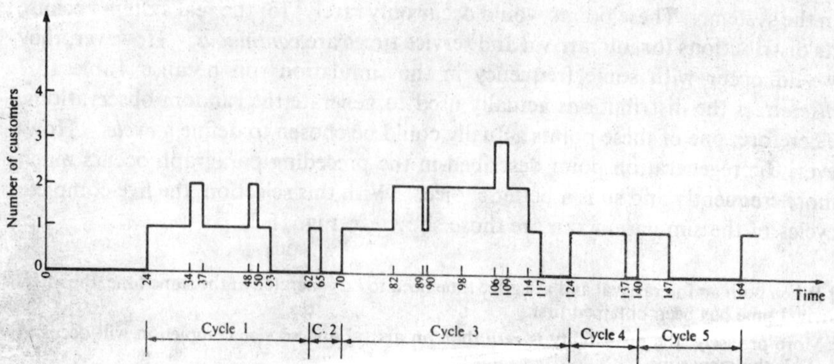

There are various types of information about the steady-state behavior of the system that can be obtained from this simulation run, including point estimates and confidence intervals for the expected number of customers in the system, the expected waiting time, and so on. In each case it is only necessary to use the corresponding statistics from the respective cycles and the lengths of the cycles. We shall first present the general statistical expressions for the cycle method and then apply them to this example.

Statistical Formulas

Formally speaking, the statistical problem for the cycle method is to obtain estimates of the expected value of some random variable X of interest. This is to be done by calculating a statistic Y for each cycle such that

$$E(X) = \frac{E(Y)}{E(Z)},$$

where the random variable Z is an appropriate measure of the *size* of the cycle. Thus, if n complete cycles are generated during the simulation run, the data gathered are $Y_1, Y_2, \ldots, Y_n$ and $Z_1, Z_2, \ldots, Z_n$ for the respective cycles.

Letting $\bar{Y}$ and $\bar{Z}$ respectively denote the sample averages for these two sets of data, the corresponding *point estimate* of $E(X)$ would be obtained from the formula

$$\text{est}\,\{E(X)\} = \frac{\bar{Y}}{\bar{Z}}$$

To obtain a *confidence interval estimate* of $E(X)$, it is first necessary to calculate several quantities from the data. These include the *sample variances*

$$s_{11} = \frac{1}{n-1}\sum_{i=1}^{n}(Y_i - \bar{Y})^2 = \frac{1}{n-1}\sum_{i=1}^{n} Y_i^2 - \frac{1}{n(n-1)}\left(\sum_{i=1}^{n} Y_i\right)^2,$$

$$s_{22} = \frac{1}{n-1}\sum_{i=1}^{n}(Z_i - \bar{Z})^2 = \frac{1}{n-1}\sum_{i=1}^{n} Z_i^2 - \frac{1}{n(n-1)}\left(\sum_{i=1}^{n} Z_i\right)^2$$

and the combined *sample covariance*

$$s_{12} = \frac{1}{n-1}\sum_{i=1}^{n}(Y_i - \bar{Y})(Z_i - \bar{Z}) = \frac{1}{n-1}\sum_{i=1}^{n} Y_i Z_i - \frac{1}{n(n-1)}\left(\sum_{i=1}^{n} Y_i\right)\left(\sum_{i=1}^{n} Z_i\right).$$

Let α be the constant such that $(1 - 2\alpha)$ is the desired *confidence coefficient* for the confidence interval, and then look up K_α in Table A5.1 (see Appendix 5) for the normal distribution. Set

$$c = \frac{K_\alpha^2}{n}$$

and

$$d = \sqrt{(\bar{Y}\bar{Z} - cs_{12})^2 - (\bar{Y}^2 - cs_{11})(\bar{Z}^2 - cs_{22})}.$$

If n is not too small, a close approximation[1] of the desired *confidence interval estimate* of $E(X)$ is then given by

$$\frac{(\overline{Y}\overline{Z} - cs_{12}) - d}{\overline{Z}^2 - cs_{22}} \leq E(X) \leq \frac{(\overline{Y}\overline{Z} - cs_{12}) + d}{\overline{Z}^2 - cs_{22}};$$

that is, the probability is approximately $(1 - 2\alpha)$, so that the end points of this interval will surround the actual value of $E(X)$.

Application of the Statistical Formulas to the Example

Consider first how to estimate the *expected waiting time* for a customer *before* beginning service (denoted by W_q in Chap. 9). Thus the random variable X now would represent a customer's waiting time excluding service, so

$$W_q = E(X).$$

The corresponding information gathered during the simulation run is the *actual* waiting time incurred by the respective customers. Therefore, for each cycle the summary statistic Y would be the *sum of the waiting times*, and the size of the cycle Z would be the *number of customers*, so that

$$W_q = \frac{E(Y)}{E(Z)}.$$

For cycle 1, a total of three customers are processed, so $Z_1 = 3$. The first customer incurs no waiting before beginning service, the second waits 3 units of time (from 34 to 37), and the third waits 2 units (from 48 to 50), so $Y_1 = 5$. Proceeding similarly for the other cycles, the data for the problem are

$$\begin{aligned} Y_1 &= 5, & Z_1 &= 3 \\ Y_2 &= 0, & Z_2 &= 1 \\ Y_3 &= 34, & Z_3 &= 5 \\ Y_4 &= 0, & Z_4 &= 1 \\ Y_5 &= 0, & Z_5 &= 1 \\ \overline{Y} &= 7.8, & \overline{Z} &= 2.2. \end{aligned}$$

Therefore the *point estimate* of W_q is

$$\text{est}\{W_q\} = \frac{7.8}{2.2} = 3\frac{6}{11}.$$

To obtain a 95 percent *confidence interval estimate* of W_q, the above formulas are first used to calculate

$$s_{11} = 219.20,\ s_{22} = 3.20,\ s_{12} = 24.80.$$

[1] This approximation is valid only if $Z^2 - cs_{22} > 0$ and the expression inside the radical sign for d also is positive.

Since $(1 - 2\alpha) = 0.95$, $\alpha = 0.025$, so that $K_\alpha = 1.96$ from Table A5.1. Consequently,

$$c = 0.72832, \; d = 15.77.$$

The resulting confidence interval is

$$-5.92 \le W_\text{J} \le 6.64;$$

that is,

$$W_\text{J} \le 6.64.$$

Now suppose that this simulation run is to be used to estimate P_0, the probability of having *zero* customers in the system. (The theoretical value is known to be $P_0 = 1 - \lambda/\mu = 1 - (1/15)/(1/10) = 1/3$.) The corresponding information obtained during the simulation run is the fraction of time during which the system is empty. Therefore the summary statistic Y for each cycle would be the *total time* during which *no* customers are present, and the size Z would be the *length* of the cycle, so that

$$P_0 = \frac{E(Y)}{E(Z)}.$$

The length of cycle 1 is 38 (from 24 to 62), so that $Z_1 = 38$. During this time the system is empty from 53 to 62, so that $Y_1 = 9$. In this manner, the following data would be obtained for this problem:

$$\begin{aligned} Y_1 &= 9, & Z_1 &= 38 \\ Y_2 &= 5, & Z_2 &= 8 \\ Y_3 &= 7, & Z_3 &= 54 \\ Y_4 &= 3, & Z_4 &= 16 \\ Y_5 &= 17, & Z_5 &= 24 \\ \bar{Y} &= 8.2, & \bar{Z} &= 28. \end{aligned}$$

Thus the *point estimate* of P_0 is

$$\text{est}\,\{P_0\} = \frac{8.2}{28} = 0.293.$$

By calculating

$$s_{11} = 29.20, \; s_{22} = 334, \; s_{12} = 17, \; c = 0.72832, \; d = 149.42,$$

a 95 percent *confidence interval estimate* of P_0 is found to be

$$0.125 \le P_0 \le 0.678.$$

(The wide range of this interval indicates that a much longer simulation run would be needed to obtain a relatively precise estimate of P_0.)

By redefining Y appropriately, the same approach also can be used to estimate other probabilities involving the number of customers in the system. However, since this number never exceeded 3 during this simulation run, a much longer run would be needed if the probability involves larger numbers.

The other basic queueing-theory expected values defined in the terminology and notation part of Sec. 9.2 (W, L_q, L) can be estimated from the estimate of W_q by using the relationships between L and W, given in Sec. 9.2. However, they can also be estimated directly from the results of the simulation run. For example, since the *expected number of customers waiting to be served* is

$$L_q = \sum_{n=2}^{\infty} (n-1)P_n,$$

it can be estimated by defining

$$Y = \sum_{n=2}^{\infty} (n-1)T_n,$$

where T_n is the *total time* that exactly n customers are in the system during the cycle. (This definition actually is *equivalent* to the definition used when estimating W_q.) In this case Z would be defined as when estimating any P_n, namely, the *length* of the cycle. The resulting *point estimate* of L_q then turns out to be simply the point estimate of W_q multiplied by the actual *average arrival rate* for the complete cycles observed.

It is also possible to estimate *higher moments* of these probability distributions by redefining Y accordingly. For example, the *second moment* of the *number of customers waiting to be served* (N_q),

$$E(N_q^2) = \sum_{n=2}^{\infty} (n-1)^2 P_n,$$

can be estimated by redefining

$$Y = \sum_{n=2}^{\infty} (n-1)^2 T_n.$$

Subtracting the *square* of the estimated *first moment* (L_q) then provides an estimate of the *variance*.

Finally, we should mention that it was unnecessary to generate the first *interarrival* time (24) for the simulation run summarized in Table 15.8 and Fig. 15.3 because this time played no role in the statistical analysis. It is more efficient with the cycle method to just start the run at the regeneration point.

15.5 CONCLUSIONS

There have been numerous applications of simulation in a wide variety of contexts. Some example are listed below to illustrate the great versatility of this technique:

1. Simulation of the operations at a large airport by an airlines company to test changes in company policies and practices (e.g., amounts of maintenance capacity, berthing facilities, spare aircraft, and so on).

2. Simulation of the passage of traffic across a junction with time-sequenced traffic lights to determine the best time sequences.

3. Simulation of a maintenance operation to determine the optimal size of repair crews.

4. Simulation of the flux of uncharged particles through a radiation shield to determine the intensity of the radiation that penetrates the shield.

5. Simulation of steel-making operations to evaluate changes in operating practices and the capacity and configuration of the facilities.

6. Simulation of the United States economy to predict the effect of economic policy decisions.

7. Simulation of large-scale military battles to evaluate defensive and offensive weapon systems.

8. Simulation of large-scale distribution and inventory control systems to improve the design of these systems.

9. Simulation of the overall operation of an entire business firm to evaluate broad changes in the policies and operation of the firm and also to provide a business game for training executives.

10. Simulation of a telephone communications system to determine the capacity of the respective components that would be required to provide satisfactory service at the most economical level.

11. Simulation of the operation of a developed river basin to determine the best configuration of dams, power plants, and irrigation works that would provide the desired level of flood control and water-resource development.

12. Simulation of the operation of a production line to determine the amount of in-process storage space that should be provided.

We have focused in this chapter on the use of simulation for predicting the *steady-state* behavior of systems whose state changes only at discrete points in time. However, by having a series of runs begin with the prescribed *starting conditions*, it can also be used to describe the *transient* behavior of a proposed system. Furthermore, by using differential equations, it has been applied with considerable success to systems whose state changes *continuously* with time.

Simulation is indeed a very versatile tool. However, it is by no means a panacea. Simulation is inherently an imprecise technique. It provides only *statistical estimates* rather than exact results, and it only *compares alternatives* rather than generating the optimal one. Furthermore, simulation is a *slow and costly* way to study a problem. It usually requires a large amount of time and expense for analysis and programming, in addition to considerable computer running time. Simulation models tend to become unwieldy, so that the number of cases that can be run and the accuracy of the results obtained often turn out to be very inadequate. Finally, simulation yields only *numerical data* about the performance of the system, so that it provides no additional insight into the cause-and-effect relationships within the system except for the clues that can be gleaned from these numbers (and from the analysis required to construct the simulation model). Therefore it is very expensive to conduct a sensitivity analysis of the parameter values assumed by the model. The only possible way would be to conduct new series of simulation runs with different parameter values, which would tend to provide relatively little information at a relatively high cost.

Simulation provides a way of *experimenting* with proposed systems or policies without actually implementing them. Sound statistical theory should be used in designing these experiments. Surprisingly long simulation runs often are needed to obtain *statistically significant* results. However, *variance-reducing techniques* can be very helpful in reducing the length of the run needed.

Several *tactical* problems arise when applying traditional statistical estimation procedures to simulated experiments. These include prescribing appropriate *starting conditions*, determining when a *steady-state condition* has essentially been reached, and dealing with *statistically dependent* observations. These problems can be eliminated by instead using the recently developed *cycle method* of statistical analysis. However, there are some restrictions on when this method can be applied.

Simulation unquestionably has an important place in the theory and practice of operations research. It is an invaluable tool for use on those problems where analytical techniques are inadequate.

Selected References

1 Emshoff, James R. and Roger L. Sisson: *Design and Use of Computer Simulation Models*, MacMillan, New York, 1970.
2 Kleijnen, J. P. C.: *Statistical Techniques in Simulation*, Marcel Dekker, New York, 1973.
3 Meier, Robert C., William T. Newell, and Harold L. Pazer: *Simulation in Business and Economics*, Prentice-Hall, Englewood Cliffs, N.J., 1969.
4 Mihram, G. Arthur: *Simulation: Statistical Foundations and Methodology*, Academic Press, New York, 1972.
5 Naylor, Thomas H.: *Computer Simulation Experiments with Models of Economic Systems*, Wiley, New York, 1971.
6 ———, Joseph L. Balintfy, Donald S. Burdick, and Kong Chu: *Computer Simulation Techniques*, Wiley, New York, 1966.

Problems

(Random numbers needed to do these problems manually should be obtained from Table 15.1. For each part, use the digits *consecutively* starting from the front of the top row to form *three-digit* random numbers 096, 569, 665, ...)

1 Use the *mixed congruential method* to generate the following sequences of random numbers:

(*a*) A sequence of 10 *one-digit* random numbers such that $x_{n+1} \equiv (x_n + 3)$ (modulo 10) and $x_0 = 2$.

(*b*) A sequence of eight random numbers between 0 and 7 such that $x_{n+1} \equiv (5x_n + 1)$(modulo 8) and $x_0 = 4$.

(*c*) A sequence of five *two-digit* random numbers such that $x_{n+1} \equiv (61x_n + 27)$ (modulo 100) and $x_0 = 40$.

2 Use the *mixed congruential method* to generate a sequence of five *two-digit* random numbers such that $x_{n+1} \equiv (21x_n + 53)$(modulo 100) and $x_0 = 33$.

3 Use the *mixed congruential method* to generate the following sequences of random numbers:

(*a*) A sequence of five random numbers between 0 and 31 such that $x_{n+1} \equiv (9x_n + 15)$(modulo 32) and $x_0 = 21$.

(*b*) A sequence of three *three-digit* random numbers such that $x_{n+1} \equiv (301x_n + 503)$(modulo 1,000) and $x_0 = 700$.

4 Use the one-digit random numbers—6, 3, 5, 0, 8—to generate random observations for each of the following situations:

(*a*) Throwing an unbiased coin.

(*b*) Throwing a die.

(*c*) The color of a traffic light found by a randomly arriving car when it is green 50 percent of the time, yellow 10 percent of the time, and red 40 percent of the time.

5 Generate five random observations from a *uniform distribution* between −20 and +30.

6 Suppose that random observations are needed from the *triangular distribution* whose probability density function is

$$f(x) = \begin{cases} 2x, & \text{if } 0 \le x \le 1 \\ 0, & \text{otherwise.} \end{cases}$$

(*a*) Derive an expression for each random observation as a function of the random decimal number *r*.

(*b*) Generate five random observations.

7 Generate three random observations from each of the following probability distributions:

(*a*) The *uniform distribution* from 25 to 50.

(*b*) The distribution whose probability density function is

$$f(x) = \begin{cases} \frac{1}{4}x^3, & \text{if } 0 \le x \le 2 \\ 0, & \text{otherwise.} \end{cases}$$

(*c*) The distribution whose probability density function is

$$f(x) = \begin{cases} \frac{1}{50}(x - 10), & \text{if } 10 \le x \le 20 \\ 0 & \text{otherwise.} \end{cases}$$

8 Generate three random observations from each of the following probability distributions:

(*a*) The random variable X has $P\{X=0\}=\frac{1}{5}$. Given $X \neq 0$, it has a uniform distribution between -1 and 3.
(*b*) The distribution whose probability density function is

$$f(x)=\begin{cases} x, & \text{if } 0 \leq x \leq 1 \\ 2-x, & \text{if } 1 \leq x \leq 2. \end{cases}$$

(*c*) The *geometric distribution* with parameter $p=\frac{1}{3}$, so that

$$P\{X=k\}=\begin{cases} \dfrac{1}{3}\left(\dfrac{2}{3}\right)^{k-1}, & \text{if } k=1, 2, \ldots \\ 0, & \text{otherwise.} \end{cases}$$

9 Generate three random observations from a *normal distribution* with mean $=2$ and standard deviation $=10$. (Use $n=12$ for each observation.)

10 Generate four random observations from a *normal distribution* with mean $=0$ and standard deviation $=1$. (Use $n=3$ for each observation.) Then use these four observations to generate two random observations from a *chi-square distribution* with 2 degrees of freedom.

11 Generate two random observations from each of the following probability distributions:

(*a*) The exponential distribution with mean $=4$.
(*b*) The Erlang distribution with mean 4 and shape parameter $k=2$ (that is, standard deviation $=2\sqrt{2}$).
(*c*) The normal distribution with mean $=4$ and standard deviation $=2\sqrt{2}$. (Use $n=6$ for each observation.)

12 The game of craps requires the player to throw two dice one or more times until a decision has been reached as to whether he wins or loses. He wins if the first throw results in a sum of 7 or 11 or, alternatively, if the first sum is 4, 5, 6, 8, 9, or 10 and the same sum reappears before a sum of 7 has appeared. Conversely, he loses if the first throw results in a sum of 2, 3, or 12 or, alternatively, if the first sum is 4, 5, 6, 8, 9, or 10 and a sum of 7 appears before the first sum reappears.

(*a*) Simulate 5 plays of this game to start the process of estimating the probability of winning.
(*b*) For a large number of plays of the game, the proportion of wins has *approximately* a *normal distribution* with mean $=0.493$ and standard deviation $=0.5/\sqrt{n}$. Use this information to calculate the number of simulated plays that would be required to have a probability of at least 0.95 that the proportion of wins will be less than 0.5.

13 Consider the first single-server version of the queueing-theory model with Poisson input and exponential service times that was discussed in Sec. 9.6 and Example 2, Sec. 15.1. Suppose that the mean arrival rate is 10 per hour and the mean service rate is 15 per hour and that it is desired to estimate the expected waiting time before service begins by using simulation.

(*a*) Starting with the system empty, use *next-event incrementing* to perform the simulation until two service completions have occurred.
(*b*) Starting with the system empty, use *fixed-time incrementing* (with 1 minute as the time unit) to perform the simulation until two service completions have occurred.
(*c*) Write a computer simulation program with *next-event incrementing* for this problem. Use the *cycle method* with 100 cycles to obtain a point estimate and 95 percent confidence interval for the steady-state expected waiting time before service begins. Compare with the theoretical value.
(*d*) Write a computer simulation program with *fixed-time incrementing* and 0.1 minutes as the time unit. Use the *cycle method* with 100 cycles to obtain a point estimate and 95 percent confidence interval for the steady-state expected waiting time before service begins. Compare with the theoretical value.

14 Consider the probability distribution whose probability density function is

$$f(x) = \begin{cases} \dfrac{1}{x^2}, & \text{if } 1 \leq x \leq \infty \\ 0, & \text{otherwise.} \end{cases}$$

The problem is to perform a simulated experiment, with the help of variance-reducing techniques, for estimating the mean of this distribution. To provide a standard of comparison, also derive the mean analytically.

For each of the following cases, generate 10 observations and calculate the resulting estimate of the mean:

(*a*) Use the *crude Monte Carlo method.*
(*b*) Use *stratified sampling* with *three* strata: $0 \leq F(x) \leq 0.6$, $0.6 < F(x) \leq 0.9$, $0.9 < F(x) \leq 1$, with 3, 3 and 4 observations, respectively.
(*c*) Use the *method of complementary random numbers.*

15 One product produced by a certain company requires that bushings be drilled into a metal block and that cylindrical shafts be inserted into the bushings. The shafts are required to have a radius of at least 1.0000 inches, but as little larger than this as possible. In actuality, the probability distribution of what the radius of a shaft will be (in inches) has the probability density function

$$f_S(x) = \begin{cases} 500e^{-5000(x-1.0000)}, & \text{if } x \geq 1.0000 \\ 0, & \text{otherwise.} \end{cases}$$

Similarly, the probability distribution of what the radius of a bushing will be (in inches) has the probability density function

$$f_B(x) = \begin{cases} 200, & \text{if } 1.0000 \leq x \leq 1.0050 \\ 0, & \text{otherwise.} \end{cases}$$

The clearance between a bushing and a shaft is the difference in their radii. Since they are selected at random, there occasionally is interference (i.e., negative clearance) between a bushing and a shaft that were to be mated. The objective is to determine how frequently this will happen under the current probability distribution.

Perform a simulated experiment for estimating the probability of interference. Notice that almost all cases of interference will occur when the radius of the bushing is much closer to 1.0000 inch than to 1.0050 inches. Therefore it appears that an efficient experiment would generate most of the simulated bushings from this critical portion of the distribution. Take this into account in part (*b*). For each of the following cases, generate 10 observations and calculate the resulting estimate of the probability of interference:

(*a*) Use the *crude Monte Carlo method.*
(*b*) Develop and apply a *stratified sampling* approach to this problem.
(*c*) Use the *method of complementary random numbers.*

16 Simulation is being used to study a system whose measure of performance X will be partially determined by the outcome of a certain external factor. This factor has three possible outcomes (unfavorable, neutral, and favorable) that will occur with equal probability (1/3). Since the favorable outcome would greatly increase the spread of possible values of X, this outcome is more critical than the others for estimating the mean and variance of X. Therefore a *stratified sampling* approach has been adopted, with four random observations of the value of X generated under the favorable outcome, two generated under the neutral outcome, and one generated under the unfavorable outcome—as shown below.

Outcome of external factor	*Simulated values of X*
Favorable	7, 3, 1, 9
Neutral	4, 2
Unfavorable	2

(*a*) Develop the resulting estimate of $E(X)$.
(*b*) Develop the resulting estimate of $E(X^2)$.

17 A certain single-server queueing system has been simulated, with the following sequence of waiting times before service for the respective customers. Use the *cycle method* to obtain a point estimate and 90 percent confidence interval for the steady-state expected waiting time before service.

(*a*) 0, 5, 4, 0, 2, 0, 3, 1, 6, 0.
(*b*) 0, 2, 7, 3, 0, 4, 2, 0, 0, 5, 1, 3, 0, 2, 5, 1, 0.

18 A company has been having a maintenance problem wth a certain complex piece of equipment. This equipment contains four identical vacuum tubes that have been the cause of the trouble. The problem is that the tubes fail fairly frequently, thereby forcing the equipment to be shut down while making a replacement. The current practice is to replace tubes only when they fail. However, a proposal has been made to replace all four tubes whenever any one of them fails to reduce the frequency with which the equipment must be shut down. The objective is to compare these two alternatives on a cost basis.

The pertinent data are the following. For each tube, the operating time until failure has approximately a *uniform distribution* from 1,000 to 2,000 hours. The equipment must be shut down for 1 hour to replace one tube or for 2 hours to replace all four tubes. The total cost associated with shutting down the equipment and replacing tubes is $20/hour plus $10 for each new tube.

(*a*) Starting with four new tubes, simulate the operation of the two alternative policies for 10,000 hours of simulated time.

(*b*) Use the data from part (*a*) to make a preliminary comparison of the two alternatives on a cost basis.

(*c*) For the *proposed* policy, describe an appropriate *regeneration point* for defining cycles that will permit applying the *cycle method* of statistical analysis. Explain why the cycle method can not be applied to the *current* policy.

(*d*) For the *proposed* policy, use the *cycle method* to obtain a point estimate and 95 percent confidence interval for the steady-state *expected cost per hour* from the data obtained in part (*a*).

(*e*) Write a computer simulation program for the two alternative policies. Then repeat parts (*a*), (*b*), and (*d*) on the computer, with 100 cycles for the *proposed* policy and 110,000 hours of simulated time (including a stabilization period of 10,000 hours) for the current policy.

19 A manufacturing company has two planers for cutting flat surfaces in large work pieces of two different types. The time required to perform each job varies somewhat, depending largely upon the number of passes that must be made. In particular, for both types of work pieces the time required by a planer has approximately the following probability distribution:

Time, in min	*Probability*
10	0.30
20	0.25
30	0.18
40	0.12
50	0.08
60	0.045
70	0.015
80	0.007
90	0.003

Every half-hour one work piece of *both* types is brought to the planer department.

Unfortunately, the planer department has had a difficult time keeping up with its work load. Frequently there are a number of work pieces waiting for a free planer. This has seriously disrupted the production schedule for the subsequent operations, thereby greatly increasing the cost of inprocess inventory as well as the cost of idle equipment and resulting lost production. Therefore the proposal has been made to obtain one additional planer to relieve this bottleneck.

It is estimated that the total incremental cost (including capital recovery cost) associated with obtaining and operating another planer would be $40/hour. (This takes into account the fact that even with an additional planer the total running time for all the planers will remain the same.) It is also estimated that the total cost associated with work pieces having to wait to be processed is $50 per work piece per hour and $20 per work piece per hour for work pieces of the first and second types, respectively. Because of this difference in costs, work pieces of the first type always are given priority over those of the second type. In other words, if a planer becomes free when work pieces of both types are waiting, a work piece of the first type always is chosen to be processed next.

(*a*) Starting with all planers idle waiting for work pieces to arrive momentarily, use *next-event incrementing* to simulate the operation of the two alternative policies (the status quo or obtaining one additional planer) for 3 hours of simulated time.

(*b*) Describe an appropriate *regeneration point* for defining cycles that will permit applying the *cycle method* of statistical analysis to this problem.

(*c*) Write a computer simulation program for the two alternative policies. Use the *cycle method* with 100 cycles each to compare the two alternatives on a cost basis.

20 Select any of the typical applications of simulation listed in Sec. 15.5 and develop a simulation model for this type of problem.

Part 3

Advanced Topics in Mathematical Programming

16 Algorithms for Linear Programming

The key to the extremely widespread use of linear programming is the availability of an exceptionally efficient algorithm—the simplex method—that will routinely solve the large-sized problems which typically arise in practice. However, the simplex method is only part of the arsenal of algorithms regularly used by linear programming practitioners. Chapter 3 described several special classes of linear programming for which *streamlined* versions of the simplex method are available (as illustrated by the *transportation simplex method* in Sec. 3.2). Section 4.2 mentioned that production computer codes *adapt* the simplex method to a more convenient matrix form. Section 4.3 pointed out how certain *modifications* or *extensions* of the simplex method are particularly useful for sensitivity analysis. Thus all these algorithms are *variants* of the simplex method as it was presented in Chap. 2. Consequently, they also are exceptionally efficient.

This chapter focuses on five particularly important algorithms based on the simplex method. In particular, the next five sections present the *upper bound technique* (a streamlined version of the simplex method for dealing with variables having upper bounds), the *dual simplex method* (a modification particularly useful for sensitivity analysis), *parametric programming* (an extension for systematic sensitivity analysis), the *revised simplex method* (an adaptation for computer implementation), and the *decomposition principle* (a streamlined version for multidivisional problems).

16.1 THE UPPER BOUND TECHNIQUE

At the end of Sec. 3.5 we discussed the fact that it is common for some or all of the *individual* x_j variables to have *upper bound constraints*

$$x_j \leq u_j,$$

where u_j is a positive constant representing the maximum *feasible* value of x_j. (The right-hand side of Fig. 3.20 shows the resulting *special structure* of the functional constraints.) However, we also pointed out in Sec. 4.2 that the most important determinant of computation time for the simplex method is the *number of functional constraints*, whereas the number of *nonnegativity* constraints are relatively unimportant. Therefore, having a large number of upper bound constraints among the functional constraints would greatly increase computational effort. The *upper bound technique* avoids this by removing the upper bound constraints from the functional constraints and treating them separately, essentially like nonnegativity constraints. Roughly speaking, this technique simply applies the simplex method in the usual way to the *remainder* of the problem (i.e., without the upper bound constraints) but with the one additional restriction that each new basic feasible solution is also required to satisfy the upper bound constraints.

To implement this idea, note that a decision variable x_i with an upper bound constraint ($x_j \leq u_j$) can always be replaced by

$$x_j = u_j - y_j,$$

where y_j would then be the decision variable. In other words, you have a choice between letting the decision variable be the amount *above zero* (x_j) or the *amount below* u_j ($y_j = u_j - x_j$). (We shall refer to x_j and y_j as *complementary* decision variables.) Since

$$0 \leq x_j \leq u_j,$$

it also follows that

$$0 \leq y_j \leq u_j.$$

Thus at any point during the simplex method you can either

1. Use x_j, where $0 \leq x_j \leq u_j$

or

2. Replace x_j by $(u_j - y_j)$, where $0 \leq y_j \leq u_j$.

The upper bound technique uses the following rule to make this choice:

Rule: Begin with choice 1.

If $x_j = 0$, then use choice (1), so x_j is *nonbasic*.

If $x_j = u_j$, then use choice (2), so $y_j = 0$ is nonbasic.

Switch choices only when the other extreme value of x_j is reached.

Therefore, whenever a *basic* variable reaches its upper bound, you would switch choices and use its *complementary* decision variable as the new nonbasic variable (the leaving basic variable) for identifying the new basic feasible solution. Thus the one substantive modification being made in the simplex method is in the rule for selecting the *leaving basic variable*.

Recall that the simplex method selects as the leaving basic variable the one which first becomes infeasible by going negative as the entering basic variable is increased. The modification now made is to select instead the variable that first becomes infeasible *in any way*, either by going negative or by going over the upper bound, as the entering basic variable is increased. (Notice that one possibility is that the *entering* basic variable may become infeasible first by going over its upper bound, so that its *complementary* decision variable becomes the leaving basic variable.) If the leaving basic variable reached zero, then proceed as usual with the simplex method. However, if it reached its upper bound instead, then switch choices and make its complementary decision variable the leaving basic variable.

To illustrate, consider the problem

$$\text{Maximize} \quad Z = 2x_1 + x_2 + 2x_3,$$

subject to

$$\begin{aligned} 4x_1 + x_2 \qquad &= 12 \\ -2x_1 \qquad + x_3 &= 4 \end{aligned}$$

and

$$\begin{aligned} 0 \le x_1 &\le 4 \\ 0 \le x_2 &\le 15 \\ 0 \le x_3 &\le 6. \end{aligned}$$

Thus all three variables have upper bound constraints ($u_1 = 4$, $u_2 = 15$, $u_3 = 6$). The two equality constraints are already in the appropriate form for identifying the initial basic feasible solution ($x_1 = 0$, $x_2 = 12$, $x_3 = 4$), so x_2 and x_3 can be used as the initial basic variables without introducing artificial variables. However, these variables then need to be eliminated algebraically from the objective function to obtain the initial Eq. (0), as shown below:

$$\begin{array}{rl} Z - 2x_1 - x_2 - 2x_3 &= 0 \\ + \quad (4x_1 + x_2 \qquad &= 12) \\ + 2(-2x_1 \qquad + x_3 &= 4) \\ \hline (0) \quad Z - 2x_1 \qquad\qquad &= 20 \end{array}$$

Thus the initial *entering basic variable* is x_1. Since the upper bound constraints are not to be included, the *entire* initial set of equations and the corresponding calculations for selecting the leaving basic variables are

			Maximum feasible value of x_1
(0)	$Z - 2x_1$	$= 20$	$x_1 \le 4$ (since $u_1 = 4$)
(1)	$4x_1 + x_2$	$= 12$	$x_1 \le \frac{12}{4} = 3$
(2)	$-2x_1 \qquad + x_3$	$= 4$	$x_1 \le \frac{6-4}{2} = 1 \leftarrow \text{min}$ (since $u_3 = 6$)

The maximum feasible value of x_1 column shows how much the entering basic variable x_1 can be *increased* from zero before some basic variable (including x_1) becomes infeasible. The maximum value given next to Eq. (0) is just the upper bound constraint for x_1. For Eq. (1), since the coefficient of x_1 is *positive*, *increasing* x_1 to 3 *decreases* the basic variable in this equation (x_2) from 12 to its *lower* bound of *zero*. For Eq. (2), since the coefficient of x_1 is *negative*, *increasing* x_1 to 1 *increases* the basic variable in this equation (x_3) from 4 to its *upper* bound of 6. Since this last maximum value of x_1 is the smallest, x_3 provides the *leaving* basic variable. However, since x_3 reached its *upper* bound, replace x_3 by $(6 - y_3)$, so that $y_3 = 0$ becomes the new *nonbasic* variable for the next basic feasible solution and x_1 becomes the new basic variable in Eq. (2). This leads to the following changes in this equation:

$$\begin{aligned}
(2)\ -2x_1 \quad &+ \ x_3 = 4 \\
\rightarrow -2x_1 + (6 - &\ y_3) = 4 \\
\rightarrow -2x_1 \quad &- \ y_3 = -2 \\
\rightarrow \quad x_1 \quad &+ \frac{1}{2} y_3 = 1
\end{aligned}$$

Therefore, after eliminating x_1 algebraically from the other equations, the *second* complete set of equations become

$$\begin{aligned}
(0)\ Z \quad &+ \ y_3 = 22 \\
(1) \quad x_2 &- 2y_3 = 8 \\
(2) \quad x_1 &+ \frac{1}{2} y_3 = 1.
\end{aligned}$$

The resulting basic feasible solution is $x_1 = 1$, $x_2 = 8$, $y_3 = 0$. By the *stopping rule*, it also is an optimal solution, so $x_1 = 1$, $x_2 = 8$, $x_3 = 6 - y_3 = 6$ is the desired solution to the original problem.

16.2 THE DUAL SIMPLEX METHOD

The *dual simplex method* can be thought of as the *mirror image* of the simplex method. This is best explained by referring to Tables 2.41 and 2.42 and Fig. 2.7. The simplex method deals directly with *suboptimal* basic solutions and moves toward an optimal solution by striving to satisfy the *condition for optimality* (the stopping rule). By contrast, the dual simplex method deals directly with *superoptimal* basic solutions and moves toward an optimal solution by striving to achieve *feasibility*. Furthermore, the dual simplex method deals with a problem as if the simplex method were being applied simultaneously to its dual problem. By making their *initial* basic solutions *complementary*, the two methods would move in complete sequence, obtaining *complementary* basic solutions on each iteration.

The dual simplex method is very useful in certain special types of situations. Ordinarily it is easier to find an initial basic feasible solution than an initial superoptimal basic solution. However, it is occasionally necessary to introduce many *artificial* variables to artificially construct an initial basic feasible solution. In such cases it may be easier to begin with a superoptimal basic solution and use the dual simplex method. Furthermore, fewer iterations may be required when it is not necessary to drive many artificial variables to zero.

As mentioned several times in Sec. 4.3, another important primary application of the dual simplex method is in conjunction with sensitivity analysis. Suppose that an optimal solution has been obtained by the simplex method but that it becomes necessary (or of interest for sensitivity analysis) to make minor changes in the model. If the formerly optimal basic solution is *no longer feasible* (but still satisfies the condition for optimality), you can immediately apply the dual simplex method by starting with this *superoptimal* basic solution. This usually would lead to the new optimal solution much more quickly than by solving the new problem from the beginning with the simplex method.

The rules for the dual simplex method are very similar to those for the simplex method. In fact, once they are started, the only difference is in the criteria used for selecting the entering and leaving basic variables and for testing for optimality (feasibility). To start the dual simplex method, all the coefficients in Eq. (0) must be nonnegative (so that the basic solution is superoptimal). The basic solutions investigated will be infeasible (except for the last one) only because some of the variables are negative. The method continues to decrease the value of the objective function, always retaining *nonnegative coefficients* in Eq. (0), until all the variables are nonnegative. Such a basic solution is feasible (it satisfies all the equations) and is, therefore, optimal by the simplex method criterion of nonnegative coefficients in Eq. (0). The details of the dual simplex method are now summarized.

Summary of Dual Simplex Method

Initialization step Introduce slack variables as needed to construct a set of equations describing the problem. Find a basic solution such that the coefficients in Eq. (0) are zero for basic variables and nonnegative for nonbasic variables. Go to the stopping rule.

Iterative step

Part 1 Determine the leaving basic variable: Select the basic variable with the largest negative value.

Part 2 Determine the entering basic variable: Select the nonbasic variable whose coefficient in Eq. (0) reaches zero first as an increasing multiple of the equation containing the leaving basic variable is added to Eq. (0). This is done by checking the nonbasic variables with negative coefficients in that equation (the one containing the leaving basic variable) and selecting the one with the smallest ratio of the Eq. (0) coefficient to the absolute value of the coefficient in that equation.

Part 3 Determine the new basic solution: Starting from the current set of equations, solve for the basic variables in terms of the nonbasic variables by the Gauss-Jordan method of elimination (see Appendix 4). Set the nonbasic variables equal to zero, and each basic variable (and Z) equals the new right-hand side of the one equation in which it appears (with a coefficient of $+1$).

Stopping rule Determine if this solution is feasible (and therefore optimal): Check if all the basic variables are nonnegative. If they are, then this solution is feasible, and therefore optimal, so stop. Otherwise, go to the iteration step.

To fully understand the dual simplex method it is important to notice that the method proceeds just as if the simplex method were being applied to the complementary basic solutions in the dual problem. (In fact, this was the motivation for constructing the method as it is.) Part 1, determining the leaving basic variable, is equivalent to determining the entering basic variable in the dual problem. The variable with the largest negative value corresponds to the largest negative coefficient in Eq. (0) of the dual problem (see Table 2.34). Part 2, determining the entering basic variable, is equivalent to determining the leaving basic variable in the dual problem. The coefficient in Eq. (0) that reaches zero first corresponds to the variable in the dual problem which reaches zero first. The two criteria for optimality are also complementary.

We shall now illustrate the dual simplex method by applying it to the *dual problem* for the *Wyndor Glass Co.* (see Table 2.25). Normally this method is applied directly to the problem of concern (a "primal" problem). However, we have chosen this problem because you have already seen the simplex method applied to *its* dual problem (namely, the primal problem) in Table 2.25, so you can compare the two. To facilitate the comparison, we shall continue denoting the decision variables in the problem being solved by y_i rather than x_j.

In *maximization* form, the problem to be solved is

$$\text{Maximize} \quad Z = -4y_1 - 12y_2 - 18y_3,$$

subject to

$$\begin{aligned} y_1 \qquad + 3y_3 &\geq 3 \\ 2y_2 + 2y_3 &\geq 5 \end{aligned}$$

and

$$y_1 \geq 0, y_2 \geq 0, y_3 \geq 0.$$

After converting the functional constraints to $\leq$ form and introducing slack variables, the initial set of equations are those shown for iteration 0 in Table 16.1. Notice that all the coefficients in Eq. (0) are nonnegative, so the solution would be optimal if it were feasible. The initial basic solution is $y_1 = 0$, $y_2 = 0$, $y_3 = 0$, $y_4 = -3$, $y_5 = -5$, with $Z = 0$, which is not feasible because of the negative values. The leaving basic variable is y_5 $(5 > 3)$, and the entering basic variable is y_2 $(12/2 < 18/2)$, which leads to the second set of equations shown after iteration 1 in Table 16.1. The corresponding basic solution is $y_1 = 0$, $y_2 = 5/2$,

Table 16.1 Dual Simplex Method Applied to Wyndor Glass Co. Dual Problem

Iteration	Basic variable	Eq. no.	Coefficient of: Z	y_1	y_2	y_3	y_4	y_5	Right side
0	Z	0	1	4	12	18	0	0	0
	y_4	1	0	−1	0	−3	1	0	−3
	y_5	2	0	0	−2	−2	0	1	−5
1	Z	0	1	4	0	6	0	6	−30
	y_4	1	0	−1	0	−3	1	0	−3
	y_2	2	0	0	1	1	0	$-\frac{1}{2}$	$\frac{5}{2}$
2	Z	0	1	2	0	0	2	6	−36
	y_3	1	0	$\frac{1}{3}$	0	1	$-\frac{1}{3}$	0	1
	y_2	2	0	$-\frac{1}{3}$	1	0	$\frac{1}{3}$	$-\frac{1}{2}$	$\frac{3}{2}$

$y_3 = 0, y_4 = -3, y_5 = 0$, with $Z = -30$, which is not feasible. The next leaving basic variable is y_4, and the entering basic variable is y_3 ($6/3 < 4/1$), which leads to the final set of equations in Table 16.1. The corresponding basic solution is $y_1 = 0, y_2 = 3/2, y_3 = 1, y_4 = 0, y_5 = 0$, with $Z = -36$, which is feasible and therefore optimal.

Notice that the optimal solution for the *dual* of this problem is $x_1^* = 2$, $x_2^* = 6$, $x_3^* = 2$, $x_4^* = 0$, $x_5^* = 0$, as was obtained in Table 2.25 by the simplex method. We suggest that you now trace through Tables 16.1 and 2.25 simultaneously and compare the complementary steps for the two mirror image methods.

16.3 PARAMETRIC LINEAR PROGRAMMING

At the end of Sec. 4.3 we described *parametric linear programming* and its use for conducting sensitivity analysis systematically by gradually changing various model parameters simultaneously. We shall now present the algorithmic procedure, first for the case where the c_j parameters are being changed and then where the b_i parameters are varied.

Systematic Changes in the c_j Parameters

For this case the *objective function* of the ordinary linear programming model

$$Z = \sum_{j=1}^{n} c_j x_j$$

is replaced by

$$Z(\theta) = \sum_{j=1}^{n} (c_j + \alpha_j \theta) x_j,$$

where the α_j are given input constants representing the *relative* rates at which the coefficients are being changed. Therefore, gradually increasing θ from zero changes the coefficients at these relative rates. The values assigned to the α_j may represent interesting simultaneous changes of the c_j for systematic sensitivity analysis of the effect of increasing the magnitude of these changes. They may also be based on how the coefficients (e.g., unit profits) would change together with respect to some factor measured by θ. This factor might be uncontrollable, e.g., the *state of the economy*. However, it may also be under the control of the decision maker, e.g., the amount of personnel and equipment to shift from some of the activities to others. For any given value of θ, the optimal solution of the corresponding linear programming problem can be obtained by the simplex method. This may have been done already for the original problem where $\theta = 0$. However, the objective is to *find the optimal solution* of the modified linear programming problem [maximize $Z(\theta)$ subject to the original constraints] *as a function of* θ. Therefore the solution procedure will need to be able to determine when and how the optimal solution changes (if it does) as θ increases from zero to any specified positive number. This is portrayed graphically in Fig. 16.1, which shows how $Z^*(\theta)$, the objective function value for the optimal solution (given θ), changes as θ increases. $Z^*(\theta)$ always has this *piecewise linear* and *convex*[1] form (see Prob. 16), where the corresponding optimal solution changes just at the values of θ where the slope changes.

The solution procedure is based directly upon the sensitivity analysis procedure for investigating changes in the c_j parameters (see cases 2*a* and 3, Sec. 4.3). The only basic difference is that the changes now are expressed in

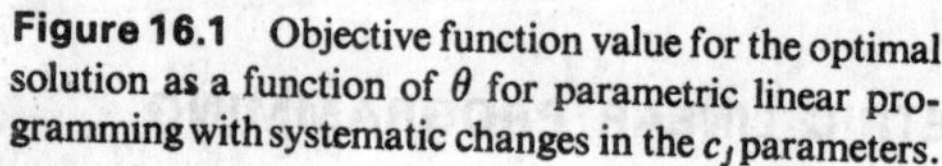
Figure 16.1 Objective function value for the optimal solution as a function of θ for parametric linear programming with systematic changes in the c_j parameters.

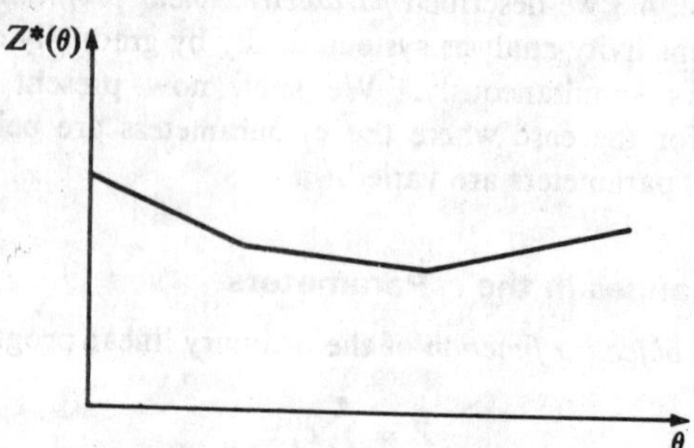

[1] See Appendix 1 for a definition and discussion of *convex* functions.

terms of θ rather than as specific numbers. To illustrate, suppose that $\alpha_1 = 2$ and $\alpha_2 = -1$ for the *Wyndor Glass Co.* problem (see Sec. 2.1 and Table 4.4), so that

$$Z(\theta) = (3 + 2\theta)x_1 + (5 - \theta)x_2 .$$

Beginning with the *final* simplex tableau for $\theta = 0$ (Table 4.4), its Eq. (0),

$$(0) \qquad Z + \frac{3}{2}x_4 + x_5 = 36,$$

would first have these changes added into it on the left-hand side:

$$(0) \qquad Z - 2\theta x_1 + \theta x_2 + \frac{3}{2}x_4 + x_5 = 36.$$

Since both x_1 and x_2 are basic variables [appearing in Eqs. (3) and (2), respectively], they both then need to be eliminated algebraically from Eq. (0):

$$\begin{aligned} Z - 2\theta x_1 + \theta x_2 + \frac{3}{2}x_4 + x_5 &= 36 \\ +2\theta \text{ times Eq. (3)} & \\ -\ \theta \text{ times Eq. (2)} & \end{aligned}$$

$$(0) \qquad Z + \left(\frac{3}{2} - \frac{7}{6}\theta\right)x_4 + \left(1 + \frac{2}{3}\theta\right)x_5 = 36 - 2\theta.$$

The *stopping rule* says that the current basic feasible solution will *remain* optimal as long as these coefficients of the nonbasic variables remain *nonnegative*:

$$\frac{3}{2} - \frac{7}{6}\theta \geq 0, \text{ for } 0 \leq \theta \leq \frac{9}{7},$$

$$1 + \frac{2}{3}\theta \geq 0, \text{ for all } \theta \geq 0.$$

Therefore, after increasing θ past $\theta = 9/7$, x_4 would need to be the *entering basic variable* for another *iteration* of the simplex method to find the new optimal solution. Then θ would be increased further until another coefficient goes negative and so on until θ has been increased as far as desired.

This entire procedure is now summarized, and the example is completed in Table 16.2.

Summary of Parametric Programming Procedure for Systematic Changes in the c_j Parameters

Step 1 Solve the problem with $\theta = 0$ by the simplex method.

Step 2 Use the sensitivity analysis procedure (cases 2*a* and 3, Sec. 4.3) to introduce the $\Delta c_j = \alpha_j \theta$ changes into Eq. (0).

Step 3 Increase θ until one of the nonbasic variables has its coefficient in Eq. (0) go negative (or until θ has been increased as far as desired).

Step 4 Use this variable as the entering basic variable for an iteration of the simplex method to find the new optimal solution. Return to step 3.

Table 16.2 The c_j Parametric Programming Procedure Applied to Wyndor Glass Co. Example

Range of θ	Basic variable	Eq. no.	Coefficient of: Z	x_1	x_2	x_3	x_4	x_5	Right side	Optimal solution
$0 \le \theta \le \frac{9}{7}$	$Z(\theta)$	0	1	0	θ	0	$\frac{9-7\theta}{6}$	$\frac{3+2\theta}{3}$	$36-2\theta$	$x_4=0$, $x_5=0$
	x_3	1	0	0	0	1	$\frac{1}{3}$	$-\frac{1}{3}$	2	$x_3=2$
	x_2	2	0	0	1	0	$\frac{1}{2}$	0	6	$x_2=6$
	x_1	3	0	1	0	0	$-\frac{1}{3}$	$\frac{1}{3}$	2	$x_1=2$
$\frac{9}{7} \le \theta \le 5$	$Z(\theta)$	0	1	0	0	$\frac{-9+7\theta}{2}$	0	$\frac{5-\theta}{2}$	$27+5\theta$	$x_3=0$, $x_5=0$
	x_4	1	0	0	0	3	1	-1	6	$x_4=6$
	x_2	2	0	0	1	$-\frac{3}{2}$	0	$\frac{1}{2}$	3	$x_2=3$
	x_1	3	0	1	0	1	0	0	4	$x_1=4$
$\theta \ge 5$	$Z(\theta)$	0	1	0	$-5+\theta$	$3+2\theta$	0	0	$12+8\theta$	$x_2=0$, $x_3=0$
	x_4	1	0	0	2	0	1	0	12	$x_4=12$
	x_5	2	0	0	2	-3	0	1	6	$x_5=6$
	x_1	3	0	1	0	1	0	0	4	$x_1=4$

Systematic Changes in the b_i Parameters

For this case the one modification made in the original linear programming model is that b_i is replaced by $(b_i + \alpha_i \theta)$, for $i = 1, 2, \ldots, m$, where the α_i are given input constants. Thus, the problem becomes

$$\text{Maximize} \quad Z(\theta) = \sum_{j=1}^{n} c_j x_j,$$

subject to

$$\sum_{j=1}^{n} a_{ij}x_j \le b_i + \alpha_i\theta, \text{ for } i = 1, 2, \ldots, m,$$

and

$$x_j \ge 0, \text{ for } j = 1, 2, \ldots, n.$$

The goal is to identify the optimal solution as a function of θ. With this formulation, the corresponding objective function value $Z^*(\theta)$ always has the *piecewise linear* and *concave*[1] form shown in Fig. 16.2. (See Prob. 17.) The set of basic variables in the optimal solution still changes only where the slope of $Z^*(\theta)$ changes, but now the values of these variables change as a (linear) function of θ between the slope changes.

The solution procedure summarized below is very similar to that presented in the preceding section for the c_j. The reason is that changing the b_i is equivalent to changing the coefficients in the objective function of the *dual* model. Therefore the procedure for the primal problem is exactly *complementary* to simultaneously applying the procedure for systematic changes in the c_j parameters to the *dual* problem. Consequently, the *dual simplex method* (see Sec. 16.2) now would be used to obtain each new optimal solution, and the applicable sensitivity analysis case (see Sec. 4.3) now is case 1, but these are the only differences.

Summary of Parametric Programming Procedure for Systematic Changes in the b_i Parameters.

Step 1 Solve the problem with $\theta = 0$ by the simplex method.

Step 2 Use the sensitivity analysis procedure (case 1, Sec. 4.3) to introduce the $\Delta b_i = \alpha_i\theta$ changes into the right-side column.

Step 3 Increase θ until one of the basic variables has its value in the right-side column go negative (or until θ has been increased as far as desired).

Figure 16.2 Objective function value for the optimal solution as a function of θ for parametric linear programming with systematic changes in the b_i parameters.

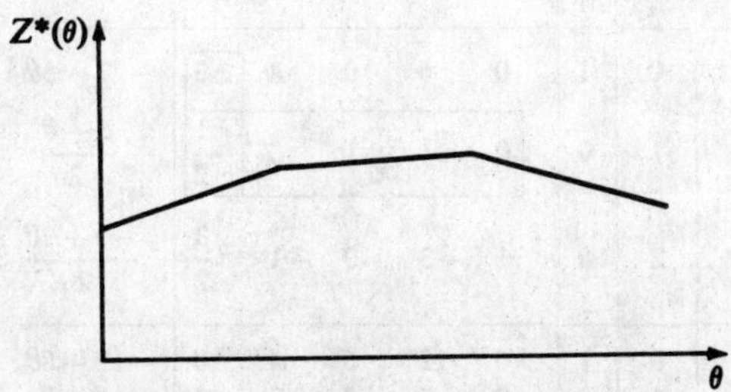

[1] See Appendix 1 for a definition and discussion of *concave* functions.

Step 4 Use this variable as the leaving basic variable for an iteration of the dual simplex method to find the new optimal solution. Return to step 3.

To illustrate this procedure in a way that demonstrates its *duality* relationship with the procedure for systematic changes in the c_j parameters, we shall now apply it to the *dual* problem for the *Wyndor Glass Co.* (see Table 2.25). In particular, suppose that $\alpha_1 = 2$ and $\alpha_2 = -1$, so that the functional constraints become

$$y_1 \qquad + 3y_3 \geq 3 + 2\theta, \text{ or } -y_1 \qquad - 3y_3 \leq -3 - 2\theta$$
$$2y_2 + 2y_3 \geq 5 - \theta, \text{ or } \qquad -2y_2 - 2y_3 \leq -5 + \theta.$$

Thus the *dual* of this problem is just the example considered in Table 16.2.

This problem with $\theta = 0$ has already been solved in Table 16.1, so we begin with the *final* simplex tableau given there. Using the sensitivity analysis expressions for case 1, Sec. 4.3, we find that

$$\Delta y_0^* = \sum_{i=1}^{2} \Delta b_i y_i^* = -2\theta(2) + \theta(6) = 2\theta,$$

$$\Delta b_1^* = \sum_{i=1}^{2} \Delta b_i s_{1i}^* = -2\theta\left(-\frac{1}{3}\right) - \theta(0) = \frac{2\theta}{3},$$

$$\Delta b_2^* = \sum_{i=1}^{2} \Delta b_i s_{2i}^* = -2\theta\left(\frac{1}{3}\right) + \theta\left(-\frac{1}{2}\right) = -\frac{7\theta}{6}$$

Table 16.3 The b_i Parametric Programming Procedure Applied to Dual of Wyndor Glass Co. Example

Range of θ	Basic variable	Eq. no.	Coefficient of Z	y_1	y_2	y_3	y_4	y_5	Right side	Optimal solution
$0 \leq \theta \leq \frac{9}{7}$	$Z(\theta)$	0	1	2	0	0	2	6	$-36 + 2\theta$	$y_1 = y_4 = y_5 = 0$
	y_3	1	0	$\frac{1}{3}$	0	1	$-\frac{1}{3}$	0	$\frac{3+2\theta}{3}$	$y_3 = \frac{3+2\theta}{3}$
	y_2	2	0	$-\frac{1}{3}$	1	0	$\frac{1}{3}$	$-\frac{1}{2}$	$\frac{9-7\theta}{6}$	$y_2 = \frac{9-7\theta}{6}$
$\frac{9}{7} \leq \theta \leq 5$	$Z(\theta)$	0	1	0	6	0	4	3	$-27 - 5\theta$	$y_2 = y_4 = y_5 = 0$
	y_3	1	0	0	1	1	0	$-\frac{1}{2}$	$\frac{5-\theta}{2}$	$y_3 = \frac{5-\theta}{2}$
	y_1	2	0	1	-3	0	-1	$\frac{3}{2}$	$\frac{-9+7\theta}{2}$	$y_1 = \frac{-9+7\theta}{2}$
$\theta \leq 5$	$Z(\theta)$	0	1	0	12	6	4	0	$-12 - 8\theta$	$y_2 = y_3 = y_4 = 0$
	y_5	1	0	0	-2	-2	0	1	$-5 + \theta$	$y_5 = -5 + \theta$
	y_1	2	0	1	0	3	-1	0	$3 + 2\theta$	$y_1 = 3 + 2\theta$

need to be added to the respective entries in the right-side column of this tableau. Therefore the two basic variables

$$y_3 = \frac{3 + 2\theta}{3}$$

$$y_2 = \frac{9 - 7\theta}{6}$$

remain nonnegative for $0 \le \theta \le 9/7$. Increasing θ past $\theta = 9/7$ requires making y_2 a *leaving basic variable* for another *iteration* of the dual simplex method and so on, as summarized in Table 16.3.

We suggest that you now trace through Tables 16.2 and 16.3 simultaneously to note the *duality* relationship between the two procedures.

16.4 THE REVISED SIMPLEX METHOD

The original simplex method described in Chap. 2 is a straightforward algebraic procedure. However, this way of executing the algorithm is not the most efficient computational procedure for electronic digital computers because it computes and stores many numbers that are not needed at the current iteration and which may not become relevant for decision making at subsequent iterations. The only pieces of information relevant at each iteration are the coefficients of the nonbasic variables in Eq. (0), the coefficients of the entering basic variable in the other equations, and the right-hand side of the equations. It would be very useful to have a procedure that could obtain this information efficiently without computing and storing all the other coefficients.

These considerations motivated the development of the *revised simplex method.* This method was designed to accomplish exactly the same things as the original simplex method, but in a way that is more efficient for execution on a digital computer. Thus it is a streamlined version of the original procedure. It computes and stores only the information that is currently needed, and it carries along the essential data in a more compact form.

The revised simplex method explicitly uses *matrix* manipulations, so it is necessary to describe the problem in matrix notation. (See Appendix 3 for a review of matrices.) Using the *matrix form*, the general model for linear programming given in Sec. 2.2 becomes

$$\text{Maximize} \quad Z = \mathbf{cx},$$

subject to

$$\mathbf{Ax} \le \mathbf{b} \text{ and } \mathbf{x} \ge \mathbf{0},$$

where **c** is the row vector

$$\mathbf{c} = [c_1, c_2, \ldots, c_n],$$

x, **b**, and **0** are the column vectors such that

$$\mathbf{x} = \begin{bmatrix} x_1 \\ x_2 \\ \vdots \\ x_n \end{bmatrix}, \mathbf{b} = \begin{bmatrix} b_1 \\ b_2 \\ \vdots \\ b_m \end{bmatrix}, \mathbf{0} = \begin{bmatrix} 0 \\ 0 \\ \vdots \\ 0 \end{bmatrix},$$

and **A** is the matrix

$$\mathbf{A} = \begin{bmatrix} a_{11} & a_{12} & \cdots & a_{1n} \\ a_{21} & a_{22} & \cdots & a_{2n} \\ \vdots & \vdots & & \vdots \\ a_{m1} & a_{m2} & \cdots & a_{mn} \end{bmatrix}.$$

Now introduce the column vector of slack variables

$$\mathbf{x}_s = \begin{bmatrix} x_{n+1} \\ x_{n+2} \\ \vdots \\ x_{n+m} \end{bmatrix},$$

so that the constraints become

$$[\mathbf{A}, \mathbf{I}] \begin{bmatrix} \mathbf{x} \\ \mathbf{x}_s \end{bmatrix} = \mathbf{b} \text{ and } \begin{bmatrix} \mathbf{x} \\ \mathbf{x}_s \end{bmatrix} \geq \mathbf{0},$$

where **I** is the $m \times m$ identity matrix, and the vector **0** now has $(n + m)$ elements.

Recall that the general approach of the simplex method is to obtain one *basic feasible solution* after another until the optimal solution is reached. One of the key features of the revised simplex method involves the way in which it obtains basic feasible solutions. In matrix notation, a basic solution is the solution of the m equations

$$[\mathbf{A}, \mathbf{I}] \begin{bmatrix} \mathbf{x} \\ \mathbf{x}_s \end{bmatrix} = \mathbf{b},$$

in which n of the $(n + m)$ elements of

$$\begin{bmatrix} \mathbf{x} \\ \mathbf{x}_s \end{bmatrix},$$

the *nonbasic variables*, are set equal to *zero*. Eliminating these n variables by equating them to zero leaves a set of m equations in m unknowns (the *basic variables*). This set of equations can be denoted by

$$\mathbf{B}\mathbf{x}_B = \mathbf{b},$$

where the vector of basic variables

$$x_B = \begin{bmatrix} x_{B1} \\ x_{B2} \\ \vdots \\ x_{Bm} \end{bmatrix}$$

is obtained by *eliminating* the *nonbasic variables* from

$$\begin{bmatrix} \mathbf{x} \\ \mathbf{x}_s \end{bmatrix},$$

and the basis matrix

$$\mathbf{B} = \begin{bmatrix} B_{11} & B_{12} & \cdots & B_{1m} \\ B_{21} & B_{22} & \cdots & B_{2m} \\ \vdots & \vdots & & \vdots \\ B_{m1} & B_{m2} & \cdots & B_{mm} \end{bmatrix}$$

is obtained by *eliminating* the columns corresponding to *coefficients of nonbasic variables* from $[\mathbf{A}, \mathbf{I}]$. (In addition, the elements of $\mathbf{x}_B$, and therefore the columns of $\mathbf{B}$, may be placed in a different order when executing the simplex method.) To solve $\mathbf{B}\mathbf{x}_B = \mathbf{b}$, both sides would be premultiplied by $\mathbf{B}^{-1}$†:

$$\mathbf{B}^{-1}\mathbf{B}\mathbf{x}_B = \mathbf{B}^{-1}\mathbf{b},$$

so that the basic solution is

$$\mathbf{x}_B = \mathbf{B}^{-1}\mathbf{b}.$$

Letting $\mathbf{c}_B$ be the vector obtained by *eliminating* the *coefficients* of *nonbasic variables* from $[\mathbf{c}, \mathbf{0}]$ and reordering the elements to match $\mathbf{x}_B$, the value of the objective function for this basic solution is then

$$Z = \mathbf{c}_B\mathbf{x}_B = \mathbf{c}_B\mathbf{B}^{-1}\mathbf{b}.$$

To illustrate, consider again the *Wyndor Glass Co.* problem presented in Sec. 2.1 and solved by the original simplex method in Table 2.25. In this case

$$\mathbf{c} = [3, 5], [\mathbf{A}, \mathbf{I}] = \begin{bmatrix} 1 & 0 & 1 & 0 & 0 \\ 0 & 2 & 0 & 1 & 0 \\ 3 & 2 & 0 & 0 & 1 \end{bmatrix}, \mathbf{b} = \begin{bmatrix} 4 \\ 12 \\ 18 \end{bmatrix}, \mathbf{x} = \begin{bmatrix} x_1 \\ x_2 \end{bmatrix}, \mathbf{x}_s = \begin{bmatrix} x_3 \\ x_4 \\ x_5 \end{bmatrix}.$$

Referring to Table 2.25, the sequence of basic feasible solutions obtained by the simplex method (original or revised) are the following:

Iteration 0

$$\mathbf{x}_B = \begin{bmatrix} x_3 \\ x_4 \\ x_5 \end{bmatrix}, \mathbf{B} = \begin{bmatrix} 1 & 0 & 0 \\ 0 & 1 & 0 \\ 0 & 0 & 1 \end{bmatrix} = \mathbf{B}^{-1}, \text{ so } \begin{bmatrix} x_3 \\ x_4 \\ x_5 \end{bmatrix} = \begin{bmatrix} 1 & 0 & 0 \\ 0 & 1 & 0 \\ 0 & 0 & 1 \end{bmatrix} \begin{bmatrix} 4 \\ 12 \\ 18 \end{bmatrix} = \begin{bmatrix} 4 \\ 12 \\ 18 \end{bmatrix},$$

$$\mathbf{c}_B = [0,0,0], \text{ so } Z = [0,0,0] \begin{bmatrix} 4 \\ 12 \\ 18 \end{bmatrix} = 0.$$

† The simplex method only introduces basic variables such that $\mathbf{B}$ is *nonsingular*, so that $\mathbf{B}^{-1}$ always will exist.

Iteration 1

$$\mathbf{x}_B = \begin{bmatrix} x_3 \\ x_2 \\ x_5 \end{bmatrix}, \mathbf{B} = \begin{bmatrix} 1 & 0 & 0 \\ 0 & 2 & 0 \\ 0 & 2 & 1 \end{bmatrix}, \mathbf{B}^{-1} = \begin{bmatrix} 1 & 0 & 0 \\ 0 & \frac{1}{2} & 0 \\ 0 & -1 & 1 \end{bmatrix},$$

so

$$\begin{bmatrix} x_3 \\ x_2 \\ x_5 \end{bmatrix} = \begin{bmatrix} 1 & 0 & 0 \\ 0 & \frac{1}{2} & 0 \\ 0 & -1 & 1 \end{bmatrix} \begin{bmatrix} 4 \\ 12 \\ 18 \end{bmatrix} = \begin{bmatrix} 4 \\ 6 \\ 6 \end{bmatrix},$$

$$\mathbf{c}_B = [0,5,0], \text{ so } Z = [0,5,0] \begin{bmatrix} 4 \\ 6 \\ 6 \end{bmatrix} = 30.$$

Iteration 2

$$\mathbf{x}_B = \begin{bmatrix} x_3 \\ x_2 \\ x_1 \end{bmatrix}, \mathbf{B} = \begin{bmatrix} 1 & 0 & 1 \\ 0 & 2 & 0 \\ 0 & 2 & 3 \end{bmatrix}, \mathbf{B}^{-1} = \begin{bmatrix} 1 & \frac{1}{3} & -\frac{1}{3} \\ 0 & \frac{1}{2} & 0 \\ 0 & -\frac{1}{3} & \frac{1}{3} \end{bmatrix},$$

so

$$\begin{bmatrix} x_3 \\ x_2 \\ x_1 \end{bmatrix} = \begin{bmatrix} 1 & \frac{1}{3} & -\frac{1}{3} \\ 0 & \frac{1}{2} & 0 \\ 0 & -\frac{1}{3} & \frac{1}{3} \end{bmatrix} \begin{bmatrix} 4 \\ 12 \\ 18 \end{bmatrix} = \begin{bmatrix} 2 \\ 6 \\ 2 \end{bmatrix},$$

$$\mathbf{c}_B = [0,5,3], \text{ so } Z = [0,5,3] \begin{bmatrix} 2 \\ 6 \\ 2 \end{bmatrix} = 36.$$

The last preliminary before summarizing the revised simplex method is to show the *matrix form* of the set of equations appearing in the simplex tableau for any iteration of the original simplex method. For the *original* set of equations, the matrix form is

$$\begin{bmatrix} 1 & -\mathbf{c} & \mathbf{0} \\ \mathbf{0} & \mathbf{A} & \mathbf{I} \end{bmatrix} \begin{bmatrix} Z \\ \mathbf{x} \\ \mathbf{x}_s \end{bmatrix} = \begin{bmatrix} 0 \\ \mathbf{b} \end{bmatrix}.$$

After any subsequent iteration, $\mathbf{x}_B = \mathbf{B}^{-1}\mathbf{b}$ and $Z = \mathbf{c}_B\mathbf{B}^{-1}\mathbf{b}$, so the right-hand side of these equations has become

$$\begin{bmatrix} Z \\ \mathbf{x}_B \end{bmatrix} = \begin{bmatrix} 1 & \mathbf{c}_B\mathbf{B}^{-1} \\ \mathbf{0} & \mathbf{B}^{-1} \end{bmatrix} \begin{bmatrix} 0 \\ \mathbf{b} \end{bmatrix} = \begin{bmatrix} \mathbf{c}_B\mathbf{B}^{-1}\mathbf{b} \\ \mathbf{B}^{-1}\mathbf{b} \end{bmatrix}.$$

Therefore the algebraic operations on *both* sides of the original set of equations has been equivalent to premultiplying them by this same matrix. Since

$$\begin{bmatrix} 1 & \mathbf{c}_B\mathbf{B}^{-1} \\ \mathbf{0} & \mathbf{B}^{-1} \end{bmatrix} \begin{bmatrix} 1 & -\mathbf{c} & \mathbf{0} \\ \mathbf{0} & \mathbf{A} & \mathbf{I} \end{bmatrix} = \begin{bmatrix} 1 & \mathbf{c}_B\mathbf{B}^{-1}\mathbf{A} - \mathbf{c} & \mathbf{c}_B\mathbf{B}^{-1} \\ \mathbf{0} & \mathbf{B}^{-1}\mathbf{A} & \mathbf{B}^{-1} \end{bmatrix},$$

the desired matrix form of the *set of equations after any iteration is*

$$\begin{bmatrix} 1 & \mathbf{c}_B\mathbf{B}^{-1}\mathbf{A} - \mathbf{c} & \mathbf{c}_B\mathbf{B}^{-1} \\ \mathbf{0} & \mathbf{B}^{-1}\mathbf{A} & \mathbf{B}^{-1} \end{bmatrix} \begin{bmatrix} Z \\ \mathbf{x} \\ \mathbf{x}_s \end{bmatrix} = \begin{bmatrix} \mathbf{c}_B\mathbf{B}^{-1}\mathbf{b} \\ \mathbf{B}^{-1}\mathbf{b} \end{bmatrix}.$$

For example, consider the *final* set of equations resulting from iteration 2 for the *Wyndor Glass Co.* problem. Using the B^{-1} given above,

$$\mathbf{B}^{-1}\mathbf{A} = \begin{bmatrix} 1 & \frac{1}{3} & -\frac{1}{3} \\ 0 & \frac{1}{2} & 0 \\ 0 & -\frac{1}{3} & \frac{1}{3} \end{bmatrix} \begin{bmatrix} 1 & 0 \\ 0 & 2 \\ 3 & 2 \end{bmatrix} = \begin{bmatrix} 0 & 0 \\ 0 & 1 \\ 1 & 0 \end{bmatrix},$$

$$\mathbf{c}_B\mathbf{B}^{-1} = [0,5,3] \begin{bmatrix} 1 & \frac{1}{3} & -\frac{1}{3} \\ 0 & \frac{1}{2} & 0 \\ 0 & -\frac{1}{3} & \frac{1}{3} \end{bmatrix} = \left[0, \frac{3}{2}, 1\right],$$

$$\mathbf{c}_B\mathbf{B}^{-1}\mathbf{A} - \mathbf{c} = [0,5,3] \begin{bmatrix} 0 & 0 \\ 0 & 1 \\ 1 & 0 \end{bmatrix} - [3,5] = [0,0].$$

Since $\mathbf{x}_B = \mathbf{B}^{-1}\mathbf{b}$ and $Z = \mathbf{c}_B\mathbf{B}^{-1}\mathbf{b}$ have already been found above, this gives the following set of equations:

$$\left[\begin{array}{c|ccc|ccc} 1 & 0 & 0 & 0 & \frac{3}{2} & 1 \\ \hline 0 & 0 & 0 & 1 & \frac{1}{3} & -\frac{1}{3} \\ 0 & 0 & 1 & 0 & \frac{1}{2} & 0 \\ 0 & 1 & 0 & 0 & -\frac{1}{3} & \frac{1}{3} \end{array}\right]\begin{bmatrix} Z \\ x_1 \\ x_2 \\ x_3 \\ x_4 \\ x_5 \end{bmatrix} = \begin{bmatrix} 36 \\ 2 \\ 6 \\ 2 \end{bmatrix},$$

as shown in the *final* simplex tableau in Table 2.25.

There are two key implications from this matrix form of the set of equations. The first is that *only* $\mathbf{B}^{-1}$ needs to be derived to be able to calculate all the numbers in the simplex tableau from the *original parameters* ($\mathbf{A}$, $\mathbf{b}$, $\mathbf{c}_B$) of the problem. Second, *any one* of these numbers (except $Z = \mathbf{c}_B\mathbf{B}^{-1}\mathbf{b}$) can be obtained by performing *only part* of a matrix multiplication. Therefore the *required numbers* to perform an iteration of the simplex method can be obtained as needed *without* expending the computational effort to obtain *all* the numbers.

Summary of Revised Simplex Method

Initialization step Same as for original simplex method.

Iterative step

Part 1 Determine the entering basic variable: Same as for original simplex method.

Part 2 Determine the leaving basic variable: Same as for original simplex method, except calculate *only* the numbers required to do this.

Part 3 Determine the new basic feasible solution: Derive $\mathbf{B}^{-1}$ and set $\mathbf{x}_B = \mathbf{B}^{-1}\mathbf{b}$.

Stopping rule Determine whether this solution is optimal: Same as for original simplex method, except calculate *only* the numbers required to do this [the coefficients of the *nonbasic variables* in Eq. (0)].

In part 3 of the iterative step, $\mathbf{B}^{-1}$ could be derived each time by using a standard computer routine for inverting a matrix. However, since $\mathbf{B}$ (and therefore $\mathbf{B}^{-1}$) changes so little from one iteration to the next, it is much more efficient to derive the new $\mathbf{B}^{-1}$ (denote it by $\mathbf{B}_{\text{new}}^{-1}$) from the $\mathbf{B}^{-1}$ at the preceding iteration (denote it by $\mathbf{B}_{\text{old}}^{-1}$). (For the *initial* basic feasible solution,

$\mathbf{B} = \mathbf{I} = \mathbf{B}^{-1}$.) The method for doing this is based directly upon the interpretation of the elements of $\mathbf{B}^{-1}$ (the coefficients of the slack variables in the current equations 1, 2, ..., m) presented in Sec. 2.11 and the procedure used by the original simplex method to obtain the new set of equations from the preceding set. To describe the method formally, let x_k be the *entering basic variable*, a'_{ik} be the coefficient of x_k in the *current* Eq. (i) for $i = 1, 2, \ldots, m$ (these coefficients are calculated in part 2 of the iterative step), and r be the number of the equation containing the *leaving basic variable*. Recall that the new set of equations [excluding Eq. (0)] can be obtained from the preceding set by subtracting a'_{ik}/a'_{rk} times Eq. (r) from Eq. (i), for $i = 1, 2, \ldots, r-1, r+1, \ldots, m$, and then dividing Eq. (r) by a'_{rk}. Therefore the element in row i and column j of $\mathbf{B}_{\text{new}}^{-1}$ is

$$(\mathbf{B}_{\text{new}}^{-1})_{ij} = \begin{cases} (\mathbf{B}_{\text{old}}^{-1})_{ij} - \dfrac{a'_{ik}}{a'_{rk}} (\mathbf{B}_{\text{old}}^{-1})_{rj}, & \text{if } i \neq r \\ \dfrac{1}{a'_{rk}} (\mathbf{B}_{\text{old}}^{-1})_{rj}, & \text{if } i = r. \end{cases}$$

This is expressed in matrix notation as

$$\mathbf{B}_{\text{new}}^{-1} = \mathbf{E}\mathbf{B}_{\text{old}}^{-1},$$

where the matrix $\mathbf{E}$ is an identity matrix, except that its rth column is replaced by the vector

$$\boldsymbol{\eta} = \begin{bmatrix} \eta_1 \\ \eta_2 \\ \vdots \\ \eta_m \end{bmatrix}, \text{ where } \eta_i = \begin{cases} -\dfrac{a'_{ik}}{a'_{rk}}, & \text{if } i \neq r \\ \dfrac{1}{a'_{rk}}, & \text{if } i = r. \end{cases}$$

Thus $\mathbf{E} = [\mathbf{U}_1, \mathbf{U}_2, \ldots, \mathbf{U}_{r-1}, \eta, \mathbf{U}_{r+1}, \ldots, \mathbf{U}_m]$, where the m elements of each of the $\mathbf{U}_i$ column vectors are zeros except for a one in the ith position.

We shall illustrate the revised simplex method by applying it to the *Wyndor Glass Co.* problem. The *initial* basic variables are the slack variables $\mathbf{x}_B = \begin{bmatrix} x_3 \\ x_4 \\ x_5 \end{bmatrix}$. Since the *initial* $\mathbf{B}^{-1} = \mathbf{I}$, no calculations are needed to obtain the numbers required to identify the entering basic variable x_2 $(-c_2 = -5 < -3 = -c_1)$ and the leaving basic variable x_4 $(a_{12} = 0,\ b_2/a_{22} = 12/2 < 18/2 = b_3/a_{32}$, so $r = 2)$. Thus the new set of basic variables is

$$\mathbf{x}_B = \begin{bmatrix} x_3 \\ x_2 \\ x_5 \end{bmatrix}.$$

To obtain the new $\mathbf{B}^{-1}$,

$$\boldsymbol{\eta} = \begin{bmatrix} -\dfrac{a_{12}}{a_{22}} \\ \dfrac{1}{a_{22}} \\ -\dfrac{a_{32}}{a_{22}} \end{bmatrix} = \begin{bmatrix} 0 \\ \dfrac{1}{2} \\ -1 \end{bmatrix},$$

so

$$\mathbf{B}^{-1} = \begin{bmatrix} 1 & 0 & 1 \\ 0 & \dfrac{1}{2} & 0 \\ 0 & -1 & 1 \end{bmatrix} \begin{bmatrix} 1 & 0 & 0 \\ 0 & 1 & 0 \\ 0 & 0 & 1 \end{bmatrix} = \begin{bmatrix} 1 & 0 & 0 \\ 0 & \dfrac{1}{2} & 0 \\ 0 & -1 & 1 \end{bmatrix},$$

so that

$$\begin{bmatrix} x_3 \\ x_2 \\ x_5 \end{bmatrix} = \begin{bmatrix} 1 & 0 & 0 \\ 0 & \dfrac{1}{2} & 0 \\ 0 & -1 & 1 \end{bmatrix} \begin{bmatrix} 4 \\ 12 \\ 18 \end{bmatrix} = \begin{bmatrix} 4 \\ 6 \\ 6 \end{bmatrix}.$$

To test whether this solution is optimal, the coefficients of the *nonbasic variables* (x_1 and x_4) in Eq. (0) are calculated. Performing only the relevant parts of the matrix multiplications,

$$\mathbf{c}_B\mathbf{B}^{-1}\mathbf{A} - \mathbf{c} = [0,5,0] \begin{bmatrix} 1 & 0 & 0 \\ 0 & \dfrac{1}{2} & 0 \\ 0 & -1 & 1 \end{bmatrix} \begin{bmatrix} 1 & - \\ 0 & - \\ 3 & - \end{bmatrix} - [3,-] = [-3,-],$$

$$\mathbf{c}_B\mathbf{B}^{-1} = [0,5,0] \begin{bmatrix} - & 0 & - \\ - & \dfrac{1}{2} & - \\ - & -1 & - \end{bmatrix} = \left[-, \frac{5}{2}, -\right].$$

Since the coefficient of x_1 is negative, this solution is *not* optimal.

Using these coefficients, the next iteration begins by identifying x_1 as the *entering basic variable*. To determine the *leaving basic variable*, it is necessary to calculate the *other* coefficients of x_1:

$$\mathbf{B}^{-1}\mathbf{A} = \begin{bmatrix} 1 & 0 & 0 \\ 0 & \dfrac{1}{2} & 0 \\ 0 & -1 & 1 \end{bmatrix} \begin{bmatrix} 1 & - \\ 0 & - \\ 3 & - \end{bmatrix} = \begin{bmatrix} 1 & - \\ 0 & - \\ 3 & - \end{bmatrix}.$$

Using the right-side column for the current basic feasible solution (the value of $\mathbf{x}_B$) given above, the ratios $4/1 > 6/3$ indicate that x_5 is the leaving basic variable, so the new set of basic variables is

$$\mathbf{x}_B = \begin{bmatrix} x_3 \\ x_2 \\ x_1 \end{bmatrix}, \text{ with } \boldsymbol{\eta} = \begin{bmatrix} -\dfrac{a'_{11}}{a'_{31}} \\ -\dfrac{a'_{21}}{a'_{31}} \\ \dfrac{1}{a'_{31}} \end{bmatrix} = \begin{bmatrix} -\dfrac{1}{3} \\ 0 \\ \dfrac{1}{3} \end{bmatrix}.$$

Therefore the new $\mathbf{B}^{-1}$ is

$$\mathbf{B}^{-1} = \begin{bmatrix} 1 & 0 & -\dfrac{1}{3} \\ 0 & 1 & 0 \\ 0 & 0 & \dfrac{1}{3} \end{bmatrix} \begin{bmatrix} 1 & 0 & 0 \\ 0 & \dfrac{1}{2} & 0 \\ 0 & -1 & 1 \end{bmatrix} = \begin{bmatrix} 1 & \dfrac{1}{3} & -\dfrac{1}{3} \\ 0 & \dfrac{1}{2} & 0 \\ 0 & -\dfrac{1}{3} & \dfrac{1}{3} \end{bmatrix},$$

so that

$$\begin{bmatrix} x_3 \\ x_2 \\ x_1 \end{bmatrix} = \begin{bmatrix} 1 & \dfrac{1}{3} & -\dfrac{1}{3} \\ 0 & \dfrac{1}{2} & 0 \\ 0 & -\dfrac{1}{3} & \dfrac{1}{3} \end{bmatrix} \begin{bmatrix} 4 \\ 12 \\ 18 \end{bmatrix} = \begin{bmatrix} 2 \\ 6 \\ 2 \end{bmatrix}.$$

Applying the stopping rule, the coefficients of the *nonbasic variables* (x_4 and x_5) in Eq. (0) are calculated as

$$\mathbf{c}_B \mathbf{B}^{-1} = [0,5,3] \begin{bmatrix} - & \dfrac{1}{3} & -\dfrac{1}{3} \\ & \dfrac{1}{2} & 0 \\ - & -\dfrac{1}{3} & \dfrac{1}{3} \end{bmatrix} = \left[-, \dfrac{3}{2}, 1\right].$$

Since both coefficients are nonnegative, the current solution ($x_1 = 2$, $x_2 = 6$, $x_3 = 2$, $x_4 = 0$, $x_5 = 0$) is optimal and the procedure terminates.

Although the above describes the essence of the revised simplex method, we should point out that minor modifications may be made to improve the efficiency of execution on electronic computers. For example, $\mathbf{B}^{-1}$ may be obtained as the product of the previous $\mathbf{E}$ matrices. This only requires storing the $\boldsymbol{\eta}$ column of $\mathbf{E}$ and the number of the column, rather than the $\mathbf{B}^{-1}$ matrix, at each iteration. If magnetic tape rather than core storage must be used, this "product form" of the basis inverse may be the most efficient.

You should also note that the preceding discussion was limited to the case of linear programming problems fitting *our standard form* given in Sec. 2.2. However, the modifications for other forms are relatively straightforward. The *initialization step* would be conducted just as for the original simplex method (see Sec. 2.10). When this involves introducing artificial variables to obtain an initial basic feasible solution (and to thereby obtain an *identity matrix* as the *initial basis matrix*), these variables would be included among the m elements of $\mathbf{x}_s$.

We shall now summarize the advantages of the revised simplex method over the original simplex method. One is that the number of arithmetic computations may be less. This is especially true when the $\mathbf{A}$ matrix contains a large number of zero elements (which usually is the case for the large problems arising in practice). The amount of information that must be stored at each iteration is less, sometimes considerably so. The revised simplex method also permits the control of round-off errors inevitably generated by digital computers. This can be done by periodically obtaining the current $\mathbf{B}^{-1}$ by directly inverting $\mathbf{B}$. Furthermore, some of the postoptimality problems discussed in Sec. 4.3 can be handled more conveniently when the revised simplex method is used. For all these reasons, the revised simplex method is usually preferable to the original simplex method when using a digital computer.

16.5 THE DECOMPOSITION PRINCIPLE FOR MULTIDIVISIONAL PROBLEMS

In Sec. 3.5 we discussed the special class of linear programming problems called *multidivisional problems* and their special *angular structure* (see Fig. 3.17). We also mentioned that the streamlined version of the simplex method called the *decomposition principle* provides an effective way of exploiting this special structure to solve very large problems. (This approach also is applicable to the *dual* of the class of *multitime-period problems* presented in Sec. 3.6.) We shall now describe and illustrate this procedure.

The basic approach is to reformulate the problem in a way that greatly reduces the number of functional constraints and then to apply the *revised simplex method.* Therefore we need to begin by giving the *matrix form* of multidivisional problems:

$$\text{Maximize} \quad Z = \mathbf{cx},$$

subject to

$$\mathbf{Ax} \leq \mathbf{b}\dagger \text{ and } \mathbf{x} \geq \mathbf{0},$$

† The following discussion would not be changed substantially if $\mathbf{Ax} = \mathbf{b}$.

where the **A** matrix has the angular structure

$$\mathbf{A} = \begin{bmatrix} \mathbf{A}_1 & \mathbf{A}_2 & \cdots & \mathbf{A}_N \\ \mathbf{A}_{N+1} & \mathbf{0} & \cdots & \mathbf{0} \\ \mathbf{0} & \mathbf{A}_{N+2} & \cdots & \mathbf{0} \\ \vdots & \vdots & & \vdots \\ \mathbf{0} & \mathbf{0} & \cdots & \mathbf{A}_{2N} \end{bmatrix},$$

where the $\mathbf{A}_i$ ($i = 1, 2, \ldots, 2N$) are matrices, and the $\mathbf{0}$ are null matrices. Expanding, this can be rewritten as

$$\text{Maximize} \quad Z = \sum_{j=1}^{N} \mathbf{c}_j \mathbf{x}_j,$$

subject to

$$[\mathbf{A}_1, \mathbf{A}_2, \ldots, \mathbf{A}_N, \mathbf{I}]\begin{bmatrix} \mathbf{x} \\ \mathbf{x}_s \end{bmatrix} = \mathbf{b}_0, \quad \begin{bmatrix} \mathbf{x} \\ \mathbf{x}_s \end{bmatrix} \geq \mathbf{0},$$

$$\mathbf{A}_{N+j}\mathbf{x}_j \leq \mathbf{b}_j \text{ and } \mathbf{x}_j \geq \mathbf{0}, \text{ for } j = 1, 2, \ldots, N,$$

where $\mathbf{c}_j$, $\mathbf{x}_j$, $\mathbf{b}_0$, and $\mathbf{b}_j$ are vectors such that $\mathbf{c} = [\mathbf{c}_1, \mathbf{c}_2, \ldots, \mathbf{c}_N]$,

$$\mathbf{x} = \begin{bmatrix} \mathbf{x}_1 \\ \mathbf{x}_2 \\ \vdots \\ \mathbf{x}_N \end{bmatrix}, \quad \mathbf{b} = \begin{bmatrix} \mathbf{b}_0 \\ \mathbf{b}_1 \\ \vdots \\ \mathbf{b}_N \end{bmatrix},$$

and where $\mathbf{x}_s$ is the vector of slack variables for the first set of constraints. This structure suggests that it may be possible to solve the overall problem by doing little more than solving the N *subproblems* of the form

$$\text{Maximize} \quad Z_j = \mathbf{c}_j \mathbf{x}_j,$$

subject to

$$\mathbf{A}_{N+j}\mathbf{x}_j \leq \mathbf{b}_j \text{ and } \mathbf{x}_j \geq \mathbf{0},$$

thereby greatly reducing computational effort. After some reformulation, this approach can indeed be used.

Assume that the set of feasible solutions for each subproblem is a bounded set (i.e., none of the variables can approach infinity). Although a more complicated version of the approach can still be used otherwise, this assumption will simplify the discussion.

The set of points $\mathbf{x}_j$ such that $\mathbf{x}_j \geq \mathbf{0}$ and $\mathbf{A}_{N+j}\mathbf{x}_j \leq \mathbf{b}_j$ constitute a *convex set*[1] with a finite number of extreme points. Therefore, under the assumption that the set is bounded, any point in the set can be represented as a weighted average of the extreme points. To express this mathematically, let n_j be the number of extreme points, and denote these points by $\mathbf{x}_{jk}^*$ for $k = 1, 2, \ldots, n_j$.

[1] See Appendix 1 for a definition and discussion of *convex sets*.

Then any solution $\mathbf{x}_j$ to subproblem j which satisfies the constraints $\mathbf{A}_{N+j}\mathbf{x}_j \leq \mathbf{b}_j$ and $\mathbf{x}_j \geq 0$ also satisfies the equation

$$\mathbf{x}_j = \sum_{k=1}^{n_j} \rho_{jk}\mathbf{x}_{jk}^*$$

for some combination of the ρ_{jk} such that

$$\sum_{k=1}^{n_j} \rho_{jk} = 1$$

and $\rho_{jk} \geq 0$ $(k = 1, 2, \ldots, n_j)$. Furthermore, this is not true for any $\mathbf{x}_j$ that is not a feasible solution for subproblem j. (You may have shown these facts for Prob. 11, Chap. 2.) Therefore this equation for $\mathbf{x}_j$ and the constraints on the ρ_{jk} provide a method for representing the feasible solutions to subproblem j without using any of the original constraints. Hence the overall problem can now be reformulated with far fewer constraints as

$$\text{Maximize} \quad Z = \sum_{j=1}^{N} \sum_{k=1}^{n_j} (\mathbf{c}_j\mathbf{x}_{jk}^*)\rho_{jk},$$

subject to

$$\sum_{j=1}^{N} \sum_{k=1}^{n_j} (\mathbf{A}_j\mathbf{x}_{jk}^*)\rho_{jk} + \mathbf{x}_s = \mathbf{b}_0, \ \mathbf{x}_s \geq \mathbf{0}, \ \sum_{k=1}^{n_j} \rho_{jk} = 1, \text{ for } j = 1, 2, \ldots, N,$$

and

$$\rho_{jk} \geq 0, \text{ for } j = 1, 2, \ldots, N \text{ and } k = 1, 2, \ldots, n_j.$$

This formulation is completely equivalent to the one given earlier. However, since it has far fewer constraints, it should be solvable with much less computational effort. The fact that the number of variables (which are now the ρ_{jk} and the elements of $\mathbf{x}_s$) is much larger does not matter much computationally if the *revised simplex method* is used. The one apparent flaw is that it would be tedious to identify all the $\mathbf{x}_{jk}^*$. Fortunately, it is not necessary to do this when using the revised simplex method. The procedure is outlined below.

Let $\mathbf{A}'$ be the matrix of constraint coefficients for this reformulation of the problem, and let $\mathbf{c}'$ be the vector of objective function coefficients. (The individual elements of $\mathbf{A}'$ and $\mathbf{c}'$ are determined only when they are needed.) As usual, let $\mathbf{B}$ be the current basis matrix, and let $\mathbf{c}_B$ be the corresponding vector of basic variable coefficients in the objective function. For a portion of the work required for the stopping rule and part 1 of the iterative step, the revised simplex method is to find the minimum element of $(\mathbf{c}_B\mathbf{B}^{-1}\mathbf{A}' - \mathbf{c}')$, the vector of coefficients of the *original* variables (the ρ_{jk} in this case) in the *current* Eq. (0). Let $(z_{jk} - c_{jk})$ denote the element in this vector corresponding to ρ_{jk}. Let m_0 denote the number of elements of $\mathbf{b}_0$. Let $(\mathbf{B}^{-1})_{1;m_0}$ be the matrix consisting of the first m_0 columns of $\mathbf{B}^{-1}$, and let $(\mathbf{B}^{-1})_i$ be the vector consisting of the ith column of $\mathbf{B}^{-1}$. Then $(z_{jk} - c_{jk})$ reduces to

$$\begin{aligned} z_{jk} - c_{jk} &= \mathbf{c}_B(\mathbf{B}^{-1})_{1;m_0}\mathbf{A}_j\mathbf{x}_{jk}^* + \mathbf{c}_B(\mathbf{B}^{-1})_{m_0+j} - \mathbf{c}_j\mathbf{x}_{jk}^* \\ &= (\mathbf{c}_B(\mathbf{B}^{-1})_{1;m_0}\mathbf{A}_j - \mathbf{c}_j)\mathbf{x}_{jk}^* + \mathbf{c}_B(\mathbf{B}^{-1})_{m_0+j}. \end{aligned}$$

Since $\mathbf{c}_B(\mathbf{B}^{-1})_{mo+j}$ is independent of k, the minimum value of $(z_{jk} - c_{jk})$ over $k = 1, 2, \ldots, n_j$ can be found as follows. Recall that the $\mathbf{x}_{jk}^*$ are just the basic feasible solutions for the set of constraints $\mathbf{x}_j \geq \mathbf{0}$ and $\mathbf{A}_{N+j}\mathbf{x}_j \leq \mathbf{b}_j$ and that the simplex method identifies the basic feasible solution which minimizes (or maximizes) a given objective function. Therefore, solve the linear programming problem

$$\text{Minimize} \quad W_j = (\mathbf{c}_B(\mathbf{B}^{-1})_{1;mo}\mathbf{A}_j - \mathbf{c}_j)\mathbf{x}_j + \mathbf{c}_B(\mathbf{B}^{-1})_{mo+j},$$

subject to

$$\mathbf{A}_{N+j}\mathbf{x}_j \leq \mathbf{b}_j \text{ and } \mathbf{x}_j \geq \mathbf{0}.$$

The optimal value of W_j (denoted by W_j^*) is the desired minimum value of $(z_{jk} - c_{jk})$ over k. Furthermore, the optimal solution for $\mathbf{x}_j$ is the corresponding $\mathbf{x}_{jk}^*$.

Therefore the first step at each iteration requires solving N linear programming problems of the above type to find W_j^* for $j = 1, 2, \ldots, N$. In addition, the *current* Eq. (0) coefficients of the elements of $\mathbf{x}_s$ that are *nonbasic* variables would be found in the usual way as the elements of $\mathbf{c}_B(\mathbf{B}^{-1})_{1;mo}$. If all these coefficients [the W_j^* and the elements of $\mathbf{c}_B(\mathbf{B}^{-1})_{1;mo}$] are *nonnegative*, the current solution is *optimal* by the stopping rule. Otherwise, the *minimum* of these coefficients is found, and the corresponding variable is selected as the new *entering basic variable*. If that variable is ρ_{jk}, then the solution to the linear programming problem involving W_j has identified $\mathbf{x}_{jk}^*$, so that the original constraint coefficients of ρ_{jk} are now identified. Hence the revised simplex method can complete the iteration in the usual way.

Assuming that $\mathbf{x} = \mathbf{0}$ is feasible for the original problem, the *initialization step* would use the corresponding solution in the reformulated problem as the *initial basic feasible solution*. This involves selecting the initial *set of basic variables* (the elements of $\mathbf{x}_B$) to be the elements of $\mathbf{x}_s$ and the one variable ρ_{jk} for each subproblem j ($j = 1, 2, \ldots, N$) such that $\mathbf{x}_{jk}^* = \mathbf{0}$. Following the initialization step, the above procedure is repeated for a succession of iterations until the optimal solution is reached. The optimal values of the ρ_{jk} are then substituted into the equations for the $\mathbf{x}_j$ for the optimal solution to conform to the original form of the problem.

To illustrate this procedure, consider the problem

$$\text{Maximize} \quad Z = 4x_1 + 6x_2 + 8x_3 + 5x_4,$$

subject to

$$\begin{aligned} x_1 + 3x_2 + 2x_3 + 4x_4 &\leq 20 \\ 2x_1 + 3x_2 + 6x_3 + 4x_4 &\leq 25 \\ x_1 + x_2 \qquad\qquad\quad &\leq 5 \\ x_1 + 2x_2 \qquad\qquad\quad &\leq 8 \\ 4x_3 + 3x_4 &\leq 12 \end{aligned}$$

and

$$x_j \geq 0, \text{ for } j = 1, 2, 3, 4.$$

Thus, the A matrix is

$$\mathbf{A} = \left[\begin{array}{cc|cc} 1 & 3 & 2 & 4 \\ 2 & 3 & 6 & 4 \\ \hline 1 & 1 & 0 & 0 \\ 1 & 2 & 0 & 0 \\ \hline 0 & 0 & 4 & 3 \end{array}\right],$$

so that $N = 2$ and

$$\mathbf{A}_1 = \begin{bmatrix} 1 & 3 \\ 2 & 3 \end{bmatrix}, \mathbf{A}_2 = \begin{bmatrix} 2 & 4 \\ 6 & 4 \end{bmatrix}, \mathbf{A}_3 = \begin{bmatrix} 1 & 1 \\ 1 & 2 \end{bmatrix}, \mathbf{A}_4 = [4,3].$$

In addition,

$$\mathbf{c}_1 = [4,6], \mathbf{c}_2 = [8,5],$$

$$\mathbf{x}_1 = \begin{bmatrix} x_1 \\ x_2 \end{bmatrix}, \mathbf{x}_2 = \begin{bmatrix} x_3 \\ x_4 \end{bmatrix}, \mathbf{b}_0 = \begin{bmatrix} 20 \\ 25 \end{bmatrix}, \mathbf{b}_1 = \begin{bmatrix} 5 \\ 8 \end{bmatrix}, \mathbf{b}_2 = [12].$$

To prepare for demonstrating how this problem would be solved, we shall first examine its two subproblems individually and then construct the reformulation of the overall problem. Thus *subproblem 1* is

$$\text{Maximize} \quad Z_1 = [4,6]\begin{bmatrix} x_1 \\ x_2 \end{bmatrix},$$

subject to

$$\begin{bmatrix} 1 & 1 \\ 1 & 2 \end{bmatrix}\begin{bmatrix} x_1 \\ x_2 \end{bmatrix} \le \begin{bmatrix} 5 \\ 8 \end{bmatrix} \quad \text{and} \quad \begin{bmatrix} x_1 \\ x_2 \end{bmatrix} \ge \begin{bmatrix} 0 \\ 0 \end{bmatrix},$$

so that its set of feasible solutions is as shown in Fig. 16.3.

It can be seen that this subproblem has four *extreme points* ($n_1 = 4$). One of these is the origin, considered the "first" of these extreme points, so

$$\mathbf{x}_{11}^* = \begin{bmatrix} 0 \\ 0 \end{bmatrix}, \mathbf{x}_{12} = \begin{bmatrix} 5 \\ 0 \end{bmatrix}, \mathbf{x}_{13} = \begin{bmatrix} 2 \\ 3 \end{bmatrix}, \mathbf{x}_{14} = \begin{bmatrix} 0 \\ 4 \end{bmatrix},$$

where $\rho_{11}, \rho_{12}, \rho_{13}, \rho_{14}$ are the respective weights on these points.

Figure 16.3 Subproblem 1 for example illustrating the decomposition principle.

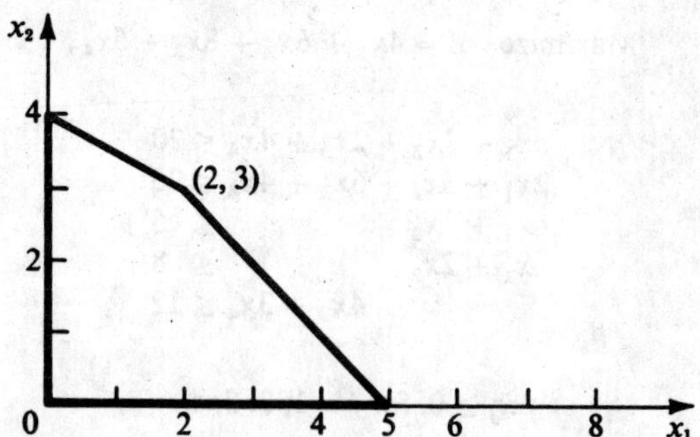

Similarly, *subproblem 2* is

$$\text{Maximize} \quad Z_2 = [8,5]\begin{bmatrix} x_3 \\ x_4 \end{bmatrix},$$

subject to

$$[4,3]\begin{bmatrix} x_3 \\ x_4 \end{bmatrix} \le [12] \text{ and } \begin{bmatrix} x_3 \\ x_4 \end{bmatrix} \ge \begin{bmatrix} 0 \\ 0 \end{bmatrix},$$

and its set of feasible solutions is shown in Fig. 16.4. Thus its three extreme points are

$$\mathbf{x}_{21}^* = \begin{bmatrix} 0 \\ 0 \end{bmatrix}, \mathbf{x}_{22}^* = \begin{bmatrix} 3 \\ 0 \end{bmatrix}, \mathbf{x}_{23}^* = \begin{bmatrix} 0 \\ 4 \end{bmatrix},$$

where $\rho_{21}, \rho_{22}, \rho_{23}$ are the respective weights on these points.

By performing the $\mathbf{c}_j \mathbf{x}_{jk}^*$ vector multiplications and the $\mathbf{A}_j \mathbf{x}_{jk}^*$ matrix multiplications, the following reformulated version of the overall problem can be obtained:

$$\text{Maximize} \quad Z = 20\rho_{12} + 26\rho_{13} + 24\rho_{14} + 24\rho_{22} + 20\rho_{23},$$

subject to

$$\begin{aligned} 5\rho_{12} + 11\rho_{13} + 12\rho_{14} + 6\rho_{22} + 16\rho_{23} + x_{s1} \qquad &= 20 \\ 10\rho_{12} + 13\rho_{13} + 12\rho_{14} + 18\rho_{22} + 16\rho_{23} \qquad + x_{s2} &= 25 \\ \rho_{11} + \rho_{12} + \rho_{13} + \rho_{14} &= 1 \\ \rho_{21} + \rho_{22} + \rho_{23} &= 1 \end{aligned}$$

and

$$\begin{aligned} &\rho_{1k} \ge 0, \text{ for } k = 1, 2, 3, 4, \\ &\rho_{2k} \ge 0, \text{ for } k = 1, 2, 3, \\ &x_{si} \ge 0, \text{ for } i = 1, 2. \end{aligned}$$

Figure 16.4 Subproblem 2 for example illustrating the decomposition principle.

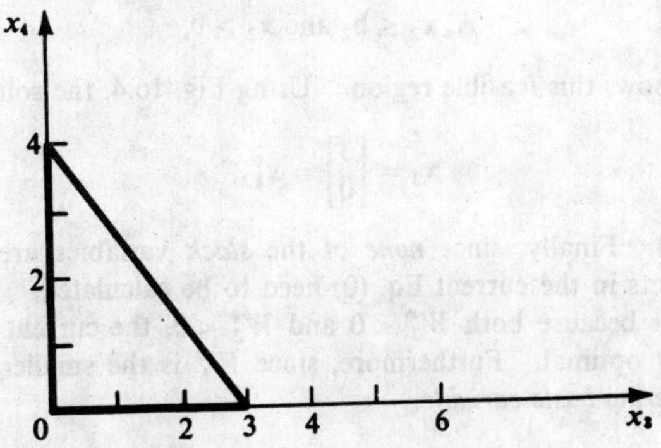

However, we should emphasize that the complete reformulation normally is *not* constructed *explicitly*; rather, just parts of it are generated as needed during the progress of the revised simplex method.

To begin solving this problem, the *initialization step* selects x_{s1}, x_{s2}, ρ_{11}, and ρ_{21} to be the initial basic variables, so that

$$\mathbf{x}_B = \begin{bmatrix} x_{s1} \\ x_{s2} \\ \rho_{11} \\ \rho_{21} \end{bmatrix}.$$

Therefore, since $\mathbf{A}_1\mathbf{x}_{11}^* = \mathbf{0}$, $\mathbf{A}_2\mathbf{x}_{21}^* = \mathbf{0}$, $\mathbf{c}_1\mathbf{x}_{11}^* = \mathbf{0}$, and $\mathbf{c}_2\mathbf{x}_{21}^* = \mathbf{0}$, then

$$\mathbf{B} = \begin{bmatrix} 1 & 0 & 0 & 0 \\ 0 & 1 & 0 & 0 \\ 0 & 0 & 1 & 0 \\ 0 & 0 & 0 & 1 \end{bmatrix} = \mathbf{B}^{-1}, \quad \mathbf{x}_B = \mathbf{b}' = \begin{bmatrix} 20 \\ 25 \\ 1 \\ 1 \end{bmatrix}, \quad \mathbf{c}_B = [0,0,0,0]$$

for the initial basic feasible solution.

To begin testing for optimality, let $j = 1$, and solve the linear programming problem

$$\text{Minimize} \quad W_1 = (\mathbf{0} - \mathbf{c}_1)\mathbf{x}_1 + 0 = -4x_1 - 6x_2,$$

subject to

$$\mathbf{A}_3\mathbf{x}_1 \leq \mathbf{b}_1 \text{ and } \mathbf{x}_1 \geq \mathbf{0},$$

so the feasible region is that shown in Fig. 16.3. Using Fig. 16.3 to solve graphically, the solution is

$$\mathbf{x}_1 = \begin{bmatrix} 2 \\ 3 \end{bmatrix} = \mathbf{x}_{13}^*,$$

so that $W_1^* = -26$.

Next, let $j = 2$, and solve the problem

$$\text{Minimize} \quad W_2 = (\mathbf{0} - \mathbf{c}_2)\mathbf{x}_2 + 0 = -8x_3 - 5x_4,$$

subject to

$$\mathbf{A}_4\mathbf{x}_2 \leq \mathbf{b}_2 \text{ and } \mathbf{x}_2 \geq \mathbf{0},$$

so Fig. 16.4 shows this feasible region. Using Fig. 16.4, the solution is

$$\mathbf{x}_2 = \begin{bmatrix} 3 \\ 0 \end{bmatrix} = \mathbf{x}_{22}^*,$$

so $W_2^* = -24$. Finally, since *none* of the *slack* variables are *nonbasic*, no more coefficients in the current Eq. (0) need to be calculated. It can now be concluded that because both $W_1^* < 0$ and $W_2^* < 0$, the current basic feasible solution is *not* optimal. Furthermore, since W_1^* is the smaller of these, ρ_{13} is the new *entering basic variable*.

For the revised simplex method to now determine the *leaving basic variable*, it is first necessary to calculate the column of $\mathbf{A}'$ giving the *original* coefficients of ρ_{13}. This column is

$$\mathbf{A}'_k = \begin{bmatrix} \mathbf{A}_1\mathbf{x}^*_{13} \\ 1 \\ 0 \end{bmatrix} = \begin{bmatrix} 11 \\ 13 \\ 1 \\ 0 \end{bmatrix}.$$

Proceeding in the usual way to calculate the *current* coefficients of ρ_{13} and the right-side column,

$$\mathbf{B}^{-1}\mathbf{A}'_k = \begin{bmatrix} 11 \\ 13 \\ 1 \\ 0 \end{bmatrix}, \mathbf{B}^{-1}\mathbf{b}' = \begin{bmatrix} 20 \\ 25 \\ 1 \\ 1 \end{bmatrix}.$$

Considering just the strictly positive coefficients, the minimum ratio of the right side to the coefficient is the 1/1 in the third row, so that $r = 3$; that is, ρ_{11} is the new *leaving basic variable*. Thus the new values of $\mathbf{x}_B$ and $\mathbf{c}_B$ are

$$\mathbf{x}_B = \begin{bmatrix} x_{s1} \\ x_{s2} \\ \rho_{13} \\ \rho_{21} \end{bmatrix}, \mathbf{c}_B = [0,0,26,0].$$

To find the new value of $\mathbf{B}^{-1}$, set

$$\mathbf{E} = \begin{bmatrix} 1 & 0 & -11 & 0 \\ 0 & 1 & -13 & 0 \\ 0 & 0 & 1 & 0 \\ 0 & 0 & 0 & 1 \end{bmatrix},$$

so

$$\mathbf{B}^{-1}_{\text{new}} = \mathbf{E}\mathbf{B}^{-1}_{\text{old}} = \begin{bmatrix} 1 & 0 & -11 & 0 \\ 0 & 1 & -13 & 0 \\ 0 & 0 & 1 & 0 \\ 0 & 0 & 0 & 1 \end{bmatrix}.$$

The stage is now set for again testing whether the current basic feasible solution is optimal. In this case

$$W_1 = (\mathbf{0} - \mathbf{c}_1)\mathbf{x}_1 + 26 = -4x_1 - 6x_2 + 26,$$

so the minimum feasible solution from Fig. 16.3 is again

$$\mathbf{x}_1 = \begin{bmatrix} 2 \\ 3 \end{bmatrix} = \mathbf{x}^*_{13},$$

with $W_1^* = 0$. Similarly,

$$W_2 = (\mathbf{0} - \mathbf{c}_2)\mathbf{x}_2 + 0 = -8x_3 - 5x_4,$$

so the minimizing solution from Fig. 16.4 is again

$$\mathbf{x}_2 = \begin{bmatrix} 3 \\ 0 \end{bmatrix} = \mathbf{x}_{22}^*,$$

with $W_2^* = -24$. Finally, there are no nonbasic slack variables to be considered. Since $W_2^* < 0$, the current solution is not optimal, and ρ_{22} is the new *entering basic variable.*

Proceeding with the revised simplex method,

$$\mathbf{A}'_k = \begin{bmatrix} \mathbf{A}_2\mathbf{x}_{22}^* \\ 0 \\ 1 \end{bmatrix} = \begin{bmatrix} 6 \\ 18 \\ 0 \\ 1 \end{bmatrix},$$

so

$$\mathbf{B}^{-1}\mathbf{A}'_k = \begin{bmatrix} 6 \\ 18 \\ 0 \\ 1 \end{bmatrix}, \mathbf{B}^{-1}\mathbf{b}' = \begin{bmatrix} 9 \\ 12 \\ 1 \\ 1 \end{bmatrix}.$$

Therefore the minimum positive ratio is 12/18 from the second row, so $r = 2$; that is, x_{s2} is the new *leaving basic variable.* Thus

$$\mathbf{E} = \begin{bmatrix} 1 & -\frac{1}{3} & 0 & 0 \\ 0 & \frac{1}{18} & 0 & 0 \\ 0 & 0 & 1 & 0 \\ 0 & -\frac{1}{18} & 0 & 1 \end{bmatrix},$$

$$\mathbf{B}_{\text{new}}^{-1} = \mathbf{E}\mathbf{B}_{\text{old}}^{-1} = \begin{bmatrix} 1 & -\frac{1}{3} & -\frac{20}{3} & 0 \\ 0 & \frac{1}{18} & -\frac{13}{18} & 0 \\ 0 & 0 & 1 & 0 \\ 0 & -\frac{1}{18} & \frac{13}{18} & 1 \end{bmatrix}, \mathbf{x}_B = \begin{bmatrix} x_{s1} \\ \rho_{22} \\ \rho_{13} \\ \rho_{21} \end{bmatrix},$$

and $\mathbf{c}_B = [0,24,26,0]$.

Now test whether the new basic feasible solution is optimal. Since

$$W_1 = \left([0,24,26,0]\begin{bmatrix} 1 & -\frac{1}{3} \\ 0 & \frac{1}{18} \\ 0 & 0 \\ 0 & -\frac{1}{18} \end{bmatrix}\begin{bmatrix} 1 & 3 \\ 2 & 3 \end{bmatrix} - [4,6]\right)\begin{bmatrix} x_1 \\ x_2 \end{bmatrix} + [0,24,26,0]\begin{bmatrix} -\frac{20}{3} \\ -\frac{13}{18} \\ 1 \\ \frac{13}{18} \end{bmatrix}$$

$$= \left(\left[0, \frac{4}{3}\right]\begin{bmatrix} 1 & 3 \\ 2 & 3 \end{bmatrix} - [4,6]\right)\begin{bmatrix} x_1 \\ x_2 \end{bmatrix} + \frac{26}{3}$$

$$= -\frac{4}{3}x_1 - 2x_2 + \frac{26}{3},$$

Fig. 16.3 indicates that the minimum feasible solution is again

$$\mathbf{x}_1 = \begin{bmatrix} 2 \\ 3 \end{bmatrix} = \mathbf{x}_{13}^*,$$

so $W_1^* = \frac{2}{3}$. Similarly,

$$W_2 = \left(\left[0, \frac{4}{3}\right]\begin{bmatrix} 2 & 4 \\ 6 & 4 \end{bmatrix} - [8,5]\right)\begin{bmatrix} x_3 \\ x_4 \end{bmatrix} + 0$$

$$= 0x_3 + \frac{1}{3}x_4,$$

so the minimizing solution from Fig. 16.4 now is

$$\mathbf{x}_2 = \begin{bmatrix} 0 \\ 0 \end{bmatrix} = \mathbf{x}_{21}^*,$$

and $W_2^* = 0$. Finally, $\mathbf{c}_B(\mathbf{B}^{-1})_{1;m_0} = [-, \frac{4}{3}]$. Therefore, since $W_1^* \geq 0$, $W_2^* \geq 0$, and $\mathbf{c}_B(\mathbf{B}^{-1})_{1;m_0} \geq \mathbf{0}$, the current basic feasible solution is *optimal*. To identify this solution, set

$$\mathbf{x}_B = \begin{bmatrix} x_{s1} \\ \rho_{22} \\ \rho_{13} \\ \rho_{21} \end{bmatrix} = \mathbf{B}^{-1}\mathbf{b}' = \begin{bmatrix} 1 & -\frac{1}{3} & -\frac{20}{3} & 0 \\ 0 & \frac{1}{18} & -\frac{13}{18} & 0 \\ 0 & 0 & 1 & 0 \\ 0 & -\frac{1}{18} & \frac{13}{18} & 1 \end{bmatrix}\begin{bmatrix} 20 \\ 25 \\ 1 \\ 1 \end{bmatrix} = \begin{bmatrix} 5 \\ \frac{2}{3} \\ 1 \\ \frac{1}{3} \end{bmatrix},$$

so

$$\mathbf{x}_1 = \begin{bmatrix} x_1 \\ x_2 \end{bmatrix} = \sum_{k=1}^{4} \rho_{1k} \mathbf{x}_{1k}^* = \mathbf{x}_{12}^* = \begin{bmatrix} 2 \\ 3 \end{bmatrix},$$

$$\mathbf{x}_2 = \begin{bmatrix} x_3 \\ x_4 \end{bmatrix} = \sum_{k=1}^{3} \rho_{2k} \mathbf{x}_{2k}^* = \frac{1}{3} \begin{bmatrix} 0 \\ 0 \end{bmatrix} + \frac{2}{3} \begin{bmatrix} 3 \\ 0 \end{bmatrix} = \begin{bmatrix} 2 \\ 0 \end{bmatrix}.$$

Thus, an optimal solution for this problem is $x_1 = 2$, $x_2 = 3$, $x_3 = 2$, $x_4 = 0$, with $Z = 42$.

16.6 CONCLUSIONS

This chapter has presented five particularly important algorithms for linear programming practitioners. Mathematical programming computer packages usually include most of them, and they are widely used. Since their basic structure is largely based upon the simplex method as presented in Chap. 2, they retain the exceptional computational efficiency to handle very large problems of the sizes described in Sec. 4.2.

The *revised simplex method* provides an effective way of adapting the simplex method for computer implementation. It also is easy to modify to incorporate these other algorithms.

The *dual simplex method* and *parametric linear programming* are especially valuable for sensitivity analysis, although they also can be very useful in other contexts as well.

The *upper bound technique* and the *decomposition principle* provide ways of streamlining the simplex method for certain rather common classes of problems. They can greatly reduce the computational effort for large problems. Various other special-purpose algorithms also have been developed to exploit the special structure of particular classes of problems (such as those discussed in Chap. 3), and this is an active area of ongoing research.

Selected References

1 Dantzig, George B.: *Linear Programming and Extensions*, Princeton University Press, Princeton, N.J., 1963.

2 Gass, Saul I.: *Linear Programming: Methods and Applications*, 3d ed., McGraw-Hill, New York, 1969.

3 Lasdon, Leon S.: *Optimization Theory for Large Systems*, Macmillan, New York, 1970.

4 Orchard-Hays, William: *Advanced Linear-Programming Computing Techniques*, McGraw-Hill, New York, 1968.

5 Simmonnard, Michel: *Linear Programming* (trans. from French by William S. Jewell), Prentice-Hall, Englewood Cliffs, N.J., 1966.

Problems

1 Use the *upper bound technique* to solve the *Wyndor Glass Co.* problem presented in Sec. 2.1.

2 Use the *upper bound technique* to solve the problem

$$\text{Maximize} \quad Z = x_1 + 3x_2 - 2x_3,$$

subject to

$$\begin{aligned} x_2 - 2x_3 &\leq 1 \\ 2x_1 + x_2 + 2x_3 &\leq 8 \\ x_1 &\leq 1 \\ x_2 &\leq 3 \\ x_3 &\leq 2 \end{aligned}$$

and

$$x_1 \geq 0,\ x_2 \geq 0,\ x_3 \geq 0.$$

3 Use the upper bound technique to solve the following problems:

(*a*) $$\text{Maximize} \quad Z = 2x_1 + 3x_2,$$

subject to

$$\begin{aligned} -x_1 + x_2 &\leq \frac{1}{2} \\ x_1 &\leq 1 \\ x_2 &\leq 1 \end{aligned}$$

and

$$x_1 \geq 0,\ x_2 \geq 0.$$

(*b*) $$\text{Maximize} \quad Z = 5x_1 + 3x_2 - 2x_3 + 2x_4,$$

subject to

$$\begin{aligned} 2x_1 + 2x_2 + x_3 + 2x_4 &\leq 5 \\ 4x_1 + 2x_2 - 3x_3 + x_4 &\leq 5 \end{aligned}$$

and

$$0 \leq x_j \leq 1, \text{ for } j = 1, 2, 3, 4.$$

4 Use the *upper bound technique* to solve the linear programming model given in Prob. 16(*b*), Chap. 4.

5 Use the *dual simplex method* to solve each of the following linear programming models:

(*a*) Model given in Prob. 15, Chap. 2.
(*b*) Model given in Prob. 20, Chap. 2.

6 Use the *dual simplex method* to solve the problem

$$\text{Minimize} \quad Z = 5x_1 + 2x_2 + 4x_3,$$

subject to

$$\begin{aligned} 3x_1 + x_2 + 2x_3 &\geq 4 \\ 6x_1 + 3x_2 + 5x_3 &\geq 10 \end{aligned}$$

and

$$x_1 \geq 0,\ x_2 \geq 0,\ x_3 \geq 0.$$

7 Consider the problem

$$\text{Maximize} \quad Z = 15x_1 + 10x_2,$$

subject to

$$\begin{aligned} x_1 + x_2 &\le 10 \\ 3x_1 + x_2 &\le 20 \\ 5x_1 + 3x_2 &\le 45 \end{aligned}$$

and

$$x_1 \ge 0, x_2 \ge 0.$$

(*a*) Solve by the *original simplex method* (in tabular form). Identify the *complementary* basic solution for the dual problem obtained at each iteration.
(*b*) Solve the *dual* of this problem by the *dual simplex method*. Compare the resulting sequence of basic solutions with the complementary basic solutions obtained in part (*a*).

8 Consider the example for case 1 of sensitivity analysis given in Sec. 4.3, where Table 4.4 is modified by changing b_2 from 12 to 24 and so changing the respective entries in the right-side column to 54, 6, 12, and −2. Starting from this revised simplex tableau, use the *dual simplex method* to obtain the new optimal solution shown in Table 4.5. Show your work.

9 Consider Prob. 18(*a*) and (*b*), Chap. 4. Use the *dual simplex method* to obtain the new optimal solution for each of these two cases.

10 Use *both* the *upper bound technique* and the *dual simplex method* to solve the *Nori & Leets Co.* problem given in Sec. 2.4 for controlling air pollution.

11 Consider the problem

$$\text{Maximize} \quad Z(\theta) = 8x_1 + 24x_2,$$

subject to

$$\begin{aligned} x_1 + 2x_2 &\le 10 \\ 2x_1 + x_2 &\le 10 \end{aligned}$$

and

$$x_1 \ge 0, x_2 \ge 0.$$

Suppose that $Z(\theta)$ represents profit and that it is possible to modify the objective function somewhat by an appropriate shifting of key personnel between the two activities. In particular, suppose that the unit profit of activity 1 can be increased above 8 (to a maximum of 18) at the expense of decreasing the unit profit of activity 2 below 24 by twice the amount. Thus $Z(\theta)$ can actually be represented as

$$Z(\theta) = (8 + \theta)x_1 + (24 - 2\theta)x_2,$$

where θ is also a decision variable such that $0 \le \theta \le 10$.

(*a*) Find the optimal solution to the original form of the problem by the simplex method. Then use *parametric linear programming* to find the optimal solution, and the optimal value of $Z(\theta)$, as a function of θ, for $0 \le \theta \le 10$. Also indicate graphically what this algebraic procedure is doing.

(*b*) Determine the optimal value of θ. Then indicate how this optimal value could have been identified directly by solving only two ordinary linear programming problems. (*Hint:* A convex function achieves its maximum at an end point.)

12 Use *parametric linear programming* to find the optimal solution of the following problem as a function of θ, for $0 \leq \theta \leq 20$:

$$\text{Maximize} \quad Z(\theta) = (30 + 3\theta)x_1 + (40 - 2\theta)x_2 + 20x_3,$$

subject to

$$\begin{aligned} 3x_1 + 3x_2 + x_3 &\leq 20 \\ 2x_1 + 4x_2 + 3x_3 &\leq 30 \\ 6x_1 + x_2 + x_3 &\leq 20 \end{aligned}$$

and

$$x_1 \geq 0,\ x_2 \geq 0,\ x_3 \geq 0.$$

13 Consider the problem

$$\text{Maximize} \quad Z(\theta) = (7 + 2\theta)x_1 + (12 + \theta)x_2 + (10 - \theta)x_3,$$

subject to

$$\begin{aligned} x_1 + x_2 + x_3 &\leq 20 \\ 2x_1 + 2x_2 + x_3 &\leq 30 \end{aligned}$$

and

$$x_1 \geq 0,\ x_2 \geq 0,\ x_3 \geq 0.$$

(*a*) Use *parametric linear programming* to find the optimal solution for this problem as a function of θ, for $\theta \geq 0$.
(*b*) Construct the dual model for this problem. Then find the optimal solution for this dual problem as a function of θ, for $\theta \geq 0$, by the method described in Sec. 16.3.2. Indicate graphically what this algebraic procedure is doing. Compare the basic solutions obtained with the complementary basic solutions obtained in part (*a*).

14 Use the *parametric linear programming* procedure for making systematic changes in the b_i to find the optimal solution for the following problem as a function of θ, for $0 \leq \theta \leq 25$:

$$\text{Maximize} \quad Z(\theta) = 2x_1 + x_2,$$

subject to

$$\begin{aligned} x_1 \phantom{{}+x_2} &\leq 10 + 2\theta \\ x_1 + x_2 &\leq 25 - \theta \\ x_2 &\leq 10 + 2\theta \end{aligned}$$

and

$$x_1 \geq 0,\ x_2 \geq 0.$$

Indicate graphically what this algebraic procedure is doing.

15 Use the *parametric linear programming* procedure for making systematic changes in the b_i to find the optimal solution for the following problem as a function of θ, for $0 \leq \theta \leq 20$:

$$\text{Maximize} \quad Z(\theta) = 21x_1 + 12x_2 + 18x_3 + 15x_4,$$

subject to

$$\begin{aligned} 6x_1 + 3x_2 + 6x_3 + 3x_4 &\leq 30 + \theta \\ 6x_1 - 3x_2 + 12x_3 + 6x_4 &\leq 78 - \theta \\ 9x_1 + 3x_2 - 6x_3 + 9x_4 &\leq 135 - 2\theta \end{aligned}$$

and

$$x_j \geq 0, \text{ for } j = 1, 2, 3, 4.$$

Then identify the value of θ that gives the largest optimal value of Z.

16 Consider the $Z^*(\theta)$ function shown in Fig. 16.1 for *parametric linear programming* with systematic changes in the c_j parameters.

(*a*) Explain why this function is *piecewise linear.*
(*b*) Show that this function must be *convex.*

17 Consider the $Z^*(\theta)$ function shown in Fig. 16.2 for *parametric linear programming* with systematic changes in the b_i parameters.

(*a*) Explain why this function is *piecewise linear.*
(*b*) Show that this function must be *concave.*

18 Let

$$Z^* = \max\left\{\sum_{j=1}^{n} c_j x_j\right\},$$

subject to

$$\sum_{j=1}^{n} a_{ij} x_j \leq b_i, \text{ for } i = 1, 2, \ldots, m,$$

and

$$x_j \geq 0, \text{ for } j = 1, 2, \ldots, n,$$

(where the a_{ij}, b_i, and c_j are fixed constants), and let $(y_1^*, y_2^*, \ldots, y_m^*)$ be the corresponding optimal dual solution. Then let

$$Z^{**} = \max\left\{\sum_{j=1}^{n} c_j x_j\right\},$$

subject to

$$\sum_{j=1}^{n} a_{ij} x_j \leq b_i + k_i, \text{ for } i = 1, 2, \ldots, m,$$

and

for $j = 1, 2, \ldots, n$,

where $k_1, k_2, \ldots, k_m$ are given constants. Show that

$$Z^{**} \leq Z^* + \sum_{i=1}^{m} k_i y_i^*.$$

19 Use the *revised simplex method* to solve the linear programming model given in Prob. 8, Chap. 2.

20 Use the *revised simplex method* to solve the linear programming model given in Prob. 9, Chap. 2.

21 Use the *revised simplex method* to solve the problem

$$\text{Maximize} \quad Z = 5x_1 + 8x_2 + 7x_3 + 4x_4 + 6x_5,$$

subject to

$$\begin{aligned} 2x_1 + 3x_2 + 3x_3 + 2x_4 + 2x_5 &\leq 20 \\ 3x_1 + 5x_2 + 4x_3 + 2x_4 + 4x_5 &\leq 30 \end{aligned}$$

and

$$x_j \geq 0, \text{ for } j = 1, 2, 3, 4, 5.$$

22 Use the *revised simplex method* to solve each of the following linear programming models:

(*a*) Model given in Prob. 25, Chap. 2.
(*b*) Model given in Prob. 27, Chap. 2.

23 Suppose that information is also desired about the *dual* problem when applying the *revised simplex method.*

(*a*) How would the *optimal solution* for the dual problem be identified?
(*b*) After obtaining the basic feasible solution at each iteration, how would the *complementary basic solution* in the dual problem be identified?

24 Explain how the *revised simplex method* can be modified to perform the *dual simplex method* in matrix form. In particular, indicate how the required information would be obtained to apply the stopping rule, identify the leaving basic variable and entering basic variable, and derive the new $\mathbf{B}^{-1}$ for each iteration.

25 Use the *revised simplex method* to conduct the specified *sensitivity analysis* for Prob. 19(*a*), (*b*), (*d*), (*e*), (*g*), Chap. 4.

26 Use the *revised simplex method* to conduct the specified *sensitivity analysis* for Prob. 20(*a*), (*b*), (*d*), (*f*), Chap. 4.

27 Use the *revised simplex method* to solve the linear programming model in nonstandard form given in Prob. 16, Chap. 2.

28 Use the *revised simplex method* to solve the linear programming model in nonstandard form given in Prob. 19, Chap. 2.

29 Use the *decomposition principle* to solve the *Wyndor Glass Co.* problem presented in Sec. 2.1.

30 Consider the *multidivisional problem*

$$\text{Maximize} \quad Z = 10x_1 + 5x_2 + 8x_3 + 7x_4,$$

subject to

$$\begin{aligned} 6x_1 + 5x_2 + 4x_3 + 6x_4 &\leq 40 \\ 3x_1 + x_2 \qquad\qquad\qquad &\leq 15 \\ x_1 + x_2 \qquad\qquad\qquad &\leq 10 \\ x_3 + 2x_4 &\leq 10 \\ 2x_3 + x_4 &\leq 10 \end{aligned}$$

and

$$x_j \geq 0, \text{ for } j = 1, 2, 3, 4.$$

(*a*) Explicitly construct the complete *reformulated* version of this problem in terms of the ρ_{jk} decision variables that would be generated (as needed) and used by the *decomposition principle.*

(*b*) Use the *decomposition principle* to solve this problem.

31 Using the *decomposition principle, begin* solving the *Good Foods Corp.* multidivisional problem presented in Sec. 3.5 by executing the first *two* iterations.

17 Integer Programming

17.1 INTRODUCTION

In many practical problems the decision variables make sense only if they have integer values. For example, it is often necessary to assign men, machines, and vehicles to activities in integer quantities. This restriction is a difficult one to handle mathematically. However, some progress has been made in developing solution procedures for the case of *linear programming* problems subjected to this *additional restriction* that the decision variables must have integer values.

In practice, a common approach to *integer linear programming* problems has been to use the simplex method (thereby ignoring the integer restriction) and then rounding off the noninteger values to integers in the resulting solution. Although this is often adequate, there are pitfalls in this approach. One is that the optimal linear programming solution is *not necessarily feasible* after it is rounded off. Often it is difficult to see in which way the rounding should be done to retain feasibility. It may even be necessary to change the value of some variables by 1 or more units after rounding off. To illustrate, suppose that some of the constraints are

$$-x_1 + x_2 \le 3\frac{1}{2}$$

$$x_1 + x_2 \le 16\frac{1}{2}$$

and that the simplex method has identified the optimal noninteger solution as $x_1 = 6\frac{1}{2}$, $x_2 = 10$. Notice that it is impossible to round off x_1 to 6 or 7 (or any other integer) and retain feasibility. This can only be done by also changing the integer value of x_2. It is easy to imagine how such difficulties can be compounded when there are tens or hundreds of constraints and variables.

Even if the optimal linear programming solution is rounded off successfully, there remains another pitfall. There is no guarantee that this rounded-off solution will be the optimal integer solution. In fact, it may even be far from optimal in terms of the value of the objective function. This is illustrated by the following problem:

$$\text{Maximize} \quad Z = x_1 + 5x_2,$$

subject to the restrictions

$$\begin{aligned} x_1 + 10x_2 &\le 20 \\ x_1 \qquad &\le 2 \end{aligned}$$

and

$$x_1 \text{ and } x_2 \text{ are } \textit{nonnegative integers.}$$

Since there are only two decision variables, this problem can be depicted graphically, as given in Fig. 17.1. Either the graph or the simplex method may be used to find that the optimal linear programming solution is $x_1 = 2$, $x_2 = 9/5$, with $Z = 11$. If a graphical solution were not available (which it would not be with more than three decision variables), then the variable with the noninteger value $x_2 = 9/5$ would normally be rounded off in the feasible direction to $x_2 = 1$. The resulting integer solution is $x_1 = 2$, $x_2 = 1$, which yields $Z = 7$. Notice that this is far from the optimal solution $(x_1, x_2) = (0,2)$, where $Z = 10$.

For these reasons it would be useful to have an efficient solution procedure for obtaining an optimal solution to integer linear programming problems. A considerable number of algorithms have been developed for this purpose. Unfortunately, none possess computational efficiency that is even remotely comparable to the *simplex method* (except on special types of problems), so they ordinarily are limited to relatively small problems having perhaps a few dozen variables. Therefore this remains an active area of research, and progress continues to be made in developing more efficient algorithms.

Figure 17.1 Illustrative integer programming problem.

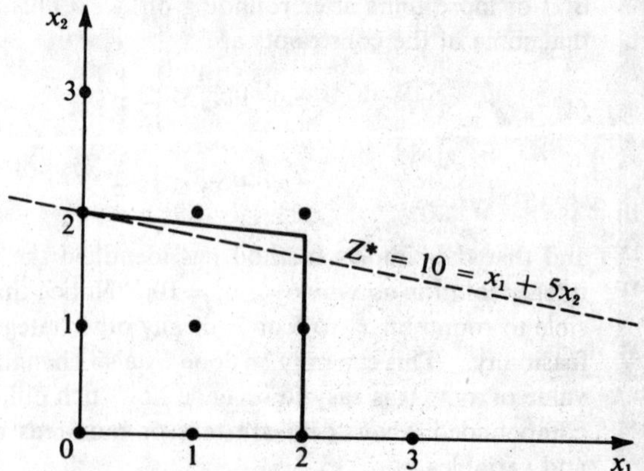

Many people feel that the most promising mode for integer programming algorithms is to use the *branch-and-bound technique* and related ideas to *implicitly enumerate* the feasible integer solutions, and we shall focus on this approach. The next section presents the branch-and-bound technique in a general context. Section 17.3 then describes a branch-and-bound algorithm for the important special class of integer linear programming problems where *all* the variables are restricted to be *either* zero or 1. Section 17.4 presents another algorithm of the same type for general *mixed* integer linear programming (where only some of the variables are restricted to be integer). We then discuss in Sec. 17.5 how mixed integer programming can be used to formulate certain special types of constraints and cost functions for mathematical programming problems.

17.2 THE BRANCH-AND-BOUND TECHNIQUE

Since any bounded integer programming problem has only a finite number of feasible solutions, it is natural to consider using some kind of *enumeration procedure* for finding an optimal solution. Unfortunately, this finite number can be, and usually is, very large. For example, if there are only 10 variables, and each one has 10 feasible values, then there can be as many as 10^{10} feasible solutions. Despite the fact that today's digital computers can perform approximately 1 million elementary arithmetic operations (additions or subtractions) per second, exhaustive enumeration would be prohibitively time consuming for problems as large as this. Therefore it is imperative that any enumeration procedure be cleverly structured so that only a tiny fraction of the feasible solutions actually need be examined. For example, dynamic programming (see Chap. 6) provides one such kind of procedure for many problems having a finite number of feasible solutions (although it is not particularly efficient for most integer programming problems). Another such approach is provided by the *branch-and-bound technique*. This technique, and variations of it, have been applied with some success to a number of problems, *including* integer programming problems.

The basic idea of the branch-and-bound technique is the following. Suppose (to be specific) that the objective function is to be *minimized*. Assume that an *upper bound* on the optimal value of the objective function is available. (This usually is the value of the objective function for the best feasible solution identified thus far.) The first step is to *partition* the set of all feasible solutions *into several subsets*, and, for each one, a *lower bound* is obtained for the value of the objective function of the solutions within that subset. Those subsets whose lower bounds exceed the current upper bound on the objective function value are then excluded from further consideration. (A subset that is excluded for this or other legitimate reasons is said to be *fathomed*.) One of the *remaining* subsets, say, the one with the smallest lower bound, is then *partitioned* further *into several subsets*. Their lower bounds are obtained in turn and used as before to exclude some of these subsets from further consideration. From *all* the *remaining* subsets, another one is selected for further partitioning and so on. This process is repeated again and again until a feasible solution is found such that the corresponding value of the objective function is no greater than the lower bound for any subset.

Summary of Branch-and-Bound Technique

Initialization step Begin with the *entire* set of solutions under consideration (including any *infeasible* solutions that can not conveniently be eliminated) as the only "remaining subset." Set $Z_U = \infty$.

Branch step Use some *branch rule* to select *one* of the *remaining* subsets (those neither fathomed nor partitioned) and partition it into two or more new subsets of solutions.

Bound step For each new subset, obtain a *lower bound* Z_L on the value of the objective function for the feasible solutions in the subset.

Fathoming step For each new subset, exclude it from further consideration if

1. $Z_L \geq Z_U$,

or

2. The subset is found to contain no feasible solutions,

or

3. The best feasible solution in the subset has been identified (so Z_L corresponds to its objective function value); if $Z_L < Z_U$, then reset $Z_U = Z_L$, store this solution as the *incumbent* solution, and reapply condition (1) to *all remaining* subsets.

Stopping rule Stop the procedure when there are *no remaining* (unfathomed) subsets; the current *incumbent* solution is *optimal.*[1] Otherwise, return to the branch step.

If the objective is to *maximize* rather than minimize the objective function, the procedure is unchanged *except* that the roles of the upper and lower bounds are reversed. Thus Z_U would be replaced by Z_L and vice versa, ∞ becomes $-\infty$, and the directions of the inequalities would be reversed.

The *branch* and *bound steps* allow considerable flexibility in designing a specific algorithm for the problem of interest, and they have an important effect on the computational efficiency of the algorithm. The two most popular *branch rules* for selecting a subset to partition are the best bound rule and the newest bound rule. The *best bound rule* says to select the subset having the *most favorable bound* (the smallest lower bound in the case of minimization) because this subset would seem to be the most promising one to contain an optimal solution. The *newest bound rule* says to select the *most recently created* subset that has not been fathomed, breaking a tie between subsets created at the same time by taking the one with the most favorable bound. The advantages of this rule are less

[1] If there is no incumbent solution (that is, Z_U still equals ∞), then the problem possesses no feasible solutions.

cumbersome bookkeeping and greater opportunity to obtain the bounds efficiently (as you will see in Secs. 17.3 and 17.4). The method selected for obtaining the bounds should represent a careful compromise between the *tightness* of the bounds and computational effort.

We shall now illustrate this approach by applying it to an *assignment problem* (see Sec. 3.4) having the *cost table* shown in Table 17.1.

Table 17.1 Cost Table for Assignment Problem Illustrating Branch-and-bound technique

		Assignment			
		1	*2*	*3*	*4*
	A	94	1	54	68
Assignee	*B*	74	10	88	82
	C	62	88	8	76
	D	11	74	81	21

Thus the objective is to assign each of the four assignees to its unique assignment in such a way as to *minimize* the sum of the four corresponding entries in the cost matrix. There are 4! (=24) feasible solutions. A natural way of partitioning these solutions into subsets is to specify one or more of the assignments. For example, if A were assigned to assignment 1, then there would be 3! possible solutions, corresponding to the six ways in which B, C, and D can be assigned uniquely to assignments 2, 3, and 4, respectively.

To apply the branch-and-bound technique to this problem it is necessary to be able to efficiently establish a tight *lower bound* Z_L on the total cost for any of the solutions in a given subset of the feasible solutions. One way of doing this is to add the *minimum* possible cost of the respective assignments without worrying about whether or not this corresponds to a feasible solution (where each assignee is assigned *uniquely* to an assignment). Thus, such a lower bound over all feasible solutions is the sum of the minimum of the respective columns of the cost matrix, $11 + 1 + 8 + 21 = 41$. Similarly, if A were assigned to assignment 1, then the lower bound for the resulting subset of six feasible solutions would be the cost of this assignment plus the sum of the minimum costs (ignoring row A) for the last three columns, $94 + (10 + 8 + 21) = 133$. (This coincidently happens to correspond to a feasible solution.)

To begin, the 24 feasible solutions would be partitioned into, say, the four subsets corresponding to the four possible ways in which assignment 1 can be made. The corresponding lower bounds (Z_L) are 133 (as obtained above) for the $A - 1$ subset, $74 + 1 + 8 + 21 = 104$ for the $B - 1$ subset, $62 + 1 + 54 + 21 = 138$ for the $C - 1$ subset, and $11 + 1 + 8 + 68 = 88$ for the $D - 1$ subset. Since this second lower bound (104) happens to correspond to a *feasible* solution, 104 also is an *upper bound* Z_U on the total cost for the optimal solution, and this solution becomes the current *incumbent* solution. These results are summarized

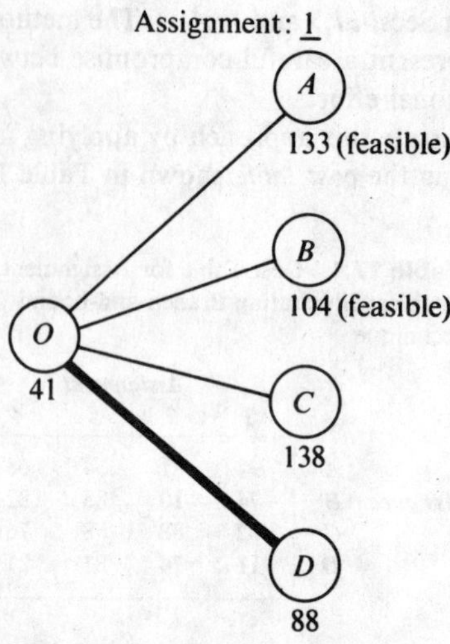

Figure 17.2 Results from the first iteration of the branch-and-bound technique for the assignment problem example.

by the "tree" (as defined in Chap. 5) shown in Fig. 17.2, where the numbers give the lower bound Z_L for each subset.

Since the lower bound $Z_L \geq Z_U = 104$ for the first three subsets, the 18 feasible solutions that include the corresponding assignments ($A - 1$, $B - 1$, or $C - 1$) are excluded from further consideration. This leaves just the fourth subset that has not been fathomed, so it is automatically selected as the first subset to be partitioned further into smaller subsets. This partitioning is done by designating both $D - 1$ and assignment 2 in the three possible ways. Thus the first such subset is the set of the (two) feasible solutions that include $D - 1$ and $A - 2$, and its lower bound is $11 + 1 + (8 + 76) = 96$. Similarly, the lower bound for the subset whose solutions include $D - 1$ and $B - 2$ is $11 + 10 + (8 + 68) = 97$. Since this bound (97) corresponds to a feasible solution, and 97 is less than the current upper bound (104) for the problem, reset $Z_U = 97$ and store this solution ($D - 1$, $B - 2$, $C - 3$, $A - 4$) as the new *incumbent* solution. The lower bound for the third new subset is $11 + 88 + (54 + 68) = 221$, so it is ignored henceforth. The tree shown in Fig. 17.3 has now been obtained.

Since only the first new subset has not yet been fathomed, it is selected next for further partitioning. This partitioning divides the subset into its two individual feasible solutions. Their total costs are $11 + 1 + 88 + 76 = 176$ and $11 + 1 + 8 + 82 = 102$, respectively, both of which exceed the current upper bound (97), so these two solutions are discarded. Therefore there now are no remaining subsets that have not been fathomed, so the current *incumbent* solution ($D - 1$, $B - 2$, $C - 3$, $A - 4$) is *optimal*.

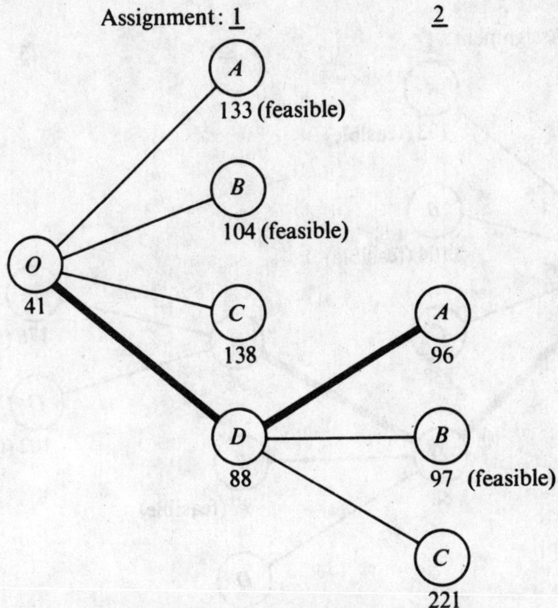

Figure 17.3 Results from the second iteration of the branch-and-bound technique for the assignment problem example.

This sequence of iterations is summarized in Fig. 17.4 and in Table 17.2. At the last iteration, the best lower bound and upper bound are equal, so the feasible solution corresponding to this upper bound is the desired optimal solution.

Table 17.2 Summary of Results for The Branch-and-bound Technique Applied to The Assignment Problem Example

Iteration	*Best* Z_L	Z_U
0	41	$+\infty$
1	88	104
2	96	97
3	97	97

In general, the branch-and-bound technique can be described in terms of a tree such as that shown in Figs. 17.2 to 17.4. The origin corresponds to the set of all feasible solutions. This set is partitioned into several subsets, usually by designating the respective values of one of the decision variables. Each value corresponds to a node at the end of a branch out of the origin. Associated

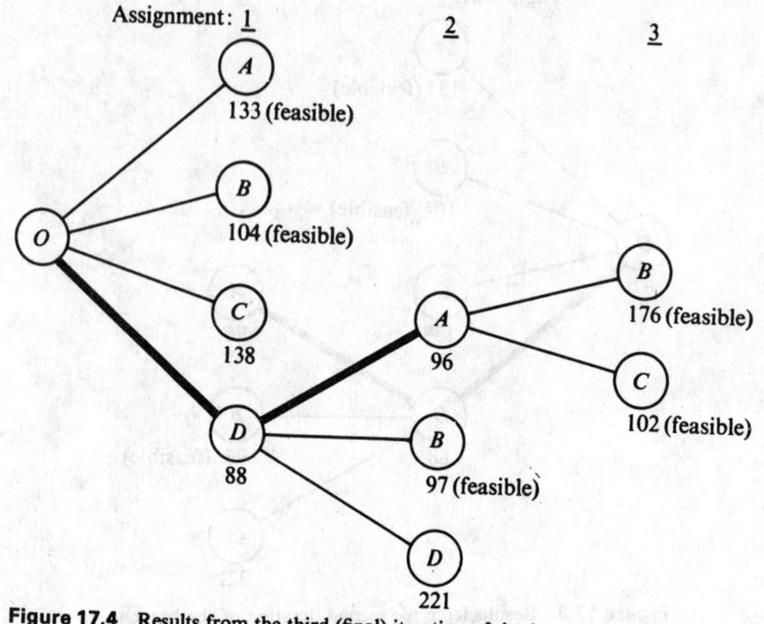

Figure 17.4 Results from the third (final) iteration of the branch-and-bound technique for the assignment problem example.

with each node is a lower bound on the value of the objective function for the feasible solutions that can be reached from that node. Assuming the best bound rule is being used, the branches out of the node with the smallest lower bound are then constructed, and a lower bound is obtained for the node at the end of each of these branches. From among all the nodes that form the end points of the tree, the one with the smallest lower bound is chosen for constructing the next set of branches and associated bounds. This process of branching and bounding is repeated again and again, each time adding new branches to the tree, until the end-point node having the smallest lower bound corresponds to a complete feasible solution. This solution is then known to be an optimal solution, and the procedure is completed.

Finally, it should be noted that rather than finding an optimal solution, the branch-and-bound technique can also be used to find a *nearly optimal* solution, generally with much less computational effort. This is done merely by terminating the procedure the first time that the smallest lower bound Z_L is within a prespecified percentage (or quantity) of the current upper bound Z_U for the problem (in the case of minimization). The feasible solution corresponding to the upper bound is then the desired suboptimal solution such that the resulting value of the objective function is guaranteed to be within the prespecified amount of the optimal value.

17.3 A BRANCH-AND-BOUND ALGORITHM FOR BINARY LINEAR PROGRAMMING

Many integer linear programming problems have the special feature that *all* the variables are restricted to just *two* values: zero or 1. The reason is that an integer decision variable frequently is used simply to indicate whether some possible action is to be undertaken ($x = 1$) or not ($x = 0$), where the level of the activity (if undertaken) is fixed, so only two values are needed. For example, the decision involved might be whether to undertake a particular research and development project, whether to use a particular site for a new manufacturing plant, whether to assign a certain job to a particular machine, and so forth.

Furthermore, when a few of the original decision variables require more than two possible values, they are sometimes replaced by a *binary representation* to reduce the entire problem to a binary (zero-1) form. Specifically, if the bounds on an integer variable x are

$$0 \le x \le u, \text{ where } 2^{N-1} < u \le 2^N,$$

then each feasible value of x can be expressed uniquely as

$$x = \sum_{i=0}^{N} 2^i y_i,$$

where the y_i variables are restricted to be *either* zero or 1. Therefore the x variable can be replaced throughout the problem by this summation involving $(N + 1)$ *binary variables.*

For these reasons considerable attention has been focused in recent years on developing efficient algorithms for the *binary linear programming problem*, i.e., the linear programming problem with the additional restriction that all the variables are *binary variables.* A convenient form in which to treat this problem is

$$\text{Minimize} \quad Z = \sum_{j=1}^{n} c_j x_j,$$

subject to

$$\sum_{j=1}^{n} a_{ij} x_j \ge b_i, \text{ for } i = 1, 2, \ldots, m,$$

and

$$x_j = 0 \text{ or } 1, \text{ for } j = 1, 2, \ldots, n,$$

where $0 \le c_1 \le c_2 \le \cdots \le c_n$. This condition on the c_j parameters actually is not restrictive because if $c_j < 0$, originally, then x_j can be replaced by $(1 - x'_j)$ where $x'_j = 0$ or 1, so that x'_j will have a *positive* coefficient in the objective function. All the variables can then be reordered as needed to place these coefficients in increasing order.

Roughly speaking, with the problem in this form the general objective of an algorithm should be to make the variables *zero* as much as the constraints will allow but to give preference to using the initial variables when it is necessary to set some variables equal to 1. Therefore it would seem sensible to first check whether it is feasible (and so optimal) to set *all* the variables to zero; if not, then check just setting $x_1 = 1$, then just $x_1 = 1$, $x_2 = 1$ and so forth.

Using roughly this idea, we shall now present a *branch-and-bound* algorithm for the binary linear programming problem. It is a slightly simplified version of Balas' **additive algorithm**[1], which has formed the basis for much of the algorithmic development on this problem. (The name *additive* comes from the fact that all the arithmetic operations are simple additions or subtractions.)

This algorithm defines subsets of solutions by *assigning values* to some of the variables, say $(x_1, x_2, \ldots, x_N)$. [We shall always let N denote the number of assigned variables for the subset currently under consideration and refer to the value of $(x_1, x_2, \ldots, x_N)$ as the *current partial solution.* Any complete solution $(x_1, x_2, \ldots, x_N, x_{N+1}, \ldots, x_n)$ starting out in this way is then called a *completion* of this partial solution.] If the *branch step* selects the partial solution $(x_1, x_2, \ldots, x_N)$ for partitioning, it is partitioned into *two* new subsets (partial solutions) by setting $x_{N+1} = 1$ and $x_{N+1} = 0$. The *newest bound rule* is used to make this selection.

For the *bound step*, the lower bound Z_L for a partial solution $(x_1, x_2, \ldots, x_N)$ is just

$$Z_L = \begin{cases} \sum_{j=1}^{N} c_j x_j, & \text{if } x_N = 1 \\ \sum_{j=1}^{N-1} c_j x_j + c_{N+1}, & \text{if } x_N = 0. \end{cases}$$

[The reason for adding c_{N+1} if $x_N = 0$ is that the algorithm would be calculating this bound only if it had previously found that $(x_1, x_2, \ldots, x_{N-1}, x_N = 0, \ldots, x_n = 0)$ is *infeasible*. This occurs while conducting test 3 of the fathoming step for the previous partial solution $(x_1, x_2 \ldots, x_M)$, where $M = \max\{j \mid x_j = 1\}$.] Therefore the bound always is *smaller* (or equal) for $x_N = 1$ than $x_N = 0$, so the newest bound rule *always* selects the $x_N = 1$ partial solution first if neither has been fathomed. Because of this, the *fathoming step* is not even applied to the $x_N = 0$ partial solution until after the $x_N = 1$ partial solution has been fathomed (perhaps by fathoming all its subsequent subsets).

The *fathoming step* is applied to a partial solution as follows. Test 1 $(Z_L \geq Z_U)$ is straightforward. Test 2 (the subset is found to contain no feasible solutions) is conducted by seeing whether any *individual* constraint can not be satisfied by completions of the partial solution. Therefore the partial solution is fathomed if

$$\sum_{j=1}^{N} a_{ij} x_j + \sum_{j=N+1}^{n} \max\{a_{ij}, 0\} < b_i, \text{ for some } i = 1, 2, \ldots, m,$$

[1] Egon Balas, "An Additive Algorithm for Solving Linear Programs with Zero-One Variables," *Operations Research,* **13**(4): 517–546, July–August, 1965.

since $\max\{a_{ij}, 0\} = \max\{a_{ij}x_j \mid x_j = 0 \text{ or } 1\}$. Test 3 (the best feasible solution in the subset is found) is conducted by seeing whether the solution corresponding to the lower bound Z_L (namely, the partial solution plus $x_{N+1} = 1 - x_N$ and the rest of the variables equal to zero) actually is feasible. Therefore, the third way in which the partial solution can be fathomed is if

$$\sum_{j=1}^{N} a_{ij}x_j + a_{i,N+1}(1 - x_N) \geq b_i, \text{ for all } i = 1, 2, \ldots, m.$$

If this occurs and $Z_L < Z_U$, then the instructions for the branch-and-bound technique would be followed in resetting $Z_U = Z_L$ and storing this solution as the current incumbent solution.

Given these ways to attempt to fathom the current partial solution, Fig. 17.5 summarizes the order in which partial solutions would be considered.

Figure 17.5 Flow diagram for the additive algorithm for binary linear programming.

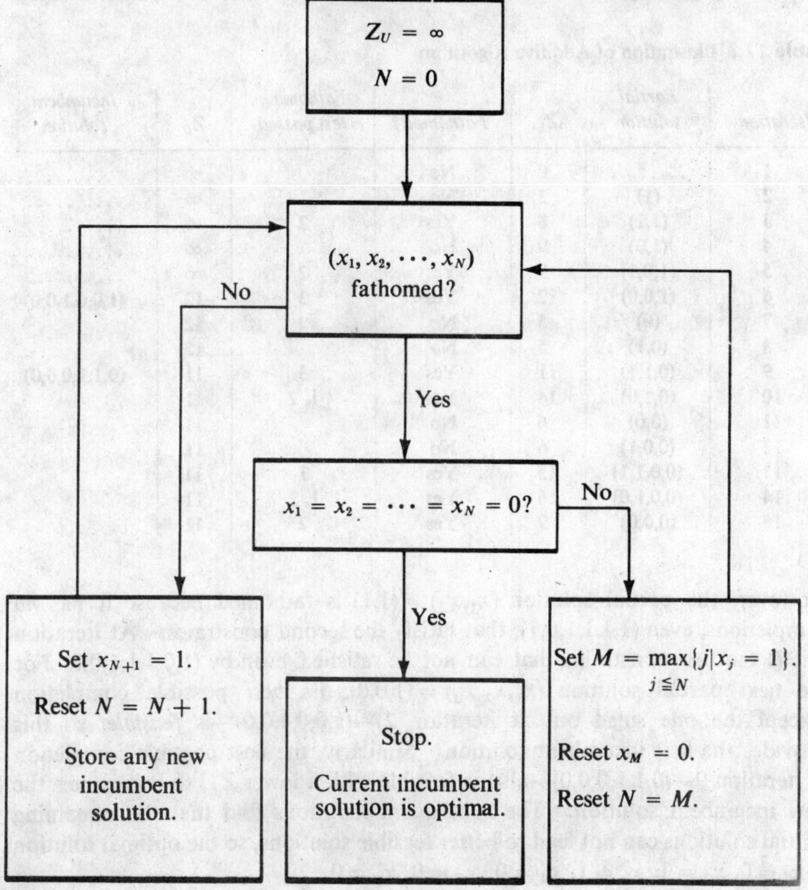

We shall now illustrate this algorithm by applying it to the problem

$$\text{Minimize} \quad Z = 3x_1 + 5x_2 + 6x_3 + 9x_4 + 10x_5 + 10x_6,$$

subject to

$$\begin{aligned} -2x_1 + 6x_2 - 3x_3 + 4x_4 + x_5 - 2x_6 &\geq +2 \\ -5x_1 - 3x_2 + x_3 + 3x_4 - 2x_5 + x_6 &\geq -2 \\ 5x_1 - x_2 + 4x_3 - 2x_4 + 2x_5 - x_6 &\geq +3 \end{aligned}$$

and

$$x_j = 0 \text{ or } 1, \text{ for } j = 1, 2, \ldots, 6.$$

The results are summarized in Table 17.3. Thus the complete set of solutions ($N = 0$) can not be fathomed at iteration 1 [$Z_L \leq Z_U$, each constraint can be satisfied, but (0, 0, . . ., 0) is infeasible], nor can the partial solution $x_1 = 1$ at iteration 2 [$Z_L \leq Z_U$, it can satisfy each constraint, but (1, 0, . . ., 0) is infeasible].

Table 17.3 Illustration of Additive Algorithm

Iteration	*Partial solution*	Z_L	*Fathomed?*	*Fathoming test passed*	Z_U	*Incumbent solution*
1	....	0	No		∞	....
2	(1)	3	No		∞	....
3	(1,1)	8	Yes	2	∞	....
4	(1,0)	9	No		∞	....
5	(1,0,1)	9	Yes	2	∞	....
6	(1,0,0)	12	Yes	3	12	(1,0,0,1,0,0)
7	(0)	5	No		12	
8	(0,1)	5	No		12	
9	(0,1,1)	11	Yes	3	11	(0,1,1,0,0,0)
10	(0,1,0)	14	Yes	1, 2	11	
11	(0,0)	6	No		11	
12	(0,0,1)	6	No		11	
13	(0,0,1,1)	15	Yes	1	11	
14	(0,0,1,0)	16	Yes	1, 2	11	
15	(0,0,0)	9	Yes	2	11	

However, the partial solution $(x_1,x_2) = (1,1)$ is fathomed because it has *no* completions, even (1,1,1,1,0,1), that satisfy the second constraint. At iteration 5 it is the first constraint that can not be satisfied, even by (1,0,1,1,1,0). For the next partial solution $(x_1,x_2,x_3) = (1,0,0)$, its *best* possible completion (except the one ruled out at iteration 2)—(1,0,0,1,0,0)—is *feasible*, so this provides the first incumbent solution. Similarly, the best possible completion at iteration 9—(0,1,1,0,0,0)—also is feasible with a lower Z_L, so it becomes the new incumbent solution. The subsequent iterations find that the remaining partial solutions can not lead to better feasible solutions, so the optimal solution is $x_1 = 0$, $x_2 = 1$, $x_3 = 1$, $x_4 = 0$, $x_5 = 0$, $x_6 = 0$.

As you can see from Table 17.3, the *newest bound rule* requires only a minimum of bookkeeping. It also may reduce the computational effort for an iteration. In particular, if a partial solution is not fathomed, then its lower *bound* needs to be incremented by only one term for the next partial solution. The *fathoming step* also is expedited.

However, it has been found that test 2 in the fathoming step is not always very effective in finding that a partial solution has no feasible completions, particularly when the problem has a considerable number of constraints. Frequently, different completions of a partial solution will satisfy individual constraints even though *no* completion satisfies all of them. Therefore much of the more recent algorithmic development has been concerned with improving this part of the fathoming step. The most notable improvement has involved using *linear programming* to obtain a single *surrogate constraint* that effectively combines the m original functional constraints.[1]

17.4 A BRANCH-AND-BOUND ALGORITHM FOR MIXED INTEGER LINEAR PROGRAMMING

We shall now consider the general *mixed integer linear programming* problem, where *some* of the variables (say I of them) are restricted to integer values (but not necessarily just 0 and 1), but the rest are ordinary continuous variables. In *minimization form*, this problem is

$$\text{Minimize} \quad Z = \sum_{j=1}^{n} c_j x_j,$$

subject to

$$\sum_{j=1}^{n} a_{ij} x_j \geq b_i, \text{ for } i = 1, 2, \ldots, m,$$

and

$$x_j \text{ integer, for } j = 1, 2. \ldots, I \ (I \leq n),$$

$$x_j \geq 0, \quad \text{for } j = 1, 2, \ldots, n.$$

(When $I = n$, this becomes the *pure* integer linear programming problem.)

Section 17.3 described how the *additive algorithm* is able to solve a *special case* of this problem ($I = N$ and all $x_j \leq 1$) by making just a few simple calculations for each partial solution. Without this simple structure it is no longer possible to obtain a reasonable lower bound Z_L and conduct strong fathoming tests with so little computational effort. However, this same information *can* still be obtained in a reasonably efficient way by using linear programming (the simplex or dual simplex method). We shall now describe one version of an

[1] A. M. Geoffrion, "An Improved Implicit Enumeration Approach for Integer Programming," *Operations Research*, 17(3): 437–454, May–June, 1969.

algorithm for doing this developed by Dakin[1], based on a pioneering branch-and-bound algorithm by Land and Doig.[2]

This algorithm is quite similar in structure to the additive algorithm. It again fits directly into the format for the branch-and-bound technique presented in Sec. 17.2. It also uses the *newest bound rule* to select the next subset of solutions for partitioning. It then partitions this subset into *two* new subsets. However, since the variables now may have more than two possible values, this partitioning now is done by dividing the possible values of some variable into two intervals. (Consequently, the *same variable* can eventually be partitioned more than once.)

The algorithm begins by ignoring the integer restriction and using the simplex method to solve the corresponding linear programming problem. If the resulting solution has integer values for all the x_j for $j = 1, 2, \ldots, I$, then it is the desired optimal solution. Otherwise, the *branch step* (at each iteration) finds the first such variable that is not integer valued, say x_j, such that

$$k < x_j < k + 1,$$

where k is an integer. It then partitions the current subset of solutions into the two new subsets:

1. Solutions in which $x_j \leq k$,
2. Solutions in which $x_j \geq k + 1$.

The *bound step* then obtains the lower bound Z_L for each of these subsets by again ignoring the integer restriction and solving the resulting linear programming problem (including the new constraint). However, rather than resolving each of these problems from the beginning, it just uses the sensitivity analysis procedure (see case 4 in Sec. 4.3) by applying the *dual simplex method* (see Sec. 16.2) starting from the basic solution that was optimal before introducing the new constraint. (Note that the *newest bound rule* increases the opportunity for reoptimizing efficiently in this way.) The fathoming step then merely checks the new optimal (linear programming) solution obtained by the dual simplex method. In particular, the new subset is fathomed if

1. $Z_L \geq Z_U$,

or

2. The dual simplex method finds that no feasible solutions exist,

or

3. The optimal solution obtained has integer values for all the x_j such that $j = 1, 2, \ldots, I$.

[1] R. J. Dakin, "A Tree Search Algorithm for Mixed Integer Programming Problems," *Computer Journal*, **8**(3): 250–255, 1965.

[2] A. H. Land and A. G. Doig, "An Automatic Method of Solving Discrete Programming Problems," *Econometrica*, **28**: 497–520, 1960.

In this last case, if $Z_L < Z_U$, then reset $Z_U = Z_L$ and store this solution as the *incumbent* solution. [However, condition (1) does not need to be reapplied to the remaining subsets until they would otherwise be selected by the newest bound rule.] When all the unpartitioned subsets have been fathomed, the current incumbent solution then is the desired optimal solution.

For example, suppose that this algorithm is applied to the problem considered in Sec. 17.1 (see Fig. 17.1). The optimal linear programming solution is $(x_1,x_2) = (2, 9/5)$, so that

$$1 < x_2 < 2.$$

Therefore the complete set of solutions is partitioned into the two subsets:

1. Solutions in which $x_2 \leq 1$,
2. Solutions in which $x_2 \geq 2$.

For the first subset, its optimal linear programming solution is $(x_1, x_2) = (2,1)$, which is integer valued, so this subset is fathomed and this solution becomes the first *incumbent* solution. For the second subset, its linear programming problem has only one feasible solution, $(x_1, x_2) = (0,2)$, but it is integer valued, so this subset is also fathomed. Furthermore, this solution is better than the incumbent solution, so it becomes the new incumbent solution. However, there now are no unpartitioned subsets left that have not been fathomed, so $(x_1, x_2) = (0,2)$ must be optimal for the integer linear programming problem.

17.5 FORMULATION POSSIBILITIES THROUGH MIXED INTEGER PROGRAMMING

Pure and mixed integer programming problems arise naturally in a wide variety of contexts, so algorithms like those presented in the preceding sections are valuable for solving these problems. However, another important application of these algorithms is for solving *other* problems that can be *reformulated* as integer programming problems. In particular, problems are sometimes encountered that fit into the linear programming format (or a more general mathematical programming format) *except* for some minor disparity. Fortunately, certain formulation possibilities are available for circumventing some of these disparities. These involve introducing one or more *artificial variables* that are *restricted to be integers*. This reduces the problem to a mixed integer programming problem (or to a pure integer programming problem if the original variables are also restricted to be integers) in the desired format. Therefore, as progress continues in the development of efficient algorithms, this approach is attaining considerable practical importance.

Some of the cases that can be handled by this approach are discussed next.

Either-or Constraints

Consider the important case where a choice can be made between two constraints, so that one must hold but not necessarily both. For example, there may be a choice as to which of two resources to use for a certain purpose, so that it is only necessary for one of the two resource availability constraints to hold mathematically. To illustrate the approach to such situations, suppose that one of the requirements in the overall problem is that

$$\begin{aligned} \text{Either} \quad & 3x_1 + 2x_2 \le 18 \\ \text{or} \quad & x_1 + 4x_2 \le 16. \end{aligned}$$

This requirement must be reformulated to fit it into the linear programming format where all specified constraints must hold. Let M be an extremely large number. Then this requirement can be rewritten as

$$\begin{aligned} &\text{Either} \begin{cases} & 3x_1 + 2x_2 \le 18 \\ \text{and} & x_1 + 4x_2 \le 16 + M \end{cases} \\ &\text{or} \begin{cases} & 3x_1 + 2x_2 \le 18 + M \\ \text{and} & x_1 + 4x_2 \le 16 \end{cases} \end{aligned}$$

because adding M to the right-hand side of such constraints has the effect of eliminating them. (This assumes that the set of feasible solutions for the overall problem is a bounded set and M is sufficiently large enough so that it will not eliminate any feasible solutions.) This formulation is equivalent to the set of constraints

$$\begin{aligned} 3x_1 + 2x_2 &\le 18 + y\,M \\ x_1 + 4x_2 &\le 16 + (1 - y)\,M \\ y &= 0 \text{ or } 1, \end{aligned}$$

which can be expressed in a *mixed integer linear programming* format as

$$\begin{aligned} 3x_1 + 2x_2 - My &\le 18 \\ x_1 + 4x_2 + My &\le 16 + M \\ y &\le 1 \\ y &\ge 0 \\ \text{and } y \text{ is an integer.} \end{aligned}$$

Since the new artificial variable y must be either zero or 1, this formulation guarantees that one of the original constraints must hold while the other one is eliminated in effect. This new set of constraints would then be appended to the other constraints in the overall problem before attempting to solve it by a mixed integer programming algorithm.

A formal presentation of this approach is given in the next section for a more general case.

K out of N Constraints Must Hold

Now consider the case where, given a set of N possible constraints, it is only required that some K of these constraints must hold. (Assume $K < N$.) Thus this is a direct generalization of the case considered in the preceding section for which $K = 1$ and $N = 2$. Denote these N constraints by

$$\begin{aligned} f_1(x_1, x_2, \ldots, x_n) &\le d_1 \\ f_2(x_1, x_2, \ldots, x_n) &\le d_2 \\ &\vdots \\ f_N(x_1, x_2 \ldots, x_n) &\le d_N. \end{aligned}$$

Then, applying the logic used in the preceding section, an equivalent formulation of this requirement is

$$\begin{aligned} f_1(x_1, x_2, \ldots, x_n) &\le d_1 + My_1 \\ f_2(x_1, x_2, \ldots, x_n) &\le d_2 + My_2 \\ &\vdots \\ f_N(x_1, x_2, \ldots, x_n) &\le d_N + My_N \\ \sum_{i=1}^{N} y_i &= N - K \\ y_i &\le 1 \\ y_i &\ge 0 \end{aligned}$$

and y_i is an integer, for $i = 1, 2, \ldots, N$,

where M is an extremely large number. Since the constraints on the y_i guarantee that K of these artificial variables will equal zero and those remaining will equal 1, K of the original constraints will be unchanged and the rest will, in effect, be eliminated.

Functions with N Possible Values

Consider the situation where a given function is required to take on any one of N given values. Denote this requirement by

$$f(x_1, x_2, \ldots, x_n) = d_1, \text{ or } d_2, \ldots, \text{ or } d_N.$$

One special case is where this function is

$$f(x_1, x_2, \ldots, x_n) = \sum_{j=1}^{n} a_j x_j,$$

as on the left-hand side of a linear programming constraint. Another special case is where $f(x_1, x_2, \ldots, x_n) = x_j$ for a given value of j, so the requirement becomes that x_j must take on any one of N given values.

The equivalent *mixed integer programming* formulation of this requirement is the following:

$$f(x_1, x_2, \ldots, x_n) = \sum_{i=1}^{N} d_i y_i$$

$$\sum_{i=1}^{N} y_i = 1$$

$$y_i \leq 1$$

$$y_i \geq 0$$

and y_i is an integer, for $i = 1, 2, \ldots, N$.

This is an equivalent formulation because exactly one y_i must equal 1, and the others must equal zero.

The Fixed-Charge Problem

It is quite common to incur a fixed charge or "setup cost" when undertaking an activity. In such cases the total cost of the activity is the sum of a variable cost related to the level of the activity and this setup cost required to initiate the activity. Frequently the variable cost will be at least approximately proportional to the level of the activity. In other words, if x_j denotes the level of activity j, the approximate total cost of activity j often will be $(k_j + c_j x_j)$ if $x_j > 0$, whereas the cost will be zero if $x_j = 0$. Were it not for the setup cost k_j, this cost structure would suggest the possibility of a *linear programming* formulation for determining the optimal levels of the competing activities. Fortunately, even with the k_j, *mixed integer linear programming* may still be used.

Let

$$Z = f_1(x_1) + f_2(x_2) + \cdots + f_n(x_n),$$

where

$$f_j(x_j) = \begin{cases} k_j + c_j x_j, & \text{if } x_j > 0 \\ 0, & \text{if } x_j = 0, \end{cases}$$

and where x_j is constrained to be nonnegative, for $j = 1, 2, \ldots, n$. (Notice that Z would be a linear programming objective function if $k_j = 0$ for $j = 1, 2, \ldots, n$.) Assume that $k_j \geq 0$ for $j = 1, 2, \ldots, n$. Suppose that the problem of interest is to

$$\text{Minimize} \quad Z,$$

subject to

given linear programming constraints.

How can this problem be reformulated into the mixed integer linear programming format when some or all of the k_j are strictly positive?

Notice that

$$Z = \sum_{j=1}^{N} (c_j x_j + k_j y_j),$$

where

$$y_j = \begin{cases} 1, & \text{if } x_j > 0 \\ 0, & \text{if } x_j = 0. \end{cases}$$

Hence it is only necessary to find linear or integer constraints which ensure that the y_j will take on the correct values. To begin, it is clear that necessary constraints include

$$y_j \le 1$$
$$y_j \ge 0$$
and y_j is an integer, for $j = 1, 2, \ldots, n$.

Next, let M be an extremely large number that exceeds the maximum feasible value of any $x_j (j = 1, 2, \ldots, n)$. Then the constraints,

$$x_j \le M y_j, \text{ for } j = 1, 2, \ldots, n,$$

will ensure that $y_j = 1$ rather than zero whenever $x_j > 0$. The one difficulty remaining is that these constraints leave y_j free to be either zero or 1 when $x_j = 0$. Fortunately this difficulty is automatically resolved because of the nature of the objective function. Recall that $k_j \ge 0$. The case where $k_j = 0$ can be ignored because y_j can then be deleted from the formulation. So consider the only other case, namely, where $k_j > 0$. When $x_j = 0$, so that the constraints permit a choice between $y_j = 0$ and $y_j = 1$, $y_j = 0$ must yield a smaller value of Z than $y_j = 1$. Therefore, since the objective is to minimize Z, an algorithm yielding an optimal solution would always choose $y_j = 0$ when $x_j = 0$.

To summarize, we have found that an equivalent formulation of the problem is

$$\text{Minimize } Z = \sum_{j=1}^{n} (c_j x_j + k_j y_j),$$

subject to

the original constraints, plus

$$x_j - M y_j \le 0$$
$$y_j \le 1$$
$$y_j \ge 0$$
and y_j is an integer, for $j = 1, 2, \ldots, n$.

17.6 CONCLUSIONS

Integer programming problems arise frequently because some or all of the decision variables must be restricted to integer values. These problems are more difficult than without the integer restriction, so the algorithms available for integer linear programming are generally much less efficient than the simplex method. The most important determinant of computation time is the number of *integer variables*. Unless the problem has a particularly simple special structure, it probably can be solved only if it has no more than a few dozen integer variables (somewhat more with just binary variables).

Computer codes for integer programming algorithms now are commonly available in mathematical programming software packages. These algorithms usually are based on the *branch-and-bound* technique and variations thereof. Some of the early algorithms used another approach involving the successive introduction of additional constraints (cutting planes) that would eliminate more and more noninteger solutions (including the current optimal linear programming solution) but not any integer solutions, until finally the new optimal linear programming is integer valued. However, these *cutting plane* algorithms met with only limited success that depended strongly upon the spcial structure of the problem. A related approach involving the application of *mathematical group theory* now is being explored and seems promising.

Practical problems often are much larger than can be handled by any of these algorithms. In these cases it is common to simply apply the simplex method and then round the optimal linear programming solution to a feasible integer solution. However, this approach is sometimes quite unsatisfactory because it may be difficult (or impossible) to find a feasible integer solution in this way, and the solution found may be far from optimal. Considerable progress now is being made in developing *efficient heuristic procedures* for finding feasible integer solutions for these problems that are not necessarily optimal but usually will be better than can be found by simple rounding.

There has been some investigation into developing algorithms for integer *nonlinear* programming, but considerably less progress thus far than for integer linear programming.

Mixed integer programming also is useful for incorporating certain special types of constraints or functions into a problem that otherwise fits a linear programming (or mathematical programming) format.

Selected References

1 Garfinkel, Robert S. and George L. Nemhauser: *Integer Programming*, Wiley, New York, 1972.

2 Geoffrion, A. M. and R. E. Marsten: "Integer Programming Algorithms: A Framework and State-of-the-Art Survey," *Management Science*, **18**(9): 465–491, May 1972.

3 Hu, T. C.: *Integer Programming and Network Flows*, Addison-Wesley, Reading, Mass., 1969.

4 Lawler, E. L. and D. E. Wood: "Branch-and-Bound Methods: A Survey," *Operations Research*, **14**(4): 699–719, 1966.

5 Mitten, L. G.: "Branch-and-Bound Methods: General Formulation and Properties," *Operations Research*, **18**(1): 24–34, January–February, 1970.

Problems

1 Consider the assignment problem with the following cost table:

		Assignment				
		1	*2*	*3*	*4*	*5*
	1	39	65	69	66	57
	2	64	84	24	92	22
Assignee	*3*	49	50	61	31	45
	4	48	45	55	23	50
	5	59	34	30	34	18

Use the *branch-and-bound technique* to find the set of assignments that minimizes total cost.

(*a*) Use the *best bound rule.*
(*b*) Use the *newest bound rule.*

2 Use the *branch-and-bound technique* (with the *best bound rule*) to solve the following assignment problems:

(*a*) Problem 18, Chap. 3.
(*b*) Problem 19, Chap. 3.

3 Five jobs need to be done on a certain machine. However, the setup time for each job depends upon which job immediately preceded it, as shown by the following table:

		Setup Time *Job*				
		1	*2*	*3*	*4*	*5*
	None	5	3	8	7	4
	1	..	9	13	8	12
Immediately	2	8	..	15	11	13
preceding job	3	5	12	..	9	8
	4	13	7	10	..	5
	5	14	11	9	13	..

The objective is to schedule the *sequence* of jobs that minimizes the sum of the resulting setup times.

(*a*) Design a *branch-and-bound algorithm* for sequencing problems of this type by specifying how the branch, bound, and fathoming steps would be performed.
(*b*) Use this algorithm to solve this problem.

4 Consider the integer programming problem

$$\text{Maximize} \quad Z = 80x_1 + 60x_2 + 40x_3 + 20x_4 - (7x_1 + 5x_2 + 3x_3 + 2x_4)^2,$$

subject to

$$x_j = 0 \text{ or } 1, \text{ for } j = 1, 2, 3, 4.$$

Given the values of the first k variables $(x_1, \ldots, x_k)$, where $k = 0, 1, 2$, or 3, an upper bound on the value of Z that can be achieved by the corresponding feasible solutions is

$$\sum_{j=1}^{k} c_j x_j - \left(\sum_{j=1}^{k} d_j x_j\right)^2 + \sum_{j=k+1}^{4} \max\left\{0, c_j - \left[\left(\sum_{i=1}^{k} d_i x_i + d_j\right)^2 - \left(\sum_{i=1}^{k} d_i x_i\right)^2\right]\right\},$$

where $c_1 = 80$, $c_2 = 60$, $c_3 = 40$, $c_4 = 20$, $d_1 = 7$, $d_2 = 5$, $d_3 = 3$, $d_4 = 2$. Use this bound and the *best bound rule* to solve the problem by the *branch-and-bound technique.*

5 Use *Balas' additive algorithm* described in Sec. 17.3 to solve the problem

$$\text{Minimize} \quad Z = 5x_1 + 6x_2 + 7x_3 + 8x_4 + 9x_5,$$

subject to

$$\begin{aligned} 3x_1 - x_2 + x_3 + x_4 - 2x_5 &\geq 2 \\ x_1 + 3x_2 - x_3 - 2x_4 + x_5 &\geq 0 \\ -x_1 - x_2 + 3x_3 + x_4 + x_5 &\geq 1 \end{aligned}$$

and

$$x_j = 0 \text{ or } 1, \text{ for } j = 1, 2, \ldots, 5.$$

6 Use *Balas' additive algorithm* described in Sec. 17.3 to solve the problem

$$\text{Maximize} \quad Z = 2x_1 - x_2 + 5x_3 - 3x_4 + 4x_5,$$

subject to

$$\begin{aligned} 3x_1 - 2x_2 + 7x_3 - 5x_4 + 4x_5 &\leq 6 \\ x_1 - x_2 + 2x_3 - 4x_4 + 2x_5 &\leq 0 \end{aligned}$$

and

$$x_j = 0 \text{ or } 1, \text{ for } j = 1, 2, \ldots, 5.$$

7 Consider the illustrative problem presented in Sec. 17.1 (see Fig. 17.1).

(*a*) Use a *binary representation* of the variables to reformulate the problem as a *binary linear programming* problem.

(*b*) Use *Balas' additive algorithm* described in Sec. 17.3 to solve this binary linear programming problem.

8 Use *Dakin's algorithm* described in Sec. 17.4 to solve the problem

$$\text{Minimize} \quad Z = 3x_1 + 2x_2,$$

subject to

$$\begin{aligned} 3x_1 + x_2 &\geq 6 \\ x_1 + x_2 &\geq 3 \end{aligned}$$

and

$$x_1 \geq 0, x_2 \geq 0$$
$$x_1, x_2 \text{ are integers.}$$

9 Consider the integer linear programming problem

$$\text{Maximize} \quad Z = 11x_1 + 4x_2,$$

subject to

$$\begin{aligned} -x_1 + 2x_2 &\le 4 \\ 5x_1 + 2x_2 &\le 16 \\ 2x_1 - x_2 &\le 4 \end{aligned}$$

and

$$x_1 \ge 0,\ x_2 \ge 0$$
$$x_1,\ x_2 \text{ are integers.}$$

(*a*) Solve this problem graphically. Compare the value of Z for the optimal solution with that obtained by rounding the optimal linear programming solution to the nearest integer solution.

(*b*) Solve this problem by *Dakin's algorithm* described in Sec. 17.4.

10 Consider the integer linear programming problem

$$\text{Maximize} \quad Z = 4x_1 - 2x_2 + 7x_3,$$

subject to

$$\begin{aligned} x_1 \phantom{{}+x_2} + 5x_3 &\le 10 \\ x_1 + x_2 - x_3 &\le 1 \\ 6x_1 - 5x_2 \phantom{{}-x_3} &\le 0 \end{aligned}$$

and

$$x_1 \ge 0,\ x_2 \ge 0,\ x_3 \ge 0$$
$$x_1,\ x_2,\ x_3 \text{ are integers.}$$

Suppose that the simplex method has been applied to this problem to initially obtain the optimal linear programming solution. The resulting final set of equations is the following:

$$\begin{aligned}
&(0) \quad Z + \frac{17}{12}x_4 + \frac{1}{12}x_5 + \frac{5}{12}x_6 = 14\tfrac{1}{4} \\
&(1) \quad x_3 + \frac{11}{60}x_4 - \frac{1}{12}x_5 - \frac{1}{60}x_6 = 1\tfrac{3}{4} \\
&(2) \quad x_2 + \frac{1}{10}x_4 + \frac{1}{2}x_5 - \frac{1}{10}x_6 = 1\tfrac{1}{2} \\
&(3) \quad x_1 + \frac{1}{12}x_4 + \frac{5}{12}x_5 + \frac{1}{12}x_6 = 1\tfrac{1}{4}.
\end{aligned}$$

Thus the optimal linear programming solution is $(x_1, x_2, x_3) = (1\tfrac{1}{4}, 1\tfrac{1}{2}, 1\tfrac{3}{4})$.

(*a*) Demonstrate by trial and error that a feasible (integer) solution can not be obtained by rounding off the optimal linear programming solution in any way.

(*b*) Solve this problem by *Dakin's algorithm* described in Sec. 17.4.

11 Use *Dakin's algorithm* described in Sec. 17.4 to solve the mixed integer linear programming problem

$$\text{Minimize} \quad Z = 5x_1 + x_2 + x_3 + 2x_4 + 3x_5,$$

subject to

$$\begin{aligned} x_2 - 5x_3 + x_4 + 2x_5 &\geq -2 \\ 5x_1 - x_2 \qquad\qquad + x_5 &\geq \ \ 7 \\ x_1 + x_2 + 6x_3 + x_4 \qquad &\geq \ \ 4 \end{aligned}$$

and

$$\begin{aligned} &x_j \geq 0, \quad \text{for } j = 1, 2, 3, 4, 5, \\ &x_j \text{ integer, for } j = 1, 2, 3. \end{aligned}$$

12 Consider the following mathematical model:

$$\text{Minimize } Z = f_1(x_1) + f_2(x_2),$$

subject to the restrictions

1. Either $x_1 \geq 10$ or $x_2 \geq 10$.
2. At least one of the following inequalities hold:

$$\begin{aligned} 2x_1 + x_2 &\geq 15 \\ x_1 + x_2 &\geq 15 \\ x_1 + 2x_2 &\geq 15. \end{aligned}$$

3. $|x_1 - x_2| = 0$, or 5, or 10.
4. $x_1 \geq 0, x_2 \geq 0$,

where

$$f_1(x_1) = \begin{cases} 20 + 5x_1, & \text{if } x_1 > 0 \\ 0, & \text{if } x_1 = 0, \end{cases}$$

$$f_2(x_2) = \begin{cases} 12 + 6x_2, & \text{if } x_2 > 0 \\ 0, & \text{if } x_2 = 0. \end{cases}$$

Formulate this problem as a *mixed integer linear programming* problem.

13 Consider the following mathematical model:

$$\text{Maximize } Z = 3x_1 + f(x_2) + 4x_3 + g(x_4),$$

subject to the restrictions,

1. $2x_1 - x_2 + x_3 + 3x_4 \leq 15$.
2. At least one of the following two inequalities hold:

$$\begin{aligned} x_1 + x_2 + x_3 + x_4 &\leq 10 \\ 3x_1 - x_2 - x_3 + x_4 &\leq 20. \end{aligned}$$

3. At least two of the following four inequalities hold:

$$\begin{aligned} 5x_1 + 3x_2 + 3x_3 - x_4 &\leq 30 \\ 2x_1 + 5x_2 - x_3 + 3x_4 &\leq 30 \\ -x_1 + 3x_2 + 5x_3 + 3x_4 &\leq 30 \\ 3x_1 - x_2 + 3x_3 + 5x_4 &\leq 30. \end{aligned}$$

4. $x_3 = 2$, or 3, or 4.
5. $x_j \geq 0 \; (j = 1, 2, 3, 4)$,

where

$$f(x_2) = \begin{cases} -10 + 2x_2, & \text{if } x_2 > 0 \\ 0, & \text{if } x_2 = 0, \end{cases}$$

and

$$g(x_4) = \begin{cases} -5 + 3x_4, & \text{if } x_4 > 0 \\ 0, & \text{if } x_4 = 0. \end{cases}$$

Formulate this problem as a ***mixed integer linear programming*** problem.

14 An airlines company is considering the purchase of new long-, medium-, and short-range jet passenger airplanes. The purchase price would be \$6,700,000 for each long-range plane, \$5,000,000 for each medium-range plane, and \$3,500,000 for each short-range plane. The Board of Directors has authorized a maximum commitment of \$150,000,000 for these purchases. Regardless of which airplanes are purchased, air travel of all distances is expected to be sufficiently large enough so that these planes would be utilized at essentially maximum capacity. It is estimated that the net annual profit (after subtracting capital recovery costs) would be \$420,000 per long-range plane, \$300,000 per medium-range plane, and \$230,000 per short-range plane.

It is predicted that enough trained pilots will be available to the company to man 30 new airplanes. If only short-range planes were purchased, the maintenance facilities would be able to handle 40 new planes. However, each medium-range plane is equivalent to $1\frac{1}{3}$ short-range planes, and each long-range plane is equivalent to $1\frac{2}{3}$ short-range planes in terms of their use of the maintenance facilities.

The information given above was obtained by a preliminary analysis of the problem. A more detailed analysis will be conducted subsequently. However, using the above data as a first approximation, management wishes to know how many planes of each type should be purchased to maximize profit.

(*a*) Formulate the ***integer linear programming*** model for this problem.
(*b*) Use ***Dakin's algorithm*** described in Sec. 17.4 to solve this model.

18 Nonlinear Programming

The fundamental role of *linear programming* in operations research is accurately reflected by the fact that it is the focus of *four* chapters and is used in several others. However, a key assumption of linear programming is that *all* its functions (objective function and constraint functions) are *linear*. Although this assumption essentially holds for numerous practical problems, it frequently does not. We described in Sec. 4.1 how it is *sometimes* possible to *reformulate* nonlinearities into a linear programming format. Nevertheless, it often is necessary to deal directly with *nonlinear programming problems*, so we now turn our attention to this important area.

In one general form, the *nonlinear programming* problem is to find $\mathbf{x} = (x_1, x_2, \ldots, x_n)$ so as to

$$\text{Maximize } f(\mathbf{x}),$$

subject to

$$g_i(\mathbf{x}) \leq b_i, \text{ for } i = 1, 2, \ldots, m,$$

and

$$\mathbf{x} \geq \mathbf{0},$$

where $f(\mathbf{x})$ and the $g_i(\mathbf{x})$ are given functions of the n decision variables. No algorithm is available that will solve *every* specific problem fitting this format. However, by making various assumptions about these functions, substantial progress has been made for some important special cases of this problem, and research is continuing very actively. This is a large area, and we shall not have space to survey it completely. However, we shall present some fundamental results in the next section and then describe an important algorithm for each of two basic special cases in Secs. 18.2 and 18.3.

18.1 THE KUHN-TUCKER CONDITIONS

Before considering algorithms it is necessary to learn how to recognize an *optimal solution* to a nonlinear programming problem. This section gives the so-called Kuhn-Tucker conditions, which describe such optimal solutions.

What are the characteristics of optimal solutions to nonlinear programming problems? Classical calculus provides some motivation for the answer to this question. To begin, consider the case where there are *no* constraints (not even nonnegativity constraints), and the objective function is differentiable. If the objective function contains only *one variable*, it is well known (see Appendix 2) that $x_1 = x_1^*$ can maximize $f(x_1)$ only if $df/dx_1 = 0$ at $x_1 = x_1^*$, where this is also a *sufficient condition* if $f(x_1)$ is a *concave function* (as defined in Appendix 1). Similarly, Appendix 2 indicates that if the function contains *several variables*, then $\mathbf{x}^* = (x_1^*, x_2^*, \ldots, x_n^*)$ can maximize $f(\mathbf{x})$ only if $\partial f/\partial x_j = 0$ at $x_j = x_j^*$ for $j = 1, 2, \ldots, n$. This becomes a *sufficient condition* if $f(\mathbf{x})$ is a *concave function*. Now suppose that the nonnegativity constraints $x_j \geq 0$ $(j = 1, 2, \ldots, n)$ are introduced. The only revision that must be made in the above statement is that if $x_j^* = 0$, then the condition $\partial f/\partial x_j = 0$ at $x_j = x_j^*$ is replaced by the condition $\partial f/\partial x_j \leq 0$ at $x_j = x_j^*$.

Unfortunately, it becomes much more difficult to characterize an optimal solution if the other constraints involving the $g_i(\mathbf{x})$ functions are also introduced. The difficulty is that increasing x_j may require changing other variables to avoid violating the constraints, so it is no longer sufficient to just look at the $\partial f/\partial x_j$ $(j = 1, 2, \ldots, n)$. However, Kuhn and Tucker derived the results[1] for this case that are analogous to those given above for simpler cases. Their basic result is embodied in the following theorem.

THEOREM 18.1 Assume that $f(\mathbf{x}), g_1(\mathbf{x}), g_2(\mathbf{x}), \ldots, g_m(\mathbf{x})$ are *differentiable* functions satisfying certain regularity conditions.[2] Then

$$\mathbf{x}^* = (x_1^*, x_2^*, \ldots, x_n^*)$$

can be an *optimal* solution to the nonlinear programming problem only if there exist m numbers, $u_1, u_2, \ldots, u_m$, such that *all* of the following conditions are satisfied:

$$\left.\begin{array}{l} 1.\quad \dfrac{\partial f}{\partial x_j} - \displaystyle\sum_{i=1}^{m} u_i \frac{\partial g_i}{\partial x_j} \leq 0 \\ 2.\quad x_j^*\left(\dfrac{\partial f}{\partial x_j} - \displaystyle\sum_{i=1}^{m} u_i \frac{\partial g_i}{\partial x_j}\right) = 0 \end{array}\right\} \text{at } x_j = x_j^*, \text{ for } j = 1, 2, \ldots, n.$$

[1] H. W. Kuhn and A. W. Tucker, "Nonlinear Programming," in Jerzy Neyman (ed.), *Proceedings of the Second Berkeley Symposium on Mathematical Statistics and Probability*, University of California Press, Berkeley, pp. 481–492, 1951.

[2] *Ibid*, p. 483.

$$\left.\begin{array}{ll} 3. & g_i(\mathbf{x}^*) - b_i \le 0 \\ 4. & u_i\,(g_i(\mathbf{x}^*) - b_i) = 0 \end{array}\right\} \text{for } i = 1, 2, \ldots, m.$$

5. $x_j^* \ge 0,$ for $j = 1, 2, \ldots, n.$
6. $u_i \ge 0,$ for $i = 1, 2, \ldots, m.$

These conditions are commonly referred to as the *Kuhn-Tucker conditions.* The u_i are somewhat analogous to the *dual variables* of linear programming, and they have a comparable economic interpretation. (However, the u_i actually arose in the mathematical derivation as generalized Lagrange multiplers.) Conditions (3) and (5) do nothing more than help ensure the feasibility of the solution. The other conditions eliminate most of the feasible solutions as possible candidates for the optimal solution. However, it should be noted that satisfying these conditions does not guarantee that the solution is optimal. Just like the analogous condition for an unconstrained function that its partial derivatives be zero, these conditions are only *necessary*, and *not sufficient*, for optimality. However, just as before, if certain additional *convexity* assumptions are satisfied, these conditions do become sufficient to guarantee optimality. Kuhn and Tucker proved the following extension of the theorem.

COROLLARY Assume that $f(\mathbf{x})$ is a *concave function* and that $g_1(\mathbf{x}), g_2(\mathbf{x}), \ldots, g_m(\mathbf{x})$ are *convex functions* satisfying the regularity conditions. Then $\mathbf{x}^* = (x_1^*, x_2^*, \ldots, x_n^*)$ is an *optimal solution* if and only if *all* the conditions of the theorem are satisfied.

EXAMPLE To illustrate the formulation and application of the Kuhn-Tucker conditions, consider the two-variable nonlinear programming problem

$$\text{Maximize} \quad f(\mathbf{x}) = \ln(x_1 + x_2),$$

subject to

$$x_1 + 2x_2 \le 5$$

and

$$x_1 \ge 0, x_2 \ge 0,$$

where *ln* denotes *natural logarithm.* Thus $m = 1$ and $g_1(\mathbf{x}) = x_1 + 2x_2$, so $g_1(\mathbf{x})$ is *convex.* Furthermore, it is easily verified (see Appendix 1) that $f(\mathbf{x})$ is *concave.* Hence the corollary to Theorem 17.1 applies, so any optimal solution can definitely be obtained by solving the Kuhn-Tucker conditions. These conditions are

(1*a*) $$\frac{1}{x_1 + x_2} - u_1 \le 0.$$

(2*a*) $$x_1\left(\frac{1}{x_1 + x_2} - u_1\right) = 0.$$

(1*b*) $$\frac{1}{x_1 + x_2} - 2u_1 \le 0.$$

(2*b*) $$x_2\left(\frac{1}{x_1 + x_2} - 2u_1\right) = 0.$$

(3) $$x_1 + 2x_2 - 5 \le 0.$$

(4) $$u_1(x_1 + 2x_2 - 5) = 0.$$

(5) $$x_1 \ge 0, x_2 \ge 0.$$

(6) $$u_1 \ge 0.$$

To solve these conditions, note that $x_1 + x_2$ must be *strictly positive* because $(x_1 + x_2)^{-1}$ is not even defined at $x_1 + x_2 = 0$. Therefore, $u_1 > 0$ from condition (1), so that $x_1 + 2x_2 - 5 = 0$ from condition (4). Furthermore, condition (1*a*) then implies that condition (1*b*) must hold with a *strict* inequality, so that $x_2 = 0$ in condition (2*b*). Hence $x_1 = 5$ and $u_1 = 1/5$, so that $(x_1, x_2, u_1) = (5,0,1/5)$ satisfy all the conditions. Consequently, $x^* = (5,0)$ is an optimal solution for the nonlinear programming problem.

You can check this optimal solution by using the fact that maximizing $\ln(x_1 + x_2)$ is *equivalent* to maximizing $x_1 + x_2$ (since ln is a monotone strictly increasing function).

For problems more complicated than this example, it may be difficult, if not essentially impossible, to derive the optimal solution *directly* from the Kuhn-Tucker conditions. Nevertheless, these conditions still provide valuable clues as to the identity of the optimal solution, and they also permit checking whether a proposed solution may be optimal. Furthermore, there are many valuable *indirect* applications of the Kuhn-Tucker conditions. You will see one of these in the next section.

18.2 QUADRATIC PROGRAMMING

The term "quadratic programming" now conventionally refers to the problem of maximizing (or minimizing) a *quadratic objective function* subject to *linear constraints*. Thus the quadratic programming problem differs from the linear programming problem only in that the *objective function* also includes x_j^2 and $x_j x_k (j \ne k)$ terms. In short, the problem is to find $x_1, x_2, \ldots, x_n$ so as to

$$\text{Maximize} \quad \left\{\sum_{j=1}^{n} c_j x_j - \frac{1}{2} \sum_{j=1}^{n} \sum_{k=1}^{n} q_{jk} x_j x_k\right\},$$

subject to

$$\sum_{j=1}^{n} a_{ij} x_j \le b_i, \text{ for } i = 1, 2, \ldots, m,$$

and

$$x_j \ge 0, \text{ for } j = 1, 2, \ldots, n,$$

where the q_{jk} are given constants such that $q_{jk} = q_{kj}$.

Several algorithms have been developed for the special case of the quadratic programming problem where the objective function is a *concave* function. (A way to verify it is a concave function is to verify the equivalent condition that

$$\sum_{j=1}^{n} \sum_{k=1}^{n} q_{jk} x_j x_k \geq 0$$

for all values of $x_1, x_2, \ldots, x_n$. Mathematically speaking, this equivalent condition is that the q_{jk} are the elements of a *positive semidefinite* matrix.) We shall describe one[1] of these that has been particularly popular because it only requires using the *simplex method* with a slight modification.

The first step for this algorithm is to formulate the *Kuhn-Tucker conditions* for the problem. A convenient form for expressing them for this case is

$$\sum_{k=1}^{n} q_{jk} x_k + \sum_{i=1}^{m} a_{ij} y_{n+i} - y_j = c_j, \quad \text{for } j = 1, 2, \ldots, n,$$

$$\sum_{j=1}^{n} a_{ij} x_j + x_{n+i} = b_i, \quad \text{for } i = 1, 2, \ldots, m,$$

$$x_j \geq 0, \quad \text{for } j = 1, 2, \ldots, n+m,$$

$$y_j \geq 0, \quad \text{for } j = 1, 2, \ldots, n+m,$$

$$x_j y_j = 0, \quad \text{for } j = 1, 2, \ldots, n+m,$$

where the y_{n+i} are the u_i of the preceding section, and where the y_j $(j=1, 2, \ldots, n)$ and the x_j $(j = n+1, \ldots, n+m)$ are slack variables. (You are asked in Prob. 2 to verify that these indeed are one form of the Kuhn-Tucker conditions). Since the objective function is assumed to be concave and the constraint functions are linear and therefore convex, the corollary to Theorem 18.1 applies. Thus $(x_1, x_2, \ldots, x_n)$ is *optimal* if and only if there exist values of $x_{n+1}, \ldots, x_{n+m}, y_1, \ldots, y_{n+m}$ such that $(x_1, \ldots, x_{n+m}, y_1, \ldots, y_{n+m})$ satisfies all these conditions. The problem is thereby reduced to finding a *feasible solution* to these conditions.

Now notice the key fact that, with the exception of the last restriction ($x_j y_j = 0$ for $j = 1, 2, \ldots, n+m$), these Kuhn-Tucker conditions are nothing more than *linear programming constraints* involving $2(n+m)$ variables. Furthermore, this $x_j y_j = 0$ restriction simply says that it is not permissible for both x_j and y_j to be *basic variables* when considering (nondegenerate) basic feasible solutions. Therefore the problem reduces to finding an *initial basic feasible solution* to any linear programming problem having these constraints, subject to this additional restriction on the identity of the basic variables. (This

[1] Philip Wolfe, "The Simplex Method for Quadratic Programming," *Econometrica,* **27**:382–398, 1959. This paper develops both a "short form" and a "long form" of the algorithm. We present a version of the *short form,* which assumes that the objective function is *strictly* concave.

"initial" basic feasible solution may be the only feasible solution in this case.) The initial basic variables for the second group of equations,

$$\sum_{j=1}^{n} a_{ij} x_j + x_{n+i} = b_i \qquad (i = 1,2, \ldots, m),$$

would be the x_{n+i} (assuming the b_i are positive). However, since most or all of the c_j normally are positive, it is not obvious what the initial basic variables should be for the other equations:

$$\sum_{k=1}^{n} q_{jk} x_k + \sum_{i=1}^{m} a_{ij} y_{n+i} - y_j = c_j \qquad (j = 1, 2, \ldots, n).$$

The standard linear programming technique when there is not an obvious initial basic feasible solution is to introduce *artificial variables* that are eventually forced to equal zero (see Sec. 2.10.). Let $z_1, z_2, \ldots, z_n$ be these artificial variables, where the only (initial) restriction on them is

$$z_j \geq 0, \text{ for } j = 1, 2, \ldots, n.$$

These equations are then (except when the coefficient of z_j is -1 when $c_j < 0$)

$$\sum_{k=1}^{n} q_{jk} x_k + \sum_{i=1}^{m} a_{ij} y_{n+i} - y_j + z_j = c_j, \text{ for } j = 1, 2, \ldots, n.$$

This technique provides an *artificial* initial basic feasible solution, namely, $z_j = c_j$ (for $j = 1, 2, \ldots, n$), $x_{n+i} = b_i$ (for $i = 1, 2, \ldots, m$), $x_j = 0$ (for $j = 1, 2, \ldots, n$), and $y_j = 0$ (for $j = 1, 2, \ldots, n + m$). However, a feasible solution to this artificial problem is feasible for the real problem if and only if $z_j = 0$ for $j = 1, 2, \ldots, n$. Therefore, $\Sigma_{j=1}^{n} z_j$ must be decreased to *zero* to obtain the desired feasible solution. To do this, start with the artificial initial basic feasible solution given above and apply a *modification* of the *simplex method* to the following problem:

$$\text{Minimize } \sum_{j=1}^{n} z_j,$$

subject to

$$\sum_{k=1}^{n} q_{jk} x_k + \sum_{i=i}^{m} a_{ij} y_{n+i} - y_j + z_j = c_j, \text{ for } j = 1, 2, \ldots, n$$

$$\sum_{j=1}^{n} a_{ij} x_j + x_{n+i} = b_i, \qquad \text{for } i = 1, 2, \ldots, m$$

and

$$x_j \geq 0, \qquad \text{for } j = 1, 2, \ldots, n + m$$

$$y_j \geq 0, \qquad \text{for } j = 1, 2, \ldots, n + m$$

$$z_j \geq 0, \qquad \text{for } j = 1, 2, \ldots, n.$$

The *modification* is that y_j is not permitted to become a basic variable whenever x_j is already a basic variable, and vice versa, for $j = 1, 2, \ldots, n+m$. This ensures that $x_j y_j = 0$ for each value of j. When the optimal solution

$$(x_1^*, \ldots, x_{n+m}^*, y_1^*, \ldots, y_{n+m}^*, z_1 = 0, \ldots, z_n = 0)$$

is obtained to this problem, $(x_1^*, \ldots, x_n^*)$ is the desired optimal solution to the original quadratic programming problem.

EXAMPLE We shall now illustrate this approach on the problem

$$\text{Maximize} \quad \{5x_1 + x_2 - (x_1 - x_2)^2\},$$

subject to

$$x_1 + x_2 \le 2$$

and

$$x_1 \ge 0, x_2 \ge 0.$$

Since $(x_1 - x_2)^2 = \frac{1}{2}(2x_1^2 - 2x_1x_2 - 2x_2x_1 + 2x_2^2)$, we obtain $q_{11} = 2, q_{12} = -2$, $q_{21} = -2$, and $q_{22} = 2$. Thus the problem to be solved by the modification of the simplex method is

$$\text{Minimize} \quad z_1 + z_2,$$

subject to

$$\begin{aligned} 2x_1 - 2x_2 \quad + y_3 \quad - y_1 + z_1 \quad &= 5 \\ -2x_1 + 2x_2 \quad + y_3 - y_2 \quad + z_2 &= 1 \\ x_1 + x_2 + x_3 \quad &= 2 \end{aligned}$$

and

$$\text{all } x_j \ge 0, y_j \ge 0, z_j \ge 0.$$

The resulting solution is $x_1 = \frac{3}{2}$, $x_2 = \frac{1}{2}$, $y_3 = 3$, with the rest of the variables zero. (We suggest that you verify this by showing that $x_1 = \frac{3}{2}$, $x_2 = \frac{1}{2}$, $u_1 = 3$ satisfy the Kuhn-Tucker conditions for this problem when they are written in the form given in Sec. 18.1.) Therefore the optimal solution to the original problem is $x_1 = \frac{3}{2}$, $x_2 = \frac{1}{2}$.

18.3 CONVEX PROGRAMMING

The *convex programming* problem is the special case of the nonlinear programming problem where $f(\mathbf{x})$ is a *concave* function and all the $g_i(\mathbf{x})$ are *convex* functions. These assumptions greatly simplify the problem. The convexity of the $g_i(\mathbf{x})$ functions implies that the set of feasible solutions is a *convex set*. This property and the concavity of $f(\mathbf{x})$ imply that any *local optimum* is also a *global optimum*; i.e., any feasible solution which maximizes $f(\mathbf{x})$ over the feasible solutions in its immediate neighborhood also maximizes $f(\mathbf{x})$ over the entire set of feasible solutions. Therefore, rather than having to find and compare a large (possibly infinite) number of local optima, it is only necessary to find one local, and therefore global, optimum.

A considerable number of algorithms have been developed for convex programming. Most use the *gradient* of the objective function in some way to obtain a sequence of solutions leading toward the optimal solution. Therefore, before describing one of the algorithms, we shall first discuss the relevance of the gradient.

Role of the Gradient

Assuming the objective function $f(\mathbf{x})$ is differentiable, it possesses a *gradient* denoted by $\nabla f(\mathbf{x})$ at each point $\mathbf{x}$. In particular, the gradient at a specific point $\mathbf{x} = \mathbf{x}'$ is the *vector* whose elements are the respective *partial derivatives* evaluated at $\mathbf{x} = \mathbf{x}'$, so that

$$\nabla f(\mathbf{x}') = \left(\frac{\partial f}{\partial x_1}, \frac{\partial f}{\partial x_2}, \ldots, \frac{\partial f}{\partial x_n}\right) \text{ at } \mathbf{x} = \mathbf{x}'.$$

The significance of the gradient is that the (infinitesimal) change in $\mathbf{x}$ which *maximizes* the rate at which $f(\mathbf{x})$ increases is the change that is *proportional* to $\nabla f(\mathbf{x})$. To express this idea geometrically, the "direction" of the gradient, $\nabla f(\mathbf{x}')$, is interpreted as the *direction* of the directed line segment (arrow) from the origin $(0,0, \ldots, 0)$ to the point $(\partial f/\partial x_1, \partial f/\partial x_2, \ldots, \partial f/\partial x_n)$, where $\partial f/\partial x_j$ is evaluated at $x_j = x_j'$. Therefore it may be said that the rate at which $f(\mathbf{x})$ increases is maximized if (infinitesimal) changes in $\mathbf{x}$ are in the *direction* of the gradient $\nabla f(x)$. Since the objective is to find the feasible solution *maximizing* $f(\mathbf{x})$, it would seem expedient to attempt to move in the direction of the gradient as much as possible.

If the problem had *no* constraints, this interpretation of the gradient suggests that an efficient *search procedure* should keep moving in the direction of the gradient until it (essentially) reaches an optimal solution $\mathbf{x}^*$, where $\nabla f(\mathbf{x}^*) = \mathbf{0}$. However, it normally would not be practical to change $\mathbf{x}$ *continuously* in the direction of $\nabla f(\mathbf{x})$ because this would require continuously *reevaluating* the $\partial f/\partial x_j$ and changing the direction of the path. Therefore a better approach is to keep moving in a *fixed* direction until $f(\mathbf{x})$ stops increasing and then recalculate the gradient to determine the new direction in which to move. With this approach, each *iteration* involves changing the *current* point $\mathbf{x}$ as follows:

$$\text{Reset} \quad \mathbf{x} = \mathbf{x} + t^* \nabla f(\mathbf{x}),$$

where t^* is the positive value of t that *maximizes* $f(\mathbf{x} + t\nabla f(\mathbf{x}))$; that is,

$$f(\mathbf{x} + t^* \nabla f(\mathbf{x})) = \max_{t \geq 0} f(\mathbf{x} + t\nabla f(\mathbf{x})).$$

The iterations of this **gradient search procedure** would continue until $\nabla f(\mathbf{x}) = \mathbf{0}$ (within a small tolerance).

The most difficult part of this procedure usually is to find t^*, the value of t that maximizes f in the direction of the gradient, at each iteration. Since $\mathbf{x}$ and $\nabla f(\mathbf{x})$ have fixed values for the maximization, this problem should be viewed as maximizing a *concave* function of a *single variable* t. Therefore classical optimization methods for such functions (see Appendix 2) are applicable, so it may be possible to obtain an analytical solution by setting the derivative with respect to t equal to zero and solving. Alternatively, it is quite straightforward for this kind of function to find t^* (within a small tolerance) by *trial and error*. Various methods are available[1] for doing this *systematically* in an efficient way.

To illustrate the *gradient search procedure*, consider the two-variable problem

$$\text{Maximize} \quad f(\mathbf{x}) = 2x_1x_2 + 2x_2 - x_1^2 - 2x_2^2.$$

Thus

$$\frac{\partial f}{\partial x_1} = 2x_2 - 2x_1,$$

$$\frac{\partial f}{\partial x_2} = 2x_1 + 2 - 4x_2.$$

It also can be verified (see Appendix 1) that $f(\mathbf{x})$ is *concave*. To begin the procedure, the initial trial solution can be selected arbitrarily. Suppose $\mathbf{x} = (0,0)$ is selected. Since the respective partial derivatives are 0 and 2 at this point, the gradient is

$$\nabla f(0,0) = (0,2).$$

Therefore, for the first iteration,

$$\text{Reset} \quad \mathbf{x} = (0,0) + t^*(0,2) = (0,2t^*).$$

Since

$$f(0, 2t^*) = \max_{t\geq 0} f(0, 2t) = \max_{t\geq 0}\{4t - 8t^2\},$$

and

$$\frac{d}{dt}\{4t - 8t^2\} = 4 - 16t = 0,$$

it follows that

$$t^* = \frac{1}{4}, \text{ so } \mathbf{x} = \left(0, \frac{1}{2}\right).$$

For this new point, the gradient is

$$\nabla f\left(0, \frac{1}{2}\right) = (1,0).$$

[1] Douglass J. Wilde, *Optimum Seeking Methods*, chap. 2, Prentice-Hall, Englewood Cliffs, N.J., 1964.

Thus, for the second iteration,

$$\text{Reset} \quad \mathbf{x} = \left(0, \frac{1}{2}\right) + t^*(1,0) = \left(t^*, \frac{1}{2}\right),$$

where

$$f\left(t^*, \frac{1}{2}\right) = \max_{t \geq 0} f\left(t, \frac{1}{2}\right) = \max_{t \geq 0}\left\{t - t^2 + \frac{1}{2}\right\},$$

$$\frac{d}{dt}\left\{t - t^2 + \frac{1}{2}\right\} = 1 - 2t = 0,$$

so

$$t^* = \frac{1}{2}, \text{ and } \mathbf{x} = \left(\frac{1}{2}, \frac{1}{2}\right).$$

Continuing in this fashion, the subsequent points would be $(\frac{1}{2}, \frac{3}{4})$, $(\frac{3}{4}, \frac{3}{4})$, $(\frac{3}{4}, \frac{7}{8})$, $(\frac{7}{8}, \frac{7}{8})$, . . . , as shown in Fig. 18.1. Since these points are converging to $\mathbf{x}^* = (1,1)$, this is the optimal solution, as verified by the fact that

$$\nabla f(1,1) = (0,0).$$

As Fig. 18.1 suggests, the gradient search procedure usually *zig zags* rather than moving in a straight line to the optimal solution. Some modifications of the procedure have been developed that *accelerate* movement toward the optimum by taking this typical behavior into account.

If $f(\mathbf{x})$ were *not* a *concave* function, the gradient search procedure still would converge to a *local* maximum. The only change in the description of the procedure for this case is that t^* now would correspond to the *first local maximum* of $f(\mathbf{x} + t\,\nabla f(\mathbf{x}))$ for positive values of t.

Figure 18.1 Illustration of the gradient search procedure.

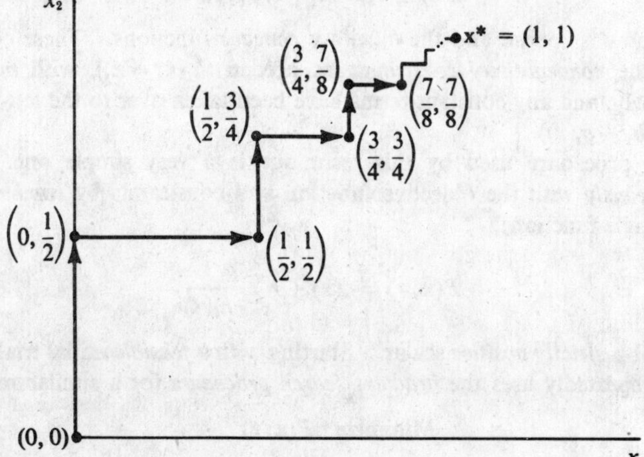

If the objective were to *minimize* $f(\mathbf{x})$ instead, one change in the procedure would be to move in the *opposite* direction of the gradient at each iteration. In other words, the rule for obtaining the next point now would be

$$\text{Reset} \quad \mathbf{x} = \mathbf{x} - t^* \nabla f(\mathbf{x}).$$

The only other change is that t^* now would be the positive value of t that *minimizes* $f(\mathbf{x} - t\nabla f(\mathbf{x}))$; that is,

$$f(\mathbf{x} - t^* \nabla f(\mathbf{x})) = \min_{t \geq 0} f(\mathbf{x} - t\nabla f(\mathbf{x})).$$

(This is the form of the gradient search procedure that will be used by the convex programming algorithm described below.)

We have described the gradient search procedure under the assumption that the optimization problem has *no* constraints. This is the *only* case for which it is designed, so it is *not* directly applicable to *convex programming*, where constraints are an important part of the problem. However, several algorithms have been developed that *adapt* the procedure in different ways to take the constraints into account. One widely used algorithm does this by applying the procedure (without modification) to a *sequence* of *unconstrained* minimization problems, where the resulting sequence of optimal solutions *converges* to an optimal solution for the convex programming problem—as we shall now describe.

The Sequential Unconstrained Minimization Technique (SUMT)

The sequential unconstrained minimization technique assumes that the convex programming problem has been reformulated in the *minimization* form

$$\text{Minimize} \quad g(\mathbf{x}),$$

subject to

$$h_i(\mathbf{x}) \geq 0, \text{ for } i = 1, 2, \ldots, m,$$

so $g(\mathbf{x})$ now is *convex* and the $h_i(\mathbf{x})$ are *concave* functions. These constraints *include* the *nonnegativity constraints* as needed ($h_i(\mathbf{x}) = x_j$), with m adjusted accordingly, and any constant terms have been taken over to the left-hand side ($h_i(\mathbf{x}) = b_i - g_i(\mathbf{x})$).

The procedure used by this technique is a very simple one. It deals *simultaneously* with the objective function and constraints by *combining* them into a single function:

$$P(\mathbf{x}; r) = g(\mathbf{x}) + r\sum_{i=1}^{m} \frac{1}{h_i(\mathbf{x})},$$

where r is a *strictly positive* scalar. Starting with a *feasible* initial trial solution, it then repeatedly uses the *gradient search procedure* (or a similar method) to

$$\text{Minimize} \quad P(\mathbf{x}; r)$$

for successively smaller values of r approaching zero. The resulting minimizing solutions converge to an optimal solution for the original problem.

The key to this technique is that each $1/h_i(\mathbf{x})$ approaches *infinity* as $h_i(\mathbf{x})$ approaches *zero* from above. Therefore, by starting with an initial trial solution such that $h_i(\mathbf{x}) > 0$ for all i, it is *guaranteed* that the gradient search procedure will find a minimizing solution of $P(\mathbf{x}; r)$ that is *feasible* for the original problem In effect,

$$r\sum_{i=1}^{m} \frac{1}{h_i(\mathbf{x})}$$

is a *boundary repulsion term* (also called a *penalty function*) that prevents the gradient search procedure from crossing (or even reaching) the *boundary* of the feasible region where one or more $h_i(\mathbf{x}) = 0$.

However, if an *optimal* solution for the original problem lies on or sufficiently near the boundary of the feasible solution, the boundary repulsion term also will prevent this solution from being the minimizing solution of $P(\mathbf{x}; r)$. This is the reason for repeatedly minimizing $P(\mathbf{x}; r)$ for successively *smaller* values of r. As r approaches zero, $P(\mathbf{x}; r)$ approaches $g(\mathbf{x})$, so the minimizing solution of $P(\mathbf{x}; r)$ converges to the desired optimal solution. Therefore, only enough minimizing solutions need to be obtained to permit extrapolating to this limiting solution.

Useful information is available for guiding the decision on when this extrapolating should be done. In particular, if $\bar{\mathbf{x}}$ is a minimizing solution of $P(\mathbf{x}; r)$, then

$$g(\bar{\mathbf{x}}) - r\sum_{i=1}^{m} \frac{1}{h_i(\bar{\mathbf{x}})} \leq g(\mathbf{x}^*) \leq g(\bar{\mathbf{x}}),$$

where $\mathbf{x}^*$ is the (unknown) *optimal* solution for the original problem. Thus $g(\bar{\mathbf{x}})$ can not exceed $g(\mathbf{x}^*)$ by more than the value of the boundary repulsion term for $\bar{\mathbf{x}}$. Therefore it would be reasonable to extrapolate to the optimal solution whenever the resulting maximum error is considered to be sufficiently small.

Selected References 1 and 2 present a detailed coverage of the theory and implementation of SUMT and related methods, including extensions to other cases.

EXAMPLE To illustrate SUMT, consider the two-variable problem

$$\text{Minimize} \quad g(\mathbf{x}) = \frac{(x_1 + 1)^3}{3} + x_2 .$$

subject to

$$x_1 \geq 1$$
$$x_2 \geq 0.$$

Thus $h_1(\mathbf{x}) = x_1 - 1$ and $h_2(\mathbf{x}) = x_2$. Therefore

$$P(\mathbf{x}; r) = \frac{(x_1 + 1)^3}{3} + x_2 + r\left[\frac{1}{x_1 - 1} + \frac{1}{x_2}\right].$$

This problem is sufficiently simple enough so that the minimizing solution of $P(\mathbf{x}; r)$ can be derived analytically:

$$\frac{\partial P}{\partial x_1} = (x_1 + 1)^2 - \frac{r}{(x_1 - 1)^2} = 0, \quad \text{so} \quad (x_1^2 - 1)^2 = r,$$

$$\frac{\partial P}{\partial x_2} = 1 - \frac{r}{x_2^2} = 0,$$

so

$$\bar{x}_1 = (\sqrt{r} + 1)^{1/2}, \bar{x}_2 = \sqrt{r}.$$

Thus, if the gradient search procedure were still used, it would obtain essentially this solution at each iteration.

A typical sequence of values of r for the iterations would be $r = 1, 10^{-2}, 10^{-4}, 10^{-6}, \ldots$. Using this sequence gives the results summarized in Table 18.1,

Table 18.1 Illustration of Sequential Unconstrained Minimization Technique

Iteration	r	$\bar{x}_1$	$\bar{x}_2$	$g(\bar{\mathbf{x}}) - r\sum_{i=1}^{m} \frac{1}{h_i(\bar{\mathbf{x}})}$	$g(\bar{\mathbf{x}})$
1	1	1.4142	1	2.27	5.69
2	10^{-2}	1.0488	0.1	2.66	2.97
3	10^{-4}	1.0050	0.01	2.67	2.70
4	10^{-6}	1.0005	0.001	2.67	2.67
		↓	↓	↓	↓
		1	0	2.67	2.67

where the last two columns give the lower and upper bound on $g(\mathbf{x}^*)$. After iteration 4, these two bounds coincide to two decimal places, so $\bar{\mathbf{x}}$ must be extremely close to optimal. It also seems clear that the sequence of solutions is converging to the boundary values of the two variables. Therefore the *optimal* solution must be $\mathbf{x}^* = (1,0)$, as can be verified from the Kuhn-Tucker conditions (or by inspection in this case).

18.4 CONCLUSIONS

Practical optimization problems frequently involve *nonlinear* behavior that must be taken into account. It is sometimes possible to *reformulate* these nonlinearities to fit into a linear programming format. However, the best approach often is to use a *nonlinear programming* formulation.

In contrast to the simplex method for linear programming, there is no efficient all-purpose algorithm that can be used to solve *all* nonlinear programming problems. In fact, some of these problems can not be solved by *any* method in a very satisfactory manner. However, considerable progress has been made for some important classes of problems, including *quadratic programming* and *convex programming*. A variety of algorithms are available for these cases that frequently perform reasonably well.

Nonlinear programming remains a very active research area.

Selected References

1 Bracken, Jerome and Garth P. McCormick: *Selected Applications of Nonlinear Programming*, Wiley, New York, 1968.
2 Fiacco, Anthony V. and McCormick: *Nonlinear Programming: Sequential Unconstrained Minimization Techniques*, Wiley, New York, 1968.
3 Luenberger, David G.: *Introduction to Linear and Nonlinear Programming*, Addison-Wesley, Reading, Mass., 1973.
4 Mangasarian, Olvi L.: *Nonlinear Programming*, McGraw-Hill, New York, 1969.
5 Wilde, Douglass J. and Charles S. Beightler: *Foundations of Optimization*, Prentice-Hall, Englewood Cliffs, N.J., 1967.
6 Zangwill, Willard I.: *Nonlinear Programming: A Unified Approach*, Prentice-Hall, Englewood Cliffs, N.J., 1969.

Problems

1 Consider the nonlinear programming problem given in Prob. 15, Chap. 4. Verify that $(x_1, x_2) = \left(\frac{2}{\sqrt{3}}, \frac{3}{2}\right)$ is an optimal solution for this problem by applying the *Kuhn–Tucker conditions.*

2 Derive the *Kuhn–Tucker conditions* for the quadratic programming problem. Show that they can be expressed as given in Sec. 18.2.

3 Consider the nonlinear programming problem given in Prob. 7, Chap. 6. Determine whether $(x_1, x_2) = (1,2)$ can be optimal by applying the *Kuhn–Tucker conditions.*

4 Use the Kuhn–Tucker conditions to derive the optimal solution for each of the following problems:

(*a*) Maximize $\{2x_1 - x_1^3 + x_2\}$,

subject to

$$x_1 + x_2 \leq 1$$

and

$$x_1 \geq 0, x_2 \geq 0.$$

(*b*) Maximize $\{x_1 + 2x_2\}$,

subject to

$$x_1^2 + x_2^2 \leq 1$$
$$2x_1 + x_2 \leq 2$$

and

$$x_1 \geq 0, x_2 \geq 0.$$

5 Consider the quadratic programming problem

$$\text{Maximize} \quad \{4x_1 - x_1^2 + 8x_2 - x_2^2\},$$

subject to

$$x_1 + x_2 \leq 2$$

and

$$x_1 \geq 0, x_2 \geq 0.$$

(*a*) Use the ***Kuhn–Tucker conditions*** to derive the optimal solution.
(*b*) Now suppose that this problem is to be solved by the procedure described in Sec. 18.2. Formulate the ***equivalent problem*** that is to be solved by a modification of the simplex method.
(*c*) Solve the problem as formulated in part (*b*).

6 Consider the quadratic programming problem

$$\text{Maximize} \quad \{10x_1 + 4x_2 - x_1^2 + 4x_1x_2 - 5x_2^2\},$$

subject to

$$x_1 + x_2 \leq 6$$
$$4x_1 + x_2 \leq 18$$

and

$$x_1 \geq 0, x_2 \geq 0.$$

Suppose this problem is to be solved by the procedure described in Sec. 18.2.
(*a*) Formulate the ***equivalent problem*** that is to be solved by a modification of the simplex method.
(*b*) Solve the problem as formulated in part (*a*).

7 Starting from the initial trial solution $(x_1, x_2) = (0,0)$, use the ***gradient search procedure*** to solve the problem

$$\text{Maximize} \quad f(\mathbf{x}) = 2x_1x_2 + 8x_2 - 12x_1 - 2x_1^2 - x_2^2.$$

8 Starting from the initial trial solution $(x_1, x_2) = (0,0)$, use the ***gradient search procedure*** to solve each of the following problems:

(*a*) Maximize $f(\mathbf{x}) = x_1x_2 + 3x_2 - x_1^2 - x_2^2$.
(*b*) Minimize $f(\mathbf{x}) = x_1^2x_2^2 - 10x_1x_2^2 - 2x_1^2x_2 + 20x_1x_2 + x_1^2 + 25x_2^2$.

9 Use the ***sequential unconstrained minimization technique*** to solve the problem

$$\text{Minimize} \quad g(\mathbf{x}) = x_1^2 - 6x_1 + 9 + 2x_2,$$

subject to

$$x_1 \geq 3$$
$$x_2 \geq 3.$$

[Derive the minimizing solution of $P(\mathbf{x}; r)$ analytically, and use the same sequence of values of r as in Table 18.1.]

10 Use the *sequential unconstrained minimization technique* to solve the problem

$$\text{Minimize} \quad g(\mathbf{x}) = x_1^2 + x_2^2 + x_1 + x_2 - x_1x_2,$$

subject to

$$x_1 \geq 0.$$

[Use the *gradient search procedure* to obtain the minimizing solution of $P(\mathbf{x}; r)$ at each iteration, with $r = 1, 10^{-2}, 10^{-4}$. Begin with the initial trial solution $(x_1, x_2) = (1,1)$, and then begin each of the next two iterations with the minimizing solution from the preceding iteration.]

19 Operations Research in Perspective

19.1 INTRODUCTION

The bulk of this book has been devoted to the mathematical methods of operations research. This is quite appropriate because these quantitative techniques form the main part of what is known about operations research. However, it does not imply that practical operations research studies are primarily mathematical exercises. As a matter of fact, the mathematical analysis often represents only a relatively small part of the total effort required. The purpose of this chapter is to place things into better perspective by describing all the major phases of a typical operations research study.

One way of summarizing the usual phases of an operations research study is the following[1]:

1. Formulating the problem.
2. Constructing a mathematical model to represent the system under study.
3. Deriving a solution from the model.
4. Testing the model and the solution derived from it.
5. Establishing controls over the solution.
6. Putting the solution to work: implementation.

Each of these phases will be discussed in turn in the following sections.

[1] Russell L. Ackoff, "The Development of Operations Research as a Science," *Operations Research*, 4:265f, 1956.

19.2 FORMULATING THE PROBLEM

In contrast to textbook examples, most practical problems are initially communicated to an operations research team in a vague, imprecise way. Therefore the first order of business is to study the relevant system and develop a well-defined statement of the problem to be considered. This includes determining such things as the appropriate objectives, the constraints on what can be done, interrelationships between the area to be studied and other areas of the organization, the possible alternative courses of action, time limits for making a decision and so on. This process of problem formulation is a crucial one because it greatly affects how relevant the conclusions of the study will be. It is difficult to extract a "right" answer from the "wrong" problem! Therefore this phase should be executed with considerable care, and the initial formulation should be continually reexamined in the light of new insights obtained during the later phases.

Determining the appropriate objectives is a very important aspect of problem formulation. To do this it is necessary to first identify the person (or persons) who will be making the decisions concerning the system under study and then to probe into all his pertinent objectives relative to the problem. After eliciting the decision maker's objectives, they should be analyzed and edited to identify the ultimate objectives that encompass the others, to determine the relative importance of these ultimate objectives and, to state them precisely in a way that does not eliminate worthwhile goals and alternatives.

By its nature, operations research is concerned with the welfare of the entire organization rather than that of only certain of its components. Thus an operations research study seeks solutions that are optimal for the overall organization rather than suboptimal solutions that are best for only one component. Therefore the objectives that are formulated should ideally be those of the entire organization. However, this is not always convenient to do. Many problems primarily concern only a portion of the organization, so the analysis would become unwieldy if the stated objectives were too general and if explicit consideration were given to all side effects on the rest of the organization. Granted that operations research takes the viewpoint of the overall organization, this does not imply that each problem should be broadened into a study of the entire organization. Instead, the objectives used in the study should be as specific as they can be while still encompassing the main goals of the decision maker and maintaining a reasonable degree of consistency with the higher level objectives of the organization. Side effects on other segments of the organization must then be considered only to the extent that there are questions of consistency with these higher level objectives.

One possible approach to circumventing the problem of suboptimization discussed above is to use long-run profit maximization as the sole objective. At first glance this approach appears to have considerable merit. In particular, the objective of long-run profit maximization is specific enough to be used conveniently, and yet it seems to be broad enough to encompass the basic goal of most organizations. In fact, some people tend to feel that all other legitimate objectives can be translated into this one. However, this is such an oversimplification that considerable caution is required! A number of studies have found that instead of profit maximization, the goal of satisfactory profits combined with other objectives is characteristic of American corporations. In particular, typical objectives might be to maintain stable profits, increase (or maintain) one's share of the market, product diversification, maintain stable prices, improve worker morale, maintain family control of the business, and increase company prestige. These objectives might be compatible with long-run profit maximization, but the relationship is sufficiently obscure that it may not be convenient to incorporate them into this one objective. Furthermore, there are additional considerations involving social responsibilities that are distinct from the profit motive. The five parties affected by a business firm are (1) the owners (stockholders), who desire profits (dividends, stock appreciation, and so on; (2) the employees, who desire steady employment at reasonable wages; (3) the customers who desire a reliable product at a reasonable price; (4) the vendors, who desire integrity and a reasonable selling price for their goods; and (5) the government and, hence, the nation, which desires payment of fair taxes and consideration of the national interest. All five parties make essential contributions to the firm, and the firm should not be viewed as the exclusive servant of any one party for the exploitation of the others. Therefore, although granting that management's prime responsibility is to make profits, its broader social responsibilities also must be recognized.

19.3 CONSTRUCTING A MATHEMATICAL MODEL

After formulating the decision maker's problem, the next phase is to reformulate this problem into a form that is convenient for analysis. The conventional operations research approach for doing this is to construct a mathematical model that represents the essence of the problem.

Mathematical models have many advantages over a verbal description of the problem. One obvious advantage is that a mathematical model describes a problem much more concisely. This tends to make the overall structure of the problem more comprehensible, and it helps to reveal important cause-and-effect relationships. In this way it indicates more clearly what additional data are relevant to the analysis. It also facilitates dealing with the problem in its entirety and considering all its interelationships simultaneously. Finally, a mathematical model forms a bridge to the use of high-powered mathematical techniques and electronic computers to analyze the problem.

On the other hand, there are pitfalls to be avoided when using mathematical models. Such a model is necessarily an abstract idealization of the problem, and approximations and simplifying assumptions generally are required if the model is to be tractable. Therefore care must be taken to ensure that the model remains a valid representation of the problem. The proper criterion for judging the validity of a model is whether or not it predicts the relative effects of the alternative courses of action with sufficient accuracy to permit a sound decision. Therefore it is not necessary to include unimportant details or factors that have approximately the same effect for all the alternative courses of action considered. It is not even necessary that the absolute magnitude of the measure of effectiveness be approximately correct for the various alternatives, provided that their relative values (i.e., the differences between their values) are sufficiently precise. Thus, all that is required is that there be a high *correlation* between the prediction by the model and what would actually happen in the real world. To ascertain whether this requirement is satisfied or not, it is important to do considerable testing and consequent modifying of the model, which will be the subject of Sec. 19.5.

A crucial step in formulating the mathematical model is constructing the objective function. This requires developing a quantitative measure of effectiveness relative to each objective. If more than one objective has been formulated for the study, it is then necessary to tranform and combine the respective measures into a composite measure of effectiveness. This composite measure would sometimes be something tangible (e.g., profit) corresponding to a higher goal of the organization, or it would sometimes need to be abstract (e.g., "utility"). In the latter case the task of developing this measure tends to be a complex one requiring a careful comparison of the objectives and their relative importance. After developing the composite measure of effectiveness, the objective function is then obtained by expressing this measure as a mathematical function of the decision variables.

19.4 DERIVING A SOLUTION

After formulating a mathematical model for the problem under consideration, the next phase in an operations research study is to derive a solution from this model. Since most of this book has been devoted to the subject of how to obtain solutions for various important types of mathematical models, little needs to be said about it here. However, it may be worthwhile to discuss briefly the nature of such solutions.

A common theme in operations research is the search for an "optimal," or best, solution. Indeed, many procedures have been developed, and are presented in this book, for finding such solutions for certain kinds of problems. However, it needs to be recognized that these solutions are optimal only with respect to the model being used. Since the model necessarily is an idealized rather than exact representation of the real problem, there can not be any Utopian guarantee tha the optimal solution for the model will prove to be the best possible solution that could have been implemented for the real problem. With the many imponderables and uncertainties associated with most real problems, this is only to be expected. However, if the model is well formulated and tested, the resulting solution should tend to be a good approximation to the ideal course of action for the real problem. Therefore, rather than be deluded into demanding the impossible, the test of the practical success of an operations research study should be whether it provides a better guide for action than can be obtained by other means.

The eminent management scientist Herbert Simon has intoduced the concept that the goal of an operations research study should be to "satisfice" rather than optimize. In other words, the appropriate goal is to find a good answer, one that the decision maker considers a satisfactory guide for action in a reasonable period of time, rather than to search for an optimal solution. Or to put this in another way that reconciles the two viewpoints, the goal should be to conduct the study in an optimal manner, regardless of whether this involves finding an optimal solution to the model or not. Thus, in addition to considering the composite measure of effectiveness in the model, one should also consider the cost of the study and the disadvantages of delaying its completion and then attempt to maximize the net benefits resulting from the study. In recognition of this concept, operations research teams occasionally use only "heuristic" procedures (i.e., intuitively designed procedures that do not guarantee an optimal solution) to find a good "suboptimal" solution. This is especially the case when the time or cost required to find an optimal solution for an adequate model of the problem would be very large.

The discussion thus far has implied that an operations research study seeks to find only one solution (which may or may not be required to be optimal). In fact, this is often not the case. An optimal solution for the original model may be far from ideal for the real problem. Therefore it is common to obtain a sequence of solutions that comprise a series of improving approximations to the ideal course of action. Thus the apparent weaknesses in the initial solution are used to suggest improvements in the model, its input data, and perhaps the solution procedure. (Sensitivity analysis also may be conducted to determine which input parameters are most critical in determining the solution and therefore require more careful estimation.) A new solution is then obtained, and the cycle is repeated. This process continues until the improvements in the succeeding solutions become too small to warrant continuation. Even then, a number of alternative solutions (perhaps solutions that are optimal for one of several plausible versions of the model and its input data) may be presented to the decision maker for the final selection. This would normally be done whenever the final choice among these decisions should be based on considerations that are best left to the judgment of the decision maker.

Ways in which the model and its solution are evaluated and improved will be discussed in the next section.

19.5 TESTING THE MODEL AND SOLUTION

One of the first lessons of operations research is that it is not generally sufficient to rely solely on one's intuition. This applies not only in obtaining a solution to a problem but also in evaluating the model that has been formulated to represent this problem. As indicated in Sec. 19.3, the proper criterion for judging the validity of a model is whether or not it predicts the relative effects of the alternative courses of action with sufficient accuracy to permit a sound decision. No matter how plausible the model may appear to be, it should not be accepted on faith that this condition is satisfied. Given the difficulty of communicating and understanding all the aspects and subtleties of a complex operational problem, there is a distinct possibility that the operations research team either has not been given all the true facts of the situation or has not interpreted them properly. For example, an important factor or interrelationship may not have been incorporated into the model, or perhaps certain input parameters have not been estimated accurately.

Before undertaking more elaborate tests, it is well to begin by checking for obvious errors or oversights in the model. Reexamining the formulation of the problem and comparing it with the model may help to reveal any such mistakes. Another useful check is to make sure that all the mathematical expressions are dimensionally consistent in the units they use. Additional insight into the validity of the model can sometimes be obtained by varying the input parameters and/or the decision variables and checking if the output from the model behaves in a plausible manner. This is often especially revealing when the parameters or variables are assigned extreme values near their maxima or minima. Finally, either the operations research team or the decision maker may detect shortcomings in the solution yielded by the model that will suggest particular omissions or errors in the model.

A more systematic approach to testing the model is to use a "retrospective" test. When it is applicable, this test involves using historical data to reconstruct the past and then determining how well the model and the resulting solution would have performed if it had been used. Comparing the effectiveness of this hypothetical performance with what actually happened then indicates whether using this model tends to yield a significant improvement over current practice or not. It may also indicate areas where the model has shortcomings and requires modifications. Furthermore, by using alternative solutions from the model and determining their hypothetical historical performances, considerable evidence can be gathered regarding how well the model predicts the relative effects of alternative courses of actions. On the other hand, a disadvantage of retrospective testing is that it uses the same data that guided the formulation of the model. The crucial question is whether or not the past is truely representative of the future. If it is not, then the model might perform quite differently in the future than it would have in the past.

To circumvent this disadvantage of retrospective testing, it is sometimes useful to temporarily continue the status quo. This provides new data that were not available when the model was constructed. These data are then used in the same ways as described above to evaluate the model.

If the final solution is used repeatedly, it is important to continue checking the model and solution after the initial implementation to make sure that they remain valid. The establishment of such controls is the subject of the next section.

19.6 ESTABLISHING CONTROL OVER THE SOLUTION

Suppose that after a series of tests and consequent improvements an acceptable model and solution are developed. Suppose further that this solution is to be used repeatedly. It is evident that this one remains a valid solution for the real problem only as long as this specific model remains valid. However, conditions are constantly changing in the real world. Therefore changes might occur that would indeed invalidate this model; e.g., the values of the input parameters may change significantly. If this should happen, it is vital that it be detected as soon as possible, so that the model, its solution, and the resulting course of action can be modified accordingly. Thus, whenever a solution and the resulting strategy for future action are applied repeatedly, this solution must be controlled in a way such as that described below.

In addition to maintaining a general surveillance of the situation, it is often worthwhile to establish systematic procedures for controlling the solution. To do this it is necessary to identify the critical input parameters of the model, i.e., those parameters subject to changes that would significantly affect the solution. This is done by sensitivity analysis, whereby the respective parameters are varied over their possible values to determine the degree of variation in the resulting solution. Next, a procedure is established for detecting statistically significant changes in each of these critical parameters. This can sometimes be done by the process control charts used in statistical quality control. Finally, provision is made for adjusting the solution and consequent course of action whenever such a change is detected.

19.7 IMPLEMENTATION

The last phase of an operations research study is to implement the final solution as approved by the decision maker. This phase is a critical one because it is here, and only here, that the benefits of the study are reaped. Therefore it is important for the operations research team to participate in launching this phase, both to make sure that the solution is accurately translated into an operating procedure and to rectify any flaws in the solution that are then uncovered.

The success of the implementation phase depends a great deal upon the support of both top management and operating management (or their counterparts in nonbusiness organizations). Therefore the operations research team should encourage the active participation of management in formulating the problem and evaluating the solution. Obtaining the guidance of management is valuable in its own right for identifying relevant special considerations and thereby avoiding potential pitfalls during these phases. However, by making management a party to the study, this also serves to enlist their active support for its implementation.

The implementation phase involves several steps. First, the operations research team gives operating management a careful explanation of the solution to be adopted and how it relates to operating realities. Next, these two parties share the responsibility for developing the procedures required to put this solution into operation. Operating management then sees that a detailed indoctrination is given to the personnel involved, and the new course of action is initiated. Finally, if the nature of the problem permits it, the initial experience with this course of action is used by the operations research team to detect modifications that should be made in the future.

In concluding this discussion of the major phases of an operations research study, it should be emphasized that there are many exceptions to the "rules" prescribed above. By its very nature, operations research (i.e., research on operations) requires considerable ingenuity and innovation, so it is impossible to write down any standard procedure that should always be followed by operations research teams. Rather, the above description may be viewed as a "model" that roughly represents how successful operations research studies are conducted.

Selected References

1 Ackoff, Russell and Patrick Rivett: *A Manager's Guide to Operations Research*, Wiley, New York, 1963.

2 Arrow, Kenneth J.: "Decision Theory and Operations Research," *Operations Research*, **5**:765–774, 1957.

3 Huysmans, Jan H. B. M.: The Implementation of Operations Research, Wiley, New York, 1970.

4 Miller, David W. and Martin K. Starr: *Executive Decisions and Operations Research*, 2d ed., Prentice-Hall, Englewood Cliffs, N.J., 1969.

5 Shuchman, Abe: *Scientific Decision Making in Business* (Readings in Operations Research for Nonmathematicians), parts I and II, Holt, Rinehart, and Winston, New York, 1963.

Appendixes

1 Convexity

The concept of convexity is frequently used in operations research work. Therefore the properties of convex (or concave) functions and convex sets are introduced in turn below.

DEFINITION A function of a single variable, say, $f(x)$ is a *convex function* if, for each pair of values of x, say, x' and x'',

$$f[\lambda x'' + (1-\lambda)x'] \leq \lambda f(x'') + (1-\lambda)f(x')$$

for all values of λ such that $0 \leq \lambda \leq 1$. It is a *strictly convex function* if $\leq$ can be replaced by $<$. It is a *concave function* (or a *strictly concave function*) if this statement holds when $\leq$ is replaced by $\geq$ (or by $>$).

This definition also has an enlightening geometrical interpretation. Consider the graph of the function $f(x)$ drawn as a function of x. Then $[x', f(x')]$ and $[x'', f(x'')]$ are two points on the graph of $f(x)$, and $[\lambda x'' + (1-\lambda)x',\ \lambda f(x'') + (1-\lambda)f(x')]$ represents the various points on the line segment between these two points when $0 \leq \lambda \leq 1$. Thus the original inequality in the definition indicates that this line segment lies entirely above or on the graph of the function. Therefore $f(x)$ is convex if, for each pair of points on the graph of $f(x)$, the line segment joining these two points lies entirely above or on the graph of $f(x)$. In other words, $f(x)$ is convex if it is "always bending upward." To be more precise, if $f(x)$ possesses a second derivative everywhere, then $f(x)$ is convex if and only if $d^2f(x)/dx^2 \geq 0$ for all values of x [for which $f(x)$ is defined]. Similarly, $f(x)$ is strictly convex when $d^2f(x)/dx^2 > 0$, concave when $d^2f(x)/dx^2 \leq 0$, and strictly concave when $d^2f(x)/dx^2 < 0$. Some examples are given in Figs. A1.1 to A1.4.

The concept of a convex function also generalizes to functions of more than one variable. Thus if $f(x)$ is replaced by $f(x_1, x_2, \ldots, x_n)$, the definition given above still

Figure A1.1 A convex function.

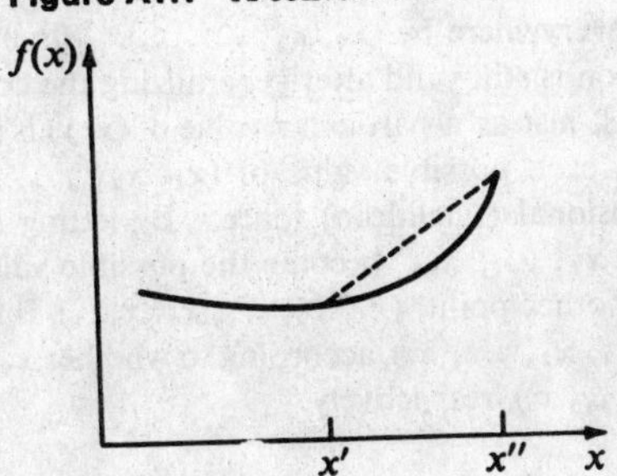

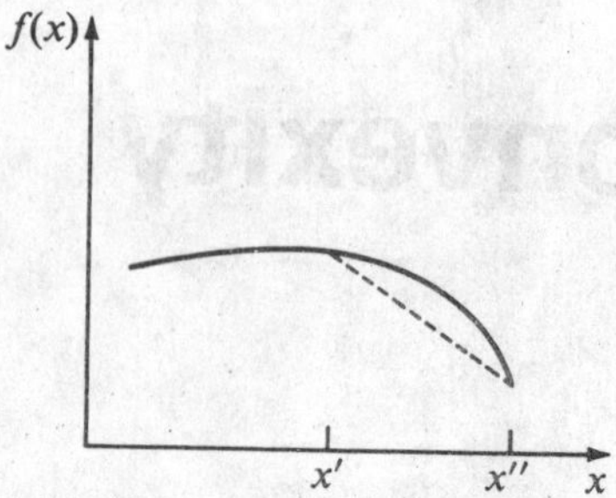

Figure A1.2 A concave function.

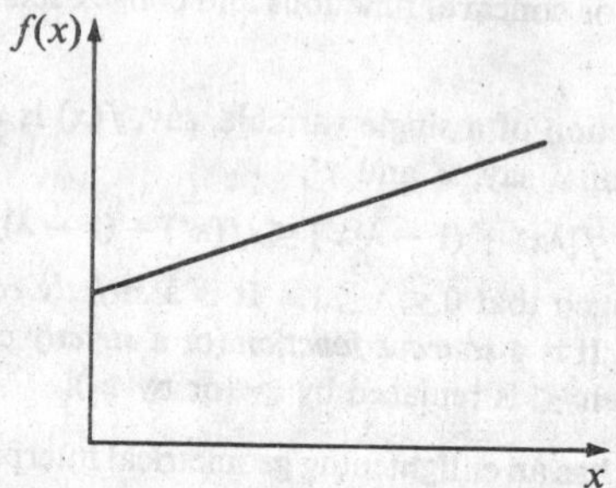

Figure A1.3 A function that is both convex and concave.

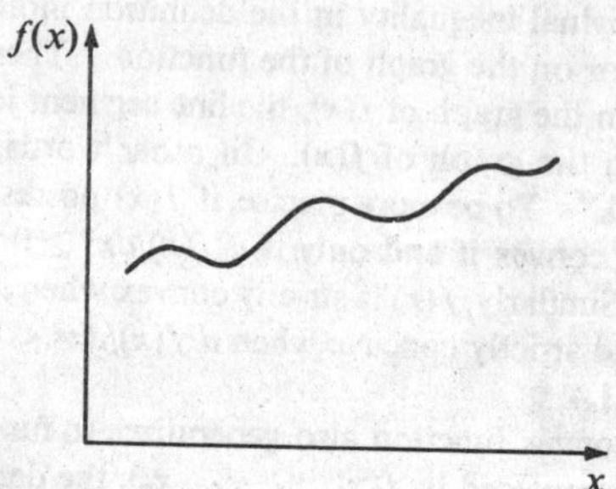

Figure A1.4 A function that is neither convex nor concave.

applies if x is replaced everywhere by $(x_1, x_2, \ldots, x_n)$. Similarly, the corresponding geometrical interpretation is still valid after generalizing the concepts of "points" and "line segments." Thus, just as a particular value of (x, y) is interpreted as a point in two-dimensional space, each possible value of $(x_1, x_2, \ldots, x_m)$ may be thought of as a point in m-dimensional (Euclidean) space. By letting $m = n + 1$, the "points on the graph of $f(x_1, x_2, \ldots, x_n)$" become the possible values of $(x_1, x_2, \ldots, x_n, f(x_1, x_2, \ldots, x_n))$. Another point, $(x_1, x_2, \ldots, x_n, x_{n+1})$, is said to lie above, on, or below the graph of $f(x_1, x_2, \ldots, x_n)$, according to whether x_{n+1} is larger, equal to, or smaller than $f(x_1, x_2, \ldots, x_n)$, respectively.

Definition The *line segment* joining any two points $(x_1', x_2', \ldots, x_m')$ and $(x_1'', x_2'', \ldots, x_m'')$ is the collection of points

$$(x_1, x_2, \ldots, x_m) = [\lambda x_1'' + (1 - \lambda)x_1', \lambda x_2'' + (1 - \lambda)x_2', \ldots, \lambda x_m'' + (1 - \lambda)x_m'],$$

such that $0 \leq \lambda \leq 1$.

Thus a line segment in m-dimensional space is a direct generalization of a line segment in two-dimensional space. For example, if

$$(x_1', x_2') = (2,6), (x_1'', x_2'') = (3,4),$$

then the line segment joining them is the collection of points

$$(x_1, x_2) = [3\lambda + 2(1 - \lambda), 4\lambda + 6(1 - \lambda)],$$

where $0 \leq \lambda \leq 1$.

Definition $f(x_1, x_2, \ldots, x_n)$ is a *convex function* if, for each pair of points on the graph of $f(x_1, x_2, \ldots, x_n)$, the line segment joining these two points lies entirely above or on the graph of $f(x_1, x_2, \ldots, x_n)$. It is a *strictly convex function* if this line segment actually lies entirely above this graph except at the end points of the line segment. *Concave* and *strictly concave* functions are defined in exactly the same way, except that "above" would be replaced by "below."

Just as the second derivative can be used (when it exists everywhere) to check whether a function of a single variable is convex or not, so second partial derivatives can be used to check functions of several variables, although in a more complicated way. For example, if there are two variables, then $f(x_1, x_2)$ is convex if and only if

(1) $$\frac{\partial^2 f(x_1, x_2)}{\partial x_1^2} \frac{\partial^2 f(x_1, x_2)}{\partial x_2^2} - \left[\frac{\partial^2 f(x_1, x_2)}{\partial x_1 \, \partial x_2}\right]^2 \geq 0,$$

(2) $$\frac{\partial^2 f(x_1, x_2)}{\partial x_1^2} \geq 0,$$

and

(3) $$\frac{\partial^2 f(x_1, x_2)}{\partial x_2^2} \geq 0,$$

for all possible values of (x_1, x_2), assuming that these partial derivatives exist everywhere. It is strictly convex if $\geq$ can be replaced by $>$ in all three conditions [but now condition (3) is superfluous and can be omitted because it is implied by the other two conditions], whereas $f(x_1, x_2)$ is concave if $\geq$ can be replaced by $\leq$ in conditions (2) and (3). When there are more than two variables, the conditions foe convexity are a generalization of them. In mathematical terminology, $f(x_1, x_2, \ldots, x_n)$ is convex if and only if its "$n \times n$ Hessian matrix is positive semidefinite" for all possible values of $(x_1, x_2, \ldots, x_n)$.

Thus far convexity has been treated as a general property of a function. However, many nonconvex functions do satisfy the conditions for convexity over certain intervals for the respective variables. Therefore it is meaningful to talk about a function being "convex over a certain region." For example, a function is said to be convex within a neighborhood of a specified point if its second derivative (or partial derivatives) satisfy the conditions for convexity at that point. This concept is useful in Appendix 2.

Finally, two particularly important properties of convex functions should be mentioned. First, if $f(x_1, x_2, \ldots, x_n)$ is a convex function, then $g(x_1, x_2, \ldots, x_n) = -f(x_1, x_2, \ldots, x_n)$ is a concave function, and vice versa. Second, the sum of convex functions is a convex function. To illustrate,

$$f_1(x_1) = x_1^4 + 2x_1^2 - 5x_1$$

and

$$f_2(x_1, x_2) = x_1^2 + 2x_1x_2 + x_2^2$$

are both convex functions, as the reader can verify by calculating their second derivatives. Therefore the sum of these functions,

$$f(x_1, x_2) = x_1^4 + 3x_1^2 - 5x_1 + 2x_1x_2 + x_2^2,$$

is a convex function, whereas its negative,

$$g(x_1, x_2) = -x_1^4 - 3x_1^2 + 5x_1 - 2x_1x_2 - x_2^2,$$

is a concave function.

The concept of a convex function leads quite naturally to the related concept of a *convex set*. Thus, if $f(x_1, x_2, \ldots, x_n)$ is a convex function, then the collection of points that lie above or on the graph of $f(x_1, x_2, \ldots, x_n)$ form a convex set. Similarly, the collection of points that lie below or on the graph of a concave function is a convex set. These cases are illustrated in Figs. A1.5 and A1.6 for the case of a single independent variable. Furthermore, convex sets have the important property that, for

Figure A1.5 Example of a convex set determined by a convex function.

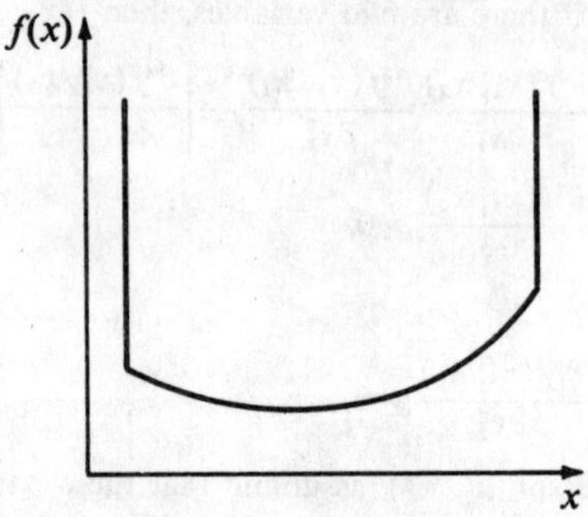

Figure A1.6 Example of a convex set determined by a concave function.

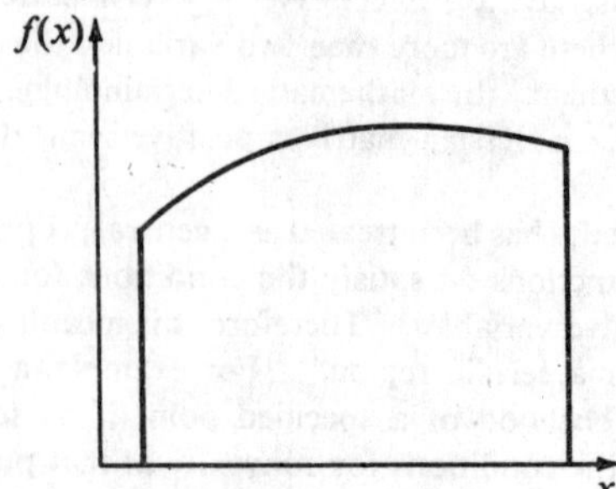

any given group of convex sets, the collection of points that lie in all of them is also a convex set. Therefore the collection of points that lie both above or on a convex function and below or on a concave function is a convex set, as illustrated in Fig. A1.7. Thus convex sets may be viewed intuitively as a collection of points whose "bottom boundary" is a convex function and whose "top boundary" is a concave function. To be a bit more precise, a convex set may be defined as follows:

DEFINITION A *convex set* is a collection of points such that, for each pair of points in the collection, the entire line segment joining these two points is also in the collection.

The distinction between nonconvex sets and convex sets is illustrated in Figs. A1.8 and A1.9. Thus the set of points shown in Fig. A1.8 is not a convex set because there exist many pairs of these points, for example, (1,2) and (2,1), such that the line segment between them does not lie entirely within the set. This is not the case for the set in Fig. A1.9, which is convex.

In conclusion, the useful concept of an ***extreme point*** of a convex set needs to be introduced.

Figure A1.7 Example of a convex set determined by both convex and concave functions.

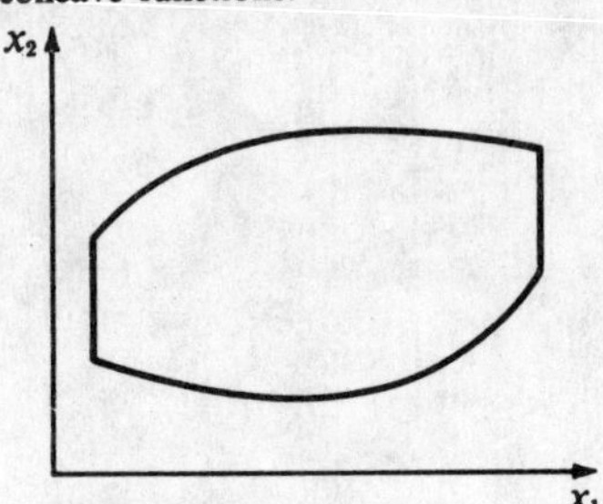

Figure A1.8 Example of a set that is not convex.

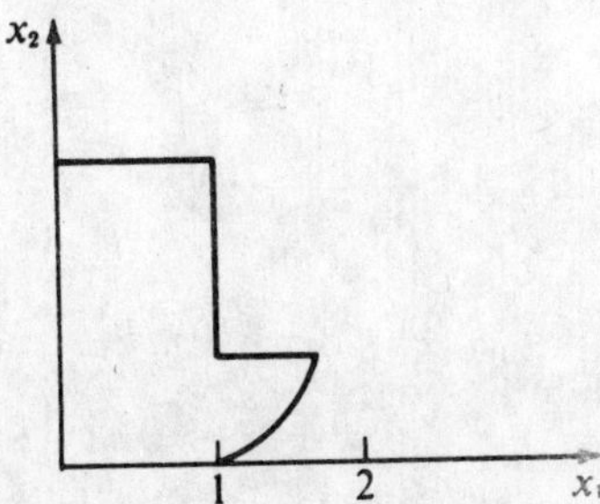

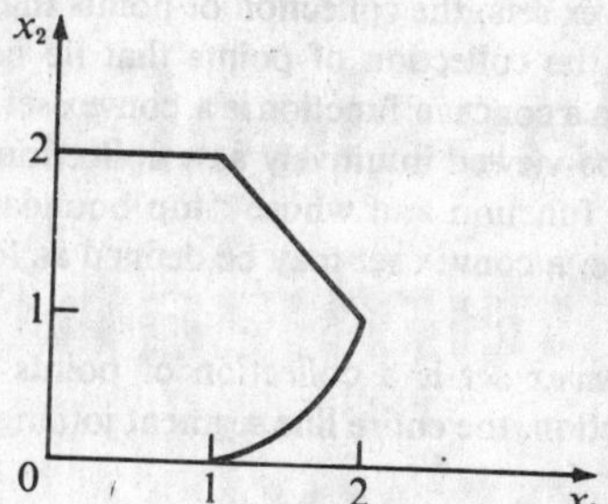

Figure A1.9 Example of a convex set.

Definition An *extreme point* of a convex set is a point in the set that does not lie on any line segment which joins two other points in the set.

Thus the extreme points of the convex set in Fig. A1.9 are (0,0), (0,2), (1,2), (2,1), (1,0) and all the infinite number of points on the boundary between (2,1) and (1,0). If this particular boundary were a straight line instead, then the set would have only the five listed extreme points.

2 Classical Optimization Methods

This appendix briefly reviews the classical methods of calculus for finding a solution that maximizes or minimizes (1) a function of a single variable, (2) a function of several variables, and (3) a function of several variables subject to constraints on the values of these variables. It is assumed that the functions considered possess continuous first and second derivatives and partial derivatives everywhere.

Consider a function of a single variable, such as that shown in Fig. A2.1. A necessary condition for a particular solution, $x = x^*$, to be either a minimum or a maximum is that

$$\frac{df(x)}{dx} = 0 \text{ at } x = x^*.$$

Thus in Fig. A2.1 there are five solutions satisfying these conditions. To obtain more information about these five so-called *critical points*, it is necessary to examine the second derivative. Thus, if

$$\frac{d^2f(x)}{dx^2} > 0 \text{ at } x = x^*,$$

Figure A2.1 A function having several maxima and minima.

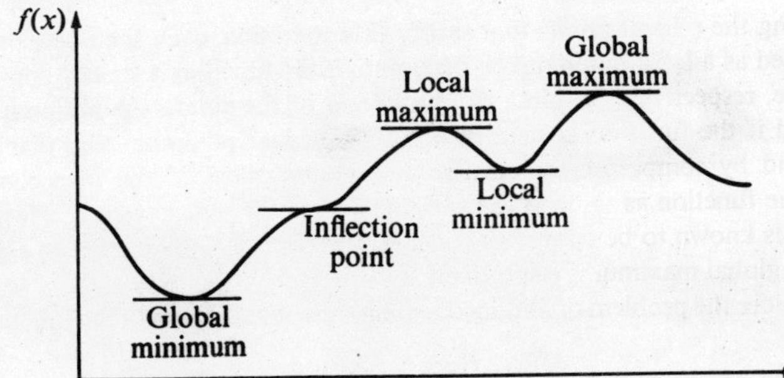

then x^* must be at least a *local minimum* [that is, $f(x^*) \leq f(x)$ for all x sufficiently close to x^*]. Using the language introduced in Appendix 1, this says that x^* must be a local minimum if $f(x)$ is strictly convex within a neighborhood of x^*. Similarly, a sufficient condition for x^* to be a *local maximum* (given that it satisfies the necessary condition) is that $f(x)$ is strictly concave within a neighborhood of x^* (that is, the second derivative is negative at x^*). If the second derivative is zero, the issue is not resolved (the point may even be an inflection point), and it is necessary to examine higher derivatives.

To find a global minimum [i.e., a solution x^* such that $f(x^*) \leq f(x)$ for all x], it is necessary to compare the local minima and identify the one that yields the smallest value of $f(x)$. If this value is less than $f(x)$ as $x \to -\infty$ and as $x \to +\infty$ (or at the end points of the function, if it is only defined over a finite interval), then this point is a global minimum. Such a point is shown in Fig. A2.1, along with the global maximum identified in an analogous way.

However, if $f(x)$ is known to be either a convex or concave function (see Appendix 1 for a description of such functions), the analysis becomes much simpler. In particular, if $f(x)$ is a convex function, such as shown in Fig. A1.1, then any solution x^*, such that

$$\frac{df(x)}{dx} = 0 \text{ at } x = x^*,$$

is known automatically to be a global minimum. In other words, this condition is not only a necessary but a sufficient condition for a global minimum of a convex function. If this function actually is strictly convex, then this solution must be the only global minimum. (However, if the function is either always decreasing or always increasing, so the derivatve is nonzero for all values of x, then there will be no global minimum at a finite value of x.) Otherwise, there could be a tie for the global minimum over a single interval where the derivative is zero. Similarly, if $f(x)$ is a concave function, then having

$$\frac{df(x)}{dx} = 0 \text{ at } x = x^*$$

becomes both a necessary and sufficient condition for x^* to be a global maximum.

The analysis for an unconstrained function of several variables, $f(x_1, x_2, \ldots, x_n)$, is similar. Thus a necessary condition for a solution $(x_1, x_2, \ldots, x_n) = (x_1^*, x_2^*, \ldots, x_n^*)$ to be either a minimum or a maximum is that

$$\frac{\partial f(x_1, \ldots, x_n)}{\partial x_j} = 0 \text{ at } (x_1, \ldots, x_n) = (x_1^*, \ldots, x_n^*), \text{ for } j = 1, 2, \ldots, n.$$

After identifying the critical points that satisfy this condition, each such point would then be classified as a local minimum or maximum if the function is strictly convex or strictly concave, respectively, within a neighborhood of the point. (Additional analysis is required if the function is neither one.) The global minimum and maximum would be found by comparing the relative minima and maxima and then checking the value of the function as some of the variables approach $-\infty$ or $+\infty$. However, if the function is known to be convex or concave, then a critical point must be a global minimum or a global maximum, respectively.

Now consider the problem of finding the minimum or maximum of the function

$$f(x_1, x_2, \ldots, x_n),$$

subject to the restriction that $(x_1, x_2, \ldots, x_n)$ must satisfy all the equations

$$g_1(x_1, x_2, \ldots, x_n) = b_1$$
$$g_2(x_1, x_2, \ldots, x_n) = b_2$$
$$\vdots$$
$$g_m(x_1, x_2, \ldots, x_n) = b_m,$$

where $m < n$. For example, if $n = 2$ and $m = 1$, the problem might be to

$$\text{Maximize } f(x_1, x_2) = x_1^2 + 2x_2,$$

subject to

$$g(x_1, x_2) = x_1^2 + x_2^2 = 1.$$

In this case (x_1, x_2) is restricted to be on the circle of radius 1, whose center is at the origin, so that the goal is to find the point on this circle which yields the largest value of $f(x_1, x_2)$. This example is soon solved, after outlining a general approach to the problem.

A classical method of dealing with this problem is the *method of Lagrange multipliers.* This procedure begins by formulating the Lagrangean function

$$h(x_1, x_2, \ldots, x_n, \lambda_1, \lambda_2, \ldots, \lambda_m) = f(x_1, x_2, \ldots, x_n) - \sum_{i=1}^{m} \lambda_i[g_i(x_1, x_2, \ldots, x_n) - b_i],$$

where the new variables $\lambda_1, \lambda_2, \ldots, \lambda_m$ are called *Lagrange multipliers.* Notice the key fact that for the permissible values of $(x_1, x_2, \ldots, x_n)$, $g_i(x_1, x_2, \ldots, x_n) - b_i = 0$ for all i. Thus $h(x_1, x_2, \ldots, x_n, \lambda_1, \lambda_2, \ldots, \lambda_m) = f(x_1, x_2, \ldots, x_n)$. Therefore it can be shown that if $(x_1, x_2, \ldots, x_n, \lambda_1, \lambda_2, \ldots, \lambda_m) = (x_1^*, x_2^*, \ldots, x_n^*, \lambda_1^*, \lambda_2^*, \ldots, \lambda_m^*)$ is a local or global minimum or maximum for the unconstrained function $h(x_1, x_2, \ldots, x_n, \lambda_1, \lambda_2, \ldots, \lambda_m)$, then $(x_1^*, x_2^*, \ldots, x_n^*)$ is a corresponding critical point for the original problem. As a result, the method now reduces to analyzing $h(x_1, x_2, \ldots, x_n, \lambda_1, \lambda_2, \ldots, \lambda_m)$ by the procedure described above for unconstrained functions. Thus the $(n + m)$ partial derivatives would be set equal to zero; that is,

$$\frac{\partial h}{\partial x_j} = \frac{\partial f}{\partial x_j} - \sum_{i=1}^{m} \lambda_i \frac{\partial g_i}{\partial x_j} = 0, \qquad \text{for } j = 1, 2, \ldots, n,$$

$$\frac{\partial h}{\partial \lambda_i} = -g_i(x_1, x_2, \ldots, x_n) + b_i = 0, \text{ for } i = 1, 2, \ldots, m,$$

and then the critical points would be obtained by solving these equations for $(x_1, x_2, \ldots, x_n, \lambda_1, \lambda_2, \ldots, \lambda_m)$. Notice that the last m equations are equivalent to the constraints in the original problem, so only permissible solutions are considered. After further analysis to identify the global minimum or maximum of $h(\cdot)$, the resulting value of $(x_1, x_2, \ldots, x_n)$ is then the desired solution to the original problem.

It should be pointed out that from a practical computational viewpoint the method of Lagrange multipliers is not a particularly powerful procedure. It is often essentially impossible to solve the equations to obtain the critical points. Furthermore, even when they can be obtained, the number of critical points may be so large (often infinite) that it is impractical to attempt to identify a global minimum or maximum. However, for certain types of small problems, this method can sometimes be used successfully. To illustrate, consider the example introduced above. In this case

$$h(x_1, x_2) = x_1^2 + 2x_2 - \lambda[x_1^2 + x_2^2 - 1],$$

so that

$$\frac{\partial h}{\partial x_1} = 2x_1 - 2\lambda x_1 = 0.$$

$$\frac{\partial h}{\partial x_2} = 2 - 2\lambda x_2 = 0,$$

$$\frac{\partial h}{\partial \lambda} = -[x_1^2 + x_2^2 - 1] = 0.$$

The first equation implies that either $\lambda = 1$ or $x_1 = 0$. If $\lambda = 1$, then the other two equations imply that $x_2 = 1$ and $x_1 = 0$. If $x_1 = 0$, then the third equation implies that $x_2 = \pm 1$. Therefore the two critical points for the original problem are $(x_1, x_2) = (0,1)$ and $(0, -1)$. Thus it is apparent that these points are the global maximum and minimum, respectively.

In presenting the classical optimization methods described above, it has been assumed that the reader already is familiar with derivatives and how to obtain them. However, there is a special case of importance in operations research work that warrants additional explanation, namely, the derivative of an integral. In particular, consider how to find the derivative of the function

$$F(y) = \int_{g(y)}^{h(y)} f(x,y)\, dx,$$

where $g(y)$ and $h(y)$ are the limits of integration expressed as functions of y. To begin, suppose that these limits of integration are constants, so that $g(y) = a$ and $h(y) = b$, respectively. For this special case it can be shown that, given the regularity conditions assumed at the beginning of this appendix, the derivative is simply

$$\frac{d}{dy} \int_a^b f(x, y)\, dx = \int_a^b \frac{\partial f(x, y)}{\partial y}\, dx.$$

For example, if $f(x, y) = e^{-xy}$, $a = 0$, and $b = \infty$, then

$$\frac{d}{dy} \int_0^\infty e^{-xy}\, dx = \int_0^\infty (-x)e^{-xy}\, dx = -\frac{1}{y^2}$$

at any positive value of y. Thus the intuitive procedure of interchanging the order of differentiation and integration is valid for this case. However, finding the derivative becomes a little more complicated than this when the limits of integration are functions. In particular,

$$\frac{d}{dy} \int_{g(y)}^{h(y)} f(x, y)\, dx = \int_{g(y)}^{h(y)} \frac{\partial f(x, y)}{\partial y}\, dx + f(h(y), y)\frac{dh(y)}{dy} - f(g(y), y)\frac{dg(y)}{dy},$$

where $f(h(y), y)$ is obtained by writing out $f(x, y)$ and then replacing x wherever it appears by $h(y)$, and similarly for $f(g(y), y)$. To illustrate, if $f(x, y) = x^2y^3$, $g(y) = y$, and $h(y) = 2y$, then

$$\frac{d}{dy} \int_y^{2y} x^2y^3\, dx = \int_y^{2y} 3x^2y^2\, dx + (2y)^2y^3(2) - y^2y^3(1) = 14y^5$$

at any positive value of y.

3 Matrices and Matrix Manipulations

A matrix is defined to be a rectangular array of numbers. For example,

$$\mathbf{A} = \begin{bmatrix} 2 & 5 \\ 3 & 0 \\ 1 & 1 \end{bmatrix}$$

is a 3×2 matrix (where 3×2 denotes "3 by 2") because it is a rectangular array of numbers with three rows and two columns. The numbers in the rectangular array are called the "elements" of the matrix. For example,

$$\mathbf{B} = \begin{bmatrix} 1 & 2.4 & 0 & \sqrt{3} \\ -4 & 2 & -1 & 15 \end{bmatrix}$$

is a 2×4 matrix whose elements are 1, 2.4, 0, $\sqrt{3}$, -4, 2, -1, and 15. Thus, in more general terms,

$$\mathbf{A} = \begin{bmatrix} a_{11} & a_{12} & \cdots & a_{1n} \\ a_{21} & a_{22} & \cdots & a_{2n} \\ \vdots & \vdots & & \vdots \\ a_{m1} & a_{m2} & & a_{mn} \end{bmatrix} = \|a_{ij}\|$$

is an $m \times n$ matrix, where $a_{11}, \ldots, a_{mn}$ represent the numbers that are the elements of this matrix; $\|a_{ij}\|$ is shorthand notation for identifying the matrix whose element in row i and column j is a_{ij} for every $i = 1, 2, \ldots, m$ and $j = 1, 2, \ldots, n$.

Since matrices do not possess a numerical value, they can not be added, multiplied, and so on as if they were individual numbers. However, it is sometimes desirable to perform certain manipulations on arrays of numbers. Therefore rules have been developed for performing operations on matrices that are analogous to arithmetic operations. To describe these, let $\mathbf{A} = \|a_{ij}\|$ and $\mathbf{B} = \|b_{ij}\|$ be two matrices having the same number of rows and the same number of columns. Then $\mathbf{A}$ and $\mathbf{B}$ are said to be "equal"; that is, $\mathbf{A} = \mathbf{B}$, if and only if all of the corresponding elements are equal; that is, $a_{ij} = b_{ij}$ for all i and j. The operation of multiplying a matrix by a number (denote this number by k) is performed by multiplying each element of the matrix by k, so that

$$k\mathbf{A} = \|ka_{ij}\|.$$

For example,

$$3\begin{bmatrix} 1 & \frac{1}{3} & 2 \\ 5 & 0 & -3 \end{bmatrix} = \begin{bmatrix} 3 & 1 & 6 \\ 15 & 0 & -9 \end{bmatrix}.$$

To "add" **A** and **B**, simply add the corresponding elements, so that

$$\mathbf{A}+\mathbf{B} = \|a_{ij}+b_{ij}\|.$$

To illustrate,

$$\begin{bmatrix} 5 & 3 \\ 1 & 6 \end{bmatrix} + \begin{bmatrix} 2 & 0 \\ 3 & 1 \end{bmatrix} = \begin{bmatrix} 7 & 3 \\ 4 & 7 \end{bmatrix}.$$

Similarly, "subtraction" is done as

$$\mathbf{A}-\mathbf{B} = \mathbf{A}+(-1)\mathbf{B},$$

so that

$$\mathbf{A}-\mathbf{B} = \|a_{ij}-b_{ij}\|.$$

For example,

$$\begin{bmatrix} 5 & 3 \\ 1 & 6 \end{bmatrix} - \begin{bmatrix} 2 & 0 \\ 3 & 1 \end{bmatrix} = \begin{bmatrix} 3 & 3 \\ -2 & 5 \end{bmatrix}.$$

Note that, with the exception of multiplication by a number, all the above operations are defined only when the two matrices involved are of the same size. However, all of them are straightforward because they only involve performing the same comparison or arithmetic operation on the corresponding elements of the matrices.

There exists one additional elementary operation that has not been defined, multiplication, but it is considerably more complicated. To find the element in row i, column j of the matrix resulting from "multiplying" **A** times **B**, it is necessary to multiply each element in row i of **A** by the corresponding element in column j of **B** and then to add these products. Therefore this matrix multiplication is defined if and only if the number of columns of **A** equals the number of rows of **B** because this is required to perform the specified element-by-element multiplication. Thus, if **A** is an $m \times n$ matrix and **B** is an $n \times r$ matrix, then their product is

$$\mathbf{AB} = \left\| \sum_{k=1}^{n} a_{ik} b_{kj} \right\|.$$

To illustrate,

$$\begin{bmatrix} 1 & 2 \\ 4 & 0 \\ 2 & 3 \end{bmatrix} \begin{bmatrix} 3 & 1 \\ 2 & 5 \end{bmatrix} = \begin{bmatrix} 1(3)+2(2) & 1(1)+2(5) \\ 4(3)+0(2) & 4(1)+0(5) \\ 2(3)+3(2) & 2(1)+3(5) \end{bmatrix} = \begin{bmatrix} 7 & 11 \\ 12 & 4 \\ 12 & 17 \end{bmatrix}$$

On the other hand, if one attempts to multiply these matrices in the reverse order, the resulting product

$$\begin{bmatrix} 3 & 1 \\ 2 & 5 \end{bmatrix} \begin{bmatrix} 1 & 2 \\ 4 & 0 \\ 2 & 3 \end{bmatrix}$$

is not even defined. Even when both **AB** and **BA** are defined,

$$\mathbf{AB} \neq \mathbf{BA}$$

in general. Thus matrix multiplication should be viewed as a specially designed operation whose properties are quite different from those of arithmetic multiplication. To motivate why this special definition was adopted, consider the following system of equations:

$$\begin{aligned} 2x_1 - x_2 + 5x_3 + x_4 &= 20 \\ x_1 + 5x_2 + 4x_3 + 5x_4 &= 30 \\ 3x_1 + x_2 - 6x_3 + 2x_4 &= 20. \end{aligned}$$

Rather than writing these equations "longhand" as shown here, they can be written much more concisely in matrix form as

$$\mathbf{Ax} = \mathbf{b},$$

where

$$\mathbf{A} = \begin{bmatrix} 2 & -1 & 5 & 1 \\ 1 & 5 & 4 & 5 \\ 3 & 1 & -6 & 2 \end{bmatrix}, \mathbf{x} = \begin{bmatrix} x_1 \\ x_2 \\ x_3 \\ x_4 \end{bmatrix}, \mathbf{b} = \begin{bmatrix} 20 \\ 30 \\ 20 \end{bmatrix}.$$

It is this kind of "multiplication" for which matrix multiplication is designed.

Carefully note that matrix division is not defined.

Although the matrix operations described above do not possess certain of the properties of arithmetic operations, they do satisfy the following laws:

$$\begin{aligned} \mathbf{A} + \mathbf{B} &= \mathbf{B} + \mathbf{A}, \\ (\mathbf{A} + \mathbf{B}) + \mathbf{C} &= \mathbf{A} + (\mathbf{B} + \mathbf{C}), \\ \mathbf{A}(\mathbf{B} + \mathbf{C}) &= \mathbf{AB} + \mathbf{AC}, \\ \mathbf{A}(\mathbf{BC}) &= (\mathbf{AB})\mathbf{C} \end{aligned}$$

when the relative sizes of these matrices are such that the indicated operations are defined.

Another type of matrix operation, which has no arithmetic analog, is the transpose operation. This operation involves nothing more than interchanging the rows and columns of the matrix, which is frequently useful for performing the multiplication operation in the desired way. Thus, for any matrix $\mathbf{A} = \|a_{ij}\|$, its transpose $\mathbf{A}^T$ is

$$\mathbf{A}^T = \|a_{ji}\|.$$

For example, if

$$\mathbf{A} = \begin{bmatrix} 2 & 5 \\ 1 & 3 \\ 4 & 0 \end{bmatrix},$$

then

$$\mathbf{A}^T = \begin{bmatrix} 2 & 1 & 4 \\ 5 & 3 & 0 \end{bmatrix}.$$

Zero and 1 are numbers that play a special role in arithmetic. There also exist special matrices that play a similar role in matrix theory. In particular, the matrix "one" is the "identity matrix" **I**, which is a square matrix whose elements are zeros except for ones along the main diagonal. Thus

$$\mathbf{I} = \begin{bmatrix} 1 & 0 & 0 & \dots & 0 \\ 0 & 1 & 0 & \dots & 0 \\ 0 & 0 & 1 & \dots & 0 \\ \vdots & & & & \\ 0 & 0 & 0 & \dots & 1 \end{bmatrix}$$

The number of rows or columns of **I** can be specified as desired. The analogy of **I** to "one" follows from the fact that for any matrix **A**,

$$\mathbf{IA} = \mathbf{A} = \mathbf{AI},$$

where **I** is assigned the appropriate number of rows and columns in each case for the multiplication operation to be defined. Similarly, the matrix "zero" is the so-called "null matrix" **0**, which is a matrix of any size whose elements are all zeros. Thus

$$\mathbf{0} = \begin{bmatrix} 0 & 0 & \dots & 0 \\ 0 & 0 & \dots & 0 \\ \vdots & \vdots & & \vdots \\ 0 & 0 & \dots & 0 \end{bmatrix}$$

Therefore, for any matrix **A**,

$$\mathbf{A} + \mathbf{0} = \mathbf{A},\ \mathbf{A} - \mathbf{A} = \mathbf{0},\ \text{and}\ \mathbf{0A} = \mathbf{0} = \mathbf{A0},$$

where **0** is the appropriate size in each case for the operations to be defined.

On certain occasions it is useful to partition a matrix into several smaller matrices called "submatrices." For example, one possible way of partitioning a 3 × 4 matrix would be

$$\mathbf{A} = \left[\begin{array}{c|ccc} a_{11} & a_{12} & a_{13} & a_{14} \\ \hline a_{21} & a_{22} & a_{23} & a_{24} \\ a_{31} & a_{32} & a_{33} & a_{34} \end{array}\right] = \begin{bmatrix} a_{11} & \mathbf{A}_{12} \\ \mathbf{A}_{21} & \mathbf{A}_{22} \end{bmatrix},$$

where

$$\mathbf{A}_{12} = [a_{12} \quad a_{13} \quad a_{14}],\ \mathbf{A}_{21} = \begin{bmatrix} a_{21} \\ a_{31} \end{bmatrix},\ \mathbf{A}_{22} = \begin{bmatrix} a_{22} & a_{23} & a_{24} \\ a_{32} & a_{33} & a_{34} \end{bmatrix}.$$

Rather than perform operations element by element on such partitioned matrices, they can instead be done in terms of the submatrices, provided the partitionings are such that the operations are defined. For example, if **B** is a partitioned 4 × 1 matrix such that

$$\mathbf{B} = \left[\begin{array}{c} b_1 \\ \hline b_2 \\ b_3 \\ b_4 \end{array}\right] = \begin{bmatrix} b_1 \\ \mathbf{B}_2 \end{bmatrix},$$

$$\mathbf{AB} = \left[\begin{array}{c} a_{11} \quad b_1 \quad + \quad \mathbf{A}_{12} \quad \mathbf{B}_2 \\ \hline \mathbf{A}_{21} \quad b_1 \quad + \quad \mathbf{A}_{22} \quad \mathbf{B}_2 \end{array}\right].$$

A special kind of matrix that plays an important role in matrix theory is that having either a single row or a column. Such matrices are often referred to as "vectors." Thus

$$\mathbf{x} = [x_1, x_2, \ldots, x_n]$$

is a "row" vector, and

$$\mathbf{x} = \begin{bmatrix} x_1 \\ x_2 \\ \vdots \\ x_n \end{bmatrix}$$

is a "column" vector. These vectors also would sometimes be called "*n* vectors" to indicate that they have *n* elements. For example,

$$\mathbf{x} = \left[1, 4, -2, \frac{1}{3}, 7\right]$$

is a "5 vector."

One reason vectors play an important role in matrix theory is that any $m \times n$ matrix can be partitioned into either *m*-row vectors or *n*-column vectors, and important properties of the matrix can be analyzed in terms of these vectors. To amplify, consider a set of *n* vectors, $\mathbf{x}_1, \mathbf{x}_2, \ldots, \mathbf{x}_m$, of the same type (i.e., they are either all row vectors or all column vectors).

DEFINITION A set of vectors $\mathbf{x}_1, \mathbf{x}_2, \ldots, \mathbf{x}_m$ is said to be *linearly dependent* if there exist *m* numbers (denoted by $c_1, c_2, \ldots, c_m$), some of which are not zero, such that

$$c_1\mathbf{x}_1 + c_2\mathbf{x}_2 + \cdots + c_m\mathbf{x}_m = 0.$$

Otherwise, the set is said to be *linearly independent*.

To illustrate, if $m = 3$ and

$$\mathbf{x}_1 = [1, 1, 1]$$
$$\mathbf{x}_2 = [0, 1, 1]$$
$$\mathbf{x}_3 = [2, 5, 5],$$

then

$$2\mathbf{x}_1 + 3\mathbf{x}_2 - \mathbf{x}_3 = 0,$$

so that

$$\mathbf{x}_3 = 2\mathbf{x}_1 + 3\mathbf{x}_2.$$

Thus $\mathbf{x}_1, \mathbf{x}_2, \mathbf{x}_3$ would be linearly dependent because one of them is a linear combination of the others. However, if $\mathbf{x}_3$ were changed to

$$\mathbf{x}_3 = [2, 5, 6]$$

instead, then $\mathbf{x}_1, \mathbf{x}_2, \mathbf{x}_3$ would be linearly independent.

DEFINITION The *rank* of a set of vectors is the largest number of linearly independent vectors that can be chosen from the set.

Continuing the above example, the rank of the set of vectors $\mathbf{x}_1$, $\mathbf{x}_2$, $\mathbf{x}_3$, was 2, but it became 3 after changing $\mathbf{x}_3$.

DEFINITION A *basis* for a set of vectors is a collection of linearly independent vectors taken from the set such that every vector in the set is a linear combination of the vectors in the collection (i.e., every vector in the set equals the sum of certain multiples of the vectors in the collection).

To illustrate, $\mathbf{x}_1$ and $\mathbf{x}_2$ constituted a basis for $\mathbf{x}_1$, $\mathbf{x}_2$, $\mathbf{x}_3$ in the above example before $\mathbf{x}_3$ was changed.

THEOREM A3.1 A collection of r linearly independent vectors chosen from a set of vectors is a basis for the set if and only if the set has rank r.

Given the above results regarding vectors, it is now possible to present certain important concepts regarding matrices.

DEFINITION The *row rank* of a matrix is the rank of its set of row vectors. The *column rank* of a matrix is the rank of its set of column vectors.

For example, if the matrix **A** is

$$\mathbf{A} = \begin{bmatrix} 1 & 1 & 1 \\ 0 & 1 & 1 \\ 2 & 5 & 5 \end{bmatrix},$$

then its row rank was shown above to be 2. Note that the column rank of **A** is also 2. This is no coincidence, as the following general theorem indicates.

THEOREM A3.2 The row rank and column rank of a matrix are the same.

Thus it is only necessary to speak of "the rank" of a matrix.

The final concept to be discussed is that of the "inverse" of a matrix. For any nonzero number k, there exists a reciprocal or inverse, $k^{-1} = 1/k$, such that

$$kk^{-1} = k^{-1}k = 1.$$

Is there an analogous concept that is valid in matrix theory? In other words, for a given matrix **A** other than the null matrix, does there exist a matrix $\mathbf{A}^{-1}$ such that

$$\mathbf{A}\mathbf{A}^{-1} = \mathbf{A}^{-1}\mathbf{A} = \mathbf{I}?$$

If **A** is not a square matrix (i.e., if the number of rows and columns of **A** differ), the answer is "never," because these matrix products would necessarily have a different number of rows for the multiplication to be defined (so that the "equality" operation would not be defined). However, if **A** is square then the answer is "under certain circumstances," as indicated in Theorem A3.3.

DEFINITION A matrix is called *nonsingular* if its rank equals both the number of rows and the number of columns. Otherwise, it is called *singular*.

Thus, only square matrices can be nonsingular. A useful way of testing for nonsingularity is provided by the fact that a square matrix is nonsingular if and only if its determinant is nonzero.

THEOREM A3.3 (*a*) If **A** is nonsingular, there is a unique nonsingular matrix $\mathbf{A}^{-1}$, called the inverse of **A**, such that $\mathbf{AA}^{-1} = \mathbf{I} = \mathbf{A}^{-1}\mathbf{A}$.

(*b*) If **A** is nonsingular and **B** is a matrix for which either $\mathbf{AB} = \mathbf{I}$ or $\mathbf{BA} = \mathbf{I}$, then $\mathbf{B} = \mathbf{A}^{-1}$.

(*c*) Only nonsingular matrices have inverses.

To illustrate, consider the matrix

$$\mathbf{A} = \begin{bmatrix} 5 & -4 \\ 1 & -1 \end{bmatrix}.$$

Notice that the rank of **A** is 2, so it is nonsingular. Therefore **A** must have an inverse, which happens to be

$$\mathbf{A}^{-1} = \begin{bmatrix} 1 & -4 \\ 1 & -5 \end{bmatrix}.$$

Hence,

$$\mathbf{AA}^{-1} = \begin{bmatrix} 5 & -4 \\ 1 & -1 \end{bmatrix} \begin{bmatrix} 1 & -4 \\ 1 & -5 \end{bmatrix} = \begin{bmatrix} 1 & 0 \\ 0 & 1 \end{bmatrix}$$

and

$$\mathbf{A}^{-1}\mathbf{A} = \begin{bmatrix} 1 & -4 \\ 1 & -5 \end{bmatrix} \begin{bmatrix} 5 & -4 \\ 1 & -1 \end{bmatrix} = \begin{bmatrix} 1 & 0 \\ 0 & 1 \end{bmatrix}$$

4 Simultaneous Linear Equations

Consider the system of simultaneous linear equations

$$\begin{aligned} a_{11}x_1 + a_{12}x_2 + \cdots + a_{1n}x_n &= b_1, \\ a_{21}x_1 + a_{22}x_2 + \cdots + a_{2n}x_n &= b_2, \\ &\vdots \\ a_{m1}x_1 + a_{m2}x_2 + \cdots + a_{mn}x_n &= b_m. \end{aligned}$$

It is commonly assumed that this system has a solution, and a unique solution, if and only if $m = n$. However, this is an oversimplification. This raises the question "Under what conditions will these equations have a simultaneous solution?" "Given that they do, when will there be only one such solution?" "If there is a unique solution, how can it be identified in a systematic way?" These are the questions to be explored in this appendix. The discussion of the first two questions assumes that the reader is familiar with the basic information about matrices reviewed in Appendix 3.

The above system of equations can also be written in matrix form as

$$\mathbf{Ax} = \mathbf{b},$$

where

$$\mathbf{A} = \begin{bmatrix} a_{11} & a_{12} & \cdots & a_{1n} \\ a_{21} & a_{22} & \cdots & a_{2n} \\ & \vdots & & \\ a_{m1} & a_{m2} & \cdots & a_{mn} \end{bmatrix}, \quad \mathbf{x} = \begin{bmatrix} x_1 \\ x_2 \\ \vdots \\ x_n \end{bmatrix}, \quad \mathbf{b} = \begin{bmatrix} b_1 \\ b_2 \\ \vdots \\ b_m \end{bmatrix}.$$

The first two questions can be answered immediately in terms of the properties of these matrices. First, the system of equations possesses at least one solution if and only if the rank of **A** equals the rank of **[A, b]**. (Notice that this is guaranteed if the rank of **A** equals m.) This follows immediately from the definitions of rank and linear independence because if the rank of **[A, b]** exceeds the rank of **A** by 1 (the only other possibility), then **b** is linearly independent of the column vectors of **A** (that is, **b** can not equal any linear combination **Ax** of these vectors). Second, given that these ranks are equal, there are then two possibilities. If the rank of **A** is n (its maximum possible value), then the system of equations will possess exactly one solution. [This follows from Theorem A3.1, the definition of a basis, and part (*b*) of Theorem A3.3.] If the rank of **A** is less than n, then there will exist an infinite number of solutions. (This follows from the fact that for any basis of the column vectors of **A**, the x_j corresponding to column vectors not in this basis can be assigned any value, and there will still exist a solution for the other variables as before.) Finally, it should be noted that if **A** and **[A, b]** have a common rank r such that $r < m$, then $(m - r)$ of the equations must be linear combinations of the other ones, so that these $(m-r)$ redundant equations can be deleted without affecting the solution(s).

Now consider how to find a solution to the system of equations. Assume for the moment that $m=n$ and $\mathbf{A}$ is nonsingular, so that a unique solution exists. This solution can be obtained by the *Gauss-Jordan method of elimination*, which proceeds as follows. To begin, eliminate the first variable from all but one (say, the first) of the equations by adding an appropriate multiple of this equation to each of the others. (For convenience, this one equation would be divided by the coefficient of this variable, so that the final value of this coefficient is 1.) Next, proceed in the same way to eliminate the second variable from all equations except one new one (say, the second). Then repeat this for the third variable, the fourth variable, and so on, until each of the n variables remains in only one of the equations and each of the n equations contains exactly one of these variables. The desired solution can then be read from the equations directly.

To illustrate the Gauss-Jordan method of elimination, consider the following system of linear equations:

$$\begin{aligned}
&(1) & x_1 - x_2 + 4x_3 &= 10\\
&(2) & -x_1 + 3x_2 \qquad &= 10\\
&(3) & 2x_2 + 5x_3 &= 22.
\end{aligned}$$

The method begins by eliminating x_1 from all but the first equation. This is done simply by adding Eq. (1) to Eq. (2), which yields

$$\begin{aligned}
&(1) & x_1 - x_2 + 4x_3 &= 10\\
&(2) & 2x_2 + 4x_3 &= 20\\
&(3) & 2x_2 + 5x_3 &= 22.
\end{aligned}$$

The next step is to eliminate x_2 from all but the second equation. Begin this by dividing Eq. (2) by 2, so that x_2 will have a coefficient of $+1$, as shown below:

$$\begin{aligned}
&(1) & x_1 - x_2 + 4x_3 &= 10\\
&(2) & x_2 + 2x_3 &= 10\\
&(3) & 2x_2 + 5x_3 &= 22.
\end{aligned}$$

Then add Eq. (2) to Eq. (1), and subtract two times Eq. (2) from Eq. (3), which yields:

$$\begin{aligned}
&(1) & x_1 \qquad + 6x_3 &= 20\\
&(2) & x_2 + 2x_3 &= 10\\
&(3) & x_3 &= 2.
\end{aligned}$$

The final step is to eliminate x_3 from all but the third equation. This requires subtracting six times Eq. (3) from Eq. (1) and subtracting two times Eq. (3) from Eq. (2), which yields:

$$\begin{aligned}
&(1) & x_1 \qquad\qquad &= 8\\
&(2) & x_2 \qquad &= 6\\
&(3) & x_3 &= 2.
\end{aligned}$$

Thus the desired solution is $(x_1,x_2,x_3)=(8,6,2)$, and the procedure is completed.

Now consider briefly what happens if the Gauss-Jordan method of elimination is applied when $m \neq n$ and/or $\mathbf{A}$ is singular. As discussed earlier, there are three possible cases to consider. First, if the rank of $[\mathbf{A}, \mathbf{b}]$ exceeds the rank of $\mathbf{A}$ by 1, then there will not exist any solution to the system of equations. In this case, the Gauss-Jordan method would obtain an equation such that the left-hand side has vanished (i.e., all the coefficients of the variables are zero), whereas the right-hand side is nonzero. This is the signpost indicating that no solution exists, so there is no reason to proceed further. The second case is where both of these ranks are equal to n, so that a unique solution exists. This implies that $m \geq n$. If $m = n$, then the previous assumptions must hold and no difficulty arises. Therefore, suppose that $m > n$, so that there are $(m - n)$ redundant equations. In this case, all these redundant equations would be eliminated (i.e., both the left-hand and right-hand sides would become zero) during the process of executing the Gauss-Jordan method, so the unique solution would be identified, just as before. The final case is where both these ranks are equal to r, where $r < n$, so that the system of equations possesses an infinite number of solutions. In this case, at the completion of the Gauss-Jordan method each of r variables would remain in only one of the equations, and each of the r equations (any additional equations would have vanished) would contain exactly one of these variables. However, each of the other $(n - r)$ variables would either have vanished or would remain in some of the equations. Therefore, any solution obtained by assigning arbitrary values to the $(n - r)$ variables, and then identifying the respective values of the r variables in the usual way, would be a solution to the system of simultaneous equations. Equivalently, the transfer of these $(n - r)$ variables to the right-hand side of the equations (either before or after the method is executed) would identify the solution for the r variables as a function of these "extra" variables.

5 Tables

Table A5.1† Areas under The Normal Curve from K_α to ∞

$$P\{\text{normal} \geq K_\alpha\} = \int_{K_\alpha}^{\infty} \frac{1}{\sqrt{2\pi}} e^{-x^2/2}\, dx = \alpha$$

$K\alpha$	.00	.01	.02	.03	.04	.05	.06	.07	.08	.09
0.0	.5000	.4960	.4920	.4880	.4840	.4801	.4761	.4721	.4681	.4641
0.1	.4602	.4562	.4522	.4483	.4443	.4404	.4364	.4325	.4286	.4247
0.2	.4207	.4168	.4129	.4090	.4052	.4013	.3974	.3936	.3897	.3859
0.3	.3821	.3783	.3745	.3707	.3669	.3632	.3594	.3557	.3520	.3483
0.4	.3446	.3409	.3372	.3336	.3300	.3264	.3228	.3192	.3156	.3121
0.5	.3085	.3050	.3015	.2981	.2946	.2912	.2877	.2843	.2810	.2776
0.6	.2743	.2709	.2676	.2643	.2611	.2578	.2546	.2514	.2483	.2451
0.7	.2420	.2389	.2358	.2327	.2296	.2266	.2236	.2206	.2177	.2148
0.8	.2119	.2090	.2061	.2033	.2005	.1977	.1949	.1922	.1894	.1867
0.9	.1841	.1814	.1788	.1762	.1736	.1711	.1685	.1660	.1635	.1611
1.0	.1587	.1562	.1539	.1515	.1492	.1469	.1446	.1423	.1401	.1379
1.1	.1357	.1335	.1314	.1292	.1271	.1251	.1230	.1210	.1190	.1170
1.2	.1151	.1131	.1112	.1093	.1075	.1056	.1038	.1020	.1003	.0985
1.3	.0968	.0951	.0934	.0918	.0901	.0885	.0869	.0853	.0838	.0823
1.4	.0808	.0793	.0778	.0764	.0749	.0735	.0721	.0708	.0694	.0681
1.5	.0668	.0655	.0643	.0630	.0618	.0606	.0594	.0582	.0571	.0559
1.6	.0548	.0537	.0526	.0516	.0505	.0495	.0485	.0475	.0465	.0455
1.7	.0446	.0436	.0427	.0418	.0409	.0401	.0392	.0384	.0375	.0367
1.8	0359	.0351	.0344	.0336	.0329	.0322	.0314	.0307	.0301	.0294
1.9	.0287	.0281	.0274	.0268	.0262	.0256	.0250	.0244	.0239	.0233
2.0	.0228	.0222	.0217	.0212	.0207	.0202	.0197	.0192	.0188	.0183
2.1	.0179	.0174	.0170	.0166	.0162	.0158	.0154	.0150	.0146	.0143
2.2	.0139	.0136	.0132	.0129	.0125	.0122	.0119	.0116	.0113	.0110
2.3	.0107	.0104	.0102	.00990	.00964	.00939	.00914	.00889	.00866	.00842
2.4	.00820	.00798	.00776	.00755	.00734	.00714	.00695	.00676	.00657	.00639
2.5	.00621	.00604	.00587	.00570	.00554	.00539	.00523	.00508	.00494	.00480
2.6	.00466	.00453	.00440	.00427	.00415	.00402	.00391	.00379	.00368	.00357
2.7	.00347	.00336	.00326	.00317	.00307	.00298	.00289	.00280	.00272	.00264
2.8	.00256	.00248	.00240	.00233	.00226	.00219	.00212	.00205	.00199	.00193
2.9	.00187	.00181	.00175	.00169	.00164	.00159	.00154	.00149	.00144	.00139

$K\alpha$	.0	.1	.2	.3	.4	.5	.6	.7	.8	.9
3	.00135	$.0^3968$	$.0^3687$	$.0^3483$	$.0^3337$	$.0^3233$	$.0^3159$	$.0^3108$	$.0^4723$	$.0^4481$
4	$.0^4317$	$.0^4207$	$.0^4133$	$.0^5854$	$.0^5541$	$.0^5340$	$.0^5211$	$.0^5130$	$.0^6793$	$.0^6479$
5	$.0^6287$	$.0^6170$	$.0^7996$	$.0^7579$	$.0^7333$	$.0^7190$	$.0^7107$	$.0^8599$	$.0^8332$	$.0^8182$
6	$.0^9987$	$.0^9530$	$.0^9282$	$.0^9149$	$.0^{10}777$	$.0^{10}402$	$.0^{10}206$	$.0^{10}104$	$.0^{11}523$	$.0^{11}260$

† From Frederick E. Croxton, *Tables of Areas in Two Tails and in One Tail of the Normal Curve*. Copyright 1949 by Prentice Hall, Inc., Englewood Cliffs, N.J.

Table A5.2† 100 α Percentage Points of Student's t Distribution
P {Student's t with ν degrees of freedom $\geq$ tabled value} $= \alpha$

ν \ α	0.40	0.25	0.10	0.05	0.025	0.01	0.005	0.0025	0.001	0.0005
1	0.325	1.000	3.078	6.314	12.706	31.821	63.657	127.32	318.31	636.62
2	.289	0.816	1.886	2.920	4.303	6.965	9.925	14.089	22.327	31.598
3	.277	.765	1.638	2.353	3.182	4.541	5.841	7.453	10.214	12.924
4	.271	.741	1.533	2.132	2.776	3.747	4.604	5.598	7.173	8.610
5	0.267	0.727	1.476	2.015	2.571	3.365	4.032	4.773	5.893	6.869
6	.265	.718	1.440	1.943	2.447	3.143	3.707	4.317	5.208	5.959
7	.263	.711	1.415	1.895	2.365	2.998	3.499	4.029	4.785	5.408
8	.262	.706	1.397	1.860	2.306	2.896	3.355	3.833	4.501	5.041
9	.261	.703	1.383	1.833	2.262	2.821	3.250	3.690	4.297	4.781
10	0.260	0.700	1.372	1.812	2.228	2.764	3.169	3.581	4.144	4.587
11	.260	.697	1.363	1.796	2.201	2.718	3.106	3.497	4.025	4.437
12	.259	.695	1.356	1.782	2.179	2.681	3.055	3.428	3.930	4.318
13	.259	.694	1.350	1.771	2.160	2.650	3.012	3.372	3.852	4.221
14	.258	.692	1.345	1.761	2.145	2.624	2.977	3.326	3.787	4.140
15	0.258	0.691	1.341	1.753	2.131	2.602	2.947	3.286	3.733	4.073
16	.258	.690	1.337	1.746	2.120	2.583	2.921	3.252	3.686	4.015
17	.257	.689	1.333	1.740	2.110	2.567	2.898	3.222	3.646	3.965
18	.257	.688	1.330	1.734	2.101	2.552	2.878	3.197	3.610	3.922
19	.257	.688	1.328	1.729	2.093	2.539	2.861	3.174	3.579	3.883
20	0.257	0.687	1.325	1.725	2.086	2.528	2.845	3.153	3.552	3.850
21	.257	.686	1.323	1.721	2.080	2.518	2.831	3.135	3.527	3.819
22	.256	.686	1.321	1.717	2.074	2.508	2.819	3.119	3.505	3.792
23	.256	.685	1.319	1.714	2.069	2.500	2.807	3.104	3.485	3.767
24	.256	.685	1.318	1.711	2.064	2.492	2.797	3.091	3.467	3.745
25	0.256	0.684	1.316	1.708	2.060	2.485	2.787	3.078	3.450	3.725
26	.256	.684	1.315	1.706	2.056	2.479	2.779	3.067	3.435	3.707
27	.256	.684	1.314	1.703	2.052	2.473	2.771	3.057	3.421	3.690
28	.256	.683	1.313	1.701	2.048	2.467	2.763	3.047	3.408	3.674
29	.256	.683	1.311	1.699	2.045	2.462	2.756	3.038	3.396	3.659
30	0.256	0.683	1.310	1.697	2.042	2.457	2.750	3.030	3.385	3.646
40	.255	.681	1.303	1.684	2.021	2.423	2.704	2.971	3.307	3.551
60	.254	.679	1.296	1.671	2.000	2.390	2.660	2.915	3.232	3.460
120	.254	.677	1.289	1.658	1.980	2.358	2.617	2.860	3.160	3.373
∞	.253	.674	1.282	1.645	1.960	2.326	2.576	2.807	3.090	3.291

† Reproduced from Table 12 of *Biometrika Tables for Statisticians*, vol. I, 3d ed., 1966, by permission of the Biometrika Trustees.

Table A5.3† 100 α Percentage Points of the Chi-square Distribution
P\{chi square with ν degrees of freedom $\geq$ tabled value\} $= \alpha$

ν \ α	0.995	0.99	0.975	0.95	0.90	0.75	0.50
1	$.0^{4}393$	$.0^{3}157$	$.0^{3}982$	.00393	.0158	.102	.455
2	.0100	.0201	.0506	.103	.211	.575	1.386
3	.0717	.115	.216	.352	.584	1.213	2.366
4	.207	.297	.484	.711	1.064	1.923	3.357
5	.412	.554	.831	1.145	1.610	2.675	4.351
6	.676	.872	1.237	1.635	2.204	3.455	5.348
7	.989	1.239	1.690	2.167	2.833	4.255	6.346
8	1.344	1.646	2.180	2.733	3.490	5.071	7.344
9	1.735	2.088	2.700	3.325	4.168	5.899	8.343
10	2.156	2.558	3.247	3.940	4.865	6.737	9.342
11	2.603	3.053	3.816	4.575	5.578	7.584	10.341
12	3.074	3.571	4.404	5.226	6.304	8.438	11.340
13	3.565	4.107	5.009	5.892	7.042	9.299	12.340
14	4.075	4.660	5.629	6.571	7.790	10.165	13.339
15	4.601	5.229	6.262	7.261	8.547	11.036	14.339
16	5.142	5.812	6.908	7.962	9.312	11.912	15.338
17	5.697	6.408	7.564	8.672	10.085	12.792	16.338
18	6.265	7.015	8.231	9.390	10.865	13.675	17.338
19	6.844	7.633	8.907	10.117	11.651	14.562	18.338
20	7.434	8.260	9.591	10.851	12.443	15.452	19.337
21	8.034	8.897	10.283	11.591	13.240	16.344	20.337
22	8.643	9.542	10.982	12.338	14.041	17.240	21.337
23	9.260	10.196	11.688	13.091	14.848	18.137	22.337
24	9.886	10.856	12.401	13.848	15.659	19.037	23.337
25	10.520	11.524	13.120	14.611	16.473	19.939	24.337
26	11.160	12.198	13.844	15.379	17.292	20.843	25.336
27	11.808	12.879	14.573	16.151	18.114	21.749	26.336
28	12.461	13.565	15.308	16.928	18.939	22.657	27.336
29	13.121	14.256	16.047	17.708	19.768	23.567	28.336
30	13.787	14.953	16.791	18.493	20.599	24.478	29.336
40	20.707	22.164	24.433	26.509	29.051	33.660	39.335
50	27.991	29.707	32.357	34.764	37.689	42.942	49.335
60	35.535	37.485	40.482	43.188	46.459	52.294	59.335
70	43.275	45.442	48.758	51.739	55.329	61.698	69.334
80	51.172	53.540	57.153	60.391	64.278	71.145	79.334
90	59.196	61.754	65.647	69.126	73.291	80.625	89.334
100	67.328	70.065	74.222	77.929	82.358	90.133	99.334
K_α	−2.576	−2.326	−1.960	−1.645	−1.282	−0.6745	0.000

† Abridged from Table 8 of *Biometrika Tables for Statisticians*, vol. I, 3d ed., 1966, by permission of the Biometrika Trustees.

Table A5.3 100 α Percentage Points of the Chi-square Distribution
P{chi square with ν degrees of freedom $\geq$ tabled value} = α (*Continued*)

0.25	0.10	0.05	0.025	0.01	0.005	0.001	α / ν
1.323	2.706	3.841	5.024	6.635	7.879	10.828	1
2.773	4.605	5.991	7.378	9.210	10.597	13.816	2
4.108	6.251	7.815	9.348	11.345	12.838	16.266	3
5.385	7.779	9.488	11.143	13.277	14.860	18.467	4
6.626	9.236	11.070	12.832	15.086	16.750	20.515	5
7.841	10.645	12.592	14.449	16.812	18.548	22.458	6
9.037	12.017	14.067	16.013	18.475	20.278	24.322	7
10.219	13.362	15.507	17.535	20.090	21.955	26.125	8
11.389	14.684	16.919	19.023	21.666	23.589	27.877	9
12.549	15.987	18.307	20.483	23.209	25.188	29.588	10
13.701	17.275	19.675	21.920	24.725	26.757	31.264	11
14.845	18.549	21.026	23.337	26.217	28.300	32.909	12
15.984	19.812	22.362	24.736	27.688	29.819	34.528	13
17.117	21.064	23.685	26.119	29.141	31.319	36.123	14
18.245	22.307	24.996	27.488	30.578	32.801	37.697	15
19.369	23.542	26.296	28.845	32.000	34.267	39.252	16
20.489	24.769	27.587	30.191	33.409	35.718	40.790	17
21.605	25.989	28.869	31.526	34.805	37.156	43.312	18
22.718	27.204	30.144	32.852	36.191	38.582	43.820	19
23.828	28.412	31.410	34.170	37.566	39.997	45.315	20
24.935	29.615	32.671	35.479	38.932	41.401	46.797	21
26.039	30.813	33.924	36.781	40.289	42.796	48.268	22
27.141	32.007	35.172	38.076	41.638	44.181	49.728	23
28.241	33.196	36.415	39.364	42.980	45.558	51.179	24
29.339	34.382	37.652	40.646	44.314	46.928	52.620	25
30.434	35.563	38.885	41.923	45.642	48.290	54.052	26
31.528	36.741	40.113	43.194	46.963	49.645	55.476	27
32.620	37.916	41.337	44.461	48.278	50.993	56.892	28
33.711	39.087	42.557	45.722	49.588	52.336	58.302	29
34.800	40.256	43.773	46.979	50.892	53.672	59.703	30
45.616	51.805	55.758	59.342	63.691	66.766	73.402	40
56.334	63.167	67.505	71.420	76.154	79.490	86.661	50
66.981	74.397	79.082	83.298	88.379	91.952	99.607	60
77.577	85.527	90.531	95.023	100.425	104.215	112.317	70
88.130	96.578	101.879	106.629	112.329	116.321	124.839	80
98.650	107.565	113.145	118.136	124.116	128.299	137.208	90
109.141	118.498	124.342	129.561	135.807	140.169	149.449	100
+0.6745	+1.282	+1.645	+1.960	+2.326	+2.576	+3.090	K_α

For $\nu > 100$ take

$$\chi^2 = \nu\left\{1 - \frac{2}{9\nu} + K_\alpha\sqrt{\frac{2}{9\nu}}\right\}^3 \quad \text{or} \quad \chi^2 = \frac{1}{2}\{K_\alpha + \sqrt{(2\nu - 1)}\}^2,$$

according to the degree of accuracy required. K_α is the standardized normal deviate corresponding to α, and is shown in the bottom line of the table.

Table A5.4[†] Summation of Terms of the Poisson Distribution
1,000 P {Poisson with parameter $\lambda \leq c$}

c \ λ	0.01	0.02	0.03	0.04	0.05	0.06	0.07	0.08	0.09
0	990	980	970	961	951	942	932	923	914
1	1000	1000	1000	999	999	998	998	997	996
2				1000	1000	1000	1000	1000	1000

c \ λ	0.10	0.15	0.20	0.25	0.30	0.35	0.40	0.45	0.50
0	905	861	819	779	741	705	670	638	607
1	995	990	982	974	963	951	938	925	910
2	1000	999	999	998	996	994	992	989	986
3		1000	1000	1000	1000	1000	999	999	998
4							1000	1000	1000

c \ λ	0.55	0.60	0.65	0.70	0.75	0.80	0.85	0.90	0.95	1.00
0	577	549	522	497	472	449	427	407	387	368
1	894	878	861	844	827	809	791	772	754	736
2	982	977	972	966	959	953	945	937	929	920
3	998	997	996	994	993	991	989	987	984	981
4	1000	1000	999	999	999	999	998	998	997	996
5			1000	1000	1000	1000	1000	1000	1000	999
6										1000

c \ λ	1.05	1.10	1.15	1.20	1.25	1.30	1.35	1.40	1.45	1.50
0	350	333	317	301	287	273	259	247	235	223
1	717	699	681	663	645	627	609	592	575	558
2	910	900	890	879	868	857	845	833	821	809
3	978	974	970	966	962	957	952	946	940	934
4	996	995	993	992	991	989	988	986	984	981
5	999	999	999	998	998	998	997	997	996	996
6	1000	1000	1000	1000	1000	1000	999	999	999	999
7							1000	1000	1000	1000

c \ λ	1.55	1.60	1.65	1.70	1.75	1.80	1.85	1.90	1.95	2.00
0	212	202	192	183	174	165	157	150	142	135
1	541	525	509	493	478	463	448	434	420	406
2	796	783	770	757	744	731	717	704	690	677
3	928	921	914	907	899	891	883	875	866	857
4	979	976	973	970	967	964	960	956	952	947
5	995	994	993	992	991	990	988	987	985	983
6	999	999	998	998	998	997	997	997	996	995
7	1000	1000	1000	1000	1000	999	999	999	999	999
8						1000	1000	1000	1000	1000

[†] Reproduced by permission from *Tables for Multiple-Server Queueing Systems Involving Erlang Distributions*, Frederick S. Hillier and Frederick D. Lo, Technical Report #14, NSF GK-2925, Department of Operations Research, Stanford University, December 28, 1971.

Table A5.4 Summation of Terms of the Poisson Distribution
1,000 P {Poisson with parameter $\lambda \leq c$} (*Continued*)

c \ λ	2.10	2.20	2.30	2.40	2.50	2.60	2.70	2.80	2.90	3.00
0	122	111	100	091	082	074	067	061	055	050
1	380	355	331	308	287	267	249	231	215	199
2	650	623	596	570	544	518	494	469	446	423
3	839	819	799	779	758	736	714	692	670	647
4	938	928	916	904	891	877	863	848	832	815
5	980	975	970	964	958	951	943	935	926	916
6	994	993	991	988	986	983	979	976	971	966
7	999	998	997	997	996	995	993	992	990	988
8	1000	1000	999	999	999	999	998	998	997	996
9			1000	1000	1000	1000	999	999	999	999
10							1000	1000	1000	1000

c \ λ	3.10	3.20	3.30	3.40	3.50	3.60	3.70	3.80	3.90	4.00
0	045	041	037	033	030	027	025	022	020	018
1	185	171	159	147	136	126	116	107	099	092
2	401	380	359	340	321	303	285	269	253	238
3	625	603	580	558	537	515	494	473	453	433
4	798	781	763	744	725	706	687	668	648	629
5	906	895	883	871	858	844	830	816	801	785
6	961	955	949	942	935	927	918	909	899	889
7	986	983	980	977	973	969	965	960	955	949
8	995	994	993	992	990	988	986	984	981	979
9	999	998	998	997	997	996	995	994	993	992
10	1000	1000	999	999	999	999	998	998	998	997
11			1000	1000	1000	1000	1000	999	999	999
12								1000	1000	1000

c \ λ	4.10	4.20	4.30	4.40	4.50	4.60	4.70	4.80	4.90	5.00
0	017	015	014	012	011	010	009	008	007	007
1	085	078	072	066	061	056	052	048	044	040
2	224	210	197	185	174	163	152	143	133	125
3	414	395	377	359	342	326	310	294	279	265
4	609	590	570	551	532	513	495	476	458	440
5	769	753	737	720	703	686	668	651	634	616
6	879	867	856	844	831	818	805	791	777	762
7	943	936	929	921	913	905	896	887	877	867
8	976	972	968	964	960	955	950	944	938	932
9	990	989	987	985	983	980	978	975	972	968
10	997	996	995	994	993	992	991	990	988	986
11	999	999	998	998	998	997	997	996	995	995
12	1000	1000	999	999	999	999	999	999	998	998
13			1000	1000	1000	1000	1000	1000	999	999
14									1000	1000

Table A5.4 Summation of Terms of the Poisson Distribution
1,000 $P\{\text{Poisson with parameter } \lambda \leq c\}$ (*Continued*)

c \ λ	5.10	5.20	5.30	5.40	5.50	5.60	5.70	5.80	5.90	6.00
0	006	006	005	005	004	004	003	003	003	002
1	037	034	031	029	027	024	022	021	019	017
2	116	109	102	095	088	082	077	072	067	062
3	251	238	225	213	202	191	180	170	160	151
4	423	406	390	373	358	342	327	313	299	285
5	598	581	563	546	529	512	495	478	462	446
6	747	732	717	702	686	670	654	638	622	606
7	856	845	833	822	809	797	784	771	758	744
8	925	918	911	903	894	886	877	867	857	847
9	964	960	956	951	946	941	935	929	923	916
10	984	982	980	977	975	972	969	965	961	957
11	994	993	992	990	989	988	986	984	982	980
12	998	997	997	996	996	995	994	993	992	991
13	999	999	999	999	998	998	998	997	997	996
14	1000	1000	1000	1000	999	999	999	999	999	999
15					1000	1000	1000	1000	1000	1000

c \ λ	6.10	6.20	6.30	6.40	6.50	6.60	6.70	6.80	6.90	7.00
0	002	002	002	002	002	001	001	001	001	001
1	016	015	013	012	011	010	009	009	008	007
2	058	054	050	046	043	040	037	034	032	030
3	143	134	126	119	112	105	099	093	087	082
4	272	259	247	235	224	213	202	192	182	173
5	430	414	399	384	369	355	341	327	314	301
6	590	574	558	542	527	511	495	480	465	450
7	730	716	702	687	673	658	643	628	614	599
8	837	826	815	803	792	780	767	755	742	729
9	909	902	894	886	877	869	860	850	840	830
10	953	949	944	939	933	927	921	915	908	901
11	978	975	972	969	966	963	959	955	951	947
12	990	989	987	986	984	982	980	978	976	973
13	996	995	995	994	993	992	991	990	989	987
14	998	998	998	997	997	997	996	996	995	994
15	999	999	999	999	999	999	998	998	998	998
16	1000	1000	1000	1000	1000	999	999	999	999	999
17						1000	1000	1000	1000	1000

Table A5.4 Summation of Terms of the Poisson Distribution
1,000 P\{Poisson with parameter $\lambda \leq c$\} (*Continued*)

c \ λ	7.10	7.20	7.30	7.40	7.50	8.00	8.50	9.00	9.50	10.00
0	001	001	001	001	001	000	000	000	000	000
1	007	006	006	005	005	003	002	001	001	000
2	027	025	024	022	020	014	009	006	004	003
3	077	072	067	063	059	042	030	021	015	010
4	164	156	147	140	132	100	074	055	040	029
5	288	276	264	253	241	191	150	116	089	067
6	435	420	406	392	378	313	256	207	165	130
7	584	569	554	539	525	453	386	324	269	220
8	716	703	689	676	662	593	523	456	392	333
9	820	810	799	788	776	717	653	587	522	458
10	894	887	879	871	862	816	763	706	645	583
11	942	937	932	926	921	888	849	803	752	697
12	970	967	964	961	957	936	909	876	836	792
13	986	984	982	980	978	966	949	926	898	864
14	994	993	992	991	990	983	973	959	940	917
15	997	997	996	996	995	992	986	978	967	951
16	999	999	999	998	998	996	993	989	982	973
17	1000	1000	999	999	999	998	997	995	991	986
18			1000	1000	1000	999	999	998	996	993
19						1000	999	999	998	997
20							1000	1000	999	998
21									1000	999
22										1000

c \ λ	10.5	11.0	11.5	12.0	12.5	13.0	13.5	14.0	14.5	15.0
0	000	000	000	000	000	000	000	000	000	000
1	000	000	000	000	000	000	000	000	000	000
2	002	001	001	001	000	000	000	000	000	000
3	007	005	003	002	002	001	001	000	000	000
4	021	015	011	008	005	004	003	002	001	001
5	050	038	028	020	015	011	008	006	004	003
6	102	079	060	046	035	026	019	014	010	008
7	179	143	114	090	070	054	041	032	024	018
8	279	232	191	155	125	100	079	062	048	037
9	397	341	289	242	201	166	135	109	088	070
10	521	460	402	347	297	252	211	176	145	118
11	639	579	520	462	406	353	304	260	220	185
12	742	689	633	576	519	463	409	358	311	268
13	825	781	733	682	628	573	518	464	413	363
14	888	854	815	772	725	675	623	570	518	466
15	932	907	878	844	806	764	718	669	619	568
16	960	944	924	899	869	835	798	756	711	664
17	978	968	954	937	916	890	861	827	790	749
18	988	982	974	963	948	930	908	883	853	819
19	994	991	986	979	969	957	942	923	901	875
20	997	995	992	988	983	975	965	952	936	917
21	999	998	996	994	991	986	980	971	960	947
22	999	999	998	997	995	992	989	983	976	967
23	1000	1000	999	999	998	996	994	991	986	981
24			1000	999	999	998	997	995	992	989
25				1000	999	999	998	997	996	994
26					1000	1000	999	999	998	997
27							1000	999	999	998
28								1000	999	999
29									1000	1000

Table A5.4 Summation of Terms of the Poisson Distribution
1,000 *P*{Poisson with parameter $\lambda \leq c$} (*Continued*)

c \ λ	16	17	18	19	20	21	22	23	24	25
1	000	000	000	000	000	000	000	000	000	000
2	000	000	000	000	000	000	000	000	000	000
3	000	000	000	000	000	000	000	000	000	000
4	000	000	000	000	000	000	000	000	000	000
5	001	001	000	000	000	000	000	000	000	000
6	004	002	001	001	000	000	000	000	000	000
7	010	005	003	002	001	000	000	000	000	000
8	022	013	007	004	002	001	001	000	000	000
9	043	026	015	009	005	003	002	001	000	000
10	077	049	030	018	011	006	004	002	001	001
11	127	085	055	035	021	013	008	004	003	001
12	193	135	092	061	039	025	015	009	005	003
13	275	201	143	098	066	043	028	017	011	006
14	368	281	208	150	105	072	048	031	020	012
15	467	371	287	215	157	111	077	052	034	022
16	566	468	375	292	221	163	117	082	056	038
17	659	564	469	378	297	227	169	123	087	060
18	742	655	562	469	381	302	232	175	128	092
19	812	736	651	561	470	384	306	238	180	134
20	868	805	731	647	559	471	387	310	243	185
21	911	861	799	725	644	558	472	389	314	247
22	942	905	855	793	721	640	556	472	392	318
23	963	937	899	849	787	716	637	555	473	394
24	978	959	932	893	843	782	712	635	554	473
25	987	975	955	927	888	838	777	708	632	553
26	993	985	972	951	922	883	832	772	704	629
27	996	991	983	969	948	917	877	827	768	700
28	998	995	990	980	966	944	913	873	823	763
29	999	997	994	988	978	963	940	908	868	818
30	999	999	997	993	987	976	959	936	904	863
31	1000	999	998	996	992	985	973	956	932	900
32		1000	999	998	995	991	983	971	953	929
33			1000	999	997	994	989	981	969	950
34				999	999	997	994	988	979	966
35				1000	999	998	996	993	987	978
36					1000	999	998	996	992	985
37						999	999	997	995	991
38						1000	999	999	997	994
39							1000	999	998	997
40								1000	999	998
41									999	999
42									1000	999
43										1000

Table A5.5† 1 Percentage Points of the F Distribution; Table of $F_{0.01;\nu_1,\nu_2}$

$P\{F$ with ν_1 and ν_2 degrees of freedom $\geq$ tabled value$\} = \alpha$

Degrees of freedom for the denominator (ν_2) \ Degrees of Freedom for the numerator (ν_1)	1	2	3	4	5	6	7	8	9	10	12	15	20	24	30	40	60	120	∞
1	4052	4999.5	5403	5625	5764	5859	5928	5981	6022	6056	6106	6157	6209	6235	6261	6287	6313	6339	6366
2	98.50	99.00	99.17	99.25	99.30	99.33	99.36	99.37	99.39	99.40	99.42	99.43	99.45	99.46	99.47	99.47	99.48	99.49	99.50
3	34.12	30.82	29.46	28.71	28.24	27.91	27.67	27.49	27.35	27.23	27.05	26.87	26.69	26.60	26.50	26.41	26.32	26.22	26.13
4	21.20	18.00	16.69	15.98	15.52	15.21	14.98	14.80	14.66	14.55	14.37	14.20	14.02	13.93	13.84	13.75	13.65	13.56	13.46
5	16.26	13.27	12.06	11.39	10.97	10.67	10.46	10.29	10.16	10.05	9.89	9.72	9.55	9.47	9.38	9.29	9.20	9.11	9.02
6	13.75	10.92	9.78	9.15	8.75	8.47	8.26	8.10	7.98	7.87	7.72	7.56	7.40	7.31	7.23	7.14	7.06	6.97	6.88
7	12.25	9.55	8.45	7.85	7.46	7.19	6.99	6.84	6.72	6.62	6.47	6.31	6.16	6.07	5.99	5.91	5.82	5.74	5.65
8	11.26	8.65	7.59	7.01	6.63	6.37	6.18	6.03	5.91	5.81	5.67	5.52	5.36	5.28	5.20	5.12	5.03	4.95	4.86
9	10.56	8.02	6.99	6.42	6.06	5.80	5.61	5.47	5.35	5.26	5.11	4.96	4.81	4.73	4.65	4.57	4.48	4.40	4.31
10	10.04	7.56	6.55	5.99	5.64	5.39	5.20	5.06	4.94	4.85	4.71	4.56	4.41	4.33	4.25	4.17	4.08	4.00	3.91
11	9.65	7.21	6.22	5.67	5.32	5.07	4.89	4.74	4.63	4.54	4.40	4.25	4.10	4.02	3.94	3.86	3.78	3.69	3.60
12	9.33	6.93	5.95	5.41	5.06	4.82	4.64	4.50	4.39	4.30	4.16	4.01	3.86	3.78	3.70	3.62	3.54	3.45	3.36
13	9.07	6.70	5.74	5.21	4.86	4.62	4.44	4.30	4.19	4.10	3.96	3.82	3.66	3.59	3.51	3.43	3.34	3.25	3.17
14	8.86	6.51	5.56	5.04	4.69	4.46	4.28	4.14	4.03	3.94	3.80	3.66	3.51	3.43	3.35	3.27	3.18	3.09	3.00
15	8.68	6.36	5.42	4.89	4.56	4.32	4.14	4.00	3.89	3.80	3.67	3.52	3.37	3.29	3.21	3.13	3.05	2.96	2.87
16	8.53	6.23	5.29	4.77	4.44	4.20	4.03	3.89	3.78	3.69	3.55	3.41	3.26	3.18	3.10	3.02	2.93	2.84	2.75
17	8.40	6.11	5.18	4.67	4.34	4.10	3.93	3.79	3.68	3.59	3.46	3.31	3.16	3.08	3.00	2.92	2.83	2.75	2.65
18	8.29	6.01	5.09	4.58	4.25	4.01	3.84	3.71	3.60	3.51	3.37	3.23	3.08	3.00	2.92	2.84	2.75	2.66	2.57
19	8.18	5.93	5.01	4.50	4.17	3.94	3.77	3.63	3.52	3.43	3.30	3.15	3.00	2.92	2.84	2.76	2.67	2.58	2.49
20	8.10	5.85	4.94	4.43	4.10	3.87	3.70	3.56	3.46	3.37	3.23	3.09	2.94	2.86	2.78	2.69	2.61	2.52	2.42
21	8.02	5.78	4.87	4.37	4.04	3.81	3.64	3.51	3.40	3.31	3.17	3.03	2.88	2.80	2.72	2.64	2.55	2.46	2.36
22	7.95	5.72	4.82	4.31	3.99	3.76	3.59	3.45	3.35	3.26	3.12	2.98	2.83	2.75	2.67	2.58	2.50	2.40	2.31
23	7.88	5.66	4.76	4.26	3.94	3.71	3.54	3.41	3.30	3.21	3.07	2.93	2.78	2.70	2.62	2.54	2.45	2.35	2.26
24	7.82	5.61	4.72	4.22	3.90	3.67	3.50	3.36	3.26	3.17	3.03	2.89	2.74	2.66	2.58	2.49	2.40	2.31	2.21
25	7.77	5.57	4.68	4.18	3.85	3.63	3.46	3.32	3.22	3.13	2.99	2.85	2.70	2.62	2.54	2.45	2.36	2.27	2.17
26	7.72	5.53	4.64	4.14	3.82	3.59	3.42	3.29	3.18	3.09	2.96	2.81	2.66	2.58	2.50	2.42	2.33	2.23	2.13
27	7.68	5.49	4.60	4.11	3.78	3.56	3.39	3.26	3.15	3.06	2.93	2.78	2.63	2.55	2.47	2.38	2.29	2.20	2.10
28	7.64	5.45	4.57	4.07	3.75	3.53	3.36	3.23	3.12	3.03	2.90	2.75	2.60	2.52	2.44	2.35	2.26	2.17	2.06
29	7.60	5.42	4.54	4.04	3.73	3.50	3.33	3.20	3.09	3.00	2.87	2.73	2.57	2.49	2.41	2.33	2.23	2.14	2.03
30	7.56	5.39	4.51	4.02	3.70	3.47	3.30	3.17	3.07	2.98	2.84	2.70	2.55	2.47	2.39	2.30	2.21	2.11	2.01
40	7.31	5.18	4.31	3.83	3.51	3.29	3.12	2.99	2.89	2.80	2.66	2.52	2.37	2.29	2.20	2.11	2.02	1.92	1.80
60	7.08	4.98	4.13	3.65	3.34	3.12	2.95	2.82	2.72	2.63	2.50	2.35	2.20	2.12	2.03	1.94	1.84	1.73	1.60
120	6.85	4.79	3.95	3.48	3.17	2.96	2.79	2.66	2.56	2.47	2.34	2.19	2.03	1.95	1.86	1.76	1.66	1.53	1.38
∞	6.63	4.61	3.78	3.32	3.02	2.80	2.64	2.51	2.41	2.32	2.18	2.04	1.88	1.79	1.70	1.59	1.47	1.32	1.00

† Reproduced from Table 18 of Biometrika *Tables for Statisticians*, vol. I, 3d ed., 1966, by permission of the Biometrika Trustees.

$F_{0.99,\nu_1,\nu_2} = 1/F_{0.01,\nu_2,\nu_1}$

Table A5.5 2.5 Percentage Points of the F Distribution; Table of $F_{0.025;\nu_1,\nu_2}$
$P\{F$ with ν_1 and ν_2 degrees of freedom $\geq$ tabled value$\} = \alpha$ *(Continued)*

Degrees of freedom for the denominator (ν_2) \ ν_1	Degrees of freedom for the numerator (ν_1)																		
ν_2	1	2	3	4	5	6	7	8	9	10	12	15	20	24	30	40	60	120	∞
1	647.8	799.5	864.2	899.6	921.8	937.1	948.2	956.7	963.3	968.6	976.7	984.9	993.1	997.2	1001	1006	1010	1014	1018
2	38.51	39.00	39.17	39.25	39.30	39.33	39.36	39.37	39.39	39.40	39.41	39.43	39.45	39.46	39.46	39.47	39.48	39.49	39.50
3	17.44	16.04	15.44	15.10	14.88	14.73	14.62	14.54	14.47	14.42	14.34	14.25	14.17	14.12	14.08	14.04	13.99	13.95	13.90
4	12.22	10.65	9.98	9.60	9.36	9.20	9.07	8.98	8.90	8.84	8.75	8.66	8.56	8.51	8.46	8.41	8.36	8.31	8.26
5	10.01	8.43	7.76	7.39	7.15	6.98	6.85	6.76	6.68	6.62	6.52	6.43	6.33	6.28	6.23	6.18	6.12	6.07	6.02
6	8.81	7.26	6.60	6.23	5.99	5.82	5.70	5.60	5.52	5.46	5.37	5.27	5.17	5.12	5.07	5.01	4.96	4.90	4.85
7	8.07	6.54	5.89	5.52	5.29	5.12	4.99	4.90	4.82	4.76	4.67	4.57	4.47	4.42	4.36	4.31	4.25	4.20	4.14
8	7.57	6.06	5.42	5.05	4.82	4.65	4.53	4.43	4.36	4.30	4.20	4.10	4.00	3.95	3.89	3.84	3.78	3.73	3.67
9	7.21	5.71	5.08	4.72	4.48	4.32	4.20	4.10	4.03	3.96	3.87	3.77	3.67	3.61	3.56	3.51	3.45	3.39	3.33
10	6.94	5.46	4.83	4.47	4.24	4.07	3.95	3.85	3.78	3.72	3.62	3.52	3.42	3.37	3.31	3.26	3.20	3.14	3.08
11	6.72	5.26	4.63	4.28	4.04	3.88	3.76	3.66	3.59	3.53	3.43	3.33	3.23	3.17	3.12	3.06	3.00	2.94	2.88
12	6.55	5.10	4.47	4.12	3.89	3.73	3.61	3.51	3.44	3.37	3.28	3.18	3.07	3.02	2.96	2.91	2.85	2.79	2.72
13	6.41	4.97	4.35	4.00	3.77	3.60	3.48	3.39	3.31	3.25	3.15	3.05	2.95	2.89	2.84	2.78	2.72	2.66	2.60
14	6.30	4.86	4.24	3.89	3.66	3.50	3.38	3.29	3.21	3.15	3.05	2.95	2.84	2.79	2.73	2.67	2.61	2.55	2.49
15	6.20	4.77	4.15	3.80	3.58	3.41	3.29	3.20	3.12	3.06	2.96	2.86	2.76	2.70	2.64	2.59	2.52	2.46	2.40
16	6.12	4.69	4.08	3.73	3.50	3.34	3.22	3.12	3.05	2.99	2.89	2.79	2.68	2.63	2.57	2.51	2.45	2.38	2.32
17	6.04	4.62	4.01	3.66	3.44	3.28	3.16	3.06	2.98	2.92	2.82	2.72	2.62	2.56	2.50	2.44	2.38	2.32	2.25
18	5.98	4.56	3.95	3.61	3.38	3.22	3.10	3.01	2.93	2.87	2.77	2.67	2.56	2.50	2.44	2.38	2.32	2.26	2.19
19	5.92	4.51	3.90	3.56	3.33	3.17	3.05	2.96	2.88	2.82	2.72	2.62	2.51	2.45	2.39	2.33	2.27	2.20	2.13
20	5.87	4.46	3.86	3.51	3.29	3.13	3.01	2.91	2.84	2.77	2.68	2.57	2.46	2.41	2.35	2.29	2.22	2.16	2.09
21	5.83	4.42	3.82	3.48	3.25	3.09	2.97	2.87	2.80	2.73	2.64	2.53	2.42	2.37	2.31	2.25	2.18	2.11	2.04
22	5.79	4.38	3.78	3.44	3.22	3.05	2.93	2.84	2.76	2.70	2.60	2.50	2.39	2.33	2.27	2.21	2.14	2.08	2.00
23	5.75	4.35	3.75	3.41	3.18	3.02	2.90	2.81	2.73	2.67	2.57	2.47	2.36	2.30	2.24	2.18	2.11	2.04	1.97
24	5.72	4.32	3.72	3.38	3.15	2.99	2.87	2.78	2.70	2.64	2.54	2.44	2.33	2.27	2.21	2.15	2.08	2.01	1.94
25	5.69	4.29	3.69	3.35	3.13	2.97	2.85	2.75	2.68	2.61	2.51	2.41	2.30	2.24	2.18	2.12	2.05	1.98	1.91
26	5.66	4.27	3.67	3.33	3.10	2.94	2.82	2.73	2.65	2.59	2.49	2.39	2.28	2.22	2.16	2.09	2.03	1.95	1.88
27	5.63	4.24	3.65	3.31	3.08	2.92	2.80	2.71	2.63	2.57	2.47	2.36	2.25	2.19	2.13	2.07	2.00	1.93	1.85
28	5.61	4.22	3.63	3.29	3.06	2.90	2.78	2.69	2.61	2.55	2.45	2.34	2.23	2.17	2.11	2.05	1.98	1.91	1.83
29	5.59	4.20	3.61	3.27	3.04	2.88	2.76	2.67	2.59	2.53	2.43	2.32	2.21	2.15	2.09	2.03	1.96	1.89	1.81
30	5.57	4.18	3.59	3.25	3.03	2.87	2.75	2.65	2.57	2.51	2.41	2.31	2.20	2.14	2.07	2.01	1.94	1.87	1.79
40	5.42	4.05	3.46	3.13	2.90	2.74	2.62	2.53	2.45	2.39	2.29	2.18	2.07	2.01	1.94	1.88	1.80	1.72	1.64
60	5.29	3.93	3.34	3.01	2.79	2.63	2.51	2.41	2.33	2.27	2.17	2.06	1.94	1.88	1.82	1.74	1.67	1.58	1.48
120	5.15	3.80	3.23	2.89	2.67	2.52	2.39	2.30	2.22	2.16	2.05	1.94	1.82	1.76	1.69	1.61	1.53	1.43	1.31
∞	5.02	3.69	3.12	2.79	2.57	2.41	2.29	2.19	2.11	2.05	1.94	1.83	1.71	1.64	1.57	1.48	1.39	1.27	1.00

$F_{0.975,\nu_1,\nu_2} = 1/F_{0.025,\nu_2,\nu_1}$

Table A5.5 5 Percentage Points of the F Distribution: Table of $F_{0.05;\,\nu_1\,\nu_2}$

$P\{F$ with ν_1 and ν_2 degrees of freedom $\geq$ tabled value$\} = \alpha$ (*Continued*)

Degrees of freedom for the denominator (ν_2) \ Degrees of freedom for the numerator (ν_1)	1	2	3	4	5	6	7	8	9	10	12	15	20	24	30	40	60	120	∞
1	161.4	199.5	215.7	224.6	230.2	234.0	236.8	238.9	240.5	241.9	243.9	245.9	248.0	249.1	250.1	251.1	252.2	253.3	254.3
2	18.51	19.00	19.16	19.25	19.30	19.33	19.35	19.37	19.38	19.40	19.41	19.43	19.45	19.45	19.46	19.47	19.48	19.49	19.50
3	10.13	9.55	9.28	9.12	9.01	8.94	8.89	8.85	8.81	8.79	8.74	8.70	8.66	8.64	8.62	8.59	8.57	8.55	8.53
4	7.71	6.94	6.59	6.39	6.26	6.16	6.09	6.04	6.00	5.96	5.91	5.86	5.80	5.77	5.75	5.72	5.69	5.66	5.63
5	6.61	5.79	5.41	5.19	5.05	4.95	4.88	4.82	4.77	4.74	4.68	4.62	4.56	4.53	4.50	4.46	4.43	4.40	4.36
6	5.99	5.14	4.76	4.53	4.39	4.28	4.21	4.15	4.10	4.06	4.00	3.94	3.87	3.84	3.81	3.77	3.74	3.70	3.67
7	5.59	4.74	4.35	4.12	3.97	3.87	3.79	3.73	3.68	3.64	3.57	3.51	3.44	3.41	3.38	3.34	3.30	3.27	3.23
8	5.32	4.46	4.07	3.84	3.69	3.58	3.50	3.44	3.39	3.35	3.28	3.22	3.15	3.12	3.08	3.04	3.01	2.97	2.93
9	5.12	4.26	3.86	3.63	3.48	3.37	3.29	3.23	3.18	3.14	3.07	3.01	2.94	2.90	2.86	2.83	2.79	2.75	2.71
10	4.96	4.10	3.71	3.48	3.33	3.22	3.14	3.07	3.02	2.98	2.91	2.85	2.77	2.74	2.70	2.66	2.62	2.58	2.54
11	4.84	3.98	3.59	3.36	3.20	3.09	3.01	2.95	2.90	2.85	2.79	2.72	2.65	2.61	2.57	2.53	2.49	2.45	2.40
12	4.75	3.89	3.49	3.26	3.11	3.00	2.91	2.85	2.80	2.75	2.69	2.62	2.54	2.51	2.47	2.43	2.38	2.34	2.30
13	4.67	3.81	3.41	3.18	3.03	2.92	2.83	2.77	2.71	2.67	2.60	2.53	2.46	2.42	2.38	2.34	2.30	2.25	2.21
14	4.60	3.74	3.34	3.11	2.96	2.85	2.76	2.70	2.65	2.60	2.53	2.46	2.39	2.35	2.31	2.27	2.22	2.18	2.13
15	4.54	3.68	3.29	3.06	2.90	2.79	2.71	2.64	2.59	2.54	2.48	2.40	2.33	2.29	2.25	2.20	2.16	2.11	2.07
16	4.49	3.63	3.24	3.01	2.85	2.74	2.66	2.59	2.54	2.49	2.42	2.35	2.28	2.24	2.19	2.15	2.11	2.06	2.01
17	4.45	3.59	3.20	2.96	2.81	2.70	2.61	2.55	2.49	2.45	2.38	2.31	2.23	2.19	2.15	2.10	2.06	2.01	1.96
18	4.41	3.55	3.16	2.93	2.77	2.66	2.58	2.51	2.46	2.41	2.34	2.27	2.19	2.15	2.11	2.06	2.02	1.97	1.92
19	4.38	3.52	3.13	2.90	2.74	2.63	2.54	2.48	2.42	2.38	2.31	2.23	2.16	2.11	2.07	2.03	1.98	1.93	1.88
20	4.35	3.49	3.10	2.87	2.71	2.60	2.51	2.45	2.39	2.35	2.28	2.20	2.12	2.08	2.04	1.99	1.95	1.90	1.84
21	4.32	3.47	3.07	2.84	2.68	2.57	2.49	2.42	2.37	2.32	2.25	2.18	2.10	2.05	2.01	1.96	1.92	1.87	1.81
22	4.30	3.44	3.05	2.82	2.66	2.55	2.46	2.40	2.34	2.30	2.23	2.15	2.07	2.03	1.98	1.94	1.89	1.84	1.78
23	4.28	3.42	3.03	2.80	2.64	2.53	2.44	2.37	2.32	2.27	2.20	2.13	2.05	2.01	1.96	1.91	1.86	1.81	1.76
24	4.26	3.40	3.01	2.78	2.62	2.51	2.42	2.36	2.30	2.25	2.18	2.11	2.03	1.98	1.94	1.89	1.84	1.79	1.73
25	4.24	3.39	2.99	2.76	2.60	2.49	2.40	2.34	2.28	2.24	2.16	2.09	2.01	1.96	1.92	1.87	1.82	1.77	1.71
26	4.23	3.37	2.98	2.74	2.59	2.47	2.39	2.32	2.27	2.22	2.15	2.07	1.99	1.95	1.90	1.85	1.80	1.75	1.69
27	4.21	3.35	2.96	2.73	2.57	2.46	2.37	2.31	2.25	2.20	2.13	2.06	1.97	1.93	1.88	1.84	1.79	1.73	1.67
28	4.20	3.34	2.95	2.71	2.56	2.45	2.36	2.29	2.24	2.19	2.12	2.04	1.96	1.91	1.87	1.82	1.77	1.71	1.65
29	4.18	3.33	2.93	2.70	2.55	2.43	2.35	2.28	2.22	2.18	2.10	2.03	1.94	1.90	1.85	1.81	1.75	1.70	1.64
30	4.17	3.32	2.92	2.69	2.53	2.42	2.33	2.27	2.21	2.16	2.09	2.01	1.93	1.89	1.84	1.79	1.74	1.68	1.62
40	4.08	3.23	2.84	2.61	2.45	2.34	2.25	2.18	2.12	2.08	2.00	1.92	1.84	1.79	1.74	1.69	1.64	1.58	1.51
60	4.00	3.15	2.76	2.53	2.37	2.25	2.17	2.10	2.04	1.99	1.92	1.84	1.75	1.70	1.65	1.59	1.53	1.47	1.39
120	3.92	3.07	2.68	2.45	2.29	2.17	2.09	2.02	1.96	1.91	1.83	1.75	1.66	1.61	1.55	1.50	1.43	1.35	1.25
∞	3.84	3.00	2.60	2.37	2.21	2.10	2.01	1.94	1.88	1.83	1.75	1.67	1.57	1.52	1.46	1.39	1.32	1,22	1.00

$F_{0.95,\,\nu_1,\,\nu_2} = 1/F_{0.05,\,\nu_2,\,\nu_1}$

Answers to Selected Problems

Chapter 2

1 $(x_1, x_2, x_3) = (26.19, 54.76, 20)$, with $Z = \$1,742.86$.
5 $(x_1, x_2) = (13,5)$; $Z = 31$.
8 $(x_1, x_2, x_3) = (0,10,6\frac{2}{3})$; $Z = 70$.
14 $(x_1, x_2) = (2,1)$; $Z = 7$.
17 $(x_1, x_2) = (-\frac{8}{7}, \frac{18}{7})$; $Z = \frac{80}{7}$.
20 $(x_1, x_2, x_3) = (\frac{4}{5}, \frac{9}{5}, 0)$, with $Z = 7$.

25

Complementary basic solutions

Primal	Z	*Dual*
(0,0,20,10) (feasible)	0	(0,0,−6,−8) (infeasible)
(4,0,0,6) (feasiable)	24	($1\frac{1}{5}$,0,0,$-5\frac{3}{5}$) (infeasible)
($2\frac{1}{2}$,$3\frac{3}{4}$,0,0) (feasible and optimal)	45	($\frac{1}{2}$,$3\frac{1}{2}$,0,0) (feasible and optimal)
(0,5,10,0) (feasible)	40	(0,4,−2,0) (infeasible)
(0,10,0,−10) (infeasible)	80	(4,0,14,0) (feasible)
(10,0,−30,0) (infeasible)	60	(0,6,0,4) (feasible)

28 Maximize $8y_1 + 6y_2$,
subject to
$$\begin{aligned} y_1 + 3y_2 &\le 2 \\ 4y_1 + 2y_2 &\le 3 \\ 2y_1 \quad\quad &\le 1 \\ y_1 \ge 0,\ y_2 &\ge 0. \end{aligned}$$

31 Minimize $5y_1 + 4y_2 + 6y_3$,
subject to
$$\begin{aligned} 2y_1 - 4y_2 + \ \ y_3 &= 1 \\ y_1 - \ \ y_2 + 3y_3 &= 2 \\ -3y_1 + y_2 \qquad\quad &= -1 \\ y_1 \ge 0,\ y_2 \ge 0,\ y_3 &\ge 0. \end{aligned}$$

Chapter 3

1 Let x_{ij} be the shipment from plant i to distribution center j. Then $x_{13} = 2$, $x_{14} = 10$, $x_{22} = 9$, $x_{23} = 8$, $x_{31} = 10$, $x_{32} = 1$; cost \$20,200.
4 (Answer in millions of acres) England → 70 oats; France → 110 wheat; Spain → 15 wheat, 60 barley, 5 oats.
7 (*a*) $x_{11} = 3, x_{12} = 2, x_{22} = 1, x_{23} = 1, x_{33} = 1, x_{34} = 2$; three iterations to reach optimality.

(*b*) and (*c*) $x_{11}=3,\ x_{12}=0,\ x_{13}=0,\ x_{14}=2,\ x_{23}=2,\ x_{32}=3$; already optimal.

10 $x_{11}=10,\ x_{12}=15,\ x_{22}=0,\ x_{23}=5,\ x_{25}=30,\ x_{33}=20,\ x_{34}=10,\ x_{44}=10$; cost = 77.40.

14 $x_{14}=20,\ x_{16}=50,\ x_{23}=10,\ x_{24}=10,\ x_{25}=60,\ x_{37}=60$.

19 Back → David, breast → Tony, butterfly → Chris, freestyle → Carl; time = 126.2.

22

Master problem	*Subproblem 1*	*Subproblem 2*
$3x_1+2x_2\le 18$	$x_1\le 4$	$2x_2\le 12$

26

Constraint	x_3	x_6	x_7	x_1	x_2	x_4	x_5	x_8	x_9	x_{10}
1	0	0	0	3	1	0		0		
2	−1	0	0	1	2					
3	0	0	0			1	5			
4	1	−1	−1	0		2	−1	0		
5	0	0	0			0	1			
6	1	1	1	0				1	3	2
7	0	0	0					2	−1	1

Chapter 4

18

Part	New Basic Solution (x_1,x_2,x_3,x_4,x_5)	Feasible	Optimal
(*a*)	(0,30,0,0,−30)	No	No
(*b*)	(0,20,0,0,−10)	No	No
(*c*)	(0,10,0,0,60)	Yes	Yes
(*d*)	(0,20,0,0,10)	Yes	Yes
(*e*)	(0,20,0,0,10)	Yes	Yes
(*f*)	(0,10,0,0,40)	Yes	No
(*g*)	(0,20,0,0,10)	Yes	Yes
(*h*)	(0,20,0,0,10, $x_6=-10$)	No	No
(*i*)	(0,20,0,0,0)	Yes	Yes

Chapter 5

1 (*a*) $0\to A\to B\to D\to T$ or $0\to A\to B\to E\to D\to T$, with length = 16.

4 (*a*) {(0, *A*); (*A*, *B*); (*B*,*C*); (*B*, *E*); (*E*, *D*); (*D*, *T*)}, with length = 18.

6 (*a*)

Arc	(1,2)	(1,3)	(1,4)	(2,5)	(3,4)	(3,5)	(3,6)	(4,6)	(5,7)	(6,7)
Flow	4	4	1	4	1	0	3	2	4	5

9

Event	1	2	3	4	5	6	7	8	9	10
Earliest time	0	6	3	5	10	10	11	14	13	20
Latest time	0	7	3	6	11	10	13	14	15	20
Slack	0	1	0	1	1	0	2	0	2	0

Critical path: $1\to 3\to 6\to 8\to 10$

Chapter 6

1 Store 1 → 0 crates; store 2 → 2 crates, store 3 → 3 crates; profit = \$21.

4 (a) Spend 3 million for phase 1, 2 million for phase 2, and 0 for phase 3; share = 7.7 percent.

(b) Spend 3.153 million for phase 1, 1.847 million for phase 2, and 0 for phase 3; share = 7.57 percent.

7 $x_1 = -2 + \sqrt{13} \approx 1.6056$, $x_2 = 5 - \sqrt{13} = 1.3944$; $Z = 32.739$.

10 Produce 2 on first production run; if none acceptable, produce 2 on second run. Expected cost = \$575.

Chapter 7

1 Player I: strategy 2; player II: strategy 1.

4 (a) Politician I: issue 2; politician II: issue 2.

(b) Politician I: issue 1; politician II: issue 2.

(c) Minimax criterion says politician I can use any issue, but issue 1 offers him his only chance of winning if politician II is not "smart."

7 (a) $(x_1, x_2) = (\frac{2}{5}, \frac{3}{5})$; $(y_1, y_2, y_3) = (\frac{1}{5}, 0, \frac{4}{5})$; $v = \frac{8}{5}$.

10 Minimize $-x_4$,

subject to

$$
\begin{aligned}
5x_1 + 2x_2 + 3x_3 - x_4 &\geq 0\\
4x_2 + 2x_3 - x_4 &\geq 0\\
3x_1 + 3x_2 \qquad\quad - x_4 &\geq 0\\
x_1 + 2x_2 + 4x_3 - x_4 &\geq 0\\
-x_1 - x_2 - x_3 \qquad\quad &= -1\\
x_1 \geq 0,\ x_2 \geq 0,\ x_3 \geq 0,\ x_4 &\geq 0.
\end{aligned}
$$

Chapter 8

1 (a) The six colored sides.

(b) $P\{X=0\} = P\{X=1\} = P\{X=2\} = \frac{1}{3}$.

(c) $E[Y] = \frac{14}{3}$.

4 (a) $k = \theta + 1$.

(b) $F_X(b) = b\theta$ for $b \leq \theta$ and $F_X(b) = b(1+\theta) - \theta$ for $\theta \leq b \leq 1$.

(c) $E[X] = \frac{1}{2}(1 + \theta - \theta^2)$;

(d) no.

7 (a)

k	-2	-1	0	1	2
$P\{X=k\}$	$\frac{1}{10}$	$\frac{2}{10}$	$\frac{3}{10}$	$\frac{1}{10}$	$\frac{3}{10}$

(c) $E[X] = \frac{3}{10}$.

10 (a) $P\{X \geq 25\} = 0.527$ and $P\{X = 20\} = 0.051$.

(b) $P\{\text{shortage}\} = 0.137$.

13 (a) $E[V] = 45$ and $\sigma_Z = 0.121$; (b) $P\{Z \geq 45.2\} = 0.0495$.

16 $n = 28$.

19

	k	0	1	2	3
(a)	$P\{X_1 = k\}$	$\frac{1}{2}$	$\frac{1}{2}$	0	0
	$P\{X_2 = k\}$	$\frac{1}{8}$	$\frac{3}{8}$	$\frac{1}{2}$	0
(b)	$P\{X_1 = k \mid X_2 = 2\}$	$\frac{1}{4}$	$\frac{3}{4}$	0	0
(e)	$P\{X_1 + X_2 = k\}$	$\frac{1}{8}$	$\frac{1}{4}$	$\frac{1}{4}$	$\frac{3}{8}$

(*c*) No.
(*d*) $E[X_1] = \frac{1}{2}$; var $[X_1] = \frac{1}{4}$.
$E[X_2] = \frac{11}{8}$; var $[X_2] = \frac{31}{64}$.

22 (*a*) All states belong to the same recurrent class.

26 (*b*) $\pi_0 = \pi_1 = \pi_2 = \pi_3 = \pi_4 = \frac{1}{5}$.

28 (*a*) $\pi_0 = 0.182, \pi_1 = 0.285, \pi_2 = 0.368, \pi_3 = 0.165$.
(*b*) 31.42.

Chapter 9

1 Input source: population having hair; customers: customers needing haircuts; queue: customers waiting for a barber; service discipline: FIFO; service mechanism—barber(s).

4 (*a*) 0.135.
(*b*) 0.270.
(*c*) 0.0527.

6 (*b*) $P_0 = \frac{2}{5}, P_n = (\frac{3}{5})(\frac{1}{2})^n$.
(*c*) $L = \frac{6}{5}, L_q = \frac{3}{5}, W = \frac{1}{25}, W_q = \frac{1}{50}$.

10 $\frac{31}{32}$.

16 (*a*) 0.429.
(*b*) 0.154.
(*c*) 0.072.

18

Part	P_0	P_1	P_2	P_3	*E (not running)*
(*a*)	0.493	0.329	0.146	0.032	0.718
(*b*) (*i*)	0.333	0.222	0.148	0.099	2.000
(*b*) (*ii*)	0.415	0.277	0.185	0.123	1.015
(*c*)	0.546	0.364	0.081	0.009	0.553

22 (*a*) W_q (exponential) $= 2W_q$ (constant) $= (\frac{8}{5})W_q$ (Erlang).
(*b*) W_q (new) $= \frac{1}{2}W_q$ (old) and L_q (new) $= L_q$ (old) for all distributions.

24 Current policy: $L = 1$; proposed policy: $L = \frac{13}{16}$.

28 (*a*) $W = \frac{1}{2}$.
(*b*) $W_1 = 0.20, W_2 = 0.35, W_3 = 1.10$.
(*c*) $W_1 = 0.125, W_2 = 0.3125, W_3 = 1.250$.

31

Service distribution	P_0	P_1	P_2	L
Erlang	0.561	0.316	0.123	0.561
Exponential	0.571	0.286	0.143	0.571

Chapter 10

2 (*a*) $E[WC] = 16$.
(*c*) $E[WC] = 26\frac{1}{2}$.

7 Status quo: $E[TC] = 50$; proposal: $E[TC] = 70.75$; keep status quo.

9 (*a*) Crew size = 2.
(*b*) Crew size = 3.

10 $\mu = 1.15$ minimizes $E[TC]$.

13 (*a*) $E[T] = \dfrac{6.8r}{v}$.

(*c*) $E[T] = \dfrac{16r}{21}$.

16 One doctor: $E[TC] = 624.80$; two doctors: 92.95; have only one doctor.

19 (*a*) $\beta = 0.80$.

(*b*) $\underline{\rho} = 0.479$, $\bar{\rho} = 1.336$.

(*c*) $\underline{L} = 0.919$, $\bar{L} = \infty$; $\underline{L}_q = 0.440$, $\bar{L}_q = \infty$; $\underline{P}_0 = 0$, $\bar{P}_0 = 0.521$.

Chapter 11

1 (*a*) $t = \sqrt{5} = 2.24$, $Q = 20\sqrt{5} = 44.72$.

(*b*) $t = \sqrt{6} = 2.45$, $Q = 20\sqrt{6} = 48.98$.

4 $t = \sqrt{62/5} = 3.52$, $Q = 8000\sqrt{62/5} = 28{,}160$.

7 $t = 86.75$ months, $Q = 694{,}000$ gallons.

10 Produce 13 units in period 1.

13 Produce 7 units in period 1 and 7 units in period 3.

16 Produce 3 units in preiod 1 and 4 units in period 3.

19 Produce 1,867 loaves.

21 $(s, S) = (2{,}5)$.

24 (*a*) $G(y) = (3/10)y + 45e^{-y/25} - 15/2$.

(*b*) $(k, Q) = (10{,}100)$ policy.

27 If $x \le 38$, order $38 - x$ units; otherwise, do not order.

30 If $x \le 2$, order $2 - x$ units; otherwise, do not order.

33 If $x \le y°$, order $y° - x$ units; otherwise, do not order.
$y° = \mu - c(1 - \alpha)/2$.

36 Forecast of sales for fourth period is 3139.2.

Chapter 12

1 Use "slow" service when no or one customers are present and "fast" service when two customers are present.

2 Minimize $2y_{01} + 6y_{02} + 2y_{11} + 6y_{12} + 22y_{21} + 26y_{22}$,
subject to
$$y_{01} + y_{02} - (\tfrac{1}{2}y_{01} + \tfrac{3}{10}y_{11} + \tfrac{1}{2}y_{02} + \tfrac{2}{5}y_{12}) = 0$$
$$y_{11} + y_{12} - (\tfrac{1}{2}y_{01} + \tfrac{1}{2}y_{11} + \tfrac{3}{5}y_{21} + \tfrac{1}{2}y_{02} + \tfrac{1}{2}y_{12} + \tfrac{4}{5}y_{22}) = 0$$
$$y_{21} + y_{22} - (\tfrac{2}{10}y_{11} + \tfrac{2}{5}y_{21} + \tfrac{1}{10}y_{12} + \tfrac{1}{5}y_{22}) = 0$$
$$y_{01} + y_{02} + y_{11} + y_{12} + y_{21} + y_{22} = 1$$
$$y_{ik} \ge 0 \text{ for } i = 0, 1, 2, \text{ and } k = 1, 2.$$

7 State 1: attempt ace; state 2: attempt lob.

8 Minimize $-\tfrac{1}{8}y_{01} + \tfrac{7}{24}y_{02} + \tfrac{1}{2}y_{11} + \tfrac{5}{12}y_{12}$,
subject to
$$y_{01} + y_{02} - (\tfrac{3}{8}y_{01} + y_{11} + \tfrac{7}{8}y_{02} + y_{12}) = 0$$
$$y_{11} + y_{12} - (\tfrac{5}{8}y_{01} + \tfrac{1}{8}y_{02}) = 0$$
$$y_{01} + y_{02} + y_{11} + y_{12} = 1$$
$$y_{ik} \ge 0 \text{ for } i = 0, 1 \text{ and } k = 1, 2.$$

13 Reject \$600 offers and accept \$800 or \$1,000 offer.

14 Minimize $60(y_{01} + y_{11} + y_{21}) - 600y_{02} - 800y_{12} - 1{,}000y_{22}$,
subject to
$$y_{01} + y_{02} - (0.99)(\tfrac{5}{8})(y_{01} + y_{11} + y_{21}) = \tfrac{5}{8}$$
$$y_{11} + y_{12} - (0.99)(\tfrac{1}{4})(y_{01} + y_{11} + y_{21}) = \tfrac{1}{4}$$
$$y_{21} + y_{22} - (0.99)(\tfrac{1}{8})(y_{01} + y_{11} + y_{21}) = \tfrac{1}{8}$$
$$y_{ik} \ge 0 \text{ for } i = 0, 1, 2 \text{ and } k = 1, 2.$$

15 After three iterations, approximation is, in fact, the optimal policy given in 13.
22 Use fertilizer B regardless of crop quality.
23 Minimize $\quad -6400(y_{01}+y_{11})-7200(y_{02}+y_{12})$,
subject to $\quad y_{01}+y_{02}-(\frac{1}{2})(\frac{3}{5}y_{01}+\frac{3}{5}y_{11}+\frac{4}{5}y_{02}+\frac{4}{5}y_{12})=\frac{1}{2}$
$\quad y_{11}+y_{12}-(\frac{1}{2})(\frac{2}{5}y_{01}+\frac{2}{5}y_{11}+\frac{1}{5}y_{02}+\frac{1}{5}y_{12})=\frac{1}{2}$
$\quad y_{ik}\geq 0$ for $i=0$, 1 and $k=1$, 2.
24 After three iterations, approximation is optimal policy given in Prob. 22.
32 Use fertilizer B in all four periods regardless of crop quality.
39 In periods 1 to 3 do nothing when the machine is in states 0 or 1, overhaul when machine is in state 2, and replace when in state 3. In period 4 do nothing when machine is in state 0, 1, or 2, and replace when in state 3.

Chapter 13

1 Paths are $\{x_1, x_2\}$ and $\{x_1, x_3\}$.
$\Phi(x_1, x_2, x_3)=\max[x_1x_2, x_1x_3]=x_1\max[x_2, x_3]=x_1[1-(1-x_2)(1-x_3)]$.
3 $R(p_1, p_2, p_3)=p_1[1-(1-p_2)(1-p_3)]$.
6 (*a*) Paths are $\{x_1, x_3\}$ and $\{x_2, x_4\}$.
Cuts are $\{x_1, x_2\}$, $\{x_1, x_4\}$, $\{x_2, x_3\}$, $\{x_3, x_4\}$.
(*b*) $R(p_1, p_2, p_3)=1-(1-p_1p_3)(1-p_2p_4)=0.9639$ when $p_i=0.9$.
(*c*) Upper bound = exact system reliability.
Lower bound $=(1-q_1q_2)(1-q_1q_4)(1-q_2q_3)(1-q_3q_4)=0.9606$ when $p_i=0.9$.
10 (*a*) $0.607\leq R(\frac{1}{4})\leq 1$.
(*b*) $0\leq R(1)\leq 0.202$.

Chapter 14

1 (*a*) a_2: order 20.
(*b*) 89,000.
(*c*) a_3: order 25.
4 (*a*) Guess coin 1.
(*b*) heads: coin 2; tails: coin 1.
7 Bayes' procedure without seismic soundings is a_1 with expected loss of $-$\$68,000.

Seismic sounding	*Bayes' action*	*E (loss)*	$Q_X(x)$
1	a_1	$-137{,}700$	0.360
2	a_1	$-\ 67{,}925$	0.260
3	a_2	$-\ 33{,}000$	0.210
4	a_2	$-\ 33{,}000$	0.170

Value of seismic soundings is \$781, so they should not be used.

Chapter 15

1 (*a*) 5, 8, 1, 4, 7, 0, 3, 6, 9, 2.
4 (*a*) Assigning numbers 0, 1, 2, 3, 4 to heads and 5, 6, 7, 8, 9 to tails gives the sequence $T\ H\ T\ H\ T$.
6 $x=\sqrt{r}$.
11 (*a*) $x=-4\ln(1-r)$.
(*b*) $x=-2\ln[(1-r_1)(1-r_2)]$.
(*c*) $x=4\sum_{i=1}^{6} r_i-8$.

14 Use first 10 three-digit decimals from Table 15.1 and generate observations from $x_i = \dfrac{1}{1 - r_i}$.

Method:	*Analytic*	*Monte Carlo*	*Stratified sampling*	*Complementary numbers*
Mean:	∞	4.3969	8.7661	3.812

17 (*a*) est$\{W_q\} = 2\frac{1}{3}$ and $P\{1.324 \leq W_q \leq 2.971\} = 0.90$.

Chapter 16

2 $(x_1, x_2, x_3) = (1,3,1)$ with $Z = 8$ is optimal.
6 $(x_1, x_2, x_3) = (\frac{2}{3},2,0)$ with $Z = \frac{22}{3}$ is optimal.

9

Part	*New optimal solution*	*Value of z*
(*a*)	$(x_1, x_2, x_3, x_4, x_5) = (0,0,9,3,0)$	117
(*b*)	$(x_1, x_2, x_3, x_4, x_5) = (0,5,5,0,0)$	90

11 (*a*)

Range of θ	*Optimal solution*	*Z(θ)*
$0 \leq \theta \leq 2$	$(x_1, x_2) = (0,5)$	$120 - 10\theta$
$2 \leq \theta \leq 8$	$(x_1, x_2) = (\frac{10}{3},\frac{10}{3})$	$\dfrac{320 - 10\theta}{3}$
$8 \leq \theta$	$(x_1, x_2) = (5,0)$	$40 + 5\theta$

14

	Optimal solution		
Range of θ	x_1	x_2	*Z(θ)*
$0 \leq \theta \leq 1$	$10 + 2\theta$	$10 + 2\theta$	$30 + 6\theta$
$1 \leq \theta \leq 5$	$10 + 2\theta$	$15 - 3\theta$	$35 + \theta$
$5 \leq \theta \leq 25$	$25 - \theta$	0	$50 - 2\theta$

21 $(x_1, x_2, x_3, x_4, x_5) = (0,5,0,\frac{5}{2},0)$ with $Z = 50$ is optimal.
23 (*a*) The elements of the optimal dual solution are the cost coefficients of the slack variables (or original basic variables) in the optimal tableau; that is, $y^* = c_B B^{-1}$.
30 (*b*) $(x_1, x_2) = \frac{1}{3}(0,0) + \frac{2}{3}(5,0) = (\frac{10}{3},0)$, $(x_3, x_4) = (5,0)$, and $Z = 73\frac{1}{3}$ is the optimal solution.

Chapter 17

1

Assignment	1	2	3	4	5
Assignee	1	3	2	4	5

4 $(x_1, x_2, x_3, x_4) = (0,1,1,0)$ with $Z = 36$.
6 $(x_1, x_2, x_3, x_4, x_5) = (0,0,1,1,1)$, with $Z = 6$.

10 (*b*) $(x_1, x_2, x_3) = (0,0,2)$, with $Z = 14$.
15 (*b*) (long, medium, short) = (14,0,16), with profit of \$9,560,000.

Chapter 18

3 (x_1, x_2) can not be optimal.
5 (*a*) $(x_1, x_2) = (0, 2)$ is optimal.
(*b*) Minimize $z_1 + z_2$,

$$\begin{array}{llr}\text{subject to} & 2x_1 - y_1 + y_3 + 4z_1 & = 4 \\ & 2x_2 - y_2 + y_3 + 8z_2 & = 8 \\ & x_1 + x_2 + x_3 & = 2 \\ & x_1 \geq 0,\ x_2 \geq 0,\ x_3 \geq 0,\ y_1 \geq 0,\ y_2 \geq 0,\ y_3 \geq 0,\ z_1 \geq 0,\ z_2 \geq 0. & \end{array}$$

(*c*) $(x_1, x_2, x_3, y_1, y_2, y_3, z_1, z_2) = (0, 2, 0, 0, 0, 4, 0, 0)$ is optimal.
9 $(x_1, x_2) = \left[3 + \left(\frac{r}{2}\right)^{1/3}, 3 + \left(\frac{r}{2}\right)^{1/2}\right]$ minimizes $P(x; r)$, so that $(x_1, x_2) = (3,3)$ is optimal.

Index